KU-541-164

GOOD HOUSEKEEPING
Cookery Book

GOOD HOUSEKEEPING

Cookery Book

completely revised edition
with many new recipes and
69 colour plates

compiled by
THE GOOD HOUSEKEEPING INSTITUTE

BOOK CLUB ASSOCIATES
London

This edition published 1978 by
Book Club Associates
by arrangement with
Ebury Press

Reprinted 1980

Edited by Gill Edden

Colour photographs by
Melvin Grey (including cover), Stephen Baker, Bryce Attwell, Anthony Blake, Barry Bullough, White Fish Authority

Drawings by Gwen Simpson

Photography accessories by
David Mellor, Gered, Wedgwood and Spode, Craftsman Potter

Filmset in England by BAS Printers Limited, Wallop, Hampshire, and
printed and bound in Italy by
New Interlitho, S.p.a., Milan

Contents

Contents

Colour plates

Colour plates

Foreword

The *Good Housekeeping Cookery Book* first appeared in 1948. It was an immediate success and has remained so ever since. It has gone into numerous editions and here once again is the newest and completely updated version full of delicious, easy-to-follow tested recipes.

It is an ideal book for anyone interested in the art of cookery. Its clear explanations of all the basic and more advanced cookery skills make it particularly easy to use. It is indispensable for family cooking with homely, traditional English fare as well as interesting quick and easy recipes. It's a mine of information and ideas for entertaining with its simple and more exotic party dishes, including many authentic foreign recipes and a guide to choosing wines. It is also an invaluable reference book with chapters giving practical information on home freezing, preserving, bread making, simple nutrition, menu planning and party giving, all updated to include the latest information on these important aspects of cookery. So too are the glossaries of herbs, spices, cheeses, fruit and vegetables which are now available in such great variety.

Obviously a comprehensive book of this kind needs to cover all the latest developments in technology and food processing and you will find the information on such things as yeast cookery, home freezing and food storage includes the most up to date guidance available.

We have included imperial and metric measures in order to make this book useful to as many people as possible. You can follow the recipes using pounds, ounces and pints or kilos, grams, and litres as you wish. The recipes have been tested in both measurements and whichever column of figures you follow you should get excellent results. Don't compare the measurements, don't mix them, just make your choice and stick to it.

The new colour pictures and line drawings are all designed to give you, the reader, as much help as possible to make your cooking perfect.

As always, the Good Housekeeping Institute's team of experts are here to help you in every way they can. Please get in touch with us at the address below if you need any advice or information about the recipes in this book.

Good Housekeeping Institute
National Magazine House
72 Broadwick Street
London W1V 2BP

Conversion to Metric Measurements

The recipes in this book were not converted by rule of thumb from imperial versions, but were tested and written up using metric weights and measures, based on a 25 g unit instead of the ounce (28.35 g). Slight adjustments to this basic conversion standard were necessary in some recipes to achieve satisfactory cooking results.

If you want to convert your own recipes from imperial to metric, we suggest you use the same 25 g unit, and use 500 ml in place of 1 pint, with the British Standard 5-ml and 15-ml spoons replacing the old variable teaspoons and tablespoons; these adaptations will, however, give a slightly smaller recipe quantity and may require a shorter cooking time.

Note: sets of British Standard metric measuring spoons are available in the following sizes – 2.5 ml, 5 ml, 10 ml and 15 ml.

When measuring milk it is more convenient to use the exact conversion of 568 ml *(1 pint)*.

For more general reference, the following tables will be helpful.

Metric Conversion Scale

CAPACITY		MASS		LENGTH	
¼ pint	= 142 ml	1 oz	= 28.35 g	1 in	= 2.54 cm
½ pint	= 284 ml	2 oz	= 56.7 g	6 in	= 15.2 cm
1 pint	= 568 ml	4 oz	= 113.4 g	100 cm	= 1 metre
½ litre	= 0.88 pints	8 oz	= 226.8 g		= 39.37 in
1 litre	= 1.76 pints	12 oz	= 340.2 g		
		16 oz	= 453.6 g		
		1 kilogram	= 2.2 lb		

Note: ml = millilitre (s); cm = centimetre (s); g = gram (s)

Oven Temperature Scales

°CELSIUS SCALE	ELECTRIC SCALE °F	GAS OVEN MARKS
110°C	225°F	¼
130	250	½
140	275	1
150	300	2
170	325	3
180	350	4
190	375	5
200	400	6
220	425	7
230	450	8
240	475	9

SERVINGS

All recipes give 4 servings unless otherwise indicated.

Cooking terms and basic methods

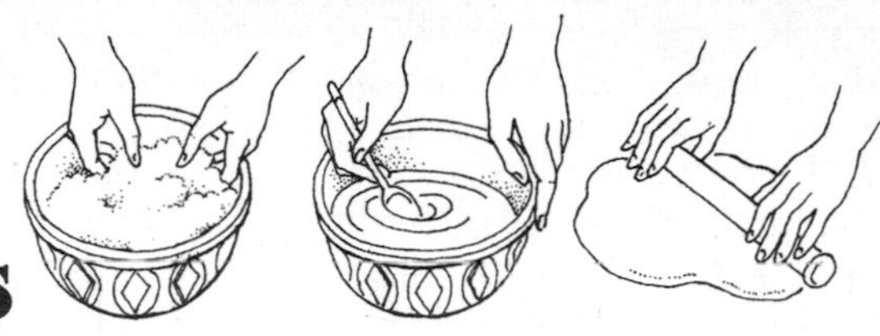

Amandine Almond finish or garnish for a savoury dish.

Anti pasti Italian equivalent of a hot or cold hors d'oeuvre.

Aspic jelly Savoury jelly used for setting and garnishing savoury dishes.

Au gratin Coated with a sauce, sprinkled with browned breadcrumbs (and sometimes with grated cheese) and browned under the grill or in the oven. The food is usually served in the dish in which it has been cooked.

Bain marie A flat, open vessel, half-filled with water, which is kept at a temperature just below boiling point; used to keep sauces, soups, etc, hot without further cooking, also used to prevent over-heating of baked custards and other egg dishes whilst cooking.

Baking Cooking in the oven by dry heat. This is the method of cooking used for most cakes, biscuits and pastries and for many other dishes.

Baking blind Baking flans, tarts and tartlets without a filling. Line the flan ring or pie dish with pastry and trim the edges. Cut a round of greased greaseproof paper slightly larger than the pastry case, place it greased side down inside the pastry and half-fill it with raw haricot beans, rice or stale crusts of bread. Bake as directed in the recipe.

Barding Covering the breast of poultry or game birds with pieces of bacon fat to prevent the flesh from drying up during roasting.

Basting Moistening meat, poultry or game during roasting by spooning over it the juices and melted fat from the tin. This prevents the food from drying out, adds extra flavour and improves the appearance.

Bath chap The cheek and jaw-bone of the pig, salted and smoked. Thus called because those coming from Bath were first known.

Beating Agitating an ingredient or mixture by vigorously turning it over and over with an upward motion, so as to introduce air; a spoon, fork, whisk or electric mixer may be used.

Raw meat is often beaten with a rolling pin or something similar to break down the fibres and make the meat more tender for cooking.

Béchamel A rich, white sauce, one of the four basic types.

Beurre manié A liaison of butter and flour kneaded together to a paste. Used for thickening soups or stews after the cooking is complete. Whisk a little of the paste into the hot liquid and bring back to the boil, adding a little more until the required thickness is reached.

Binding Adding a liquid, egg or melted fat to a dry mixture to hold it together.

Black Jack Name given to caramel, burnt sugar; sometimes used for colouring brown soups, brown sauce and gravies.

Blanching Treating food with boiling water in order to whiten it, preserve its natural colour, loosen the skin or remove a flavour which is too strong. Vegetables are blanched before freezing to destroy harmful bacteria. Two methods are:
1 To plunge the food into boiling water; use this method for skinning tomatoes.
2 To bring it to the boil in the water; used to whiten veal and sweetbreads or to reduce the saltiness of kippers and pickled meat.

Blanquette A stew usually made of veal or fowl, with a white sauce enriched with cream and egg yolks.

Blender A powerful electric machine comprising a goblet with sharp rotating blades, for purééing and grinding cooked and some raw ingredients. Quickly reduces most ingredients.

Blending Mixing flour, cornflour, rice flour and similar ground cereals to a smooth cream with a cold liquid (milk, water or stock) before a boiling liquid is added; this is done in the preparation of soups, stews, puddings, gravies, to prevent lumps forming.

Boiling Cooking in liquid – stock, water or milk – at a temperature of 100°C *(212°F)*. The chief foods that are boiled are vegetables, rice, pasta and suet puddings; syrups and glazes that need to be reduced in quantity and thickened are also boiled. Meat, poultry and fish, though put into boiling water, are actually simmered – fast boiling during the entire cooking time makes them shrink and lose flavour and they tend to become less digestible.

Boning Removal of bones from meat or poultry before rolling or stuffing.

Bouchée Small puff pastry patty, cut about 4 cm *($1\frac{1}{2}$ in)* round, traditionally a mouthful only.

Bouquet garni A small bunch of herbs tied together in muslin and used to give flavour to stews and casseroles. A simple bouquet garni consists of a sprig each of parsley and thyme, a bayleaf, 2 cloves and a few peppercorns.

Bourguignonne Applied to dishes in which a Burgundy wine and small braised button onions are used, eg a classic boeuf bourguignonne.

Braising A method of cooking which is a combination of roasting and stewing. Cuts of meat, poultry and game which are too coarse to roast are cooked by this method; vegetables can also be braised. A casserole or pan with a tightly fitting lid is used, so that little juice is lost through evaporation. The food is put on a bed of vegetables (a mirepoix) with just enough liquid to cover the vegetables and to keep the food moist.

Brining Immersing food (mainly meat or fish which is to be pickled and vegetables which are to be preserved) in a salt and water solution.

Brioche A light French yeast mixture, an enriched dough baked in deep fluted patty tins and finished with a knob of dough on top. A favourite for continental breakfast eaten warm, with coffee.

Brochette Skewer, spit.

Broiling The American term for grilling.

Browning Giving a dish (usually already cooked) an appetising golden brown colour by placing it under the grill or in a hot oven for a short time.

Brûlée The French for burnt, applied to a sugar crust on a custard base, grilled to a caramel.

Brut Unsweetened – a term used to describe dry wines.

Canapés Appetisers, consisting as a rule of slices of bread cut into various sizes – usually quite small – used plain or fried, topped with savoury tidbits.

Caramel A substance obtained by heating sugar syrup very slowly in a thick pan until it is a rich brown colour; used for flavouring cakes and puddings and for lining pudding moulds. When heated to a dark brown colour, caramel forms the basis of gravy browning.

Carbonade A rich stew or braise of meat, generally beef, including beer.

Casserole A baking dish with a tightly fitting lid, used for cooking stews and vegetables in the oven. The food is usually served straight from the dish.

Chantilly Served with whipped cream, generally slightly sweetened and often flavoured with vanilla.

Charlotte A custard dish, the classic being charlotte russe which is a cream set with thin biscuits. An adaptation is apple charlotte, a plain mould lined with bread dipped in butter, filled with thick apple purée and baked.

Chasseur Hunter-style, cooked with mushrooms, shallots and white wine.

Chaudfroid A jellied sauce with a béchamel base, used for masking cold fish, poultry and game.

Chilling Cooling food, without freezing, in a refrigerator.

Chining Severing the rib bones from the backbone by sawing through the ribs close to the spine. Joints such as loin or neck of lamb, mutton, veal or pork are best chined instead of merely being chopped through the backbone, as this makes them easier to carve into conveniently sized chops or cutlets.

Chopping Dividing food into very small pieces. The ingredient is placed on a chopping board and a very sharp knife is used with a quick up-and-down action.

Chowder A thick American soup, a cross between a soup and a stew, frequently based on fish.

Chow-chow Name of a kind of pickle.

Clarifying Clearing or purifying. The term is used to describe the process of freeing fat from water, meat juices or salt, so that it may be used for frying or making cakes such as Genoese sponge.

To clarify dripping

Melt the fat and strain it into a large basin to remove any large particles. Now pour over it 2–3 times its own bulk of boiling water, stir well and allow to cool; the clean fat will rise to the top. When it has solidified, lift it off, dab the underside with muslin or kitchen paper and scrape off any sediment.

To clarify butter or margarine

Heat it gently until it melts, then continue to heat slowly, without browning, until all bubbling ceases (this shows the water has been driven off). Remove from the heat and let it stand for a few minutes for the salt and sediment to settle then gently pour off the fat. If there is much sediment, strain the fat through the muslin, but this is seldom necessary.

Coating 1 Covering food which is to be fried with flour, egg and breadcrumbs, batter, etc.

Coating 2 Covering food which is cooked or ready to serve with a thin layer of mayonnaise, sauce, etc.

Cocotte Small earthenware ovenproof container in single portion size.

Coddling A method of soft-boiling eggs; they are put into a pan of boiling water, withdrawn from the heat and allowed to stand for 8–10 minutes.

Colander Perforated metal or plastic basket for draining.

Compote Fruit stewed in a sugar syrup and served either hot or cold.

Concassé Roughly chopped.

Conserve Whole fruit jam.

Consistency The term used to describe the texture of a dough, batter or cake mixture.

Cordon Bleu An ancient culinary distinction awarded to especially skilful female cooks who passed an examination under the French government 1578–1830. It consisted of a medal suspended on a dark blue ribbon.

Cornstarch The American name for cornflour.

Creaming The beating together of fat and sugar to resemble whipped cream in colour and texture, ie until pale and fluffy. This method of mixing is used for cakes and puddings containing a high proportion of fat.

Crimping 1 Slashing a fish at intervals, in order to make it easier for the heat to penetrate the flesh.

Crimping 2 Trimming cucumber and similar foods in such a way that the slices appear to be deckled.

Crimping 3 Decorating the double edge of a pie or tart or the edge of a shortbread by pinching it at regular intervals with the fingers, giving it a fluted effect.

Croquette A mixture of meat, fish, poultry or potatoes, bound together and formed into a roll or cork shape, then coated with egg and breadcrumbs and fried in deep fat.

Croûte 1 A large round or finger of toasted bread, about 0.5 cm *(¼ in)* thick, on which game and some entrées and savouries are served.

Croûte 2 A pastry crust.

Croûtons Small pieces of bread which are fried or toasted and served as an accompaniment to soup or as a garnish.

Curd 1 The solid part of soured milk or junket.

Curd 2 A creamy preserve made from fruit – usually lemons or oranges, with sugar, eggs and butter.

Curdle To cause fresh milk or sauce to separate when acid is present and excessive heat applied. Also applied to creamed mixtures when the egg is beaten in too much at a time or cold from the refrigerator.

Cure To preserve fish, meat or poultry by salting, drying or smoking.

Dariole The name of a small, narrow mould with sloping sides, used for setting creams and jellies and for baking or steaming puddings and madeleines.

Daube A term for meats and poultry which are braised.

Deep fat Hot fat or oil in which food can be totally immersed for frying.

Devilled Food which has been grilled or fried with sharp, hot seasonings.

Dice To cut into small cubes.

Dough A thick mixture of uncooked flour and liquid, often combined with other ingredients. The term is not confined to a typical yeast dough, but can include mixtures such as pastry, scones and biscuits.

Dredging The action of sprinkling food lightly and evenly with flour, sugar, etc. Fish and meat are often dredged with flour before frying, while cakes, biscuits, pancakes, etc may be sprinkled with fine sugar to improve their appearance. A pierced container of metal or plastic (known as a dredger) is usually used.

Dress To pluck, draw and truss as applied to poultry and game, or the neat presentation of a cooked dish in the way of garnishes.

Dressing Sauce for a salad.

Dripping The fat obtained from roasted meat during cooking or from small pieces of new fat that have been rendered down (see Rendering).

Dropping consistency The term used to describe the texture of a cake or pudding mixture before cooking. To test, fill a spoon with the mixture and hold it on its side above a basin – the mixture should fall in 5 seconds without you having to jerk the spoon.

Dusting Sprinkling lightly with flour, sugar, spices or seasoning.

Egg-and-crumbing A method of coating fish, cutlets, rissoles, croquettes, etc, before they are fried or baked. Have a beaten egg on a plate and some fresh white or dry breadcrumbs on a piece of kitchen paper. Dip the fish or other food in the egg and lift it out, letting it drain for a second or two. Transfer it to the crumbs and tip the paper until the food is well covered. Press in the crumbs, then shake to remove any surplus.

En croûte Encrusted, wrapped or enclosed in pastry before cooking.

En papillote Wrapped in greased paper or foil, in which the food is cooked and sent to the table; usually fish, meat or birds.

Entrée A hot or cold, dressed, savoury dish consisting of meat, poultry, game, fish, eggs or vegetables, served complete with sauce and garnish; for example, cutlets, fillets, croquettes, quenelles.

Escalope A slice of meat (usually veal) cut from the top of the leg. Escalopes are generally egged, crumbed and fried.

Espagnole A rich brown sauce, one of the four basic types.

Faggot A little bunch of flavouring herbs, alternative to bouquet garni; a savoury dish, usually baked, comprising pork offal, onion and breadcrumbs, also known as savoury ducks.

Farce, forcemeat Stuffing used for meat, fish or vegetables. A farce is based on meat, bacon, etc, while the basic forcemeat is made from breadcrumbs, suet, onion and herbs.

Farina Fine flour made from wheat, nuts and potatoes.

Fillet A term used for the undercut of a loin of beef, veal, pork or game, for boned breasts of poultry and birds and for boned sides of fish.

Fines herbes A mixture of chopped herbs, usually parsley, tarragon, chives and chervil.

Flaking 1 Separating cooked fish into individual flakes.

Flaking 2 See Scalloping.

Flambé Used to describe a dish flavoured with flamed alcohol. Alcohol (usually brandy or sherry) is ignited and allowed to burn either on the finished dish, eg Christmas pudding, or in the pan during cooking, eg veal flambé.

Folding in (sometimes called cutting and folding) Combining a whisked or creamed mixture with other ingredients so that it retains its lightness; it is a method used for certain cake mixtures and for meringues and soufflés. The mixture must be folded very lightly and must not be agitated more than absolutely necessary, because with every movement some of the air bubbles are broken down. This cannot be done with an electric mixer.

Fondue A dish cooked on the table, usually over a spirit heater. A Swiss fondue is a traditional mixture of melted cheeses and wine, served with cubes of bread for dunking. A fondue bourguignonne is cubes of meat deep fried in oil and served with cold dips and relishes.

Fool Cold dessert consisting of puréed fruit and whipped cream and sometimes custard.

Freezing Preserving food by chilling and storing at 0°C *(32°F)*.

Fricassee A white stew of chicken, rabbit or veal finished with cream and egg yolks.

Frosting A method of decorating the rim of a glass in which a cold drink is to be served. Coat the edge with whipped egg white, dip into caster sugar and allow to dry.

Frothing Dredging the surface of roasts, generally with flour, and briskly heating to a brown colour in a hot oven.

Frying The process of cooking food in hot fat or oil. There are two main methods, as below.

Shallow frying
Only a small quantity of fat is used, in a shallow pan. This method is used for steak, chops, sausages, fish steaks, white fish such as sole, and pancakes – all these need only sufficient fat to prevent them sticking to the pan. Made-up dishes such as fish cakes can also be shallow fried, but need enough fat to half-cover them. In most cases the food requires a suitable coating.

Deep frying
The food is cooked in sufficient fat to cover it completely. The method is used for batter-coated fish, whitebait, chipped potatoes, doughnuts and made-up dishes such as croquettes and fritters. A deep pan and wire basket are needed, with enough fat, about 900 g–1.4 kg *(2–3 lb)* to come about three-quarters up the pan; clarified beef fat, lard and oil are suitable. The fat must be pure and free from moisture, to avoid spurting or boiling over, and it must be heated to the right temperature, or the food will be either grease-sodden or burnt. If the fat is strained into a basin, jug or wide-necked jar and covered, it may be stored in a cool place for further use; with care it can be used many times and kept for months.

Fumet The flavour or essence of game or fish; any lightly flavoured concentrated substance used to impart a rich flavour to certain dishes or sauces.

Galantine A dish of white meat, boned, sometimes stuffed, rolled, pressed and glazed to be served cold.

Garnish An edible decoration, such as parsley, watercress, hard-boiled egg or lemon, added to a savoury dish to improve the appearance and flavour.

Génoise A sponge cake, a whisked egg mixture enriched by the addition of melted butter. As Genoese.

Gill Liquid measure equivalent to 142 ml *(¼ pt)*.

Glace An ice, a concentrated jellied stock (meat glaze) or an icing.

Glaze Beaten egg, egg white, milk, syrup, thick jelly, meat glaze, etc, used to give a glossy surface to certain sweets and to savouries such as galantines; the glaze improves both appearance and flavour. The tops of pies and buns are brushed with glaze to improve the finished appearance; an egg glaze is usually applied before baking, a sugar and water glaze afterwards. The meat glaze used for savouries is meat stock reduced by rapid boiling.

Goujon Gudgeon. Also small fish fried as a garnish or strips of fish egged, crumbed and fried.

Goulash An Austro-Hungarian stew consisting of beef or veal in a rich brown sauce flavoured with paprika.

Granita A half-frozen water ice.

Grating Shaving foods such as cheese and vegetables into small shreds. Foods to be grated must be firm and cheese should be allowed to harden.

Greque, à la Greek-style. Cooking, especially vegetables, in stock, with olive oil, sometimes dressed with vinegar.

Griddle Flat, heavy, metal plate, usually with a hoop handle, for baking breads, scones, cakes on top of the cooker.

Grilling The process of cooking foods by direct heat under a grill or over a hot fire. Good quality tender meat (steak, chops), whole fish (eg herring, trout) and fish cutlets and fillets are the foods most usually cooked in this way, together with tomatoes, mushrooms, pineapple rings and apple rings used as accompaniments. Some cooked dishes are put under the grill to give them a brown top surface or to heat them through before they are served. The grill should be well heated before use and adjusted as required during cooking.

Grilse A young salmon in its second or third year after its first return from the sea.

Grinding The process of reducing hard foodstuffs such as nuts and coffee beans to small particles by means of a food mill, grinder or electric blender.

Grissini Italian bread sticks.

Gros-sel Coarse salt.

Gugelhupf Sweetened yeast cake, lightly spliced with dried fruit and baked in a fluted tin.

Hamburger An American minced meat cake, fried or grilled, often served in a soft bun.

Hanging Suspending meat or game in a cool, dry place to tenderise and develop the flavour.

Hard sauce Creamed butter and sugar flavoured with brandy, rum or whisky, chilled until firm, served with hot puddings; also known as brandy or rum butter.

Hors d'oeuvre Small dishes served cold, usually before the soup, to act as an appetiser; hors d'oeuvre are generally small and piquant.

Hulling Removal of the calyx from soft fruit such as strawberries, raspberries and loganberries.

Icing Covering for cakes or pastry made with sugar and white of egg or sugar and water, flavoured and coloured to taste.

Infusing A means of extracting flavour from spices and herbs. The usual method of making an infusion is to pour on boiling liquid, cover and leave to stand in a warm place without further cooking or heating.

Jardinière Garnished with diced mixed spring vegetables, plus green peas, cauliflower sprigs, etc.

Julienne Garnished with fine strips of mixed vegetables.

Jugged Meat such as hare stewed in a tall, covered pot until very tender and a rich brown colour.

Jus The natural juices from roast meats used as the basis of gravy.

Kebab Cubes of meat, marinaded and cooked on a skewer.

Kneading Working a dough firmly, using the knuckles for bread-making, the finger-tips in pastry-making. In both cases the outside of the dough is drawn into the centre.

Kosher Prepared according to orthodox Jewish law.

Langues de chats Literally cats' tongues; small, thin, flat, crisp biscuits.

Larding Inserting small strips of fat bacon into the flesh of game birds, poultry and meat before cooking to prevent it drying out when roasting. A special larding needle is used.

Liaison A thickening agent, such as flour, cornflour, arrowroot, rice flour or egg yolk; used for thickening or binding sauces and soups.

Leaven The ingredient which causes dough to rise, eg yeast, baking powder.

Lukewarm Moderately warm; about blood heat, approximately 38°C *(100°F)*.

Macédoine A mixture of fruits or vegetables cut into even-sized dice, generally used as a decoration or garnish. The fruits may alternatively be set in a jelly.

Mâche Lambs lettuce or corn salad.

Macerate To soften foods by soaking in a liquid.

Marinade A blend of oil, wine, vinegar and seasonings used to give flavour to and tenderise meat, game, etc; the process of steeping in marinade. (Also marinate.)

Marmite Earthenware stock pot.

Masking 1 Covering or coating a cooked meat or similar dish with savoury jelly, glaze or sauce.

Masking 2 Coating the inside of a mould with jelly.

Medallions Small rounds of meat, fish or pâté.

Meringue Egg white whisked until stiff, mixed with caster sugar and dried in a cool oven till crisp.

Meunière Cooked in butter, seasoned with salt, pepper and lemon juice and finished with parsley, usually of fish.

Mincing Chopping or cutting into small pieces with a knife or, more commonly, in a mincing machine or electric mixer.

Mirabelle Small yellow plum used as a pie filling, or a liqueur from the same fruit.

Mirepoix A mixture of carrot, celery and onion, often including some ham or bacon, cut into large pieces, lightly fried in fat and used as a bed on which to braise meat.

Mixed herbs These mostly consist of a blend of dried parsley, tarragon, chives, thyme and chervil, but other variations may occur in certain recipes. See also Fines herbes.

Mocca A blend of chocolate and coffee.

Navarin A stew of mutton or lamb, turnips being the principal garnish.

Neapolitan A mousse-type dessert or ice cream moulded in layers.

Noisettes Neatly trimmed, round or oval shapes of lamb, mutton or beef, not less than 1 cm *(½ in)* thick.

Panada A thick binding sauce (25 g, *1 oz*, fat and 25 g, *1 oz*, flour to 150 ml, *¼ pt*, liquid) made by the roux method and used for binding croquettes and similar mixtures.

Panetone Cake-like bread with raisins, served in Italy at Christmas.

Parboiling Part boiling; the food is boiled for part of the normal cooking time, then finished by some other method.

Parfait A light, cream-enriched ice cream dessert, often a purée of fresh fruit is added.

Paring Peeling or trimming, especially vegetables.

Pasteurising Sterilising milk by heating to 60–82°C *(140–180°F)* to destroy bacteria.

Pastry wheel Small serrated wheel used for cutting pastry or biscuit mixtures, leaving a zig-zag edge.

Pasty Small savoury pastry pie made without a dish on a baking sheet, eg Cornish pasty.

Pâte Pastry, especially pâte sucrée, a sweet flan pastry.

Pâté A minced or finely cut savoury mixture, either smooth or rough textured, often with a liver base, cooked in a terrine, casserole or wrapped in pastry.

Patty A small pie or vol-au-vent, often of puff pastry.

Paupiettes Slices of meat rolled with forcemeat, or rolled fillets of fish such as plaice or sole.

Pectin Substance found in fruit and vegetables, necessary for setting jams and jellies. Commercial pectin prepared from apples is sold in bottles.

Petits fours Very small fancy cakes, often iced, and almond biscuits, etc, served at the end of a formal meal.

Petits pois Small green peas.

Pimiento Red Spanish pepper-pod with a sweet, pungent flavour.

Pintado Guinea fowl.

Piping Forcing cream, icing or butter out of a special icing bag through a nozzle, to decorate cakes, etc. Also used for potatoes, some cake mixtures and meringues. The bag may be made of cotton, nylon, plastic or greaseproof paper.

Piquant Sharp of flavour, stimulating, pungent or sour.

Pith The white cellular lining under the rind of citrus fruit, next to the flesh.

Plat du jour Dish of the day.

Plucking Removing feathers from poultry and game.

Poaching Cooking in an open pan at simmering point with sufficient seasoned liquid to cover. Usually applied to eggs, fish and some meat dishes, eg quenelles.

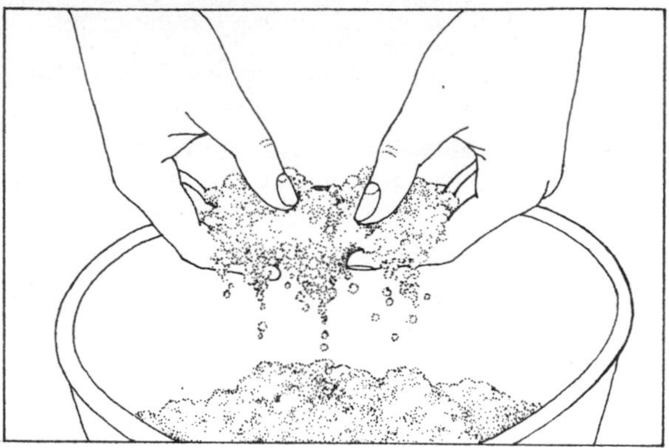

Rubbing-in

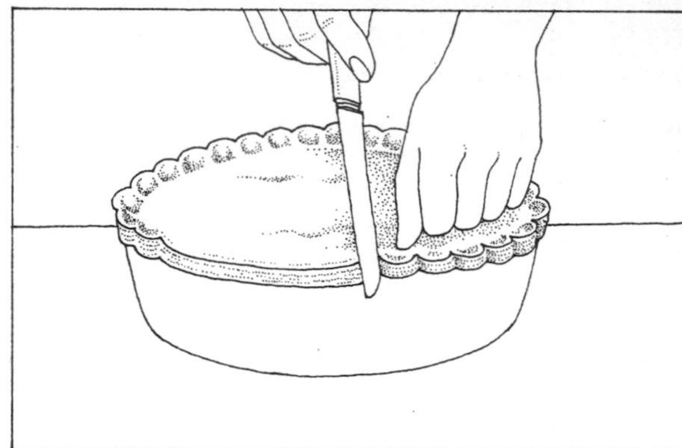

Scalloping

Pope's eye The name given to a small circle of fat in the centre of a leg of mutton or pork, also prime rump steak in Scotland.

Potage A thick soup.

Pot roasting A method of cooking meat in a saucepan with fat and a very small amount of liquid; it is particularly good for small and less tender cuts.

Praline Sweetmeat of almonds coated in caramellised sugar.

Praliné Flavoured with burnt almonds.

Preserving Keeping food in good condition by refrigeration, freezing, heat, chemicals, pickling or crystallising.

Prosciutto Raw smoked ham of Italian origin.

Pulp To reduce food to a soft consistency by crushing or cooking, also the fleshy area of fruit or vegetables.

Quenelles A fine, light forcemeat of fish, poultry, meat or eggs, shaped in balls or ovals, poached and used to garnish soups or entrées or served as a main course.

Ramekin Small oven-ware dish; a cheese tartlet.

Raspings Fine crumbs made from stale bread; used for coating foods for frying and for au gratin dishes. The bread is first dried in a cool oven, then crushed.

Ratafia Miniature macaroon; essence of bitter almonds; a liqueur.

Réchauffé A term applied to re-heated leftover foods.

Reducing The process of boiling a liquid (especially when making a soup, sauce or syrup) in an uncovered pan, in order to evaporate surplus liquid and give a more concentrated result.

Refreshing A process used by French cooks when preparing vegetables. After the vegetables have been cooked, cold water is poured over them to preserve the colour; they are then re-heated before serving.

Relish Sharp, spicy sauce.

Rendering Extracting fat from meat trimmings, etc, by cutting them up small and heating in a cool oven at 160°C *(300°F)* mark 1 until the fat has melted out, or by boiling them in an uncovered pan with very little water until the water is driven off and the fat is melted; the fat is then strained into a basin.

Rennet An extract from calves' stomachs. It contains rennin and is used for curdling or coagulating milk for junket and for cheese-making.

Rice paper Edible paper made from the pith of a Chinese tree, used when baking macaroon and other almond mixtures, including nougat.

Roulade Meat roll, rolled meat, chocolate cake or soufflé-type mixture served in a roll.

Roux A mixture of equal amounts of fat and plain flour, cooked together to form the basis for sauce and for thickening sauces and stews.

Rubbing in A method of incorporating fat into flour, used in making shortcrust pastry, plain cakes and biscuits, when a short texture is required. Cut the fat into small pieces in the flour, then rub it into the flour with the fingertips.

Rusks Fingers or slices of bread dried in a slow oven.

Salmi A ragout or stew, usually of game.

Sauté Food tossed in shallow fat. The vegetables used in making soups, stews and sauces may be sautéed without browning to improve their flavour without spoiling the colour of the finished dish. Sauté potatoes are boiled, cut in slices and cooked in a little fat until they are a light golden brown.

Scalding The process of pouring boiling water over food to clean it, to loosen hairs (eg from a joint of pork) or to remove the skin (eg tomatoes and peaches). The food must not be left in boiling water or it will begin to cook.

The term also means the heating of milk to just below boiling point to retard souring.

Scallion Spring onion without a bulb, used in salads.

Scalloped Baked in a scallop shell or similar container; the food is often previously cooked and is usually combined with a creamy sauce, topped with breadcrumbs and surrounded with a border of piped potato.

Scalloping A means of decorating the double edge of the pastry covering of a pie. Make close horizontal cuts with a knife round the edge of the pie, giving a flaked effect, then, with the back of the knife, pull the edge up vertically at regular intervals to form scallops. Traditionally these should be close together for a sweet pie and wider apart for a savoury one.

Scaloppine A small escalope of veal.

Scoring Making shallow, parallel cuts in the surface of food to improve its flavour or appearance or to help it cook more quickly.

Searing Browning meat quickly in a little hot fat before grilling or roasting.

Seasoning Salt, pepper, spices, herbs, etc, added to give a palatable depth of flavour.

Seasoned flour Used for dusting meat and fish before frying or stewing. Mix about 30 ml *(2 level tbsps)* flour with about 5 ml *(1 level tsp)* salt and a good sprinkling of pepper. Either pat it on to the food or dip the pieces in the flour and shake them gently before cooking.

Shredding Slicing a food such as cheese or raw vegetables into very fine pieces. A sharp knife or coarse grater is usually used.

Sieving Rubbing or pressing food (eg cooked vegetables) through a sieve; a wooden spoon is used to force it through.

Sifting Shaking a dry ingredient through a sieve or flour sifter, to remove lumps and aerate dry ingredients.

Simmering Keeping a liquid just below boiling point, at about 96°C *(205°F)*. First bring the liquid to the boil, then adjust the heat so that the surface of the liquid is kept just moving or 'shivering'; bubbling indicates the temperature is too high.

Skewer Metal or wooden pointed stick, used to hold the shape of meat, poultry or fish during cooking.

Skimming Taking off the surface of stock, gravy, stews, etc, or scum from other foods (eg jams) while they are cooking. A piece of kitchen paper or a metal spoon may be used.

Smoking Curing of food by exposure to wood smoke.

Sousing Pickling in brine or vinegar.

Spit The rotating metal rod or skewer used for impaling meat, poultry or game for cooking over an open barbecue or under a grill.

Spring-form mould Shallow baking tin with hinged sides and loose base, held together with a clamp or pin.

Steaming An economical method of cooking food in the steam from rapidly boiling water. There are several ways of steaming, according to the equipment that is available, see page 297.

Steeping The process of pouring hot or cold water over food and leaving it to stand, either to soften it or to extract its flavour and colour.

Sterilisation The action of destroying bacteria, usually by application of heat.

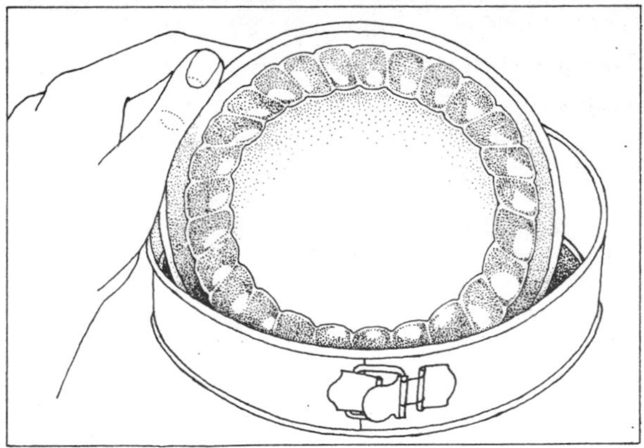

A spring-form mould

Stewing A long, slow method of cooking in a liquid which is kept at simmering point; particularly suitable for coarse-fibred foods. The liquid is served with the food, so that none of the flavour is wasted. A good strong pan or casserole with a tightly fitting lid is best for stews; it is important that the temperature is kept below boiling point, as actual boiling causes the food either to become tough or to break up.

Stirring Mixing with a circular action using a fork, spoon or spatula.

Stock The liquid produced when meat, bones, poultry, fish or vegetables are simmered in water with herbs and flavourings for several hours, to extract their flavour.

Straining Separating liquids from solids using a sieve, colander or muslin.

Stuffing Savoury mixture used to fill poultry, meat, fish, vegetables, etc.

Sweating Cooking a food (usually a vegetable) very gently in melted fat until it exudes its juices.

Syrup A concentrated solution of sugar in water, used in making water ices, drinks and fruit dishes. Golden syrup is a by-product of sugar refining. Maple syrup is extracted from the North American sugar maple.

Tammy To strain soups, sauces, etc, through a fine woollen cloth.

Tepid Approximately at blood heat. Tepid water is obtained by adding 2 parts cold water to 1 part boiling water.

Terrine China or earthenware dish used for pâtés and potted meats, also general term for food cooked in a terrine.

Thickening Giving body to soups, sauce or gravies by the addition of flour, cornflour or arrowroot.

Timbale Thimble-shaped mould for the preparation of savoury mixtures; foods shaped in such a mould.

Truffle A rare fungus of the same family as the mushroom. Either black or white (rarely red). Truffles are used mostly for garnishing.

Trussing Tying or skewering a bird into a compact shape before cooking.

Tube pan Ring shaped tin for baking.

Turnover Sweet or savoury pasty made by folding over a round or square of rolled out pastry into a semi-circle or triangle and baking on a flat baking sheet.

Tutti-frutti Italian name for a mixture of fruits such as candied fruits in an ice cream dessert.

Vanilla sugar Sugar in which a vanilla pod has been left to infuse.

Vol-au-vent A round or oval case made of puff pastry and filled with diced meat, poultry, game or fish in a well flavoured sauce.

Water bath See Bain marie.

Whey Part of milk that remains liquid when the rest forms curds; used in cheese making, also a cooling drink.

Whipping or whisking Beating air rapidly into a mixture either by hand, using an egg beater or whisk, or with a rotary whisk or with an electric mixer.

Whisk Hoops of metal in a rounded shape, used to incorporate air into a mixture.

Zest The coloured part of orange and lemon peel, containing the oil that gives the characteristic flavour. To obtain zest, remove the rind very thinly, with no pith, by grating. If it is required for a sweet dish, it can be rubbed off with a lump of sugar.

Zester A gadget used to scrape away the zest from citrus fruit.

Appetisers and savouries

We have gathered together in this chapter recipes for (a) the simple titbits eaten with a drink before a meal; (b) the hors d'oeuvre taken as the first course of a meal; (c) the savouries served at the end of a fairly formal dinner; (d) the canapés and other savouries suitable for serving with drinks or at a cocktail party.

PRE-MEAL NIBBLERS

These titbits should be piquant, small and manageable. Avoid anything that is sticky or crumbles at a touch. You can buy many nibblers which are easily stored until needed – most of them ready to serve. Here are some popular titbits, followed by a few recipes for home-made ones. See also Savouries with Drinks, pages 31–38.

Potato crisps Plain or with various flavours, such as cheese and onion. Serve them cold or, even better, heat them for 5–10 minutes in the oven at 220°C (425°F) mark 7.

Salted nuts Peanuts, cashews, almonds and mixed nuts can be bought ready salted. To prepare nuts at home, heat 60–90 ml *(4–6 tbsps)* oil in a shallow pan, add 100 g *(¼ lb)* shelled nuts and cook until golden brown, turning frequently. Drain on crumpled kitchen paper and sprinkle with salt; coarse sea salt is especially good.

Devilled nuts Prepare as for salted nuts but sprinkle with a very little cayenne pepper and some salt.

Savoury biscuits, crackers and straws There are innumerable varieties, some flavoured with cheese, others with tomato, onion, Marmite and so on. 'Cheese Footballs' and 'Twiglets' are particularly popular.

Onions Small cocktail onions are available in various colours. Serve them on their own or use as a garnish for canapés and savouries.

Olives You can buy olives loose or bottled in brine – of every shape and size. They can be green – the large Seville Queens or the smaller stuffed manzanilles with centres of pimiento, anchovy, hazelnuts, almonds or onions – or black and unstuffed, smooth, shiny, crinkly, soft fleshed or the bitter and pricey cracked ones from Cyprus. Probably the most sought after are the little kalamata olives from Greece; they come packed in cans with oil and vinegar, expensive but delicious. Always buy loose olives from sources with a good turnover.

Gherkins Sold loose and in jars.

Nuts and bolts

225 g *(8 oz)* assorted unsweetened breakfast cereals
2 pkts pretzel sticks, halved
75 g *(3 oz)* mixed nuts
10 ml *(2 level tsps)* salt
1.25 ml *(¼ level tsp)* pepper
45 ml *(3 tbsps)* melted butter

Mix all the ingredients together, put on a baking sheet and bake in the oven at 180°C *(350°F)* mark 4 for 15 minutes, until golden in colour. Any remaining nuts and bolts can be stored in an airtight tin.

Cheese straws

100 g *(4 oz)* plain flour
salt and cayenne pepper
50 g *(2 oz)* butter
50 g *(2 oz)* mature Cheddar cheese, grated
1 egg yolk
cold water to mix

Season the flour with the salt and cayenne. Rub in the butter to give the texture of fine crumbs. Mix in the cheese and the egg yolk and enough cold water to give a stiff dough. Roll out the pastry thinly and trim to oblongs 18 cm *(7 in)* long and 6.5 cm *(2½ in)* wide. Place on a greased baking sheet and cut each into straws 6.5 cm *(2½ in)* long and 0.5 cm *(¼ in)* wide, separating them as you cut. Roll out the remaining pastry and cut rounds with a 5-cm *(2-in)* plain cutter, then cut out the centre rounds with a 4-cm *(1½-in)* plain cutter; put on to the baking sheet. Bake in the oven at 200°C *(400°F)* mark 6 for 10–15 minutes, until pale golden in colour. Remove from the oven and cool slightly on the tray before cooling completely on a wire rack. Dust the ends of the straws with paprika pepper and put a few into each ring before serving.

Stuffed prunes or dates

Remove the stones from some plump Californian prunes or dessert dates and stuff the cavity with well seasoned cream cheese.

STARTERS AND HORS D'OEUVRE

These can be a single ingredient, simply served (for example, sliced Continental sausage, oysters), or a selection, set out either on individual plates or on a large platter or a trolley. If you are serving *hors d'oeuvre variés*, choose ingredients that are well contrasted to each other in appearance, flavour and texture. It is usual to include some meat, some fish and some vegetables and/or salad, with perhaps rice, pasta or a pulse vegetable; often a pickle, relish or chutney is added to give a piquant note. The hors d'oeuvre should contrast with, not echo, the other courses, and the portions should be small (except when you are serving mixed hors d'oeuvre as the main course in an informal lunch or supper).

Tomato, fruit or vegetable juice makes another popular and very easy starter course.

Hors d'Oeuvre Variés

A mixed hors d'oeuvre might include four or five chosen from the following list:

Sardines
Anchovies
Rollmop herrings
Shrimps
Garlic, salami or other sausage
Gherkins
Olives
Beetroot
Radishes
Potato salad
Tomato salad
Onion salad
Russian salad
Cole slaw salad
Sweet corn and red pepper salad
Rice salad
Egg mayonnaise
Relish or chutney

Fresh fruit

Melon cocktail

Cut the top off the melon, remove the seeds and scoop out the flesh. Cut into cubes and mix with strawberries, raspberries, orange segments or any other fresh fruit. Dredge with sugar, sprinkle with a little brandy or fruit liqueur and chill. Serve in glasses or return the mixture to the chilled shell of the melon.

Melon balls

Cut the top off the melon, remove the seeds from the centre and scoop out the flesh with a Parisian cutter (melon baller) or a teaspoon. Dredge the melon balls with sugar, sprinkle with Madeira or sherry and chill. Serve in small bowls or stemmed glasses, set if possible in crushed ice.

Melon slices

Chill a melon thoroughly and cut into wedge-shaped slices. Remove the seeds and loosen the flesh from the skin. Cut the flesh at right angles to the skin into wedge-shaped pieces. Leave on the skin. Serve with ground ginger and caster sugar or with wedges of lemon.

Grapefruit

Cut each grapefruit in half and cut round each half, loosening the flesh from the outer skin. Cut between the segments to loosen the flesh from the membranes, sprinkle with sugar and chill before serving. If liked, decorate the centre with a maraschino or glacé cherry.

Ortaniques and ugli fruit may be served in the same way.

Spiced hot grapefruit

Prepare some grapefruit as in the previous recipe. Mix 30 ml *(2 level tbsps)* brown sugar and 7.5 ml *(1½ level tsps)* ground cinnamon, sprinkle over the grapefruit and dot with butter. Grill lightly under a medium grill until the sugar has melted and the grapefruit is heated through; serve hot.

Florida cocktail

2 small grapefruit
2 large oranges
curaçao or any orange liqueur
sugar

Working over a plate, prepare the grapefruit as follows: remove all the skin, peeling the fruit with a sawing action and cutting deep enough to show the pulp. Holding the fruit in one hand, remove the flesh of each segment by cutting down at the side of the membrane and then scraping the segment off the membrane on the opposite side on to the plate.

Repeat the process for the oranges. Mix the segments, together with any of the juice collected on the plate. Add curaçao or other liqueur and sugar to taste. Divide the fruit between 4 glasses and pour a little juice into each. Serve chilled.

Dressed avocados *see colour plate facing p. 65*

avocados (allow half per person)
lemon juice
French dressing or tomato vinaigrette or garlic cream dressing (see below), or shrimps or other shellfish, plus thin mayonnaise or soured cream and seasoning
lettuce leaves (optional)

Cut open the avocados lengthwise, using a stainless steel knife and making a deep cut through the flesh, up to the stone and entirely encircling the fruit. Separate the halves by gently rotating them in opposite directions and discard the stone. Brush the cut surfaces with lemon juice. Serve with one of the following dressings spooned into the hollow of each avocado-half, or fill the hollow with shelled shrimps, prawns, flaked crab or lobster meat, moistened with thin mayonnaise or well seasoned soured cream. If you wish, serve the avocados on lettuce leaves.

Tomato vinaigrette Using a container with a tightly fitting lid, shake together 150 ml *(¼ pt)* salad oil, 60 ml *(4 tbsps)* red wine vinegar, 1.25 ml *(¼ level tsp)* salt, a little freshly ground pepper, 1.25 ml *(¼ level tsp)* dry mustard, 2.5 ml *(½ level tsp)* caster sugar and 15 ml *(1 tbsp)* tomato ketchup. *Serves 6.*

Garlic cream dressing Using a container with a tightly fitting lid, shake together 60 ml *(4 tbsps)* garlic vinegar, 150 ml *(¼ pt)* single cream, 2.5 ml *(½ level tsp)* salt, a little freshly ground pepper, 1 clove of garlic, skinned and crushed, 1.25 ml *(¼ level tsp)* caster sugar and 15 ml *(1 tbsp)* chopped parsley. *Serves 6.*

Avocado creams *see colour plate facing p. 65*

2 avocados, about 350 g *(12 oz)* each
grated rind of ½ lemon
45 ml *(3 tbsps)* lemon juice
150 ml *(¼ pt)* thick mayonnaise
5 ml *(1 level tsp)* finely grated onion
1.25 ml *(¼ level tsp)* white pepper
2.5 ml *(½ level tsp)* salt
15 ml *(3 level tsps)* powdered gelatine
150 ml *(¼ pt)* water
142-ml *(5-fl oz)* carton double cream
2 egg whites
For garnish
1 small avocado
lemon juice
watercress sprigs

Peel and stone 2 avocados and roughly cut the flesh into pieces. Put it in an electric blender with the lemon rind, juice and mayonnaise. Purée until really smooth. Turn the purée into a large bowl and stir in the onion and seasoning. Dissolve the gelatine in the measured water. Cool it a little, then stir in 30–45 ml *(2–3 tbsps)* of avocado purée; return this to the bulk, stirring.

Whip the cream until it holds shape; whisk the egg whites until stiff but not dry. Fold the cream, then the egg whites, into the avocado. Divide the mixture between 8 small avocado-shaped or soufflé dishes. Chill for about 2 hours. Garnish with slices of skinned avocado, brush with lemon juice and decorate with watercress sprigs. *Serves 8.*

Note If you have no blender, a Mouli Baby can be used to purée the avocado, but to get a really smooth texture beat afterwards with a rotary whisk.

Fish hors d'oeuvre

Anchovies
Drain and serve on a bed of lettuce, garnished with the chopped white and sieved yolk of a hard-boiled egg.

Sardines
Drain and serve on a bed of lettuce, garnished with strips of pimiento and chopped parsley. They can be coated with a French dressing or mayonnaise, if not canned in a sauce.

Rollmop or soused herrings
Serve with the liquor in which they were cooked; garnish with chopped parsley or thin onion rings.

Smoked cod's roe
If bought whole, skin, slice and serve on small leaves of lettuce; if a jar of cod's roe is used, spoon it out on to the individual plates. Serve with thin brown bread and butter, lemon wedges and freshly ground black pepper.

Smoked eel
Arrange on a bed of lettuce and serve with thin brown bread and butter, lemon wedges and freshly ground black pepper or horseradish relish.

Smoked haddock
Poach and skin the haddock and serve coated with mayonnaise, on a bed of lettuce; garnish with sliced cucumber or cucumber cones. Serve cold.

Smoked trout
Remove the skin from the body of the fish, but leave the head and tail intact. Serve with lemon wedges and horseradish sauce. Alternatively, skin the fish, remove the fillets from the bone and serve on lettuce leaves, with lemon and brown bread. Smoked mackerel is served in a similar way.

Smoked salmon
Serve thinly sliced, with thin brown bread and butter, lemon wedges and paprika pepper.

Fresh salmon
Cold poached salmon can be divided into small portions, dressed with mayonnaise and served on a bed of lettuce. Garnish with cucumber slices or cones.

Whitebait
See page 78 for method of cooking. Serve with wedges of lemon and garnish each portion with a sprig of parsley.

Potted shrimps

150 g *(5 oz)* picked shrimps
100 g *(4 oz)* melted butter
pinch ground mace
pinch cayenne pepper
pinch ground nutmeg
clarified butter

Heat the shrimps very slowly in the butter, but without allowing them to come to the boil. Add the seasonings, then pour the shrimps into small pots or glasses. Leave them to become quite cold and cover each pot with a little clarified butter. Refrigerate. Use within a few days.

Unless the pots are really attractive, turn the shrimps out on to individual plates lined with a few lettuce leaves, but try to retain the shape of the pot. Serve at room temperature with lemon wedges, brown bread or Melba toast and freshly ground pepper.

Oysters

Oysters should be served on the half shell and if possible on a bed of chopped ice. Thin brown bread and butter, slices of lemon and cayenne or freshly ground black pepper are the correct accompaniments. Tabasco sauce may also be served with them. See also page 90.

Smoked (canned) oysters Remove from the can and drain. Serve with thin brown bread and butter, lemon wedges and freshly ground black pepper.

Caviar

This is served ice-cold from the container it comes in, embedded in cracked ice or turned out into a glass dish in ice, with freshly made toast or crisp biscuits and chilled butter. Lemon juice may be sprinkled over it if you wish or serve wedges of lemon. Alternatively, spread the caviar directly on croûtes of fried bread or toast and sprinkle with a few grains of cayenne pepper.

Caviar is the roe of the sturgeon and the true caviar is the most expensive food in the world. In colour it is always a soft grey to grey black and the quality is judged by the size of the eggs, also the less salt the better the caviar. The finest comes from Russia or the Caspian Sea – red caviar is much cheaper than the black and is often replaced by lumpfish roe.

Fish cocktail

100–175 g *(4–6 oz)* **peeled prawns or shrimps or flaked crab or lobster meat**
½ lettuce, washed and shredded
30 ml *(2 tbsps)* **mayonnaise**
30 ml *(2 tbsps)* **tomato ketchup**
30 ml *(2 tbsps)* **single cream**
salt and pepper
squeeze of lemon juice or a dash of Worcestershire sauce
cucumber slices, capers or lemon wedges to garnish

Use either fresh or frozen prawns or shrimps; crab meat may be either fresh or canned – if fresh, use only the white meat; lobster may be either fresh or canned. Line some small glasses with shredded lettuce. Mix the remaining ingredients to make a dressing. Combine the fish and dressing, pile into the glasses and garnish.

Snails à la bourguignonne

1 can snails (about 20)
300 ml *(½ pt)* **white wine**
1 onion stuck with cloves
2 cloves garlic, skinned and crushed
150 ml *(¼ pt)* **brandy**
bouquet garni
salt and butter

For garlic butter
100 g *(4 oz)* **softened butter**
½ shallot, skinned and finely chopped
1 clove garlic, skinned and crushed
5–10 ml *(1–2 tsps)* **chopped parsley**
good pinch of mixed spice
salt and pepper

Remove the snails from the can and place in a pan with the rest of the ingredients. Simmer gently for 1 hour, remove from the heat and allow to cool in the liquor. Meanwhile, mix the ingredients for the garlic butter, blending well. Put a snail into each shell, fill up with butter and put the shells in an ovenproof dish. Bake them in the oven at 230°C *(450°F)* mark 8 for 10 minutes and serve hot.

Note: If shells are not provided with the can of snails, simmer the snails as before, put them in an ovenproof dish, place the butter over and round them and bake as above.

Stuffed eggs with pâté

6 eggs, hard-boiled
100 g (*¼ lb*) soft liver pâté
salt and pepper
stoned green olives

Cut the eggs in half lengthwise and carefully remove the yolks. Press the yolks through a nylon sieve into a bowl, add the pâté and beat well. Season with salt and pepper. Pipe the pâté mixture into the egg white 'shells' using a 1-cm (*½-in*) plain vegetable nozzle. Garnish with slices of green olive.

Eggs in jellied consommé (Oeufs en gelée)

396-g (*14-oz*) can consommé
2.5 ml (*½ level tsp*) powdered gelatine
30 ml *2 tbsps*) dry sherry
5 ml (*1 tsp*) Worcestershire sauce
5 ml (*1 tsp*) lemon juice
175 g (*6 oz*) coarse pâté
6 eggs

Put the consommé in a saucepan. Sprinkle the gelatine over and heat very gently to dissolve it. Off the heat, stir in the sherry, Worcestershire sauce and lemon juice. Cool. Place a little pâté in the bases of 6 150-ml (*¼-pt*) individual dishes. Make a 'well' in the centre to hold the eggs. Bring a saucepan of salted water to the boil. Put the eggs in the pan, and return it to the boil and cook for 6 minutes. Cool the eggs quickly and shell them. Put the eggs in ramekins and pour over consommé to almost fill the dishes. Reserve a little for later use. When the jelly around the eggs has set, use the remaining consommé to glaze the top of the egg. Chill until set. Serve with hot, buttered toast. *Serves 6.*

Curry stuffed eggs

5 ml (*1 tsp*) very finely chopped onion
5 ml (*1 level tsp*) concentrated curry sauce
50 g (*2 oz*) cooked ham, very finely chopped
60 ml (*4 tbsps*) thick mayonnaise
6 eggs, hard-boiled
salt and pepper
parsley for garnish

In a bowl combine the onion, curry sauce, ham and mayonnaise. Cut the eggs in half lengthwise, scoop out the yolks carefully and add to the bowl. Beat with a wooden spoon until well blended. Adjust seasoning. Pile the mixture back into the egg whites, garnish each with a tiny sprig of parsley.

Oeufs à l'indienne

50 g (*2 oz*) butter
100 g (*4 oz*) onion, skinned and very finely chopped
5 ml (*1 level tsp*) dried celery flakes
5 ml (*1 level tsp*) curry powder
100 ml (*4 fl oz*) thick mayonnaise
30 ml (*2 tbsps*) top of the milk
1 eating apple, peeled, cored and finely chopped
Tabasco sauce
salt and pepper
4 eggs, hard-boiled
watercress to garnish

Melt the butter in a small pan, add the onion and celery flakes. Sauté until really tender then stir in the curry powder; cook for 2 minutes. Cool, chop again until pulpy. Combine the mayonnaise with the top of the milk, curried onion and apple. Season to taste with Tabasco, salt and pepper. Halve the eggs, place on individual plates and mask with the sauce. Garnish with watercress.

Stuffed anchovy eggs

4 hard-boiled eggs, shelled
4–6 anchovy fillets, chopped
4–6 capers, chopped
lettuce
15 ml (*1 tbsp*) finely chopped parsley
mayonnaise

Cut the eggs in half lengthwise, remove the yolks and mash to a smooth paste with the anchovies and capers. Replace the mixture in the egg whites, arrange on a bed of lettuce and garnish with the parsley. Serve with mayonnaise.

Egg mayonnaise

Follow the recipe on page 241, but serve on individual dishes, allowing 1 egg per person.

Vegetables

Jerusalem artichokes
Prepare and cook in the usual way (see page 207), allowing 3–4 per person. Serve cold, tossed in mayonnaise or soured cream, sprinkled with cayenne pepper, or serve hot, with Hollandaise sauce (page 200).

Globe artichokes
Prepare and cook in the usual way (see page 207), allowing 1 per person. Serve with melted butter or French dressing (page 244).

Corn-on-the-cob
Prepare in the usual way (see page 216), allowing 1 per person. Serve hot with melted butter.

Tomato and onion salad
A mixture of sliced tomato and finely chopped onion, dressed with French dressing, is an excellent starter.

Peperoni mediterrani

2 medium sized red peppers
2 medium sized green pappers
4 tomatoes, thinly sliced
2 small cloves garlic, skinned and crushed
75 g *(3 oz)* onion, skinned and thinly sliced
4 anchovies
5 ml *(1 level tsp)* dried oregano
salt
ground pepper
olive oil
chopped parsley

Halve the peppers, removing stem and seeds; place the halves side by side in a serving dish. Fill each pepper cavity with tomato slices, a little crushed garlic and thin onion slices. Place thin, scissor-snipped strips of anchovy on top. Sprinkle over the oregano and a little salt and pepper. Spoon oil on top so that each pepper 'cup' is well moistened. Bake at 200°C *(400°F)* mark 6 for about 40 minutes until the peppers look wrinkled and the other vegetables are browned and soft. Cool at room temperature before serving. Garnish with lots of chopped parsley.

PÂTÉ

A pâté is essentially a purée of meats (chiefly liver), well seasoned and cooked slowly. Pâté is served cold and usually with toast or brown bread and butter. There are many varieties, the most famous – and expensive – being Pâté de Foie Gras, made from the livers of specially fattened geese. Most restaurants and hotels of any standing which offer French-type food have their own version, usually shown on the menu as 'Pâté Maison'.

French-style pâté maison

100 g *(¼ lb)* bacon rashers, rinded
700 g *(1½ lb)* calves' or lambs' liver
225 g *(½ lb)* chicken livers
1 clove garlic, skinned and crushed
1 egg, beaten
30 ml *(2 tbsps)* double cream
10 ml *(2 tsps)* brandy
salt and pepper

Line a 900-g *(2-lb)* loaf tin or terrine with the rashers of bacon. Mince the two kinds of liver and add the garlic, egg, cream, brandy and seasoning to taste. Mix well, place in the tin and cover with foil. Stand the tin in a dish with sufficient water to come half way up the sides and bake in the oven at 170°C *(325°F)* mark 3 for about 2 hours. Allow to cool, cover with a plate, put a weight on top to press the pâté and chill overnight. Turn it out of the mould just before serving, garnish as desired and slice thinly.

Mixed meat pâté

175–225 g *(6–8 oz)* **bacon rashers, rinded**
100 g *(¼ lb)* **lambs' liver, chopped**
100 g *(¼ lb)* **lean raw pork, minced**
100 g *(¼ lb)* **sausage meat**
105 ml *(7 tbsps)* **fresh white breadcrumbs**
15 ml *(1 tbsp)* **milk**
1 small onion, skinned and finely chopped
a little beaten egg
1 small glass of brandy
salt and pepper
a good pinch of ground nutmeg
225 g *(8 oz)* **cold roast chicken, duck or game, sliced**

Line a 900-g *(2-lb)* loaf tin or terrine with the rashers of bacon. Mix together the liver, pork, sausage meat, breadcrumbs, milk, onion, beaten egg, brandy and seasonings. Fill the tin, starting with a layer of the sliced poultry or game, alternating it with the sausage mixture and finishing with a layer of sliced meat. Cover with foil, place the tin in a shallow dish of water and bake in the oven at 170°C *(325°F)* mark 3 for 2½–3 hours. Remove from the oven, cover with a plate, put a weight on top to press the loaf and chill overnight. Turn the loaf out and serve sliced.

Potted beef

450 g *(1 lb)* **stewing steak, cut into 1-cm** *(½-in)* **cubes**
150 ml *(¼ pt)* **stock**
1 clove
1 blade of mace
salt and pepper
50 g *(2 oz)* **butter, melted**
fresh bay leaves, optional

Put the meat in a casserole with the stock, clove, mace and seasoning. Cover and cook in the oven at 180°C *(350°F)* mark 4 for 2½–3 hours, until tender. Remove the clove and mace and drain off the stock, setting it aside. Mince the meat twice or place it in a blender and blend for several minutes, until smooth. Add half the melted butter and sufficient of the reserved stock to moisten. Press it into small glass dishes, cover with the remainder of the melted butter and chill. Serve garnished with fresh bay leaves if possible.

As this potted meat does not contain a preservative, it will only keep for a few days in a refrigerator or for 2 days in a cool larder.

Chicken liver pâté

700 g *(1½ lb)* **chicken livers**
75 g *(3 oz)* **butter**
1 medium sized onion, skinned and finely chopped
1 large clove garlic, skinned and crushed
15 ml *(1 tbsp)* **double cream**
30 ml *(2 level tbsps)* **tomato paste**
45 ml *(3 tbsps)* **sherry or brandy**
melted butter, optional

Rinse the chicken livers and dry thoroughly on kitchen paper. Fry them in the butter until they change colour. Reduce the heat, add the onion and garlic, cover and cook for 5 minutes. Remove from the heat and cool. Add the cream, tomato paste and sherry or brandy. Purée in a blender or press through a sieve. Turn into individual dishes. Cover tops with melted butter if you wish. Chill. *Serves 10.*

Peter's pâté

450 g *(1 lb)* **pigs' liver**
50 g *(2 oz)* **butter**
1 onion, skinned and chopped
100 g *(¼ lb)* **streaky bacon, rinded and diced**
100 g *(¼ lb)* **belly pork, diced**
1 clove garlic, skinned and crushed
25 ml *(1½ level tbsps)* **tomato paste**
good pinch black pepper
good pinch garlic salt
good pinch dried basil
good pinch salt
60 ml *(4 tbsps)* **red wine**
grated rind of ¼ lemon
2 bayleaves

Remove the skin and any gristle from the liver. Melt the butter in a saucepan and fry the onion. Add all the other ingredients, cover and cook slowly for about 1½ hours. Remove the bayleaves and drain the meat, retaining the liquor. Mince the meat finely and stir in the liquor. Press the mixture into a 700-ml *(1¼-pt)* ovenproof dish. Cover and cook in the oven at 180°C *(350°F)* mark 4 for 30 minutes; remove from the oven and allow to cool. *Serves 8.*

Liver and meat pâté

700 g ***(1½ lb)*** **lambs' liver**
225 g ***(½ lb)*** **chicken livers**
225 g ***(½ lb)*** **lean veal**
450 g ***(1 lb)*** **belly of pork, rinded and boned**
100 g ***(4 oz)*** **onion, skinned**
2 cloves of garlic, skinned
10 ml ***(2 level tsps)*** **salt**
2.5 ml ***(½ level tsp)*** **freshly ground black pepper**
5 ml ***(1 level tsp)*** **dried basil**
30 ml ***(2 tbsps)*** **brandy**
225 g ***(½ lb)*** **streaky bacon rashers, rinded**

Mince the lamb and chicken livers, veal, pork, onion and garlic. Blend in the salt, pepper, basil and brandy. Stretch the bacon rashers by drawing the blade of a knife along their length. Use the rashers to line the sides and base of a 2-l *(3½-pt)* loaf tin, or similar-sized ovenproof dish or terrine. Spoon in the minced meats, and cover with more bacon. Put the tin in a dish with water to come halfway up the sides of the tin. Lightly top with foil and cook in the oven at 180°C *(350°F)* mark 4 for 2½–3 hours. When cool, weight down and leave until cold in the refrigerator or other cold place. *Serves 8–10.*

Hunter's pâté

450 g ***(1 lb)*** **fat streaky bacon rashers, rinded**
450 g ***(1 lb)*** **rabbit or hare flesh**
450 g ***(1 lb)*** **belly of pork, trimmed**
225 g ***(½ lb)*** **pig's liver**
225 g ***(½ lb)*** **pork sausage meat**
225 g ***(½ lb)*** **garlic sausage**
100 g ***(4 oz)*** **onion, skinned**
45 ml ***(3 tbsps)*** **sherry**
30 ml ***(2 tbsps)*** **chopped parsley**
30 ml ***(2 level tbsps)*** **dried sage**
salt and freshly ground pepper

Grill or fry the bacon rashers until they begin to colour. Cut the rabbit or hare meat into small pieces. Put the pork, liver, sausage meat, garlic sausage and onion through the mincer. Mix in the rabbit pieces, sherry, parsley and sage, and season well with salt and pepper. Line a 2-l *(3½-pt)* loaf tin with the bacon. Turn the pâté mixture into the prepared tin and fold the bacon edges over the mixture. Cover with kitchen foil. Place the tin in a dish with water to come halfway up the sides of the tin. Cook in the oven at 170°C *(325°F)* mark 3 for about 3 hours. Cool in the tin. Unmould, and serve cut in thick slices.
Serves 10.

Duck terrine with orange *see colour plate facing p. 145*

2-kg ***(4½-lb)*** **oven-ready duck**
450 g ***(1 lb)*** **belly pork**
225 g ***(½ lb)*** **pork fat**
1 orange
225 g ***(½ lb)*** **onion, skinned and finely chopped**
1 clove garlic, skinned and crushed
60 ml ***(4 tbsps)*** **red wine**
30 ml ***(2 tbsps)*** **chopped parsley**
5 ml ***(1 level tsp)*** **ground mace**
5 ml ***(1 level tsp)*** **salt**
good pinch ground pepper
1 orange for garnish

Cut away the skin and fat layer from the duck and remove the flesh – about 700 g *(1½ lb)*. Remove the rind and any bones from the belly pork. Pass all the meat and pork fat twice through a fine mincer. Grate the rind from the orange. Remove all pith and membrane, collecting any juice and cut the flesh into small dice.

Combine the minced meats, orange rind, chopped orange and any juice, and all remaining ingredients, except the garnish. Press the pâté into an earthenware terrine, pie or soufflé dish. Cover with foil; put the dish in another dish with water to come halfway up the sides. Cook in the oven at 170°C *(325°F)* mark 3 for about 3 hours.

Strain off the juices and skim off the surface fat. Reduce these to a glaze and pour the juices over the pâté. Cover and weight down. Refrigerate until cold.

Peel the remaining orange. Slice it thinly and use half slices to garnish the dish. *Serves 8.*

Rillettes de porc

900 g ***(2 lb)*** **belly or neck of pork, rinded and boned**
salt
450 g ***(1 lb)*** **back pork fat**
1 clove garlic, skinned and bruised
bouquet garni
freshly ground black pepper

Rub the meat well with the salt and leave it to stand for 4–6 hours. Then cut it into thin strips along the grooves from where the bones were removed. Put these strips into an ovenproof dish, with the pork fat also cut into small strips. Bury a bruised clove of garlic and a bouquet garni in the centre, season with a little pepper; add 75 ml *(5 tbsps)* water. Cover with a lid and cook at 150°C *(300°F)* mark 2, for about 4 hours. Discard the bouquet garni and garlic and season well. Strain the fat from the meat and when well drained, partly pound it then pull it into fine shreds with two forks. Pile lightly into a glazed earthenware or china jar. Pour the fat over the top. Cover with foil. Keep in a cool place.

Rillettes should be soft-textured, so allow to come to room temperature before serving.

Fresh salmon pâté

50 g *(2 oz)* butter
50 g *(2 oz)* flour
400 ml *(¾ pt)* milk
1 bayleaf
salt and pepper
1.25 ml *(¼ level tsp)* ground nutmeg
225 g *(½ lb)* fresh haddock fillet, skinned
450 g *(1 lb)* fresh salmon, skinned and boned
grated rind and juice of 1 lemon
15 ml *(1 tbsp)* chopped parsley
2 eggs, beaten
melted butter
parsley sprigs and lemon for garnish

Melt the butter in a pan, remove from the heat and stir in the flour; cook for 2–3 minutes. Slowly add the milk, beating after each addition. Add the bayleaf, salt, pepper and nutmeg, and boil gently for 2–3 minutes. Discard the bayleaf. Finely chop or mince the haddock and 350 g *(12 oz)* of the salmon. Add to the sauce. Stir in the lemon rind and juice, parsley and eggs. Butter 6–8 individual soufflé dishes (100-ml, *3½-fl oz*, capacity) and divide the mixture between them. Brush the tops with melted butter. Slice the remainder of the salmon and decorate the tops. Place the dishes in a large roasting tin or similar tin and pour in enough water to come halfway up the dishes. Cook in the oven at 150°C *(300°F)* mark 1–2 for about 40 minutes. Chill in the refrigerator. Garnish with parsley and lemon, and serve Melba toast separately. *Serves 6–8.*

Smoked fish pâté

Smoked salmon mousse

see colour plate between pp. 528 and 529

300 ml *(½ pt)* milk
1 small carrot, pared and chopped
1 small onion, skinned and halved
3 parsley stalks
6 peppercorns
40 g *(1½ oz)* butter
25 g *(1 oz)* flour
100 g *(4 oz)* smoked salmon trimmings
25 ml *(5 level tsps)* powdered gelatine
400 ml *(¾ pt)* chicken stock
juice of ½ lemon
30 ml *(2 level tbsps)* mayonnaise
142-ml *(5-fl oz)* carton double cream
salt and freshly ground black pepper

Pour the milk into a saucepan, add the carrot, onion, parsley stalks and peppercorns. Bring to the boil, remove from the heat and allow to infuse for 15 minutes. Melt the butter in another saucepan, stir in the flour and cook for 1–2 minutes without browning. Off the heat, add the strained milk gradually, then bring to the boil and cook, stirring, for ½ minute. Cover the sauce with greaseproof paper and let it cool. Chop the smoked salmon coarsely.

Dissolve the gelatine in some of the stock, add the rest of the stock and allow it to cool. Fold this into the white sauce. Add the smoked salmon, lemon juice and mayonnaise. Beat the cream lightly and fold it into the sauce mixture. Pour the mixture into a 15-cm *(6-in)* soufflé dish or 1.1-l *(2-pt)* rigid polythene container. Leave to set. Dip the container in hot water and invert on to a serving plate. Garnish with lemon and small rolls of smoked salmon. Serve with Melba toast. *Serves 6.*

Smoked fish pâté

198-g *(7-oz)* can smoked codling fillets or kipper fillets
175 g *(6 oz)* butter
pinch cayenne pepper
30 ml *(2 tbsps)* finely chopped capers
30 ml *(2 tbsps)* chopped parsley
15 ml *(1 tbsp)* medium dry sherry
15 ml *(1 tbsp)* lemon juice
salt and freshly ground pepper and nutmeg
25 g *(1 oz)* butter, melted
cucumber slices to garnish

Drain and flake the fish, removing any bones and dark skin. Cream the butter well and add the cayenne by degrees, to taste. Beat in the fish, capers, parsley, sherry and lemon juice. Season to taste with salt, pepper and nutmeg. Spoon the mixture either into small individual pots or into one soufflé dish. Spread it evenly, and top with a little extra melted butter. Chill. Garnish with cucumber, and serve Melba toast separately. *Serves 6–8.*

Taramasalata

225 g *(8 oz)* smoked cod's roe, skinned
180 ml *(12 tbsps)* olive oil
juice and grated rind of 1 lemon
5 ml *(1 tsp)* grated onion
15 ml *(1 tbsp)* chopped parsley
freshly ground black pepper

Put the roe in a bowl with half the oil and leave for 10 minutes. Blend in an electric blender until smooth, gradually adding the lemon juice and remaining oil. Turn the mixture into a bowl, then stir in the lemon rind, onion, parsley and ground pepper.

Note Canned cod's roe cannot be substituted for smoked in this recipe. For a less rich mixture add a few fresh breadcrumbs. *Serves 8.*

AFTER-DINNER SAVOURIES

These are usually hot. Like hors d'oeuvre, they should be piquant or distinctively flavoured, making a good contrast to the main course, and they should be small.

Angels on horseback

4 rounds of bread, about 5 cm *(2 in)* in diameter
25 g *(1 oz)* butter
2 rashers streaky bacon, rinded
4 oysters
a little cayenne pepper
lemon juice
watercress

Fry the bread until golden in the butter. Flatten the rashers with the knife blade and cut in half. Put an oyster in the middle of each piece of bacon, sprinkle with cayenne pepper and a squeeze of lemon juice and roll the bacon round the oyster; secure each with a cocktail stick or small wooden skewer to keep it rolled. Place one roll on top of each croûte of bread and bake in the oven at 200°C *(400°F)* mark 6 for about 15 minutes, or until the bacon is lightly cooked. Serve at once, garnished with a little watercress.

Devils on horseback

4 blanched almonds, optional
olive oil
salt and cayenne pepper
4 large, plump Californian prunes
2 thin rashers of streaky bacon
4 rounds of bread, about 5 cm *(2 in)* in diameter
25 g *(1 oz)* butter
watercress

Fry the almonds for 2–3 minutes in a little oil, until they are golden brown, and toss them in a little salt and cayenne pepper. Remove the stones from the prunes and put the almonds in their place. Cut the rind off the bacon, flatten the rashers with a knife blade, cut in half and roll around the prunes; secure with a cocktail stick or small wooden skewer and cook under a medium grill, turning them until all the bacon is golden brown. Meanwhile, fry the bread for 2–3 minutes in the butter, until golden. Put a prune on each piece, garnish with watercress and serve at once.

Scallops and bacon

8 scallops, prepared
salt and pepper
lemon juice
8 rashers of streaky bacon
tartare sauce

Sprinkle the scallops with salt, pepper and lemon juice. Remove the rind from the bacon, wrap one rasher round each scallop and secure with a cocktail stick. Grill under a moderate heat until cooked through – about 5 minutes on each side. Serve with tartare sauce (page 200).

Mushrooms on toast

225 g *(½ lb)* mushrooms
15 ml *(1 tbsp)* lemon juice or 5 ml *(1 tsp)* Worcestershire sauce
25 g *(1 oz)* butter
salt and pepper
a little cream or top of the milk
fingers of hot toast
chopped parsley

Chop the mushrooms, put them in a small pan, just cover with water and add the lemon juice or sauce, with the butter; season to taste. Cook gently until the water has evaporated, then keep hot. Just before serving, stir in the cream or top of the milk, place the mixture on the fingers of toast and garnish with a little chopped parsley.

Chicken livers on toast

75–100 g *(3–4 oz)* chicken livers
seasoned flour
butter for frying
4 rounds of bread about 5 cm *(2 in)* in diameter
½ glass of sherry or Madeira
50 g *(2 oz)* sliced mushrooms, optional

Wash and dry the livers, cut them in small pieces and coat with the seasoned flour. Melt some butter in a frying pan and fry the bread for 2–3 minutes, until golden; remove it from the pan. Add more butter, put in the prepared livers and stir them over the heat until browned. Add the sherry or Madeira, mix well and cook slowly for 10–15 minutes. Serve the livers on the croûtes of fried bread. If the mushrooms are used, cook them with the livers.

Welsh rarebit

Make in the usual way (see page 264) and serve hot, garnished with parsley or paprika pepper.

Scotch woodcock

1 slice of bread
butter
60-g *(2-oz)* can anchovies
knob of butter
30–45 ml *(2–3 tbsps)* milk
1 large egg
salt and pepper
pieces of canned pimiento or paprika pepper to garnish

Toast the bread, remove the crusts, butter the toast and cut it into triangles. Reserve 2 anchovy fillets for garnish, sieve the rest and spread on the toast triangles. Melt the butter in a saucepan. Whisk together the milk, egg and seasoning, pour into the pan and stir slowly over a gentle heat until the mixture begins to thicken. Remove from the heat and stir until creamy. Spread the mixture on top of the anchovy toast, garnish with thin strips of anchovy fillet and add pieces of pimiento or a sprinkling of paprika.

Note Gentleman's Relish may be used to replace the sieved anchovies.

Cheese meringues

2 egg whites
30 ml *(2 level tbsps)* grated Parmesan cheese
salt and cayenne pepper
fat for deep frying
parsley or watercress to garnish

Whisk the egg whites stiffly and fold in the cheese and seasonings. Heat the fat to 180°C *(350°F)* or until a 2.5-cm *(1-in)* cube of bread turns brown in 60 seconds. Drop in 15 ml *(1 tbsp)* of the cheese mixture at a time and cook until golden brown – 2–3 minutes. Drain well on crumpled kitchen paper and serve hot, garnished with watercress or parsley.

Soft roe savoury

12 herring roes
butter for frying
4 fingers of bread
salt and pepper
a squeeze of lemon juice
parsley

Wash the roes, dry them well and fry gently in some butter for 8–10 minutes, until golden. Remove them from the pan and drain on crumpled kitchen paper. Add more butter to the pan and fry the bread fingers for 2–3 minutes, until golden. Place the roe mixture on the fried bread, season, add a squeeze of lemon juice and garnish with a sprig of parsley.

Hot cheese soufflé

See recipe on page 253.

SAVOURIES WITH DRINKS

Walnut pairs

75 g *(3 oz)* full-fat cream cheese
onion salt
paprika pepper
100 g *(4 oz)* shelled walnut halves

Beat the cream cheese until soft. Season to taste with onion salt and paprika pepper. Use this spread to sandwich the walnut halves together. *Makes 20–24.*

Talmouse

212-g *(7½-oz)* pkt frozen smoked haddock fillets
150 ml *(¼ pt)* thick white sauce
salt and pepper
lemon juice
368-g *(13-oz)* pkt frozen puff pastry, thawed
beaten egg to glaze

Cook the fish as directed on the packet. Discard any skin and bones; flake the flesh. Bind with the white sauce and season to taste with salt, pepper and lemon juice. Roll out the pastry thinly and using a 7.5-cm *(3-in)* cutter stamp out as many rounds as possible, including re-rolling. Brush the rim of each with beaten egg. Place a little of the fish mixture in the centre of each. Shape up the pastry into tricorns and brush with more beaten egg. Place on a dampened baking sheet and bake in the oven at 200°C *(400°F)* mark 6 for 20 minutes or until golden. Serve hot. *Makes about 30.*

Pâté pop-ins

75 g *(3 oz)* well drained gherkins
225 g *(½ lb)* garlic-flavoured pâté

Finely chop the gherkins. Divide the garlic pâté into about 24 portions, shape each into a small ball and toss lightly in chopped gherkin. Chill, and serve on cocktail sticks. *Makes about 24.*

Pâté whirls *see colour plate facing p. 32*

For the base
10 slices from a small white loaf
75 g *(3 oz)* butter

For the topping
225 g *(8 oz)* smooth pâté
100 g *(4 oz)* butter, softened
½ small clove garlic, skinned and crushed
salt and pepper
parsley

Remove the crusts from the bread, squaring up the slices, and cut each into 4 small squares (giving 40 in all). Melt the 75 g *(3 oz)* butter. Brush 2 baking sheets with butter and put the bread on to them. Brush the bread squares with the remaining butter and bake in the oven for about 15 minutes, at 220°C *(425°F)* mark 7, until golden brown. Leave to cool on a wire rack.

Cream the pâté with the butter and garlic and adjust the seasoning. Using a forcing bag fitted with a large star vegetable nozzle, pipe whirls of the pâté on to the crisp squares. Garnish each with a minute piece of parsley. *Makes 40.*

Note If you wish, use garlic pâté and omit the crushed garlic; use Ritz-type crackers instead of home-made crisp squares. If using crackers, prepare within 1 hour of serving, to prevent them softening.

Sausage pielets

200 g *(7 oz)* shortcrust pastry, made with 200 g *(7 oz)* flour etc (see page 351)
225 g *(½ lb)* bacon rashers, rinded
450 g *(1 lb)* pork sausage meat
salt and freshly ground black pepper
1 egg, beaten
212-g *(7½-oz)* pkt frozen puff pastry, thawed

Roll out the shortcrust pastry thinly and use it to line 15 deep patty tins. Finely dice the bacon, fry until the fat runs, then stir it into the sausage meat; season well. Spoon the mixture into the pastry cases. Brush the pastry edges with beaten egg. Roll out the puff pastry and stamp out 15 lids (keep the pastry trimmings to use as decoration). Place the lids over the sausage meat and seal the edges. Brush the lids with egg, then add the pastry decoration. Bake in the oven at 230°C *(450°F)* mark 8 for about 30 minutes. Serve hot. *Makes 15.*

Cheese medallions *see colour plate facing p. 32*

100 g *(4 oz)* unsalted butter
100 g *(4 oz)* Gouda cheese, grated
1 egg yolk
salt and paprika pepper
100 g *(4 oz)* plain flour
beaten egg
cress to garnish

For the filling
50 g *(2 oz)* unsalted butter
100 g *(4 oz)* Gouda cheese, grated

Beat the butter to a cream; gradually add the cheese, egg yolk, salt and paprika to taste, then work in the flour. When well blended, wrap the dough and put it in a cold place for 1–2 hours until of rolling consistency. Roll out on a floured surface to 0.3–0.5 cm *(⅛–¼ in)* thick. Stamp into rounds with a 2.5-cm *(1-in)* plain cutter. Place the rounds well apart on lightly greased baking sheets, glaze with beaten egg and bake in oven at 200°C *(400°F)* mark 8 for about 10 minutes, until beginning to colour; cool on a wire rack. (Handle with care.)

To make the filling, cream the butter and gradually beat in the cheese. Before serving, sandwich the medallions together in pairs with the filling, and garnish each with cress. *Makes 50 pairs.*

Cheese and olive pick-ups

100 g *(¼ lb)* blue cheese
100 g *(¼ lb)* cottage cheese
15 ml *(1 tbsp)* chopped or snipped chives
50 g *(2 oz)* black olives, finely chopped
15 ml *(1 tbsp)* brandy
50 g *(2 oz)* nibbed almonds, browned
buttered cracker biscuits

Blend the cheeses together. Work in the chives, olives and brandy and shape into a roll about 2.5 cm *(1 in)* across. Roll in the nuts, coating evenly, and chill on a plate. Just before serving, slice with a sharp knife and serve on buttered crackers. *Makes 30–36.*

Pickle dillies

8 thin slices of brown or white bread from a large loaf
softened butter
dill pickle
225 g *(½ lb)* Cheddar or Cheshire cheese, finely grated

Stamp out rounds from the bread slices, using a 4-cm *(1½-in)* cutter. Lightly butter – 25 g *(1 oz)* should be sufficient. Place 1–2 thick slices of drained pickle on top of each. Sprinkle some grated cheese on top of the pickle. Put under a hot grill until the cheese is bubbling. *Makes about 36.*

Cherry bacon roll-ups

226-g *(8 oz)* bottle maraschino cherries
12–15 rashers streaky bacon, rinded

Drain the cherries; cook the bacon until the fat becomes transparent, then cut each rasher into 2–3 pieces. Roll each piece of bacon round a cherry, and arrange on skewers. Grill for a further 2–3 minutes, until crisp and golden brown on all sides. Remove the skewers and serve the roll-ups on cocktail sticks. *Makes about 36.*

Cocktail sausages

Allow 3–4 sausages per person. Since cocktail sausages are sometimes difficult to buy and are usually very expensive, we suggest that you get chipolatas and twist and cut each of them into two; 225 g *(½ lb)* chipolatas yields 16 cocktail sausages.

To cook, place in a single layer in a baking tin and bake in the oven at 200°C *(400°F)* mark 6 for about 30 minutes, until golden. To keep hot, cover the tin with foil and reduce the oven temperature. To serve, drain on kitchen paper and spear on cocktail sticks.

Sardine pyramids

2 106-g *(3¾-oz)* cans sardines, drained
lemon juice
salt and pepper
20–24 small cracker biscuits
chopped parsley or paprika to garnish

Remove the sardine tails, then mash the flesh with a little of the sardine oil, and with lemon juice and seasoning to taste. Mound some sardine mixture on to each cracker biscuit and make a cross on the top, using a skewer dipped in the finely chopped parsley or the paprika. *Makes 20–24.*

Pâté whirls (p. 31), Cheese medallions (p. 32), Baby quiches (p. 33), Cream cheese boats (p. 37), Anchovy twists (p. 37), Savoury horns (p. 38), Pimiento dip (p. 40).

Asparagus rolls

2 small brown loaves
450 g *(1 lb)* butter, softened
salt and pepper
2 283-g *(10-oz)* cans asparagus tips, drained

Remove all the crusts from the loaves and slice the bread very thinly – it may prove easier to butter the bread before cutting; chilling the loaf also helps. Sprinkle each slice with salt and pepper and roll up with an asparagus tip inside. Store wrapped in foil until required but preferably serve the day they are made. *Makes about 50.*

Smoked salmon pinwheels

1 large white loaf
225 g *(½ lb)* butter, softened
350 g *(¾ lb)* smoked salmon, thinly sliced
lemon juice
freshly ground black pepper

Remove the crusts from the loaf and cut the bread into thin slices lengthwise. Butter each slice and cover with salmon; sprinkle with lemon juice and season with pepper. Roll up from the long side, wrap in foil and chill for a short time before slicing. *Makes about 48.*

Baby quiches *see colour plate facing p. 32*

100 g *(4 oz)* shortcrust pastry (made with 100 g, *4 oz*, flour etc)
75 g *(3 oz)* matured Cheddar cheese, grated
150 ml *(¼ pt)* milk
1 large egg
1.25 ml *(¼ level tsp)* mixed dried herbs or 5 ml *(1 tsp)* chopped fresh parsley
salt and pepper

Roll out the pastry and use it to line 12–14 5-cm *(2-in)* patty tins. Divide the cheese between the pastry cases. Lightly whisk together the milk, egg and herbs or parsley; season to taste. Spoon the mixture evenly over the cheese. Bake in the oven at 180°C *(350°F)* mark 4 for 20–25 minutes. Serve warm. *Makes 12–14.*

Salt beef pinwheels

75 g *(3 oz)* full-fat cream cheese
15 ml *(1 level tbsp)* creamed horseradish
5 slices salt beef

Blend the cheese and horseradish. Lay out the slices of salt beef on a flat surface and spread equally with horseradish mixture. Roll each slice up as you would with a Swiss roll and chill until firm. Wrap and keep in a cool place. Slice with a sharp knife, and serve with or without cocktail sticks. *Makes 20–24.*

Spicy bacon rolls

25 g *(1 oz)* butter
1.25 ml *(¼ level tsp)* dried thyme
1 clove garlic, skinned and crushed
225 g *(½ lb)* chicken livers
225 g *(½ lb)* lean streaky bacon rashers

Melt the butter, gently stir in the thyme, garlic and chicken livers and cook for 10 minutes, until firm. Rind and stretch the bacon rashers, then cut in half. Drain the chicken livers and wrap each one (or part of one, depending on size) in a piece of bacon. Thread on fine skewers and bake for about 10 minutes at 220°C *(425°F)* mark 7; reduce the heat to the lowest setting and keep the rolls warm until required. Serve hot, on cocktail skewers. *Makes about 30.*

Grape pairs

225 g *(½ lb)* white grapes
100 g *(4 oz)* soft cream cheese

Make a small slit in each grape, but don't cut right through; discard the pips. Fill each grape with a little cream cheese, and serve on cocktail sticks. *Makes about 40.*

Bouchées

368-g *(13-oz)* pkt puff pastry, thawed
beaten egg to glaze

Roll out the pastry to 0.5 cm *(¼ in)* thick and cut out 24 5-cm *(2-in)* rounds, using a plain cutter and re-rolling as required. Place the rounds on wetted baking sheets and brush with beaten egg. Using a 4-

Cream of curry soup (p. 52), Lentil and bacon soup (p. 50), Watercress soup (p. 47).

cm *(1¼-in)* plain cutter, mark a circle in the centre of each, but don't cut right through. Leave to stand in a cool place for 5–10 minutes. Bake in the oven at 230°C *(450°F)* mark 8 for about 20 minutes, until well risen and golden brown. Remove the centres, and either use the cases hot or cool them on a wire rack and use cold. *Makes 24.*

Note When making bouchées for a party, it is far better to heat up the fillings at the last moment and fill the empty cases (warmed up in the oven), than to fill the pastry cases and then reheat them.

Here is a selection of fillings, each enough to fill 24 bouchée cases.

Mushroom Melt a knob of butter in a small pan and sauté 75 g *(3 oz)* button mushrooms, roughly chopped. Put on one side, wipe the pan and melt a further 25 g *(1 oz)* butter. Stir in 45 ml *(3 level tbsps)* flour and cook for 1 minute. Slowly beat in 150 ml *(¼ pt)* milk and bring to the boil, stirring; cook for about 2 minutes. Fold in the mushrooms and enough single cream or top of the milk to give a thick pouring consistency – about 45 ml *(3 tbsps)*. Season to taste with salt, pepper and a dash of Worcestershire sauce.

Prawn Sauté 100 g *(4 oz)* shelled prawns to replace the mushrooms and add 5 ml *(1 tsp)* chopped parsley and a little lemon juice instead of the Worcestershire sauce.

Chicken Sauté 1 small skinned and finely chopped onion to replace the mushrooms; replace the Worcestershire sauce by Tabasco, and add 100 g *(4 oz)* diced cooked chicken meat before re-heating.

Savoury choux

50 g *(1½ oz)* butter or margarine
150 ml *(¼ pt)* water
120 ml *(8 level tbsps)* plain flour
2 eggs, lightly beaten
fillings, see below

Use the fat, water, flour and eggs to make choux pastry, see page 355. Using a 1-cm *(½-in)* plain vegetable nozzle, pipe about 24 small walnut-sized balls of paste on to greased baking sheets. Bake in the oven at 200°C *(400°F)* mark 6 for 15–20 minutes, until golden brown and crisp. Remove from the oven and make a short slit in the side of each to let out the steam. If necessary, return the cases to the oven to dry out completely. Either spoon or pipe the filling into the cases. *Makes about 24.*

Fillings 1 Cream together 100 g *(4 oz)* cream cheese and 50 g *(2 oz)* softened butter; add 5 ml *(1 tsp)* lemon juice and salt and pepper to taste.

2 Cream together 100 g *(4 oz)* cream cheese, 50 g *(2 oz)* softened butter and 10 ml *(2 level tsps)* tomato paste, add a few drops of Worcestershire sauce and seasoning to taste.

3 Cream 175 g–225 g *(6–8 oz)* butter with 10 ml *(2 tsps)* anchovy essence and pepper to taste.

Savoury butters for canapés

These 'anchor' the toppings and prevent the bases from becoming soggy; if smooth they can be piped on top of canapés or savouries for decoration. Make them at least a few hours beforehand and leave in a cool place to become firm before you use them.

With 100 g *(4 oz)* butter use one of the following flavouring ingredients:

Anchovy butter 6 anchovies, mashed with a fork.

Green butter 50 g *(2 oz)* chopped watercress.

Blue cheese butter 50 g *(2 oz)* soft blue cheese.

Tomato butter 30 ml *(2 level tbsps)* tomato ketchup (or 10 ml, *2 level tsps*, tomato paste and 5 ml, *1 level tsp*, sugar).

Lobster butter 50 g *(2 oz)* lobster coral.

Golden butter Sieved yolks of 2 hard-boiled eggs.

Curry butter 10 ml *(2 level tsps)* curry powder.

Ham butter 100 g *(4 oz)* minced cooked ham.

Sardine butter 4 sardines, mashed with a fork.

Onion butter 30 ml *(2 level tbsps)* finely grated onion.

Maître d'hôtel (parsley) butter 30 ml *(2 tbsps)* finely chopped parsley and a squeeze of lemon juice, with salt and cayenne pepper.

Pimiento butter 30 ml *(2 level tbsps)* sieved canned pimiento.

Horseradish butter 30 ml *(2 level tbsps)* creamed horseradish.

Cream cheese spreads for canapés

These too can also be used for decorating canapés and small savouries. Use 75 g *(3 oz)* softened cream cheese and blend with one of the following flavourings:

Pimiento cheese 15 ml *(1 tbsp)* sieved canned pimiento.

Guava cheese 1½ mashed canned guavas and 2.5 ml *(½ level tsp)* salt.

Ham cheese 25 g *(1 oz)* finely chopped or minced ham.

Chive cheese 15 ml *(1 tbsp)* finely chopped chives.

Tuna cheese 30–45 ml *(2–3 level tbsps)* finely mashed tuna fish mixed with 5 ml *(1 tsp)* vinegar or 15 ml *(1 tbsp)* mayonnaise.

Toppings and decorations for canapés

Put one or more of the following toppings on the base after spreading with a savoury butter or cheese spread:
Thin slices of cold meat, rolled or chopped.
Flaked fish or very small whole fish.
Hard-boiled eggs, sliced, quartered or chopped.
Slices or segments of cheese or grated cheese.
Small leaves of lettuce or watercress.
Rings or segments of tomato.
Thin slices of cucumber, flat or in cones.
Cooked beetroot, diced or sliced.
Segments of fruit such as pineapple.
Whole or chopped nuts.

The canapés can be decorated with piped savoury butter or any simple savoury garnish. For a more formal occasion, the canapés may then be finished with a thin coating of aspic jelly – in which case they should be served fairly quickly, so that the base does not become soggy. The first two recipes over illustrate typical ways of assembling the savouries.

Tomato canapés

Spread croûtes of fried bread with onion butter, put a ring of tomato on top of each and decorate each with ½ a black olive or a sprig of parsley.

Ham canapés

Spread croûtes of fried bread with chive cheese and add a small piece of lettuce to each. Put a small roll of ham in the centre of the lettuce. Pipe chive cheese round the base of the canapés. As a garnish, place a thin strip of pimiento over each ham roll, at right angles to it.

Camembert canapés

Make and butter some toast and cut into long, narrow fingers about 7.5 cm *(3 in)* by 1 cm *(½ in)*. Cut fingers of Camembert cheese to the same shape but slightly smaller. Place the cheese strips on top of the fingers of toast and cook under a very hot grill for 2–3 minutes, until bubbly and golden brown. Sprinkle the top with paprika pepper and serve immediately.

Pâté canapés

Cut rounds of bread about 4 cm *(1½ in)* in diameter and fry in butter for 2–3 minutes until golden brown; drain on crumpled kitchen paper. Spread the croûtes with soft liver pâté and decorate the top of each with a slice of stuffed olive.

Devilled crab canapés

15 ml *(1 tbsp)* finely chopped onion
knob of butter
92-g *(3¼-oz)* can crab meat
5 ml *(1 tsp)* Worcestershire sauce or a good dash of Tabasco sauce
pinch of dry mustard
30 ml *(2 tbsps)* white sauce or double cream
parsley or paprika for garnish

Fry the onion lightly in the butter for 5 minutes, until golden brown. Drain and add to the crab meat; stir in the seasonings and sauce or cream. Use as a topping for 24 croûtes of fried bread. Decorate each with a sprig of parsley or sprinkle with paprika.

Ham fingers

2 slices of bread
butter for frying
75 g *(3 oz)* cooked ham, finely chopped
2 eggs, beaten
30 ml *(2 tbsps)* milk
salt and pepper

Fry the bread in some butter for 2–3 minutes, until golden; cut into fingers. Add more butter to the pan and fry the ham gently for 2–3 minutes. Whisk the eggs with the milk and seasoning, pour the mixture into the pan and stir slowly over a gentle heat until it begins to thicken; remove from the heat and stir until creamy. Pile on to the fried bread and serve at once.

Anchovy toasts

2 slices of bread
knob of butter
a squeeze of lemon juice
5 fillets of anchovy, chopped
a little pepper
a pinch each of ground nutmeg and ground mace
parsley

Toast the bread and cut it into fingers. Melt the butter, add a squeeze of lemon juice, the anchovies, pepper, nutmeg and mace. Beat well and rub through a sieve. Spread this mixture on the fingers of toast and decorate with sprigs of parsley.

Similar savouries can be made with sardines or herrings.

Cream cheese boats *see colour plate facing p. 32*

100 g *(4 oz)* cheese pastry, made with 100g *(4 oz)* flour etc (see page 352)
75 g *(3 oz)* flavoured cream cheese (see page 35)
paprika

Line some boat-shaped moulds with the pastry. Prick the bottom of the pastry well and bake blind (see page 357) in the oven at 200°C *(400°F)* mark 6 for 10–15 minutes, until golden brown. Cool on a wire rack. Pile the cheese mixture into the cases and smooth with a knife. Garnish with lines of paprika.

Anchovy twists *see colour plate facing p. 32*

trimmings of flaky pastry
60-g *(2-oz)* can anchovies
1 egg, beaten

Roll out the pastry and cut it into thin finger lengths 10 cm by 0.5 cm *(4 in by ¼ in)*. Rinse the anchovies in cold water, dry and cut in half lengthwise. Place a half on each piece of pastry and twist the fillet and pastry together. Put on to a baking sheet, brush the pastry with egg and bake in the oven at 200°C *(400°F)* mark 6 for about 10 minutes, until golden brown.

Cheese dartois

1 egg, beaten
25 g *(1 oz)* butter, melted
50 g *(2 oz)* Cheddar cheese, grated
salt and pepper
100 g *(4 oz)* flaky pastry (see page 354), or 212-g *(7½-oz)* pkt frozen puff pastry, thawed
beaten egg to glaze

Mix the beaten egg, butter and cheese to a smooth cream and season well. Roll out the pastry thinly into a 33-cm *(13-in)* square, cut it in half and place one half on a baking tray. Spread the cheese mixture over the pastry to within 0.5 cm *(¼ in)* of each edge. Damp the edges with water and cover with the remaining pastry. Glaze with the beaten egg and mark the pastry into fingers. Bake in the oven at 200°C *(400°F)* mark 6 for about 10–15 minutes, until well risen and golden brown. Cut into fingers before serving. *Makes 20–24.*

Anchovy dartois

100 g *(4 oz)* flaky pastry (see page 354), or 212-g *(7½-oz)* pkt frozen puff pastry, thawed
60-g *(2-oz)* can anchovies, drained
25 g *(1 oz)* butter, softened
1 egg, beaten
pepper
beaten egg to glaze

Roll out the pastry as for cheese dartois. Mash the anchovies with a fork, blend to a smooth cream with the butter and egg and season with pepper. Continue as before. *Makes 20–24.*

Curry puffs

100 g *(4 oz)* flaky or rough puff pastry (see page 354), or 212-g *(7½-oz)* pkt frozen puff pastry, thawed
150 ml *(¼ pt)* picked shrimps or 113-g, *4-oz*, pkt frozen shrimps, chopped
150 ml *(¼ pt)* thick curry-flavoured white sauce (page 193)
beaten egg

Roll out the pastry thinly and cut into rounds, using a 4-cm *(1½-in)* plain cutter. Mix the shrimps with enough curry sauce to bind and put a little of this mixture into the centre of half the pastry rounds. Moisten the edges with water and place another pastry round on top of each. Seal the edges and flake them. Brush over with egg and bake in the oven at 230°C *(450°F)* mark 8 for 10–15 minutes, until golden brown. *Makes about 40.*

York fingers

50 g *(2 oz)* Cheddar cheese
trimmings of puff pastry or ½ a 212-g *(7½-oz)* pkt frozen puff pastry, thawed
beaten egg
a little finely grated cheese
50 g *(2 oz)* minced ham
10 ml *(2 tsps)* horseradish sauce
paprika pepper

Cut the cheese into very thin flakes and roll out the pastry thinly. Put the flakes of cheese on top of the pastry, fold it over and roll out thinly again. Cut into fingers about 1 cm *(½ in)* wide and 7.5 cm *(3 in)* long, brush with beaten egg and sprinkle with a little grated cheese. Bake in the oven at 230°C *(450°F)* mark 8 until golden brown – 10–15 minutes – and allow to cool. Mix the ham with the horseradish sauce and spread on the fingers. Sprinkle with paprika pepper before serving. *Makes about 40.*

Savoury horns *see colour plate facing p. 32*

Roll out some puff pastry thinly and cut into long strips 0.5 cm (*¼ in*) wide. Damp one edge of each strip with water and wind it round a cream horn case, overlapping the pastry slightly each time. Brush with beaten egg and bake in the oven at 230°C (*450°F*) mark 8 for 10–15 minutes. Remove from the cases, cool and fill with a mixture of a flavoured cream cheese or a thick white sauce and chopped mushrooms, chicken or ham.

Cheese aigrettes

These are little balls of cheese-flavoured choux pastry which are fried in deep fat. Follow the recipe on page 264, but make the aigrettes extra small and serve them hot, sprinkled with a little grated Parmesan cheese.

Savoury éclairs

Make very small éclairs, and fill them with a savoury mixture as described for savoury choux, page 34. (For éclair recipe, see page 391.)

Blini

15 ml (*1 level tbsp*) dried yeast
300 ml (*½ pt*) milk, warmed
350 ml (*12 oz*) plain flour, sifted
3 eggs, separated
30 ml (*2 tbsps*) cream
pinch of salt
fat for frying
butter, soured cream, caviar or smoked fish for filling

Dissolve the yeast in the milk, mix into a dough with 175 g (*6 oz*) flour and leave to prove in a warm place for 2 hours. Add the remaining flour, egg yolks, cream and salt to the dough and mix well to make a thickish batter. Add the stiffly beaten egg whites and leave for ½ hour. Make tiny pancakes, spread the cooked pancakes with the chosen filling. Serve at once.

DIPS AND DUNKS

A dip is a soft, well flavoured mixture, hot or cold, and a dunk is a bite-size portion of something firm or crisp which can be dipped into it.

A hot dip usually has a base of white sauce to which various seasonings and flavourings can be added, while many of the cold ones are based on cream cheese.

To use as dunks you can buy small savoury biscuits, gristicks, potato crisps and so on, or you can cut French bread into small chunks or prepare celery curls, raw carrot sticks or radish roses (see page 234). For something a little more substantial, offer cooked chipolata sausages, fried scampi, tiny meat balls or cubes of grilled marinaded steak – fix them firmly on cocktail sticks so that they can be dipped into the savoury mixture.

Mexican fire

knob of butter
25 ml *(1½ level tbsps)* **flour**
150 ml *(¼ pt)* **milk**
salt and pepper
1.25 ml *(¼ level tsp)* **dry mustard**
1.25 ml *(¼ level tsp)* **chili powder**
100 g *(4 oz)* **Gruyère cheese, finely chopped**
15 ml *(1 level tbsp)* **chopped green pepper, optional**

Melt the fat, stir in the flour and cook for 2–3 minutes. Stir in the milk, gradually bring to the boil and continue to stir until the sauce thickens; add the seasonings. Remove from the heat and add the cheese and the green pepper (if used). Stir until the cheese has melted and serve hot with scampi.

Devil's dip

25 g *(1 oz)* **butter**
45 ml *(3 level tbsps)* **flour**
2.5 ml *(½ level tsp)* **curry powder**
300 ml *(½ pt)* **stock or milk**
2.5 ml *(½ level tsp)* **cayenne pepper**
10 ml *(2 tsps)* **vinegar**
142-ml *(¼-pt)* **carton double cream**

Melt the butter in a pan, stir in the flour and curry powder and cook for 2–3 minutes. Gradually stir in the stock or milk, bring to the boil and continue to stir until it thickens; add the cayenne pepper and vinegar. If the dip is to be served hot, pour a little sauce into the cream, blend to a smooth cream, return the mixture to the pan and re-heat, without boiling. For a cold dip, cool the sauce, whip the cream and fold it in. Serve with carrot sticks, chipolatas or meat balls.

Hot mustard dip

15 ml *(1 tbsp)* **French mustard**
10 ml *(2 level tsps)* **made English mustard**
30 ml *(2 tbsps)* **vinegar**
25 g *(1 oz)* **butter**
45 ml *(3 level tbsps)* **flour**
300 ml *(½ pt)* **stock**
15 ml *(1 tbsp)* **cream, optional**

Blend the mustards and vinegar together. Melt the butter in a pan and stir in the flour. Cook for 2–3 minutes, stir in the stock, bring to the boil and stir until the mixture thickens. Remove from the heat and add the prepared mustard. Serve hot. If a milder flavour is preferred, stir in the cream just before serving with chipolatas, meat balls or potato crisps.

Chive dip

100 g *(4 oz)* **cream cheese**
30 ml *(2 tbsps)* **chopped chives**
15 ml *(1 tbsp)* **cream or top of the milk, if necessary**

Blend all the ingredients to a soft cream. Serve with chipolatas, cubed steak, French bread or vegetable dunks.

Blue cheese dip

100 g *(4 oz)* **Danish Blue or Roquefort cheese, softened**
75 g *(3 oz)* **cream cheese, softened**
15 ml *(1 tbsp)* **lemon juice**
2.5 ml *(½ level tsp)* **salt**

Blend all the ingredients to a smooth cream and serve with chunks of French bread or vegetable dunks.

Garlic dip

100 g *(4 oz)* cream cheese
1 clove garlic, skinned and crushed
15 ml *(1 tbsp)* cream or top of the milk, if necessary
salt and pepper

Blend the ingredients to a soft cream and season to taste. (Garlic salt may be used instead of crushed garlic.) Serve with sausage or meat titbits, French bread or vegetable dunks.

Pimiento dip *see colour plate facing p. 32*

100 g *(4 oz)* cream cheese
15 ml *(1 tbsp)* cream or top of the milk, if necessary
½ green pepper, finely chopped
½ red pepper, finely chopped
salt and pepper

Blend the cream cheese and cream or milk to a soft cream. Stir in the green and red peppers and season to taste. Serve with scampi, savoury biscuits or French bread.

Miniature meat balls (for dunking)

225 g *(½ lb)* raw minced beef
½ small onion, skinned and grated
1 egg yolk to bind
salt and pepper
egg and breadcrumbs to coat

Combine the ingredients and shape into small balls about the size of marbles. Coat with egg and breadcrumbs, put on a baking sheet and bake for 30 minutes in the oven at 180°C *(350°F)* mark 4. Alternatively, fry for about 5 minutes in deep fat, hot enough to brown a 2.5-cm *(1-in)* cube of bread in 60 seconds; drain well on crumpled kitchen paper and push them on to cocktail sticks before serving.

Scampi dunk

200 g *(7 oz)* frozen scampi
beaten egg and breadcrumbs
deep fat for frying

Thaw out the scampi and dry well, then coat with beaten egg and the breadcrumbs. Heat the fat until it will brown a 2.5-cm *(1-in)* cube of bread in 60 seconds and fry the scampi until they are a light golden brown. Drain them on crumpled kitchen paper and serve hot, on cocktail sticks, with Pimiento or Mexican Fire dip.

Soups

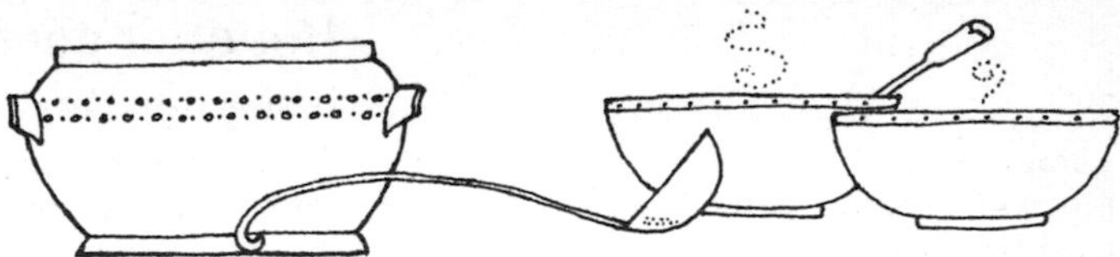

Soup may be thin and clear, thickened, or so crammed with meat, vegetables, pasta or rice that it almost qualifies as solid food and makes a really filling meal. We mostly think of soup as being savoury, but there are fruit soups. Soup can be a luxury dish, like lobster bisque or the real turtle soup served at a Lord Mayor's Banquet (the recipe for which is not given here), or it may have an economical basis of vegetable trimmings and bone stock. The main ingredient of soup is generally a stock made from meat, poultry, vegetables or fish, plus whatever ingredient is needed to give the characteristic flavour. Extras can be added to improve the taste, the food value and the look of a soup. Egg yolks, cream, grated cheese, croûtons and chopped parsley are among the many suitable garnishes, while toast, bread or rolls can be served with soup to add bulk.

Numbers of serving are not given for each recipe as the finished amount may vary, but allow 200 ml *(⅓ pt)* soup per portion.

Stock

Good full-bodied stock is the foundation of great soups, whether it is used as the basis of a soup recipe, or to give added richness to packet or canned soups. There are numerous ready-made stock preparations – the most popular probably being bouillon (stock) cubes, which save much time and trouble. Don't forget that these are well seasoned and inclined to be salty – so add any extra seasoning after checking the flavour at the final stage. We include several recipes for home-made stocks. First of all we give a general recipe for a stock that you can make from the bones of a roast joint or a bird. Stock can be made from a definite recipe or adapted to take in a variety of ingredients as they come to hand – trimmings and scraps of meat, more fresh bones, if wished, poultry giblets, bacon rinds, meat juices. A roast chicken or turkey carcass will produce excellent stock. As a rough guide allow about double the weight in water to solids. This basic bone stock is suitable for most soups, as it is fairly light-coloured; you can put in a little browning if you wish to make it darker. Otherwise, brown stock is used for dark soups and chicken or white stock for light-coloured ones.

Consommé requires a really well flavoured brown stock. The test of a good bone/meat stock is that when it cools it sets to jelly. The concentrated stock can be diluted with water or vegetable water before use if you wish. A large saucepan or a pressure cooker is required to make stock; some people keep a special stockpot, but this is really more of a catering practice. If you keep stock in a cool place, the larder for instance, boil it up each day. If you store it in the fridge it is sufficient to boil it up every 2–3 days to keep it fresh.

Stock can also be kept in the freezer as a useful standby. Freeze only well reduced, concentrated stock – the less space it takes up in the freezer the better. When cool but not jellied, skim off any fat, pour the stock into rigid containers or use a pre-former (see page 469). Seal well and freeze. It is a good idea to pour some into ice cube trays – useful when only a small amount is needed. Store for up to 2 months as cubes, 3 months for larger amounts. Either thaw for 1–2 hours at room temperature or heat from frozen until boiling point is reached.

Bouquet garni

Most soups are improved by the addition of a small bunch of herbs, called a 'faggot' or 'bouquet garni'. The herbs can be made into a small bunch or (if dried) tied up in muslin, so that they are easily removed before the soup is served. Bouquets garnis are available ready packed in muslin or paper sachets. The combination of herbs is very much a matter of choice. At its simplest, a bouquet garni can be a sprig of thyme, some stalks of parsley and a bay leaf. For long slow meat stews, more aromatic bouquets are often used, with mixtures like chervil, basil, tarragon, rosemary and dried celery seed.

We give two examples.

Traditional bouquet garni

1 bayleaf
1 sprig of parsley
1 sprig of thyme
few peppercorns
} **tied in a small piece of leek leaf or muslin**

You can, of course, choose other herbs or include some dried mixed herbs.

Bouquet garni

(Using dried herbs)

1 small bayleaf
pinch of dried mixed herbs
6 peppercorns
1 clove
pinch of dried parsley

Tie the herbs together in a small square of muslin with string or cotton, leaving a long end free to tie the bouquet garni to the handle of the pan.

Basic bone stock

900 g *(2 lb)* meat bones, fresh or from cooked meat
cold water
2 onions
2 sticks celery
2 carrots
5 ml *(1 level tsp)* salt
3 peppercorns
bouquet garni or sprig of parsley and thyme, bayleaf, blade of mace, etc.

Wash the bones and chop them up. If using a pressure cooker add 1.4 l *(2½ pt)* water, bring to the boil and skim off any skum. Add roughly chopped vegetables, salt, peppercorns and herbs. Bring to high *(15-lb)* pressure and cook for 1–1¼ hours. If you are using marrow bones, increase the water to 1.7 l *(3 pt)* and cook for 2 hours. Reduce pressure at room temperature.

In an ordinary pan use 2 l *(3½ pt)* water. After skimming, add vegetables, etc, and simmer, well covered, for 5–6 hours. Strain the stock, which should yield about 1.1 l *(2 pt)*; when cold remove all traces of fat.

Brown stock

450 g *(1 lb)* marrow bone or knuckle of veal, chopped
450 g *(1 lb)* shin of beef, cut into pieces
1.7 l *(3 pt)* water
bouquet garni
1 carrot, pared and sliced
1 medium onion, skinned and sliced
1 stick celery, sliced
2.5 ml *(½ level tsp)* salt

To give a good flavour and colour, brown the bones and meat in the oven (exact temperature not important) before using them. Put in a pan with the water, herbs, vegetables and salt, bring to the boil, skim and simmer covered for 5–6 hours. Makes about 1.4 l *(2½ pt)*. Pressure cook on high *(15-lb)* pressure as for basic bone stock, using 1.4 l *(2½ pt)* water.

Note For a more economical brown stock, use 900 g *(2 lb)* bones, omit the shin of beef and fry the onion until well browned.

White stock

900 g *(2 lb)* knuckle of veal, chopped
2.3 l *(4 pt)* cold water
little lemon juice
1 onion, skinned and sliced
2 carrots, pared and sliced
bouquet garni
5 ml *(1 level tsp)* salt

Put the bones in a large pan, add the water and lemon juice, bring to the boil and remove any scum that rises. Add the vegetables, bouquet garni and salt, reboil, cover and simmer for 5–6 hours. Strain and when cold remove any fat. Makes about 1.7 l *(3 pt)*; ideal for light-coloured soups.

Chicken stock

Break down the carcass and bones of a carved roast chicken and include any skin, chicken scraps, etc. Add about 1.1 l *(2 pt)* water, flavouring vegetables and herbs if you wish. Pressure cook at high *(15-lb)* for 45–60 minutes. Or, in an ordinary pan, use 1.4–1.7 l *(2½–3 pt)* water and simmer for 3 hours.

Fish stock

1 cod's head or fish bones and trimmings
cold water
salt
bouquet garni
1 onion, skinned and sliced

Clean the cod's head or wash the fish trimmings. Put in a saucepan, cover with water, add some salt, bring to the boil and skim. Reduce the heat and add the bouquet garni and onion. Cover, simmer for 20 minutes and strain. Use on the same day, or store in the refrigerator for not more than 2 days.

CONSOMME AND VARIATIONS

Classic consommé

1.1 l *(2 pt)* brown stock (cold)
100 g *(¼ lb)* lean beefsteak, eg rump
150 ml *(¼ pt)* cold water
1 carrot, pared and quartered
1 small onion, skinned and quartered
bouquet garni
1 egg white
salt
10 ml *(2 tsps)* dry sherry, optional

A completely clear, well flavoured broth, made from good brown stock. Both the stock and the utensils must be quite free from any trace of grease, to prevent droplets of fat forming on the surface of the soup.

Remove any fat from the stock. Shred the meat finely and soak it in the 150 ml *(¼ pt)* water for 15 minutes. Put the meat and water, vegetables, stock and bouquet garni into a deep saucepan; lastly add the egg white. Heat gently and whisk continuously until a thick froth starts to form. Stop whisking and bring to the boil. Reduce the heat immediately, cover and simmer for 2 hours. If the liquid boils too rapidly, the froth will break and cloud the consommé.

Scald a clean cloth or jelly bag, wring it out, tie it to the four legs of an up-turned stool and place a bowl underneath. Pour the soup through, keeping the froth back at first with a spoon, then let it slide out on to the cloth. Again pour the soup through the cloth and through the filter of egg white.

The consommé should now be clear and sparkling. Re-heat it, add salt if necessary and if you like a little sherry to improve the flavour, but add nothing that would make the liquid cloudy.

Consommé may be served hot or cold, plain or varied by the addition of one of the following garnishes – in which case the consommé takes its name from the garnish. Cold consommé should be lightly jellied. To prevent the soup becoming cloudy, rinse the garnish in water and add it to the hot consommé just before it is served.

Canned consommé is a very useful standby, and is made quite acceptable by the addition of dry sherry or Madeira and garnishing as for home made consommé.

Consommé julienne

Cut small quantities of vegetables such as carrot, turnip and celery into thin strips and boil separately; rinse the garnish before adding it to the soup.

Consommé à la royale

The garnish consists of steamed savoury egg custard cut into tiny fancy shapes. Make the custard by mixing 1 egg yolk, 15 ml *(1 tbsp)* stock, milk or cream and salt and pepper to taste; strain it into a small greased basin, cover with foil or greaseproof paper and stand the basin in a saucepan containing enough hot water to come half-way up its sides. Steam the custard slowly until it is firm; turn it out, cut into thin slices and from these cut the fancy shapes.

Consommé à la jardinière

Prepare a mixture of vegetables such as carrots and turnips, cut into pea shapes or finely diced, tiny sprigs of cauliflower, green peas and so on. Cook in boiling salted water, rinse and add as above.

Consommé à la brunoise

Prepare a mixture of carrot and turnip (cut into small dice) and celery and leek (sliced neatly), cook in boiling salted water, rinse and add as above.

Consommé au riz

Allow 15 ml *(1 tbsp)* long grain rice per 600 ml *(1 pt)* of consommé. Cook in boiling salted water for 15 minutes; rinse and add it to the consommé just before serving.

Consommé à l'italienne

Cook some Italian soup pasta (tiny letters, shells, stars or wheels) in boiling salted water until tender. Rinse, drain and add to the consommé just before serving.

Consommé princesse

Add asparagus tips, cooked and drained.

CREAM SOUPS

Cream soups have a smooth, creamy texture, achieved by adding cream or egg yolks or more frequently by thickening them with flour, cornflour or some similar cereal. They can be made with any kind of stock or with milk and may contain vegetables, meat, poultry or fish.

Using cream

To prevent curdling, put the cream in a basin, add a little of the hot soup, then stir into the saucepan of soup. Re-heat but don't boil.

Using flour or other fine cereal

When adding flour as a thickening, at the end of cooking, blend it to a thin cream with a little cold milk or other liquid, add a little of the hot soup, then stir it into the saucepan of soup, bring back to the boil and boil for a few minutes, until thickened. Or use beurre manié see page 11.

Using egg yolks

Mix the egg yolks with a little milk or cream. Slowly add a little of the soup, mixing well. Strain the mixture back into the soup, away from the heat. Don't re-heat or you may curdle the egg. (It won't matter if the soup already contains flour, as it will be less likely to curdle.)

Adjusting the consistency

If the soup is too stiff after the thickening has been added, stir in more stock or milk. If it is too thin, boil the soup until it is sufficiently reduced (provided it does not contain egg yolks – see above).

Cream of artichoke soup

900 g *(2 lb)* **Jerusalem artichokes**
2 slices of lemon
900 ml *(1½ pt)* **cold water**
25 g *(1 oz)* **butter**
100 g *(4 oz)* **onion, skinned and chopped**
30 ml *(2 level tbsps)* **cornflour**
400 ml *(¾ pt)* **milk**
25 ml *(1½ tbsps)* **lemon juice**
30 ml *(2 tbsps)* **chopped parsley**
7.5 ml *(1½ level tsps)* **salt**
white pepper
113-ml *(4-fl oz)* **carton single cream**

Wash the artichokes well and put them in a large saucepan with the lemon slices. Cover with water, bring to the boil and cook until tender, about 20 minutes. Drain off the water and reserve 600 ml *(1 pt)*. Allow the artichokes to cool before peeling away the skins. Roughly mash them. Melt the butter in a clean saucepan, add the onion and fry until soft but not coloured. Stir in the cornflour, reserved artichoke water and milk. Stir in the artichokes. Bring the sauce to the boil, stirring. Cook for 2–3 minutes, then sieve the soup or purée in an electric blender. Return the soup to the saucepan. Stir in the lemon juice, parsley, seasoning and cream. Bring to serving temperature. Garnish with croûtons.

Cream of asparagus soup

1 large bundle of asparagus
½ onion, skinned and sliced
600 ml *(1 pt)* white stock
50 g *(2 oz)* butter
45 ml *(3 level tbsps)* flour
salt and pepper
300 ml *(½ pt)* milk
45 ml *(3 tbsps)* cream

Wash and trim the asparagus, discarding the woody part of the stem, and cut the remainder into short lengths, keeping a few tips for garnish. Cook the tips for about 5–10 minutes in boiling salted water. Put the rest of the asparagus, the onion, 150 ml *(¼ pt)* of the stock and the butter in a saucepan, cover and simmer for about 20 minutes until the asparagus is soft. Blend the flour and the remaining stock to a smooth cream. Stir in a little of the hot soup and return this mixture to the pan; bring to the boil, stirring until it thickens. Cook for a further 2–3 minutes. Season to taste and sieve the soup or purée it in an electric blender. Stir in the remaining milk and the cream, re-heat and garnish with asparagus tips.

Cream of cucumber soup

1 large or 2 medium sized cucumbers
25 g *(1 oz)* butter
1 blade of mace
600 ml *(1 pt)* white stock
568 ml *(1 pt)* milk
2 egg yolks
45 ml *(3 tbsps)* cream
salt and pepper

Peel and slice the cucumber, discarding the stalk end (which might give a bitter flavour). Scald in boiling water and strain. Melt the butter and add the cucumber, the mace and stock, bring to the boil, cover and simmer for about 20 minutes, until soft. Sieve the soup or purée it in an electric blender and return it to the pan. Add the milk to the purée and bring to the boil. Mix the egg yolks and cream together, stir in a little of the hot liquid and stir it into the soup. Season to taste and re-heat, without boiling.

Cream of carrot soup

450 g *(1 lb)* carrots, pared and chopped
a stick of celery, scrubbed and chopped
¼ small turnip, peeled and chopped
¼ onion, skinned and sliced
1 rasher bacon, rinded and chopped
25 g *(1 oz)* butter
900 ml *(1½ pt)* white stock
bouquet garni
salt and pepper
45 ml *(3 level tbsps)* flour
150 ml *(¼ pt)* milk
30 ml *(2 tbsps)* cream
chopped parsley

Lightly fry the vegetables and bacon in the butter for about 5–7 minutes, until soft but not coloured. Add the stock, bouquet garni, salt and pepper. Cover and allow to simmer gently for about 1 hour, or until the vegetables are soft. Remove the bouquet garni and sieve the soup or purée it in an electric blender and return it to the pan. Blend the flour and milk to a smooth cream. Stir in a little of the hot liquid and add the mixture to the pan. Bring it to the boil, stirring until it thickens and cook for 2–3 minutes; re-season if necessary and add the cream and parsley. Bring to serving temperature but do not boil after adding the cream.

Cream of celery soup

1 large head of celery, trimmed and sliced
1 medium sized onion, skinned and sliced
25 g *(1 oz)* butter
1.1 l *(2 pt)* white stock or milk and stock mixed
salt and pepper
bouquet garni
45 ml *(3 level tbsps)* flour
150 ml *(¼ pt)* milk
45 ml *(3 tbsps)* cream
chopped parsley

Lightly fry the celery and onion in the butter for 5–7 minutes, until soft but not coloured. Add the liquid, seasoning and bouquet garni, bring to the boil, cover and simmer for about 1 hour, until the vegetables are quite soft. Remove the bouquet garni. Sieve the soup or purée it in an electric blender and return it to the pan. Blend the flour and milk to a smooth cream. Stir in a little of the hot soup and add the mixture to the pan. Bring to the boil, stirring until it thickens. Cook for 2–3 minutes, re-season if necessary and add the cream and freshly chopped parsley just before serving.

Cream of chicken soup

45 ml *(3 level tbsps)* flour
150 ml *(¼ pt)* milk
1.1 l *(2 pt)* chicken stock
100 g *(4 oz)* cooked chicken meat, diced
salt and pepper
5 ml *(1 tsp)* lemon juice
grated nutmeg
30 ml *(2 tbsps)* cream

Blend the flour with a little of the milk to a smooth cream. Boil the stock and pour it on to the blended mixture, stirring well. Return it to the pan and simmer gently for about 20 minutes. Stir in the chicken meat, seasoning, lemon juice and a little nutmeg. Mix the rest of the milk with the cream and stir it into the soup; re-heat without boiling.

The stock can be made from the carcass of a roast chicken and the meat can be the trimmings from it. (See page 42.) Alternatively, chicken bouillon cubes and ready-cooked chicken can be used.

Crème Dubarry

1 firm white cauliflower
40 g *(1½ oz)* butter
45 ml *(3 level tbsps)* flour
900 ml *(1½ pt)* white stock
salt, pepper and nutmeg
142-ml *(5-fl oz)* carton cream

Divide the cauliflower into sprigs, discarding the green leaves, and wash in salted water. Melt the butter, stir in the flour and cook for 2–3 minutes. Remove the pan from the heat and gradually stir in the stock, bring to the boil and continue to stir until it thickens. Add the cauliflower (reserving a dozen well-shaped pieces) and salt and pepper, cover and simmer for about 30 minutes. Meanwhile, cook the remaining cauliflower in salted water for 10–15 minutes, until soft but not broken. Sieve the soup or purée it in an electric blender, re-season if necessary and add a pinch of grated nutmeg. Re-heat the soup, stir in the cream and serve garnished with the cauliflower sprigs.

Cream of leek and potato soup

4 medium sized leeks, sliced and thoroughly washed
1 small onion, skinned and sliced
3 medium sized potatoes, peeled and sliced
25 g *(1 oz)* butter
1.1 l *(2 pt)* white stock
salt and pepper
45 ml *(3 tbsps)* cream

Lightly fry the vegetables in the butter for about 5 minutes, until soft but not coloured. Add the stock, cover and simmer for about 45 minutes until the vegetables are cooked. Sieve the soup or purée it in an electric blender and return it to the pan. Re-heat, re-season if necessary and stir in the cream just before serving.

Cream of green pea soup

1 small onion, skinned and chopped
25 g *(1 oz)* butter
400 ml *(¾ pt)* white stock
900 g *(2 lb)* peas, shelled, or about 450 g *(1 lb)* frozen peas
600 ml *(1 pt)* béchamel sauce (pouring consistency), see page 196
30 ml *(2 tbsps)* cream
a pinch of sugar
salt and pepper

Lightly fry the onion in the butter for about 5 minutes, until soft but not coloured. Add the stock, bring to the boil, add the peas (saving a few for garnish – cook separately), cover and cook until soft – 20–30 minutes for shelled peas, or as directed on the packet for frozen. Sieve the soup or purée it in an electric blender, add it to the béchamel sauce and heat through. Stir in the cream and sugar and adjust the seasoning. Serve garnished with the remaining peas.

A sprig of mint can be added to the peas while they are cooking or a little freshly chopped mint can be used as a garnish; or use frozen minted peas.

Cream of mushroom soup

225 g *(½ lb)* mushrooms, sliced
1 small onion, skinned and sliced
300 ml *(½ pt)* white stock
25 g *(1 oz)* butter
45 ml *(3 level tbsps)* flour
400 ml *(¾ pt)* milk
salt and pepper
45 ml *(3 tbsps)* cream

Cook the mushrooms and onion in the stock, covered, for about ½ hour; sieve or purée them in an electric blender. Melt the butter, stir in the flour and cook for 2–3 minutes. Remove the pan from the heat and gradually stir in the milk; bring to the boil and continue to stir until it thickens. Add the mushroom purée and seasoning and simmer for 15 minutes. Allow to cool slightly and stir in the cream. Re-heat without boiling and if you wish, serve it with a garnish of lightly fried sliced mushrooms.

Cream of onion soup

700 g *(1½ lb)* onions, skinned and sliced
25 g *(1 oz)* butter or margarine
900 ml *(1½ pt)* white stock
bouquet garni
45 ml *(3 level tbsps)* flour
150 ml *(¼ pt)* milk
salt and pepper
45–60 ml *(3–4 tbsps)* cream

Lightly fry the onions in the butter for about 5 minutes, until soft but not coloured. Add the stock and bouquet garni, cover, bring to the boil and simmer for about 45 minutes, until the onions are cooked. Remove the bouquet garni. Sieve the soup or purée it in an electric blender, return it to the saucepan and re-heat. Blend the flour and milk to a smooth cream, stir in a little of the hot soup and return the mixture to the pan: season, bring to the boil, stirring until it thickens, and cook for a further 2–3 minutes. Stir in the cream just before serving.

Note For brown onion soup, use brown (beef) stock and brown the onions very slowly in the fat for about 20 minutes before adding the stock.

Cream of pumpkin soup

2 small onions, skinned and sliced
1 pumpkin, weight about 1.4 kg *(3 lb)*, peeled, seeded and chopped
50 g *(2 oz)* butter
600 ml *(1 pt)* white stock
45 ml *(3 level tbsps)* flour
568 ml *(1 pt)* milk
salt and pepper
little grated cheese
45 ml *(3 tbsps)* cream
chopped parsley to garnish

Lightly fry the onions and pumpkin in the butter for about 5 minutes, do not colour. Add the stock, cover and simmer for about 1 hour, or until the vegetables are soft. Sieve or purée the soup in an electric blender and return it to the pan. Blend the flour with a little of the milk to a smooth cream. Add the rest of the milk to the soup and re-heat. Stir a little of the soup into the blended flour and milk and return this mixture to the pan; bring to the boil, stirring until it thickens, and cook for a further 2–3 minutes. Season, stir in the cheese and cream and sprinkle with parsley before serving.

Cream of tomato soup

1 stick of celery, scrubbed and chopped
1 carrot, pared and sliced
1 small onion, skinned and chopped
1 rasher of bacon, rinded and chopped
25 g *(1 oz)* butter
30 ml *(2 level tbsps)* flour
700 g *(1½ lb)* tomatoes, quartered
600 ml *(1 pt)* white or brown stock
bouquet garni
salt, pepper and a pinch of sugar
30 ml *(2 tbsps)* cream
chopped chervil, basil or parsley to garnish

Lightly fry the celery, carrot, onion and bacon in the butter for 5 minutes, until soft but not coloured. Sprinkle in the flour and stir. Add the quartered tomatoes, stock and bouquet garni, cover and cook gently for about 30 minutes, until soft. Remove the bouquet garni and sieve the soup or purée it in an electric blender and sieve to remove the seeds. Return it to the pan with the seasonings, add the cream and re-heat, but don't let it boil. Garnish with freshly chopped chervil or basil, when in season – otherwise use chopped parsley.

If the tomatoes lack flavour, add a little tomato paste. Canned tomatoes can be used to replace the fresh ones; drain off the liquor and make it up to 600 ml *(1 pt)* with stock. When fresh celery is not available, use a few flakes of dried celery.

Watercress soup *see colour plate facing p. 33*

100 g *(4 oz)* butter
50 g *(2 oz)* plain flour
750 ml *(1¼ pt)* chicken or veal stock
300 ml *(½ pt)* milk
salt and freshly ground black pepper
75 g *(3 oz)* onions, skinned and chopped
2 bunches watercress

Melt 75 g *(3 oz)* of the butter in a pan and stir in the flour. Cook over a gentle heat for 1–2 minutes, stirring. Remove from the heat and stir in the stock and milk. Return to the heat and bring to the boil, stirring continuously. Simmer gently for 3 minutes. Season with salt and pepper. Sauté the onion in the remaining 25 g *(1 oz)* butter until soft. Wash and trim the watercress, leaving some of the stem, then roughly chop it and add it to the onion. Cover with a lid and sauté for a further 4 minutes. Stir the sauté vegetables into the sauce, sieve or purée in an electric blender, then adjust seasoning and re-heat.

Avocado soup *see colour plate facing p. 65*

25 g *(1 oz)* butter
25 g *(1 oz)* flour
150 ml *(¼ pt)* milk
900 ml *(1½ pt)* chicken stock
1.25 ml *(¼ level tsp)* salt
freshly ground black pepper
1 small green pepper, seeded and chopped
1 ripe avocado
chopped parsley or snipped chives for garnish

Melt the butter, stir in the flour and cook gently over a low heat for about 3 minutes, without browning. Remove from the heat and add the milk, beating. Gradually add the stock, stirring, along with the salt, pepper and green pepper. Simmer, covered, for 15 minutes. Halve, stone and peel the avocado. Mash the flesh to a smooth cream. Blend some of the thickened stock with the avocado and stir back into the pan. Simmer the soup for a few minutes but do not boil it. Strain to remove the green pepper. Serve garnished with parsley or chives.

Cream of lemon soup

25 g *(1 oz)* butter or margarine
100 g *(4 oz)* onions, skinned and sliced
100 g *(4 oz)* carrots, pared and sliced
1 l *(1¾ pt)* turkey or chicken stock
1 large lemon
1 bouquet garni
15 ml *(1 level tbsp)* arrowroot
salt and freshly ground black pepper
142-ml *(5-fl oz)* carton single cream

Melt the butter in a large saucepan. Add the sliced vegetables and cook gently until tender, stirring frequently. Pour over the stock, bring to the boil, reduce the heat and simmer. Using a vegetable peeler, thinly pare the rind from the lemon. Pour boiling water over the rind and leave for 1 minute; drain. Add the rind, juice of the lemon and bouquet garni to the pan contents. Cover and cook for 1 hour or until the vegetables are really soft. Remove the bouquet garni. Purée the soup a little at a time in an electric blender. In a clean pan, blend the arrowroot with a little of the soup then add the remainder, stirring. Bring to the boil, stirring. Adjust seasoning before adding the cream. Reheat but do not boil.

MEAT SOUPS

Kidney soup with dumplings

225 g *(½ lb)* ox kidney
seasoned flour
1 onion, skinned and finely chopped
40 g *(1½ oz)* dripping
1.1 l *(2 pt)* brown stock
small bouquet garni
30 ml *(2 level tbsps)* flour
gravy browning, optional
herb dumplings, see page 57

Skin the kidney, wiping it if necessary. Cut it in half, discarding the fatty core, and toss in seasoned flour. Fry the prepared kidney and onion in the dripping for 5 minutes, or until lightly browned. Chop the kidney finely, return it to the pan and pour in the stock gradually, stirring well. Add the herbs, cover and simmer for 1½ hours, skimming and stirring occasionally. When the kidney is tender, blend the flour to a smooth cream with a little water. Stir in a little of the hot soup and add the mixture to the pan. Colour it if you wish with a little gravy browning. Re-boil, stirring, until the soup thickens. Add the dumplings and cook for a further 15–20 minutes, until the dumplings are cooked.

Scotch broth

700 g *(1½ lb)* neck of mutton or shin of beef
2.3 l *(4 pt)* water
salt and pepper
1 carrot and 1 turnip, peeled and chopped
1 onion, skinned and chopped or diced
2 leeks, thinly sliced and washed
45 ml *(3 level tbsps)* pearl barley
15 ml *(1 tbsp)* finely chopped parsley

Cut up the meat and remove any fat, put it in a pan, cover with the water, add some salt and pepper, bring slowly to boiling point, cover and simmer for 1½ hours. Add the vegetables and the barley. Cover and simmer for about 1 hour until the vegetables and barley are soft. Remove any fat on the surface with a spoon or with kitchen paper and serve the soup garnished with parsley.

Traditionally, the meat is served with a little of the broth and the remaining broth is served separately.

Oxtail soup

1 oxtail, jointed
25 g *(1 oz)* butter
2 onions, skinned and chopped
1 carrot, pared and sliced
2 sticks of celery, trimmed and sliced
2 l *(3½ pt)* brown stock
25 g *(1 oz)* lean ham or bacon, chopped
bouquet garni
salt and pepper
45 ml *(3 level tbsps)* flour
a little port, optional
a squeeze of lemon juice

Wash and dry the oxtail and trim off any excess fat. Fry the pieces of oxtail in the butter with the vegetables for 5 minutes, until evenly browned. Just cover with the stock and bring to the boil. Add the chopped ham or bacon, bouquet garni and seasoning. Cover the saucepan and simmer gently for about 4 hours, or until the tail meat is tender. As oxtail is very fatty, it is necessary to skim the soup occasionally with a metal spoon. Strain the soup, remove the meat from the bones and cut it up neatly. Return the meat and strained liquor to the pan and re-heat. Blend the flour and a little water or port to a smooth cream. Stir in a little of the hot liquid and add the mixture to the pan. Bring to the boil, stirring until it thickens, and cook for about 5 minutes. Add a squeeze of lemon juice and seasoning to taste before serving.

This 'hearty' soup can be made into a meal in itself by adding some small dumplings (see recipe page 57), putting them in 20 minutes before the end of the cooking time.

Pot-au-feu

1 kg *(2¼ lb)* lean beef (brisket, flank or topside)
3 l *(5¼ pt)* water
salt and pepper
1 carrot, pared and quartered
1 turnip, peeled and quartered
1 onion, skinned and quartered
1 parsnip, peeled and quartered
2 small leeks, quartered and washed
2 stalks of celery, trimmed and quartered
1 small cabbage, washed and halved
bouquet garni
30 ml *(2 level tbsps)* seed pearl tapioca

Tie the meat securely to keep it in one piece, put into a large saucepan, add the water and 10 ml *(2 level tsps)* salt, cover and simmer for 2 hours. Add the vegetables (except the cabbage) and the bouquet garni and cook for another 2 hours. Put the cabbage into the pan and continue cooking for a final ½ hour, or until it is soft. Strain off most of the liquid, put into a pan, bring to the boil, sprinkle in the tapioca and simmer for about 15 minutes, or until the tapioca clears. The meat can be served separately, with the vegetables and any remaining cooking liquid. Adjust seasoning before serving.

Chicken broth

1 small boiling chicken
2 l *(3½ pt)* cold water
10 ml *(2 level tsps)* salt
1.25 ml *(¼ level tsp)* pepper
1 onion, skinned and halved
50 g *(2 oz)* each carrot and celery, diced
30 ml *(2 level tbsps)* long grain rice
chopped parsley

Wash the bird, cut it in half, put it into a large pan, cover with water and add the seasoning and vegetables. Bring to the boil, cover and simmer for 3–3½ hours, adding more water if necessary. Strain, then remove any grease from the top of the broth with a metal spoon or by drawing a piece of kitchen paper across the surface of the liquid. Return the broth to the pan, bring to the boil, sprinkle in the rice and simmer for 15–20 minutes, until the rice is soft. Serve sprinkled with chopped parsley. Some of the meat can be finely chopped and added to the broth, the rest being used in made-up dishes (eg fricassee).

The broth can also be made with a chicken or turkey carcass instead of a whole chicken, when it will need to be simmered for about 2 hours.

Cock-a-leekie

1 boiling fowl – about 1 kg *(2¼ lb)*
1 l *(1¾ pt)* stock or water
4 leeks, cleaned and sliced
salt and pepper
6 prunes, optional

Cover the fowl with stock or water and add the leeks and seasoning. Bring to the boil, cover and simmer for 3½ hours, until tender. Remove the chicken from the stock, carve off the meat and cut it into fairly large pieces. Serve the soup with the chicken pieces in it, or serve the soup on its own, with the chicken as a main course.

If prunes are used, soak them overnight in cold water, halve and stone them and add to the stock 30 minutes before the end of the cooking.

Lentil and bacon soup *see colour plate facing p. 33*

175 g *(6 oz)* lentils
1.4 l *(2½ pt)* stock
1 clove garlic, skinned and crushed
1 clove
salt and pepper
200 g *(7 oz)* lean bacon rashers, rinded and diced
226 *(8 oz)* can tomatoes
100 g *(4 oz)* onions, skinned and chopped
450 g *(1 lb)* potatoes, peeled and diced
30 ml *(2 tbsps)* lemon juice

For garnish
crisply fried bacon rolls, chopped parsley, grated cheese or croûtons

Wash the lentils and put them in a saucepan with the stock. Add the garlic, clove, salt, pepper, bacon, tomatoes and onion. Bring to the boil, cover and simmer for about 1 hour, until the lentils and bacon are soft. Add the potatoes and cook for a further 20 minutes. Remove the clove, pour the soup into a sieve or electric blender and purée it until smooth. Add the lemon juice and re-heat to serving temperature.

VEGETABLE SOUPS

(See also Cream Soups)

Chunky courgette soup

100 g *(4 oz)* haricot beans
salt
350 g *(12 oz)* potatoes
225 g *(8 oz)* courgettes, trimmed
350 g *(12 oz)* leeks, washed
1 clove garlic, skinned and crushed
30 ml *(2 tbsps)* oil
50 g *(2 oz)* butter
1.1 l *(2 pt)* chicken or veal stock
freshly ground black pepper
2.5 ml *(½ level tsp)* dried basil
100 g *(4 oz)* Cheddar cheese, grated
chopped parsley

Soak the beans overnight in water. Next day drain and place the beans in a saucepan, cover with salted fresh water and simmer, covered, for 1½ hours. Drain. Peel and dice the potatoes, slice the courgettes into chunky slices about 0.5 cm *(¼ in)* thick. Chop the leeks finely. Combine the garlic with the leeks. Heat the oil and fry the potato first for 2–3 minutes. Drain, using a slotted spoon, and put them in a large saucepan. Sauté the leeks for about 5 minutes, stirring frequently, drain and add to the potato. Lastly melt the butter, add the courgettes and cook for about 5 minutes. Add to the pan with the beans. Pour over the stock, add seasoning and basil.

Simmer, covered for 1½ hours, until the vegetables are tender. Sprinkle cheese over the soup during the last 15 minutes of cooking. Check seasoning. Garnish with chopped parsley.

Split pea soup

225 g *(½ lb)* dried green split peas
1.7 l *(3 pt)* water
2 pig's trotters, split
1 marrow bone
salt and pepper
225 g *(½ lb)* peeled potatoes, sliced
3 leeks, sliced and washed
3 sticks green celery, sliced
celery leaves, chopped
chopped parsley
about 175 g *(6 oz)* Frankfurter sausage

Wash the peas and soak in 900 ml *(1½ pt)* water overnight. In a covered pan simmer the trotters and chopped marrow bone in the remaining measured water for 1 hour. Add the peas and soaking water. Continue to cook until the peas are soft – about 1 hour more. Season well.

Add the sliced potatoes, leeks, including green part, and celery 40 minutes before the end of the cooking time.

Remove the marrow bone and trotters, scrape out the meat and put it back into the soup. Thin the soup if necessary with a little extra stock. Adjust the seasoning and stir in the chopped celery leaves and parsley, along with sliced sausage as required. Reheat to serve. This nourishing meat soup is served with hunks of crisp French bread.

Minestrone

½ leek, shredded and washed
1 onion, skinned and finely chopped
1 clove garlic, skinned and crushed
25 g *(1 oz)* butter
1 l *(1¾ pt)* white stock
1 carrot, pared and cut in thin strips
1 turnip, peeled and cut in thin strips
1 stick of celery, trimmed and thinly sliced
45 ml *(3 tbsps)* shortcut macaroni
¼ cabbage, washed and finely shredded
3 runner beans, thinly sliced
45 ml *(3 tbsps)* fresh or frozen peas
5 ml *(1 level tsp)* tomato paste or 4 tomatoes, skinned and diced
1–2 rashers of bacon, rinded, chopped and fried
salt and pepper
grated Parmesan cheese

Lightly fry the leek, onion and garlic in the melted butter for 5–10 minutes, until soft. Add the stock, bring to the boil, add the carrot, turnip, celery and macaroni and simmer, covered, for 20–30 minutes. Add the cabbage, beans and peas, cover and simmer for a further 20 minutes. Stir in the tomato paste or tomatoes, bacon and seasoning to taste. Bring back to the boil. Serve the grated Parmesan cheese in a separate dish.

Winter hotchpotch

225 g *(8 oz)* Jerusalem artichokes
450 g *(1 lb)* carrots, pared
225 g *(8 oz)* turnips, peeled
2 onions, skinned, or 2 leeks, cleaned
2–3 sticks of celery, trimmed
½ small cabbage, washed
1 rasher of bacon, rinded and chopped
75 g *(3 oz)* dripping or butter
bouquet garni
brown stock or water
salt and pepper
100 g *(4 oz)* macaroni, in small pieces
chopped parsley
grated cheese

Peel the artichokes, cut them into slices and then strips and keep in water to which 10 ml *(2 tsps)* lemon juice has been added to prevent discoloration. Cut the rest of the vegetables (except the cabbage) into fairly small pieces. Coarsely shred the cabbage. Fry the bacon lightly, add the fat and when it is melted, fry the vegetables (except the cabbage) for about 10 minutes, until soft but not coloured. Add the bouquet garni and enough stock or water to cover. Season well, cover and simmer for ¾–1 hour. Add the cabbage and macaroni and cook for a further 20–30 minutes, adding more liquid as required. When all the ingredients are soft, remove the bouquet garni and re-season if necessary. Serve sprinkled with freshly chopped parsley and grated cheese.

If preferred, the cabbage can be shredded and added just before serving, instead of being cooked in the soup; this gives a pleasant crispness.

Golden vegetable soup

175 g *(6 oz)* potatoes
175 g *(6 oz)* turnips
175 g *(6 oz)* carrots
175 g *(6 oz)* onion
175 g *(6 oz)* celery
900 ml *(1½ pt)* unseasoned bone or chicken stock
salt and freshly ground black pepper
bouquet garni
25 g *(1 oz)* butter or margarine
Parmesan cheese, celery leaves for garnish

Peel the potatoes, turnips and carrots. Skin the onions and finely chop, finely slice the celery. Grate the potatoes, turnips and carrots into a large pan, add the onion, celery and stock together with 5 ml *(1 level tsp)* salt, pepper and a bouquet garni. Bring to the boil, reduce the heat, cover and simmer for about 1 hour. Adjust the seasoning, add the butter and when melted serve the soup with a dusting of grated Parmesan cheese and snipped celery leaves.

SPECIAL SOUPS

French onion soup

225 g (*½ lb*) onions, skinned and sliced
50 g (*2 oz*) butter
30 ml (*2 level tbsps*) flour
900 ml (*1½ pt*) brown stock
salt and pepper
bayleaf
slices of French bread
grated Gruyère cheese

Fry the onions in the butter for 5–10 minutes, until browned. Stir in the flour, mixing well. Pour in the stock gradually, season, add the bayleaf, bring to the boil and simmer in a covered pan for 30 minutes. Remove the bayleaf. Put a slice of bread into each individual soup bowl, pour on the soup and top with cheese. Alternatively, put all the soup into a flameproof casserole, float the slices of bread on it, cover with grated cheese and put under the grill or in a hot oven until the cheese is melted and bubbling.

Note Gruyère is the cheese traditionally used in this soup. Cheddar could be used as an alternative.

Canadian cheese soup

225 g (*½ lb*) potatoes, peeled
225 g (*½ lb*) onions, skinned
50 g (*2 oz*) carrots, pared
50 g (*2 oz*) celery, diced
300 ml (*½ pt*) water
600 ml (*1 pt*) rich turkey or chicken stock
100 g (*4 oz*) mature Cheddar cheese
45 ml (*3 tbsps*) single cream
salt and pepper
30 ml (*2 tbsps*) chopped parsley

Finely slice or dice the potatoes, onion and carrot. Place in a saucepan with the celery and water. Bring to the boil, reduce the heat, cover and simmer for about 20 minutes until the vegetables are tender. Add the rest of the ingredients except the parsley and reheat without boiling. Adjust seasoning, sprinkle in the parsley and serve.

Almond soup

30 ml (*2 tbsps*) olive oil
100 g (*4 oz*) blanched almonds, finely chopped
15 ml (*1 level tbsp*) chopped onion
2.5 ml (*½ level tsp*) crushed garlic
5 ml (*1 tsp*) chopped parsley
105 ml (*7 level tbsps*) fresh white breadcrumbs
1.1 l (*2 pt*) chicken stock
salt and pepper

Heat the oil and slowly cook the almonds, onion, garlic and parsley, stirring all the time. Do not brown. Stir in the breadcrumbs and cook slowly for a further 3 minutes. Pour on the stock, season, cover and simmer for 15 minutes.

Cream of curry soup *see colour plate facing p. 33*

30 ml (*2 level tbsps*) ground almonds
30 ml (*2 level tbsps*) desiccated coconut
150 ml (*¼ pt*) boiling water
1 medium sized onion, skinned and chopped
50 g (*2 oz*) butter
45 ml (*3 level tbsps*) flour
15 ml (*1 level tbsp*) curry paste
1 l (*1¾ pt*) stock
50 g (*2 oz*) seedless raisins
strip of lemon rind
bayleaf
15 ml (*1 level tbsp*) cornflour
1 small apple, peeled, cored and sliced
50 ml (*2 fl oz*) double cream

Soak the ground almonds and the coconut for 30 minutes in the boiling water, drain and reserve the liquor. Lightly fry the onion in 25 g (*1 oz*) butter until soft but not browned. Stir in the flour and curry paste and cook for 1 minute. Stir in the stock, raisins, lemon rind and bayleaf, bring to the boil, cover and simmer for 20 minutes.

At the end of the cooking time, remove the bayleaf and lemon rind and stir in the liquor from the nuts and the cornflour, blended with water to a cream. Bring to the boil and allow to thicken. Meanwhile fry the apple slices in the remaining butter. Finally, just before serving, stir in the double cream. Serve garnished with the fried apple slices.

Bortsch

6 small raw beetroot (about 1 kg, *2¼ lb*), peeled
2 medium sized onions, skinned and chopped
2.2 l *(4 pt)* seasoned beef stock
30 ml *(2 tbsps)* lemon juice
90 ml *(6 tbsps)* dry sherry
seasoning
soured cream, chives (optional)

Grate the beetroot coarsely and put it together with the onion in a pan with the stock. Bring to the boil and simmer without a lid for 45 minutes. Strain and add the lemon juice and sherry. Adjust seasoning. Serve either chilled well or hot with a whirl of soured cream and chopped chives.

Fifteen-minute bortsch

283-g *(10-oz)* can sliced beetroot (this should not be in vinegar)
425-g *(15-oz)* can consommé
lemon juice
salt and pepper
soured cream

Drain the beetroot and put it in an electric blender, with the consommé. Blend until smooth, then pour it into a saucepan. Sharpen the flavour with lemon juice and season well. Bring to the boil and serve hot, with a spoonful of soured cream in each soup cup.

Cauliflower and bacon soup

100 g *(4 oz)* butter
1 onion, skinned and finely chopped
2 carrots, pared and finely diced
2 potatoes, peeled and finely diced
225 g *(8 oz)* cauliflower, in florets
2 sticks celery, finely diced
900 ml *(1½ pt)* chicken stock
salt
ground black pepper
4 rashers lean bacon
4 small slices white bread
100 g *(4 oz)* Gouda cheese

Melt 50 g *(2 oz)* butter in a large pan and gently fry all the vegetables for 5 minutes. Add the stock, bring to the boil and cover, simmer for 20 minutes; season. Melt the remaining 50 g *(2 oz)* butter. Remove the rind from the bacon, roughly chop it and fry gently for 4–6 minutes. Drain well before adding to the soup. Fry the bread in the pan until crisp and golden. Drain well on kitchen paper. Place the soup in a flameproof tureen or casserole and arrange the bread to float on top. Cover the bread with sliced cheese and grill until the cheese melts and browns slightly. Serve immediately.

German potato soup

700 g *(1½ lb)* potatoes
75 g *(3 oz)* carrots
1 stick celery
1 leek
100 g *(4 oz)* onion
100 g *(4 oz)* smoked bacon, rinded and diced
1.1 l *(2½ pt)* water
5 ml *(1 level tsp)* salt
freshly ground black pepper
2.5 ml *(½ level tsp)* dried marjoram
2.5 ml *(½ level tsp)* dried fines herbes
1 sprig parsley with stem
5 ml *(1 tsp)* chopped parsley
100 g *(4 oz)* German sausage, chopped
croûtons

Prepare the vegetables and cut them neatly into dice or slices. In a saucepan, fry the bacon over a low heat to extract the fat. Add the vegetables and sauté for 2–3 minutes. Cover with water. Season with salt, pepper, marjoram and *fines herbes*. Bring to the boil, add the parsley sprig, cover then simmer until all the vegetables are well cooked – about 45 minutes. Using a sieve or electric blender, purée the soup. Add the chopped parsley and German sausage. Reheat in a clean pan to serving temperature and garnish with croûtons. Alternatively omit the chopped sausage and serve alongside German smoked sausages and mustard.

FISH SOUPS AND CHOWDERS

Fish chowder

1 onion, skinned and sliced
2 rashers of bacon, rinded and chopped
knob of butter
3 potatoes, peeled and sliced
450 g *(1 lb)* fresh haddock, skinned and cubed
425-g *(15-oz)* can tomatoes
600 ml *(1 pt)* fish stock
salt and pepper
1 bayleaf
2 cloves
chopped parsley to garnish

Lightly fry the onion and bacon in the butter for about 5 minutes, until soft but not coloured. Add the potatoes and the fish. Sieve the tomatoes with their juice, add them to the fish stock, combine with the fish mixture and add seasoning and flavourings. Cover and simmer for ½ hour, until all the fish is soft but still in shape. Remove the bayleaf and cloves and sprinkle with parsley before serving.

Curried cod chowder

700 g *(1½ lb)* cod fillet or any white fish
900 ml *(1½ pt)* cold water
salt and freshly ground black pepper
225 g *(8 oz)* potatoes, peeled
50 g *(2 oz)* butter
175 g *(6 oz)* onions, skinned and chopped
175 g *(6 oz)* celery, trimmed and chopped
2.5 ml *(½ level tsp)* mild curry powder
45 ml *(3 level tbsps)* flour
300 ml *(½ pt)* creamy milk
chopped parsley and chives

Wipe the fish with a damp cloth. Put it in the base of a large saucepan. Pour cold water over and season it. Bring it almost to the boil, remove from the heat and skim off the surface froth; carefully lift the fish, using a fish slice, on to a plate. Remove the skin and bones and flake the fish into bite-sized portions. Leave to one side. Strain and reserve the fish stock. Cut the potato into small dice and bring them to the boil in salted water. Cook until tender, drain and reserve.

Melt the butter in a large flameproof casserole. Stir in the onions and celery. Cook slowly until soft but not brown. Add the curry powder and flour. Gradually blend in the fish stock and milk. Bring to the boil and cook for 2–3 minutes. Reduce the heat to a simmer before adding the potatoes and fish, check the seasoning. Garnish with chopped parsley and chives. Serve with warm French bread.

Bouillabaisse

900 g *(2 lb)* mixed fish: eg John Dory, red mullet, whiting, mackerel, rock salmon, gurnet, bass, crawfish or lobster, crab, prawns, eel or conger eel
2–3 onions, skinned and sliced
1 stick celery, trimmed and chopped
150 ml *(¼ pt)* olive oil
225 g *(½ lb)* tomatoes, skinned and sliced
2 cloves garlic, skinned and crushed
1 bayleaf
pinch of dried thyme and fennel (if available)
few sprigs of parsley
finely shredded rind of ½ an orange
salt and pepper
pinch of saffron (if available)
French bread

This is a traditional dish from the South of France. The authentic version is made from at least 8 different types of fish, many of which are available only along the Mediterranean coasts. However, any variety of white and shell fish can be used to give quite a good imitation. The French themselves differ about the traditional recipe and indeed get quite heated about it!

Have the fish cleaned, skinned and cut in fairly thick pieces; have the shell fish removed from the shells. Lightly fry the onions and celery in the oil for about 5 minutes, until soft but not coloured. Stir in the tomatoes, garlic, herbs, orange rind and seasoning. Put all the firmer-fleshed fish in a layer over the vegetables, just cover with water (in which the saffron has been dissolved, if used), bring to the boil and boil for about 8 minutes. Add the softer-fleshed fish and continue cooking for a further 5–8 minutes, until all the ingredients are cooked but still in shape.

The bouillabaisse can be served as a complete dish, or the cooking liquid can be strained off and served in individual bowls containing a slice of French bread – the fish is then served separately.

In some areas sliced potatoes are included in the bed of vegetables; the cooking liquid is sometimes enriched with 2 egg yolks and 45–60 ml *(3–4 tbsps)* cream, blended together and added just before serving.

Lobster bisque

1 cooked hen lobster
1 l *(1¾ pt)* fish stock or water
1 small carrot, pared and sliced
1 small onion, skinned and sliced
1 bayleaf
sprig of parsley
salt and pepper
25 g *(1 oz)* butter
45 ml *(3 level tbsps)* flour
squeeze of lemon juice
little cream
½ glass white wine
lobster butter

Scrub the shell thoroughly. Remove the lobster meat from the shell and cut it into neat pieces, reserving the coral for lobster butter (see below). Break up the shell and cook it, covered, with the stock, vegetables, herbs and seasoning for ¾–1 hour, then strain off the liquid. Melt the butter, stir in the flour and cook for 2–3 minutes. Remove the pan from the heat and gradually stir in the lobster stock, bring to the boil and continue to stir until it thickens; cook for a further 3 minutes. Add the lemon juice, cream and wine. Re-season if necessary. Add the pieces of lobster meat and whisk in the lobster butter.

Lobster butter
Remove the coral from a cooked lobster, wash and dry it in a cool oven, without allowing it to change colour. Pound it in a mortar with double its weight in butter, season to taste and rub it through a fine nylon sieve.

Shrimp or prawn chowder

1 large onion, skinned and sliced
knob of butter
200 ml *(7 fl oz)* boiling water
3 medium sized potatoes, peeled and diced
salt and pepper
198-g *(7-oz)* can peeled shrimps or prawns, drained weight 113 g *(4 oz)*
568 ml *(1 pt)* milk
50 g *(2 oz)* cheese, grated
15 ml *(1 tbsp)* chopped parsley

Lightly fry the onion in the butter for about 5 minutes, until soft but not coloured. Add the boiling water, potatoes and seasoning. Cover and simmer gently for 15–20 minutes, or until the potatoes are just cooked. Add the shrimps and the milk and re-heat. Stir in the grated cheese and parsley and serve with crusty bread or toast.

CHILLED SOUPS

Chilled cucumber soup

1 small onion, skinned and sliced
900 ml *(1½ pt)* white stock
1 large cucumber, peeled and roughly chopped
sprig of mint
15 ml *(1 level tbsp)* cornflour
45 ml *(3 tbsps)* cream
salt and pepper
edible green colouring

Simmer the onion for 15 minutes in a pan with the stock. Add the cucumber (saving a little for garnish) and mint; cover, simmer for about 20 minutes or until the cucumber is cooked. Sieve the soup or purée it in an electric blender, return it to the pan and re-heat. Blend the cornflour with a little cold water to a smooth cream. Stir in a little of the hot soup, add the mixture to the pan and bring to the boil, stirring until it thickens. Cook for a further 2–3 minutes. Stir in the cream and adjust the seasoning. Tint the soup delicately with green colouring, pour it into a large bowl, cover and chill. Serve sprinkled with small cucumber dice or shredded mint.

Chilled asparagus soup

Follow the recipe for cream of asparagus soup on page 45, but after sieving the cooked soup, pour it into a large bowl, cover and chill. Before serving, stir in the remaining milk and the cream and garnish with the asparagus tips.

Crème vichyssoise

4 leeks, cleaned and sliced
1 onion, skinned and sliced
50 g *(2 oz)* butter
1 l *(1¾ pt)* white stock
2 potatoes, peeled and thinly sliced
salt and pepper
200 ml *(7 fl oz)* cream
chopped chives to garnish

Lightly fry the leeks and onion in the butter for about 10 minutes, until soft but not coloured. Add the stock and potatoes. Season, cover and cook until the vegetables are soft. Sieve the soup or purée it in an electric blender, stir in the cream, with more seasoning if necessary, and chill. Sprinkle with chives before serving.

Gazpacho *see colour plate facing p. 64*

1 medium cucumber
450 g *(1 lb)* fully ripened tomatoes
100 g *(4 oz)* green pepper, seeded
50–100 g *(2–4 oz)* onions, skinned
1 clove garlic, skinned
45 ml *(3 tbsps)* oil
45 ml *(3 tbsps)* wine vinegar
425-g *(15-oz)* can tomato juice
30 ml *(2 level tbsps)* tomato paste
1.25 ml *(¼ level tsp)* salt

Wash and roughly chop the cucumber, tomatoes, pepper, onion and garlic. Mix all the ingredients together in a basin. Purée them in an electric blender in small portions. Return the purée to the bowl and add a few ice cubes. Serve the soup with very finely diced green pepper, and croûtons.

Jellied consommé

Jellied consommé is a good soup for summer days. Use the 'classic' recipe given on page 43 and leave the soup to cool and set. Serve it broken up, in individual dishes. It can also be made from the quick recipe if 15 ml *(1 level tbsp)* powdered gelatine is dissolved in a little water and added to each 1.1 l *(2 pt)* soup before it is chilled.

Variations

1. Add 30–45 ml *(2–3 tbsps)* chopped herbs (chives, parsley and tarragon) to 1.1 l *(2 pt)* consommé. Garnish with whipped cream which has been flavoured with curry powder or sprinkled with toasted almonds.
2. Add 30–45 ml *(2–3 tbsps)* chopped mint leaves to 1.1 l *(2 pt)* consommé. Garnish with whipped cream mixed with chopped mint.

CANNED AND PACKET SOUP VARIATIONS

An interesting soup can be quickly made by combining two cans or packets of soup or adding other ingredients.

Oxtail and tomato

Use a can of each and add lemon juice or sherry to taste; serve with grated cheese or toast.

Pea and asparagus

Use a can of each soup and serve sprinkled with 45 ml *(3 tbsps)* chopped shelled shrimps.

Pea and tomato

Use a can of each. Grill 4 bacon rashers till crisp, chop them (alternatively, mince 50 g *(2 oz)* cooked ham), and sprinkle over the soup before serving.

Celery and mushroom

Use a can of each soup. Serve garnished with soured cream and sprinkled with chopped chives or with about 25 g *(1 oz)* sliced and lightly fried mushrooms.

Quick minestrone
Mix a can of vegetable beef broth with one of tomato soup. Add 25 g *(1 oz)* short-cut macaroni and simmer for about 15 minutes, until it is cooked. Serve sprinkled with grated Parmesan cheese.

Chicken and almond
Fry 15 ml *(1 tbsp)* each of finely chopped onion, parsley and blanched almonds in a knob of butter for 5 minutes. Add a can of cream of chicken soup and simmer for 10 minutes.

SOUP ACCOMPANIMENTS AND GARNISHES

Certain soups have a recognised accompaniment or garnish, but with the others you can ring the changes on a variety of simple and more elaborate finishing touches. Some of them, like dumplings, also give more 'body', turning the soup into a main course.

Mushrooms Slice thinly and lightly fry in a little butter for 3–5 minutes, until soft but not coloured.

Onions Fried onion rings give a good flavour. Cut them thinly, dip in egg white or milk and fry until golden brown and crisp in a little dripping, bacon fat or butter; add to the soup just before serving.

Leek Fried chopped leek adds flavour to potato soup.

Cucumber Slice very finely and serve with soup of any flavour, but especially with chicken.

Bacon Rind some lean rashers, cut into small strips or dice and fry lightly. These are most suitable for thick soups. Alternatively, grill the bacon until just crisp, crumble roughly and sprinkle over the soup.

Sausages and sausage meat Left-over cooked sausages go well with vegetable soups such as spinach. Cut in rounds and heat in the soup. Make sausage meat into small balls and cook in the soup for 20 minutes.

Melba toast Traditionally this is made by toasting 0.5-cm *(¼-in)* slices of bread, splitting them through the middle and toasting the uncooked surfaces. Ready cut thin-sliced bread is ideal.

Alternatively, cut stale bread into very thin slices, lay them on baking sheets and dry off in the bottom of a very slow oven until they are crisp and curled. Before serving, brown them slightly under a very slow grill.

Croûtons Fried: Cut bread into 0.5–1-cm *(¼–½-in)* cubes and fry quickly in lard or oil until crisp and golden.

Toasted: Cut slices of toast into 0.5–1-cm *(¼–½-in)* dice. Serve croûtons separately or sprinkle them over the soup.

Rice Left-over dry boiled rice may be added to soup shortly before it is served, together with freshly chopped parsley or chives. Rice may also be cooked in the actual soup or broth; give it about ¼ hour's cooking.

Macaroni, tagliatelle and spaghetti These are good with minestrone and any thin soup. Break them into short lengths, cook separately for about 15 minutes, drain and add to the soup. Italian soup pasta in the shape of letters, shells, stars and wheels can also be used – add about 10–15 minutes before the soup is served. Allow 25–50 g *(1–2 oz)* pasta to 1.1 l *(2 pt)* of soup.

Noodles Cook them in the soup or separately in boiling water for about 15 minutes.

Celery Pick the leaves from the ends of the centre stems and wash well; serve one or two sprigs in each bowl of soup.

Lemon Thin slices are delicious with many of the clear soups and with tomato soups.

Cheese Freshly grated hard cheese is a pleasant accompaniment to almost any vegetable soup. Grated cheese is usually served separately, but may also be sprinkled on the soup just before it is served. A little of some chopped fresh herb, eg parsley, can be mixed with the cheese for added colour.

Dumplings Either plain or herb-flavoured dumplings may be added to almost any meat or vegetable soup, to make it more substantial. To make herb dumplings, mix 100 g *(4 oz)* self raising flour, 50 g *(2 oz)* shredded or chopped suet, ½ small onion, skinned and finely grated, 2.5 ml *(½ level tsp)* mixed dried herbs, salt and pepper, with sufficient cold water to make an elastic dough. Divide into about 16 portions, roll into small balls, using a little flour, add to the soup and simmer for about 15–20 minutes. For plain dumplings, omit the onion and herbs.

Fish

A common way of grouping fish is into sea and fresh-water types. Another classification, which cuts across these two groups, is into white and oily fish. White fish have a low fat content and characteristic white flesh; familiar examples are cod, haddock, hake, sole, plaice and turbot. Oily fish have a high fat content and their flesh is usually darker; the best known are herring, mackerel, sprat, eel and salmon. Shellfish – lobster, scampi, shrimps and so on – make a separate group. Fish is a good source of protein and the oily fish also supply vitamins A and D.

Sea fish

Anchovies
Small fish which are filleted and cured then packed in either bottles or cans in brine or olive oil. They are used, in small amounts only as they are very salty, in appetisers and cocktail nibblers, as a pizza topping and in salade niçoise. They also make anchovy butter (see page 34) for use in savouries and sandwiches and as a spread for toast.

Bass
In season May to August. Bass is not unlike salmon in shape, but the flesh is very white. Large bass, which have a good flavour, are usually poached or baked; small fish can be grilled or fried.

Bloater
See page 61

Bream (sea)
At its best from June to December. A round, coarse skinned fish with lean, firm, white flesh and a rather delicate flavour. Bream is often stuffed and baked but may also be poached, fried or grilled.

Brill
In season all the year, but at its best from April to August. A flat fish with a good flavour and texture resembling those of turbot. The flesh is firm and slightly yellowish, avoid any with a bluish tinge. It may be poached, served cold with mayonnaise, or cooked like turbot.

Catfish
In season September to February. A round fish, with slightly pink, firm flesh. Decapitated and skinned at port. Best used for soups and stews.

Cod, codling
In season all the year, but at its best from October to May. A large, round fish with close, white flesh, somewhat lacking in flavour, but improved if cooked with herbs, vegetables or a stuffing. Cod can be grilled, baked or fried in batter and may be used in made-up dishes such as fish pie.

Salt cod tends to be uninteresting cooked alone but is good made up with other well flavoured ingredients. Often used in continental recipes. Buy salt cod fillets that are thick and the flesh white; when not fresh salt cod takes on a yellow appearance. To use, soak for 24 hours in cold water, changing the water several times. Drain and remove any skin and bones before cooking.

Coley (Saithe)
Available all the year round. A meaty fish, part of the cod family; takes particularly well to ingredients with robust flavours; added moisture overcomes its tendency to dryness. Its greyish flesh turns whiter during cooking.

Conger eel
At its best from March to October. The flesh is white and firm, with a good flavour, though coarser and more oily than fresh-water eel. Conger eels are prepared and cooked like the common (fresh-water) eel, and are often used for hors d'oeuvre.

Dab
Small, white fleshed fish of the plaice family, excellent either fried or baked.

Flounder
In season from February to September. Flounders resemble plaice, but have not such a good texture and flavour; cook in the same ways.

Gurnet, gurnard
In season from July to April. A small fish with a large, bony head and firm, white flesh of good flavour. Cook as for haddock.

Haddock
At its best from September to February. A round fish, distinguished from cod by the dark streak which runs down the back and the two black 'thumb marks' above the gills. Haddock has firm, white flesh and may be cooked by any method suitable for white fish; it is useful for made-up dishes.

Hake
In season all the year, but at its best from June to January. Hake is somewhat like cod in shape, but has a closer white flesh and a better flavour; it is cooked like cod.

Halibut
In season all the year, but best from August to April. Halibut is a very large flat fish with an excellent flavour and like turbot is regarded as one of the 'good class' fish. It is usually baked or grilled, but may also be cooked by any recipe suitable for turbot or cod.

Herring
In season all the year, but best from June to December. Fairly small, round, oily fish with creamy coloured flesh of distinctive flavour. Herrings are usually grilled, fried or sautéed. Though they are generally sold whole the fishmonger will fillet them for you on request. Herrings are also sold prepared in various ways, the main ones being listed on page 61

Salt herring is gutted and preserved in wooden casks between layers of salt. Salt herrings are usually sold at delicatessen counters.

Rollmops and bismarcks are boned herrings marinaded in spiced vinegar. Rollmops are rolled with chopped onions, gherkins and peppercorns. Bismarcks are flat fillets covered with finely sliced onion.

Canned herrings are most popular in tomato sauce. Canned kippers and bloaters are available too, as are herring roes.

Huss
This used to be known as rock salmon; it is of the dogfish family and sold skinned. The firm flesh has a tinge of pink. It is especially popular fried but also good matched with strongish flavours and vegetables.

John dory
In season from October to December. An ugly fish, with very large jaws and a body that is nearly oval in shape; it has firm, white flesh with a good flavour. After the head and fins have been removed the fish can be poached or baked whole, but it is more usually filleted and cooked according to any recipe for sole.

Mackerel
In season from October to July, but at its best during April, May and June. A fairly small, round, oily fish rather bigger than a herring, with characteristic blue-black markings on the back, creamy coloured flesh and a distinctive flavour. It can be left whole or filleted and cooked by any method suitable for herrings. Mackerel must be eaten very fresh.

Monk fish
A firm fleshed fish with a texture not unlike lobster; sold in fillets – the head is very ugly – it is excellent fried, baked or poached.

Mullet (grey)
At its best from July to February. This is larger and coarser than red mullet and is suitable for baking, poaching and grilling.

Pilchard
Most pilchards are caught off the coasts of Devon and Cornwall and are sold canned. Fresh pilchards can be grilled or fried whole. A small, round, oily fish.

Plaice
In season all the year round, but best towards the end of May. Plaice has soft, white flesh and a very delicate flavour. You can cook it whole or filleted, by most methods, including steaming, frying, grilling and baking.

Red fish (Norway haddock)
These have a flattened body with bright orange-red skin with dark blotches. Sold whole and filleted, the flesh is lean, firm and of good flavour. Excellent for soup but can be cooked like bream.

Salmon trout
In season from March to August. This resembles salmon, but when cooked has slightly pinker flesh; it has not quite such a good flavour, so is cheaper. Salmon trout is cooked whole and is usually poached or baked; it may be served hot or cold.

Sardine
Sardines are strictly speaking young pilchards, but the name is also applied to the young of other fish (eg, sprats and herrings) which are canned in olive oil or tomato sauce. Fresh sardines can be grilled or fried as for sprats.

Skate
In season from September to April. Only the 'wings' or side parts of this large white fish are eaten. Cook by poaching or frying.

Smelt
In season from June to September. A small round, silvery fish with a delicate flavour. To prepare smelts, make a small cut with scissors just below the gills and gently press out the entrails, then wash the fish well. Leave the heads on. Smelts are usually fried, but larger ones may be baked.

Sole
In season all the year round. The true 'Dover' sole is easily distinguished by its dark, brownish grey back skin from the lemon, witch and Torbay soles. It is considered one of the finest flat fish. The flesh is firm and delicate, with a delicious flavour. The skin of the lemon sole is lighter in colour and its shape is more pointed than that of the Dover sole. The flesh is more stringy and has less flavour. Witch sole has slightly greyish skin but the flesh is similar to that of lemon sole.

Sole can be cooked by most methods, especially, grilling, frying, baking and steaming, and is the basis of many classic fish dishes.

Sprat
In season from November to March. A fairly small, round fish of the same family as the herring. To prepare sprats, wash them and draw them through the gills, as for smelts. Fry or grill.

Sturgeon
In season from August to March, although not usually available in this country. The hard roe of various members of the sturgeon family is known as caviare when salted.

Turbot
In season all the year, but at its best from March to August. Turbot has creamy white flesh with a delicious flavour and is considered to be the finest of the flat fish. It is usually cut in steaks and grilled or baked – very often with wine.

Whitebait
At their best in May, June and July. Very small silvery fish, the fry of various kinds, chiefly herring and sprat. They are fried whole and served as the first course of a meal.

Whiting
In season all the year, but at its best from December to March. A round fish with a delicate flavour. Cook it whole or in fillets, by any of the usual methods.

Fresh-water fish

Carp
In season October to February. A round fish. If small it may be grilled or fried, but when larger it is better stuffed and baked. To counteract the somewhat muddy flavour which the flesh tends to have, soak the fish in salted water for 3–4 hours and rinse well before cooking.

Char
Belongs to the salmon family and has a fine flavour. Cook as for trout.

Fresh water eel
A long, slender fish. The skin is grey-black and the firm white flesh is full flavoured. At its best in the autumn and early winter, the common eel is always sold alive and should be cooked soon after killing. The fishmonger will kill and skin an eel whole. To cook cut into pieces and then braise, casserole, deep-fry or steam.

Grayling
In season when trout are not, like trout they make good eating.

Perch
Should be eaten very fresh. Prepare as carp; treat the dorsal fins with respect as they can wound. To fillet for frying, plunge the fish into boiling water with lemon juice and scrape off the scales first; for poaching, cook first then remove the skin and scales.

Pike
Although on the dry side, pike has an excellent flavour. Those of a similar size to perch are preferable (up to 900 g, *2 lb*) – large pike tend to be tough. The bones are dangerous as they do not dissolve in the stomach. Taint from mud can be removed by soaking in cold water for a few hours but if possible avoid washing too much as the film on the skin helps to tenderise. Cook with care as the flesh breaks up easily; hence its value for making quenelles and stuffings.

Salmon
In season in England and Scotland from February to August and Ireland January to September, but is imported and sold frozen all year round. When buying a whole fish look for a small head and broad shoulders as the head represents up to one-fifth of the weight. A round fish, the scales are bright and silvery, the flesh deep pink when raw and pale pink when cooked; it is firm and rich – 100 g *(4 oz)* being an average helping. When home-caught, this expensive fish has such a delicious flavour and excellent texture that the simplest cooking is the best. Buy whole, in pieces, as steaks or cutlets. Canadian, Norwegian, Alaskan and Japanese salmon tend to be less tender and delicate but can be made interesting with sauces.

Trout

Rainbow trout is available all the year round, fresh and frozen. The flesh is delicate and white. Grill, bake in foil or poach.

River or brown trout is best from March to September, but not widely available. Its flesh is considered superior to that of rainbow trout. Best grilled or fried.

Smoked fish

Haddock and cod

Smoked fillets of haddock and cod are frequently taken from large fish and may be coarse textured. They are dyed, often to a bright orange yellow. Cod is skinned but haddock has the skin left on. Cook as finnan haddock.

Finnan haddock are named after the village of Findon near Aberdeen. Before smoking the fish are split and lightly brined but not usually dyed. They are a light straw colour after smoking and darken during cooking.

Smokies are haddock or whiting with the heads cut off and the bodies left round. Originally smokies came from Arbroath and had a very dark appearance but are now smoked mechanically and lighter in colour. To reheat (they are already cooked by hot smoking), brush with butter and heat in the oven or under the grill. Split and add a piece of butter, close and heat until the butter melts.

Golden fillets are small haddocks, beheaded, split and boned before smoking. Cook as finnan haddock, adjusting the time to their size.

Smoked cod's roe is sliced and served on lettuce, with lemon wedges and fingers of toast, as an appetiser.

Herrings

Kipper is the most popular variety of smoked herring. The fish are split, lightly brined and then smoke-cured over wood chips. Kippers can be bought with the bone in, ready boned or in 'boil-in-the-bag' packs. All these can be had either fresh or frozen.

Buckling is a whole, smoked herring. It is smoked longer and at a higher temperature than a kipper, so the flesh of buckling becomes lightly cooked during smoking.

Bloater is a lightly smoked, dry salted, whole herring. Bloaters do not keep as long as other types of smoked herring and they should be served within 24 hours of buying.

Red herring is heavily smoked and highly salted. Although they make excellent snacks and hors d'oeuvre, red herrings are rarely seen these days as they are mostly exported.

Mackerel

Mackerel are smoked whole and ready for eating.

Salmon

Scotch smoked salmon is the best quality, Canadian and Pacific smoked salmon are slightly drier. Good smoked salmon should be moist and a deep pink colour. It can be bought fresh, frozen or canned and is served sliced very thinly.

Shellfish

Clam

In season all year round, but best in autumn. Sold live in its shell. Usually eaten raw like oysters. Otherwise cook as for mussels. Also available canned and smoked.

Cockles

Available all year round, but best September to April. Usually sold cooked and shelled. Can be used in dishes in place of mussels or oysters, or eaten plain with vinegar.

Crab

At its best from May to August. Can also be bought canned and frozen. Crabs are usually sold ready boiled and many fishmongers will also prepare and dress them. The edible portion of the crab consists of two parts – the white flesh of the claws and legs and the 'brown' meat, usually a combination of the liver and roe mixed with a little breadcrumb to give a smooth consistency.

Crawfish

Often called the spiny lobster, it resembles a lobster without the big claws, and is prepared and cooked like that fish. Also obtainable canned and frozen.

Crayfish

A fresh water crustacean, in season from September to April. Crayfish resemble miniature lobsters. They have a delicate flavour and the smaller ones can be used for soups and garnishes, while the larger ones can be served hot in a cream sauce or cold with salad and brown bread and butter.

To prepare crayfish, wash them well and remove the intestinal tube under the tail, using a pointed knife. Place the fish in salted water and cook for about 10 minutes after the liquid has reached boiling point.

Dublin Bay prawns

Just one of the many common names for the Norway Lobster (Nephrops norvegicus). Can be cooked whole as lobster and served cold with mayonnaise, alternatively the peeled uncooked tail meat (scampi) can be fried or used in hot dishes, take care not to overcook.

Lobster
In season all the year round, but at their best in the summer months; lobsters are sometimes difficult to obtain from December to April. Like crabs, lobsters are usually sold ready boiled. Lobster meat may also be bought ready prepared in cans or frozen whole.

They may be served hot, grilled or in such classic dishes as Lobster Newburg or Thermidor. The remains may be curried, scalloped or served up in the form of patties or omelettes, but there is really nothing to equal plainly dressed lobster, or lobster mayonnaise.

Mussels
In season from September to March. It is not advisable to collect mussels from around the tide lines. They must be alive when bought – discard any with gaping shells, scrub thoroughly and remove byssus threads before cooking. Wash in several changes of water. The last water should be absolutely clean.

Oysters
In season from September to April. When oysters are bought, the shells should be firmly closed. Oysters can be served raw 'on the shell' or cooked in various ways – in patties, as oysters au gratin, or added to steak and kidney pudding. Oysters usually live in the mouth of a river or in a bay near the shore, cultivated ones being reared in special beds. There are many varieties of oyster. In this country the smaller ones from Essex and Kent beds are the best for eating raw, while Portuguese oysters or the large American Blue Points (now also cultivated in the British Isles) are used for cooking.

When you buy oysters, they should come from a reliable source, as if they are not absolutely fresh they may cause poisoning.

Prawns
Obtainable all the year round, but at their best from February to October. Also sold canned, bottled and frozen. Fresh prawns are usually sold boiled in the shell. Frozen prawns come from different areas around the world. Choose those from cold water fishing grounds for cocktails and salads. Use warm water prawns for cooked dishes – curry, sauces etc.

Scallops
In season from October to March and at their best in January and February. Frozen scallops are obtainable at any time of the year. The roe of scallops should be a bright orange colour and the flesh white. They are delicious fried with bacon or served in a cheese sauce.

Scampi
Italian name for Norway Lobster, known as langoustine in France, cigala in Spain, but all the same hard shelled crustacean related to the lobster. Peeled tail meat sold frozen with or without breadcrumb coating. See Dublin Bay prawn entry.

Shrimps
Fresh shrimps, pink or brown, are available nearly all the year round; they may also be bought frozen, or potted in butter. The fresh ones are usually sold ready boiled. Shrimps may be served in the same ways as prawns, but being cheaper, they are also used in fish sauces, chowders and casseroles. Potted shrimps are served as a 'starter' and should ideally be warmed before serving to melt the butter and bring out the full flavour of shrimps and spices.

Whelks
Available all year round, but best September to February. Usually sold cooked and shelled, eaten plain with vinegar.

Winkles
Available all year round, but best October to May. Sold cooked, with or without shell, eaten plain with vinegar.

Buying fish

Fresh fish
Buy fish when it is in season and at its best. Some kinds can be bought all the year round, others have a close season (usually covering the spawning period).

Frozen fish
Most frozen fish is of high quality, there is no waste and it is quick to cook. The freezing does not affect the flavour or the food value. Frozen fish can be bought in a variety of ways – whole, filleted, in cutlets, or as fingers or cakes. Shellfish are also available.

Use it like fresh fish; but follow the manufacturers' individual instructions concerning the storage, thawing and cooking.

Cleaning fish

Whole fish
Remove any scales, using a knife and scraping from tail to head, with frequent rinsing.

To remove the entrails from round fish such as herrings or trout, make a slit along the abdomen from the gills half-way to the tail, draw out the insides and clean away any blood. Rub with a little salt to remove the black skin.

With flat fish, such as sole and plaice, open the cavity which lies in the upper part of the body under the gills and clean out the entrails in the same way.

Cut off the fins and gills, if the fish is to be served whole. The head and tail may be cut off if you prefer; if the head is left on, take out the eyes. Rinse the fish in cold water.

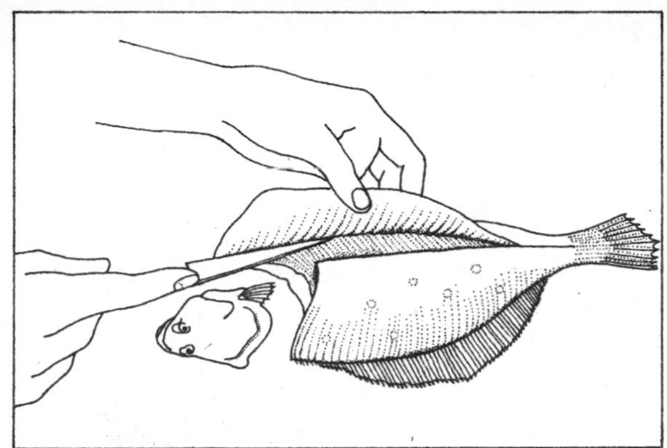

Filleting flat fish

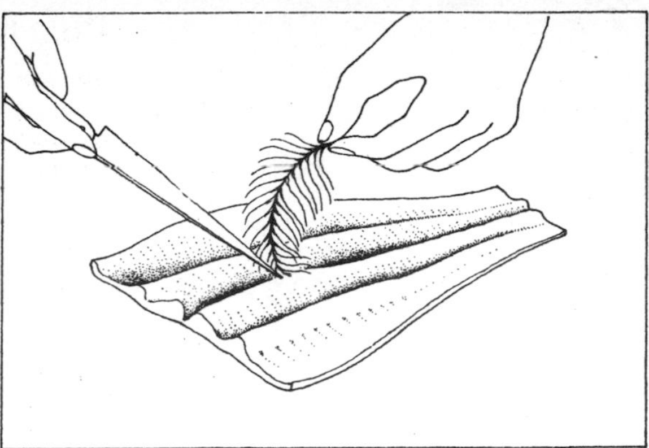

Filleting herring and mackerel

Fillets and cutlets

Wash and wipe with a paper towel.

Skinning fish

Whole flat fish (eg sole)

Wash the fish and cut off the fins. Make an incision across the tail, slip the thumb between the skin and flesh and loosen the dark skin round the sides of the fish. Hold the fish down firmly with one hand and with the other take hold of the skin and draw it off quickly, upwards towards the head. The white skin can be removed in the same way, but unless the fish is particularly large, it is generally left on.

Fillets of flat fish

Lay the fillet on a board, skin side down, salt the fingers and hold the tail end of the skin firmly with the fingers. Then separate the flesh from the skin by sawing with a sharp knife from side to side, pressing the flat of the blade against the flesh. Keep the edge of the blade close to the skin while cutting, but don't press it down at too sharp an angle or the skin will be cut.

Round fish

These are more usually cooked with the skin on, but if you want them skinned, start from the head.

Cut off a narrow strip of skin along the spine and cut across the skin just below the head; loosen the skin under the head with the point of a sharp knife, dip the fingers in salt and gently pull the skin down towards the tail, working carefully to avoid breaking the flesh. Skin the other side of the fish in the same way.

Filleting fish

Flat fish (eg plaice)

Four fillets are taken from the fish, two from each side. Using a small, sharp, pointed knife, make an incision straight down the back of the fish, following the line of the bone. Insert the knife under the flesh and carefully remove it with long, clean strokes. Take the first fillet from the left-hand side of the fish, working from head to tail, then turn the fish round and cut off the second fillet from tail to head. Fillet the other side of the fish in the same way. When you have finished, no flesh should be left on the bone.

Round fish (eg haddock)

Cut along the centre of the back to the bone, using a sharp knife, and cut along the abdomen of the fish. Remove the flesh cleanly from the bones, working from the head down, pressing the knife against the bones and working with short, sharp strokes. Remove the fillet from the other side in the same way. If the fish is large, cut the fillets into serving-size pieces. Skin the fillets or not, as preferred.

Herring and mackerel

Cut off the head, tail and fins. Split the fish open along the underside, remove the entrails and rub off the black inner skin, using a little salt on the fingers. Put the fish on a board, cut side down, and press lightly with the fingers down the middle of the back to loosen the bone. Turn the fish over and ease the backbone up with the fingers, removing with it as many of the small bones as possible. If the fish contains roes, remove these before filleting it (to cook and serve with the fish or separately, as you prefer).

Poached fish

Suitable for: Fillets, steaks or small whole fish – halibut, turbot, brill, haddock, flounder, salmon, salmon trout, smoked haddock, kippers.

Although we sometimes speak of 'boiling' fish, true boiling spoils it and it should actually be poached – that is, simmered in the liquid. The cooking may be done either in a saucepan on top of the stove or in a shallow covered casserole in the oven at 180°C *(350°F)* mark 4.

Whole fish and large pieces are usually cooked on top of the stove, completely covered with the liquid. This may be salted water, flavoured with some of the following: parsley sprigs, a small piece of onion and/or carrot, a few mushroom stalks, a squeeze of lemon juice, a bayleaf or some peppercorns. For the more classic dishes you can cook whole fish such as trout and large pieces such as salmon or turbot in court bouillon (see below).

Heat the liquid until it is simmering, put in the fish, cover and simmer very gently until tender, allowing 10–15 minutes per 450 g *(1 lb)*, according to the thickness of the cut, or about 20 minutes in all for a small piece. Drain the fish, place on a hot dish and serve with a sauce made from the cooking liquid (see pages 193 to 197). Alternatively, serve the poached fish cold, in aspic or with a mayonnaise dressing (see page 245). Fish fillets are often cooked in the oven and they need be only half-covered with cold liquid – whether seasoned milk and water, cider or dry white wine – which is then used as basis for a sauce to accompany the cooked fish.

Court bouillon for poached fish

1 litre *(1¾ pt)* water (or dry white wine and water mixed)
1 small carrot, pared and sliced
1 small onion, skinned and sliced
1 small stalk of celery, scrubbed and chopped (optional)
15 ml *(1 tbsp)* vinegar or lemon juice
few sprigs of parsley
½ bayleaf
3–4 peppercorns
10 ml *(2 level tsps)* salt

Place all the ingredients in a pan and simmer for about ½ hour. Allow to cool and if preferred, strain the liquid before using it.

Making lemon twists to garnish fish

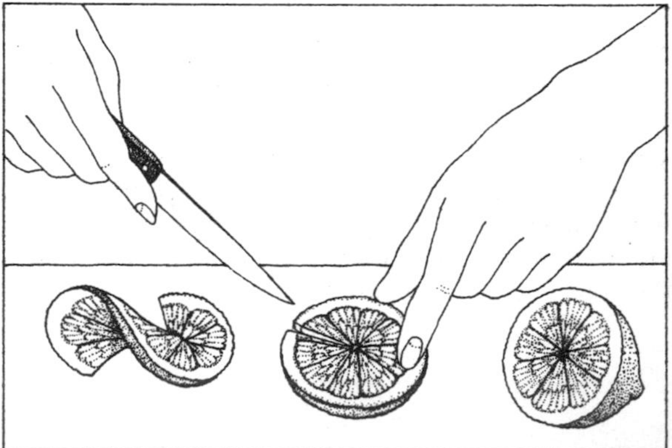

Gazpacho (p. 56).

Steamed fish

Suitable for: Thin fillets of sole, plaice

Wash and wipe the fish and lay it on a greased plate; dot with a few pieces of butter, add 15 ml *(1 tbsp)* milk and a little salt and pepper, cover with another plate and place over a pan of boiling water. Cook for 10–15 minutes. The liquid round the fish plus a little milk can be made into a sauce – for instance, parsley, shrimp, egg or cheese. (See Sauces chapter.)

Grilled fish

Suitable for: Small fish, thin fillets and thicker cuts – sole, plaice, halibut, turbot, hake, brill, cod, haddock, flounder, salmon, salmon trout, trout, herring, mackerel, smoked haddock, kippers

Wash the fish. If it is whole, remove the scales and fins. When it is too plump to allow the heat to penetrate easily (eg herring, mackerel) make 3–4 diagonal cuts in the body on each side.

White fish such as plaice, halibut, sole, cod and haddock should be brushed with oil or melted butter to prevent drying, but oily ones like herrings, mackerel and salmon do not need it.

Thin fillets or steaks can be cooked by grilling on one side only, but thicker pieces or whole fish should be turned once (use a fish slice or palette knife) to ensure thorough cooking on both sides.

Cook under a moderate heat, allowing 4–5 minutes for thin fillets, 10–15 minutes for thicker fillets, steaks and small whole fish; adjust the times as necessary according to the size and thickness of the fish.

Serve with maître d'hôtel or melted butter, lemon wedges and parsley.

Shallow-fried fish

Suitable for: Fillets, steaks and small whole fish – sole, plaice, dabs, bass, bream, cod, haddock, mackerel, herring, trout, perch, pike – also for fish cakes, etc.

Coat the fish with seasoned flour or with egg and breadcrumbs. Heat some shallow fat gently until it is fairly hot – if you let it smoke it is too hot. Lard or oil is usually used, but for fish cooked *à la meunière* (see below), butter is essential. Put in the piece of fish so that the side which you wish to be uppermost when it is served goes down first into the fat or oil. Cook gently and when the first side is browned, turn the fish and cook the other side. Allow about 10 minutes in all, according to thickness. Use a slice or palette knife to turn fish and to lift it out of the pan. Drain well on crumpled kitchen paper and serve with lemon and parsley or maître d'hôtel butter.

Fish à la meunière

Suitable for: Fillets or whole fish – sole, plaice, trout, pike, perch

Shallow-fry the fish in butter. When it is cooked, transfer it to a hot dish. Lightly brown a little extra butter in the frying pan, add a squeeze of lemon juice and pour it over the fish. Garnish with chopped parsley.

Avocado soup (p. 48), Dressed avocado with tomato vinaigrette (p. 21), Avocado cream (p. 21).

Deep-fried fish

Suitable for: Fillets coated with batter or egg and breadcrumbs, small whole fish – cod, haddock, hake, whiting, coley, gurnet, skate, sprats, smelts, fresh sardines, whitebait; also fish cakes, etc

You will need a deep pan with a wire basket (except for batter-coated fish), and enough fat or oil to come about half-way up the pan. Clarified dripping, lard and cooking oil are suitable. The fat must be pure and free from moisture. Heat the fat to 177°–188°C *(350°–370°F)*. A simple way to test it is to put in a 2.5-cm *(1-in)* cube of bread, which should brown in 60 seconds. If the fat is too cool, the fish will be soggy; if it is too hot, the outside will brown before the inside is cooked. While the fat is heating coat the fish with egg and breadcrumbs or batter (see page 310). Lower the fish gently into the fat, using the basket for egg-and-crumbed pieces; cook only a little at a time, to avoid lowering the temperature. As soon as the fish is golden brown – 5–10 minutes – lift it out and drain it really well on crumpled kitchen paper before serving. The fat may be strained into a clean basin and kept for future use.

Baked fish

Suitable for: Fillets, steaks, cuts from large fish and small whole fish – cod, haddock, hake, whiting, sole, plaice, turbot, halibut, salmon

Wash and wipe the fish and prepare according to type.

Put in a stuffing if you wish and place the fish in an ovenproof dish. Add 45–60 ml *(3–4 tbsps)* milk or white or red wine and a bouquet garni (or a small piece of onion and ½ a bayleaf). Cover with a lid or foil and bake in the oven at 180°C *(350°F)* mark 4, unless otherwise directed in a particular recipe, until tender – allow 10–20 minutes for fillets, 20 minutes for steaks, 25–30 minutes for small whole fish.

Alternatively, wrap the prepared fish in buttered foil and add a squeeze of lemon juice and a sprinkling of salt and pepper. Wrap it loosely and put it on a baking sheet. Bake in the oven at 180°C *(350°F)* mark 4, allowing about 20 minutes for steak and 6–10 minutes per 450 g *(1 lb)* plus 6–10 minutes over for large pieces, according to size unless otherwise directed in a particular recipe.

SEA FISH RECIPES

Haddock with cheese sauce

700 g *(1½ lb)* haddock fillets or any white fish
salt and pepper
150 ml *(¼ pt)* milk
25 g *(1 oz)* butter or margarine
45 ml *(3 level tbsps)* flour
175 g *(6 oz)* cheese, grated

Wash and wipe the fish, cut it into 4 even-sized pieces, place them in a saucepan, just cover with cold water and add a little salt. Cover the pan, bring slowly to the boil, turn off the heat and leave covered for 5 minutes. Drain off the liquid, retaining 150 ml *(¼ pt)*, and mix it with the milk. Remove the skin from the fish, keep the pieces as whole as possible and put them in a shallow ovenproof dish to keep warm. Melt the fat, stir in the flour and cook for 2–3 minutes.

Remove from the heat and gradually stir in the milk and fish stock. Bring to the boil and stir until the sauce thickens. Remove from the heat, stir in 100 g *(4 oz)* cheese and season to taste; pour the sauce over the fish and sprinkle with the remaining cheese. Place under a hot grill until golden and bubbling.

Haddock julienne

700 g *(1½ lb)* haddock or cod fillet
25 g *(1 oz)* butter
salt and pepper
ground coriander
juice of ½ lemon
50 g *(2 oz)* onion, skinned
2 tomatoes, skinned and seeded
25 g *(1 oz)* Cheddar cheese, grated
5 ml *(1 level tsp)* arrowroot
chopped parsley

Remove the skin from the fillet. Cut the fish into 4 portions. Use half the butter to well grease a shallow ovenproof serving dish. Arrange the fish in a single layer, with salt, pepper and a very little coriander. Pour over the lemon juice. Cut the onion thinly into rings. Cut the tomato flesh into strips. In a small frying pan, melt the rest of the butter; slowly fry the onion until soft and beginning to colour. Combine with the tomato and cheese.

Spoon the onion mixture evenly over each fillet. Cover and cook in the oven at 190°C *(375°F)* mark 5 for 20 minutes.

In a small pan, blend the arrowroot with 15 ml *(1 tbsp)* water, add the drained-off fish liquor and bring to the boil, stirring. Pour it over the fish and serve garnished with chopped parsley.

Haddock baked in cream

700 g *(1½ lb)* fresh haddock fillet
1 onion, skinned and finely chopped
juice of ½ a lemon
5 ml *(1 tsp)* Worcestershire sauce
salt and pepper
142-ml *(5-fl oz)* carton single cream

Wash and skin the fish, place it in a greased ovenproof dish and sprinkle with the onion. Mix the lemon juice, Worcestershire sauce, seasoning and cream and pour over the fish. Cover with a lid or foil and bake in the oven at 180°C *(350°F)* mark 4 for 20–30 minutes, or until the fish and onions are cooked. (Don't worry if the cream curdles.)

Stuffed cod steaks

4 cod steaks (or cutlets)
½ onion, skinned and finely chopped
100 g *(4 oz)* streaky bacon, rinded and chopped
knob of butter
2 tomatoes, skinned and chopped
50 g *(2 oz)* fresh white breadcrumbs
salt and pepper
about 150 ml *(¼ pt)* milk

Wash and wipe the fish, trim off the fins and remove the central bone with a sharp-pointed knife; place the fish in a greased ovenproof dish. Fry the onion and bacon gently in the butter for about 5 minutes, until soft; stir in the tomatoes and crumbs. Season well and add enough milk to bind the mixture. Fill the centre of each steak with this stuffing, and fix the flaps of fish with wooden cocktail sticks to secure the stuffing. Pour 30–45 ml *(2–3 tbsps)* milk round the fish, cover with a lid or foil and bake in the oven at 180°C *(350°F)* mark 4 for about 20 minutes.

As an alternative filling use veal forcemeat made with 50 g *(2 oz)* breadcrumbs (see page 183) or the following mixture.

Cheese and tomato stuffing for cod

2 large tomatoes, skinned and chopped
75 g *(3 oz)* cheese, grated
50 g *(2 oz)* fresh white breadcrumbs
5 ml *(1 level tsp)* dried mixed herbs or sage
salt and pepper
milk to bind

Mix all the ingredients together.

Cheese grilled fish

4 fish steaks or fillets (eg cod, haddock) weighing about 700 g *(1½ lb)*
½ small onion, skinned and grated
100 g *(4 oz)* cheese, grated
50 g *(2 oz)* butter
5 ml *(1 level tsp)* dry mustard
salt and pepper
2 tomatoes, sliced

Wash, wipe and trim the fish steaks and remove the centre bones with a sharp-pointed knife. Mix the remaining ingredients (except the tomatoes) until well blended. Place the steaks on the grill rack and grill under a medium heat for about 5 minutes, turn them and grill for a further 3 minutes. Spread the cheese mixture over the fish and lay 1–2 slices of tomato on each steak. Grill for a final 3–5 minutes, until the cheese topping is golden and the tomatoes are cooked.

Plaki

225 g *(½ lb)* onions, skinned and finely chopped
olive oil
4 ripe tomatoes, skinned and sliced
chopped parsley
salt and pepper
1 kg *(2¼ lb)* white fish, filleted
lemon juice
1 clove garlic, skinned and crushed
1 tomato and 1 lemon for garnish

Fry the onions in a little oil until tender but not coloured, add the tomatoes and parsley. Season. Arrange the fish in a lightly buttered ovenproof dish, sprinkle with lemon juice. Add the crushed garlic to the onion mixture and spoon over the fish. Bake at 220°C *(425°F)* mark 7 for about 15 minutes. Garnish with slices of tomato and lemon. *Serves 4–6.*

Fish pellao

700 g *(1½ lb)* cod fillet
50 g *(2 oz)* ghee or butter
5 ml *(1 level tsp)* turmeric
2.5 ml *(½ level tsp)* chili powder
5–10 ml *(1–2 level tsps)* garam masala (see note)
10 ml *(2 tsps)* lemon juice
2 onions, skinned and sliced
225 g *(½ lb)* long grain rice
1 l *(1¾ pt)* water
2 bayleaves
tomatoes to garnish

Skin the fish, wipe it and cut into cubes. Melt half the ghee or butter and add the turmeric, chili powder and garam masala; fry for 5 minutes and add the lemon juice. Cook the fish in this mixture for 10–15 minutes, then remove and place on a plate. Melt the remaining fat in a second pan and fry the onions until pale golden brown. Add the washed rice and continue frying for 3–5 minutes. Add the gravy mixture from the first pan, with the water and bayleaves, and cook for 20–30 minutes by which time the liquid will be absorbed and the rice tender. Add the fish, stir gently and serve garnished with sliced raw tomato.

Note Garam masala is a flavouring made by mixing 5 ml *(1 level tsp)* each of ground cloves, ground cinnamon, ground black pepper, cumin seeds and ground cardamom seeds.

Mint and cucumber fish salad *see colour plate facing p. 128*

900 g *(2 lb)* fresh cod fillet (the thick end is the best choice)
juice of ½ lemon
salt
½ cucumber
30 ml *(2 tbsps)* freshly chopped mint
30 ml *(2 tbsps)* freshly chopped parsley

For French dressing
90 ml *(6 tbsps)* olive oil
30 ml *(2 tbsps)* vinegar
salt and freshly ground black pepper
mustard

For garnish
25–50 g *(1–2 oz)* peeled prawns
lemon wedges
sprigs of mint

Wash and skin the fish and cut it into three or four pieces. Sprinkle with lemon juice and salt. Steam or gently poach until just cooked (the flakes should separate easily and look milky white all through). Leave the fish covered until quite cold. Flake the fish very coarsely into a large bowl, removing any stray bones. Wash the cucumber, cut it into small dice and add to the fish. Tip in the chopped mint and parsley. Stir the French dressing ingredients together in a basin and pour over the salad. Using two spoons, lift and turn the salad until all the ingredients are combined and coated with dressing. Take care not to break up the natural flakes of fish. Pile the mixture into individual dishes and garnish each one with prawns, lemon wedges and sprigs of mint. Alternatively, serve in a large salad bowl accompanied by mayonnaise, tossed green salad and French bread.

Fish and cider casserole

700 g ***(1½ lb)*** **fillet of cod or haddock**
2 onions, skinned and finely chopped
225 g ***(½ lb)*** **tomatoes, skinned and sliced**
150 ml ***(¼ pt)*** **dry cider**
5 ml ***(1 level tsp)*** **dried sage or mixed herbs**
salt and pepper
45 ml ***(3 tbsps)*** **fresh white breadcrumbs**
45 ml ***(3 tbsps)*** **grated cheese, optional**

Wash and skin the fish, cut it into 4 pieces and place it in a casserole. Cover with onion and tomato and pour the cider round the fish. Sprinkle with the herbs and seasoning, cover with a lid or foil and bake in the oven at 170°C *(325°F)* mark 3 for 20–30 minutes, until tender. Remove the lid, sprinkle the fish with the crumbs and cheese (if used) and brown under a hot grill before serving.

Fish steaks Catalan style

4 175-g ***(6-oz)*** **steaks white fish**
25 g ***(1 oz)*** **butter**
15 ml ***(1 tbsp)*** **oil**
175 g ***(6 oz)*** **onion, skinned and sliced**
60 ml ***(4 level tbsps)*** **tomato paste**
30 ml ***(2 level tbsps)*** **flour**
300 ml ***(½ pt)*** **water**
150 ml ***(¼ pt)*** **dry white wine**
30-g ***(1-oz)*** **can anchovies, drained and chopped**
50 g ***(2 oz)*** **black olives**
30 ml ***(2 tbsps)*** **capers**
salt and pepper

Wipe the fish and remove the fins and black skin. Heat the butter and oil and quickly brown the fish on both sides. Drain and keep to one side. Sauté the onion in the same pan until soft. Add the tomato paste and flour. Cook for 1 minute. Stir in the water, wine, anchovies, olives and capers. Adjust seasoning to taste and bring to the boil.

Replace the fish in the sauce, reduce the heat and simmer for about 15 minutes, until the fish flakes.

Salt cod in sauce

450 g ***(1 lb)*** **salt cod**
2 large onions, skinned and finely chopped
2 cloves garlic, skinned and crushed
30 ml ***(2 tbsps)*** **olive oil**
cayenne pepper
2 tomatoes, skinned and chopped
5 ml ***(1 tsp)*** **chopped parsley**
1 stick celery, chopped
2 egg yolks, beaten

Soak the fish in cold water for 24 hours, changing the water 2–3 times. Poach the cod gently in water for 10–15 minutes and cut it into convenient-sized pieces, removing bones. Fry the onions and garlic in oil until brown and tender. Add some cayenne, the tomatoes, parsley and celery, pour in 400 ml *(¾ pt)* boiling water and simmer for a few minutes. Add the pieces of fish, baste with the mixture, then simmer gently. When the fish is tender, take it off the heat and add the beaten egg yolks, pouring them in at several different places; shake the pan gently to mix, then slide the fish and sauce carefully into a shallow casserole to serve.

Waterzooi de poisson

700 g ***(1½ lb)*** **cod fillet**
3 sticks celery, roughly chopped
25 g ***(1 oz)*** **butter**
5 ml ***(1 level tsp)*** **salt**
freshly ground black pepper
3 egg yolks
60 ml ***(4 tbsps)*** **double cream**
10 ml ***(2 level tsps)*** **cornflour**
chopped parsley
rye bread

Remove any dark skin from the fish by making an incision in the flesh, holding the skin and firmly pulling away in one movement. Cut the fish into large pieces about 4 cm *(1½ in)* square. Put them in a saucepan and cover with cold water. Add the celery, butter and seasoning. Poach gently for about 8–10 minutes, until the flesh flakes easily when pierced with a fork. Carefully remove the fish using a draining spoon and put it in a serving dish. Scatter the celery over. Cover and keep warm. Strain the fish liquid then rapidly boil it down to about 600 ml *(1 pt)*. Remove from the heat. Beat the egg yolks with the cream and cornflour until smooth. Stir in a little hot fish stock, then add this to the pan contents. Do not boil, but stir continuously until thickened. Cook for 2–3 minutes. Adjust the seasoning if necessary and pour the sauce over the fish. Garnish with chopped parsley. Serve rye bread alongside. *Serves 6.*

Fried whiting

Clean, wash and skin the whiting, removing the eyes but not the head of the fish; dry well in a cloth. A few minutes before the whiting are to be fried, remove them from the cloth and if you wish put the tail of each fish into its mouth. Brush the fish over with beaten egg, roll them in breadcrumbs and shake off any loose crumbs. Heat some deep fat until it will brown a 2.5-cm *(1-in)* cube of bread in 1 minute; fry the whiting for 5–10 minutes, handling them carefully, as they break easily. Drain well on crumpled kitchen paper, garnish with fried parsley and serve with anchovy or other suitable sauce.

Whiting casserole

225 g *(8 oz)* carrots, pared
225 g *(8 oz)* celery, trimmed
75 g *(2½ oz)* butter
25 g *(1 oz)* whole almonds, blanched and split
25 g *(1 oz)* long grain rice
900 ml *(1½ pt)* light stock
226-g *(8-oz)* can tomatoes
grated rind and juice of ½ lemon
45 ml *(3 level tbsps)* flour
100 g *(¼ lb)* mushrooms, quartered
4 whiting, filleted, skinned and cut into cubes
salt and pepper
chopped parsley

Roughly chop the carrot and celery. Melt 40 g *(1½ oz)* butter in a flameproof casserole and sauté the carrots, celery, almonds and rice until the almonds are browned.

Add the stock, tomatoes with their liquid, lemon rind and juice. Cover and simmer for 15 minutes. Cream the flour with 25 g *(1 oz)* butter and whisk in small pieces into the sauce to thicken it. Add the quartered mushrooms and cubes of whiting and simmer for a further 10 minutes. Season to taste.

Sprinkle with chopped parsley and serve with creamed potatoes.

Gebakken schol fillet uit de pan

5 plaice fillets, 175 g *(6 oz)* each, skinned
7.5 ml *(1½ level tsps)* salt
juice of 1 lemon
40 g *(1½ oz)* butter
6 rashers of streaky bacon, rinded
45 ml *(3 level tbsps)* plain flour
1.25 ml *(¼ level tsp)* dill seeds
1.25 ml *(¼ level tsp)* ground nutmeg
freshly ground black pepper
50 g *(2 oz)* Gouda cheese, grated
75 g *(3 oz)* white breadcrumbs
30 ml *(2 tbsps)* chopped almonds
50 g *(2 oz)* butter

Season both sides of the plaice fillets with salt and lemon juice. Leave in a shallow dish for 30 minutes. Melt the butter in a wide shallow flameproof casserole, large enough to hold the fish in a single layer. Tilt the dish to coat the sides with butter. Fry the bacon gently in the butter until lightly browned. Drain well and keep to one side. Pat the fish fillets dry and fold lengthwise in half. Roll them in flour and sprinkle with dill seeds and nutmeg. Arrange side by side in the buttered dish. Top with bacon and season. Mix the cheese, breadcrumbs and almonds together. Scatter this mixture over the fish and dot with pats of butter. Cook covered, on the stove top over a gentle heat, for about 15 minutes, then uncover and put under a preheated grill to brown the topping. Serve with lemon wedges. *Serves 5.*

Stuffed rolled plaice

2 hard-boiled eggs, shelled and chopped
50 g *(2 oz)* cheese, grated
15 ml *(1 tbsp)* chopped parsley
75 g *(3 oz)* fresh white breadcrumbs
50 g *(2 oz)* butter, melted
salt and pepper
2 whole plaice, filleted and skinned

Mix the eggs with the cheese, parsley and 50 g *(2 oz)* of the breadcrumbs. Bind with the butter and add seasoning. Spread this mixture over the skinned side of the fillets and roll them up, starting from the tail end; secure them if necessary with a wooden cocktail stick. Place the fillets close together in a buttered shallow ovenproof dish, sprinkle with the remaining breadcrumbs and bake uncovered in the oven at 180°C *(350°F)* mark 4 for about 20 minutes, until the fish is tender and the breadcrumbs crisp on top. The liquid that comes from the fish as it cooks can be strained off and used with milk to make a white or parsley sauce to serve with the fish. (See pages 195, 196.)

Fried fillets of plaice

Allow 2 fillets per person. Wash and wipe them and dip into seasoned flour; shake off any excess and dip the fish into beaten egg and then in dry white or golden breadcrumbs to cover. Put into shallow hot butter or lard, skin side uppermost, and fry for 3–5 minutes; turn them once and fry for a further 2–3 minutes; until crisp and golden. Drain on crumpled kitchen paper and serve with wedges of lemon and tartare sauce. Deep fat fry if you prefer.

Sole meunière

4 small soles, skinned
seasoned flour
75 g *(3 oz)* butter
15 ml *(1 tbsp)* chopped parsley
juice of 1 lemon
lemon slices to garnish

Cut off the fins from the soles and wipe the fish; coat them with seasoned flour. Heat 50 g *(2 oz)* butter in the frying pan, put the fish in upper side first and fry gently for about 5 minutes, until brown. Turn them over carefully and continue frying for a further 5 minutes, or until they are tender and golden. Drain on crumpled kitchen paper and place on a hot serving dish. Wipe the pan clean, melt the remaining butter and heat until lightly browned. Add the parsley and lemon juice and pour immediately over the fish. Garnish with thin slices or wedges of lemon.

Note Although it is more traditional to cook the fish on the bone, fillets of sole can be used. Plaice and other white fish can also be cooked à la meunière.

Sole colbert

1 small sole per person
seasoned flour
beaten egg
dry breadcrumbs
deep fat for frying
maître d'hôtel butter (see page 35)

Have the heads cut off the fish and the black skin removed. Wash and wipe the soles. With a sharp knife make a cut down the centre of the backbone on one side of the fish. Raise the fillets on this side only away from the bone to form a pocket. Then with the points of scissors cut the backbone through just below the head and above the tail, so that it may be more easily removed after the fish is cooked. Dip the soles in seasoned flour and coat with beaten egg and breadcrumbs. Heat the fat in a large, wide pan until it will brown a 2.5-cm *(1-in)* cube of bread in 1 minute; fry the fish for about 10 minutes and drain on crumpled kitchen paper. Using scissors or a knife, cut the backbone and ease it from the cooked fish. Fill the centre cavity of each fish with maître d'hôtel butter and serve at once.

Sole véronique

2 sole, filleted
2 shallots (or 2–3 slices of onion), skinned and chopped
2–3 button mushrooms, sliced
few sprigs of parsley
½ bayleaf
salt and pepper
150 ml *(¼ pt)* dry white wine, eg Graves, Chablis
150 ml *(¼ pt)* water
100 g *(4 oz)* white grapes
knob of butter
30 ml *(2 level tbsps)* flour
about 150 ml *(¼ pt)* milk
a squeeze of lemon juice
30 ml *(2 tbsps)* single cream

Trim off the fins, wash and wipe the fillets and lay them in a shallow ovenproof dish with the shallots, mushrooms, herbs, salt and pepper, wine and water. Cover with foil or a lid and bake in the oven at 180°C *(350°F)* mark 4 for about 15 minutes or until tender. Simmer the grapes for a few minutes in a little water or extra white wine, peel them and remove the pips. Meanwhile, strain the liquid from the fish and reduce it slightly by boiling rapidly; keep the fish warm. Melt the butter, stir in the flour and cook for 2–3 minutes. Remove the pan from the heat and gradually stir in the reduced fish liquor, made up to 300 ml *(½ pt)* with milk. Bring to the boil and continue to stir until the sauce thickens. Remove from the heat and stir in most of the grapes, the lemon juice and the cream. Pour over the fish and serve decorated with the remaining grapes.

Note Plaice fillets may be cooked in the same way.

Sole bonne femme

2 soles, filleted
2 shallots (or 2–3 slices of onion), skinned and finely chopped
100 g *(4 oz)* button mushrooms
45 ml *(3 tbsps)* dry white wine, eg Graves, Chablis
15 ml *(1 tbsp)* water
salt and pepper
1 bayleaf
40 g *(1½ oz)* butter
30 ml *(2 level tbsps)* flour
about 150 ml *(¼ pt)* milk
30–45 ml *(2–3 tbsps)* cream

Trim off the fins, wash and wipe the fillets and fold each in three. Put the shallot or onion in the bottom of an ovenproof dish, with the stalks from the mushrooms, finely chopped. Cover with the fish fillets, pour round them the wine and water, sprinkle with salt and pepper and add the bayleaf. Cover with foil or a lid and bake in the oven at 180°C *(350°F)* mark 4 for about 15 minutes, until tender. Strain off the cooking liquid and keep the fish warm.

Fry the mushroom caps lightly in half the butter. Melt the remaining butter, stir in the flour and cook for 2–3 minutes. Remove the pan from the heat and gradually stir in the cooking liquid from the fish, made up to 300 ml *(½ pt)* with milk. Bring to the boil and continue to stir until the sauce thickens, remove from the heat and stir in the cream. Pour the sauce over the fish and serve garnished with the mushroom caps.

Note The classic sole bonne femme may next be coated with hollandaise sauce and browned under a hot grill before being served, but the recipe given here is the one more usually followed. Plaice and other white fish can also be cooked in this way.

Mousseline of sole with prawns

450 g *(1 lb)* fillets of sole, skinned and chopped
50 g *(2 oz)* shelled prawns
1 egg white, beaten
1.25 ml *(¼ level tsp)* each salt, white pepper
400 ml *(¾ pt)* double cream
3 egg yolks
75 g *(3 oz)* unsalted butter, softened
10 ml *(2 tsps)* lemon juice
5 ml *(1 level tsp)* tomato paste
whole prawns, optional
mushrooms, see below

Combine the chopped fish with the prawns, egg white and seasoning. Purée half the mixture in an electric blender with 150 ml *(¼ pt)* cream, stopping to scrape down the goblet. Remove the purée from the goblet, repeat with the rest of the fish and another 150 ml *(¼ pt)* cream. Oil six 150-ml *(¼-pt)* ovenproof soufflé dishes and press the mixture well down into the dishes. Chill, covered, for 3 hours then cook in a water bath at 150°C *(300°F)* mark 2 for 30–40 minutes. Turn out on to a wire rack to drain. Keep warm. In double boiler, combine the yolks, a knob of butter and the lemon juice. Stir until of coating consistency. Off the heat, slowly beat in the rest of the butter and the tomato paste. Lightly whip the remaining cream. Fold into sauce, return to the heat to thicken, without boiling. Place the moulds on a warm dish; mask with sauce. Garnish with prawns, mushrooms and snipped parsley. *Serves 6.*

Poached mushrooms
Bring to the boil 100 g *(4 oz)* button mushrooms, 5 ml *(1 tsp)* lemon juice, pinch of salt, knob of butter and 150 ml *(¼ pt)* water. Boil until the liquid evaporates.

Fritto misto

1 small sole, skinned and filleted
seasoned flour
beaten egg
fresh white breadcrumbs
100 g *(4 oz)* shelled frozen prawns
French dressing, optional, see page 244
1 whiting
200 g *(7 oz)* whitebait, optional
oil for frying
fritter batter (see below)
lemon wedges and endive to garnish
rémoulade sauce (see opposite)

Cut the sole into long, thin strips, dip in seasoned flour, then in beaten egg and breadcrumbs. Leave in a cool place to set the coating. Dip the prawns in a little French dressing, if you wish, then drain. Fillet the whiting, skin, and cut each fillet lengthwise into 2 or 3 strips; dip in seasoned flour. Toss the whitebait in seasoned flour.

To fry, heat the oil in a deep pan to 190°C *(375°F)*. Dip the whiting into the batter and twist the strips before placing them in the oil; when they are beginning to brown, add the sole and then the prawns, dipped in the batter. When all are golden brown, drain on absorbent kitchen paper and keep warm. Quickly reheat the oil and fry the whitebait until crisp. Pile a selection of fish on each of four warm plates and garnish. Serve the rémoulade sauce separately.

Fritter batter Sift together 75 g *(3 oz)* plain flour and a pinch of salt; stir in about 90 ml *(6 tbsps)* water and 15 ml *(1 tbsp)* corn oil.

Beat until smooth. Just before using, fold in a stiffly beaten egg white.

Rémoulade sauce Into 150 ml *(¼ pt)* mayonnaise, fold 2.5 ml *(½ level tsp)* each of French and English mustards, 5 ml *(1 level tsp)* each of chopped capers, gherkin, parsley and chervil, and 1 anchovy fillet, finely chopped.

Fillets of sole dugléré

2 sole, filleted, or 8 fillets of plaice
1–2 shallots, skinned and chopped
½ bayleaf
few sprigs of parsley
150 ml *(¼ pt)* white wine
150 ml *(¼ pt)* water
salt and pepper
25 g *(1 oz)* butter
45 ml *(3 level tbsps)* flour
45 ml *(3 tbsps)* single cream
2 tomatoes, skinned and diced, with seeds removed
10 ml *(2 tsps)* chopped parsley

Rinse and dry the fish, remove the dark skin and put in an ovenproof dish with the shallots, herbs, wine, water, salt and pepper. Cover with foil or a lid and bake in the oven at 180°C *(350°F)* mark 4 for about 15 minutes, or poach gently on top of the cooker, until tender. Strain off the cooking liquid and keep the fish warm. Melt the butter, stir in the flour and cook for 2–3 minutes. Remove the pan from the heat and gradually stir in the cooking liquid from the fish. Bring to the boil and continue to stir until the sauce thickens. Remove from the heat and stir in the cream, tomatoes and parsley. Adjust the seasoning if necessary and pour over the fish.

Note Most white fish can be cooked dugléré style.

Fried sole with orange

4 sole, skinned
seasoned flour
50 g *(2 oz)* butter
1 small orange, skinned and sliced
15 ml *(1 tbsp)* sherry
7.5 ml *(1½ tsps)* tarragon vinegar
chopped parsley

Rinse and dry the fish. Coat them with seasoned flour and fry gently, one at a time, in about 40 g *(1½ oz)* of the butter, turning them once to brown and cook the second side; keep them warm. Meanwhile combine the orange slices and any juice, the sherry and vinegar and heat very gently. When all the fish are cooked, arrange them on a heated serving dish and keep hot. Clean out the pan and brown the remaining butter lightly. Place the orange slices in a line down the centre of the fish, add the liquid in which they were heated to the browned butter in the pan and pour over the fish. Serve at once, garnished with chopped parsley.

Note Plaice may be cooked in the same way.

Grilled halibut or turbot

Allow 175 g *(6 oz)* fish per person. Wash and trim the fish, wipe and place on a greased grill grid. Brush with melted butter and sprinkle with salt and pepper. Grill gently for about 15 minutes altogether, turning the pieces once, brushing the second side with butter and sprinkling with salt and pepper. Serve with grilled mushrooms and a tomato or other well flavoured sauce.

Baked halibut with wine

4 pieces of halibut, about 700 g *(1½ lb)*
½ small onion, skinned and chopped
50 g *(2 oz)* lean streaky bacon, rinded and chopped
25 g *(1 oz)* butter
15 ml *(1 level tbsp)* flour
225–350 g *(½–¾ lb)* ripe tomatoes, skinned and chopped, or a 425-g *(15-oz)* can of tomatoes, drained
45 ml *(3 tbsps)* dry white wine
salt, pepper, a pinch of sugar
½ bayleaf
3–4 peppercorns

Rinse and dry the fish and place it in a greased ovenproof dish. Fry the onion and bacon in the butter until soft but not brown – about 5 minutes – and stir in the flour. Add the tomatoes, wine, seasonings and flavourings and pour over the fish. Cover with foil and bake in the oven at 180°C *(350°F)* mark 4 for about 20 minutes, or until the fish is tender. Remove the bayleaf and peppercorns before serving.

Halibut or turbot mornay

4 pieces of turbot or halibut, about 700 g (*1½ lb*)
2–3 slices of lemon
2–3 sprigs of parsley
½ bayleaf
salt and pepper
about 300 ml (*½ pt*) milk
25 g (*1 oz*) butter
45 ml (*3 level tbsps*) flour
100 g (*4 oz*) cheese, grated

Rinse, dry and trim the fish, place it in a shallow ovenproof dish and add the lemon, parsley, bayleaf, salt, pepper and half the milk. Cover with foil or a lid and bake in the oven at 180°C (*350°F*) mark 4 for about 20 minutes, or until the fish is tender. Drain off and retain the liquid and keep the fish warm. Melt the fat, stir in the flour and cook for 2–3 minutes. Remove the pan from the heat and gradually stir in the cooking liquid, made up to 300 ml (*½ pt*) with more milk. Bring to the boil and continue to stir until the sauce thickens; remove the pan from the heat and stir in 75 g (*3 oz*) of the cheese, with extra seasoning if necessary. Pour the sauce over the fish, sprinkle with the remaining cheese and brown in the oven or under a hot grill.

With spinach (florentine)
The fish can be baked as above and placed on a bed of chopped spinach (cooked in the usual way) before being coated with the sauce.

Turbot with crab sauce

4 pieces of turbot or halibut, about 700 g (*1½ lb*)
2–3 slices of onion
few sprigs of parsley
½ bayleaf
salt and pepper
150 ml (*¼ pt*) dry white wine
knob of butter
30 ml (*2 level tbsps*) flour
about 150 ml (*¼ pt*) milk
92-g (*3¼-oz*) can crab meat
60–120 ml (*4–8 tbsps*) Parmesan cheese, grated

Wash and trim the fish, place it in a shallow ovenproof dish with the onion, parsley, bayleaf and seasoning and pour in the wine. Cover the fish and bake it in the oven at 180°C (*350°F*) mark 4 until tender – about 20 minutes, depending on the thickness of the fish. Drain off and retain the cooking liquid and keep the fish warm.

Melt the butter, stir in the flour and cook for 2–3 minutes. Remove the pan from the heat and gradually stir in the cooking liquid, made up to 300 ml (*½ pt*) with milk. Bring it to the boil and continue to stir until the sauce thickens. Add the flaked crab meat and continue cooking for a further 2–3 minutes. Pour the sauce over the fish in an ovenproof dish, sprinkle with the cheese and brown it under a hot grill.

Mullet in tomato sauce

4 red mullet, whole and cleaned
30 ml (*2 level tbsps*) seasoned flour
oil or butter for frying
30 ml (*2 tbsps*) fresh white breadcrumbs
15 ml (*1 tbsp*) chopped parsley

For the sauce
½ onion, skinned and finely chopped
1 clove garlic, skinned and crushed, optional
25 g (*1 oz*) butter
450 g (*1 lb*) tomatoes, skinned and quartered
salt and pepper
10 ml (*2 level tsps*) sugar
1 bayleaf

First make the sauce. Fry the onion and the garlic (if you are using it) in the butter for about 5 minutes, until soft but not coloured. Add the tomatoes, salt, pepper, sugar and bayleaf, cover with a lid and simmer gently until soft and pulped – about ½ hour; remove the bayleaf.

Rinse the fish and dry them well. Dip them in seasoned flour and fry them in shallow fat until tender, turning them once and allowing 6–8 minutes in all. Place half the tomato sauce in a shallow ovenproof dish, lay the fish on top, then cover with the rest of the sauce; sprinkle with the breadcrumbs and brown under a hot grill. Sprinkle with parsley and serve at once.

Grilled mullet

4 mullet, whole and cleaned
60 ml (*4 tbsps*) oil
60 ml (*4 tbsps*) vinegar
piece of onion, skinned and finely chopped
few peppercorns
½ bayleaf or a few parsley stalks
tomato sauce (see page 202)

Rinse the fish and dry them well. Put them in a dish with the oil, vinegar and flavourings and leave them to marinade for about 1 hour, turning them several times. Drain the fish and put them on a greased grill grid. Cook under a medium heat for about 10 minutes, basting with some of the marinade and turning them once. Serve with tomato sauce.

Fried skate

700–900 g *(1½–2 lb)* prepared skate
seasoned flour
beaten egg and dry breadcrumbs
fat for frying

Preparation of skate

The 'wings' of young small skate are often sold whole, but those of larger fish are usually sold cut in slices. Pieces of small skate can be cooked without any preparation, but larger skate, which tend to be rather tough and flavourless, are better if first simmered in salted water or court bouillon (see page 64) until just tender, skinned and cut into pieces measuring about 5–7.5 cm *(2–3 in)*. They can then be fried or cooked in any way you wish.

Frying

Drain the skate well, coat with seasoned flour, egg and crumbs and fry it gently for 5 minutes on each side in shallow fat (or for 5 minutes in all, in deep fat), until the pieces are tender and golden. Serve with cut lemon and a sharp-flavoured sauce such as tartare (see page 200).

Skate in batter

700–900 g *(1½–2 lb)* skate
coating batter (see page 310)
deep fat for frying

Prepare the skate as described in the recipe above and dip it in the coating batter. Fry in deep fat for about 5 minutes, until crisp and golden. Drain on crumpled kitchen paper and serve with tartare or any sharp sauce. If preferred, the raw skate can be marinaded before being coated with the batter. Make the marinade (see below), allow the fish to stand in it for 2–3 hours, drain the pieces well and continue cooking as above.

Marinade Combine 30 ml *(2 tbsps)* olive oil, 15 ml *(1 tbsp)* lemon juice, a little chopped onion and a little chopped parsley, with salt and pepper to taste.

Skate with black butter

700–900 g *(1½–2 lb)* skate
50 g *(2 oz)* butter
15 ml *(1 tbsp)* vinegar
10 ml *(2 tsps)* capers
10 ml *(2 tsps)* chopped parsley

Simmer the fish in salted water or court bouillon until tender, drain and keep it warm. Heat the butter until lightly browned. Add the vinegar and capers, cook for a further 2–3 minutes and pour it over the fish. Sprinkle with the parsley and serve at once.

Skate Toledo *see colour plate facing p. 97*

25 g *(1 oz)* butter
1 clove garlic, optional
1 large onion, cut into rings
1 large green pepper, thinly sliced
175 g *(6 oz)* long grain rice
400 ml *(¾ pt)* chicken stock
4 large tomatoes, skinned and roughly chopped
freshly ground black pepper
2 wings of skate, about 1.4 kg *(2½ lb)* (any other white fish would be equally suitable)
seasoned flour
cooking oil
chopped parsley

Melt the butter in a frying pan and add the crushed clove of garlic if used. Add the onion and pepper and cook gently without browning for about 5 minutes. Stir in the rice and chicken stock. Simmer steadily, stirring occasionally, until the rice is cooked and all the liquid absorbed – 15–20 minutes. Just before the rice is cooked stir in the chopped tomatoes. Season well with freshly ground black pepper.

While the rice is cooking wash and dry the fish and cut each wing into two or three pieces. Coat thoroughly in seasoned flour.

Heat 1 cm *(½ in)* of cooking oil in a frying pan and fry the fish quickly on both sides until pale golden brown, about 5 minutes. Drain on kitchen paper.

Pile the rice mixture in the centre of a serving dish surrounded by the fish, sprinkled with chopped parsley. *Serves 3.*

Herrings in oatmeal (Fried)

Remove the heads, tails and fins and bone the herrings. Clean the flesh by rubbing with a little salt, then rinse and dry it well. Sprinkle with salt and pepper and coat with fine oatmeal, pressing it well into the fish on both sides. Fry in a small amount of lard or butter in a frying pan, turning the fish once, until brown on both sides. Drain well on kitchen paper and serve with lemon and parsley.

Grilled herrings

Cut off the heads and fins, clean the fish but leave whole. Wash and wipe them, make 2–3 diagonal cuts in the flesh on both sides of the fish and sprinkle with salt and pepper. Brush with oil or melted butter and cook on a greased grill grid for 10–15 minutes under a moderate heat, turning the fish once, until thoroughly cooked on both sides. Grilled herrings are good with mustard, horseradish or curry sauce (see pages 195, 201, 202).

Soused herrings

4 large or 6–8 small herrings, cleaned and boned
salt and pepper
1 small onion, skinned and sliced into rings
6 peppercorns
1–2 bayleaves
few parsley stalks
150 ml (*¼ pt*) malt vinegar
150 ml (*¼ pt*) water

Trim off the heads, tails and fins, remove the bones and sprinkle the fish with salt and pepper. Roll up from the head end and secure with wooden cocktail sticks. Pack them into a fairly shallow ovenproof dish and add the onion, peppercorns and herbs. Pour in the vinegar and enough water to almost cover the fish. Cover with greaseproof paper or foil and bake in the oven at 180°C *(350°F)* mark 4 for about ¾ hour, or until tender. Leave the herrings to cool in the cooking liquid before serving as an appetiser or with salad.

Note If you wish, the tails can be left on the fish; when the rolled fish are put in the dish, the tails are arranged pointing upwards. Herrings can also be soused whole.

Herrings braised in wine

½ bottle red wine
thick slices of onion, carrot and celery
1 bayleaf
bouquet garni
6 peppercorns
salt and pepper
6 herrings, cleaned with heads, tails and fins removed
sauté button mushrooms and small onions, and some parsley

Put the wine, sliced vegetables, herbs, peppercorns and seasoning in a saucepan, cover and simmer for 30 minutes. Arrange the herrings in a single layer in an ovenproof dish. Strain the liquor over them, until almost covered – add a little water, if necessary. Cover the dish and cook in the oven at 170°C *(325°F)* mark 3 for about 1 hour. Serve the herrings in the liquor, garnished with the sauté mushrooms and onions and with sprigs of parsley. *Serves 6.*

Herring roes

The roes can be left in the fish or removed and served separately. Herring roes can also be bought separately.

Roes on toast

Wash the roes and dip them in seasoned flour (see page 17). Brush them over with melted butter and grill on a greased grid, turning them once to ensure even cooking – allow about 8–10 minutes altogether. Serve on hot toast, sprinkled with cayenne pepper if you wish, and accompanied by lemon.

Roe fritters

Wash the roes, then dip them in an ordinary coating batter (see page 310).

Fry in deep fat until crisp and golden, drain well and serve with lemon wedges.

Mackerel or herrings calaisienne

4 mackerel or herrings, cleaned, with heads, tails and fins removed

For the stuffing
½ onion, skinned and chopped
1 hard-boiled egg, shelled and chopped
15 ml *(1 tbsp)* chopped parsley
50 g *(2 oz)* fresh white breadcrumbs
grated rind of ½ lemon, optional
salt and pepper
milk to mix

Bone the herrings. Mix the rest of the ingredients to make a stuffing and fill the fish with it; place them in an ovenproof dish with 30–45 ml *(2–3 tbsps)* water, cover and bake them in the oven at 180°C *(350°F)* for 20–30 minutes. Serve with tomato sauce.

If the fish have soft roes, these can be chopped and mixed with the stuffing.

Grilled, fried or soused mackerel

Follow the recipes for herrings.

Grilled mackerel with orange *see colour plate facing p. 129*

3 medium sized fresh mackerel

For marinade
150 ml *(¼ pt)* oil
75 ml *(5 tbsps)* white wine
few drops Tabasco sauce
salt and freshly ground black pepper

For garnish
50 g *(2 oz)* black olives
2 oranges, peeled and sliced into rings
fresh bayleaves

Clean, gut and wash the mackerel and remove the heads. Make two slanting incisions with a sharp knife across both sides of each fish. Lay the mackerel in the grill pan and pour over the mixed oil, wine and seasonings. Leave the fish in the marinade for two hours, turning occasionally. Put the pan under a preheated grill and cook the fish for 5–8 minutes on each side, depending on thickness. When cooked, lift the mackerel carefully on to a serving dish. Pour over the juices from the pan and when the fish are quite cold, garnish with olives, orange rings and bay leaves. *Serves 3.*

Stuffed mackerel fillets

175 g *(6 oz)* cooking apple, peeled and cored
75 g *(3 oz)* celery
25 g *(1 oz)* butter
4 medium sized gherkins, chopped
2.5 ml *(½ level tsp)* dried thyme
5 ml *(1 tsp)* vinegar
45 ml *(3 level tbsps)* fresh white breadcrumbs
salt and pepper
2 large mackerel, filleted
150 ml *(¼ pt)* pure apple juice
5 ml *(1 level tsp)* arrowroot
5–10 ml *(1–2 tsps)* sugar
gherkin fans for garnish

Chop the apple and celery. Melt the butter in a saucepan and cook the apple and celery together until the apple is pulpy. Add the gherkins, thyme, vinegar, breadcrumbs and seasoning to taste. Mix well.

Spread the stuffing over the fish fillets and fold each in half. Put them in an ovenproof dish and bake, uncovered, at 180°C *(350°F)* mark 4 for 25–30 minutes.

Blend a little apple juice with the arrowroot and sugar. Warm the remaining juice and add the blended arrowroot. Bring to the boil to thicken. Glaze the mackerel with some of the sauce, garnish with gherkin fans and serve the remaining sauce separately. *Serves 2–4.*

Baked mackerel with orange and lemon stuffing

4 mackerel, cleaned

For the stuffing
1 large orange, peeled
¼ onion, skinned and finely chopped
50 g *(2 oz)* fresh white breadcrumbs
15 ml *(1 tbsp)* chopped parsley
juice of 1 lemon
salt and pepper to taste

Trim off the heads and tails, wash and wipe the fish and remove the backbones. Chop the flesh of the orange (on a plate to retain the juice) and mix with the onion, crumbs, parsley, lemon juice, salt and pepper. Fill the fish with the stuffing and place them in a greased ovenproof dish; add 30–45 ml *(2–3 tbsps)* water and cover with a lid or foil. Bake in the oven at 180°C *(350°F)* mark 4 for 20–30 minutes, until the fish are tender. Drain well and serve with an orange salad.

Mackerel in cream sauce

4 mackerel
bunch of parsley
little butter
30 ml *(2 level tbsps)* flour
fat for frying
salt
150 ml *(¼ pt)* water
142-ml *(5-fl oz)* carton soured cream

Wash the fish, fillet them and sprinkle the fillets with chopped parsley and a few flakes of butter. Roll up the fillets and tie them with fine string, toss them in flour and fry in a saucepan until brown. Add salt to taste, the water and the soured cream and let them simmer gently in the covered pan for 10 minutes. Remove the strings and serve the fillets with the liquor poured over.

Fish and potato casserole

2 large salt herrings
450 g *(1 lb)* boiled potatoes, sliced
15 ml *(1 tbsp)* chopped onion or spring onion
30 ml *(2 tbsps)* melted butter
3 eggs
568 ml *(1 pt)* milk
2.5 ml *(½ level tsp)* pepper
60 ml *(4 tbsps)* dried breadcrumbs

Soak the fish for 6 hours, skin and bone them and cut in long strips. Butter a baking dish and put in a layer of potato, then one of herring, with a little onion; repeat, finishing with a potato layer, and pour the melted butter over the top. Beat the eggs, add the milk and pepper, pour into the baking dish and sprinkle with breadcrumbs. Bake in the oven at 180°C *(350°F)* mark 4 for 30–40 minutes, or until browned. *Serves 6.*

Canned salmon may be used instead of salt herring to make this dish.

Fried whitebait

Wash the whole fish and dry them in a cloth. Put 30–45 ml *(2–3 level tbsps)* flour in a dry cloth and toss the whitebait in it a few at a time. Put them in a frying basket. Heat some deep fat until it will brown a 2.5-cm *(1-in)* cube of bread in 1 minute. Fry the whitebait for 2–3 minutes, until lightly browned, then drain them on crumpled kitchen paper. Sprinkle with salt, garnish with lemon and parsley and serve with brown bread and butter.

Devilled whitebait

45 ml *(3 level tbsps)* plain flour
2.5 ml *(½ level tsp)* curry powder
1.25 ml *(¼ level tsp)* ground ginger
1.25 ml *(¼ level tsp)* dry mustard
1.25 ml *(¼ level tsp)* garlic salt
pinch cayenne pepper

Sift together the above ingredients and use to coat the whitebait, then fry as above.

Fried sprats

Prepare and fry as for whitebait, but allow 4–5 minutes frying.

Savoury fish cakes

450 g *(1 lb)* potatoes, peeled
75 g *(3 oz)* onion, skinned and chopped
450 g *(1 lb)* coley, skinned
25 g *(1 oz)* butter or margarine
2.5 ml *(½ tsp)* anchovy essence
30 ml *(2 tbsps)* chopped parsley
5 ml *(1 tsp)* Worcestershire sauce
salt, pepper
1 egg, separated
fresh breadcrumbs for coating

Cook the potatoes and onion in boiling, salted water until tender. Drain and mash. Sauté the roughly chopped coley in 25 g *(1 oz)* butter for 10 minutes then flake it finely. Combine with the potato, anchovy essence, parsley, Worcestershire sauce, salt, pepper and egg yolk. Allow to go cold.

Form the fish mixture into 8 cakes using floured hands. Dip in lightly beaten egg white, then in breadcrumbs, patting them well into the surface. Deep or shallow fry until crisp and golden.

Note The crumbed cakes can be left in the refrigerator for an hour or so before frying.

Puff-top supper pie

100 g *(4 oz)* each celery, carrot and onion
75 g *(3 oz)* butter
a few parsley stalks
2 bayleaves
700 g *(1½ lb)* huss, boned
400 ml *(¾ pt)* milk
30 ml *(2 level tbsps)* flour
celery salt and freshly ground black pepper
1 egg yolk
15 ml *(1 tbsp)* single cream
75 g *(3 oz)* red Leicester cheese, grated
212-g *(7½-oz)* pkt frozen puff pastry, thawed
beaten egg to glaze

Prepare and dice the vegetables and sauté in 50 g *(2 oz)* butter with the parsley and bayleaves. Cover and leave over a gentle heat until quite tender.

Cut the fish in large cubes, sauté quickly with the vegetables until the fish is opaque. Pour the milk over, bring to the boil, cover and simmer for 10 minutes. Remove the parsley and bayleaves and drain off the liquor and set it aside.

Melt the rest of the butter in a clean saucepan, stir in the flour and cook for 1 minute, add the fish liquor and bring to the boil, stirring. Add the fish and vegetables and adjust seasoning with celery salt and pepper. Combine the egg yolk and cream and stir them into the fish. Transfer to a shallow 1.4-l *(2½-pt)* ovenproof dish, leave to go cold and sprinkle with cheese.

Roll out the pastry to 0.5 cm *(¼ in)* thick and cut out 5-cm *(2-in)* fluted rounds. Overlap these along one side of the dish, right against the rim, then brush with beaten egg. Bake at 230°C *(450°F)* mark 8 for 30 minutes. *Serves 4–6.*

Coley with oriental sauce

25 g *(1 oz)* butter
175 g *(6 oz)* onion, skinned and chopped
1 clove garlic, skinned and crushed
3 sticks celery, thinly sliced
63-g *(2¼-oz)* can tomato paste
45 ml *(3 level tbsps)* concentrated curry sauce
400 ml *(¾ pt)* light stock
50 g *(2 oz)* sultanas
25 g *(1 oz)* desiccated coconut
1 large piece stem ginger, finely chopped
30 ml *(2 level tbsps)* redcurrant jelly
15 ml *(1 level tbsp)* cornflour
30 ml *(2 tbsps)* lemon juice
900 g *(2 lb)* coley fillet, skinned
1 small onion, skinned and finely sliced
chopped parsley

Melt the butter in a large shallow pan. Add the onions, garlic and celery. Cook until soft and transparent. Stir in the next three ingredients, bring to the boil, then reduce to a simmer. Add the sultanas, coconut, ginger and redcurrant jelly. Cook, covered, for 30 minutes. Blend the cornflour with the lemon juice. Stir it into the sauce, bring to the boil, then simmer for 10 minutes.

Wipe the fish, remove any bones and cut it into large pieces. Stir the fish into the curry sauce, cover and simmer for about 20 minutes, stirring occasionally, until fish is cooked. Try not to break up the fish. Carefully pour into serving dish. Decorate with raw onion rings and parsley and serve with warm poppadums. *Serves 6–8.*

MADE-UP FISH DISHES

Many of these dishes require flaked cooked fish, which is prepared as follows. Wash the fish, put it in a pan, just cover with cold water, milk or milk and water, add a little salt and cover with a lid. Bring slowly to the boil, turn off the heat and leave the fish covered for 5 minutes. Drain off the liquid (this can be used alone or with an equal amount of milk if water only was used, for making a sauce). Skin the fish, flake roughly and remove any bones.

Fish pie

450 g *(1 lb)* cod fillet or any other white fish
700–900 g *(1½–2 lb)* potatoes
40 g *(1½ oz)* butter
150 ml *(¼ pt)* milk, plus 45 ml *(3 tbsps)*
45 ml *(3 level tbsps)* flour
30 ml *(2 tbsps)* chopped parsley
salt and pepper
50 g *(2 oz)* cheese, grated

Cook and flake the fish, retaining 150 ml *(¼ pt)* of the cooking liquid. Boil and mash the potatoes in the usual way, add a knob of butter and 45 ml *(3 tbsps)* milk and beat with a wooden spoon until creamy. Melt the remaining butter, stir in the flour and cook for 2–3 minutes. Remove the pan from the heat and gradually stir in the fish liquid and 150 ml *(¼ pt)* milk; bring it to the boil. When the sauce has thickened, remove it from the heat and stir in the flaked fish, the parsley and seasoning to taste. Pour the mixture into an ovenproof dish and cover with the creamed potatoes, sprinkle with the cheese and bake in the oven at 200°C *(400°F)* mark 6 for about 30 minutes, until the pie is well heated through and the cheese golden.

The parsley sauce can be replaced by a white sauce to which one of the following has been added:
100 g *(4 oz)* mushrooms, chopped and lightly fried
or 100 g *(4 oz)* peeled shrimps
or 50–100 g *(2–4 oz)* grated cheese.

Russian fish pie

225 g *(½ lb)* white fish, eg cod, haddock
25 g *(1 oz)* butter
45 ml *(3 level tbsps)* flour
150 ml *(¼ pt)* milk
30 ml *(2 tbsps)* chopped parsley
salt and pepper
1 hard-boiled egg, shelled and chopped
212-g *(7½-oz)* pkt frozen puff or 100 g *(4 oz)* home-made flaky pastry, (page 354) made with 100 g *(4 oz)* flour, etc
beaten egg to glaze

Cook and flake the fish (see page 79), retaining 150 ml *(¼ pt)* of the cooking liquid. Melt the butter, stir in the flour and cook for 2–3 minutes. Remove the pan from the heat and gradually stir in the fish liquid mixed with the milk. Bring it to the boil and continue to stir until the sauce thickens. Mix half the sauce with the flaked fish, parsley, salt, pepper and chopped egg.

Roll out the pastry thinly into a fairly large square and place it on a baking sheet. Put the filling in the centre in a square shape, brush the edges of the pastry with beaten egg and draw them up to the middle to form an envelope shape. Press the edges well together and flake and scallop them (see page 17). Brush the pie with beaten egg and bake in the oven at 200°C *(400°F)* mark 6 for about 30 minutes, until golden. Serve with the remaining parsley sauce.

Curried fish

700 g *(1½ lb)* filleted cod, haddock or similar white fish, skinned
1 large onion, skinned and chopped
25 g *(1 oz)* butter
15 ml *(1 level tbsp)* curry powder
60 ml *(4 level tbsps)* flour
300 ml *(½ pt)* chicken stock
300 ml *(½ pt)* milk
1 small apple, skinned, cored and chopped
2 tomatoes, skinned and chopped
25–50 g *(1–2 oz)* sultanas
salt
boiled rice
lemon wedges

Cut the fish into 2.5-cm *(1-in)* cubes. Fry the onion gently in the butter for 5 minutes without browning. Stir in the curry powder, fry it for 2–3 minutes, add the flour and cook for a further 2–3 minutes. Remove the pan from the heat, stir in the stock and milk gradually and bring to the boil, stirring until the sauce thickens. Add the apple, tomatoes, sultanas, salt and pepper; cover and simmer for 15 minutes.

Add the fish, stir and simmer for a further 10 minutes, or until the fish is tender. Add more salt and pepper if necessary and serve with boiled rice and lemon wedges.

Scalloped fish with cheese

148-g *(5¼-oz)* pkt instant potato
75 g *(3 oz)* butter
1 egg, beaten
450 g *(1 lb)* cod or other white fish fillet
1 bayleaf
50 g *(2 oz)* plain flour
150 ml *(¼ pt)* milk
300 ml *(½ pt)* fish stock
100 g *(4 oz)* mature Cheddar cheese, grated
juice of ½ a lemon
salt and freshly ground pepper
parsley sprigs and lemon wedges

Make up the potato following the packet instructions. Add 25 g *(1 oz)* butter and the egg. Poach the fish in sufficient water to cover, adding the bayleaf. When it is tender, strain off and reserve the fish liquor. Discard any bones and skin from the fish. Melt the remaining butter in a saucepan and stir in the flour; cook for 1 minute. Add the milk all at once, with the fish stock, off the heat. Whisk or beat well, return the pan to the heat and bring to the boil, stirring. Add the cheese to the sauce, with the lemon juice and seasoning to taste. Spoon the potato into a piping bag fitted with a large vegetable nozzle. Butter 4–6 large natural scallop shells and pipe potato round each outside edge. Divide the fish between the shells. Spoon the sauce over and bake in the oven at 200°C *(400°F)* mark 6 for about 30 minutes or reheat under a moderate grill until the sauce is bubbling and the potato golden. Garnish with parsley and lemon. *Serves 4–6.*

Fish provençale

1 onion, skinned and chopped
1 small green pepper, seeded and chopped
50–75 g *(2–3 oz)* **streaky bacon, chopped**
25 g *(1 oz)* **butter**
450 g *(1 lb)* **fillet of cod, haddock or whiting, skinned**
seasoned flour
425-g *(15-oz)* **can tomatoes, drained**
1 bayleaf
10 ml *(2 level tsps)* **sugar**
salt and pepper

Fry the onion, pepper and bacon gently in the butter for 5–10 minutes, until soft but not coloured. Wash and dry the fish and cut it into 2.5-cm *(1-in)* cubes. Toss the fish in seasoned flour and fry with the vegetables for a further 2–3 minutes. Stir in the tomatoes, bayleaf, sugar and seasoning, bring to the boil, stirring gently, cover with a lid and simmer for 10–15 minutes, until the fish and vegetables are cooked. Serve with boiled rice.

Fish cakes

225 g *(½ lb)* **fish, eg cod, haddock**
450 g *(1 lb)* **potatoes, peeled and cut up**
25 g *(1 oz)* **butter**
15 ml *(1 tbsp)* **chopped parsley**
salt and pepper
milk or beaten egg to bind
1 egg, beaten, to coat
dry breadcrumbs
fat for frying

Cook and flake the fish (see page 79). Boil and drain the potatoes and mash with the butter. (Alternatively, use 225 g *(½ lb)* left-over mashed potatoes or instant potato). Mix the fish with the potatoes, parsley and salt and pepper to taste, binding if necessary with a little milk or egg. Form the mixture into a roll on a floured board, cut it into 8 slices and shape into cakes. Coat them with egg and crumbs, fry in hot fat (deep or shallow) until crisp and golden; drain well. Vary the flavour of the cakes by using smoked haddock, herrings, canned tuna or salmon instead of white fish.

As fish cakes tend to be dry, serve with a sauce such as tomato or parsley.

Fish quenelles

225 g *(½ lb)* **cod or any similar white fish – pike is the classic choice**
25 g *(1 oz)* **butter**
45 ml *(3 level tbsps)* **flour**
60 ml *(4 tbsps)* **milk**
1 egg, beaten
15 ml *(1 tbsp)* **cream**
salt and pepper

Cook the fish (see page 79) and purée it in an electric blender. Melt the fat, stir in the flour and cook for 2–3 minutes. Remove the pan from the heat and gradually stir in the milk. Return the pan to the heat and stir until the sauce thickens. Remove from the heat and stir in the fish, egg, cream and a generous amount of salt and pepper.

Grease a large frying pan, three-quarters fill it with water and heat to simmering point. Using 2 wetted spoons, make the fish mixture into egg-shaped or oval pieces, put into the pan and simmer for about 10 minutes, basting well, until the quenelles are swollen and just set. Remove them from the pan with a slotted spoon and serve coated with a well flavoured sauce.

SMOKED FISH RECIPES

Poached smoked haddock

Cut the fins from the fish and if the fish is large, cut it into serving-sized pieces. Place in a frying pan (or large saucepan), barely cover with milk or milk and water, sprinkle with pepper and simmer gently for 10–15 minutes, or until tender. Alternatively, cook in the oven, adding a knob of butter. The haddock can be served topped with a poached egg.

Creamed haddock with cheese

450 g *(1 lb)* **smoked haddock**
40 g *(1½ oz)* **butter**
60 ml *(4 level tbsps)* **flour**
300 ml *(½ pt)* **milk**
100 g *(4 oz)* **cheese, grated**
salt and pepper
chopped parsley to garnish

Wash and trim the fish, put it in a pan, cover with water and bring to the boil slowly. Turn out the heat, cover with a lid and leave to stand for 5–10 minutes, until the fish is tender. Drain off the liquid, retaining 150 ml *(¼ pt)* and skin and flake the fish. Melt the butter, stir in the flour and cook for 2–3 minutes. Remove from the heat and gradually stir in the fish liquid, made up to 400 ml *(¾ pt)* with the milk. Bring to the boil and continue to stir until the sauce thickens. Remove from the heat and add remaining ingredients. Serve on buttered toast or boiled rice. Sprinkle with chopped parsley before serving.

Grilled smoked haddock

Trim the fish, put it in a basin, cover with boiling water and soak for 5 minutes; drain well. Place the fish on the grill grid, skin side uppermost, and grill under a medium heat for about 3–5 minutes, depending on its thickness. Turn the fish, brush with a little melted butter or oil, sprinkle with pepper and grill for a further 3–5 minutes, until tender. Serve topped with a knob of butter.

Smoked haddock gougère

For choux paste
75 g *(3 oz)* **butter**
200 ml *(7 fl oz)* **water**
100 g *(4 oz)* **plain flour, sifted**
3 standard eggs, lightly beaten

For filling
450 g *(1 lb)* **smoked haddock**
large knob butter
100 g *(4 oz)* **onion, skinned and chopped**
25 g *(1 oz)* **flour**
300 ml *(½ pt)* **milk**
10 ml *(2 tsps)* **capers**
2 hard-boiled eggs, peeled and chopped
2 tomatoes, skinned and seeded
salt and pepper
lemon juice
15 ml *(1 level tbsp)* **fresh white breadcrumbs**
15 ml *(1 level tbsp)* **grated cheese**

For the choux, bring the butter and water to the boil. Shoot in all the flour at once; beat well until the mixture leaves the sides of the pan. Cool it slightly, then beat in the eggs. Using a 1-cm *(½-in)* plain nozzle, pipe the mixture in 2 circles (one on top of the other) round the bottom of each of 4 12.5-cm *(5-in)* diameter 200 ml *(7 fl oz)* ovenproof dishes. Bake at 220°C *(425°F)* mark 7 for about 25 minutes. Poach the fish in water to cover for 10 minutes. Drain, flake and discard the bones. Melt the butter in saucepan and sauté the onion. Stir in the flour and cook for 1 minute. Add the milk and cook, still stirring, until the sauce thickens. Stir in the capers, eggs, fish and strips of tomato. Season well; add lemon juice to taste.

Spoon the mixture into the centre of the gougère. Combine the crumbs and cheese, sprinkle over and cook for a further 10 minutes in the oven. Garnish with chopped parsley.

Note Golden fillets could be used instead of haddock.

Haddock soufflé

225 g *(½ lb)* **smoked haddock (or white fish such as cod, haddock)**
30 ml *(2 level tbsps)* **cornflour**
300 ml *(½ pt)* **milk**
knob of butter
50–75 g *(2–3 oz)* **cheese, grated**
1–2 eggs, separated
salt and pepper

Grease a 1.1-l *(2-pt)* ovenproof dish. Cook and flake the fish (see page 79). Blend the cornflour with 30 ml *(2 tbsps)* of the cold milk and boil the remainder with the butter; pour on to the blended cornflour, stirring well. Return the mixture to the pan and heat until boiling, stirring until the sauce thickens. Remove from the heat, add the cheese, fish and egg yolks and season well. Whisk the egg whites stiffly and fold into the fish mixture. Pour into the dish and bake in the oven at 200°C *(400°F)* mark 6 for about 20 minutes, until well risen and golden. Serve immediately, for the mixture sinks as it cools.

Kedgeree

450 g *(1 lb)* smoked haddock
175 g *(6 oz)* long grain rice
2 hard-boiled eggs
75 g *(3 oz)* butter or margarine
salt and cayenne pepper
chopped parsley

Cook and flake the fish (see page 79). Cook the rice in the usual way and drain if necessary. Shell the eggs, chop one and slice the other into rings. Melt the butter or margarine in a saucepan, add the fish, rice, chopped egg, salt and cayenne and stir over a moderate heat for about 5 minutes, until hot. Pile it on a hot dish and garnish with lines of chopped parsley and the sliced egg.

Kippers

Grilling Dot with butter, sprinkle with salt and pepper and grill gently for 4–5 minutes on each side.

Baking For the least smell, wrap in foil, and pop in the oven at 190°C *(375°F)* mark 5 for 10–15 minutes.

Poaching Place in a frying pan, cover with boiling water and simmer until tender – about 5 minutes. Serve with a knob of butter on each kipper.

Jug method Place in a jug of boiling water and leave in a warm place for 5–10 minutes.

Bloaters

Cut off heads, tails and fins and remove the bone. With a sharp knife, make 3 slashes along one side of each fish. Brush with a little melted butter or oil. Very lightly grill bloaters on both sides and then fill slashes with a little French mustard. Sprinkle some fresh breadcrumbs over and add extra melted butter. Brown under a hot grill.

FRESH-WATER FISH RECIPES

Salmon

900 g *(2 lb)* piece of salmon

Foil-baked method

Pre-heat the oven to 150°C *(300°F)* mark 1–2. Wipe the fish, removing the fins, etc. Butter a large piece of foil thoroughly. Place the fish in the centre and season it lightly with salt and pepper. Package the foil loosely and put it on a baking sheet. Bake for about 1 hour, depending on the thickness of the fish. Cool in the foil, unwrap and remove the skin. Carefully lift the flesh from the bones.

Slow-cooking method

Prepare the fish as above. Fill a fish kettle or large saucepan with sufficient water to almost cover the salmon. Add 150 ml *(¼ pt)* white wine, a bayleaf, a sprig of parsley, salt and 2–3 peppercorns. Bring this to the boil and simmer for 10 minutes. Lower in the salmon, and boil gently for 3 minutes. Take the fish kettle from the heat, remove the lid and leave on one side until cold. Lift out the fish, remove the skin and, if you wish, lift the flesh from the bones. *Serves 4–6.*

salmon steaks, cutlets

Cutlets should be cut about 2 cm *(¾ in)* thick. If they are very large, serve one between two people rather than ask for the steaks to be cut thinly. Wipe the fish, and remove any blood from the backbone area. Close the flaps and, to keep the pieces a good shape, secure with a cocktail stick. When individual portions of cold salmon are required for coating with mayonnaise, and especially for small numbers, it is sometimes easier to cook cutlets. After cooking, carefully ease away the bones, remove the skins and portion the fish as required.

To poach
Place the fish in a deep frying pan (preferably not a saucepan, as a shallow utensil makes removal of the fish much easier), with court bouillon to cover (see page 64). Cover the pan with a lid and simmer gently for 5–10 minutes. To ensure the fish is cooked, penetrate the thickest part of the flesh with a skewer. If cooked, the flesh will offer no resistance to the skewer. Serve hot or cold.

To bake
Line a baking sheet with a larger piece of foil, and butter the surface. Place the prepared salmon on the foil. Dot each steak with butter and season with salt, pepper and lemon juice. Package loosely and cook in the oven at 170°C *(325°F)* mark 3 for 20–40 minutes, according to the thickness of the fish. Serve with maître d'hôtel butter or hollandaise sauce or garnish with poached diced cucumber, sliced lemon and parsley sprigs. If it is to be eaten cold, leave it to cool still wrapped in the foil.

To grill
Season the prepared fish with salt and pepper and brush well with melted butter. Cook it on a greased grid under a medium heat. When the top side is cooked, and tinged light brown, brush with more butter and continue to cook for about 10–20 minutes altogether. Serve hot; traditional accompaniments are poached diced cucumber, new potatoes and asparagus or peas.

Salmon trout

Although a sea fish, this is generally considered as being very similar to the salmon. It is however usually much smaller, so it is cooked whole. Salmon trout can be poached in salted water or court bouillon or baked in foil (see baked salmon). It can be served cold with mayonnaise and salad and is also ideal for coating with aspic for serving at a formal buffet.

Whole salmon trout or grilse

Cooked on top of the stove
For this you need a fish kettle or similar large utensil. Prepare a court bouillon (see page 64); lower in the cleaned fish and reduce the heat. The stock should only just show signs of movement—the bubbles should not be allowed to break. Allow 10 minutes per 450 g *(1 lb)* for the first 2.5 kg *(6 lb)* plus 8 minutes per 450 g *(1 lb)* for the next 2.5 kg *(6 lb)*. Leave the fish in the liquor for 10 minutes, then if it is to be served hot, lift it out (most fish kettles have a rack which makes this easy). If the fish is to be served cold (see salmon in aspic), leave it in the liquor until lukewarm.

Note If the fish kettle does not have a rack, wrap the fish in muslin or buttered greaseproof paper to avoid spoiling it when it is lifted.

Oven-poached
Clean the fish, leaving on the head and tail, but removing the eyes. Curl the fish round to fit a large roasting tin. Pour over it a mixture of 1

part dry white wine and 1 part water, with slices of onion, peppercorns, a bayleaf and a slice of lemon. The liquid should come halfway up the fish. Cover the dish with buttered foil, but don't let the foil touch the fish. Cook in the oven at 170°C *(325°F)* mark 3 for about 10 minutes per 450 g *(1 lb)*; a fish weighing 1.7–2.5 kg *(3½–4½ lb)* will take 45–60 minutes. Baste occasionally. Leave to cool in the liquor, basting occasionally, and glaze as in salmon in aspic.

Salmon mousse

2 210-g *(7½-oz)* cans salmon
about 300 ml *(½ pt)* milk
25 g *(1 oz)* butter
45 ml *(3 level tbsps)* flour
2 eggs, separated
142-ml *(5-fl oz)* carton double cream, lightly whipped
30 ml *(2 tbsps)* tomato ketchup
5 ml *(1 tsp)* anchovy essence
5 ml *(1 tsp)* lemon juice
salt and pepper
20 ml *(4 level tsps)* powdered gelatine
60 ml *(4 tbsps)* warm water
slices of cucumber to garnish

Drain the juice from the salmon and make it up to 300 ml *(½ pt)* with milk. Remove the skin and bones from the fish and mash the flesh until smooth. Melt the butter, stir in the flour and cook for 2–3 minutes. Remove the pan from the heat and gradually stir in the salmon liquid and milk. Bring to the boil and continue to stir until the sauce thickens. Remove from the heat and add the egg yolks. Allow the sauce to cool slightly and stir in the cream, ketchup, essence, lemon juice and seasoning to taste and add it to the salmon.

Dissolve the gelatine in the water by putting it in a small basin in a pan of hot water; stir it into the salmon mixture. Whisk the egg whites stiffly and fold these into the mixture. Pour it into an 18-cm *(7-in)* soufflé dish and leave to set in a cool place. Garnish with slices of cucumber before serving.

Salmon à la King

439-g *(15½-oz)* can salmon
50 g *(2 oz)* butter
3 sticks celery, chopped
1 green pepper, seeded and chopped
45 ml *(3 level tbsps)* flour
2.5 ml *(½ level tsp)* salt
5 ml *(1 level tsp)* garlic salt, optional
milk
100 g *(4 oz)* button mushrooms, sliced
1 canned red pimiento, chopped

Drain the salmon, reserving the liquid, and break the fish into chunks, removing any bone and skin. Heat the butter and fry the celery and green pepper for 3–4 minutes. Add the flour, salt and garlic salt (if used) and cook gently for 2–3 minutes. Make the salmon liquid up to 300 ml *(½ pt)* with milk and gradually add to the vegetable mixture, stirring well. Bring to the boil and simmer for 2–3 minutes. Add the salmon, mushrooms and pimiento and cook for a further 5 minutes.

Serve with rice or toast croûtons.

Salmon in aspic

1 small salmon or salmon trout
400 ml *(¾ pt)* aspic jelly
radishes, cucumber, parsley, olives, tomato skins, shrimps, etc., to garnish

Have the fish cleaned but left whole. Poach or bake it in the usual way (see pages 64, 66). Leave it to cool, then remove the skin from the body, leaving on the head and tail. Make up the aspic according to the makers' instructions and when it is just beginning to thicken, coat the fish thinly. Decorate the fish, using thin rings of radish, strips of cucumber skin or thin cucumber slices, diamonds or strips of tomato skin, rings of olive, sprigs of parsley, picked shrimps, etc. Cover with further layers of aspic until the decoration is held in place. Serve with a mixed salad and mayonnaise.

Notes For a really professional finish and to ease carving, the salmon bones should be removed before the fish is glazed. Loosen the flesh along the ridge of the backbone and use scissors to cut the bone through just below the head and above the tail. Gently pull and ease out the bone. (To lift the fish, easing it on to the flat part of your arm is the simplest method.) Probably the easiest way to carry out the glazing is on a wire cooling tray, with a large plate underneath to catch the drips of aspic as they fall through. When the aspic has set, transfer the fish carefully to a large dish. Leave any remaining aspic to set, chop it on damp greaseproof paper and use as a garnish.

Truite au bleu

This is suitable only for freshly killed river trout. Clean them immediately, leaving the fish whole and the heads on; put them in a saucepan with 30 ml *(2 tbsps)* boiling vinegar and cover with boiling court bouillon (see page 64). The fish will curl round, which is quite usual. Reduce the heat and simmer for about 15 minutes, or until tender. Serve with melted butter to which lemon juice has been added.

Trout and almonds

4 trout, about 100–150 g *(4–5 oz)* each
seasoned flour
175 g *(6 oz)* butter
50 g *(2 oz)* blanched almonds, cut in slivers
juice of ½ lemon

Clean the fish, but leave the heads on. Wash and wipe them and coat with seasoned flour. Melt 100 g *(4 oz)* butter in a large frying pan and fry the fish in it two at a time, turning them once, until they are tender and golden on both sides – 12–15 minutes. Drain and keep them warm on a serving dish. Clean out the pan and melt the remaining butter; add the almonds and heat until lightly browned, add a squeeze of lemon juice and pour over the fish. Serve at once, with lemon.

Trout in aspic

See salmon in aspic, page 85. This is a good dish for a formal buffet.

Trout in cream

4 trout
juice of 1 lemon
15 ml *(1 tbsp)* chopped chives
15 ml *(1 tbsp)* chopped parsley
142-ml *(5-fl oz)* carton single cream
30 ml *(2 tbsps)* white breadcrumbs
a little melted butter

Have the fish cleaned (the heads can be left on or removed). Wash and wipe the fish, lay them in a greased shallow ovenproof dish and sprinkle with the lemon juice, herbs and about 15 ml *(1 tbsp)* water. Cover with foil and bake in the oven at 180°C *(350°F)* mark 4 for 10–15 minutes, or until tender. Heat the cream gently and pour it over the fish, sprinkle with the breadcrumbs and melted butter and brown under a hot grill. Serve at once.

Baked carp and mushrooms

4 cross-cut pieces of carp, about 700 g *(1½ lb)*
100 g *(4 oz)* button mushrooms, sliced
15 ml *(1 tbsp)* chopped parsley
½ small onion, skinned and finely chopped
salt and pepper
150 ml *(¼ pt)* red wine
150 ml *(¼ pt)* water
15 ml *(1 level tbsp)* cornflour

Clean the fish well; soak it in several changes of salted water and then wash in vinegar and water. Remove the scales and dry it. Put it in a greased ovenproof dish and add the mushrooms, chopped parsley and onion, salt, pepper, wine and water. Cover with a lid or foil and bake in the oven at 180°C *(350°F)* mark 4 for about 30 minutes, or until tender. Remove the fish, spoon the mushroom mixture over it and keep it warm. Strain and retain 300 ml *(½ pt)* of the cooking liquid. Blend the cornflour with a little cold water and stir it into the cooking liquid; put it into a pan and bring it to the boil, stirring all the time until it thickens. Cook for a further 1–2 minutes and adjust the seasoning if necessary. Serve the fish coated with this sauce.

Perch meunière

Cook fillets of perch as for sole meunière (page 71), allowing 6–8 minutes cooking time.

Baked pike

Scale, clean and wash the fish, stuff with veal forcemeat (see page 183) and put in a greased ovenproof dish. Brush the fish with melted butter and sprinkle with salt, pepper, a little chopped parsley and a few fresh white breadcrumbs. Cover with a lid or foil and bake in the oven at 180°C *(350°F)* mark 4 for about ¾–1 hour (depending on the size of the fish) until tender. Serve with anchovy sauce (see page 194).

Note The foil can be removed for the last ¼ hour to brown the crumbs, if you wish.

Pike meunière

Cook pike fillets as for sole meunière (page 71), allowing about 10 minutes cooking time, according to the size of the fish.

Stewed eels

700–900 g *(1½–2 lb)* eels, prepared
salt and pepper
squeeze of lemon juice
few sprigs of parsley
40 g *(1½ oz)* butter
60 ml *(4 level tbsps)* flour
300 ml *(½ pt)* milk
30 ml *(2 tbsps)* chopped parsley

To prepare the eels Eels are sold alive and should be cooked as soon after killing as possible. The task of preparing eels is best left to the fishmonger, but to prepare them yourself, cut off the head, turn back the skin at the head end and peel it off with a sharp pull. Split open the body and remove the backbone. Clean well and wash the eels in salted water.

Cooking Cut the eels into 5-cm *(2-in)* pieces, cover with water and add the seasoning, lemon juice and sprigs of parsley.

Simmer for about ¾ hour, until tender. Drain and retain 300 ml *(½ pt)* of the cooking liquid and keep the fish warm. Melt the fat, stir in the flour and cook for 2–3 minutes. Remove the pan from the heat and gradually stir in the cooking liquid from the fish with the milk. Bring to the boil and continue to stir until the sauce thickens. Remove from the heat, stir in the parsley, add seasoning to taste and serve the eels coated with this sauce.

Calamares fritos

450 g *(1 lb)* squid (ink-fish)
175 g *(6 oz)* plain flour
2 large eggs
salt and pepper
about 90 ml *(6 tbsps)* cold water
oil for frying
sliced lemon and parsley for garnish

Wash the fish and discard the tentacles, ink sac and any bony parts. Slice the fleshy body into rings 0.5–1 cm *(¼–½ in)* thick. Dry on absorbent paper. Make a batter by beating the flour, eggs and seasoning with enough water to give a coating consistency. Heat about 2.5 cm *(1 in)* oil in a large saucepan and cook the pieces of squid, a few at a time, for 5–8 minutes; drain on kitchen paper as they are fried. Add more oil to the pan and reheat. Dip the squid, a few pieces at a time, into the batter and deep-fry them, turning the pieces once, until golden and crisp. Drain well. Serve garnished with lemon slices and parsley.

SHELLFISH RECIPES

Dressed crab

A crab is usually sold ready cooked; in fact, many fishmongers will prepare and dress it as well. If it is bought alive, cook it as follows: wash it, place in cold salted water, bring slowly to boiling point and boil fairly quickly for 10–20 minutes, according to size – don't overcook it, or the flesh will become hard and thready. Allow to cool in the water. To give extra flavour, you can add a few parsley stalks, a bayleaf, a few peppercorns and a very little lemon juice or vinegar to the cooking water.

Lay the cooked crab on its back, hold the shell firmly with one hand and the body (to which the claws are attached) in the other hand and pull apart.

Take the shell part and use a spoon to remove the stomach bag (which lies just below the head); discard this. Carefully scrape all the meat from the shell into a basin and reserve it – this is called the soft or dark meat. Knock away the edge of the shell up as far as the dark line round the rim. Wash and if necessary scrub the shell; dry it and rub with a little oil to give a gloss.

Add 15–30 ml *(1–2 tbsps)* fresh breadcrumbs to the brown meat, season with salt, pepper and lemon juice and add a little chopped parsley; pack the mixture into the sides of the prepared shell, leaving a space in the middle for the white meat.

Take the body section and remove from it all the greyish-white frond-like pieces (called the 'dead men's fingers'), which are inedible. Crack the claws (except the very tiny ones) with a weight and take out all the flesh or white meat from both claws and body. Use the handle of a teaspoon or a skewer to reach into the crevices and take care not to get splinters of shell amongst the meat. Season the flesh with salt, pepper, cayenne and vinegar and pile it into the centre of the shell.

Decorate the crab with a little paprika and chopped parsley and lay it on a bed of lettuce, garnished with the small claws.

Crab with avocado

1 large avocado
lemon juice
white meat from 1 crab or 2 92-g *(3¼-oz)* cans crab meat
1 shallot, skinned and chopped
30 ml *(2 tbsps)* tomato ketchup
30 ml *(2 tbsps)* salad cream
15–30 ml *(1–2 tbsps)* single cream
salt and pepper to taste

Cut the avocado in half lengthwise and remove the stone; scoop out the flesh, dice it and dip at once in lemon juice. If canned crab meat is used, drain it well. Mix the crab with the remaining ingredients, stir in the drained avocado and adjust the seasoning if necessary.

Serve on a bed of lettuce or watercress, with tomato wedges; if it is to be used as an appetiser, place it in individual glasses on a bed of shredded lettuce. As this is a rich combination of ingredients, only small servings are needed.

Crab gratiné

1 medium sized crab, cooked (225 g, *8 oz*, crab meat)
50 g *(2 oz)* breadcrumbs
100 g *(4 oz)* cheese, grated
1.25 ml *(¼ level tsp)* dry mustard
2.5 ml *(½ level tsp)* cayenne pepper
2.5 ml *(½ level tsp)* salt
1.25 ml *(¼ level tsp)* pepper
few drops of Worcestershire sauce
about 45 ml *(3 tbsps)* single cream or top of the milk
2 bananas
knob of butter

Prepare the crab in the usual way. Mix the flaked white and dark meats with the breadcrumbs, cheese and seasonings. Add sufficient cream to bind to a fairly soft consistency. Replace the mixture in the cleaned shell and bake in the oven at 200°C *(400°F)* mark 6 for about 20 minutes. Place the shell and claws on a bed of watercress and garnish with slices of banana fried in the butter till lightly browned.

Lobster, simply served

Connoisseurs consider that lobster is best served quite simply with an oil and vinegar dressing or mayonnaise.

A lobster is generally sold ready boiled, but if it has been bought alive, cook it as for crab, allowing 15–25 minutes according to size and taking care not to overcook it, as the flesh tends to become hard and thready. A 900-g *(2-lb)* lobster yields about 350 g *(12 oz)* meat.

First twist off the large claws and crack them without injuring the flesh. Remove the smaller claws, which are used only for garnishing. Cut off the head. Split the lobster right down the middle of the body from the head to tail, using a strong pointed knife. Remove the intestine (which looks like a small vein running through the centre of the tail), the stomach, which lies near the head, and the spongy-looking gills, which are not edible.

Stand the head upright on a dish, arrange the cracked claws and split tail round it and garnish with parsley or salad. Serve the oil and vinegar dressing or mayonnaise separately.

Lobster mayonnaise

See page 242.

Grilled lobster

Split the lobster lengthwise and remove the intestine, stomach and gills. Brush the shell and flesh over with oil and grill the flesh side for 8–10 minutes, then turn the lobster and grill the shell side for 5 minutes. Dot the flesh with small pieces of butter, sprinkle with a little salt and cayenne pepper and serve with melted butter or with shrimp or other suitable sauce.

Lobster Newburg

2 small cooked lobsters, weighing 225 g *(½ lb)* each
25 g *(1 oz)* butter
white, cayenne and paprika pepper
salt
60 ml *(4 tbsps)* Madeira or sherry
2 egg yolks
142-ml *(5-fl oz)* carton single cream
buttered toast or boiled rice
chopped parsley to garnish

Cut the lobsters in half, carefully detach the tail meat in one piece and cut it into fairly thin slices. Crack the claws and remove the meat as unbroken as possible. Melt the butter in a frying pan, lay the lobster in the pan, season well and heat very gently for about 5 minutes, without colouring. Pour the Madeira or sherry over and continue to cook a little more quickly until the liquid is reduced by half. Beat the egg yolks with a little seasoning and add the cream. Take the lobster off the heat, pour the cream mixture over and mix gently over a slow heat till the sauce reaches the consistency of cream. Adjust the seasoning, pour at once on to hot buttered toast or boiled rice and sprinkle with parsley.

Note As an alternative, make Prawns Newburg, using 225 g *(8 oz)* peeled prawns or shrimps.

Lobster Thermidor

2 small cooked lobsters, 225 g *(½ lb)* each
50 g *(2 oz)* butter
15 ml *(1 tbsp)* chopped shallot
10 ml *(2 tsps)* chopped parsley
5–10 ml *(1–2 tsps)* chopped tarragon
60 ml *(4 tbsps)* dry white wine
300 ml *(½ pt)* béchamel sauce (see page 196)
45 ml *(3 level tbsps)* grated Parmesan cheese
mustard, salt and paprika pepper

Remove the lobster meat from the shells, chop the claw and head meat roughly and cut the tail meat into thick slices. Melt half the butter in a saucepan and add the shallot, parsley and tarragon. After a few minutes add the wine and simmer for 5 minutes. Add the béchamel sauce and simmer until it is reduced to a creamy consistency. Add the lobster meat to the sauce, with 30 ml *(2 tbsps)* of the cheese, the remaining butter, in small pieces, and mustard, salt and paprika to taste. Arrange the mixture in the shells, sprinkle with the remaining cheese and put under the grill to brown the top quickly. Serve at once.
Serves 2.

Oysters au naturel

Always buy oysters from a reliable source. If not absolutely fresh they may cause poisoning. It is possible to keep oysters alive for a day or two until they are required. Place them in a deep pan with the deeper shell on the bottom, cover with salt water, allowing 175–200 g salt to 4.5 l water *(6–7 oz salt to 1 gal water)*, and keep in a cool place. Change the water daily and sprinkle fine oatmeal in the water after it has been changed. When the oysters are required, scrub them, then open as follows: hold each in a cloth or glove in the palm of one hand, with the deeper shell downwards, and prise open the shells at the hinge, work the point of the knife into the hinge between the shell and cut the ligament (a special knife may be obtained for this purpose).

Remove the beard from each and loosen the oysters, leaving them in the half-shell. Season lightly and serve with brown bread and butter, lemon wedges and Tabasco sauce.

Oysters au gratin

oysters – at least 3 per person
15 ml *(1 tbsp)* single cream per serving
15 ml *(1 level tbsp)* grated Parmesan cheese per serving

Open the oysters (see Oysters au naturel), remove the beard and loosen the oysters, but leave them in the half-shell. Pour the cream over, sprinkle with the cheese and cook for 3–4 minutes under a hot grill, until golden and bubbling.

Oyster patties

Make little vol-au-vent cases (see page 357) and make some white sauce. Open the oysters (see Oysters au naturel), remove the beard, chop the oysters roughly and add them to the white sauce. Fill the patty cases and heat in the oven at 180°C *(350°F)* mark 4 for about 10 minutes.

Coquilles St. Jacques

8 large fresh scallops, or 225 g *(½ lb)* frozen, thawed
bouquet garni (parsley, bayleaf, thyme)
150 ml *(¼ pt)* dry white wine
150 ml *(¼ pt)* water
100 g *(4 oz)* butter
30 ml *(2 tbsps)* lemon juice
50 g *(2 oz)* onion, skinned and chopped
100 g *(4 oz)* button mushrooms, chopped
75 ml *(4½ level tbsps)* flour
1 egg yolk
60 ml *(4 tbsps)* double cream
salt and freshly ground black pepper
25 g *(1 oz)* fresh white breadcrumbs
watercress, for garnish
lemon wedges, for garnish
brown bread and butter, for serving

If using fresh scallops, first open the shells. Rest the hinge on a flat surface. Insert a sturdy small knife into the small opening to be found on either side of the shell just above the hinge. Prise open slightly, keeping the knife close against the flat shell to prevent mutilating the scallop, and sever the muscle attaching it to the shell. Discard the black sac and shell trimmings. Remove the scallop and wash and polish the shells for later use. (If you are using frozen scallops, empty shells can usually be obtained from a fishmonger.) Tip the prepared scallops into a pan, add the bouquet garni and pour over the wine and water. Bring to the boil, cover with a lid and simmer for 10–15 minutes until the scallops are tender when pricked.

Melt 25 g *(1 oz)* butter in a small pan with 15 ml *(1 tbsp)* lemon juice and stir in the onion and mushrooms. Cover with a lid and cook gently without colouring for 10 minutes. Strain off juices and reserve.

Drain the scallops and remove the bouquet garni. Cut the scallops into bite-size pieces. Melt half the remaining butter in a pan, remove from the heat and stir in the flour. Return to the heat and cook for 1–2 minutes without colouring, stirring continuously. Stir in the stock from the scallops and the juice from the mushrooms a little at a time, bring to the boil and simmer for 3 minutes.

Blend together the egg yolk and cream, add a little of the hot sauce, blend and pour back into the bulk of the sauce, whisking. Gently reheat the sauce but do not boil. Stir in the scallops, mushrooms and onion. Season to taste.

Melt the remaining butter in a small pan and use a little to brush the insides of the scallop shells. Blend the remainder with the breadcrumbs. Off the heat, stir in 10 ml *(2 tsps)* lemon juice. Divide the scallops and sauce between the shells. Sprinkle with the crumbs and brown under a preheated grill.

Garnish with watercress and lemon wedges. Serve with thinly sliced brown bread and butter.

Scallops au gratin

8 scallops, prepared
400 ml *(¾ pt)* milk
40 g *(1½ oz)* butter
60 ml *(4 level tbsps)* flour
100 g *(4 oz)* cheese, grated
salt and pepper
browned crumbs

Grease 4 individual dishes or deep scallop shells. Cut each scallop into 2–3 pieces and simmer in a little of the milk until tender – about 10 minutes. Drain, reserving the milk, and make this up to 400 ml *(¾ pt)* with the remaining milk.

Melt the butter in the pan, stir in the flour and cook for 2–3 minutes. Remove the pan from the heat and gradually stir in the milk. Bring it to the boil and continue to stir until it thickens. Add 75 g *(3 oz)* of the cheese and some salt and pepper. Divide the fish between the dishes or shells and pour the sauce over. Mix the crumbs with the rest of the cheese and sprinkle over the top; brown under a hot grill.

Scallop fricassee

8 scallops, prepared
milk
40 g *(1½ oz)* butter
60 ml *(4 level tbsps)* flour
salt and pepper
lemon wedges and parsley to garnish

Cook the scallops gently in a little water for about 10 minutes. Drain them, reserving the liquor, and make this up to 400 ml *(¾ pt)* with milk; keep the scallops hot. Melt the butter in a saucepan, stir in the flour and cook for 2–3 minutes. Remove the pan from the heat, gradually stir in the milk, bring to the boil, continue to stir until it thickens and season to taste. Arrange the scallops in a dish, pour the sauce over them and garnish with lemon wedges and parsley.

Fried scampi

225 g *(8 oz)* scampi or Dublin Bay prawns
seasoned flour
100 g *(4 oz)* plain flour
pinch of salt
15 ml *(1 tbsp)* oil
1 egg, separated
30–45 ml *(2–3 tbsps)* water or milk and water
fat for deep frying

If fresh scampi or prawns are used, discard their heads, remove the flesh from the shells and remove the dark veins; if frozen, allow to defrost, then drain well. Dip the prawns in the seasoned flour. Mix the plain flour, salt, oil and egg yolk with sufficient liquid to give a stiff batter which will coat the back of the spoon; beat until smooth. Just before cooking, whisk the egg white stiffly and fold it into the batter. Dip the scampi in the batter. Heat the fat until a cube of bread dropped into it takes 20–30 seconds to brown. Fry the scampi a few at a time until they are golden brown, drain and serve with tartare or tomato sauce.

Alternatively, the scampi can simply be coated with beaten egg and fresh breadcrumbs and fried until golden brown.

Scampi provençale

1 onion, skinned and finely chopped
1 clove garlic, skinned and finely chopped
25 g *(1 oz)* butter or 45 ml *(3 tbsps)* cooking oil
450 g *(1 lb)* tomatoes, peeled and chopped, or 425-g *(15-oz)* can tomatoes, drained
60 ml *(4 tbsps)* dry white wine
salt and pepper
pinch of sugar
15 ml *(1 tbsp)* chopped parsley
225 g *(8 oz)* frozen scampi, thawed

Fry the onion and garlic gently in the butter or oil for about 5 minutes, until soft but not coloured. Add the tomatoes, wine, seasoning, sugar and parsley, stir well and simmer gently for about 10 minutes. Drain the scampi well, add to the sauce and continue simmering for about 5 minutes, or until they are just heated through. Serve with crusty French bread or boiled rice.

Prawn mousse

150 ml *(¼ pt)* aspic jelly, made as directed on the packet
225 g *(8 oz)* shelled prawns
568 ml *(1 pt)* milk
1 small onion, skinned and quartered
1 carrot, pared and quartered
1–2 cloves
1 bayleaf
3–4 peppercorns
40 g *(1½ oz)* butter
60 ml *(4 level tbsps)* flour
2 eggs, separated
salt and pepper
20 ml *(4 level tsps)* powdered gelatine
150 ml *(¼ pt)* dry white wine or stock

Make up the aspic jelly, pour a thin layer into a 1.1-l *(2-pt)* jelly mould, adding a few prawns for decoration, and leave to set. Put the milk, onion, carrot, cloves, bayleaf and peppercorns into a covered pan, bring to the boil, turn off the heat and leave to cool for about 15 minutes, until the milk is well flavoured. Melt the butter, stir in the flour and cook for 2–3 minutes. Remove the pan from the heat and gradually stir in the milk (strained of the vegetables and herbs). Bring to the boil and continue to stir until the sauce thickens. Remove from the heat, cool slightly and stir in the egg yolks and seasoning to taste. Dissolve the gelatine in the wine or stock in a basin over a pan of hot water and stir it into the sauce. Add the remaining prawns, roughly chopped, and leave in a cool place until the mixture begins to set. Whisk the egg whites stiffly, fold them in, turn the mixture into the prepared mould and leave to set. Unmould and serve with salad.

Shrimps can of course be substituted for prawns in this dish.

Prawns with bean sprouts

175 g *(6 oz)* shelled prawns
45 ml *(3 tbsps)* sherry
45 ml *(3 tbsps)* oil
2.5 ml *(½ level tsp)* salt
175 g *(6 oz)* bean sprouts
25 ml *(1½ tbsps)* soy sauce
2.5 ml *(½ level tsp)* sugar

Soak the prawns in the sherry for 1½ hours. Heat the oil, add the drained prawns and the salt and fry for 2 minutes. Add the bean sprouts and fry for 1 minute. Add the soy sauce and sugar, mixing well. Serve with plain boiled rice. *Serves 2.*

Prawns Creole

1 small onion, skinned and finely chopped
1 small green pepper, seeded and finely chopped
25 g *(1 oz)* butter
30–45 ml *(2–3 level tbsps)* flour
425-g *(15-oz)* and 226-g *(8-oz)* can tomatoes, roughly chopped
5 ml *(1 level tsp)* each dried rosemary, thyme and oregano
salt and pepper
5–10 ml *(1–2 level tsps)* sugar
225 g *(8 oz)* peeled prawns

Fry the onion and pepper gently in the butter for 5–10 minutes, until soft. Stir in the flour and gradually add the tomatoes, herbs, salt and pepper and sugar. Simmer gently for about 15 minutes, until the sauce has thickened and the flavours have blended. Add the prawns and cook for a further 5 minutes to heat them through. Serve with boiled rice. Shrimps can be used instead of prawns; frozen shrimps or prawns can also be used – allow them to thaw and drain well before adding them.

Moules marinières

4 dozen mussels, about 3.4 l *(6 pt)*
butter
4 shallots or 1 medium onion, skinned and finely chopped
½ bottle dry white wine
chopped parsley
2 sprigs thyme, if available
1 bayleaf
freshly ground black pepper
flour

Put the mussels in a large bowl and under running water scrape off the mud, barnacles, seaweed and 'beards' with a small sharp knife. Discard any that are open or even just loose (unless a tap on the shell makes them close), or any that are cracked. Rinse again until there is no trace of sand in the bowl. Melt a large knob of butter and sauté the shallot until soft but not coloured. Add the wine, a small handful chopped parsley, the thyme, bayleaf and several turns of pepper from the mill. Simmer covered for 10 minutes. Add the drained mussels a handful at a time. Cover and 'steam', shaking often until the shells open; this will take about 5 minutes. Holding the mussels over the saucepan to catch the juices, remove the top shells, and place the mussels in warm wide soup plates. Keep them warm. Strain the liquor and reduce it by half by fast boiling. Thicken it a little by adding a small knob of soft butter creamed with 10 ml *(2 level tsps)* flour whisked in in small pieces. Adjust the seasoning. When the sauce is cooked pour it over the mussels. Sprinkle with freshly chopped parsley and serve at once.

Moules à la bruxelloise

25 g *(1 oz)* butter
3 sticks celery, finely sliced
100 g *(4 oz)* onion, skinned and chopped
1 clove garlic, skinned and crushed
1 l *(2 pt)* mussels
2 bayleaves
2 blades mace
5 ml *(1 level tsp)* salt
150 ml *(¼ pt)* dry white wine
15 ml *(1 tbsp)* chopped parsley
bread

Melt the butter in a medium sized pan. Fry the celery and onion until the onion looks transparent, remove from the heat and stir in the garlic. Wash the mussels as in moules marinières and scrub the shells well. Discard any open ones.

Cover with 400 ml *(¾ pt)* water, add bayleaves, mace and salt. Bring to the boil and cook for a few minutes, until the shells open. Any that remain closed should be thrown away. Strain off the liquid and reserve 300 ml *(½ pt)*. To the fried vegetables, add the mussel stock, wine and mussels. Cover and boil rapidly for about 7 minutes. Uncover, arrange the mussels in a shallow serving dish and pour the juices over. Serve immediately, sprinkled with chopped parsley. Use crusty bread to soak up the juices.

The sauce may be thickened if you wish with a little beurre manié, but usually it is left thin.

Escargots à la bourguignonne

1 can escargots (20 snails), with shells

For garlic butter
75 g *(3 oz)* butter
1 shallot, skinned and finely chopped
1 clove garlic, skinned and crushed
5 ml *(1 tsp)* chopped parsley
pinch of mixed spice
salt and pepper

Soften the butter and work in the remaining ingredients, seasoning to taste. Drain the snails and push each one into a shell. Fill up the shells with garlic butter, place them in snail dishes or an ovenproof dish and put in the oven at 220°C *(425°F)* mark 7 for 10 minutes until thoroughly hot. Serve at once. *Serves 3.*

Cockles, winkles and whelks

These small shellfish must be washed free of sand and then soaked for 2–3 hours before they are cooked. The most usual way of serving is to eat them cold, sprinkled with vinegar.

Cockles are cooked in a pan with a little water; heat gently, shaking the pan to prevent burning, for about 5 minutes, until the shells open.

Winkles and whelks can be simmered in boiling salted water until tender.

Meat

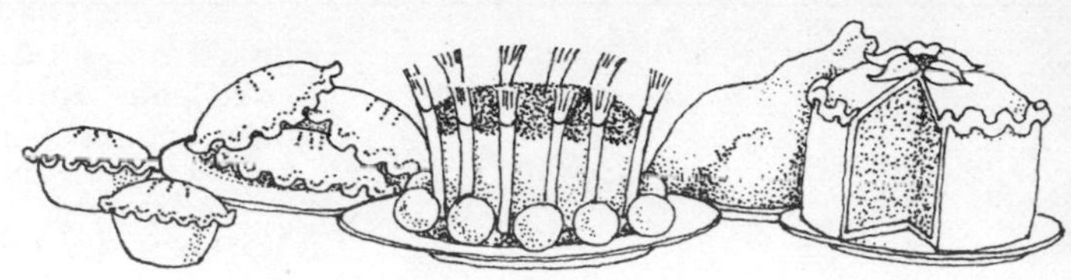

Meat not only makes the basis of a good, satisfying meal, but it also supplies us with protein, some of the B vitamins and iron; the fat, which is of high energy value, helps to give the meat some of its characteristic flavour.

The price of meat varies according to the type of cut, the most expensive joints being those parts which are least exercised and are therefore usually tender. These cuts can be roasted, fried or grilled, while the tougher parts need slower methods of cooking to soften them. The cheaper cuts are, however, just as nutritious as the dearer ones and have just as good a flavour.

Choice of meat

Modern methods of transport and cold storage have done away with 'seasons' for meat and you can buy lamb, beef, and pork at any time of the year.

Most butchers sell both fresh home-killed meats and chilled and frozen imported ones. Imported meat is less expensive than that from our own farms and the quality and flavour may not always be quite so excellent, but it is usually satisfactory.

Frozen meat is generally thawed out by the butcher and sold ready to cook. If, however, it is still icy when you buy it, let it thaw out at room temperature before cooking it – don't put it in a hot place or pour hot water over it to speed the process, as some of the flavour is then lost. Cook it as for fresh meat.

Find a butcher who sells meat in prime condition for cooking; even the highest quality meat, if sold without being properly hung, will be flavourless and tough when cooked. Don't be afraid to ask the butcher's advice – he is an expert and will be able to help you select the best cut for your particular purpose.

Generally speaking, choose meat which has no undue amount of fat; what fat there is should be firm and free from dark marks or discoloration. Lean meat should be finely grained, firm and slightly elastic and it should have a fine marbling of fat through it.

Storing meat

Never store meat still in its wrapping paper; either unwrap it and put it on a plate or wrap it in thin plastic leaving the ends open for ventilation. Don't wash meat unless absolutely necessary; it is best merely to wipe the surface with a damp cloth to remove any blood, sawdust and so on.

Store meat in a cool place – immediately below the freezing unit of the refrigerator is ideal. In some refrigerators a special meat drawer or container is available and meat need not be wrapped or covered but can be put straight into this compartment. Although the low controlled temperature means that uncooked meat can be kept for 3–4 days, a refrigerator must not be regarded as a storage place for long periods – the low temperature only slows down the process of deterioration and does not completely prevent it. Minced raw meat, sausages and offal are particularly perishable and they should be used within a day of being purchased.

When no refrigerator is available, store the meat in a cool well-ventilated place, lightly wrapped to protect it from flies.

Cooked meats which are put into a refrigerator should be wrapped to prevent drying. Leftover stews and casseroles should first be allowed to cool and then be put into the refrigerator or a cool larder in a covered dish. Re-heat such dishes very thoroughly before using them the next day.

Roasting meat

This can be carried out in two ways, the oven method being the commoner.

In the oven

Meat is roasted either at the traditional high temperature in a hot oven at 220°C *(425°F)* mark 7, when the joint is seared quickly on the outside, giving a good, meaty flavour, or at a lower temperature, 190°C *(375°F)* mark 5 when the joint is more moist, there is less shrinkage and (since the fibres are broken down) the meat is more tender, though some people consider that the flavour is not quite so good.

Arrange the shelves in the oven so that the meat is in the centre. Put the joint in the roasting tin so that the largest cut surfaces are exposed and the thickest layer of fat is on top; this automatically bastes the joint. If the fat is rather meagre, top the meat with 50 g *(2 oz)* dripping or lard. Don't prick the meat with a fork or anything sharp while it is cooking or you will lose some of the juices. If you turn or lift the joint, use two spoons.

Basting If the hot fat and juices from the tin are spooned over the joint several times during the cooking period, the flavour is improved and the meat is moist and juicy.

Frothing Sprinkling with flour and salt $\frac{1}{4}$ hour before the cooking is finished gives a crisp outside.

Roasting on a grid

If the meat is cooked on a rack or grid standing inside a roasting tin, the finished result will be less fatty.

Roasting in a closed tin

Using a covered tin produces a moist joint (and incidentally keeps the inside of the oven clean). However, the meat is pale in colour and doesn't have such a good flavour as when it is roasted in an open tin. You can remove the lid during the last half-hour of the cooking time to crisp and brown the joint.

Roasting in foil

If the meat is wrapped in aluminium foil before it is put in the roasting tin it will be moist and tender and will not shrink so much. However, foil wrapping has the same effect as roasting in a closed tin and the meat will not develop so much flavour and colour. The foil should therefore be opened during the last half-hour of the cooking time, so that the joint can become crisp and brown.

Roasting wraps and bags

The main purpose of these is to keep the oven clean while the meat roasts. The bag or wrap also collects the meat juices together, and if a little flour is sprinkled inside the bag before inserting the meat, you have ready-made gravy at the end of the cooking time. The packets usually recommend cooking times and temperatures – usually up to 200°C *(400°F)* mark 6. Instructions suggest piercing or slitting the bag or wrap before cooking, to allow for expansion of air. To obtain crisp, browned meat, the wrap or bag should be opened during the last half-hour of the cooking time.

Roasting on a spit

The latest roasting method is in effect a return to the older ways. Cookers are available with an attached spit roaster, or you can buy one separately. A joint roasted on an open spit has a much better flavour than oven-roast meat; spit-roasting in the oven, however, shows little difference from ordinary oven-roasting. (See section on Rôtisserie Cooking, page 576).

Meat thermometers

Some people find a meat thermometer a great help when roasting meat. Insert it into the thickest part of the joint before this is put into the oven. When the thermometer registers the required internal temperature (see chart below), the meat will be correctly cooked. The thermometer is particularly useful with beef, ensuring that you can have it rare, medium or well-done, to your particular taste. (It is, of course, still necessary to work out the approximate length of cooking time, in order to know at what time cooking should be started.) Make sure the thermometer does not touch the bone.

A thermometer is essential if you are cooking meat from frozen, see page 475).

Using a meat thermometer

Beef:		
Rare	60°C *(140°F)*	Very rare when hot, but ideal when cold.
	75°C *(160°F)*	Brown meat, but bloody juices running from it, pale pinkish tinge when cold.
Well done	77°C *(170°F)*	Well cooked. Tends to be dry when cold.
Very well done	82°C *(180°F)*	Fibres breaking up; fat rendered down.
Veal:	82°C *(180°F)*	Moist, pale meat
Lamb:	82°C *(180°F)*	Moist, brown meat.
Pork:	89°C *(190°F)*	Moist, pale meat.

Pot roasting

This method of cooking joints of meat in a covered pan is particularly suitable for small, compact pieces and for cuts which are inclined to be tough, such as breast of mutton (boned, stuffed and rolled); brisket ; stuffed sheep's heart.

Braising

Braising is a combination of stewing, steaming and roasting. The meat is cooked in a saucepan or casserole, over a bed of vegetables, with just sufficient liquid to keep it moist. This gives a good flavour and texture to meat that otherwise would be tough and flavourless. To give a 'roast' flavour, bake or roast the meat in the oven at 220°C *(425°F)* mark 7 for the last $\frac{1}{2}$ hour of the cooking time. If it is already being cooked in the oven, merely remove the lid from the pan and increase the temperature. Boned and stuffed joints are particularly good braised.

Stewing

A long, slow method of cooking in a liquid which is kept at simmering point 96°C *(205°F)*; it is particularly suitable for cheaper pieces of meat. The meat is cut up and vegetables are usually added. Since all the liquid is served, none of the flavour or food value is lost. A good, strong pan or casserole is needed to avoid burning; it should have a tightly fitting lid to prevent evaporation. Keep the temperature below boiling point – this is important, as boiling often causes meat to become tough.

To obtain a good colour when making a brown stew, the meat and vegetables are fried in hot fat until they are lightly browned before the liquid is added.

Boiling

Although, technically speaking, boiling is cooking in a liquid at 100°C *(212°F)* meat is actually simmered at about 96°C *(205°F)* to prevent shrinkage and loss of flavour and to keep it tender. Root vegetables are usually added to give extra flavour. The joint is barely covered with cold water, brought slowly to boiling point, covered with a tightly fitting lid and simmered gently throughout the whole of the cooking time given in the particular recipe.

Grilling

A quick method of cooking food under a grill or over a hot fire, which is suitable only for the best-quality types of meats – chiefly tender chops, steaks, liver, kidneys, gammon and back rashers. The poorer cuts remain tough, as the fibres cannot be broken down quickly enough. Season the meat with salt and pepper and brush it with melted fat or oil before cooking. The grill should be made really hot before the cooking is begun.

Many meats are greatly improved if they are first marinaded for at least 2 hours. Mix 2 parts salad oil with 1 part vinegar or lemon juice, add a little chopped onion and some salt and pepper and keep turning the meat in this mixture.

Frying

Another quick method of cooking – in hot fat or oil instead of by radiant heat. Only the better quality meats should be fried – see those suggested above for grilling.

Pickling meat

Silverside or brisket of beef, leg or belly of pork, ox tongue and pig's head are particularly suited to pickling or salting. The only equipment required is a large earthenware crock, bowl or basin or a polythene bowl or pail, with a board or lid to keep out the dust.

Home pickling is best done in cold weather. Trim and wash the meat, then rub it over with salt to remove all traces of blood. Of the two methods given below, the first is the easier, but the second gives a more interesting flavour to the meat.

Wet pickle

Put 4.5 l *(1 gal)* water, 700 g *(1½ lb)* bay or common salt, 30 ml *(2 level tbsps)* saltpetre and 175 g *(6 oz)* brown sugar in a large pan, bring to the boil and boil for 15–20 minutes, skimming carefully. Strain the liquid into the container you are using, allow to cool, put in the meat and cover.

Dry pickle

Pound 225 g *(½ lb)* bay salt, mix with 225 g *(½ lb)* common salt, 225 g *(½ lb)* brown sugar, 20 ml *(4 level tsps)* saltpetre, 20 ml *(4 level tsps)* ground black pepper and 5 ml *(1 level tsp)* allspice. Rub the meat daily with this mixture, leaving it meantime in the covered container.

Pickling time

A thick cut of beef needs about 10 days, whereas a thinner cut, or a pig's head split in half, may be sufficiently salted in 4–5 days.

Cooking pickled meat

Remove the meat from the pickle and wash it thoroughly in cold water. If you wish, soak it for 1 hour in cold water before cooking. Tie the meat up neatly if necessary, put it into a pan of cold water, bring slowly to the boil and skim. Add some sliced carrot, turnip and onion, a few peppercorns and a bouquet garni and let the water simmer very gently until the meat is tender; allow 1 hour per 450 g *(1 lb)* for joints up to 1.5 kg *(3 lb)*, a total of 3–4 hours for joints weighing 2–2.5 kg *(4–5 lb)*. (The liquid may be used for making soups.)

Carving meat

When a joint is well carved the meat looks attractive and goes further. Luckily, carving is an art most people can acquire, given a good knife. Your butcher will prepare the joint in the easiest way to carve if he knows how it is to be served. For example, a joint that includes part of the backbone (eg loin) can be 'chined' – that is, cut through the ribs close to the backbone. The chump (ie leg) bone is also cut away. The loose piece of bone that is left can be removed before carving. When preparing meat for cooking, don't use wooden skewers, which swell and become difficult to remove.

Equipment

A long-bladed, sharp knife is essential. To restore the sharpness, use a steel or a patent sharpener. The correct way to use a steel is to draw each side of the blade in turn smoothly down and across with rapid strokes, holding the blade at an angle of 45° to the steel. Careless sharpening can inflict permanent damage on the knife or your finger!

Some modern stainless steel knives have a hollowed out, grooved blade; these do not often require sharpening and are perhaps easier for an inexperienced person to use, but the skilful carver usually prefers a

Prawn vol-au-vent (p. 357).

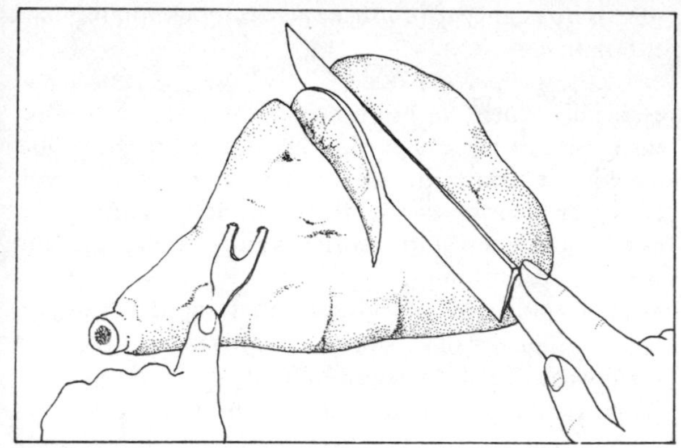

Carving a leg of lamb

plain blade.

A sharp two-pronged fork will hold the meat steady; it must have a metal guard to protect the hand, lest the knife should slip.

Keep the carving set separate from other cutlery, or the knife may become dulled.

A modern meat dish with sharp prongs to hold the joint steady is a great help. Put the meat on the dish with little or no fat and little garnishing; gravy should be served separately. Place the dish on the table close to the carver and well away from other dishes.

Technique

The meat is usually best when cut across the grain, though sometimes with meat that is very tender – for example, the undercut – the joint is cut with the grain. The carver needs to know the make-up of each joint – where the bone is to be found and how lean and fat are distributed.

It is much easier to carve standing up. Use long, even strokes, keeping the blade at the same angle, to give neat, uniform slices. As you carve, move the knife to and fro, cutting cleanly without bearing down on the meat, which presses out the juices. Serve the carved slices of meat on to very hot plates, or it will cool surprisingly quickly.

Beef and veal (except fillet) are carved very thinly, pork and lamb are cut in slices about 0.5 cm *(¼ in)* thick. When cutting a joint with a bone, take the knife right up to this so that eventually the bone is left quite clean.

Sirloin of beef Stand the joint on its back with the fillet uppermost; remove the strings. Carve the fillet, loosening each slice from the bone with the knife-tip; turn the joint over and carve in long slices right up to the bone.

Rib of beef Stand the joint on edge on the bone. Slice downwards along the full length of the joint, cutting each slice down to the bone and slanting a little away from the cut edge, so that the bone is left clean. Support the slices with the fork to prevent their breaking.

Boneless joints of beef Carve across the grain, usually horizontally. In the case of a long piece of roast fillet, however, you will need to carve downwards.

Stuffed breast of lamb or veal Cut downwards in fairly thick slices, right through the joint.

Fillet of veal The bone is usually removed and replaced by stuffing. Cut across the grain (ie, horizontally) into medium-thick slices, right across the joint.

If the bone has been left in, cut the meat down to it on one side, then turn the joint over and do the same on the underside.

Leg of lamb Begin by cutting a wedge-shaped slice from the centre of the meatier side of the joint. Carve slices from each side of the cut, gradually turning the knife to get larger slices and ending parallel to the bone. Turn the joint over and carve in long slices.

Shoulder of lamb Cut a thick wedge-shaped slice from the centre of the meatiest side of the joint. Carve small slices from each side down to the shank and the shoulder-bone. Turn the joint over and carve in long slices.

Best end of neck of lamb Cut the joint right through, downwards, into cutlets. (This is easier if it has previously been chined.)

Saddle of lamb First carve the meat from the top of the joint in long slices, cutting downwards to and parallel with the backbone. Do this at each side of the bone, taking about 4 slices. Then carve diagonal slices from either side of the saddle.

Loin of pork Sever the chined bone from the chop bones and put to one side. Divide into chops by cutting between the bones and the scored crackling.

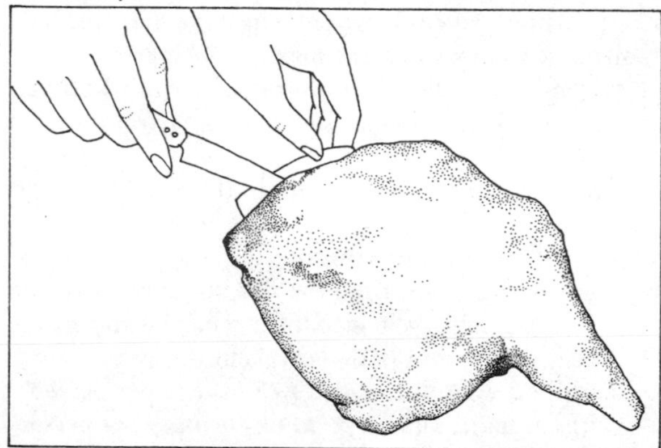

An alternative method of preparing a shoulder of lamb for easy carving. Before cooking insert knife and ease meat away from blade bone; after roasting, twist and remove the bone. Carve downwards until the bone is reached then turn the joint over and continue carving the other side.

Skate Toledo (p. 75).

Boned and rolled pork Remove the string from each part of the joint as it is carved. Cut through the crackling where it was scored half-way along the joint. Lift off the crackling and cut into pieces. Carve the meat into slices.

Leg of pork Use the point of the knife to cut through the crackling; it is usually easier to remove it and then divide it into portions. Carve as for leg of lamb, but medium-thick.

Spare rib of pork Cut between the score marks into moderately thick slices.

Texturized vegetable protein

Otherwise known as novel protein, TVP is derived from cotton seed, peanuts, sesame seed, oats, sunflower seed and soya bean – the last being the most prolific. As a natural protein in its own right, this new non-synthetic food has a nutritional value almost identical to meat though short in one or two essential amino acids. Since in most people's diet it will not replace but supplement meat this doesn't matter.

For some time vegetarians and health food followers have used vegetable protein in place of animal in their diet in appetising meatless stews, as a stuffing for cannelloni, to prepare lasagne and similar dishes and because you don't expect meat they are quite acceptable. Only recently has there been large scale technological research designed to produce a generally acceptable mass alternative to meat.

In the proportion of 25% TVP to 75% meat and especially when it's in granule form which integrates easily into dishes designed to use minced meat, people would not know that there was anything different. However, chunks are slightly more tricky to disguise as their regular shape and small cut is more easily picked out from diced fresh meat.

It is important to know whether the TVP is pre-seasoned, plenty of seasoning is important, introduce a variety of vegetables in casseroles or stews, curry bases are particularly acceptable, and do not rely on the size of TVP pieces for appearance or total taste. When using TVP in recipes it is important to remember that it has greater absorption powers than fresh meat and so it is well to check on the liquid and adjust accordingly. Reconstitute TVP according to manufacturers' directions. Because TVP is pre-cooked, it needs less cooking time than fresh meat (extra cooking doesn't help to tenderise) and so sauces and other basic mixtures are best cooked for a while before the TVP is added.

As a meat-extender, ground TVP is suitable for incorporation with fresh mince in burgers, cottage pie, meat balls, bolognese sauce. Certainly it would be a good idea to have a pack in the cupboard to stretch a dish if unexpected visitors appear. Generally speaking for replacement value 25 g *(1 oz)* TVP is equal to 100 g *(4 oz)* fresh mince.

BEEF

1. The lean should be bright red, the fat a creamy-yellow.
2. There should be small flecks of fat through the lean; this fat (called 'marbling') helps to keep the lean moist and tender when the meat is cooking.
3. Avoid meat with a line of gristle between lean and fat, which usually suggests it has come from an old animal.
4. The quantities to allow refer to the weight of meat as bought.

Cuts and method of cooking

Sirloin A large joint from the ribs, usually roasted on the bone. Can also be boned, fillet removed and rolled. It is very tender and has an excellent flavour.

With bone, allow 225–350 g *(8–12 oz)* per person.

Without bone, allow 175–225 g *(6–8 oz)* per person.

Rib A fairly large joint, next to the sirloin and without the undercut. It can be bought on the bone or boned and rolled, and is roasted. Can also be used for pot roasting, braising and boiling.

Quantities as for sirloin.

Topside A lean joint, usually boned and rolled and therefore economical. It can be roasted, but braising or pot roasting are more suitable methods as topside can be lacking in flavour and is not as tender as sirloin.

Allow 175–225 g *(6–8 oz)* per person.

Brisket Can be sold on or off the bone and is often salted. It is rather a fatty joint but has a good flavour. Brisket can be slow-roasted or braised; when salted, it should be boiled.

With bone, allow 225–350 g *(8–12 oz)* per person.

Without bone, allow 175–225 g *(6–8 oz)* per person.

Silverside A boneless joint. Needs long, slow cooking, such as boiling or braising. Often salted and cooked as traditional boiled beef and carrots.

Allow 175–225 g *(6–8 oz)* per person.

Aitch-bone A cheaper joint, but has a large bone and tends to be rather fatty on the top of the joint. Usually roasted, but also boiled or braised. Sometimes salted and then boiled. Also sold boned and rolled.

Allow 350 g *(12 oz)* per person on the bone.

Flank A cheaper cut, known as thick or thin flank, that comes from the belly of the animal and tends to be coarse. Needs slow, moist cooking, such as stewing, braising or pot roasting.

Allow 175–225 g *(6–8 oz)* per person.

Leg and shin Cheap cuts containing a lot of bone, but quite lean and with a good flavour. Long, slow cooking is needed, such as stewing. They can be used for curries, goulash, stews, meat pies and puddings.

Allow 175–225 g *(6–8 oz)* per person.

Chuck or blade steak A cheaper cut, without bone, taken from the shoulder. Fairly lean and suitable for stewing, casseroles, pies and so on.

Allow 175–225 g *(6–8 oz)* per person.

Rump, fillet, entrecôte steak, etc See steaks, page 101.

Roast beef

Wipe the meat, trim it if necessary, then weigh it and calculate the cooking time, allowing 20 minutes per 450 g *(1 lb)* plus 20 minutes if the meat is on the bone; 25 minutes per 450 g *(1 lb)* plus 25 minutes if boned and rolled. Put the meat in a roasting tin so that the thickest layer of fat is uppermost and the cut sides are exposed to the heat. Add about 50 g *(2 oz)* dripping if the meat is lean. Put the joint in the middle of the oven and cook at 220°C *(425°F)* mark 7 uncovered for the calculated time, basting from time to time with the juices from the tin. Serve slightly rare, accompanied by Yorkshire pudding, horseradish sauce, thin brown gravy and vegetables as desired.

To roast meat more slowly, which tends to give a moister joint, prepare and cook at 190°C *(375°F)* mark 5 allowing 27 minutes per 450 g *(1 lb)* plus 27 minutes for joints on the bone; 33 minutes per 450 g *(1 lb)* plus 33 minutes for boned and rolled joints.

Suitable joints – Sirloin, rib, rump, topside, aitch-bone.

Yorkshire pudding

Make up 300 ml *(½ pt)* pouring batter, see page 307. Put 25 g *(1 oz)* dripping or lard in a tin measuring about 18 cm *(7 in)* square and place it towards the top of the oven preheated to 220°C *(425°F)* mark 7. When the fat in the tin shows a haze and is really hot, pour in the batter and return to the oven to cook for 40–45 minutes.

Note It is necessary to cook a batter in a tin to get a crisp puffed up result: cooked in a pie dish or flameproof ware, a batter tends to become soggy.

For individual puddings or popovers, use 50 g *(2 oz)* flour, a pinch of salt, 1 egg, 150 ml *(¼ pt)* milk and cook for 15–20 minutes. This quantity will fill a 4-cup Yorkshire pudding pan or, alternatively 10–12 patty tins.

Pot roast of beef

1.6 kg *(3½ lb)* topside or brisket, in a piece
salt and pepper
25 g *(1 oz)* fat or oil
2–3 cloves
1 onion, skinned
300 ml *(½ pt)* water

Use a heavy based pan on top of the stove or an iron or heavy enamelled casserole with a well fitting lid in the oven. Season the meat on all sides and fry it in the hot fat or oil in the pan or casserole until lightly browned all over. Stick the cloves into the onion, add it to the meat, with the water, cover and cook over a gentle heat for about 3 hours, or until the meat is tender, turning it occasionally. Alternatively, cook the meat in the oven at 150°C *(300°F)* mark 2. If you wish, a few thickly sliced vegetables such as onions, carrots, parsnips or turnips can be added about 1 hour before cooking is complete. Remove the meat, lay the vegetables in the bottom of the casserole or pan, then replace the meat on top of the vegetables, cover and continue cooking. Serve the meat hot, surrounded by any vegetables which were added.

To make a gravy, pour off any excess fat, add 300 ml *(½ pt)* stock or vegetable water to the casserole and stir round to mix in any browned residue sticking to the bottom. Bring to the boil, season well and serve. Clear gravy is the more usual choice, but it can be thickened by adding 15–20 ml *(3–4 level tsps)* flour or cornflour, blended with the stock or water.

Braised beef

1.6 kg *(3½ lb)* topside, silverside or rolled rib of beef, in a piece
salt and pepper
15 ml *(1 tbsp)* fat or oil
3–4 onions, skinned and sliced
3–4 carrots, pared and left whole or sliced
1 small turnip, pared and quartered
1–2 sticks celery, trimmed and sliced
1 parsnip, pared and quartered
2–3 bacon rinds
1 bayleaf
few parsley stalks
3–4 peppercorns

Meat can be braised on top of the cooker in a solid based pan or in a casserole in the oven set at 170°C *(325°F)* mark 3. The container must have a tightly fitting lid. Season the meat well on all sides and fry in the hot fat or oil until lightly browned all over. Remove it and fry the vegetables and bacon rinds in the same fat or oil until lightly browned. Pour off the excess fat. Add the bayleaf, parsley stalks and peppercorns, more seasoning and water to come about three-quarters up the vegetables. Put the meat on to the bed of vegetables, cover with a lid and simmer until the meat is tender. Allow about 2 hours for meat up to 1.4 kg *(3 lb)* and 25 minutes per 450 g *(1 lb)* plus 25 minutes for larger pieces. Baste 2 or 3 times during the cooking. Remove the lid and turn the oven up to 220°C *(425°F)* mark 7 for ½ hour until the meat is brown. Serve sliced, with a gravy made from the cooking liquid – left clear or thickened with a little blended flour or cornflour, 10 ml *(2 level tsps)* to 300 ml *(½ pt)* liquid.

Stewing steak can be sliced and braised as above for about 2 hours.

Boiled beef and carrots with herb dumplings

1.8-kg *(4-lb)* piece of fresh brisket or silverside
30 ml *(2 level tsps)* salt per 450 g *(1 lb)* meat
bouquet garni
3–4 onions, skinned and left whole
4–6 small carrots, pared and left whole or sliced
2–3 leeks, or 1–2 sticks of celery, cleaned and cut in 5-cm *(2-in)* lengths
1 small turnip, pared and quartered

For the dumplings
100 g *(4 oz)* self raising flour
salt
2.5 ml *(½ level tsp)* mixed dried herbs
50 g *(2 oz)* shredded suet

To calculate the cooking time, allow 30 minutes per 450 g *(1 lb)* and 30 minutes over for meat up to 1.4 kg *(3 lb)*; 45 minutes per 450 g *(1 lb)* for joints any larger than this – ie 3 hours for a 1.8-kg *(4-lb)* piece. Put it in a large pan with the salt and enough water to cover, bring slowly to the boil, skim off any scum that rises, add the bouquet garni, cover with a lid, reduce the heat and leave to simmer. Three-quarters of an hour before the cooking is complete, add the vegetables and continue cooking.

To make the dumplings, combine all the ingredients and bind with water to give an elastic dough; divide into 10–12 small pieces and roll into balls. Add to the pan about ¼ hour before cooking is complete, cover and simmer for 15–20 minutes, or until the dumplings swell and rise to the top of the pan. If the pan is rather full, pour off some of the cooking liquid into a separate pan, bring this to the boil, drop in the dumplings and cook as above. Remove the bouquet garni and serve the meat hot, surrounded by the vegetables and dumplings. Any meat left over is excellent used cold for sandwiches or served with salad.

Salted brisket, silverside or belly of pork can also be cooked in this way. If very salty, soak for 3–4 hours before cooking, rinse, then cover with fresh water and proceed as for unsalted meat, but allow 1 hour per 450 g *(1 lb)* for joints up to 1.4 kg *(3 lb)* and 3–4 hours for joints weighing 1.8–2.3 kg *(4–5 lb)*.

Spiced silverside

1.8-kg *(4-lb)* piece salted silverside
1 onion, skinned and sliced
2 carrots, pared and sliced
1 small turnip, pared and sliced
1–2 sticks of celery, trimmed and chopped
8 cloves
100 g *(4 oz)* soft brown sugar
2.5 ml *(½ level tsp)* dry mustard
5 ml *(1 level tsp)* ground cinnamon
juice of 1 orange

Soak the meat for several hours or overnight, then rinse it, put in a large pan with the vegetables, cover with water and bring slowly to the boil. Remove any scum, cover with a lid and simmer until tender, allowing about 1 hour for 450 g *(1 lb)*, 2–3 hours for 1–1.4 kg *(2–3 lb)* and 3–4 hours for 1.8–2.3 kg *(4–5 lb)*. Allow to cool in the liquid. Drain, put into a roasting tin and stick the cloves into the fat. Mix together the remaining ingredients and spread over the meat. Bake in the oven at 180°C *(350°F)* mark 4 for ¾–1 hour, basting from time to time. Serve hot or cold. If you wish, you can press the meat after cooking it until tender. Fit it snugly into a casserole or foil-lined tin, spoon a few spoonfuls of the liquor over and place a board or plate on top, with a heavy weight. Leave in a cold place.

STEAKS

Rump The joint next to the sirloin and one of the commonest cuts used for grilling or frying. The 'point' is considered the best part for tenderness and flavour.

Fillet The undercut of the sirloin, probably one of the best-known and the most expensive of the cuts used for grilling and frying. Very tender, although it usually has less flavour than rump. The 'centre' or 'eye' of the fillet is considered the best part. The fillet is often cut and shaped into small rounds, known as Tournedos, weighing about 125 g *(5 oz)* each.

A *filet mignon* is a small round steak, weighing about 75 g *(3 oz)*, cut from the end of the fillet.

Chateaubriand A thick slice taken from the middle of the fillet, generally regarded as the most superb cut of all. It can weigh about 350 g *(12 oz)*. Grill and serve with maître d'hôtel butter.

Sirloin (or Contre-filet) Cut into two parts. Porterhouse steak is cut from the thick end of the sirloin, giving a large juicy piece that can weight 850 g *(30 oz)*; when it is cooked on the bone it is called T-bone steak in the United States. *Minute steak* is a very thin steak from the upper part of the sirloin, weighing 125–150 g *(5–6 oz)*, without any trimmings of fat.

Entrecôte By definition this is the part of the meat between the ribs of beef, but a slice cut from the sirloin or rump is often served under this name.

Preparation of steaks

Very little need be done. Trim the steak to a good shape if necessary and wipe it well. Salt and pepper or 'seasoned' salt and 'seasoned' pepper can be sprinkled over the meat before cooking; if there is doubt as to its tenderness the steak can be beaten with a rolling pin or steak hammer.

Cooking steaks

To grill Brush with melted butter or oil and put under a pre-heated grill. Cook under a medium heat, turning them regularly and using a blunt tool so as not to pierce the meat and allow juices to escape.

To fry If the steak is large, brown it quickly on both sides in shallow oil or melted butter, then reduce the heat and cook gently for the remaining time. With small steaks, fry over medium heat for half the cooking time on one side, then turn them and cook for remaining time.

Cooking times for steaks (in minutes)

Thickness	*Rare*	*Medium Rare*	*Well-done*
2 cm *(¾ in)*	5	9–10	12–15
2.5 cm *(1 in)*	6–7	10	15
4 cm *(1½ in)*	10	12–14	18–20

To serve A piece of maître d'hôtel butter (page 35), placed on each steak before it is served, is the traditional but not invariable accompaniment. Other accompaniments are matchstick or chipped potatoes, grilled tomatoes and mushrooms.

Steak Diane

4 pieces of fillet steak, 0.5 cm *(¼ in)* thick
25 g *(1 oz)* butter
30 ml *(2 tbsps)* oil
30 ml *(2 tbsps)* Worcestershire sauce
15 ml *(1 tbsp)* lemon juice
15 ml *(1 tbsp)* grated onion
10 ml *(2 tsps)* chopped parsley

Fry the steaks in the butter and oil for 1–2 minutes on each side. Remove them (keeping them hot) and add the Worcestershire sauce and lemon juice to the juices in the pan. Stir well and warm through; add the onion and parsley and cook gently for 1 minute.

Serve the sauce spooned over the steaks.

Mustard steaks

4 fillet steaks, 175–225 g *(6–8 oz)* each
salt and pepper
50 g *(2 oz)* butter
142 ml *(¼ pt)* double cream
10 ml *(2 tsps)* French mustard

Sprinkle the steaks with salt and pepper and fry in hot butter for 3–5 minutes on each side. Drain and keep hot. Carefully pour the cream into the remaining butter and meat juices and cook without boiling until thick; stir in the mustard and pour the mixture over the steaks immediately before serving.

Gaelic steak flambé

50 g *(2 oz)* butter
30 ml *(2 tbsps)* oil
1 medium sized onion, skinned and finely chopped
4 fillet or entrecôte steaks, about 1 cm *(½ in)* thick
freshly ground black pepper and salt
30 ml *(2 tbsps)* chopped parsley
30 ml *(2 tbsps)* Irish whiskey
freshly cooked asparagus spears

Melt the butter with the oil in a large frying pan. Add the onion and sauté gently for about 5 minutes, until just beginning to colour. Rub the steaks well with pepper and put them in the pan. Fry quickly for about 2 minutes on each side (the time depends on whether you prefer steak rare, medium or well done). Add some salt and the parsley. Pour the whiskey over and ignite it. When the flames die down turn the steaks over and continue to cook for about 30 seconds.

Serve at once, with asparagus.

Carpet bag steak

700–900 g *(1½–2 lb)* rump or fillet steak, in a piece
12 raw oysters
50 g *(2 oz)* mushrooms, finely sliced, optional
salt and cayenne pepper
olive oil or butter

Choose a piece of the very best rump or fillet steak, cut at least 5 cm *(2 in)* thick. Slit the steak through its thickness so that it opens like a book. Fill with the raw oysters, cover these with the mushrooms (if used) and sprinkle with a very little salt and some cayenne pepper. Sew up with fine white string, so that neither the filling nor the juice can escape. Rub the steak over on both sides with oil or melted butter and grill under a quick grill for 5–6 minutes on each side. When the meat has browned, finish cooking for a further 10 minutes or so, according to the degree of 'rareness' desired.

Steak Sauternes

75 g *(3 oz)* butter
60 ml *(4 tbsps)* Sauternes or any other sweet white wine
60 ml *(4 tbsps)* stock or water
100 g *(4 oz)* mushrooms, sliced
50 g *(2 oz)* cooked ham, chopped
4 fillet steaks, 175–225 g *(6–8 oz)* each

Melt 25 g *(1 oz)* of the butter and add the wine and stock or water. Add the mushrooms and ham and simmer gently for 8–10 minutes. Meanwhile fry the steaks in the remaining butter, turning them once and cooking for 3–7 minutes on each side, according to taste. Pour the wine sauce over the steaks.

Note If you like, toast some rounds of bread the size of the steaks and place the meat on these before pouring the sauce over. A few of the mushrooms can be kept whole, fried with the steaks and used as an additional garnish.

Fondue bourguignonne

175–225 g *(6–8 oz)* fillet or rump steak per person
oil for frying
finely chopped onion or shallot
finely chopped parsley
chutney, optional
roughly chopped pineapple, optional
dips (see below)

This dish is cooked at the table, each guest cooking his own meat.

Cut the steak into 2.5-cm *(1-in)* cubes with a sharp knife; arrange it on plates. Put on the table a metal container of oil over a spirit stove, to heat to around 190°C *(375°F)*.

Give each guest a long-handled wooden skewer or two-pronged fondue fork for spearing the meat cubes, which they cook in the hot oil and then cool a little, or transfer to a second fork. The cooked cube of meat is then dipped in one of the sauces given below, then in a mixture of chopped onion and parsley. Chopped chutney and pineapple also make a good mixture for this purpose. Have crusty bread as an accompaniment and, if you wish, offer two or more of the following as side dishes: chopped banana, sliced gherkins, sliced olives.

Horseradish dip Whisk together 90 ml *(6 tbsps)* whipped cream, 45 ml *(3 tbsps)* horseradish sauce and some freshly ground black pepper.

Curry dip Mix together 45 ml *(3 tbsps)* home-made mayonnaise, 45 ml *(3 tbsps)* whipped cream, 5 ml *(1 level tsp)* curry powder and 5 ml *(1 tsp)* chutney sauce.

Paprika dip Beat 75 g *(3 oz)* cream cheese until soft, combine with 60 ml *(4 tbsps)* home-made mayonnaise, 5 ml *(1 level tsp)* paprika and 3 gherkins, finely chopped.

Tomato dip Mix together 45 ml *(3 tbsps)* home-made mayonnaise, 45 ml *(3 tbsps)* whipped cream, 30 ml *(2 tbsps)* tomato ketchup, 10 ml *(2 level tsps)* tomato paste and a good dash of Worcestershire sauce.

Mustard dip Blend 7.5 ml *(1½ level tsps)* dry mustard with 10 ml *(2 tsps)* port. Add 45 ml *(3 tbsps)* home-made mayonnaise and 60–90 ml *(4–6 tbsps)* whipped cream.

Hollandaise or tartare sauce (see page 200) may also be used.

Boeuf stroganoff

700 g *(1½ lb)* rump steak, thinly sliced
45 ml *(3 level tbsps)* seasoned flour
50 g *(2 oz)* butter
1 onion, skinned and sliced thinly
225 g *(½ lb)* mushrooms, sliced
salt and pepper
300 ml *(½ pt)* soured cream

Beat the steak, trim it, cut it into strips 0.5 cm *(¼ in)* by 5 cm *(2 in)* and coat with the seasoned flour. Fry the meat in 25 g *(1 oz)* butter till golden brown – about 5–7 minutes. Cook the onion and mushrooms in the remaining 25 g *(1 oz)* butter for 3–4 minutes, season to taste and add to the beef. Warm the soured cream and stir it into the meat mixture. Serve with plain boiled or buttered rice.

Fillet of beef Wellington (beef en croûte)

1.8 kg *(4 lb)* fillet of beef
freshly ground black pepper
100 g *(4 oz)* butter
225 g *(8 oz)* button mushrooms
175 g *(6 oz)* smooth liver pâté
2 368-g *(13-oz)* pkts frozen puff pastry, thawed
beaten egg to glaze

Trim and tie up the fillet at intervals to retain its shape. Season with pepper. Melt 50 g *(2 oz)* butter in a large frying pan. When foaming, add the meat and fry briskly on all sides to colour. Press down with a wooden spoon while frying to seal the surface well. Roast at 210°C *(425°F)* mark 7 for 20 minutes then chill the beef and remove the string. Slice the mushrooms and sauté them in remaining butter until soft; leave them to go cold then blend with the pâté. Place the pastry blocks on top of each other, then roll out to a large rectangle about 45.5 by 38 cm *(18 by 15 in)* and 0.5 cm *(¼ in)* thick. Egg-glaze the pastry centre. Place the meat over the glaze and spread pâté over the meat surface. Cut the pastry diagonally from the outer corners inward, to within 1 cm (*½ in*) of each corner of the meat. Trim the corners from the end 38-cm (*15-in*) flaps to make them square-sided and fold them up over the meat. On each side flap make diagonal cuts at 2.5-cm (*1-in*) intervals. Lightly egg-glaze and plait the strips alternately over the fillet. Use the pastry trimmings to neaten the end. Chill until the pastry is firm; just before baking brush with egg. Cook at 210°C (*425°F*) mark 7 for about 50 minutes, covering with foil half-way through the cooking. *Serves 8.*

Beef olives *see colour plate facing p. 160*

8 thin slices of topside
seasoned flour
30 ml (*2 tbsps*) oil
400 ml (*¾ pt*) stock or water
2 onions, sliced

For the stuffing
50 g (*2 oz*) shredded suet
50 g (*2 oz*) ham or bacon, chopped
100 g (*4 oz*) fresh breadcrumbs
10 ml (*2 tsps*) chopped parsley
1.25 ml (*¼ level tsp*) mixed dried herbs
grated rind of ½ lemon
salt and pepper
beaten egg to mix

Combine the ingredients for the stuffing and bind with the egg. Spread each slice of meat with stuffing, roll up, secure with fine string and toss in seasoned flour. Heat the fat or oil in a frying pan and brown the beef olives lightly, remove and place in a casserole. Add 30 ml (*2 level tbsps*) of the seasoned flour to the frying pan, brown well, gradually add the stock and bring it to the boil; season to taste and pour over the olives. Add the onion slices, divided into rings, cover and cook in the oven at 180°C (*350°F*) mark 4 for 1½ hours. Remove the strings before serving the beef olives.

Flemish steaks *see colour plate between pp. 112 and 113*

4 pieces chuck steak, about 750 g (*1½ lb*)
45 ml (*3 tbsps*) oil
salt and pepper
3 medium sized onions, skinned and sliced
large knob butter
100 g (*4 oz*) button mushrooms
flour
1 bottle lager
30 ml (*2 level tbsps*) demerara sugar
1 clove garlic, skinned and crushed

Marinade the meat overnight in the oil with a little seasoning. Sauté the onions in the butter until lightly coloured and put them in a casserole, with the mushrooms. Drain the steaks and coat them with flour; fry lightly in the pan in which the onions were sautéed, adding any remaining marinading oil. Put the steaks on top of the vegetables in the casserole. Mix together the lager, sugar, garlic and some salt and pepper and pour over the meat. Cover and cook in the oven at 150°C (*300°F*) mark 1–2 for 3½–4 hours.

When they are available, use 12 small pickling onions instead of the 3 larger onions – left whole they taste delicious and they look attractive when the dish is served.

Boeuf bourguignonne

900 g (*2 lb*) topside
30 ml (*2 tbsps*) fat or oil
100-g (*4-oz*) piece of streaky bacon, rinded and diced
15 ml (*1 level tbsp*) flour
45 ml (*3 tbsps*) brandy
50 ml (*¼ pt*) burgundy or other red wine
150 ml (*¼ pt*) stock
pinch of thyme
½ bayleaf
1 clove garlic, skinned and chopped
salt and pepper
6–8 shallots or tiny onions, skinned and left whole

Cut the meat into 5-cm (*2-in*) squares. Heat 15 ml (*1 tbsp*) of the fat or oil in a large pan and fry the meat until browned, a few pieces at a time; drain and put in a large ovenproof casserole. Fry the bacon in the fat remaining in the pan, add the flour and allow to brown, stirring occasionally. Transfer to the casserole. Warm the brandy in a small pan, ignite and pour it over the meat while it is still flaming. Add the wine and stock, thyme, bayleaf and garlic, and season well with salt and pepper. Cover and cook in the oven at 170°C (*325°F*) mark 3 for 2 hours. Melt the remaining fat or oil in a small pan, add the shallots and brown them; drain thoroughly and add to the meat. Turn the oven down to 150°C (*300°F*) mark 2 and cook for a further ½ hour until the meat is tender. Remove the bayleaf before serving.

This classic French dish needs no additional vegetables except creamy mashed potatoes.

Carbonade of beef

900 g *(2 lb)* stewing steak, cut into 1-cm *(½-in)* cubes
salt and pepper
50 g *(2 oz)* fat or oil
75 g *(3 oz)* lean bacon, rinded and chopped
60 ml *(4 level tbsps)* plain flour
300 ml *(½ pt)* beer
300 ml *(½ pt)* stock or water
30–45 ml *(2–3 tbsps)* vinegar
450 g *(1 lb)* onions, skinned and chopped
1 clove garlic, skinned and chopped
bouquet garni

Season the meat and fry in the fat or oil until brown – about 5 minutes. Add the bacon and continue cooking for a few minutes. Remove the meat and bacon from the pan, stir in the flour and brown lightly. Gradually add the beer, stock and vinegar, stirring continuously until the mixture thickens. Fill a casserole with layers of meat, bacon, onion and garlic. Pour the sauce over and add the bouquet garni. Cover and cook for 3½–4 hours in the oven at 150°C *(300°F)* mark 2. Add a little more beer while cooking, if necessary. Just before serving, remove the bouquet garni. Serve with plain boiled potatoes.

Goulash

700 g *(1½ lb)* stewing steak, cut into 1-cm *(½-in)* cubes
45 ml *(3 level tbsps)* seasoned flour
2 medium sized onions, skinned and chopped
1 green pepper, seeded and chopped
30 ml *(2 tbsps)* fat or oil
10 ml *(2 level tsps)* paprika
45 ml *(3 level tbsps)* tomato paste
little grated nutmeg
salt and pepper
50 g *(2 oz)* flour
300 ml *(½ pt)* stock
2 large tomatoes, skinned and quartered
bouquet garni
150 ml *(¼ pt)* beer

Coat the meat with seasoned flour. Fry the onions and pepper lightly in the fat or oil for about 3–4 minutes. Add the meat and fry lightly on all sides until golden brown – about 5 minutes. Add the paprika and fry for about a minute longer. Stir in the tomato paste, nutmeg, seasoning and flour and cook for a further 2–3 minutes. Add the stock, tomatoes and bouquet garni, put into a casserole and cook in the oven at 170°C *(325°F)* mark 3 for 1½–2 hours. Add the beer, cook for a few minutes longer and remove the bouquet garni. Serve with sauerkraut and caraway-flavoured dumplings (page 57), or with a green salad.

Swiss steak

700 g *(1½ lb)* chuck or blade steak
45 ml *(3 level tbsps)* seasoned flour
4 medium sized onions, skinned and sliced
50 g *(2 oz)* fat or oil
1–2 stalks of celery, scrubbed and chopped
1 clove garlic, skinned and crushed
396-g *(14-oz)* can tomatoes or 450 g *(1 lb)* tomatoes, skinned and quartered
15 ml *(1 level tbsp)* tomato paste

Trim the meat, cut it into 8 portions and coat with seasoned flour. Brown the onions lightly for about 5 minutes in half of the fat or oil; remove them from the pan. Add the rest of the fat or oil to the pan, brown the steak on both sides for 2–3 minutes and reduce the heat. Add the celery, garlic, tomatoes, paste and onions, stir, cover and simmer very gently for 2 hours.

Beefsteak casserole

700 g *(1½ lb)* stewing steak
45 ml *(3 level tbsps)* seasoned flour
2 onions, skinned and sliced
3 carrots, pared and sliced
2–3 potatoes, peeled and sliced
ground nutmeg
salt and pepper
396-g *(14-oz)* can tomatoes
stock

Cut the steak into 2.5-cm *(1-in)* cubes and coat with seasoned flour. Put into a casserole with layers of sliced onions, carrots and potatoes, sprinkling each layer with a pinch of nutmeg and some seasoning. Add the tomatoes and enough stock to come halfway up the ingredients, cover and cook in the oven at 170°C *(325°F)* mark 3 for about 2½ hours.

A few peas may be included, if you like towards the end of the cooking time.

Brown stew

700 g *(1½ lb)* stewing steak
30 ml *(2 tbsps)* fat or oil
2 onions, skinned and sliced
2 carrots, pared and sliced
60 ml *(4 level tbsps)* flour
900 ml *(1½ pt)* stock
salt and pepper
bouquet garni

Cut the meat into 1-cm *(½-in)* cubes. Heat the fat or oil in a frying pan and fry the onions and carrots until browned. Remove from the pan and fry the meat until browned. Put the meat and vegetables in a casserole. Add the flour to the fat remaining in the pan, stir well and add the stock gradually; bring to the boil, season and add to the casserole, with the bouquet garni. Cover and cook in the oven at 170°C *(325°F)* mark 3 for about 2 hours.

Remove the bouquet garni before serving.

Beef with green peppers

450 g *(1 lb)* cooked beef
45 ml *(3 tbsps)* cooking oil
5 ml *(1 level tsp)* salt
pepper
1 scallion or spring onion, cut into 1-cm *(½-in)* pieces
1 clove garlic, skinned and chopped
3 green peppers, seeded and sliced
3 sticks of celery, trimmed and sliced
300 ml *(½ pt)* chicken stock

For the thickening
10 ml *(2 level tsps)* cornflour
150 ml *(¼ pt)* water
5 ml *(1 tsp)* soy sauce

Slice the beef; heat the oil in a pan, add the seasonings and when very hot sauté the beef for 1 minute, stirring constantly. Add the scallion, garlic and green peppers, stir once or twice, then slowly add the celery and stock. Cover the pan, turn down the heat and simmer for 10 minutes. Add the thickening and when the gravy is thick and smooth, put the mixture into a shallow bowl and serve at once.

Rich beef casserole

700 g *(1½ lb)* chuck or blade steak
30 ml *(2 tbsps)* fat or oil
1 large onion, skinned and sliced
2 green peppers, seeded and sliced
150 ml *(¼ pt)* red wine
30 ml *(2 level tbsps)* tomato paste
salt and pepper
170-g *(6-oz)* pkt frozen corn kernels

Cut the meat into 2.5-cm *(1-in)* cubes. Heat the fat or oil and fry the onion until golden brown; remove and place in a casserole. Fry the peppers lightly and add to the onions in the casserole. Fry the meat until brown – about 5 minutes. Add the wine and tomato paste and season to taste. Mix well and add to the vegetables in the casserole. Cover and cook in the oven at 170°C *(325°F)* mark 3 for about 2 hours, then add the corn kernels and continue cooking for a further 10–15 minutes.

Steak and mushroom pie

450 g *(1 lb)* stewing steak
30 ml *(2 level tbsps)* seasoned flour
1 onion, skinned and sliced
water
100 g *(4 oz)* mushrooms
212-g *(7½-oz)* pkt frozen puff pastry, thawed
beaten egg to glaze

Wipe the meat, cut it into small, even pieces and coat with seasoned flour. Put the meat and sliced onion into a pan and just cover with water. Bring to the boil, reduce the heat and simmer for 1½–2 hours or until the meat is tender. Alternatively, the meat can be cooked for 2 hours in a covered casserole in the oven at 170°C *(325°F)* mark 3. Leave it to cool.

Put the meat and mushrooms into a 1-l *(2-pt)* pie dish with enough of the gravy to half fill it. Roll out the pastry 2.5 cm *(1 in)* larger than the top of the dish. Cut off a 1-cm *(½-in)* strip from round the edge of the pastry and put this strip round the damped rim of the dish. Damp the edges of the pastry with water and put on the top of the pie, without stretching the pastry; trim if necessary and flake the edges. Decorate if you wish and brush with beaten egg. Bake in the oven at 220°C *(425°F)* mark 7 for 20 minutes. Reduce the heat to 180°C *(350°F)* mark 4 and cook for about a further 20 minutes.

Variations

Add one of the following, omitting the mushrooms, if liked:

1. 100 g *(4 oz)* lambs' kidneys: wipe and core, removing any skin, cut into small pieces and add to the meat in the pie dish before covering with the pastry. *See colour plate between pp. 112 and 113.*
2. 2–3 carrots, pared and sliced: add to the meat in the pie dish before covering with the pastry.

Steak and kidney pudding

225 g *(8 oz)* suetcrust pastry (see page 352), made with 225 g *(8 oz)* flour etc
225–350 g *(½–¾ lb)* stewing steak, cut into 2-cm *(¾-in)* cubes
100 g *(¼ lb)* kidney
30 ml *(2 level tbsps)* seasoned flour
1 onion, skinned and chopped
water

Half fill a steamer or large saucepan with water and put it on to boil. Grease a 900-ml *(1½-pt)* pudding basin. Cut off a quarter of the pastry to make the lid and roll out the remainder into a round large enough to line the basin. Coat the meat with the seasoned flour. Remove the skin and core from the kidneys, cut into slices and coat with seasoned flour. Fill the basin with the meat, kidney, onion and 45 ml *(3 tbsps)* water. Roll out the pastry for the lid to a round the size of the top of the basin and damp the edge of it. Place on top of the meat and seal the edges of the pastry well. Cover with greased greaseproof paper or foil and steam for about 4 hours.

Variation

The meat can be prepared and stewed with the onion for about 2 hours earlier in the day or the previous night before being used for the filling. In this case reduce the steaming time to 1½–2 hours.

Cornish pasties

350 g *(12 oz)* chuck or blade steak
100 g *(4 oz)* raw potato, peeled and diced
1 small onion, skinned and chopped
salt and pepper
350 g *(12 oz)* shortcrust pastry (see page 351), made with 350 g *(12 oz)* flour etc

Cut the steak into small pieces, add the potato and onion and season well. Divide the pastry into four and roll each piece into a round about 20 cm *(8 in)* in diameter. Divide the meat mixture between the pastry rounds, damp the edges, draw the edges of the pastry together to form a seam across the top and flute the edges with the fingers. Place on a baking sheet and bake in the oven at 220°C *(425°F)* mark 7 for 15 minutes to brown the pastry, then reduce the heat to 170°C *(325°F)* mark 3 and cook for a further hour. Serve hot or cold.

Curried beef

450 g *(1 lb)* stewing steak, cut into 2-cm *(¾-in)* cubes
50 g *(2 oz)* fat or oil
2 large onions, skinned and sliced
1 cooking apple, peeled and chopped
15 ml *(1 level tbsp)* curry powder
45 ml *(3 level tbsps)* flour
600 ml *(1 pt)* stock or water
salt and pepper
30 ml *(2 tbsps)* chutney
50 g *(2 oz)* sultanas
2 tomatoes, skinned and chopped
squeeze of lemon juice

Fry the meat in the fat or oil until brown. Drain well and put into a casserole. Fry the onions and apple in the fat remaining in the pan, and add to the meat. Fry the curry powder, add the flour and cook together for 2–3 minutes. Add the stock gradually and bring to the boil; add the seasoning and remaining ingredients and cook for 2–3 minutes, then pour over the meat. Cover the casserole and cook gently in the oven at 170°C *(325°F)* mark 3 for 2 hours. Adjust the seasoning as required and serve the curry with boiled rice.

Note Cold roast beef can be used in a curry. Prepare the sauce as above and add the cubed meat just before putting the dish in the oven; it will need only 30–40 minutes' cooking. Alternatively, make a curry sauce (see page 201), add the meat and simmer for 10–15 minutes until the beef is heated through.

Curried mince

50 g *(2 oz)* fat or oil
2 medium sized onions, skinned and chopped
1 green pepper, seeded and sliced
1 cooking apple, peeled and chopped
15 ml *(1 level tbsp)* curry powder
15 ml *(1 level tbsp)* flour
300 ml *(½ pt)* stock
15 ml *(1 tbsp)* chutney
50 g *(2 oz)* sultanas
450 g *(1 lb)* raw minced beef
lemon slices for garnish

Heat half of the fat or oil and fry the onions, green pepper and apple until brown. Remove from the frying pan and put into a saucepan. To the fat remaining in the pan add the curry powder and flour and cook together for 2–3 minutes; gradually add the stock, bring to the boil and cook for 1–2 minutes. Stir in the chutney and sultanas, then add to the saucepan and simmer for 20 minutes. Cook the mince in the remaining fat and add to the sauce; continue to simmer the mince for 15 minutes. Serve in a shallow dish with boiled rice and lemon slices to garnish.

Calcutta beef curry

5 ml *(1 level tsp)* ground coriander
5 ml *(1 level tsp)* ground turmeric
5 ml *(1 level tsp)* ground chili
pinch black pepper
pinch ground ginger
300 ml *(½ pt)* coconut milk, see below
1 onion, skinned and sliced
1 clove of garlic, skinned and crushed
25 g *(1 oz)* butter
450 g *(1 lb)* stewing steak, cubed
300 ml *(½ pt)* stock
salt and lemon juice

Mix the powdered ingredients and make into a paste with a little of the coconut milk. Fry the onion and garlic in the butter until tender and add the paste, then fry for a further 3–4 minutes. Add the meat and stock, bring slowly to the boil and simmer for about 2 hours. Add the remaining coconut milk, some salt and lemon juice and serve at once, accompanied by boiled rice and a fruit or vegetable sambal.

Coconut milk Traditionally made from fresh coconut, but a good substitute can be gained by infusing 15–30 ml *(1–2 level tbsps)* desiccated coconut in about 300 ml *(½ pt)* boiling water, then squeezing out the liquid through a fine tea strainer.

Dry beef curry

15 ml *(1 level tbsp)* ground coriander
5 ml *(1 level tsp)* ground turmeric
1.25 ml *(¼ level tsp)* ground chili
2.5 ml *(½ level tsp)* ground cumin
pinch of ground cinnamon
2 cloves
1 bayleaf
15 ml *(1 tbsp)* vinegar diluted with 15 ml *(1 tbsp)* water
50 g *(2 oz)* butter
1 onion, skinned and finely chopped
1 clove garlic, skinned and finely chopped
5 ml *(1 level tsp)* curry paste
450 g *(1 lb)* stewing steak, cut into 1-cm *(½-in)* cubes
300 ml *(½ pt)* stock or water
salt

Mix the spices and diluted vinegar to form a paste. Melt the butter and fry the onion and garlic. Then fry the spices and curry paste thoroughly, stirring constantly. Add the meat and cook slowly for about 1 hour, stirring occasionally. Add the stock, cover and cook gently for another hour, till the liquid is absorbed. Adjust the seasoning, if necessary, and serve with boiled rice or lentil dhal and sambals (see below).

Sambals

Boiled rice is a traditional accompaniment to curry but there are also many other side dishes, known as sambals, without which no curry is considered really complete.

Some can be bought ready to eat and others need some preparation. They are usually served in small dishes. For a few examples see below.

Chapattis Large unleavened girdle cakes which can be bought from delicatessens and shops specialising in Eastern foods.

Pappadums Thin water-like biscuits that can be bought in tins. To cook, fry one at a time in a little hot fat until crisp, holding them down with a spoon as they swell in cooking; alternatively heat for 1–2 minutes under a hot grill.

Gherkins Use whole or sliced.

Melon Cut into cubes, removing skin and pips.

Bananas Peel and slice thinly. Sprinkle with lemon juice to prevent browning.

Green pepper Slice, removing seeds and membranes.

Tomatoes Slice thinly.

Onion Skin and slice thinly.

Relishes Such as chutney, guava jelly, preserved ginger, pickled mangoes, olives, grated coconut.

See also page 277 for various rice accompaniments.

Indian wafers (Puris)

100 g *(4 oz)* plain wholemeal flour
knob of ghee or butter (see note)
pepper and salt
60 ml *(4 tbsps)* water
fat for frying

Put the flour in a small bowl and rub in the fat; season with pepper and salt. Gradually work in just sufficient water to give a pliable dough and knead well. If time permits, cover and leave for an hour. Roll out wafer-thin between sheets of non-stick (silicone) paper, then cut out rounds about 8 cm *(3 in)* in diameter; if they are not to be fried at once, cover them lightly with a damp cloth. Fry in hot fat, one or two at a time – drop the raw puri into the fat by slithering it on to the side quickly and hold it down with a wide draining slice, pressing lightly to distribute the air – this produces the characteristic balloon shape. Turn the puris once, remove carefully, drain on absorbent paper and serve at once.

Note Ghee is a form of clarified butter available from stores selling Indian foods. The butter is treated with steam to remove impurities.

Lentil purée (Dhal)

100 g *(4 oz)* red lentils
300 ml *(½ pt)* cold water
pepper and salt
1 medium sized onion, skinned
fat for frying
25 g *(1 oz)* butter or dripping

There is no need to soak the lentils. Wash them, put them into the cold water, add pepper and salt and let them cook steadily for about 1–1½ hours, adding more water if they get too dry. Meanwhile, chop the onion finely and fry it. When the lentils are tender, remove them from the heat and stir vigorously. Add the butter or dripping and the fried onion and stir over the heat to blend well. Serve with curry.

Plain Indian girdle cakes (Chapattis)

200 g *(½ lb)* plain wholemeal flour
100 g *(¼ lb)* plain white flour
water

Take a large deep dish and knead the flour in it with water to make a soft dough; meanwhile heat the girdle. Take small pieces of the dough and roll them first into small balls the size of an apple, then flatten them with a rolling-pin on a pastry board or marble slab, into thin discs the size of a pancake. Cook them on the greased girdle on both sides. Before taking each cake off the girdle press it gently with a clean cloth to exclude all the air. When the air has escaped, put the chapattis into a clean basket, to keep warm. Ideally, they should be served hot direct from the girdle, to eat with curry as a substitute for rice, or as a second course after curry and rice.

Madras curry

50 g *(2 oz)* almonds, chopped
50 g *(2 oz)* butter or fat
2 onions, skinned and chopped
1 clove garlic
5 ml *(1 level tsp)* ground coriander
5 ml *(1 level tsp)* ground black pepper
2.5 ml *(½ level tsp)* chili seasoning
2.5 ml *(½ level tsp)* ground cardamom
2.5 ml *(½ level tsp)* ground cumin
small piece of cinnamon stick
2.5 ml *(½ level tsp)* ground cloves
10 ml *(2 level tsps)* flour
600 ml *(1 pt)* stock or water
450 g *(1 lb)* meat, cut small
10 ml *(2 level tsps)* ground turmeric
5 ml *(1 level tsp)* sugar
salt
juice of 1 lemon

Cover the almonds with 150 ml *(¼ pt)* boiling water and leave for 15 minutes, then strain the infusion. Melt the fat and lightly fry the onion and garlic. Add the spices and flavourings (except the turmeric) and the flour and cook for 5 minutes. Add the stock and meat and simmer till tender – 1½–2 hours. Add the almond infusion, turmeric, sugar and salt to taste and simmer for ¼ hour; finally, add the lemon juice.

Cottage pie
(Shepherd's pie)

900 g *(2 lb)* potatoes
45 ml *(3 tbsps)* milk
knob of butter
salt and pepper
1 large onion, skinned and chopped
little dripping
450 g *(1 lb)* cold cooked beef, minced
stock
30 ml *(2 tbsps)* chopped parsley or 10 ml *(2 level tsps)* mixed dried herbs

Boil the potatoes, drain and mash them with the milk, butter and seasoning. Fry the onion in a little dripping for about 5 minutes and mix in the minced meat, with a little stock, seasoning and parsley or mixed herbs. Put the prepared meat mixture into an ovenproof dish and cover the top with mashed potato. Mark the top with a fork and bake for 25–30 minutes in the oven at 190°C *(375°F)* mark 5 until the surface is crisp and browned.

Variations

1. Add a 226-g *(8-oz)* can of tomatoes, drained and chopped.
2. Add a small can of baked beans.
3. Mix 15–30 ml *(1–2 tbsps)* pickle with the meat or put it in a layer at the bottom of the dish.
4. Use 450 g *(1 lb)* fresh minced beef in place of the cooked meat; in this case, add it to the onion in the frying pan and cook for about 15 minutes, stirring well, before adding the stock, etc, and putting the mixture into the ovenproof dish.
5. Top the mashed potatoes with a little grated cheese before baking the pie.

Note There is much controversy about cottage and shepherd's pies. Some people say that shepherd's pie is made only with lamb; others say that cottage pie is made with minced meat and shepherd's pie with sliced meat.

Hamburgers

450 g *(1 lb)* lean beef, eg chuck, shoulder or rump steak
½ onion, skinned and grated, optional
salt and pepper
melted butter or oil for coating or a little fat for shallow frying

Choose lean meat and have it minced finely by the butcher. Mix well with the onion (if used) and a generous amount of salt and pepper. Shape lightly into 6–8 round flat cakes. To cook, brush sparingly with melted butter or oil and grill for 4–6 minutes turning once, or fry in a little fat in a frying pan, turning them once and allowing the same amount of time.

Hamburgers can be served rare or well done, according to personal preference, hence the variation in cooking time.

Variations

Traditionally, hamburgers contain no other ingredients, but they can be varied as follows:

1. Add any of the following when mixing the hamburgers:
   50–100 g *(2–4 oz)* grated cheese
   15 ml *(1 tbsp)* sweet pickle
   5–10 ml *(1–2 level tsps)* made mustard
   5 ml *(1 level tsp)* dried mixed herbs
   15 ml *(1 tbsp)* chopped parsley
   50 g *(2 oz)* mushrooms, sliced
   2–3 tomatoes, skinned and chopped.
2. Make the hamburgers into thin cakes and wrap each with a rasher of bacon secured with a cocktail stick, then grill gently, turning them frequently.

Savoury mince

1 onion, skinned and quartered
2 carrots, pared and quartered
2 sticks of celery, scrubbed
450 g *(1 lb)* cold cooked beef
298-g *(10½-oz)* can oxtail soup or 150 ml *(¼ pt)* beef stock
salt and pepper
30 ml *(2 level tbsps)* curry powder
50 g *(2 oz)* raisins or sultanas

Mince together the vegetables and meat (or if preferred dice the vegetables and mince the meat). Put them into a pan and stir in enough of the soup and stock to give a really moist mixture. Add the seasoning, curry powder and raisins or sultanas, cover with a lid and simmer gently for 20–30 minutes, until the vegetables are soft and the flavours well blended. Stir from time to time, as the mixture tends to stick slightly; add more soup or stock if it becomes too thick. Serve with chipped or boiled potatoes – or as a sauce over pasta or rice.

Hussar's salad

about 225 g *(½ lb)* cold cooked meat
1–2 cooked beetroots
6–8 cold cooked potatoes
1 apple
few cocktail onions and gherkins
mayonnaise
French mustard
salt and pepper
1–2 hard-boiled eggs

Dice the meat. Chop the beetroots, potatoes, apple, onions and some of the gherkins. Reserve a little of the beetroot for garnishing; combine the rest with the potato, apple, onion and chopped gherkin, mix with some mayonnaise and add French mustard and seasonings to taste. Place the salad on a meat dish and garnish with mayonnaise, the remaining beetroot and gherkins and the sliced hard-boiled eggs.

The exact quantities are not important in this salad, which is a good way of serving leftovers. Cubed cucumber is also sometimes included.

Smyrna sausages

2 small slices white bread
milk
450 g *(1 lb)* minced beef
2 small onions, skinned and minced
little chopped parsley and mint
1.25 ml *(¼ level tsp)* ground cumin or mixed spice
1 egg, beaten
45–60 ml *(3–4 tbsps)* butter or oil
45–60 ml *(3–4 tbsps)* plain flour
150 ml *(¼ pt)* puréed tomatoes
5 ml *(1 level tsp)* sugar
150 ml *(¼ pt)* white wine
150 ml *(¼ pt)* water
salt and pepper

Remove the crusts from the bread, soak the soft part in a little milk and squeeze it almost dry. Place the meat in a basin and mix with half the minced onion, the soaked bread, chopped parsley and mint and the cumin or spice. Bind with the egg and knead well.

Shape the meat mixture into small sausage shapes about 5 cm *(2 in)* long and fry them lightly in a little butter or oil until the meat changes colour. Place them carefully in a saucepan. Meanwhile prepare the tomato sauce; fry the remaining minced onion in butter until soft but not brown; add the flour, tomato purée, sugar, wine, water, salt and pepper and simmer for a few minutes. Pour the sauce on to the sausages in their saucepan and simmer all together for ½–¾ hour, until the meat is cooked. Serve hot.

Stuffed vine leaves

425-g *(15-oz)* can vine leaves
45 ml *(3 tbsps)* lard or olive oil
450 g *(1 lb)* minced meat
1–2 onions, thinly sliced
60 ml *(4 tbsps)* cooked rice
little chopped parsley
little tomato sauce
salt and pepper
juice of 1 lemon

Remove the vine leaves from the can and drain off the brine. Put 30 ml *(2 tbsps)* of the lard or oil in a frying pan with the meat, onions, rice, parsley, sauce and seasonings, mix well and fry. Add the lemon juice and stuff the vine leaves with the mixture, securing with skewers or fine string. Put in a saucepan with a little water, the remaining lard or oil and a little more sauce if desired and cook over a low heat until the gravy has reduced considerably.

This stuffing can also be used for aubergines, peppers, tomatoes and so on.

Rissoles

225–350 g *(8–12 oz)* cooked minced beef
½ small onion, skinned and grated
450 g *(1 lb)* potatoes, boiled and mashed
15 ml *(1 tbsp)* sweet pickle or table sauce
salt and pepper
beaten egg
dry breadcrumbs for coating
shallow fat for frying

Mix the meat, onion and potatoes and add the pickle or sauce and a generous amount of seasoning. Stir until well blended. Turn on to a floured board, form into a roll and cut into slices about 2.5 cm *(1 in)* thick. Shape these into round cakes, coat with the beaten egg and then with crumbs. Fry on both sides in the fat until golden. Drain well on absorbent paper before serving.

Variations

1. Replace the minced meat by a can of corned beef, finely chopped.
2. Omit the pickle or sauce and season with 15 ml *(1 tbsp)* chopped parsley, 5 ml *(1 level tsp)* mixed dried herbs or 5–10 ml *(1–2 level tsps)* curry powder.

Stuffed pancakes

125 g *(4 oz)* plain flour
pinch of salt
1 egg
300 ml *(½ pt)* milk or milk and water
savoury mince (see page 111)
fat for frying

Make a batter by mixing the flour and salt and beating in the egg and about 30 ml *(2 tbsps)* of the milk or milk and water until a smooth mixture is obtained. Gradually beat in the remaining liquid to give a creamy batter. Make the savoury mince mixture and keep it warm. Melt just enough fat in a thick based frying pan to coat the base thinly and when it is hot pour in just enough batter to cover the base of the pan – about 30–45 ml *(2–3 tbsps)*. Cook over a medium heat until brown underneath, then turn, using a palette knife, and brown the second side. Keep the pancakes hot on a plate in a warm oven and when they are all made, spread with the filling, roll up and serve at once.

As a variation, place the stuffed pancakes on an ovenproof dish, sprinkle generously with grated cheese and brown under the grill before serving.

Country pie *see colour plate between pp. 112 and 113*

900 g *(2 lb)* potatoes, peeled
25 g *(1 oz)* butter
45 ml *(3 tbsps)* milk
salt and pepper
25 g *(1 oz)* lard
100 g *(4 oz)* onion, skinned and chopped
450 g *(1 lb)* minced beef
100 g *(4 oz)* lean bacon rashers, rinded and minced
15 ml *(1 level tbsp)* flour
150 ml *(¼ pt)* beef stock
225 g *(½ lb)* small tomatoes, skinned
112-g *(4-oz)* pkt frozen peas

Boil the potatoes, cream with the butter and milk and season to taste. Heat the lard in a frying pan and fry the onion until golden brown. Add the minced beef and bacon and cook gently, mixing with a fork, for 5 minutes. Season, add the flour and mix well. Stir in the stock, bring to the boil, reduce the heat and simmer for 5 minutes. Place half the mince mixture in the base of a 1.4-l *(2½-pt)* ovenproof casserole. Arrange the tomatoes on top, then add the peas and the remaining mince. Pipe on the creamed potato (using a piping bag fitted with a large star vegetable nozzle). Bake in the oven at 200°C *(400°F)* mark 6 for 40 minutes, until golden on top.

Pork chops with orange (p. 129), Caramelled potatoes (p. 225).
(Overleaf) Country pie (above), Steak and mushroom pie (p. 107), Flemish steaks (p. 104).

London double-crust pie

50 g *(2 oz)* mushrooms, sliced
1 small onion, skinned and sliced
50 g *(2 oz)* fat or oil
5 ml *(1 level tsp)* curry powder
450 g *(1 lb)* raw minced beef
150 ml *(¼ pt)* gravy
salt and pepper
200 g *(7 oz)* shortcrust pastry (see page 351), made with 200 g *(7 oz)* flour, etc

Fry the mushrooms and onion gently in the fat or oil until just soft – about 5 minutes. Stir in the curry powder and cook for a further 2–3 minutes, add the meat and heat it through; add the gravy and seasoning. Roll out half the pastry and line a 20.5-cm *(8-in)* pie dish with it; put in the filling. Roll out the remaining half of the pastry to make a lid, put over the filling, seal the edges well, trim and scallop. Bake in the oven at 200°C *(400°F)* mark 6 for 30 minutes, until the pastry is golden brown. Reduce the temperature to 180°C *(350°F)* mark 4 and cook for a further 15–20 minutes.

Beef-stuffed cabbage leaves

25 g *(1 oz)* butter
450 g *(1 lb)* lean minced beef
10 ml *(2 tsps)* chopped parsley
little chopped mint, optional
60 ml *(4 level tbsps)* cooked rice
½ onion, skinned and grated
salt and pepper
pinch dried mixed herbs
pinch ground mixed spice
about 600 ml *(1 pt)* stock
12 medium sized cabbage leaves

Melt the butter, add the meat and cook until brown. Add the parsley, mint (if used), rice, onion, seasonings and flavourings and 150 ml *(¼ pt)* of the stock. Continue cooking for 5 minutes, until the stock is absorbed.

Blanch the cabbage leaves by dipping them in boiling water for 2 minutes; drain well. Place a spoonful of filling in the centre of each leaf and roll up, tucking in the ends to form a neat 'package'. Place the rolls closely together in a casserole. Bring the stock to the boil and pour over enough stock to half cover. Cover with a lid and cook in the oven at 180°C *(350°F)* mark 4 for about 45 minutes.

Chili con carne

700 g *(1½ lb)* raw minced beef
15 ml *(1 tbsp)* fat or oil
1 large onion, skinned and chopped
1 green pepper, seeded and chopped, optional
425-g *(15-oz)* can tomatoes
salt and pepper
15 ml *(1 level tbsp)* chili powder
15 ml *(1 tbsp)* vinegar
5 ml *(1 level tsp)* sugar
30 ml *(2 level tbsps)* tomato paste
425-g *(15-oz)* can red kidney beans

Fry the beef in the fat or oil until lightly browned, then add the onion and pepper and fry for 5 minutes, until soft. Stir in the tomatoes and add the seasoning and chili powder blended with the vinegar, sugar and tomato paste. Cover and simmer for 30–40 minutes, or until tender. Add the kidney beans 10 minutes before the cooking time is completed.

Note Add chili powder very judiciously – some of it is very hot. American chili powder is generally a milder pre-mixed seasoning, based on ground Mexican chili, so look for this type.

Aubergine moussaka

2 aubergines, sliced
45–60 ml *(3–4 tbsps)* olive oil
4–5 medium sized onions, skinned and sliced
450 g *(1 lb)* minced beef or lamb, raw
4 tomatoes, peeled and sliced
150 ml *(¼ pt)* stock
45 ml *(3 level tbsps)* tomato paste
2 eggs
45 ml *(3 tbsps)* milk
45 ml *(3 tbsps)* cream
salt and pepper

Fry the aubergines in half of the oil for about 4–5 minutes, then arrange them in the bottom of an ovenproof dish. Fry the onions and meat until lightly browned – about 5 minutes. Place layers of onion and minced meat on top of the aubergines and lastly add the slices of tomato. Mix the stock and tomato paste and pour into the dish. Bake in the oven at 180°C *(350°F)* mark 4 for about 30 minutes. Beat together the eggs, milk and cream, season well and pour this mixture over the meat. Put it back into the oven for 15–20 minutes, until the sauce is set and the mixture is firm and golden brown.

Liver Mexican (p. 143).

Meat loaf

450 g *(1 lb)* raw minced beef
100 g *(¼ lb)* sausage meat
1 onion, skinned and finely chopped
5 ml *(1 level tsp)* dried mixed herbs
30 ml *(2 tbsps)* tomato ketchup
15 ml *(1 tbsp)* table sauce
salt and pepper
105 ml *(7 tbsps)* white breadcrumbs
1 egg, beaten

Grease a 1-l *(1¾-pt)* loaf tin. Mix together the meats, onion, herbs, sauces and seasoning and add the breadcrumbs. Beat with a fork until well blended, then add the egg and beat again. Pack firmly into the tin and cover with foil or greaseproof paper. Bake in the oven at 180°C *(350°F)* mark 4 for 1–1¼ hours, or until the meat is tender and the loaf begins to shrink from the sides of the tin. Serve sliced, either hot with gravy or cold with salad.

Aberdeen sausage

450 g *(1 lb)* stewing beef
100 g *(4 oz)* streaky bacon rashers, rinded
100 g *(4 oz)* onion, skinned
100 g *(4 oz)* rolled oats
10 ml *(2 tsps)* Worcestershire sauce
1 egg, beaten
5 ml *(1 level tsp)* salt
freshly ground black pepper
15 ml *(1 tbsp)* chopped parsley

Trim the meat where necessary to remove surplus fat. Put the meat, bacon and onions twice through a mincer. Add the remaining ingredients and mix well. Shape into a long thick sausage and wrap in oiled foil. Fold the foil lightly across the top and twist the ends together. Put the sausage on a baking sheet and bake in the oven at 150°C *(300°)* mark 2 for about 2 hours. Gently remove the foil and serve hot in thick slices, accompanied by a tomato sauce.

LAMB

1. The younger the animal the paler the flesh; in a young lamb it is light pink, while in a mature animal it is light red.
2. A slight blue tinge to the bones suggests that the animal is young.
3. Imported lamb has a firm white fat, while English lamb (available only in spring and early summer) has creamy-coloured fat.

Cuts and methods of cooking

Loin A prime cut, usually roasted (or served as chops): can be cooked on the bone or boned, stuffed and rolled. Allow 350 g *(¾ lb)* on the bone, 125–175 g *(4–6 oz)* if boned, per person.

Leg Another good roasting cut.

Allow 350 g *(¾ lb)* on the bone per person.

The meat can be cut from the bone for use in pies, stews, kebabs, and so on.

Shoulder A large joint, with more fat but often with more flavour than leg. Usually roasted. Shoulder meat can also be cut from the bone, as for leg.

Allow 350 g *(¾ lb)* on the bone per person.

Best end of neck The cut next to the loin. Very good roasted, or it can be divided into cutlets.

Allow 350 g *(¾ lb)* per person.

Chops Cut from the loin, those nearest the leg being known as chump chops. Suitable for grilling, frying and casseroles.

Allow 1–2 chops per person.

Cutlets From the best end of neck; they have a small eye of lean meat and a long bone; suitable for grilling and frying.

Allow 1–2 cutlets per person.

Breast A rather fatty cut, therefore generally quite cheap. Usually boned, stuffed and rolled; it can be slow-roasted or braised, stewed or boiled.

Allow 225–350 g *(½–¾ lb)* on the bone per person.

Middle and scrag end Cheap cuts with rather a high proportion of bone and fat, but with a good flavour.

Suitable for stews and casseroles.

Allow 225–350 g *(½–¾ lb)* on the bone per person.

Accompaniments to lamb

With roast lamb and grilled chops serve mint sauce or jelly; with roast mutton, red-currant jelly or onion sauce.

With boiled leg of mutton, caper sauce is traditional.

Roast lamb

Trim the meat if necessary, then weigh it and calculate the cooking time, allowing 20 minutes per 450 g *(1 lb)* plus 20 minutes. If it is boned and rolled, allow 25 minutes per 450 g *(1 lb)* plus 25 minutes.

Put the meat into a roasting tin with the thickest layer of fat on top and add dripping if the joint is very lean. Put in the oven at 220°C *(425°F)* mark 7 and cook uncovered, basting from time to time with the juices from the tin. Cook for the calculated time and serve well done, accompanied by mint sauce, new or roast potatoes, peas or a green vegetable and a slightly thickened gravy.

To roast lamb in a moderate oven, at 180°C *(350°F)* mark 4, allow 30–35 minutes per 450 g *(1 lb)* for joints on the bone, 40–45 minutes per 450 g *(1 lb)* if boned and rolled.

Crown roast of lamb

2 pieces of best end of neck, each with 6–7 cutlets
dripping if needed
cutlet frills or potato balls

For the stuffing
50 g *(2 oz)* **onion, skinned and finely chopped**
50 g *(2 oz)* **celery, finely chopped**
225 g *(8 oz)* **fresh breadcrumbs, toasted**
1 egg, slightly beaten
pinch garlic powder
225 g *(8 oz)* **cooked long grain rice (about 75 g,** *3 oz* **raw)**
25 g *(1 oz)* **butter**
10 ml *(2 level tsps)* **curry powder**
salt and pepper

If possible, the pieces of best end should be taken from opposite sides of the animal though this is not essential. They should be chopped, not chined, and sliced between the bones to about halfway down, the ends of the bones being scraped clean. Trim neatly and bend round with the meaty side inwards to form a crown, securing it with skewers and string. Twist some pieces of foil round the exposed bones to prevent them burning. Mix all the ingredients for the stuffing and insert into the prepared crown. Roast in the oven at 180°C *(350°F)* mark 4 allowing 30 minutes per 450 g *(1 lb)* plus 30 minutes. Before serving, remove the foil and place small cutlet frills on the ends of the bones.

Variations

Replace the above stuffing with sausage meat or sage and onion stuffing. Alternatively leave the centre unstuffed (fill it with foil to keep the shape during the cooking) and fill it just before serving with cooked vegetables – diced carrots, peas, or small potatoes garnished with parsley butter.

Guard of honour

2 best ends of neck of lamb (6–7 cutlets each), about 2½ kg *(5 lb)* **total weight**

Ask the butcher to chine the joints. Remove the chine bone. With a sharp knife, cut through the flesh about 2.5 cm *(1 in)* from the end of the cutlet bones. Remove the fat and meat from the bone ends and scrape them clean. Interlace the best ends to form an arch, fat side outside, then fasten together with string. Cover the bone tips with foil to prevent them burning. Season with salt and pepper. Place in a roasting tin and roast in oven at 180°C *(350°F)* mark 4 for about 1½ hours. Remove the foil and place the joint on a serving dish..

Alternatively, ask the butcher in advance to prepare the guard of honour for you.

Rolled stuffed breast of lamb *see colour plate facing p. 193*

Joints containing a good percentage of bone can be boned (the butcher will usually do this), then rolled and tied into shape before being roasted in the usual way. They can if you wish be stuffed before being rolled – this gives added flavour and helps to make the joints go further.

Spread the boned-out joint flat on a board, sprinkle with salt and pepper and rub the seasonings into the meat. Make up some veal forcemeat or any other suitable stuffing (see pages 183 to 186) and spread this over the meat. Roll up the meat loosely, to allow the stuffing to expand during cooking. Tie it in several places with fine string to hold it in shape. Weigh it and calculate the cooking time, allowing 25–30 minutes per 450 g *(1 lb)* plus 25 minutes. Place the meat in the roasting tin, putting it on a grill grid or meat trivet if it is fatty, and cook in the oven at 180°C *(350°F)* mark 4 for the calculated time, until well done. Remove the strings and serve sliced fairly thickly, accompanied by a thickened gravy.

Any extra stuffing can be cooked in a separate small dish and served with the joint. Other cuts of lamb suitable for stuffing are shoulder and best end of neck; they are cooked as for breast.

Lamb en croûte

2.2 kg *(4½-lb)* leg of lamb, boned
150 ml *(¼ pt)* red wine
450 g *(1 lb)* pork sausage meat
100 g *(¼ lb)* bacon rashers, rinded and chopped
15 ml *(1 tbsp)* pistachio nuts, blanched and chopped
salt and freshly ground black pepper
25 g *(1 oz)* butter
225 g *(½ lb)* onions, skinned and sliced
sprig of thyme or a little dried thyme
1 bayleaf
3 parsley stalks
1 clove garlic, skinned and crushed
425-g *(15-oz)* can consommé
450 g *(1 lb)* ready-made puff pastry
beaten egg to glaze
a little flour
cornflour
braised celery heads and butter-glazed carrots to garnish

Marinade the lamb in the wine for 2–3 hours, turning it occasionally. Combine the sausage meat, bacon and nuts and season well. Remove the meat from the wine and dry on absorbent paper. Stuff the cavity with the sausage meat and sew up both ends with string. Fry the meat in the butter to seal the surface, then place in a casserole. Reheat the butter, add the onions, sauté, and add to the casserole with the thyme, bayleaf, parsley, garlic, marinade and consommé. Cover, and cook in the oven at 170°C *(325°F)* mark 3 for 2 hours. Take the meat from the dish (reserving the juices) and allow to cool.

Roll the pastry out into an oblong 50 cm by 25 cm *(20 in by 10 in)*. Brush the meat surface with beaten egg and dust with flour. Place the lamb in the centre and make a parcel by folding the short ends over, sealing them with beaten egg; draw the long edges over and seal. Turn on to a baking sheet, sealed side down. Decorate with the pastry trimmings, brush with beaten egg and bake in the oven at 230°C *(450°F)* mark 8 for about 45 minutes, covering with foil if in danger of over-browning. Garnish with braised celery heads and carrots glazed with butter. To make gravy, strain the juices and remove the fat with layers of absorbent paper. The yield should be about 600 ml *(1 pt)*. Thicken in the usual way with about 30 ml *(2 level tbsps)* cornflour. *Serves 10.*

Forest gyuvech (Bulgarian stew)

450 g *(1 lb)* middle neck lamb
450 g *(1 lb)* stewing veal
50 g *(2 oz)* butter
2 small onions, skinned and sliced
226-g *(8-oz)* can tomatoes
½ fresh chili
salt
paprika
400 ml *(¾ pt)* stock
225 g *(½ lb)* green or red peppers, seeded and sliced
100 g *(¼ lb)* mushrooms, sliced
1 clove garlic, skinned and crushed
chopped mint
100 g *(4 oz)* long grain rice
chopped parsley
black pepper

Chop the lamb and cut the veal into 2.5-cm *(1-in)* pieces; melt the butter and fry the meat until it begins to brown. Add the onions, fry for a few minutes, then add half the tomatoes and the chili. Season with salt and paprika, add the stock and bring to the boil. Simmer gently, uncovered, until the meat is nearly tender (about 30 minutes). Add the thinly sliced peppers, the mushrooms, garlic and some chopped mint, with the rest of the tomatoes and the rice. Cook for a further 15–20 minutes. Serve topped with a sprinkling of chopped parsley and a turn of black pepper from the mill.

Daube d'agneau

1.4 kg *(3 lb)* **leg of lamb**
600 ml *(1 pt)* **red wine**
100 g *(4 oz)* **onion, skinned and chopped**
3 medium sized carrots, diced
5 ml *(1 level tsp)* **salt**
1.25 ml *(¼ level tsp)* **black pepper**
5 sprigs parsley
2 sprigs thyme
1 bayleaf
75 ml *(5 tbsps)* **olive oil**
225 g *(½ lb)* **salt pork**
1 pig's foot, split
2 cloves garlic, skinned and crushed
4 firm red tomatoes, quartered

Put the lamb in a heavy gauge polythene bag, or in one thin bag inside another. Place it in a large bowl and put into the bag the wine, onion, carrot, seasoning and herbs. Pour over the olive oil and marinade overnight. Scrub the rind of the salt pork. Put it in a pan with the pig's foot, cover with water and bring to the boil. Pour off the water and stand it in fresh cold water overnight.

Next day put the lamb and its marinade in a deep casserole. Cut the rind off the pork and scissor-snip it into small squares. Cut the flesh into narrow strips. Add with the pig's foot, garlic and two tomatoes to the lamb. Cover tightly. Cook in the oven at 150°C *(300°F)* mark 2 for about 3½ hours. Baste the joint occasionally.

Skim the surface fat from the juices. Remove the lamb and keep it warm. Strain the diced vegetables and spoon them round the joint. Reduce the pan juices by a quarter by fast boiling and pour them over the meat. Garnish with tomato quarters, skinned and seeded. *Serves 6.*

Barbecued lamb

1 shoulder of lamb, about 1.6 kg *(3½ lb)*
5 ml *(1 level tsp)* **each of dry mustard, ground ginger, salt and pepper**
2 cloves garlic, skinned and crushed
flour

For the barbecue sauce
60 ml *(4 tbsps)* **Worcestershire sauce**
60 ml *(4 tbsps)* **brown table sauce**
60 ml *(4 tbsps)* **mushroom ketchup**
10 ml *(2 level tsps)* **sugar**
15 ml *(1 tbsp)* **vinegar**
45 ml *(3 tbsps)* **melted butter**
cayenne pepper
salt
150 ml *(¼ pt)* **water**
1 small onion, skinned and thinly sliced

Trim off any excess fat from the shoulder of lamb. Mix the mustard, ginger, salt, pepper and garlic well together and rub into the surface of the meat. Sprinkle the meat with flour and put it in a roasting tin. Blend the sauce ingredients well together, adding the sliced onion last, and pour over the meat. Cook in the oven at 220°C *(425°F)* mark 7 for 30 minutes, then lower the heat to 180°C *(350°F)* mark 4 and continue to cook, allowing 27 minutes per 450 g *(1 lb)*. Baste the joint with the sauce two or three times during the cooking, adding a little more water to the sauce if needed.

Boiled leg of lamb with caper sauce

1 small 1.4-kg *(3-lb)* **leg of lamb**
10 ml *(2 level tsps)* **salt**
water to cover
2 onions, skinned and halved
3–4 whole carrots, pared (halved if they are large)
1 small turnip, pared and quartered
1–2 sticks of celery, trimmed and halved
caper or onion sauce (see pages 194 and 195)

Trim the joint, removing any excess fat, then weigh the meat and calculate the time required for cooking, allowing 25–30 minutes per 450 g *(1 lb)* plus 25 minutes over. Put the meat in a large saucepan with the salt and cold water to cover. Bring it to the boil, skim off any scum which rises, then add the vegetables; reduce the heat and cover the pan with a lid. Simmer until the meat is tender, drain the meat from the cooking liquid and serve it hot, coated with the caper or onion sauce. If preferred, the vegetables can be added to the saucepan about ¾ hour before the cooking is completed and may then be served as an accompaniment to the meat.

Middle neck of lamb can also be cooked this way.

Fried lamb chops

Fry the chops in a little dripping or lard, turning them frequently; allow about 15 minutes in all.

Grilled lamb chops

Brush the chops with melted butter or oil and cook under a high heat for 1 minute on each side, then reduce to a moderate heat and cook, turning them from time to time, until browned – 10–12 minutes in all.

Smothered lamb chops

4 lamb chops
4 thin slices of lemon (with rind left on)
2 onions, skinned and sliced
1 green pepper, sliced
salt and pepper
396-g *(14-oz)* can tomatoes
chopped parsley

Put the chops in an ovenproof dish and top each with a slice of lemon. Add the onions and green pepper. Season, pour the canned tomatoes round the chops and cook in the oven at 200°C *(400°F)* mark 6 for 45 minutes. Sprinkle with chopped parsley before serving.

Mixed grill

4 best end of neck lamb chops
225 g *(½ lb)* chipolata sausages
2 lamb's kidneys
4 rashers of bacon
4 tomatoes
4 mushrooms
salt and pepper
melted butter or oil

Trim the chops, separate the sausages, skin, halve and core the kidneys, trim the rind from the bacon, halve the tomatoes and trim the ends of the mushroom stalks. Sprinkle the chops, kidneys, tomatoes and mushrooms with salt and pepper. Brush them all with fat or oil. Heat the grill and put the tomatoes (cut side up) and the mushrooms (stalks up) in the grill pan, where they will be basted by the juices from the other food and will cook without further attention. Place the grill grid in the grill pan and put on the chops, sausages and kidneys. Cook them under a medium heat, allowing 14–16 minutes altogether and turning the food on the grid frequently to ensure even cooking. The kidneys will probably be cooked first, so remove these and keep them warm. Replace them by the bacon rashers and cook for a further 3–5 minutes. If the grill is small and all the food has to be cooked separately, heat the oven to a low temperature to keep the food warm as it cooks.

Serve the food on a large plate, with a simple garnish of watercress. Traditional accompaniments are chipped or matchstick potatoes, and for more formal occasions maître d'hôtel butter.

Note Small pieces of fillet or rump steak are often substituted for the lamb chop; calf's or lamb's liver is sometimes included in a grill.

Lamb paprika

8 middle or best end of neck chops
40 g *(1½ oz)* butter
225 g *(½ lb)* onions, skinned and chopped
450 g *(1 lb)* tomatoes, peeled and sliced
15 ml *(1 tbsp)* chopped parsley
5–10 ml *(1–2 level tsps)* paprika pepper
salt
142 ml *(¼ pt)* soured cream or yoghurt

Trim off any excess fat from the chops. Heat the butter, brown the chops on both sides and remove from the pan. Fry the onions in the fat until golden brown – about 5 minutes. Add the tomatoes, parsley, paprika and salt to taste, replace the chops, cover and simmer gently for 1 hour, or bake in a covered casserole in the oven at 170°C *(325°F)* mark 3 for 1½ hours. Stir in the cream or yoghurt, re-season and reheat without boiling.

Noisettes of lamb

These are prepared from a whole best end of neck. Ask the butcher to chine the meat, but not to cut through the rib bones. Remove the chine bones, skin the meat and remove all rib bones. Season the inside of the meat with salt, freshly ground pepper and herbs and roll it up tightly, starting from the thick end towards the flap and wrapping this round. Tie securely at 4-cm *(1½-in)* intervals. Using a sharp knife, cut up in portions, with the string coming in the centre of each one. Cook as for chops, allowing 5 minutes longer cooking time. Remove the strings before serving.

Irish stew

8 middle neck chops
900 g *(2 lb)* potatoes, peeled and sliced
2 large onions, skinned and sliced
salt and pepper
chopped parsley

Trim some of the fat from the chops. Place alternate layers of vegetables and meat in a saucepan, seasoning with salt and pepper and finishing with a layer of potatoes. Add sufficient water to half cover. Cover with a lid and simmer very slowly for 3 hours. Serve sprinkled with chopped parsley.

Alternatively, cook the stew in a casserole in the oven at 190°C *(375°F)* mark 5 for 2½–3 hours.

If you use scrag end of neck for Irish stew it makes an economical dish.

Lancashire hot-pot

8 middle neck chops
225 g *(½ lb)* onions, skinned and sliced
2 lamb's kidneys, skinned and diced, optional
450 g *(1 lb)* potatoes, peeled and sliced
salt and pepper
300 ml *(½ pt)* stock
25 g *(1 oz)* lard or dripping

Remove any excess fat from the chops and put them in a casserole. Add the onions, the kidneys (if used) and lastly the potato; season well. Pour on the stock and brush the top of the potato with the melted lard or dripping. Cover and cook in the oven at 170°C *(325°F)* mark 3 for 2 hours, or until the meat and potatoes are tender. Remove the lid and brown the top layer of potatoes in the oven at 220°C *(425°F)* mark 7 for 20 minutes.

Note Some people prefer to use chunky pieces of potato for the topping instead of the slices suggested in this recipe.

Lancashire hot-pot is traditionally made containing oysters. Allow 1 shelled oyster to each lamb chop, putting the oysters on top of the chops in the casserole.

Blanquette d'agneau

700 g *(1½ lb)* diced lean shoulder of lamb
100 g *(¼ lb)* carrots, pared and sliced
100 g *(¼ lb)* onions, skinned and sliced
2 sticks of celery, trimmed and sliced
small bayleaf
5 ml *(1 level tsp)* dried thyme
salt and pepper
300 ml *(½ pt)* stock or water
30 ml *(2 tbsps)* butter, softened
45 ml *(3 level tbsps)* flour
1 egg yolk
30 ml *(2 tbsps)* cream or milk
chopped parsley to garnish

Put the meat, carrots, onions, celery, flavourings and seasonings in a large pan. Cover with stock or water, put the lid on and simmer for 1½ hours. Blend together the softened butter and flour; when they are thoroughly mixed, add to the stew in small knobs and stir until thickened; simmer for 10 minutes, adding more liquid if necessary. Blend together the egg yolk and cream, add to the stew and reheat without boiling. Garnish with parsley before serving.

Haricot lamb

100 g *(4 oz)* haricot beans
1 kg *(2¼ lb)* best end of neck or breast of lamb in a piece
30 ml *(2 tbsps)* oil
2 onions, skinned and sliced
1 turnip, pared and sliced
5 ml *(1 level tsp)* salt
pepper
15 ml *(1 tbsp)* Worcestershire sauce

Soak the beans overnight in cold water. Cut the meat into serving-size pieces, trimming off any excess fat, and fry it in the hot oil for 2–3 minutes, until browned. Add the onions and turnip and fry for a further 2–3 minutes. Pour on just sufficient boiling water to cover the meat. Add the drained beans, salt and pepper, cover with a lid and simmer for 2–2½ hours, or cook in the oven at 170°C *(325°F)* mark 3 for 2½–3 hours. Stir in the Worcestershire sauce just before serving.

Navarin of lamb

1 kg *(2¼ lb)* best end of neck or shoulder of lamb
30 ml *(2 tbsps)* oil
5 ml *(1 level tsp)* sugar
15 ml *(1 level tbsp)* flour
900 ml *(1½ pt)* stock or water
30 ml *(2 tbsps)* tomato paste
salt and pepper
bouquet garni
4 onions, skinned and quartered
4 carrots, pared and sliced
1–2 turnips, pared and quartered
8 small, even sized potatoes, peeled
chopped parsley

This is a traditional dish of French origin.

Trim the meat and cut into 2.5-cm *(1-in)* cubes. Fry it lightly on all sides in the oil. If there is too much fat at this stage, pour off a little to leave 15–30 ml *(1–2 tbsps)*. Stir in the sugar and heat until it browns slightly, then add the flour, stirring until this also cooks and browns. Remove from the heat, stir in the stock gradually, then bring to the boil and add the tomato paste, seasoning and bouquet garni. Cover, reduce the heat and simmer for about 1 hour. Remove the bouquet garni, add the onions, carrots and turnips and continue cooking for another ½ hour. Finally, add the potatoes and continue cooking for about 20 minutes, until tender.

Serve the meat on a heated serving dish, surrounded by the vegetables and garnished with the parsley.

Note A 112-g *(4-oz)* packet of frozen peas can also be added to the mixture about 10 minutes before it is served.

Lamb cutlets navarre

4 lamb cutlets
salt and pepper
25 g *(1 oz)* lard
225-g *(½-lb)* slice of gammon, diced
1 onion, skinned and chopped
450 g *(1 lb)* tomatoes, skinned and chopped
225 g *(½ lb)* chipolata sausages

Season the cutlets with salt and pepper and fry them in the lard; when they are browned, transfer them to a casserole. Fry the gammon and onion in the same fat. When the onion is golden brown, add the tomatoes, season and cook for a further 10 minutes. Pour this sauce over the cutlets, cover the casserole and cook in the oven at 180°C *(350°F)* mark 4 for 20–30 minutes. Fry the sausages separately. Place the cutlets in a hot dish and garnish with the sausages, or if you prefer add the sausages to the casserole.

Colonial goose

1.8-kg *(4-lb)* leg of lamb
1 sheep's kidney, skinned and chopped
2 rashers of bacon, rinded and chopped
175 g *(6 oz)* fresh white breadcrumbs
5 ml *(1 level tsp)* mixed dried herbs
1 small onion, skinned and chopped
1 medium sized apple, cored and chopped
1 medium sized tomato, skinned and chopped
5 ml *(1 level tsp)* salt
pepper
1 egg, beaten
25 g *(1 oz)* butter, melted

Have the meat boned and remove any surplus fat. Combine all the remaining ingredients to make a stuffing. Stuff the meat, roll it up and tie securely or sew up with thread. Place the joint in a roasting tin and cook in the oven at 190°C *(375°F)* mark 5, allowing 20 minutes per 450 g *(1 lb)* and 30 minutes over. Serve either hot or cold.

Breton roast lamb

1 leg of lamb, weighing 1.4–1.8 kg *(3–4 lb)*
salt and pepper
1 clove garlic, sliced lengthwise into 2–3 pieces
fat
225 g *(½ lb)* haricot beans, soaked overnight
1 onion, skinned
bouquet garni

Rub the lamb with salt and pepper; cut several slits in the flesh close to the bone and insert the pieces of garlic. Place the joint in a roasting tin with the fat and cook in the oven at 180°C *(350°F)* mark 4, allowing 30–35 minutes per 450 g *(1 lb)*. The meat should not be overbrowned when cooked, but juicy and pink. Meanwhile cook the haricot beans by simmering them in salted water with the whole onion and the bouquet garni – about 45 minutes. Serve them round the joint, with some of the gravy from the roasting tin poured over. *Serves 6–8.*

Kebabs

thick slice of lamb taken from the leg – approx 700 g *(1½ lb)*
45 ml *(3 tbsps)* olive oil
15 ml *(1 tbsp)* lemon juice
salt and pepper
1 clove garlic, skinned and crushed
4 small tomatoes, halved, optional
8 button mushrooms
few bayleaves, optional
2 small onions, quartered, optional
melted butter

Remove all fat and gristle from the meat and cut it into 2.5-cm *(1-in)* cubes. Marinade for 2 hours (or preferably overnight) in the olive oil, lemon juice, seasoning and crushed garlic. Thread 8 skewers alternately with meat cubes, halved tomatoes, if used, and whole mushrooms. If you like, a bayleaf or an onion quarter may be placed on each side of the meat pieces, to give more flavour. Brush with melted butter and cook under a low grill for 10–15 minutes, turning the kebabs about 3 times, until the meat is tender. Serve on plain boiled rice, with lemon.

Lamb's kidneys may also be added; allow ½ to 1 kidney per person, removing the core. Rolled streaky bacon rashers are another good addition to kebabs. For added flavour, include in the marinade some herbs such as dried marjoram and chopped fresh parsley.

VEAL

1. As veal comes from a young animal the flesh should be comparatively light in colour – fine-textured, pale pink, soft and moist; avoid really flabby, wet meat.
2. If the flesh looks bluish or mottled it generally means it comes from an older animal.
3. The fat – of which there is very little – should be firm and pinkish or creamy white.
4. Veal has a lot of bone in proportion to the meat and this makes excellent jellied stock or gravy when it is boiled – it gives the special flavour to veal stews and fricassees.

Cuts of veal and methods of cooking

Leg is a prime cut and is usually roasted, often being boned and stuffed before cooking.

Allow 225–350 g *(½–¾ lb)* with bone for each person.

Fillet, which is usually the most expensive cut, is sold in the piece for roasting; like leg, it is usually boned and stuffed before cooking. It can also be cut into thin slices or escalopes, which are beaten thin and generally fried.

Allow 125–175 g *(4–6 oz)* boned for each person.

Loin Another prime cut for roasting, either on the bone or boned, stuffed and rolled.

Allow 225–350 g *(½–¾ lb)* with bone for each person.

Chops The loin can be divided into chops, those from the bottom end, which have a small round bone in the centre, being known as chump chops. They are suitable for grilling or frying.

Allow 1 per person.

Cutlets Prime cuts from the top or neck end of the loin; they are grilled, fried or braised.

Allow 1–2, according to size, for each person.

Shoulder is an awkward shape and is therefore often quite cheap, although when boned and stuffed it is quite suitable for roasting. Portions of shoulder meat, taken off the bone, are often sold for pies, stews and fricassees.

Allow 450 g *(1 lb)* with bone, 125–175 g *(4–6 oz)* without bone, per person.

Knuckle This cheap cut from the foreleg is good for boiling and stewing and the meat from it can be used for making pies. It can also be boned, stuffed and then braised.

Allow 450 g *(1 lb)* with bone, 125–175 g *(4–6 oz)* without bone, per person.

Best end of neck This fairly cheap cut is good value; it can be boned and stuffed or cooked on the bone.

It is suitable for roasting, braising and stewing.

Allow about 450 g *(1 lb)* with bone, 125–175 g *(4–6 oz)* without bone, per person.

Breast A fairly cheap cut, which is usually boned, stuffed and roasted and has a good flavour.

Allow about 450 g *(1 lb)* with bone, 125–175 g *(4–6 oz)* without bone, per person. It can be served cold as a veal mould.

Pie veal Consists of trimmings and small pieces of shoulder, breast, neck or knuckle, bought ready cut up for use.

Roast veal

Trim the joint, then weigh and calculate the cooking time, allowing 25 minutes per 450 g *(1 lb)* plus 25 minutes if the meat is on the bone, 30 minutes per 450 g *(1 lb)* plus 30 minutes if the joint is boned and rolled. Season well and bake in the oven at 220°C *(425°F)* mark 7 for the calculated time, basting frequently; serve well done. Carve in thick slices and serve accompanied by bacon rolls, veal forcemeat and gravy.

Veal can be a little dry and insipid, so to improve the flavour cover the joint with some strips of streaky bacon or stuff it with forcemeat (see page 183).

The meat will be more moist if baked in a closed tin or wrapped in foil, although the appearance is not so good.

Veal escalopes

When cooking escalopes by any of the three methods described below it is not advisable to have more than 2 in the pan at once as they are difficult to turn over.

Fried escalopes (Wiener schnitzel)

Allow 1 escalope per person and get the butcher to beat it until really thin. Coat with beaten egg and fresh white breadcrumbs, patting them on well. Melt 50 g *(2 oz)* butter in a large frying pan and fry the veal gently (about 5 minutes on each side). Drain well on kitchen paper and serve with wedges of lemon and a green salad. If you wish, garnish with thin strips of anchovy fillet and chopped hardboiled egg.

Escalopes with Parmesan cheese

Prepare and coat the escalopes as above, then fry gently in butter for about 3 minutes on each side or until just tender. Cover each escalope with a thin slice of cooked ham and 15 ml *(1 level tbsp)* grated Parmesan cheese. Spoon a little of the butter over the cheese, cover the pan with a lid or large plate and cook for a further 2–3 minutes, until the cheese just melts. Serve at once.

Escalope with Marsala and cheese

Coat each escalope with seasoned flour and fry gently in 50 g *(2 oz)* butter until just tender and golden (3 minutes on each side). Stir into the pan 30–45 ml *(2–3 tbsps)* Marsala (or sherry or Madeira) and sprinkle each escalope with 15 ml *(1 level tbsp)* grated Parmesan cheese. Spoon some of the butter-wine mixture over, cover the pan with a lid or plate and cook gently for a further 2–3 minutes, until the cheese just melts.

Escalopes fines herbes

60 ml *(4 level tbsps)* flour
salt and pepper
4 escalopes of veal
50 g *(2 oz)* butter
10 ml *(2 level tsps)* tomato paste
1 wineglass sherry
1 wineglass red wine
50 g *(2 oz)* mushrooms, sliced
2.5 ml *(½ level tsp)* mixed dried herbs
60 ml *(4 tbsps)* single cream
226-g *(8-oz)* can tomatoes, drained and chopped
50 g *(2 oz)* cheese, grated

Mix 45 ml *(3 tbsps)* flour with some salt and pepper and coat the meat with this. Heat 25 g *(1 oz)* of the butter in a frying pan and fry the escalopes gently for 5 minutes on each side; remove them and keep hot. Add the remaining flour to the frying pan, stir in the tomato paste, sherry and red wine and bring the mixture slowly to the boil; add the sliced mushrooms, mixed dried herbs and lastly the cream. Season as required and cook very gently for about 5 minutes, without letting the sauce come to the boil.

Heat the remaining butter in a pan, add the canned tomatoes and heat through. Pour the mixture into a dish, put the meat on top, pour the sauce over, sprinkle with the grated cheese and brown under the grill.

Fresh tomatoes may be used instead of canned ones; skin and chop them.

Veal birds

4 veal escalopes
2 rashers of streaky bacon, rinded
knob of butter
½ small onion, skinned and chopped
15 ml *(1 level tbsp)* flour
226-g *(8-oz)* can tomatoes

For the forcemeat
1 thick slice bread
pinch of thyme or mixed dried herbs
salt and pepper
grated rind of ½ lemon
beaten egg or milk to mix

Begin by making the forcemeat. Make the bread into crumbs, add the herbs, salt, pepper and lemon rind and bind with the egg or milk.

Have the escalopes beaten thin, cut each rasher of bacon in half and spread out until thin with the flat of a knife. Lay a piece of bacon on each escalope and add a quarter of the forcemeat. Roll up each escalope and secure by wrapping round with sewing cotton. Fry the 'birds' in the fat until lightly browned (about 4 minutes), remove them and fry the onion lightly, then stir in the flour and the tomatoes made up to 300 ml *(½ pt)* with water. Add seasoning and bring this sauce to the boil. Add the 'birds', cover, then reduce the heat and simmer gently for about 1½ hours, or until tender.

Stuffed veal escalopes

4 slices veal fillet
salt
1 egg, beaten
50 g *(2 oz)* butter
50 g *(2 oz)* cooked peas
50 g *(2 oz)* cooked ham, chopped
15 ml *(1 level tbsp)* flour
15 ml *(1 tbsp)* milk
60 ml *(4 level tbsps)* fresh white breadcrumbs
100 g *(4 oz)* fat for frying

Trim the meat, beat lightly and season with salt. Scramble the egg in a pan with the butter, peas and ham, spread a little of this mixture on each piece of veal, fold the meat in half and secure with a small skewer. Coat the meat with the flour, then dip each piece in the milk and roll it in the breadcrumbs. Fry in the hot fat until lightly browned – 10–15 minutes.

Veal à la crème flambé

4 escalopes
salt and pepper
15 ml *(1 tbsp)* lemon juice
40 g *(1½ oz)* butter
6 mushrooms
45 ml *(3 tbsps)* brandy
60 ml *(4 tbsps)* double cream
small sprigs of parsley to garnish

Flatten the escalopes and season with salt, pepper and some of the lemon juice. Melt 25 g *(1 oz)* of the butter and fry the escalopes until brown – about 5 minutes on each side. Remove them from the pan and keep them warm on a serving dish. Add the chopped mushroom stalks to the fat remaining in the pan and cook for 3 minutes. Add 30 ml *(2 tbsps)* of the brandy and set it alight. When the flames have died down, pour in the cream and the rest of the lemon juice. Stir well to loosen any residue from the pan and cook without boiling until the sauce has thickened; season it to taste and strain it over the escalopes. Slice the mushrooms and fry them lightly in the rest of the butter. Add 15 ml *(1 tbsp)* brandy and ignite it. Garnish the escalopes with the flamed mushroom slices and some tiny sprigs of parsley.

Stuffed veal escalopes en papillote

4 thin escalopes of veal
50 g *(2 oz)* mushrooms, chopped
100 g *(4 oz)* white breadcrumbs
2 tomatoes, skinned and diced
pinch of mixed herbs
4 bacon rashers, diced
40 g *(1½ oz)* butter, melted

Lay the escalopes out flat on a board. Mix the mushrooms, breadcrumbs, tomatoes and herbs together in a bowl. Fry the diced bacon lightly and mix with the other ingredients. Bind the mixture with the melted butter. Place a spoonful of stuffing on one half of each escalope and fold the other half over, pressing the edges together. Wrap each escalope in buttered double greaseproof paper or foil, twisting the ends to secure it. Put on a baking sheet and cook in the oven at 190°C *(375°F)* mark 5 for 30–40 minutes, or until tender. Remove the papers before serving.

Veal with paprika

4 rashers streaky bacon, rinded and diced
2 medium sized onions, skinned and sliced
30 ml *(2 tbsps)* oil
700 g *(1½ lb)* shoulder of veal, boned and cubed
300 ml *(½ pt)* chicken stock
20 ml *(4 level tsps)* paprika
175 g *(6 oz)* button mushrooms
25 g *(1 oz)* butter
142 ml *(¼ pt)* soured cream
30 ml *(2 tbsps)* flaked almonds, lightly roasted

Fry the bacon until crisp and remove from the pan. Fry the onions in the bacon fat until soft and golden brown – about 5 minutes. Discard the bacon fat and heat the oil in the pan, then brown the meat a few cubes at a time. Put the bacon, onions and veal in a 2-l *(3½-pt)* casserole. Pour on the stock, mixed with the paprika, cover and cook for 1 hour in the oven at 180°C *(350°F)* mark 4. Meanwhile fry the mushrooms in the butter. Add to the veal, with the soured cream. Return the casserole to the oven and cook for a further ½ hour. Check the seasoning, sprinkle the almonds on top and serve accompanied by plain noodles or boiled potatoes.

Blanquette of veal

700 g *(1½ lb)* lean veal (from shoulder or knuckle), cubed
2 onions, skinned and chopped
2 carrots, pared and chopped
squeeze of lemon juice
bouquet garni
salt and pepper
25 g *(1 oz)* butter
45 ml *(3 level tbsps)* flour
1 egg yolk
30–45 ml *(2–3 tbsps)* cream
lemon wedges and bacon rolls to garnish

Put the meat, onions, carrots, lemon juice, bouquet garni and seasoning into a large pan with enough water to cover. Put on the lid and simmer gently for about 1½ hours, until the meat is tender. Strain off the cooking liquid, retaining 600 ml *(1 pt)* and keep the meat and vegetables warm. Melt the butter, stir in the flour and cook for 2–3 minutes, stirring all the time. Adjust the seasoning, remove from the heat and when slightly cooled stir in the egg yolk and cream. Pour over the meat and vegetables and before serving reheat without boiling for a further 5 minutes, to allow the flavours to blend. Serve with lemon wedges and bacon rolls.

Italian veal casserole

700 g *(1½ lb)* boned leg of veal
2 cloves garlic, skinned and chopped
60 ml *(2 tbsps)* oil
salt and pepper
225 g *(½ lb)* tomatoes, skinned and chopped
10 ml *(2 level tsps)* tomato paste
150 ml *(¼ pt)* white wine
2 sprigs of rosemary
strip of lemon rind

Slice the meat or cut it into small pieces. Fry the chopped garlic in the oil until golden brown – about 2 minutes. Add the meat, salt and pepper and continue cooking until the meat is golden brown – about 8–10 minutes. Stir in the tomatoes, tomato paste, wine, rosemary and lemon rind and just enough water to cover. Pour into a casserole, cover tightly and cook in the oven at 180°C *(350°F)* mark 4 for about 1 hour, or until the meat is tender.

Cherry-stuffed veal

3 kg *(6½ lb)* breast of veal, boned (about 2.5 kg, *5 lb*, after boning)
225 g *(½ lb)* lean back bacon, in a piece
175 g *(6 oz)* glacé cherries
little rosemary
oil
garlic salt (or a clove of garlic and ordinary salt)

Lay the veal on a chopping board. Cut the meat where it tapers and pull back the flap to make an oblong shape. Remove the rind from the bacon, cut the bacon in quarters along the length of the rinded fat, and then in half at right angles to the first cut. Lay the strips of bacon at intervals along the meat, parallel to the width. Position the cherries between the bacon, with the rosemary. Roll up from the short side. Secure in position with skewers before tying neatly and firmly with string. Place in a small roasting tin, brush with oil, dust with garlic salt (or halve the skinned garlic clove and rub it over the veal, then dust with salt). Roast in the oven at 200°C *(400°F)* mark 6 for ½ hour, reduce the temperature to 180°C *(350°F)* mark 4 and cook for about a further 2½ hours. Cover with foil or 2 layers of greaseproof paper, previously wetted, if the meat is in danger of over-browning. *Serves 12.*

Veal fricassee

225 g *(½ lb)* back bacon, cut in 2 thick rashers
700 g *(1½ lb)* stewing veal, cubed
50 g *(2 oz)* butter
15 ml *(1 tbsp)* oil
½ small onion, skinned and finely chopped
300 ml *(½ pt)* white stock or water
salt and pepper
30 ml *(2 level tbsps)* flour
15–30 ml *(1–2 tbsps)* lemon juice

A good standby for all occasions. Add your own personal touch with herbs, or use half stock and half dry white wine for cooking. Alternatively, use half the stated amount of stock for cooking and replace the other half by milk, added at the end.

Rind the bacon, trim off any excess fat and cut into pieces the same size as the veal. Fry the veal and bacon very lightly in 25 g *(1 oz)* butter and the oil, but do not colour. Lift them out and place in a 1.7-l *(3-pt)* casserole. Fry the onion in the remaining fat until transparent but not brown and add to the veal. Pour the stock over the meat, season, cover and cook in the oven at 180°C *(350°F)* mark 4 for 1½ hours, or until tender. Strain off the liquor and keep the veal and bacon hot in the casserole. Melt the remaining butter, stir in the flour and cook for 2–3 minutes. Gradually stir in the strained liquor, bring to the boil and boil for 2–3 minutes, stirring all the time. Add the lemon juice and re-check the seasoning. Pour the sauce over the veal.

Osso bucco

1 kg *(2¼ lb)* shin of veal
salt and pepper
50 g *(2 oz)* butter
1 medium sized onion, skinned and finely chopped
1 carrot, pared and thinly sliced
1 stalk of celery, scrubbed and thinly sliced
150 ml *(¼ pt)* dry white wine
15 ml *(1 level tbsp)* flour
400 ml *(¾ pt)* stock
225 g *(½ lb)* tomatoes, skinned and chopped
pinch of dried rosemary
15 ml *(1 tbsp)* chopped parsley to garnish
1 clove garlic, skinned and finely chopped
grated rind of ½ lemon

Ask your butcher to saw the veal into 5-cm *(2-in)* pieces. Season with salt and pepper. Melt the butter, brown the veal all over and remove from the pan. Add a little more butter if necessary and fry the onion, carrot and celery until they are golden brown. Drain off any excess fat, return the meat to the pan and add the wine. Cover and simmer gently for 20 minutes. Blend the flour with a little stock to a smooth cream, add the remainder of the stock and add to the meat. Add the tomatoes and rosemary, cover tightly and continue to simmer for a further 1½ hours, or until the meat is tender. Arrange in a deep serving dish and sprinkle with a mixture of parsley, garlic and lemon rind. Serve with risotto (see page 279) and a dressed green salad.

Raised veal and ham pie

450 g *(1 lb)* hot-water crust (see page 355)
350 g *(¾ lb)* pie veal, diced
100 g *(¼ lb)* ham, chopped
15 ml *(1 tbsp)* chopped parsley
grated rind and juice of 1 lemon
salt and pepper
little stock or water
1 hard-boiled egg
beaten egg to glaze
jelly stock

Make a pastry case as described on page 357. Mix the veal, ham, parsley, lemon rind and juice, season with salt and pepper and moisten with a little stock or water. Half fill the pastry case with this mixture, put the hard-boiled egg in the centre, add the remaining meat mixture, cover and decorate the pie. Make a small hole in the centre with a sharp knife, to allow you to test whether the meat is cooked and to fill with jelly stock when cooked. Glaze the top with a little beaten egg and tie a greaseproof paper band round the pie. Bake in the oven at 220° C *(425°F)* mark 7 for 15–20 minutes, then reduce the heat to 180° C *(350°F)* mark 4 and continue cooking for a further 1½ hours or longer, until the meat feels tender when tested with a skewer. When cold, fill the pie up with jelly stock made by dissolving 10 ml *(2 level tsps)* gelatine in 300 ml *(½ pt)* chicken stock. Leave to set.

Veal balls

1 kg *(2¼ lb)* veal, minced
50 g *(2 oz)* onion, skinned and finely chopped
50 g *(2 oz)* fresh white breadcrumbs
2 eggs, beaten
30 ml *(2 tbsps)* olive oil
15 ml *(1 tbsp)* wine vinegar
15 ml *(1 tbsp)* finely chopped parsley
2.5–5 ml *(½–1 tsp)* chopped mint
2.5 ml *(½ level tsp)* dried oregano
2 cloves garlic, skinned and crushed
30 ml *(2 tbsps)* boiling water
salt and pepper
flour for coating
oil or lard for frying

For the tomato sauce
175 g *(6 oz)* onion, skinned and sliced
30 ml *(2 tbsps)* olive oil
450 g *(1 lb)* ripe tomatoes, skinned and chopped
5 ml *(1 level tsp)* sugar
1.25 ml *(¼ level tsp)* ground cinnamon
300 ml *(½ pt)* stock or water
salt and pepper

Combinc all thc ingredients for the veal balls and divide into walnut-sized balls. Flour a baking sheet, place the balls in a single layer and roll them in the flour by shaking the tray backwards and forwards a few times. Fry them in hot fat until evenly browned – about 5 minutes. Drain. For the sauce, sauté the onion in the oil until soft and add the rest of the ingredients. Simmer the sauce until soft, put through a sieve and return it to the pan, with the veal balls. Simmer, covered, for a further 15 minutes.

Vitello tonnato

Note This has to be prepared the day before it is served.

700 g *(1½ lb)* boned leg of veal
1 small carrot, pared and sliced
1 onion, skinned and quartered
1 stick of celery, trimmed and chopped
4 peppercorns
5 ml *(1 level tsp)* salt
99-g *(3½-oz)* can tuna
4 anchovy fillets
150 ml *(¼ pt)* olive oil
2 egg yolks
pepper
15 ml *(1 tbsp)* lemon juice
capers and lemon slices for garnish

Tie the meat into a neat roll and put into a saucepan with the bone, if you have it, carrot, onion, celery, peppercorns, salt and some water. Bring to the boil, cover and simmer until tender – about 1 hour. Remove the meat and cool it. Meanwhile, mash together the tuna, anchovy fillets and 15 ml *(1 tbsp)* olive oil. Break down the fish with a wooden spoon, then stir in the egg yolks and pepper. Press it through a sieve into a small basin and add the lemon juice. Stir in the remaining oil a little at a time, beating well after each addition. Continue until the sauce resembles thin cream. Cut the meat into slices, arrange in a shallow dish and coat completely with the sauce. Cover and leave overnight. Serve cold, with a garnish of capers and lemon slices. *Serves 4–6.*

Saltimbocca alla romana

8 thin slices of veal
lemon juice
freshly ground black pepper
8 fresh sage or basil leaves or ground marjoram
8 thin slices of prosciutto
butter
30 ml *(2 tbsps)* Marsala
1-cm *(½-in)* squares of day-old bread, fried

Ask the butcher to flatten the veal into pieces about 13 cm by 10 cm *(5 in by 4 in)* or do it yourself by putting the veal between sheets of waxed paper and using a flat mallet or chopper. Season each piece with lemon juice and pepper. Place a sage or basil leaf or some marjoram in the centre and cover with a slice of prosciutto cut to fit. Roll up and fix firmly with a cocktail stick. Melt enough butter to cover the base of a frying pan; gently fry the veal rolls until golden brown – don't overheat the butter. Add the Marsala, bring to simmering point, cover the pan and simmer gently until the veal rolls are tender. Serve with the juices poured over and surround with the fried croûtons and some beans or peas.

Note Prosciutto is a special Italian smoked ham.

Veal chops en papillote

8 veal chops 1 cm *(½ in)* **thick**
60 ml *(4 tbsps)* **olive oil**
10 ml *(2 tsps)* **chopped parsley**
10 ml *(2 tsps)* **chopped onion**
30 ml *(2 tbsps)* **chopped chives**
100 g *(¼ lb)* **mushrooms, thinly sliced**
butter
salt and black pepper

Marinade the chops in the oil for 12 hours. Mix the parsley, onion and chives with the mushrooms. Cut 8 pieces of kitchen parchment paper or foil, each large enough to wrap a chop completely, spread with butter and sprinkle with the herb and mushroom mixture. Place a chop on each paper, cover with another layer of the herb mixture, season well and wrap up firmly. Bake in the oven at 200°C *(400°F)* mark 6 for 20 minutes, until tender. Serve the chops still encased in the papers. *Serves 8.*

Roast veal with beer

1.4 kg *(3 lb)* **loin of veal**
50 g *(2 oz)* **dripping or lard**
salt and pepper
2–3 carrots, pared and sliced
2–3 onions, skinned and sliced
300 ml *(½ pt)* **beer**
1 bayleaf
2 cloves
15 ml *(1 level tbsp)* **flour**

Spread the meat thickly with the dripping or lard and put it in a meat tin; season with salt and pepper. Add the carrots and onions, and roast in the oven at 220°C *(425°F)* mark 7 for 30 minutes. Pour the beer over the meat, add the bayleaf and cloves and return it to the oven. Turn down the heat to 190°C *(375°F)* mark 5 and cook the meat until tender, basting frequently – allow 30 minutes per 450 g *(1 lb)*. When the meat is cooked place it on a serving dish. Blend the flour with the juices in the tin, heat until boiling, then strain over the meat.

PORK

1. The lean part of pork should be pale pink, moist and slightly marbled with fat.
2. There should be a good outer layer of firm, white fat, with a thin, elastic skin; if the joint is to be roasted, get the butcher to score the rind.
3. The bones should be small and pinkish (which denotes a young animal.)
4. Although pork was considered seasonal at one time, it can now be bought all the year round; prices, however, vary considerably, so check up before buying.

Cuts and methods of cooking

Leg Prime joint but rather large, so it is often cut into two. Roasted on the bone, or boned and stuffed.

Allow 225–350 g *(½–¾ lb)* with bone per person; 125–175 g *(4–6 oz)* without bone.

Fillet A lean, expensive cut taken from the top of the hind leg, with a central bone. It is best roasted and can be cooked on the bone or boned and stuffed.

Pork fillet (tenderloin) is also obtainable in the piece or as fairly thin slices, which can be roasted, grilled, fried or casseroled.

Allow 225–350 g *(½–¾ lb)* with bone per person; 125–175 g *(4–6 oz)* without bone.

Loin An expensive but prime cut, suitable for roasting; often includes the kidney. It can be cooked on the bone or boned and stuffed.

Allow 225–350 g *(½–¾ lb)* with bone per person; 125–175 g *(4–6 oz)* without bone.

Spare rib Fairly lean and moderately priced. Good for roasting, but can also be cut up for braising and stewing.

Allow 225–350 g *(½–¾ lb)* with bone per person.

Chops Usually consist of the cut-up loin and often include the kidney. They can be grilled, fried or casseroled.

Allow 1 per person.

Cutlets A more unusual cut, these are taken from the sparerib and have little or no bone; they are usually lean. Cooked as for chops.

Allow 1–2 per person.

Blade Another cut for roasting on the bone.

Allow 225–350 g *(½–¾ lb)* per person.

Hand and Spring The foreleg, suitable for roasting, boiling and stewing.

Allow 350 g *(¾ lb)* per person.

Belly A fatty cut, sometimes sold salted and usually

boiled and served cold. Can also be roasted.

Allow 125–175 g *(4–6 oz)* per person.

Spare ribs (American and North-country style) are from the belly and are removed in one piece, leaving the meat between the rib bones. Usually barbecued.

Accompaniments for pork

Apple (or gooseberry) sauce is the most usual accompaniment, with sage and onion stuffing when appropriate. Try baked or fried apples or cranberry or redcurrant jelly as an alternative.

Roast pork

Trim the joint, then weigh it and calculate the cooking time; roast at 220°C *(425°F)* mark 7, allowing 25 minutes per 450 g *(1 lb)* plus 25 minutes if the meat is on the bone; if the meat is rolled, it is better cooked at 190°C *(375°F)* mark 5 for 30–35 minutes per 450 g *(1 lb)* plus 35 minutes.

Rub the scored rind with oil and salt to give crisp crackling. Put the joint into the roasting tin (on a grill grid or meat trivet if it is fatty). Bake in the oven for the calculated time and serve well done (pork should never look pink when cooked), with apple or gooseberry sauce, sage and onion stuffing and thickened gravy.

Boned loin is particularly good stuffed with an apple and prune stuffing before roasting (see page 185).

Roast crown of pork

This is an interesting dish for a special party. It requires 6 ribs from each side of a loin of pork; ask your butcher to scrape the ends of the bones, as for cutlets, but do *not* separate the chops. The sections of meat are turned so that the bones are on the outside and the two pieces are then fastened together with string to form a circle. Put forcemeat in the centre and cover the ends of the bones with greased greaseproof paper or foil to stop them from burning. Cook in the oven at 190°C *(375°F)* mark 5, allowing 30–35 minutes per 450 g *(1 lb)* plus 25 minutes; baste frequently. When the meat is cooked remove the paper or foil and put a small, white, parboiled onion or a new potato on each bone.

Sage-and-bacon stuffed pork

1 kg *(2¼ lb)* loin of pork (boned weight)
225 g *(½ lb)* sweet-cure back bacon rashers, rinded
12 fresh or dried sage leaves
oil and salt

Have the pork rind scored deeply and evenly. Place the joint on a flat surface, fat side down, and cut the flesh to open it out a little. Lay the rashers over the flesh and place sage leaves at intervals. Roll up carefully and secure firmly with string, parcel fashion. Weigh, then put in a roasting tin. Rub the rind well with oil and salt. Roast in the oven at 190°C *(375°F)* mark 5 for 30–35 minutes per 450 g *(1 lb)* stuffed weight, plus 30 minutes over. Remove the strings, place the meat on a serving dish and keep it warm while the gravy is being made. *Serves 6.*

Baked pork chops with pineapple

4 pork chops
salt and pepper
226-g *(8-oz)* can pineapple rings
brown sugar

Trim the chops, put them in an ovenproof dish and season. Pour in enough pineapple juice to come halfway up the chops, cover with a lid or foil and bake in the oven at 180°C *(350°F)* mark 4 for about 45 minutes, till tender. Uncover, garnish each chop with a pineapple ring, sprinkle with a little brown sugar and return them to the oven for 5–10 minutes, until the sugar has just melted.

Mint and cucumber fish salad (p.68).

Fried pork chops

Trim the chops, removing any extra fat. Fry the chops slowly in a little dripping, oil or lard, turning them frequently, for about 20 minutes.

The chops may first be egg-and-breadcrumbed.

Pork chops with orange *see colour plate facing p. 112*

4 large pork chump chops, rinded
30 ml *(2 level tbsps)* seasoned flour
oil for frying
2 large thin-skinned oranges
60 ml *(4 level tbsps)* soft, light brown sugar
15 ml *(1 tbsp)* cornflour
150 ml *(¼ pt)* dry white wine
300 ml *(½ pt)* orange juice
1 medium sized onion, skinned and sliced
watercress to garnish

Coat the chops in seasoned flour. Heat just enough oil in a large frying pan to cover the base. Fry the chops quickly on either side until well browned. Drain and place in a shallow casserole, large enough to take the chops in a single layer. Remove the rind and all traces of white pith from the oranges. Slice, discarding the pips, and cut each slice in half; sprinkle with 30 ml *(2 tbsps)* sugar. Blend the cornflour with a little wine; add the rest of the wine, the orange juice and sugar. Bring to the boil, stirring, and pour over the chops. Arrange the sliced onion over the chops, cover tightly and cook in the oven at 180°C *(350°F)* mark 4 for 1¼–1½ hours. Remove the lid; arrange the orange slices over the onion and cook for a further 15–20 minutes, basting occasionally. Before serving, reduce the liquor, if you wish, by boiling, then adjust the seasoning and garnish with watercress.

Boston baked beans

250–350 g *(9–12 oz)* haricot beans
225 g *(½ lb)* fat salt belly of pork
2 medium sized onions, skinned and sliced
7.5 ml *(1½ level tsps)* dry mustard
5–10 ml *(1–2 level tsps)* salt
good pinch of pepper
15 ml *(1 level tbsp)* sugar
30 ml *(2 tbsps)* black treacle
15–30 ml *(1–2 tbsps)* cider vinegar
pinch ground cinnamon
pinch ground cloves

Wash the beans, cover with cold water and leave to soak overnight. Drain, saving the water. Cut the pork into 2.5-cm *(1-in)* cubes. Put the beans, onions and pork into a large ovenproof casserole, pour in just enough water to cover the beans and stir in the remaining ingredients. Cover closely and cook in the oven at 150°C *(300°F)* mark 1–2 for 8–9 hours. Stir occasionally, adding more water if the beans dry out while cooking.

Braised pork chops

4 thick pork chops
50 g *(2 oz)* fat or oil
1 onion, skinned and thinly sliced
1 carrot, pared and thinly sliced
bouquet garni
150 ml *(¼ pt)* white wine
150 ml *(¼ pt)* stock
100 g *(¼ lb)* mushrooms, sliced
150 ml *(¼ pt)* milk and water
salt and pepper
15 ml *(1 level tbsp)* plain flour

Trim the chops, brown on both sides in the fat or oil, remove them and lightly fry the onion and carrot for 5 minutes; remove and place in a casserole with the chops on top. Add the bouquet garni, wine and stock and cook in the oven at 180°C *(350°F)* mark 4 for 1 hour. Meanwhile put the mushrooms in a pan with the milk and water, season, cover and simmer for 5 minutes. Blend the flour with the fat left in the frying pan to make a roux. Drain off the liquid from the casserole and that from the mushrooms and add gradually to the roux, stirring until the sauce has boiled. Add the mushrooms and pour over the chops in the casserole.

Pork chops with apple and prune stuffing

4 pork chops
apple and prune stuffing: use about a quarter of the amounts given in recipe on page 185, but include at least ½ an egg

Trim the chops. Place a portion of stuffing on each chop, put into a greased baking tin and cover with greaseproof paper or foil. Cook in the oven at 200°C *(400°F)* mark 6 for 1 hour, or until tender.

Grilled mackerel with orange (p. 77).

Grilled pork chops with apple rings

4 pork chops
olive oil
1 cooking apple, peeled and cored and sliced

Trim the chops and brush with olive oil. Place the rings of apple in the base of the grill pan and put the chops on the grid. Grill the chops for 8–10 minutes on each side under a medium grill, making sure that they are well cooked; when they are done, place on a serving dish. Put the apple rings on to the grid and brown very lightly. Arrange between the chops on the serving dish.

Casserole of pork

8 slices of belly of pork – 700 g *(1½ lb)*
2 onions, skinned and sliced
1 large cooking apple, peeled, cored and diced
300 ml *(½ pt)* stock
gravy browning, salt, pepper
30 ml *(2 level tbsps)* flour
2 carrots, pared and sliced

Trim the excess fat from the belly of pork. Layer the onions and apple in a casserole and overlap the slices of pork on top. Colour the stock with a few drops of gravy browning, add some seasoning and pour over the meat. Cover and cook in the oven at 170°C *(325°F)* mark 3 for 2 hours; skim off any excess fat. Blend the flour with a little cold water, stir in the liquid from the casserole and return it to the casserole, with the carrots. Cover and cook for a further hour.

Barbecued spare-ribs

30 ml *(2 tbsps)* oil
175 g *(6 oz)* onion, skinned and chopped
1 clove garlic, skinned and crushed
30 ml *(2 level tbsps)* tomato paste
60 ml *(4 tbsps)* malt vinegar
1.25 ml *(¼ level tsp)* dried thyme
1.25 ml *(¼ level tsp)* chili seasoning
45 ml *(3 level tbsps)* honey
1 beef stock cube
1 kg *(2¼ lb)* spare-ribs (American cut)

Heat the oil in a saucepan, add the onion and sauté until clear. Add the flavourings, honey and beef cube, dissolved in 150 ml *(¼ pt)* hot water. Bubble the mixture gently for 10 minutes. Place the spare-ribs in a roasting tin in a single layer. Brush with a little of the sauce; roast in the oven at 190°C *(375°F)* mark 5 for ½ hour. Pour off the fat and spoon the remaining sauce over the meat; cook for a further 1–1¼ hours.

Normandy pork

900 g *(2 lb)* fillet of pork
30 ml *(2 level tbsps)* seasoned flour
300 ml *(½ pt)* dry white wine
225 g *(½ lb)* button mushrooms, sliced
40 g *(1½ oz)* butter
30 ml *(2 tbsps)* brandy
30 ml *(2 tbsps)* chopped parsley
142 ml *(¼ pt)* double cream
salt and pepper

Cut the pork into pieces about the size and shape of potato chips and toss these in the seasoned flour. Bring the wine to the boil, add the mushrooms and simmer, covered, for 10–15 minutes. Brown the pork in the hot butter. Warm the brandy in a small pan, set it alight and when the flames die down, pour it over the meat. Add the wine and mushrooms to the pork and simmer, covered, for ½ hour, or until the meat is tender. Strain the pork and mushrooms, put in a serving dish and keep warm. Add the parsley and cream to the juices in the pan and check the seasoning. Simmer without boiling until the sauce thickens and pour it over the pork. Serve with rice and green salad. *Serves 6.*

Pork roll

450 g *(1 lb)* lean pork, cubed
450 g *(1 lb)* lean ham, cubed
15 ml *(1 tbsp)* finely chopped onion
150 ml *(¼ pt)* thick white sauce
1 egg
salt and pepper
pinch of dried rosemary
thinly cut rashers of back bacon, rinded
little vinegar

Mince the pork, ham and onion twice. (Alternatively ask the butcher to mince the meat for you.) Blend these ingredients very thoroughly with the white sauce, egg, seasoning and rosemary. Shape into a roll on a floured surface. Lay the rashers of bacon overlapping each other on a piece of greased foil so that they will well cover the surface of the roll. Lay the pork mixture over the rashers, reshape the roll in the foil fold the foil over and seal the edges tightly. Boil gently for 2½ hours in water to which a little vinegar and salt have been added. (A saucer or similar shallow utensil, placed on the base of the pan, will prevent the roll from coming directly in contact with the metal.) Remove the roll from the pan, leave to cool and remove the foil. Serve with the attractive pattern of the bacon uppermost.

For a special effect, glaze with a thin coating of aspic jelly and garnish with sliced radish. *Serves 6.*

Spanish pork

700 g *(1½ lb)* pork fillet, sliced
30 ml *(2 level tbsps)* seasoned flour
2 medium sized onions, skinned and sliced
50 g *(2 oz)* fat or oil
2 green peppers, seeded and sliced
100 g *(¼ lb)* mushrooms, sliced
396-g *(14-oz)* can tomatoes
salt and pepper

Coat the slices of pork with seasoned flour. Fry the onions in the fat or oil, then add the pork and fry until browned – 3–4 minutes; transfer it to a casserole. Fry the peppers and mushrooms until tender – 5–6 minutes – and add the tomatoes. Add to the meat in the casserole, season, cover and cook in the oven at 180°C *(350°F)* mark 4 for 1½ hours.

Pork ragout

2 onions, skinned and sliced
50 g *(2 oz)* fat or oil
900 g *(2 lb)* shoulder of pork, boned and cubed
2 small green peppers, seeded and sliced
2 cloves of garlic, skinned and crushed
150 ml *(¼ pt)* red wine
150 ml *(¼ pt)* stock or water
1.25 ml *(¼ level tsp)* chili seasoning
5 ml *(1 level tsp)* celery salt
1 bayleaf
salt and pepper
45 ml *(3 tbsps)* long grain rice
99-g *(3½-oz)* pkt sage and onion stuffing mix

Cook the onions gently in the fat or oil for about 5 minutes; remove from the pan and brown the meat in the remaining fat for 8–10 minutes; drain off any excess fat. Return the onions to the pan with the peppers, garlic, wine, stock, chili powder, celery salt, bayleaf and seasoning. Cover and simmer for 1½ hours, or until the meat is tender. Meanwhile cook the rice in boiling salted water for 15–20 minutes and drain well. Make up the sage and onion stuffing according to the directions on the packet, shape into 12 small balls and fry till pale golden brown – 3–4 minutes. Add to the meat with the rice just before serving.

Sweet-sour pork balls

450 g *(1 lb)* pork, minced
1 clove garlic, skinned and crushed
60 ml *(4 level tbsps)* flour
50 g *(2 oz)* fresh white breadcrumbs
salt and pepper
1 egg yolk
25 g *(1 oz)* lard

For the sauce
75 g *(3 oz)* sugar
60 ml *(4 tbsps)* cider vinegar
45 ml *(3 tbsps)* soy sauce
30 ml *(2 level tbsps)* cornflour
300 ml *(½ pt)* water
1 green pepper, blanched and cut in thin strips
225 g *(½ lb)* tomatoes, skinned and quartered
312-g *(11-oz)* can crushed pineapple

Mix the pork, garlic, 15 ml *(1 level tbsp)* of the flour, the breadcrumbs, salt and pepper; add the egg yolk and mix well. Form into 24 balls and toss in the remaining flour. Heat the lard in a frying pan, add the balls and fry gently for 20 minutes, turning them frequently until golden.

Meanwhile, put the sugar, vinegar and soy sauce in a saucepan. Blend the cornflour with the water and add to the pan. Bring to the boil, stirring; simmer gently for 5 minutes, then add the green pepper, tomatoes and pineapple. Simmer for a further 5 minutes. To serve, put the pork balls into a warmed casserole and pour the sauce over. Serve with fried rice and a green salad.

Raised pork pie

700 g *(1½ lb)* **pie pork, cubed**
400 ml *(¾ pt)* **chicken stock, made from a cube**
200 g *(7 oz)* **hot-water crust pastry (see page 355), made with 200 g** *(7 oz)* **flour etc**
15 ml *(1 tbsp)* **chopped parsley**
salt and pepper

The day before
Put the meat in a pan with the stock, cover and simmer for 1 hour, or until tender. Drain it and leave in a cool place until required. Boil the stock rapidly until it measures 300 ml *(½ pt)*; cool.

The next day
Mould three-quarters of the pastry into a shell about 10 cm *(4 in)* in diameter (see page 357). Put the cold cooked meat in the pastry case with the parsley and seasoning. Remove any fat from the top of the stock (which should have set to a soft jelly) and add a few spoonfuls of the liquid to the meat. Use the remaining quarter of the pastry to make the lid for the pie. Using a sharp knife make a small hole in the top of the pastry to pour the stock through when cooked. Bake it in the oven at 220°C *(425°F)* mark 7 for 15 minutes, reduce the temperature to 180°C *(350°F)* mark 4 and cook for a further 40 minutes. Remove the paper band and cook for another 20 minutes. Leave the pie until cold, then melt the remaining jellied stock and fill it up. If the stock does not set well, add 5–10 ml *(1–2 level tsps)* powdered gelatine and dissolve it in the stock over a gentle heat. Leave the pie until quite set before cutting it.

Bigos

(Polish cabbage and meat)

225 g *(½ lb)* **leg or shoulder pork**
flour
100 g *(¼ lb)* **Polish ham, smoked or salt**
50 g *(2 oz)* **flat mushrooms**
450 g *(1 lb)* **sauerkraut, bottled or canned**
1 bayleaf
450 g *(1 lb)* **firm cabbage heart, shredded**
100 g *(¼ lb)* **streaky bacon rashers, rinded**
1 large onion, skinned and chopped
50 g *(2 oz)* **Polish sausage, skinned and diced**
30 ml *(2 level tbsps)* **tomato paste**
150 ml *(¼ pt)* **red wine**
1 clove garlic, skinned
salt and pepper

Cut the pork into 5-cm *(2-in)* pieces and dredge with flour; cut the ham and mushrooms into strips. Drain the sauerkraut, put into a pan with the bayleaf and 300 ml *(½ pt)* water, bring to the boil and simmer for ½ hour. Meanwhile, put the cabbage and mushrooms into a second pan, add 300 ml *(½ pt)* water and cook as for the sauerkraut. Cut the bacon in pieces and fry in its own fat, then add to the sauerkraut. Fry the onion in the bacon fat until golden and add to the sauerkraut. Add more fat to the pan if necessary, and fry the pork until golden; add this to the sauerkraut. Simmer for about 1 hour, until the pork is quite tender. About 30 minutes before the dish is to be served, add the cabbage, sausage, tomato paste, wine and crushed garlic, and season to taste.

Bigos should be just juicy, not swimming in liquid. If necessary, a little extra boiling water can be added during the cooking. Serve with rye bread or floury boiled potatoes. *Serves 4–6.*

Fillet de porc chasseur

1 kg *(2¼ lb)* **pork fillet**
30 ml *(2 tbsps)* **oil**
75 g *(2½ oz)* **butter**
225 g *(8 oz)* **onions, skinned and chopped**
225 g *(8 oz)* **button mushrooms**
45 ml *(3 level tbsps)* **flour**
150 ml *(¼ pt)* **beef stock**
150 ml *(¼ pt)* **white wine**
salt
freshly ground black pepper
chopped parsley
croûtons

Cut the pork into 3–4-cm *(1¼–1½ in)* pieces. Heat the oil in a frying pan, add the pork and cook quickly to brown and seal the surface. Remove from pan, transfer to an ovenproof casserole. Heat 50 g *(2 oz)* butter in the frying pan, add the onions and cook slowly until soft. Add the mushrooms and quickly sauté. Remove while still crisp and place over the meat. Blend the flour into the remaining pan juices, adding remaining butter and gradually add the stock and wine. Blend to a smooth consistency. Bring to the boil and simmer for 2–3 minutes. Adjust seasoning and pour into the casserole.

Cover and cook in the oven at 180°C *(350°F)* mark 4 for about 1¾ hours until pork is fork tender. Serve sprinkled liberally with chopped parsley. Garnish with croûtons or sliced, toasted French bread. *Serves 6.*

Pork with plums

4 pork chops
225 g *(½ lb)* fresh plums
30 ml *(2 level tbsps)* sugar
ground cinnamon
4 cloves
1 glass red wine
salt and pepper

Trim any excess fat from the chops and heat the trimmings to extract some fat. Use this to fry the chops until lightly but evenly browned. Stew the plums with the sugar and just enough water to prevent the fruit from burning. Pass them through a sieve. Put the chops in a shallow ovenproof dish in a single layer; add a pinch of cinnamon and the cloves to the plum pureé and pour over the chops. Add the wine; season with salt and pepper, cover, and bake in the oven at 180°C *(350°F)* mark 4 for 1 hour, adding a little water if necessary during the cooking.

Breaded pork trotters

4 fresh or lightly pickled pig's trotters
salt and pepper
1 clove
1 bayleaf
1 stick celery, trimmed and cut up
100 g *(4 oz)* fresh white breadcrumbs
1 onion, skinned and minced
fat for deep frying
chopped parsley

Wash the trotters, place in tepid water with the salt, pepper, clove, bayleaf and celery and simmer gently for 2½ hours. Cut each trotter in half and remove the bones. Mix the breadcrumbs and onion and season with salt and pepper. Dip the hot trotters in this mixture, then fry in the hot fat. Sprinkle with parsley and serve with mustard or horseradish cream.

Pig's trotters in Madeira

4 pig's trotters, trimmed
1 onion, skinned and sliced
1 carrot, pared and sliced
½ leek, sliced
1 clove garlic
pinch dried thyme
pinch dried rosemary
pinch pepper
2 bayleaves
400–600 ml *(¾–1 pt)* white wine
30 ml *(2 tbsps)* olive oil
3 tomatoes, skinned and chopped
30 ml *(2 level tbsps)* tomato paste
Madeira wine

Halve the trotters, wash them well and leave to soak for some hours in cold water. Drain and put in a casserole with the vegetables, herbs and pepper. Cover with white wine and leave to marinade for 3 days in the refrigerator. Drain the trotters, parboil them, drain and add the marinade, vegetables, olive oil, tomatoes and tomato paste; simmer gently for 4 hours. Strain the sauce and flavour with Madeira wine. Dish up the trotters and serve with the sauce, accompanied by noodles.

Frikadeller

450 g *(1 lb)* lean pork, cubed
1 small onion, skinned and quartered
salt and pepper
30 ml *(2 level tbsps)* plain flour
1 egg, beaten
a little milk
fat for deep frying

Mince the meat and onion twice. Add salt and pepper and stir in the flour, egg and enough milk to give a mixture that is soft but will hold its shape; roll it into small balls. Heat the fat until it will brown a cube of bread in 1 minute and cook the meat balls until brown, for about 6 minutes. Drain on kitchen paper and serve with a tomato sauce (page 202).

Catalonian sausage

450 g *(1 lb)* smoked garlic sausage, in the piece
knob of lard
100 g *(4 oz)* salt pork, finely diced
90 ml *(6 tbsps)* finely chopped spring onions
90 ml *(6 tbsps)* dry white wine
90 ml *(6 tbsps)* water
10 ml *(2 tsps)* chopped fresh mint
1 bayleaf
2.5 ml *(½ level tsp)* salt
freshly ground black pepper
700 g *(1½ lb)* shelled broad beans, cooked
30 ml *(2 tbsps)* finely chopped parsley

Cut the sausage into 0.5-cm *(¼-in)* thick slices, then cut into quarters. Melt the lard in a flameproof casserole. Add the salt pork and cook until crisp and golden brown. Drain on kitchen paper. Add the spring onions to the fat in the pan and cook for about 5 minutes until the onions are soft but not brown. Pour in the wine and water, add the quartered sausage, diced pork, mint, bayleaf, salt and pepper. Bring to the boil over high heat, reduce to low, then simmer, covered, for about 20 minutes. Add the beans and parsley, then simmer uncovered, stirring frequently, for about 10 minutes. *Serves 4 to 6.*

Pork baked on sauerkraut

1.4-kg *(3-lb)* loin of pork, salted and chined
709-g *(25-oz)* can of sauerkraut, drained
25 g *(1 oz)* dripping
1 large onion, skinned and sliced
1 bayleaf
few juniper berries
few caraway seeds
300 ml *(½ pt)* stock or water
pinch of sugar

Remove the skin from the pork; trim off most of the fat. Place the sauerkraut in a dish large enough to take the meat. Melt the dripping in a frying pan and sauté the onion for a few minutes. Then add it to the sauerkraut, with the bayleaf, juniper berries, caraway seeds, stock and sugar. Put the meat on top, fat side uppermost. Cover and cook in the oven at 170°C *(325°F)* mark 3 for about 1¾ hours. Serve with boiled potatoes or potato dumplings (page 227).

Note Unsalted pork can be used if the butcher cannot salt it for you.

Marinaded pork

900 g *(2 lb)* pork fillet
oil for frying
15 ml *(1 level tbsp)* cornflour
300 ml *(½ pt)* stock
15 ml *(1 tbsp)* tomato paste
15 ml *(1 tbsp)* chopped parsley
parsley sprigs to garnish

For the marinade
150 ml *(¼ pt)* dry white wine
45 ml *(3 tbsps)* vinegar
4 cloves garlic, skinned and crushed
1.25 ml *(¼ level tsp)* ground cloves
2.5 ml *(½ level tsp)* dried marjoram
freshly ground black pepper

Mix together the wine, vinegar and seasonings for the marinade. Cut the pork into thin strips and leave in the marinade for about 6 hours. Drain off and reserve the liquid. Heat the oil and brown the meat. Pour off the fat, add the marinade and simmer gently for about 45 minutes, adding a little more white wine or stock if necessary. Blend the cornflour with the stock and add to the meat mixture, stirring until boiling. Cook for a further 2 minutes, then add the tomato paste and chopped parsley. Stir to blend, and cook for a further 10 minutes. Serve garnished with parsley sprigs. *Serves 6.*

Tortière

1 onion, skinned and chopped
knob of lard
225 g *(½ lb)* pork shoulder, minced
1 clove garlic, skinned and crushed
150 ml *(¼ pt)* water
salt and pepper
dash of grated nutmeg or ground mace
little summer savory, if available
250 g *(9 oz)* shortcrust pastry, made with 250 g *(9 oz)* flour etc (see page 351)

Fry the onion in the melted lard until soft but not coloured. Add the meat and garlic and continue frying to seal the meat. Add the water and cook without the lid until the meat mixture is almost tender and the texture thick; if necessary, add more water during the cooking to prevent sticking. Add seasonings and flavourings to taste and leave to cool. Make up the pastry and use to line a 23-cm *(9-in)* pie plate or deep sandwich tin; reserve some pastry for the lid. Spoon the pork mixture into the pastry case and top with a pastry lid. Seal the edges and make a slit to let steam escape. Bake in the oven at 230°C *(450°F)* mark 8 for 10 minutes. Reduce the heat to 180°C *(350°F)* mark 4 and bake for a further 40 minutes. Serve hot, with spicy tomato sauce (see pages 202, 203).

Note French-Canadian families traditionally serve this pie at Christmas and New Year.

Nasi goreng

100 g *(4 oz)* **onion, skinned and chopped**
1 clove garlic, skinned and crushed
50 g *(2 oz)* **butter**
225 g *(8 oz)* **long grain rice**
2.5 ml *(½ level tsp)* **ground coriander**
2.5 ml *(½ level tsp)* **caraway seeds**
2.5 ml *(½ level tsp)* **chili seasoning**
5 ml *(1 level tsp)* **curry powder**
15 ml *(1 tbsp)* **soy sauce**
450 g *(1 lb)* **cooked pork, diced**
225 g *(½ lb)* **frozen peas, freshly cooked**
1 egg
30 ml *(2 tbsps)* **water**
salt and pepper
tomato wedges

Fry the onion and garlic until soft in the butter. Meanwhile boil the rice until cooked but still firm. Drain, rinse under cold water. Stir the spices and soy sauce into the onion. Cook for 1–2 minutes. Stir in the meat, heat thoroughly; add the cooked rice, blending all the ingredients.

When the meat and rice are thoroughly heated, add the peas. Break one egg into a bowl, whisk lightly, add 30 ml *(2 tbsps)* water and salt and pepper. Lightly grease the base of a frying pan and pour in the omelette mixture. When set, turn it out on to a warm, greased baking sheet. Cut into strips.

Turn the nasi goreng into a serving dish. Decorate the top with a lattice of omelette. Garnish with tomato wedges.

BACON

Bacon is made by curing fresh pork. Pigs for bacon are specially bred to have small bones, a long back, small shoulders and large plump gammons. Most bacon today is cured traditionally by a combination of brine injection and dry salting followed by immersion in brine and a period of maturation. When mature the sides have a pale cream rind with pink meat and the characteristic bacon flavour.

Some bacon goes through the additional process of smoking. This browns the rind and gives the meat a firmer texture and a smoked flavour. In the old days smoked bacon was prized for its good keeping qualities but this is not so important today except when freezing bacon.

One of the best things about bacon joints from the cook's point of view is that they are mostly boned and prepared before being sold so there is very little waste. Bacon joints are equally good hot or cold and any left over makes excellent savouries or supper dishes, so once you have cooked the joint it will give several good meals with little extra trouble. Rashers are an excellent standby for meals throughout the day.

Good bacon has a pleasant fresh aroma. The fat should be white and firm with the lean areas pinky in colour, firm with a good bloom without being soft. Rind a good pale cream colour if unsmoked. The rind of smoked bacon is light or dark golden brown depending on regional preference. Unsmoked bacon is sometimes called 'green' or 'pale' bacon.

Cuts of bacon

These vary from one part of the country to another. Many localities have their own method of cutting and selling so that it is difficult to generalise or to describe all available cuts. In some areas gammon is referred to as 'ham', but see separate entry for Ham, page 137.

Back bacon A prime rasher with a good eye of lean and a distinct layer of fat. Used for frying and grilling and can also be bought in the piece for boiling.

Streaky Narrow rashers in which lean and fat are mixed. It is good for grilling and frying and provides plenty of fat for frying bread, eggs, etc., can also be boiled in the piece.

Middle cut or through cut Long rashers in which back and streaky are joined. Sold flat or rolled. Good value for family meals and usually priced between back and streaky. Makes a handsome roast or boiling joint with stuffing.

Bacon chops Boneless rib back chops cut between 0.5–1 cm *(¼–½ in)* or thicker. Quick to fry or grill.

Gammon steaks and rashers Gammon steaks about 1 cm *(½ in)* thick, usually 100–225 g *(4–8 oz)*, almost circular in shape, are the leanest and most expensive cut for grilling and frying. Thinner gammon rashers are just as lean, more economical.

Collar Prime collar is one of the best boiling and baking joints and is good for braising. Whole joints weigh 3.6 kg *(8 lb)* but are usually sold in small pieces; end of collar which weighs about 900 g *(2 lb)* is an inexpensive cut. Collar rashers are substantial and meaty.

Forehock Whole hocks can be very inexpensive bought bone in, and weigh about 3.2–3.6 kg *(7–8 lb)* including knuckle. Can be boiled or roasted, knuckle used for soup, bacon pieces. Small boneless forehock joints 700–900 g *(1½ or 2 lb)* are popular boiling pieces, especially prime forehock.

Gammon The most prized part of the bacon side for leanness, flavour and fine texture of the meat, little fat. Often sold as a cooked meat. Whole or half gammons popular for weddings, special occasions. Smaller joints, usually boneless, are middle gammon, corner gammon, slipper gammon. Gammon knuckle is considerably meatier than forehock knuckle.

Bacon pieces Useful when available for providing fat pieces to lard very lean joints of meat and poultry. Cheaper than ordinary rashers. Can be used in pies, flans, to flavour stews.

Bacon in the bag

Joints are sometimes sold ready packed in film bags with special instructions for cooking. They can be cooked without the bag being removed; this has the advantage of keeping the joint a good shape and retaining the natural juices of the meat. Unlike vacuum packs of bacon, the film bag does not extend the keeping qualities of the contents.

Vacuum packed bacon

Bacon is widely sold in vacuum packets which are hygienic and convenient both for the customer and the shop-keeper, though usually more expensive than equivalent cuts bought unpacked. Mostly rashers but also small joints and gammon steaks. Vacuum packing extends the keeping qualities of bacon and packets are usually marked with a 'sell by' or 'use by' date. Once opened use and treat as loose bacon.

Special cures

In addition to the traditional cure outlined above, there are others for which varying names are used such as 'tender cure' and 'sweet cure'. Cook as for green bacon or follow instructions provided by manufacturers.

Storage of bacon

Store bacon at a cool temperature in the refrigerator or larder. Wrap closely in aluminium foil or cling film. This applies to joints not in a bag or vacuum packet and rashers bought loose. Do not use greaseproof paper which is porous and allows the bacon to dry out, causing surface saltiness. Refrigerate for up to 1 week.

Preparing rashers

Rind rashers thinly with kitchen scissors or a sharp knife unless, of course, the bacon is bought already rinded. Remove any bone. Thick rashers or chops should be snipped at intervals along the fat edge to help them remain flat and attractive looking during the cooking process. If you suspect that chops or other thick bacon or gammon slices are salty, soak them or poach them in water for a few minutes, throw away the water and cook as desired. Very salt bacon should also be blanched before it is used in large amounts in made up dishes or the flavour may be too strong.

For bacon rolls, use thin cut rashers and remove the rind. Stretch the rashers by stroking along the length with a heavy knife. Either roll up the whole rasher or cut each in half crosswise before rolling.

Cooking rashers

Streaky or back For frying, lay the bacon rashers in a cold pan, with the lean parts over the fat; for grilling arrange them in the reverse way. Lean rashers are better brushed with fat or oil for grilling. Cook quickly to obtain a crisp effect, slowly if you prefer the rashers softer. Thread bacon rolls on a skewer and grill until crisp for 3–5 minutes, turn once.

Gammon Choose rashers that are not less than 0.5 cm (*¼ in*) thick. Cut off the rind with scissors and clip the fat at intervals. Grilling is the ideal way of cooking. Pre-heat the grill at medium. Put the rashers on to a lightly greased grill grid, brush with melted butter or a little oil and cook under a medium heat for about 5 minutes. Turn them, brush the second side with butter or oil and continue for a further 5–10 minutes until tender. For a special finish after cooking the first side, spread the second side with any of the following before grilling: melted butter and a sprinkling of brown sugar – preferably soft brown – marmalade sharpened with a little vinegar or lemon juice, brown sugar mixed with a pinch of dry mustard or ground ginger and moistened with orange or pineapple juice. Serve with grilled apple or pineapple rings basted and grilled towards the end of the cooking.

To boil bacon joints

The need to soak bacon joints is considerably reduced by milder cures. Today more and more housewives find soaking unnecessary. If soaking is preferred, do not allow more than 2–3 hours. Overnight soaking, if done at all should be reserved for larger joints – 8 hours is sufficient. A more practical method with an average size joint if you are worried about saltiness is to place the piece of bacon in cold water to cover, bring to the boil, throw away the water and start again with fresh cold water. Cooking – weigh the bacon joint, then calculate the cooking time, allowing 20–25 minutes per 450 g (*1 lb*) plus 20 minutes over. If you are cooking a joint 4.5 kg (*10 lb*) or over, allow 15–20 minutes per 450 g (*per 1 lb*) plus 15 minutes. Place the bacon in a large pan, skin side down, cover with cold water and bring slowly to the boil, skimming off any scum that forms. Time the cooking from this point. Cover and simmer until cooked. For extra flavour add 2 onions, skinned and quartered, 2 carrots pared and quartered, 1 bay leaf and 4 peppercorns. When the bacon is cooked, ease away the rind and serve the joint hot with a sauce such as parsley, or after removing from the liquid remove rind and press browned breadcrumbs into the fat, when cold serve with salad, in sandwiches or to partner chicken or turkey.

To bake and glaze a bacon joint – weigh the joint, calculate the cooking time and boil as above for half the cooking time, then drain and wrap in kitchen foil. Place on a baking sheet and now bake in the centre of the oven at 180°C (*350°F*) mark 4 until ½ hour before cooking time is complete. Raise the oven temperature to 220°C *(425°F)* mark 7. Undo the foil, remove the rind from the bacon, score the fat in diamonds, stud with cloves and sprinkle the surface with demerara sugar, pat in. Return the joint to the oven until crisp and golden. *See colour plate facing p. 192.*

Alternative glazes for a 2-kg *(4-lb)* joint

Spiced marmalade and honey In a small basin blend together 60 ml *(4 level tbsps)* fine shred marmalade, 75 ml *(5 tbsps)* clear honey and 4–5 drops Tabasco sauce. Brush a little glaze over the bacon fat 30 minutes before the end of cooking time, use about one-third. Return to the oven for 10 minutes before applying the second glaze. Don't use the glaze that has run into the pan as this will dull the shine. Repeat with the final third.

Sharp honey In a small saucepan warm 15 ml *(1 tbsp)* clear honey and 30 ml *(2 tbsps)* vinegar. Strip off bacon rind. Pour the glaze over the bacon fat. Sprinkle with equal quantities of mixed brown sugar and golden brown breadcrumbs. Return to oven, basting frequently.

Cider Strip the rind off the bacon. Pour 150 ml *(¼ pt)* cider over. Mix 100 g *(4 oz)* brown sugar with 5 ml *(1 level tsp)* dry mustard and press into bacon fat and continue baking, basting frequently. Honey can be used instead of the sugar to give a richer flavour.

HAM

Ham, strictly speaking, is the leg of a pig cut from the whole carcass and then cured and matured individually. When selecting a ham choose a short, thick leg without too much fat with a thin rind. More often than not hams are cooked prior to purchase but if not soak for about 12 hours or more depending on the type of ham (one that has been hung for a long time and is very dry may need 24 hours). Scrape and brush the ham to remove rust and trim off any coloured parts – bloom is the sign of a good ham. To cook a York ham follow directions supplied or cook as for gammon. A popular finish after cooking is to score the rinded fat in triangles, baste with a few tablespoonfuls of sherry, port or madeira then thickly coat with soft brown sugar. Put in the oven at 230°C *(450°F)* mark 8 until a golden crust forms – about 15 minutes.

Amongst the best known of the cooking hams – apart from smoked ham which is eaten raw – are:

York ham is dry-salt cured and lightly smoked, cut by the oyster bone and rounded off. Average weight 7–9 kg *(16–24 lb)*.

Wiltshire ham A long cut, straw coloured and mild cured.

Bradenham ham is small and expensive and processed in molasses instead of brine. This 'Chippenham cure' turns the skin black and the meat rather red. To cook soak for 48–72 hours, drain, put in fresh cold water, add 450 g *(1 lb)* black treacle and simmer a 6 kg *(14 lb)* ham for about 4 hours. Cool in the cooking liquid.

Suffolk sweet-cured ham is similar to Bradenham but the processing is different.

Irish peat-cured ham is cured in a similar way to York ham but finished with peat smoke.

Jambon de Paris is similar to York ham either very lightly smoked or not at all.

Jambon de Bayonne is salted and then smoked with herbs. Eat raw or use in cooking but never boil.

Mainz, Westphalian and Parma ham are mostly eaten raw as an hors d'oeuvre cut wafer thin.

Bath chap Pigs' cheeks, chops, chaps or jowls cured and usually smoked. Each half-head is divided into two, the upper jaw or eye pieces and the lower jaw or Bath Chap. The former is triangular and plump, the latter is rather more meaty and contains half the tongue. Being rather fat they are very suitable for serving cold with chicken, turkey or ox tongue. Generally speaking Bath Chaps are bought ready cooked, otherwise soak overnight and then simmer until tender.

Braised bacon

piece of gammon, collar or forehock bacon
1 onion, skinned and sliced
4 carrots, pared and sliced
½ turnip, pared and sliced
2 sticks of celery, trimmed and sliced
45 ml *(3 tbsps)* oil
stock
bouquet garni
salt and pepper

Soak the bacon or gammon for 1 hour (or overnight if you think it is likely to be very salty). Boil it for half the cooking time, allowing 20–25 minutes per 450 g *(1 lb)* plus 20 minutes over. Lightly fry the vegetables in the hot fat or oil for 3–4 minutes. Put them in a casserole, put the bacon on top and add enough stock to cover the vegetables. Add the bouquet garni and the seasoning, cover and cook in the oven at 180°C *(350°F)* mark 4 for the remainder of the cooking time. Half an hour before the bacon is done, remove the rind and continue cooking, uncovered, for the final 30 minutes. Remove the bouquet garni.

Parsley sauce goes well with this, or you can thicken the vegetable liquid with a little cornflour.

Bacon-burgers

225 g *(8 oz)* lean bacon
1 medium sized onion, skinned
1.25 ml *(¼ level tsp)* dry mustard
1.25 ml *(¼ level tsp)* grated nutmeg
pepper
beaten egg
fat for frying

Mince the bacon and onion or chop finely. Mix the bacon, onion, mustard, nutmeg and a good shake of pepper. Add enough egg to make the mixture bind together, turn on to a floured board and shape into 8 thin cakes. Fry in the hot fat for 6–7 minutes, turning the cakes 2 or 3 times with a fork and spoon, until they are cooked through and golden brown.

Bacon and egg pie

200 g *(7 oz)* shortcrust pastry (see page 351), made with 200 g *(7 oz)* flour etc
4 rashers bacon, rinded and chopped
4 eggs
60 ml *(4 tbsps)* milk
salt and pepper
2 tomatoes, or 4 mushrooms, sliced, optional

Line an 18-cm *(7-in)* deep pie plate with half the pastry; roll out the remaining pastry to form a lid. Fry the bacon lightly in its own fat until transparent; spread over the base of the pie. Whisk the eggs and add the milk and seasoning. Pour over the bacon and add the tomatoes or mushrooms (if used). Damp the edges of the pastry and cover with the lid, pressing the edges well together; flake and scallop the edge. Brush the top of the pie with the little egg that remains in the basin. Bake the pie on a baking sheet in the oven at 220°C *(425°F)* mark 7 for 15 minutes, then reduce the temperature to 180°C *(350°F)* mark 4 and cook for a further 30 minutes. Serve hot or cold.

Bacon pasties

1 onion, skinned and chopped
4 tomatoes, skinned and chopped
175 g *(6 oz)* streaky bacon, rinded and chopped
2.5 ml *(½ level tsp)* dried mixed herbs
salt and pepper
250 g *(9 oz)* shortcrust pastry (see page 351), made with 250 g *(9 oz)* flour etc
little milk to glaze

Mix together the onion, tomatoes, bacon, herbs and seasoning. Roll out the pastry and cut into 4 rounds, using a small saucepan lid as a cutter. Put a quarter of the meat mixture in the centre of each round of pastry, wet the edges of the pastry, draw them up and press firmly together over the top of the pasty; crimp the edges with your fingers and brush the pasty with milk. Place on a baking sheet and cook in the oven at 220°C *(425°F)* mark 7 for about 15 minutes, or until the pastry begins to brown, then lower the heat to 170°C *(325°F)* mark 3 and bake for another 45 minutes.

Bacon roly-poly

250 g *(9 oz)* suetcrust pastry (see page 352), made with 250 g *(9 oz)* flour etc
2.5 ml *(½ level tsp)* salt
450 g *(1 lb)* cooked bacon, minced or finely chopped
1 onion, skinned and finely chopped
5 ml *(1 level tsp)* dried sage or mixed herbs
15 ml *(1 tbsp)* sweet pickle, optional
1 egg, beaten, optional
few canned tomatoes, optional

Put the pastry on a floured board and roll it out into an oblong 30 cm by 15 cm *(12 in by 6 in)*. Mix the remaining ingredients together (omitting the salt if the bacon is very salty, and binding the mixture if necessary with a beaten egg or a few chopped canned tomatoes). Spread the filling over the pastry to within 1 cm *(½ in)* of the edges. Damp the edges and roll up like a Swiss roll, starting from one short end, wrap in greased greaseproof paper or foil and seal well. Steam for 2–2½ hours over rapidly boiling water. Serve with tomato or parsley sauce (pages 196, 202).

Caramelled gammon

2 gammon rashers cut 1 cm *(½ in)* thick, rinded
226-g *(8-oz)* can pineapple rings
40 g *(1½ oz)* butter
60 ml *(4 level tbsps)* demerara sugar

Trim the rashers, snip the fat at intervals and cut each rasher in half. Drain the pineapple rings, retaining the juice. Poach the rashers in a little water for 1–2 minutes and throw away the water. Fry the rashers in the butter until golden brown on both sides – about 2 minutes. Remove the rashers and cool the remaining butter; add the pineapple juice and sugar, dissolve over a low heat and bring to the boil. Return the rashers to the pan, reduce the heat, cover and simmer for about 20 minutes, or until tender. Arrange the rashers on a serving dish. Reduce the liquor by boiling rapidly. Add the pineapple rings and heat through, arrange them on top of the rashers and pour the glaze over them. Serve with fluffy rice.

Bacon in cider

1.1 kg *(2½ lb)* collar bacon joint
300 ml *(½ pt)* cider
1 small onion
1 carrot
bayleaf
bouquet garni
peppercorns
toasted breadcrumbs

Bring the bacon to the boil in cold water. Drain and place the joint in cider and enough cold water to cover. Add onion, carrot, bayleaf, bouquet garni and a few peppercorns. Bring back to the boil, reduce heat and simmer joint for 20 minutes per 450 g *(1 lb)* and 20 minutes over. Drain joint, remove string and rind. Coat with toasted breadcrumbs. Serve cold.

Ham and asparagus mould

300 ml *(½ pt)* aspic jelly, made according to directions on packet
298-g *(10½-oz)* can asparagus tips
20 ml *(4 level tsps)* powdered gelatine
30 ml *(2 tbsps)* cold water
75 g *(3 oz)* granulated sugar
20 ml *(4 level tsps)* dry mustard
2.5 ml *(½ level tsp)* salt
3 eggs, slightly beaten
200 ml *(7 fl oz)* vinegar
284 ml *(½ pt)* single cream
450 g *(1 lb)* cooked ham, cut into 2.5-cm *(1-in)* slivers
watercress and tomato

Line a 900-ml *(1½-pt)* mould with aspic jelly (see page 325) and decorate the sides with some asparagus tips. Dissolve the gelatine in the cold water. Mix the sugar, mustard and salt together and add to the eggs. Heat the vinegar just to boiling point and gradually add the egg to it. Return the mixture to the heat and cook slowly till it thickens but does not boil. Remove from the heat, add the dissolved gelatine and chill, stirring occasionally, until the mixture thickens. Add the cream, the ham and the rest of the asparagus, cut into small pieces. Pour into the prepared mould and chill until firm. Unmould and garnish with watercress and tomato wedges.

Ham and leeks au gratin

8 medium-sized leeks
50 g *(2 oz)* butter
75 ml *(5 tbsps)* flour
568 ml *(1 pt)* milk
salt and pepper
100 g *(4 oz)* Cheddar cheese, grated
8 thin slices of cooked ham or bacon
browned breadcrumbs

Trim, wash and clean the leeks, put into boiling, salted water and boil gently for 20 minutes, until soft. Drain and keep warm. Meanwhile, melt about three-quarters of the butter, stir in the flour and cook for 2–3 minutes. Gradually add the milk, stirring well to avoid lumps. Bring to the boil, stirring all the time, and simmer for about 5 minutes. Season and add 75 g *(3 oz)* of the cheese. Wrap each leek in a slice of ham, place in an ovenproof dish and coat with sauce. Top with breadcrumbs and the rest of the cheese. Dot with the remaining butter and brown under the grill.

Gammon Montmorency

1 onion, skinned and chopped
1 carrot, pared and sliced
2 rashers of bacon, rinded and chopped
45 ml *(3 tbsps)* oil
50 g *(2 oz)* flour
600 ml *(1 pt)* stock, made from a cube
15 ml *(1 level tbsp)* tomato paste
bouquet garni
15 ml *(1 tbsp)* sherry or cider
24 sweet black cherries
4 thick gammon rashers
little oil
15 ml *(1 level tbsp)* red-currant jelly
15 ml *(1 level tbsp)* horseradish cream

Fry the onion, carrot and bacon in the oil till golden brown – about 5 minutes. Remove the vegetables, draining the fat back into the pan, then stir in the flour and cook for 3–4 minutes until well browned, to give the sauce a good colour. Gradually stir in the stock, return the vegetables and add the tomato paste, bouquet garni and sherry or cider. Bring to the boil and simmer, stirring occasionally, for 30 minutes. Alternatively, pour the sauce into a casserole and put in the oven at 150°C *(300°F)* mark 2 for 2 hours. Stone the cherries. Trim the gammon rashers and snip the edges. Fifteen minutes before serving the meal, brush the rashers with oil and grill for 7–10 minutes under a medium grill.

Meanwhile strain the sauce and return it to the pan. Turn the rashers over, brush with more oil and grill for a further 7 minutes. Stir the jelly and horseradish cream into the sauce, bring to the boil and simmer for 4 minutes. Add the cherries and heat through. Serve the rashers with the sauce poured over them.

Bacon stewpot

700 g *(1½ lb)* lean unsmoked collar joint
40 g *(1½ oz)* butter or margarine
225 g *(8 oz)* leeks, sliced and washed
1 small onion, skinned and chopped
30 ml *(2 level tbsps)* plain flour
400 ml *(¾ pt)* unseasoned stock
100 g *(4 oz)* carrots, pared and sliced
pepper
210-g *(7½-oz)* can butter beans
15 ml *(1 tbsp)* chopped fresh parsley

Remove rind and any excess fat or gristle from the bacon. Cut meat into 1.5-cm *(¾-in)* cubes. Place in a pan of cold water and bring slowly to the boil. Drain well. Melt butter in a saucepan, add leeks and onion and cook gently until soft but not brown. Stir in the flour and cook for a minute. Off the heat gradually add the stock. Bring to the boil, stirring. Cook for a further minute. Add carrots, bacon and pepper. Cover pan and cook gently for 1¼ hours. Drain butter beans and add to the stew with the parsley. Heat through for about 5 minutes before serving.

Gammon and apricot casserole

25 g *(1 oz)* lard
700 g *(1½ lb)* lean gammon, cut into 1-cm *(½-in)* cubes
1 large onion, skinned and roughly chopped
175 g *(6 oz)* long grain rice
600 ml *(1 pt)* unseasoned chicken stock
75 g *(3 oz)* dried apricots, roughly chopped
1 bayleaf
salt and pepper

Melt the lard in a pan and fry the gammon on all sides to seal. Remove the meat from the pan and place in a casserole. Add the onion to the remaining fat and fry gently for 3 minutes, stir in the rice and cook for a further 3 minutes. Add the stock to the pan, bring to the boil, add the apricots, bayleaf, salt and pepper. Pour over the gammon and mix well. Cover the casserole and cook in the oven at 170°C *(325°F)* mark 3 for 1¼–1½ hours. Fork the rice through from time to time.

Scalloped gammon and potatoes

2 thick gammon rashers (about 225 g, *8 oz*, each)
water
25 g *(1 oz)* butter
100 g *(¼ lb)* mushrooms, stalked and sliced
1 bayleaf
1 or 2 stalks of celery
450 g *(1 lb)* potatoes, peeled and thickly sliced
parsley

Rind the gammon rashers and snip the fat at intervals. In a shallow flameproof casserole, cover gammon with water, bring to the boil, pour off the water. Put gammon on one side. Melt the butter in the casserole, sauté mushrooms until just soft. Drain and put on one side. Return gammon to the casserole, add the bayleaf and celery, cut in pieces. Pour over 300 ml *(½ pt)* water. Cover and simmer on the top of the cooker for ½ hour. Discard bayleaf and celery. Lift gammon and place sliced potato underneath. Cook, covered until potatoes are soft – the water should nearly be absorbed, about 25 minutes. Top each rasher with sautéed mushrooms, return to heat to re-heat mushrooms. Garnish with parsley. *Serves 2–3.*

Bacon chops en croûte

15 ml *(1 level tbsp)* plain flour
5 ml *(1 level tsp)* soft brown sugar
5 ml *(1 level tsp)* dry mustard
freshly ground black pepper
4 bacon chops, rinded
few drops Tabasco sauce
226-g *(8-oz)* can pineapple rings, drained
175 g *(6 oz)* Bel Paese cheese, cut into 4 slices
368-g *(13-oz)* pkt frozen puff pastry, thawed

Mix together the flour, sugar, mustard and pepper in a small polythene bag. Toss the bacon chops in this mixture, one at a time. Place the bacon on a board, sprinkle each chop with a little Tabasco sauce, place a pineapple ring in the centre and top with a slice of cheese. Roll out the pastry thinly. Cut into 4 squares, large enough to encase the chops. Place a chop in the centre of each piece of pastry. Moisten the edges of the pastry and fold over to cover the meat completely. Seal well together. Place on a baking sheet. Chill for 30 minutes. Cook in the oven at 220°C *(425°F)* mark 7 for ¾–1 hour.

Middle cut roast bacon

1.4 kg *(3 lb)* middle cut bacon joint

For stuffing
50 g *(2 oz)* butter
100 g *(4 oz)* fresh white breadcrumbs
30 ml *(2 tbsps)* chopped parsley
grated rind of 1 lemon
10 ml *(2 level tsps)* dried thyme
½ beaten egg
pepper

Bring bacon to the boil in cold water. Drain and cover with fresh cold water. Boil again, reduce heat and simmer for 20 minutes. Meanwhile melt butter and stir in the stuffing ingredients. Drain joint, remove string, strip off the rind and remove any brown from underneath with a sharp knife. Place the stuffing in the centre of the joint, re-roll making a good round, tie with string. Score fat in a criss-cross design, place in roasting tin and cook in the oven at 180°C *(350°F)* mark 4 for 1 hour. *Serves 6.*

OFFAL

There are various parts of an animal which do not fit into the category of 'joints' and a lot of delicious things come under the not very pleasing heading of 'offal'. The favourite is perhaps liver, with kidney and oxtail almost as popular.

Liver

Ox or bullock liver, which is fairly cheap, has a strong flavour and is often rather tough and coarse textured, so that it is best used in a casserole or stew rather than for frying or grilling.

Calf's liver, the best and most expensive, is very tender and delicate in flavour. It can be lightly grilled or fried, but over-cooking makes it hard and dry.

Lamb's liver is a little cheaper than calf's liver and has a stronger flavour. It is excellent for grilling and frying, as well as for casseroles and stews.

Pig's liver is cheaper than lamb's or calf's liver, but it has a very pronounced flavour and a soft texture that many people dislike. It is best casseroled or stewed and makes excellent pâté.

Allow 125 g *(4 oz)* liver for each person.

Kidney

Delicious grilled with bacon or devilled and served on toast, but equally good made into a rich stew with rice or used as an ingredient in a casserole, pie or pudding.

Ox or bullock kidney is usually the cheapest and has a fairly strong flavour. It needs slow, gentle cooking to make it tender, so should be stewed, casseroled, used in curries, pies and so on, rather than fried or grilled. A whole kidney, consisting of many joined lobes, weighs about 700 g *(1½ lb)*.

Allow about 125 g *(4 oz)* kidney for each person.

Calf's kidney is more tender and delicate in flavour than ox kidney, but is used in same ways.

1 kidney will serve 1–2 persons.

Lamb's kidneys These are usually the best, being small, well-flavoured and tender enough to grill or fry, either whole or in halves. The thin skin and white 'core' should be removed before cooking.

Allow 2 whole kidneys for each person.

Pig's and sheep's kidneys are similar to lamb's kidneys, but are slightly larger and generally not quite so tender. They can be halved and grilled or fried, or they may be used in stews, curries or casseroles.

Allow 1–2 per person, depending on their size.

Heart

Though somewhat neglected nowadays, hearts can be used to make a variety of economical and savoury dishes.

Ox or bullock heart is the largest and tends to be rather tough unless cooked long and slowly. It can be par-boiled whole and then roasted, or cut up and braised or used in stews, but in any case it needs strong seasonings and flavourings. When cooked whole, ox heart is often stuffed with a savoury forcemeat.

An ox heart may weigh about 1.5–2 kg *(3–4 lb)* and is enough for 4–6 people. It can also be bought sliced, for use in stews, casseroles and similar dishes.

Calf's heart is small and more tender, but still needs slow cooking to make it enjoyable. It may be roasted, braised or stewed.

One calf's heart will serve 2 people.

Lamb's heart The smallest kind, one of which serves only 1 person. More tender than calf's or ox heart, it has a finer flavour and is usually stuffed and either roasted or braised.

Sweetbreads

These take a little time to prepare, but the results are worth the effort. Either fried or braised, they make a delicious change.

Ox or bullock's sweetbreads are usually the cheapest

and need slow, gentle cooking, in either a stew or a casserole, to make them tender.

Calf's sweetbreads These are more expensive and more tender, but are also best stewed or casseroled.

Lamb's sweetbreads The most expensive and tender, with a fine delicate flavour. They can be fried, stewed or casseroled.

Allow 125 g *(4 oz)* sweetbreads per person.

Oxtail

This has a high proportion of bone and is generally rather fatty, so it is not highly priced. Its flavour is excellent and when cooked long and slowly it makes rich, hearty and delicious stews and soup. Choose an oxtail with bright red flesh and creamy white fat.

One will generally make a good stew for 4 people.

Tripe

This can be of different texture, known as 'blanket' or 'honeycomb', from the first or the second stomach respectively. Tripe is usually sold 'dressed', that is, cleaned and par-boiled.

Allow 125–175 g *(4–6 oz)* per person.

Tongue

Often sold pickled or salted, in which case the cooking time is halved.

Ox tongue A tongue weighs about 1.8 kg *(4 lb)* and is usually salted, cooked whole and served cold and sliced.

Calf's tongue Weighs 450–900 g *(1–2 lb)*. Usually salted. Several tongues are often pressed together after cooking and served cold and sliced. They can, however, also be served hot.

Lamb's tongues These weigh only 125–150 g *(4–5 oz)* each. Usually served hot.

Allow about 125 g *(4 oz)* cooked tongue per person.

Brains

Calf's brains are considered the best; they are served poached, with a sauce. Lamb's brains are more often used for stews, etc., but can be cooked separately as for calf's brains.

Allow 1 'set' of brains per person.

Liver and onions

450 g *(1 lb)* onions, skinned and chopped
25 g *(1 oz)* fat or oil
salt and pepper
2.5 ml *(½ level tsp)* dried sage or mixed herbs, optional
450 g *(1 lb)* calf's or lamb's liver

Fry the onions lightly in the hot fat or oil until they begin to colour, then add the seasoning (and the herbs, if used). Cover the frying pan with a lid or large plate and simmer very gently for about 10 minutes until the onions are soft. Meanwhile wash and trim the liver and cut it into thin strips. Add to the onions, increase the heat slightly and continue cooking for about 5–10 minutes, stirring all the time, until the liver is just cooked. Remove it from the pan, drain and serve with boiled rice.

Liver, bacon and mushrooms

450 g *(1 lb)* calf's or lamb's liver
1–2 onions, skinned and chopped
4 rashers of lean bacon, rinded and chopped
25 g *(1 oz)* fat or oil
100 g *(4 oz)* mushrooms, sliced

Wash the liver and cut it into thin strips. Fry the onions and bacon in the hot fat or oil for 5 minutes, or until soft, then add the sliced mushrooms and strips of liver and continue frying over a gentle heat, stirring from time to time, until the meat is just cooked – about 5–10 minutes.

Drain very well before serving, as this dish is inclined to be rather greasy.

Liver Marsala

450 g *(1 lb)* calf's or lamb's liver
lemon juice
seasoned flour
50 g *(2 oz)* butter
45 ml *(3 tbsps)* Marsala
150 ml *(¼ pt)* stock
whole grilled tomatoes, matchstick potatoes and parsley to garnish

Wash and slice the liver. Sprinkle it with the lemon juice and coat with seasoned flour. Melt the butter in a frying pan and fry the liver quickly on both sides until lightly browned. Stir in the Marsala and stock and simmer until the meat is just cooked and the sauce syrupy. Arrange the liver on a serving dish and garnish with the tomatoes, potatoes and parsley.

Ragout of liver

450 g *(1 lb)* lamb's liver
60 ml *(4 level tbsps)* seasoned flour
4 rashers bacon, rinded and chopped
25 g *(1 oz)* fat or oil
400 ml *(¾ pt)* stock
100 g *(4 oz)* long grain rice
30 ml *(2 tbsps)* sultanas
1 apple, peeled and grated
5 ml *(1 level tsp)* tomato paste

Wash the liver, cut it into small pieces and coat with the seasoned flour. Fry the liver and bacon in the fat or oil until golden brown, for about 5 minutes. Add the stock to the pan and bring to the boil, stirring to prevent burning. Add the rice, sultanas, apple and tomato paste and simmer for 20 minutes, until the rice is cooked and all the stock is absorbed.

Liver terrine

450 g *(1 lb)* pig's liver
100 g *(¼ lb)* fat bacon
4 eggs, beaten
1 clove garlic, skinned and crushed
150 ml *(¼ pt)* thick white sauce
salt and pepper
12 rashers streaky bacon, rinded

Mince the liver and fat bacon finely, then put the mixture through the mincer again and finally sieve it, to ensure a really smooth result. Mix it with the beaten eggs, crushed garlic, sauce and seasoning to taste. Line a 1-l *(2-pt)* terrine with bacon rashers, fill up with the liver mixture and place in a dish containing enough cold water to come halfway up the sides of the terrine. Bake in the oven at 170°C *(325°F)* mark 3 for 2 hours. Cover the top of the liver mixture with greaseproof paper or foil. Press evenly and leave for 24 hours in a cold place before serving. Serve cold and sliced, with toast and butter and crisp lettuce.

Liver Mexican *see colour plate facing p. 113*

450 g *(1 lb)* lamb's liver
30 ml *(2 level tbsps)* seasoned flour
50 g *(2 oz)* fat or oil
2 onions, skinned and sliced
225 g *(½ lb)* tomatoes, skinned and sliced
1 red pepper, seeded and sliced
45 ml *(3 level tbsps)* plain flour
300 ml *(½ pt)* stock
salt and pepper
100 g *(4 oz)* long grain rice

Wash the liver, slice it, toss in seasoned flour, fry lightly in the hot fat or oil for 5 minutes, then put into a casserole. Fry the onions, tomatoes and red pepper (reserving a few slices of pepper) for 5 minutes and add to the liver. Stir the flour into the fat left in the pan and gradually add the stock; bring to the boil, stirring all the time, season well, pour over the liver and cook in the oven at 180°C *(350°F)* mark 4 for ¾ hour. Meanwhile cook the rice in boiling salted water. Serve the liver on the rice and garnish with the sliced pepper.

Fried liver, Chinese style

450 g *(1 lb)* lamb's liver
10 ml *(2 level tsps)* cornflour
30 ml *(2 tbsps)* sherry
3–4 slices of fresh ginger
1 small onion, skinned and finely chopped
25 g *(1 oz)* dried mushrooms, or 4 fresh mushrooms
175 g *(6 oz)* canned bamboo shoots
oil for frying
10 ml *(2 tsps)* soy sauce

Cut the liver up small and mix with the cornflour, sherry, ginger, and onion. If dried mushrooms are used, soak in hot water until soft, then cut them up small. Cut the bamboo shoots into strips. Heat the oil, fry the liver quickly over a strong heat and add the vegetables. Stir till every piece is golden, then pour in the soy sauce and serve hot.

Note The entire cooking of this dish should take only 7–8 minutes.

Portuguese liver sauté

450 g *(1 lb)* calf's or lamb's liver
1 clove garlic, skinned and crushed
60 ml *(4 tbsps)* white wine vinegar
1 bayleaf
few peppercorns
45 ml *(3 tbsps)* oil
150 ml *(¼ pt)* stock
10 ml *(2 level tsps)* cornflour

Slice the liver very thinly and marinade it overnight with the garlic, vinegar, bayleaf and peppercorns. Drain the liver very thoroughly, reserving the marinade. Heat the oil in a frying pan; when it is just hot, fry the liver until lightly browned and just cooked through – this should be done quickly. Keep the liver warm on a serving dish.

To the dripping in the pan add the marinade and the stock, blended with the cornflour; stir to loosen the drippings from the pan, bring to the boil and boil for 1–2 minutes. Pour over the liver and serve at once, with boiled or fried sliced potatoes.

Savoury liver

450 g *(1 lb)* **lamb's liver**
50 g *(2 oz)* **fresh white breadcrumbs**
15 ml *(1 tbsp)* **fresh chopped parsley**
5 ml *(1 level tsp)* **dried mixed herbs**
45 ml *(3 level tbsps)* **shredded suet**
salt and pepper
grated rind of ½ lemon
little egg or milk to mix
4 rashers streaky bacon, rinded
150 ml *(¼ pt)* **stock or water**

Wash the liver and cut it into slices 1 cm *(½ in)* thick. Arrange it in a flat tin or casserole. Make a stuffing by mixing together the breadcrumbs, parsley, herbs, suet, seasoning and lemon rind. Bind together with a little egg or milk. Spread the stuffing on the liver and place a rasher of bacon on top of each slice of liver and stuffing. Pour in the stock or water and cover the tin with foil. Cook in the oven at 180°C *(350°F)* mark 4 for ½–¾ hour, until the liver is tender, removing the cover for the final ¼ hour to crisp the bacon.

Grilled kidneys

Allow 1–2 lamb's or pig's kidneys per person, according to size. Wash the kidneys, cut in half and cut out the core. Thread them on to a skewer, cut side uppermost, brush over with oil and sprinkle with salt and pepper. Cook under a hot grill, uncut side first and then cut side, so that the juices gather in the cut side. Serve on fried bread, with grilled or fried bacon, or with fried or diced potatoes.

Kidneys with sherry

25 g *(1 oz)* **butter**
1 onion, skinned and chopped
2 cloves garlic, skinned and crushed
30 ml *(2 level tbsps)* **flour**
300 ml *(½ pt)* **stock**
30 ml *(2 tbsps)* **chopped parsley**
1 bayleaf
30 ml *(2 tbsps)* **oil**
8 lamb's kidneys, prepared
75 ml *(5 tbsps)* **dry sherry**
salt and pepper

Heat the butter and sauté the onion until clear. Add the garlic, sprinkle in the flour and stir to blend. Gradually add the stock, stirring until thick and smooth. Add the parsley and bayleaf and leave over a low heat. Heat the oil, add the kidneys and brown evenly; transfer them to the sauce, draining carefully. Add the sherry to the pan drippings and bring to the boil, add to the kidneys and mix all together. Simmer for 5 minutes, remove the bayleaf and adjust the seasoning. Serve on a bed of rice. *Serves 3–4.*

Rognoni Tripolata

450 g *(1 lb)* **lamb's kidneys**
25 g *(1 oz)* **butter**
grated rind of ½ lemon
1.25 ml *(¼ level tsp)* **salt**
freshly ground pepper
15 ml *(1 level tbsp)* **cornflour**
150 ml *(¼ pt)* **beef stock**
30 ml *(2 tbsps)* **Marsala**
10 ml *(2 tsps)* **lemon juice**
chopped parsley

Skin the kidneys and cut them in half. Remove the core and slice thinly. Melt the butter in a pan, add lemon rind, salt and pepper. Sauté gently for 2–3 minutes. Cream the cornflour with 45 ml *(3 tbsps)* stock, blend together with the rest of the stock before adding to kidneys. Cook gently for about 10 minutes, stirring occasionally. Increase the heat to thicken the sauce. Cook for 2–3 minutes. Remove from the heat and stir in the Marsala and lemon juice. Serve on hot noodles, sprinkle over with chopped parsley.

Kidneys in red wine

50 g *(2 oz)* **butter**
1 onion, skinned and chopped
4–6 lamb's kidneys
45 ml *(3 level tbsps)* **flour**
150 ml *(¼ pt)* **red wine**
150 ml *(¼ pt)* **stock**
bouquet garni
15 ml *(1 level tbsp)* **tomato paste**
salt and pepper
50 g *(2 oz)* **mushrooms, sliced**

Melt the butter and fry the onion until golden brown. Wash, skin and core the kidneys and cut them into small pieces, add to the pan and cook for 5 minutes, stirring occasionally. Stir in the flour, pour in the wine and stock and bring slowly to the boil, then add the bouquet garni, tomato paste and some salt and pepper. Simmer for 5 minutes. Add the mushrooms and simmer for a further few minutes. Remove the bouquet garni before serving and check the seasoning. Serve with plain boiled rice or creamed potatoes. *Serves 2–3.*

Poacher's pie (p. 182).
(Overleaf) Roast pheasant (p. 175).

6
20198

Rognons sautés Turbigo *see colour plate facing p. 161*

15 lamb kidneys
26 pickling onions
175 g *(6 oz)* butter
350 g *(¾ lb)* mini pork sausages
350 g *(¾ lb)* button mushrooms, halved
45 ml *(3 level tbsps)* flour
10–15 ml *(2–3 level tsps)* tomato paste
45 ml *(3 tbsps)* sherry
600 ml *(1 pt)* brown stock
2 bayleaves
salt
freshly ground black pepper
6 slices white bread
oil
chopped parsley

Skin the kidneys, cut them in half lengthways and core. Pour boiling water over the onions, leave for 2–3 minutes, drain and peel. Heat a large frying pan with 25 g *(1 oz)* butter. Cook the sausages until brown on all sides, remove them from the pan, wipe the pan clean, add 75 g *(3 oz)* butter and cook the onions and mushrooms over brisk heat for 3–4 minutes, shaking the pan. Add these to the sausages. Add the remaining butter; when it is foaming, put in the kidneys and sauté briskly until evenly coloured (about 5 minutes). Add to sausages. Strain the fat and return it to the pan. Stir the flour, tomato paste, sherry and stock into the juices. Bring to the boil, stirring. Add the bayleaves, seasoning and sausages, etc. Cover and simmer for 20–25 minutes. Trim the bread into small triangles. Fry in oil until golden brown. Drain well and serve around the kidneys. Scatter parsley over. *Serves 6.*

Curried kidneys

Lambs' kidneys may be cooked in the sauce given for Curried Beef (page 107), but since they are very rich, a smaller quantity is required, and they should be served in a border of noodles or rice. Use 225 g *(½ lb)* kidneys, finely chopped, and halve the quantities for the sauce ingredients; cook for about ½ hour, or until the kidney is tender.

Stuffed heart casserole

4 small lamb's hearts
100 g *(4 oz)* fresh white breadcrumbs
1 medium sized onion, skinned and finely chopped
45 ml *(3 tbsps)* melted butter
10 ml *(2 level tsps)* dried mixed herbs
salt and pepper
30 ml *(2 level tbsps)* seasoned flour
25 g *(1 oz)* fat or oil
600 ml *(1 pt)* stock
1 onion, skinned and sliced
4 sticks of celery, trimmed and sliced
100 g *(¼ lb)* carrots, pared and sliced
15 ml *(1 tbsp)* cider, optional

Wash the hearts, slit open, remove any tubes or gristle and wash again. Fill with a stuffing made from the breadcrumbs, onion, melted butter, mixed herbs and seasonings. Tie the hearts firmly into their original shape with string, coat with seasoned flour and brown quickly in the hot fat or oil. Place in a casserole with the stock, cover and bake in the oven at 170°C *(325°F)* mark 3 for 2½ hours, turning them frequently. Add the onion, celery, carrots and cider (if used) for the last 45 minutes of the cooking time.

Rich casseroled heart

1 ox heart, weighing 1–1.4 kg *(2¼–3 lb)*
45 ml *(3 tbsps)* oil
2 onions, skinned and sliced
45 ml *(3 level tbsps)* flour
300 ml *(½ pt)* stock
salt and pepper
225 g *(½ lb)* carrots, pared and grated
½ small swede, peeled and grated
rind of 1 orange
6 walnuts, chopped

Cut the heart into 1-cm *(½-in)* slices, removing the tubes, and wash it well. Fry the slices of meat in the oil till slightly browned and put into a casserole. Fry the onions and add to the casserole. Add the flour to the remaining fat and brown slightly. Pour in the stock, bring to the boil and simmer for 2–3 minutes, then strain over the slices of heart in the casserole; cover and cook for 3½–4 hours in the oven at 150°C *(300°F)* mark 2, adding the carrots and swede after 2½–3 hours. Pare the rind from the orange, shred it finely, cook in boiling water for 10–15 minutes, then drain. Add the walnuts and orange rind to the casserole 15 minutes before the cooking is completed. Alternatively, replace the orange rind and walnuts by a 226-g *(8-oz)* can tomatoes (chopped up).

Duck terrine with orange (p. 27).

Queue de boeuf aux olives noires

2 oxtails, jointed
cold water
30–45 ml *(2–3 tbsps)* olive oil
90 ml *(6 tbsps)* brandy, warmed
200 ml *(⅓ pt)* dry white wine
stock or water
bouquet garni (bayleaves, thyme, parsley, orange peel, and a clove of garlic, skinned and crushed)
225 g *(½ lb)* black olives, stoned
beurre manié (see page 11)
350–450 g *(12–16 oz)* long grain rice

Put the oxtail in a bowl, cover with cold water and leave for 2 hours. Drain and dry the oxtail on kitchen paper.

Heat the oil in a frying pan (or better still, a flameproof casserole). Seal a few pieces of meat at a time. If a frying pan is used, transfer the contents to a heatproof casserole. Warm the brandy, ignite it and pour it over the oxtail. When the flames have died down, add the wine and let it bubble rapidly for a few minutes. Add just sufficient stock or water to cover the meat. Add the bouquet garni, cover, and cook in the oven at 150°C *(300°F)* mark 1–2 for 3 hours. Pour the liquor off into a bowl. Remove the bouquet garni. Keep the liquor and meat separately in the refrigerator overnight. The next day, remove the fat from the liquor, bring to the boil and pour over the oxtail. Add the olives, cover and cook on top of the stove for another 1–1½ hours, until the meat comes easily away from the bones. Thicken the juices with beurre manié. Serve with boiled rice. *Serves 6–8.*

Oxtail casserole

1 oxtail, jointed
25 g *(1 oz)* fat or oil
2 onions, skinned and sliced
45 ml *(3 level tbsps)* plain flour
400 ml *(¾ pt)* stock
pinch of dried, mixed herbs
bayleaf
2 carrots, pared and sliced
10 ml *(2 tsps)* lemon juice
salt and pepper

Fry the oxtail in the fat or oil until golden brown, then place it in a casserole. Fry the onions and add to the meat. Sprinkle the flour into the fat and brown it, add the stock gradually and bring to the boil, then pour over the meat. Add the herbs, carrots and lemon juice, season, cover and cook in the oven at 190°C *(375°F)* mark 5 for ½ hour, then reduce to 150°C *(300°F)* mark 1 and simmer very gently for a further 2½–3 hours.

Casserole of lamb's tongues

4 lamb's tongues
25 g *(1 oz)* fat or oil
1 onion, skinned and sliced
1 carrot, pared and grated
4 large tomatoes, skinned and sliced
15 ml *(1 tbsp)* chopped parsley
salt and pepper
stock

Wash the tongues and trim if necessary. Fry the onion golden brown in the fat or oil and place it in a casserole. Add the tongues, carrot, tomatoes, parsley and seasoning and just enough stock to cover. Cook in the oven at 150°C *(350°F)* mark 4 for 1½ hours. If preferred, the tongues may be skinned and then reheated in the liquor before serving. Grilled or baked bacon rolls make a good garnish for this dish.

Boiled ox tongue

Before cooking a pickled tongue, soak it in cold water for several hours (overnight if the tongue has been smoked). Skewer it into a convenient shape if very large and put it into a pan with water to cover, bring gradually to the boil and drain. Add flavouring ingredients such as pared and sliced carrot, onion, turnip, a few peppercorns and a bouquet garni; cover with fresh cold water, bring to the boil and simmer until tender – 2½–3 hours if pickled, 4½–6 hours if fresh; skim from time to time. Plunge it into cold water, then skin it, taking out any bones or pieces of gristle.

To serve cold Put the tongue into a convenient-sized cake tin (an 18-cm *(7-in)* tin is required for a 2.6-kg *(6-lb)* tongue). Fill up with a little of the stock, put a plate on top, weigh down with a heavy object and leave to set. Turn out and garnish.

To serve hot Sprinkle the skinned tongue with browned crumbs and garnish with sliced lemon and parsley. Serve with parsley or tomato sauce.

Note For method of salting a fresh tongue, see Pickling Meat page 96.

Fried sweetbreads

Allow 450 g *(1 lb)* lamb's or calf's sweetbreads for 4 people. Soak them for about 3–4 hours in cold water, drain and put into a pan. Cover them with water and the juice of ½ a lemon, bring slowly to the boil, then simmer for 5 minutes. Drain and leave in cold water until they are firm and cold, then strip off any stringy unwanted tissues.

Press the sweetbreads well between absorbent paper, slice and dip into beaten egg and crumbs. Cut a few rashers of streaky bacon into strips and fry lightly until just crisp; drain and keep hot, then fry the sweetbreads in the same fat until golden. Toss the bacon and sweetbreads together and serve at once, with tartare or tomato sauce.

Creamed sweetbreads

450 g *(1 lb)* sweetbreads, prepared as for fried sweetbreads
½ onion, skinned and chopped
1 carrot, pared and chopped
few parsley stalks
½ bayleaf
salt and pepper
40 g *(1½ oz)* butter
60 ml *(4 level tbsps)* flour
300 ml *(½ pt)* milk
squeeze of lemon juice
chopped parsley to garnish

Put the sweetbreads, vegetables, herbs and seasoning in a pan with water to cover and simmer gently until tender – ¾ to 1 hour. Drain and keep hot, retaining 300 ml *(½ pt)* of the cooking liquid. Melt the butter, stir in the flour and cook for 2–3 minutes. Remove the pan from the heat and gradually stir in the sweetbread liquid and the milk. Bring to the boil and continue to stir until it thickens, season well and add a squeeze of lemon juice. Reheat the sweetbreads in the sauce and serve sprinkled with the parsley.

Lancashire tripe and onions

450 g *(1 lb)* dressed tripe
225 g *(8 oz)* shallots
568 ml *(1 pt)* milk
salt and pepper
pinch of grated nutmeg
½ bayleaf, optional
25 g *(1 oz)* butter
45 ml *(3 level tbsps)* flour
chopped parsley

Simmer the tripe, shallots, milk, seasonings and bayleaf (if used) in a covered pan for about 2 hours, or until tender. Alternatively, cook in a casserole in the centre of the oven at 150°C *(300°F)* mark 2 for 3 hours. Strain off the liquid and measure 600 ml *(1 pt)*. Melt the butter, stir in the flour and cook for 2–3 minutes. Remove the pan from the heat and gradually stir in the cooking liquid. Bring to the boil and continue to stir until it thickens. Add the tripe and shallots and reheat. Adjust the seasoning, sprinkle with parsley and serve with pieces of toast or boiled potatoes.

Tripe Romana

700 g *(1½ lb)* dressed tripe
30 ml *(2 tbsps)* vinegar
30 ml *(2 tbsps)* oil
50 g *(2 oz)* butter
100 g *(4 oz)* mushrooms, sliced
1 large or 2 small onions, skinned and sliced
45 ml *(3 level tbsps)* flour
396-g *(14-oz)* can tomatoes, made into a purée
salt and pepper
50 g *(2 oz)* fresh breadcrumbs
113-g *(4-oz)* pkt frozen peas

Cut the tripe into narrow strips 5 cm *(2 in)* long and soak for 30 minutes in the mixed vinegar and oil. Melt 40 g *(1½ oz)* of the butter and fry the mushrooms and onions for 3–4 minutes. Remove the vegetables, add the flour to the pan and brown slightly. Pour in the tomato purée and season to taste. Grease a casserole and cover the base with half the tripe. Add the mushrooms and onions and sprinkle on half the crumbs. Place another layer of tripe on this, pour the sauce over, sprinkle the top with the remaining crumbs and dot with the rest of the butter. Bake in the uncovered dish in the oven at 200°C *(400°F)* mark 6 for 25–35 minutes. Towards the end of the time, cook the peas and use to garnish the tripe.

Tripe à la mode de Caen

1 kg *(2¼ lb)* dressed tripe
1–2 cow heels
salt and pepper
2 bayleaves
2 sprigs thyme
2 sprigs parsley
4 large onions, skinned
4 cloves
4 leeks, sliced
2 carrots, pared and sliced
600 ml *(1 pt)* cider or dry white wine
45 ml *(3 tbsps)* brandy, optional

Wash the tripe very thoroughly and blanch it, then cut it into small pieces; divide up the cow heels. Put both into a casserole with the seasonings, herbs, onions (each stuck with a clove) and the leeks and carrots. Add the cider or wine and the brandy (if used), cover and cook in the oven at 150°C *(300°F)* mark 1–2 for 6 hours. This dish may be left overnight; remove the fat from the surface and take out the cow heel bones and the herbs before reheating for serving. *Serves 6.*

Brains in black butter sauce

4 pairs of lamb's brains
15 ml *(1 tbsp)* vinegar
salt
100 g *(4 oz)* butter
15 ml *(1 tbsp)* wine vinegar
black pepper
chopped parsley

Wash the brains and soak for an hour in cold water. Remove as much of the skin and membrane as possible and put the brains into a pan with the vinegar, 2.5 ml *(½ level tsp)* salt and enough water to cover well. Bring to simmering point and cook gently for 15 minutes; put into cold water, then dry on a towel. Heat half of the butter in a frying pan, add the brains, brown on all sides and put on to a very hot dish. Add the rest of the butter and heat it until dark brown, without allowing it to burn. Add the wine vinegar and pour over the brains; sprinkle with salt, pepper and parsley.

Creamed brains

Cook as for creamed sweetbreads, page 147, preparing them in the same way, but simmer for 10–15 minutes only.

Pressed ox cheek

1 ox cheek
1 cow heel
salt
few peppercorns
bouquet garni
ground allspice, optional

Clean the cheek and cow heel, put in a pan and cover with cold water; bring to the boil and discard the water. Add salt, the peppercorns and bouquet garni and fresh cold water to cover, bring to simmering point and simmer for about 3 hours, till the meat will fall easily from the bone. Drain and shred the meat. Add some seasoning and a little allspice if you wish, pack closely into a bowl or mould, cover and weight down. When it is cold, turn it out and serve with salad.

Pickled pig's head

See pickling meat, page 96.

Brawn

½ pickled or fresh pig's head or calf's head
bouquet garni
6 peppercorns
1 large onion, skinned
pieces of carrot and turnip, pared
salt
pepper and ground nutmeg
1 hard-boiled egg, sliced

Wash the head thoroughly, making sure the ear and nostrils are clean; soak it in salted water for about 1 hour. Cut off the ear and remove the brains. Scald the ear, scrape it free of hair and wash well. Place the head in a large pan with the ear, bouquet garni, peppercorns, vegetables and 5 ml *(1 level tsp)* salt if the head is pickled, 10 ml *(2 level tsps)* if it is fresh. Cover with water, bring to the boil, skim, cover and allow to cook very slowly until the meat is tender – about 2–3 hours. Strain off the liquid, remove the meat from the bones and cut it into small pieces. Skin the tongue and slice it thinly. Cut the ear into strips. Skim off the fat from the remaining liquid, add the brains, tied up in muslin, then boil until the liquid is reduced to half. Chop the brains and add to the meat. Season the mixed meats well with salt, pepper and nutmeg. Garnish the bottom of a mould or cake tin with sliced egg, pack the meat in tightly and pour some of the liquid over. Put a saucer and a weight on it and leave till cold and set. When the brawn is required for use, dip the mould into hot water and turn the brawn out on to a dish.

SAUSAGES AND CANNED MEATS

The sausage is a convenient way of utilising odd scraps of meat that are too 'bitty' and diverse to make a proper cut or joint. Good quality, well flavoured sausages make endless excellent meals or snacks.

Pork and beef sausages are the two commonest types in this country, but there are all kinds of local variations in different regions – black and white 'puddings', smoked sausage, breakfast sausage and so on, some of which are ready-cooked and make good snacks and sandwiches. Supermarkets and delicatessens offer an enormous variety of continental sausages.

Beef and pork sausages Pork sausages are more expensive and more delicately flavoured than beef, which have a distinctive taste that is not popular with everybody. Each kind is sold both in the normal 8-to-the-450 g *(1 lb)* size and as the thinner 16-to-the-450 g *(1 lb)* chipolatas. The actual mixture is usually the same, but the thick sausages need longer, slower cooking if they are not to split; chipolatas sometimes look more attractive and appeal to people who like plenty of nice crisp, brown 'outside'.

Skinless sausages cook quickly and are good for casseroles, pies and made-up dishes and for people who do not like sausage skins, but they are apt to be dry.

Sausage meat, which can be bought by weight, is very useful for stuffing, for sausage rolls and for such dishes as Scotch eggs.

Frankfurters, delicately flavoured smoked boiling sausages of minced pork with slight garlic seasoning.

Simmer for 5 minutes in water just off the boil or grill for 4 minutes, turning once.

Fried sausages

Melt a little fat in the frying pan, add the sausages and fry for 15–20 minutes, keeping the heat low to prevent them burning and turning them once or twice to brown them evenly.

Grilled sausages

Heat the grill to hot, put the sausages on the grill rack in the pan and cook until one side is lightly browned, then turn them; continue cooking and turning them frequently for about 15–20 minutes, until the sausages are well browned.

Baked sausages

Heat the oven to 200°C *(400°F)* mark 6. Put the sausages in a greased baking tin and cook in the centre of the oven for 30 minutes.

Alternatively, make kilted sausages by wrapping rinded streaky bacon rashers round pairs of chipolatas and baking in the same way at 190°C *(375°F)* mark 5.

Sausage cakes

Mix 450 g *(1 lb)* sausage meat with 1 grated onion and 5 ml *(1 level tsp)* mixed dried herbs. Divide the mixture into 8 and shape each portion into a round cake. Heat 25 g *(1 oz)* fat or oil in a frying pan and fry the cakes over a low heat for 10 minutes; turn them and fry the other side until crisp and brown.

Sausage bean feast

439-g *(15½-oz)* can baked beans
30 ml *(2 tbsps)* tomato ketchup
15 ml *(1 level tbsp)* soft brown sugar
2.5 ml *(½ level tsp)* prepared mustard
225 g *(½ lb)* Frankfurters, sliced

Combine all the ingredients in a casserole and bake uncovered in the oven at 180°C *(350°F)* mark 4 for 30–40 minutes.

Sausage casserole

100 g *(¼ lb)* streaky bacon
225 g *(½ lb)* chipolata sausages
225 g *(½ lb)* apples, peeled, cored and sliced
225 g *(½ lb)* tomatoes, skinned and sliced
1 green pepper, seeded and sliced
45 ml *(3 tbsps)* stock or water
salt and pepper

Cut the rind off the bacon and wrap each slice around 2 sausages, fry them (or brown lightly under the grill) and place in a casserole. Arrange the apples, tomatoes and pepper in layers on top of the sausages and bacon, add the stock and seasoning and cook in the oven at 200°C *(400°F)* mark 6 for about 40 minutes.

Spanish sausages

1 onion, skinned and sliced
45 ml *(3 tbsps)* fat or oil
450 g *(1 lb)* sausages
1 green pepper, seeded and sliced
10 ml *(2 level tsps)* salt
1 bayleaf
2 cloves
396-g *(14-oz)* can tomatoes or tomato juice
5 ml *(1 level tsp)* sugar
45 ml *(3 level tbsps)* flour
90 ml *(6 tbsps)* water

Lightly fry the onion in the hot fat or oil for 2–3 minutes. Add the sausages and brown lightly, add the rest of the ingredients, except the flour and water, cover and simmer for 30 minutes. Blend the flour and water to a smooth cream, stir in a little of the hot liquid, add this mixture to the pan and bring to the boil, stirring until it thickens. Remove the bayleaf and cloves before serving.

Sausage pie

2 onions, skinned and chopped
2–3 potatoes, peeled and thinly sliced
salt and pepper
450 g *(1 lb)* sausage meat
5 ml (1 level tsp) dried sage or mixed herbs
150 g *(5 oz)* shortcrust pastry (see page 351), made with 150 g *(5 oz)* flour etc

Put the vegetables into salted water, cover and bring slowly to the boil, then drain. Put them into a 20.5-cm *(8-in)* pie plate, and cover with the sausage meat, divided into small pieces, then add a generous amount of seasoning and the herbs. Roll out the pastry to form a lid and cover the pie with it; making a double edge so that it will not brown too much. Bake in the oven at 200°C *(400°F)* mark 6 for about 10–15 minutes, until the pastry begins to brown, then reduce the heat to 180°C *(350°F)* mark 4 and cook for about 30 minutes longer, until the vegetables and meat are tender.

Sausage rolls

200 g *(7 oz)* shortcrust pastry (see page 351), made with 200 g *(7 oz)* flour etc
225 g *(8 oz)* sausage meat
flour
milk to glaze

Roll the pastry out thinly into an oblong, then cut it lengthwise into 2 strips. Divide the sausage meat into 2 pieces, dust with flour, and form into 2 rolls the length of the pastry. Lay a roll of sausage meat down the centre of each strip, brush down the edges of the pastry with a little milk, fold one side of the pastry over the sausage meat and press the two edges firmly together. Seal the long edges together by flaking (see page 13). Brush the length of the two rolls with milk, then cut each into slices 4–5 cm *(1½–2 in)* long. Place on a baking sheet and bake in the oven at 200°C *(400°F)* mark 6 for 15 minutes; to cook the meat thoroughly, reduce the temperature to 180°C *(350°F)* mark 4 and cook for a further 15 minutes.

Good sausage rolls can be made with bought puff pastry, fresh or frozen. Use a 212-g *(7½-oz)* packet and allow it to reach room temperature (which will take about 2 hours) before rolling it out, then it will be easier to handle. Make the rolls as above, but heat the oven to 180°C *(350°F)* mark 4 and bake for a further 15 minutes.

Toad in the hole

125 g *(4 oz)* plain flour
2.5 ml *(½ level tsp)* salt
1 egg
300 ml *(½ pt)* milk and water
450 g *(1 lb)* skinless sausages

Sift the flour and salt into a bowl. Add the egg and half the liquid. Gradually stir in the flour and beat until smooth; stir in the remaining liquid. Grease a shallow ovenproof dish or Yorkshire pudding tin, put in the sausages and pour in the batter. Bake in the oven at 220°C *(425°F)* mark 7 for 40–45 minutes, or until the batter is well risen and golden brown.

Sausage flan

150 g *(5 oz)* shortcrust pastry (see page 351), made with 150 g *(5 oz)* flour etc
1 onion, skinned and chopped
½ green pepper, seeded and chopped
100 g *(4 oz)* streaky bacon, rinded and chopped
30 ml *(2 tbsps)* butter or oil
450 g *(1 lb)* sausage meat
1 egg, beaten
5 ml *(1 level tsp)* dried mixed herbs
salt and pepper

Line a 20.5-cm *(8-in)* metal pie plate or sandwich cake tin with the pastry, making a double edge. Fry the onion, pepper and bacon in the fat for 5 minutes, until soft. Drain well and add to the sausage meat, binding the mixture with the egg and the herbs and seasoning. Turn it into the pastry case and bake in the oven at 190°C *(375°F)* mark 5 for 30–40 minutes, until the filling is cooked and begins to shrink slightly from the pastry.

This flan can be served either hot or cold. As it is fairly rich it is best accompanied by tomatoes, a green vegetable or perhaps a mixed salad.

Corned beef casserole

1 kg *(2¼ lb)* potatoes, peeled
salt and pepper
1 medium sized onion, skinned and chopped
45 ml *(3 tbsps)* oil
439-g *(15½-oz)* can baked beans
340-g *(12-oz)* can corned beef, cubed

Cook the potatoes in boiling salted water for about 20 minutes, until just soft; drain and dice. Fry the onion in the oil until pale golden brown – about 5 minutes. Add the diced potatoes and continue to fry until they are golden brown. Remove a quarter of the onion and potato from the pan. Add the baked beans and corned beef, mix and season well. Put the mixture into a casserole and spoon the remaining onion and potato over the top. Bake in the oven at 190°C *(375°F)* mark 5 for 20 minutes.

Curry beefburgers

450 g *(1 lb)* potatoes, peeled
1 medium sized onion, skinned and chopped
45 ml *(3 tbsps)* oil
5–10 ml *(1–2 level tsps)* curry powder
340-g *(12-oz)* can corned beef, cubed
salt and pepper
fat for shallow frying

Cook the potatoes in boiling salted water for 20 minutes until soft. Drain and mash them. Fry the onion in the oil until soft and pale golden brown. Add the curry powder and continue to cook for a further 2–3 minutes. Stir the meat and the onion mixture into the mashed potato and season well. Let the mixture cool and then shape into 8 cakes. Fry in shallow fat until golden brown and drain on kitchen paper before serving.

Luncheon meat fritters

340-g *(12-oz)* can luncheon meat
125 g *(4 oz)* flour
pinch of salt
1 egg
150 ml *(¼ pt)* milk
fat or oil for deep frying

Cut the meat into thick slices. Put the flour and salt into a bowl. Add the egg and half the milk and beat well to make a smooth batter; gradually stir in the rest of the milk. Dip the luncheon meat slices in the batter and fry until crisp and golden in deep fat that will brown a cube of bread in 40–50 seconds. Drain on kitchen paper before serving. Before the meat is coated with batter, a little made mustard or tomato sauce may be spread on the slices.

Poultry

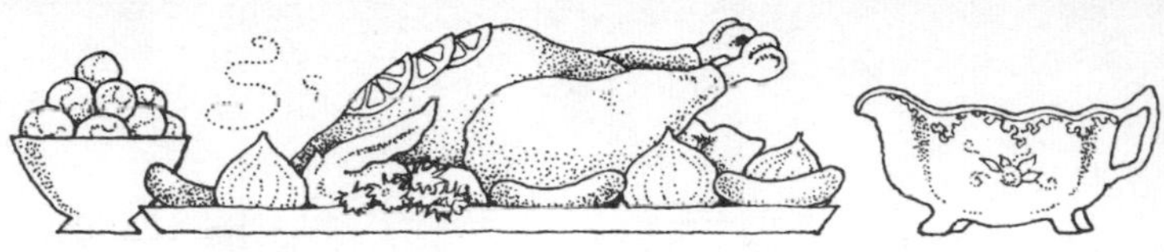

Poultry includes chickens (fowls), guinea fowls, ducks, geese and turkeys. Quite a lot of it is frozen, which means there is a good all-the-year-round supply (see notes below on frozen poultry). Most poultry is sold ready for cooking – that is, cleaned, plucked and trussed. Both fresh and frozen chicken and ducks, and occasionally turkeys, are available in separate joints as well as whole.

Hanging and storing
Poultry should be hung for 2–3 days after killing before it is cooked. In cold weather it can if necessary be hung for about a week, but unlike game it is not kept until it is 'high'. Poultry is usually plucked before hanging (see below), though this is not essential, but the inside should be left in. Hang the bird by the feet in a cool airy larder and protect it from flies, using muslin if the larder is not fly-proof. If poultry is to be put in a refrigerator, remove the inside and wrap the bird loosely or put it in a covered dish.

Plucking and singeing
Poultry is usually plucked, or at least rough-plucked, immediately after killing, as the feathers are much easier to remove while the bird is still warm. If many feathers remain, spread a piece of old sheeting or a large piece of paper on the floor or table and pluck on to this. Holding the bird firmly, take 2–3 feathers at a time and pull them sharply towards the head – that is, in the opposite direction to that in which they lie. Don't try to pluck handfuls at a time, or you may tear the skin. Large wing feathers are firmly attached and need to be plucked singly, with pliers if necessary. After the actual feathers have all been plucked, down (such as that on a goose) and any hairs can be singed off. Hold the bird over an open flame (gas burner, lighted taper or a piece of burning paper), turning it quickly.

Drawing
In older birds the leg sinews need removing. Cut a small slit with a sharp-pointed knife in the leg just above the claw and parallel with the leg bone, exposing the sinews. Slip a skewer under one of them, then, holding the foot firmly, pull on the skewer to draw out the sinew from the flesh. There are 4–5 sinews in each leg and they must be taken out singly.

Unless the bird is very young it is usual to cut off the feet and the easiest way of doing this is to sever the leg at the joint; bend the foot back, insert the knife in the joint and cut through. (The feet can be added to giblet stock).

To cut off the head, first cut through the skin of the neck about 5 cm *(2 in)* from the body. Slip back the skin and cut off the neck close to the trunk. (The neck is kept for stock, but the head is discarded.)

Slit the skin of the neck a little way down the back of the bird – far enough to let you get your fingers inside and to loosen the windpipe and gullet, which simplifies drawing. Cut round the vent at the tail end with scissors or a sharp knife, taking care not to puncture the entrails. Make the hole large enough to get your fingers inside the body. Take hold of the gizzard (the large, oval, muscular organ containing food and grit) and draw out all the entrails, including the lungs, windpipe and gullet. Reserve the giblets (heart, gizzard and liver) and any fat – there is always plenty on a goose. Discard the rest of the entrails, burning them if possible. Wipe out the inside of the bird with a clean, damp cloth.

The giblets
Cut out the gall-bladder from the liver, keeping it intact, and discard it; discard also the flesh on which it rested, as this may have a bitter flavour. Carefully cut through the flesh of the gizzard up to but not through the crop, peel off the flesh and discard the crop.

Giblet stock
Wash the liver, gizzard and heart. Wash and scald the feet, remove the scales and nip off the claws. Put them all in a saucepan, cover with water and stew gently for $\frac{3}{4}$–1 hour, to make a stock that can be used for gravy or soup.

Boning
To bone a chicken for a galantine or similar purpose, first cut off the neck and feet as above and cut off the end joints of the wings. Start boning at the neck. Using a small, sharp knife and keeping it close to the bone, separate the flesh from the bone. To bone the wings, cut through from inside where the wing joins the body, then work down the bone, scraping the flesh from it and turning the wing inside out; repeat with the other wing. Continue to work down the body, boning the legs in the same manner as the wings. Finally, turn the bird right side out.

Stuffing and trussing
For stuffing recipes and method, see pages 183 to 186.

The object of trussing is to keep the bird a good shape so that it will be easy to carve. A trussing needle (a long needle with an eye large enough to take fine string) is useful, but failing this, use a skewer and some fine string. First fold the neck skin under the body and fold the tips of the wings back towards the backbone so that they hold the neck skin in position; set the bird on its back and press the legs well into the side, thus raising the breast. Make a slit in the skin above the vent and put the tail (the 'parson's nose') through this.

Thread the needle with a length of string and insert it close to the second joint of the right wing; push it right through the body, passing it out so as to catch the corresponding joint on the left side. Insert the needle again in the first joint of the left wing, pass it through the flesh at the back of the body, catching the tips of the wings and the neck skin, and pass it out through the first joint of the wing on the right side. Tie the ends of the string in a bow.

To truss the legs, re-thread the needle and insert it through the gristle at the right side of the parson's nose. Pass the string over the right leg, over the left leg, through the gristle at the left side of the parson's nose, carry it behind the parson's nose and tie the ends of the string firmly to keep all in place.

When using a skewer, insert it right through the body of the bird just below the thigh bone and turn the bird over on to its breast. First, catching in the wing tips, pass the string under the ends of skewer and cross it over the back. Turn the bird over and tie the ends of the string together round the tail, at the same time securing the drumsticks.

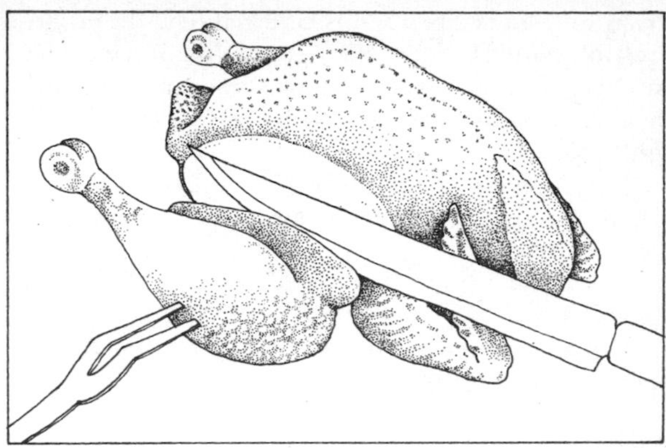

Carving off the leg

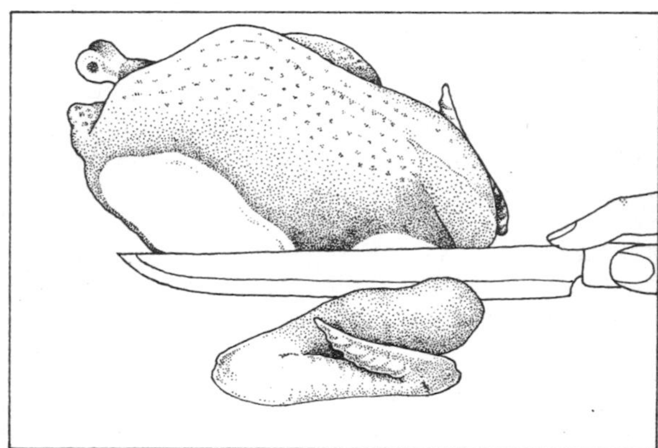

Carving off the wing

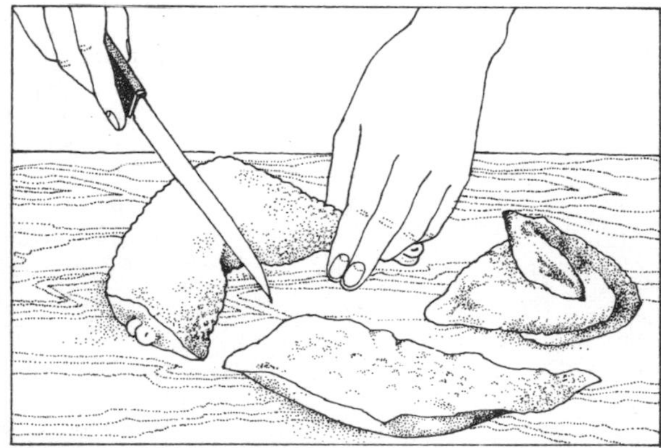

Jointing a chicken into portions

Frozen poultry

Poultry and game birds must be thawed completely before cooking (see page 476).

The giblets are usually wrapped in polythene and placed inside the body cavity, so remove them before cooking the bird. Frozen birds are usually sold trussed, ready for stuffing.

Carving poultry

Place the bird so that one wing is towards your left hand, with the breast diagonally towards you.

Steadying the bird with the flat of the knife held against the breast, prise the leg outwards with the fork, thus exposing the thigh joint – one clean cut through the joint will then sever the leg. It is usual to divide the thigh from the drumstick by cutting through the joint and in a big bird the thigh is further divided. Hold the wing with the fork and cut through the outer layer of the breast, judging the direction of the cut so that the knife enters the wing joint. Gently ease the wing away from the body of the bird and firmly cut through the joint gristle. Repeat for the other wing. Cut the breast in thin slices, parallel with the breastbone. When stuffing has been cooked in a bird, it is sliced from the front of the breast; the rest is scooped out with a spoon.

Chicken

When buying a fresh (non-frozen) bird, feel the tip of the breast-bone with the thumb and finger. In a young bird this is soft and flexible; if it is hard and rigid the bird is probably too old to roast satisfactorily and will have to be steamed or boiled. Look at the feet also – in a young bird they are smooth with small (not coarse) scales and with short spurs.

Many different terms have been used at times to classify chickens, but the main categories seen nowadays are:

Poussins
Very small chickens 450–900 g *(1–2 lb)* 6–8 weeks old; one serves 1–2 people.

Broilers
Small birds, 1.1–1.6 kg *(2½–3½ lb)* 12 weeks old; one serves 3–4 people. (Frozen chickens are usually broilers.)

Large roasters
Generally young cockerels or hens, but may be capons. 'Young roasters' are 1.8–2.3 kg *(4–5 lb)* and one serves 5–6 people.

Boiling fowls
Older, tougher birds; 1.8–3.2 kg *(4–7 lb)*. They should be 18 months old, but may in some cases be older. Usually served in casseroles, etc; allow 75–125 g *(3–4 oz)* meat per person.

Capons
Young cockerels that have been castrated and specially fattened. They weigh 3.6–4.6 kg *(8–10 lb)* and one serves 6–10 people.

Note All weights given are for oven-ready birds.

Accompaniments for chicken

Bacon rolls
Roll up rashers of rinded streaky bacon, thread on a skewer and grill until crisp – 3–5 minutes.

Forcemeat balls
See page 183.

Thin gravy
Pour off all the fat except 15 ml *(1 tbsp)* from the roasting tin. Sprinkle in 60 ml *(4 level tbsps)* flour and stir in 300 ml *(½ pt)* giblet stock (see page 152). Bring to the boil, stirring, season with salt and pepper and add a touch of gravy browning, if necessary. The finely chopped chicken liver may be included to give a richer flavour.

Roast chicken

If the bird is frozen, allow it to thaw out completely, then remove the bag of giblets. Wash the inside of the bird and stuff it at the neck end before folding the neck skin over. To add flavour you can put an onion, a thick lemon wedge or a knob of butter in the body of the bird. Brush the chicken with melted butter or oil and sprinkle with salt and pepper. Put in a shallow roasting tin. A few strips of streaky bacon may be laid over the breast to prevent it from becoming too dry. Bake in the oven at 200°C *(400°F)* mark 6, basting from time to time and allowing 20 minutes per 450 g *(1 lb)* plus 20 minutes. Put a piece of paper over the breast if the flesh shows signs of becoming too brown. Alternatively, wrap the chicken in foil before roasting; allow the same cooking time, but open the foil for the final 15–20 minutes, to allow the bird to brown.

Serve with roast potatoes and a green vegetable or – for a change – a tossed green salad. Bacon rolls, forcemeat balls, small chipolata sausages, bread sauce and thin gravy (see page 152) are the usual accompaniments.

Note An older bird should first be steamed or boiled for about 2 hours, to make it tender; it is best to do this the previous day, so that the chicken gets cold before it is stuffed. Roast for ½–¾ hour at 200°C *(400°F)* mark 6 to make it crisp, brown and really hot.

French-style roast chicken

1.1–1.4-kg *(2½–3-lb)* oven-ready chicken
75 g *(3 oz)* butter
salt and pepper
5–6 sprigs of tarragon or parsley
melted butter
2 rashers bacon, rinded
300 ml *(½ pt)* chicken stock

Prepare the bird as for ordinary roasting. Cream the butter with a good sprinkling of salt and pepper and put the butter and sprigs of herb inside the bird. Brush the breast with melted butter and cover with the rashers of bacon. Place the bird in a roasting tin and add the stock. Bake in the oven at 190°C *(375°F)* mark 5, basting with the stock every 15 minutes. Remove the bacon during the last 15 minutes of the cooking to brown the breast. Retain the stock to make gravy.

Note Half the stock may be replaced by 150 ml *(¼ pt)* dry white wine.

Baked chicken joints

Coat the joints with flour or egg and breadcrumbs. Melt 50–75 g *(2–3 oz)* butter or bacon dripping in a baking tin, put the joints in and bake in the oven at 200°C *(400°F)* mark 6 for 45 minutes, turning them once and basting occasionally.

Fried chicken

Cut a small bird in halves or quarters, a larger one into neat joints (or buy ready-cut pieces). Season with salt and pepper and coat all over with flour. Fry in hot fat, turning the pieces so that they brown on all sides, then reduce the heat; allow 15 minutes on each side. Serve with potatoes and a green vegetable such as broccoli.

Alternatively, season the joint and dip them in egg and breadcrumbs before frying. For a change, garnish the fried chicken with parsley and serve with a gravy or tomato sauce (see pages 197, 202). Another variation is to pile the pieces in a napkin-lined basket and garnish with rings of raw onion or green pepper.

Chicken Maryland

1–1.4-kg *(2–3-lb)* oven-ready chicken, jointed
45 ml *(3 level tbsps)* seasoned flour
1 egg, beaten
dry breadcrumbs
50 g *(2 oz)* butter
15–30 ml *(1–2 tbsps)* oil
4 bananas
sweet corn fritters
4 rashers of streaky bacon

Divide the chicken into fairly small portions, coat with seasoned flour, dip in beaten egg and coat with breadcrumbs. Fry the chicken in the butter and oil in a large frying pan until lightly browned. Continue frying gently, turning the pieces once, for about 20 minutes, or until tender. Alternatively, fry them in deep fat for 5–10 minutes. The fat should be hot enough to brown a 2.5-cm *(1-in)* cube of bread in 60–70 seconds. Serve the chicken with fried bananas, corn fritters and bacon rolls.

Fried bananas
Peel and slice the bananas lengthways and fry gently for about 3 minutes in a little hot butter or lard, until lightly browned.

Corn fritters
Make up a batter from 100 g *(4 oz)* flour, a pinch of salt, 1 egg and 150 ml *(¼ pt)* milk (see page 310). Fold in a 312-g *(11-oz)* tin sweetcorn kernels, drained. Fry in spoonfuls in a little hot fat until crisp and golden, turning them once. Drain well on crumpled kitchen paper.

Bacon rolls See page 154.

Chicken with cheese and cider sauce

4 joints chicken
100 g *(4 oz)* **butter**
small piece of onion, skinned and chopped
pinch of dried thyme
150 ml *(¼ pt)* **stock**
45 ml *(3 level tbsps)* **cornflour**
150 ml *(¼ pt)* **dry cider**
30–45 ml *(2–3 tbsps)* **single cream**
100 g *(4 oz)* **strong Cheddar cheese, grated**
salt and pepper
10 ml *(2 level tsps)* **mild mustard**

Fry the chicken joints in the hot butter, turning them frequently, until tender – about 20 minutes. Remove them, put into an ovenproof dish and keep hot. Meanwhile simmer the onion with a good pinch of thyme in the stock until tender – about 10 minutes. Strain the stock and return it to the pan. Blend the cornflour with a little cold water; add a little of the hot stock and mix, then return the mixture to the pan. Bring to the boil, stirring all the time, and stir in the cider. Remove the pan from the heat and stir in the cream and half the cheese and the seasonings. Pour sauce over the chicken portions, sprinkle with the remaining cheese and grill under a very hot grill until golden brown.

Chicken julienne

450 g *(1 lb)* **chicken meat, cooked**
40 g *(1½ oz)* **butter**
40 g *(1½ oz)* **flour**
300 ml *(½ pt)* **rich chicken stock**
300 ml *(½ pt)* **milk**
30 ml *(2 tbsps)* **lemon juice**
25 g *(1 oz)* **cheese, grated**
pinch of dried rosemary
salt and pepper
25 g *(1 oz)* **flaked almonds, toasted**
175–225 g *(6–8 oz)* **long grain rice**
15–30 ml *(1–2 tbsps)* **chopped parsley**
a lemon twist and a parsley sprig for garnish

Cut the carved chicken into long, narrow strips and place them in a shallow ovenproof dish. Melt the butter, stir in the flour and cook for several minutes. Slowly add the stock and milk, beating well; bring to the boil, stirring, and cook gently for 2–3 minutes. Add the lemon juice, cheese and rosemary. Adjust the seasoning (remembering that the chicken meat will dilute the sauce's flavour). Pour the sauce over the chicken and sprinkle with the nuts.

Cover and cook in the oven at 180°C *(350°F)* mark 4 for about 30 minutes. Serve in a border of parsley rice (see below) garnished with a lemon twist and a sprig of parsley.

Parsley rice Cook the rice in boiling salted water until just tender; rinse and drain it well. If you wish, this can be done early in the day, or even the day before. Parcel the cold, well separated rice in kitchen foil, with a few shavings of butter, and re-heat in the oven alongside the chicken dish for about 40 minutes. Add the parsley and toss lightly.

Suprêmes of chicken

4 suprêmes (chicken breasts), skinned
30 ml *(2 level tbsps)* **seasoned flour**
1 egg, beaten
50 g *(2 oz)* **fresh white breadcrumbs**
25 g *(1 oz)* **butter**
15 ml *(1 tbsp)* **oil**
300 ml *(½ pt)* **well flavoured white sauce (see pages 193 to 194)**
squeeze of lemon juice
1 egg yolk
15 ml *(1 tbsp)* **cream**

Trim the suprêmes and coat with seasoned flour; dip them in the beaten egg and then in breadcrumbs. Fry best side first in the butter and oil, turn them once and cook for about 20 minutes altogether. Remove them from the pan, drain on crumpled kitchen paper and keep them hot. Mix the sauce, lemon juice, egg yolk and cream and reheat without boiling, re-season if necessary and pour over the chicken.

Suprêmes are excellent served cold with a salad and are ideal for packed meals.

Poussins in a basket

4 poussins
100 g *(4 oz)* **melted butter**
salt and pepper
2 onions, skinned and sliced, optional
watercress

Split the birds down the back. Trim off the legs and the wings at the first joint, open out the birds and flatten as much as possible. Brush all over with melted butter and season lightly. Grill under a medium heat turning once or twice, for about 20 minutes, or until the poussins are tender. Serve on a napkin in a basket, garnished with the onion rings and watercress.

Chicken Kiev

4 large chicken breasts, skinned (about 225 g, *8 oz*, each with bone)
100 g *(4 oz)* butter
grated rind of ½ lemon
15 ml *(1 tbsp)* lemon juice
salt and pepper
15 ml *(1 tbsp)* chopped parsley
1 clove garlic, skinned and crushed
25 g *(1 oz)* seasoned flour
1 egg, beaten
100 g *(4 oz)* fresh white breadcrumbs
oil for deep frying

Using a small sharp knife, carefully work the flesh off the bone. Take care to keep the flesh in one piece. With a slightly damped heavy knife beat out each piece.

Work together the butter, lemon rind, juice, salt, pepper, parsley and garlic. Place it on a sheet of non-stick or waxed paper, form into a roll and chill until firm. Cut into 4 pieces and place one on each piece of chicken; roll up, folding the ends in to enclose the butter completely, and secure with cocktail sticks.

Coat in seasoned flour, then in beaten egg and breadcrumbs, patting the crumbs well in. Chill till required.

Heat the oil to 160°C *(325°F)*. Place 2 chicken portions in a frying basket and carefully lower into the oil; fry for about 15 minutes and drain. Fry the remaining chicken. Serve at once, on a bed of savoury rice.

Grilled chicken

Young and tender birds (such as poussins or small broilers) and chicken joints are suitable for grilling. Split a whole bird down the back, but without cutting through the skin of the breast; flatten it out, removing the breast-bone and breaking the joints where necessary. Skewer the legs and wings closely to the body, keeping the bird flat. A frozen bird should of course be allowed to thaw first. Joints require no special preparation.

Brush the chicken over with olive oil or melted butter, sprinkle with salt and pepper and place in the pan on a greased grid, skin side down. Grill under a moderate heat for 20 minutes, turn over and grill for a further 20–30 minutes, basting. Serve with a thin gravy made from the giblets (see page 154) and garnish with watercress.

Alternatively, sprinkle the chicken with a mixture of finely chopped onion, parsley and breadcrumbs, after brushing it with oil or butter; when it is cooked, garnish it with watercress and serve with brown or tomato sauce (see pages 197, 202).

Almond chicken

1 roasting chicken, jointed and skinned, or 4 chicken joints, skinned
1 egg, beaten
100 g *(4 oz)* ground almonds
50 g *(2 oz)* butter

Brush the joints with egg and roll them in the ground almonds, pressing these well in. Melt the butter in a shallow roasting tin and bake the chicken in this in the oven at 200°C *(400°F)* mark 6 for ¾–1 hour, until tender; baste once or twice during the cooking. Serve with a green or mixed salad.

Alternatively, serve with almond sauce. To make this, shred 50 g *(2 oz)* blanched almonds, brown in a knob of butter, season with salt and pepper and add 150 ml *(¼ pt)* double cream; heat, but do not boil.

Chicken ramekins

knob of butter
100 g *(4 oz)* cooked chicken, minced
2 mushrooms, chopped
2 eggs, separated
30 ml *(2 tbsps)* cream
salt and pepper

Grease 4 ramekins with the butter. Mix the chicken and mushrooms and bind with the egg yolks and cream; season to taste with salt and pepper. Whisk the egg whites stiffly and fold into the chicken mixture. Divide this mixture between the ramekins, place the ramekins on a baking sheet and cook in the oven at 180°C *(350°F)* mark 4 for 15–20 minutes. Serve at once. The chicken mixture need not be cooked in separate dishes, but can be put into a greased 600-ml *(1-pt)* soufflé dish, baked in the oven at 200°C *(400°F)* mark 6 for 25–30 minutes and served as a savoury.

Devilled poussins

4 poussins
little cayenne pepper
2.5 ml *(½ level tsp)* black pepper
10–15 ml *(2–3 tsps)* Worcestershire sauce
10–15 ml *(2–3 level tsps)* made mustard
10–15 ml *(2–3 tsps)* vinegar
45–60 ml *(3–4 tbsps)* oil

Split the birds down the back and open them out. Blend all the remaining ingredients and when smooth spread the mixture on the poussins. Place them under a medium heat and grill, turning them once or twice, for about 20 minutes, until tender.

Chicken parcels

4 chicken quarters
50 g *(2 oz)* melted butter
3 medium sized onions, skinned and sliced
60 ml *(4 level tbsps)* demerara sugar
5–10 ml *(1–2 tsps)* vinegar
paprika pepper

Cut 4 pieces of foil each large enough to cover a portion of chicken. Brush each piece of chicken with melted butter, dip the slices of onion in the sugar and divide them between the pieces of foil. Place the chicken portions on top of the onion and sprinkle with vinegar and paprika. Lightly fold the foil over the chicken, place the parcels on a baking sheet or in an ovenproof dish and bake in the oven at 200°C *(400°F)* mark 6 for about 45 minutes, or until the chicken is tender. Remove the pieces from the foil and serve topped with the onion.

Boiled chicken

Prepare the bird as described on page 152. Tie the legs together and fold the wings under the body. Rub the bird over with lemon juice to preserve the colour, put it in a large pan and just cover with cold water; add a little salt, an onion stuck with 3–4 cloves, a carrot and bouquet garni. Bring to the boil, cover and simmer for 3–4 hours if the bird is a boiling fowl; for a younger chicken, 45 minutes is enough. Drain the bird and keep it hot while making a parsley, egg or white sauce with 300 ml *(½ pt)* chicken stock and 300 ml *(½ pt)* milk. Serve the chicken coated with the sauce. Many people like to serve boiled ham as an accompaniment, to give extra flavour. Alternatively, the bird may be served cold, either whole and coated with a chaudfroid sauce (page 197), or sliced and accompanied by salad. It makes excellent sandwiches. The meat from a boiled chicken is often used to make a fricassee: take the flesh from the bones, dice it and mix with a white sauce made with half milk and half chicken stock. (For a somewhat more elaborate version, see the next recipe.)

Chicken fricassee

1.1-kg *(2½-lb)* oven-ready boiling chicken, jointed
2 medium sized onions, skinned and finely chopped
2 carrots, pared and finely sliced
100 g *(¼ lb)* mushrooms, sliced
water
bouquet garni
salt and pepper
50 g *(2 oz)* butter
50 g *(2 oz)* flour
4 rashers streaky bacon, rinded and rolled
1 egg yolk
45 ml *(3 tbsps)* cream
juice of ½ lemon
chopped parsley

Place the chicken joints, vegetables, just enough water to cover and the bouquet garni in a large saucepan. Add salt and pepper and bring slowly to the boil; simmer gently for 1 hour, or until the chicken is tender. When the chicken is cooked, remove it from the heat, strain off the stock and put it on one side. Remove the chicken meat from the bones and cut it into cubes. Melt the butter, stir in the flour, cook for 2–3 minutes and remove from the heat. Measure off 600 ml *(1 pt)* of the strained stock, gradually stir it into the roux, bring to the boil and continue to stir until the sauce thickens. Add the meat and vegetables and heat through for about 2 minutes.

Grill the bacon rolls. Blend together the egg yolk and cream, add a little of the sauce to the mixture and blend to a smooth cream. Return the blended mixture to the sauce and heat through gently, without boiling. Add the lemon juice. Pour the fricassee into a serving dish and garnish with the bacon rolls and chopped parsley.

Chicken à la king

50 g *(2 oz)* butter
100 g *(4 oz)* mushrooms, sliced
½ green pepper, chopped (or 1 small canned pimiento, chopped)
40 g *(1½ oz)* flour
400 ml *(¾ pt)* milk or milk and chicken stock, mixed
225–350 g *(8–12 oz)* diced cooked chicken
salt and pepper
paprika or ground nutmeg
15–30 ml *(1–2 tbsps)* sherry, optional

Melt the butter and fry the mushrooms and pepper until soft. Stir in the flour, cook for 2–3 minutes, remove from the heat and stir in the milk gradually. Bring the sauce to the boil and continue to stir until it thickens. Add the chicken, season to taste and add the sherry, if you wish. Serve with boiled rice or buttered noodles or as a snack with toast or crisp rolls.

Chicken Marengo

4 chicken joints
45–60 ml *(3–4 tbsps)* oil
2 carrots, pared and sliced
1 stick of celery, trimmed and chopped
1 onion, skinned and chopped
50 g *(2 oz)* streaky bacon, rinded and chopped
45 ml *(3 level tbsps)* flour
300 ml *(½ pt)* chicken stock
425-g *(15-oz)* can tomatoes
30 ml *(2 tbsps)* sherry
salt and pepper
bouquet garni
100 g *(¼ lb)* mushrooms, sliced
chopped parsley

Fry the chicken joints in the oil for about 5 minutes, until golden brown, remove them from the pan and put into a casserole. Fry the vegetables and bacon in the oil for about 5 minutes until golden brown; remove them from the pan. Stir the flour into the remaining fat, cook for 2–3 minutes and gradually stir in the stock; bring to the boil and continue to stir until it thickens. Return the vegetables to the pan and add the tomatoes, sherry, salt and pepper. Pour this sauce over the chicken joints, add the bouquet garni and sliced mushrooms and cook in the oven at 180°C *(350°F)* mark 4 for ¾–1 hour, until the chicken joints are tender. Remove them to a warm serving dish. Strain the sauce from the casserole over them and sprinkle with chopped parsley.

Chicken everglades

4 chicken joints
25 g *(1 oz)* butter
15 ml *(1 tbsp)* oil
4 slices cooked ham
100 g *(4 oz)* mushrooms, sliced
100-g *(4-oz)* pkt frozen peas
1 clove garlic, skinned and crushed
45 ml *(3 level tbsps)* flour
400 ml *(¾ pt)* dry white wine
150 ml *(¼ pt)* stock or water
salt and pepper

Fry the chicken joints in the butter and oil for about 5 minutes, until golden brown. Put them in a casserole and cover each with a slice of ham. Fry the mushrooms in the oil and butter for about 5 minutes, remove from the pan and add to the casserole, with the peas and crushed garlic. Stir the flour into the fat remaining in the pan and cook for 2–3 minutes. Stir in the wine and stock or water gradually, bring to the boil and stir until it thickens; season with salt and pepper and pour over the chicken joints. Cover and cook in the oven at 180°C *(350°F)* mark 4 for ¾–1 hour, until the chicken joints are tender.

Casserole of chicken

2 medium sized onions, skinned and sliced
2 sticks celery, trimmed and chopped
100 g *(4 oz)* mushrooms, sliced
50 g *(2 oz)* bacon, rinded and chopped
15 ml *(1 tbsp)* oil
25 g *(1 oz)* butter
4 chicken joints
45 ml *(3 level tbsps)* flour
400 ml *(¾ pt)* chicken stock
425-g *(15-oz)* can tomatoes, drained
salt and pepper

Lightly fry the onions, celery, mushrooms and bacon in the oil and butter for about 5 minutes, until golden brown. Remove them from the pan with a slotted spoon and use them to line the bottom of the casserole. Fry the chicken joints in the oil and butter for 5 minutes, until golden brown. Put the chicken in the casserole on the bed of vegetables. Stir the flour into the remaining fat and cook for 2–3 minutes; gradually stir in the stock and bring to the boil. Continue to stir until the mixture thickens then add the tomatoes, with salt and pepper to taste. Pour this sauce over the chicken joints, cover and cook in the oven at 180°C *(350°F)* mark 4 for ¾–1 hour, until the chicken is tender.

Chicken and bacon casserole *see colour plate facing p. 257*

4 large chicken joints
30 ml *(2 level tbsps)* flour
freshly ground black pepper
45 ml *(3 tbsps)* corn oil
25 g *(1 oz)* butter
4 rashers of back bacon, rinded
1 small onion, 50 g *(2 oz)*, skinned and finely chopped
1 chicken stock cube
300 ml *(½ pt)* water
4 large tomatoes, skinned and quartered
fried croûtons and chopped parsley for garnish

Remove the skin from the chicken and discard it. Put the flour and some pepper into a large paper bag and toss the chicken joints in it, two at a time, to coat them well. Heat the oil and butter together in a large frying pan or, better still, use a flameproof casserole which will take the joints in a single layer. Fry the joints until browned. Drain and put on one side. Pour off the excess fat. Add the bacon, cut in narrow strips, and fry gently until the fat starts to run. Add the onion and continue to fry until it is beginning to brown. Stir in any excess flour left from coating the chicken, add the crumbled stock cube and gradually stir in the water. Bring to the boil, stirring, and add the tomatoes. At this stage, turn the mixture into a wide, shallow casserole, if a flameproof one was not used for the initial cooking. Arrange the chicken, flesh side down, in the casserole, and cover tightly. Cook in the oven at 170°C *(325°F)* mark 3 for about 1¼ hours, until the chicken is fork-tender. Keep the chicken joints warm while reducing the liquor to a glaze by fast boiling. Arrange the chicken in the casserole and spoon the reduced liquor over. Garnish with fried croûtons and chopped parsley.

Coq au vin

75 g *(3 oz)* bacon, rinded and chopped
175 g *(6 oz)* mushrooms, wiped and sliced
16 button onions, skinned
knob of butter
15 ml *(1 tbsp)* oil
1 roasting chicken, jointed
60 ml *(4 tbsps)* brandy
45 ml *(3 level tbsps)* flour
400 ml *(¾ pt)* red wine
150 ml *(¼ pt)* stock
15 ml *(1 level tbsp)* sugar
bouquet garni
pinch of nutmeg
salt and pepper

Fry the bacon, mushrooms and onions in the butter and oil for about 3–4 minutes, until lightly browned; remove from the pan. Fry the chicken for 8–10 minutes, until golden brown and sealed all over. Pour brandy over the chicken, remove the pan from the heat and 'flame' it by igniting the liquid in the saucepan with a match. Remove the chicken when the flames have died down and place it in a casserole. Stir the flour into the fat remaining in the pan and cook for 2–3 minutes. Stir in the wine and stock gradually, bring to the boil and continue to stir until the mixture thickens; add sugar, herbs and seasonings. Add the browned vegetables to the casserole and pour the sauce over the chicken. Cover and cook in the oven at 180°C *(350°F)* mark 4 for ¾–1 hour, until tender. Before serving, remove the bouquet garni.

Galantine of chicken

1 boiling chicken
salt and pepper
350 g *(12 oz)* sausage meat
2 hard-boiled eggs, shelled and sliced
50 g *(2 oz)* cooked ham, chopped
50 g *(2 oz)* pressed tongue, chopped
150–300 ml *(¼–½ pt)* aspic jelly
sliced cucumber, olives, egg, to garnish

Bone the bird as described on page 152. When all the bones are removed, spread out the bird and sprinkle the flesh with salt and pepper. Cover the body of the bird with the sausage meat, pushing it inside the wings and legs so that they regain their original shape. Arrange the sliced eggs, ham and tongue over the sausage meat and season again. Wrap the cut ends of the skin over one another to make a neat shape, as like that of the original bird as possible. Using a large bodkin or trussing needle and a piece of string, sew the skin in place.

Wrap the bird in a clean cloth, tie firmly, put in a large pan and cover with salted water. Put on the lid and simmer for about 2 hours, or until tender. When the chicken is cooked, remove it from the pan and re-shape. When it is cold, remove the cloth, coat with aspic jelly (made according to the manufacturer's instructions), decorate with slices of cucumber, stuffed olives, hard-boiled egg, and cover with more aspic jelly; leave to set. Serve sliced with salad.

Beef olives (p. 104).

Chicken chasseur

4 chicken joints
15 ml *(1 level tbsp)* seasoned flour
15 ml *(1 tbsp)* oil
25 g *(1 oz)* butter
1 onion, skinned and chopped
50 g *(2 oz)* mushrooms, wiped and sliced
2 tomatoes, skinned, seeded and diced
150 ml *(¼ pt)* espagnole sauce (see page 198)
30 ml *(2 tbsps)* white wine
salt and pepper
chopped parsley

Coat the chicken joints in seasoned flour and fry in the oil and butter for about 5 minutes, until golden brown. Remove the chicken joints from the pan and put into a casserole. Fry the onion and mushrooms in the oil and butter for 5 minutes, until golden brown; add the tomatoes, espagnole sauce, wine, salt and pepper and pour over the chicken joints. Cover and cook in the oven at 180°C *(350°F)* mark 4 for ¾–1 hour, until tender. Place the chicken joints on a serving dish, pour the sauce over them and sprinkle with chopped parsley before serving.

Chinese chicken

4 chicken joints
90 ml *(6 tbsps)* soy sauce
90 ml *(6 tbsps)* sherry
5 ml *(1 level tsp)* sugar
2 spring onions, skinned and chopped
45 ml *(3 level tbsps)* flour
deep fat for frying

Soak the chicken joints in a marinade of the soy sauce, sherry, sugar and chopped onions for about 1 hour. Drain the chicken and dip each piece in flour. Heat some deep fat until it will brown a 2.5-cm *(1-in)* cube of bread in 60 seconds. Fry the chicken for about 8–10 minutes, until golden brown. Serve with plain boiled rice to which has been added a little of the marinade. (Any marinade left over can be used for flavouring other sauces or soups.)

Instead of deep-frying the chicken joints, you can fry them for about 20 minutes in 50 g *(2 oz)* butter and 15 ml *(1 tbsp)* oil in a frying pan covered with a lid.

Curried chicken

1 chicken, jointed and skinned
30 ml *(2 level tbsps)* seasoned flour
2 onions, skinned and sliced
50 g *(2 oz)* butter
1 apple, cored and chopped
10 ml *(2 level tsps)* curry powder
150 ml *(¼ pt)* stock
little lemon juice
10 ml *(2 tsps)* sweet chutney
1 tomato, sliced

Coat the chicken with flour. Lightly fry the onions in the butter, then add the chicken and fry until golden brown. Add the apple, curry powder and remaining flour, stir well and fry for 1–2 minutes. Add the stock, lemon juice and chutney and mix together. Cover the pan and simmer till the chicken is cooked and the sauce thickens – about 40 minutes. Serve with rice or a pilau (see page 281) and garnish with tomato slices.

If you use cooked chicken, omit the preliminary frying.

Chicken and cranberry curry *see colour plate facing p. 225*

350 g *(12 oz)* cooked chicken
50 g *(2 oz)* lard
1 large onion, skinned and chopped
1 clove garlic, skinned and crushed
15 ml *(1 level tbsp)* flour
25 ml *(1½ level tbsps)* curry powder
30 ml *(2 level tbsps)* tomato paste
juice of 1 lemon
226-g *(8-oz)* can whole berry cranberry sauce
300 ml *(½ pt)* water
2.5 ml *(½ level tsp)* salt
3 whole cloves
1 bayleaf
175–225 g *(6–8 oz)* long grain rice, cooked
25 g *(1 oz)* flaked almonds, toasted

Cut the chicken into 2.5-cm *(1-in)* pieces. Heat the lard in a large frying pan and fry the onion slowly until golden brown; add the crushed garlic. Remove the pan from the heat and stir in the flour, curry powder, tomato paste, lemon juice and cranberry sauce; stir well. Gradually add the water, stirring continuously. Return the pan to the heat and bring to the boil, stirring. Add the salt, cloves and bayleaf, cover the pan and simmer for 30 minutes, stirring occasionally. Add the chicken to the sauce and heat through while the rice is cooking. Discard the cloves and bayleaf. Serve the chicken in the centre of a border of rice, with a garnish of toasted flaked almonds.

Note A 900-g *(2-lb)* oven-ready bird yields about 350 g *(12 oz)* meat.

Rognons sautés Turbigo (p. 145).

Chicken mousse

150 ml *(¼ pt)* aspic jelly
slices of cucumber and thin strips of tomato and lemon rind to garnish
350 g *(12 oz)* cooked chicken, minced
150 ml *(¼ pt)* béchamel sauce, see page 196
30–45 ml *(2–3 tbsps)* mayonnaise
salt and pepper
284-ml *(10-fl oz)* carton double or whipping cream, whipped

Line a 900-ml *(1½-pt)* mould or some individual moulds with a little aspic jelly and allow it to set. Decorate with a few slices of cucumber and strips of tomato and lemon rind, spoon a little more jelly over and allow to set. Mix the chicken, béchamel sauce and mayonaise and add the remainder of the aspic jelly. Season well. When on the point of setting, fold in the whipped cream. Turn the mixture into the mould or moulds and leave to set. When it is cold and firm, turn out and garnish with slices of cucumber and strips of tomato and lemon rind.

Chicken 'Dopyaza'

4 chicken joints, skinned
5 ml *(1 level tsp)* ground ginger
5 ml *(1 level tsp)* salt
900 g *(2 lb)* onions, skinned
1 clove of garlic, skinned
75 g *(3 oz)* butter
seeds of 1 cardamom
15 ml *(1 level tbsp)* ground turmeric
25 ml *(1½ level tbsps)* ground cumin
15 ml *(1 level tbsp)* ground coriander
400 ml *(¾ pt)* yoghurt
300 ml *(½ pt)* water
8 peppercorns

If possible, use an enamelled iron casserole. Wipe the chicken joints, prick with a fine skewer, rub in the ginger and salt and leave for ½ hour. Roughly chop 450 g *(1 lb)* of the onions and crush the garlic. Fry the chopped onions in the fat until evenly browned, then add the garlic; remove the onion and drain it. Cook the cardamom seeds in the fat for 1 minute. Place the chicken in the fat with the turmeric, cumin, coriander and yoghurt and cook until the yoghurt is almost absorbed. Pound the cooked onions (or pulp them in an electric blender), add the water and pour over the chicken joints. Slice the rest of the onions thinly, put on top with the peppercorns, cover the pan tightly and cook in the oven at 170°C *(325°F)* mark 3 for 1 hour.

The name dopyaza means 'twice onion' and as a general rule in these curries onions should be added in two different forms at two stages of the cooking, as in this recipe. However, a number of authentic recipes do not follow this method.

Chicken with walnuts

1.5-kg *(3¼-lb)* oven-ready chicken
1 large carrot, pared
1 onion, skinned
1 bayleaf
salt and pepper

For the walnut sauce
50 g *(2 oz)* butter
175 g *(6 oz)* walnut halves
225 g *(½ lb)* onions, skinned and sliced
300 ml *(½ pt)* natural yoghurt
1.25 ml *(¼ level tsp)* paprika
150 ml *(¼ pt)* chicken stock

Place the chicken in a large saucepan and cover with cold water. Cut the carrot and onion into thick slices and add to the pan, together with the bayleaf and some salt and pepper. Bring to the boil, then cover, reduce the heat and simmer for 1½ hours. Leave the bird to cool in the stock for 1 hour. Remove and discard the skin from the chicken. Cut the chicken meat into largish pieces.

Heat the butter in a frying pan, add 50 g *(2 oz)* of the walnut halves and fry gently until light golden brown, then remove from the pan. Add the onions and sauté until soft, but don't allow to brown; add the yoghurt, paprika and chicken stock. Place the remaining walnuts in an electric blender until finely ground (or put through a Mouli grater), then add to the sauce. Add the walnut halves and the chicken, heat through and check the seasoning. Serve with buttered courgettes.

Chicken chaudfroid

150 ml *(¼ pt)* aspic jelly
1 cooked chicken, skinned
150 ml *(¼ pt)* béchamel sauce, see page 196
cucumber, pickled walnuts, radish and strips of lemon rind to garnish

Make up the aspic as directed on the packet and leave it until it has almost reached setting point. Place the cold chicken on a cooling rack over a tray or large plate. Add half the aspic to the béchamel sauce, stir in lightly and allow it to thicken but not set. (Keep the remaining aspic in a basin which is standing in a bowl of warm water.) Coat the chicken by pouring the sauce steadily over it to give a smooth, even surface;

allow the excess to run off and collect in the tray. Decorate the chicken with strips of cucumber skin, pieces of pickled walnut, slices of radish and strips of lemon rind, then carefully spoon over it the remaining aspic (which should be at setting point), so that the coated bird is completely covered but the decoration is not disturbed.

Boer chicken pie

1.4-kg *(3-lb)* oven-ready chicken
900 ml *(1½ pt)* water
15 ml *(1 level tbsp)* salt
5 ml *(1 tsp)* whole allspice
5 ml *(1 tsp)* whole peppercorns
2 bayleaves
3 carrots, pared and sliced
2 onions, skinned and quartered
2 sticks of celery, sliced
5 sprigs of parsley
50 g *(2 oz)* thinly sliced cooked ham
2 hard-boiled eggs
25 g *(1 oz)* butter
45 ml *(3 level tbsps)* flour
30–45 ml *(2–3 tbsps)* sherry
15 ml *(1 tbsp)* lemon juice
5 ml *(1 level tsp)* sugar
pinch of ground mace
pinch of pepper
1 egg yolk
250 g *(9 oz)* shortcrust pastry, ie made with 250 g *(9 oz)* flour etc (see page 351)
egg to glaze

This delicious pie can be prepared early in the day, kept in a cool place and baked just before it is required. Quarter the chicken, put it in a large pan with the water, salt, allspice, peppercorns, bayleaves, vegetables and parsley sprigs (tied together). Cover and simmer for ½ hour, or until the vegetables are tender but not over-done. Take out the vegetables and chicken and strain the stock. Cut the vegetables up small; cut the meat from the chicken bones in large chunks. Put into a large pie dish alternate layers of chicken, vegetables, quarter-slices of ham, folded over, and sliced hard-boiled egg.

Melt the butter and gradually stir in the flour, 300 ml *(½ pt)* of the stock, the sherry, lemon juice, sugar, mace and pepper. Cook until the sauce is thick and smooth. Beat the egg yolk well, stir slowly into the sauce and heat gently, stirring, till thick, but don't boil. Pour this sauce over chicken and vegetables; cool. Cover the pie with pastry, then, using a sharp knife, cut a short line from the centre towards each of the four corners and fold each pastry triangle back, leaving an open square. Brush the pastry over with beaten egg to glaze and bake in the oven at 220°C *(425°F)* mark 7 for 25 minutes.

Puff top chicken pie

1.8-kg *(4-lb)* oven-ready chicken
1 small onion, skinned and halved
1 carrot, peeled
1 leek, washed and trimmed or 1 stick celery, scrubbed
6 peppercorns
salt

For the sauce
50 g *(2 oz)* butter
175 g *(6 oz)* onion, skinned and chopped
225 g *(8 oz)* sweet red peppers, seeded and chopped
50 g *(2 oz)* green chilies, halved and seeded
60 ml *(4 level tbsps)* flour
100 g *(4 oz)* Cheddar cheese, grated
salt, black pepper
396-g *(13-oz)* pkt frozen puff pastry, thawed
1 egg, beaten

Simmer the chicken in sufficient water to cover with the vegetables, peppercorns and salt for about 2 hours. Remove the chicken, reduce the liquor to 600 ml *(1 pt)* by rapid boiling and then strain. Melt the butter in a saucepan, fry the chopped onion, peppers and chilies for 10 minutes; if you prefer the chilies may be removed at this stage.

Carve the chicken, cutting it into fork size pieces, and discard the skin. Place the meat in a 1.7-l *(3-pt)* pie dish with a funnel. Blend the flour into the fried vegetables and slowly add the strained stock, stirring continuously. Bring to the boil. When the liquid has thickened add the cheese and adjust the seasoning. Spoon over the chicken and allow to cool. Roll out the puff pastry and use to cover the filled pie dish. Knock up and scallop the edge and score the top of the pastry into diamonds with a knife, glaze with beaten egg, place on a baking sheet and cook in the oven at 230°C *(450°F)* mark 8 for 30 minutes. Reduce the heat to 170°C *(325°F)* mark 3 and cook for a further 30 minutes.

Danish chicken

1.4-kg *(3-lb)* oven-ready chicken
clove of garlic, skinned and halved
salt and freshly ground pepper
pinch of ground ginger
75 g *(3 oz)* butter
300 ml *(½ pt)* water
1 medium sized green pepper, seeded and cut in thin rings
2 tomatoes, skinned and thickly sliced
142-ml *(5-fl oz)* carton double cream
50 g *(2 oz)* Samsoe cheese, grated

Remove the skin from the chicken; cut the chicken into 8 pieces. Rub these with garlic, then season with salt, pepper and ginger. Melt the butter in a large pan, add the chicken pieces and fry, turning the pieces until browned all over. Add the water and bring to the boil, then reduce the heat; cover and simmer for 30–40 minutes, until tender. Place the drained chicken joints in a serving dish and keep warm. Add the peppers to the stock in the pan and cook until soft – about 5 minutes – then add the tomatoes and cook for a further few minutes. Drain the vegetables and spoon them over the chicken. Add the cream to the juices in the pan and pour over the chicken. Sprinkle with the cheese and place under a hot grill until golden brown. Serve with crisp French bread or plain boiled rice.

Swedish chicken salad

1.6-kg *(3½-lb)* oven-ready chicken, roasted
175 g *(6 oz)* long grain rice
1 green eating apple
1 red eating apple
2 bananas
lemon juice
142-ml *(5-fl oz)* carton double cream
200 ml *(⅓ pt)* home-made mayonnaise or lemon mayonnaise (see page 245)
5 ml *(1 level tsp)* curry powder
salt and pepper
watercress to garnish

When the chicken is cold, carve it into slices and cut into strips.

Meanwhile, cook, drain and cool the rice. Core and thinly slice the apples; peel and thickly slice the bananas. Sprinkle both with lemon juice. Whip the cream to the consistency of the mayonnaise and lightly fold it in. Add the curry powder. Fold in the chicken, apple and banana. Add more lemon juice and adjust the seasoning to taste. Pile on a bed of rice, or mix with rice. Garnish with watercress. *Serves 6.*

Pakistan curry

100 g *(¼ lb)* creamed coconut in a block
568 ml *(1 pt)* milk
100 g *(¼ lb)* blended white vegetable fat
450 g *(1 lb)* onions, skinned
little green ginger, chopped
10 ml *(2 level tsps)* curry powder
10 ml *(2 level tsps)* flour
10 ml *(2 level tsps)* salt
45 ml *(3 level tbsps)* ground almonds
141-g *(5-oz)* can tomato paste
2 141-g *(5-oz)* cartons plain yoghurt
1.6-kg *(3½-lb)* oven-ready chicken, boned and cut into 6 portions

Grate the coconut and put it in a bowl, pour the milk over and leave to soak for ½ hour. Heat the fat in a flameproof casserole over a low heat. Cut the onions into rings and sauté in the fat until soft, but don't allow to brown. Add the ginger, curry powder, flour, salt and ground almonds. Mix well and simmer gently for 10 minutes. Add the tomato paste and mix well.

Strain the coconut from the milk. Add the flavoured milk and the yoghurt to the curry sauce and mix well. Place the chicken portions in the sauce, cover the casserole and cook in the oven at 170°C *(325°F)* mark 3 for 1½–2 hours, until tender. Serve with cooked rice. *Serves 6.*

Brazilian chicken Rio

3 oranges
4 chicken portions
salt
2.5 ml *(½ level tsp)* paprika
50 g *(2 oz)* butter
30 ml *(2 level tbsps)* flour
7.5 ml *(½ level tbsp)* soft brown sugar
1.25 ml *(¼ level tsp)* ground ginger

Pare the rind from 1 orange, free of all white pith, and cut the rind into fine shreds. Squeeze the juice from the rinded orange and 1 other, then add water to make up to 300 ml *(½ pt)*. Divide each chicken joint into two; sprinkle with salt and paprika. Melt the butter in a large, deep frying pan, add the chicken and brown well. Remove the chicken joints. Stir the flour into the dripping in the pan, together with the sugar and ginger; blend well. Stir in the orange juice and rind, bring to the boil and boil for 2–3 minutes. Check the seasoning. Return the chicken to the sauce, cover, and simmer for about 45 minutes, until the chicken is tender. Peel the third orange and divide into segments, free of membrane. Add to the chicken during the last 5 minutes of the cooking time. Serve with plain boiled rice.

Poulet en cocotte *see colour plate facing p. 224*

1.4–1.6-kg *(3–3½-lb)* oven-ready chicken
salt and freshly ground pepper
75 g *(3 oz)* butter
225 g *(8 oz)* lean back bacon, in one slice
450 g *(1 lb)* potatoes, peeled
3 sticks of celery, trimmed and sliced
450 g *(1 lb)* small new carrots, scraped
50 g *(2 oz)* button mushrooms
25 g *(1 oz)* shelled walnuts
chopped parsley

For the stuffing
100 g *(4 oz)* sausage meat
30 ml *(2 level tbsps)* white breadcrumbs
1 chicken liver, chopped
30 ml *(2 tbsps)* chopped parsley

Mix all the stuffing ingredients together in a bowl until well blended. Stuff the chicken at the neck end, plump up and secure with a skewer; truss the bird as for roasting and season well. Melt the butter in a large frying pan, add the chicken and fry, turning it until well browned all over. Place the chicken and butter in a large ovenproof casserole. Rind the bacon and cut into 2-cm *(¾-in)* cubes. Add to the casserole, cover, and cook in the oven at 180°C *(350°F)* mark 4 for 15 minutes. Meanwhile cut the potatoes into 2.5-cm *(1-in)* dice. Remove the casserole from the oven and baste the chicken. Surround it with the vegetables and walnuts, turning them in the fat; season. Return the casserole to the oven and cook for a further 1½ hours. Garnish with chopped parsley. Have a plate to hand for carving the bird. Serve the vegetables and juices straight from the casserole.

Poulet à l'estragon

1.4-kg *(3-lb)* oven-ready chicken
½ lemon, sliced
2.5 ml *(½ level tsp)* salt
freshly ground black pepper
1.25 ml *(¼ level tsp)* dried tarragon or 5 ml *(1 tsp)* chopped fresh tarragon
3 carrots, pared and quartered
1 small onion, skinned and quartered
1 bayleaf
2 sprigs parsley
400 ml *(¾ pt)* chicken stock
90 ml *(6 tbsps)* white wine

For sauce
25 g *(1 oz)* butter
30 ml *(2 level tbsps)* flour
2.5 ml *(½ level tsp)* dried tarragon
2 egg yolks
75 ml *(5 tbsps)* single cream
salt

Cut chicken into 8 small joints. Put them in a large pan together with the giblets and the next 10 ingredients. Bring to the boil, cover and simmer on top of the stove for about 30 minutes, or until the chicken is cooked. Remove the chicken joints from the pan; discard the giblets, remove the skin from the joints, transfer the joints to a serving dish and keep hot. Strain the liquor into a measuring jug and make up to 400 ml *(¾ pt)* with water if necessary. Heat the butter in a pan; blend in the flour and cook for 1 minute. Gradually add the chicken liquor and bring to the boil, stirring. Add the tarragon and simmer for 3 minutes. Blend together the egg yolks and cream. Add 60 ml *(4 tbsps)* sauce to the egg mixture and then return it to the pan. Adjust the seasoning and pour the sauce over the chicken pieces.

Catalonian chicken

1.4-kg *(3-lb)* oven-ready chicken
seasoned flour
50 g *(2 oz)* butter
30 ml *(2 tbsps)* vegetable oil
12 small onions, skinned
25 ml *(1½ level tbsps)* flour
300 ml *(½ pt)* chicken stock
30 ml *(2 tbsps)* white wine, optional
10 ml *(2 level tsps)* tomato paste
salt and pepper
12 chestnuts
225 g *(½ lb)* chipolata sausages
fried bread for garnish

Cut the chicken into 8 portions and dip in seasoned flour. Heat the butter and oil in a frying-pan, add the chicken and brown well. Remove from the pan and drain. Brown the onions in the fat, then place in the base of a 1.5–2-l *(3½–4-pt)* casserole. Sprinkle the flour over the drippings in the frying pan and stir in the chicken stock, white wine and tomato paste. Place the chicken joints on the onions and pour thickened stock over; season. Cover casserole and cook in the oven at 180°C *(350°F)* mark 4 for 1 hour.

Meanwhile, prepare and cook the chestnuts. Fry the sausages and cut each in three pieces. Add the chestnuts and sausage to the chicken about 10 minutes before the end of the cooking time. Thicken the gravy slightly if necessary. Garnish with the fried bread. *Serves 4–6.*

Chicken piri-piri

2 fresh or dried red chilies, seeded and sliced
1.25 ml *(¼ level tsp)* **dried tarragon**
1.25 ml *(¼ level tsp)* **dried marjoram**
1.25 ml *(¼ level tsp)* **dried basil**
1.25 ml *(¼ level tsp)* **dried thyme**
1 small bayleaf, crushed
30 ml *(2 tbsps)* **raisins, stoned**
salt and freshly ground pepper
150 ml *(¼ pt)* **olive oil**
30 ml *(2 tbsps)* **lemon juice**
1 poussin or spring chicken, about 1 kg *(2¼ lb)*

Make the 'piri-piri' marinade by putting all the ingredients except the chicken in a bowl and leaving to stand for 2 hours. Split the chicken down the back, but don't separate the halves entirely. Press it out flat, using a weight if necessary. Fix with crossed skewers to maintain a good shape during the grilling. Brush the chicken inside and out with some of the marinade. Cook cage-side uppermost under a moderate grill for 15 minutes; turn the chicken and baste at intervals until it is cooked through – about 20 minutes. Serve on a bed of plain boiled rice, with a garnish of lemon wedges and parsley sprigs. *Serves 2.*

Sweet-sour chicken

25 g *(1 oz)* **fat**
2 cloves garlic, skinned and crushed
1 chicken breast, sliced
4 chicken livers, quartered
2 carrots, pared
1 cucumber, peeled
2 tomatoes, skinned
1 onion, skinned
283-g *(10-oz)* **can condensed chicken soup**
15 ml *(1 level tbsp)* **flour**
30 ml *(2 level tbsps)* **sugar**
45 ml *(3 tbsps)* **soy sauce**
45 ml *(3 tbsps)* **vinegar**

Heat the fat and sauté the garlic without browning. Add the chicken breast and livers. Slice the carrot. Split the cucumber lengthwise and cut into matchstick shaped pieces 0.5 cm *(¼ in)* thick. Cut the tomatoes and the onion into small wedges. Add to the meat mixture, with the soup, cover and simmer until tender – about 20–30 minutes. Blend the remaining ingredients and pour over the chicken mixture, then cook for 2–3 minutes. Serve in a bowl, with rice or noodles.

Pollo cacciatore

1.5-kg *(3¼-lb)* **oven-ready chicken**
45 ml *(3 tbsps)* **oil**
25 g *(1 oz)* **butter**
225 g *(½ lb)* **onions, skinned and sliced**
1 clove garlic, skinned and crushed
396-g *(14-oz)* **can tomatoes**
30 ml *(2 tbsps)* **chopped parsley**
1.25 ml *(¼ level tsp)* **dried basil**
2.5 ml *(½ level tsp)* **salt**
freshly ground pepper
150 ml *(¼ pt)* **red wine**
chopped parsley to garnish

Remove and discard the skin from the chicken. Divide the chicken into 8 portions. Heat the oil and butter in a large saucepan. Fry the chicken a few pieces at a time until golden brown all over; remove from the pan when brown, then fry the remaining pieces. Add the onion to the pan and fry until golden brown. Add the garlic, tomatoes, parsley, basil, salt and pepper and bring to the boil. Return the chicken joints to the pan, add the wine, bring to the boil, cover, then reduce the heat and simmer for 40–45 minutes, until the chicken is tender. Serve sprinkled with chopped parsley.

Chicken with oysters

1.4-kg *(3-lb)* **oven-ready chicken, cut into eight joints**
5 ml *(1 level tsp)* **salt**
2.5 ml *(½ level tsp)* **pepper**
100 g *(4 oz)* **butter**
150 g *(¼ pt)* **milk**
1.25 ml *(¼ level tsp)* **dried sage**
225 g *(½ lb)* **shelled oysters, drained**
142-ml *(5-fl oz)* **carton double cream**
2.5 ml *(½ level tsp)* **dried basil**

Sprinkle the chicken with half the salt and pepper. Heat the butter in a large pan and sauté the chicken pieces (uncovered) for 10 minutes, turning them once. Put into an ovenproof dish, pour the milk over the top and sprinkle with the rest of the salt and pepper, and the sage. Cover with a lid or aluminium foil and bake in the oven at 190°C *(375°F)* mark 5 for 1¼ hours. Uncover the dish, add the oysters, cream and basil, cover and bake for a further 15 minutes or until the sauce is hot. Serve in soup plates, with a fork and spoon. *Serves 6.*

Mexican chicken

1.4-kg *(3-lb)* oven-ready chicken
30 ml *(2 level tbsps)* seasoned flour
60 ml *(4 tbsps)* oil
1 medium sized onion, skinned and chopped
396-g *(14-oz)* can tomatoes
mole, if available–see note
170-g *(6 oz)* can pimientos, drained
2 chicken stock cubes
8 stuffed olives
175 g *(6 oz)* long grain rice
salt and pepper
225 g *(½ lb)* pork chipolata sausages
113-g *(4-oz)* pkt frozen peas
small whole tomatoes or watercress for garnish

Cut the chicken into 8 pieces and toss in seasoned flour, coating well. Heat the oil in a large saucepan, brown the chicken well, drain and set aside. Add the onion to the pan and brown it. Drain the tomatoes and make the juice up to 400 ml *(¾ pt)* with water. To the saucepan add the tomato juice, mole, pimientos, crumbled stock cubes, olives, rice, seasoning and sausages, cut into 1-cm *(½-in)* slices. Mix well. Arrange the chicken joints on top. Cover and simmer for 30 minutes, occasionally lifting the rice with a fork to prevent sticking. Add the peas and simmer for a further 15 minutes, or until the chicken is tender. Serve garnished with small whole baked or grilled tomatoes or watercress.

Note Mole, the Mexican chili sauce which is the traditional ingredient for this dish, is available from delicatessen counters.

Braised chicken with mushrooms

1.4-kg *(3-lb)* oven-ready chicken
15 ml *(1 tbsp)* soy sauce
15 dried mushrooms, soaked
1 medium sized bamboo shoot
2 water chestnuts
oil for deep frying
5 slices of fresh ginger
5 ml *(1 level tsp)* salt
900 ml *(1½ pt)* water
2.5 ml *(½ level tsp)* sugar
pinch of pepper
2 onion stalks, cut into 2-cm *(¾-in)* pieces
10 ml *(2 level tsps)* cornflour mixed with 45 ml *(3 tbsps)* water

Cut the chicken in half and rub it inside and out with soy sauce. Slice the mushrooms, bamboo shoot and water chestnuts into shreds. Put about 2 cm *(¾ in)* oil into a deep frying pan and when it is very hot fry the chicken on each side for 2 minutes; drain the chicken and set aside. Drain off the oil. In the oily pan sauté the ginger with the salt for 1 minute; add the water, sliced mushrooms, water chestnuts, bamboo shoot, sugar, pepper and onion stalks. Place the chicken in this mixture, cover, lower the heat and simmer for 30 minutes. Remove the chicken, take out the bones and chop the meat into small pieces and arrange on a serving dish. Stir the blended cornflour into the gravy and when it is clear and thick, pour the whole mixture over the chicken and serve at once.

Chinese chicken and vegetable dish

450 g *(1 lb)* uncooked chicken meat
45 ml *(3 tbsps)* oil
5 ml *(1 level tsp)* salt
30 ml *(2 tbsps)* soy sauce
270-g *(9½-oz)* can bean sprouts, drained
2–3 sticks celery, sliced
50 g *(2 oz)* button mushrooms
100 g *(4 oz)* canned pineapple pieces, drained
150 ml *(¼ pt)* chicken stock
15 ml *(1 level tbsp)* cornflour
salt and pepper
50 g *(2 oz)* flaked almonds, toasted

Cut the chicken meat into 2.5-cm *(1-in)* cubes. Heat the oil in a large frying pan and add the chicken and salt. Sauté for 3–5 minutes. Add the soy sauce and blend well. Add the bean sprouts, celery, mushrooms, pineapple and stock; cover, and simmer for 15 minutes. Blend the cornflour with a little water and stir into the chicken. Bring slowly to the boil, stirring. Season to taste and sprinkle with the toasted almonds. Serve with plain boiled rice. *Serves 3–4.*

GUINEA FOWL

These are available all the year round, but are at their best from February to June. A guinea fowl has grey plumage and white spots and is usually of about the same size as a pheasant, though it can be as large as a small chicken. When choosing one, look out for the same points as in a fresh chicken, especially a plump breast and smooth-skinned feet. An average-sized bird will serve 4 people.

Guinea fowl needs to be hung for some time after killing. All methods for cooking chicken or pheasant (see pages 175 to 176) are applicable, especially braising or casserolling, but take care to use plenty of fat when roasting it, otherwise the flesh will be dry.

Roast guinea fowl

Singe, draw and wipe the bird and truss it for roasting (see page 152). Roast in the oven at 200°C *(400°F)* mark 6 for 45–60 minutes, or longer according to size, basting frequently with butter or dripping. Garnish with watercress and serve with thin gravy and orange or mixed green salad or with bread sauce.

Casserole of Guinea Fowl, Salmi Of Guinea Fowl

Cook as for casserole of pheasant and salmi of partridges respectively (page 175).

DUCK

The name 'duckling' applies to a bird between 6 weeks and 3 months old. Ducklings are more commonly eaten than fully grown ducks.

Choose a young bird with soft, pliable feet; the feet and the bill should be yellow. It should weigh at least 1.5 kg *(3 lb)* otherwise the proportion of bone is too high. Allow about 450 g *(1 lb)* dressed weight per person.

Roast duck

Pluck, draw and truss as for chicken (see page 152), but do not draw the wings across the back; tie the legs with fine string.

A young duckling does not require stuffing, but it is usual to stuff an older bird with sage and onion stuffing at the tail end. Sprinkle the breast with salt and pepper. Cook in the oven at 190°C *(375°F)* mark 5, allowing 30 minutes per 450 g *(1 lb)*. Remove the trussing strings and skewers; serve the bird garnished with watercress and accompanied by apple sauce, potatoes, peas and thin brown gravy. Orange salad is also a favourite accompaniment for roast duck.

Wild Duck See page 178.

Duck with cherries *see colour plate facing p. 256*

1 roasting duck
knob of butter
salt
300 ml *(½ pt)* stock
1 orange
3–4 sugar lumps
40 g *(1½ oz)* caster sugar
1 wineglass port
450 g *(1 lb)* red cherries, stoned
600 ml *(1 pt)* espagnole sauce (see page 198) or good gravy

Rub the breast of the duck with the butter and sprinkle with salt. Put the duck in the roasting tin with the stock and cook in the oven at 190°C *(375°F)* mark 5 for 30 minutes per 450 g *(1 lb)*, basting occasionally with the liquid. Meanwhile, rub the skin of the orange with the sugar lumps to obtain the zest and put the lumps in a pan with the caster sugar and the port. Squeeze the orange and add the juice to the sugar in the pan; allow the sugar to dissolve slowly, add the cherries, cover and simmer gently for about 5 minutes.

The duck should still be slightly pink when cooked; remove it from the oven and leave whole or joint. Place the duck on a serving dish and keep hot. Strain the syrup from the cherries and keep the fruit hot. Add the syrup to the espagnole sauce and spoon some of the mixture over the duck. Arrange the cherries on the serving dish and serve the sauce separately.

Duck with apricots *see colour plate between pp. 528 and 529*

see colour plate between pp. 528 and 529

1 duck, about 2.3–2.6 kg *(5–6 lb)*, oven-ready weight
100 g *(4 oz)* dried apricots
grated rind and juice of 1 orange
150 ml *(¼ pt)* water
1 onion, skinned and finely chopped
40 g *(1½ oz)* flour
400 ml *(¾ pt)* stock
30 ml *(2 level tbsps)* demerara sugar
salt and pepper
425-g *(15-oz)* can apricot halves
60 ml *(4 tbsps)* brandy
25 g *(1 oz)* walnuts, chopped

Roast the duck in the oven at 190°C *(375°F)* mark 5 for 30 minutes per 450 g *(1 lb)*, basting occasionally. Meanwhile, gently stew the dried apricots in the orange juice with the rind and water for 20 minutes until soft; purée in an electric blender or sieve. Remove the cooked duck from the roasting tin, joint it and place the pieces in a casserole. Drain the excess fat from the tin and fry the onion until just coloured. Add the flour and continue cooking, stirring, for 3 minutes. Gradually add the stock, apricot purée and sugar; boil for 2–3 minutes stirring. Season to taste and pour over duck.

Heat the apricot halves with their juice and the brandy in a saucepan, drain and serve on top of the duck. Top with chopped walnuts. *Serves 6.*

Duck in red wine

1 oven-ready duck, about 2.3–2.6 kg *(5–6 lb)*
½ clove garlic, skinned and crushed
50 g *(2 oz)* flour
400 ml *(¾ pt)* red wine
50 g *(2 oz)* mushrooms, sliced
bayleaf
sprigs of parsley
2.5 ml *(½ level tsp)* dried thyme
5 ml *(1 level tsp)* salt
450 g *(1 lb)* small onions, skinned
450 g *(1 lb)* small carrots, scraped

Remove the skin and fat from the duck and put them with the giblets into a pan; cover with water and simmer for 1 hour. Skim off the fat from the surface and let the stock cool. Cut the duck into joints. Heat 30 ml *(2 tbsps)* of the duck fat in a pan, then brown the duck joints on all sides. Remove them from the fat and put in a casserole. Add the crushed garlic to the fat, fry for 1 minute and stir in the flour. Add the stock, wine, mushrooms, herbs and salt. Bring to the boil, stirring constantly until the sauce thickens. Put the onions and carrots into the casserole, pour the sauce over, cover and cook in the oven at 180°C *(350°F)* mark 4 for about 1 hour, until tender. *Serves 4–6.*

Duck with bigarade sauce

1 roasting duck
knob of butter
salt and pepper
150 ml *(¼ pt)* white wine
4 oranges (use bitter oranges when available)
1 lemon
15 ml *(1 level tbsp)* sugar
15 ml *(1 tbsp)* vinegar
30 ml *(2 tbsps)* brandy
15 ml *(1 level tbsp)* cornflour
1 bunch watercress

Rub the breast of the duck with the butter and sprinkle with salt. Put the duck in the roasting tin with the wine and cook in the oven at 190°C *(375°F)* mark 5 for 30 minutes per 450 g *(1 lb)*, basting occasionally with the wine. Squeeze the juice from 3 of the oranges and the lemon and grate the rind from 1 orange. Melt the sugar in a pan with the vinegar and heat until it is a dark brown caramel. Add the brandy and the juice of the oranges and lemon to the caramel and simmer gently for 5 minutes. Cut the remaining orange into segments.

When the duck is cooked, remove it from the roasting tin, joint it and place the pieces on a serving dish. Drain the excess fat from the roasting tin and add the grated rind and the orange sauce to the sediment. Blend the cornflour with a little water, stir it into the pan juices, return the tin to the heat, bring to the boil and cook for 2–3 minutes, stirring. Season and pour the sauce over the joints. Garnish with orange wedges and watercress.

Duck and orange casserole

1 duck, jointed
seasoned flour
knob of fat
100 g *(¼ lb)* mushrooms, sliced
2 onions, skinned and chopped
25–50 g *(1–2 oz)* flour
400 ml *(¾ pt)* stock
150 ml *(¼ pt)* orange juice
1 orange

Coat the duck joints with the seasoned flour. Fry the duck in the fat for 8–10 minutes, until well browned, and transfer to a casserole. Fry the mushrooms and onions lightly in the hot fat for about 3 minutes, remove from the pan and add to the casserole. Stir the flour into the remaining fat and brown it over a very low heat, stirring all the time. Remove from the heat, gradually stir in the stock and orange juice and bring to the boil; continue to stir until it thickens. Pour over the duck, cover and cook in the oven at 180°C *(350°F)* mark 4 for 1 hour, until the duck is tender.

Pare off the coloured part of the orange rind with a vegetable peeler and cut it into very thin strips. Divide the orange itself into segments, removing any pith or pips. Simmer the strips of rind in water until tender – about 5 minutes; drain well and sprinkle over the cooked duck joints. Garnish with the orange segments before serving.

GOOSE

Geese are available all the year round, but are at their best from December to March. A 4.5-kg *(10-lb)* oven-ready bird will serve 7–8 people.

A young bird, which has more tender flesh, is recognised by soft, yellow feet and a yellow bill; the fat should be yellow and the flesh pinkish in colour.

Preparation and trussing

Pluck the bird (see page 152) and remove the stumps from the wings. Cut off the feet and the wing tips at the first joint. Cut off the head, then, forcing back the neck skin, cut off the neck where it joins the back. Draw the bird as described for other poultry and clean the inside with a cloth wrung out in hot water. Put a thick fold of cloth over the breast-bone and flatten it with a mallet or rolling pin. Stuff with sage and onion stuffing or a fruit stuffing. (See pages 183 to 186.)

Working with the breast side uppermost and tail end away from you, pass a skewer through one wing, then through the body and out again through the other wing. Pass a second skewer through the end of the wing joint on one side, through the thick part of the leg, through the body and out the other side in the same way. Pass a third skewer through the loose skin near the end of the leg through the body and out the other side in the same way.

Enlarge the vent, pass the tail through it and fix with a small skewer. Wind string round the skewers, keeping the limbs firmly in position, but avoid passing the string over the breast of the goose. Tuck the neck skin in under the string.

Roast goose

Sprinkle the bird with salt, put in a baking tin on a rack or trivet (as goose tends to be fatty) and cover with the fat taken from inside, then with greased paper. A sour apple put in the roasting tin during the cooking adds flavour to the gravy.

To cook by the fast method, roast at 200°C *(400°F)* mark 6 for 15 minutes per 450 g *(1 lb)* plus 15 minutes, basting frequently. To cook by the slow method, roast at 180°C *(350°F)* mark 4 for 25–30 minutes per 450 g *(1 lb)*. Remove the paper for the last 30 minutes, to brown the bird.

Serve with giblet gravy (made in the roasting tin after the fat has been poured off) and apple or gooseberry sauce (pages 201, 202). Apple rings which have been dipped in lemon juice, brushed with oil and lightly grilled also make an attractive garnish.

Salmi of goose

Cook as for salmi of partridge, page 175.

TURKEY

Turkeys are now available all the year round, but are of course especially abundant at Christmas time.

Choose a bird that is plump and white-fleshed; short spurs and smooth black legs are signs that it is young.

A 4.5–5.9-kg *(10–13-lb)* oven-ready turkey will serve 13–15 people.

A 7.3–9-kg *(16–20-lb)* oven-ready turkey will serve 20–30 people.

An oven-ready turkey of 4 kg *(9 lb)* is equivalent to one of 5.4 kg *(12 lb)* undressed weight.

For general preparation, see pages 152 to 153.

Frozen turkeys

These should first be allowed to thaw out completely, preferably slowly (see page 476).

Roast turkey

It is usual to stuff the neck end of a turkey with veal forcemeat or chestnut stuffing; allow 450 g *(1 lb)* made stuffing for a bird of up to 6.3 kg *(14 lb)*; twice this amount for a larger bird. For the body cavity, sausage meat or sausage stuffing is generally used – allow 450–900 g *(1–2 lb)*, according to size. (Recipes will be found on pages 183 to 186.)

Make the turkey as plump and even in shape as possible, then truss it with the wings folded under the body and the legs tied together. Before cooking the bird, spread it with softened dripping or butter; the breast may also be covered with strips of fat bacon. If you are going to cook it by the quick method (see below) it is best to wrap the bird in aluminium foil to prevent the flesh drying and the skin hardening. Foil is not recommended for the slow method of cooking, as it tends to give a steamed rather than a roast bird.

For the slow method roast at 170°C *(325°F)* mark 3; for the quick method cook at 230°C *(450°F)* mark 8, calculating the time according to the chart below. Calculate to be ready 30 minutes before serving. If the turkey is cooked, lower the heat and keep the bird hot. If not, continue cooking. Unless the bird is cooked in foil, baste it regularly, turning it round once to ensure even browning. Foil, if used, should be unwrapped for the last ½ hour, so that the bird may be well basted and then left to become crisp and golden.

Garnish and accompaniments

Small sausages, forcemeat balls (see page 183), rolls of bacon and watercress may be used to garnish the turkey. Serve it with brown gravy and bread sauce. Cranberry or some other sharp sauce can also be served. Sliced tongue or ham is a favourite accompaniment.

Weight	*Hours-slow method*	*Hours-quick method*
2.7–3.6 kg *(6–8 lb)*	3–3½	2¼–2½
3.6–4.5 kg *(8–10 lb)*	3½–3¾	2½–2¾
4.5–5.4 kg *(10–12 lb)*	3¾–4	2¾
5.4–6.3 kg *(12–14 lb)*	4–4¼	3
6.3–7.3 kg *(14–16 lb)*	4¼–4½	3–3¼
7.3–8.2 kg *(16–18 lb)*	4½–4¾	3¼–3½
9–10 kg *(20–22 lb)*	4¾–5	3½–3¾

Devilled turkey drumsticks

Cut the drumsticks from a cooked turkey. (Other fair-sized portions can be used in the same way.) Score with a sharp knife, then brush with melted butter. To prepare the devilled mixture, mix on a plate 5 ml *(1 level tsp)* each of French and English mustard, 10 ml *(2 tsps)* finely chopped chutney, a pinch of ground ginger and a little pepper, salt and cayenne. Spread this mixture over and into the cuts and leave the turkey legs for 1 hour or longer. Grill them on a greased grid under a medium heat until crisp and brown, turning them regularly to ensure even cooking. Serve garnished with watercress.

Blanquette of turkey

225 g *(½ lb)* cooked turkey
1 medium sized onion, skinned and chopped
40 g *(1½ oz)* butter
45 ml *(3 level tbsps)* flour
400 ml *(¾ pt)* chicken stock
salt and pepper
pinch of mace
1 egg yolk
30 ml *(2 tbsps)* cream
10 ml *(2 tsps)* lemon juice

Remove all the skin and bone from the turkey meat and cut it into cubes. Cook the onion lightly in the butter for 5 minutes without colouring; stir in the flour and cook for a further 2–3 minutes. Gradually stir in the stock, bring to the boil and continue stirring until it thickens. Add the turkey meat, season well, add the mace and heat the turkey thoroughly. Remove the sauce from the heat. Blend the egg yolk, cream and lemon juice to a smooth cream; stir in a little of the sauce, return the blended mixture to the pan and reheat without boiling. Turn the blanquette into a serving dish and serve with small triangles of fresh toast. *Serves 2.*

Turkey fricassee

See chicken fricassee, page 158.

Turkey à la king

See chicken à la king, page 159.

Turkey cacciatora

1 small onion, skinned and chopped
1 clove garlic, skinned and chopped
1 carrot, pared and thinly sliced
1 bayleaf
olive or cooking oil
120-g *(4½-oz)* can tomato juice
salt and pepper
225 g *(½ lb)* cooked turkey, cut in cubes
15 ml *(1 level tbsp)* flour
pinch of dried basil and pinch of ground allspice, mixed
30 ml *(2 tbsps)* red wine
112-g *(4-oz)* pkt frozen peas

A delicious way of using up turkey left overs.

Cook the onion, garlic, carrot and bayleaf in 30 ml *(2 tbsps)* oil for about 10 minutes. Add the tomato juice and season with salt and pepper, then simmer for 20 minutes. Remove the bayleaf. Coat the cubed turkey with flour, basil and allspice. Fry it gently in a little more oil. Pour the tomato sauce over the turkey, add the wine and peas and simmer for 10 minutes. Serve poured over a bed of cooked macaroni. *Serves 2.*

Game

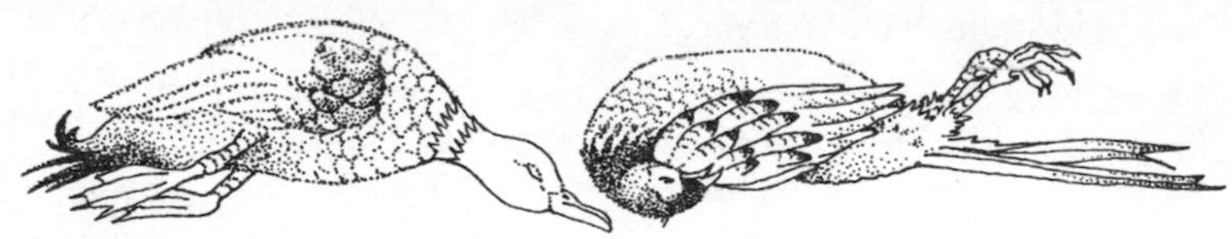

Game is a name given to wild birds and animals which are hunted and killed for food, but which at certain times of the year are protected by law. For the sake of convenience we also deal in this chapter with pigeons (though strictly speaking only wood or wild pigeons count as game) and with rabbits, since they so closely resemble hares from the cookery point of view.

Game seasons

We give here the period when the bird or animal is most likely to be available in the shops.

Rabbits, pigeons not protected, sold all the year.

Black Grouse (Capercaillie, Blackgame) August 20th – December 20th (September 1st – December 20th Somerset, Devon, New Forest)

Duck, Wild August – February

Scottish Grouse August 12th – December 10th

Ptarmigan (Mountain Grouse) August 20th – December 10th

Partridge September 1st – February 1st

Pheasant October 1st – January 31st (England) October 1st – December 10th (Scotland)

Plover August 20th – December 10th

Quail All year, best June – September

Snipe August 12th – December 20th

Mallard September 1st – January 31st

Teal September 1st – December 20th

Wild Goose November – December

Woodcock October 1st – December 20th

Hare August 1st to end February

Venison All year; at its best October – March

Game birds

Buying game and other birds

Try to choose a young bird. The plumage is a guide, as all young birds have soft even feathers. With pheasants and partridge, the long wing feathers are V-shaped in a young bird, as distinct from the rounded ones of an older bird. Smooth, pliable legs, short spurs and a firm, plump breast are other points to look for. Ask whether the bird has been hung (see below), as some poulterers do this.

Hanging and preparations

All game birds need to be hung up by the neck, without being plucked or drawn, before being cooked, or the flesh will be tough and tasteless. The time for hanging depends on the weather and on your taste, varying from a week in 'muggy' weather to 2 – 3 weeks in frosty weather. Four days is usually long enough for partridge.

Keep the bird in a cold, dry, airy place and examine it from time to time, especially any that has been shattered when shot, or has got wet, or has been packed up for any length of time before hanging, as such birds do not keep so well. For most people the bird is sufficiently mature when the tail or breast feathers will pluck out easily. With a pheasant, the flesh on the breast begins to change colour and the bird smells 'gamey'. Pluck, draw and truss the bird as for poultry (see page 152), but leave the feet on and don't draw the sinews from the legs. Some birds, such as snipe, have the head left on and are not drawn before being roasted – see the individual recipes. The larger birds may be jointed like a chicken before being cooked.

Cooking

Generally speaking, the more simply game is cooked, the better. For a young bird, there is no better way than roasting, but for older birds, which are likely to be tough if plainly roasted, braising or casseroling is a better method.

Game birds lack fat, so it is usual to cover the breast before roasting with pieces of fat bacon (this is called 'barding') and to baste frequently with butter or margarine during the cooking. When the bird is nearly cooked, the bacon can be removed; the breast is then dredged with flour and basted (this is called 'frothing') in order to brown it. Sometimes a knob of butter or a piece of juicy steak is put inside the bird before roasting.

Accompaniments

Thin gravy Served with roast game. To make it, add 150 ml (*¼ pt*) water or meat stock to the roasting tin and with a spoon rub down any cooking juices left in the tin; bring to the boil and boil for 2–3 minutes. Remove all grease from the surface with a metal spoon, season to taste and strain before serving.

Fried crumbs Fry 50–100 g *(2–4 oz)* fresh white breadcrumbs in 25 g *(1 oz)* butter until golden brown. Stir from time to time to ensure even browning.

Game chips See page 224.

Carving game
A pheasant or other game bird, if large, is carved in the same general manner as a chicken. Partridges, pigeons and birds of similar size are usually cut in half. If very small, the whole bird may be served as one portion; woodcock, snipe and quail are among the birds which are served whole, on the toast on which they were cooked. Special poultry shears are available for cutting birds in half; failing these, use the game carver or a short, pointed kitchen knife, by inserting the point of the knife in the neck end of the breast and cutting firmly through the bird in the direction of the breast-bone and tail.

Roast grouse

After hanging, pluck, draw and truss the bird, season inside and out and lay some fat bacon over the breast. Put a knob of butter inside the bird and place it on a slice of toast. Roast in the oven at 200°C *(400°F)* mark 6 for 40 minutes, basting frequently. After 30 minutes, remove the bacon, dredge the breast with flour and baste well.

Remove the trussing strings before serving the bird on the toast on which it was roasted. Garnish with watercress and serve with thin gravy, bread sauce, fried crumbs and matchstick potatoes. A lettuce or watercress salad may also be served. *Serves 1–2.*

Roast partridge

Select a young bird; pluck, draw and truss it, season the inside with pepper and salt, replace the liver and add a knob of butter. Cover the breast with pieces of fat bacon. Roast the bird in the oven at 230°C *(450°F)* mark 8 for 10 minutes, then reduce the temperature to 200°C *(400°F)* mark 6 and roast for a further 20–30 minutes, according to size; partridge must be well done. Baste frequently during cooking.

The usual accompaniments are fried crumbs or game chips and a tossed salad, or bread sauce, or orange sauce. A garnish of lemon quarters and watercress (seasoned and sprinkled with a few drops of vinegar) is often added. *Serves 1–2.*

Partridge with cabbage

2 partridges, plucked, drawn and trussed
butter or bacon fat
1 firm cabbage
175 g *(6 oz)* streaky bacon, rinded
salt and pepper
1 carrot, pared and roughly chopped
1 onion, skinned
2–3 cloves
bouquet garni
boiling stock
smoked sausages, optional

This is one of the best ways of serving old partridges; the red-legged type can be cooked very well in this manner. Fry the partridges in butter or bacon fat until golden brown. Cut the cabbage in quarters, removing the outside leaves and any hard pieces of stalk, wash it well, cook for 5 minutes in boiling salted water, then drain. Line a casserole with the bacon and lay half the cabbage over it, with seasoning to taste. Put the partridges on the top, with the carrot, onion stuck with the cloves and the bouquet garni; add the rest of the cabbage and more seasoning. Cover with stock, put on a lid and cook in the oven at 180°C *(350°F)* mark 4 for 1–1½ hours, or until the birds are tender.

As a variation, 1–2 lightly fried smoked sausages are sometimes added to the casserole before it is put into the oven. To serve, remove the partridges, bacon and sausages (if used) from the casserole, cut the birds into neat joints and the sausages into pieces; remove the carrot, onion and bouquet garni and cut the cabbage in shreds with a sharp knife. Serve the cabbage with the pieces of partridge on top of it and the bacon and sausage around.

Casserole of partridge

2 medium sized onions, skinned and sliced
2 sticks of celery, trimmed and sliced
100 g *(4 oz)* mushrooms, sliced
100 g *(4 oz)* bacon, rinded and chopped
15 ml *(1 tbsp)* cooking oil
25 g *(1 oz)* butter
2 partridges, plucked, drawn and jointed
45 ml *(3 level tbsps)* flour
400 ml *(¾ pt)* stock
396-g *(14-oz)* can tomatoes
salt and pepper
150 ml *(¼ pt)* red wine

Fry the onions, celery, mushrooms and bacon in the oil and butter for about 5 minutes, until golden brown. Remove from the pan with a slotted spoon and line the bottom of a casserole with them. Fry the partridge joints in the oil and butter for about 5 minutes, until golden brown. Remove from the pan with the slotted spoon and put in the casserole on the bed of vegetables. Stir the flour into the fat remaining in the pan and cook for 2–3 minutes. Gradually stir in the stock, bring to the boil and continue to stir until it thickens. Add the tomatoes, salt, pepper and wine, pour the sauce over the partridge joints, cover and cook in the oven at 180°C *(350°F)* mark 4 for 1 hour, until the partridge joints are tender.

Salmi of partridge

2 partridges, lightly roasted
1 shallot, skinned and chopped
1 orange, peeled and sectioned
150 ml *(¼ pt)* stock
300 ml *(½ pt)* espagnole sauce
150 ml *(¼ pt)* red wine
few white grapes, skinned and pipped
red-currant jelly

Remove the skin from the partridges; cut off the leg and wing joints and put aside. Break the carcasses into small pieces and put in a pan with the shallot, thinly pared orange rind and stock. Simmer together for ½ hour. Strain the stock from the pan, put it with the espagnole sauce, wine and partridge joints into a saucepan and simmer until the joints are heated through – about 10 minutes. Arrange the joints on a serving dish and boil the sauce until it is reduced to a syrupy consistency. Pour it over the partridges and garnish with the grapes and sections of orange. Serve with red-currant jelly.

Roast pheasant *see colour plate between pp. 144 and 145*

Pheasant requires to be well hung, otherwise the flesh is dry and tasteless; it needs on an average 10–11 days – rather less should the weather be 'muggy', up to 3 weeks if frosty.

Pluck, draw and truss the bird and cover the breast with strips of fat bacon. Roast in the oven at 230°C *(450°F)* mark 8 for 10 minutes, then reduce the temperature to 200°C *(400°F)* mark 6 and continue cooking for 30–40 minutes, according to the size of the bird, basting frequently with butter. About 15 minutes before the cooking is completed, remove the bacon, dredge the breast of the bird with flour, baste well and finish cooking. Remove the trussing strings, put the pheasant on a hot dish and garnish with watercress. Serve with thin gravy, bread sauce, fried crumbs and chipped potatoes; a tossed green salad may also be served. *Serves 2–3.*

Casserole of pheasant

1 pheasant, plucked, drawn and jointed
15 ml *(1 tbsp)* oil
25 g *(1 oz)* butter
100 g *(4 oz)* mushrooms, sliced
50 g *(2 oz)* flour
300 ml *(½ pt)* chicken stock
150 ml *(¼ pt)* orange juice
150 ml *(¼ pt)* very dry white wine
1 orange

Fry the pheasant on both sides in the oil and butter for 5–6 minutes, until well browned. Remove from the pan with a slotted spoon and transfer to a 1.1-l *(2-pt)* casserole. Fry the mushrooms lightly for 4–5 minutes, remove from the pan with a slotted spoon and add to the casserole. Stir the flour into the fat remaining in the pan and cook for 2–3 minutes. Remove the pan from the heat and gradually pour in the stock, orange juice and white wine; bring to the boil, stirring until it thickens, and pour into the casserole. Cook for 1 hour in the oven at 180°C *(350°F)* mark 4 until the pheasant is tender.

Meanwhile peel the zest from the orange with a vegetable peeler and cut it into thin strips with a sharp knife. Divide the orange itself into segments. Simmer the strips of rind in water until they are soft and sprinkle over the casserole before serving. Garnish with the orange segments.

Pheasant à l'américaine

1 young pheasant
50 g *(2 oz)* butter, melted
salt and pepper
100 g *(4 oz)* fresh breadcrumbs
cayenne pepper
4 thin rashers of bacon, rinded
4 tomatoes, halved
100 g *(4 oz)* button mushrooms
bunch of watercress, washed

Slit the pheasant down the back and flatten it; brush it with melted butter and dust with salt and pepper. Grill lightly for 5 minutes under a medium heat, sprinkle with the breadcrumbs and dust with cayenne. Continue to grill for about 20 minutes, turning the bird frequently. Roll up the rashers of bacon and grill them, with the tomatoes and button mushrooms, for 3–5 minutes, until cooked. Serve the pheasant with the bacon rolls, tomatoes, mushrooms and watercress arranged around it.

Pheasant with chestnuts

1 pheasant, plucked, drawn and jointed
15 ml *(1 tbsp)* olive oil
25 g *(1 oz)* butter
225 g *(½ lb)* chestnuts, peeled
2 medium sized onions, skinned and sliced
45 ml *(3 level tbsps)* flour
400 ml *(¾ pt)* stock
1 wineglass Burgundy
salt and pepper
grated rind and juice of ½ orange
10 ml *(2 tsps)* red-currant jelly
bouquet garni
chopped parsley

Fry the pheasant in the oil and butter for about 5–6 minutes until golden brown. Remove from the pan with a slotted spoon and put in a casserole. Fry the chestnuts and onions in the oil and butter for about 5 minutes, until golden brown, and add to the pheasant. Stir the flour into the remaining fat and cook for 2–3 minutes. Remove the pan from the heat and add the stock and wine gradually; bring to the boil and continue to stir until it thickens. Season and pour over the pheasant. Add the orange rind and juice, red-currant jelly and bouquet garni, cover and cook in the oven at 180°C *(350°F)* mark 4 for 1 hour, until the pheasant is tender. Remove the bouquet garni before serving and adjust the seasoning to taste, if necessary. Sprinkle with chopped parsley.

Salmi of pheasant

Make as for salmi of partridge, substituting 1 pheasant for 2 partridges.

Roast pigeon

Select young birds for roasting. Pluck and draw them, singe if necessary and truss them. Spread with some softened butter and tie a piece of fat bacon over the breasts. Roast in the oven at 230°C *(450°F)* mark 8 for 15–20 minutes, according to size, basting well and removing the bacon before cooking is completed, to allow the breast to brown. Add a garnish of watercress and serve gravy or a sauce separately. If you prefer, the pigeons may be halved before serving. *A pigeon serves 1.*

Pigeons à la française

4 large pigeons
salt and pepper
60 ml *(4 tbsps)* cooking oil
90 ml *(6 tbsps)* dry sherry
175 g *(6 oz)* button onions, skinned
1 lettuce, washed and shredded
454-g *(1-lb)* pkt frozen peas
1.25 ml *(¼ tsp)* mint (not peppermint) essence
knob of butter
10 ml *(2 level tsps)* flour

Halve the pigeons and season with salt and pepper. Fry them in the oil, flesh side down, until golden brown. Drain, and place in a flameproof casserole. Pour the sherry over, add the onions, cover tightly and cook in the oven at 170°C *(325°F)* mark 3 for about 1½ hours. About ½ hour before the end of the time add the lettuce, peas and mint essence. Return the dish to the oven and cook until the peas are tender. Thicken the juices with the butter and flour creamed to a paste and added a little at a time; bring to the boil, stirring. Serve with sauté potatoes and baked tomatoes. Failing mint essence, use minted peas or add a little fresh mint.

Casserole of pigeon

4 pigeons, plucked, drawn and jointed
30–45 ml *(2–3 tbsps)* oil
50 g *(2 oz)* bacon, rinded and chopped
2 carrots, pared and sliced
1 onion, skinned and chopped
45 ml *(3 level tbsps)* flour
600 ml *(1 pt)* chicken stock
15 ml *(1 level tbsp)* tomato paste
salt and pepper

Fry the pigeon joints in the oil for about 5 minutes, until golden brown, remove from the pan with a slotted spoon and put in a casserole. Fry the bacon, carrots and onion in the remaining oil for about 5 minutes, until golden brown. Remove the vegetables from the pan with a slotted spoon and add to the casserole. Stir the flour into the remaining fat in the pan and cook for 2–3 minutes. Remove the pan from the heat and gradually stir in the stock. Bring to the boil, continue to stir until it thickens and add the tomato paste and seasoning. Pour the sauce over the pigeon joints, cover and cook in the oven at 170°C *(325°F)* mark 3 for about 1½ hours, or until the pigeons are tender.

Tipsy pigeons

8 black olives
60 ml *(4 tbsps)* dry sherry
2 pigeons, plucked and drawn
30 ml *(2 tbsps)* oil
1 large onion, skinned and sliced
100 g *(4 oz)* bacon, rinded and chopped
4 slices of garlic sausage
45 ml *(3 level tbsps)* flour
300 ml *(½ pt)* chicken stock
30 ml *(2 tbsps)* brandy
salt and pepper

Marinade the olives in the sherry for 2 hours. Fry the pigeons in the oil until golden brown – about 5 minutes. Remove from the pan with a slotted spoon and put in a casserole. Fry the onion, bacon and garlic sausage in the remaining fat until golden brown – about 5 minutes. Remove from the pan with a slotted spoon and add to the casserole, with the sherry and olives. Stir the flour into the fat remaining in the pan and cook for 2–3 minutes. Gradually stir in the stock, bring to the boil and stir until it thickens. Add the brandy, season and pour the sauce over the pigeons. Cover and cook in the oven at 170°C *(325°F)* mark 3 for 1½ hours, until tender. *Serves 2.*

Quail

Pluck and singe the birds but do not draw, as they are eaten whole. Cut off the head and neck and take out the crop. Place each bird on a round of fried bread and cover the breast with thin rashers of fat bacon. Roast in the oven at 220°C *(425°F)* mark 7 for about 25 minutes, basting with butter. Serve on the bread with the bacon; thin gravy, fried crumbs and chipped potatoes are usual accompaniments. *Allow 1 quail per person.*

Creamed quail casserole

4 quail
seasoned flour
50 g *(2 oz)* butter
100 g *(4 oz)* button mushrooms
60 ml *(4 tbsps)* dry sherry
salt and pepper
150 ml *(¼ pt)* soured cream
chopped parsley

Coat the quail in the seasoned flour. Melt the butter in a flameproof casserole and brown the birds evenly. Add the mushrooms and sauté them, then add the sherry and seasoning. Cover and cook in the oven at 190°C *(375°F)* mark 5 for 40 minutes. Stir in the soured cream, adjust the seasoning and serve sprinkled with chopped parsley.

Capercaillie

A game bird, also called 'Cock o' the wood' or 'Wood grouse'. It is in fact similar to grouse and may be cooked in the same way. *Serves 1.*

Ptarmigan

A small wild bird of the grouse family; it has not such a good flavour as grouse, but may be treated in the same way. *Serves 1.*

Wild geese

These do not make particularly good eating. Cook them as for farmyard geese, but since the flesh is drier, put plenty of fat bacon or lard over the breast.

Wild duck

Hang for a short time only, then pluck, draw and truss like a domestic duck. Spread with softened butter and roast in the oven at 220°C *(425°F)* mark 7, basting frequently. Allow 20 minutes for teal, 30 minutes for mallard and widgeon – they should on no account be over-cooked. After half the cooking time, pour a little port or orange juice over the birds. Garnish with watercress and serve with thin gravy and orange salad or with bigarade sauce (see page 199).
A teal will serve 1–2 people; other wild ducks as a rule will serve 2–3 people.

Woodcock, snipe, plover

Pluck and singe the birds. Don't draw them, but skin the head and neck and remove the eyes before trussing. Cover each bird all over with softened butter, then put it on a round of toast. Cover the breast with rashers of fat bacon and roast in the oven at 190°C *(375°F)* mark 5 for 15–20 minutes. Serve the birds on the toast, garnished with lemon and watercress. Thin gravy, fried crumbs and game chips (or if preferred, a salad) are the usual accompaniments.
Allow 1 bird per person.

Raised game pie

350 g *(¾ lb)* hot-water crust pastry, ie made with 350 g *(¾ lb)* flour etc (see page 355)
350 g *(12 oz)* sausage meat
100 g *(4 oz)* lean ham, cut into small cubes
175 g *(6 oz)* lean chuck steak, cut into small cubes
the meat of 1 cooked pheasant or 2 pigeons, cut into small pieces
salt and pepper
beaten egg
150–300 ml *(¼–½ pt)* stock

Make the pastry and cover it with a basin or a cloth to prevent a skin forming on it. Shape the pie case by hand as described on page 357. (Alternatively use the cake tin method, see below.) Line the base and sides of the pie with sausage meat, to hold the pastry in a good shape. Mix the ham, steak and pheasant or pigeon meat, season well, and fill the pie with the mixture. Put on the lid and finish as described on page 357. Bake in the oven at 220°C *(425°F)* mark 7 for 15–20 minutes, reduce the oven temperature to 180°C *(350°F)* mark 4 and bake for a further 1½ hours, or until the meat is tender when tested with a skewer. If the top of the pie appears to be over-browning, cover it with a piece of greaseproof paper. Remove the pie from the oven and cool. Pour the cold but liquid stock through the hole in the top and leave the pie to get cold. Top up with more stock if necessary.

Cake tin method
If you have an 18-cm *(7-in)* cake tin with a loose base, the pie may be baked in this. Line the tin with three-quarters of the pastry rolled out 0.5 cm *(¼ in)* thick, fill it as above and put on the lid. When the pie has cooked for 1½ hours, remove it from the tin and brush the top and sides with beaten egg. Put it on a baking sheet, and cook for a further 30 minutes, until golden brown.

Game pie

A simple game pie can be made with bottled or canned game, combined with sauce and flavourings as above. Put the game mixture into a pie dish and cover with a 212-g *(7½-oz)* packet of bought puff pastry. Finish and cook as for steak and mushroom pie on page 106.

Rich game casserole

1 can or bottle of pheasant or other game
400 ml *(¾ pt)* espagnole sauce (see page 198)
60 ml *(4 tbsps)* port wine
12 button mushrooms
a little fat
6 glacé cherries

This is a good recipe for use when game is not in season.
Divide the bird into joints and remove the skin. Put the pieces into a heavy, flameproof casserole. Cover with the sauce, wine and mushroom stalks and simmer slowly for about 30 minutes. Sauté the mushroom caps in the fat. Arrange the pieces of game on a hot dish. Strain the sauce, skim off any excess fat and pour the sauce over the joints. Garnish with the sauté mushrooms and the cherries.

VENISON

The meat of the red deer, venison is inclined to be tough. It should be hung for 1–2 weeks, according to the weather, in a cool, airy place and wiped occasionally with a cloth to remove moisture. Test it at intervals by running a skewer through the haunch – as soon as a slight 'high' smell is noticeable, the venison is ready for cooking. The best joints are the saddle, haunch and shoulder. Before cooking they should be marinaded, as the meat tends to be dry. The usual accompaniments are red-currant jelly, braised chestnuts and a port wine sauce.

Marinade for venison

2 carrots, pared and chopped
2 small onions, skinned and chopped
1 stick celery, trimmed and chopped
6 peppercorns
parsley stalks, washed
bayleaf
3 blades mace
red wine

Place the vegetables and flavourings in a large container, put in the venison and add sufficient wine to half-cover it. Leave to soak for 12 hours, turning the meat over in the marinade 2 or 3 times. Remove the meat and cook as desired. Boil the marinade to reduce it by half; strain, and use to make gravy.

Roast venison

The best joint for roasting is the saddle, but for a smaller piece use the loin or a fillet cut from the saddle. To keep the joint as moist as possible, it was traditional to cover the joint with a paste made by mixing flour and water to a stiff dough (allow about 1.4 kg *(3 lb)* flour to a saddle) and rolling it out to 1 cm *(½ in)* thick; nowadays the meat is usually brushed generously with melted fat or oil and loosely wrapped in foil. Roast in the oven at 170°C *(325°F)* mark 3, allowing 25 minutes per 450 g *(1 lb)*; 20 minutes before the cooking is completed, remove the foil or the paste, dredge the joint with flour and return it to the oven to brown. Serve hot, with a thickened gravy and red-currant or cranberry jelly.

Stewed venison

700 g *(1½ lb)* shoulder of venison or other stewing part, cut in 1-cm *(½-in)* cubes
90 ml *(6 level tbsps)* seasoned flour
50 g *(2 oz)* dripping or lard
2 onions, skinned and chopped
2 carrots, pared and sliced
300 ml *(½ pt)* stock
150 ml *(¼ pt)* red wine
salt and pepper
bouquet garni
10 ml *(2 tsps)* vinegar

Toss the meat in the seasoned flour. Fry it in the fat for 8–10 minutes, until well browned, remove from the pan, draining well, and put in a casserole. Fry the vegetables in the fat for about 5 minutes, until golden brown, remove from the pan, again draining well, and put them into the casserole. Stir the rest of the seasoned flour into the fat remaining in the pan and cook slowly until brown. Remove the pan from the heat and gradually stir in stock and wine; bring to the boil and continue stirring until it thickens. Pour the sauce over the venison, season and add the bouquet garni and vinegar. Cover and cook in the oven at 170°C *(325°F)* mark 3 for 2–2½ hours, until the meat is tender. Remove the bouquet garni before serving the venison.

HARES

A hare should be hung by the feet (without being paunched) for 7–10 days, to improve the flavour; it is usually sold already hung, but if you hang it yourself, put a bowl under the nose to collect the blood, which is used to thicken the gravy. In some shops cut joints of hare are sold.

Skinning, paunching and trussing

Cut off the feet at the first joint. Loosen the skin round the back legs. Hold the end of one leg and bend at the joint – the flesh can then be grasped and the skin pulled off. Do the same with the other legs. Draw off the skin from the head, cutting it through at ears and mouth, and cut out the eyes with a sharp knife. Wipe the whole of the body with a clean damp cloth – don't wash it. Place the hare on paper. Using kitchen scissors, snip the skin at the fork and cut it up to the breast-bone; open the paunch by cutting the inside skin in the same direction. Draw out and burn the entrails. Reserve the kidneys. Detach the liver, taking care not to puncture the gall-bladder; cut this out from the liver, keeping it intact, and discard; cut away also the flesh on which it rested, as it may taste bitter.

Cut the diaphragm and draw out the lungs and heart; catch in a basin the blood which will have collected. Discard the lungs, but keep the heart.

Cut the sinews in the hind legs at the thigh, bring the legs forward and press closely against the body. Bend forelegs back in the same way. Fix with 2 fine metal skewers or use a trussing needle and string.

Jointing

Remove the legs. Cut the back into several pieces, giving the back of the knife a sharp tap with a hammer to cut through the bone. Cut off the head and cut the ribs in two lengthwise. (The head, split in two, may be included in a stew.)

Roast hare

Very young hares may be roasted whole, but for larger hares the body alone is used, being known as saddle or baron of hare. Cut off the saddle close to the shoulders (reserve the rest of the hare to jug or make into soup). Prepare some veal forcemeat (see page 183). If you wish, the heart, liver and kidneys may be added to the forcemeat; wash them well, put into a pan of cold water, bring to boiling point, strain and chop finely. Stuff the hare, fold the skin over and sew in position. Lay slices of fat bacon over the back, cover with greased greaseproof paper, put in a tin with some knobs of dripping and roast in the oven at 180°C *(350°F)* mark 4 for 1½–2 hours, according to size. Baste frequently, as the flesh is apt to be dry. Fifteen minutes before the cooking is completed, remove the paper and bacon, baste the hare and allow to brown. Remove the skewers and string before dishing up. Serve with thick gravy and red-currant or guava jelly.

Jugged hare

1 hare
50 g *(2 oz)* bacon, rinded and chopped
25 g *(1 oz)* lard or dripping
1 onion, skinned and stuck with 2 cloves
1 carrot, pared and sliced
1 stick celery, trimmed and sliced
900 ml *(1½ pt)* stock
bouquet garni
juice of ½ lemon
45 ml *(3 level tbsps)* flour
15 ml *(1 tbsp)* red-currant jelly
150 ml *(¼ pt)* port or red wine, optional
salt and pepper

Prepare the hare as described, retaining the blood; wipe and joint. Fry the joints with the bacon in the lard until they are lightly browned (about 5 minutes). Transfer to a deep casserole and add the vegetables, enough stock to cover the joints, the bouquet garni and lemon juice. Cover and cook in the oven at 170°C *(325°F)* mark 3 for 3–4 hours, or until tender.

A few minutes before serving, blend the flour with a little cold water to a smooth cream, stir in the blood of the hare and add to the casserole, with the jelly and wine (if used). Adjust seasoning. Reheat without boiling and serve with red-currant jelly and forcemeat balls (see page 183).

RABBITS

Rabbits, both fresh and frozen, are usually sold cleaned and skinned; otherwise, you should follow the directions given for hares. The paunching should be done within a few hours of killing.

Rabbits may be cooked in almost any way suitable for other types of meat, especially hares, though only very young ones should be roasted or fried. They can be fricasseed, braised or made into a pie.

To make the flavour of a rabbit less strong, wash it and soak in salted water for 1–2 hours before it is cut up and cooked.

Fricassee of rabbit

1 rabbit, jointed
1 large onion, skinned and stuck with 3 cloves
100 g *(¼ lb)* bacon, rinded and chopped
bouquet garni
600 ml *(1 pt)* stock
25 g *(1 oz)* butter
45 ml *(3 level tbsps)* flour
2 onions, skinned and sliced
150 ml *(¼ pt)* white wine
2 egg yolks
salt and pepper
grated nutmeg
sliced lemon and toast squares

Place the rabbit joints in a saucepan with the large onion, bacon and bouquet garni; add the stock and simmer for about 45 minutes. Melt the butter, add the flour and cook for 2–3 minutes. Strain the stock from the rabbit and stir gradually into the flour; bring to the boil and continue to stir till it thickens. Add the rabbit, bacon and sliced onions and simmer until the onions are soft – about 30 minutes. Blend the wine and egg yolks together to a smooth cream, add a little of the sauce and return the blended mixture to the pan; add salt, pepper and a little grated nutmeg and allow to heat through, but do not boil. Place the rabbit joints on a serving dish and pour the sauce over them. Garnish with lemon slices and small squares of toast or border with rice.

Poacher's pie *see colour plate facing p. 144*

200 g *(7 oz)* shortcrust pastry, ie made with 200 g *(7 oz)* flour etc (see page 351)
4 rabbit joints, chopped
2 potatoes, peeled
1 leek, trimmed and washed
3–4 rashers bacon, rinded and chopped
salt and pepper
15 ml *(1 tbsp)* chopped parsley
1.25 ml *(¼ level tsp)* mixed dried herbs
stock or water
beaten egg to glaze

Make the pastry. Wash the rabbit pieces; slice the potatoes and leek. Fill a pie dish with alternate layers of rabbit, bacon and vegetables, sprinkling each layer with seasoning and herbs. Half-fill the dish with stock or water, cover with the pastry and make a hole in the centre to let the steam escape. Decorate with leaves made from the pastry trimmings and brush with egg. Bake in the oven at 220°C *(425°F)* mark 7 until the pastry is set, then reduce the temperature to 170°C *(325°F)* mark 3 and cook for about 1¼ hours, until the meat is tender.
Note This recipe may be used for individual pies if you prefer.

Sweet-sour rabbit with prunes

1-kg *(2¼-lb)* prepared rabbit, jointed
300 ml *(½ pt)* dry white wine
175 g *(6 oz)* onions, skinned and sliced
300 ml *(½ pt)* chicken stock
1 bayleaf
30 ml *(2 tbsps)* red-currant jelly
a few peppercorns
8 whole prunes, stoned
50 g *(2 oz)* seedless raisins
15 ml *(1 tbsp)* malt vinegar
cornflour
salt and freshly ground black pepper
chopped parsley and fried almonds for garnish

Marinade the cleaned and jointed rabbit overnight in the wine with the onions. Discard the onions, place the rabbit and wine in a flameproof casserole and add the chicken stock, bayleaf, red-currant jelly and a few peppercorns; bring to the boil. Submerge the prunes and raisins in the liquor, cover the casserole tightly and cook in the oven at 170°C *(325°F)* mark 3 for about 1½ hours, until the rabbit is really tender and the prunes plump.

Remove the meat and discard the bones. Strain the liquor into a clean pan retaining the prunes and raisins; add the vinegar, blended with 10 ml *(2 level tsps)* cornflour, adjust the seasoning and boil for 1–2 minutes. Arrange the rabbit, prunes and raisins in a clean hot casserole and pour the thickened juices over. Garnish with parsley and fried almonds.
Note If you wish, discard the raisins before serving.

Rabbit hot-pot

1 rabbit
45 ml *(3 level tbsps)* seasoned flour
2–3 medium sized onions, skinned and sliced
450 g *(1 lb)* potatoes, peeled
chopped parsley
stock or water

Wash and joint the rabbit, dry, then toss the pieces in seasoned flour. Slice the onions and cut the potatoes into quarters or eighths, according to size. Place a layer of onions in a large casserole, put the rabbit on top, sprinkle liberally with chopped parsley and cover with onion and potato. Add the liquid, nearly covering the rabbit, cover the dish and bake in the oven at 170°C *(325°F)* mark 3 for 2–2½ hours. Remove the cover a short time before serving, to brown the potatoes.

Rabbit stew

1-kg *(2¼-lb)* rabbit, jointed
10 ml *(2 level tsps)* salt
5 ml *(1 level tsp)* pepper
50 g *(2 oz)* butter or margarine
1 onion, skimmed and sliced
300 ml *(½ pt)* chicken stock
150 ml *(¼ pt)* white wine
150 ml *(¼ pt)* tomato purée
5 ml *(1 level tsp)* sugar
30 ml *(2 level tbsps)* flour
30 ml *(2 tbsps)* chopped parsley

Season the rabbit pieces with some of the salt and pepper and brown in the butter. Add the onion, stock, wine and remaining seasoning and simmer, covered, for ¾–1 hour. Remove the rabbit pieces and onion and keep hot. Stir the tomato purée and sugar into the liquid. Blend the flour with 30 ml *(2 tbsps)* cold water, add to the mixture and cook till thickened. Replace the rabbit and onion and add the parsley, then simmer covered, till heated through. Arrange on a large dish and sprinkle with more parsley if you wish.

Stuffings

Stuffing, sometimes called forcemeat, serves a triple purpose – it fills up the cavity in a boned joint or in a bird, helping to retain its good shape; it adds flavour; it makes a small joint or bird go further. Assemble the ingredients well ahead, but don't mix with liquid or egg or stuff the meat or bird until you want to cook it; it is not safe to leave stuffing around – even in the refrigerator – for more than 2–3 hours.

Most stuffings start with a base of one of the following:

Sausage-meat

Breadcrumbs
Make these from bread 2–3 days old. An electric blender will cope with fresh bread if you are stuck.

Rice
Boil it in salted water, rinse and dry before using.
To this basis add a fat (butter, dripping, oil or, most commonly, chopped suet); a little moisture and/or egg to bind; herbs and seasonings to give flavour and perhaps vegetables or fruits of various kinds.

Suet
Fresh butcher's suet on the whole gives a better flavour but packet shredded suet is less time consuming as it is ready prepared. Butcher's suet should be chopped finely, dusting with a little flour to prevent it sticking. Any membranes in the suet are then more easily removed after chopping. Packet suet should be used as fresh as possible, buy as required.

Reminders
Don't have the stuffing too wet or it becomes stodgy, nor yet too dry, or it will become crumbly and fall apart. Season a stuffing well.

Don't stuff a joint or bird too tightly, for when the stuffing absorbs juices from the flesh during the cooking, it expands and might burst the skin or come out. It is better to cook any surplus stuffing in a separate casserole or baking tin. Sometimes it is rolled into small balls and cooked round a joint.

Roll a stuffed joint such as breast of lamb and tie in several places with fine string to hold the shape during cooking. In the case of a leg or shoulder that has been boned and stuffed, press it into the correct shape and if necessary tie with fine string. Remove all strings before carving.

When stuffing a bird, put the forcemeat in loosely at the neck end, under the flap of skin, taking care to give the breast a plump, rounded shape. If you wish, a turkey can have a different stuffing in each end. Put a knob of butter, a wedge of lemon or an onion in the body of the bird to keep the flesh moist. Truss the bird firmly.

Note It is not advisable to stuff meat or poultry prior to home freezing.

Veal forcemeat

100 g *(4 oz)* lean veal
75 g *(3 oz)* lean bacon, rinded
1 small onion, skinned and finely chopped
25 g *(1 oz)* butter
75 g *(3 oz)* fresh white breadcrumbs
1 large mushroom, wiped and chopped
5 ml *(1 level tsp)* finely chopped parsley
salt, pepper, cayenne and ground mace
1 egg, beaten

Pass the mixed veal and bacon twice through a mincer, then beat them well in a bowl. Lightly fry the onion in a little of the butter, until soft but not coloured – 2–3 minutes; add to the meat. Add the breadcrumbs, mushroom, the remaining butter, parsley and seasonings and lastly the beaten egg. Mix well; if the mixture is too stiff, add a little milk.

Use for veal or lamb; double the quantities for a 6-kg *(13-lb)* turkey.

Sage and onion stuffing

2 large onions, skinned and chopped
25 g *(1 oz)* butter
100 g *(4 oz)* fresh white breadcrumbs
10 ml *(2 level tsps)* dried sage
salt and pepper

Put the onions in a pan of cold water, bring to the boil and cook until tender – about 10 minutes. Drain well, add the other ingredients and mix well. Use with pork.

Herb (parsley) stuffing

50 g *(2 oz)* bacon, rinded and chopped
45 ml *(3 tbsps)* shredded suet
100 g *(4 oz)* fresh white breadcrumbs
15 ml *(1 tbsp)* chopped parsley
10 ml *(2 level tsps)* dried mixed herbs or 30 ml *(2 tbsps)* freshly chopped mixed herbs
grated rind of ½ lemon
1 small egg, beaten
salt and pepper
milk or stock to bind

Fry the bacon in its own fat without browning; drain it on absorbent paper. Mix it with the suet, breadcrumbs, parsley, herbs, lemon rind, egg and seasoning and enough milk or stock to bind the mixture together. Use for stuffing a joint of lamb or veal or a chicken. Double the quantities for stuffing the neck end of a turkey.

Sufficient for an average-sized joint or chicken.

Nut stuffing

50 g *(2 oz)* shelled walnuts
45 ml *(3 tbsps)* shelled cashew nuts
6 shelled Brazil nuts
50 g *(2 oz)* butter
2 small onions, skinned and finely chopped
100 g *(4 oz)* mushrooms, finely chopped
pinch of dried mixed herbs
15 ml *(1 tbsp)* chopped parsley
175 g *(6 oz)* fresh white breadcrumbs
1 large egg, beaten
giblet stock to moisten
seasoning

Finely chop the nuts. Melt the butter and sauté the onion for 5 minutes. Add the mushrooms and sauté for a further 5 minutes. Toss together the nuts, mixed herbs, parsley and breadcrumbs. Stir in the mushroom mixture with the beaten egg. If necessary, moisten with stock. Season to taste with salt and freshly ground black pepper.

This is sufficient for a 4–4.5-kg *(9–10-lb)* turkey.

Chestnut stuffing

50 g *(2 oz)* bacon, rinded and chopped
100 g *(4 oz)* fresh white breadcrumbs
5 ml *(1 tsp)* chopped parsley
25 g *(1 oz)* butter, melted
grated rind of 1 lemon
225 g *(8 oz)* chestnut purée (see note)
salt and pepper
1 egg, beaten

Fry the bacon gently in its own fat for about 3–5 minutes, until crisp. Drain and add the rest of the ingredients, binding with the beaten egg.

This stuffing is suitable for a 4.5-kg *(10-lb)* turkey.

Note Chestnut purée may be made from fresh, dried or canned chestnuts, or use canned unsweetened chestnut purée.

Fresh chestnuts To peel, snip the brown outer skins with a pair of scissors or sharp knife and place the chestnuts in a pan of boiling water for 3–5 minutes. Lift out a few at a time and peel off both the brown and inner skins. To cook, simmer gently in a little chicken stock until tender – they will take 35–40 minutes. 450 g *(1 lb)* fresh chestnuts gives 350 g *(12 oz)* peeled, and when cooked as above and then puréed yields about 400 g *(14 oz)* unsweetened purée.
Whole canned, unsweetened – use as fresh cooked chestnuts.
Canned purée, unsweetened – use as fresh cooked purée.

Dried chestnuts Reconstituted, dried chestnuts can be used as fresh, cooked chestnuts. To prepare, soak overnight in cold water, then simmer in stock or milk until tender – about 40 minutes. 450 g *(1 lb)* dried chestnuts gives 900 g *(2 lb)* whole chestnuts.

Sausage stuffing

1 large onion, skinned and chopped
450 g *(1 lb)* pork sausage meat
10 ml *(2 tsps)* chopped parsley
5 ml *(1 tsp)* dried mixed herbs
25 g *(1 oz)* fresh white breadcrumbs
salt and pepper

Mix all the ingredients together.

Use with chicken, or turkey, adapting the quantities as necessary. This stuffing is sufficient for a 4–4.5-kg *(9–10-lb)* oven-ready turkey.

Bacon or ham stuffing

¼ onion, skinned and chopped
15 ml *(1 tbsp)* dripping
2 mushrooms, chopped
50–75 g *(2–3 oz)* cooked bacon or ham, chopped
25 g *(1 oz)* fresh white breadcrumbs
salt and pepper
little dry mustard
few drops of Worcestershire sauce
beaten egg or milk to bind

Lightly fry the onion in the dripping for 1–2 minutes; add the mushrooms and bacon or ham and fry until the onion is soft but not coloured. Remove from the heat and add the crumbs, seasonings and sauce and bind with beaten egg or milk. Use as a stuffing for vegetables, tomatoes, small marrows, peppers, etc. This quantity is sufficient for a 1.4-kg *(3¼-lb)* chicken.

Apple and celery stuffing

50 g *(2 oz)* bacon, rinded and chopped
25 g *(1 oz)* butter
2 onions, skinned and chopped
2 sticks of celery, trimmed and chopped
4 medium sized cooking apples, peeled, cored and sliced
75 g *(3 oz)* fresh white breadcrumbs
30 ml *(2 tbsps)* chopped parsley
sugar to taste
salt and pepper

Fry the bacon in the butter for 2–3 minutes until golden brown and remove from the pan with a slotted spoon. Fry the onions and celery for 5 minutes and remove from the pan with the slotted spoon. Fry the apples for 2–3 minutes, until soft. Mix all the ingredients together.

Use with duck or pork, or make double the quantity and use for goose.

Apple and prune stuffing

100 g *(4 oz)* prunes, soaked and stoned
225 g *(8 oz)* cooking apples, peeled and cored
100 g *(4 oz)* cooked rice
50 g *(2 oz)* shredded suet
50 g *(2 oz)* almonds, blanched and chopped
salt and pepper
juice and grated rind of ½ lemon
1 egg, beaten

Cut the prunes into quarters and roughly chop the apples. Mix the fruit, rice, suet and nuts, season to taste, add the lemon rind and juice and bind with beaten egg.

Use for pork.

Rice stuffing

50 g *(2 oz)* rice, cooked
1 chicken liver, chopped
1 small onion, skinned and chopped
50 g *(2 oz)* raisins
50 g *(2 oz)* almonds, blanched and chopped
30 ml *(2 tbsps)* chopped parsley
25 g *(1 oz)* butter, melted
salt and pepper
1 egg, beaten, optional

Combine all the ingredients, season and bind them well together.

Use for chicken, meat, fish or vegetables.

Tomato stuffing

2 large tomatoes, skinned and chopped
½ red pepper, seeded and finely chopped
½ clove garlic, skinned and crushed
45 ml *(3 tbsps)* fresh white breadcrumbs
knob of butter, melted
salt and pepper

Mix the ingredients together and bind with the juice from the tomatoes and the melted butter. Season well.

Use instead of veal forcemeat for baked stuffed liver.

Mushroom stuffing

100 g *(4 oz)* **mushrooms, chopped**
1 small onion, skinned and chopped
25 g *(1 oz)* **butter or margarine**
15 ml *(1 tbsp)* **chopped parsley**
salt and pepper
100 g *(4 oz)* **fresh white breadcrumbs**
beaten egg

Lightly fry the mushrooms and onion in the fat for 2–3 minutes until soft but not coloured. Add the parsley, seasoning and breadcrumbs and bind with a little beaten egg.

Use to stuff a goose or turkey; double these amounts for a 4.5-kg *(10-lb)* bird. The mixture may also be used to stuff tomatoes or green peppers, but for this purpose the amount of breadcrumbs should be reduced to 50 g *(2 oz)*.

Brazilian stuffing

½ onion, skinned and chopped
30 ml *(2 tbsps)* **oil**
½ clove garlic, skinned and crushed
½ green pepper, seeded and chopped
2 tomatoes, skinned and chopped
30 ml *(2 tbsps)* **sultanas**
4 olives, sliced
50 g *(2 oz)* **rice, cooked**
salt and pepper

Lightly fry the onion in the oil for 2–3 minutes, until soft but not coloured. Add the remaining ingredients, season well and mix thoroughly.

Use with pork.

Apricot stuffing

175 g *(6 oz)* **fresh white breadcrumbs**
100 g *(4 oz)* **dried apricots, finely chopped**
50 g *(2 oz)* **salted peanuts, finely chopped**
15 ml *(1 tbsp)* **chopped parsley**
50 g *(2 oz)* **butter**
175 g *(6 oz)* **onion, skinned and finely chopped**
juice and grated rind of 1 small orange
5 ml *(1 level tsp)* **curry powder**
2.5 ml *(½ level tsp)* **salt**
freshly ground black pepper
1 small egg, beaten

Place the breadcrumbs in a bowl and add the apricots, peanuts and parsley. Melt the butter in a small saucepan, add the onion and orange rind, cover and cook gently until soft. Remove from the pan and add to the breadcrumbs. Sprinkle in the curry powder and cook gently for 1 minute. Pour 45 ml *(3 tbsps)* orange juice over and bubble gently for 30 seconds. Blend the curried orange juice into the breadcrumbs. Season well with salt and pepper, and bind all together with beaten egg.

This is ideal with duck, and also good with other birds or breast of lamb.

Herbs spices and other flavourings

HERBS

Name	*Characteristics*	*Used particularly for*	*Other dishes*
Balm	Fragrant leaves, with lemon scent and flavour	Punches, fruit drinks, fish, poultry and ham dishes. Makes an excellent tisane	Soups, sauces, marinades, stuffings
Basil or Sweet Basil	Pungent, sweet; has a flavour of cloves and orange peel, with a minty aftertaste. Use sparingly. Cooking enhances its flavour; does not lose pungency when dried	Tomatoes	Cold rice salads; lamb's liver, lamb chops; basil butter; egg canapés; tomato soup; beef stews; asparagus; green beans; broccoli; green salads
Bay	A strong, sweet and spicy flavour, sometimes called musky; it becomes stronger when dried. Leaves may be used straight from the tree, or dried. Use sparingly	Included in *bouquets garnis,* meat and fish casseroles, marinades for poultry and game. Remove before serving dish	Tomato juice; aspic dishes; Bolognese sauce; soups; stocks; stews; soused herrings. Infuse in milk to be used for sauces. Sweet dishes, especially milk puddings
Borage	Both leaves and blue flowers are used; they give a faint, slightly salty cucumber flavour	To flavour claret cup and iced drinks; the flowers make a pretty garnish, either fresh or candied	Salads, fruit salads
Capers	Pickled flower-buds of the evergreen caper bush. On no account should these be confused with the poisonous fruits of the Caper Spurge; this is a biennial weed whose fruits resemble the caper	Sauce served with boiled mutton and some fish	Mayonnaise, salads, tartare sauce, stuffings, sandwich spreads
Chervil	Delicate, sweet taste, fragrant aroma. Use similarly to parsley. May be used generously. Has the power of bringing out the flavour of other herbs when mixed with them	Sauces, such as parsley, hollandaise; for salads; with green vegetables and new potatoes. Important ingredient of *fines herbes* and often included in *bouquets garnis*	Blends well with egg, cheese and chicken dishes. Sprinkle on buttered vegetables, soups, stews, casseroles
Chives	Member of the onion family the tender, narrow leaves being used. They are delicately flavoured and slightly oniony; best used fresh	Flavouring salads and dressings; used chopped, minced or scissor-snipped	As garnish for soups and other savoury dishes; cottage cheese, cream cheese; jacket or mashed potatoes
Dill	Two forms of the same plant – weed and seed. Mild, aromatic, slightly sweet caraway flavour. Use fairly generously. More pungent when dried	Seed in pickles, cucumber and soured cream, in lemon butter; weed with grilled or poached fish, eg salmon, halibut	Use the seed in cheese spreads and dips, potato salad, cucumber sandwiches, cole slaw, bread rolls, apple pie, and with veal, pork, sprinkled on rye bread. Weed is pleasant on new potatoes, scrambled eggs, lamb stew, veal, pork kidneys

Name	*Characteristics*	*Used particularly for*	*Other dishes*
Fennel	The seeds and the feathery leaves can be used; both are sweet, with flavour resembling aniseed or liquorice. Use seeds fairly generously, but remember they are more pungent when dried	Boiled fish, oily fish – counteracts the richness; tie the seeds in muslin; sauces; salad dressings	Use seeds with roast pork; beef stews, with apples in any form. In Scandinavian countries it is used fresh as a garnish
Garlic	Bulb of a plant of the onion family; each bulb is really a collection of smaller ones, called 'cloves'. Will keep for months in a dry place; not impaired when some cloves are removed. Has a powerful acrid taste; use sparingly. Available also minced, powdered and as garlic salt and pepper	Soups, stews, re-heated savoury dishes, curries, sauces, gravies, pâtés, dips, pizza	Salad dressings – mere suggestion only – it is often sufficient to rub the bowl round, with a cut clove; garlic butter; garlic bread
Horseradish	Plant with a pungent, acrid-flavoured root, which is grated for use and eaten raw	Flavouring sauce or cream to serve with roast beef and with smoked or freshwater fish	Include in sandwiches. Use to flavour salad dressing
Lemon thyme	Aromatic plant with a lemon flavour	Flavouring stuffings, (especially for veal), for egg recipes, salads, fish dishes; a basic herb for *bouquets garnis*	Sometimes used as a substitute for true lemon flavour; use with roast lamb, carrots, mushrooms and potatoes
Marjoram	Spicy, slightly bitter, nutmeg flavour. Can replace basil in meat dishes. Use rather sparingly; more pungent when dried	Sprinkled over meat especially pork – roast, stewed, grilled, fried – and in meat soups, pizza, sausages. Interchangeable with oregano	In stuffing for meat, poultry, and fish, with buttered vegetables, cream soups, salads, French dressing, scrambled eggs, omelettes
Mint	One of the most widely grown herbs; about 14 varieties (eg spearmint, Apple and Bowles mint, peppermint). Less pungent when dried	Mint sauce to serve with lamb; flavouring for new potatoes and peas. Mint jelly is a popular alternative to sauce	Other vegetables, tomatoes, pea soup, scrambled eggs. Garnish for wine and fruit cups; cream cheese, salads and dressings
Oregano	Sometimes known as wild marjoram; used widely in Italian cookery. Strong, distinctive flavour	Interchangeable with marjoram as flavouring for meats, sausages, soups, pizza and other Italian dishes, tomatoes	In salads, dressings, buttered vegetables, cheese spreads, egg dishes, marinades
Parsley	Mild, pleasant flavour. Very widely employed, and may be used quite generously; most of the flavour is in the stalks	Essential ingredient in *bouquets garnis, fines herbes*. Sauces for boiled ham and bacon, fish, chicken; soups. Garnish for many savoury dishes	Mashed and new potatoes; egg dishes; rissoles; stuffings; parsley butter; cottage cheese; cream cheese; salads
Rosemary	Pungent, aromatic, sweet. Use with care. Less pungent when dried	Roast lamb (sprinkle over before cooking), lamb stews; poultry	With veal chops or steaks, cold meats and fish; in creamy soups, marinades and dressings. Also used in scones and sweet dishes
Sage	Bold flavour, slightly bitter: use sparingly. Good with rich, oily meats – said to aid digestion	Pork (including sausages) and stuffings for pork, veal, duck; in Italian and Provençal dishes	Minced meat; fish dishes; spinach, beans, aubergines, Brussels sprouts, onions. Delicious with cream cheese; consommé; green salads; egg dishes
Savory	Two varieties – summer and winter. Distinctive but pleasant pungent, peppery flavour. Use with care. Keeps flavour when dried	Omelettes, beans of all kinds	Eggs, tomato sauce, veal, pork pies, sausages, turkey, fish (use with marjoram and/or thyme). Summer variety, in conserves and syrups; vegetables; cheese; soups

Name	*Characteristics*	*Used particularly for*	*Other dishes*
Sorrel	Wild plant with strongly acid flavour. Use sparingly, when young and fresh. Can be cultivated	Lettuce and other salads and some sauces; egg dishes	May be cooked like spinach, or mixed with it. Can be used to make a soup
Tarragon	Two culinary types – French and Russian. Strong aromatic flavour; use sparingly. Less flavour when dried	One of the *fines herbes*. Used in sauces such as hollandaise, béarnaise, tartare; wine vinegar; marinades; with egg dishes	With fish and shellfish; salads; chicken dishes such as fricassees; meat stews; tarragon butter; in a sauce for ham; in aspic glazes
Thyme	Strong, pungent, aromatic, rather clovelike. Many varieties. Use sparingly. More aromatic when dried	Meat – beef, lamb, veal – rub it in before roasting. A basic herb in *bouquets garnis*	Soups, stuffings and forcemeat for mutton and chicken; with hare. Use with wine-cooked dishes; in bread sauce with lemon; on carrots, onions, mushrooms

SPICES

Name	*Description*	*Uses, etc*
Allspice (also called pimento and Jamaican pepper)	Small dried berries resembling smooth peppercorns. Aroma recalls that of cloves, cinnamon and nutmeg	Whole: Meats; broths; pickles; chutney; marinades; poached fish Ground: Pickles; relishes; soups; sauces; vegetables; beef stews; baked ham; lamb; boiled fish; oyster stew; cakes; milk puddings; fruit pies
Aniseed (Anise)	Small seeds of the anise plant, which contain a volatile oil with a warm, sweet, aromatic taste and odour	Salad dressings; with sugar and butter on carrots, red cabbage; cheese; fish and shellfish; sweets; rolls; cakes; biscuits; pastry for pies and tarts; baked apples; liqueurs and cordials; (also has certain medicinal uses)
Caraway seed	Small, brown and hard; curved in shape, tapering at the ends. Pleasant, slightly sharp liquorice-like flavour	Soups; salads; sauerkraut; cabbage; turnips; asparagus; potatoes; tomatoes; cheeses (especially cream cheese and fondue); omelettes; pork dishes; meats and stews; rye bread; biscuits; muffins; rolls and cakes; much used in mid-European and Jewish cookery
Cardamom seed	Member of the ginger family. Available with or without the pod and whole or ground. Use seed sparingly. Strong, bitter-sweet, slightly lemony flavour	Ingredient of most curry powders; pickles; green pea soup; curries; beef and pork dishes; with sweet potato, pumpkin, apples; bread, buns, biscuits and cakes; iced melon; custard; rice pudding
Cayenne	Prepared from the smallest, hottest chilies, which vary in colour from red to yellow. A very hot, slightly sweet, pungent pepper, always sold ground	Use (with restraint) to flavour meats and sauces especially barbecue and devilled recipes, eggs, fish, and vegetables in curries; cheese sauces and pastry, chicken croquettes, cheese and vegetable soups
Celery seeds	Aromatic seeds of a plant related to vegetable celery. Slightly bitter celery flavour. Sold whole or ground	Pickles; chutney; meat and fish dishes; salads; bread; marinades, dressings and dips
Chilies (powdered)	The whole chili pepper, crushed or ground. Hot, nippy flavour. (Not to be confused with chili powder)	Whole: Pickling; chutneys and ketchups; Mexican dishes. Crushed or ground: Soups; tomato dishes; casseroles; spaghetti and meat sauces

Name	*Description*	*Uses, etc*
Cinnamon	Pungent, sweet spice, available as bark (rolled in slender 'sticks') or ground	Ground: Preserving; eggnog; ham and pork; buns; cakes; gingerbread; milk puddings; fruit pies; Christmas pudding; pumpkin pie; cinnamon sugar – on toast and sweet dishes. Sticks: Pickling and preserving; mulled wine; beef stews; stewed fruit; compotes
Clove	Available whole or ground. Distinctive pungent aroma	Ground: Sweet vegetables; meat stews; baked goods; mincemeat and Christmas puddings; milk puddings Whole: Used to stud ham and pork; fruit punch and mulled wines; soups and stews; pickling fruits; pumpkins; spinach; apple pies and puddings
Coriander seed	Mild, sweet, delicately flavoured, with a hint of orange; available whole or ground. Used in every curry powder formula	Use whole in pickling spice. Use crushed in pea soup; rub on pork before roasting; crushed in casseroles and curries; poultry stuffing; apple pies; baked goods
Cumin seed	In appearance and aroma similar to caraway. Available whole and ground. One of the chief ingredients in chilli and curry powder	Pickles; chutney; cheese dishes; soups; cabbage; rice; Mexican and Eastern dishes; curries; minced beef and meat loaves; kebabs; chicken; pork; fish dishes; fruit pies
Fenugreek	A leguminous plant resembling celery in flavour, but pleasantly bitter like burnt sugar	The ground seeds are used in curry powder; chutneys; pickles; sauces
Ginger	Whole root ginger is available fresh or dried, or the root is dried and ground to a fine powder. Stem (or green) ginger is sometimes canned in brine, more usually crystallised or preserved in syrup. Flavour is hot and sweet; root ginger needs cooking to release the true depth of flavour	Whole root: marinades, curries, sauces and chutneys. Ground: curries, sauces, preserves, cake-making and sprinkled on melon. Stem: When crystallised or preserved in syrup is a confection rather than a spice, though ginger in syrup is an important ingredient in Chinese cookery. Canned green ginger used as an alternative to whole root ginger
Juniper berries	The fruit of the Juniper tree – small, dark purple-blue berries, aromatic, with a pine tang. Crush to release the maximum flavour	A flavouring agent for gin, use in stuffing for game and with pork and mutton, or in casseroles using similar ingredients; pâtés and sauerkraut
Mace	The membrane or aril surrounding the nutmeg. Used ground or in 'blade' form. Exotic, mild nutmeg flavour	Ground: Tomato juice; chutneys; cream of chicken soup; sauces; cheese dishes; veal; lamb; beef; fish dishes; light fruit cakes; gingerbread; whipped cream; mulls and hot punches Blade: Pickles and preserves; stewed fruits; fruit salad; béchamel sauce
Mustard	One of the oldest condiments known. It comes from the black or white seeds of the mustard plant. Black seeds give aroma and white give pungency; most mustards are a combination of both. Available as whole seeds or ground mustard flour. The special flavours that differentiate the various types are produced by the liquid used to moisten the flour	Use to flavour dressings and sauces, pickles, meat and cheese dishes, especially Welsh rarebit, and as a condiment to accompany beef, ham, bacon etc.
Nutmeg	The pit or seed of the nutmeg fruit is a powerful spice with a strong aroma. Available ground and whole (for grating as required). Nutmeg loses its scent and flavour quickly once ground	Chicken and cream soups; sprinkle on buttered corn, spinach, carrots, beans, sprouts; eggnog; cheese dishes; fish cakes; chicken or veal fricassee; doughnuts; custards; puddings; spice cake; biscuits; milk puddings

Name	*Description*	*Uses, etc*
Paprika	A ground red pepper from the capsicum family. There are two varieties, with a sweet mild flavour or with a slight bite. The best is known as Szegediner. Buy little and often as it does not keep	A 'garnish' spice – used to give an appetising appearance to salads, fish, meat, chicken, soup; eggs; vegetables, canapés, cheese dishes; goulash
Pepper (See also Cayenne and Paprika)	Most widely-used spice. It promotes the appetite and digestive processes. Fresh peppercorns are available in bottles or cans. White: Berries are picked when fully ripe and the kernels are usually ground. Black: The unripe berries are cured (dried) until dark brown or black. Available whole or ground. Stronger and more aromatic than white. Coralline is made from a mild variety of red pepper, finely ground	General seasoning agent. Used in manufacture of food products, especially in curing meats and seasoning sausages. Whole blade peppercorns are at their best freshly ground. Choose white pepper for light coloured sauces as it does not discolour them. Coralline: Generally used for decorating
Poppy seeds	Small deep-blue seeds of a type of poppy, with a mild but distinctive nutty flavour	Dips, spreads; onion soup; salads and dressings; peas, potatoes, carrots; egg dishes; cheese; pasta dishes; bread, rolls, cakes, biscuits; continental and Jewish pastries
Saffron	Made from the flower stigmas of a type of crocus; available whole or ground into a yellow powder with aromatic, slightly bitter taste	Used for flavouring and colouring bouillabaise; chicken soups; rice and paella; cream cheese; scrambled eggs; fish sauces; traditional cakes and buns. Expensive but normally only a pinch needed
Sesame seeds	The seeds of a herbaceous plant widely grown and used in the East. The oil expressed from them is highly regarded for culinary use. Rich, sweet, slightly burnt flavour that can be heightened by toasting before use	Fry seeds in butter and add to green salads, mashed potatoes, cream cheese; toast seeds and sprinkle on fish, cooked chicken, fruit salads; add to pastry on meat pies; sprinkle on uncooked scones, biscuits, rolls
Turmeric	Dried and ground roots of a plant of the ginger family. Yellow-orange colour; aromatic, slightly bitter flavour	An essential ingredient in curry powder. Also used in pickles and relishes; can be used for colouring cakes, rice, etc.

HERB AND SPICE MIXTURES AND OTHER FLAVOURINGS

Name	*Description*	*Uses, etc*
Barbecue Spice	Includes chilies, cumin, garlic, cloves, paprika, salt and sugar	Use to sprinkle on grilled or barbecued foods – steaks, hamburgers, kebabs, cutlets, poultry, fish. Add to marinades and soups. Sprinkle on green beans, baked beans. Gives an unusual fillip to plain stews and casseroles
Bouquet garni	A small bunch of herbs either tied together or, if dried, tied up in a piece of muslin. Traditionally, this includes a bayleaf, a sprig of parsley and a sprig of thyme. A dried bouquet garni can include a bayleaf, a pinch of mixed herbs, 6 peppercorns, 1 clove and a pinch of dried parsley. The dried variety can now be purchased ready made up in suitable quantities	Soups, stews, stocks
Chili powder / seasoning (not to be confused with powdered chili)	Blend of spices, with chili pepper as basic ingredient, plus ground cumin seed, ground oregano, powdered garlic, and usually salt. Other spices may be added, eg ground cloves. Much less pungent than powdered chili	Basic seasoning for chili con carne. Good in shellfish and oyster cocktail sauces, with hard-boiled and scrambled eggs, minced meat or hamburgers, vegetable and meat soups, salads, barbecue sauces

Name	*Description*	*Uses, etc*
Curry powder	Rich golden powder, a blend of many spices – cayenne, coriander, turmeric, cumin, ginger, mace, clove, cardamom, fenugreek and pepper. Very distinctive flavour; the degree of 'heat' depends on the blend	For curry sauce to serve with eggs, fish, shrimps, poultry, meat, vegetables; French dressing, mayonnaise, soups, salted nuts
Curry paste	Same spices and uses as curry powder, but mixed to a thick paste with either clarified butter or vinegar	
Celery salt	Table salt plus ground celery seed	Used in soups, stews, salads, meat and poultry dishes. (Reduce ordinary salt proportionately)
Fines herbs	A combination of chervil, tarragon, chives and parsley in equal proportions	Used mainly in omelettes; add also to meat dishes, fish, soups, salads and stuffings for poultry
Garlic salt	Table salt plus powdered garlic	Use discreetly to improve the flavour of meat dishes, salads, and sauces (reduce ordinary salt proportionately)
Mixed herbs	A combination of herbs, usually marjoram or oregano, tarragon, sage, thyme, parsley	Soups; meat; poultry and fish dishes; stuffings
Mixed spice	A blend of ground sweet spices – cloves, allspice, cinnamon	Use with stewed fruits and puddings, fruit and spice cakes, biscuits, pancakes, conserves
Onion salt	Table salt plus powdered onion	Used in any dishes where onion flavour is required – soups, casseroles, meat dishes, sauces; add to bread dough for onion bread. (Reduce ordinary salt proportionately)
Salt	A mineral. Sea salt (Maldon salt) and bay salt come from the sea and have a clean fresh taste and attractive appearance. Rock salt is mined or pumped up from salt beds. Coarse salt is stronger than the more common free-flowing variety. Table salts have magnesium carbonate added to help them run more freely, and some are iodized	An essential condiment in all cooking and one that is often combined with spices for extra seasoning power
Seasoning salts	Specially blended seasonings for fish, chicken, steak, salads. Consist usually of salt, monosodium glutamate, sugar, herbs, spices, calcium stearate	Sprinkle directly on to meats, or in sauces, stews, soups, salad dressings, marinades, etc. (Reduce ordinary salt proportionately)
Seasoned pepper	Mixture of black pepper, spices and sugar	For flavouring and garnishing savoury dishes, and as a condiment
Vanilla	The pods of a climbing orchid grown mainly in Mexico and France. Buy it as an essence of which only a few drops are needed at a time, or buy whole pods which can be used several times	Leave a pod in the caster sugar jar and it will impart flavour over a long period of time. Vanilla marries well with chocolate dishes and also flavours custards and ice cream

NOTE: Sodium Glutamate (Monosodium Glutamate) is a pure white powder or crystals, extracted from a cereal source. It has a slightly sweet-salty taste, and when added to such foods as meat, poultry and fish it intensifies or enhances their natural flavour. It is therefore being increasingly added to manufactured meat, fish and other savoury products, and is present in many Chinese foods. If taken to excess, it can cause an unpleasant but usually short-lived sensation or condition which has been given the name of Kwok's disease. In any case it is not a good idea to add sodium glutamate to too many savoury dishes, as it tends to make everything taste rather similar. However, it is a useful standby for improving the flavour of soups and so on that might otherwise be a little lacking in taste and character. Sodium glutamate is available for domestic use as a powder, sold under such names as 'Ac'cent', and occurs as an ingredient in some special blended seasonings.

Glazed bacon joint (p. 137).

Sauces

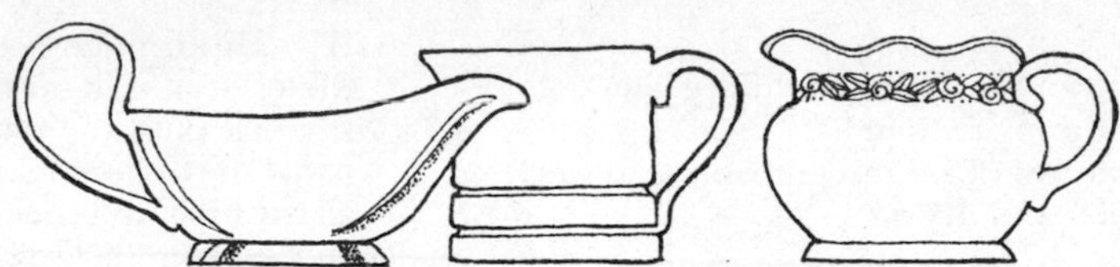

A well-made sauce – which can be quite simple – improves the flavour and appearance of many dishes. Sometimes, indeed, the sauce *makes* the dish, as in eggs mornay.

For white sauces the liquid used is usually milk or milk and white stock; for brown sauces meat stock and/or vegetable water give a good flavour; for a sauce to serve with fish the fish bones can be used to make a stock which is used in combination with milk. The method of making stocks is given on page 41; however, nowadays a chicken or beef bouillon cube is often used to make a quick substitute for traditional stock.

When a sauce is thickened with flour (preferably plain) it may be made in one of two ways, known as the roux and the blended methods:

A roux is made by melting the butter (or other fat), adding the flour, mixing thoroughly and cooking until they are well combined; in the case of a brown sauce the roux is cooked until it is an even golden brown colour, but for a white sauce it is not allowed to colour. The liquid is then added gradually, the sauce being stirred well after each addition, then cooked to reach the required consistency. (Beginners will find it easier if they take the pan off the heat to add the liquid.)

With the blended method, the cornflour (or flour) and a little of the cold liquid are blended to a creamy mixture, the rest of the liquid is brought to the boil and stirred gradually into the blended flour and the sauce is then cooked and stirred for a few minutes.

The white sauce recipe below shows how to vary the proportion of ingredients to give sauces of different consistencies for different purposes.

You can prepare a sauce early in the day (pressing a piece of damped greaseproof paper on to its surface to prevent a skin forming) and re-heat it when needed.

SAVOURY SAUCES

Vast as the number of individual savoury sauces may be, most of them can be divided into white (simple or rich), brown and egg sauces, plus a group of miscellaneous ones such as mint sauce.

A roux based flour sauce is always preferable to a cornflour base when making anything beyond a simple parsley sauce, as cornflour gives a more glutinous consistency. Cornflour sauces are best served sweet.

WHITE SAUCES

Simple white sauce – roux method

I – Pouring consistency

20 g *(¾ oz)* **butter or margarine**
30 ml *(2 level tbsps)* **flour**
300 ml *(½ pt)* **milk or milk and stock**
salt and pepper

Melt the fat, add the flour and stir with a wooden spoon until smooth. Cook over a gentle heat for 2–3 minutes, stirring until the mixture (called a roux) begins to bubble. Remove from the heat and add the liquid gradually, stirring after each addition to prevent lumps forming. Bring the sauce to the boil, stirring continuously, and when it has thickened, cook for a further 1–2 minutes. Add salt and pepper to taste.

II – Coating consistency

25 g *(1 oz)* **butter or margarine**
45 ml *(3 level tbsps)* **flour**
300 ml *(½ pt)* **milk or milk and stock**
salt and pepper

Make the sauce as above.

For a thick coating sauce increase the quantities to 40 g *(1½ oz)* butter, 60 ml *(4 level tbsps)* flour.

Rolled stuffed breast of lamb (p.115).

III – Binding consistency (panada)

50 g *(2 oz)* **butter or margarine**
50 g *(2 oz)* **flour**
300 ml *(½ pt)* **milk or milk and stock**
salt and pepper

Melt the fat, add the flour and stir well. Cook gently for 2–3 minutes, stirring, until the roux begins to bubble and leave the sides of the pan. Off the heat, add the liquid gradually, bring to the boil, stirring all the time, and cook for 1–2 minutes after it has thickened; add salt and pepper to taste. This very thick sauce is used for binding mixtures such as croquettes.

Simple white sauce – blending method

I – Pouring consistency

25 ml *(1½ level tbsps)* **cornflour**
300 ml *(½ pt)* **milk**
knob of butter
salt and pepper, or sugar

Put the cornflour in a basin and blend with 15–30 ml *(1–2 tbsps)* milk to a smooth cream. Heat the remaining milk with the butter until boiling; pour on to the blended mixture, stirring all the time to prevent lumps forming. Return the mixture to the pan and bring to the boil, stirring continuously with a wooden spoon. Cook for 1–2 minutes after the mixture has thickened, to make a white, glossy sauce. Add salt and pepper to taste before serving. Or add sugar to taste for a sweet sauce.

II – Coating consistency

Increase the quantity of cornflour to 30 ml *(2 level tbsps)*.

Simple white sauce, all-in-one method

25 g *(1 oz)* **soft tub margarine**
25 g *(1 oz)* **plain flour**
seasoning
300 ml *(½ pt)* **milk**

Put all the ingredients together in a medium sized saucepan. Whisking all the time over a moderate heat, bring to the boil and continue cooking for 2–3 minutes. For variations add the flavouring ingredient in the usual way.

Anchovy sauce

300 ml *(½ pt)* **white sauce, made with half milk and half fish stock**
5–10 ml *(1–2 tsps)* **anchovy essence**
squeeze of lemon juice
red colouring, optional

Make the sauce and when it has thickened, remove it from the heat and stir in anchovy essence to taste, then lemon juice and a few drops of colouring (if used) to tint a dull pink.

Serve with fish.

Caper sauce

300 ml *(½ pt)* **white sauce**
15 ml *(1 tbsp)* **capers**
5–10 ml *(1–2 tsps)* **vinegar from the capers, or lemon juice**
salt and pepper

Make the sauce, using all milk or – to give a better flavour – half milk and half liquid in which the lamb was boiled. When the sauce has thickened stir in the capers and vinegar or lemon juice. Season well.

Re-heat for 1–2 minutes, before serving with boiled lamb (see page 117).

Egg sauce

300 ml *(½ pt)* **white sauce**
1 egg, hard-boiled and shelled
5–10 ml *(1–2 tsps)* **chopped chives, optional**

In making the sauce, use all milk or (if possible), half fish stock and half milk. Chop the egg and add with the chives. Season well and re-heat for 1–2 minutes.

Serve with poached or steamed fish or kedgeree.

Fish sauce

Make a white sauce using half milk and half liquid in which the fish was cooked. This gives a well flavoured sauce that can be used instead of plain white sauce for any fish dish. Any additional flavouring can then be added.

Lemon sauce

rind and juice of 1 lemon
300 ml *(½ pt)* white sauce, using half milk and half chicken or fish stock
5–10 ml *(1–2 level tsps)* sugar
salt and pepper

Simmer the lemon rind in the milk and stock for 5 minutes; strain and use the liquid to make a white sauce. When it has thickened, stir in the lemon juice and sugar and season to taste.

Serve with fish or chicken.

This sauce is quite sharp; if preferred, reduce the lemon juice or counteract it by stirring in 15–30 ml *(1–2 tbsps)* single cream just before serving. Add tarragon sparingly for a lemon and tarragon sauce.

Cheese sauce

300 ml *(½ pt)* white sauce
50–100 g *(2–4 oz)* mature cheese, grated
pinch of dry mustard
pinch of cayenne pepper, optional
salt and pepper

Make the sauce and when it has thickened remove from the heat and stir in the cheese and seasonings. Do not reboil, or the cheese will be over-cooked – there is sufficient heat in the sauce to melt the cheese.

Serve with vegetables, eg, cauliflower or leeks, eggs, fish or pasta.

Mushroom sauce

300 ml *(½ pt)* white sauce
50–75 g *(2–3 oz)* button mushrooms, sliced
knob of butter
salt and pepper

Make the sauce in the usual way. Lightly fry the mushrooms in the butter until soft but not coloured. Fold into the sauce and season to taste.

Serve with fish, meat or eggs.

Mustard sauce

300 ml *(½ pt)* white sauce
15 ml *(1 level tbsp)* dry mustard
10 ml *(2 level tsps)* sugar
15 ml *(1 tbsp)* vinegar

Make the sauce using all milk or half milk and half stock from the fish (or a chicken bouillon cube). Blend the mustard, sugar and vinegar to a smooth cream and stir into the sauce.

Serve with fish.

To vary the flavour, use some of the many different mustard mixes now available, adapting the amount added to taste.

Onion sauce

2 onions, skinned and chopped
300 ml *(½ pt)* white sauce, using half milk and half onion liquor
grated rind of ½ lemon, optional
salt and pepper

Cover the onions with salted water, bring to the boil and simmer until soft – about 10–15 minutes. Drain well and retain the liquor. Use half this and half milk as the basis of the white sauce. When it has thickened, stir in the cooked onion. Add the grated lemon rind and season to taste.

Serve with lamb, tripe or freshly hard-boiled eggs.

Parsley sauce

300 ml *(½ pt)* white sauce
15–30 ml *(1–2 tbsps)* chopped parsley
salt and pepper
squeeze of lemon juice, optional

Make the sauce using half milk and half stock (if available). When it has thickened, stir in the parsley and seasonings. Don't re-boil or the parsley may turn the sauce green.

Serve with fish or boiled or braised bacon or pour it over vegetables.

Shrimp sauce

rind of 1 lemon
1 small bayleaf
300 ml *(½ pt)* white sauce
50 g *(2 oz)* frozen, canned or potted shrimps
salt and pepper

Simmer the lemon rind and bayleaf for 5 minutes in the liquid from which the sauce is to be made (this can be milk or milk and stock, if available). Strain and use to make the white sauce. When it has thickened stir in the shrimps, season to taste and reheat for 1–2 minutes.

Serve with fish.

RICH WHITE SAUCES

Béchamel sauce

300 ml *(½ pt)* milk
1 shallot, skinned and sliced, or a small piece of onion, skinned
small piece of carrot, pared and cut up
½ stick celery, scrubbed and cut up
½ bayleaf
3 peppercorns
25 g *(1 oz)* butter
45 ml *(3 level tbsps)* flour
salt and pepper

Put the milk, vegetables and flavourings in a saucepan and bring slowly to the boil. Remove from the heat, cover and leave to infuse for about 15 minutes. Strain the liquid and use this with the butter and flour to make a roux sauce (see page 193). Season to taste before serving.

This classic sauce is the basis of many other sauces and a few examples are given below.

Aurore sauce

300 ml *(½ pt)* béchamel sauce
15–30 ml *(1–2 level tbsps)* tomato paste
25 g *(1 oz)* butter
salt and pepper

Make the sauce and when it has thickened, blend the tomato paste with the butter, stir in a little at a time and season to taste.

Serve with eggs, chicken or fish.

Mornay sauce

300 ml *(½ pt)* béchamel sauce
50 g *(2 oz)* Parmesan, Gruyère or mature Cheddar cheese, grated
paprika pepper
salt and pepper

Make the sauce and when it has thickened remove from the heat and stir in the cheese and seasonings. Do not re-heat or the cheese will become overcooked and stringy.

Serve with eggs, chicken or fish.

Soubise sauce

225 g *(½ lb)* onions, skinned and chopped
25 g *(1 oz)* butter
a little stock or water
300 ml *(½ pt)* béchamel sauce
salt and pepper

Cook the onions gently in the butter and a small amount of stock or water until soft – about 10–15 minutes. Sieve or purée in an electric blender and stir the purée into the sauce, with seasoning to taste; reheat for 1–2 minutes.

Serve with meat.

Chaudfroid sauce (white)

40 ml *(2½ level tbsps)* **aspic jelly powder**
150 ml *(¼ pt)* **hot water**
10 ml *(2 level tsps)* **powdered gelatine**
300 ml *(½ pt)* **béchamel sauce**
100–150 ml *(⅛–¼ pt)* **single cream**
salt and pepper

Put the aspic jelly powder in a small basin and dissolve it in the hot water. Stand the basin in a pan of hot water, sprinkle in the gelatine and stir until it has dissolved, taking care not to overheat the mixture. Stir into the warm béchamel sauce, beat well and add the cream and extra salt and pepper if necessary. Strain the sauce and leave to cool, stirring frequently so that it remains smooth and glossy. Use when at the consistency of thick cream, for coating chicken, fish or eggs.

Note A simpler chaudfroid sauce can be made by adding 150 ml *(¼ pt)* melted aspic jelly to 300 ml *(½ pt)* warm béchamel sauce; beat well, strain, cool and use as above.

Velouté sauce

knob of butter
about 30 ml *(2 level tbsps)* **flour**
400 ml *(¾ pt)* **chicken or other light stock**
30–45 ml *(2–3 tbsps)* **single cream**
few drops of lemon juice
salt and pepper

Melt the butter, stir in the flour and cook gently, stirring well, until the mixture is pale fawn colour. Stir in the stock gradually, bring to the boil, stirring all the time, and simmer until slightly reduced and syrupy. Remove from the heat and add the cream, lemon juice and seasoning.

Serve with poultry, fish or veal.

Suprême sauce

300 ml *(½ pt)* **velouté sauce**
1–2 egg yolks
30–45 ml *(2–3 tbsps)* **single or double cream**
knob of butter
squeeze of lemon juice
salt and pepper

Make the velouté sauce, remove from the heat and stir in the egg yolks and cream. Add the butter a little at a time, the lemon juice and seasoning to taste. Reheat if necessary but don't re-boil, or the sauce will curdle.

Serve with poultry or fish. Suprême sauce is sometimes used in meat and vegetable dishes.

BROWN SAUCES

The main brown sauces are gravy (which is really a simple brown sauce), espagnole sauce and its variations, and demi-glace sauce, again with variations.

Gravy

A rich brown gravy is served with all roast joints—thin with roast beef and thick with other meats. If the gravy is properly made in the baking tin, there should be no need to use extra colouring.

Remove the joint from the tin and keep it hot while making the gravy.

Thin gravy

Pour the fat very slowly from the tin, draining it off carefully from one corner and leaving the sediment behind. Season well with salt and pepper and add 300 ml *(½ pt)* hot vegetable water or stock (which can be made from a bouillon cube). Stir thoroughly with a wooden spoon until all the sediment is scraped from the tin and the gravy is a rich brown; return the tin to the heat and boil for 2–3 minutes. Serve very hot.

This is the 'correct' way of making thin gravy, but some people prefer to make a version of the thick gravy given below, using half the amount of flour.

Thick gravy
Leave 30 ml *(2 tbsps)* of the fat in the tin, add 15 ml *(1 level tbsp)* flour (preferably shaking it from a flour dredger, which gives a smoother result), blend well and cook over the heat until it turns brown, stirring continuously. Slowly stir in 300 ml *(½ pt)* hot vegetable water or stock and boil for 2–3 minutes. Season well, strain and serve very hot.

Notes
1. If the gravy is greasy (due to not draining off enough fat) or thin (due to adding too much liquid), it can be corrected by adding more flour, although this weakens the flavour.
2. When gravy is very pale, a little gravy browning may be added.
3. Meat extracts are sometimes added to give extra taste; however, they do tend to overpower the characteristic meat flavour. A sliced carrot and onion cooked with the meat in the gravy will give extra 'body' to the taste without impairing it. 15 ml *(1 tbsp)* cider or wine added at the last moment does wonders.

Espagnole sauce

1 rasher streaky bacon, rinded and chopped
25 g *(1 oz)* butter
1 shallot, skinned and chopped, or a small piece of onion, chopped
60 ml *(4 tbsps)* mushroom stalks, chopped
1 small carrot, pared and chopped
30–45 ml *(2–3 level tbsps)* flour
300 ml *(½ pt)* beef stock
bouquet garni
30 ml *(2 level tbsps)* tomato paste
salt and pepper

This classic brown sauce is used as a basis for many other savoury sauces.

Fry the bacon in the butter for 2–3 minutes, add the vegetables and fry for a further 3–5 minutes, or until lightly browned. Stir in the flour, mix well and continue frying until it turns brown. Remove from the heat and gradually add the stock (which if necessary can be made from a stock cube), stirring after each addition. Return the pan to the heat and stir until the sauce thickens; add the bouquet garni, tomato paste and salt and pepper. Reduce the heat and allow to simmer very gently for 1 hour, stirring from time to time to prevent it sticking; alternatively, cook in the oven at 170°C *(325°F)* mark 3 for 1½–2 hours. Strain the sauce, re-heat and skim off any fat, using a metal spoon. Re-season if necessary.

15 ml *(1 tbsp)* sherry may be added just before the sauce is served.

Demi-glace sauce

150 ml *(¼ pt)* clear beef gravy or jellied stock from under beef dripping
300 ml *(½ pt)* espagnole sauce

Add the gravy to the sauce and boil (uncovered) until the sauce has a glossy appearance and will coat the back of the spoon with a shiny glaze.

This is a simplified version of the classic demi-glace, but gives quite a satisfactory result for ordinary use.

Serve with dishes made from beef.

Piquant sauce

2 shallots or a small piece of onion, skinned and finely chopped
knob of butter
150 ml *(¼ pt)* wine vinegar
300 ml *(½ pt)* espagnole or demi-glace sauce
2–3 gherkins, finely chopped
15 ml *(1 tbsp)* chopped parsley

Fry the shallots or onion in the butter for about 10 minutes, until really soft but not browned. Add the vinegar and boil rapidly until reduced by about half. Stir in the sauce and simmer for 15 minutes. Add the gherkins and parsley and serve without further cooking.

Serve with pork or any cold meat.

Bigarade sauce

300 ml *(½ pt)* espagnole sauce
juice of 1 orange
juice of 1 lemon
30–45 ml *(2–3 tbsps)* port
pinch of sugar
salt and pepper

Heat the espagnole sauce, stir in the fruit juices and port and simmer (uncovered) for 10 minutes; add a little sugar if the sauce is too sharp and adjust the seasoning.

Serve with roast duck.

Réforme sauce

45–60 ml *(3–4 tbsps)* vinegar
6 peppercorns
300 ml *(½ pt)* espagnole sauce
30–45 ml *(2–3 tbsps)* port
15 ml *(1 tbsp)* red-currant jelly

Put the vinegar and peppercorns into a pan and boil rapidly (uncovered) until reduced by half. Stir in the espagnole sauce, port and jelly, simmer for 10–15 minutes and strain.

Serve with lamb cutlets or fillet of beef.

Madeira or Marsala sauce

Add up to 150 ml *(¼ pt)* Madeira or Marsala to 300 ml *(½ pt)* espagnole sauce (coating consistency) and reheat but don't re-boil. The juice and extracts from the meat tin can also be reduced and added, to give extra flavour.

Serve with any meat or game.

Chaudfroid sauce – brown

40 ml *(2½ level tbsps)* aspic jelly powder
150 ml *(¼ pt)* hot water
10 ml *(2 level tsps)* powdered gelatine
400 ml *(¾ pt)* espagnole sauce
Madeira, sherry or port to taste
salt and pepper

Dissolve the aspic jelly powder in the hot water. Sprinkle in the gelatine and stir over a gentle heat until it dissolves. Warm the espagnole sauce and beat in the aspic and gelatine mixture. Add wine to taste and extra salt and pepper if necessary. Strain the sauce and allow to cool, beating it from time to time so that it remains smooth and glossy. When it reaches the consistency of thick cream, use to coat game, duck or cutlets.

Robert sauce

1 small onion, skinned and finely chopped
25 g *(1 oz)* butter
150 ml *(¼ pt)* dry white wine
15 ml *(1 tbsp)* wine vinegar
300 ml *(½ pt)* espagnole or demi-glace sauce
5–10 ml *(1–2 level tsps)* mild made mustard
pinch of sugar
salt and pepper

Fry the onion gently in the butter for about 10 minutes without browning. Add the wine and vinegar and boil rapidly until reduced by half. Stir in the sauce and simmer for 10 minutes. Add the mustard, a little sugar and extra seasoning if necessary.

Serve with pork.

Raisin sauce

30 ml *(2 level tbsps)* sugar
30 ml *(2 tbsps)* vinegar
300 ml *(½ pt)* espagnole sauce
50 g *(2 oz)* stoned raisins
60 ml *(4 tbsps)* red wine

Dissolve the sugar in the vinegar and boil until syrupy and slightly caramelised. Take the pan from the heat and gradually add the sauce and the raisins. Reheat and simmer for about 5 minutes or until the raisins are plump.

This sauce is very rich and tends to be rather thick, so just before serving thin it down with red wine until the desired consistency is obtained.

Serve with tongue, beef or game.

EGG SAUCES

Hollandaise

30 ml *(2 tbsps)* wine or tarragon vinegar
15 ml *(1 tbsp)* water
2 egg yolks
75–100 g *(3–4 oz)* butter
salt and pepper

Put the vinegar and water in a small pan and boil until reduced to about 15 ml *(1 tbsp)*; cool slightly. Put the egg yolks in a basin and stir in the vinegar. Put over a pan of hot water and heat gently, stirring all the time, until the egg mixture thickens (never let the water go above simmering point). Divide the butter into small pieces and gradually whisk into the sauce; add seasoning to taste. If the sauce is too sharp add a little more butter – it should be slightly piquant, almost thick enough to hold its shape and warm rather than hot when served.

Serve with salmon and other fish dishes, asparagus, or broccoli.

Béarnaise sauce

60 ml *(4 tbsps)* wine or tarragon vinegar
1 shallot, skinned and chopped
few sprigs of fresh tarragon, chopped
2 egg yolks
75 g *(3 oz)* butter
salt and pepper

Put the vinegar, shallot and tarragon in a small saucepan over a gentle heat and reduce by boiling to about 15 ml *(1 tbsp)*. Cool slightly and stir into the egg yolks in a basin and cook over a pan of simmering water until slightly thickened (as for hollandaise sauce, above). Whisk in the butter a little at a time, then season to taste. The sauce should be slightly thicker than hollandaise and with a more piquant flavour.

Serve with steaks or grills.

Note 15 ml *(1 tbsp)* vinegar can be replaced by 15 ml *(1 tbsp)* water – this gives a slightly less piquant sauce which some people prefer.

Mayonnaise

This is strictly speaking an egg sauce, but as it is served with salads, the recipe is given under salad dressings on page 245.

Tartare sauce

150 ml *(¼ pt)* mayonnaise
5 ml *(1 tsp)* chopped fresh tarragon or chives
10 ml *(2 tsps)* chopped capers
10 ml *(2 tsps)* chopped gherkins
10 ml *(2 tsps)* chopped parsley
15 ml *(1 tbsp)* lemon juice or tarragon vinegar

Mix all the ingredients well, then leave the sauce to stand for at least 1 hour before serving, to allow the flavours to blend.

Serve with fish.

OTHER SAVOURY SAUCES

Sauce provençale

50 g *(2 oz)* mushrooms, chopped
45 ml *(3 tbsps)* finely chopped shallots
1 clove garlic, skinned and chopped
30 ml *(2 tbsps)* cooking oil
300 ml *(½ pt)* well flavoured stock
150 ml *(¼ pt)* cider
5 ml *(1 level tsp)* tomato paste
salt and freshly ground black pepper
bouquet garni

Fry the mushrooms, shallots and garlic in the oil until soft but not browned. Add the stock, cider, tomato paste, salt, pepper and bouquet garni. Bring to the boil and simmer uncovered for 15–20 minutes. Remove the bouquet garni before serving. Serve with fish.

Apple sauce

450 g *(1 lb)* cooking apples, peeled and cored
25 g *(1 oz)* butter
little sugar

Slice the apples and boil gently in an open saucepan with 30–45 ml *(2–3 tbsps)* water until soft and thick – about 10 minutes. Beat to a pulp with a wooden spoon or potato masher, then if you wish sieve or purée in an electric blender. Stir in the butter and add a little sugar if the apples are very tart.

Serve with pork or sausages.

Bread sauce

1 medium sized onion
2 cloves
400 ml *(¾ pt)* milk
salt
few peppercorns
½ small bayleaf
knob of butter
75 g *(3 oz)* fresh white breadcrumbs

Skin the onion and stick the cloves into it, put it in a saucepan with the milk, salt and peppercorns and bayleaf, bring almost to boiling point and leave in a warm place for about 20 minutes, in order to extract the flavour from the onion. Remove the peppercorns and bayleaf and add the butter and breadcrumbs. Mix well and allow to cook very slowly for about 15 minutes, then remove the onion.

If you prefer, remove the onion before adding the breadcrumbs, but a better flavour is obtained by cooking it with the crumbs, as this allows the taste of the onion to penetrate them.

Serve with roast chicken, turkey or pheasant.

Barbecue sauce

50 g *(2 oz)* butter
1 large onion, skinned and chopped
5 ml *(1 level tsp)* tomato paste
30 ml *(2 tbsps)* vinegar
30 ml *(2 level tbsps)* demerara sugar
10 ml *(2 level tsps)* dry mustard
30 ml *(2 tbsps)* Worcestershire sauce
150 ml *(¼ pt)* water

Melt the butter and fry the onion for 5 minutes, or until soft. Stir in the tomato paste and continue cooking for a further 3 minutes. Blend the remaining ingredients to a smooth cream and stir in the onion mixture. Return the sauce to the pan and simmer uncovered for a further 10 minutes.

Serve with chicken, sausages, hamburgers or chops.

Chestnut sauce

225 g *(½ lb)* chestnuts, peeled
300 ml *(½ pt)* stock
small piece of onion, skinned
small piece of carrot, pared
40 g *(1½ oz)* butter
45 ml *(3 level tbsps)* flour
salt and pepper
30–45 ml *(2–3 tbsps)* single cream

Put the peeled nuts into a pan with the stock and vegetables, cover, simmer until soft and mash or sieve. Melt the butter and stir in the flour to form a roux, then add the chestnut purée and bring to the boil, stirring – the sauce should be thick, but it may be necessary at this point to add a little milk or extra stock. Season well with salt and pepper, remove from the heat and stir in the cream. Re-heat without boiling and serve at once, with turkey or other poultry.

Curry sauce

2 medium sized onions, skinned
25 g *(1 oz)* dripping or butter
15 ml *(1 level tbsp)* curry powder
5 ml *(1 level tsp)* curry paste
15 ml *(1 level tbsp)* rice flour or ordinary flour
1 clove garlic, skinned and crushed
200 ml *(7 fl oz)* stock or coconut milk
salt
little cayenne pepper
30 ml *(2 tbsps)* chutney
15 ml *(1 tbsp)* single cream, optional

Slice the onions and chop them finely. Melt the fat, fry the onions golden brown and add the curry powder, paste and rice (or ordinary) flour. Cook for 5 minutes, then add the garlic, pour in the stock or coconut milk and bring to the boil. Add the seasonings and chutney, cover and simmer for 30–40 minutes. This sauce is improved by the addition of the cream immediately before use and less curry powder may be used for those who prefer a mild dish.

Note The rice flour and ordinary flour can be omitted, since a curry is thickened by reduction of the liquid and by long, slow simmering.

Cranberry sauce

225 g *(½ lb)* sugar
300 ml *(½ pt)* water
225 g *(½ lb)* cranberries

Dissolve the sugar in the water and boil for 5 minutes. Add the cranberries and simmer for about 10 minutes or until the berries burst. Cool before serving. A little port can be added for additional flavour.

Serve with turkey.

Gooseberry sauce

225 g *(½ lb)* gooseberries, topped and tailed
25 g *(1 oz)* butter
30–60 ml *(2–4 level tbsps)* sugar

Stew the fruit in as little water as possible, until soft and pulped. Beat well, then sieve or purée in a blender. Add the butter and a little sugar if the fruit is very sour.

Serve with mackerel.

Horseradish cream

30 ml *(2 tbsps)* grated fresh horseradish
10 ml *(2 tsps)* lemon juice
10 ml *(2 level tsps)* sugar
pinch of dry mustard, optional
150 ml *(¼ pt)* double cream

Mix the horseradish, lemon juice, sugar and mustard. Whip the cream until it just leaves a trail, then fold in the horseradish mixture.

Serve with beef, trout or mackerel.

Cumberland sauce

1 orange
1 lemon
60 ml *(4 level tbsps)* red-currant jelly
60 ml *(4 tbsps)* port
10 ml *(2 level tsps)* arrowroot
10 ml *(2 tsps)* water

Pare the rind thinly from the orange and lemon, free of all the white pith. Cut it in fine strips, cover with water and simmer for 5 minutes. Squeeze the juice from both fruits. Put the red-currant jelly, orange juice and lemon juice in a pan, stir until the jelly dissolves, simmer for 5 minutes and add the port. Blend the arrowroot and water to a smooth cream and stir in the red-currant mixture. Return the sauce to the pan and reheat, stirring until it thickens and clears. Drain the strips of rind and add to the sauce.

Serve with ham, venison and lamb.

Spicy raisin sauce

75 g *(3 oz)* stoned raisins
2 cloves
300 ml *(½ pt)* water
75 g *(3 oz)* brown sugar
5 ml *(1 level tsp)* cornflour
salt and pepper
25 g *(1 oz)* butter
10 ml *(2 tsps)* lemon juice

Put the raisins and cloves in a saucepan with the water, bring to the boil and simmer uncovered for about 10 minutes; remove the cloves and add the sugar and cornflour, blended to a cream with a little cold water and seasoned with a pinch of salt and pepper. Stir well as the mixture thickens. Finally, add the butter and lemon juice.

Serve with grilled gammon rashers.

Tomato sauce
(Made from fresh tomatoes)

1 small onion, skinned and chopped
1 small carrot, pared and chopped
25 g *(1 oz)* butter
25 ml *(1½ level tbsps)* flour
450 g *(1 lb)* cooking tomatoes, quartered
300 ml *(½ pt)* chicken stock
½ bayleaf
1 clove
5 ml *(1 level tsp)* sugar
salt and pepper

Lightly fry the onion and carrot in the butter for 5 minutes. Stir in the flour and add the tomatoes, stock, bayleaf, clove, sugar, salt and pepper. Bring to the boil, cover and simmer for 30–45 minutes, or until the vegetables are cooked. Sieve, reheat and re-season if necessary.

Serve with croquettes, cutlets, rechauffés or any savoury dish.

Note If you wish, add 10 ml *(2 level tsps)* tomato paste to give a full flavour and better colour. 15–60 ml *(1–4 tbsps)* dry white wine or dry sherry may also be added just before serving.

Tomato sauce
(Made from canned tomatoes)

½ onion, skinned and chopped
2 rashers of bacon, rinded and chopped
knob of butter
25 ml *(1½ level tbsps)* **flour**
396-g *(14-oz)* **can tomatoes**
1 clove, ½ bayleaf and a few sprigs of rosemary, or 5 ml *(1 level tsp)* **mixed dried herbs**
pinch of sugar
salt and pepper

Fry the onion and bacon in the butter for 5 minutes. Stir in the flour and gradually add the tomatoes with their juice, also the flavourings and seasoning. Simmer gently for 15 minutes, then sieve and if necessary re-season.

Serve as for fresh tomato sauce.

Mint sauce

small bunch of mint, washed
10 ml *(2 level tsps)* **sugar**
15 ml *(1 tbsp)* **boiling water**
15–30 ml *(1–2 tbsps)* **vinegar**

Put the mint leaves only with the sugar on a board and chop finely. Put in a sauceboat, add the boiling water and stir until the sugar is dissolved. Stir in vinegar to taste. The sauce should be left for 1 hour before being served.

Mint sauce is served with lamb.

Port wine sauce

150 ml *(¼ pt)* **clear gravy or juices from roast lamb or venison**
15–30 ml *(1–2 level tbsps)* **red-currant jelly**
60 ml *(4 tbsps)* **port wine**

Put all the ingredients in a pan, stir well and simmer in an open pan for 5 10 minutes, until clear and syrupy.

Serve with roast lamb or venison.

SWEET SAUCES

White sauce

20 g *(¾ oz)* **butter or margarine**
about 30 ml *(2 level tbsps)* **flour**
300 ml *(½ pt)* **milk**
25 ml *(1½ level tbsps)* **sugar**

I – Roux method

Make a roux sauce (see page 193) and when it has thickened, add the sugar to taste.

25 ml *(1½ level tbsps)* **cornflour**
300 ml *(½ pt)* **milk**
about 25 ml *(1½ level tbsps)* **sugar**

II – Blended method

Make a blended sauce (see page 194) and when it has thickened, add the sugar to taste.

For those who like a thicker sauce, the proportions for a coating sauce (see page 194) can be used. This will be necessary if you add cream, rum or any other form of liquid when the sauce has been made.

Variations on white sauce (roux or blended)

Flavour with any of the following when the sauce has thickened:

5 ml *(1 level tsp)* mixed spice or ground nutmeg.
30 ml *(2 level tbsps)* jam
grated rind of ½ an orange or lemon.
30 ml *(2 tbsps)* single cream.
15–30 ml *(1–2 tbsps)* rum.
1 egg yolk (the sauce must be reheated but not re-boiled).

Chocolate sauce

15 ml *(1 level tbsp)* cornflour
15 ml *(1 level tbsp)* cocoa powder
30 ml *(2 level tbsps)* sugar
300 ml *(½ pt)* milk
knob of butter

Blend the cornflour, cocoa and sugar with enough of the measured milk to give a thin cream. Heat the remaining milk with the butter until boiling and pour on to the blended mixture, stirring all the time to prevent lumps forming. Return the mixture to the pan and bring to the boil, stirring until it thickens; cook for a further 1–2 minutes.

Serve with steamed or baked sponge puddings.

Note The cornflour and cocoa may be replaced by 30 ml *(2 level tbsps)* chocolate-flavoured cornflour.

Custard sauce

25 ml *(1½ level tbsps)* custard powder
25–30 ml *(1½–2 level tbsps)* sugar
300 ml *(½ pt)* milk

Blend the custard powder and sugar with a little of the measured cold milk to a smooth cream. Boil the rest of the milk and stir into the blended mixture. Return the sauce to the boil, stirring all the time until it thickens.

Serve hot with puddings or pies.

Note Cold thick custard is often used in cold sweets, eg, fruit fool; for this thicker consistency use 30–40 ml *(2–2½ level tbsps)* custard powder.

Egg custard sauce

1½ eggs or 3 yolks
15 ml *(1 level tbsp)* sugar
300 ml *(½ pt)* milk
few strips of thinly pared lemon rind or ½ vanilla pod, split

Whisk the eggs and sugar lightly. Warm the milk and lemon rind and leave to infuse for 10 minutes. Pour the milk on to the eggs and strain the mixture into the top of a double boiler or into a thick-based saucepan. Stir over a very gentle heat until the sauce thickens and lightly coats the back of the spoon. Do not boil.

Serve hot or cold, with fruit sweets.

Jam sauce

60 ml *(4 tbsps)* jam, sieved
150 ml *(¼ pt)* water or fruit juice
10 ml *(2 level tsps)* arrowroot
30 ml *(2 tbsps)* cold water
squeeze of lemon juice, optional

Warm the jam and water and simmer for 5 minutes. Blend the arrowroot and cold water to a smooth cream and stir in the jam mixture. Return the sauce to the pan and heat, stirring, until it thickens and clears. Add the lemon juice before serving.

Serve hot with steamed or baked puddings or cold over ice cream.

Note A thicker sauce is made by just melting the jam on its own over a gentle heat and adding a little lemon juice.

Red wine sauce

30 ml *(2 level tbsps)* granulated sugar
300 ml *(½ pt)* water
thinly pared rind of ½ lemon
150 ml *(¼ pt)* red wine
60 ml *(4 tbsps)* seedless bramble jam
20 ml *(4 level tsps)* arrowroot
30 ml *(2 tbsps)* lemon juice

Put the sugar, water, lemon rind, wine and jam in a saucepan. Bring slowly to the boil and simmer for 5 minutes. Remove the lemon rind. Blend the arrowroot with the lemon juice and stir it into the sauce. Bring to the boil, stirring, reduce the heat and cook until thickened.

Serve with fruit, ice cream or sponge puddings.

Syrup sauce

60–75 ml *(4–5 tbsps)* golden syrup
45 ml *(3 tbsps)* water
juice of ½ lemon

Warm the syrup and water, stir well and simmer for 2–3 minutes; add the lemon juice.

Serve with steamed or baked sponge puddings.

Fruit sauce

425-g *(15-oz)* can fruit
10 ml *(2 level tsps)* arrowroot or cornflour
squeeze of lemon juice, optional

Strain the juice from the fruit. Sieve the fruit, make up to 300 ml *(½ pt)* with juice and heat until boiling. Blend the arrowroot with a little more juice until it is a smooth cream and stir in the puréed fruit. Return mixture to pan and heat gently, continuing to stir, until the sauce thickens and clears. A squeeze of lemon juice or 15 ml *(1 tbsp)* of rum, sherry or fruit liqueur may be added just before serving. Good with meringue sweets, cold soufflés, ice creams, hot baked puddings and steamed puddings.

Lemon or orange sauce

grated rind and juice of 1 large lemon or orange
water
15 ml *(1 level tbsp)* cornflour
30 ml *(2 level tbsps)* sugar
knob of butter
1 egg yolk, optional

Make up the fruit rind and juice with water to 300 ml *(½ pt)*. Blend the cornflour and sugar with a little of the liquid to a smooth cream. Boil the remaining liquid and stir into the mixture. Return it to the pan and bring to the boil, stirring until the sauce thickens and clears. Add the butter. Cool, beat in the egg yolk (if used) and reheat, stirring, without boiling.

Serve hot or cold, as for fruit sauce.

Brandy butter (Hard sauce)

75 g *(3 oz)* butter
75 g *(3 oz)* caster sugar
30–45 ml *(2–3 tbsps)* brandy

Cream the butter until pale and soft. Beat in the sugar gradually and add the brandy a few drops at a time, taking care not to allow the mixture to curdle. The finished sauce should be pale and frothy. Pile it up in a small dish and leave to harden before serving.

Traditionally served with Christmas pudding and mince pies.

Note If you prefer a less granular texture, use sifted icing sugar or half icing and half caster sugar.

Rum butter

Make this as brandy butter, above, but use soft brown sugar, replace the brandy by 60 ml *(4 tbsps)* rum and include the grated rind of half a lemon and a squeeze of lemon juice.

Mousseline sauce

1 egg
1 egg yolk
45 ml *(3 level tbsps)* sugar
15 ml *(1 tbsp)* sherry
60 ml *(4 tbsps)* single cream

Place all the ingredients in a basin over a pan of boiling water and whisk until pale and frothy and of a thick creamy consistency.

Serve at once over light steamed or baked puddings, fruit, fruit sweets or Christmas pudding.

Sabayon sauce (cold)

50 g *(2 oz)* caster sugar
60 ml *(4 tbsps)* water
2 egg yolks, beaten
grated rind of ½ lemon
juice of 1 lemon
30 ml *(2 tbsps)* rum or sherry
30 ml *(2 tbsps)* single cream

Dissolve the sugar in the water and boil for 2–3 minutes, until syrupy. Pour slowly on to the yolks, whisking until pale and thick. Add the lemon rind, lemon juice and rum or sherry and whisk for a further few minutes. Fold in the cream and chill well.

Serve with cold fruit sweets.

ICE CREAM SAUCES

The following are used mainly with ice cream and in sundaes.

Chocolate sauce

50 g *(2 oz)* plain chocolate
knob of butter
15 ml *(1 tbsp)* milk
5 ml *(1 tsp)* vanilla essence

Melt the chocolate and butter in a basin standing in a pan of warm water. Stir in the milk and vanilla essence and serve straight away over ice cream.

Rich chocolate sauce

175 g *(6 oz)* plain chocolate
large knob of butter
45 ml *(3 tbsps)* milk
45 ml *(3 level tbsps)* golden syrup
15 ml *(1 tbsp)* coffee essence

Put the broken up chocolate in a basin over a pan of hot water. Add the rest of the ingredients and heat gently until melted and warm. Beat well before serving.

Coffee sauce

100 g *(4 oz)* demerara or granulated sugar
30 ml *(2 tbsps)* water
300 ml *(½ pt)* strong black coffee

Put the sugar and water in a heavy based pan and dissolve over a gentle heat, without stirring. Bring to the boil and boil rapidly until the syrup becomes golden in colour. Add the coffee and stir until the 'caramel' has dissolved. Boil for a few minutes, until syrupy. Allow to cool, and serve poured over ice cream.

Butterscotch sauce

25 g *(1 oz)* butter
30 ml *(2 level tbsps)* brown sugar
15 ml *(1 tbsp)* golden syrup
45 ml *(3 tbsps)* chopped nuts
squeeze of lemon juice, optional

Warm the butter, sugar and syrup until well blended. Boil for 1 minute and stir in the nuts and lemon juice.

Melba sauce

60 ml *(4 tbsps)* red-currant jelly
75 g *(3 oz)* sugar
150 ml *(¼ pt)* raspberry purée, from 225 g *(½ lb)* raspberries, sieved
10 ml *(2 level tsps)* arrowroot or cornflour
15 ml *(1 tbsp)* cold water

Mix the jelly, sugar and raspberry purée and bring to the boil. Blend the arrowroot with the cold water to a smooth cream, stir in a little of the raspberry mixture, return the sauce to the pan; bring to the boil, stirring with a wooden spoon until it thickens and clears. Strain and cool.

Vegetables

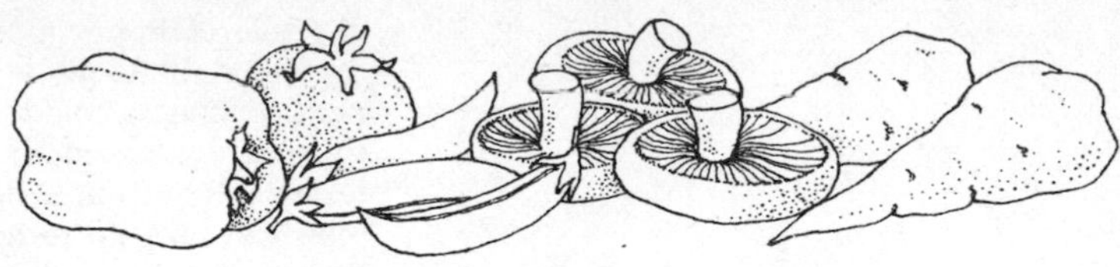

Vegetables are essential in the diet because of their importance as a source of vitamins B and C and carotene, which is a precursor of vitamin A. They are also rich in minerals, particularly iron and calcium. Generally speaking vegetables have a low calorific value which is to some an additional advantage. The cellulose in vegetables has a stimulating effect on the intestinal tract. In the main leafy vegetables are richer in vitamin C than root vegetables, potatoes being one of the exceptions.

Most vegetables are served as an accompaniment to other dishes, but some (for instance globe artichokes) make a good appetiser and there are various dressed vegetables which can form a course in themselves, either after the roast at a formal meal (eg dressed asparagus) or as a main dish for an informal lunch or supper (eg cauliflower cheese).

Storing and preparation

Keep vegetables in a cool, airy place – for example in a vegetable rack placed in a cool larder or in the vegetable compartment of the refrigerator. Green vegetables should be used as soon as possible after gathering, while their vitamin C value is at its highest.

All vegetables should be prepared as near to the time of cooking as possible, to retain both flavour and vitamin C content. Generally speaking when cooking vegetables allow about 5 ml *(1 level tsp)* salt per 600 ml *(1 pt)* water.

Serving vegetables

Serve them as soon as they are cooked – they deteriorate when they are kept hot. Have them slightly under-cooked rather than over-cooked, and drain them well, if boiled. (You can press green vegetables to squeeze out the water.) It's worth remembering that fresh from the garden young vegetables usually need less cooking time.

Serve fried vegetables very hot and don't cover them with a lid or they will become soggy.

A sprinkling of salt and pepper improves most vegetables – especially fried ones, where no salt is used in the cooking process. Add a knob of butter to boiled and steamed vegetables.

A sprinkling of chopped herbs added before serving also improves vegetables – try parsley on carrots, mint on peas, tarragon on courgettes. A little grated nutmeg gives an interesting flavour to cabbage.

A well flavoured white or cheese sauce makes a change with such vegetables as cauliflower, marrow, leeks and onions, broad beans and carrots. (For recipes see pages 193 to 195.)

A platterful of assorted vegetables, arranged in rows or circles, looks attractive and is a good accompaniment to boiled meat.

ARTICHOKE (JERUSALEM)

Scrub the artichokes; using a stainless steel knife or peeler, peel them quickly and immediately plunge them into cold water, keeping them under the water as much as possible to prevent discoloration. A squeeze of lemon juice (or a few drops of vinegar) added to the water helps to keep them a good colour. Cook in boiling salted water to which a little lemon juice (or vinegar) has been added until just tender, 15–20 minutes. Alternatively cook with the skin on and peel after cooking but by this method they do darken a little. Drain, garnish with finely chopped parsley and serve with melted butter or a white, cheese or hollandaise sauce (see pages 193, 195, 200).

Allow 175–225 g (6–8 oz) per portion.

ARTICHOKES (GLOBE)

The artichokes should be of a good green colour, with tightly clinging, fleshy leaves – leaves that are spreading and fuzzy, or purplish centres indicate over-maturity. Cut off the stem close to the base of the leaves and take off the outside layer of leaves and any others which are dry or discoloured. As globe artichokes have close-growing leaves, they need soaking in cold water for about ½ hour, to ensure that they are thoroughly cleaned; drain well. Cook in boiling salted water until the leaves will pull out easily – 20–40 minutes, depending on size. Large ones can take up to 60 minutes. Drain upside-down. Serve with melted butter or hollandaise sauce (see page 200).

Globe artichokes may also be served cold with a vinaigrette dressing (see page 244). When eating them, pull off the leaves with the fingers; the soft end of each leaf is dipped in the sauce and sucked. When you reach the centre, remove the choke (or soft flowery part), if it has not already been taken out, and eat the bottom, which is the chief delicacy, with a knife and fork.

Allow 1 artichoke per person.

Stuffed globe artichokes

4 globe artichokes, trimmed and washed
½ small onion, skinned and finely chopped
2 mushrooms, finely chopped
knob of butter, about 15 g *(½ oz)*
50 g *(2 oz)* **cooked ham, chopped**
10 ml *(2 level tsps)* **fresh breadcrumbs**
beaten egg to bind
salt and pepper

Cook the artichokes in boiling salted water for 20–40 minutes, until the leaves will pull out easily; drain and remove the inner leaves and the chokes. Lightly fry the onion and the mushrooms in the butter for about 5 minutes and add the other ingredients, using enough beaten egg to bind. Season the mixture and fill the artichokes with it. Put them into a greased ovenproof dish, cover with greased paper and bake in the oven at 190°C *(375°F)* mark 5 for 10–15 minutes.

Artichokes à la lyonnaise

4 globe artichokes
lemon juice
30 ml *(2 tbsps)* **oil**
1 onion, skinned and chopped
4 rashers bacon, rinded and chopped
45 ml *(3 level tbsps)* **flour**
400 ml *(¾ pt)* **stock**
150 ml *(¼ pt)* **dry white wine**
salt and pepper

Prepare the artichokes by removing the stalks level with the leaves, and trim the tops from the outer leaves. Wash several times in water, then leave to soak in fresh cold water for 30 minutes; drain. Place in boiling water, sharpened with lemon juice, and boil until the leaves can easily be pulled away (20–40 minutes). Meanwhile heat the oil in a saucepan and sauté the onion and bacon until lightly browned. Stir in the flour and cook for a few minutes. Gradually add the stock, stirring until smooth and thick. Stir in the wine and season well with salt and pepper. Drain the artichokes, and serve with the wine sauce.

ASPARAGUS

Cut off the woody end of the stalks and scrape the white part lightly, removing any coarse spines. Tie in bundles of even thickness, with all the heads together, and place upright in a saucepan of boiling water. The water should be almost to the tips. Cover the tips with foil, bring the water to the boil, reduce the heat and cook gently for 10–15 minutes. Alternatively, cradle the heads in a band of foil, so that they cook in the steam only. Lay the bundles in the bottom of a saucepan with the heads all pointing in the same direction and cook as before. Don't overcook asparagus – it is better to have to discard more of the stem part than to have the tips mushy.

Drain and untie the bundles before serving with melted butter or hollandaise sauce (see page 200). To eat, hold a stick by the stem end and dip the tip in the butter or sauce. It is not usual to eat the stem end.

Asparagus may also be served cold, with a vinaigrette dressing or with mayonnaise (pages 244, 245).

Allow 8–12 stems per portion.

Fried aubergines with parsley (p. 209), Cauliflower niçoise (p. 215).
(Overleaf) Grapefruit and prawn salad (p. 242), Tomato salad (p. 235), Green salad (p. 235), Cucumber salad (p. 235), Mushroom salad (p. 236), Cream cheese and celery salad (p. 240).

CLOVES
MACE

Asparagus with cheese dressing

Cook the asparagus as above and cut off the inedible part of the stalks. Place the tips in a vegetable dish and sprinkle with finely grated Parmesan cheese or a mixture of Gruyère and Parmesan. Pour over them melted butter, with salt and pepper and 5 ml *(1 tsp)* lemon juice to every 30 ml *(2 tbsps)* melted butter.

AUBERGINE OR EGG PLANT

A long, oval vegetable with a shiny purple skin. Aubergines should be of uniform colour, firm, smooth and free from blemishes. Cut off the stem and small leaves which surround it; wash the vegetable and if necessary peel it. Aubergines are usually fried or stuffed and baked.

Allow about 175 g (6 oz) per portion.

Fried aubergines with parsley *see colour plate facing p. 208*

4 aubergines – 700 g *(1½ lb)*
salt and freshly ground pepper
flour, optional
60–75 ml *(4–5 tbsps)* cooking oil
50 g *(2 oz)* butter
small clove garlic, skinned and crushed
30 ml *(2 tbsps)* chopped parsley

Wipe the aubergines and discard stem and calyx; peel if you wish. Cut into 1-cm *(½-in)* slices and sprinkle with salt; leave for ½–1 hour, drain well, wipe, and if you like, dip into flour. Heat half the oil and butter and fry the aubergines a few slices at a time until brown and tender (adding the remaining oil and butter as required); drain and keep hot in a serving dish. Finally, pour off all but 15 ml *(1 tbsp)* of the pan drippings and add the crushed garlic and parsley. Spoon over the aubergines, and add some pepper. Serve as an accompaniment.

Stuffed aubergines

2 medium sized aubergines
50 g *(2 oz)* cooked ham, chopped
15 ml *(1 tbsp)* chopped parsley
1 tomato, skinned and chopped
50 g *(2 oz)* fresh breadcrumbs
½ onion, skinned and grated
salt and pepper
100 g *(4 oz)* Cheddar cheese, grated
little stock or beaten egg to bind (if necessary)

Wash the aubergines and remove the stalks. Cut in half lengthways and scoop out the flesh from the centre of each, leaving a 0.5-cm *(¼-in)* thick 'shell'.

Make the stuffing by combining the ham, parsley, tomato, crumbs, onion, seasoning and 50 g *(2 oz)* of the cheese with the roughly chopped aubergine flesh. Moisten with a little stock or beaten egg and fill the aubergine shells. Sprinkle with the remaining grated cheese, cover with a lid or foil and bake in the oven at 200°C *(400°F)* mark 6 for 15–20 minutes, until cooked. Uncover and cook for a further 5–10 minutes, until crisp and brown on top. Serve hot with a cheese or tomato sauce (see pages 195 or 202).

Aubergine fiesta

450 g *(1 lb)* aubergines
boiling water
396-g *(14-oz)* can tomatoes, drained
25 g *(1 oz)* butter
1 clove garlic, skinned and crushed
1.25 ml *(¼ level tsp)* salt
freshly ground pepper
340-g *(12-oz)* can whole-kernel sweet corn
50 g *(2 oz)* Parmesan cheese, grated
chopped parsley for garnish

Peel the aubergines, cut into 2.5-cm *(1-in)* slices and cut each slice into 4 triangular chunks. Put in a saucepan, cover with boiling water and boil gently for 5 minutes; drain well. Roughly chop the tomatoes. Butter the inside of an ovenproof dish and put in the aubergines, tomatoes, garlic, seasoning and corn. Sprinkle evenly with the cheese. Bake uncovered in the oven at 200°C *(400°F)* mark 6 for about 20 minutes, until the sauce is bubbly and the cheese has melted. Garnish with the chopped parsley.

Anna potatoes (p. 225), Potato croquettes (p. 225).

Baked aubergines

Wash the aubergines and cut into slices about 1 cm (*½ in*) thick. Salt and drain as for fried aubergines. Lay them in a buttered shallow ovenproof dish. Sprinkle thickly with white breadcrumbs, season well with salt and pepper, pour a little melted butter over and bake in the oven at 200°C (*400°F*) mark 6 for 15 minutes. Serve with tomato sauce.

Ratatouille *see colour plate facing p. 288*

30 ml (*2 tbsps*) **oil**
15 g (*½ oz*) **butter**
2 large onions, skinned and sliced
1 large aubergine, washed and chopped
4 tomatoes, skinned and chopped
4 courgettes, washed and sliced
1 green or red pepper, seeded and sliced
1 clove garlic, skinned and crushed
30 ml (*2 level tbsps*) **tomato paste**
salt and pepper
30 ml (*2 tbsps*) **chopped parsley**

Heat the oil and butter in a flameproof casserole and add the prepared vegetables, seasoning and garlic. Stir well, cover tightly and put in the oven at 180°C (*350°F*) mark 4 for 1–1¼ hours, or until cooked. Serve garnished with parsley.

BEANS (BROAD)

Use only young beans.

Shell and cook in boiling salted water until soft – 15–20 minutes. If you wish, serve with parsley sauce.

When broad beans are very young and tender – that is, when the pods are only a few inches long and the beans inside very small – the whole pods may be cooked and eaten.

Allow 225–350 g (½–¾ lb) beans per portion (weight as bought).

BEANS (FRENCH AND RUNNER)

Top, tail and string the beans. Slice runner beans thinly; French beans may be left whole. Cook in boiling salted water until tender but still slightly crisp – young beans 8–12 minutes, larger beans 15–20 minutes. Remove any scum that rises to the top with a spoon. Drain and toss with salt and pepper and a knob of butter before serving. To keep the colour of French beans, plunge them into cold water when cooked then drain and reheat in melted butter.

Allow 100–125 g (¼–½ lb) per portion.

Runner beans with carrots

225 g (*½ lb*) **young carrots, pared and thinly sliced**
salt and pepper
450 g (*1 lb*) **runner beans, stringed and thinly sliced**
30 ml (*2 tbsps*) **oil**

Put 2.5 cm (*1 in*) of water in a strong saucepan, add the carrots, salt and pepper and cook for 5 minutes, with the lid on. Add the beans and oil and continue cooking for about a further 12 minutes, or until soft.

BEETROOT

Cut off the stalks 2.5 cm (*1 in*) or so above the root, then wash the beetroots, taking care not to damage the skin or they will 'bleed' when boiled. Boil in salted water until soft; the time depends on the age and freshness, small early beetroots will take about 30 minutes, larger older ones about 1½ hours. When they are cooked, peel off the skin and cut the beets into cubes or slices. Serve hot, coated with a white sauce, or cold, sliced and in a little vinegar.

Beetroots can be cooked in a much shorter time if peeled and sliced when raw and cooked until tender in a small amount of liquid in a covered saucepan. Again, the time taken varies, the average being ½ hour. Serve in the liquor in which the beetroots were cooked, or use the liquor to make a sauce, instead of milk.

Allow 100–175 g (4–6 oz) when served as an accompaniment.

Glazed beetroots

12 small beetroots, cooked
25 g *(1 oz)* butter
5 ml *(1 level tsp)* sugar
salt and pepper
grated rind of 1 lemon
5 ml *(1 tsp)* chopped chives
10 ml *(2 tsps)* chopped parsley
juice of ½ lemon
15 ml *(1 tbsp)* capers

Remove the skin, stalks and root end from the beetroots. Melt the butter in a saucepan and add the beetroots, sugar, salt, pepper and lemon rind. Toss the beetroots in the pan over a medium heat until they are well coated; add the remaining ingredients, heat through and serve.

BROCCOLI

There are several varieties of this vegetable, the chief ones being:

White broccoli, with a fairly large flower head, which is cooked and served in the same way as cauliflower. Buy by the head, judging by size.

Purple broccoli and calabrese (a green sprouting broccoli), which have a more delicate flavour. They are cooked like cauliflower, but take only 10–15 minutes, although steaming takes a little longer it does retain the maximum flavour. Serve plain, buttered or with hollandaise sauce (see page 200).

Allow 175–225 g (6–8 oz) per serving.

BRUSSELS SPROUTS

Wash the sprouts, removing any discoloured leaves, and cut a cross in the stalks. Cook in boiling salted water until soft – 10–15 minutes. Drain, return them to the pan and re-heat with salt and pepper and a knob of butter.

Allow 100–175 g (4–6 oz) per person.

Brussels sprouts and chestnuts

This mixture is especially good to serve with Christmas poultry.

Allow half the amount of chestnuts to Brussels sprouts. Put the chestnuts into cold water and bring to the boil. Remove both the outside and inside skins. Put the nuts in a saucepan, cover with a little stock and add a stick of celery and 5 ml *(1 level tsp)* sugar. Bring to the boil and allow to simmer gently until the nuts are soft – about 35–40 minutes. Remove the celery and drain the nuts. Cook the Brussels sprouts separately in boiling salted water for 8–10 minutes. Mix the cooked nuts and sprouts together and toss in butter.

CABBAGE

Savoy and Dutch

Remove the coarse outer leaves, cut the cabbage in half and take out the hard centre stalk. Wash thoroughly, shred finely and cook rapidly in about 2.5 cm *(1 in)* of boiling salted water for about 5–10 minutes, or until cooked. Alternatively cook in wedges for about 15 minutes.

Drain well and toss with a knob of butter, a sprinkling of pepper and a pinch of grated nutmeg (optional). Serve at once.

Allow 175–225 g (6–8 oz) per portion.

Spring greens

Separate the leaves and cut off the base of any thick stems. Wash well and shred roughly. Cook as for cabbage. Chop before serving if you wish.

Allow 225 g (½ lb) per portion.

Red cabbage

Cook as for Savoy or Dutch Cabbage (above), but add 15 ml *(1 tbsp)* vinegar to the water to improve the flavour; allow 15–20 minutes.

For pickled red cabbage, see page 452.

Chinese leaves (or cabbage)

Resembles a cross between a very pale, whitish-green cos lettuce, and a head of celery, though much larger and considerably heavier than both. Each head weighs from 900 g to 2.5 kg *(2–5 lb)*. Chinese leaves have a distinctive taste, extremely delicate and best described as predominately that of juicy cabbage, with more than a hint of celery. Keeping quality is good up to a week in the refrigerator. Chinese leaves are a useful addition to the ranks of vegetables available mid-November until early June, with a break of about 1 month in April. They serve a double purpose as they may be cooked or eaten raw as a salad base. To cook, shred the amount required, plunge into boiling salted water and continue boiling quickly until tender – about 5 minutes. Drain well, toss with butter and finely chopped parsley or a sprinkling of nutmeg. In salads it is preferable to use the inner leaves as an alternative to lettuce or cabbage in a slaw mixture.

Fried cabbage

½ a Dutch cabbage
25 g *(1 oz)* butter
15 ml *(1 tbsp)* oil
2.5–5 ml *(½–1 level tsp)* salt

Wash the cabbage and shred it finely. Heat the butter and oil in a heavy based frying pan, add the cabbage and cook it for 5–10 minutes, stirring all the time, until crisp but not coloured. Sprinkle lightly with salt and serve immediately.

Cabbage parcels

1 Savoy cabbage, untrimmed
50 g *(2 oz)* butter
225 g *(8 oz)* calves' liver, chopped
1 large onion, skinned and chopped
30 ml *(2 level tbsps)* tomato paste
2.5 ml *(½ level tsp)* grated nutmeg
salt and pepper
25 g *(1 oz)* flour
150 ml *(¼ pt)* milk
75 g *(3 oz)* mature Cheddar cheese, grated
pinch of mustard and cayenne
100 g *(4 oz)* long grain rice, cooked
oil for glazing

Carefully remove all perfect leaves from the cabbage. You need 10 medium sized leaves. Place them in a large saucepan, cover with cold water and bring to the boil. Reduce the heat and simmer gently for about 10 minutes. Drain and pat the leaves dry. Melt 25 g *(1 oz)* butter in a pan, add the liver and fry until firm, about 5 minutes. Add the onion and fry until tender. Stir in the tomato paste and seasonings; cool slightly. Make a white sauce, using 25 g *(1 oz)* butter, the flour and milk. Add the cheese and season, adding the mustard and cayenne. Combine the liver mixture and rice with the cheese sauce and divide the mixture between the cabbage leaves. Fold up lightly and place them in an ovenproof dish. Brush with oil. Bake in the oven at 190°C *(375°F)* mark 5 for about 30 minutes. *Serves 4–5.*

Scalloped cabbage

1 small white cabbage, washed and shredded
300 ml (*½ pt*) well seasoned white sauce
100 g (*4 oz*) grated cheese

Cook the cabbage in boiling salted water for 5–7 minutes, drain well and put in a greased ovenproof dish. Make the white sauce with half milk and half liquor from the cabbage (see page 193). Add the grated cheese, reserving 15 ml (*1 tbsp*). Heat gently until the cheese is melted and beat until smooth. Pour the sauce over the cabbage, stir lightly together, sprinkle with the remaining grated cheese and brown in the oven at 220°C (*425°F*) mark 7 or under the grill.

Bubble and squeak

leftover mashed potatoes
leftover cooked cabbage, chopped
salt and pepper
butter, dripping or lard

Mix the potatoes and cabbage together, with seasoning to taste. Heat some fat in a frying pan, put in the vegetable mixture, smooth it over and flatten with a palette knife. Fry it until it is nicely browned underneath, then turn it over and brown the underside, allowing it to heat through thoroughly.

Other cooked vegetables, such as carrot, celery and parsnip, may be added, also small cubes of cooked meat or poultry.

Braised red cabbage

1 kg (*2¼ lb*) red cabbage
2 medium sized onions, skinned and sliced
2 cooking apples, peeled, cored and chopped
10 ml (*2 level tsps*) sugar
salt and freshly ground pepper
bouquet garni
30 ml (*2 tbsps*) water
30 ml (*2 tbsps*) red wine vinegar
25 g (*1 oz*) margarine or butter

Shred the cabbage finely, discarding any discoloured outside leaves and coarse stems. Layer the cabbage in a 3.4-l (*6-pt*) casserole with the onions, apples, sugar and seasoning. Put the bouquet garni in the centre and pour the water and vinegar over. Cover tightly and cook in the oven at 200°C (*400°F*) mark 6 for 1 hour. Remove the lid and continue cooking for about 30 minutes, until the liquid is evaporated. Add butter or margarine and mix with the cabbage at the end of the cooking time. This is excellent with pork. *Serves 6.*

Note Red cabbage reheats well.

CARROTS

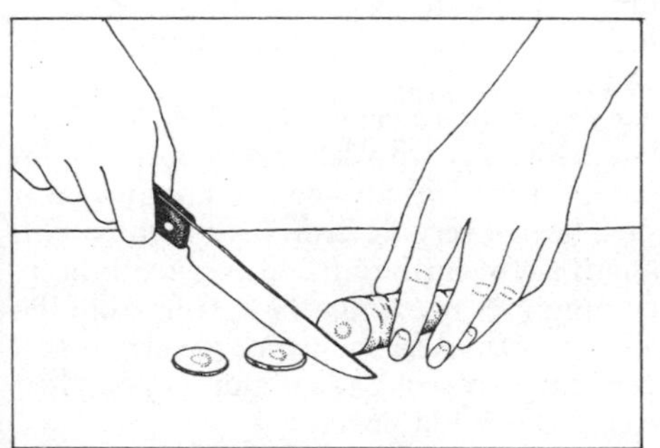

Slicing carrots into thin rounds

New Trim off the leaves, then scrape lightly with a sharp knife. As they are small, new carrots are usually cooked whole. Simmer in salted water for about 15 minutes, or until cooked. Serve tossed with a little butter, pepper and chopped parsley. Add a pinch of sugar to bring out the flavour if you wish.

Old Pare thinly and cut in one of these ways:

1. Into 0.5- or 1-cm (*¼- or ½-in*) lengthways strips.
2. Into strips and then across to small cubes.
3. Into thin rounds.

Cook and serve as for new carrots, but simmer strips and cubes for 10–15 minutes, thin slices 6–8 minutes.

Allow 100–175 g (4–6 oz) per portion.

Vichy carrots

450 g (*1 lb*) carrots, trimmed and scraped
pinch of salt
water
butter
5 ml (*1 level tsp*) sugar
freshly ground pepper
chopped parsley

Slice the carrots thinly if old, leave whole if young. Blanch old carrots in boiling water for 2 minutes. Drain. Return the carrots to the pan with 400 ml (*¾ pt*) water, salt, a knob of butter and the sugar. Bring to the boil and cook uncovered over a low heat, shaking occasionally towards the end until all the liquid has evaporated – about 45 minutes.

Serve hot, with an extra knob of butter, freshly ground pepper and a garnish of parsley.

Glazed carrots

50 g *(2 oz)* butter
450 g *(1 lb)* young carrots, scraped and left whole
3 lumps of sugar
1.25 ml *(¼ level tsp)* salt
little home-made jellied stock
freshly ground pepper
chopped parsley

Melt the butter in a saucepan. Add the carrots, sugar, salt and enough stock to come halfway up the carrots. Cook gently without a lid, shaking the pan occasionally, until soft; remove the carrots and keep them hot. Boil the liquid rapidly until it is reduced to a rich glaze. Replace the carrots in it a few at a time, turning them until all sides are well coated with glaze. Season with pepper and serve sprinkled with parsley.

Carrots in orange juice

Cook the carrots in the normal way, drain and add a knob of butter, 30 ml *(2 level tbsps)* brown sugar and the juice of 1 orange. Heat gently to melt the butter and dissolve the sugar, then simmer for 5 minutes.

CAULIFLOWER

Remove the coarse outside leaves, cut a cross in the stalk end and wash the cauliflower. Cook it stem side down in fast-boiling salted water to come half-way up for 10–15 minutes, depending on size. Drain well and serve coated with white or cheese sauce (see pages 193, 195).

The cauliflower can be divided into individual florets and cooked in fast-boiling salted water for 8–10 minutes. Drain well and serve tossed with butter and a sprinkling of pepper or coated with sauce.

A medium-sized cauliflower serves 4 people.

Cauliflower appetiser, with garlic

450 g *(1 lb)* prepared cauliflower florets
salt
vegetable oil
freshly ground black pepper
50 g *(2 oz)* seasoned flour
2 eggs, beaten
75 ml *(5 tbsps)* fresh white breadcrumbs
75 ml *(5 tbsps)* olive oil
1 clove garlic, skinned
7.5 ml *(1½ level tsps)* paprika
25 ml *(1½ tbsps)* white vinegar
40 ml *(2½ tbsps)* boiling water

Drop the florets into boiling salted water. Cook briskly, uncovered, for 8–10 minutes or until cauliflower resists only slightly when pierced. Drain on kitchen paper.

Heat a deep saucepan with about 10 cm *(4 in)* of oil to 180°C *(350°F)*. Sprinkle the florets liberally with salt and pepper. Dip in flour, then beaten egg and crumbs. Fry for about 4 minutes until golden brown. Arrange on a heated serving dish, cover lightly with foil and keep warm. In a small pan, warm the olive oil over gentle heat; add the garlic, cook for 2–3 minutes to extract the flavour from the garlic, then remove it from the pan. Add the paprika, vinegar and water to the oil, stirring continuously; cook 1–2 minutes more, then pour it over the cauliflower and serve at once.

Cauliflower au gratin

1 cauliflower, trimmed
40 g *(1½ oz)* butter
45 ml *(3 level tbsps)* flour
300 ml *(½ pt)* milk
100 g *(4 oz)* cheese, grated
salt and pepper

Cook the cauliflower in fast-boiling salted water until just tender, drain and place in an ovenproof dish. Melt the butter, stir in the flour and cook for 2–3 minutes. Remove the pan from the heat and gradually stir in the milk; bring to the boil and continue to stir until it thickens. Stir in 75 g *(3 oz)* of the cheese and season to taste. Pour over the hot cauliflower, sprinkle with the remaining cheese and brown under a hot grill. Cauliflower can also be served with an egg sauce (see page 194).

Cauliflower niçoise *see colour plate facing p. 208*

1 medium sized cauliflower
salt
1 small onion, skinned
225 g *(½ lb)* firm tomatoes, skinned
25 g *(1 oz)* butter
1 small clove garlic, skinned and crushed
freshly ground black pepper
15 ml *(1 tbsp)* chopped parsley

Divide the cauliflower head into florets and cook these in boiling salted water for about 10 minutes. Drain thoroughly. Meanwhile have ready the niçoise mixture. Slice the onion finely. Halve the tomatoes, discard the seeds and cut the flesh into squares. Melt the butter and fry the onion till soft. Lightly stir in the tomato and garlic. Heat through, and season with pepper. Arrange the cauliflower in a serving dish, then top with the tomato mixture and plenty of parsley.

CELERIAC

(The root of turnip-rooted celery)
Peel the celeriac fairly thickly; small roots may be cooked whole but larger ones should be sliced thickly or cut into dice. Cook in boiling salted water or stock until tender – 45 minutes to 1 hour. Drain well and serve with melted butter or a béchamel or hollandaise sauce (see pages 196, 200).

Celeriac may also be braised or served au gratin, it makes good fritters and soup; in a salad, serve it raw, thinly cut or grated.

Allow 100–225 g (¼–½ lb) per portion.

CELERY

Wash, scrub and cut into 5-cm *(2-in)* lengths, or slice thinly. Cook in boiling salted water until tender – 10–20 minutes depending on the coarseness of the celery. Drain well and serve with a white, parsley or cheese sauce (see pages 193 to 196).

Allow 1 head of celery per person if small, 2–3 sticks if large.

Braised celery

4 small heads celery, trimmed and scrubbed
50 g *(2 oz)* butter
well flavoured stock, preferably home-made and jellied
salt and pepper

Tie each head of celery securely to hold the shape. Fry lightly in half the butter for 5 minutes, until golden brown. Put in an ovenproof dish, add enough stock to come halfway up the celery, sprinkle with salt and pepper and add the remaining butter. Cover and cook for 1–1½ hours in the oven at 180°C *(350°F)* mark 4. Remove the strings and serve with the cooking liquid poured over; if the stock is home-made reduce it first to a glaze by fast boiling.

Celery au gratin

1 head celery, scrubbed and chopped
25 g *(1 oz)* butter
45 ml *(3 level tbsps)* flour
150 ml *(¼ pt)* milk
75 g *(3 oz)* mature cheese, grated
salt and cayenne pepper
browned breadcrumbs

Cook the celery in a little boiling salted water for 10–20 minutes until tender and drain well, keeping 150 ml *(¼ pt)* of the liquid. Melt the fat, stir in the flour and cook for 2–3 minutes. Remove the pan from the heat and gradually stir in the 150 ml *(¼ pt)* celery liquor and the milk, bring to the boil and continue to stir until the mixture thickens; add 50 g *(2 oz)* of the cheese and season to taste with salt and a few grains of cayenne pepper. Fill an ovenproof dish with alternate layers of celery and sauce. Sprinkle the top with the remaining cheese and a few browned breadcrumbs. Put under a low grill until heated through and browned.

CHICORY

These plants are grown in the dark to preserve their delicate flavour and prevent them from becoming too bitter, hence the long, thin leaves are practically white, or if coloured at all are only a pale yellowy green at the tip. When fresh the heads are crisp and the tips firm, showing no signs of green at the tip. In this country they are generally eaten raw as a salad plant, but they may also be cooked.

To prepare, cut off a thin slice from the base and, using a pointed knife, remove the core. Pull away any damaged outer leaves and wash quickly under cold water – do not soak.

To cook, plunge the heads into boiling salted water and blanch for 5 minutes. Drain and cook covered in a minimum of water, with lemon juice, a knob of butter and seasoning, for 20–30 minutes. To serve add chopped parsley or paprika. Equally good with béchamel or cheese sauce (pages 195, 196).

Allow 1–2 heads per portion when cooked.

Braised chicory

700 g *(1½ lb)* **chicory, washed**
25 g *(1 oz)* **butter**
1.25 ml *(¼ level tsp)* **grated nutmeg**
juice of 1½ lemons
150 ml *(¼ pt)* **chicken stock**
7.5 ml *(1½ level tsps)* **cornflour**
15 ml *(1 tbsp)* **cold water**
30 ml *(2 tbsps)* **cream**
salt and freshly ground black pepper
chopped parsley

Blanch the whole chicory heads in boiling salted water for 5 minutes. Drain well. Butter a large enough casserole to take the chicory in a single layer. Arrange the chicory in the base and dot with butter. Stir the nutmeg and lemon into the stock and pour over the chicory. Cover with buttered foil or a lid and cook in the oven at 170°C *(325°F)* mark 3 for about 1½ hours. Blend the cornflour with the water. Drain the juices from the casserole into a small pan, add the cornflour and bring to the boil, stirring, bubble for 1 minute. Add the cream – do not boil. Adjust seasoning. Pour over the chicory. Sprinkle with chopped parsley.

CORN ON THE COB

Choose the cobs when they are plump, well formed and of a pale golden yellow colour and cook them while still really fresh. Remove the outside leaves and silky threads, put the cobs into boiling unsalted water (salt toughens corn) and cook for 12–20 minutes, depending on their size – overcooking also makes them tough. Drain well and serve with plenty of melted butter, salt and freshly ground pepper.

Allow 1–2 cobs per portion.

COURGETTES

These are a variety of small vegetable marrow. They are normally cooked unpeeled, being either left whole or cut into rounds. They may be boiled in a minimum of water (allow 10–15 minutes), steamed or fried and are served with melted butter and chopped parsley or tarragon. Alternatively cook, dress with French dressing while still warm, then leave to go cold and serve as a salad.

Allow 100 g (¼ lb) per portion, when served as an accompaniment.

Buttered courgettes with lemon

450 g *(1 lb)* **courgettes**
salt and freshly ground black pepper
200 ml *(⅓ pt)* **water**
25 g *(1 oz)* **butter**
15 ml *(1 tbsp)* **chopped parsley or chives**
lemon juice

Trim the courgettes and thinly slice. Cook in boiling salted water for 5 minutes, drain well. Finish cooking the courgettes in melted butter and when tender but still slightly crisp add the herbs, lemon juice and freshly ground pepper to taste. *Serves 3–4.*

Courgettes with tomatoes

450 g *(1 lb)* courgettes, cut into 0.5-cm *(¼-in)* slices
salt
75 g *(3 oz)* butter
225 g *(½ lb)* tomatoes, skinned and chopped
15 ml *(1 tbsp)* chopped parsley
1 small clove garlic, skinned and crushed
pepper
2.5 ml *(½ level tsp)* sugar
50 g *(2 oz)* cheese, grated
105 ml *(7 tbsps)* fresh white breadcrumbs

Put the courgette slices into a colander, sprinkle with salt and allow to drain for about an hour; dry them well. Melt 50 g *(2 oz)* butter in a frying pan and put in the courgettes. Cook gently until soft and slightly transparent and put them in an ovenproof dish. Melt the remaining butter and cook the tomatoes, parsley, garlic, pepper and sugar until a thickish purée forms. Re-season the mixture if necessary and pour it over the courgettes. Sprinkle with the cheese and breadcrumbs and grill until golden brown.

Baked courgettes and aubergines

2 aubergines
6–7 courgettes
6–8 shallots, skinned
1 clove garlic, skinned
olive oil
salt and pepper
a little sugar
45 ml *(3 level tbsps)* tomato paste
150 ml *(¼ pt)* stock
30 ml *(2 level tbsps)* fresh white breadcrumbs
olives, to garnish

Slice the aubergines, courgettes and shallots and chop the garlic very finely. Rub an ovenproof dish with oil, put a layer of aubergine in the bottom and sprinkle with salt and pepper; now put in a layer of shallot and a little garlic, then one of courgettes. Continue like this until the dish has been filled. Mix the sugar, tomato paste and stock and pour this over the vegetables. Sprinkle with the crumbs, pour on 30 ml *(2 tbsps)* oil and bake in the oven at 180°C *(350°F)* mark 4 for 1 hour. Serve hot or cold, garnished with a few olives.

CUCUMBER

Although cucumber is usually eaten raw as a salad vegetable, it may also be cooked. To do this, peel the cucumber, cut it in half lengthwise, then into pieces about 5 cm *(2 in)* long (or cut into dice) and cook very gently in butter in a covered pan for 10–15 minutes. Serve with white sauce or melted butter.

Allow 100–175 g (4–6 oz) per portion for cooked cucumber.

ENDIVE

There are two types, the 'Curly' Endive, which has very crinkly leaves, and the 'Batavian' Endive, with much smoother leaves. Both are very pale green in colour – almost white at the heart – and of somewhat bitter flavour. In this country they are generally eaten raw as salad plants, but in France (where they are called *chicorée*) they are often served braised, like lettuce.

Allow 1 medium sized head of endive per person when it is cooked; for salad use, 1 endive will serve 4–6 people.

FENNEL

The fennel which is eaten as a vegetable is Florence fennel. It has solid white stems with a swollen base, rather resembling celery. Whole fennel may be cooked in the same way as celery and served hot; it makes an agreeable partner to fish. The young, tender side stems can be washed, peeled and thinly sliced to eat raw as an hors d'oeuvre or with cheese; grate the root coarsely and dress with a sharp dressing to serve the same way. Fennel has a slight but distinctive aniseed flavour.

Allow 1 head per person.

KALE

A green, curly leaved vegetable of the cabbage family, which does not form a head. It has a good flavour when picked young. Prepare and cook it like cabbage.

KOHL RABI

A vegetable with a stem enlarged to a turnip-like globe which grows above the ground, topped with curly green leaves. These enlarged stems should be eaten while they are small and young. Cut off the leaves and peel thickly. If the globes are small, leave them whole, otherwise cut them into thick slices or cubes. Cook in boiling salted water until soft – 30–40 minutes according to size. Serve coated with a white sauce (page 193) or glaze with butter and toss in chopped parsley. Alternatively serve as fritters, purée or au gratin.

Kohl rabi can also be served cold with vinaigrette dressing (page 244).

Allow 100–150 g (4–6 oz) per portion.

LEEKS

Remove the coarse outer leaves and cut off the tops and roots. Wash the leeks very thoroughly, splitting them down the centre to within 2.5 cm *(1 in)* or so of the base, to ensure that all grit is removed – if necessary cut them through completely to achieve this. Cook in boiling salted water until tender – 10–20 minutes. Drain very thoroughly. Serve coated with a white or cheese sauce (see pages 193, 195). As an alternative, trim, leaving on about 5 cm *(2 in)* of the green leaves, slice thinly and wash thoroughly. Blanch in boiling salted water until tender – about 5 minutes. Drain well and finish with melted butter and freshly ground black pepper. Raw, finely shredded leek makes an interesting salad.

Allow 1–3 leeks per portion, or 225–350 g ($\frac{1}{2}$–$\frac{3}{4}$ lb), depending on the amount of waste.

Braised leeks

Cook as for braised celery; allow 2–3 leeks per person.

LETTUCE

Both the cabbage and cos varieties of lettuce are used chiefly as salad vegetables. They can, however, be cooked in various ways – for example braised.

Allow 1 medium sized lettuce per person, when it is cooked. For salad use, a medium sized lettuce will serve 4 people.

Braised lettuce

Wash 2 lettuces and remove the outer leaves. Put the lettuce into a saucepan of boiling water and cook for about 2–3 minutes. Lift them out and place at once in cold water, then drain them very thoroughly, pressing lightly to remove the water. Put them into a pan with salt and pepper, a little chopped onion, a good knob of butter and just enough stock to cover. Cover the pan and simmer gently for about 45 minutes. Lift out the lettuces, drain carefully and place on a hot dish. Blend 15 ml *(1 level tbsp)* cornflour with a little cold water, stir in a little of the liquor in which the lettuces were cooked and return the mixture to the pan. Bring to the boil, stirring until it thickens and cook for a further 2–3 minutes. Pour the sauce over the lettuce and sprinkle with a little chopped parsley before serving.

VEGETABLE MARROW

Large marrows must be peeled, the seeds removed and the flesh cut into even sized pieces. Cook in a little boiling salted water until tender – 10–20 minutes – and drain well. Serve coated with a white or cheese sauce (see pages 193, 195).

Alternatively, cut the marrow into large dice; melt about 25 g *(1 oz)* butter in a saucepan, add the marrow, season and cover tightly. Cook over a low heat, shaking the pan occasionally, for 10–20 minutes. Garnish with chopped parsley.

Marrow can also be roasted in the dripping round the meat or stuffed and baked either whole or in rings.

Allow 175 g (6 oz) per portion when marrow is served as an accompaniment.

Stuffed marrow

1 vegetable marrow, about 1 kg *(2¼ lb)*
350 g *(¾ lb)* minced meat
60 ml *(4 tbsps)* fresh breadcrumbs
5–10 ml *(1–2 level tsps)* mixed herbs or 15 ml *(1 tbsp)* chopped parsley
1 onion, skinned and finely chopped
salt and pepper
1 egg, beaten
tomato sauce (see page 202)

Wash the marrow, peel, cut it in half and scoop out the seeds. Mix the meat, crumbs, herbs, onion and seasoning with a fork and add enough egg to bind the mixture together. Put this stuffing into the two halves of the marrow and place them together again. Wrap in greased greaseproof paper, put in an ovenproof dish and bake in the oven at 180°C *(350°F)* mark 4 for about 1 hour, until the marrow is done. Remove the paper and serve the marrow with a tomato sauce.

Alternatively, cut the marrow into slices 4–5 cm *(1½–2 in)* thick, remove the seeds, stand the pieces on a greased ovenproof dish and fill each with the same stuffing as used above. Cover the dish with foil and bake at the same temperature for about 55 minutes–1 hour.

Marrow and tomato casserole

1 onion, skinned and chopped
25 g *(1 oz)* butter
1 medium sized marrow, peeled and diced
425-g *(15-oz)* can tomatoes
salt and pepper
pinch of mixed herbs

Fry the onion in the butter for about 3–5 minutes, until soft but not browned. Add the marrow, tomatoes, seasoning and herbs and continue cooking over a very low heat until the marrow is tender – about 20 minutes.

MUSHROOMS

The majority of mushrooms bought today are cultivated and require only wiping before being used. Cut off and discard the earthy end of each stalk; the rest of the stalk can be included in the dish or as an ingredient in a stuffing. Field mushrooms need skinning and should be washed thoroughly to remove any mud or grit.

Allow 25–75 g (1–3 oz) per portion depending on whether the mushrooms are to be used as a garnish or a vegetable.

Baked mushrooms

Wash and drain the mushrooms, or wipe them, and place them, stalks uppermost, in a greased baking dish. Put a small pat of butter on each mushroom, season with salt and pepper and cover with greased paper. Bake in the oven at 190°C *(375°F)* mark 5 for 15–30 minutes, or until cooked.

Grilled mushrooms

Wipe the mushrooms and trim the stalks level with the caps. Melt 50 g *(2 oz)* butter for each 450 g *(1 lb)* mushrooms. Dip the caps in butter then put them in the grill pan, cap uppermost. Grill for 2 minutes. Turn them, sprinkle the gills with salt and pepper and grill for a further 2–3 minutes.

Fried mushrooms

Heat 50 g *(2 oz)* butter per 450 g *(1 lb)* mushrooms. Put in the mushrooms, stalks uppermost, season with salt and pepper and if you wish add a squeeze of lemon juice. Cover the pan and cook over a moderate heat for 4–5 minutes. Do not turn the mushrooms over, and the juice will remain in the mushrooms.

Stuffed mushrooms *see colour plate facing p. 321*

8 medium sized mushrooms
1 small onion, skinned and finely chopped
knob of butter or margarine
45 ml *(3 tbsps)* finely chopped ham or cooked bacon
75 ml *(5 tbsps)* fresh white breadcrumbs
25 g *(1 oz)* cheese, grated
5 ml *(1 tsp)* chopped parsley
beaten egg to bind
salt and pepper
4 slices of toast, buttered

Remove and chop the stalks from the mushrooms. Lightly fry the stalks and onion in the butter or margarine for 3–5 minutes, until soft but not coloured. Add the ham or bacon, breadcrumbs, cheese and parsley and enough egg to bind them all together. Stir until well mixed and hot, season to taste and pile into the mushroom caps. Put the mushrooms in a greased tin, cover with greaseproof paper or foil and bake in the oven at 190°C *(375°F)* mark 5 for 15–30 minutes. Serve on buttered toast.

Creamed mushrooms

225 g *(½ lb)* button mushrooms, washed and drained
300 ml *(½ pt)* milk
25 ml *(1½ level tbsps)* cornflour
knob of butter
15–30 ml *(1–2 tbsps)* cream
salt and pepper
squeeze of lemon juice
4 slices of toast, buttered

Simmer the mushrooms in some of the milk until just soft – about 10 minutes. Blend the cornflour to a smooth cream with the cold milk, add the milk in which the mushrooms were cooked and return the mixture to the pan; bring to the boil, stirring all the time until it thickens, and cook for a further 2–3 minutes. Stir in the butter and cream, season well and add the lemon juice. Serve on buttered toast.

ONIONS

Onions vary considerably in both size and flavour. The small white 'cocktail' onion is not much bigger than a large pea. Shallots are smaller than the average true onion, but have a stronger flavour. Spanish onions are larger but milder in flavour than the English variety.

Both the leaves and the bulbs of the young plants, known as spring onions, may be eaten in salads, but in the case of ordinary mature onions the leaves are discarded.

Allow 100–175 g (4–6 oz) per portion for cooked onions.

Boiled onions

Cut off the roots and remove the papery outside skin. Cook in boiling salted water until soft – 30–40 minutes, according to size. Drain and coat with a white or cheese sauce (see pages 193, 195).

Onions can also be boiled for 20–30 minutes, then baked for 10–15 minutes in the oven at 190°C *(375°F)* mark 5.

Glazed onions

50 g *(2 oz)* butter
450 g *(1 lb)* button onions, skinned and boiled
10 ml *(2 level tsps)* caster sugar

Heat the butter in a wide saucepan, add the onions and toss them in the fat for 2–3 minutes. Sprinkle them with the sugar and continue to shake them in the pan over a gentle heat until they are evenly glazed – about 2–3 minutes. Serve with the remaining glaze poured over.

Fried onions

lard or oil
4 large onions, skinned and sliced
salt and pepper

Heat enough lard or oil in a frying pan to cover the bottom of the pan and fry the onions slowly until golden brown and quite soft – 5–10 minutes; stir them occasionally. Drain well, season and serve hot.

Crisp fried onions

4 large onions, skinned and cut into 0.5-cm *(¼-in)* slices
a little milk
a little flour
salt and pepper
fat for deep frying

Separate the onion slices into rings and dip in milk and seasoned flour. Heat the fat so that when one onion ring is dropped in, it rises to the surface surrounded by bubbles. Gradually add the rest of the rings to the fat and fry for 2–3 minutes, until golden brown. Drain on crumpled kitchen paper, season and serve at once.

Baked onions à la francaise

450 g *(1 lb)* small white onions, skinned
salt and pepper
50 g *(2 oz)* brown sugar
300 ml *(½ pt)* brown stock
butter

Cook the onions in boiling salted water for 10 minutes. Drain and dry them. Put into a greased shallow ovenproof dish, sprinkle with salt, pepper and sugar, pour the stock round and put a knob of butter on the top of each. Bake in the oven at 190°C *(375°F)* mark 5 until the onions are soft – 10–15 minutes; baste occasionally with the stock.

Baked stuffed onions

4 medium sized onions, skinned
30 ml *(2 tbsps)* fresh breadcrumbs
salt and pepper
50 g *(2 oz)* cheese, grated
a little milk
a little butter

Cook the onions in boiling salted water for about 25 minutes, removing them before they are quite soft; drain and cool. Scoop out the centres, using a pointed knife to cut the onion top and a small spoon to remove the centres. Chop the centres finely, mix with the crumbs, seasoning and half the cheese and moisten with milk if necessary. Fill the onions and place them in a greased ovenproof dish. Put small knobs of butter on top and sprinkle with the remaining cheese. Bake in the oven at 200°C *(400°F)* mark 6 for about 35 minutes, till the onions are cooked and browned.

Serve with a white sauce (see page 193), making it with equal quantities of milk and onion liquor; season well and flavour with grated cheese. A tomato sauce makes a good alternative.

PARSNIPS

Wash the parsnips, peel off the skin, quarter and remove the hard centre cores. Cut into slices, strips or dice and leave in water till required for cooking. Cook in boiling salted water for 30 minutes, until tender. Drain and toss in butter, salt, pepper and a little grated nutmeg.

To roast parsnips, par-boil them for 5 minutes in salted water, drain and place in the fat round the joint to cook for 1 hour.

Allow 175–225 g (6–8 oz) per portion.

PEAS

The season for fresh peas lasts for about 6 weeks only, but they are sold preserved in various ways – canned, bottled, dried, accelerated freeze dried (AFD) and frozen.

Quantities to allow
For 1 average serving:
225 g *(8 oz)* peas in the pod
75 g *(3 oz)* canned, bottled or frozen peas
50 g *(2 oz)* AFD peas

Preparation and cooking

Fresh peas Shell and wash, place in boiling salted water with about 5 ml *(1 level tsp)* sugar and a sprig of mint and cook until tender; young peas will need 8–10 minutes, larger ones 15–20 minutes. Drain them, remove the mint and if you like toss the peas with a knob of butter before serving.

Petits pois This particularly small and sweet type of pea is much used in continental Europe. The peas are generally cooked with the addition of a little chopped onion and some butter – see the recipe for peas à la française, below.

Dried peas See page 227.

Mange tout (sugar peas) are pale green fleshy pods which are eaten whole with the very small under developed peas left inside. Top and tail them after washing, boil gently with just enough salted water to cover – about 5–10 minutes. Drain and finish with butter and pepper.

Peas à la française

¼ lettuce, washed and shredded finely
6 spring onions, halved and trimmed
little parsley and mint, tied together
700 g *(1½ lb)* peas, shelled
150 ml *(¼ pt)* water
25 g *(1 oz)* butter
salt and pepper
10 ml *(2 level tsps)* sugar
butter for serving

Put all the ingredients in a saucepan, cover closely and simmer until tender – about 20 minutes. Remove the parsley and mint, drain the peas well and serve with a knob of butter.

Sauté of peas

700 g *(1½ lb)* peas, shelled
25 g *(1 oz)* butter
2 small onions, skinned and sliced
salt and pepper
about 300 ml *(½ pt)* white stock
5 ml *(1 tsp)* chopped parsley

Lightly fry the peas in the butter for about 2 minutes and add the onions, salt and pepper and just enough stock to cover the peas. Cover and cook gently until tender – about 20 minutes. Do not drain, but serve the liquid with the peas. If you like, remove the lid about 10 minutes before the cooking time is completed, so that some of the water evaporates. Sprinkle the chopped parsley in just before serving.

Italian-style peas

700 g *(1½ lb)* peas, shelled
ham or chicken stock
1 small onion, skinned and finely chopped
knob of butter

Cover the peas with the stock, add the onion and simmer until the peas are tender. Strain off the stock, add the butter to the peas and toss them over a low heat. Serve hot with the pieces of onion in them.

Note If you like, add 50 g *(2 oz)* ham, cut into thin strips, with the butter.

POTATOES

Peel potatoes as thinly as possible, using either a special potato peeler or a sharp, short-bladed knife. New potatoes are scraped or brushed. Cook the potatoes as soon as you can after the peeling or scraping; if it is necessary to let them stand for a while, keep them under water, to prevent discoloration.

Allow 175–225 g (6–8 oz) per portion.

Boiled Cut the prepared potatoes into even-sized pieces, put into cold water, add 2.5 ml *(½ level tsp)* salt per 450 g *(1 lb)*, bring to the boil and simmer until tender but unbroken – 15–20 minutes for new potatoes, 20–30 minutes for old. Drain well, add a knob of butter if you wish and serve sprinkled with chopped parsley.

Mashed Boil old potatoes in the usual way, drain and dry over a low heat, then mash with a fork or a potato masher.

Creamed Mash the cooked potatoes with a knob of butter, salt and pepper to taste and a little milk. Beat them well over a gentle heat with a wooden spoon until fluffy. Serve in a heated dish, mark with a fork and sprinkle with chopped parsley.

Baked or 'jacket' potatoes Choose even-sized potatoes, scrub well, dry and prick all over with a fork. Bake in the oven at 200°C *(400°F)* mark 6 for about ¾–1 hour for small potatoes, 1–1¼ hours for large ones, or until soft when pinched. Cut a cross in the top of each potato and put in a knob of butter or a spoonful of soured cream.

To cut down the baking time the potatoes can either be boiled first for 10 minutes – they then bake in about 30 minutes – or they can be threaded on a metal skewer and baked for 40 minutes.

Roast Using old potatoes, peel in the usual way and cut into even-sized pieces. Cook in salted water for 5–10 minutes – depending on the size – and drain well. Transfer them to a roasting tin containing 100 g *(4 oz)* of hot lard or dripping, baste well and bake in the oven at 220°C *(425°F)* mark 7 for about 20 minutes; turn them and continue cooking until soft inside and crisp and brown outside – about 40 minutes altogether. Drain well on kitchen paper and serve in an uncovered serving dish, sprinkled with salt.

If preferred, do not parboil the potatoes to begin with – in this case they will take about 50–60 minutes to cook.

They can also be cooked in the roasting tin around the joint, when little or no extra fat will be needed.

Sauté Boil the potatoes until they are just cooked and cut into slices 0.5 cm *(¼ in)* thick. Fry slowly in a little hot butter or lard, turning them once so that they are crisp and golden on both sides. Drain well on kitchen paper and serve with a little chopped parsley or chives.

Chipped or French fried Cut peeled old potatoes into 0.5–1 cm *(¼–½-in)* slices and then into strips *(¼–½ in)* wide. (For speed, several slices can be put on top of one another and cut together.) Place in cold water and leave for at least ½ hour; drain well and dry with a cloth.

Heat a deep fat fryer of oil to 190°C *(375°F)* or until when one chip is dropped in, it rises to the surface at once, surrounded by bubbles. Put enough chips into the basket to about quarter-fill it and lower carefully into the fat. Cook for about 6–7 minutes. Remove the chips and drain on absorbent paper. Follow the same procedure until all the chips have been cooked. Just before serving, re-heat the fat, test to make sure it is hot enough and fry the chips rapidly for about 3 minutes, until crisp and brown. Drain well on kitchen paper and serve in an uncovered dish, sprinkled with salt.

Game chips Scrub and peel the potatoes and slice very thinly into rounds. Soak them in cold water, dry and fry in deep fat, as for chipped potatoes, but allowing a shorter cooking time – about 3 minutes for the first frying.

Potato crisps may also be bought ready prepared.

Matchstick potatoes Cut potatoes into very small chips of matchstick size. Cook like chips, but as they are very much smaller, allow a shorter cooking time – about 3 minutes at the first cooking.

Swiss Rosti

350 g *(¾ lb)* **medium to small old potatoes**
salt and pepper
40 g *(1½ oz)* **butter**

Scrub the potatoes, parboil in salted water for 7 minutes. Remove the skins. Heat the butter in a frying pan; when bubbling, coarsely grate the potatoes straight into the pan. Using a palette knife, shape the edges to form a neat round which is not too thick. Fry gently for 5–7 minutes until golden brown, then carefully turn, using a wide spatula, and brown the second side. Serve hot cut in half, with a parsley garnish. *Serves 2.*

Browned potatoes

900 g *(2 lb)* **new potatoes**
75 g *(3 oz)* **butter**
50 g *(2 oz)* **dried breadcrumbs**

Cook the potatoes until tender, then peel them. Coat with 25 g *(1 oz)* of the butter, melted, and the breadcrumbs. Heat the remaining butter in a large frying pan and brown the coated potatoes over a medium heat, turning them until they are golden and hot.

Duchesse potatoes

450 g *(1 lb)* **potatoes, boiled and drained**
50 g *(2 oz)* **butter**
1 egg
salt, pepper and grated nutmeg

Sieve or mash the potatoes, add the butter, egg and seasoning and beat well until the mixture is very smooth. Pipe into rosettes on a greased baking sheet and bake for about 25 minutes in the oven at 200°C *(400°F)* mark 6 until golden brown.

Parisienne potatoes

1 kg *(2¼ lb)* **old potatoes, peeled**
45 ml *(3 level tbsps)* **butter**
30 ml *(2 tbsps)* **oil**
salt

Using a round vegetable scoop, scoop small balls from the potatoes. Boil in salted water for 5 minutes, drain and dry well. Heat the butter and oil and fry the potatoes in it, tossing all the time until evenly browned. Season and serve.

Poulet en cocotte (p. 165).

Caramelled potatoes *see colour plate facing p. 112*

450 g *(1 lb)* small, evenly shaped potatoes, peeled
45 ml *(3 level tbsps)* sugar
25 g *(1 oz)* butter
15 ml *(1 tbsp)* hot water

Boil the potatoes for 5–10 minutes. Heat the sugar gently in a strong frying pan until it becomes a golden brown syrup, add the butter and water and stir. Put in the potatoes and shake over a gentle heat until they are evenly browned – about 10 minutes.

If small potatoes are unobtainable, use potato balls cut from large raw potatoes with a Parisian potato cutter: boil for 2–3 minutes and finish in the sugar and butter as above.

Potato croquettes *see colour plate facing p. 209*

450 g *(1 lb)* potatoes, boiled and drained
25 g *(1 oz)* butter
1 egg
5 ml *(1 tsp)* chopped parsley
salt and pepper
egg and browned crumbs for coating
fat for deep frying

Sieve or mash the potatoes and add the butter, egg, parsley and seasoning. Form the mixture into small balls or rolls and coat with egg and crumbs – twice if possible, as this helps to prevent breaking. Heat the fat so that a 2.5-cm *(1-in)* cube of bread takes 40–50 seconds to brown. Fry the croquettes for 4–5 minutes, drain well and serve immediately.

Tortilla (potato omelette)

300 ml *(½ pt)* oil
450 g *(1 lb)* old potatoes, peeled and sliced
½ onion, skinned and chopped
4 eggs
salt and freshly ground pepper

Heat the oil and fry the potato slices until lightly browned, then drain well on absorbent paper. Pour off the oil from the pan, leaving only 15 ml *(1 tbsp)*. Sauté the onion until clear. Return the potatoes to the pan. Beat the eggs with salt and pepper and pour over the vegetables. Cook over a gentle heat and complete the cooking of the top under the grill. *Serves 3–4.*

Anna potatoes *see colour plate facing p. 209*

700 g *(1½ lb)* even sized, waxy potatoes, peeled
salt and pepper
melted butter

Grease a thick cake tin and line the bottom with greased paper. Trim the potatoes so that they will give equal sized slices. Slice them very thinly and arrange a layer of slightly overlapping slices in the tin. Sprinkle with salt, pepper and melted butter.

Continue in this way until all the potatoes have been used, pressing each layer well into the tin. Cover with greaseproof paper and a lid and bake for about 1 hour in the oven at 190°C *(375°F)* mark 5 adding more butter if the potatoes begin to look dry. Turn out and serve at once.

Scalloped potatoes

4 medium sized potatoes, peeled and sliced
salt and pepper
45 ml *(3 level tbsps)* flour
25 g *(1 oz)* butter
about 150 ml *(¼ pt)* milk

Put a layer of potato in a buttered dish and sprinkle with salt and pepper. Dredge with flour and dot with butter. Repeat, then add milk until it may be seen through the top layer. Bake in the oven at 190°C *(375°F)* mark 5 for about 1¼ hours, until the potato is soft and the top golden brown.

Rissole potatoes

Using small new potatoes, scrape and boil for 5–10 minutes in salted water. Drain and dry well. Fry in a mixture of half butter and half oil, turning the potatoes frequently until they are evenly golden brown.

Chicken and cranberry curry (p. 161).

Lyonnaise potatoes

225 g (*½ lb*) onions, skinned and sliced
15–30 ml (*1–2 tbsps*) oil
450 g (*1 lb*) potatoes, sautéed (see page 224)
chopped parsley

Fry the onion slowly in the oil until golden brown – about 10 minutes. Serve in layers with the potatoes and sprinkle with the chopped parsley.

Fondant potatoes

Using large old potatoes, peel and cut into oblongs. Boil for 5–10 minutes in salted water, drain and dry well. Fry quickly on both sides in hot oil and butter. Put the potatoes into a casserole and add enough stock to come halfway up the potatoes; season. Put in the oven at 200°C (*400°F*) mark 6, with no lid and leave until the stock has evaporated – about 20–30 minutes. Brush with butter and sprinkle with chopped parsley.

Maître d'hôtel potatoes

450 g (*1 lb*) potatoes, boiled in their skins
15 ml (*1 tbsp*) olive oil
salt and pepper
chopped parsley
15 ml (*1 tbsp*) vinegar

Peel the cooked potatoes while still warm and cut into 0.5-cm (*¼-in*) slices. Heat the oil in a frying pan, add the rest of the ingredients and toss the sliced potatoes in this mixture until well heated. Serve at once.

Baked stuffed potatoes *see colour plate facing p. 289*

1 **75 g (*3 oz*) cheese, grated**
25 g (*1 oz*) butter
little milk
salt, pepper and grated nutmeg

2 **75 g (*3 oz*) bacon, scissor snipped and fried**
little milk
salt and pepper

3 **75 g (*3 oz*) smoked haddock, cooked and mashed**
5 ml (*1 tsp*) chopped parsley
5 ml (*1 tsp*) lemon juice
little milk
salt, pepper and grated nutmeg

4 **30–45 ml (*2–3 tbsps*) cream**
10 ml (*2 tsps*) chopped chives
salt

Cook as for baked potatoes (page 223), but instead of making a cross in the top, cut in halves lengthwise and scoop out the centres, taking care to keep the skins intact. Mash the potato in a basin and add one of the 4 stuffings listed. (The quantities given are sufficient for 4 potatoes.)

Mix well, pile back into the skins and fork the tops. Sprinkle with cheese or brush with a little milk and put back in the oven until hot and golden brown.

Gratin Dauphinois

900 g (*2 lb*) old potatoes, peeled
1 clove garlic, skinned and crushed
142-ml (*5-fl oz*) carton single cream
salt and freshly ground pepper
pinch of grated nutmeg
75 g (*3 oz*) Gruyère cheese, grated
watercress for garnish

Cut the potatoes into small pieces and parboil for 5 minutes; drain well and place in a lightly greased pie dish or shallow casserole. Stir the garlic into the cream, with the salt, pepper and nutmeg. Pour this seasoned cream over the potatoes and sprinkle with the cheese. Cover with foil and bake in the oven at 180°C (*350°F*) mark 4 for about 45 minutes. Remove the foil and flash the gratin under the grill to brown the cheese. Serve garnished with watercress.

Potato dumplings

1.4 kg ***(3 lb)*** **potatoes, peeled**
5 ml ***(1 level tsp)*** **salt**
2.5 ml ***(½ level tsp)*** **grated nutmeg**
50 g ***(2 oz)*** **semolina**
75 g ***(3 oz)*** **wheatmeal flour**
2 eggs, beaten
2 slices of bread
butter

Cook and sieve the potatoes and leave to become cold. Add the salt, nutmeg, semolina, flour and eggs and knead into a smooth dough. Cut the bread into small dice and fry until light brown in the hot butter.

Flour the hands, make round dumplings about the size of a fist with the potato dough and press a few of the fried croûtons into each. Put the dumplings into boiling salted water and cook them thoroughly – about 12–15 minutes. Place them on a flat dish and pour melted butter (or margarine) over them; alternatively, chop and fry some bacon and pour over the dumplings. *Serves 6.*

Vegetable samosa

225 g ***(½ lb)*** **potatoes, peeled and diced**
225 g ***(½ lb)*** **peas, shelled**
salt and pepper
225 g ***(½ lb)*** **self raising flour**
25 g ***(1 oz)*** **butter**
225 g ***(½ lb)*** **fat for deep frying**

Boil the potatoes with the peas; when cooked, drain and add salt and pepper to taste. Mix the flour, a pinch of salt, rub in butter, add cold water and make into a pastry dough. Roll out 0.3 cm *(⅛ in)* thick and cut into 8-cm *(3-in)* rounds. Add 10 ml *(2 tsps)* of the potato and pea mixture to each round, fold the pastry over and seal the edges. Fry in the hot fat till golden brown.

PULSES – DRIED VEGETABLES

Dried beans are a valuable source of protein and vitamin B and are eaten widely in countries where meat and animal proteins are in short supply.

Always use pulses that are young; those that have been kept for long periods of time rarely soften during cooking, however long they are given. Although overnight soaking does no harm there is no great advantage when the pulses are fresh, except in the case of chick peas or brown lentils. Simply cover the pulse well with water, bring to the boil and leave to stand for a couple of hours, then drain and cook in the usual way. The best time to add salt to the water is half way through the cooking time, as salt tends to slow down the softening.

Dried peas Sold either whole or split, minus the wrinkled green skin. Whole peas when cooked (about 1½ hours) and puréed make a good accompaniment for smoked meat or can be turned into a soup. Split peas are the classic base for pease pudding and are also good for soup making – cooking time about 40 minutes.

Lentils There are two varieties. The red (Egyptian) being the most common sold here, and the greenish brown (German) lentil which is much larger. The red lentil cooks quickly without soaking – about 10 minutes to give a purée. The brown lentil also cooks quickly but keeps its shape making it ideal for adding to casserole recipes; it can also be dressed as an hors d'oeuvre ingredient.

Haricot beans The traditional bean for the French cassoulet and American Boston beans. Soak, then cook slowly for about 1½ hours.

Flageolets (green flageolets) Pale green in colour and long and thin. They are grown in France and Italy and although the majority are exported to Britain they tend to be expensive.

Red kidney beans The seeds of runner beans which when mature are shelled and dried. Soak then cook for about 40 minutes.

Butter beans One of the most favoured beans for cooking. Allow about 1¼ hours. A delicious accompaniment to boiled bacon with parsley sauce.

Chick peas (garban ozos) These look like peas with a groove down one side. They are popular with Greeks and Turks as a drinks nibble – they cook them, saturate them with olive oil and then season with salt, pepper, garlic and lemon juice. Chick peas must be soaked, their cooking time varies with their age, anything from 20 minutes onwards.

Mexican beans

175 g ***(6 oz)*** **red kidney beans, cooked**
4 sticks celery, chopped
25 g ***(1 oz)*** **gherkins, chopped**
30 ml ***(2 level tbsps)*** **finely chopped onion**
60 ml ***(4 tbsps)*** **oil**
30 ml ***(2 tbsps)*** **malt vinegar**
2.5 ml ***(½ level tsp)*** **French mustard**
1.25 ml ***(¼ level tsp)*** **caster sugar**
salt and black pepper
1 Cos lettuce
a few celery leaves

Drain the kidney beans and combine in a bowl with the celery, gherkins and onion. Place the oil, vinegar, mustard, salt and pepper in a tightly lidded container. Shake well and pour over the bean mixture and fold through.

Wash and drain the lettuce, arrange to form a bed in a serving bowl. Pile the bean mixture on to the lettuce, spooning over any remaining dressing. Garnish with celery leaves.

Pease pudding

225 g ***(8 oz)*** **split peas**
salt and pepper
1 ham bone or some bacon scraps
25 g ***(1 oz)*** **butter**
1 egg, beaten
pinch of sugar

A traditional accompaniment to boiled ham or bacon. Wash the peas well, removing any discoloured ones, and soak overnight in cold water. Tie loosely in a cloth, place in a saucepan with a pinch of salt and boiling water to cover and add the bone or bacon scraps. Boil for 2–2½ hours, or until soft. Lift out the bag of peas, sieve and add the butter, egg, sugar and pepper to taste. Beat until thoroughly mixed, then tie up tightly in a floured cloth and boil for another ½ hour. Turn on to a hot plate to serve.

To give extra flavour, chopped onion or herbs may be added.

RUTABAGA

Rutabaga is a turnip-shaped root vegetable with a delicate flavour, sometimes known as yellow turnip. To prepare, pare, slice, dice or cut in strips. To cook, boil as for turnip in salted water with a little sugar for 25–40 minutes. To serve drain and add butter, mash and cream with an equal amount of fluffy potatoes, or sauté in butter.

Allow 700–900 g (1½–2 lb) for 4 people.

PUMPKIN

The best method of cooking pumpkin is to peel it, cut up (removing the seeds) and roast it round the joint like potatoes. Alternatively, cube it and boil in water for 10–15 minutes, or until soft; add salt if making a savoury dish. Another method is to put the pumpkin in cold water, bring to the boil, drain and finish the cooking in the oven, adding a knob of butter.

Cooked pumpkin may be served with cheese sauce, added to meat in a meat pie, mixed with other vegetables in cream soups, cooked and used for pumpkin pie (see page 292) or mixed with apple for apple pie – in this case use cinnamon rather than cloves for flavouring. Pumpkin can also be used in chutney.

Allow 225 g (½ lb) per portion when it is used as a vegetable.

SALISFY

White salisfy is similar to parsnip in shape; black salisfy is usually called scorzonera. Scrub the roots and scrape white salisfy quickly, placing at once in cold water to which a few drops of lemon juice or vinegar have been added; this helps to keep them a good colour. Cut into short lengths and cook in boiling salted water until tender – about 30–40 minutes. Peel scorzonera after cooking. Serve coated with a white sauce or re-heat in a béchamel sauce (see page 196).

Allow 100–175 g (4–6 oz) per portion.

SEAKALE

This resembles thin celery stalks in appearance; it is bleached and forced in the same way as celery. Wash well, cut off ends and tie into neat bundles. Cook until just tender in boiling salted water to which a squeeze of lemon juice has been added (this is to preserve the white colour) for 15–20 minutes. Drain well and remove the strings before serving with melted butter. If liked serve coated with a béchamel or hollandaise sauce (see pages 196, 200).

Seakale may also be braised or served au gratin. Cold, it may be served with a vinaigrette dressing or added to a salad. It is also eaten raw with cheese and in salads.

Allow 100–225 g (4–8 oz) per portion.

SORREL

A leafy plant with a strong acid flavour, used in small quantities to add flavour to lettuce and other salads and to sauces. It may also be puréed like spinach for serving with poached eggs, sweetbreads and some meat dishes and can be mixed with spinach to improve its flavour. The French make a soup with it. Sorrel should be picked when young and fresh.

Allow 175–225 g (6–8 oz) per portion.

SPINACH

Wash well in several waters to remove all grit and strip off any coarse stalks. Pack into a saucepan with only the water that clings to the leaves. Heat gently, turning the spinach occasionally, then bring to the boil and cook gently until tender – 5–10 minutes. Drain thoroughly and re-heat with a knob of butter and a sprinkling of salt and pepper.

Allow 225 g (½ lb) per portion.

Stuffed spinach roulade

450 g *(1 lb)* spinach
75 g *(3 oz)* butter
50 g *(2 oz)* plain flour
150 ml *(¼ pt)* milk
salt and pepper
2 eggs, separated
225 g *(8 oz)* cooked ham, chopped
30 ml *(2 tbsps)* soured cream
grated cheese
cheese sauce

Line a Swiss roll tin 23 by 30.5 cm *(9 by 12 in)* with greaseproof paper. Clean the spinach, soak it in water for 10 minutes and transfer it to a pan with no water except that which clings to the leaves. Cook it until tender – about 10 minutes – drain and sieve it. Melt 50 g *(2 oz)* of the butter, add the flour and stir well. Cook over a gentle heat for 2–3 minutes, stirring until the roux begins to bubble. Remove from the heat and add the milk gradually, stirring after each addition to prevent lumps forming. Bring the sauce to the boil and cook for 2–3 minutes. Season with salt and pepper and stir in the egg yolks and the spinach purée. Finally, whisk the egg whites until stiff and fold into the mixture. Pour it into the prepared tin and bake in the oven at 200°C *(400°F)* mark 6 for 20 minutes.

Meanwhile, make a filling by heating the ham in the remaining butter, then adding the cream. Turn the spinach roll out on to a board covered with damped paper, spread it with the filling and roll up like a Swiss roll. (This must be done whilst the spinach roll is hot.) Cover it with greased paper and reheat in the oven. Serve sprinkled with cheese and accompanied by cheese sauce.

Creamed spinach

Sieve the cooked spinach, add 15–30 ml *(1–2 tbsps)* cream and some salt and pepper and re-heat before serving.

SWEDES *(Swedish Turnips)*

A large root vegetable with yellow flesh and tough skin, obtainable from late autumn to spring. Swedes can be served as a separate vegetable and used in soups or in savoury dishes combined with bacon or cheese.

Swedes should be peeled thickly so that all the tough outer skin is removed. They may be sliced, diced or cut into fancy shapes. Keep them covered with water and cook as soon as possible after peeling. Boil till tender in a little salted water with the lid on for about 20–40 minutes (according to size and age), drain and mash with a little salt, pepper and grated nutmeg and a knob of butter. Alternatively, roast them as follows: cut in chunks or fingers and cook round the joint or in a separate tin with dripping, allowing 1–1¼ hours, according to the size of the pieces. Serve round the joint.

Allow 100–175 g (4–6 oz) per portion.

SWEET PEPPERS

Sweet peppers, both red and green, can be eaten raw as a salad vegetable. Being quite strong-flavoured, they should be sliced or chopped and only a small quantity added to the salad. Small amounts of raw peppers (again sliced or chopped) may be included in savoury dishes made with rice and macaroni. Peppers may be fried or stuffed and baked.

To prepare them, cut off the stalks, cut in half lengthwise and remove the seeds and any stringy membrane. If required for flavouring, they may then be sliced or chopped.

Allow 1 medium sized pepper per portion for cooked dishes such as stuffed or fried peppers.

Stuffed peppers *see colour plate facing p. 321*

4 green peppers, halved lengthways and seeded
1 onion, skinned and chopped
100 g *(4 oz)* bacon, chopped
40 g *(1½ oz)* butter
4 tomatoes, skinned and sliced
100 g *(4 oz)* long grain rice, boiled
salt and pepper
60 ml *(4 tbsps)* grated Cheddar cheese
50 g *(2 oz)* fresh breadcrumbs
150 ml *(¼ pt)* stock

Put the halved peppers in an ovenproof dish. Lightly fry the onion and bacon in 25 g *(1 oz)* of the butter until golden brown. Add the tomatoes, cooked rice, seasoning and half the cheese. Mix the rest of the cheese with the breadcrumbs. Put the bacon stuffing into the cases and sprinkle with the breadcrumb mixture. Pour the stock round the cases, top each with a knob of butter and cook in the oven at 190°C *(375°F)* mark 5 for 15–20 minutes, or until the pepper cases are cooked.

Sweet peppers with tomatoes

30 ml *(2 tbsps)* cooking oil
½ onion, skinned and chopped
1 clove garlic, skinned and crushed
4 tomatoes, skinned and sliced
30 ml *(2 level tbsps)* tomato paste
150 ml *(¼ pt)* dry white wine
4 peppers, seeded and thinly sliced, about 450 g *(1 lb)*
salt and pepper

Heat the oil in a large frying pan or saucepan and lightly cook the onion and garlic for 5 minutes without colouring. Add the tomatoes, tomato paste and wine and simmer for 5 minutes. Add the peppers, cover and simmer gently for 30 minutes. Season if necessary.

SWEET POTATOES

Sweet potatoes are no relation to ordinary potatoes and have a sweet, slightly perfumed flesh. They may be boiled or roasted. In America, where they are very popular, they are also served as a sweet, cooked with sugar or molasses and flavoured with cinnamon.

Allow 225 (½ lb) per portion.

Candied sweet potatoes

Boil the sweet potatoes until almost cooked, peel and cut into thick slices. Brush the slices over with melted butter and brown sugar, then bake in the oven at 220°C *(425°F)* mark 7 for 15 minutes.

SWISS CHARD

(Also known as silver beet or seakale beet)

These different names are given to a variety of beets cultivated for their 'chards' or broad mid-ribs, instead of for their roots. They are almost two vegetables in one, as the leaves and the mid-ribs can be treated separately. Trim the mid-ribs free of all green leaf, scrape, removing the stringy parts, cut into short pieces and cook as for celery, but with lemon juice in the water. When tender serve with white or cheese sauce.

The green leafy part is cooked as for spinach. Alternatively, keep the leaves whole and cook in boiling salted water for about ½ hour.

Allow 175–225 g (6–8 oz) leaves per portion or 2–3 ribs per portion.

TOMATOES

Although strictly speaking a fruit, the tomato is nearly always used as a vegetable and has come to be classed under that heading.

The characteristic flavour is probably best enjoyed when tomatoes are picked ripe and eaten raw as a salad, but they are very useful in cookery, making soups and many light savoury dishes (eg stuffed tomatoes) and giving a good flavour to such things as stews and cheese dishes. Grilled, baked and fried tomatoes make a colourful garnish for hot dishes and raw tomatoes can be used in various ways for decoration. Tomato juice is a popular refreshing drink.

To remove the skins from tomatoes, plunge them for a few seconds into boiling water, then lift them out and put them immediately into cold water; when they are cool, the skins will peel off easily with a knife. Alternatively, spear a tomato on the prongs of a fork and turn it gently over a gas jet until the skin bursts, then peel it off with a knife.

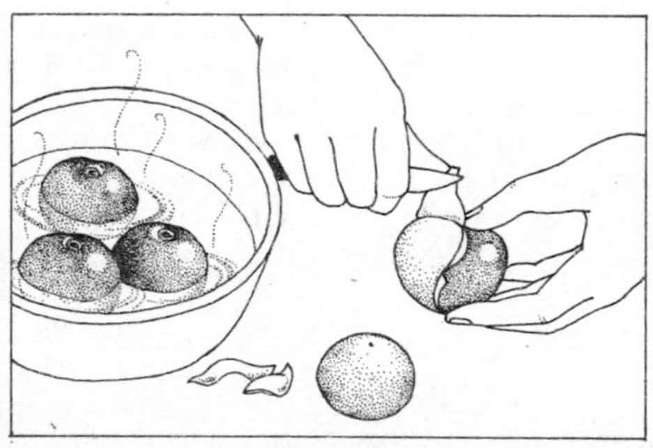

Skinning tomatoes after blanching

Grilled tomatoes

Choose even-sized ones, cut in half and place on the grill pan grid, cut side uppermost. Put a knob of butter and a sprinkling of salt and pepper on each and cook under a medium heat for 5–10 minutes, depending on their size, until soft.

Baked tomatoes

Prepare as for grilled tomatoes or if of even size leave whole and cut a cross just through the skin, on the end away from the stem. Brush with melted butter and place in a greased ovenproof dish. Add butter and seasoning, cover with foil or greaseproof paper and bake in the oven at 180°C *(350°F)* mark 4 for 10–15 minutes.

Allow 1–2 tomatoes per portion, or 450 g (1 lb) for 4 people.

Stuffed tomatoes

4 even sized tomatoes
25 g *(1 oz)* cooked ham, chopped
5 ml *(1 tsp)* chopped onion
knob of butter
30 ml *(2 tbsps)* fresh breadcrumbs
2.5 ml *(½ tsp)* chopped parsley
salt and pepper
30 ml *(2 tbsps)* grated cheese, optional

Cut a small round from each tomato at the end opposite to the stalk. Scoop out the centres. Lightly fry the ham and onion in the fat for 3 minutes. Add the crumbs, parsley, seasoning, cheese (if used) and the pulp removed from the tomatoes. Fill the tomatoes with this mixture, pile it neatly on top, put on the lids and bake in the oven at 200°C *(400°F)* mark 6 for 10–15 minutes.

TURNIPS

Peel thickly to remove the outer layer of skin and put under water to prevent discoloration. Young turnips can be left whole, older ones should be sliced or diced. Cook in salted water for about 15 minutes. If they are used whole, toss in butter or a little top of the milk, with added seasoning, or serve in a white sauce (see page 193). Old ones are mashed with salt, pepper and a knob of butter.

Allow 100–175 g (4–6 oz) per portion.

VINE LEAVES

Dolmades

1 can vine leaves
45 ml *(3 tbsps)* lard or cooking oil
450 g *(1 lb)* cooked lean meat, minced
1–2 onions, skinned and chopped
30 ml *(2 tbsps)* cooked long grain rice
chopped parsley
a little tomato sauce
salt and pepper
juice of 1 lemon

Dip the vine leaves in boiling water for 1–2 minutes and leave to drain while the stuffing is prepared. Put 30 ml *(2 tbsps)* of the lard or oil in a frying pan with the meat, onions, rice, parsley, tomato sauce and seasoning, mix well and fry. Add the lemon juice and put a small portion in the centre of each vine leaf; roll up and parcel envelope fashion. Secure if necessary with fine string or skewers. Put in a saucepan with the remaining fat or oil, a little more tomato sauce and a little water. Cook over a low heat until the sauce is well reduced.

WATERCRESS

Watercress is usually eaten raw as a salad plant or used as a garnish, but may also be cooked as for spinach and makes a good soup.

Allow 1 bunch for 4–6 people, for salad use.

Salads and salad dressings

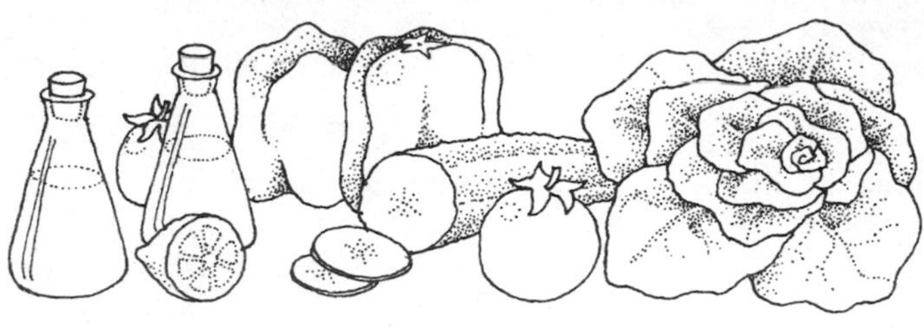

Most of us eat salads mainly because we enjoy their crisp freshness and because some of them go well with various main dishes. They also help us to achieve a well-balanced diet, for a salad usually supplies a proportion of the daily vitamin C requirement and some mineral salts. As well as the salads served as an accompaniment to another dish, there are many that form a course in themselves. The dressings (see latter part of chapter) are equally varied. A salad intended to accompany a main dish at a formal dinner or luncheon should be a very simple affair, tossed in a French dressing. Heartier salads, with mayonnaise or another rich dressing, may be served at a less formal lunch, dinner or supper, where the main course is not very substantial.

Storing salads

Trim and wash the salad plants, shake them free of surplus moisture and keep them in the salad drawer of a refrigerator, or loosely wrapped in a polythene bag at the bottom of the refrigerator.

Preparing salad ingredients

Avocados

Just before serving, slice in half, remove stone and peel, and slice. Toss in lemon juice to prevent discoloration and use in mixed salad.

Beetroot

Thinly peel the cooked beetroot (see page 210). Cut into thin slices, if the beetroots are small; grate or dice them if large. The prepared beetroot can be sprinkled with salt, pepper and a very little sugar and covered with vinegar or vinegar and water – this helps it to keep and also gives it a better flavour.

Cabbage

Wash the leaves in salted water, drain and cut into shreds with a sharp knife.

Celeriac

Wash, slice and then peel. Dice or cut into matchstick shaped pieces. Blanch in boiling, salted water for 2–3 minutes. Drain and cool. Use tossed in mayonnaise or French dressing.

Celery

Separate the sticks and wash them well in cold water, scrubbing to remove any dirt from the grooves. Slice, chop or make into curls (see page 234).

Chicory

Trim off the root end and any damaged leaves, wash the chicory in cold water and drain. Separate the slices or slice thinly across.

Chinese cabbage

Trim the root end and any damaged outer leaves, wash well. Use in salads finely shredded.

Cucumber

Wipe the skin and either leave it on if liked or peel it off thinly. Slice the cucumber finely, sprinkle with salt and leave it for about 1 hour; pour off the liquid and rinse. Alternatively, you can soak the cucumber in a little vinegar, with salt and a pinch of sugar. If you like the cucumber crisp use it when freshly sliced.

Endive

Trim off the root end, remove the coarse outer leaves, separate remaining leaves, wash and drain well.

Fennel

Trim off top stems and slice off base. Wash well in cold water and thinly slice. Fennel has a distinct aniseed flavour which is very refreshing when used in salad.

Lettuce

Remove the outer coarse leaves. Separate the inner leaves and wash them under a running cold tap or in a bowl of cold water. Drain them in a sieve or colander or shake them in a clean tea towel.

To 'revive' a withered lettuce, wash it in cold water, shake slightly to remove the excess moisture, place in a polythene bag or bowl covered with a plate and put in the bottom of the refrigerator or in any cool place. In an hour or so the leaves will have crisped up.

Mushrooms
Trim the base of the stalks. Skin or wipe and thoroughly dry, if necessary. Halve or slice thinly and use in salads.

Mustard and cress
Trim off the roots and lower parts of the stems with scissors and place the leaves in a colander or sieve. Wash them (under a fast-running cold tap if possible), turning the cress over and removing the seeds.

Peppers
Wash, cut off top to remove stalk, seeds and membrane from inside. Slice thinly and use in salads.

Radishes
Trim off the root end and leaves and wash the radishes in cold water. Slice thinly or cut into 'lilies' or 'roses' (see below).

Spring onions
Trim off the root end, remove the papery outer skin, trim the green leaves down to about 5 cm *(2 in)* of green above the white and wash.

Tomatoes
Remove the stem and wash or wipe the tomatoes. To skin them, dip in boiling water for about ½ minute, then in cold water and peel off the skin. Cut in wedges, slices or 'lilies' (see page 235).

Watercress
Trim the coarse ends from the stalks, wash the watercress and drain well before using.

Dressing the salad

The dressing can make or mar a salad. The most usual mistake is to use too much dressing, swamping the salad instead of making it appetising. No surplus dressing should be seen at the bottom of the bowl – there should be just sufficient clinging to the salad ingredients to flavour them.

Herbs in salads

Parsley is an addition to any salad. Do not chop it very finely but snip it with scissors straight on to the salad, just before serving. A few leaves of fresh mint, sage, thyme, dill or tarragon (one at a time, not all together) can be chopped and sprinkled over a salad.

Garlic
Many of those who say they dislike garlic don't really know how to use it. True, it is pungent and needs using with discretion – you will find one 'clove' ample for the average bowl of salad.

First remove the papery outside skin of the garlic clove, then crush the clove with a broad-bladed knife (do this on a plate, unless you have a board that you keep specially for onion-chopping). Scrape the crushed garlic into the salad bowl or add it to the dressing. Alternatively, use a garlic press, if you have one.

To make salad garnishes

Celery curls Cut a celery stick into strips about 1 cm *(½ in)* wide and 5 cm *(2 in)* long. Make cuts along the length of each, close together and to within 1 cm *(½ in)* of one end. Leave the pieces in cold or iced water for 1–2 hours, until the fringed strips curl. Drain well before using.

Cucumber cones Use thin slices of cucumber. Make a cut in each slice from the centre to the outer edge, then wrap one cut edge over the other to form a cone.

Crimped cucumber Run a fork down the sides of the cucumber to remove strips of peel and slice the cucumber thinly in the usual way – this gives the slices an attractive deckled edge.

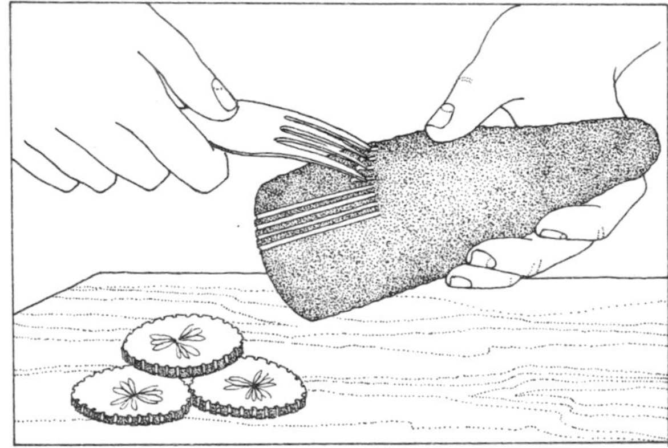

Crimping a cucumber

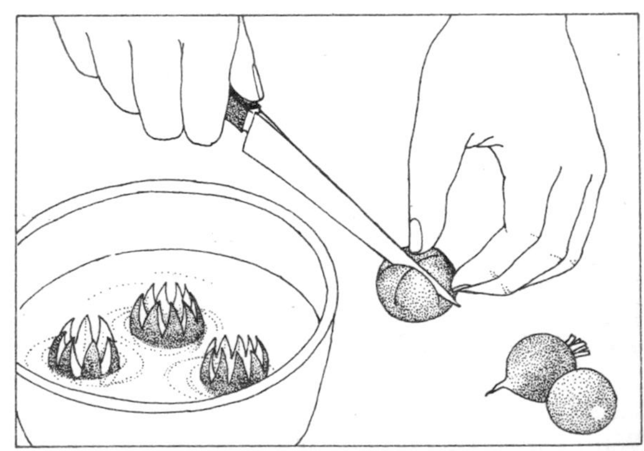

Making radish roses

Gherkin fans Use whole gherkins, choosing long, thin ones. Cut each lengthwise into thin slices, but leave these joined at one end. Fan out the strips of gherkins so that they overlap each other.

Radish roses Trim the radishes. Make 4 or 8 small, deep cuts, crossing in the centre at the root end. Leave the radishes in cold or iced water for 1–2 hours, till the cuts open to form 'petals'.

Tomato lilies Choose firm, even-sized tomatoes. Using a small sharp-pointed knife, make a series of V-shaped cuts round the middle of each, cutting right through to the centre. Carefully pull the halves apart.

Quick garnish Sprinkle finely chopped parsley on potato salad; finely chopped onion on beetroot; chopped spring onion on tomato; chopped mint, chives, tarragon or parsley on green salad.

SIDE SALADS

Green salad

see colour plate between pp. 208 and 209

Use two or more green salad ingredients, such as lettuce, cress, watercress, endive, chicory, cabbage and so on. Wash and drain them and just before serving toss lightly in a bowl with French dressing, adding a little finely chopped onion if you wish.

Sprinkle with chopped fresh parsley, chives, mint, tarragon or other herbs, as available.

Endive salad

endive, washed and trimmed
French dressing
1 hard-boiled egg, finely chopped

Prepare the endive and chill it, toss it in the dressing and sprinkle with egg. Use as an alternative to green salad.

Cucumber salad

see colour plate between pp. 208 and 209

¼ cucumber
French dressing
chopped parsley

Wipe the cucumber, peel if you wish and slice it thinly. Put the cucumber in a dish, cover with the dressing and allow to stand for about ¼ hour; serve sprinkled with the parsley.

Tomato salad

see colour plate between pp. 208 and 209

4 tomatoes
small piece of onion (or 2–3 small spring onions)
salt and pepper
French dressing
chopped parsley or chives

Wipe the tomatoes, skin them if you wish and cut in thin slices. Skin and finely chop the onion (or spring onions). Arrange the tomatoes in a dish, sprinkle with the onion and seasoning and pour the dressing over. Allow to stand for a short time and serve sprinkled with the chopped herbs.

Onion and tomato salad

2 onions, skinned and sliced
3 firm tomatoes, skinned and sliced
45–60 ml *(3–4 tbsps)* **French dressing**
chopped chives

Arrange the onions and tomatoes alternately in a shallow dish. Pour the dressing over and serve sprinkled with the chives.

Onion and mint salad

1 bunch of spring onions, sliced
small bunch of mint, chopped
15 ml *(1 level tbsp)* caster sugar
salt and pepper
vinegar

Arrange the onions and mint in layers in a small dish, sprinkling sugar and seasoning between the layers. Add enough vinegar to cover and allow to stand for about 30 minutes before serving. This is delicious with cold lamb.

Potato salad

leftover boiled potatoes
small piece of raw onion, skinned and finely chopped
salad cream to bind
finely chopped parsley or chives

The potatoes must be firm and cold. Cut them in 1-cm *(½-in)* dice, mix with the onion and add salad cream to bind the mixture together. Pile into a dish and sprinkle with parsley or chives. Allow to stand for about ½ hour before serving, so that the flavours can blend.

Carrot salad

3 large carrots, pared
1 lettuce, washed
French dressing
finely chopped parsley

Grate the carrots finely and arrange on a bed of lettuce leaves. Sprinkle with the French dressing and garnish with chopped parsley.

Dressed cauliflower

1 cauliflower, trimmed and broken into sprigs
French dressing

Cook the cauliflower in fast-boiling salted water for 10–15 minutes, until just soft. Drain well and allow to become cold. Put in a dish, pour the French dressing over and toss lightly before serving.

If you wish, you can add a garnish of chopped parsley or 1–2 rashers of streaky bacon, grilled until crisp and lightly crumbled, just before serving the salad.

Mushroom salad *see colour plate between pp. 208 and 209*

100 g *(4 oz)* mushrooms
15 ml *(1 tbsp)* lemon juice or cider vinegar
45 ml *(3 tbsps)* salad oil
15 ml *(1 tbsp)* finely chopped parsley
little freshly ground black pepper
salt

Wipe and dry the mushrooms but don't peel them; remove the stalks (keeping them to use in a stew, sauce, etc). Slice the mushrooms very thinly into a serving dish and add the lemon juice, oil, parsley and pepper. Marinade in the dressing for ½ hour and salt lightly just before serving. This is a good accompaniment salad with fish.

Orange salad

2 oranges, peeled
chopped tarragon or mint
French dressing

Divide the oranges into sections, removing all the skin, pith and pips, or cut across in thin slices, using a saw-edged knife. Put the slices into a shallow dish, sprinkle with the tarragon or mint and pour the dressing over; allow to stand for a short time before serving.

This salad can be served on a bed of watercress, small cress or endive.

Lemon salad

2 lemons
1 orange
30 ml *(2 level tbsps)* caster sugar
15 ml *(1 level tbsp)* chopped tarragon
French dressing
small, crisp lettuce leaves, washed

Dip the fruit into boiling water, peel, removing all the pith, and slice the fruit thinly. Arrange in a salad dish, sprinkling sugar and tarragon between the layers. Pour the dressing over and garnish with the lettuce leaves.

Mixed vegetable salad

A good way of using up leftover cooked vegetables. Use an assortment such as carrots, peas, potatoes, cauliflower, beetroot and turnip. Cut into even-sized pieces, toss in enough salad cream to bind the mixture and serve sprinkled with chopped parsley, chives or other fresh herbs.

Crunchy salad

1 lettuce, washed and shredded
1 bunch of watercress, washed and trimmed
1 small cauliflower, divided into florets
1 avocado, peeled, stoned and diced, optional
2 tomatoes, skinned, seeded and chopped
45 ml *(3 tbsps)* flaked almonds

For the dressing
1 clove garlic, skinned and crushed
5 ml *(1 level tsp)* salt
30 ml *(2 tbsps)* lemon juice
1.25 ml *(¼ level tsp)* sugar
1.25 ml *(¼ level tsp)* pepper
1.25 ml *(¼ level tsp)* paprika
1.25 ml *(¼ level tsp)* celery seeds
2.5 ml *(½ level tsp)* dry mustard
60 ml *(4 tbsps)* corn oil

Make the dressing by crushing the garlic and adding the remaining ingredients. Beat thoroughly (or shake in a screw-topped jar) and chill. Put the lettuce, watercress, cauliflower, avocado, tomatoes and almonds in a bowl, sprinkle the dressing over and lightly toss all together.

A general accompaniment for cold meats and excellent with pizza.

Raisin and nut salad

2 sharp dessert apples
100 g *(4 oz)* seeded raisins, chopped
50 g *(2 oz)* walnuts, chopped
salad dressing
1 bunch of watercress, washed and trimmed

Wipe the apples; don't peel them, but grate them on a clean grater into a basin. Add the chopped raisins and nuts and a little salad dressing and mix lightly. Arrange the watercress in a circle on a plate and pile the fruit mixture in the centre.

Winter salad

2 eating apples, cored and chopped
4 sticks of celery, scrubbed and chopped
1 medium sized cooked beetroot, peeled and diced
½ small onion, skinned and finely chopped
salad cream to bind
few chopped walnuts, optional

Mix the apples, celery, beetroot and onion and add sufficient salad cream to bind together. Pile on to a dish and serve sprinkled with the chopped walnuts.

Cole slaw – 1

½ hard white cabbage, washed and finely shredded
1 large carrot, pared and coarsely grated
small piece of onion, skinned and finely chopped
15 ml *(1 tbsp)* chopped parsley, optional
about 75 ml *(5 tbsps)* salad cream or mayonnaise
5 ml *(1 level tsp)* sugar
salt and pepper
few drops of vinegar or lemon juice

Combine the cabbage, carrot, onion and parsley (if used) in a large bowl. Mix the salad cream with the sugar, salt and pepper and add enough vinegar or lemon juice to sharpen the flavour. Toss with the salad in the bowl until lightly coated, adding a little more salad cream if necessary.

Cole slaw – 2

½ hard white cabbage, washed and shredded
2 sticks of celery, scrubbed and chopped
½ small onion, skinned and chopped, optional
50 g *(2 oz)* sultanas
45 ml *(3 tbsps)* chopped walnuts
salad cream

Combine the cabbage, celery, onion (if used), sultanas and nuts in a large bowl and toss lightly with just enough salad cream to bind.

Golden slaw

1 small Savoy cabbage
100–175 g *(4–6 oz)* Gruyère cheese, cut in thin strips
225 g *(½ lb)* red-skinned apples, cored and chopped
150 ml *(¼ pt)* mayonnaise
15 ml *(1 level tbsp)* prepared mustard
5 ml *(1 level tsp)* sugar
salt and pepper

Wash the cabbage well. Curl back the outer leaves, cut round the base of the heart and scoop out the heart, leaving a 'bowl'. Finely shred the cabbage heart and put in a basin with the cheese and apples. Combine the mayonnaise with the mustard, sugar and seasoning and toss the salad in this dressing until the ingredients are well coated. Serve in the scooped-out cabbage 'bowl'.

Roma salad

1 pkt Italian dressing mix
30 ml *(2 tbsps)* water
60 ml *(4 tbsps)* cider vinegar
142-ml *(5-fl oz)* carton soured cream
½ firm white cabbage, shredded
50 g *(2 oz)* salted nuts, chopped
12 dates, stoned and chopped
1 apple, cored and chopped
5 ml *(1 level tsp)* celery seeds
little paprika pepper

Put the Italian dressing mix in a large screw-topped jar, add the water and shake. Add the vinegar and soured cream and again shake very thoroughly. In a large bowl, toss together the cabbage, nuts, dates, apple and celery seeds. Pour the dressing over and mix thoroughly with a fork. Dredge lightly with paprika pepper.

This is an ideal salad to accompany cold veal and ham pie.

Salade niçoise

225 g *(½ lb)* tomatoes, skinned
½ small cucumber, thinly sliced
salt and freshly ground black pepper
5 ml *(1 tsp)* chopped basil
5 ml *(1 tsp)* chopped parsley
grated rind of 1 lemon
100 g *(4 oz)* cooked French beans
50 g *(2 oz)* black olives
½ clove garlic, finely crushed
French dressing
8 anchovy fillets, halved
brown bread and butter
quarters of lemon

Slice the tomatoes, put in layers with the cucumber on a shallow dish, season well and sprinkle with the herbs and lemon rind. Pile the French beans in the centre of the dish, scatter the stoned and chopped olives over and season again. Add the garlic to the dressing and pour over the salad. Arrange the anchovy fillets in a lattice pattern over the salad and allow to stand for about ½ hour before serving, so that the flavours blend. Serve with the bread and butter and lemon.

Filled beetroots

4 small cooked beetroots
salt and pepper
15 ml *(1 tbsp)* lemon juice
4 sticks of celery, chopped
1 orange, peeled and chopped
5 ml *(1 tsp)* horseradish sauce
5 ml *(1 level tsp)* sugar
French dressing

Peel and hollow out the beetroots, season with salt and pepper and sprinkle with lemon juice. Mix the celery and orange and fill the beetroot cups. Add the horseradish sauce and sugar to the French dressing and spoon this over the beetroots.

Pear and grape salad

2 fresh pears, peeled and halved (or 4 halved canned pears)
30 ml *(2 tbsps)* cream cheese
knob of butter
salt and pepper
5 ml *(1 tsp)* chopped chives
milk if required
100 g *(¼ lb)* black grapes, halved and pipped
1 lettuce, washed
30 ml *(2 tbsps)* French dressing

Core the pears if necessary. Blend the cream cheese, butter, seasoning and chives, adding a very little milk if necessary to soften the mixture. Put this mixture between the grape halves. Arrange each pear half on a crisp lettuce leaf, fill the hollow centres with the stuffed grapes, chill well and sprinkle with French dressing.

Waldorf salad

450 g *(1 lb)* eating apples
lemon juice
5 ml *(1 level tsp)* sugar
150 ml *(¼ pt)* mayonnaise
½ head of celery, chopped
50 g *(2 oz)* walnuts, chopped
1 lettuce

Peel and core the apples, slice one and dice the rest; dip the slices in lemon juice to prevent discoloration. Toss the diced apples with 30 ml *(2 tbsps)* lemon juice, 5 ml *(1 level tsp)* sugar and 15 ml *(1 tbsp)* mayonnaise and leave to stand for about ½ hour. Just before serving, add the celery, walnuts and remaining mayonnaise and toss together. Serve in a bowl lined with lettuce leaves and garnish with the apple slices and a few whole walnuts, if liked.

Rice salad

225 g *(½ lb)* tomatoes, skinned and quartered
225 g *(½ lb)* long grain rice, cooked and drained
100 g *(¼ lb)* French beans, cooked
100 g *(¼ lb)* frozen peas, cooked
2 sticks of celery, scrubbed and chopped
1 small dessert apple, cored and chopped
10 ml *(2 tsps)* chopped parsley
10 ml *(2 tsps)* chopped chives or 5 ml *(1 tsp)* chopped onion
French dressing (well flavoured with mustard)
1 bunch of watercress, trimmed and washed

Remove the seeds from the tomatoes, strain off any juice and cut the flesh into quarters. Put the rice (which should be quite dry) into a bowl and add the beans, peas, celery and apple. Stir with a fork, adding the parsley, chives, tomato juice and enough dressing to moisten nicely. Pile up in the centre of a dish and arrange the tomato quarters round the sides, with the watercress at each end.

Californian salad

4 tomatoes, thinly sliced
small piece of cucumber, diced
2 sticks of celery, finely chopped
salt and pepper
2 bananas, thinly sliced
2 red-skinned apples, cored and diced
juice of ½ lemon
salad cream or mayonnaise to bind
lettuce or watercress

Sprinkle the tomatoes, cucumber and celery with salt and pepper. Soak the bananas and apples in the lemon juice for about 10 minutes and drain. Mix all the ingredients together and bind lightly with the salad cream. Serve on a bed of lettuce.

MAIN-DISH SALADS

Cheese salad

French dressing
5 ml *(1 tsp)* made mustard
1 small onion, skinned and finely chopped
225 g *(½ lb)* Gruyère cheese, cut in thin strips
lettuce or watercress, washed and trimmed

Make the French dressing, add the mustard and onion and mix with the cheese. Allow to stand for 1 hour and serve on a bed of lettuce or watercress.

Cream cheese and celery salad

see colour plate between pp. 208 and 209

3 sticks of celery, scrubbed and chopped
225 g *(½ lb)* cream cheese
1 bunch of watercress, washed and trimmed
paprika

Mix the celery and cream cheese together. Arrange the watercress on a plate, pile the cheese mixture on top and serve sprinkled with a little paprika.

This simple cream cheese salad can be varied by reducing the amount of celery to 1–2 sticks and adding any of the following: 1 red-skinned apple, cored and chopped: a few canned pineapple chunks or segments of mandarin orange, drained; 30–45 ml *(2–3 tbsps)* chopped walnuts; 30 ml *(2 tbsps)* sultanas.

Salmon and rice salad

see colour plate facing p. 240

175 g *(6 oz)* long grain rice
226-g *(8-oz)* can of salmon
225 g *(½ lb)* tomatoes, skinned and chopped
60 ml *(4 tbsps)* finely chopped chives
45 ml *(3 tbsps)* double cream, whipped
90 ml *(6 tbsps)* mayonnaise
5 ml *(1 level tsp)* celery seeds, optional
grated rind of 1 lemon
salt and pepper
lettuce and radishes

Cook the rice in the usual way and allow to cool. Drain the salmon, remove the skin and bones and flake the fish; add with the tomatoes and chives to the rice and mix lightly. Fold the whipped cream into the mayonnaise and add the celery seeds (if used), with the lemon rind and salt and pepper to taste. Fold in the rice mixture and press into a 1.1-l *(2-pt)* ring mould (or jelly mould). When lightly chilled, turn out on to a plate lined with lettuce and garnish with sliced radishes.

Mixed English salad

small bunch of radishes, washed and trimmed
bunch of spring onions, washed and trimmed
1 lettuce, washed
bunch of watercress (or a box of small cress), washed and trimmed
4 tomatoes, skinned
1 cooked beetroot, peeled and diced
1 small piece of cucumber, skinned (if you wish)
2–4 hard-boiled eggs, shelled and sliced
50–100 g *(2–4 oz)* firm cheese, grated

Cut the radishes into 'roses' (see page 234). Make fine cuts down the length of the onion tops. Put the radishes and onions in iced water and leave until the radishes open and the onions curl. Put a bed of lettuce and watercress or cress on a shallow plate and arrange the remaining ingredients on top, in rows or groups.

Stuffed tomato salad

8 firm tomatoes
2 eggs, hard-boiled and shelled
60 ml *(4 tbsps)* cooked peas
15–30 ml *(1–2 tbsps)* thick salad cream
lettuce or small cress, washed and trimmed

Wipe the tomatoes and cut a slice from the top of each; remove the pulp with a small spoon, and turn the cases upside-down to drain. Chop one of the eggs and mix with the peas and salad cream. Pile into the tomato cases and serve on a bed of lettuce or cress. Cut the other egg into long wedge-shaped slices and use as a garnish.

Salmon and rice salad (above).
(Overleaf) Ravioli stuffed with spinach (p. 275).

Fruit, nut and cheese salad

200 g *(7 oz)* cream cheese
5 ml *(1 tbsp)* raisins
30 ml *(2 tbsps)* chopped walnuts
lettuce, washed
4 large canned peach halves

Beat the cheese until smooth. Put the raisins into boiling water for 1–2 minutes to soften them, drain and cool. Mix with half the nuts and the cheese. Arrange the peach halves on a bed of lettuce, hollow side up, top each with a spoonful of the cheese and raisin mixture and sprinkle with the remaining chopped nuts.

Note This cheese mixture can also be served on pineapple rings.

Tahitian salad

1 small lettuce, washed
4 pineapple rings
200 g *(7 oz)* cream cheese
chopped chives
grated coconut

Arrange the lettuce on a plate, place the rings of pineapple on it and divide the cream cheese evenly between them. Sprinkle with chopped chives and grated coconut.

Caribbean salad Replace the pineapple rings by peeled and sliced bananas (dipped in lemon juice to prevent discoloration).

Egg mayonnaise

4 hard-boiled eggs, shelled
few lettuce leaves
150 ml *(¼ pt)* mayonnaise
chopped parsley or paprika

Cut the eggs lengthways into halves. Wash and drain the lettuce and put on a shallow dish. Serve the eggs on the lettuce, cut side down; coat with the mayonnaise and garnish with parsley or paprika.

Sardine and beetroot salad

2 124-g *(4⅜-oz)* cans sardines, drained
2 eating apples, grated
1 medium sized beetroot, peeled and grated
60–90 ml *(4–6 tbsps)* salad cream
salt and pepper
squeeze of lemon juice
lettuce, washed

Mash the sardines in a bowl. Mix the apple and beetroot with the sardines, add salad cream to bind and season well, adding a little lemon juice to taste. Serve on a bed of lettuce.

Smoky bean salad

450 g *(1 lb)* smoked haddock
little milk and water
439-g *(15½-oz)* can of butter beans
lettuce, washed
1 hard-boiled egg, shelled and sliced

For the dressing
45 ml *(3 tbsps)* soured cream
15–30 ml *(1–2 tbsps)* lemon juice
15 ml *(1 tbsp)* chopped parsley
1.25 ml *(¼ level tsp)* curry powder
little freshly ground black pepper

Put the fish in a pan, cover with milk and water, put the lid on the pan, bring to the boil, turn out the heat and leave the fish to stand for 10 minutes. Drain thoroughly, remove the bones and skin, place the fish in a basin and break into large flakes, using a fork. Drain the butter beans and add to the fish. Bind carefully with dressing and serve on a bed of lettuce, garnished with slices of hard-boiled egg.

To prepare the dressing, blend the cream and lemon juice and gradually stir in the parsley, curry powder and pepper; check the seasoning. Serve as a light supper dish.

Stirred rice (p. 279).

Apple and tuna salad

198-g *(7-oz)* can tuna fish
450 g *(1 lb)* red-skinned apples
30 ml *(2 tbsps)* lemon juice
4 sticks of celery, diced
150 ml *(¼ pt)* mayonnaise or salad cream

Drain and flake the tuna fish. Core and dice the apples and sprinkle with the lemon juice. Combine the celery with the apples, tuna and mayonnaise or salad cream, tossing them together before serving.

Patio salad

198-g *(7-oz)* can of tuna fish
2–3 olives, finely chopped
225 g *(½ lb)* new potatoes, cooked and diced
225 g *(½ lb)* French beans, cooked and cut into 10-cm *(4-in)* pieces.
4 tomatoes, skinned and sliced
1 head of chicory, washed

For the dressing
5 ml *(1 level tsp)* dry mustard
15 ml *(1 tbsp)* wine vinegar
30 ml *(2 tbsps)* oil
salt and pepper

Drain off the excess oil from the tuna, flake the fish into a bowl and add the olives. Arrange the potatoes, French beans and tomatoes in layers on the serving dish, top with the tuna mixture and pour the dressing over. Garnish with the spears of chicory.

To prepare the dressing, blend the mustard and vinegar and gradually add the oil. Season to taste.

Note When chicory is unobtainable, use watercress or endive.

Shrimp salad

45–60 ml *(3–4 tbsps)* mayonnaise
300 g *(11 oz)* shelled shrimps
1 small lettuce, shredded
½ cucumber, sliced
lemon wedges

Stir the mayonnaise into the shrimps and serve on the lettuce, garnished with cucumber and lemon wedges. If frozen shrimps are used, allow them to thaw completely and drain well before using.

Grapefruit and prawn salad *see colour plate between pp. 208 and 209*

lettuce, washed
1 grapefruit, peeled
½ cucumber, peeled and diced
200 g *(7 oz)* peeled prawns
French dressing
1.25 ml *(¼ level tsp)* dried dill weed

Arrange a bed of lettuce in a shallow salad bowl. Remove the pith from the grapefruit and divide it into segments; cut each segment into three and put the juice and grapefruit flesh into a basin. Add the cucumber and the prawns, pour on some French dressing, sprinkle over the dill and mix lightly with a spoon and fork. Pile the mixture on the lettuce and garnish with a few prawn heads (if available).

Lobster mayonnaise

1 medium sized lobster, cooked
1 lettuce, washed
150 ml *(¼ pt)* mayonnaise
1 hard-boiled egg, sliced

Remove the meat from the lobster, retaining the flesh from the claws and any coral for garnishing. Flake the remaining flesh with a fork or divide it into neat pieces. Arrange the shredded outer leaves of the lettuce in a salad bowl. Mix the lobster meat with the mayonnaise and pile lightly on the lettuce leaves in the bowl. Garnish with slices of egg, the lettuce heart, divided into quarters, the claw meat of the lobster and the coral (if present).

Ham and tongue salad

113-g *(4-oz)* pkt frozen peas
3–4 tomatoes, skinned and sliced
3 sticks celery, scrubbed and chopped
100 g *(4 oz)* cooked ham, diced
100 g *(4 oz)* cooked tongue, diced
45–60 ml *(3–4 tbsps)* French dressing
lettuce, washed

Cook the peas according to the manufacturer's instructions, drain and allow to cool. Mix with the tomatoes, celery, ham and tongue and toss with the French dressing. Serve on a bed of lettuce.

Cold beef salad

200 g *(7 oz)* long grain rice
2–3 tomatoes, skinned and sliced
225 g *(8 oz)* cold cooked beef, thinly sliced
15 ml *(1 tbsp)* finely chopped onion
5 ml *(1 tsp)* made mustard
45 ml *(3 tbsps)* French dressing

Cook the rice in the usual way and allow to cool. Mix it with the tomatoes, meat and onion. Add the mustard to the French dressing and stir into the salad ingredients.

Russian salad – 1

(Using aspic jelly)

1 small cauliflower, cooked
1–2 envelopes of aspic jelly powder
60 ml *(4 tbsps)* cooked peas
30 ml *(2 tbsps)* cooked diced carrot
30 ml *(2 tbsps)* cooked diced turnip
3 potatoes, cooked and diced
1 small beetroot, cooked and diced
2 tomatoes, skinned and diced
50 g *(2 oz)* ham or tongue, diced
50 g *(2 oz)* shrimps or prawns, cooked
50 g *(2 oz)* smoked salmon, cut in strips, optional
3 gherkins, chopped
15 ml *(1 tbsp)* capers
few lettuce leaves, shredded
30–45 ml *(2–3 tbsps)* salad cream
4 olives
4 anchovy fillets

Divide the cauliflower into small sprigs. Make up the aspic jelly following the manufacturer's instructions. When it is cold, pour a little into a ring mould and turn this round until the sides are coated with jelly. Decorate with a little of the peas and diced vegetables and allow to set. Set layers of vegetables, meat, fish, gherkins and capers alternately with layers of jelly in the mould, but don't use up all the vegetables. When the mould is set, turn it out. Toss the lettuce and remaining vegetables in the salad cream and pile into the centre of the mould. Decorate with olives and anchovy fillets.

Note Failing a ring mould, use an ordinary jelly mould; the remaining salad can be served in a border round the jellied salad.

Russian salad – 2

(Without aspic jelly)

Prepare vegetables, meat and fish as above; put layers of them in a salad bowl, season with salt, pepper and a pinch of caster sugar and cover each layer with salad cream. Decorate with beetroot, olives, capers, anchovies and salmon (if used).

Curried chicken salad

175 g *(6 oz)* long grain rice
½ cooked chicken
1 small cauliflower washed and trimmed
45 ml *(3 tbsps)* French dressing
150 ml *(¼ pt)* mayonnaise
30 ml *(2 tbsps)* milk or cream
15 ml *(1 level tbsp)* curry powder
salt and pepper
1 small green pepper, seeded and cut into strips
2 sticks of celery, chopped
1–2 small onions, skinned and finely sliced
1 lettuce, washed

Cook the rice in the usual way and leave to cool. Cut the chicken meat into chunks. Divide the cauliflower into small sprigs and toss with the rice in the French dressing. Combine the mayonnaise, milk or cream, curry powder, salt and pepper in a large bowl, add the chicken and toss together. Add the rice mixture, the green pepper, the celery and the onions and serve on a bed of lettuce. Shredded coconut, salted peanuts, pineapple cubes, tomato wedges and red-currant jelly, served in small dishes, make good accompaniments.

Chicken and almond salad

50–100 g *(2–4 oz)* raisins, stoned
350 g *(12 oz)* cooked chicken meat
50 g *(2 oz)* almonds, blanched
small piece of raw onion, skinned, optional
30–45 ml *(2–3 tbsps)* single cream
30–45 ml *(2–3 tbsps)* mayonnaise or salad cream
salt and pepper
squeeze of lemon juice
15 ml *(1 tbsp)* chopped parsley
lettuce or watercress, washed and trimmed

Cover the raisins with boiling water, leave for 5 minutes and drain. Cut the chicken meat into chunks. Roughly chop the almonds and brown lightly under the grill. Grate the onion. Mix the cream, mayonnaise, seasoning, lemon juice and parsley and combine with the raisins, chicken, almonds and onion in a bowl. Serve on a bed of lettuce or watercress.

SALAD DRESSINGS

French dressing
(Sauce vinaigrette)

1.25 ml *(¼ level tsp)* salt
pinch pepper
1.25 ml *(¼ level tsp)* dry mustard
1.25 ml *(¼ level tsp)* sugar
15 ml *(1 tbsp)* vinegar
30 ml *(2 tbsps)* salad oil

Put the salt, pepper, mustard and sugar in a bowl, add the vinegar and stir until well blended. Beat in the oil gradually with a fork. The oil separates out on standing, so if necessary whip the dressing immediately before use. If you wish, store it in a salad cream bottle, shaking it up vigorously just before serving.

Note The proportion of oil to vinegar varies with individual taste, but use vinegar sparingly. Malt, wine, tarragon or any other vinegar may be used.

Variations

To the above dressing add any of the following:

clove of garlic, crushed
5–10 ml *(1–2 tsps)* chopped chives
2.5–5 ml *(½–1 level tsp)* curry powder
10 ml *(2 tsps)* chopped fresh parsley, 2.5 ml *(½ level tsp)* dried marjoram and a pinch of dried thyme
5 ml *(1 tsp)* chopped fresh parsley, 5 ml *(1 tsp)* chopped gherkins or capers, 5 ml *(1 tsp)* chopped olives
5–10 ml *(1–2 tsps)* sweet pickle
15 ml *(1 tbsp)* finely sliced or chopped stuffed olives
5–10 ml *(1–2 tsps)* Worcestershire sauce
5–10 ml *(1–2 tsps)* chopped fresh mint
15 ml *(1 tbsp)* finely chopped anchovies
pinch of curry powder, ½ hard-boiled egg, shelled and finely chopped, 5 ml *(1 tsp)* chopped onion (this is called Bombay dressing)
25 g *(1 oz)* blue-vein cheese, crumbled

Lemon and oil dressing

30–45 ml *(2–3 tbsps)* salad oil
pepper and salt
15 ml *(1 tbsp)* lemon juice

Add the oil gradually to the salt and pepper and when they are well blended, whisk in the lemon juice with a fork.

Classic mayonnaise

1 egg yolk
2.5 ml *(½ level tsp)* **dry mustard**
2.5 ml *(½ level tsp)* **salt**
1.25 ml *(¼ level tsp)* **pepper**
2.5 ml *(½ level tsp)* **sugar**
about 150 ml *(¼ pt)* **salad oil**
15 ml *(1 tbsp)* **white vinegar**

Put the egg yolk into a basin with thc seasonings and sugar. Mix thoroughly, then add the oil drop by drop, stirring briskly with a wooden spoon the whole time or using a whisk, until the sauce is thick and smooth. If it becomes too thick add a little of the vinegar. When all the oil has been added, add the vinegar gradually and mix thoroughly. If liked, lemon juice may be used instead of the vinegar.

Notes To keep the basin firmly in position, twist a damp cloth tightly round the base – this prevents it from slipping. In order that the oil may be added 1 drop at a time, put into the bottle neck a cork from which a small wedge has been cut.

Should the sauce curdle during the process of making, put another egg yolk into a basin and add the curdled sauce very gradually, in the same way as the oil is added to the original egg yolks.

Variations
Using 150 ml *(¼ pt)* mayonnaise as a basis, add a flavouring as follows:

Caper Add 10 ml *(2 tsps)* chopped capers, 5 ml *(1 tsp)* chopped pimiento and 2.5 ml *(½ tsp)* tarragon vinegar. Goes well with fish.

Celery Add 15 ml *(1 tbsp)* chopped celery and 15 ml *(1 tbsp)* chopped chives.

Cream Add 60 ml *(4 tbsps)* whipped cream. Goes well with salads containing fruit, chicken or rice.

Cucumber Add 30 ml *(3 tbsps)* finely chopped cucumber and 2.5 ml *(½ level tsp)* salt. Goes well with fish salads, especially crab, lobster and salmon.

Herbs Add 30 ml *(2 tbsps)* chopped chives and 15 ml *(1 tbsp)* chopped parsley.

Horseradish Add 15 ml *(1 tbsp)* horseradish sauce.

Piquant Add 5 ml *(1 tsp)* tomato ketchup, 5 ml *(1 tsp)* chopped olives and a pinch of paprika pepper.

Tomato Add ½ tomato, skinned and diced, 1 spring onion, chopped, 1.25 ml *(¼ level tsp)* salt and 5 ml *(1 tsp)* vinegar or lemon juice.

Blue cheese Add 25 g *(1 oz)* crumbled blue cheese.

Note All these variations can also be made using a basis of bought salad cream.

Foamy mayonnaise

2 egg yolks
salt and pepper
150 ml *(¼ pt)* **salad oil**
30 ml *(2 tbsps)* **lemon juice**
1 egg white, stiffly whisked

Cream the egg yolks and seasonings and add the oil drop by drop, stirring hard all the time until the mayonnaise is thick and smooth, then stir in the lemon juice. Put in a cool place until required; just before serving, fold in the egg white.

Thousand Islands mayonnaise

150 ml *(¼ pt)* **mayonnaise**
15 ml *(1 tbsp)* **chopped stuffed olives**
5 ml *(1 tsp)* **finely chopped onion**
1 hard-boiled egg, chopped
15 ml *(1 tbsp)* **finely chopped green pepper**
5 ml *(1 tsp)* **chopped parsley**
5 ml *(1 level tsp)* **tomato paste**

Mix all the ingredients together until evenly combined.

Cream dressing

salt
cayenne pepper
142-ml *(5-fl oz)* carton double cream
15–30 ml *(1–2 tbsps)* vinegar

Season the cream to taste and whip until thick; add the vinegar gradually and chill before using.

Soured cream dressing

142-ml *(5-fl oz)* carton soured cream
30 ml *(2 tbsps)* white vinegar
small piece of raw onion, skinned and finely chopped
2.5 ml *(½ level tsp)* sugar
5 ml *(1 level tsp)* salt
pinch of pepper

Mix all the ingredients thoroughly.

Horseradish dressing

30 ml *(2 tbsps)* bottled horseradish sauce
142-ml *(5-fl oz)* carton soured cream, whipped
5 ml *(1 level tsp)* sugar
5 ml *(1 tsp)* lemon juice
5 ml *(1 tsp)* vinegar
salt and cayenne

Mix the horseradish sauce with the cream and add the sugar, lemon juice, vinegar and seasoning to taste. Good served with roast beef.

Golden dressing

300 ml *(½ pt)* mayonnaise
2.5 ml *(½ level tsp)* salt
large pinch pepper
large pinch paprika
10 ml *(2 level tsps)* sugar
30 ml *(2 tbsps)* vinegar
30 ml *(2 tbsps)* milk
10 ml *(2 tsps)* prepared mustard
2 egg yolks

Combine the mayonnaise with the remaining ingredients until well blended.

Mustard dressing

15 ml *(1 level tbsp)* flour
pinch of cayenne pepper
25 ml *(1½ level tbsps)* sugar
5 ml *(1 level tsp)* dry mustard
2.5 ml *(½ level tsp)* salt
150 ml *(¼ pt)* milk
2 egg yolks, beaten
60 ml *(4 tbsps)* vinegar

Mix the dry ingredients to a smooth cream with a little of the cold milk. Heat the remainder of the milk and when boiling stir into the blended ingredients; return the mixture to the pan and bring to the boil, stirring all the time. Cool slightly, stir in the egg yolks and again return the pan to the heat. Cook gently until the mixture thickens, but don't let it boil. Allow to cool and stir in the vinegar.

Note A richer effect can be obtained if a little whipped cream is stirred in before serving.

Cooked salad cream

45 ml *(3 level tbsps)* flour
15 ml *(1 level tbsp)* sugar
10 ml *(2 level tsps)* dry mustard
5 ml *(1 level tsp)* salt
150 ml *(¼ pt)* milk
2 eggs, beaten
50 g *(2 oz)* butter
150 ml *(¼ pt)* vinegar
150 ml *(¼ pt)* salad oil

Mix all the dry ingredients and blend to a smooth cream with the milk. Bring to the boil, stirring all the time, cook for 1 minute and then cool. Beat in the eggs and butter, return the pan to the heat and cook until thick, but don't boil. Beat in the vinegar gradually and finally stir in the oil.

This salad dressing can be used as for mayonnaise. It can also be bottled and kept for a few days in a refrigerator – in this case, shake it well before using, as it tends to separate out on standing.

Eggs

Eggs are invaluable for a multitude of quick snacks, they are available all the year round and remain cheap compared with such food as meat and fish. They are indispensable in most cakes and in many other dishes, from sauces to hot and cold puddings. Eggs are rich in protein and fat and contain vitamin A, vitamins of the B complex and useful amounts of iron and calcium. The key to successful preparation of egg dishes is gentle cooking and, if the dish is hot, immediate serving.

Buying and storing eggs

Eggs are sold by 'grade' and the English grades are as follows:

large – 62 g *($2\frac{3}{16}$ oz)*
standard – 53.2–62 g *($1\frac{7}{8}$–$2\frac{3}{16}$ oz)*
medium – 46.1–53.2 g *($1\frac{5}{8}$–$1\frac{7}{8}$ oz)*
small – 42.5–46.1 g *($1\frac{1}{2}$–$1\frac{5}{8}$ oz)*
extra small – less than 42.5 g *(less than $1\frac{1}{2}$ oz)*.

When EEC weight grades come into operation the grades will be as follows:

Grade 1 over 70 g
Grade 2 65–70 g
Grade 3 60–65 g
Grade 4 55–60 g
Grade 5 50–55 g
Grade 6 45–50 g
Grade 7 below 45 g.
The standard egg is roughly equivalent to Grade 4.

Standard and medium eggs are perfectly suitable for most cooking.

The colour of the eggshell varies according to the breed of chicken and does not affect the egg's flavour or food value.

Store eggs in a cool place: if they are put in the refrigerator, keep them well away from the ice-box and take them out some time before using, to give them time to reach room temperature, otherwise they crack when being boiled and are also difficult to whisk. Use the refrigerator racks or boxes provided, as these are designed to protect the eggs. Don't store eggs next to cheese, fish or onions, as they absorb strong flavours.

As eggs are nowadays plentiful and relatively cheap all the year, it is not worth preserving them unless you keep your own hens and have a sudden glut of eggs. They can be preserved in waterglass, according to the instructions on the container.

To test for freshness

There is always a small air space inside an egg and this increases as the egg ages. The fresher the egg, therefore, the fuller it is, and that is the basis of the following test. Place the egg in a tumbler of cold water. If fresh and full, it lies flat at the bottom of the glass. If the egg tilts slightly, it is probably not fresh enough to boil, but will fry or scramble satisfactorily; if it floats, it is very likely to be quite bad.

Using eggs in cookery

Apart from their uses as a main dish, eggs have three main functions in cookery:

1. Emulsifying The yolk only is used as an emulsifying agent (in such mixtures as mayonnaise, for instance – see the chapter on Salads and Salad Dressings).

2. Thickening and binding Beaten eggs are used to thicken sauces (see the Sauces chapter and also custard mixtures in the Hot Puddings chapter), for binding such things as fish cakes and for coating foods which are likely to disintegrate during the cooking, such as fried fillets of fish, fritters and croquettes, etc.

3. Raising Eggs are used as a raising agent for batters and for many cakes. Where an extra light mixture is required, the egg whites are whisked separately before being added. Whisked egg whites are also used for making meringues (see page 390), soufflé omelettes, soufflés and various light, foamy sweets and icings.

Cooking eggs

Except in the case of hard-boiled eggs, the more lightly egg dishes are cooked, the better. This applies particularly to fried and baked egg dishes and to omelettes, where too long cooking makes the eggs tough. Cook custards and similar dishes containing eggs very slowly over a low heat or stand them in a water bath or use a double saucepan.

To separate an egg

Give the egg a sharp knock against the side of a basin or cup and break the shell in half – tapping it lightly two or three times is liable to crush the shell instead of breaking

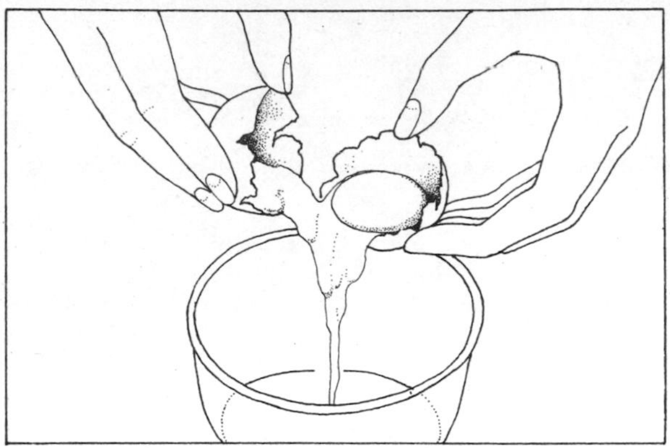

Separating the yolk from the white of an egg

it cleanly and may cause the yolk to mix into the white. Having broken the shell, pass the yolk back and forth from one half of the shell to the other, letting the white drop into the basin. Put the yolk into another basin.

If you are separating more than one egg, use a third basin for cracking the eggs (so that if any of the yolks should break, only the one white will be spoilt): put the second yolk in with the first one and tip the white in with the first white. Continue using the third basin in this way for any more eggs that may be needed.

Ducks' eggs

Ducks' eggs are larger and richer than hens' eggs. They need to be thoroughly cooked to be safe, at least 10 minutes being allowed for boiling. They can be included in cakes (except sponge mixtures) and puddings, but they should not be used for making meringues or any sweet which is cooked for only a short time or at a low temperature, nor should they be preserved or stored.

Turkey and goose eggs

These are as delicate in flavour as hens' eggs, but they are much larger. They can be cooked by any of the methods given for hens' eggs and can be used for all cakes and puddings. Allow a longer time for boiling – for soft-boiled eggs allow about 7 minutes.

Gull, plover, pheasant and guinea fowl eggs

These are usually served hard-boiled as an hors d'oeuvre. Cook them for 10–15 minutes.

Boiled eggs

Eggs should be simmered rather than boiled. Put them into boiling water, using a spoon, lower the heat and cook for 3 minutes for a light set and up to 4½ minutes for a firmer set. Alternatively, put them in cold water and bring slowly to the boil – they will then be lightly set. The water in each case should be just sufficient to cover the eggs. Fresh eggs tend to take a little longer to cook than those which are a few days old.

Hard-boiled eggs

Put the eggs into boiling water, bring back to the boil and boil gently for 10–12 minutes.

Hard-boiled eggs should be placed at once under running cold water, the shells tapped against the edge of a basin or work surface and left until they are cold: this prevents a discoloured rim forming round the outside of the yolk and enables the shell to be easily removed. Crack the shell all round by tapping on a firm surface, then peel it off.

Soft-boiled eggs (Oeufs mollets)

Soft-boiled eggs can be served hot or cold. Cold, they are fine for eggs in aspic; hot, they can be 'blanketed' in any savoury sauce. Use as an alternative to poached eggs. Put the eggs into a pan of boiling water and allow 5 minutes from the time the water comes back to the boil – small eggs may take less time. Plunge at once in cold water, leave about 8 minutes then take out of water and gently crack the shell with the back of a spoon. Carefully peel away the shell from the centre remembering that the egg is only lightly set.

Coddled eggs

Place the eggs in boiling water, cover, remove from the heat and keep in a warm place for 8–10 minutes; they will then be lightly set.

Poached eggs

The eggs may be cooked in a special poaching pan or in a frying pan, with the aid of round pastry cutters. To use an egg poacher, half-fill the lower container with water, place a small piece of butter in each cup and put over the heat; when the water boils, break the eggs into the cups, season lightly and cover the pan with the lid. Simmer gently until the eggs are set and loosen them with a knife before turning out. To use a frying pan, half-fill it with water, adding a pinch of salt or a few drops of vinegar to help the eggs keep their shape and give added flavour. Grease the required number of plain pastry cutters. Bring the water to the boil, put in the cutters and break an egg into each; or just slip the eggs into the water without rings. Cook gently until lightly set and lift out with a slotted spoon or fish slice. Drain the eggs before serving.

Fried eggs *see colour plate between pp. 272 and 273*

Melt a little dripping or lard in a frying pan. Break each egg separately into a cup and drop carefully into the hot fat. Cook gently and use a spoon to baste with the fat, so that the eggs cook evenly on top and underneath. When they are just set, remove them from the pan with a fish slice or broad palette knife. If the eggs are to be served with fried bacon, cook this first, then remove the rashers and keep them hot while frying the eggs in the hot bacon fat.

Baked eggs

Place the required number of individual ovenproof dishes or cocottes on a baking sheet, with a knob of butter in each dish. Put them in the oven for 1–2 minutes, until the butter has melted. Break an egg into each dish, sprinkle with a little salt and pepper, place in the oven at 180°C *(350°F)* mark 4 and leave until the eggs are just set – about 5–8 minutes. Garnish if you wish and serve at once.

Scrambled eggs

Melt a knob of butter in a small saucepan. Whisk 2 eggs with 30 ml *(2 tbsps)* milk or water and some salt and pepper. Pour into the saucepan and stir slowly over a gentle heat until the mixture begins to thicken. Remove from the heat and stir until creamy. Pile on to hot buttered toast and serve immediately.

Variations

Add to a 4-egg mixture one of the following ingredients:

50 g *(2 oz)* lightly fried sliced mushrooms

2 peeled tomatoes, chopped and lightly fried with a diced rasher of bacon

50 g *(2 oz)* chopped ham, tongue or other cooked meat

50 g *(2 oz)* sliced cooked pork sausages

50 g *(2 oz)* Finnan haddock (or other smoked fish), cooked, boned, skinned and flaked

50 g *(2 oz)* picked shrimps
50–75 g *(2–3 oz)* grated cheese
2.5 ml *(½ level tsp)* dried herbs or 15 ml *(1 level tbsp)* finely chopped mixed fresh herbs.

Alternatively, pile scrambled egg on one half of a slice of buttered toast and on the other half pile hot cooked mushrooms, tomatoes, green peppers or flaked boned fish.

Scrambled eggs archiduchesse

75 g *(3 oz)* butter
6 eggs, beaten
salt and paprika pepper
30–45 ml *(2–3 tbsps)* cream
50 g *(2 oz)* cooked ham, chopped
25 g *(1 oz)* mushrooms, sliced and lightly fried
fried bread
12 freshly cooked asparagus heads (or 1 small can of asparagus heated)

Melt the butter and add the eggs, seasonings and cream. Cook very slowly, stirring gently. As the mixture starts to thicken, add the ham and mushrooms. Serve on fried bread, topped with the asparagus heads.

OMELETTES

With care anyone can master the art of omelette making. Delicate handling is needed, but a little practice perfects the knack – don't be discouraged if your first two or three omelettes are not successful. Two points about omelettes that make them particularly convenient are the short time they take to make and the way they enable one to use up odds and ends – such as cooked meat, fish or vegetables – either in the omelette itself, as a filling or as an accompaniment.

Have everything ready before beginning to make an omelette, including a hot plate on which to serve it – an omelette must never wait, but rather be waited for.

The pan

Special little omelette pans are obtainable and should be kept for omelettes only. If you do not own such a pan, however, a thick-based frying pan can equally well be used. Whether of cast iron, copper, enamelled iron or aluminium, the pan should be thick, so that it will hold sufficient heat to cook the egg mixture as soon as this is put in. Thus the omelette can be in and out of the pan in about 2 minutes – one of the essentials for success; slow cooking and over-cooking both make an omelette tough. A 15–18-cm *(6–7 in)* pan takes a 2–3-egg omelette.

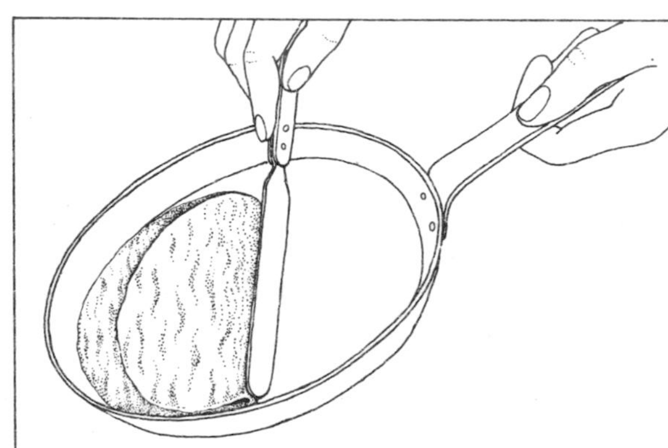

Folding an omelette

To season an omelette pan, put 15 ml *(1 level tbsp)* salt in the pan, heat it slowly, then rub well in with a piece of kitchen paper. Tip away the salt and wipe the pan with kitchen paper. To clean an omelette pan after use, don't wash it, but rub it over with kitchen paper, then with a clean cloth. Non-stick pans are ideal for omelettes and do not need seasoning.

A few minutes before you want to cook an omelette, place the pan on a very gentle heat, to ensure that it is heated evenly right to the edges – a fierce heat would cause the pan to heat unevenly. When the pan is ready for the mixture it will feel comfortably hot if you hold the back of your hand about 2.5 cm *(1 in)* away from the surface.

Note Manufacturers of non-stick pans advise that heating the empty pan will damage the surface, so add the fat before heating the pan.

Fat for greasing omelette pans

Undoubtedly butter gives the best flavour, but unsalted margarine can be used as a substitute. Bacon fat can also be used.

Types of omelette

Basically there are only two different kinds, the plain and the soufflé omelette, in which the egg whites are whisked separately and folded into the yolk mixture, giving it a fluffy texture. Plain omelettes are almost invariably savoury and soufflé omelettes are most commonly served as a sweet. There are of course many different omelette variations, achieved by the different ingredients added to the eggs or used in the filling.

Plain omelette

Allow 2 eggs per person. Whisk them just enough to break down the egg; don't make them frothy as overbeating spoils the texture of the finished omelette. Season with salt and pepper and add 15 ml *(1 tbsp)* water. Place the pan over a gentle heat and when it is hot add a knob of butter to grease it lightly. Pour the beaten eggs into the hot fat. Stir gently with the back of the prongs of a fork or wooden spatula, drawing the mixture from the sides to the centre as it sets and letting the liquid egg from the centre run to the sides. When the egg has set, stop stirring and cook for another minute until it is golden underneath and still creamy on top. Tilt the pan away from you slightly and use a palette knife to fold over a third of the omelette to the centre, then fold over the opposite third. Turn the omelette out on to the warmed plate, with the folded sides underneath, and serve at once. Don't overcook or the omelette will be tough.

Omelette fillings

Fines herbes Add 5 ml *(1 level tsp)* mixed dried herbs or 10 ml *(2 tsps)* finely chopped fresh herbs to the beaten egg mixture before cooking. Parsley, chives, chervil and tarragon are all suitable.

Cheese Grate 40 g *(1½ oz)* cheese and mix 45 ml *(3 tbsps)* of it with the eggs before cooking; sprinkle the rest over the omelette after it is folded.

Tomato Peel and chop 1–2 tomatoes and fry in a little butter in a saucepan for 5 minutes, until soft and pulpy. Put in the centre of the omelette before folding.

Mushroom Wash and slice 50 g *(2 oz)* mushrooms and cook in butter in a saucepan until soft. Put in the centre of the omelette before folding.

Bacon Rind and scissor snip 2 rashers of bacon and fry in a saucepan until crisp. Put in the centre of the omelette before folding.

Kidney Skin, core and chop 1–2 sheep's kidneys, add 5 ml *(1 tsp)* finely chopped onion and fry lightly in a little butter in a saucepan until tender. Put in the centre of the omelette before folding.

Ham or tongue Add 50 g *(2 oz)* chopped meat and 5 ml *(1 tsp)* chopped parsley to the beaten egg before cooking.

Fish Flake some cooked fish and heat gently in a little cheese sauce. Put in the centre of the omelette before folding.

Shrimp or prawn Thaw out 50 g *(2 oz)* frozen shrimps or prawns and sauté in melted butter (or use the equivalent from a can) in a saucepan, with a squeeze of lemon juice. Put into the centre of the omelette before folding.

Omelet Arnold Bennett

100 g *(4 oz)* **smoked haddock, poached (page 64)**
50 g *(2 oz)* **butter**
142-ml *(5-fl oz)* **carton double cream**
3 eggs, separated
30 ml *(2 tbsps)* **grated Parmesan cheese**
salt and freshly ground black pepper

Flake the cooked fish, removing any skin and bones. Place the fish in a saucepan with half the butter and 30 ml *(2 tbsps)* cream. Toss over a high heat until the butter melts then leave it to cool. Beat the egg yolks with 15 ml *(1 tbsp)* cream, 15 ml *(1 tbsp)* Parmesan and seasonings. Stir in the fish mixture. Stiffly whisk the egg whites and fold into the fish. Melt the remaining butter in an omelette pan and cook the omelette in the usual way but do not fold over. Slide on to a heatproof plate, top with the remaining cheese and cream blended together, then quickly bubble under a pre-heated grill. *Serves 2.*

Spanish omelette

45 ml *(3 tbsps)* **olive oil**
2 large potatoes, peeled and cut into 1-cm *(½-in)* **cubes**
2 large onions, skinned and coarsely chopped
salt and freshly ground black pepper
6 eggs, lightly beaten

In a medium sized frying pan, gently heat the olive oil. Add the potatoes and onions and season with salt and pepper. Sauté, stirring occasionally, for 10–15 minutes until golden brown. Drain off excess oil and quickly stir in the eggs. Cook for 5 minutes, shaking the pan occasionally to prevent sticking. If you wish, place under a hot grill to brown the top. Turn out on to a warmed serving plate.

Note This is a basic Spanish omelette, but other vegetables may be added, such as chopped fresh red pepper, tomatoes, peas, mushrooms, spinach. Either add them raw at the beginning or stir cooked vegetables into the eggs (peas and spinach should be added already cooked).

Soufflé omelette

2 eggs
5 ml *(1 level tsp)* **caster sugar (or salt and pepper to taste for a savoury omelette)**
30 ml *(2 tbsps)* **water**
knob butter

Separate the yolks from the whites of the eggs, putting them in different bowls. Whisk the yolks until creamy. Add the sugar (or seasoning) and the water and beat again. Whisk the egg whites until stiff but not dry. At this point place the pan containing the butter over a low heat and let the butter melt without browning. Turn the egg whites into the yolk mixture and fold in carefully, using a spoon, but don't overmix. Grease the sides of the pan with the butter by tilting it in all directions and then pour in the egg mixture. Cook over a moderate heat until the omelette is golden brown on the underside. Put under the grill until the omelette is browned on the top. Remove at once, as over-cooking tends to make it tough. Run a spatula gently round the edge and underneath the omelette to loosen it, make a mark across the middle at right angles to the pan handle, add any required filling – see suggestions below – and double the omelette over. Turn it gently on to a hot plate and serve at once. *Serves 1.*

Soufflé omelette fillings

Jam Spread the cooked omelette with warmed jam, fold it over and sprinkle with caster or icing sugar.

Rum Substitute 15 ml *(1 tbsp)* rum for half the water added to the egg yolks before cooking. Put the cooked omelette on a hot dish, pour 45–60 ml *(3–4 tbsps)* warmed rum round it, ignite and serve immediately.

Apricot Add the grated rind of an orange or tangerine to the egg yolks. Spread some thick apricot pulp over the omelette before folding it and serve sprinkled with caster sugar.

Savoury Any of the fillings already given for plain omelettes can be used for soufflé omelettes.

Baked soufflé omelette

4 eggs
30 ml *(2 level tbsps)* caster sugar
6 almonds, blanched and finely chopped
30 ml *(2 tbsps)* water
pinch of salt
knob of butter
sugar for dredging
jam or stewed fruit, optional

Separate the yolks from the whites of the eggs and whisk the yolks thoroughly with the sugar. Add the almonds and the water. Whisk the egg whites and salt stiffly and fold into the yolk mixture. Grease a shallow dish with butter and put the omelette mixture in to it. Bake in the oven at 180°C *(350°F)* mark 4 for 15–20 minutes. Sprinkle with sugar and serve at once. *Serves 2.*

A little jam or some stewed fruit may be put at the bottom of the dish before the egg mixture is added.

SOUFFLÉS

It is traditional to use a special soufflé dish, fairly shallow in depth, smooth inside and fluted outside. These are usually of plain white china, but they are also obtainable in coloured chinaware and in ovenproof glass.

The foundation soufflé mixture, or panada, consists of flour, butter and milk, in the proportions of 25 ml *(1½ level tbsps)* flour and 25 g *(1 oz)* butter to 150 ml *(¼ pt)* milk. The egg yolks are always separated from the whites and are beaten into the panada, the stiffly beaten whites being folded in as the last step. The preparation of the panada is important, for unless it is smoothly blended and thoroughly amalgamated with the egg yolks, the soufflé may be leathery. When making the panada, choose a rather large saucepan – big enough not only to beat the egg yolks in, but also to fold in the whites.

Basic soufflé mixture

3 eggs
25 g *(1 oz)* butter
25 ml *(1½ level tbsps)* flour
150 ml *(¼ pt)* milk
salt and pepper
filling (see below)

Grease a 15-cm *(6-in)* soufflé dish. Separate the eggs. Melt the butter, stir in the flour and cook for 2–3 minutes. Gradually stir in the milk and bring to the boil, stirring all the time. Cool slightly and add the filling or flavouring. Add the egg yolks one at a time, beating well, and season. Stiffly whisk the egg whites, fold these into the mixture and put it into the soufflé dish. Bake in the oven at 180°C *(350°F)* mark 4 for about 30 minutes, until well risen and brown. *Serves 2.*

Soufflé fillings and flavourings

Don't use too great a weight of filling or the soufflé will be heavy.

Ham 75 g *(3 oz)* cooked ham, luncheon meat or chopped pork and ham, finely chopped.

Fish 75 g *(3 oz)* cooked smoked haddock, finely flaked.

Mushroom 75–100 g *(3–4 oz)* mushrooms, chopped and cooked in butter until tender.

Cheese 75 g *(3 oz)* finely grated mature cheese.

Sweet See page 305; for cold soufflés, see page 335.

EGG DISHES

Eggs à la mornay

40 g *(1½ oz)* butter
45 ml *(3 level tbsps)* flour
300 ml *(½ pt)* milk
salt and pepper
50 g *(2 oz)* cheese, grated
4 eggs, hard-boiled and sliced
chopped parsley

Melt 25 g *(1 oz)* butter, stir in the flour and cook for 2–3 minutes. Remove the pan from the heat and gradually stir in the milk, bring to the boil and continue to stir until the sauce thickens. Season well and stir in 25 g *(1 oz)* of the cheese. Lay the eggs in an ovenproof dish, reserving a few slices for garnish. Pour the sauce over them, sprinkle the remaining cheese over the top, dot with shavings of butter and brown under a hot grill for a few minutes. Garnish with the slices of egg and a little chopped parsley.

Variation *see colour plate between pp. 272 and 273*
Prepare hot stuffed eggs (see recipe below), reserving a little sieved yolk; sandwich the stuffed halves together and arrange in a heatproof dish. Pour hot cheese sauce over and add a little more grated cheese; grill until golden and bubbling. Garnish with the remaining sieved egg and some watercress.

Stuffed eggs – hot

4 eggs, hard-boiled and shelled
50 g *(2 oz)* mushrooms, chopped
1 onion, skinned and chopped
40 g *(1½ oz)* margarine
300 ml *(½ pt)* tomato juice
5 ml *(1 level tsp)* sugar
salt and pepper
10 ml *(2 level tsps)* cornflour

Cut the eggs in half lengthways and remove the yolks. Lightly fry the mushrooms and onion in the hot fat for 5 minutes, until golden brown. Put half the mixture in a basin. Add the tomato juice, sugar and seasoning to the remaining mixture in the pan and cook for 5 minutes. Blend the cornflour to a smooth cream with a little water. Stir in a little of the hot tomato juice and return it to the pan; bring to the boil, stirring until it thickens, and continue cooking for 1–2 minutes. Keep this tomato sauce hot. Meanwhile mix the egg yolks with the remaining onion and mushroom mixture in the basin and use to stuff the eggs. Place on a dish and pour the tomato sauce round it.

Stuffed eggs – cold

4 eggs, hard-boiled and shelled
25 g *(1 oz)* butter
15 ml *(1 tbsp)* mayonnaise
salt and pepper
parsley

Cut the eggs in half lengthways; remove the yolks, put in a basin, mash with a fork and mix in the butter, mayonnaise and seasoning. Mix until smooth, put into a forcing bag with a 1-cm *(½-in)* star pipe and pipe back into the egg whites.

Garnish with sprigs of parsley.

Variations
Add 5 ml *(1 tsp)* anchovy essence to the yolk mixture.
Add a little minced tongue or ham to the yolk mixture.

Curried eggs

50 g *(2 oz)* butter
1 onion, skinned and finely chopped
½ apple, peeled and finely chopped
10 ml *(2 level tsps)* curry powder
30 ml *(2 level tbsps)* flour
300 ml *(½ pt)* stock or water
salt and paprika
5 ml *(1 tsp)* lemon juice
4 eggs
125 g *(4 oz)* rice, freshly cooked
chopped parsley

Melt the butter in a saucepan and lightly fry the onion until golden. Add the apple, curry powder and flour and cook for a few minutes, stirring occasionally. Add the stock gradually and season with salt and lemon juice. Bring to the boil, stirring all the time, cover and simmer for about 30 minutes. Hard-boil the eggs during the last 10 minutes of the time, shell and halve them. Place them in a hot dish and pour the sauce over.

Surround with the rice and garnish with chopped parsley and paprika.

Beefy eggs in curry sauce *see colour plate between pp. 272 and 273*

225 g *(8 oz)* lean minced beef
50 g *(2 oz)* fresh white breadcrumbs
2.5 ml *(½ level tsp)* onion salt
freshly ground black pepper
2 eggs, beaten
4 eggs, hard-boiled
flour
oil

For curry sauce
225 g *(½ lb)* onions, skinned
15 ml *(1 level tbsp)* curry powder
15 ml *(1 level tbsp)* flour
226-g *(8-oz)* can tomatoes
300 ml *(½ pt)* water
1 beef stock cube
2 caps canned red pepper (pimiento)

Blend together the beef, breadcrumbs, onion salt, pepper and 1 beaten egg. Divide into 8 portions. Cut the hard-boiled eggs in half crosswise. On a floured surface press the portions of meat into thin discs. Brush the surface of the meat with the second beaten egg. Shape the meat round the egg halves, moulding it well together free of cracks. Brush again with the egg and roll in the flour. Heat about 0.5-cm *(¼-in)* oil in a frying pan and fry the balls until evenly brown. Drain and keep them on one side. Drain off all but 30 ml *(2 tbsps)* oil, add the sliced onion and cook until soft. Stir in the curry powder and flour and cook for 5 minutes. Stir in the tomatoes with their liquid, the water and crumbled stock cube. Bring to the boil and boil for 10 minutes. Place the meat balls in a casserole, pour the sauce over, cover and cook in the oven at 180°C *(350°F)* mark 4 for about 45 minutes. Add the sliced red pepper 5 minutes before the end.

Pickled eggs

For every 6 hard-boiled eggs allow:
600 ml *(1 pt)* white wine or cider vinegar
6 cloves garlic, skinned
25 g *(1 oz)* pickling spice
small piece of orange peel
piece of mace

Boil all the ingredients (except the eggs) for 10 minutes in a heavy pan with a well fitting lid. When the mixture is cool, strain it into a wide-mouthed glass jar with a screw-lid or a tight cork. Put in the eggs (shelled but whole) and leave for at least 6 weeks before eating.

More hard-boiled eggs can be added as convenient, but they must always be covered by the liquid.

Serve as a snack or buffet dish or with salad.

Scotch eggs

4 eggs, hard-boiled and shelled
10 ml *(2 level tsps)* seasoned flour
Worcestershire sauce
225 g *(½ lb)* sausage meat
1 egg, beaten
dry breadcrumbs
deep fat
parsley

Dust the eggs with the seasoned flour. Add a few drops of Worcestershire sauce to the sausage meat and divide it into 4 equal portions. Form each quarter into a flat cake and work it round an egg, making it as even as possible, to keep the egg a good shape and making sure there are no cracks in the sausage meat. Brush with beaten egg and toss in breadcrumbs. Heat the fat until it will brown a cube of bread in 40–50 seconds. (As the sausage meat is raw, it is essential that the frying should not be hurried unduly, so the fat must not be too hot.) Fry the eggs for about 7–8 minutes. When they are golden brown on the outside, remove them from the fat and drain.

Cut the eggs in half lengthways, garnish each half with a small piece of parsley and serve either hot with tomato sauce (see page 202) or cold with a green salad.

Eggs Florentine

900 g *(2 lb)* spinach
salt and pepper
40 g *(1½ oz)* butter
45 ml *(3 level tbsps)* flour
300 ml *(½ pt)* milk
75 g *(3 oz)* cheese, grated
4 eggs

Wash the spinach well in several changes of water, put into a saucepan with a little salt and just the water that clings to the leaves, cover and cook for 10–15 minutes, until tender. Drain well, chop roughly and re-heat with a knob of butter. Melt the remaining 25 g *(1 oz)* butter, stir in the flour and cook for 2–3 minutes. Remove the pan from the heat and gradually stir in the milk; bring to the boil and continue to stir until the sauce thickens. Add 50 g *(2 oz)* cheese and season. Poach the eggs. Place the spinach in an ovenproof dish, arrange the eggs on top and pour the cheese sauce over. Sprinkle with the remaining cheese and brown under the grill.

Croque-monsieur

4 slices of bread, generously buttered
4 slices of cheese
4 thin rashers of bacon, rinded
4 tomatoes, halved
salt
4 eggs

Toast the bread on the buttered side until it is golden. Lay a slice of cheese on each piece of bread and grill until bubbly and golden in colour. Lightly grill the rashers of bacon and put on top of the cheese. Arrange the slices of bread and the tomatoes in an ovenproof dish and sprinkle with salt. Turn the grill low and put the dish under it until the tomatoes are soft and the bacon crisp. Fry the eggs, lift them out from the pan, using a slotted spoon to drain off any fat, and serve on top of the bacon.

Framed eggs

4 thick, large slices of white bread
lard or dripping
4 eggs

Remove the centre crumb from each slice of bread, leaving a 'frame' 1–2 cm *(½–¾ in)* wide. Fry the frames in the hot fat until brown, turn them over and brown the second side. Break an egg into the centre of each frame and fry until the eggs are set. Lift out with a slice or palette knife, draining off any fat, and serve on a hot plate.

Eggs baked in cream

Butter as many small ovenproof dishes or cocottes as required. Put 5 ml *(1 tsp)* cream in the bottom of each and add a light sprinkling of salt and pepper. Break 1 egg into each, sprinkle more salt and pepper on top, and cover with more cream. Place the dishes in a meat tin containing sufficient water to come half-way up the sides, cook in the oven at 180°C *(350°F)* mark 4 until the eggs are just set – about 15 minutes – and serve at once.

Eggs in baked potatoes

4 large raw potatoes, scrubbed
25 g *(1 oz)* butter
salt and pepper
30 ml *(2 tbsps)* milk
4 eggs

Mark a circle round the top of each potato with a sharp-pointed knife. Bake in the oven at 180°C *(350°F)* mark 4 for 1½–2 hours, or until soft. Remove the insides of the potatoes with a teaspoon and mash with the butter, seasoning and milk. Half-fill each potato case with the mixture, break in an egg, return the potatoes to the oven and cook until the eggs have set – about 10–15 minutes. The rest of the potato can then be either piped or forked round the top and browned under the grill.

Butter-cup scrambles *see colour plate facing p. 273*

125 g *(4½ oz)* butter
8 slices from a large thin sliced loaf
5 eggs
90 ml *(6 tbsps)* milk
freshly ground black pepper
2.5 ml *(½ level tsp)* mixed dried herbs
100 g *(4 oz)* sliced garlic sausage, chopped
2 sticks celery, sliced
2 spring onions, trimmed and chopped
50 g *(2 oz)* mature Cheddar cheese, grated

Melt 100 g *(4 oz)* of the butter and allow it to cool, but not solidify. Trim the crusts from the bread. Dip each slice in the butter. Use the bread to line 8 individual (9-cm, *3½-in*, diameter) deep Yorkshire pudding tins, leaving the corners uppermost. Brush over with any remaining butter. Bake at 200°C *(400°F)* mark 6 for 15–20 minutes. Keep these bread 'cups' warm.

Break the eggs into a bowl, add the milk, pepper and herbs. Lightly whisk. Melt the remaining butter in a heavy based saucepan. Add the beaten egg mixture. Cook over a low heat, stirring until it begins to set. Fold in the sausage, celery, onions and cheese. Check the seasoning and divide between the bread cups. Serve immediately.

Duck with cherries (p. 168).

Golden egg puffs *see colour plate facing p. 272*

700 g *(1½ lb)* potatoes, peeled weight
salt and freshly ground black pepper
50 g *(2 oz)* butter
125 g *(4½ oz)* mature Cheddar cheese, grated
45 ml *(3 tbsps)* milk
350 g *(12 oz)* onion, skinned and sliced
226-g *(8-oz)* can tomatoes
2.5 ml *(½ level tsp)* dried summer savory
Moutarde de Meaux
4 eggs

Cook the potatoes in boiling salted water until tender. Drain well, add 25 g *(1 oz)* butter, 100 g *(4 oz)* cheese and the milk. Cream until soft and fluffy. Season. Use to fill a piping bag fitted with a large star vegetable nozzle. Melt 25 g *(1 oz)* butter, add the onion; cover and sauté gently until the onion is soft. Remove the lid and put aside one-third of the onion. To the rest add the tomatoes with their juice and the savory. Increase the heat. Reduce to a pulp by fast boiling. Butter four 400-ml *(¾-pt)* ovenproof dishes. Divide the pulp between the dishes and add 5 ml *(1 tsp)* mustard to each. Pipe the potatoes in a nest over the tomato mixture, finishing at the rim. Cook in the oven at 240°C *(450°F)* mark 8 for 10 minutes. Take out and deepen the 'hollow' in the centre of each. Divide the reserved onion between the hollows and crack an egg into each. Top the egg with the reserved cheese. Return the dishes to the oven, turned down to 220°C *(425°F)* mark 7, for about 12 minutes until the eggs are just set. Serve at once.

Kipper cream roulade

210 g *(7½ oz)* boil-in-the-bag kipper or smoked haddock fillets, or a 198-g *(7-oz)* can
3 eggs, separated
30 ml *(2 tbsps)* hot water
30 ml *(2 level tbsps)* cornflour
25 g *(1 oz)* Parmesan cheese, grated
good pinch each of salt, mustard, paprika
freshly ground black pepper
45 ml *(3 tbsps)* double cream
15 ml *(1 tbsp)* lemon juice

Cook the boil-in-the-bag kippers as directed on the packet. Whisk together the egg yolks and hot water until foamy and pale yellow in colour (when the whisk is lifted it should leave a trail). Fold in the cornflour, cheese and seasonings. Stiffly whisk the egg whites and fold through. Line a shallow baking tin 28-cm by 18-cm *(11-in by 7-in)* with greaseproof paper and grease it well. Turn the egg mixture into it and bake at 200°C *(400°F)* mark 6 for about 10 minutes. Meanwhile, drain, skin and flake the kippers. Heat them gently in a saucepan with the cream, lemon juice and pepper. Then put aside to keep warm. Turn the cooked roulade on to a sheet of greaseproof paper and remove the lining paper. Spread with kipper filling and roll up. Serve at once.

Egg croquettes

40 g *(1½ oz)* butter
150 ml *(¼ pt)* water
50 g *(2 oz)* plain flour
1 egg, beaten
2.5 ml *(½ level tsp)* mild curry powder
salt and pepper
2 eggs, hard-boiled and shelled
25 g *(1 oz)* toasted chopped almonds
1 small egg, for coating
75 g *(3 oz)* fresh white breadcrumbs
fat for frying

Melt the butter in the water and bring to the boil. Remove from the heat and quickly add the flour. Beat well until paste is smooth and forms a ball. Allow to cool for a few minutes and then beat in the egg. Season well with curry powder, salt and pepper. Chop the hard boiled eggs and add with the almonds to the pan. Take heaped spoonfuls of the mixture and roll to a sausage shape on a floured surface. Pat the ends flat. Coat with beaten egg and breadcrumbs. Chill, then deep fry in oil at 150–170°C *(300–325°F)* for about 5 minutes until puffed and golden brown. Drain on kitchen paper. Serve immediately with tomato sauce (page 202). *Makes 12–14.*

Ham and egg cocottes

100 g *(4 oz)* cooked ham, cut in strips
50 g *(2 oz)* butter
100 g *(4 oz)* mushrooms, sliced
2.5 ml *(½ level tsp)* cornflour
freshly ground black pepper
4 eggs
60 ml *(4 tbsps)* double cream
50 g *(2 oz)* mature cheese, grated

Use the ham to line four individual ramekin dishes. Melt the butter and quickly sauté the mushrooms. Blend cornflour with a little water and add to the mushrooms. Cook until thickened. Season with pepper. Spoon into the ramekin dishes.

Break an egg into each dish, spoon 15 ml *(1 tbsp)* cream over and sprinkle with grated cheese. Bake at 190°C *(375°F)* mark 5 for about 15 minutes. Serve with hot buttered toast.

Chicken and bacon casserole (p. 160).

Oeufs paysanne

225 g *(8 oz)* lean bacon, in a piece
1 large onion, skinned
700 g *(1½ lb)* potatoes, peeled
60 ml *(4 tbsps)* oil
30 ml *(2 tbsps)* chopped parsley
salt and pepper
4 eggs

Rind and dice the bacon. Dice the onion and roughly dice the potatoes. Blanch the potatoes in boiling salted water for 1–2 minutes. Drain. Fry the bacon in the oil until crisp, remove and drain it on kitchen paper. Add the onion to the fat. Cook until transparent and tender, then drain. Add the onion to the bacon and place them in an ovenproof dish to keep warm. Add the potatoes to the pan fat, fry gently until cooked and golden brown. Drain and add to bacon and onion with the parsley. Toss them lightly together and season well. Keep warm. Fry eggs – a little more oil may be needed. Put the fried eggs on to potato mixture and serve at once.

Andalusian flamenco eggs

2–3 slices cooked ham
15 ml *(1 tbsp)* finely chopped onion
olive oil or butter
225 g *(½ lb)* tomatoes, skinned and sliced
225 g *(½ lb)* cooked peas
a few asparagus tips
225 g *(½ lb)* cooked potatoes, sliced
½ a green pepper, seeded and cut into strips
a little stock
225 g *(½ lb)* Continental-type sausage
4–8 eggs

Cut the ham into small pieces and fry with the onion in the oil or butter until it begins to colour. Add the other vegetables and sufficient stock to moisten, then sauté gently for a few minutes, stirring carefully. Add the sliced sausage and put the mixture into an ovenproof dish; break the eggs on top and cook in the oven at 230°C *(450°F)* mark 8 for 2–3 minutes, until the eggs are just set.

Vegetable curry with eggs *see colour plate facing p. 320*

225 g *(8 oz)* aubergine, trimmed and cubed
salt
1 small cauliflower
450 g *(1 lb)* courgettes, sliced
396-g *(14-oz)* can tomatoes
50 g *(2 oz)* butter
225 g *(8 oz)* onion, skinned and chopped
30 ml *(2 level tbsps)* concentrated curry sauce
40 g *(1½ oz)* flour
50 g *(2 oz)* cashew nuts
50 g *(2 oz)* mature cheese, grated
grated rind of 1 small lemon
6 eggs
chopped parsley

Sprinkle aubergine with salt and leave it for 30 minutes. Rinse well and pat dry. Cut the cauliflower into florets and blanch in boiling, salted water for 5 minutes. Drain, then blanch the courgettes in the same water for 4 minutes. Drain. Strain the tomatoes, make the juice up to 400 ml *(¾ pt)* with the vegetable liquor.

Melt the butter in a frying pan, sauté the onion and aubergines until slightly browned. Stir in the curry sauce and flour. Cook for 1 minute then stir in the tomato juice. Cook for a few minutes, stirring till thickened.

Put the cauliflower, courgettes and tomatoes in a large ovenproof dish and pour the aubergine mixture over. Combine the nuts, cheese and lemon rind and sprinkle over the centre. Bake at 190°C *(375°F)* mark 5 for about 25 minutes.

Meanwhile cook the eggs, timed to be ready at the same time as the curry; place them in cold water, bring to boil and cook for 8 minutes. Shell, halve and arrange hot round the curry and garnish with chopped parsley.

Eggs Bénédict

4 slices bread, cut from a barrel loaf
4 eggs
4 thin slices lean ham
150 ml *(¼ pt)* sauce hollandaise (page 200)
chopped parsley

Toast the bread on both sides. Poach the eggs (page 249), keeping the hollandaise sauce warm. Top each slice of toast with a folded slice of ham, then the hot poached egg and finally coat with hollandaise. Sprinkle with chopped parsley and serve at once.

Piperade

2 184-g ***(6½-oz)*** **cans red peppers (pimientos)**
450 g ***(1 lb)*** **tomatoes**
100 g ***(4 oz)*** **butter**
1 large onion, skinned and finely chopped
3 cloves garlic, skinned and crushed
salt and freshly ground pepper
8 eggs
60 ml ***(4 tbsps)*** **milk**
fried croûtons

Drain the peppers and shred finely. Skin the tomatoes, cut into halves, discard the seeds and roughly chop the flesh. In a medium sized pan, melt the butter; when it is frothy, add the onion and garlic and cook for 1–2 minutes, then add the peppers and simmer for 4 minutes. Add the tomatoes. Season well and leave to simmer while you beat the eggs, milk and seasoning with a fork. When the vegetables in the pan are well reduced, pour in the beaten eggs. Cook for 3–4 minutes, stirring continuously. When a soft scrambled egg is obtained, turn on to a hot serving plate, and surround with fried croûtons.

Cheese

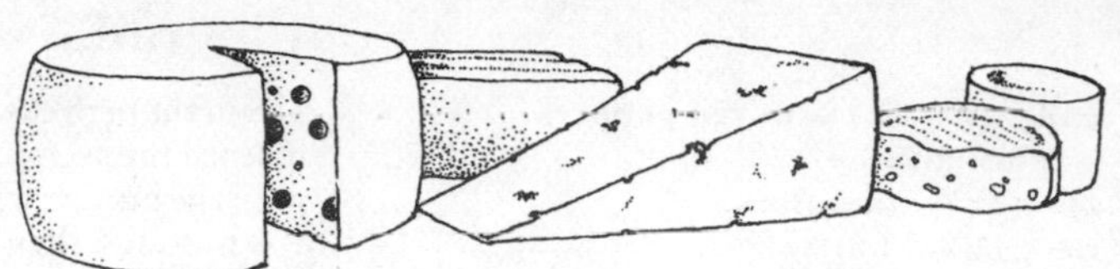

Cheese is a concentrated form of milk. During cheese-making, most of the milk protein – casein – coagulates to form a curd, usually by the action of rennet, and virtually all the butterfat of the original milk remains in the curd. Excess moisture is expressed from the curd to leave a relatively hard mass which is then allowed to mature.

The quality and the sources of the milk (whether cow's, goat's or ewe's), and the particular processes used in the making, give rise to an almost endless variety of cheeses. Local conditions of climate and vegetation and of course seasonal changes also influence the finished product. This explains why some cheeses are essentially local and cannot be produced in large quantities or under factory conditions.

British cheeses

Arran An individual rindless Dunlop cheese in a 1-kg *(2¼-lb)* pack made on the island of Arran.

Caboc originated from the Western Highlands in the fifteenth century. The recipe is believed to have been handed down from mother to daughter through the centuries. This is a very rich, soft double cream cheese rolled in oatmeal.

Caerphilly Originally a Welsh cheese, this is now made also in Somerset, Wiltshire, Devon and Dorset. It is made from whole milk, pressed only lightly and eaten in its 'green' state, when about ten days old. Caerphilly is soft and white, with a creamy mild flavour, and is best served uncooked.

Cheddar Cheddar is perhaps the best known and most widely used of the English cheeses and one of the oldest. Made originally in Somerset – where the finest Cheddar is still to be obtained.

The name 'Cheddar' is given to any cheese which undergoes the 'cheddaring' process, regardless of where it is made. Cheddar is now produced in various other parts of England and also in Scotland, Ireland, Canada, Australia and New Zealand.

English Farmhouse Cheddar is made with whole milk from a single herd of cows. The process is the same as ordinary Cheddar but Farmhouse is allowed to mature longer to produce a richer and more mellow flavour. Flavours vary from mild to quite strong and are equally good cooked or uncooked.

The mellow, slightly salty Cheddar made in Canada is similar to Farmhouse Cheddar. Its strong, mature flavour makes it excellent for cooking. Australian and New Zealand Cheddars are also widely available and are usually of a mild quality.

Cheshire Said to be the oldest English cheese, Cheshire is another very well known type. Like Cheddar, it is a hard cheese, but rather more crumbly in texture, with a mild yet mellow flavour. There are two main varieties – the red, which is coloured by the addition of vegetable dye, and the white. There is no significant difference in the flavour. Blue Cheshire is also made but is not widely available. Farmhouse Cheshire, which is made from a single herd of cows, is also available. In all its forms Cheshire cheese is equally good cooked or uncooked.

Derby A hard, close-textured cheese, mild in flavour when young. It develops a fuller flavour as it matures – at its best when it is six months old.

Sage Derby was originally made by layering with sage leaves to give a pleasant, sharp tangy flavour and speckled appearance. It must be eaten fresh or the flavour becomes very sharp. Nowadays an essence is used in place of the leaves, which gives a rather synthetic appearance but retains the flavour longer.

Dunlop A Scottish cheese made originally in Dunlop, Ayrshire, but now fairly general throughout Scotland. It is not unlike Cheddar, but moister and of a closer texture.

Gloucester Gloucester is an orange-yellow, hard cheese with a close, crumbly texture and a good rich flavour, rather similar to that of a mature Cheddar. Originally there were 'double' and 'single' Gloucesters, one being twice the size of the other, but now only the 'double' is made.

Highland Crowdie Similar to cottage cheese but more finely ground. It is high in protein and low in fat with a light, fresh flavour. Recommended as a slimmers' cheese.

Hramsa This is a soft cheese made from fresh double cream which is delicately flavoured with wild garlic. It is excellent served on savoury biscuits or made into a cheese dip with some fresh cream.

Islay is a miniature Dunlop which is excellent for melting and is best eaten when fairly mature.

Lancashire A fairly hard cheese, crumbly in texture when cut. When new it has a mild, tangy flavour, which develops considerably as it matures. It can be enjoyed cooked or uncooked, particularly the Farmhouse English variety.

Leicester A hard cheese with a mild, slightly sweet flavour and orange-red colour.

Orkney This cheese which is made in Orkney was originally made in various farms, but is now made in a modern creamery. Each cheese weighs 454 g *(1 lb)*, is similar to Dunlop cheese and is available as white cheese, red cheese and the more subtle smoked cheese.

Stilton Stilton, one of the best known of English cheeses, is made in Leicestershire, Nottinghamshire and Derbyshire. It is a white full-cream milk cheese now produced all the year round although it used to be a seasonal cheese. Stilton is semi-hard and has a blue veining, caused by a mould which in most cases is a natural growth throughout the curd, accelerated by the use of stainless steel skewers piercing the cheese to allow the mould to enter. The veins of blue mould should be evenly distributed throughout. The rind, of a dull, drab colour, should be well crinkled and regular and free from cracks. Stilton is at its best when fully ripe, that is 4–5 months after it has been made. If bought in small quantities eat it as soon as possible. A whole or half Stilton will keep well if the cut surface is covered and the cheese is kept in a dry airy larder. It needs no port or anything else added to it. It should be cut in slices from the top and not scooped out.

White Stilton bears little resemblance to Blue Stilton in flavour but it is the same cheese before the blue mould has grown into it. This is now widely available. It has a slightly crumbly texture and is white in colour without the characteristic blue-veining. This cheese has a pleasant, mild flavour.

Windsor Red A mature Cheddar cheese flavoured and coloured with English fruit wine. This produces a cheese with a red-veining and enhances the cheese to give a very mature flavour.

Wensleydale Made in the vale of Wensleydale in Yorkshire. Originally it was a double-cream cheese, cylindrical in shape, which matured until it became blue – in this form it was considered one of the best English blue cheeses, next only to Stilton. Since 1954 much of the Wensleydale production has been sold when white and in this form it is a mild, creamy-coloured cheese with a rather flaky texture. Blue Wensleydale is obtainable from specialist cheese chops.

Soft cheeses

A true soft cheese is made by coagulating milk with rennet. The addition of a 'starter' just before rennet is added ensures a clean acid flavour. The majority of soft cheeses are foreign in origin such as Camembert. English soft cheeses include York and Colwick. The British cheeses are usually marketed in a fresh or unripened state whilst the better known of those made abroad are consumed when fully mature. This requires the growth of specific bacteria and moulds to produce the desired ripening action. The British varieties of unripened soft cheese are usually made from cow's milk, but goat's milk can equally well be used.

Cream cheese can be classified as a soft cheese. Its manufacture is very similar to that described above, but it is made from cream rather than milk. A typical cream cheese is a soft bodied, unripened cheese with a rich, full and mildly acid flavour. It has a rather granular texture, buttery consistency and a high content of milk fat which gives it a creamy appearance. It is usually moulded into small cylindrical, square, rectangular or round shapes of varying sizes. There are two recognised varieties of cream cheese – single cream cheese or double cream cheese.

Single cream cheese is made from single cream with an optimum fat content of 20–25%. 1.2 litres *(2 pints)* of this cream will yield about six cheeses weighing 100–125 g *(about 4 oz)* each. Carefully prepared single cream cheese will keep for a week in a refrigerator, after which it deteriorates quickly both in flavour and appearance.

Double cream cheese is produced from cream containing about 50–55% butterfat. Usually 1.2 litres *(2 pints)* of this cream will yield eight double cream cheeses weighing 100–125 g *(about 4 oz)* each. This cheese does not keep quite as long as single cream cheese.

Acid curd cheese

Acid curd cheese is frequently classed as a soft cheese, but is fundamentally different. The curds are formed solely by the action of lactic acid upon the casein. Acid curdling is a completely different action from rennet coagulation and yields a curd of high acidity, quick drainage properties and somewhat granular texture. The cheese has a clean, acid flavour, and a slightly granular, soft, spreadable texture. It has a short shelf life and must be eaten in a fresh state.

Cottage cheese is an acid curd cheese, but is made from pasteurised, skimmed milk. The curd is cut into small cubes and slowly heated to develop the right body and texture. The whey is drained off, and the curd washed several times and cooled. The washing of the curd produces the familiar lumpy appearance of cottage cheese. Salt and single cream are then added and the cheese is packaged in cartons. The addition of the cream gives a final butterfat content of 4% in the cottage cheese. This, combined with the high moisture content gives the cheese its soft velvety texture. Cottage cheese has a short keeping quality and should be eaten while fresh.

Continental cheeses

Bel Paese A rich, creamy cheese of mild flavour, made in various parts of Italy, usually from October to June. The cheeses weigh about 2.3 kg *(5 lb)* each.

Bleu de Bresse A soft and creamy blue cheese from France with a rich, subtle flavour. It has a grey coloured rind and should not be allowed to over ripen as it develops a strong, and unpleasant flavour.

Boursin This is the brand name of a fresh cream cheese made in France usually flavoured with garlic, herbs or rolled in crushed peppercorns.

Brie A soft-textured farm cheese, produced in the north of France. It is made from whole milk and is mould-inoculated. Brie is flat and round, usually 35 cm *(14 in)* in diameter and about 2.6 kg *(6 lb)* in weight; it has a white floury crust instead of the more usual hard rind. It should be eaten fresh when soft all through. It doesn't keep well.

Camembert A French soft cheese, made of cows' milk, the curd being inoculated with a white mould. The cheese was made originally in Normandy, but is made now also in other parts of France. Camembert is at its best when it begins to get soft; if allowed to over-ripen, it develops a smell which many people find unpleasant.

Danish Blue A white softish cheese made in Denmark; it has a blue mould veining and a sharp, salty taste.

Demi-sel A fresh cream cheese, usually sold in small squares wrapped in foil. It is made in France, mainly in Normandy.

Dolcelatte A mild, blue cheese similar to Gorgonzola but slightly softer and creamier.

Edam A Dutch ball-shaped cheese, bright red outside and deep yellow inside, and about 2.3 kg *(5 lb)* in weight. It is firm and smooth in texture and has a mild flavour.

Emmenthal A Swiss cheese similar to Gruyère but larger and slightly softer in texture, with larger 'eyes'.

Esrom Made in Denmark, this is a semi-hard yellow cheese and has a pleasant, mild flavour.

Fontainebleau A French cheese of the cream type, soft and fresh; it is made in the country round Fontainebleau, mostly in the summer.

Gorgonzola A semi-hard, blue-veined sharp-flavoured cheese, made in Italy in the district round Milan.

Gouda A wheel shaped Dutch cheese, not unlike Edam in taste and texture, but flatter in shape, with a yellow skin and very much larger, approximately 5 kg *(9 lb)* in weight, and is an excellent cheese for cooking. There are also small Goudas, about 450 g *(1 lb)* in weight, known as Midget Goudas.

Gruyère A hard, large cheese, weighing anything up to 45 kg *(100 lb)*. Originally it came exclusively from Switzerland but is now made also in France, Italy and other parts of Europe. It is pale yellow in colour and is honeycombed with 'eyes' or holes, caused by the rapid fermentation of the curd; it has a distinctive and fairly sweet taste. It is served uncooked, but is also used in such classic cooked dishes as fondue.

Limburger A semi-hard, whole milk cheese made in Belgium (and also in Germany and Alsace), from December to May. It is full flavoured and strong smelling.

Mozzarella An Italian cheese, pale coloured and egg shaped. When fresh, it is very soft, dripping with buttermilk. Traditionally made from buffalo milk, it is now more often made from cows' milk. Mozzarella should be eaten fresh, as once the buttermilk has drained away the cheese dries out and becomes stodgy. Available only from specialist Continental shops. It is uninteresting to eat raw, but is splendid for pizzas, lasagnes, and other Italian dishes. Bel Paese may be used as a substitute.

Mycella This cheese gets its name from the mould mycelium which produces the blue veins. It is a full-fat cheese similar to Danish Blue but has a milder flavour.

Mysöst (Gietöst) A whey cheese, principally made from goats' milk, which is produced in Norway. It is hard and dark brown, with a sweetish flavour.

Parmesan This Italian cheese is the hardest of all. After being specially processed, the curd is broken up, heated, packed into a large mould the shape of a millstone and matured for at least two and usually three years. When it is ripe the crust is almost black, but the cheese itself should be of a pale straw colour and full of tiny holes, like pinpricks. Parmesan has a strong and distinctive flavour and is used finely grated for cooking or as a traditional accompaniment for soups such as minestrone and for rice and pasta dishes.

Petit Suisse (Petit Gervais) An unsalted cream cheese, cylindrical in shape, made in France. It is very mild in flavour. Often sold in small foil-wrapped packs.

Pommel A double-cream cheese, unsalted and not unlike Petit Suisse, which is made in France all the year round.

Pont L'Evêque A soft paste cheese with a thickish orange rind, about 10 cm *(4 in)* square and 4 cm *(1½ in)* thick. It is made practically all the year round in the Pont l'Evéque district of Normandy. The smell is stronger than the taste.

Saint Paulin A French semi-hard cheese, round in shape, it was made originally by the monks of Port du Salut, but is now made in various other parts of France. It is creamy yellow in colour and has a very mild and delicate flavour; it should be eaten while still slightly soft.

Ricotta A fragrant Italian cheese made from the whey left over when producing other cheeses. It has a delicate, smooth flavour and is very suitable for cooking in such things as ravioli or cannelloni. It can also be eaten with sugar or used layered in fruit tarts and puddings.

Roquefort This is the only ewes' milk cheese which has obtained a world-wide reputation. It is made during the lambing season in the village of Roquefort in the Cevennes mountains of France. It can be made only in this district, partly because the sheep-grazing land here is particularly suitable, but also because of the limestone caverns of Roquefort itself, which play a very important part in the maturing of the Roquefort cheese. The same mould as that used in the making of Stilton is introduced into the curd as a maturing agent. This delicious blue cheese has a sharp, pungent flavour and a soft creamy, crumbly texture. Very good for salads, mixed with the dressing.

Samsoe Named after the Danish island of Samsoe. It is a firm cheese, made from unskimmed cows' milk. It has a few irregular sized small holes and a delicate, nutty flavour. The flavour acquires greater pungency as it matures.

Smoked Cheese (Austrian) Sold in small rounds or 'sausages' wrapped in a brown skin, the cheese is a pale creamy colour. Mild and smoky in flavour, with a very smooth, soft texture, it is essentially a table cheese, excellent with wine.

Tome Is the name given to the various small cheeses produced during the summer months in Savoie. They are mostly from skimmed cows' milk.

Tome au Raisin is ripened in a mixture of grape skins, pips and stalks to give the cheese its distinctive flavour.

Tome de Savoie is cylindrical in shape and has a pleasant, light flavour resembling Saint Paulin.

The cheese course *see colour plate facing p. 385*

A cheese board or platter is one of the best ways of finishing a meal; many people prefer it to a sweet.

A cheese board should offer a variety of colours and shapes of cheeses – for instance, white, deep yellow and blue; flat, rounded or in segments.

Buy only in small quantities, as this is more economical. Have a good-sized board. With the cheese serve:

1. Biscuits – savoury or salty, plain or semi-sweet; rolls or bread – French, granary, wholemeal or rye, cut into chunks and put in a basket or on a plate.
2. Butter – in one slab or cut into small cubes.
3. Salad ingredients or crisp vegetables – lettuce, chunks of celery, leaves of chicory, wedges of tomatoes, small whole radishes, sprigs of watercress, sticks of carrot, spring onions.
4. A bowl of fresh fruit.

Storing and cooking cheese

Though cheese often requires months – sometimes years – to bring it to full maturity, once ripe it deteriorates comparatively rapidly. So buy only enough to last a few days to a week and store it in a cool place, such as a cold larder; cover it loosely to protect it from the air, but do not make it air-tight. If entirely exposed to the air, cheese will become hard and dry and if tightly covered it is likely to mould. A cheese dish with a ventilated cover is good for the purpose; otherwise, cover with an upturned bowl. If you store cheese in a refrigerator, wrap it in waxed paper or foil to prevent drying and put if possible in the door storage rack or special dairy compartment which is not as cold as the main body of the refrigerator. The soft French cheeses like Camembert and Brie should be kept in the boxes they are bought in. Their shelf life is very short and if bought in a perfect, ripe condition should be eaten that day.

If you want cheese to become hard and dry, for grating, leave it exposed to the air in a dry though cool place. It is best to hang it in a muslin bag, as then the air can circulate completely. If the cheese is left on a plate or board to dry, stand it on its rind; cheese that has no rind should be turned occasionally, otherwise the underside will remain soft and will very likely mould. Cheese that has formed mould on the surface is not necessarily spoiled – the mould should be scraped off and the cheese either used up quickly or dried for grating.

Hard cheese can be grated for cooking (use a fine grater), but a soft processed cheese should be shredded rather than grated. Very soft cheeses can be sliced and added to sauces, and so on, without grating or shredding.

When cooking cheese remember that too fierce a heat can make it stringy – it needs to melt rather than 'cook' – so when you're preparing a sauce, don't let it boil after you've added the cheese. Well matured cheese with a high fat content blends in better than a younger one, so the matured or Farmhouse varieties with their extra 'bite' are ideal. If you go for the less expensive, ordinary Cheddar you may need to zip up the taste with mustard, salt and freshly ground pepper. Adding more of a mild cheese does not give greater depth of flavour.

Among the English cheeses, Cheddar is good for baking, but for toasting you can't beat Lancashire, with Cheshire and Leicestershire close runners-up. For speciality dishes look to cheeses from other countries.

Note For information on freezing cheese see page 483.

Cheese on toast

225 g *(8 oz)* firm cheese, grated
5 ml *(1 level tsp)* dry mustard
salt and pepper
2.5–5 ml *(½–1 tsp)* Worcestershire sauce
milk to mix
sliced bread for toasting

Mix the cheese and seasonings and bind to a paste with milk. Toast the bread, only lightly on one side. Spread the cheese thickly on the lightly browned sides and cook under a hot grill until golden and bubbling.

Welsh rarebit

225 g *(8 oz)* Cheddar cheese, grated
25 g *(1 oz)* butter
5 ml *(1 level tsp)* dry mustard
salt and pepper
60 ml *(4 tbsps)* brown ale
toast

Place all the ingredients in a thick-based pan and heat very gently until a creamy mixture is obtained. Pour over the toast and put under a hot grill until golden and bubbling.

Buck rarebit
This is Welsh rarebit topped with a poached egg.

Fried cheese slices

Allow 1 slice of bread per person; fry in about 25 g *(1 oz)* butter until the first side is golden. Turn the slices and cover with a slice of Gruyère, Saint Paulin or Bel Paese. Cover the frying pan with a lid or large plate and cook gently until the cheese melts. Just before serving, crumble some crisply grilled bacon and sprinkle over the slices.

Sandwich Holstein

butter
4 slices bread cut from a round white (barrel) loaf
100 g *(4 oz)* mature cheese, sliced
2 eggs
25 g *(1 oz)* anchovies
16 capers

Butter the slices of bread and make into sandwiches with the cheese.

Melt 25 g *(1 oz)* butter in a frying pan and fry the sandwiches, turning once, until crisp and golden. Meanwhile fry the eggs. Cut anchovies in half lengthwise. Remove sandwiches from pan and top each with a fried egg. Arrange a lattice of anchovies over the eggs and garnish with capers. Serve at once.

Cheese and onion crisp

Skin 1–2 onions, slice into thin rings and parboil in salted water for 5–10 minutes. Drain well and lay on slices of buttered toast. Sprinkle with salt and pepper, crumble over some Lancashire cheese and cook under a hot grill until golden and bubbly.

Cheese aigrettes

40 g *(1½ oz)* butter
150 ml *(¼ pt)* water
50 g *(2 oz)* plain flour, sifted
2 eggs, beaten
50 g *(2 oz)* mature Cheddar cheese, grated
salt, pepper and cayenne pepper
fat for deep frying

Heat the butter and water in a saucepan until the fat dissolves and bring to the boil. Remove from the heat, add the flour all at once and beat well until the paste is smooth and leaves the sides of the pan. Allow to cool slightly, then beat in the eggs gradually. Add the cheese and season well. Heat the pan of fat and drop in teaspoonfuls of the mixture. Fry until golden, drain well on crumpled kitchen paper and serve hot.

Cheese and potato cakes

450 g ***(1 lb)*** **potatoes, boiled and mashed**
25 g ***(1 oz)*** **butter**
100 g ***(4 oz)*** **cheese, grated**
15 ml ***(1 tbsp)*** **chopped chives (or a little grated onion)**
salt and pepper
15–30 ml ***(1–2 level tbsps)*** **flour, if necessary**
beaten egg and dry breadcrumbs

Mix the potatoes with the butter, cheese, chives (or onion) and seasoning and beat until smooth, adding a little flour if necessary to make a firm mixture. Turn on to a floured board and form into a roll. Cut into 2.5-cm *(1-in)* slices and shape into round cakes. Coat with egg and dry breadcrumbs, place on a baking sheet and bake in the oven at 190°C *(375°F)* mark 5 for about 20 minutes; alternatively, fry the cakes.

These are good served with grilled bacon and tomatoes.

Cheese and potato eggs

Make up the same mixture as for cheese and potato cakes, divide it into 4 pieces and form each into a flattened round on a floured board. Have ready 4 large eggs, hard-boiled and shelled, and place one on each piece of cheese potato. Mould this round the eggs, sealing the join really well and keeping the egg shape. Brush with egg, coat with dry breadcrumbs and fry in deep fat until crisp and golden. Drain well on crumpled kitchen paper and serve hot with tomato sauce.

Cheese potatoes

4 large potatoes
25 g ***(1 oz)*** **butter**
salt and pepper
a little milk
175 g ***(6 oz)*** **cheese, grated**

Scrub the potatoes, prick the skins all over with a fork and bake in the oven at 200°C *(400°F)* mark 6 for 1–1¼ hours, or until soft when squeezed. Cut in half lengthways and scoop out the cooked potato without damaging the skins. Mash the cooked potato and beat in the butter, milk, seasoning and 100 g *(4 oz)* of the cheese. Pile the mixture into the potato skins, sprinkle the remaining cheese on top and brown under the grill or near the top of a hot oven.

Variations

1. When the mixture has been returned to the skins, cover it with strips of streaky bacon instead of with grated cheese and grill until the bacon is crisp.
2. Return most of the mixture to the cases, leaving a hollow in the centre of each. Break an egg into each hollow, surround by a border of the remaining potato and bake for a further 15 minutes (approx), or until the eggs are set.

Savoury cheese slice

1 small onion, skinned and finely chopped
100 g ***(4 oz)*** **streaky bacon, rinded and chopped**
75 g ***(3 oz)*** **butter or margarine**
225 g ***(8 oz)*** **self raising flour**
150 g ***(5 oz)*** **cheese, grated**
1 egg, beaten
a little milk (if needed)
2.5–5 ml ***(½–1 level tsp)*** **dried mixed herbs**
seasoning

Fry the onion and bacon gently for about 5 minutes in 25 g *(1 oz)* fat. Rub the remaining 50 g *(2 oz)* fat into the flour until it resembles breadcrumbs. Stir in 75 g *(3 oz)* of the cheese, then mix to a fairly soft dough with egg and some milk if necessary. Divide the dough into 2 pieces and roll out each piece into a 20-cm *(8-in)* square. Place one piece on a greased baking sheet, cover with the onion and bacon and sprinkle with the herbs and seasoning. Wet the edges and cover with the second piece of dough, pressing the edges together. Brush with milk and sprinkle with the remaining cheese. Bake in the oven at 200°C *(400°F)* mark 6 for about 20 minutes, until crisp and golden. Serve cut in fingers or wedges; eat it hot or cold.

Variation

Fry 2–3 skinned and chopped tomatoes with the onion and bacon.

Cauliflower gratinata

175 g ***(6 oz)*** **cut macaroni**
700 g ***((1½ lb)*** **cauliflower**
50 g ***(2 oz)*** **butter**
100 g ***(4 oz)*** **onion, skinned and chopped**
60 ml ***(4 level tbsps)*** **flour**
5 ml ***(1 level tsp)*** **dry mustard**
568 ml ***(1 pt)*** **milk**
salt and pepper
175 g ***(6 oz)*** **mature cheese, grated**
4 large tomatoes, sliced

Cook the macaroni in boiling, salted water then drain it. Cut the cauliflower into large florets and cook in the minimum of water until just tender. Drain.

Melt the butter and sauté the onion until transparent. Stir in the flour and mustard and cook for 1 minute. Stir in the milk and cook over a gentle heat until the sauce thickens. Season it well. Off the heat, stir in 100 g *(4 oz)* cheese.

Combine half the sauce with the macaroni. Put it in a 1.7-l *(3-pt)* buttered ovenproof serving dish. Arrange the tomato slices around the edge of the dish and pile the cauliflower in the centre. Spoon over the rest of the sauce. Top with the remaining cheese and bake at 220°C *(425°F)* mark 7 for 20 minutes. Serve at once.

Cheese and onion pie

2 onions, skinned and chopped
175 g ***(6 oz)*** **cheese, grated**
1 egg, beaten
salt and pepper
212-g ***(7½-oz)*** **pkt frozen puff pastry, thawed**

Cook the onions in boiling salted water for 5 minutes, drain well and mix with the cheese. Add nearly all the egg and season to taste. Roll out half the pastry very thinly, line an 18–20.5-cm *(7–8-in)* metal pie plate with it and pour the cheese filling into the centre. Roll out the remaining pastry to form a lid. Damp the edges of the pastry on the dish and cover with the lid, pressing the edges well together. Flake and scallop the edge and brush with the remaining egg. Bake in the oven at 200°C *(400°F)* mark 6 for about 30 minutes.

Cheese and rice soufflé

50 g ***(2 oz)*** **long grain rice**
226-g ***(8-oz)*** **can tomatoes, drained**
25 g ***(1 oz)*** **butter**
60 ml ***(4 level tbsps)*** **flour**
300 ml ***(½ pt)*** **milk**
175 g ***(6 oz)*** **cheese, grated**
3 eggs, separated
salt and pepper

Cook the rice in the usual way until just soft. Put the tomatoes into a greased 1.1-l *(2-pt)* soufflé dish or well greased large ovenproof dish. Melt the fat, stir in the flour and cook for 2–3 minutes. Remove the pan from the heat and gradually stir in the milk. Bring to the boil, stirring all the time and when the sauce has thickened, remove from the heat, stir in the cooked rice, cheese, egg yolks and seasoning to taste. Finally whisk the egg whites stiffly and fold in lightly. Pour over the tomatoes and bake in the oven at 180°C *(350°F)* mark 4 for about 50 minutes until well risen and golden. Serve immediately.

Variation

1 small sliced onion and 3–4 chopped rashers of bacon can be sautéed lightly and used with or instead of the tomatoes.

Cheese and watercress soufflé

25 g ***(1 oz)*** **butter**
25 ml ***(1½ level tbsps)*** **flour**
1.25 ml ***(¼ level tsp)*** **dry mustard**
1.25 ml ***(¼ level tsp)*** **curry powder**
150 ml ***(¼ pt)*** **milk**
½ bunch watercress, washed
3 eggs, separated
100 g ***(4 oz)*** **Gouda cheese, grated**
15 ml ***(1 tbsp)*** **snipped chives**
salt and pepper

Melt the butter and stir in the flour, mustard and curry powder. Cook 2–3 minutes then gradually stir in the milk. Cook for a further 2–3 minutes.

Discard the coarse stems from the watercress and chop the leaves. Beat the egg yolks into the sauce, then stir in the cheese, watercress and chives. Season to taste.

Whisk the egg whites stiffly and fold them through the mixture. Turn the mixture into a buttered 15-cm *(6-in)* 1.1-l *(2-pt)* soufflé dish and bake at 180°C *(350°F)* mark 4 for 30–35 minutes until well risen and golden. Serve at once. *Serves 2–3.*

Fondue

1 clove garlic, skinned and crushed
150 ml *(¼ pt)* dry white wine and a squeeze of lemon juice
225 g *(8 oz)* cheese, cut in thin strips (half Gruyère and half Emmenthal)
10 ml *(2 level tsps)* cornflour
1 liqueur glass of Kirsch
pepper and grated nutmeg

Rub the inside of a flameproof dish with the garlic, place the dish over a gentle heat and warm the wine and lemon juice in it. Add the cheese and continue to heat gently, stirring well until the cheese has melted and begun to cook. Add the cornflour and seasonings, blended to a smooth cream with the Kirsch, and continue cooking for a further 2–3 minutes; when the mixture is of a thick creamy consistency, it is ready to serve.

Traditionally, fondue is served at the table in the dish in which it was cooked, kept warm over a small spirit lamp or dish-warmer. To eat it, provide cubes of crusty bread which are speared on a fork and dipped in the fondue.

An anglicised version of fondue can be made using a strong-flavoured Cheddar or Lancashire cheese, cider instead of white wine and brandy instead of Kirsch.

Hot cheese dip

150 ml *(¼ pt)* medium dry white wine
5 ml *(1 tsp)* lemon juice
400 g *(14 oz)* Gouda cheese, grated
15 ml *(1 level tbsp)* cornflour
5 ml *(1 level tsp)* made English mustard
pepper

Put the wine and lemon juice into a heavy saucepan and heat until nearly boiling. Add the cheese and beat well with a wooden spoon.

Blend the cornflour with a little water and add to the cheese mixture, beating well. Stir in the mustard and season with pepper.

Serve at once with chunks of French bread.

Note Serve as a traditional fondue for leisurely eating. Supply each guest with a fork for spearing the bread and then dipping into the hot cheese mixture. Accompany with a well-tossed salad. *Serves 6–8.*

Cheese pudding

4–6 slices of white bread (100 g, *4 oz*)
60 ml *(4 tbsps)* dry white wine, optional
25 g *(1 oz)* butter, melted
2 eggs, beaten
300 ml *(½ pt)* milk
salt and pepper
100 g *(4 oz)* mature cheese, grated

Cut the bread into cubes and place in a 900-ml *(1½-pt)* greased ovenproof dish with the wine (if used) and the butter. Mix the eggs and milk, season well and pour over the bread mixture. Sprinkle with the cheese and bake in the oven at 190°C *(375°F)* mark 5 for about 30 minutes, until golden and well risen. Serve at once.

Pizza napoletana

about 150 ml *(¼ pt)* water
2.5 ml *(½ level tsp)* sugar
7.5 ml *(1½ level tsps)* dried yeast or 15 g *(½ oz)* fresh yeast
225 g *(½ lb)* strong plain flour
5 ml *(1 level tsp)* salt
small knob lard
cooking oil

For topping
450 g *(1 lb)* onions, skinned and chopped
2 425-g *(15-oz)* cans tomatoes, drained
10 ml *(2 level tsps)* dried marjoram
salt and pepper
100 g *(4 oz)* Bel Paese or Mozzarella cheese, cut into small dice
2 60-g *(2-oz)* cans anchovy fillets, drained
black olives

Warm the water to blood heat and dissolve the sugar in it. Sprinkle the dried yeast on and leave in a warm place until frothy. If you are using fresh yeast, blend it with the water and use at once; omit the sugar. Mix the flour and salt, rub in the lard and pour in the yeast mixture. Hand mix and beat until the dough leaves the bowl clean. Knead on a floured board until smooth and elastic. Put the dough in an oiled plastic bag, leave in a warm place until doubled in size. Turn the dough on to a floured surface and roll to a long strip. Brush with oil and roll it up like a Swiss roll.

Repeat 3 times. Grease a 30-cm *(12-in)* plain flan ring on a baking sheet, and roll out the dough to fit this (if no flan ring is available, roll out the dough to a 30-cm *(12-in)* round and place on a baking sheet. Brush with oil. Sauté the onions in a little oil until soft but not coloured. Spread to within 2 cm *(¾ in)* of the edge of the dough. Arrange the tomatoes on top, sprinkle with marjoram and seasoning and bake in the oven at 230°C *(450°F)* mark 8 for 20 minutes. Scatter the cheese over, lattice with anchovies and arrange olives in the spaces between. Cover loosely with foil and cook for a further 20 minutes. Serve hot in wedges, with a green salad. *Serves 6.*

Quick pizza *see colour plate facing p. 384*

100 g *(4 oz)* self raising flour
2.5 ml *(½ level tsp)* salt
75 ml *(5 tbsps)* cooking oil
45–60 ml *(3–4 tbsps)* water
1 small onion, skinned and chopped
396-g *(14-oz)* can tomatoes, drained and chopped, or 350 g *(¾ lb)* fresh tomatoes, skinned and chopped
5–10 ml *(1–2 level tsps)* dried mixed herbs
25 g *(1 oz)* butter
100 g *(4 oz)* cooking cheese, cut in small cubes
few olives and anchovy fillets

Mix the flour and salt and stir in 15 ml *(1 tbsp)* oil and enough water to mix to a fairly soft dough. Roll out into an 18-cm *(7-in)* round and fry on one side in the remaining oil in a large frying pan. Meanwhile make the topping by frying the onion, tomatoes and herbs in the butter. Turn the dough over and spread with the tomato mixture, the cheese, and a few sliced olives and/or anchovy fillets. Fry until the underside is golden and place under a hot grill until the cheese is golden and bubbling. Serve hot, cut in wedges – it goes well with a green salad. *Serves 2–3.*

Cheese and asparagus tart

200 g *(7 oz)* shortcrust pastry, ie made with 200 g, *(7 oz)* flour etc
25 g *(1 oz)* butter or margarine
45 ml *(3 level tbsps)* flour
300 ml *(½ pt)* milk
100 g *(4 oz)* cheese, grated
salt and pepper
340-g *(12-oz)* can green asparagus spears, drained

Line a 20.5-cm *(8-in)* flan ring or deep pie plate with the pastry. Bake 'blind' in the oven at 220°C *(425°F)* mark 7 for 15–20 minutes, until the pastry is cooked but not browned. Melt the fat in a saucepan, stir in the flour and cook for 2–3 minutes. Remove the pan from the heat and gradually stir in the milk. Bring to the boil and continue to stir until the sauce has thickened. Remove from the heat and stir in 75 g *(3 oz)* cheese and seasoning to taste. Place the drained asparagus in the pastry case, retaining a little for decoration, pour the sauce over and decorate with the remaining asparagus. Sprinkle with the remaining cheese and brown under a hot grill or in a hot oven before serving.

Fluffy cheese flan

150 g *(5 oz)* shortcrust pastry, ie made with 150 g *(5 oz)* flour etc
25 g *(1 oz)* butter or margarine
45 ml *(3 level tbsps)* flour
300 ml *(½ pt)* milk
100 g *(4 oz)* cheese, grated
salt and pepper
2 eggs, separated

Make the pastry and use it to line an 18-cm *(7-in)* pie plate or plain flan ring. Bake this case 'blind' in the oven at 220°C *(425°F)* mark 7 for 15–20 minutes or until cooked but still pale in colour. Melt the fat, stir in the flour and cook for 2–3 minutes. Remove pan from the heat and gradually stir in the milk. Bring to the boil and continue to stir until the sauce thickens. Remove from the heat and stir in 75 g *(3 oz)* of the cheese, the seasoning and egg yolks; pour into the pastry case.

Whisk the egg whites stiffly, pile on top of the flan and sprinkle with the remaining cheese. Reduce the oven to 180°C *(350°F)* mark 4 and return the flan for about 10 minutes, or until it is heated through and the meringue is golden.

Variation

Add 1 small skinned and chopped onion, lightly boiled, 50 g *(2 oz)* sliced mushrooms, lightly fried, or 2 skinned and chopped tomatoes to the sauce before putting it in the case.

Roquefort quiche *see colour plate facing p. 353*

150 g *(5 oz)* shortcrust pastry, ie made with 150 g *(5 oz)* flour etc
75 g *(3 oz)* Roquefort or other blue cheese
175 g *(6 oz)* cream cheese
2 eggs, beaten
142-ml *(5-fl oz)* carton single cream
5–10 ml *(1–2 tsps)* grated onion, or 15 ml *(1 tbsp)* chopped chives
salt and pepper

Make the pastry and use it to line an 18–20.5-cm *(7–8-in)* flan case or metal pie plate. Bake 'blind' in the oven at 220°C *(425°F)* mark 7 for 10 minutes, until the pastry is just set. Cream the two kinds of cheese and stir in the eggs, cream, onion and seasoning. Pour into the pastry case, reduce the oven temperature to 190°C *(375°F)* mark 5 and cook for about 30 minutes, until well risen and golden. Serve at once. Have a green salad as accompaniment. *Serves 4–6.*

Quiche Lorraine

150 g *(5 oz)* shortcrust pastry, ie made with 150 g *(5 oz)* flour etc
75–100 g *(3–4 oz)* lean bacon, chopped
75–100 g *(3–4 oz)* Gruyère cheese, thinly sliced
2 eggs, beaten
150 ml *(¼ pt)* single cream or creamy milk
salt and pepper

Roll out the pastry and use it to line an 18-cm *(7-in)* plain flan ring or sandwich cake tin, making a double edge. Cover the bacon with boiling water and leave for 2–3 minutes, then drain well. Put into the pastry case with the cheese, mix the eggs and cream, season well and pour into the case. Bake in the oven at 200°C *(400°F)* mark 6 for about 30 minutes, until well risen and golden.

There are many variations on this traditional dish – it can be made with bacon or cheese or both as shown. The cheese and bacon given above may be replaced by 75 g *(3 oz)* blue cheese mixed with 175 g *(6 oz)* cream cheese.

In some recipes lightly boiled rings of onions or leeks are used instead of, or as well as, the bacon.

Courgette and cheese flan

175 g *(6 oz)* plain flour
15 ml *(1 level tbsp)* grated Parmesan cheese
2.5 ml *(½ level tsp)* dry mustard
1.25 ml *(¼ level tsp)* paprika
175 g *(6 oz)* butter
450 g *(1 lb)* small courgettes
1 clove garlic, skinned and crushed
grated rind of ½ lemon
10 ml *(2 tsps)* lemon juice
salt and freshly ground black pepper
45 ml *(3 level tbsps)* flour
150 ml *(¼ pt)* milk
142-ml *(5-fl oz)* carton soured cream
1 egg, separated
175 g *(6 oz)* mature Cheddar cheese, grated
crisps, chopped chives to garnish

Sift the flour and dry ingredients together. Rub in half the butter. Add about 30 ml *(6 tsps)* cold water and knit the dough together with your fingertips. Roll it out and use to line a 23-cm *(9-in)* fluted flameproof flan dish. Bake blind at 200°C *(400°F)* mark 6 for about 25 minutes.

Trim and slice the courgettes. Blanch them for 1 minute in boiling water, then drain. Melt 50 g *(2 oz)* butter and add the next four ingredients. Season and sauté slowly till the courgettes are soft. Lift out the courgettes. Add the rest of the butter to the pan. Stir in the flour and cook a few minutes. Off the heat, stir in the milk gradually. Bring to the boil, reduce the heat and cook for a few minutes. Beat in the soured cream and beaten egg yolk. Cool slightly.

Whisk the egg white stiffly, fold it into the sauce with the cheese and check the seasoning. Spread the sauce over the base of the flan. Top with courgettes and reheat in the oven for 10–15 minutes. Scatter crushed crisps round edge, reheat for 5 minutes. Garnish with chives.

Pasta and rice

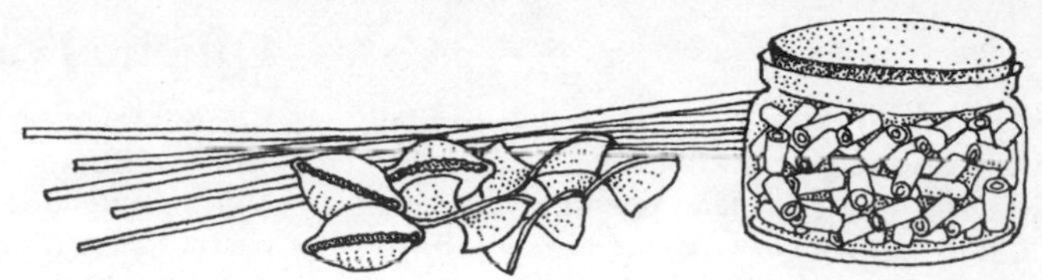

Though so different in origin and character, these two foods can play much the same part in a meal. Both are becoming steadily more popular in this country, but are still more widely used abroad, so many of the best known pasta and savoury rice recipes are borrowed from continental Europe – especially Italy – and from the East. Another Italian speciality, gnocchi, is also included in this chapter for the sake of convenience, since it is eaten at the beginning of a meal in the same way as pasta.

For desserts based on rice see the chapters on hot and cold puddings.

Pasta

Pasta, which is Italian in origin, is made from Amber durum wheat. This is finely ground down into semolina and then mixed with water to form a dough. Different colours can be accounted for by the addition of egg or spinach or because the pasta has been made from wholemeal semolina. The dough is kneaded, then extruded or pressed through a mould, and cut and dried. The different shaped dies make the different pasta – spaghetti, macaroni, lasagne etc.

Many Italian housewives still make their own supply, though if they live in a town they can buy it freshly made each day. In this country we generally buy it in packets, though some Italian shops, especially in the Soho region of London, do sell freshly made pasta (which should be used straight away). The packeted pasta sold throughout the country will keep indefinitely. The main practical difference between fresh and packeted pasta is that the former takes only about 5 minutes to cook.

Pasta shapes

You can buy a selection of the different pasta shapes in this country.

Long spaghetti is a solid rod in different thicknesses, and lengths of either 25.5 cm *(10 in)* or 51 cm *(20 in)*. Lower it into boiling water and, as it softens, curve it into the pan without breaking the rods.

Long macaroni is much thicker than spaghetti, comes in 25.5 cm *(10 in)* and 51 cm *(20 in)* lengths and has a hole through the middle.

Bucatini is quick-cook macaroni; hollow, it comes in either long or short lengths but thinner than standard macaroni.

Lasagne is either green (added spinach), plain or with egg. It comes in 5 cm *(2 in)* strips, or 10 cm *(4 in)* squares.

Long noodles are narrow, flat pasta, either 25.5 cm *(10 in)* or 51 cm *(20 in)* long.

Folded vermicelli look like very fine spaghetti and resemble a bird's nest when cooked.

Folded noodles are broad and fine. They come already bent, in a manageable mass.

Tagliatelle (fettucine) are long folded ribbons of noodles.

Ribbed rings are giant-sized solid twisted rings.

Hoops may be small, medium or large pasta circles.

Straight pipe macaroni This is the thickest tube pasta, most usually found in 2.5 cm *(1 in)* lengths. It is easier going for those who find the long pasta hard to manipulate.

Elbow macaroni comes as short, curved lengths of macaroni, in various sizes.

Alphabet letters These are shaped flat pieces of pasta often used in soups – popular with children.

Cannelloni are large, empty tubes, about 10 cm *(4 in)* long. Stuff them with meat or vegetables and serve with sauce.

Rigatoni are narrow 'stockings' ready for stuffing.

Wagon wheels is the name given to cartwheel-shaped pasta in various sizes.

Lumachine – literally 'little snails' – are small round shapes.

Spirals resemble small corkscrews.

Conchiglia are pasta shells shaped like winkles in various sizes.

Fargaletti are pasta bows and butterflies.

To cook pasta

Allow 50–75 g *(2–3 oz)* per head, as a vegetable alternative, whatever the shape. This should more than double its weight when cooked. Put the pasta in a large saucepan of fast boiling water to which you have added 5 ml *(1 level tsp)* of salt and cook uncovered for 10–15 minutes (a good 15 minutes for the wholemeal varieties). This should produce pasta cooked *al dente*–literally 'to the tooth'–which still has some bite in it and is not completely soft. A knob of butter or 15 ml *(1 tbsp)* oil added to the cooking water help to keep the pasta from sticking. Serve freshly grated Parmesan cheese separately.

Parmesan cheese
The authentic Italian flavour of this cheese is quite unique and although excellent in cooking, is expensive. Freshly grated from a piece the texture and taste are superior to that ready prepared in a drum. As an alternative you could use a dry Cheddar.

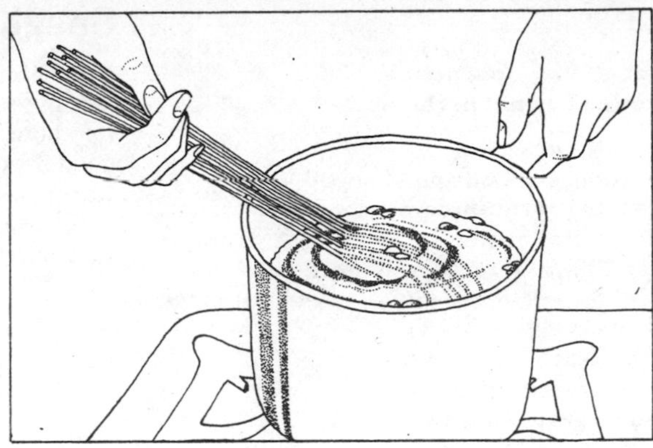

Cooking spaghetti – as the ends soften, coil them round in the pan

Spaghetti al burro
(Spaghetti with butter and Parmesan cheese)

Have a large pan of boiling salted water. Allow 50–75 g *(2–3 oz)* spaghetti per person; hold the end of the bunch of spaghetti in the water and as it softens, coil it round in the pan. Boil rapidly for 10–12 minutes, moving the spaghetti occasionally to prevent sticking, until it is just cooked. Drain well and return it to the pan with 25 g *(1 oz)* butter for 4 servings and a good sprinkling of grated Parmesan cheese. Stir and leave for a few minutes for the butter and cheese to melt. Serve with more grated cheese in a separate dish.

Any form of tubular or ribbon pasta can be cooked and served in this way.

Spaghetti alla bolognese
(Using a traditional Italian meat sauce)

225 g *(8 oz)* spaghetti
grated Parmesan cheese to serve

For the sauce
50 g *(2 oz)* bacon, chopped
knob butter
1 small onion, skinned and chopped
1 carrot, pared and chopped
1 stick celery, trimmed and chopped
225 g *(8 oz)* minced beef
100 g *(4 oz)* chicken livers, chopped
15 ml *(1 level tbsp)* tomato paste
150 ml *(¼ pt)* dry white wine
300 ml *(½ pt)* beef stock
salt and pepper
grated nutmeg

Make the sauce first. Fry the bacon lightly in the butter for 2–3 minutes, add the onion, carrot and celery and fry for a further 5 minutes until lightly browned. Add the beef and brown lightly. Stir in the chopped chicken livers. After cooking them for about 3 minutes, add the tomato paste and wine, allow to bubble for a few minutes and add the stock, seasoning and nutmeg.

Simmer for 30–40 minutes, until the meat is tender and the liquid in the sauce is well reduced. Adjust the seasoning if necessary.

Meanwhile cook the spaghetti in the usual way in fast-boiling water for about 10–12 minutes. Drain and serve on a heated dish with the sauce poured over. Serve the cheese sprinkled over the sauce or in a separate dish.

Spaghetti milanese

225 g *(8 oz)* spaghetti
grated Parmesan cheese

For the sauce
½ onion, skinned and chopped
50 g *(2 oz)* mushrooms, chopped
25 g *(1 oz)* butter
225 g *(½ lb)* tomatoes, skinned and chopped, or 425-g *(15-oz)* can tomatoes, drained
½ bayleaf
pinch dried thyme
pinch grated nutmeg
5 ml *(1 level tsp)* sugar
salt and pepper
50 g *(2 oz)* ham, chopped
50 g *(2 oz)* tongue, chopped

Fry the onion and mushrooms in the butter for 3–5 minutes, until soft. Stir in the tomatoes, herbs and seasonings, cover and simmer gently for about 20 minutes, until the sauce has thickened and developed a good flavour. Add thc ham and tongue and simmer uncovered for a further 5–10 minutes. Cook the spaghetti in fast-boiling salted water in the usual way for 10–12 minutes, drain well and mix with the sauce on a heated dish. Serve the cheese in a separate dish.

Spaghetti napolitana

225 g *(8 oz)* spaghetti
25 g *(1 oz)* butter
150–300 ml *(¼–½ pt)* tomato sauce (see page 202)
salt and pepper
25 g *(1 oz)* Parmesan cheese, grated

Cook the spaghetti in fast-boiling salted water in the usual way for 10–12 minutes. Drain and return it to the pan, with the butter, and shake it over a gentle heat for a minute or two. Serve on a heated dish, with the tomato sauce poured over it and the cheese sprinkled on top; if you prefer, the sauce and cheese may be served separately.

Spaghetti with meatballs

225 g *(8 oz)* spaghetti
Parmesan cheese

For the meatballs
450 g *(1 lb)* minced beef
1 clove garlic, skinned and crushed
1 thick slice of bread (soaked in a little milk)
2.5 ml *(½ level tsp)* dried marjoram or basil
pinch of grated nutmeg
salt and pepper
1 egg, beaten
butter for frying

For the sauce
½ onion, skinned and chopped
1 stick celery, trimmed and chopped
25–50 g *(1–2 oz)* mushrooms, chopped
425-g *(15-oz)* can tomatoes
10 ml *(2 level tsps)* tomato paste
5 ml *(1 level tsp)* sugar
salt and pepper
2.5 ml *(½ level tsp)* dried marjoram or basil

Mix the ingredients for the meatballs and bind them with the egg. Turn the mixture on to a floured board, divide into 16 pieces and form into balls.

Fry the meatballs in the butter for about 5 minutes, until lightly browned, and remove with a slotted spoon.

Fry the onion, celery and mushrooms in the same fat as the meatballs for about 6 minutes, until soft. Stir in the remaining ingredients for the sauce and add the meatballs. Cover and simmer for 30 minutes, or until the sauce is thick and the meatballs cooked. Meanwhile cook the spaghetti in fast-boiling salted water for 10–12 minutes, drain and place on a hot dish; spoon the sauce and meatballs over it and then sprinkle the Parmesan cheese on top.

Golden egg puffs (p. 257).
(Overleaf) Fried eggs (p. 249), Stuffed eggs à la mornay (p. 254), Beefy eggs in curry sauce (p. 255).

MOUTARDE DE MEAUX
IMPERARE OMNIBUS CIBIS

Spaghetti alla carbonara

350 g *(12 oz)* spaghetti
salt
2 eggs
2 egg yolks
90 ml *(6 level tbsps)* freshly grated Parmesan cheese
75 g *(3 oz)* Cheddar cheese, grated
225 g *(8 oz)* streaky bacon, rinded
6 tomatoes, skinned, seeded and chopped
142-ml *(5-fl oz)* carton single cream
30 ml *(2 tbsps)* chopped parsley
50 g *(2 oz)* butter
freshly ground black pepper

Cook the spaghetti in fast-boiling salted water until tender but not soft. Drain well. Beat together the eggs and egg yolks. Stir in half the Parmesan and half the Cheddar cheese. Scissor-snip the bacon and fry without extra fat until crisp. Stir in the chopped tomato flesh. Reduce the heat and add the cream and parsley. Allow to simmer while the spaghetti is cooking. Soften the butter in the saucepan and return the spaghetti to pan. Add the bacon and cream mixture. Toss well using 2 forks. Finally add the egg mixture. Toss well again. (The heat of the spaghetti and other ingredients will be sufficient to cook the eggs.) Adjust the seasoning and turn it into a serving dish. Sprinkle the remaining cheeses on top.

Macaroni with tomato sauce

tomato sauce made from fresh or canned tomatoes (see pages 202, 203)
225 g *(8 oz)* macaroni
knob of butter
grated Parmesan cheese

While the tomato sauce is simmering, cook the macaroni in fast-boiling salted water in the usual way for 10–15 minutes. Drain, toss it with the butter, pile on a heated dish and pour the sauce over. Sprinkle with Parmesan cheese and serve more cheese separately.

Alternatively, boil the macaroni for 10 minutes only and layer it with the sauce in a greased ovenproof dish, sprinkle with grated cheese and bake in the oven at 200°C *(400°F)* mark 6 for about 20 minutes, until bubbling and golden.

A bolognese type sauce (see spaghetti bolognese) or mediterranean sauce (see recipe page 274) can replace the tomato sauce.

Quick macaroni can also be used – cook as directed on the packet.

Macaroni with ham and eggs

175 g *(6 oz)* short cut macaroni
25 g *(1 oz)* butter
100 g *(4 oz)* cooked ham, chopped
2–3 eggs, beaten
salt and pepper
30 ml *(2 tbsps)* grated Parmesan cheese

Cook the macaroni in the usual way in fast-boiling water for 10–15 minutes, until soft, and drain it well. Fry the ham lightly for 2–3 minutes in the butter, until heated through, and stir in the drained macaroni, beaten eggs and seasoning. Stir over a gentle heat until the mixture is well blended and the eggs are just beginning to thicken. Add the cheese, mix well and serve straight away.

Quick macaroni can also be used – cook as directed on the packet.

Macaroni cheese *see colour plate facing p. 352*

175 g *(6 oz)* shortcut macaroni
40 g *(1½ oz)* butter
60 ml *(4 level tbsps)* flour
568 ml *(1 pt)* milk
salt and pepper
pinch of grated nutmeg or 2.5 ml *(½ level tsp)* made mustard
175 g *(6 oz)* mature cheese, grated
30 ml *(2 tbsps)* fresh white breadcrumbs, optional

Cook the macaroni in fast-boiling salted water for 10 minutes only and drain it well. Meanwhile melt the fat, stir in the flour and cook for 2–3 minutes. Remove the pan from the heat and gradually stir in the milk. Bring to the boil and continue to stir until the sauce thickens; remove from the heat and stir in the seasonings, 100 g *(4 oz)* of the cheese and the macaroni. Pour into an oven-proof dish and sprinkle with the breadcrumbs (if used) and the remaining cheese. Place on a baking sheet and bake in the oven at 200°C *(400°F)* mark 6 for about 20 minutes, or until golden and bubbling. Quick macaroni can also be used – cook it as directed on the packet.

Variations
Add to the sauce any of the following:
1 small onion, skinned, chopped and boiled
100 g *(4 oz)* bacon or ham, rinded, chopped and lightly fried

Butter-cup scrambles (p. 256).

½–1 green pepper, seeded, chopped and blanched
½–1 canned pimiento, chopped
1 medium sized can of salmon or tuna, drained and flaked
50 g *(2 oz)* mushrooms, sliced and lightly fried.

Pasta with mediterranean sauce

any type of pasta
2 medium sized onions, skinned and chopped
40 g *(1½ oz)* butter or 30–45 ml *(2–3 tbsps)* oil
1 clove garlic, skinned and crushed
425-g *(15-oz)* can tomatoes
63-g *(2¼-oz)* can tomato paste
5 ml *(1 level tsp)* dried marjoram or rosemary
5 ml *(1 level tsp)* sugar
salt and pepper
100 g *(4 oz)* mushrooms, sliced

Cook the pasta in the usual way. Fry the onions gently in 25 g *(1 oz)* of the butter for 5 minutes, until soft but not coloured. Stir in the garlic, tomatoes, tomato paste, herbs, sugar and seasoning, cover and simmer for 30 minutes, until the sauce is thick. Fry the mushrooms gently for about 3 minutes in the remaining knob of butter and add to the sauce. Adjust the seasoning and serve as a sauce over the pasta.

Cannelloni with cheese sauce

8 large cannelloni or 32 rigatoni
salt
100 g *(¼ lb)* mushrooms, chopped
50 g *(2 oz)* butter
184-g *(6½-oz)* can pimientos
283-g *(10-oz)* can garden peas, drained
2 cloves garlic, skinned and crushed
210-g *(7½-oz)* can salmon or tuna steak, drained and flaked
50 g *(2 oz)* fresh white breadcrumbs

For the sauce
50 g *(2 oz)* butter
60 ml *(4 level tbsps)* flour
568 ml *(1 pt)* milk
175 g *(6 oz)* Cheddar cheese, grated
salt and pepper

Cook the pasta in salted water for the time directed on the packet; drain well. Meanwhile sauté the mushrooms in the butter; add 2 caps of pimiento (diced), the peas, garlic, fish and breadcrumbs. Cook over a low heat for 5 minutes, stirring.

Make up the sauce in the usual way, using 150 g *(5 oz)* of the cheese. Stuff the pasta with the fish filling so that it protrudes slightly at each end. Arrange side by side in an ovenproof dish. Pour the sauce over. Garnish with the remainder of the pimiento, cut in strips, and scatter the rest of the cheese over. Bake in the oven at 200°C *(400°F)* mark 6 for 30 minutes, until bubbly and golden brown.

Lasagne al forno

2 425-g *(15-oz)* cans tomatoes
63-g *(2¼-oz)* can tomato paste
2.5–5 ml *(½–1 level tsp)* dried marjoram
salt and pepper
5 ml *(1 level tsp)* sugar
225 g *(8 oz)* cooked veal or ham, diced
100 g *(4 oz)* lasagne
175 g *(6 oz)* Ricotta or curd cheese
50 g *(2 oz)* Parmesan cheese
225 g *(8 oz)* Mozarella or Bel Paese cheese

Combine the canned tomatoes, tomato paste, marjoram, seasonings and sugar, simmer gently for about 30 minutes and add the veal or ham. Cook the lasagne in boiling salted water in the usual way for about 10–15 minutes (or as stated on the packet) and drain well.

Cover the base of a fairly deep ovenproof dish with a layer of the tomato and meat sauce. Add half the lasagne, put in another layer of the sauce, then cover with the cheeses, using half of each kind.

Repeat these layers with the remaining ingredients, finishing with a layer of cheese. Bake in the oven at 190°C *(375°F)* mark 5 for 30 minutes, until golden and bubbling on top. Serve at once. The tomato and meat sauce can be replaced by a bolognese sauce (see the recipe for spaghetti bolognese).

Note If neither Ricotta nor curd cheese are available use a blend of half cream cheese and half cottage cheese.

Tagliatelle con prosciutto

225 g *(8 oz)* **tagliatelle**
225 g *(8 oz)* **prosciutto ham, chopped**
butter
grated Parmesan cheese

Cook the tagliatelle in fast-boiling water in the usual way for about 10 minutes. Meanwhile lightly fry the ham in a little butter for 2–3 minutes. Drain the pasta, mix with the butter and ham and serve on a hot dish, sprinkled with the cheese.

Fried crispy noodles

450 g *(1 lb)* **noodles**
oil for deep frying

Put the noodles into boiling salted water and boil for 5 minutes, then drain; run cold water through them and drain well. Fry in deep oil for 5 minutes, until golden brown and crisp.

RAVIOLI

In Italy, supplies of ravioli and its variants are made and cooked fresh daily. In this country, freshly made ravioli can be bought in some Italian shops and restaurants, especially in the Soho neighbourhood in London. Failing this you can find ready-cooked ravioli in some delicatessen shops and it can also be bought in cans.

To cook fresh ravioli

Put the ravioli into boiling salted water, adding about 10–15 pieces at a time, and cook for 10–15 minutes (don't cook more than this at any one time, as the pieces tend to break up if the pan is crowded). Remove them with a slotted spoon and keep warm until all are cooked. Toss them with a little butter and then serve sprinkled with finely grated Parmesan cheese. As a variation, the cooked ravioli can be layered with tomato sauce (see page 202) in a greased ovenproof dish, sprinkled with grated Parmesan cheese and baked in the oven at 200°C *(400°F)* mark 6 for about 15 minutes, until golden and bubbly.

Ravioli stuffed with spinach

see colour plate between pp. 240 and 241

350 g *(12 oz)* **plain flour**
3 large eggs, beaten
1.25 ml *(¼ level tsp)* **salt**
30 ml *(2 tbsps)* **warm water**
melted butter, diced tomato, grated cheese and chopped parsley, for garnish

For filling
75 g *(3 oz)* **butter**
226-g *(8-oz)* **pkt frozen spinach, thawed and chopped**
100 g *(4 oz)* **Cheddar cheese, grated**
salt and pepper
grated nutmeg

Sift the flour on to a working top. Make a well in the centre, add the eggs, salt and water to it. Gradually incorporate the flour, knead the dough for 10 minutes then place it inside an oiled polythene bag and leave for 30 minutes. Meanwhile, melt the butter and add it to the drained spinach with the cheese. Season well. Halve the dough. Roll it out, then stretch by drawing the fingertips underneath until each half is 35.5 cm *(14 in)* by 51 cm *(20 in)*. Place 8 small mounds of spinach along the length and 6 down the breadth, equally spaced. Make 48 altogether. Brush around the mounds with water. Cover with the remaining dough. Seal around each spinach mound. Cut out with a serrated pastry wheel between the 'humps'. Boil in salted water for about 15–20 minutes; drain. Toss in melted butter with diced tomato flesh, grated cheese and chopped parsley. *Serves 8.*

GNOCCHI

This name is given to several different dishes, based on semolina, maize meal, cooked potatoes, cheese-flavoured choux pastry and even cream cheese. Some of the versions belong more to high-class French cuisine, but we give here two recipes which are met in everyday Italian cookery.

Semolina gnocchi alla Romana

568 ml *(1 pt)* milk
100 g *(4 oz)* fine semolina
salt, pepper
pinch of grated nutmeg
1–2 eggs, beaten
25 g *(1 oz)* butter
75 g *(3 oz)* grated Parmesan cheese
little butter and extra cheese for topping

Bring the milk to the boil, sprinkle in the semolina and seasonings and stir over a gentle heat until the mixture is really thick. Beat well until smooth and stir in the egg, butter and cheese. Return the pan to a low heat and stir for 1 minute. Spread this mixture, about ½–1 cm *(¼–½ in)* thick, on a shallow buttered dish and allow to cool. Cut into 2.5-cm *(1-in)* rounds or squares and arrange in a shallow greased ovenproof dish. Put a few knobs of butter over the top, sprinkle with a little extra cheese and brown under the grill or towards the top of the oven at 200°C *(400°F)* mark 6. Serve with more cheese and tomato sauce (see page 202).

Cream cheese gnocchi

225 g *(½ lb)* curd or cream cheese (traditionally Ricotta), sieved
50 g *(2 oz)* butter
60 ml *(4 level tbsps)* grated Parmesan cheese
2 eggs, beaten
50–75 g *(2–3 oz)* flour
salt and pepper
little grated nutmeg
melted butter and grated cheese to serve

Mix all the ingredients together, beat until smooth, then form into small balls or cork shapes. Roll these in flour and poach a few at a time in boiling salted water – this takes about 5 minutes, and they are ready when they rise to the top of the pan. Serve tossed in melted butter and sprinkled with grated Parmesan cheese.

RICE

Shapes of grain

There are three main kinds of rice grain – long, medium and short.

The long slender grains are fluffy and separate when cooked so they are ideal for made-up savoury rice dishes and for rice used as an accompaniment to savoury dishes such as curries and stews. Medium and short grain rice have moister, stickier grains. The medium grains are very suitable for savoury dishes where the rice needs to be moulded or bound together (eg rice rings, stuffings and croquettes). Short grain rice is used for rice puddings and other sweet rice dishes.

Types of rice

Regular milled, long grain white rice The hulls, germ, and most of the bran layers are removed. The rice is white in colour, with only a bland, very slight flavour when cooked.

Brown rice Whole unpolished grains of rice with only the inedible husk and a small amount of bran removed. It takes longer to cook than white rice (about 40 minutes), and more liquid. Apart from its fawn colour when cooked, it differs from white rice by having a more chewy texture and a pleasant, nutty flavour. It is used in savoury dishes.

Par-boiled or pre-fluffed rice Cooked before milling by a special steam pressure process, which helps to retain the natural food value. It takes longer to cook than regular milled white rice (20–25 minutes), absorbs more liquid (2½ parts water to 1 part rice). But it more easily produces a perfect result, with grains that are fluffy, separate and plump when cooked.

Pre-cooked or instant rice This is completely cooked and then dehydrated. It is useful when in a hurry as it only needs heating in boiling water for about 5 minutes or as directed on the pack. It is a very good stand-by for snacks and quick rice dishes, both savoury and sweet.

Risotto rice, known as **Arborio** is a plump Italian rice which gives risotto its essentially creamy texture, with each grain firm in the centre and slightly chewy.

Wild rice This is not actually rice, but seeds from a wild grass, used for savoury dishes. It is expensive and not widely available, but delicious for special occasions, particularly with game.

Preparing and cooking rice

Rice sold in unbranded packs or loose should be washed before it is cooked. Put it in a strainer and rinse it under the cold tap until all the loose starch (white powder) is washed off – it is this loose starch which prevents rice drying out into separate grains when cooked.

Storing and re-heating rice

The rice can be cooked in quite large quantities and any not required at once can be stored in a covered container in a refrigerator for up to a week without any deterioration, or for several days in a cool place. To re-heat it, place about 1 cm *(½ in)* water in a pan, add some salt, bring to the boil and add the rice. Cover tightly, then reduce the heat and simmer very gently for about 5 minutes.

Boiled rice

Place 225 g *(8 oz)* long grain rice in a saucepan with 600 ml *(1 pint)* water and 5 ml *(1 level tsp)* salt. Bring quickly to the boil, stir well and cover with a tightly fitting lid. Reduce the heat and simmer gently for 14–15 minutes. Remove from the heat and before serving separate out the grains gently, using a fork (The rice will not need draining.) If a drier effect is required, leave the rice covered for 5–10 minutes after it has been cooked. The grains should then be tender, but dry and quite separate. 225 g *(8 oz)* rice gives 3–4 servings. Here are some points to remember when using this method:

Don't increase the amount of water or the finished rice will be soggy.

Don't uncover the rice whilst it is cooking or the steam will escape and the cooking time will be increased.

Don't stir the rice while it is simmering – it breaks up the grains and makes them soggy. When the rice is cooked, don't leave it longer than 10 minutes before serving, or the grains will stick together.

Oven-cooked rice

Place 225 g *(8 oz)* rice in an ovenproof dish. Bring 600 ml *(1 pint)* water and 5 ml *(1 level tsp)* salt to the boil, pour over the rice and stir well. Cover tightly with a lid or foil and bake in the oven at 180°C *(350°F)* mark 4 for 35–40 minutes, or until the grains are just soft and the cooking liquid has all been absorbed by the rice.

Flavoured rice

Although rice is most usually cooked in water, it can also be cooked in other liquids to give extra flavour and variety. The water may be replaced by any of the following:
Chicken or beef stock (fresh or made from a cube).
Canned tomato juice, undiluted or used half-and-half with water.
Orange juice – used half-and-half with water.

Alternatively, rice can be flavoured as in the following recipes:

Savoury rice

Fry some chopped onion, pepper, celery or bacon in a little butter in the pan before adding the rice.

Herby rice

Add a pinch of dried herbs with the cooking liquid (eg sage, marjoram, thyme, mixed herbs).

Raisin rice

Add stoned raisins (or currants or sultanas) with the cooking liquid; a pinch of curry powder can also be added.

Variety rice

When the rice is cooked stir in any of the following: diced pineapple, chopped canned pimiento, slivered brown almonds, grated cheese, chopped fresh herbs.

Spanish rice

4 rashers streaky bacon, rinded and chopped
knob butter
1 onion, skinned and chopped
1 green pepper, seeded and chopped
225 g *(8 oz)* long grain rice
600 ml *(1 pt)* canned tomato juice
salt and pepper

Fry the bacon lightly for 2–3 minutes in the butter, add the onion and pepper and fry for about 5 minutes, until soft. Stir in the rice, liquid and seasoning, bring to the boil, cover with a lid, reduce the heat and simmer gently for 14–15 minutes. Stir lightly with a fork and serve.

Good with chicken and ham.

Curried rice

1 onion, skinned and finely chopped
25 g *(1 oz)* butter
225 g *(8 oz)* long grain rice
25–50 g *(1–2 oz)* currants or stoned raisins
2.5 ml *(½ level tsp)* curry powder
600 ml *(1 pt)* chicken or beef stock
salt and pepper
25 g *(1 oz)* blanched almonds, slivered and browned (optional)

Fry the onion in the butter for about 5 minutes, until soft. Add the rice and fry for a further 2–3 minutes, stirring all the time. Add the fruit, curry powder, stock and seasoning and bring to the boil. Stir and cover with a lid, reduce the heat and simmer gently for 14–15 minutes. Stir in the almonds (if used) and serve.

Good with meat or chicken.

Casseroled yellow rice

100 g *(4 oz)* dried apricots
225 g *(8 oz)* long grain rice
2.5 ml *(½ level tsp)* salt
75 g *(3 oz)* onion, skinned and finely chopped
25 g *(1 oz)* seedless raisins
2.5 ml *(½ level tsp)* turmeric

Scissor-snip the apricots into small dice. Place in a basin, pour over 700 ml *(1¼ pt)* boiling water. Leave to stand for 1 hour. In an ovenproof casserole, combine the rice, salt, onion, raisins and turmeric. Re-boil the water and apricots and pour on to the contents of the casserole. Stir before covering and cook in the oven at 180°C *(350°F)* mark 4 for about 45 minutes until the water is absorbed and rice tender.

Mince with rice

1 large onion, chopped
2 sticks celery, trimmed and chopped, optional
25 g *(1 oz)* butter
50 g *(2 oz)* mushrooms, sliced
450 g *(1 lb)* fresh minced meat
175–225 g *(6–8 oz)* long grain rice
425-g *(15-oz)* can tomatoes, made up to 900 ml *(1½ pt)* with stock or water
salt and pepper
pinch of dried herbs
½ bayleaf

Fry the onion and celery in the butter for 5 minutes, until soft. Stir in the mushrooms, add the meat and fry until lightly browned. Stir in the rice and continue frying for a further few minutes. Pour in the tomatoes and liquid and add the seasoning and herbs. Bring to the boil, cover and simmer gently until the meat is tender, the rice soft and the liquid absorbed. Serve with a separate dish of grated cheese (Parmesan if possible).

Variations

Fry 50 g *(2 oz)* chopped bacon or ½ a green pepper (seeded and chopped) with the other vegetables.

Use 225 g *(½ lb)* fresh tomatoes and about 15 ml *(1 level tbsp)* tomato paste, with more stock, instead of the canned tomatoes.

Stirred rice *see colour plate facing p. 241*

100 g *(4 oz)* **long grain rice, cooked**
100 g *(4 oz)* **shrimps**
50 g *(2 oz)* **butter**
50 g *(2 oz)* **raisins, seeded**
50 g *(2 oz)* **cooked ham, chopped**
6 scallions or spring onions, chopped
50 g *(2 oz)* **walnuts, blanched**
50 g *(2 oz)* **almonds, blanched**
30 ml *(2 tbsps)* **soy sauce**
2.5 ml *(½ level tsp)* **salt**

Reheat the rice by steaming or simmering in fresh water. Shell the shrimps and cut each into 4 pieces. Heat the fat, add the shrimps and stir for 1 minute. Add the raisins, ham, scallions, nuts, soy sauce and salt and stir for 2 minutes, then stir in the rice.

Fried rice

100 g *(4 oz)* **long grain rice**
2 eggs, beaten
60 ml *(4 tbsps)* **oil**
2.5 ml *(½ level tsp)* **salt**
½ onion, skinned and finely chopped
50 g *(2 oz)* **mushrooms, thinly sliced**
30 ml *(2 tbsps)* **frozen peas**
50 g *(2 oz)* **cooked ham, diced**
10 ml *(2 tsps)* **soy sauce**

Boil the rice – which should be fluffy and dry. Make a plain omelette from the eggs (see page 251), cut it into thin strips and set aside. Fry the drained rice preferably in a non-stick pan for about 5 minutes in 30 ml *(2 tbsps)* very hot oil with the salt until light golden brown, stirring gently all the time; remove from the pan and set aside. Fry the onion in the remaining oil for about 3 minutes till lightly browned, add the remaining vegetables, rice and the ham and fry lightly for a further 3 minutes stirring gently. Stir in the soy sauce and shredded omelette; serve the mixture as soon as it is hot, to accompany chicken.

RISOTTO

Risotto is the main rice dish in the north of Italy, where rice takes the place of pasta. Risotto is usually a dish complete in itself (with the exception of Milanese risotto, which is served as an accompaniment to such well-known Italian dishes as Osso Bucco).

The difference between a risotto and a pilau (see next page) is that the former is moister, being made from Italian risotto rice. In this country a long grain rice may have to be substituted for it, but the risotto should still be made more moist than a pilau.

Chicken risotto

½ boiling chicken or 2–3 good-sized chicken portions, uncooked
75 g *(3 oz)* **butter**
2 small onions, skinned and finely chopped
1 stick celery, scrubbed, trimmed and finely chopped
1 clove garlic, skinned and crushed, optional
1 green pepper, seeded and finely chopped
50 g *(2 oz)* **mushrooms, sliced**
50 g *(2 oz)* **bacon or ham, rinded and chopped**
150 ml *(¼ pt)* **dry white wine**
chicken stock
salt and pepper
chopped fresh herbs as available (eg marjoram, thyme or basil)
225 g *(8 oz)* **long grain rice**
grated Parmesan cheese

Skin the chicken, bone it and cut the flesh in strips. Melt 25 g *(1 oz)* of the butter and fry half the chopped onion gently for 5 minutes, until soft. Add the chicken, the remaining vegetables and the bacon or ham and fry for a further few minutes, stirring all the time. Add the wine and let it bubble until well reduced; just cover with chicken stock and add the seasoning and herbs. Put on the lid and leave to simmer for about 1 hour, until the chicken is really tender. Drain off the juices and make up to 600 ml *(1 pt)* with more stock if required.

Fry the remaining onion in 25 g *(1 oz)* of the remaining butter for about 5 minutes, until soft. Add the rice and stir until transparent. Add the chicken stock and bring to the boil. Cover and simmer for 10 minutes. Fold in the chicken mixture, stir well and continue cooking until the two mixtures are well blended and the liquid all absorbed. Stir in the remaining butter and some Parmesan cheese and serve.

Shellfish risotto

1 onion, skinned and finely chopped
75 g *(3 oz)* butter
225 g *(8 oz)* long grain rice
150 ml *(¼ pt)* dry white wine
900 ml *(1½ pt)* boiling chicken stock
salt and pepper
1 clove garlic, skinned and crushed, optional
225 g (8 oz) frozen scampi or prawns, thawed
grated Parmesan cheese

Prepare the risotto as above, using 50 g *(2 oz)* of the butter. Just before the rice becomes tender, gently fry the garlic (if used) and the shellfish in the remaining 25 g *(1 oz)* butter for 5 minutes. Stir into the risotto and serve with the cheese.

A few sliced button mushrooms can be fried with the shellfish or a few frozen peas or strips of canned pimiento can be added to the risotto just before the rice is cooked. Other shellfish, such as crab or lobster meat (fresh or canned) may also be used; a mixture of shellfish, with possibly a few mussels (canned or fresh) will give a more unusual touch.

Risotto alla milanese

1 onion, skinned and finely chopped
75 g *(3 oz)* butter
225 g *(8 oz)* long grain rice
150 ml *(¼ pt)* dry white wine
600 ml *(1 pt)* boiling chicken stock
salt and pepper
30–45 ml *(2–3 level tbsps)* grated Parmesan cheese

Fry the onion gently for about 5 minutes in 50 g *(2 oz)* of the butter, until it is soft and just beginning to turn golden. Add the rice and continue frying, stirring all the time, until the rice looks transparent. Pour in the wine and allow to bubble briskly until well reduced. Add the stock and the seasoning and cook covered over a moderate heat until the stock has been absorbed, about 15–20 minutes. Add the remaining butter and stir in well. The cheese can also be stirred in until it melts, or if preferred it can be served separately.

Traditionally, 25–50 g *(1–2 oz)* beef marrow is included, being fried after the onion is soft; the rice is coloured with saffron, which is dissolved in a little of the stock and added towards the end of the cooking time. If these two ingredients are omitted, the risotto should strictly speaking be called a *risotto bianco*.

Paella

6–8 mussels, fresh or bottled
50–100 g *(2–4 oz)* Dublin Bay prawns or frozen scampi
1 small cooked lobster
1 small chicken
60 ml *(4 tbsps)* olive oil
1 clove garlic, skinned and crushed
1 onion, skinned and chopped
1 green pepper, seeded and chopped
4 tomatoes, skinned and chopped
225–350 g *(8–12 oz)* long grain rice
900 ml–1.4 l *(1½–2½ pt)* chicken stock
salt and pepper
little powdered saffron
100 g *(4 oz)* frozen peas

This famous Spanish dish takes its name from the pan in which it is cooked – a shallow oval metal dish with handles at each side. There are few hard-and-fast rules about making a paella, although the following ingredients are traditionally included – chicken, lobster, shellfish of various kinds, onion, green or red peppers and rice. Paella is rather elaborate and somewhat expensive to prepare in this country, but it makes an attractive party dish. The quantities given in this recipe should serve at least 8 people.

Shell or drain the mussels and peel the prawns, if fresh. Remove the lobster meat from the shell and dice it, retaining the claws for decorating. Cut the meat from the chicken into small pieces. Put the oil into a large paella or frying pan and fry the garlic, onion and green pepper for 5 minutes, until soft but not browned. Add the tomatoes and chicken pieces and fry until the chicken is lightly browned. Stir in the rice, most of the stock, the seasoning and saffron (blended with a little of the stock). Bring to the boil, then reduce the heat and simmer for about 20–25 minutes, until the chicken is tender and the rice just cooked.

Stir in the mussels, prawns, lobster meat and peas and simmer for a final 5–10 minutes, until heated through. Serve garnished with a few extra strips of green pepper or pimiento and the lobster claws. Mussels in their shells can also be used as a garnish.

PILAU (PILAFF, PILAV)

This rice dish, which is made throughout the Middle East, somewhat resembles paella (above). It may be simply cooked, perhaps with onions, or highly spiced, with the addition of nuts, dried fruits, green ginger and so on. A pilau can be served as accompaniment to kebabs (see page 121).

Basic pilau

225 g *(8 oz)* long grain rice
50 g *(2 oz)* butter
700 ml *(1¼ pt)* boiling chicken stock
salt and pepper

Fry the rice gently in the melted butter for about 5 minutes, stirring all the time, until it looks transparent. Add the stock, pouring it in slowly, as it will tend to bubble rather a lot at first. Add the seasoning, stir well, cover with a tightly fitting lid and leave over a very low heat for about 15 minutes, until the water is absorbed and the rice grains are just soft. (The idea is that the rice should cook in its own steam, so don't stir it while it is cooking.)

Remove the lid, cover the rice with a cloth, replace the lid and leave in a warm place to dry out for at least 15 minutes before serving. (This is a traditional part of making a pilau, although not included in many European versions of this dish.)

To serve, stir lightly with a fork to separate the grains, add a knob of butter and serve at once.

Mutton pilau

450–700 g *(1–1½ lb)* loin or best end of neck of mutton or lamb
900 ml *(1½ pt)* chicken stock
175 g *(6 oz)* long grain rice
pinch ground cinnamon
pinch ground cloves
salt and pepper
50 g *(2 oz)* currants or stoned raisins
50 g *(2 oz)* butter

Trim the meat and cut it into even-sized pieces. Cover with the stock and stew until tender, then lift out, drain and keep on one side. Wash the rice well and sprinkle into the liquid in which the meat was cooked; add the spices, seasoning and currants. Bring to the boil, then cover and simmer very gently for about 15 minutes, until all the liquid is absorbed and the rice is just soft. Remove from the heat and leave covered for about 15 minutes to dry out. Fry the meat in half the butter until lightly browned and stir the remaining butter into the rice mixture. Serve the rice piled on a dish with the meat in the centre. This dish can be garnished with wedges of tomato or fried onion rings.

Liver pilau

225 g *(½ lb)* calf's liver, cut in strips
50 g *(2 oz)* butter
2 onions, skinned and finely chopped
25 g *(1 oz)* shelled peanuts or almonds
175–225 g *(6–8 oz)* long grain rice
salt and pepper
pinch of mixed spice
50 g *(2 oz)* currants
2 tomatoes, skinned and chopped
700 ml *(1¼ pt)* chicken or meat stock, boiling
little chopped parsley

Fry the liver lightly in the butter for 2–3 minutes and remove it from the fat with a slotted spoon. Fry the onions for 5 minutes in the same fat until soft but not brown. Add the nuts and rice and fry for a further 5 minutes, stirring all the time. Add the seasoning, spice, currants, tomatoes and stock, stir well, cover with a tightly fitting lid and simmer for about 15 minutes, until all the liquid has been absorbed. Stir in the liver and parsley, cover again and before serving leave for 15 minutes in a warm place (but without further cooking). The liver may if preferred be replaced by cooked leftover chicken or lamb.

Fruit

In this chapter we give notes on all the more important home-grown and imported fruits; for recipes for using them, see the chapters on Hot and Cold Puddings and those on different branches of preserving.

Apple

Apples are grown in most temperate regions, including of course Great Britain, and there are now very many varieties. They can be divided into cooking and eating types.

Cooking apples are usually larger than the eatings kinds, with firm, acid-tasting flesh that pulps easily on cooking. Some popular varieties are:

Bramley's Seedling	Early Victoria
Newton Wonder	Lord Derby
Grenadier	Warner King

Eating apples vary in size. The skin colour varies from green through yellow and russet to parti-coloured or deep red; the flesh is sweet and can be either really firm and crisp or soft and almost mealy.

Home-grown apples are available from July to November, but these are supplemented by a large number of imported apples throughout the year.

Among the many kinds of eating apple now grown, the following good varieties are widely available in the shops:

Cox's Orange Pippin	Newton Wonder (cooking and eating)
Laxton Superb	Worcester Pearmain
Jonathan	Blenheim Orange
Granny Smith	Sturmer Pippin
Golden Delicious	Millers Seedling
Winesap	Red Delicious
James Grieve	
Golden Russett	
Dunn's Seedlings	

Apricot

A stone fruit, round and about the size of a plum, with a velvety, yellowish-orange skin and fairly soft, juicy pulp of much the same colour.

Apricots should be eaten when just ripe – if under-ripe they are sour and hard, with little flavour, if over-ripe the flesh becomes soft and 'woolly'. They can be eaten plain as a dessert fruit or used – raw or cooked – in puddings, sweets, pies and preserves. The kernels of apricots have an attractive almond flavour, so a few are sometimes included in apricot preserves.

The fruit is also available in cans and dried.

In season December–February and May–August.

Avocado

The fruit of a tree from places with a sub-tropical climate. Avocados are the same shape as pears, with a fairly tough, shiny skin, which varies between dark green and brown; they have soft, oily, pale-green flesh of the consistency of butter and a large central stone.

Available nearly all the year round.

Note Avocados are normally eaten as a savoury, either as a starter or in salads, though in some tropical countries they are used in sweet dishes.

Banana

The fruit of a tropical tree. The two main types are the Jamaica or Plantain Banana – long and fairly large, with creamy-coloured flesh of little flavour – and the Canary or Dwarf Banana – smaller, with more pink-tinged flesh and a more pronounced flavour.

Bananas are imported in large bunches (called 'hands') while still green and on entering this country are ripened in special large warehouses before being distributed to the retail shops.

Bananas can be eaten raw as a dessert or in many fruit sweets. They can also be used in cooked sweets such as fritters, creole bananas, etc., and sometimes as an accompaniment to savoury dishes, eg chicken Maryland. Available all the year round.

Bilberry

Bilberries are small dark blue or mauve berries, smaller than black currants, with small seeds and a distinctive flavour. Can be sour when eaten raw, they are usually cooked in fruit puddings or pies.

Bilberries grow wild on the moors and hills in England and Wales, but those sold in the shops are usually imported from Poland.

In season July–August.

Blackberry

A small soft fruit, dark red to black in colour. Blackberries are available wild and cultivated; the cultivated ones are larger and more juicy than the wild ones and have a slightly different flavour. Blackberries can be eaten raw, stewed, included in many cooked fruit puddings and pies and made into jams or jellies (often combined with apples).

In season June–October.

Cape gooseberry
(Physalis or Chinese Lantern)
This is the berry of the Cape gooseberry, which in this country is usually grown for decoration. When ripe the berries are enclosed in a lantern-shaped case or calyx, orange-yellow in colour. They can be eaten raw, used in fruit salads or made into jams. If the case or calyx is bent back to form 'petals' round the central berry, they can be used as a decoration for formal cakes and sweets.

Canned Cape gooseberries are imported from Kenya, usually under the name of Golden Berries.

In season February–March.

Cherry
The stone fruit of a tree which is cultivated in many countries. In this country the best-known eating types are the White and the Black Heart cherries, which are large, juicy and sweet.

In season June–August.

Cherries for cooking (ie, for use in pies, puddings and jams) are the May Dukes and the Morello, which are in season July–August.

Cherry plum
A round stone fruit with a shiny red and yellow skin, rather like a large cherry. Cherry plums are rarely eaten raw, the flesh being rather mealy, but are good for stewing and bottling.

In season July–August.

Chinese gooseberry
(Kiwi fruit)
A fairly rare fruit in this country, being imported from New Zealand. It is egg-shaped, about 5 cm *(2 in)* long with a brown, hairy skin and soft, green flesh. Chinese gooseberries have a very high vitamin C content and about 30 calories per fruit.

In season July–February.

Crab apple
The common European crab is the original wild apple. A number of cultivated varieties now exist, including the Japanese and Siberian types. The small fruit have a shiny red or yellow skin and firm flesh, which is usually very sour. Crab apples are chiefly used to make jelly or other preserves.

In season September–October.

Cranberry
A small round berry, crimson or red and yellow in colour, slightly smaller than a cherry. Cranberries have a hard, mealy flesh and small seeds. As they are sour when eaten raw, they are usually stewed and used in fruit sweets, for sauce or for making cranberry jelly.

They can be grown in this country, where they ripen July–August, but are more usually imported.

Available November–February.

Currant
Black-currants
The small fruits grow in strings or clusters and are almost black when ripe. They have a rich flavour, but are usually rather sour to eat raw, so are used in puddings, pies and fruit sweets. They are often made into jams and jellies and the juice is made into a cordial.

In season June–August.

Red-currants
Similar to black-currants, but as their name suggests, they are a bright cherry red. They are used mainly for fruit sweets, puddings and pies and preserves, especially jelly. The seeds are obtrusive, so many people prefer to use red-currants only in sieved form.

White-currants
These are less common, but are similar to red-currants except in colour.

Custard apple
Originally a West Indian fruit, although most of those imported now come from Madeira. The custard apple has a soft, yellow, pulpy flesh and a tough green skin.

In season September–February.

Damson
A small roundish plum, purple to dark blue in colour, with yellow flesh. Damsons are sour, unless really ripe, and are usually stewed or used in pies and fruit puddings and for preserves, especially damson cheese.

In season August–October.

Damson plums are larger than damsons, not so pointed, with a rougher stone, and they do not have such a good flavour.

Bullaces or wild damsons are very sour and usually used only for preserves.

Date
The fruit of the date palm tree, almost oval in shape, with brown, firm, sweet flesh and a long cylindrical stone. Dessert dates are loosely packed in boxes, whole and 'on the stem', but dates of poorer quality are stoned and pressed into a solid pack, to be used for cooking purposes (for instance, in puddings, cakes and biscuits).

Dessert dates are available from September–March; cooking dates are available all the year round.

Elderberry
The fruit of the elder tree, which grows wild in hedgerows and similar places. The berries are small, round and shiny, almost black in colour, and grow in flat, spreading clusters, ripening in late summer. Elderberries are usually used only to make elderberry wine – one of the best known country wines.

Fig
There are two main varieties of fig, both of which have a large number of small seeds.

The green fig has a green skin and yellowish-green flesh.

The purple fig has a purple skin and reddish-purple flesh.

Figs can be grown outdoors in the South of England, but are more usually hothouse-grown. The majority on sale in shops are imported.

In season September–December.

Figs are also sold dried, the best-known being Smyrna and Adriatic figs.

Fresh figs are eaten raw as a dessert, but the dried ones are used chiefly as stewed fruit or in puddings.

Gooseberry
There are many varieties, round or long, hairy or smooth, cooking or dessert.

Cooking gooseberries, used in pies and puddings and for jam, etc, are usually green, very sour, with firm flesh and a fairly large number of seeds. Dessert gooseberries can be green, yellow-white or a russet colour, often with a hairy skin, and they usually have soft, pulpy, sweet flesh and large seeds.

In season May–August.

Granadilla *(See Passion fruit)*

Grape
Grapes are usually imported to this country, although some are grown in hothouses. There is a pretty constant supply (at varying prices) throughout the year.

Dessert grapes come in two main types – 'White', which are greenish-yellow, and 'Black', which are a dark purple. The white Muscat and the black Hamburg are considered the best varieties. They can be used in fruit salads and other raw fruit dishes, but are rarely served cooked. In grape-growing countries, smaller grapes are grown especially for wine-making and are also dried as raisins.

Grapefruit
A citrus fruit with a smooth, thick yellow skin, juicy, acid, yellow or pink flesh and large pips (though some are seedless). It varies in size the smallest being the size of a large orange. Grapefruit is usually eaten raw as an appetiser or in fruit sweets, but can form the basis of fruit drinks and it is also used in mixed citrus fruit marmalades. Large quantities of grapefruit are also canned, especially in the U.S.A. and West Indies, both as segments and as grapefruit juice.

Imported from various countries and available the year round.

Greengage
A fairly small, rather round plum, greenish-yellow in colour, with a very good flavour. Greengages can be eaten as a dessert fruit, used in puddings and pies or made into jam.

Some are grown in this country and supplies are also imported.

In season during July and September.

Guava
There are many varieties of this tropical fruit – some pear-shaped, some rather like tomatoes or oranges and others even fig-shaped. They have pink, fairly firm flesh and a lot of quite large seeds.

Guavas are usually made into jelly or guava cheese, but the fruit is also available in cans and the juice is bottled, alone or with other fruit juices, as a fruit cordial. The canned fruit can be used in fruit salads or in any other fruit sweets.

Japonica
The fruits of the ornamental japonica tree resemble in shape a cross between an apple and pear. They do not always ripen on the tree, if the year is not a good one, but can be picked whilst green and stored for about a month, until they begin to turn slightly yellow. They have a distinctive flavour and are often mixed with apples in a pie or when stewed, and can be made into japonica jelly.

In season in October.

Kumquat
The fruit of a small tree originating in China and Japan; it is closely related to the orange, but the fruit is about the size of a plum and oval in shape.

Kumquats are eaten fresh as a dessert, included in fruit salads and other fruit sweets and made into marmalade. They are also given a glacé or crystallised finish and can be used for cake and sweet decoration or eaten as a sweetmeat.

Fresh kumquats are available sporadically throughout the year.

Lemon
There are many varieties of this citrus fruit, which is grown in most countries with a hot climate, but the commonest is the Genoa lemon, with a fairly tough yellow rind and juicy, very acid yellow flesh.

The lemon is one of the most widely used fruits in cookery, the rind and juice being used as flavourings in fruit sweets, puddings, cakes, etc, as the main ingredient in lemon meringue pie, in fruit drinks and in preserves such as lemon curd and marmalade, as well as in many savoury dishes, sauces and so on. Lemon juice is an excellent source of pectin and is used widely in jam making.

Lemons are available all the year round.

Lime

A lime is like a small lemon in shape, with a very sharp flavour. When ripe, limes have a yellow skin, but they are usually imported to this country whilst still green.

Limes are rarely used raw in this country, being normally made into cordials or used for marmalade.

In season all year round.

Litchi *(Lychee)*

The fruit of a tree of Chinese origin, now also grown in South Africa. Litchis have a hard, red-brown scaly skin and white pulpy flesh, with a small brown stone in the centre. They have a distinctive flavour – slightly acid yet sweet.

Litchis are occasionally obtainable fresh, but are more usually sold canned in a fairly heavy sugar syrup.

In season December–February.

Loganberry

A soft fruit, dark red to purplish in colour, similar to but slightly larger than a raspberry, with a fairly hard central hull.

Loganberries can be eaten raw as a dessert or cooked in puddings, pies and preserves. They are also canned.

In season July–August.

Mandarin *(See Tangerine)*

Mango

Looks like a large irregularly shaped potato. It is green while growing, yellow when ripe. The red-yellow very juicy flesh has a delicate fragrance and taste.

Available January–September.

Medlar

There are several varieties of this fruit, but the most usual one is rather like a rosehip in shape and russet-brown in colour. Medlars are picked in November, but should be kept for 2–3 weeks, until the fruit is really soft and mellow. Although medlars can be eaten raw, they are usually made into a preserve, eg medlar cheese.

Melon

The melon is thick-skinned, hollow in the centre and has a layer of pips round the inside of the rather watery flesh (except for a water melon – see entry below). The best-known types of melon are:

Canteloup Almost round in shape, with a dark-green, segmented skin and pinkish-yellow flesh.

Tiger A segmented melon, similar to a canteloup, with striped or spotted green and yellow skin.

Charentais Small melons (each serves 1–2), with deep yellowish-green skin, deep yellow flesh, quite a pronounced, distinctive flavour and a slightly perfumed smell.

Honeydew Oval in shape, with dark-green, ridged skin or pale greenish-white skin and greenish-yellow flesh.

Ogen Small melons with yellowish-orange skin with faint green stripes, yellow flesh.

Water melon Large round or oval melons with a smooth, green skin and pinkish-red, watery flesh, in which large flat seeds are embedded. (They have no hollow in the centre.)

Available June–September.

Melon is usually served raw as an appetiser or in fruit salads, although it can be used for jam, pickles or chutney.

Mulberry

A fruit similar in shape to a blackberry, but rather larger, with red flesh, darkening to deep purple when fully ripe. They are not produced commercially, and with the disappearance of many large old gardens the trees are becoming increasingly rare.

Mulberries can be eaten raw or stewed and they can be mixed with other fruit (eg apples) to make into jam.

In season August–September.

Nectarine

This fruit is closely related to the peach, which it resembles in flavour and texture, but the skin is shiny and smooth. Nectarines can be grown in hothouses in this country, but are generally imported. They are usually eaten raw and can also replace peaches in any recipe.

In season July–August (home-grown) and December–May and August–September (imported).

Orange

The fruit of an evergreen tree grown in hot climates in many parts of the world. There are two main types, sweet and bitter.

THE SWEET ORANGE

Jaffa Large thick, rough skinned orange, deep orange in colour. Very sweet and juicy flesh. Imported from Israel. December–April

Ovals Small oval shaped orange with golden-yellow skin and flesh. Imported from Cyprus from December–April.

Navels So called because of the characteristic growth at

one end of the orange. Has very sweet and juicy flesh. Imported from Spain, Morocco and Australia. Available all year round.

Bloods This orange has red flecks in the flesh and a red tinge to the skin. Imported from Spain from February–April.

Valencia Lates Medium sized orange with thin, smooth skin. Has delicate flavour and very juicy flesh. Imported from Cyprus, Spain and Israel. Available from March–May.

Sweet oranges are usually eaten raw as a dessert and in many fruit sweets, although they can be included in cooked sweets. The rind and juice are used as a flavouring in many sweets and savoury dishes and the rind also makes a garnish. The juice of oranges is also made into many fruit drinks; sweet oranges can be mixed with other citrus fruits to make marmalade.

THE BITTER OR SEVILLE ORANGE
Has a thin rind and sour, juicy flesh. It is too bitter to eat as dessert and is used for making marmalade, wines and cordials and in sauces and relishes, especially those served with duck.

Oranges are imported all the year round, from many countries.

Ortanique
A cross between an orange and a tangerine, this fruit comes from Jamaica.

In season January–April.

Papaw
This fruit is often considered medicinal because of its high vitamin content: it has vitamins A, B, C and calcium. Large tropical fruit with smooth skin which ripens from green to yellow to orange. The pulp is orange-pink and the seed lies in the centre of the fruit.

Available all year round but very scarce.

Passion fruit *(Granadilla)*
Many different forms are grown. The American passion fruit has a hard brown skin and soft, pulpy, seedy flesh, with a refreshing distinctive flavour. The flesh is scooped out with a teaspoon and eaten with a little sugar.

Although passion fruit are only occasionally available fresh, the pulped flesh is obtainable in cans and may be used in fruit creams, jellies and fruit salads.

Peach
A round, fleshy fruit with a velvety skin, yellowish-orange, often tinged with red. The flesh is pale or deep orange-yellow. There is a fairly large central stone, which separates easily from the flesh in a 'freestone' peach; in a 'clingstone' the flesh and stone are not easily separated. Peaches are imported from various countries and are also widely sold in canned form. They can be grown in the South of England, usually in hothouses.

In season: South African – January–March; French – June–August; Italian – June–September; Home-grown – June–August.

Pear
There is a great variety of pears, both dessert and cooking types. Many are grown in this country, but large quantities are also imported.

Well-known dessert pears are Williams, Comice, Conference, Laxton's and Clapp's Favourite. Well-known cookers are Bartlett and Kieffer.

Most pears, whether dessert or cooking, are better if taken from the trees when fully formed but not yet ripe, then ripened in the house; this applies particularly to dessert pears, which soon become 'woolly' and over-ripe if not watched.

Pears can be eaten as a dessert, stewed, used in fruit sweets and made into preserves.

They can be obtained nearly all the year round, the home-grown ones being supplemented by the imported ones.

Persimmon
An imported fruit, about the size of a large tomato, with a fairly leathery, yellowish-orange skin and pulpy flesh. Some types are seedless, others have seeds.

Persimmons have an acid taste and can be used in jellies and fruit sweets and made into jams.

In season March–November.

Pineapple
A tropical fruit, almost cylindrical in shape, topped by a tuft of grey-green, pointed leaves; it has hard, ridged skin of a deep orange colour and firm yet juicy flesh, varying in colour between cream and deep yellow. The outer surface contains a large number of 'eyes' which must be cut out before the fruit can be eaten.

There are many different varieties of pineapple, varying in size and flavour. Fresh ones are imported all year round. Pineapple is widely bought in the canned form – as rings, spears, chunks and pulp; pineapple juice is also canned.

Available all the year round.

Plum
There are many different varieties of this stone fruit, varying in size and ranging in colour through gold and red to deep purple. Some are used mainly for cooking (being stewed, used in pies and puddings and made into preserves), while some may be used for both cooking and dessert.

Cooking plums Santa Rosa, Gaviora, Kelsey, Golden King.

Cooking and eating plums Victoria, Greengage Plums, Prune Plums, Czars, Pond's Seedling, Monarch.

In season: South African – January–April; Spanish – May–July; Home-grown – July–September.

Pomegranate
A fruit the size of an orange, with a hard, russet-coloured skin and red flesh containing a mass of hard seeds. The whole fruit can be served as a dessert or the juice can be added to fruit salads and fruit drinks.

In season October–November.

Prune
Prunes are dried plums and have dark brown, almost black, wrinkled flesh. Good quality plump prunes can be eaten in their dry form – they are usually stoned and stuffed with nuts, marzipan, etc, to make an appetiser or sweet. Usually, however, prunes are used in cooked fruit sweets and puddings. French plums are considered to give the finest prunes, but most of those sold in this country are imported from California; they are known as Californian or Santa Clare prunes and are available all the year round.

Quince
A fruit very similar to a japonica (see separate entry), though larger. It was widely used in cookery in the Middle Ages, but nowadays it is not very common, being usually home grown rather than sold on a commercial scale. The fruit is shaped like an apple or pear and has yellowish or russet-coloured skin, with a soft down on the outside when ripe, hard, sour flesh and a lot of seeds.

Quinces can be eaten raw, but are usually made into preserves such as marmalades and jellies. Small quantities of quince can be cooked with apples to give them added flavour.

In season September–November.

Raspberry
A soft, juicy fruit, red in colour, with a central hull. Raspberries have a delicious sweet yet slightly acid flavour. They can be eaten as a dessert, used either raw or cooked in fruit sweets, puddings and pies, or made into preserves.

In season June–September (home-grown), May–June (imported). Frozen raspberries are available all the year round.

Rhubarb
Though really the stem of a plant, this is usually classed as a fruit. 'Forced' rhubarb, which appears from December to March, is pink and tender, having a very fresh flavour. Home grown outdoor rhubarb, available from March–June, is green tinged with red, and is firmer and thicker, with a stronger, more acid flavour. Rhubarb is always cooked and is used in fruit puddings and pies and in preserves.

The leaves of rhubarb must not be eaten, as they are poisonous.

Rosehip
The fruit of the wild rose, amber-red in colour and with hairy seeds. Rose hips are inedible raw, but as they have a high vitamin C content they are made into a syrup which is given to young children.

Sloe
The fruit of the blackthorn tree, considered by many to be the originator of the modern plum. The tree grows wild in the hedgerows and the fruits, which ripen in late summer, are like small plums of a dark blue-black colour and sour taste.

Sloes are usually made into wine or used in sloe gin in this country; in continental Europe they are also made into jams.

Strawberry
Widely grown in England, strawberries are a very popular soft fruit, red in colour; the juicy flesh grows round a central hull and has small pips embedded in the outer surface.

Home grown fruit is in season from the end of April to September, and a small late crop comes along in September and October. Strawberries are also imported at other times. Frozen strawberries are obtainable all the year.

Tangerine
A small type of orange, with a thin, easily removed rind, sweet flesh and many rather large pips. Tangerines are usually served raw as a dessert, but the rind and juice can be used as a flavouring in fruit salads and other fruit sweets and in puddings or cakes. Tangerines can also be used in a mixed citrus fruit marmalade.

Clementine A form of tangerine with a closer rind, more like that of an orange. It is almost seedless and less sweet than a tangerine. In season December–February.

Mandarin Flatter in shape than a tangerine, with a thin, slightly darker orange rind and sweeter flesh. In season October–March.

Satsuma A form of seedless mandarin grown in Spain. In season October–February.

Ugli *(Tangelo)*
A cross between a tangerine and grapefruit, the size of a grapefruit but more pointed at the stem end. The ugli has a thick, loose, greenish-yellow skin and yellow flesh. It is imported from Jamaica and is in season October–November.

Hot puddings

Few other countries having anything like the range of hot puddings that have been devised in British kitchens – particularly our sponge and suet puddings, both steamed and baked, and our various fruit and other baked sweets. Perhaps the climate has had a lot to do with it – on a cold damp day there's something peculiarly comforting about a steaming-hot syrup sponge, sugared pancake or perhaps one of the many Fruit Charlotte variations.

In this chapter we include the following groups: baked puddings, sub-divided into sponges, pastry and fruit; steamed puddings, covering both sponge and suet types; milk puddings; custards; soufflés; batters (including fritters and pancakes) and waffles. For recipes for the various pastries, see pages 350 to 357.

BAKED SPONGE PUDDINGS

Plain baked sponge

75 g *(3 oz)* butter or margarine
75 g *(3 oz)* caster sugar
1 egg, beaten
150 g *(5 oz)* self raising flour
2.5 ml *(½ tsp)* vanilla essence
milk to mix

Grease 600–900-ml *(1–1½-pt)* pie dish. Cream the fat and sugar until pale and fluffy. Add the egg a little at a time, beating after each addition. Fold in the flour with the essence and a little milk to give a dropping consistency. Put into the prepared dish and bake in the oven at 180°C *(350°F)* mark 4 for 30–40 minutes, until well risen and golden. Serve with syrup sauce or custard. *Serves 3–4.*

This sponge pudding can be varied in several ways – for instance:

Jam sponge
Put 30–45 ml *(2–3 tbsps)* jam in a layer over the bottom of the greased dish before adding the sponge mixture. Serve with a jam or a sweet white sauce.

Baked castle puddings
Grease 8 small individual foil dishes or dariole moulds and put 5–10 ml *(1–2 tsps)* jam in the bottom of each. Divide the mixture between the dishes or moulds, bake for 20 minutes and serve with jam sauce.

Orange and lemon sponge
Add the grated rind of an orange or lemon to the creamed mixture and replace the milk by the fruit juice. Serve with an orange or lemon sauce.

Spicy fruit sponge
Sift 2.5 ml *(½ level tsp)* mixed spice with the flour. Add 75–100 g *(3–4 oz)* sultanas or currants and 25–50 g *(1–2 oz)* chopped glacé cherries or cut mixed peel with the flour. Serve with white sauce or custard.

Chocolate sponge
Add 45 ml *(3 level tbsps)* cocoa, sifted with the flour, or stir 25 g *(1 oz)* chocolate dots or chips into the mixture. Serve with chocolate sauce.

Coconut sponge
Replace 25 g *(1 oz)* of the flour by 25 g *(1 oz)* desiccated coconut; omit the vanilla essence.

Ratatouille (p. 210).

Ginger sponge
Sift 2.5 ml *(½ level tsp)* ground ginger with the flour, or add 2 pieces of preserved ginger, finely chopped, and 10 ml *(2 tsps)* of the ginger syrup to the mixture. Serve with a sauce made from golden syrup, thinned down with hot water.

Eve's pudding

450 g *(1 lb)* cooking apples, peeled and cored
75 g *(3 oz)* demerara sugar
grated rind of 1 lemon
15 ml *(1 tbsp)* water
75 g *(3 oz)* butter or margarine
75 g *(3 oz)* caster sugar
1 egg, beaten
125 g *(5 oz)* self raising flour
milk to mix

Slice the apples thinly into a greased 900-ml *(1½-pt)* ovenproof dish and sprinkle the demerara sugar and grated lemon rind over them. Add the 15 ml *(1 tbsp)* water. Cream the fat and sugar until pale and fluffy. Add the egg a little at a time, beating well after each addition. Fold in the flour with a little milk to give a dropping consistency and spread the mixture over the apples. Bake in the oven at 180°C *(350°F)* mark 4 for 40–45 minutes, until the apples are tender and the sponge mixture cooked.

Pineapple upside-down pudding

50 g *(2 oz)* butter
50 g *(2 oz)* brown sugar
226-g *(8-oz)* can pineapple rings, drained
100 g *(4 oz)* butter or margarine
100 g *(4 oz)* caster sugar
2 eggs, beaten
175 g *(6 oz)* self raising flour
30–45 ml *(2–3 tbsps)* pineapple juice or milk

Grease an 18-cm *(7-in)* round cake tin. Cream together the butter and brown sugar and spread it over the bottom of the tin. Alternatively, use 30–45 ml *(2–3 tbsps)* golden syrup. Arrange the rings of pineapple on this layer in the bottom of the tin. Cream together the remaining fat and sugar until pale and fluffy. Add the beaten egg a little at a time and beat well after each addition. Fold in the flour, adding some pineapple juice or milk to give a dropping consistency, and spread on top of the pineapple rings. Bake in the oven at 180°C *(350°F)* mark 4 for about 45 minutes. Turn out on to a dish and serve with a pineapple sauce made by thickening the remaining juice with a little cornflour.

Chocolate pear upside-down pudding
Use canned pear halves instead of pineapple. Substitute 25 g *(1 oz)* cocoa powder for 25 g *(1 oz)* flour in the sponge mixture.

Rhubarb ginger upside-down pudding
Cut 225–350 g *(½–¾ lb)* trimmed rhubarb into 2.5-cm *(1-in)* lengths (or peel, core and thinly slice 2 cooking apples). Arrange the fruit over the layer of creamed fat and sugar or syrup. Make up the cake mixture, using soft brown sugar instead of white, and sift 5–10 ml *(1–2 level tsps)* powdered ginger with the flour.

Lemon layer pudding

juice and grated rind of 1 lemon
50 g *(2 oz)* butter
100 g *(4 oz)* sugar
2 eggs, separated
300 ml *(½ pt)* milk
50 g *(2 oz)* self raising flour

Add the lemon rind to the butter and sugar and cream the mixture until pale and fluffy. Add the egg yolks and flour and beat well. Stir in the milk and 30–45 ml *(2–3 tbsps)* lemon juice. Whisk the egg whites stiffly, fold in and pour the mixture into a fairly large greased ovenproof dish – about 1.3-l *(2¼-pt)*. Stand the dish in a shallow tin of water and cook in the oven at 200°C *(400°F)* mark 6 for about 45 minutes, or until the top is set and spongy to the touch.

Note This pudding separates out in the cooking into a custard layer with a sponge topping.

Baked stuffed potatoes (p. 226).

Bread pudding

225 g *(8 oz)* white bread, preferably stale
300 ml *(½ pt)* milk
100 g *(4 oz)* currants, sultanas or stoned raisins
50 g *(2 oz)* mixed peel, chopped very finely
50 g *(2 oz)* shredded suet
50 g *(2 oz)* demerara sugar
5–10 ml *(1–2 level tsps)* ground mixed spice
1 egg, beaten
a little milk to mix
nutmeg, optional

Butter a 900-ml *(1½-pt)* pie dish. Remove the crusts from the bread and break the crumb into small pieces; pour the 300 ml *(½ pt)* milk over it and leave to soak for ½ hour, then beat out the lumps. Add the cleaned dried fruit, the peel, suet, sugar and spice and mix well. Add the egg, with a little extra milk if required to make the mixture of a dropping consistency. Pour it into the pie dish, grate a little nutmeg over if you wish and bake in the oven at 180°C *(350°F)* mark 4 for about 1½–2 hours. Dredge with sugar before serving.

The peel may be replaced by an extra 50 g *(2 oz)* dried fruit, if you prefer.

PASTRY SWEETS

Where a quantity such as 100 g *(4 oz)* pastry is given, this indicates pastry made with 100 g *(4 oz)* flour, not the finished weight. If ready-made pastry is intended the packet size is given.

Syrup tart

100 g *(4 oz)* shortcrust pastry, (see page 351)
90 ml *(6 tbsps)* golden syrup
50 g *(2 oz)* fresh white breadcrumbs
grated rind of ½ lemon

Roll out the pastry and line a shallow 18-cm *(7-in)* shallow pie plate. Mix together the syrup, breadcrumbs and lemon rind. Spread the mixture in the pastry case, keeping the border free. Make cuts down the border at 2.5-cm *(1-in)* intervals and fold over each strip to form a triangle. Cook in the oven at 220°C *(425°F)* mark 7 for about 20 minutes or until golden brown. Serve hot or cold.

Mincemeat lattice tart *see colour plate facing p. 448*

200 g *(7 oz)* shortcrust pastry (see page 351)
2 cooking apples, peeled and sliced thinly or grated
lemon juice
120 ml *(8 level tbsps)* mincemeat

Roll out the pastry and use it to line a 20.5-cm *(8-in)* pie plate or flan dish. Trim the edges and keep the trimmings for the lattice. Cover the bottom of the pastry case with the apples and sprinkle or brush the apples with lemon juice. Spread the mincemeat over the apples in an even layer. Roll out the remaining pastry and cut into strips 0.5 cm *(¼ in)* wide. Arrange the strips of pastry across the top of the mincemeat to form a criss-cross pattern. Bake in the oven at 200°C *(400°F)* mark 6 for about 30 minutes. Serve warm.

Dutch apple pie

700 g *(1½ lb)* cooking apples, peeled and quartered
60 ml *(4 tbsps)* water
100 g *(4 oz)* light soft brown sugar
15 ml *(1 level tbsp)* cornflour or arrowroot
2.5 ml *(½ level tsp)* salt
5 ml *(1 level tsp)* ground cinnamon
30 ml *(2 tbsps)* lemon juice
25 g *(1 oz)* butter or margarine
2.5 ml *(½ tsp)* vanilla essence
250 g *(9 oz)* shortcrust pastry (see page 351)
a little milk to glaze

Simmer the apples with the water until soft. Mix together the sugar, cornflour or arrowroot, salt and cinnamon and add to the cooked apples. Stir in the lemon juice and cook, stirring, until fairly thick. Remove from the heat, stir in the butter and essence and cool. Roll out half of the pastry and line a 22-cm *(8½-in)* greased pie plate; put the cooked apples in the pastry case. Roll out the remaining pastry to make a lid. Damp the edges of the pastry on the plate and cover with the lid, pressing the edges well together; flake and scallop the edges. Make short slashes with a knife into the centre. Brush the top with milk put the plate on a baking sheet and bake in the oven at 200°C *(400°F)* mark 6 for about 1 hour. Cover loosely with foil after 30 minutes to prevent it over-browning. Serve hot or cold, with cream or custard.

Fruit pie

700 g *(1½ lb)* cooking fruit, eg apples, plums or rhubarb
100 g *(4 oz)* sugar
15 ml *(1 tbsp)* water
250 g *(9 oz)* shortcrust pastry, (see page 351)
caster sugar

Prepare the fruit as for stewing and layer it with the sugar into a pie dish, about 1.1-l *(2-pt)* capacity. Add the water. Roll out the pastry 0.5 cm *(¼ in)* thick to the shape and size of the pie dish. Cut off a strip of the pastry wide enough to cover the rim, wet this and press the strip on. Again roll the pastry out to the size of the dish. Moisten the strip of pastry and cover with the lid, pressing the edges well together. Trim, flake and scallop the edges. Make a hole in the centre of the pastry. Bake in the oven at 200°C *(400°F)* mark 6 for 30–40 minutes until the pastry is lightly browned, and the fruit is cooked. Sprinkle with caster sugar.

Variations

1. A spice can be added with the sugar, eg 5 ml *(1 level tsp)* ground ginger with rhubarb, 5 ml *(1 level tsp)* ground cinnamon with gooseberries or plums.
2. Fruits such as apple can be given more flavour and colour by mixing them with blackberries or raspberries, when in season.

Gooseberry marshmallow tart

450 g *(1 lb)* gooseberries, topped and tailed
175 g *(6 oz)* sugar
30 ml *(2 level tbsps)* cornflour
2.5 ml *(½ level tsp)* ground cinnamon
2.5 ml *(½ level tsp)* ground nutmeg
pinch of ground cloves
200 g *(7 oz)* shortcrust pastry (see page 351)
100 g *(¼ lb)* marshmallows

Put the prepared gooseberries into a pan with a little water, stew until soft and add 100 g *(4 oz)* of the sugar. Blend the remaining sugar, the cornflour and spices with a little cold water, add to the fruit and continue to cook until the mixture thickens. Roll out the pastry and use it to line a deep 20.5-cm *(8-in)* flan case; trim the edges and crimp them. Put the cooled fruit mixture into the pastry case. Roll out the trimmings, cut into thin strips and arrange in a lattice on top of the fruit. Bake in the oven at 220°C *(425°F)* mark 7 for 25–30 minutes. Remove from the oven, place a marshmallow in each sqaure of the lattice work and return the tart to the oven for a further 5–10 minutes, to brown the marshmallows. Serve with cream or custard.

Lemon meringue pie

150 g *(5 oz)* shortcrust pastry (see page 351)
45 ml *(3 level tbsps)* cornflour
150 ml *(¼ pt)* water
juice and grated rind of 2 lemons
100 g *(4 oz)* sugar
2 eggs, separated
75 g *(3 oz)* caster sugar
glacé cherries and angelica

Roll out the pastry and use it to line an 18-cm *(7-in)* flan case or deep pie plate. Trim the edges and bake blind in the oven at 220°C *(425°F)* mark 7 for 15 minutes (see page 357). Remove the paper and baking beans and return the case to the oven for a further 5 minutes. Reduce the oven temperature to 180°C *(350°F)* mark 4. Mix the cornflour with the water in a saucepan, add the lemon juice and grated rind and bring slowly to the boil, stirring until the mixture thickens, then add the sugar. Remove from the heat, cool the mixture slightly and add the egg yolks. Pour into the pastry case. Whisk the egg whites stiffly, whisk in half the caster sugar and fold in the rest. Pile the meringue on top of the lemon filling and bake in the oven for about 10 minutes, or until the meringue is crisp and lightly browned. Decorate before serving with cherries and angelica.

Apricot amber

200 g *(7 oz)* shortcrust or flan pastry (see page 351)
425-g *(15-oz)* can apricots
2 eggs, separated
25 g *(1 oz)* butter, melted
50 g *(2 oz)* caster sugar

Roll out the pastry and use it to line a 20·5-cm *(8-in)* flan case; trim the edges and crimp. Bake blind in the oven at 220°C *(425°F)* mark 7 for 15 minutes (see page 357). Drain the apricots and sieve them. Stir the egg yolks and melted butter into the pulp and pour it into the cooked flan case. Reduce the oven temperature to 180°C *(350°F)* mark 4 and cook the flan for 15 minutes, or until the filling is lightly set. Whisk the egg whites stiffly, whisk in half the sugar and fold in the rest of the sugar. Pile on top of the apricot filling. Put the apricot amber back in the oven and cook for about 10 minutes, or until lightly browned.

Apple amber
Replace the apricots with stewed apples.

Double-crust black-currant pie

450 g *(1 lb)* black-currants
100 g *(4 oz)* sugar
30 ml *(2 level tbsps)* flour
250 g *(9 oz)* shortcrust pastry (see page 351)
milk to glaze

String, pick over and wash the fruit and mix it with the sugar and flour. Roll out half the pastry and use it to line a 22-cm *(8½-in)* greased deep pie plate. Fill the plate with the fruit mixture and roll out the remaining pastry to form a lid. Damp the edges of the pastry on the dish and cover with the lid, pressing the edges well together. Flake and scallop the edges, cut short slashes into the centre with a knife and brush the top with milk. Put the plate on a baking sheet and bake in the oven at 200°C *(400°F)* mark 6 for about 1 hour. Cover it loosely with foil after 30 minutes to prevent over-browning.

Variations
Most other fruits can be used, such as red-currants, gooseberries, apples, rhubarb, bilberries, blackberries and apples; prepare as for stewing and make up as above. With apples, gooseberries or rhubarb the grated rind of ½ a lemon or a sprinkle of ground ginger or cinnamon mixed with the sugar improves the flavour. Alternatively, 3–4 whole cloves can be used to give flavour in an apple pie.

Bakewell tart *see colour plate between pp. 432 and 433*

100 g *(4 oz)* flaky or rough puff pastry (see page 354)
15–30 ml *(1–2 tbsps)* raspberry jam
50 g *(2 oz)* butter or margarine
50 g *(2 oz)* caster sugar
grated rind and juice of ½ lemon
1 egg, beaten
75 g *(3 oz)* cake crumbs, sieved
75 g *(3 oz)* ground almonds

Roll out the pastry thinly and line a deep 18-cm *(7-in)* pie plate. Spread the bottom of the pastry with the jam. Cream the fat and sugar with the lemon rind until pale and fluffy. Add the egg a little at a time and beat after each addition. Mix together the cake crumbs and ground almonds, fold half into the mixture with a tablespoon, then fold in the rest, with a little lemon juice if necessary to give a dropping consistency. Put the mixture into the pastry case and smooth the surface with a knife. Bake in the oven at 220°C *(425°F)* mark 7 for about 15 minutes, until the tart begins to brown; reduce the temperature to 180°C *(350°F)* mark 4 and cook for a further 20–30 minutes until the filling is firm to the touch. Serve hot or cold, with cream or custard.

Pumpkin pie

The traditional Thanksgiving dessert in the United States

450 g *(1 lb)* pumpkin
200 g *(7 oz)* shortcrust pastry (see page 351)
2 eggs, beaten
100 g *(4 oz)* caster sugar
60 ml *(4 tbsps)* milk
pinch ground nutmeg
pinch ground ginger
10 ml *(2 level tsps)* ground cinnamon

Cut the pumpkin into pieces, remove any seeds and cottonwoolly inside part and cut off the outside skin. Steam the pieces of pumpkin between 2 plates over a pan of boiling water until tender – 15–20 minutes – and drain thoroughly. Mash well with a fork or purée in an electric blender.

Roll out the pastry and use it to line a 20.5-cm *(8-in)* flan case or deep pie plate; trim and decorate the edges. Beat the eggs with the sugar. Add the pumpkin, milk and spices. Blend well and pour into the pastry case. Bake in the oven at 220°C *(425°F)* mark 7 for 15 minutes, then reduce the temperature to 180°C *(350°F)* mark 4 and bake for a further 30 minutes or until the filling is set. Serve warm, with cream.

Pecan pie

100 g *(4 oz)* blended vegetable fat
25 g *(1 oz)* butter
175 g *(6 oz)* plain flour
pinch of salt
45 ml *(3 tbsps)* cold water

For the filling

3 eggs
15 ml *(1 tbsp)* milk
175 g *(6 oz)* demerara sugar
150 ml *(¼ pt)* maple or corn syrup
50 g *(2 oz)* butter, softened
2.5 ml *(½ tsp)* vanilla essence
175 g *(6 oz)* pecan nuts, halved

Cream together the white fat and butter. Gradually stir in the sifted flour and salt; cream well after each addition. Add the water and mix thoroughly with the hands. Knead lightly with extra flour, as this pastry is sticky to handle. Chill. Roll out the pastry and line a 23-cm *(9-in)* ovenproof flan dish; flute the edge. Chill this case while preparing the filling.

Beat the eggs and milk together. Boil the sugar and syrup together in a saucepan for 3 minutes. Slowly pour on to the beaten eggs and stir in the butter and essence. Use half the nuts to cover the base of the pastry case, spoon the syrup mixture over and cover with the remaining nuts. Bake in the oven at 220°C *(425°F)* mark 7 for 10 minutes. Reduce the heat to 170°C *(325°F)* mark 3 and cook for a further 45 minutes, until the filling is set. Serve warm or cold with unsweetened whipped cream. *Serves 6–8.*

Apple dumplings

250 g *(9 oz)* shortcrust pastry (see page 351)
4 even sized cooking apples
50 g *(2 oz)* sugar
milk to glaze
caster sugar

Divide the pastry into four and roll out each piece into a round 20–25 cm *(8–10 in)* across. Peel and core the apples, place one on each round and fill the centre with some of the sugar. Moisten the edges of the pastry with water, gather the edges to the top, pressing well to seal them together, and turn the dumplings over. If you wish, decorate with leaves cut from any trimmings of pastry. Brush the tops with milk. Bake on a greased baking sheet in the oven at 220°C *(425°F)* mark 7 for 10 minutes, then reduce the temperature to 170°C *(325°F)* mark 3 and continue to cook for a further 30 minutes, until the apples are soft. Dredge with caster sugar and eat hot or cold, with custard or cream.

Apfel strudel

225 g *(8 oz)* plain flour
2.5 ml *(½ level tsp)* salt
1 egg, slightly beaten
30 ml *(2 tbsps)* oil
60 ml *(4 tbsps)* lukewarm water
45 ml *(3 tbsps)* seedless raisins
45 ml *(3 tbsps)* currants
75 g *(3 oz)* caster sugar
2.5 ml *(½ level tsp)* ground cinnamon
1 kg *(2¼ lb)* cooking apples, peeled and grated
45 ml *(3 tbsps)* melted butter
100 g *(4 oz)* ground almonds
icing sugar

Put the flour and salt in a large bowl, make a well in the centre and pour in the egg and oil. Add the water gradually, stirring with a fork to make a soft, sticky dough. Work the dough in the bowl until it leaves the sides, turn it out on to a lightly floured surface and knead for 15 minutes. Form into a ball, place on a cloth and cover with a warmed bowl. Leave to 'rest' in a warm place for an hour.

Mix thoroughly the raisins, currants, sugar, cinnamon and apples.

Warm the rolling pin. Spread a clean old cotton tablecloth on the table and sprinkle lightly with 15–30 ml *(1–2 level tbsps)* flour. Place the dough on the cloth and roll out into a rectangle about 0.3 cm *(⅛ in)* thick, lifting and turning it to prevent its sticking to the cloth. Gently stretch the dough, working from the centre to the outside and using the backs of the hands, until it is paper-thin. Trim the edges to form a rectangle about 68 by 60 cm *(27 by 24 in)*. Leave to dry and 'rest' for 15 minutes.

Arrange the dough with one of the long sides towards you, brush it with melted butter and sprinkle with ground almonds. Spread the apple mixture over the dough, leaving a 5-cm *(2-in)* border uncovered all round the edge. Fold these pastry edges over the apple mixture, towards the centre. Lift the corners of the cloth nearest to you up and over the pastry, causing the strudel to roll up, but stop after each turn, to pat it into shape and to keep the roll even. Form the roll into a horseshoe shape, brush it with melted butter and slide it on to a lightly buttered baking sheet. Bake in the oven at 190°C *(375°F)* mark 5 for about 40 minutes or until golden brown. Dust with icing sugar and serve hot or cold, with cream. *Serves 6–8.*

Individual apfel strudel
Cut the rolled out dough into strips 23 cm by 15 cm *(9 in by 6 in)* and spread with the fruit mixture, leaving a 2-cm *(¾-in)* border all round the edge. Fold in the borders. Roll it up from a short side, brush with melted butter, slide it on to a lightly buttered baking sheet and bake for about 35 minutes. When you are making individual strudels, you will find the dough much easier to handle if, as each piece is cut, you put it on a damp tea towel and then spread and roll it.

Choux puffs with plum rum sauce *see colour plate facing p. 449*

For choux pastry
50 g *(2 oz)* butter
150 ml *(¼ pt)* water
75 g *(2½ oz)* plain flour, sifted together with 25 g *(1 oz)* caster sugar
2 standard eggs
icing sugar
oil for deep frying

For the sauce
700 g *(1½ lb)* eating plums
100 g *(4 oz)* granulated sugar
600 ml *(1 pt)* water
15 ml *(1 level tbsp)* cornflour
90 ml *(6 tbsps)* rum
30 ml *(2 tbsps)* lemon juice
4 firm bananas

Make up the choux pastry in the usual way (page 355). Turn the paste into a fabric piping bag fitted with a medium star vegetable nozzle and chill whilst making the sauce. Wash, dry, halve and stone the plums and cut into quarters. Dissolve the granulated sugar in the water then fast-boil for 1–2 minutes. Add one-third of the plums and purée in an electric blender. Blend the cornflour with the rum and lemon juice, add to the puréed plums, bring to the boil to thicken, stirring. Add the rest of the plums and the roughly chopped bananas. Heat oil for deep frying to 182°C *(360°F)* and then pipe 4-cm *(1½-in)* lengths of choux into the oil. Fry, in about 3 batches, for 2–3 minutes turning once until puffed and golden. Drain on absorbent paper, keep warm. To serve, dredge with icing sugar and accompany with sauce. *Serves 6.*

Cheesecake

75 g *(3 oz)* self raising flour
30 ml *(2 level tbsps)* caster sugar
pinch salt
40 g *(1½ oz)* butter
little milk
350 g *(12 oz)* curd cheese, sieved
1 egg, separated
1 egg yolk
2 lemons
50 g *(2 oz)* caster sugar
142-ml *(5-fl oz)* carton double cream

Mix together the flour, sugar and salt. Rub in the butter until the mixture resembles fine breadcrumbs. Mix to a pliable dough with a little milk. Roll out to fit base of a greased shallow 28 cm by 18 cm *(11 in by 7 in)* tin. Bake in the oven at 190°C *(375°F)* mark 5 for 25 minutes until golden brown. Beat together the curd cheese, egg yolks, grated rind of one lemon and juice of one, caster sugar and lightly whipped cream. From the remaining rind cut slivers free of white pith; cut these into fine julienne strips. Stiffly whisk the egg white and fold it into the cheese mixture. Spread over the baked pastry, scatter julienne strips over and bake for a further 30–35 minutes at 190°C *(375°F)* mark 5 until the topping is set. Serve slightly warm, cut into squares and eat with a fork.

BAKED FRUIT PUDDINGS

Rum-glazed pears

6 large, firm eating pears
finely grated rind and juice of 1 lemon
150 g *(5 oz)* granulated sugar
15 ml *(1 tbsp)* rum
15 ml *(1 level tbsp)* arrowroot
30 ml *(2 tbsps)* cold water
double cream

Peel the pears thinly, keeping the stems intact; dip them in lemon juice to prevent discoloration. Sit the pears in a single layer in a saucepan. Pour over them the rest of the lemon juice and grated rind, with sufficient water to just cover the pears up to 2.5 cm *(1 in)*. Cover the pan, bring to the boil and simmer for about 20 minutes, until the pears are tender. Meanwhile, put the sugar into a heavy-based pan and cook over a medium heat, without stirring, until it caramelises;

cool slightly. Remove the pears from the pan and gradually stir the juices from the pan and the rum into the caramel, working with a wooden spoon to remove the caramel sediment from the pan base. Blend the arrowroot with the water and gradually add to the sauce, stirring all the time; bring to the boil. Replace the pears in the juices, cover and simmer for a further 15–20 minutes. Serve hot, with plenty of double cream. *Serves 6.*

Baked apples

4 medium sized cooking apples
60 ml *(4 tbsps)* water
demerara sugar
butter

Wipe the apples and make a shallow cut through the skin round the middle of each. Core the apples and stand them in an ovenproof dish. Pour the water round them, fill each apple with sugar and top with a small knob of butter. Bake in the oven at 200°C *(400°F)* mark 6 till the apples are soft – $\frac{3}{4}$–1 hour.

Variations

1. Stuff the centre of the apples with mincemeat instead of demerara sugar.
2. Stuff the apples with currants, sultanas, stoned raisins, chopped dried apricots, mixed peel or glacé fruits or with a mixture of chopped dates and walnuts or other nuts.
3. Put a marshmallow on each apple just before the end of the cooking and return the apples to the oven to brown the topping.
4. Pack the centres with chopped dates, grated orange rind and soft brown sugar.

Meringued apples

Bake 4 apples in the usual way. Just before the end of the cooking time remove them from the oven and strip off the top half of the skin. Whisk 2 egg whites stiffly and whisk in 50 g *(2 oz)* sugar. Whisk again and fold in another 50 g *(2 oz)* sugar. Cover the apples with the meringue and return them to the oven for a further 10–15 minutes, until the meringue is crisp and pale golden brown.

Mincemeat and apple round

75 g *(3 oz)* butter or margarine
175 g *(6 oz)* self raising flour
75 g *(3 oz)* sugar
1 egg, beaten
45–60 ml *(3–4 tbsps)* milk
30–45 ml *(2–3 tbsps)* mincemeat
1 cooking apple, peeled
15 ml *(1 level tbsp)* demerara sugar

Grease a baking sheet. Rub the fat into the flour and stir in the sugar. Add the egg and sufficient milk to give a fairly firm dough, knead lightly and cut into 2 pieces. Put on a floured board and roll out one half quite thinly into a round. Transfer to the baking sheet and spread with mincemeat to within about 1 cm *($\frac{1}{2}$ in)* of the edge. Grate the apple coarsely and spread thinly over the mincemeat. Roll out the remaining dough to make a lid; damp the edges of the dough on the tray, cover with the lid and press the edges firmly. Knock up the edges and make a small slit in the centre. Brush the top with milk and sprinkle with brown sugar. Bake in the oven at 190°C *(375°F)* mark 5 for 20–25 minutes, until golden and crisp.

Fruit crumble

700 g *(1$\frac{1}{2}$ lb)* raw fruit, eg apples, plums, gooseberries, rhubarb, blackcurrants
granulated sugar
75 g *(3 oz)* margarine or butter
175 g *(6 oz)* plain flour

Prepare the fruit as for stewing and layer it in a 900-ml–1.1 l *(1$\frac{1}{2}$–2 pt)* ovenproof dish with 100–175 g *(4–6 oz)* sugar, depending on the sharpness of the fruit. Rub the fat into the flour until the mixture is the texture of fine crumbs; stir in 50 g *(2 oz)* sugar. Sprinkle the mixture on top of the prepared fruit and bake in the oven at 200°C *(400°F)* mark 6 for 30–40 minutes. Alternatively, stew the fruit before putting it in the dish and bake for 20–30 minutes. Serve with custard or cream. *Serves 4–6.*

Variations

1. Add 5 ml *(1 level tsp)* ground cinnamon, mixed spice or ginger to the flour before rubbing in the fat.
2. Add 50 g *(2 oz)* chopped crystallised ginger to the crumb mixture before sprinkling it over the prepared fruit.
3. Add the grated rind of an orange or lemon to the crumb mixture before sprinkling it on the fruit.
4. Roughly crush 30 ml *(2 tbsps)* cornflakes and add them to the rubbed-in mixture with demerara sugar in place of granulated sugar.

Apple and blackberry charlotte

450 g *(1 lb)* cooking apples, peeled
450 g *(1 lb)* blackberries
rind and juice of ½ lemon
1.25 ml *(¼ level tsp)* ground cinnamon
50 g *(2 oz)* melted butter
6 slices from a large white loaf
175–225 g *(6–8 oz)* sugar
30 ml *(2 tbsps)* bread or cake crumbs

Quarter the apples and remove the cores. Wash and pick over the blackberries. Stew the fruit in a pan with the lemon rind, juice and cinnamon. Brush a charlotte mould or a 12.5-cm *(5-in)* cake tin generously with melted butter. Cut the crusts off the bread. Trim one piece to a round the same size as the base of the tin, dip it into the melted butter and fit into the bottom of the tin. Dip the remaining slices of bread in the butter and arrange closely around the side of the tin, reserving one piece for the top. Add the sugar and crumbs to the stewed fruit, mix well and fill the tin. Cover with the remaining slice of bread, trimmed to fit the top of the mould. Cook in the oven at 190°C *(375°F)* mark 5 for about 1 hour, turn out and serve with custard or cream.

This is the traditional charlotte recipe. It is often made with apples alone; any other stewed fruit, or a mixture, may be used in the same way. For a quicker version, see rhubarb betty below.

Fruit cobbler *see colour plate between pp. 432 and 433*

225 g *(8 oz)* self raising flour
pinch of salt
50 g *(2 oz)* butter or margarine
30 ml *(2 level tbsps)* caster sugar
about 150 ml *(¼ pt)* milk
sweetened cooked fruit, eg plums, blackberries and apples, apricots, gooseberries
milk to glaze

Sift the flour and salt, rub in the fat to the texture of fine crumbs and stir in the sugar. Make a well in the centre and add sufficient milk to give a soft but manageable dough. Turn it on to a lightly floured board, knead lightly and roll out the dough to 1 cm *(½ in)* thick; cut out rounds with a 4-cm *(1½-in)* fluted cutter. Place enough cooked fruit in an ovenproof dish, to half-fill it. Arrange the rounds overlapping round the edge of the dish and glaze them with a little milk. Bake in the oven at 220°C *(425°F)* mark 7 for 10–15 minutes, until the topping is golden brown.

Rhubarb betty

700 g *(1½ lb)* rhubarb, trimmed and wiped
100 g *(4 oz)* fresh white breadcrumbs
75 g *(3 oz)* demerara sugar
75 g *(3 oz)* shredded suet
grated rind of 1 lemon, or 5 ml *(1 level tsp)* ground ginger or cinnamon
knob of butter

Grease a 900 ml–1.1 l *(1½–2 pt)* ovenproof dish. Cut the rhubarb into short lengths. Mix together the crumbs, sugar, suet and lemon rind or ginger. Put half the fruit in the dish and cover with half the crumb mixture. Add the remaining fruit and top with the remaining crumbs. Dot with the butter and bake in the oven at 180°C *(350°F)* mark 4 for about 45 minutes, or until the fruit is soft and the topping crisp.

Baked mincemeat or jam roly-poly

Make like a steamed roly-poly (see mincemeat roly-poly, page 300), but bake in the oven at 200°C *(400°F)* mark 6 for about 1 hour.

Cherries in red wine

450 g *(1 lb)* fresh red cherries
150 ml *(¼ pt)* water
75 g *(3 oz)* granulated sugar
150 ml *(¼ pt)* red wine
15 ml *(1 tbsp)* red-currant jelly
small piece cinnamon stick

Discard the cherry stalks and if you prefer remove the stones with a cherry stoner. In a pan, bring the water, sugar, wine, red-currant jelly and the cinnamon stick to the boil. Add the cherries, return it to the boil, reduce the heat and simmer, uncovered, for about 10 minutes. Use a draining spoon to take out the cherries and place them in a serving dish. Bring the juices to the boil and boil rapidly to reduce a little then strain over the cherries. Serve warm, not hot or cold, with thick cream.

STEAMED PUDDINGS

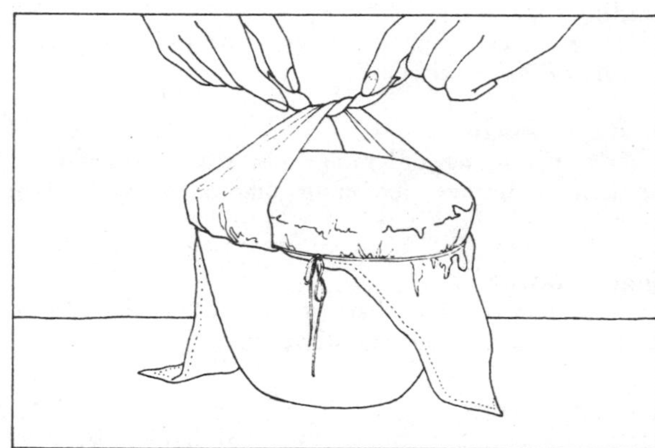

Covering a basin with a pudding cloth (see Christmas pudding, page 301)

General rules for steaming

1. Put on the steamer with the base half-filled with water so that this is boiling by the time the pudding is made. If you have no steamer, fill a large saucepan with water to come halfway up the pudding basin. Bring this to the boil.
2. Grease the pudding basin well, and put a round of greased greaseproof paper in the base.
3. Cut double greaseproof paper or a piece of foil to cover the pudding basin and grease well. If you wish put a pleat in the paper or foil to allow the pudding room to rise.
4. Fill the basin not more than two-thirds full with mixture.
5. Cover the basin tightly with the paper or foil to prevent steam or water entering. Secure with string.
6. Keep the water in the steamer boiling rapidly all the time and have a kettle of boiling water ready to top it up regularly, or the steamer will tend to boil dry. If you are using a saucepan, put an old saucer or crossed skewers in the base to keep the basin off the bottom. Keep the water gently bubbling so that the basin just wobbles. Top up as necessary from a kettle.

Plain sponge pudding

100 g *(4 oz)* butter or margarine
100 g *(4 oz)* caster sugar
2 eggs, beaten
a few drops of vanilla essence
175 g *(6 oz)* self raising flour
a little milk to mix

Half-fill a steamer or large saucepan with water and put it on to boil. Grease a 900-ml *(1½-pt)* pudding basin. Cream together the fat and sugar until pale and fluffy. Add the beaten eggs and the essence a little at a time and beat well after each addition. Using a metal spoon, fold in half the sifted flour, then fold in the rest, with enough milk to give a dropping consistency. Put the mixture into the basin, cover with greased greaseproof paper or foil and secure with string. Steam for 1½ hours. Serve with jam sauce (see page 204).

This basic recipe can be varied as follows:

Jam sponge pudding

Put 30 ml *(2 tbsps)* jam into the bottom of the greased pudding basin before adding the pudding mixture. Serve with a custard sauce or jam sauce.

Syrup sponge pudding

Put 30 ml *(2 tbsps)* golden syrup into the bottom of the basin before adding the mixture. If you wish flavour the mixture with the grated rind of a lemon.

Fruit sponge pudding
Put a shallow layer of drained canned fruit or a layer of stewed fruit in the basin before adding the pudding mixture.

Mincemeat surprise pudding *see colour plate facing p. 448*
Line the bottom and sides of the basin with a thin layer of mincemeat and fill with the pudding mixture. When the pudding is cooked, turn it out carefully so that the outside remains completely covered with the mincemeat. This pudding is sometimes known as mock Christmas pudding and makes a less rich alternative to the traditional version.

Chocolate sponge pudding
Blend 60 ml *(4 level tbsps)* cocoa powder to a smooth cream with 15 ml *(1 tbsp)* hot water; add gradually to the creamed fat and sugar. Serve with a chocolate or rum sauce (see pages 203, 204).

Jamaica pudding
Add 50–100 g *(2–4 oz)* chopped stem ginger with the flour. Serve with a syrup sauce (see page 204).

Lemon or orange sponge
Add the grated rind of 1 orange or lemon when creaming the fat and sugar. Serve with an orange, lemon or marmalade sauce (see page 205).

Cherry sponge pudding
Add 50–75 g *(2–3 oz)* halved glacé cherries with the flour. Serve with custard or sweet white sauce (see pages 203, 204).

Steamed castle puddings
Prepare an ordinary steamed sponge mixture and divide it between greased individual pudding basins or dariole moulds. Fill two-thirds full, cover each mould with greased foil and secure with string. Steam for 30–45 minutes (depending on size) over rapidly boiling water. Turn out on to a dish and serve with jam sauce (see page 204).

Duchesse pudding

100 g *(4 oz)* butter or margarine
100 g *(4 oz)* sugar
2 eggs, beaten
175 g *(6 oz)* self raising flour
30 ml *(2 tbsps)* stoned raisins
30 ml *(2 tbsps)* chopped glacé cherries
30 ml *(2 tbsps)* chopped mixed peel
30 ml *(2 tbsps)* chopped walnuts
few drops of almond essence
little milk to mix

Half-fill a steamer or large saucepan with water and put on to boil. Grease a 900-ml *(1½-pt)* pudding basin. Cream together the fat and the sugar until pale and fluffy. Add the eggs a little at a time, beating after each addition. Mix together the flour, fruit and nuts. Using a metal spoon, fold half the flour and fruit mixture into the creamed mixture, then fold in the rest. Add the almond essence and enough milk to give a dropping consistency. Put into the basin, cover with greased greaseproof paper or foil and secure with string. Steam for 1½–2 hours over rapidly boiling water. Turn the pudding out on to a dish and serve with an apricot or jam sauce.

Lafayette pudding

100 g *(4 oz)* self raising flour
75 g *(3 oz)* ground almonds
50 g *(2 oz)* fresh white breadcrumbs
100 g *(4 oz)* butter or margarine
100 g *(4 oz)* caster sugar
2 eggs, beaten
50 g *(2 oz)* glacé cherries, chopped
30–45 ml *(2–3 tbsps)* milk

Half-fill a steamer or large saucepan with water and put on to boil. Grease a 900-ml *(1½-pt)* pudding basin. Mix together the flour, ground almonds and breadcrumbs. Cream the fat and the sugar until pale and fluffy. Add the eggs a little at a time, beating after each addition. Fold in half the dry ingredients with a metal spoon; fold in the rest, with the cherries and enough milk to give a dropping consistency. Put into the greased basin, cover with greased greaseproof paper or foil and secure with string. Steam for 1½–2 hours over rapidly boiling water. Turn the pudding out on to a dish and serve with custard.

Marbled pudding

150 g ***(5 oz)*** **self raising flour**
pinch of salt
100 g ***(4 oz)*** **butter or margarine**
100 g ***(4 oz)*** **caster sugar**
2 eggs, beaten
milk to mix
grated rind of 1 lemon
30 ml ***(2 level tbsps)*** **cocoa**

Half-fill a steamer or large saucepan with water and put it on to boil. Grease a 900-ml *($1\frac{1}{2}$-pt)* pudding basin. Sift the flour and salt. Cream the fat and sugar until pale and fluffy, then add the egg a little at a time, beating well after each addition. Fold in half the flour with a metal spoon, then fold in the rest of the flour and enough milk to give a soft dropping consistency. Divide the mixture in two and add the lemon rind to one half; blend the cocoa with a little water to give a thick paste and add it to the other half. Put the two mixtures in alternate spoonfuls into the greased basin, giving the marbled effect. Cover with greased greaseproof paper or foil and steam for $1\frac{1}{2}$–2 hours. Serve with hot chocolate sauce or custard (see page 204).

Variation

The plain mixture may be tinted pink with a few drops of edible food colouring and flavoured with a little almond essence instead of grated lemon rind.

Chocolate crumb pudding

50 g ***(2 oz)*** **chocolate**
75 g ***(3 oz)*** **butter or margarine**
75 g ***(3 oz)*** **caster sugar**
1 egg, separated
2.5–5 ml ***($\frac{1}{2}$–1 tsp)*** **vanilla essence**
100 g ***(4 oz)*** **fresh white breadcrumbs**
50 g ***(2 oz)*** **self raising flour**
60–75 ml ***(4–5 tbsps)*** **milk**

Half-fill a steamer or large saucepan with water and put on to boil. Grease a 900-ml *($1\frac{1}{2}$-pt)* pudding basin. Melt the chocolate in a basin over hot water. Cream the fat and sugar until pale and fluffy and beat in the chocolate, egg yolk and vanilla essence. Mix the breadcrumbs and flour and fold half into the creamed mixture, with 30 ml *(2 tbsps)* milk. Fold in the remaining crumbs and flour and sufficient milk to give a fairly soft dropping consistency. Whisk the egg white stiffly and fold into the mixture. Turn it into the prepared basin, cover with greased greaseproof paper or foil and secure with string. Steam for $1\frac{1}{2}$–2 hours over rapidly boiling water. Turn out and serve with hot chocolate sauce (see page 204).

Steamed suet pudding

175 g ***(6 oz)*** **self raising flour**
pinch of salt
75 g ***(3 oz)*** **shredded suet**
50 g ***(2 oz)*** **caster sugar**
about 150 ml ***($\frac{1}{4}$ pt)*** **milk**

Half-fill a steamer or large saucepan with water and put on to boil. Grease a 900-ml *($1\frac{1}{2}$-pt)* pudding basin. Mix the flour, salt, suet and sugar. Make a well in the centre and add enough milk to give a soft dropping consistency. Put into the greased basin, cover with greased greaseproof paper or foil and secure with string. Steam over rapidly boiling water for $1\frac{1}{2}$–2 hours. Serve with a jam, golden syrup sauce or fruit sauce.

Variations

For a lighter pudding use 75 g *(3 oz)* self raising flour and 75 g *(3 oz)* fresh white breadcrumbs. For a richer pudding, use 1 beaten egg and about 90 ml *(6 tbsps)* milk instead of the 150 ml *($\frac{1}{4}$ pt)* milk.

Jam Put 30 ml *(2 tbsps)* red jam in the bottom of the greased pudding basin before adding the mixture.

Apple Add to the dry ingredients 225 g *($\frac{1}{2}$ lb)* cooking apples, peeled and finely chopped or grated. Serve the pudding with a sweet white sauce flavoured with a pinch of nutmeg (see page 203).

Date Add to the dry ingredients 100 g *(4 oz)* chopped dates and the grated rind of a lemon; reduce the sugar to 30 ml *(2 tbsps)*. Serve with lemon sauce (see page 205).

Apricot Add to the dry ingredients 50 g *(2 oz)* chopped dried apricots, 100 g *(4 oz)* apple, peeled and finely chopped, and the grated rind of 1 lemon.

Rich fig Add to the dry ingredients 100 g *(4 oz)* chopped dried figs, 25–50 g *(1–2 oz)* chopped blanched almonds and the grated rind of 1 lemon. Mix to a soft dropping consistency with 2 beaten eggs and 30 ml *(2 tbsps)* sherry or milk. Serve with lemon sauce or custard (see pages 204, 205).

Apple suet pudding

200 g *(7 oz)* suetcrust pastry (see page 352)
450 g *(1 lb)* cooking apples, peeled, cored and sliced
100 g *(4 oz)* sugar

Half-fill a steamer or large saucepan with water and put it on to boil. Grease a 900-ml *(1½-pt)* pudding basin. Make the pastry and roll out into a round 2.5 cm *(1 in)* larger all round than the top of the basin. Cut a quarter out of the round; with the remaining portion line the pudding basin, damping the cut edges, overlapping them and pressing well to seal. Fill the basin with the sliced apples and sugar in alternate layers. Roll out the remaining pastry to make a lid, damp the edges of the pastry in the basin and cover with the lid, pressing the edges well together. Cover with greased greaseproof paper or foil and steam for 2½ hours. Turn the pudding out on to a dish and serve with pouring custard or sweet white sauce (pages 203, 204).

Variation
Use different fruits, such as rhubarb, plums, damsons (increasing the sugar to 175 g, *6 oz*), blackberries combined with apples, or black-currants, prepared as for stewing. When the softer fruits are used, steam for only 2 hours.

Spotted Dick

75 g *(3 oz)* self raising flour
pinch of salt
75 g *(3 oz)* fresh breadcrumbs
75 g *(3 oz)* shredded suet
50 g *(2 oz)* caster sugar
175 g *(6 oz)* currants
about 60–90 ml *(4–6 tbsps)* milk

Half-fill a steamer with water and put on to boil. Mix together the flour, salt, breadcrumbs, suet, sugar and currants in a bowl. Make a well in the centre and add enough milk to give a fairly soft dough. Form into a roll on a well floured board, wrap loosely in greased greaseproof paper and then in foil, sealing the ends well.

Steam over rapidly boiling water for 1½–2 hours. Unwrap the pudding, put in a hot dish and serve with custard or with a sweet white sauce flavoured with cinnamon or grated lemon rind (see page 203). Alternatively, make the mixture of a soft dropping consistency and steam it for 1½–2 hours in a greased 900-ml *(1½-pt)* basin.

Mincemeat roly-poly

175 g *(6 oz)* suetcrust pastry (see page 352)
60–90 ml *(4–6 tbsps)* mincemeat
a little milk

Half-fill a steamer with water and put it on to boil.

Grease a piece of foil 23 by 33 cm *(9 by 13 in)*. Make the suetcrust pastry and roll it out to an oblong about 23 by 25 cm *(9 by 11 in)*. Spread the mincemeat on the pastry, leaving 0.5 cm *(¼ in)* clear along each edge. Brush the edges with milk and roll the pastry up evenly, starting from one short side. Place the roll on the greased foil and wrap the foil round the roll loosely, to allow room for expansion, but seal the edges very well. Steam the roly-poly over rapidly boiling water for

1½–2 hours. When it is cooked, remove it from the foil and serve with a custard sauce.

Jam roly-poly
Replace the mincemeat with 60 ml *(4 tbsps)* jam.

Syrup roly-poly
Replace the mincemeat with 60 ml *(4 tbsps)* golden syrup, bound with 30–45 ml *(2–3 tbsps)* fresh white breadcrumbs.

Christmas pudding – 1

350 g *(12 oz)* fresh white breadcrumbs
350 g *(12 oz)* plain flour
5 ml *(1 level tsp)* salt
2.5 ml *(½ level tsp)* ground mace
2.5 ml *(½ level tsp)* ground ginger
2.5 ml *(½ level tsp)* ground nutmeg
2.5 ml *(½ level tsp)* ground cinnamon
350 g *(12 oz)* shredded suet
225 g *(8 oz)* caster sugar
225 g *(8 oz)* soft brown sugar
225 g *(8 oz)* mixed candied peel, chopped very finely
350 g *(12 oz)* currants
225 g *(8 oz)* sultanas
550 g *(1 lb 4 oz)* stoned raisins
175 g *(6 oz)* almonds, blanched and chopped
225 g *(½ lb)* apples, peeled and chopped
grated rind and juice of 1 lemon
grated rind and juice of 1 orange
60 ml *(4 tbsps)* brandy
3 large eggs, beaten
about 150 ml *(¼ pt)* milk

Mix together in a large mixing bowl all the dry ingredients, the almonds, apples and orange and lemon rind. Mix the lemon and orange juice and the brandy with the beaten eggs and add to the dry ingredients, with enough milk to give a soft dropping consistency.

Cover the mixture lightly and leave overnight. Half-fill 3 saucepans with water and put them on to boil. Grease 3 pudding basins, 600-ml, 900-ml and 1.1-l *(1-pt, 1½-pt and 2-pt)* capacities. Stir the mixture before turning it into the prepared basins, cover with greased greaseproof paper and with a clean dry cloth or foil.

Steam over rapidly boiling water as follows:

600-ml *(1-pt)* pudding	5 hours
900-ml *(1½-pt)* pudding	7 hours
1.1-l *(2-pt)* pudding	9 hours

When the puddings are cooked, remove them from the pans and allow to cool Remove foil or cloth but leave the paper in position. Re-cover them with a fresh cloth or foil and store in a cool place.

On the day of serving steam the pudding as follows:

600-ml *(1-pt)* pudding	2 hours
900-ml *(1½-pt)* pudding	3 hours
1.1-l *(2-pt)* pudding	3 hours

Turn out on to a hot dish and serve with brandy or rum butter or a sweet white sauce flavoured with rum (see pages 203 and 205).

Note Don't put the aluminium foil directly on to the pudding, as the fruit eats into it after some weeks; this does no harm to the pudding, but the foil ceases to be watertight.

Christmas pudding – 2

450 g *(1 lb)* fresh white breadcrumbs
5 ml *(1 level tsp)* ground ginger
5 ml *(1 level tsp)* ground mixed spice
5 ml *(1 level tsp)* salt
225 ml *(8 oz)* shredded suet
225 ml *(8 oz)* brown sugar
100 g *(4 oz)* mixed chopped peel
100 g *(4 oz)* currants
100 g *(4 oz)* sultanas
450 g *(1 lb)* seedless raisins
75 g *(3 oz)* carrot, pared and grated
2 eggs, lightly beaten
45 ml *(3 tbsps)* brandy
30 ml *(2 tbsps)* milk
30 ml *(2 tbsps)* golden syrup

This is a lighter-textured pudding

Half-fill two saucepans with water and put them on to boil. Grease two 1.1-l *(2-pt)* pudding basins. Mix together all the dry ingredients. Mix the eggs, brandy, milk and syrup together and add to the dry ingredients. Let the mixture stand for an hour, then put it into the prepared basins, cover with greased greaseproof paper and foil or a pudding cloth and secure with string. Steam for 8 hours over steadily boiling water. After 8 hours, remove from the steamer and cool. Leave the greaseproof paper in position, cover with a clean dry cloth or foil and store in a cool place.

On Christmas Day steam for a further 2 hours. Turn out on to a hot dish and serve with brandy or rum butter or a white sauce flavoured with brandy or rum (see pages 203 and 205).

Scotch pudding

225 g *(8 oz)* self raising flour
100 g *(4 oz)* shredded suet
100 g *(4 oz)* currants
100 g *(4 oz)* sultanas
50 g *(2 oz)* stoned raisins
50 g *(2 oz)* mixed chopped peel or 50 g *(2 oz)* dried apricots, chopped
100 g *(4 oz)* fresh white breadcrumbs
100 g *(4 oz)* soft brown sugar
7.5 ml *(1½ level tsps)* ground mixed spice
about 300 ml *(½ pt)* milk
15 ml *(1 tbsp)* lemon juice

Half-fill a steamer or large saucepan with water and put it on to boil. Grease a 1.1-l *(2-pt)* pudding basin. Mix together all the dry ingredients and add milk and lemon juice to give a soft dropping consistency. Turn the mixture into the greased basin, cover with greased greaseproof paper or foil and secure with string. Steam for 3 hours over rapidly boiling water.

This pudding, which is an alternative to Christmas pudding, can be kept for 1–2 weeks after the first cooking; it should be covered with a clean dry cloth, foil or greaseproof paper. Re-heat by steaming for 2 hours over rapidly boiling water. Turn it out on to a dish and serve with rum or brandy butter or with a white sauce flavoured with rum (see pages 203 and 205).

Syrup ginger pudding

75 g *(3 oz)* self raising flour
5–10 ml *(1–2 level tsps)* ground ginger
pinch of salt
75 g *(3 oz)* fresh white breadcrumbs
75 g *(3 oz)* shredded suet
60–90 ml *(4–6 tbsps)* golden syrup
1 egg, beaten
milk to mix

Half-fill a steamer or large saucepan with water and put it on to boil. Grease a 900-ml *(1½-pt)* pudding basin. Sift the flour, ginger and salt into a bowl and add the breadcrumbs and suet. Warm the syrup slightly, make a well in the centre of the dry ingredients and add the syrup and beaten egg, with a little milk if necessary to give a soft dropping consistency. Turn the mixture into the greased pudding basin, cover with greased greaseproof paper or foil and secure with string. Steam over rapidly boiling water for 1½–2 hours. Turn out on to a dish and serve with a syrup sauce (see page 204).

Dumplings with apple sauce

white bread
50 g *(2 oz)* butter
2 large eggs, separated
100 g *(4 oz)* cottage cheese
45 ml *(3 tbsps)* double cream
50 g *(2 oz)* plain flour
pinch of salt
grated rind of ½ lemon
hot apple sauce

For the buttered crumbs
50 g *(2 oz)* butter
50 g *(2 oz)* stale white breadcrumbs
30 ml *(2 level tbsps)* caster sugar

Cut two thick slices off the loaf – about 100 g *(4 oz)*. Trim off the crusts and crumb the bread. Beat the butter until soft. Beat in the egg yolks one at a time. Stir in the cheese, cream and the breadcrumbs. Sift the flour with the salt and add the lemon rind; fold into the other ingredients and leave for ½ hour. Shape into about 8 small dumplings. Just before the dumplings are required, poach them very gently in simmering (not fast-boiling) salted water for about 20 minutes.

Meanwhile prepare the coating crumbs. Melt the butter and gently fry the breadcrumbs until golden; stir in the sugar. Drain the dumplings and toss them lightly in the fried crumbs. Serve at once, with apple sauce, or, when in season, with a thick purée of fresh plums.

MILK PUDDINGS

Rice pudding

45 ml *(3 tbsps)* short grain rice
30 ml *(2 level tbsps)* caster sugar
568 ml *(1 pt)* milk
knob of butter
whole nutmeg

Wash the rice and put it into a buttered 900-ml *(1½-pt)* ovenproof dish with the sugar. Pour on the milk, top with shavings of butter and grate some nutmeg on top. Bake in the oven at 150°C *(300°F)* mark 2 for about 2 hours; stir it after about ½ hour.

Variations

1. Add 50 g *(2 oz)* dried fruit to the pudding before baking.
2. Add 5 ml *(1 level tsp)* ground cinnamon or mixed spice to the pudding before baking it; omit the nutmeg.

Flaked rice, Tapioca
Make as above.

Apricot rice pudding

50 g *(2 oz)* dried apricots, or a 312-g *(11-oz)* can apricots
sugar
45 ml *(3 level tbsps)* short grain rice
568 ml *(1 pt)* milk
2 eggs, beaten

Wash the dried apricots, cover with water and soak overnight. Cook in 150 ml *(¼ pt)* water, with sugar to taste. Cook the rice and the milk gently in a thick-based pan or double saucepan until creamy stirring occasionally; this will take about 45 minutes or up to 2 hours in a double pan. Add 30 ml *(2 level tbsps)* sugar and the eggs. Drain the apricots and put them into a pie dish, reserving the juice. Pour the rice mixture on top and bake in the oven at 200°C *(400°F)* mark 6 for about 15 minutes, until heated through and lightly browned. Meanwhile boil the apricot juice until syrupy and serve with the pudding.

Lemon meringue rice pudding *see colour plate facing p. 416*

45 ml *(3 level tbsps)* short grain rice
568 ml *(1 pt)* milk
juice and thinly peeled rind of 1 lemon
1–2 eggs, separated
75 g *(3 oz)* sugar
jam

Wash the rice and put it into a thick-based or double saucepan with the milk and lemon rind. Cook gently for about 45 minutes, or up to 2 hours in a double pan, until the rice is soft and creamy. Remove the lemon rind and stir in the juice; cool the mixture slightly and beat in the egg yolks and 30 ml *(2 level tbsps)* sugar. Put a layer of jam on the bottom of a pie dish and pour on the rice. Whisk the egg whites very stiffly, whisk in half the remaining sugar and fold in the rest. Pile the meringue on the pudding and bake in the oven at 180°C *(350°F)* mark 4 for about 15 minutes, until the meringue top is lightly browned.

Semolina pudding

568 ml *(1 pt)* milk
knob of butter
60 ml *(4 level tbsps)* semolina
50 g *(2 oz)* sugar

Heat the milk and butter and sprinkle on the semolina. Continue to heat until the milk boils and the mixture thickens, and cook for a further 2–3 minutes, until the grain is clear, stirring all the time. Remove from the heat and stir in the sugar. Pour the pudding into a greased ovenproof dish and bake in the oven at 200°C *(400°F)* mark 6 for about 30 minutes, till lightly browned. (Or serve as it is without baking, allowing up to 15 minutes' cooking in the pan.)

Variations
1. Add the grated rind of an orange or lemon to the milk.
2. Pour the cooked pudding on to a layer of jam or stewed fruit before baking it as above.

Fine sago and flaked grains
Cook as for semolina, but for sago, cook for 5–10 minutes after bringing to the boil.

Spiced semolina pudding

568 ml *(1 pt)* milk
60 ml *(4 level tbsps)* semolina
75 g *(3 oz)* sugar
5–10 ml *(1–2 level tsps)* ground mixed spice
grated rind of ½ lemon
50 g *(2 oz)* currants or sultanas
2 eggs, separated

Heat the milk, sprinkle on the semolina, bring to the boil and cook for 2–3 minutes, stirring all the time. Remove from the heat and stir in half the sugar, the spice, lemon rind, dried fruit and egg yolks and pour into an ovenproof dish. Whisk the egg whites stiffly, fold in the remaining sugar and pile on top of the pudding. Bake in the oven at 200°C *(400°F)* mark 6 for 5–10 minutes, until the meringue is lightly browned.

Alternatively, add all the sugar to the pudding, fold in the whisked egg whites and bake for 15–20 minutes, or until the pudding is well risen and lightly browned.

CUSTARD AND CUSTARD SWEETS

Baking custards

Baked custard

568 ml *(1 pt)* milk
3 eggs
30 ml *(2 level tbsps)* sugar
ground nutmeg

Warm the milk in a saucepan but don't boil it. Whisk the eggs and sugar lightly in a basin; pour on the hot milk, stirring all the time. Strain the mixture into a greased ovenproof dish, sprinkle the nutmeg on top and bake in the oven at 170°C *(325°F)* mark 3 for about 45 minutes, or until set and firm to the touch.

Note The dish containing custard can be stood in a shallow tin containing water – this helps to ensure that the custard does not curdle or separate through overheating. Bake in individual dishes if preferred.

Bread and butter pudding

3–4 thin slices of bread and butter
50 g *(2 oz)* currants or sultanas
15 ml *(1 level tbsp)* caster sugar
400 ml *(¾ pt)* milk
2 eggs
ground nutmeg

Cut the bread and butter into strips and arrange, buttered side up, in layers in a greased ovenproof dish, sprinkling the layers with the fruit and sugar. Heat the milk, but do not allow it to boil. Whisk the eggs lightly and pour the milk on to them, stirring all the time. Strain the mixture over the bread, sprinkle some nutmeg on top and let the pudding stand for ¼ hour. Bake in the oven at 180°C *(350°F)* mark 4 for 30–40 minutes, until set and lightly browned.

Osborne pudding

Use brown bread and butter, spread with marmalade; omit the dried fruit.

Rich cabinet pudding

50 g *(2 oz)* glacé cherries, halved
angelica
400 ml *(¾ pt)* milk
2 eggs
30 ml *(2 level tbsps)* sugar
2.5 ml *(½ tsp)* vanilla essence
3 trifle sponge cakes
about 25 g *(1 oz)* ratafia biscuits, optional

Grease a 12.5-cm *(5-in)* round cake tin and line the bottom with greased greaseproof paper. Put a few cherries and some pieces of angelica on the bottom; when the pudding is turned out these will decorate the top. Heat the milk. Whisk the eggs and sugar and add the milk and vanilla essence, stirring well. Cut the sponge cake into small dice and crumble the ratafias, if used; put both in the tin with the rest of the cherries, strain the eggs and milk over and leave to soak for ¼ hour. Cover with greased greaseproof paper and steam over gently boiling water for about 1 hour, until set. Turn out on to a serving dish and serve with sabayon or jam sauce (see pages 204 and 205).

Queen of puddings

400 ml *($\frac{3}{4}$ pt)* milk
25 g *(1 oz)* butter
grated rind of $\frac{1}{2}$ lemon
2 eggs, separated
50 g *(2 oz)* caster sugar
75 g *(3 oz)* fresh white breadcrumbs
30 ml *(2 tbsps)* red jam

Warm the milk, butter and lemon rind. Whisk the egg yolks and half of the sugar lightly and pour on the milk, stirring well. Strain over the breadcrumbs, pour into a greased 1.1-l *(2-pt)* ovenproof dish and leave to stand for $\frac{1}{4}$ hour. Bake in the oven at 180°C *(350°F)* mark 4 for 25–30 minutes, until lightly set; remove from the oven. Warm the jam and spread it over the pudding. Whisk up the egg whites stiffly and add half the remaining sugar; whisk again and fold in the remaining sugar. Pile the meringue on top of the jam and bake for a further 15–20 minutes, until the meringue is lightly browned.

Zabaglione

6 egg yolks
50 g *(2 oz)* caster sugar
75 ml *(5 tbsps)* Marsala

Place beaten egg yolks, sugar, and Marsala in a deep basin over a pan of hot, but not boiling, water. Whisk continuously until thick and creamy. Pour at once into small glasses and serve immediately with macaroons or sponge fingers. If liked, a little fruit may be placed at the bottom of the glasses before adding the zabaglione mixture – pineapple goes particularly well.

HOT SOUFFLES

Soufflé à la vanille

50 g *(2 oz)* caster sugar
4 large eggs
60 ml *(4 level tbsps)* plain flour
300 ml *($\frac{1}{2}$ pt)* milk
2.5 ml *($\frac{1}{2}$ tsp)* vanilla essence
icing sugar, optional

Butter an 18-cm, 1.7-l *(7-in, 3-pt)* soufflé dish. Cream the sugar with one whole egg and one yolk until pale cream in colour. Stir in the flour. Pour on the milk and mix until smooth. Bring to boiling point, stirring, and simmer for 2 minutes. Cool slightly, then beat in the remaining yolks and vanilla essence. Fold in the stiffly beaten egg whites. Pour into the soufflé dish and bake for about 45 minutes at 180°C *(350°F)* mark 4, until well risen, firm to the touch and pale golden. If you wish, after 30 minutes cooking, quickly dust the soufflé with icing sugar and continue to bake.

Variations

Line the base of the buttered soufflé dish with sliced banana, previously sautéed in butter and dredged with sugar. Top with the vanilla soufflé mixture. Or omit vanilla essence and stir in the finely grated rind and juice of 1 lemon before adding the egg white. Serve with a thin orange sauce (page 205). Or marinade sliced fresh strawberries in a little sugar, orange juice and orange curaçao. Drain and retain the juice. Line the base of the soufflé dish with strawberries. Top with vanilla soufflé mixture. Serve baked soufflé with whipped cream flavoured with marinade.

Hot ginger soufflé

40 g *(1½ oz)* butter
60 ml *(4 level tbsps)* plain flour
300 ml *(½ pt)* milk
75 g *(3 oz)* caster sugar
15 ml *(1 tbsp)* brandy
pinch of ground ginger
50 g *(2 oz)* stem ginger, chopped
4 large eggs, separated
ginger syrup
double cream

Butter an 18-cm, 1.7-l *(7-in, 3-pt)* soufflé dish. Melt the butter in a saucepan, stir in the flour then gradually add the milk. Bring to the boil, stirring, then reduce the heat and cook for 2 minutes. Stir in the sugar, brandy and ginger. Beat in the egg yolks, then fold in the stiffly whisked egg whites. Turn the mixture into the soufflé dish and bake for about 45 minutes at 180°C *(350°F)* mark 4 until well risen and just firm to the touch. Serve at once. Top each serving with a spoonful of ginger syrup and unwhipped double cream.

Soufflé au liqueur

2 trifle sponge cakes
75 ml *(5 tbsps)* Grand Marnier
75 g *(2½ oz)* mixed glacé fruits
50 g *(2 oz)* butter
45 ml *(3 level tbsps)* plain flour
150 ml *(¼ pt)* milk
50 g *(2 oz)* caster sugar
3 large eggs, separated
icing sugar

Butter an 18-cm, 1.1-litre *(7-in, 2-pt)* soufflé dish. Cut the sponge cakes into cubes and soak in 15 ml *(1 tbsp)* of liqueur. Rinse the glacé fruits in very hot water. Dry and cut into small pieces. Soak in 15 ml *(1 tbsp)* liqueur. Melt the butter in a saucepan. Stir in the flour, then the milk. Bring to boiling point, stirring, and cook until the mixture leaves the sides of the pan. Remove from the heat. Beat in the sugar, egg yolks and the remaining liqueur. Lastly, fold in the stiffly beaten egg whites. Pour half the mixture into the soufflé dish, arrange the sponge and fruit on top, then pour over the remaining mixture. Bake for 35–45 minutes at 180°C *(350°F)* mark 4 until well risen, just firm to the touch and light golden brown. Dust with icing sugar and serve at once.

Soufflé au chocolat

75–100 g *(3–4 oz)* chocolate dots
30 ml *(2 tbsps)* water
400 ml *(¾ pt)* milk
50 g *(2 oz)* caster sugar
60 ml *(4 level tbsps)* plain flour
knob of butter
3 egg yolks
4 egg whites
icing sugar

Butter an 18-cm, 1.7-l *(7-in, 3-pt)* soufflé dish. Put the chocolate dots in a basin with the water and melt them over a pan of boiling water. Heat the milk, reserving a little, with the sugar and pour on to the melted chocolate. Blend the flour to a smooth paste with the remaining milk, and stir in the chocolate mixture. Return to the pan, stir over a moderate heat until boiling, then cook for 2 minutes, stirring occasionally. Add the butter, in small pieces, then leave until lukewarm. Beat in the yolks, then fold in the stiffly whisked whites. Turn the mixture into the soufflé dish. Bake at 180°C *(350°F)* mark 4 for about 45 minutes, until well risen and firm to the touch. Dust with icing sugar before serving.

Hot apricot soufflé

425-g *(15-oz)* can apricot halves, drained
40 g *(1½ oz)* butter
60 ml *(4 level tbsps)* plain flour
150 ml *(¼ pt)* milk
50 g *(2 oz)* caster sugar
4 large eggs, separated
15 ml *(1 tbsp)* apricot brandy

Butter a 17-cm, 1.7-l *(6½ in, 3 pt)* soufflé dish. Sieve the apricots. Melt the butter in a saucepan, stir in the flour, then the milk. Stir until smooth then add the apricot purée, bring to boiling point, stirring, and simmer for 2 minutes. Remove from the heat and stir in the sugar, egg yolks and liqueur. Fold in the stiffly whisked egg whites. Turn the mixture into the soufflé dish. Bake for about 45 minutes at 180°C *(350°F)* mark 4 until well risen, golden brown and just firm to the touch. Serve immediately, with a liqueur-laced thin sauce made from the juice of the apricots.

Variation

Replace apricot with apple purée, made by stewing 450 g *(1 lb)* cooking apples, cored and sliced, with 25 g *(1 oz)* butter and 30 ml *(2 tbsps)* water to a pulp, then sieve. Omit the apricot brandy and add a pinch of powdered cinnamon. Serve dusted with cinnamon sugar and accompany with thin cream.

BATTERS

There are two main types of batter which are used for hot sweets – a pouring or Yorkshire pudding batter and a coating or fritter one. The batter used for waffles is also of coating consistency, though it contains some extra ingredients.

Pouring batter

125 g *(4 oz)* plain flour
pinch of salt
1 egg
300 ml *(½ pt)* milk or two-thirds milk and one third water

For pancakes, baked batter puddings, Yorkshire pudding
Mix the flour and salt, make a well in the centre and break in the egg. Add half the liquid, gradually work in the flour using a wooden spoon and beat the mixture until it is smooth. Add the remaining liquid gradually and beat until well mixed and the surface is covered with tiny bubbles. See pancakes, page 308.

Note The batter may be used at once or left to stand in a cool place. If it is left to stand it may be necessary to add a little more milk before using.

The batter may also be beaten with an egg whisk or electric mixer.

Rich pancake batter

Follow the above recipe, but add a knob of melted butter with the liquid.

Variations

1. Add 5–10 ml *(1–2 level tsps)* icing sugar to the flour before mixing.
2. Add the grated rind of ½ a lemon or orange to the flour before mixing.

This batter can be used as the basis of crêpes Suzette.

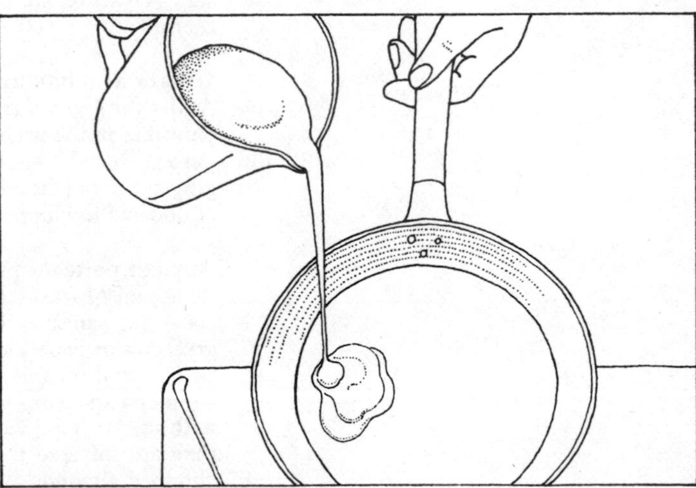

Making pancakes

Baked batter pudding

Make up 300 ml *(½ pt)* pouring batter as page 307. Put 25 g *(1 oz)* butter into a tin measuring about 18 cm *(7 in)* square and heat it in the oven, preheated to 220°C *(425°F)* mark 7. Pour in the batter and bake for about 40 minutes, until well risen. Cut into squares and serve at once with jam or syrup sauce.

Apple batter

Core and slice 450 g *(1 lb)* cooking apples, put into a 20.5-cm *(8-in)* tin and sprinkle with the grated rind of ½ a lemon and 75–100 g *(3–4 oz)* sugar. Pour in the batter and bake as above.

Apricot batter

Replace the apples by 1 large can – 822 g *(1 lb 13 oz)* of halved apricots, draining them well before use.

Pancakes

300 ml *(½ pt)* pouring batter (see page 307)
lard
caster sugar
lemon wedges

Make up the batter mixture. Heat a little lard in an 18-cm *(7-in)* heavy based, flat frying pan until really hot, running it round to coat the sides of the pan; pour off any surplus. Raise the handle-side of the pan slightly, pour a little batter in from the raised side, so that a very thin skin of batter flows over the pan; move it to and fro until the base is covered. Place over a moderate heat and leave until the pancake is golden brown. Turn it with a palette knife or by tossing and cook the second side until golden. Turn out on to sugared paper and sprinkle with sugar. Repeat, greasing the pan each time. *Makes 8 pancakes.*

If you are cooking a large number of pancakes, keep them warm by putting them as they are made between 2 plates in a warm oven. Finally, sprinkle each pancake with lemon juice, roll up and serve at once, with extra sugar and lemon wedges. Cooked pancakes will keep for up to a week if wrapped in greaseproof paper and stored in a refrigerator. Re-heat them in a hot frying pan, without any fat, turning them over once.

Jam pancakes

Spread the pancakes with jam, roll up and serve with cream.

Orange pancakes

Add the grated rind of an orange to the batter and cook in the usual way. To serve, sprinkle with sugar and pour the orange juice over them.

Ginger and banana pancakes

Add 5 ml *(1 level tsp)* ground ginger with the flour and cook the pancakes in the usual way. To make the filling, mash 1 banana per person with double cream and add some small pieces of preserved ginger. Spread the filling on the hot cooked pancakes, roll up and serve at once with whipped cream.

Apricot pancakes

Add 5 ml *(1 level tsp)* ground cinnamon to the batter mixture and cook the pancakes in the normal way. Turn out on to sugared greaseproof paper, spread with hot apricot and almond filling (see below), roll up and serve at once with cream. To make the filling, simmer 50 g *(2 oz)* chopped dried apricots in 60 ml *(4 tbsps)* water, with 50–75 g *(2–3 oz)* sugar and a good squeeze of lemon juice, until they are soft and the mixture is fairly thick; add 45 ml *(3 tbsps)* chopped almonds, lightly toasted.

Layered pancakes

Instead of rolling the pancakes, use a filling (for instance whipped cream or hot apple sauce and jam) to layer the pancakes one on top of the other. The layered pancakes are served cut in wedges, like a cake.

A mixture of hot drained canned fruit or fruit pie filling (such as peaches, apricots, strawberries and raspberries) and whipped cream, makes another delicious filling.

Surprise pancakes

Make the pancakes in the usual way, spoon some ice cream into the centre of each pancake and fold in half, like an omelette. Serve at once with jam sauce or a sauce made from sieved raspberries.

Blintzes

300 ml *(½ pt)* rich pancake mixture (see page 307)
100 g *(¼ lb)* cottage cheese
30 ml *(2 tbsps)* soured cream
1 egg, beaten
grated rind of ½ lemon
15 ml *(1 level tbsp)* icing sugar
30 ml *(2 tbsps)* raisins, plumped in boiling water
butter for frying

Make the pancake mixture. Combine the remaining ingredients (except the butter) to make the filling. Heat a little butter in a thick-based pan, cook the pancakes on one side only and keep them warm between 2 plates, cooked side uppermost. Spread a little of the filling on the cooked side of each pancake and fold over the two sides to enclose it. Melt some more butter, return the pancakes to the pan and cook until golden brown. Serve with soured cream.

Saucer pancakes

50 g *(2 oz)* butter or margarine
50 g *(2 oz)* caster sugar
2 eggs
50 g *(2 oz)* plain flour
300 ml *(½ pt)* milk, slightly warmed
jam

Cream the fat and sugar until light and fluffy. Beat in the eggs one at a time with a little of the flour. Fold in the rest of the flour. Stir in the milk (at this stage the mixture will probably curdle, but this does not matter). Half fill 6 buttered, heatproof saucers or very shallow wide patty tins with the mixture. Bake at once in the oven at 190°C *(375°F)* mark 5 for 15–20 minutes. Immediately turn the pancakes out on to sugared paper; place a teaspoonful of warm jam in each, quickly and carefully fold in half. Serve at once. *Serves 6.*

Pear and almond crêpes

For rich crêpe batter
125 g *(4 oz)* plain flour
pinch of salt
1 egg
300 ml *(½ pt)* milk
15 ml *(1 tbsp)* brandy
good knob of butter, melted
butter for frying

For filling
100 g *(4 oz)* butter
50 g *(2 oz)* icing sugar
50 g *(2 oz)* ground almonds
1.25 ml *(¼ tsp)* almond essence
grated rind of 1 lemon
425-g *(15-oz)* can pears, drained and diced
melted butter
lemon wedges

Make up as for basic batter (page 307), using flour, salt, egg and milk. Add brandy and butter. Make 8 pancakes as for basic pancakes (page 308), using a little butter for greasing the pan instead of lard or oil. Keep the pancakes warm. Cream the butter and sugar until light and fluffy. Stir in the ground almonds, almond essence, lemon rind and diced pears. Place a little filling over the lower half of each pancake, fold top half over and then in half again to form triangles. Arrange the pancakes overlapping each other in a heatproof dish; brush lightly with butter and quickly brown under a hot grill. Serve with lemon wedges.

Cinnamon-apple pancakes

see colour plate facing p. 417

300 ml (½ pt) pouring batter (see page 307)
100 g (4 oz) fresh white breadcrumbs
75 g (3 oz) butter
grated rind and juice of 1 lemon
700 g (1½ lb) cooking apples, peeled and sliced
50 g (2 oz) caster sugar
5 ml (1 level tsp) ground cinnamon
icing sugar

Make the pancakes (see page 308). Fry the crumbs in 50 g *(2 oz)* butter until golden, turning often. Place the remaining butter, lemon rind, juice, apples, sugar and cinnamon in a pan, cover and cook gently until puréed. Add the fried crumbs. Divide this mixture between the pancakes. Roll them up. Place side by side in a single layer in a hot, ovenproof dish. Cover with foil. Heat in the oven at 170°C *(325°F)* mark 3 for about 20 minutes. Dust heavily with icing sugar before serving. *Serves 4–8.*

Crêpes Suzette

butter for frying
300 ml (½ pt) rich pancake mixture (see page 307)
50 g (2 oz) sugar
50 g (2 oz) butter
juice of 2 oranges
grated rind of 1 lemon
45 ml (3 tbsps) Cointreau
30 ml (2 tbsps) brandy

Heat a little of the butter in a 15–18-cm *(6–7-in)*, thick-based frying pan, pour off the excess and cook the pancakes in the usual way; keep them flat between 2 plates in a warm place. Clean the pan, put in the sugar and heat gently, shaking the pan occasionally until the sugar has melted and turned golden brown. Remove the pan from the heat and add the butter and the orange juice. Fold each pancake in half and then in half again to form a quarter-circle. Add the Cointreau to the fruit juice, replace all the crêpes in the pan and simmer for a few minutes until reheated, spooning the sauce over them. Warm the brandy, pour it over the crêpes, ignite it and serve at once.

Basic coating batter

For fritters

125 g (4 oz) plain flour
pinch of salt
1 egg
150 ml (¼ pt) milk or milk and water

Mix together the flour and salt, make a well in the centre and break in the egg. Add half the liquid and beat the mixture until smooth. Gradually add the rest of the liquid and beat until well mixed.

Light batter

For fritters

125 g (4 oz) plain flour
pinch of salt
15 ml (1 tbsp) oil
150 ml (¼ pt) water
2 egg whites

Mix together the flour and salt, make a well in the centre and add the oil and half the water. Beat until smooth and add the remaining water gradually. Just before using, whisk the egg whites stiffly and fold them into the batter, then use the mixture straight away.

Apple fritters

Peel and core 3–4 cooking apples and cut into rings 0.5 cm *(¼ in)* thick. Dip in coating batter (use either recipe above) and fry until golden in deep fat hot enough to brown a 2.5-cm *(1-in)* cube of bread in 60–70 seconds. Drain on crumpled kitchen paper, toss in caster sugar and a little ground cinnamon and serve straight away. If you prefer, fry fritters in shallow fat, turning each one once.

Pineapple fritters

Use drained canned pineapple rings.

Banana fritters

Use small bananas, peeled and cut in half lengthways.

Fruit fritters with liqueur
Soak some pineapple rings in Kirsch or some apricot halves in rum before making into fritters.

Loukomades

For the syrup
225 g *(8 oz)* caster sugar
175 g *(6 oz)* clear honey
60 ml *(4 tbsps)* lemon juice
thinly pared rind of 1 lemon
90 ml *(6 tbsps)* water

For the fritters
20 g *($\frac{3}{4}$ oz)* fresh yeast
250 ml *(8 fl oz)* lukewarm water
350 g *(12 oz)* plain flour
2.5 ml *($\frac{1}{2}$ level tsp)* salt
90 ml *(6 tbsps)* lukewarm milk
1 egg, beaten
oil for deep frying
chopped walnuts

Put the sugar, honey, lemon juice, rind and water in a heavy saucepan and heat gently, stirring, until the sugar dissolves. Increase the heat and boil, until the syrup reaches 104°C *(220°F)*. Remove the rind and leave the syrup to cool.

Blend the fresh yeast with a little of the lukewarm water. Sift the flour and salt into a large bowl, make a well in the centre and pour in the yeast, milk and remaining water. Add the beaten egg and stir well with a spoon. Beat vigorously until the batter is smooth, and just thick enough to hold its shape. Cover with oiled polythene and leave to rise for about 45 minutes until double its size. Heat the oil to 190°C *(375°F)*. Dip a metal spoon in cold water and use it to scoop a level spoonful of batter into the oil.

Cook for 3–4 minutes. Drain on absorbent kitchen paper and keep warm. When all the fritters are cooked, pour the syrup over them and sprinkle with chopped walnuts. *Makes about 14.*

Churros

50 g *(2 oz)* butter
300 ml *($\frac{1}{2}$ pt)* water
150 g *(5 oz)* plain flour
3 large eggs
orange-flower water
oil for deep frying
a mixture of caster sugar and icing sugar for dusting the churros

Warm the butter and water in a saucepan, bring to the boil, tip in all the flour at once and beat until smooth, off the heat. Add the eggs one at a time and beat until well incorporated. Add orange-flower water to taste – about 15 ml *(1 tbsp)*. Put the mixture into a forcing bag fitted with a plain vegetable nozzle – 0.5–1 cm *($\frac{1}{4}$–$\frac{1}{2}$ in)* in diameter. Heat a pan of deep fat to about 180–190°C *(350–375°F)*. Carefully pipe lengths of the churros paste into the fat, in rings, spirals or horseshoes; cut the paste off to the required length with a knife. Fry until golden brown, turning them once. (Don't fry more than about 3 at a time, as the paste swells during the cooking). Drain thoroughly on kitchen paper and keep warm. Before serving, dredge them heavily with the mixed sugars. Serve fresh as a dessert, or like doughnuts at teatime. *Serves about 6.*

WAFFLES

These crisp, light wafers, made from a type of batter, are cooked in a special waffle iron, heated on the stove top or with its own electric element. Like omelette pans, waffle irons should never be washed, as this tends to make the batter stick. A steel-bristled brush is excellent for removing crumbs from the crevices but should not of course be used on a non-stick surface. The directions supplied with some irons state that greasing is not necessary, but if you experience any trouble with the batter sticking, brush the iron over with a little lard or clarified butter.

Unless the manufacturer advises to the contrary, season the grid of a new waffle iron before use, as this helps to prevent sticking. Just brush the grids of the cold iron thoroughly with a cooking oil or fat, heat to baking temperature and allow to cool.

The cooking time varies with different kinds of waffle irons, but as a rule 2–3 minutes is sufficient.

To make and serve waffles
Heat the iron. Prepare the batter just before it is required for cooking – it should be of the consistency of thick cream. Pour enough batter into the iron to run over the surface (a measure is usually supplied with electric waffle irons). Don't overfill, or the mixture will not be able to rise properly and will ooze out of the iron. Close the iron over the mixture and leave for 2–3 minutes to cook, turning the iron if using a non-electric type. When the

waffle is cooked it should be golden brown and crisp and easily removed from the iron – if it sticks, cook for a minute longer, until it is quite done.

Waffles are best served immediately, but if they must be kept for a few minutes, place them on a wire rack or grid in the oven or under a slow grill. (If they are piled on a plate, the steam will make them sodden.)

Maple syrup is the correct accompaniment and it is served cold. Alternatively, use golden syrup or melted butter. Waffles sandwiched with layers of jam or red-currant jelly look very attractive and are delicious as an alternative to cake for tea; the top may be sprinkled with icing sugar. Another filling is whipped cream, sweetened and flavoured with vanilla essence.

Plain waffles

125 g *(4 oz)* self raising flour
pinch of salt
15 ml *(1 level tbsp)* caster sugar
1 egg, separated
30 ml *(2 tbsps)* butter, melted
150 ml *(¼ pt)* milk
2.5 ml *(½ tsp)* vanilla essence, optional

Mix the dry ingredients together in a bowl. Add the egg yolk, melted butter, milk and essence and beat to give a smooth coating batter. Whisk the egg white stiffly and fold into the batter. Cook as above.

Serve with butter and golden or maple syrup. Alternatively, layer the waffles with whipped cream and fresh fruit such as strawberries or raspberries.

Spice waffles

Add 2.5 ml *(½ level tsp)* ground mixed spice to the dry ingredients.

Pineapple waffles

Add 100 g *(4 oz)* drained crushed pineapple to the mixture for plain waffles. Serve with a pineapple sauce made by boiling 150 ml *(¼ pt)* of the syrup from the pineapple with 50 g *(2 oz)* sugar.

American waffles

175 g *(6 oz)* plain flour
pinch of salt
15 ml *(1 level tbsp)* baking powder
30 ml *(2 level tbsps)* caster sugar
2 eggs
300 ml *(½ pt)* milk
50 g *(2 oz)* butter or margarine, melted
vanilla essence

Sift the flour, salt and baking powder into a basin and stir in the sugar. Make a well in the centre and add the egg yolks; mix in, adding the milk and melted butter alternately. Lastly, stir in the vanilla essence, whip up the egg whites very stiffly and fold in lightly. Pour the batter into the heated waffle iron and cook according to the directions given above. Serve immediately, with butter and maple or golden syrup.

Cold puddings

In this chapter we give recipes for desserts based on fruit, milk, cream and custard, for jellies, ice creams, mousses, soufflés and creams, a variety of gâteaux, pastries and refrigerator cakes, flans, meringue-based sweets – and a few which fit into none of these categories. There is also a final section on 'store-cupboard sweets'. Since cream plays a part in so many cold puddings, either as an ingredient or as decoration, we give a few notes on preparing it.

Whipped cream, whipped evaporated milk
Use double cream or whipping cream – single cream does not contain enough fat to whip stiffly. However, a little single cream may be added to double cream before it is whipped, to make it go further. Use 1 part single cream to 2 parts double. Another way of extending whipped double cream is to fold in 1 stiffly whisked egg white or whisk 15 ml *(1 tbsp)* milk with each 142 ml *(5 fl oz)* cream. Whipping cream should not be extended.

Both the whisk and the bowl must be clean and dry when you are whipping cream. The cream itself should be chilled. Take care not to over-whip – cream stiffens very quickly especially in warm weather or when the cream is not quite fresh, and it is too late when it turns to a butter consistency. Never beat too hard or too long. Use a fork for small quantities; otherwise a rotary whisk, or a small electric mixer set on low speed and used in a deep bowl gives good results. Stop every now and again to test the consistency. In most cases it is ready when the cream just holds its shape but is still floppy; at this stage the maximum amount of air is incorporated. Overbeating of cream can give a poor texture in dishes like cold soufflés and mousses, it is also more difficult to fold in evenly.

Evaporated milk is a little more trouble to whip than cream, but it will give quite satisfactory results in certain recipes. It is best to prepare it by boiling the unopened can in water for 15 minutes and then chilling it for several hours. (It is a good idea to keep 1–2 cans of the milk ready boiled in the refrigerator.)

For an even stiffer result, before whisking the evaporated milk, add 5 ml *(1 level tsp)* powdered gelatine, dissolved in 30 ml *(2 tbsps)* hot water. This helps to hold the consistency; without it evaporated milk will quickly lose its volume after whipping and will not be suitable for decorative purposes.

As an alternative to whipped cream for a topping or for piping, use one of the manufactured synthetic cream products. These can also replace cream in recipes to give bulk, but are no real alternative flavourwise.

FRUIT SWEETS

For fruit salads and similar dishes prepare the fruit as follows:

Apples and pears Peel thinly (though the skin is often left on red apples which are to be used in fruit salad); core and cut into quarters, eighths or thin slices. To prevent discoloration, put the prepared fruit at once into cold water (adding a little lemon juice if you wish), directly into lemon juice or into sugar syrup – see the fruit salad recipe, page 315.

Bananas Prepare these at the last moment, as they discolour quickly when exposed to the air. Peel, cut in slices, straight or diagonally and put at once into sugar syrup or sprinkle with lemon juice.

Oranges, tangerines, grapefruit Peel, remove all the white pith and cut the flesh into slices 0.3–0.5 cm *($\frac{1}{8}$–$\frac{1}{4}$ in)* thick. Alternatively, hold the fruit over a plate, to catch any juice that escapes and, using a sharp knife, remove all the skin with a sawing action, cutting deep enough to show the flesh. Holding the fruit in the left hand, remove the flesh of each segment in turn by cutting down at the side of the membrane and then scraping the segment off the membrane on the opposite side. Any juice collected should be added to the syrup.

Grapes Grapes can be peeled, though some people prefer them unskinned. Remove the skin with a sharp knife, or your finger nail. If the skin is obstinate, plunge the grapes into hot water for a second or two, then into

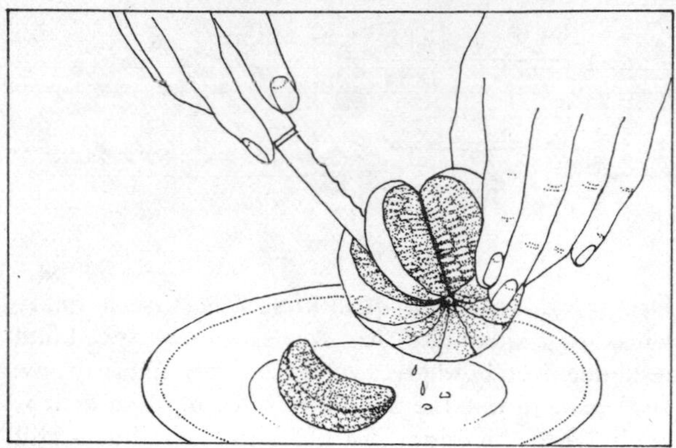
Cutting an orange into segments

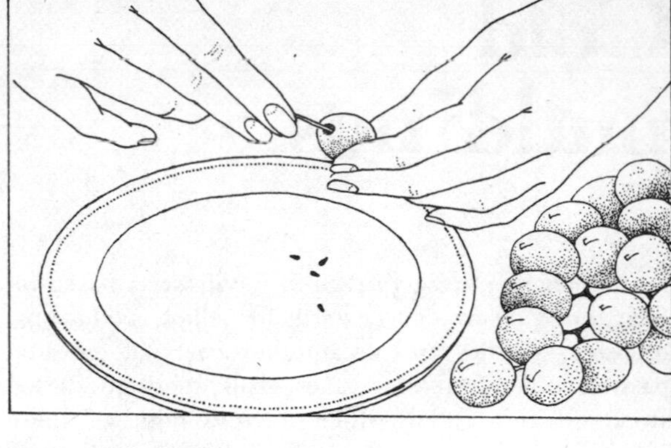
Removing the pips from grapes

cold. Make a small slit in the side of each grape and remove the pips with a fine skewer or leave the grapes whole and use the rounded end of a *new* hair grip, pushed into the stem end. Whole unskinned grapes can be cut in half and the pips then removed.

Cherries Take the cherries off the stalks and wash them well. Remove the stones, either with a cherry stoner – much the quickest way – or by making a split down one side of the cherry and removing the stone with a pointed knife.

Plums, greengages, damsons Pick over the fruit, removing the stalks, and wash it thoroughly. Very large plums may be halved and stoned before being stewed. Fresh dessert plums can be used in fruit salads; peel, stone and slice them. Keep them under sugar syrup or prepare only a short time before serving as plums discolour quickly.

Soft fruits (raspberries, strawberries, etc)
Pick over the fruit, removing any stalks and hulls; strawberries usually require washing but keep it to the minimum, preferably putting them in a sieve or colander and rinsing under the cold tap. Drain well. Put the fruit into sugar syrup or place it in a bowl and sprinkle with caster sugar.

Dried fruits See recipe for stewed dried fruit, below.

Stewed fresh fruit

75–100 g *(3–4 oz)* sugar
150 ml *(¼ pt)* water, or 300 ml *(½ pt)* for hard fruits
450 g *(1 lb)* fresh fruit, prepared

Make a syrup by dissolving the sugar in the water over a gentle heat. Add the fruit and simmer gently until it is soft but still keeps its shape. Some fruits are improved by an additional flavouring, which is usually removed before serving.

To stewed apples, add a squeeze of lemon juice, a strip of lemon rind, 1 or 2 cloves or a small piece of cinnamon stick.

To stewed pears, add 1 or 2 cloves or a small piece of cinnamon stick.

To stewed plums, add the plum kernels or a few sweet almonds.

To stewed rhubarb, add a piece of root ginger, a piece of cinnamon stick or a strip of lemon or orange rind.

Stewed dried fruit

450 g *(1 lb)* dried fruit, eg prunes, apricots, peaches, figs, apples, pears or a mixture
600 ml *(1 pt)* water
225 g *(½ lb)* demerara sugar
piece of lemon rind

Wash the fruit thoroughly, add the measured water and soak for 12 hours. Put it into a saucepan with the water in which it soaked, the sugar and lemon peel, bring to the boil and simmer gently until tender. Remove the fruit, boil the juice for a few minutes until syrupy, then strain it over the fruit.

Fruit salad

100 g *(4 oz)* sugar
300 ml *(½ pt)* water
juice of ½ lemon
selection of fruit, eg 2 red-skinned apples, 2 oranges, 2 bananas, 100 g *(4 oz)* black or green grapes

To make a syrup dissolve the sugar in the water over a gentle heat and boil for 5 minutes; cool and add the lemon juice. Prepare the fruits as required (see opposite) and put them into the syrup as they are ready. Mix them all together and if possible leave to stand for 2–3 hours before serving, to blend the flavours. Any other combinations of fresh fruits can be used, such as dessert pears, strawberries, raspberries, cherries and melon.

To give additional flavour, add to the syrup:

1. 1.25 ml *(¼ level tsp)* ground cinnamon or nutmeg or infuse a piece of cinnamon stick when preparing the syrup; this will avoid clouding the syrup.
2. 15–30 ml *(1–2 tbsps)* fruit liqueur, brandy or rum.

Fruit salad can be served in a hollowed-out melon or pineapple; in either case the flesh which has been removed should be cut into chunks and used in the salad.

Canned fruit such as apricot halves, peach slices and pineapple chunks can also be used in fruit salads, or the more exotic canned guavas and litchis. If you use canned fruit use some of the syrup from the can, sharpened with lemon juice, to replace sugar syrup.

Winter fruit salad

100 g *(4 oz)* sugar
300 ml *(½ pt)* water
pared rind and juice of 1 lemon
100 g *(4 oz)* prunes, stewed and drained
100 g *(4 oz)* dried apricots, stewed and drained
1 banana, skinned and sliced
2 oranges, skinned and segmented
1 grapefruit, skinned and segmented

Make a syrup by dissolving the sugar in the water over a gentle heat; add the lemon rind, heat and boil for 5 minutes. Add the lemon juice. If you wish, stone the prunes and halve the apricots, then strain the syrup over the prepared fruits and leave to cool.

Alternatively, use mixed dried fruit as a basis, cooking it in the usual way and adding any fresh fruit that may be available.

Gooseberry fool

450 g *(1 lb)* gooseberries, or a 566-g *(1-lb 4-oz)* can, drained
100 g *(4 oz)* sugar, optional
150 ml *(¼ pt)* custard
green food colouring
142-ml *(5-fl oz)* carton double or whipping cream, whipped
chopped nuts

Stew the fruit in 30 ml *(2 tbsps)* water, with the sugar (unless canned fruit is used). Purée the fruit, preferably using a nylon sieve or an electric blender. Fold the purée into the custard and leave it until cold. Tint it green, remembering that the colour will lighten when you add the cream. Lightly fold in the cream. Pour into glasses and decorate with chopped nuts. Serve with shortbread, sponge fingers or a plain sweet biscuit. This sweet can also be made with apples, blackberries, apricots, rhubarb, damsons or raspberries (these should not be cooked, just sieve and sweeten to taste).

Note To prepare the custard use 150 ml *(¼ pt)* milk, 15 ml *(1 level tbsp)* custard powder and 15 ml *(1 level tbsp)* sugar. Alternatively replace the custard and cream with a 284-ml *(10-fl oz)* carton double or whipping cream.

Melon with jellied blackberries

1.4 kg *(3 lb)* ripe honeydew melon
1 tablet raspberry jelly
225 g *(8 oz)* fresh plump blackberries

Cut the melon in half lengthwise, scoop out the seeds and membrane and neaten the centre cavity. Strain the seeds and reserve any melon juice. Make the melon juice up to 150 ml *(¼ pt)* with water. Dissolve the jelly tablet in the melon juice and water and chill until just on the point of setting. Spoon the blackberries through the jelly and turn into the melon halves. Chill until completely set. Cut into wedges and serve. *Serves 4–6.*

Note Frozen unsweetened blackberries are suitable. Add frozen berries to the warm jelly, this helps to speed up the setting. If using bottled fruit, include the juice as part of the liquid for the jelly.

Danish 'Peasant girl with veil'

175 g *(6 oz)* fresh breadcrumbs
75 g *(3 oz)* brown sugar
50 g *(2 oz)* butter
700 g *(1½ lb)* cooking apples, peeled, cored and sliced
juice of ½ lemon
sugar to taste
142-ml *(5-fl oz)* carton double or whipping cream
50 g *(2 oz)* chocolate, grated

Mix the crumbs and sugar together and fry in the hot butter until crisp. Cook the apples in a very little water, with the lemon juice and some sugar to taste, until they form a pulp – 10–15 minutes. Put alternate layers of the fried crumb mixture and the apple pulp into a glass dish, finishing with a layer of crumbs. When the pudding is quite cold, pour the cream on top and sprinkle with the chocolate.

Note If you wish, spread a layer of raspberry jam between the last layer of crumbs and the cream.

Strawberry foam *see colour plate between pp. 400 and 401*

225 g *(½ lb)* ripe strawberries, hulled
1 egg white
75 g *(3 oz)* icing sugar, sifted

Do not wash the strawberries, wipe only if really necessary as the berries should be very dry. Turn the berries into a deep bowl and squash with something like a stainless steel potato masher. Add the egg white and the icing sugar and with an electric beater whisk for about 10 minutes until thick and frothy – with a hand rotary whisk this will take about twice as long. Turn into glasses, piling the mixture well up. Chill for up to 6 hours before serving. Serve with single cream.

Summer pudding

30 ml *(2 tbsps)* water
150 g *(5 oz)* sugar
450 g *(1 lb)* mixed black-currants, stringed and washed, and blackberries, picked over and washed
100–175 g *(4–6 oz)* white bread, cut in thin slices
whipped cream or custard

Stir the water and sugar together and bring slowly to the boil, add the fruits and stew gently, until they are soft but retain their shape. Cut the crusts from the bread and line a 900-ml *(1½-pt)* pudding basin with the slices. Pour in the fruit and cover with more slices of bread. Place a saucer with a weight on it on top of the pudding and leave overnight in a cool place. Turn out and serve with whipped cream or custard. Other soft fruits (or a mixture) may be used in summer pudding, providing that they have a rich, strong colour – for example, raspberries, red-currants, damsons. A proportion of apple can also be included.

Strawberry shortcake

225 g *(8 oz)* self raising flour
5 ml *(1 level tsp)* baking powder
1.25 ml *(¼ level tsp)* salt
75 g *(3 oz)* butter or margarine
75 g *(3 oz)* sugar
1 egg, beaten
15–30 ml *(1–2 tbsps)* milk, optional
350–450 g *(¾–1 lb)* strawberries
45–60 ml *(3–4 level tbsps)* caster sugar for filling
142-ml *(5-fl oz)* carton double or whipping cream

Grease a deep 20.5-cm *(8-in)* sandwich tin. Sift the flour, baking powder and salt together and rub in the fat until the mixture resembles fine breadcrumbs; stir in the sugar. Add the egg a little at a time to the rubbed-in mixture until this begins to bind together; use a little milk as well if necessary. Knead the mixture lightly into a smooth, light, manageable dough.

Turn the dough on to a floured board, form into a round and roll out until it is 20.5 cm *(8 in)* across. Press it evenly into the tin and bake in the oven at 190°C *(375°F)* mark 5 for 20 minutes, or until golden and firm. Turn the cake out of the tin on to a cooling tray.

Hull and wash the strawberries and drain them well. Keep about a dozen berries whole for decorating and crush the rest with a fork in a basin, sprinkling with 30–45 ml *(2–3 level tbsps)* of the caster sugar. Whisk the cream and stir in the remaining sugar. When the cake is nearly or just cold, split, spread with half of the cream and all the crushed fruit and replace the top. Pile the remaining cream on the top of the cake and decorate with whole berries.

Apple snow

450 g *(1 lb)* cooking apples, peeled, cored and chopped
30 ml *(2 tbsps)* water
10 ml *(2 tsps)* lemon juice
25–50 g *(1–2 oz)* granulated sugar
sap green colouring, optional
2 eggs, separated

Place apples, water, lemon juice and sugar in a saucepan and cook, covered, over a medium heat until the fruit is thick and pulpy. Pass it through a nylon sieve. In a basin combine the apple purée, a few drops of green colouring and the egg yolks. Beat well and allow to cool. Stiffly whisk the egg whites then fold them into the apple purée until well blended. Turn the purée into individual glasses and chill before serving decorated with cream or grated chocolate.

Note 300 ml *(½ pt)* bottled or frozen unsweetened apple purée can be used as an alternative.

Honeyed apples

50 g *(2 oz)* dried figs, chopped
25 g *(1 oz)* almonds, blanched and chopped
45 ml *(3 tbsps)* water
100 g *(¼ lb)* honey
large knob of butter
6 medium sized cooking apples

Mix the figs and almonds. Warm together the water, honey and butter in a saucepan. Twist the stems from the apples and, starting at the stem end, peel each apple about a third of the way down; remove the core. Fill the apples with the fig and almond mixture, arrange them in a shallow baking dish and pour on the water and honey. Bake in the oven at 170°C *(325°F)* mark 3 basting often with the honey syrup, until tender but still unbroken – about 1¼ hours. Refrigerate until required. *Serves 6.*

Chinese toffied apples

3 eating apples
45 ml *(3 level tbsps)* plain flour
15 ml *(1 level tbsp)* cornflour
1 egg white
45 ml *(3 tbsps)* water
oil for deep fat frying
150 g *(5 oz)* caster sugar
75 ml *(5 tbsps)* water
15 ml *(1 tbsp)* corn oil
15 ml *(1 level tbsp)* sesame seeds

Peel and core the apples, cut into six wedges and toss in a little flour. Mix the remaining flour, cornflour, egg white and 45 ml *(3 tbsps)* water together to form a thick batter. Coat the apple pieces in this and fry in deep fat heated to correct temperature (a small cube of bread will brown in 30 seconds) until golden brown, drain. Place sugar and remaining water in a small thick saucepan; bring slowly to the boil stirring until the sugar has dissolved. Add 15 ml *(1 tbsp)* of corn oil and boil until the liquid becomes golden brown. Remove from the heat and add the apples and sesame seeds, turn until well coated. To serve dip the apple slices quickly in and out of ice cold water.

Black-currant mallow

450 g *(1 lb)* black-currants
175 g *(6 oz)* sugar
400 ml *(¾ pt)* water
25 ml *(1½ level tbsps)* powdered gelatine
1 egg white
10 marshmallows

If necessary, stem and wash the currants. Cook them in a covered pan with the sugar and water until soft – about 20 minutes. Blend the gelatine with 30 ml *(2 tbsps)* water and heat over a pan of hot water until dissolved. Sieve the cooked black-currants (or purée them in an electric blender and then sieve to remove the seeds). Stir in the prepared gelatine and cool until the consistency of egg white.

Whisk the egg white until it is stiff enough to hold peaks. Cut the marshmallows into quarters with a wetted knife or scissors and add them to the egg white in a large bowl. Gradually fold in the black-currant mixture. When evenly blended, pour into a jelly mould, leave in a cool place to set, then turn out. Serve with shortbread or similar biscuits.

Cranberry mould

450 g *(1 lb)* cranberries, fresh or frozen
225 g *(8 oz)* sugar, or according to taste
50 g *(2 oz)* cornflour
double cream for decoration

Stew the cranberries with 300 ml *(½ pt)* water, with the lid on, until tender – about 10 minutes. Sieve or purée in an electric blender and then sieve to remove the seeds. Add the sugar, using more or less according to taste; add sufficient water to make up to 500 ml *(1 pt)* with the juice. Mix the cornflour with 30 ml *(2 tbsps)* water to a fairly thin paste, add to the cooked cranberries and boil for about 2 minutes, stirring all the time. Pour the mixture into a wetted china or glass mould and leave to set. Turn out, and decorate with whipped cream.

Alternatively, put the cranberry mixture (made with 45 ml *(3 level tbsps)* instead of 50 g *(2 oz)* cornflour) into individual dishes and serve hot, with whipped or single cream.

Note In Finland, lingenberries would be used, but cranberries make a very good substitute. *Serves 4–6.*

Red-currant griestorte *see colour plate between pp. 400 and 401*

3 large eggs, separated
100 g *(4 oz)* caster sugar
grated rind and juice of ½ lemon
50 g *(2 oz)* fine semolina
15 ml *(1 level tbsp)* ground almonds
170-ml *(6-fl oz)* carton double cream
15 ml *(1 tbsp)* milk
100 g *(¼ lb)* red-currants
icing sugar

Grease and line a 20.5-cm by 30.5-cm *(8-in by 12-in)* Swiss roll tin with non-stick paper to extend above the sides. Grease the paper, sprinkle with caster sugar and a dusting of flour. Whisk the egg yolks with 100 g *(4 oz)* sugar until thick and pale. Whisk in the lemon juice. Stir in the rind, semolina and almonds mixed together. Whisk the egg whites until stiff and fold the egg yolk mixture through the whites. Turn it into the tin, level the surface and bake at 180°C *(350°F)* mark 4 for about 30 minutes until puffed and pale gold. Turn the griestorte carefully on to a sheet of non-stick paper dusted with caster sugar. Trim the long edges and roll it up loosely with the paper inside. Cool on a wire rack. To finish, whisk together the cream and milk until they just hold their shape. Unroll the griestorte – don't worry if it cracks a little – spread the cream over but not quite to the edges and sprinkle with currants, reserving a few on the stem for decoration . Roll up, pressing lightly into shape. Dust with icing sugar and decorate. Eat the same day. *Serves 6.*

Savarin with fresh fruit

45 ml *(3 tbsps)* warm milk
15 g *(½ oz)* fresh yeast
100 g *(4 oz)* plain strong flour
1.25 ml *(¼ level tsp)* salt
15 ml *(1 level tbsp)* caster sugar
2 eggs, beaten
50 g *(2 oz)* butter, softened
syrup – see below
60–90 ml *(4–6 tbsps)* warm apricot glaze
fruit salad – see below

Blend together the milk and yeast, then stir in 25 g *(1 oz)* flour. Stand the bowl in a warm place for about 20 minutes. Add the remaining flour, salt, sugar, eggs and butter and beat for 3–4 minutes. Well grease an 18-cm *(7-in)* 900-ml *(1½-pt)* metal ring mould with lard and dust with flour. Fill it with the mixture, cover and allow to rise until the tin is two-thirds full. Bake in the oven at 200°C *(400°F)* mark 6 for about 20 minutes. Cool the savarin for a few minutes, then ease it out on to a wire rack, and while still warm, prick with a fine skewer. Spoon enough syrup over to saturate, reserving the remainder. Brush with glaze and let it cool. Place the ring on a serving dish, fill and decorate with fruit. Serve with cream.

Syrup Dissolve 175 g *(6 oz)* sugar in 200 ml *(7 fl oz)* water. Add 4 strips lemon rind. Boil it for 5 minutes then cool and add 45 ml *(3 tbsps)* Kirsch.

Fruit salad Peel 1 orange and divide it into segments without membrane. Peel and slice 1 pear and 1 banana. Leave the skin on 1 red apple, core and dice it. Stone 100 g *(4 oz)* mixed grapes. Toss all the fruit in 30 ml *(2 tbsps)* lemon juice and the remaining sugar syrup.

Caramelled bananas

45 ml *(3 level tbsps)* sugar
30 ml *(2 tbsps)* water
4 ripe bananas, peeled

Make a caramel by dissolving the sugar in the water and heating until just golden brown. Arrange the bananas in the top part of a chafing dish over hot water or on a deep enamel dish over a saucepan of hot water, then pour the caramel sauce over them. Cook slowly for about 10–15 minutes, basting them constantly with the caramel. Transfer the bananas to a dish and pour the remainder of the caramel over them; serve with pouring cream and sponge fingers.

Lemon chiffon

3 eggs, separated
75 g *(3 oz)* sugar
juice of 1 lemon
grated rind of ½ lemon

Beat the egg yolks and sugar together until creamy, then gradually add the lemon juice and rind. Heat gently in a thick-based pan or the top of a double boiler, stirring all the time, until the mixture thickens – do not overheat or it will curdle. Allow to cool. Whisk the egg whites stiffly and fold into the lemon cream mixture. Pile into individual glasses and chill before serving. Eat the same day. To give extra flavour, add 30 ml *(2 tbsps)* dry white wine with the lemon juice.

Oranges à la turque

8 juicy oranges
450 g *(1 lb)* caster sugar
2 cloves

Thinly pare the rind from half the oranges, keeping it free of white pith. Cut the rind into very thin julienne strips with a sharp knife or scissors, put into a small pan and cover well with water. Cover the pan and cook until the rind is tender; strain. Cut away all the pith from these oranges, and both rind and pith from the 4 remaining oranges. (Hold them over a bowl to catch the juice.) Dissolve the sugar in 300 ml *(½ pt)* water, with the cloves. Bring to the boil and boil until caramel-coloured. Remove the pan from the heat, add 45 ml *(3 tbsps)* water and return it to a very low heat to dissolve the caramel; add the orange juice.

Arrange the oranges in a single layer in a serving dish. Top with the julienne strips and spoon the caramel syrup over. Leave for several hours in a cold place, turning the oranges occasionally. Serve the oranges sliced and then re-assembled, or whole – in this case, provide knife, fork and spoon. *Serves 4–8.*

Pears in port wine

4 large ripe pears
150 ml *(¼ pt)* port
150 ml *(¼ pt)* water
75 g *(3 oz)* sugar
rind of 1 lemon
about 30 ml *(2 tbsps)* red-currant jelly

Peel the pears, cut in quarters lengthwise and remove the cores. Make a syrup from the port, water, sugar and lemon rind. Add the pears and simmer gently until tender. Remove the fruit, add the red-currant jelly to the syrup and boil rapidly until it is well reduced. Place 4 pear quarters in each glass and strain the syrup over. Allow to cool and serve with cream.

Liqueured peaches

4 yellow peaches
300 ml *(½ pt)* water
100 g *(4 oz)* sugar
thinly peeled lemon rind
30 ml *(2 tbsps)* maraschino or orange liqueur

Put the peaches into boiling water, remove and skin with a stainless steel knife; cut in half and remove the stones. Put the water, sugar and lemon rind in a pan, dissolve the sugar and bring to the boil. Add the peaches and poach very gently for about 10 minutes, until just soft. Drain carefully. Reduce the syrup to about one-third, strain and stir in the liqueur; pour this over the peaches and chill. A quicker way which requires no cooking is to use canned whole or halved peaches; add the liqueur to the syrup with a little lemon juice to sharpen it and pour over the peaches. Leave to marinade for at least 1 hour.

Brandied apricots

450 g *(1 lb)* fresh ripe apricots
300 ml *(½ pt)* water
100 g *(4 oz)* sugar
thinly peeled lemon rind
45 ml *(3 tbsps)* brandy

Make as above, poaching the apricots for 5–10 minutes.

Rødgrød

600 ml *(1 pt)* red-currant purée, made from 900 g *(2 lb)* fresh fruit or 2 425-g *(15-oz)* cans
600 ml *(1 pt)* raspberry purée, made from 900 g *(2 lb)* fresh fruit or 2 425-g *(15-oz)* cans
45 ml *(3 level tbsps)* arrowroot
caster sugar
browned shredded almonds and double cream to decorate

Mix the fruit purées. Blend the arrowroot with a little of the purée, bring the remainder to boiling point, stir into the blended mixture and return it all to the pan. Bring to the boil again, cook for 2–3 minutes and sweeten to taste. Allow to cool before pouring into individual glasses. Top with shredded almonds and whipped cream. *Serves 6.*

MILKY AND CUSTARD SWEETS

Creamed rice

50 g *(2 oz)* short grain pudding rice
568 ml *(1 pt)* milk
30 ml *(2 level tbsps)* sugar
flavouring or other addition (see below)

Put the rice, milk and sugar into a thick-based pan or in the top of a double boiler, cover and cook very gently for about 30 minutes or up to 2 hours in a double pan, until creamy. Remove the lid after half the time and cook uncovered for the remainder of the time, stirring the pudding occasionally. Allow to cool and finish in one of the following ways:

Dairy creamed rice
Whip a 142-ml *(5-fl oz)* carton double or whipping cream and fold into the pudding just before serving.

Fudge rice
Fold 50 g *(2 oz)* chopped fudge into the pudding just before serving.

Honey pudding
When making the pudding, use 15 ml *(1 tbsp)* honey instead of sugar; serve with chopped nuts.

Fruit rice
Drain the fruit from a small can and roughly chop if necessary. Fold it into the pudding just before serving.

Chocolate rice
Fold 50 g *(2 oz)* coarsely grated chocolate or 50 g *(2 oz)* chocolate chips into the cooled rice pudding and top with more chocolate when serving.

Vegetable curry with eggs (p. 258).

Lemon creamed rice with cinnamon

75 g *(3 oz)* short grain pudding rice
900 ml *(1½ pt)* milk
45 ml *(3 level tbsps)* sugar
thinly pared rind of 1 lemon
3 egg yolks
cinnamon sugar

Wash the rice in cold water and drain well. Put the rice, milk, sugar and lemon rind in a saucepan and mix well. Cook very slowly over a low heat until thick and creamy – about 45 minutes. Discard the lemon rind. Stir in the beaten egg yolks and reheat but don't boil. Turn the mixture into a shallow dish. When it is cold but not chilled, sprinkle with cinnamon sugar. *Serves 5–6.*

Peach condé

rice pudding, made as above, using 568 ml *(1 pt)* milk
425-g *(15-oz)* can peach halves
120 ml *(8 tbsps)* red-currant jelly
15 ml *(1 tbsp)* peach juice
lemon juice

Divide the rice pudding between 4 sundae glasses. Drain the peach halves thoroughly and arrange the halves on top of the rice, cut side down. Heat the red-currant jelly with the peach and lemon juice, stirring until smooth and slightly thickened. Pour over the peaches and leave to cool before serving. Alternatively coat the peaches with melba sauce (see page 206).

Ground rice mould

568 ml *(1 pt)* milk
40 g *(1½ oz)* ground rice
25 g *(1 oz)* sugar
whole nutmeg

Heat all except 60 ml *(4 tbsps)* of milk. Blend the ground rice with the reserved milk to a smooth thin paste. When the milk has reached boiling point pour it over the paste, stirring. Return to pan, add the sugar and bring to the boil, stirring all the time. Cook gently for 4–6 minutes until the rice is clear. Add grated nutmeg to taste. Allow to cool and serve in a dish with fruit or a fruit sauce or set in a 600-ml *(1-pt)* mould and turn out when cold.

Cornflour mould

60 ml *(4 level tbsps)* cornflour
568 ml *(1 pt)* milk
strip of lemon rind
30–60 ml *(2–4 level tbsps)* sugar

Blend the cornflour to a smooth cream with 15–30 ml *(1–2 tbsps)* of the milk. Boil the remaining milk with the lemon rind and strain it on to the blended mixture, stirring well. Return the mixture to the pan and bring to the boil, stirring all the time, until it thickens. Cook for a further 2–3 minutes and add sugar to taste. Pour into a wetted jelly mould and leave to set. Turn out when cold and serve with fruit or jam sauce (see pages 204, 205).

Orange mould
Substitute orange for lemon rind.

Chocolate mould
Mix 15 ml *(1 level tbsp)* cocoa with the blended cornflour or add 50 g *(2 oz)* melted chocolate to the cooked mixture. Omit the lemon rind and add a few drops of vanilla essence.

Coffee mould
Add 15–30 ml *(1–2 tbsps)* coffee essence or 5–10 ml *(1–2 level tsps)* instant coffee to the cooked mixture. Omit the lemon rind.

Caramel custard

125 g *(4½ oz)* sugar
150 ml *(¼ pt)* water
568 ml *(1 pt)* milk
4 eggs

Put 100 g *(4 oz)* of the sugar and the water into a small pan and dissolve the sugar slowly; bring to the boil without stirring until it caramelises, ie becomes a rich golden brown colour. Pour the caramel into a 15-cm *(6-in)* cake tin which has been heated slightly, turning

Stuffed mushrooms (p. 220), Stuffed peppers (p. 230).

the tin until the bottom is completely covered. Warm the milk, pour on to the lightly whisked eggs and remaining sugar and strain over the cooled caramel. Place the tin in a shallow tin of water and bake in the oven at 170°C *(325°F)* mark 3 for about 1 hour until set. Leave in the tin until quite cold (preferably until the next day) before turning out.

Note Individual custards are easier to turn out. Divide the above mixture between 6 150-ml *(¼-pt)* caramel coated tins. Cook for about 45 minutes.

Egg custard tart

150 g *(5 oz)* shortcrust pastry ie made with 150 g *(5 oz)* flour etc (see page 351)
2 eggs
30 ml *(2 level tbsps)* sugar
300 ml *(½ pt)* milk
a little grated or ground nutmeg

Roll out the pastry, use it to line a fairly deep 18-cm *(7-in)* pie plate or flan case and decorate the edge. Place on a baking sheet. Whisk the eggs lightly with the sugar; warm the milk and pour on to the egg mixture. Strain the custard into the pastry case and sprinkle the top with nutmeg. Bake in the oven at 220°C *(425°F)* mark 7 for about 10 minutes, until the pastry begins to brown. Reduce the oven temperature to 180°C *(350°F)* mark 4 and continue cooking for about 20 minutes, or until the custard is just set. Serve cold.

Note If you have trouble with the crust rising when making a custard tart, this is probably due to a small break forming in the pastry. To avoid this (1) don't stretch the pastry when lining the pie plate; (2) brush the lined pie plate with raw egg white before adding the custard.

Junket

This centuries-old sweet is made by adding rennet to milk. The rennet (which is prepared from the digestive juices of the calf) contains an enzyme that acts on the protein in milk and sets it, forming junket or 'curds and whey'. The enzyme is most active at blood heat, so the milk must be warmed to this temperature before the rennet is added. Don't overheat the milk, or the enzyme will be destroyed, and don't chill it too rapidly, or the enzyme may become inactive and prevent the junket setting. Junket should not be disturbed until it is served – once it is cut, the whey tends to run out and separate from the curds, spoiling the texture. (Incidentally, any leftover junket that has separated out can be used to make curd cheesecakes.)

Note Rennet is sold as a liquid or in a tablet without added colouring; there are also commercial preparations of rennet in powder, tablet and liquid form, which are already coloured and flavoured. Store rennet in a cool, dry place.

Simple junket

568 ml *(1 pt)* rich milk (not Long Life)
15–30 ml *(1–2 level tbsps)* caster sugar
5 ml *(1 tsp)* liquid rennet
flavouring (see below)

Warm the milk to blood heat (that is, just warm to the finger) and stir in the sugar until it is dissolved. Add the rennet, stir, pour the mixture at once into serving dishes and put in a warm place to set. Chill lightly before serving.

Nutmeg
Sprinkle grated or ground nutmeg over the surface of the junket.

Vanilla, almond, raspberry
Add a few drops of the essence to the milk, with a few drops of the appropriate vegetable colouring.

Rum
Add 5–10 ml *(1–2 tsps)* rum to the milk.

Note Use rennet in powdered or tablet form according to the directions on the pack.

Choc-au-rhum

175 g *(6 oz)* plain chocolate
3 large eggs, separated
15 ml *(1 tbsp)* rum
142-ml *(5-fl oz)* carton double cream, whipped
grated chocolate or finely chopped nuts

Melt the chocolate in a bowl over a pan of hot water. Beat the yolks into the melted chocolate and add the rum. Whisk the whites until stiff and carefully fold into the chocolate mixture. Chill and serve in small sundae glasses, topped with whipped cream and grated chocolate or chopped nuts.

Sherry trifle *see colour plate facing p. 513*

8 trifle sponge cakes
jam
150 ml *(¼ pt)* medium sherry
6 macaroons, crushed
400 ml *(¾ pt)* custard
284-ml *(10-fl oz)* carton double cream, whipped
sugar and flavouring
glacé cherries, angelica and cream to decorate

Split the sponge cakes, spread them with jam and arrange in a glass dish, then pour the sherry over and leave to soak for ½ hour. Sprinkle the macaroons over the sponge cakes and pour on the warm, not hot, custard. Cover the dish with a plate to prevent a skin forming and leave until cold. Sweeten and flavour the cream to taste and spread most of it over the custard. Decorate with the rest of the cream, piped, the cherries and angelica (or with ratafias, almonds, etc.). Fruit juice such as orange may replace some or all of the sherry, if you prefer. *Serves 6.*

SYLLABUB

This old English sweet was traditionally made with milk straight from the cow poured from a height over wine, brandy, cider or ale; this gave a frothy mixture, which was sweetened to taste and flavoured with spices and spirit. Nowadays, there are numerous variants, but we give two popular versions, using dairy cream instead of milk.

Syllabub made with wine

2 egg whites
100 g *(4 oz)* caster sugar
juice of ½ lemon
150 ml *(¼ pt)* sweet white wine
284-ml *(10-fl oz)* carton double cream, whipped
crystallised lemon slices

Whisk the egg whites stiffly and fold in the sugar, lemon juice, wine and cream. Pour the mixture into individual glasses and chill for several hours before serving. Decorate with the lemon slices. The mixture will separate out as it stands.

Everlasting syllabub

juice and grated rind of 1 lemon
75 g *(3 oz)* caster sugar
15–30 ml *(1–2 tbsps)* brandy
30 ml *(2 tbsps)* sherry (sweet or dry)
284-ml *(10-fl oz)* carton double cream, whipped

Soak the lemon rind in the juice for 2–3 hours, then add the sugar, brandy and sherry. Add to the whipped cream, mixing until it is all evenly blended. Serve with sponge fingers or spoon it over crushed macaroons.

Syllabub trifle

450 g *(1 lb)* strawberries, fresh or frozen, thawed
225 g *(½ lb)* green grapes, seeded
175 g *(6 oz)* macaroons
3 egg whites
175 g *(6 oz)* caster sugar
150 ml *(¼ pt)* dry white wine
juice of ½ lemon
30 ml *(2 tbsps)* brandy
284-ml *(10-fl oz)* carton double cream
strawberries to decorate

Arrange the strawberries and grapes alternately round the base of a glass dish. Cover with a single layer of macaroons (reserving about 10 for decoration). Layer with the remaining fruit and macaroons. Stiffly whisk the egg whites, gradually add half the sugar and re-whisk until the meringue holds its shape, then fold in the remaining sugar. Pour the wine, lemon juice and brandy over, folding the liquids into the egg whites. Whisk the cream until it just holds its shape and use a little to fill the macaroons reserved as decoration.

Fold the frothy meringue mixture through the rest of the cream. Pour over the fruit and allow to stand for several hours in a cool place, to let the macaroons become moistened. Just before serving, place the cream-filled macaroons and a few berries on top. *Serves 6–8.*

This trifle, based on a syllabub mixture, is the traditional version.

JELLIES AND JELLY SWEETS

The simplest way of making a jelly is of course with a proprietary jelly tablet or crystals, but you can also use unflavoured gelatine; this is usually sold in powdered form, though it is sometimes found in sheets and occasionally in flakes or strips.

To make up a proprietary jelly, add liquid according to the manufacturer's instructions. With plain gelatine a 10-g *(½-oz)* sachet is needed to set 500 ml *(1 pt)* liquid just stiff enough to be moulded. If the weather is hot and you have no refrigerator, you will need to increase the amount of gelatine by 5–10 ml *(1–2 level tsps)*. When a refrigerator is available, it is better to use only the minimum amount of gelatine, or the jelly may be too stiff. Most brands of powdered gelatine are packed in small inner envelopes, each containing enough to set 500 ml *(1 pt)* of liquid under normal conditions. Otherwise, reckon that 15 ml *(3½ level tsps)* weighs approximately 10 g *(½ oz)*. If sheet gelatine is preferred, base the proportions on approximately 3 sheets to set 500 ml *(5 sheets to set 1 pt)*. Before sheet, flake or strip gelatine is used, it should be soaked in cold water to cover until just pliable – about 10 minutes is generally long enough – drain and dissolve as for powdered gelatine. Powdered gelatine does not need to be soaked beforehand.

Making a jelly

1. Treat proprietary jelly tablets or crystals as directed on the packet.
2. Weigh or measure gelatine accurately; soak it if necessary (see above). Dissolve powdered gelatine (or soaked leaf gelatine) in about 45 ml *(3 tbsps)* of the measured liquid in a basin standing in hot water. When using powdered gelatine, put the measured water in a small bowl or cup and sprinkle the gelatine over it before heating.
3. Warm the required amount of liquid (water, fruit juice, wine etc) and if necessary sweeten, flavour and colour it.
4. Quickly stir the dissolved gelatine into the warmed liquid (the two should be as nearly as possible at the same temperature). When adding gelatine to a cold mixture, it is best to add a little of the cold mixture to the warm, not hot, gelatine and then return it to the bulk, to avoid 'roping' (uneven setting) or premature setting.
5. Pour the mixture into a wetted mould or individual moulds, put in a cool place and when it is nearly cold, transfer to a refrigerator.

Special points

Milk jellies Dissolve the gelatine in water as already described, leave until luke-warm and then add the cold milk.

Jellies containing fruit, etc If adding solid ingredients, stir them in when the jelly is just beginning to set. Alternatively, follow the recipe given on page 326 for fruit set in jelly.

Pineapple jelly Fresh pineapple juice makes a delicious jelly, but since it contains an enzyme which breaks down gelatine and destroys its setting powers, the juice must first be boiled for 2–3 minutes, to kill the enzyme.

To set jellies quickly Put the mixture into small moulds or individual containers; if ice is available, pack some round the moulds. Alternatively make up the jelly with only half the recipe quantity of hot liquid and add ice cubes to make up the rest; as the ice melts, the jelly cools and sets.

All jellied desserts are best not served straight from the refrigerator. Allow them to 'come to' at room temperature for about 1 hour.

To line or mask a mould with jelly

First prepare any decorations (eg sliced glacé cherries and pistachio nuts, cut angelica). Fill a large basin with chips of ice and nest the wetted jelly mould in it. Pour 30–45 ml *(2–3 tbsps)* cold but liquid jelly into the mould and rotate this slowly until the inside is evenly coated. Continue pouring in and setting cold liquid jelly until the whole surface is lined with a layer about 0.3 cm *(⅛ in)* thick. Using 2 fine skewers, dip the pieces of cherry, etc, into liquid jelly and place in position in the mould, allowing each piece to set firmly. Finally, pour a thin coating over the whole and allow to set before adding the cream mixture or other filling.

To unmould a jelly

Fill a basin with very hot water. Wet the serving plate or dish. Draw the tip of a knife or finger round the rim of the mould. Immerse mould for 1–2 seconds in water. Place plate in position on top of mould. Hold in position with both hands, quickly reverse, give one or two sharp shakes and the jelly can be felt to transfer its weight on to the plate. If obstinate, dip it in the water again; porcelain moulds often need a second immersion. If the mould is not centred on the plate gently ease it into place on the wet surface.

Chopped jelly for use as a decoration

The jelly should be very clear and it must be chopped coarsely but cleanly, so that the light is refracted from the cut surfaces as from the facets of a jewel. To achieve this, use a wetted knife on wet greaseproof paper. The more coarsely the jelly is chopped, the better the effect; finely chopped jelly has a slightly opaque appearance.

Packet jelly variations

1. Make the jelly in the usual way, pour a little into the bottom of individual glasses and add a little fresh or drained canned fruit, if you wish, Leave the remaining jelly in a basin in a cool place until it begins to set round the edges; pour into a large bowl and whisk hard until pale and fluffy. Pour the whipped jelly over that already in the glasses and leave to set.
2. Make a jelly in the usual way, pour it into a divided ice-cube tray and place a piece of fruit in each division. Put the tray in the refrigerator until the jelly has set, then remove the divisions and serve the squares of jelly piled up with cream or ice cream.
3. Make a jelly in the usual way, but using only enough water to make 400 ml *(¾ pt)* and leave until it begins to set. Meanwhile, whisk the contents of a can of cream (or evaporated milk), add to the jelly and whisk the two together until pale and fluffy. Pour into glasses and leave to set. Decorate with desiccated coconut, chopped walnuts or grated chocolate.
4. Make a jelly using the juice from a can of fruit (making up the amount if necessary with a little water) and adjusting the extra sweetness with lemon juice. Leave the jelly until it begins to set, then whisk as above. Chop the fruit if it is in large pieces, but keep a few whole pieces for decoration; fold it into the jelly, pour the mixture into individual dishes and leave to set. Decorate with the whole fruit.
5. Make a lemon jelly using ginger ale; decorate with cream and pieces of preserved or candied ginger.

Orange jelly

75 g *(3 oz)* lump sugar
1 lemon
3 oranges
20 ml *(4 level tsps)* powdered gelatine
300 ml *(½ pt)* cold water

Rub the lump sugar on the rind of the lemon and 1 of the oranges to extract the zest. In a saucepan, sprinkle the gelatine over the water, add the sugar and dissolve over a low heat, do not boil. Squeeze the juice from the fruit and strain it; if necessary, add water to make up to 150 ml *(¼ pt)*. Add the strained juice to the gelatine mixture and strain through a piece of muslin into a wetted mould. Leave to set.

Clear lemon jelly

4 lemons
whites and shells of 2 eggs
45 ml *(3 level tbsps)* powdered gelatine
175 g *(6 oz)* lump sugar
900 ml *(1½ pt)* cold water
3 cloves
2-cm *(¾-in)* stick cinnamon

Wash the lemons and the eggs. Pare the rind in thin strips from 3 of the lemons and squeeze the juice of 4, adding water if necessary to make up to 300 ml *(½ pt)*. Put the lemon rind, lemon juice, gelatine, sugar and water, together with the cloves and cinnamon, into a large saucepan. Lastly, add the egg whites and the crushed eggshells, place over a gentle heat and start to whisk at once. Continue to whisk the mixture until nearly boiling, by which time there should be a thick froth on the surface. Stop whisking and allow the froth to rise and crack, then reduce the heat and simmer gently for 5 minutes.

Before straining the jelly, pour boiling water through a jelly-bag into a basin below, to warm the cloth and basin. (This prevents the jelly setting before straining is complete.) Empty the water from the basin, then carefully pour the jelly through the cloth, allowing it to drip into the basin below. The whites and shells of the eggs, as well as the cloth, serve to filter the jelly. It is a good idea to have a second warm basin ready to place under the jelly-bag, as the first jelly to come through should be refiltered to make it crystal-clear. Avoid shaking the jelly. When the jelly is nearly cold, pour it into a wetted mould and leave to set, then turn out.

Fruit set in jelly

Make up some lemon jelly (see above – or use a packet jelly) and prepare a variety of fresh fruits such as black grapes, bananas, cherries, sections of oranges, raspberries and pieces of pineapple. Pour about 2.5 cm *(1 in)* of jelly into the mould and arrange a few fruits in this. Allow the jelly to set. Add more jelly and fruit and again allow to set. Continue until the mould is completely filled.

For a professional look, let each portion of jelly that is poured into the mould set completely before more is added, otherwise the fruit will move.

Claret jelly

300 ml *(½ pt)* water or raspberry juice
300 ml *(½ pt)* claret
50 g *(2 oz)* sugar
rind and juice of ½ lemon
20 ml *(4 level tsps)* powdered gelatine
cochineal, optional

Slowly bring all the ingredients except the cochineal to simmering point – do not boil. Strain through muslin, add a few drops of cochineal if necessary to improve the colour and pour into a wetted mould. When the jelly is set, turn out and serve with cream. Claret (and other wine jellies) may be cleared if you wish with egg whites and shells, as for clear lemon jelly, page 325.

Honeycomb mould

2 large eggs, separated
568 ml *(1 pt)* milk
45 ml *(3 level tbsps)* sugar
few drops vanilla essence
20 ml *(4 level tsps)* powdered gelatine
30 ml *(2 tbsps)* water

Make a custard with the egg yolks, milk and sugar (see page 204) and flavour with vanilla then leave to cool. Dissolve the gelatine in the water and add it to the custard. Whisk the egg whites very stiffly and fold lightly into the cool custard mixture. Pour into a glass dish or mould put in a cool place and turn out when set. Serve with chocolate sauce (page 204) or with stewed fruit (or jam) and cream.

Note This mixture separates into layers.

Lemon fluff

2 large juicy lemons
3 eggs, separated
125 g–150 g *(4–5 oz)* caster sugar
10 ml *(2 level tsps)* powdered gelatine
45 ml *(3 tbsps)* water
45–60 ml *(3–4 tbsps)* double or whipping cream
grated chocolate for decoration

Finely grate the rind of the lemons free of white pith and squeeze out the juice (about 90 ml, *6 tbsps*). Whisk the yolks and sugar together in a deep bowl until thick and creamy. Gradually whisk in the lemon juice. Dissolve the gelatine in the water, in a small bowl over hot water. Cool it slightly and whisk into the lemon mixture. When it is beginning to set, fold in the stiffly whisked egg whites and lemon rind, using a metal spoon. Divide between four sundae glasses. Leave to set. Serve decorated with swirls of lightly whipped cream and grated chocolate.

Orange snow

30 ml *(2 level tbsps)* **powdered gelatine**
75 ml *(5 tbsps)* **cold water**
300 ml *(½ pt)* **boiling water**
75 g *(3 oz)* **sugar**
45 ml *(3 tbsps)* **lemon juice**
150 ml *(¼ pt)* **orange juice**
3 egg whites, stiffly whisked

Soak the gelatine in the cold water, add the boiling water and sugar and dissolve over gentle heat. Add the fruit juices and put in a cold place until cold but not set. Whisk until light and frothy, fold in the stiffly whipped egg whites and put into a wetted mould. Leave to set, then turn out on to a flat plate.

Milk jelly

50 g *(2 oz)* **caster sugar**
3 thin strips of lemon rind
568 ml *(1 pt)* **milk**
20 ml *(4 level tsps)* **powdered gelatine**
45 ml *(3 tbsps)* **water**

Add the sugar and lemon rind to the milk and allow to infuse for 10 minutes over a gentle heat. Let it cool. Dissolve the gelatine in the water over a gentle heat and add the cooled milk. Strain into a wetted mould and leave to set.

Lemon cheesecake *see colour plate facing p. 496*

1½ pkts of lemon jelly
60 ml *(4 tbsps)* **water**
2 eggs, separated
300 ml *(½ pt)* **milk**
grated rind of 2 lemons
90 ml *(6 tbsps)* **lemon juice**
450 g *(1 lb)* **cottage cheese**
15 ml *(1 level tbsp)* **caster sugar**
142-ml *(5-fl oz)* **carton double cream, whipped**
glacé cherries and mint sprigs

For the crumb base
100 g *(4 oz)* **digestive biscuits**
50 g *(2 oz)* **caster sugar**
50 g *(2 oz)* **butter, melted**

Put the jelly and water in a small pan and warm gently over a low heat, stirring until dissolved. Beat together the egg yolks and milk, pour on to the jelly, stir and return the mixture to the heat for a few minutes without boiling. Remove from the heat and add the lemon rind and juice. Sieve the cottage cheese and stir it in to the jelly or put jelly and cottage cheese in an electric blender and purée until smooth; turn the mixture into a bowl. Whisk the egg whites stiffly, add the 15 ml *(1 tbsp)* sugar and whisk again until stiff; fold into the cool cheese mixture.

Fold in the cream. Put the mixture into 20.5-cm *(8-in)* spring-release cake tin fitted with a tubular base.

Crush the biscuits and stir in the sugar and butter. Use to cover the cheese mixture, pressing it on lightly; chill. Turn the cheesecake out carefully, and decorate with cherries and mint sprigs. *Serves 8.*

ICES AND ICED PUDDINGS

Bought ice cream is so widely available that it is more and more commonly used to make quick cold sweets, very often in combination with fruit in some form. If you occasionally like a richer ice cream, with more individual flavour, you can make some at home, using a special pail-type freezer or ice-cream maker, a refrigerator or home freezer. You can also experiment with the range of delicious water ices, sorbets and so on, which are not normally available in retail shops.

There are several varieties of both cream and water ices and here is a list of the commonest:

Cream ices These are seldom made entirely of cream, but any of the following mixtures gives a good result: equal parts of cream and custard (the best being egg custard made with yolks only); cream and fruit purée; cream and egg whites. If necessary, the cream may be replaced by unsweetened evaporated milk, a home-made cream substitute or a commercial preparation. Flavourings and colourings are added as required – the more economical the mixture, the more important the flavouring.

Water ices The foundation is a sugar-and-water syrup, usually flavoured with fruit juice or purée; wine or liqueur is frequently included.

Sherbets A true sherbet is a water ice in which whipped egg white is included, giving a fluffy texture.

Sorbets Semi-frozen ices, sometimes flavoured with liqueur; because of their softness they are not moulded but are served in tall goblets or glasses. Strictly speaking, a sorbet should precede the roast in a full dinner, the idea being that it clears the palate; nowadays, however, a sorbet is quite often served as part of the sweet course.

Mousses These are made from a very light frozen mixture – custard, cream, fruit purée or a combination of these. They usually contain stiffly beaten egg whites, which give them their lightness and fluffy texture. When the mixture contains gelatine it may be merely chilled instead of frozen.

Parfaits A rather rich form of mousse, with a light texture due to the inclusion of whipped egg white; cream and fruit syrup are also included.

Sundaes Various combinations of ice cream, fruit syrup, fresh or canned fruit and nuts.

Bombes and iced puddings A bombe is an iced pudding frozen in a special bomb-shaped mould; it is made of a single ice cream mixture or a combination of two or more. The finished bombe is usually served on a round of sponge cake and is fairly elaborately decorated with cream, fruit and so on. Other iced puddings are made in large or small fancy moulds similar to jelly moulds, but with tight-fitting lids.

To mould bombes and other iced puddings

In the case of a plain mixture, first half-freeze it to a mushy consistency; this is not necessary for mousses and parfaits. Pack the mixture into the chilled mould, filling it to the brim and leaving no air spaces. Press the lid on firmly, place the mould in the frozen food compartment of the refrigerator with the control turned to the coldest setting, and leave undisturbed for about 2 hours or longer, or use a freezer.

Before unmoulding the pudding, have ready any rounds of sponge cake, fruit or decorations that may be needed. Dip the mould in tepid water for a few seconds, take off the lid, invert the bombe on to the prepared dish and decorate it quickly. Serve at once.

Making a bombe with two mixtures Chill the mould, line it to a thickness of about 2.5 cm *(1 in)* with one of the half-frozen mixtures, put the other mixture in the centre, then fill up with the first mixture. Good combinations are: vanilla and raspberry; coffee and vanilla; chocolate and orange. Finish the bombe as described above.

Neapolitan ice cream Use a square or oblong mould and fill with layers of half-frozen mixture in 3 colours – the most usual are brown (chocolate), white (vanilla) and pink (raspberry). Finish as above.

Freezing a mousse or parfait mixture

Chill the mould. The mixture must be quite cold, but need not be half-frozen. Put it into the mould, cover with waxed paper, put on the lid and freeze as above. Allow 4 hours or longer in a refrigerator.

Making ice cream

Modern refrigeration makes it all easy, though for the creamiest mixtures there is still nothing to beat the old churning method which gives the smoothest texture and practically no unwanted ice crystals. For those who don't find it a strain on their energy and patience, the results are certainly worth it; with a big churn and 15–20 minutes' hand-turning you will get superb ice-cream that, once made, will safely store for about a month in the home freezer.

The more up-to-date way is to use a small electric churn. To use these you still need a refrigerator for the churn to stand in, as well as an extra electric point to plug in the churn.

The churning method gives a greater bulk from the same amount of mixture than other ways of making ice: about half as much again.

Eight pointers to fool proof results:

1. Freezing reduces sweetness and flavour, so adjust accordingly and with care. Too much sugar and the mixture won't freeze properly: too little and it will be hard, rocky and unpleasant.
2. Use evaporated milk as a substitute for cream only when you're combining it with strong flavours.
3. Use maximum freezing power whatever method you employ – the quicker the mixture freezes, the better the texture. Everything should be cold to start with – equipment as well as each one of the ingredients.
4. Set the dial of the frozen food compartment in an ordinary refrigerator at maximum for about an hour before you need to freeze the mixture. Stir the mixture every 30 minutes until half-frozen and mushy, then leave for 2–3 hours to mature.

   Don't forget to return the dial to normal afterwards, or other foods in the fridge could suffer as a result.
5. If you use a home freezer, set the dial to fast freeze about an hour ahead. Put mixture in a mixing bowl and freeze until mushy. Whisk it thoroughly, then return the mixture to the freezer until firm – in an ice-cube tray, or in a deeper container if you want to use a scoop for serving.
6. Ice-creams made in the home freezer are best if only a proportion of cream is used. Too much gives a grainy texture. Fast freezing in the home freezer usually eliminates the need for frequent stirring between times.
7. Once the ice-cream is made, let it 'come to' and mellow in the body of the fridge a little while before serving. Rock-hard ices are never pleasant, though they can be served at a firmer stage if they're having a hot sauce accompaniment.
8. Chill serving dishes and dip scoops or spoons in cold water before portioning. It makes the job easier.

To serve ice cream

Use a special ice cream scoop, if available, to serve the ices; failing this, use a soup spoon, dipping it in tepid water before scooping up the ice. Put the ices on small plates or saucers or in glass dishes, stemmed glasses or silver cups.

The simplest way of serving ice cream is with wafer biscuits – plain oblongs, rolled fingers, sugary fantails and so on. A cold fruit syrup or a hot sauce may be added. You can also combine ice cream with fruit, nuts and other ingredients. A favourite sweet consists of meringue cases sandwiched together with ice cream.

Rich vanilla ice cream

150 ml *(¼ pt)* milk
45 ml *(3 level tbsps)* sugar
1 egg, beaten
2.5–5 ml *(½–1 tsp)* vanilla essence
142-ml *(5-fl oz)* carton double cream, half-whipped

Heat the milk and sugar and pour on to the egg, stirring. Return the mixture to the saucepan and cook it over a gentle heat, stirring all the time until the custard thickens; strain it and add the vanilla essence. Allow to cool, fold in the half-whipped cream, pour into a freezing container and freeze.

Chocolate
Add 90 ml *(6 tbsps)* grated plain chocolate, melted.

Coffee
Add 10 ml *(2 level tsps)* instant coffee, dissolved in 5 ml *(1 tsp)* hot water.

Banana
Add 2 small bananas, mashed or puréed.

Ginger
Add 45 ml *(3 tbsps)* chopped preserved ginger, and 15 ml *(1 tbsp)* ginger syrup.

Orange ice cream

284-ml *(10-fl oz)* carton double or whipping cream
300 ml *(½ pt)* orange juice
caster sugar
sections of mandarin orange
wafers

Whip the cream until it holds its shape. Stir in 150 ml *(¼ pt)* orange juice and add a further 150 ml *(¼ pt)* a little at a time. Add sufficient sugar to make the mixture taste slightly oversweet. Half-freeze, stir well, then complete the freezing. Serve with mandarin orange sections and sugared fan-tail wafers.

Fruit ice cream

small can evaporated milk
225 g *(8 oz)* fresh raspberries or a 425-g *(15-oz)* can, drained
50 g *(2 oz)* sugar, if fresh raspberries are used

Boil the unopened can of milk in water for 15 minutes and chill thoroughly for several hours. Sieve the raspberries to make 150 ml *(¼ pt)* purée; add the sugar. Whip the milk until stiff and fold in the sweetened purée; freeze as usual. The raspberries may be replaced by sieved strawberries, bananas or cooked dried apricots.

Strawberry liqueur ice cream

142-ml *(5-fl oz)* carton double or whipping cream, whipped
225 g *(8 oz)* strawberries, puréed to give 150 ml *(¼ pt)*
2.5 ml *(½ tsp)* vanilla essence
15 ml *(1 tbsp)* rum or maraschino
50 g *(2 oz)* sugar, if fresh strawberries are used

Mix the cream with all the other ingredients, pour into the freezing container and freeze for ¾–1 hour. Turn out and whisk until smooth, then return the mixture to the container and freeze until firm.

Variations

1. Use raspberries instead of strawberries (in this case the purée may need sieving to remove the pips).
2. Use a can of pineapple; drain off the juice from the can and crush the pineapple pieces well before adding to the cream, or use a can of crushed pineapple.

Praline bombe

100 g *(4 oz)* granulated sugar
150 ml *(¼ pt)* hot water
4 egg yolks, beaten
100 g *(4 oz)* almond toffee, crushed
5 ml *(1 tsp)* vanilla essence
pinch of salt
284-ml *(10-fl oz)* carton double or whipping cream, whipped
600 ml *(1 pt)* vanilla ice cream

Put the sugar into a saucepan and heat very gently until coffee-coloured: add the hot water, re-dissolve the caramel and cool. Put the egg yolks in the top of a double saucepan or in a bowl and pour on the caramel. If a bowl is used, stand it over a pan of hot water. Stir until the mixture is thick. Cool, add the crushed toffee, vanilla essence and salt and fold in the cream. Pour this praline mixture into a freezing container and freeze until half-set. Line a pudding basin or bombe mould with vanilla ice cream and fill it with the half-frozen praline mixture (see directions for making bombes). Freeze, and turn out just before serving.

Iced raspberry soufflé

see colour plate between pp. 400 and 401

10 ml *(2 level tsps)* cornflour
300 ml *(½ pt)* milk
75 g *(3 oz)* caster sugar
2 eggs, beaten
225 g *(8 oz)* fresh raspberries, hulled
170-ml *(6-fl oz)* carton double cream
chocolate cornets (see below)
fresh raspberries
mint sprigs

Choose four small straight-sided soufflé dishes measuring 7.5 cm *(3 in)* across the top and holding about 105 ml *(7 tbsps)* water. Other dishes of a similar type and size could also be adapted. Fit a strip of non-stick paper long enough to fit round the outside of the dish and slightly overlapping, to extend 2.5 cm *(1 in)* above the rim. Secure paper with paperclips, pulling it tightly into place. Put the dishes on a flat baking sheet. Blend the cornflour with 30 ml *(2 tbsps)* of the cold milk. In a small pan, dissolve the sugar in the remaining milk over a low heat. Pour on to the blended cornflour, stirring. Pour slowly on to the beaten eggs, whisking. Return to the pan and cook for a few minutes without boiling. Allow the mixture to cool. Sieve the raspberries to remove the seeds and stir into the cornflour sauce. Leave covered until cold. Whisk the cream until it just holds its shape, and is the same consistency as the cornflour mixture. Then fold the cornflour mixture evenly through the whisked cream. Spoon into the prepared soufflé dishes so that the mixture comes about 1 cm *(½ in)* above the rim. Freeze until firm but not solid, either in a home freezer or the frozen food compartment of a refrigerator, set at lowest. Just before serving remove the paper collar and decorate with chocolate cornets, fresh raspberries and mint sprigs.

Chocolate cornets Cut non-stick paper into 10-cm *(4-in)* squares then cut each into 2 triangles. With the base towards you fold the right-hand corner up to the top point of the triangle and then turn the paper round to take in the other point. Slightly overlap the points and secure with a staple or fold the tips over. Melt 50–75 g *(2–3 oz)* chocolate in a small basin over a pan of hot, not boiling, water. Spoon a little of the chocolate, cool but still flowing, in the centre of each paper cornet, turn the cornet to evenly coat the sides. Chill, recoat if necessary. When set carefully peel away the paper. Store in a cool place.

WAYS WITH BOUGHT ICE CREAM

A block of ice cream can be dressed up in many ways, either by combining it with other ingredients or by serving it with a sauce (see page 206 for additional recipes).

Banana split

vanilla ice cream
4 bananas
60 ml *(4 tbsps)* melba or red jam sauce (see pages 204, 206)
25 g *(1 oz)* shelled walnuts or blanched almonds, chopped

Put portions of ice cream in 4 shallow dishes. Peel the bananas, cut in half lengthwise and put a piece on either side of the ice cream. Spoon some of the sauce over, sprinkle with nuts and serve at once.

Peach melba

vanilla ice cream
425-g *(15-oz)* can peach halves, drained
60 ml *(4 tbsps)* melba sauce (see page 206)
whipped cream
30 ml *(2 tbsps)* chopped shelled walnuts

Put portions of ice cream in 4 individual glasses, add 2 peach halves to each and spoon some of the sauce over. Decorate the top with cream and nuts and serve at once.

Belle Hélène pears

425-g *(15-oz)* can pear halves
vanilla ice cream
chocolate sauce (see page 206)
whipped cream

Drain the juice from the can of pears. Put portions of ice cream in 4 individual glasses, add a pear half to each and pour some of the chocolate sauce over. Decorate with cream and serve at once.

Baked Alaska

18-cm *(7-in)* round sponge cake
312-g *(11-oz)* can fruit (eg raspberries), drained
483-ml *(17-fl oz)* block of ice cream
3–4 egg whites
100–175 g *(4–6 oz)* caster sugar

Pre-heat the oven to 230°C *(450°F)* mark 8. Place the sponge cake on a flat ovenproof dish and spoon over it just enough fruit juice to moisten the cake. Put the ice cream in the centre of the cake and pile the fruit on top. Whisk the egg whites stiffly, whisk in half the sugar, then fold in the remaining sugar. Pile this meringue mixture over the cake, covering the cake, ice cream and fruit completely and taking the meringue down to the dish. Place in the oven immediately and cook for 2–3 minutes, or until the outside of the meringue just begins to brown. Serve at once.

Variations

1. Use fresh crushed fruit, eg strawberries, when in season.
2. Sprinkle 15–30 ml *(1–2 tbsps)* sherry or rum over the cake before the ice cream is added.

Ice cream cake

18-cm *(7-in)* sponge sandwich cake
jam (eg cherry, black-currant)
483-ml *(17-fl oz)* block of ice cream
142-ml *(5-fl oz)* carton double cream, whipped

Split the sponge cake and spread one half with jam. Cover with the ice cream, piling it up in the centre. Cut the other half of the cake into wedges and arrange round the cake so that they open at the centre to show the ice cream. Fill the gaps between the wedges with the cream, piping or forking it in place.

Variation
Replace the jam by crushed fresh fruit in season (eg raspberries, strawberries) and serve decorated with whole fruits.

Knickerbocker glory

¼ pkt red jelly
¼ pkt yellow jelly
210-g *(7½-oz)* can peach slices, chopped
210-g *(7½-oz)* can pineapple chunks
483-ml *(17-fl oz)* block of vanilla ice cream
142-ml *(5-fl oz)* carton double cream, whipped
4 glacé cherries

Make up the jellies as directed on the packet, allow to set and then chop them. Put small portions of the chopped fruit in the bottom of tall sundae glasses. Cover this with a layer of red jelly. Put a scoop of ice cream on top and add a layer of yellow jelly. Repeat, then finish with a layer of cream and a cherry. *Serves 4–6.*

Raspberry-honey sundae

Layer fresh raspberries, ice cream, chopped nuts and if you wish some raspberry purée, in tall glasses. Pour over the mixture a honey (or other) sauce, and top with whipped cream. Serve with biscuits.

Honey sauce Melt 50 g *(2 oz)* butter and stir in 7.5 ml *(1½ level tsps)* cornflour. Gradually add 100–175 g *(4–6 oz)* thin honey. Bring to the boil and cook for a minute or two. Use warm not hot.

Chocolate nut sundae

Put a scoop of vanilla ice cream in each sundae glass and coat with chocolate sauce (see page 206). Pipe a whirl of cream on top and sprinkle with chopped walnuts.

Ice cream with peach sauce

Skin 4 ripe peaches, crush the flesh with a stainless steel fork and press through a nylon sieve. Put this purée into a small pan with 10 ml *(2 tsps)* rum and 5 ml *(1 tsp)* almond essence, sweeten to taste with icing sugar and heat slowly until warm but not boiling. Pour over portions of vanilla ice cream.

Ice cream with marshmallow sauce

100 g *(4 oz)* sugar
45 ml *(3 tbsps)* water
8 marshmallows cut up small
1 egg white
vanilla essence
red colouring, optional
coffee or chocolate ice cream

Dissolve the sugar in the water and boil for 5 minutes. Add the marshmallows and stir until melted. Whip the egg white stiffly and gradually fold in the marshmallow mixture. Flavour with vanilla to taste and tint pink if desired. Serve at once over the portions of ice cream.

WATER ICES AND SORBETS

As already mentioned, the basis of a water ice is a syrup made from sugar and water, to which some fruit juice or purée and a small quantity of egg white are added.

For a sorbet the ingredients are similar, but the proportion of egg white is greater. The consistency is therefore much softer, so a sorbet cannot be moulded.

Lemon water ice

225 g *(8 oz)* caster sugar
600 ml *(1 pt)* water
rind and juice of 3 lemons
1 egg white, whisked

Dissolve the sugar in the water over a low heat, add the thinly pared lemon rind and boil gently for 10 minutes; leave to cool. Add the lemon juice and strain the mixture into the freezing container and leave to half-freeze to a mushy consistency. Turn the mixture into a bowl, fold in the egg white, mixing thoroughly, replace in the container and re-freeze.

Orange water ice

100 g *(4 oz)* caster sugar
300 ml *(½ pt)* water
15 ml *(1 tbsp)* lemon juice
grated rind of 1 orange
grated rind of 1 lemon
juice of 3 oranges and 1 lemon, mixed (about 300 ml, *½ pt*)
1 egg white, whisked

Dissolve the sugar in the water over a low heat, bring to the boil and boil gently for 10 minutes. Add 15 ml *(1 tbsp)* lemon juice. Put the grated fruit rinds in a basin, pour the boiling syrup over and leave until cold. Add the mixed fruit juices and strain into the freezing container. Freeze to a mushy consistency. Turn the mixture into a bowl; fold in the egg white, mixing thoroughly, replace in the container and freeze.

Other flavours of water ices (eg raspberry, strawberry) can be made by adding 300 ml *(½ pt)* fruit purée and the juice of ½ a lemon to 300 ml *(½ pt)* of the syrup; continue as above.

Fruit sorbet

Follow a water ice recipe, but add twice the amount of egg white, which will give a much softer consistency. Freeze the mixture in the freezing compartment of the refrigerator, with the control at the normal setting, until the sorbet is sufficiently stiff for serving; spoon it into glasses.

MOUSSES

Black-currant mousse

225 g *(½ lb)* fresh black-currants, or 425-g *(15-oz)* can black-currants, drained and puréed
caster sugar to taste
4 egg yolks
142-ml *(5-fl oz)* carton double cream, whipped
2 egg whites, whisked

Cook fresh black-currants with 30 ml *(2 tbsps)* water until soft enough to put through a sieve or purée in an electric blender. This should give 150 ml *(¼ pt)* purée. Put the purée, sugar and egg yolks into a large bowl, stand this over a saucepan of hot water and whisk until thick and creamy – the mixture should be stiff enough to retain the impression of the whisk for a few seconds. Remove from the heat and whisk until cool. Fold in the whipped cream and the egg whites, pour the mixture into a shallow dish or some individual soufflé dishes, refrigerate and serve the same day. *Serves 4–6.*

Note For a plainer mousse, omit the egg yolks and mix the fruit purée with 150 ml *(¼ pt)* custard (see page 204) without heating. Then fold in the cream and egg whites and continue as above.

Raspberry mousse

2 425-g *(15-oz)* cans raspberries, drained, or 450 g *(1 lb)* fresh raspberries, sieved to make 300 ml *(½ pt)* purée
caster sugar to taste
142-ml *(5-fl oz)* carton double or whipping cream, whipped
20 ml *(4 level tsps)* powdered gelatine
45 ml *(3 tbsps)* water or raspberry juice
2 egg whites, whisked
whipped cream for decoration

Mix the raspberry purée, sugar and cream. Put the gelatine and the water or fruit juice in a basin, stand the basin in a pan of hot water and heat gently until the gelatine is dissolved; allow to cool slightly. Pour into the raspberry mixture in a steady stream, stirring the mixture all the time, and fold in the whisked egg whites. Pour into a dish and leave in a cool place to set. Decorate with whipped cream.

Pineapple cheesecake mousse *see colour plate facing p. 401*

3 eggs, separated
grated rind and juice of 1 lemon
75 g *(3 oz)* granulated sugar
350 g *(12 oz)* cream cheese
369-g *(13¼-oz)* can crushed pineapple
20 ml *(4 level tsps)* powdered gelatine
45 ml *(3 tbsps)* water
142-ml *(5-fl oz)* carton double cream
macaroons
glazed pineapple, see below

In a basin over hot water, whisk together the egg yolks, lemon rind, juice and sugar until pale and creamy. Remove the basin from the heat and continue whisking from time to time until cool. Beat the cream cheese with a little of the egg mixture, then add it to the bulk. Stir in the contents of the can of pineapple. Dissolve the gelatine in the water in the usual way. Stir it into the pineapple mixture. Half whip the cream and fold it in. Stiffly whisk the egg whites and fold these into the mixture. Turn the mousse into a 2.3-l *(4-pt)* shallow ring mould and chill. Turn it out and decorate with macaroons and glazed pineapple. *Serves 8.*

Glazed pineapple Turn the contents of a 439-g *(15½-oz)* can of fancy cut pineapple into a frying pan. Bring to the boil and boil until the syrup has reduced and the pan is nearly dry.

Pineapple snow

425-g *(15-oz)* can pineapple rings
10 ml *(2 level tsps)* powdered gelatine
2 eggs, separated
50 g *(2 oz)* caster sugar
glacé cherries and angelica to decorate

Drain the pineapple rings, keeping 2 or 3 for decoration. Cut the remaining rings in half and place in the base of a fruit dish. Measure 150 ml *(¼ pt)* of the juice into a small basin, sprinkle the gelatine over, and put the basin over a pan of hot water to dissolve the gelatine. Meanwhile, whisk the egg yolks and sugar until thick and creamy. Gradually beat in the juice and gelatine mixture. Leave till on the point of setting. Whisk the egg whites until they hold their shape, and lightly fold into the pineapple mixture. Turn this into the dish and chill for 1–2 hours. Before serving, decorate with the remaining pineapple rings, glacé cherries and little strips or diamonds of angelica.

Passionfruit mousse

3 eggs, separated
10 ml *(2 level tsps)* sugar
10 ml *(2 level tsps)* powdered gelatine
150 ml *(¼ pt)* hot water
juice of 1 lemon
150 ml *(¼ pt)* milk
425-g *(15-oz)* can passion fruit, drained
halved grapes or glacé cherries to decorate
whipped cream

Put the egg yolks and sugar in a basin and beat lightly. Dissolve the gelatine in the water and add to the mixture, with the lemon juice and milk; stir in the passion fruit pulp. Leave to stand until on the point of setting, then whisk well. Lastly fold in the stiffly beaten egg whites, pour the mixture into a glass dish or individual glasses and chill well. Decorate with halved grapes or glacé cherries and serve with whipped cream.

Blender berry cheese mousse *see colour plate between pp. 400 and 401*

caster sugar
150 ml (*¼ pt*) water
100 g (*¼ lb*) black-currants
100 g (*¼ lb*) red-currants
powdered gelatine
100 g (*¼ lb*) raspberries
1 orange
1 lemon
142-ml (*5-fl oz*) carton soured cream
350 g (*12 oz*) cottage cheese
2 eggs, separated
142-ml (*5-fl oz*) carton double cream

In a saucepan, dissolve 25–50 g (*1–2 oz*) sugar in the water. Add the prepared currants and cook slowly until the fruit is just tender, not mushy. Meanwhile in a cup or small bowl, sprinkle 10 ml (*2 level tsps*) gelatine over 30 ml (*2 tbsps*) water and leave for a few minutes. Off the heat, stir the gelatine into the currants until dissolved. Cool and add the hulled raspberries. When beginning to set, pour into a 1.7-l (*3-pt*) ring mould and chill. Grate the rind from the orange and the lemon free of white pith. Using a large electric blender, combine the rind, orange and lemon juice, 50 g (*2 oz*) caster sugar, the soured cream, cottage cheese and egg yolks and blend until smooth. In the cup or small bowl dissolve 25 ml (*1½ level tbsps*) gelatine with 45 ml (*3 tbsps*) water over hot water in usual way. Add to the mixture in the blender, switch on for a few seconds. Turn it into a bowl. Whip the double cream until it holds its shape and fold it into the cheese mixture. Stiffly whisk the egg whites, add 25 g (*1 oz*) sugar and whisk again. Fold into the bulk of the mixture, then pour into a ring mould. Chill until set and unmould to serve. *Serves 8–10.*

COLD SOUFFLÉS

To prepare the soufflé dish

Cut a strip of double greaseproof paper long enough to go right round the soufflé dish with the ends overlapping slightly and deep enough to reach from the bottom of the dish to about 7 cm (*2¾ in*) above the top. Tie the paper round the outside of the dish with string, or stick it with adhesive tape, so that it fits closely to the rim of the dish and prevents any mixture escaping. The soufflé will then set at least 2.5 cm (*1 in*) above the rim and after the paper is removed will appear to have risen like a baked soufflé.

To take off the paper when the soufflé has set, remove the string and ease the paper away from the mixture with a knife dipped in hot water.

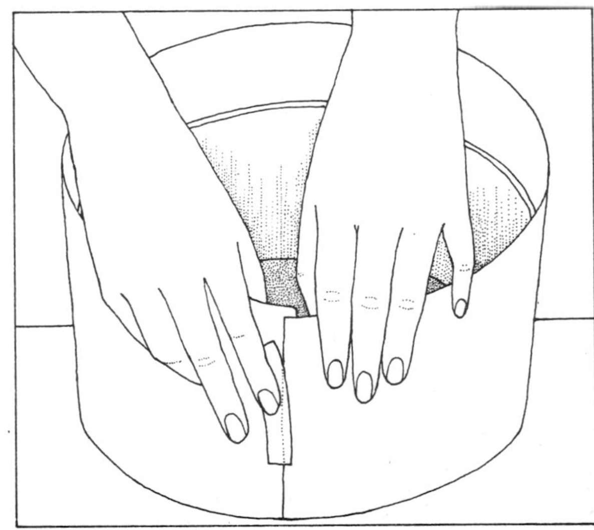

Preparing a soufflé dish

Size guide to soufflé dishes

As the depths of different soufflé dishes vary within the diameter we give both measurements below. It's important to use the correct dish, to enable the mixture to 'rise' properly above the rim.

12.5-cm (*5-in*), 500-ml (*1-pt*) dish, 3-egg quantity. *Serves 4.*

15-cm (*6-in*), 1.1-l (*2-pt*) dish, 6-egg quantity. *Serves 6–8.*

16-cm (*6½-in*), 1.4-l (*2½-pt*) dish, 9-egg quantity. *Serves 8–10.*

Soufflé milanaise (lemon) *see colour plate facing p. 481*

grated rind of 3 lemons
90 ml *(6 tbsps)* lemon juice
100 g *(4 oz)* caster sugar
4 egg yolks
45 ml *(3 tbsps)* cold water
15 ml *(1 level tbsp)* powdered gelatine
170-ml *(6-fl oz)* carton double cream, chilled
4 egg whites

To decorate
142-ml *(5-fl oz)* carton double cream
angelica leaves, mimosa balls

Prepare a 13.5-cm *(5½-in)* 900-ml *(1½-pt)* soufflé dish. Place it on a baking sheet for easier handling. Finely grate the lemon rind free of white pith into a large deep bowl, add the juice, sugar and egg yolks. Place the bowl over a saucepan of hot (but not fast boiling) water and whisk the ingredients until pale in colour and of the consistency to coat the back of a wooden spoon – about 10 minutes. Remove the bowl from the heat and whisk from time to time while the mixture cools.

Spoon the measured cold water into a cup or small basin. Sprinkle the gelatine across the surface of the water. Stand the basin in a pan with water to come half way up, and heat the water until the gelatine has completely dissolved. Remove the basin from the water and cool it a little. When combining dissolved gelatine with a soufflé mixture, it is wise to add a few spoonfuls of the cool but not cold mixture to the gelatine (they should be the same temperature). Then whisk this into the rest of the mixture. By doing so, you will prevent any risk of 'roping' – a lumpy texture occurring. Chill until the mixture is the consistency of unbeaten egg white or until the edge shows signs of setting. As the mixture cools, scrape the bowl down with a rubber spatula to keep an even texture. If at this stage the egg is insufficiently set, the soufflé may separate out later, leaving a heavy jellied layer in the base.

Whip the chilled cream until it just holds its shape, but is still light and floppy. Whisk the whites until they are stiff but not dry-looking. Fold the cream through the lemon mixture using a large metal spoon in a figure-of-eight movement. Then when no cream is visible, fold in the egg whites a little at a time. Keep the mixture light, and stop folding as soon as the egg whites are evenly combined. Turn the mixture into the prepared dish and leave to set – minimum time about 3 hours in the refrigerator. If it is to be left overnight, place a piece of plastic film across the top of the paper collar to prevent a skin forming.

To serve, take the soufflé from the refrigerator about an hour before required. To remove the paper collar, first remove the fastening, then place a small knife between the folded paper and, with your other hand, gently pull the collar away with slight pressure from the knife against the soufflé edge. Very little soufflé mixture should adhere to the paper. Whip the cream for the decoration until it just holds its shape. Spoon it into a fabric forcing bag fitted with a small star vegetable nozzle, and pipe a series of shells round the edge. Finish with angelica leaf shapes and mimosa balls. *Serves 4–6.*

Coffee soufflé

75–90 ml *(5–6 tbsps)* fresh strong black coffee
100 g *(4 oz)* caster sugar
4 egg yolks
45 ml *(3 tbsps)* cold water
15 ml *(1 level tbsp)* powdered gelatine
170-ml *(6-fl oz)* carton double cream
4 egg whites

To decorate
142-ml *(5-fl oz)* carton double cream
coarsely grated chocolate or sugar coffee beans

Prepare a 13.5-cm *(5½-in)* 900 ml *(1½-pt)* soufflé dish. Place it on a baking sheet for easier handling. Make the coffee using 45 ml *(3 level tbsps)* ground coffee and 150 ml *(5 fl oz)* water in the usual way. Put the coffee, sugar and egg yolks in a large deep bowl. Place the bowl over a saucepan of hot water (but not fast boiling) and whisk the ingredients until pale in colour and of the consistency to coat a wooden spoon – about 10 minutes. Remove the bowl from the heat and whisk from time to time while the mixture cools. Spoon the measured cold water into a cup or small basin. Sprinkle the gelatine across the surface of the water. Stand the basin in a pan with water to come half way up, and heat the water until the gelatine has completely dissolved. Remove the basin from the water and cool it a little. When combining dissolved gelatine with a soufflé mixture, it is wise to add a few spoonfuls of the cool but not cold mixture to the gelatine (they should

Singin' Hinny (p. 381), Drop scones (p. 381), Cheese scones (p. 380), Wholemeal scone round (p. 380). (Overleaf) Glazed pineapple gâteau (p. 393), Coconut frosted ring (p. 367), Caraway cobbler ring cake (p. 367), Orange peel kugelhupf (p. 368), Butterscotch gâteau (p. 370).

be the same temperature). Then whisk this into the rest of the mixture. By doing so, you will prevent any risk of 'roping' – a lumpy texture occurring. Chill until the mixture is the consistency of unbeaten egg white or until the edge shows signs of setting. As the mixture cools, scrape the bowl down with a rubber spatula to keep an even texture. If at this stage the egg is insufficiently set, the soufflé may separate out later, leaving a heavy jellied layer in the base.

Whip the chilled cream until it just holds its shape, but is still light and floppy. Whisk the whites until they are stiff but not dry-looking. Fold the cream through the coffee mixture using a large metal spoon in a figure-of-eight movement. Then when no cream is visible, fold in the egg whites a little at a time. Keep the mixture light, and stop folding as soon as the egg whites are evenly combined. Turn the mixture into the prepared dish and leave to set – minimum time, about 3 hours in the refrigerator. If it is to be left overnight, place a piece of plastic film across the top of the paper collar to prevent a skin forming.

To serve, take the soufflé from the refrigerator about an hour before required. To remove the paper collar, first remove the fastening, then place a small knife between the folded paper and, with your other hand, gently pull the collar away with slight pressure from the knife against the soufflé edge. Very little soufflé mixture should adhere to the paper. Whip the cream for the decoration until it just holds its shape. Spoon it into a fabric forcing bag fitted with a small star vegetable nozzle, and pipe a series of shells round the edge. Finish with grated chocolate or sugar coffee beans. *Serves 4 6.*

Orange liqueur soufflé

grated rind of 2 oranges
60 ml *(4 tbsps)* **orange juice**
30 ml *(2 tbsps)* **Grand Marnier**
100 g *(4 oz)* **caster sugar**
4 egg yolks
45 ml *(3 tbsps)* **cold water**
15 ml *(1 level tbsp)* **powdered gelatine**
170-ml *(6-fl oz)* **carton double cream**
4 egg whites

To decorate
142-ml *(5-fl oz)* **carton double cream**
slices of fresh orange and walnut halves

Prepare a 13.5-cm *(5½-in)* 900 ml *(1½-pt)* soufflé dish. Place it on a baking sheet for easier handling. Finely grate the orange rind free of white pith into a large deep bowl, add the orange juice, liqueur, sugar and egg yolks. Place the bowl over a saucepan of hot water and whisk the ingredients until pale and of a coating consistency – about 10 minutes. Remove the bowl from the heat and whisk from time to time whilst the mixture cools. Spoon the measured cold water into a cup or small basin. Sprinkle the gelatine across the surface of the water. Stand the basin in a pan with water to come half way up, and heat the water until the gelatine has completely dissolved. Remove the basin from the water and cool it a little. When combining dissolved gelatine with a soufflé mixture, it is wise to add a few spoonfuls of the cool but not cold mixture to the gelatine (they should be the same temperature). Then whisk this into the rest of the mixture. By doing so, you will prevent any risk of 'roping' – a lumpy texture occurring. Chill until the mixture is the consistency of unbeaten egg white or until the edge shows signs of setting. As the mixture cools, scrape the bowl down with a rubber spatula to keep an even texture. If at this stage the egg is insufficiently set, the soufflé may separate out later, leaving a heavy jellied layer in the base. Whip the chilled cream until it just holds its shape, but is still light and floppy. Whisk the whites until they're stiff but not dry looking. Fold the cream through the orange mixture using a large metal spoon in a figure-of-eight movement. Then when no cream is visible, fold in the egg whites a little at a time. Keep the mixture light, and stop folding as soon as the egg whites are evenly combined. Turn into the prepared dish and leave to set – minimum time, about 3 hours in the refrigerator. If it is to be left overnight, place a piece of plastic film across the top of the paper collar to prevent a skin forming.

To serve, take the soufflé from the refrigerator about an hour before required. To remove the paper collar, first remove the fastening, then

Victoria sandwich cake (p. 365), Sultana almond lattice cake (p. 369), Queen cakes (p. 369), Coconut tart (p. 365).

place a small knife between the folded paper and, with your other hand, gently pull the collar away with slight pressure from the knife against the soufflé edge. Very little soufflé mixture should adhere to the paper. Whip the cream for the decoration until it just holds its shape. Spoon it into a fabric forcing bag fitted with a small star vegetable nozzle, and pipe a series of shells round the edge. Finish with orange slices and walnuts, in pieces or chopped. *Serves 4–6.*

Chocolate soufflé

3 large eggs, separated
75 g *(3 oz)* caster sugar
75 g *(3 oz)* plain chocolate
30 ml *(2 tbsps)* water
15 ml *(1 level tbsp)* powdered gelatine
15 ml *(1 tbsp)* brandy
284-ml *(10-fl oz)* carton double cream

Prepare a 12.5-cm *(5-in)* 500 ml *(1-pt)* soufflé dish. Whisk the egg yolks and caster sugar together in a deep bowl over a pan of hot water, until thick and creamy. Remove from the heat and continue whisking on and off until cool. Melt the chocolate in a bowl over hot water. Put the measured water in a small bowl, sprinkle gelatine over, stand this in a pan with water to come half way up and heat gently until the gelatine is dissolved. Allow it to cool slightly and pour it into the egg mixture in a steady stream, stirring the mixture all the time. Stir the melted chocolate with the brandy into the egg mixture. Cool until the mixture is nearly setting. Lightly whip half the cream and fold it into the chocolate mixture. Whisk the egg whites in a clean bowl until stiff but not dry and quickly, lightly and evenly fold them into the mixture. Pour at once into the prepared soufflé dish and allow to set. When the soufflé is set, whip up the rest of the chilled cream, remove the paper and pipe 6–8 whirls of cream around the top edge and decorate with curls of chocolate or coarsely grated chocolate.

Cold raspberry soufflé

4 eggs, separated
100 g *(4 oz)* caster sugar
300 ml *(½ pt)* fresh raspberry purée
15 ml *(1 level tbsp)* powdered gelatine
30 ml *(2 tbsps)* water
15 ml *(1 tbsp)* curaçao, optional
142-ml *(5-fl oz)* carton double cream
142-ml *(5-fl oz)* carton single cream
whole raspberries and cream for decoration

Prepare a 15–18-cm *(6–7-in)* 1.1-l *(2-pt)* soufflé dish. Put the egg yolks and sugar in a large deep bowl over a pan of hot water. Whisk until thick and pale in colour. Add the raspberry purée and continue to whisk until it begins to thicken. Remove from the heat and stir in the gelatine dissolved in the usual way in the water and the liqueur. Allow the mixture to cool until just beginning to set, whisking occasionally. Meanwhile, whisk the creams together until thick but not stiff. Lightly fold the cream through the raspberry mixture, followed by the whisked egg whites. Turn the mixture into the soufflé dish and leave to set. Remove the paper collar. Decorate with whipped cream and whole berries. *Serves 6–8.*

Note For the purée, put 450 g *(1 lb)* fresh or thawed frozen raspberries through a nylon sieve. For a gooseberry soufflé, cook 450 g *(1 lb)* berries in the minimum of water, when soft sieve as for raspberries. If necessary increase sugar slightly.

Cold pineapple soufflé

425-g *(15-oz)* can crushed pineapple
25 ml *(1½ level tbsps)* powdered gelatine
4 large eggs, separated
75 g *(3 oz)* caster sugar
30 ml *(2 tbsps)* whisky
142-ml *(5-fl oz)* carton single cream
142-ml *(5-fl oz)* carton double cream
chopped pistachio nuts and whipped cream for decoration.

Prepare a 15-cm *(6-in)* 900-ml *(1½-pt)* soufflé dish. Drain the pineapple. Reserve 60 ml *(4 tbsps)* juice and pour it into a small bowl. Sprinkle over the gelatine. Place the bowl in a pan with hot water and dissolve the gelatine. Whisk the egg yolks, sugar and whisky in a large deep basin over a pan of hot water until they are thick and pale. Remove the basin from the heat and add the crushed pineapple. Add a little pineapple mixture to the gelatine and pour back into the soufflé mixture, whisking. Leave to cool, whisking occasionally.

When the mixture is not quite cold, whisk the creams together until thick and floppy. Fold into the cool, but not set, pineapple base. Whisk the egg whites until stiff but not dry, pour the pineapple cream base over the whites and fold in lightly. Turn the whole mixture into the prepared soufflé dish and chill. To serve, remove the paper collar, decorate the edges with pistachio nuts and top with piped cream. *Serves 6.*

CREAMS

This name is given to three groups of sweets. In 'whole' creams, dairy cream is the main ingredient. 'Custard' creams are based on a half-and-half mixture of custard and dairy cream. 'Fruit' creams consist essentially of half fruit purée and half cream (or a mixture of cream and custard). We give an example of each type of cream, followed by some recipes using the different kinds.

Whole cream – basic recipe

10 ml *(2 level tsps)* **powdered gelatine**
30–45 ml *(2–3 tbsps)* **water**
50 g *(2 oz)* **sugar**
5 ml *(1 tsp)* **vanilla essence**
568-ml *(1-pt)* **carton double cream, half-whipped**

Use a 900-ml *(1½-pt)* jelly mould or a basin. Sprinkle the gelatine over the water in a small basin, stand this in a pan of hot water and heat gently until the gelatine is dissolved. Fold the sugar and vanilla essence into the cream. Add a spoonful or two of cream to the gelatine, then quickly fold it into the bulk of the cream. When the mixture is just on the point of setting, pour quickly into the mould and leave to set. Unmould just before serving, see page 325.

Variations
Replace the vanilla essence by one of the following:

Almond 2.5 ml *(½ tsp)* almond essence.

Coffee 15–20 ml *(3–4 level tsps)* instant coffee, dissolved in 10 ml *(2 tsps)* hot water.

Chocolate 50–75 g *(2–3 oz)* chocolate, melted.

Custard cream – basic recipe

300 ml *(½ pt)* **pouring egg custard (see page 204)**
5–10 ml *(1–2 tsps)* **vanilla essence**
10 ml *(2 level tsps)* **powdered gelatine**
30 ml *(2 tbsps)* **water**
284-ml *(10-fl oz)* **carton double cream, whipped**

Use a 900-ml *(1½-pt)* jelly mould (or a basin). Make up the custard in the usual way, using extra sugar to make a well sweetened mixture, add the vanilla essence and stir occasionally as it cools. To prevent a skin forming, press a piece of wetted greaseproof paper down on to the surface of the custard. Put the gelatine and the water in a basin, stand this in a pan of hot water and heat gently until the gelatine is dissolved; allow to cool slightly. Pour into the custard in a steady, thin stream, stirring the mixture all the time. Fold in the cream, check the sweetness and when the mixture is just on the point of setting, pour into the wetted mould and leave to set. Unmould just before serving.

Ginger cream
Add 50 g *(2 oz)* preserved ginger, chopped.

Italian cream
Omit the vanilla and add 15 ml *(1 tbsp)* brandy or curaçao.

Strawberry cream

450 g *(1 lb)* fresh strawberries or 2 432-g *(15¼-oz)* cans, drained
sugar to taste
10 ml *(2 level tsps)* powdered gelatine
30–45 ml *(2–3 tbsps)* water or fruit juice
284-ml *(10-fl oz)* carton double cream, whipped, or 142-ml *(5-fl oz)* carton cream and 150 ml *(¼ pt)* custard

Use a 900-ml *(1½-pt)* jelly mould or a basin. Sieve the strawberries to make 300 ml *(½ pt)* purée; add sugar as necessary.

Put the gelatine and the water or fruit juice in a basin, stand this in a pan of hot water and heat gently until the gelatine is dissolved. Allow to cool slightly. Pour it into the purée in a steady stream, stirring the mixture all the time. Fold in the cream (and the custard if used). When the mixture is just on the point of setting, pour it quickly into the wetted mould and leave to set. Unmould just before serving.

Variations *see colour plate facing p. 480*
Use raspberry or apricot purée, or 300 ml *(½ pt)* fresh orange juice, or a mixture of raspberries and redcurrants.

Orange cream

15 ml *(1 level tbsp)* powdered gelatine
100 g *(4 oz)* sugar
1.25 ml *(¼ level tsp)* salt
1.25 ml *(¼ level tsp)* ground cinnamon
4 eggs, separated
400 ml *(¾ pt)* milk
3 large oranges
45 ml *(3 tbsps)* dry sherry
15 ml *(1 tbsp)* lemon juice
142-ml *(5-fl oz)* carton double cream, whipped
25 g *(1 oz)* walnuts, chopped

Put the gelatine, sugar, salt, cinnamon and egg yolks in the top of a double saucepan and mix together. Add the milk, then cook over boiling water, stirring until thickened. Turn the mixture into a bowl and place in the refrigerator until beginning to set.

Meanwhile, grate the rind of 1 orange; peel this orange and 1 more, divide into wedges and cut each wedge in half crosswise. Place in a bowl and pour the sherry over; allow to stand in the refrigerator.

When the egg mixture is beginning to set, combine it with the lemon juice, oranges in sherry, whipped cream and the grated rind of 1 orange. Stiffly beat the egg whites and fold into the above mixture. Pile into a glass dish and sprinkle the top with chopped walnuts. Chill lightly and peel and slice the third orange and use for decoration. *Serves 8.*

Banana chartreuse

300 ml *(½ pt)* lemon jelly
4 bananas, thinly sliced
15 ml *(1 tbsp)* finely chopped pistachio nuts
284-ml *(10-fl oz)* carton double cream, half-whipped
25 g *(1 oz)* caster sugar
10 ml *(2 tsps)* lemon juice
5 ml *(1 level tsp)* powdered gelatine
30 ml *(2 tbsps)* cold water

Mask a plain 600-ml *(1-pt)* soufflé dish or cake tin with a thin layer of lemon jelly (see page 325). Line the mould entirely with half the sliced banana, dipping each piece in a little cold jelly. Fill the spaces with the nuts and coat the inside with another thin layer of jelly. Sieve the remaining banana and add to the half-whipped cream, together with the sugar and lemon juice. Dissolve the gelatine in the water over a gentle heat and add to the cream mixture; pour into the prepared mould and allow to set. Turn out the chartreuse carefully and if you wish decorate it with any remaining jelly, neatly chopped.

Charlotte russe

600 ml *(1 pt)* lemon jelly (135-g *(4¾-oz)* tablet)
few diamonds of angelica
300 ml *(½ pt)* milk
1 vanilla pod
45 ml *(3 tbsps)* water
10 ml *(2 level tsps)* powdered gelatine
3 egg yolks
30 ml *(2 level tbsps)* caster sugar
10–12 soft sponge fingers
142-ml *(5-fl oz)* carton double cream

Pour a little jelly into a 12.5-cm *(5-in)* 900-ml *(1½-pt)* sloping-sided russe tin. Allow to set. Arrange a pattern of angelica over and set carefully with a little more jelly. Place remaining jelly in a basin and leave to set.

Heat the milk in a saucepan with the vanilla, do not boil; leave to infuse for 10 minutes.

Put the water in a small bowl, sprinkle the gelatine over and leave to swell up. Beat the egg yolks and sugar, pour the strained milk over and return it to the pan. Cook gently to a coating consistency. Add the gelatine and stir until dissolved, then cool the mixture until beginning to set.

Arrange the sponge fingers (trimmed down each side) side by side round the tin. Lightly whip the cream until floppy and fold it into the custard. Turn at once into the tin. Trim the fingers level with the mixture and place the trimmings over the top. Chill until set. Turn out as for a jelly and decorate with the remaining jelly, chopped. *Serves 6.*

Note If packet jelly is used, add lemon juice as part of measured water to sharpen.

Chocolate refrigerator cake

24–26 soft sponge fingers
175 g *(6 oz)* caster sugar
30 ml *(2 level tbsps)* cornflour
400 ml *(¾ pt)* milk
284-ml *(10-fl oz)* carton double or whipping cream
50 g *(2 oz)* unsweetened chocolate
2 egg yolks
25 g *(1 oz)* butter
5 ml *(1 level tsp)* powdered gelatine
10 ml *(2 tsps)* water
toasted flaked almonds to decorate

Line a loaf tin measuring about 23 × 12.5 × 6.5 cm *(9 × 5 × 2½ in)* with non-stick paper. Arrange a layer of sponge fingers to cover the base and sides. Blend the sugar and cornflour in a saucepan; gradually stir in the milk and half the cream. Break up the chocolate, add to the milk and bring slowly to the boil, stirring. Boil gently for 2–3 minutes, stirring, cool for a few minutes and beat in the egg yolks. Cook for 1 minute and beat in the butter. Sprinkle the gelatine over the water and stir into the mixture. Cool, stirring occasionally. When the mixture is beginning to thicken, pour half of it over the sponge fingers. Cover with another layer of sponge fingers, then spoon the remaining mixture over these. Trim the tops of the fingers level with the filling and use the trimmings to make a final layer.

Leave overnight in the refrigerator. To serve, turn out on to a flat dish. Whip the rest of the cream, cover the top of the cake with it and strew with the almonds.

Strawberry refrigerator cake

225 g *(½ lb)* strawberries, hulled
150 ml *(¼ pt)* fresh orange juice
45 ml *(3 tbsps)* curaçao
30 ml *(2 level tbsps)* icing sugar
30 ml *(2 tbsps)* golden syrup
2 egg yolks, beaten
75 g *(3 oz)* butter
30 boudoir biscuits
142-ml *(5-fl oz)* carton double cream
60 ml *(4 tbsps)* single cream
whole strawberries to decorate

Slice the strawberries. Mix the orange juice, curaçao and sugar; pour over the fruit and leave for ½ hour. Heat the syrup over a gentle heat, bring to the boil, then allow to cool for a minute. Pour in a thin stream on to the egg yolks, whisking all the time; continue to whisk until pale and creamy. Cream the butter until soft, then beat in the egg syrup a little at a time. Drain the fruit. One by one dip 10 boudoir biscuits in the orange marinade; arrange side by side on a sheet of non-stick paper. Cover with a layer of half the butter filling. Top with half the marinaded strawberries. Add another layer of 10 biscuits and top with the remaining butter mixture and strawberries. Finally, top with a layer of biscuits (all the marinade should now have been used up). Wrap the cake in paper and chill. Half an hour before it is required, whisk the creams together until the mixture is thick enough to hold its shape; mask the cake, and decorate with whole berries.

Crème brûlée

284-ml *(10-fl oz)* carton double cream
284-ml *(10-fl oz)* carton single cream
1 vanilla pod
60–75 ml *(4–5 level tbsps)* caster sugar
4 egg yolks

Half-fill the base of a double boiler with water. Pour the creams into the top pan, stir, then add the vanilla pod. Place the double pan over a moderate heat. Warm the cream mixture slowly to scalding point – about 52°C *(125°F)*. If a jam thermometer is not available, use the little finger – a pricking sensation will tell you the mixture is scalding. Remove vanilla pod. In a small bowl, cream 15 ml *(1 level tbsp)* of the measured sugar with the egg yolks, using either a rotary whisk or a wooden spoon, until the mixture is thick and pale. Pour the warmed cream on to the egg yolks, stir well and return to the boiler. Continue to heat gently, stirring continuously (do not boil) until the mixture thickens enough to coat the back of the wooden spoon. Strain the custard into a shallow ovenproof serving dish to give a depth of 3–4 cm *(1¼–1½ in)*. Place on a baking sheet in the oven at 170°C *(325°F)* mark 3 for 5–8 minutes until a skin forms on the top. Leave the custard cream to cool, then chill in the refrigerator for several hours, preferably overnight. Pre-heat the grill. Dust the top of the cream evenly with the remaining sugar. Slip under the hot grill and brown the sugar until it caramelises. Remove from the heat and chill for 2–3 hours before serving.

GÂTEAUX AND PASTRIES

Mille-feuilles gâteau

100 g *(4 oz)* puff or rough puff pastry, made with 100 g *(4 oz)* flour etc (see page 354), or a 212-g *(7½-oz)* pkt frozen puff pastry, thawed
450 g *(1 lb)* fresh raspberries
caster sugar
284-ml *(10-fl oz)* carton double cream, whipped
pale green glacé icing (see page 384)
45 ml *(3 tbsps)* roughly chopped walnuts

Roll out the pastry very thinly (this is easier to do if it is rolled between sheets of waxed paper) and cut into three 15-cm *(6-in)* rounds. Place on wetted baking sheets, prick and bake at 230°C *(450°F)* mark 8 for 8–10 minutes, until crisp and golden brown. Cool on a cooling rack.

Reserve a few raspberries for decoration and crush and sweeten the remainder. Sandwich the pastry rounds together with layers of cream and raspberries, cover the top with glacé icing and decorate with raspberries and nuts.

Any other soft fruit can be used in the same way.

Mille-feuilles slices

212-g *(7½-oz)* pkt frozen puff pastry, thawed
30–45 ml *(2–3 tbsps)* raspberry jam
142-ml *(5-fl oz)* carton double cream, whipped
glacé icing (see page 384)
15–30 ml *(1–2 tbsps)* chopped nuts

Roll the pastry into a strip 0.5 cm *(¼ in)* thick, 10 cm *(4 in)* wide and 30.5 cm *(12 in)* long. Brush the baking sheet with water, lay the pastry on it and cut it from side to side in strips 5 cm *(2 in)* wide, but don't separate the slices. Bake in the oven at 230°C *(450°F)* mark 8 for about 10 minutes. Separate the strips and cool them; split each into two and sandwich them together in threes or fours with jam and cream. Cover the tops with icing and sprinkle chopped nuts at each end. *Makes 6.*

Note Ready-made pastry should be rolled thinner than home-made.

Gâteau St. Honoré

100 g *(4 oz)* shortcrust or flan pastry, made with 100 g *(4 oz)* flour, etc (see page 351)
choux pastry, using 120 ml *(8 level tbsps)* plain flour (see page 355)
1 egg, beaten, to glaze
2 egg yolks
50 g *(2 oz)* caster sugar for filling
25 ml *(1½ level tbsps)* plain flour
20 ml *(4 level tsps)* cornflour
300 ml *(½ pt)* milk
5 ml *(1 tsp)* vanilla essence
3 egg whites, stiffly whisked
142-ml *(5-fl oz)* carton double cream, whipped
45 ml *(3 level tbsps)* caster sugar for syrup
45 ml *(3 tbsps)* water
angelica and glacé cherries

Roll the shortcrust or flan pastry into an 18-cm *(7-in)* round, prick well and put on a lightly greased baking sheet. Brush a 1-cm *(½-in)* band round the edge with beaten egg. Using a 1-cm *(½-in)* plain nozzle, pipe a circle of choux paste round the edge of the pastry and brush it with beaten egg. With the remaining choux paste pipe about 20 walnut-sized rounds on to the baking sheet. Brush these with beaten egg and bake both the flan and the choux balls in the oven at 190°C *(375°F)* mark 5 for about 35 minutes or until well risen and golden brown. Cool on a rack.

Meanwhile prepare the pastry cream filling. Cream the egg yolks with the 50 g *(2 oz)* caster sugar until pale, add the flours, with a little of the milk, and mix well. Heat the remainder of the milk with the vanilla essence almost to boiling point; pour on to the egg mixture, return this to the pan and bring to the boil, stirring all the time. Boil for a further 2–3 minutes, then turn the mixture into a bowl to cool. Whisk with a rotary beater till smooth, then fold in the egg whites. Pipe some whipped cream inside the cold choux paste buns, reserving a little for the top of the gâteau.

Dissolve the 45 ml *(3 level tbsps)* sugar in the water and boil until the edge just begins to turn straw-coloured. Dip the tops of the choux paste buns in this syrup, using a skewer or tongs to hold them. Use the remainder of the syrup to stick the buns on to the choux pastry border. Fill the centre of the gâteau with the pastry cream mixture and cover this with the remaining cream. Decorate with angelica and cherries.

Profiteroles *see colour plate facing p. 512*

choux pastry, using 120 ml *(8 level tbsps)* plain flour (see page 355)
142-ml *(5-fl oz)* carton double cream, whipped
icing sugar
chocolate sauce (see page 206, or below)

Using a 1 cm *(½ in)* plain vegetable nozzle, pipe small balls of pastry about the size of a walnut on to wetted baking sheets. Bake in the oven at 220°C *(425°F)* mark 7 until crisp – 15–20 minutes. Allow to cool. Make a hole in the bottom of each profiterole and fill with whipped cream. Dust with icing sugar and pile them into a pyramid. Pour a little chocolate sauce over and serve the rest separately. As an alternative to the sauce recipe on page 206, melt 100 g *(4 oz)* Menier chocolate over a very low heat, gradually stir in a small can of evaporated milk and beat well.

Black Forest gâteau *see colour plate between pp. 528 and 529*

4 eggs
100 g *(4 oz)* caster sugar
100 g *(4 oz)* plain flour
454-g *(1-lb)* can black cherries
15 ml *(1 level tsp)* arrowroot
30 ml *(2 tbsps)* kirsch
cream

For the crème au beurre filling
75 g *(3 oz)* sugar
60 ml *(4 tbsps)* water
2 egg yolks, lightly beaten
100–175 g *(4–6 oz)* butter, preferably unsalted
100 g *(4 oz)* plain chocolate

Grease two 20.5-cm *(8-in)* sandwich tins and dust with flour and sugar. Put eggs and sugar in a large deep bowl, stand this over a pan of hot water and whisk until light and creamy – mixture should be quite stiff. Remove from heat and whisk until cold. Sift the flour over the mixture and fold in very lightly. Divide the mixture between the tins and bake at 190°C *(375°F)* mark 5 for 25–30 minutes. Turn out and cool on a wire rack. For the crème au beurre, place the sugar in a heavy based saucepan, add the water and leave over low heat to dissolve. Bring to the boil and boil steadily for 2–3 minutes (110°C, *225°F*, on a sugar thermometer). Pour the syrup in a thin stream on to the egg yolks, whisking until the mixture is thick and cold. Cream the butter in large bowl; gradually add the egg mixture. Melt 50 g *(2 oz)* chocolate in a bowl over hot water and beat it into the crème au beurre mixture. Split the cakes and sandwich them together with crème au beurre; spread the remaining crème round the edges of the layers.

Grate 50 g *(2 oz)* plain chocolate coarsely on to greaseproof paper and roll the gâteau edge in it so it is completely covered with chocolate. To decorate, drain a 454-g *(1-lb)* can of black cherries (keep juice) and arrange them on top of the gâteau. Blend 15 ml *(1 level tbsp)* arrowroot with the juice and boil, stirring. Add 30 ml *(2 tbsps)* Kirsch and glaze the cherries with a brush. Whip the cream and pipe in whirls around the edge.

Spicy halva

175 g *(6 oz)* sugar
150 ml *(¼ pt)* water
100 g *(4 oz)* butter
100 g *(4 oz)* semolina
50 g *(2 oz)* stoned raisins
grated rind of 1 orange
50 g *(2 oz)* ground almonds
4–5 cardamom seeds
ground cinnamon

Put the sugar and water into a pan and when the sugar has dissolved, bring to the boil; boil until the syrup thickens, then remove it from the heat. Melt the butter, shower in the semolina, stir and brown it, then add the raisins, orange rind, ground almonds and cardamom seeds. Finally add the syrup and cook the mixture over a low heat, stirring all the time, until it is thick. Pour into wetted moulds and when cool, turn out and serve sprinkled with ground cinnamon.

FLANS

Flans are not only pretty and good to eat, but they also have the advantage that most if not all of the cooking can be done beforehand.

In addition to the conventional flan cases of pastry and sponge cake, uncooked flan cases can be made from mixtures based on crumbled biscuits, cornflakes and so on – see recipes below.

Pastry flan cases

See pages 351, 356.

Sponge flan cases

Grease 21.5-cm *(8½-in)* sponge flan tin and dust it with a mixture of flour and caster sugar. If you wish you can place a round of greased greaseproof paper on the raised part of the flan tin to prevent sticking. Make a fatless sponge cake mixture (see page 371), using 2 eggs, 50 g *(2 oz)* caster sugar and 50 g *(2 oz)* plain flour; pour it into the tin and bake in oven above the centre at 220°C *(425°F)* mark 7 for about 10 minutes, until well risen, golden and just firm to the touch.

Loosen the edge carefully, turn the flan case out on to a wire rack and leave to cool.

Biscuit crust flan cases

175 g *(6 oz)* wheatmeal or plain biscuits
75 g *(3 oz)* melted butter

Grease a shallow 20.5-cm *(8-in)* pie plate, flan dish or sandwich cake tin. Crush the biscuits with a rolling pin and bind together with the melted butter. Spoon the crumbs into the plate, flan dish or tin, pressing it firmly into shape to make a shell. Chill or leave in a cool place until set.

Variations

1. Replace 25 g *(1 oz)* of the crumbs by 25 g *(1 oz)* desiccated coconut or chopped nuts.
2. Add the grated rind of 1 lemon.
3. Add 5–10 ml *(1–2 level tsps)* ground ginger or mixed spice.
4. Bind the crumbs with 75–100 g *(3–4 oz)* chocolate and a walnut-sized knob of butter, melted together.
5. Use gingernut biscuits and bind with melted plain chocolate.

Cornflake crust flan case

75 g *(3 oz)* cornflakes
50 g *(2 oz)* butter
50 g *(2 oz)* sugar
15 ml *(1 tbsp)* golden syrup

Grease a shallow 18-cm or 20.5-cm *(7- or 8-in)* pie plate or sandwich tin. Crush the cornflakes roughly in your hands. Heat the remaining ingredients until melted and bubbling, pour over the cornflakes in a basin and stir until well blended. Line the plate or tin with the mixture, pressing it firmly in place. Chill or leave in a cool place to set.

Fresh fruit flan filling

225 g *(½ lb)* fresh fruit, eg strawberries, raspberries
red-currant jelly or ½ pkt red jelly

Pick over the fruit, wash it if necessary and arrange in the flan case. Make a glaze by melting 30–45 ml *(2–3 tbsps)* red-currant jelly with about 15 ml *(1 tbsp)* water or by making up ½ pkt table jelly; pour the glaze over the fruit when it begins to thicken.

Note Adapt the quantity to suit the size of flan case.

Canned fruit flan filling

425-g *(15-oz)* can fruit
15 ml *(1 level tbsp)* cornflour
150 ml *(¼ pt)* fruit juice

Arrange the drained fruit in the flan case, filling it well. Blend the cornflour with a little of the fruit juice to a smooth cream. Boil the rest and stir into the blended cornflour. Return this mixture to the pan and bring to the boil, stirring until a clear thickened glaze is obtained. Spoon over the fruit to coat it evenly.

Note Adapt the quantity to suit the size of flan case.

Plum and almond open tart

150 g *(5½ oz)* plain flour
45 ml *(3 level tbsps)* caster sugar
3 egg yolks
100 g *(4 oz)* softened, unsalted butter
7.5 ml *(1½ level tsps)* grated lemon rind
50 g *(2 oz)* ground almonds
50 g *(2 oz)* fresh breadcrumbs
700 g *(1½ lb)* small firm plums, halved and stoned
175 g *(6 oz)* red-currant jelly

Sift the flour and sugar into a basin. Incorporate the egg yolks and beat in the butter, a little at a time. Sprinkle over this the lemon rind then knead to a smooth, pliable dough and gather it into a ball; wrap the dough in greaseproof paper and chill for 30 minutes. Line a 25.5-cm *(10-in)* loose-bottomed French fluted flan ring with the pastry; chill for about 30 minutes until quite firm. Combine the almonds and breadcrumbs and sprinkle over the base of the flan. Lay plum halves on top in concentric circles. Bake at 190°C *(375°F)* mark 5 for about 45–60 minutes, until the plums are tender and the pastry cooked. Heat the jelly in a saucepan and allow it to cool before glazing over the fruit, using a pastry brush. Leave the tart to cool before serving, but do not refrigerate. *Serves 8–10.*

Frangipane flan

19-cm *(7½-in)* baked shortcrust flan case
15–20 ml *(3–4 level tsps)* cornflour
400 ml *(¾ pt)* milk
4 egg yolks
30 ml *(2 level tbsps)* caster sugar
75 g *(3 oz)* ground almonds
almond essence

For the fruit layer and topping
100 g *(¼ lb)* white grapes, skinned, halved and seeded
2 oranges, peeled and segmented
1 banana, peeled and sliced
caster sugar
50 g *(2 oz)* flaked almonds, toasted

Make the flan case in the usual way. Mix the cornflour to a smooth paste with a little of the milk. Put the remainder on to heat; stir in the cornflour paste and cook, stirring, until thick and smooth. Remove from the heat and beat in the egg yolks one at a time. Continue cooking over a gentle heat until the mixture thickens. Remove from the heat and stir in the caster sugar, ground almonds and a few drops of almond essence. Cover, and leave until cold.

Arrange the fruits in the pastry case. Spread the frangipane cream mixture over and pile into a pyramid shape. Just before serving dust thickly with caster sugar. With a red-hot skewer, brand the sugar to caramelise it – reheat the skewer after marking each line. Sprinkle with the almonds.

Norwegian almond flan

150 g *(5 oz)* plain flour
75 g *(2½ oz)* butter
75 g *(2½ oz)* caster sugar
1 small egg

For the filling
100 g *(4 oz)* ground almonds
100 g *(4 oz)* icing sugar, sifted
1 large egg, separated
almond essence

Put the flour into a bowl, rub in the fat and stir in the sugar. Mix with beaten egg to form a stiff dough; add a little water if necessary. Chill. Grease a deep 20.5-cm *(8-in)* straight-sided sandwich tin or flan ring. Line with pastry, prick the base and knock up the edge. Knead together the pastry offcuts, roll out thinly and cut into narrow strips. Blend the ground almonds, icing sugar, egg yolk and a few drops of essence together; whisk the egg white until stiff and fold into the mixture. Turn this filling into the lined tin. Lattice with the pastry strips. Bake in the oven at 220°C *(425°F)* mark 7 for 15 minutes, then reduce the temperature to 150°C *(300°F)* mark 2 and cook for a further 30 minutes. Serve cut in wedges, with whipped cream if you like. *Serves 6.*

Note This rich pie is traditionally served cold, but it is equally good hot.

Chocolate peppermint crisp flan

3 egg yolks
100 g *(4 oz)* caster sugar
30 ml *(2 tbsps)* crème de menthe
10 ml *(2 level tsps)* powdered gelatine
30 ml *(2 tbsps)* water
few drops of green colouring
142-ml *(5-fl oz)* carton double or whipping cream, whipped
biscuit crust case made with gingernuts and chocolate (see above)

Whisk the egg yolks, add the sugar and crème de menthe and continue whisking until the mixture thickens. Sprinkle the gelatine over the water in a small basin, stand this in a pan of hot water and heat gently until the gelatine has dissolved; allow to cool slightly and gradually whisk into the egg mixture. Fold in the colouring and cream. When the filling is beginning to set, pour into the biscuit crust case. Chill before serving.

Belgian tart

225 g *(8 oz)* butter
50 g *(2 oz)* caster sugar
30 ml *(2 tbsps)* oil
few drops vanilla essence
1 egg, beaten
450 g *(1 lb)* plain flour
5 ml *(1 level tsp)* baking powder
1.25 ml *($\frac{1}{4}$ level tsp)* salt
apricot or raspberry jam, warmed
icing sugar

Grease and line a loose-bottomed 20.5-cm *(8-in)* round cake tin. Soften the butter and cream with the sugar, beat well and add the oil, vanilla essence and egg. Sift the flour, baking powder and salt and fold into the creamed mixture. Knead lightly. Using a coarse grater, grate half the mixture into the tin, covering the bottom completely. Spread with the warmed jam and cover with the rest of the mixture, grated as before. Bake in the oven at 180°C *(350°F)* mark 4 for about $1\frac{1}{4}$ hours. When the tart is done, sprinkle sifted icing sugar over the top while it is still hot and turn it out of the tin when cold. Serve with whipped cream or pouring cream. *Serves 6.*

Polish cheese cake

For the topping
225 g *(8 oz)* cream cheese
6 egg yolks
50 g *(2 oz)* butter, melted
225 g *(8 oz)* caster sugar
little vanilla essence
glacé icing

For the pastry
100 g *(4 oz)* butter
225 g *(8 oz)* plain flour
50 g *(2 oz)* sugar
1 egg yolk

Tie the cream cheese in muslin and squeeze out the moisture. When the cheese is dry, grate or crumble it into a mixing bowl. Add the egg yolks, melted butter, sugar and a little vanilla essence and beat thoroughly until the mixture is quite smooth. Rub the butter into the flour, add the sugar and work in the egg, with a little water if necessary to give a firm but manageable dough. Roll out and use to cover the base of a 20.5-cm *(8-in)* square cake tin. Place the cheese mixture on top and bake in the oven at 180°C *(350°F)* mark 4 for about 1 hour. Leave it to cool in the tin until the topping is set. Turn it out and coat with glacé icing. When set cut it into squares.

MERINGUE SWEETS

Meringue flan case

3 egg whites
175 g *(6 oz)* caster sugar

Draw a 20.5-cm *(8-in)* circle on a sheet of silicone (non-stick) paper and place the paper on a baking sheet. Whisk the egg whites until stiff, whisk in half the sugar until stiff, then fold in the remaining sugar. Spread some of the meringue over the circle to form the base of the flan. Using a large star vegetable nozzle pipe the remainder to form the edge of the flan, or make a rim with the aid of a spoon. Bake in the oven at 130°C *(250°F)* mark $\frac{1}{4}$–$\frac{1}{2}$ for 1$\frac{1}{2}$–2 hours, or until dry. Leave to cool on a rack, remove the paper and fill (see below).

Alternatively, make 7.5-cm *(3-in)* individual meringue flan cases, cooking these for about the same time.

Cases made from meringue cuite

2 egg whites
125 g *(4$\frac{1}{2}$ oz)* icing sugar

Line a baking sheet with silicone (non-stick) paper or use greaseproof paper very lightly greased with oil. Place the egg whites and icing sugar in a basin over a pan of boiling water and whisk until the mixture forms a meringue stiff enough to hold a shape. Put this mixture in piles on the prepared baking sheet, hollowing it in the centre to make 4 nest-like shapes. (Alternatively, if you have the time or inclination, pipe the mixture, using a small star vegetable nozzle.) Put the cases in the oven at 150°C *(300°F)* mark 1 and dry out for about 1 hour.

Fillings for meringue cases

1. Fresh fruit mixed with whipped sweetened cream.
2. Canned fruit in a glaze of jam.
3. Grate the rind from 1 orange and squeeze out the juice. Squeeze the juice from a lemon. Mix the grated rind and juices and make up to 300 ml *($\frac{1}{2}$ pt)* with water. Blend 30 ml *(2 level tbsps)* custard powder and 15 ml *(1 level tbsp)* sugar with a little of the juice, heat the rest and pour it on to the blended mixture, then return it to the pan, stirring until it thickens. Cool slightly and add 2 of the egg yolks left from making the meringue mixture.
4. Make up a packet of lemon pie filling, using slightly less water than usual, and fold in 2 egg yolks. (This is a very quickly made filling.)

Pavlova

3 egg whites
175 g *(6 oz)* caster sugar
2.5 ml *($\frac{1}{2}$ tsp)* vanilla essence
2.5 ml *($\frac{1}{2}$ tsp)* vinegar
5 ml *(1 level tsp)* cornflour
284-ml *(10-fl oz)* carton double cream, whipped
fresh strawberries, raspberries, Chinese gooseberries or canned passion fruit, drained

Draw an 18-cm *(7-in)* circle on silicone (non-stick) paper and place the paper on a baking sheet. Beat the egg whites till very stiff, then beat in the sugar gradually. Beat in the vanilla essence, vinegar and cornflour. Spread the meringue mixture over the circle and bake in the oven at 150°C *(300°F)* mark 1–2 for about 1 hour, till firm. Leave to cool, then carefully remove the paper. Invert the meringue on to a flat plate, pile the cream on it and arrange the fruit on top.

STORE-CUPBOARD SWEETS

Given a reasonable stock of packet preparations, canned fruit and so on, you can always whip up a sweet in a few minutes. Here are some ideas, including a few recipes that take a little longer to prepare.

1. Make up a half-packet of 2 different-flavoured blancmange powders and pour them in alternate layers into glass dishes. Suggested combinations: chocolate and banana; strawberry and vanilla; butterscotch and vanilla.
2. Make up a packet of instant pudding or blancmange and fill individual glasses with alternate layers of pudding and jam or canned, stewed or fresh fruit. Try raspberry instant pudding or blancmange with canned raspberries or raspberry jam; butterscotch or chocolate with bananas or pineapple; vanilla with mandarin or fresh orange.
3. Chop some praline or nut brittle and fold it into a butterscotch or vanilla instant pudding. Pour into dishes and finish with a border of chopped praline.
4. Make up 2 packets of lemon pie filling. Whisk up 2 egg whites and fold them lightly into the lemon filling. Pile in individual glasses and if liked combine in layers with mandarin oranges. Serve decorated with grated chocolate or thread coconut.
5. Pile cold canned creamed rice into individual dishes, cover with a layer of softened raspberry jam and top with a peach or pear half.
6. Mix canned creamed rice with a little sherry or the grated rind of an orange or lemon. Pile in glasses in layers with some jam or canned fruit and top with whipped cream.

Caramel banana crunch

175 g *(6 oz)* digestive biscuits
15 ml *(1 level tbsp)* caster sugar
75 g *(3 oz)* melted butter
1 pkt caramel blancmange powder
568 ml *(1 pt)* milk
142-ml *(5-fl oz)* carton double cream, lightly whipped
2 bananas, peeled and sliced
whipped cream, toasted coconut and pistachio nuts to decorate

Crush the biscuits, stir in the sugar and butter and press the mixture into a 20.5-cm *(8-in)* pie dish to make a crust. Bake in the oven at 180°C *(350°F)* mark 4 for 8–10 minutes and leave to cool. Make up the blancmange using the milk; cool, stirring frequently to prevent a skin forming and to keep the mixture smooth. When it is almost cold, fold in the lightly whipped cream and one of the sliced bananas. Spoon into the case and level off; chill thoroughly. Before serving, decorate with whipped cream, toasted coconut, pistachio nuts and the remaining sliced banana.

Choc mallow

100 g *(4 oz)* plain chocolate
25 g *(1 oz)* butter
2 eggs, separated
20 marshmallows
whipped cream

Put the chocolate in a basin which is standing over a pan of hot water and heat until it is melted. Add the butter, egg yolks and marshmallows and continue to cook, stirring all the time until the mixture is smooth; add 15 ml *(1 tbsp)* hot water. Remove from the heat. Stiffly whisk the egg whites, fold into the mixture and whisk until well blended. Divide between individual glasses and chill. To serve, top with cream.

Jamaican crunch pie

150 g *(5 oz)* gingernuts
75 g *(2½ oz)* butter, melted
142-ml *(5-fl oz)* carton double cream
198-g *(7-oz)* can sweetened condensed milk
90 ml *(6 tbsps)* lemon juice
pared rind of 1 lemon
glazed lemon slices

Crumb the gingernuts in the blender and mix into the melted butter. Work the crumbs with the back of the spoon to form a shell in a 19-cm *(7½-in)* pie plate (or a flan ring placed on a flat plate). Put the remaining ingredients, except the lemon slices, into the blender and mix well or whisk well together by hand. Pour into the gingernut base and refrigerate overnight. Prepare the glazed lemon slices by poaching 8 thick slices of lemon in a frying pan with just enough water to cover them. When they are tender, remove and drain, then pour over them a syrup made by dissolving 75 g *(3 oz)* sugar in the liquid in a frying pan and boiling rapidly to a thick syrup. Allow the slices to cool and use to decorate the pie. Serve well chilled.

Coffee crackle *see colour plate facing p. 400*

70 g *(2½ oz)* butter
30 ml *(2 level tbsps)* golden syrup
75 g *(3 oz)* rice crispies
15 ml *(1 level tbsp)* powdered gelatine
30 ml *(2 tbsps)* coffee essence
15 ml *(1 tbsp)* water
400 ml *(¾ pt)* milk
142-ml *(5-fl oz)* carton single cream
two 70-g *(2½-oz)* pkts coffee Supreme Dessert Whip
142-ml *(5-fl oz)* carton double cream
15 ml *(1 tbsp)* milk
bought chocolate syrup

In a saucepan, melt the butter and golden syrup together. Add the rice crispies. Toss together until the crispies are evenly coated. Leave to one side. Grease and line the base and sides of a 2.3-l *(4-pt)* Charlotte mould – for lining the sides use short strips of paper to fit the tin snugly. Press the crispies mixture on to the base and sides of the tin with the back of a spoon – tilt the mould at an angle to do this satisfactorily. Chill until firm, then turn out the mould carefully and ease off the paper. Place the shell on a serving plate. Dissolve the gelatine in the coffee essence and water. Whisk the milk, single cream and dessert mix until thick. Fold the warm dissolved gelatine into a little of the whisked mixture. Add it to the rest, then chill for 1 hour. Carefully spoon it into the crispy shell and level the surface. Lightly tie a band of ribbon round for support. Whip the double cream with 15 ml *(1 tbsp)* milk until it just holds its shape. Spread this over the filling. Drizzle some chocolate syrup over and draw a skewer through to 'marble'. Serve quickly. *Serves 6–8.*

Pineapple velvet

1 lemon jelly
142-ml *(5-fl oz)* carton double cream, lightly whipped
312-g *(11-oz)* can crushed pineapple
almonds, chopped and toasted

Make up the lemon jelly, using 400 ml *(¾ pt)* water. When it is on the point of setting, whisk until light and fluffy. Fold in the cream and pineapple, pour into individual glasses and leave to set. Decorate with the almonds before serving.

Pastry making

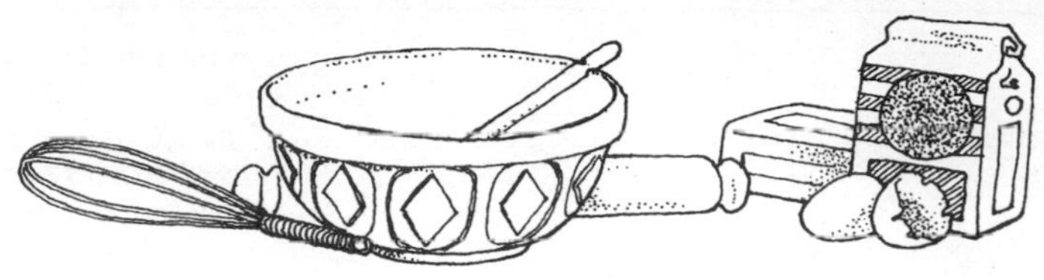

For almost all pastry making you need cool working conditions – in fact, the richer the pastry, the cooler they should be. To keep the pastry cool, handle it as little as possible and use only the fingertips or a pastry blender for rubbing in the fat. Except for choux pastry and hot-water crust, use cold water for mixing. The rich flaky and puff pastries will be improved if you leave them in a cool place between the successive rollings and before baking.

Here are other points to watch:

Add the water cautiously, using only enough to make the mixture bind without becoming sticky – sticky dough leads to hard pastry. Use the barest minimum of flour on the rolling pin and board, or you will alter the proportions of the ingredients. Roll pastry lightly and as little as possible.

Avoid stretching pastry when putting it into a tin or over the top of a pie, for it will shrink back during the baking and spoil the finished shape.

The ingredients

Flour Plain flour is generally recommended, but you can obtain quite good results with a shortcrust pastry by using self-raising flour, though this will give a softer, more crumbly texture.

Fat Butter, margarine and lard are the fats most commonly used, but proprietary vegetable shortenings (both blended and whipped up) and pure vegetable oils can give excellent results. Remember to follow the maker's directions, as sometimes a smaller quantity is recommended in proportion to the flour than is usual with other kinds of fat. Generally speaking the firmer block margarines should be used for traditional rubbing in, a special recipe is given for using 'luxury' or 'table' soft tub margarines.

For shortcrust pastry, butter, margarine, lard or vegetable fat can be used alone but margarine tends to give a firmer pastry which is more yellow in colour. Good results are achieved with a mixture of fats – butter or margarine with lard. For the richer pastries it is better to keep to the fat specified in the recipe.

Liquid Generally, allow about 5 ml *(1 tsp)* liquid per 25 g *(1 oz)* flour to bind short pastry to a stiff dough and 15 ml *(1 tbsp)* to bind suet or flaky pastries to an elastic dough.

THE SHORT PASTRIES

Shortcrust pastry

This, which is probably the most widely used pastry, is made by the 'rubbing-in' method. It is quick and simple to produce and forms the basis of a wide range of sweet and savoury dishes.

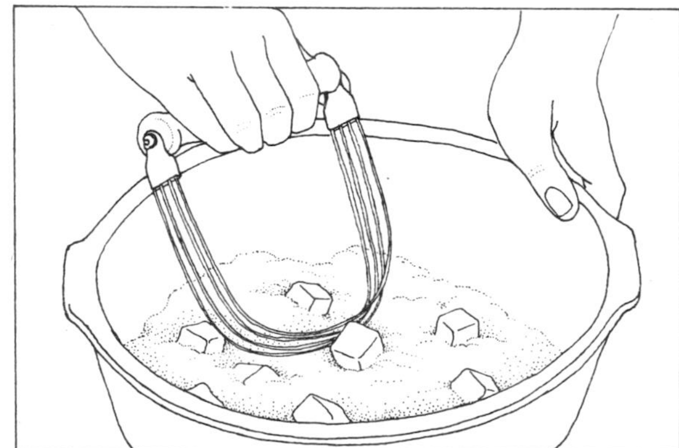

Using a pastry blender

Flan pastry

A slightly richer pastry, made by the same method as shortcrust. It is usually sweetened and is ideal for flan cases, small tartlets and other sweet pastries; if the sugar is omitted, it can be used for savoury flans and tarts.

Pâte sucrée (sugar pastry)

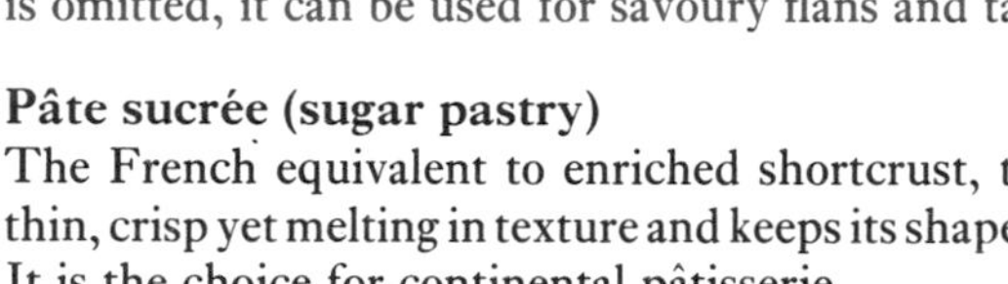

The French equivalent to enriched shortcrust, this is thin, crisp yet melting in texture and keeps its shape well. It is the choice for continental pâtisserie.

Cheese pastry

There are two methods of making this: the less rich version, being easier to handle and less liable to crack when shaped, is better for pies, tarts and flans, while the richer one is better for small savouries, such as party and cocktail 'nibblers'.

Use a hard, dry, well flavoured mature cheese, such as Cheddar, Cheshire or Parmesan, and grate it finely.

Shortcrust pastry

250 g *(9 oz)* plain flour
pinch salt
125 g *(4½ oz)* fat – half lard, half block margarine or butter
about 45 ml *(9 tsps)* water

Mix the flour and salt together. Cut the fat into small knobs and add it. Using both hands, rub the fat into the flour between finger and thumb tips. After 2–3 minutes there will be no lumps of fat left and the mixture will look like fresh breadcrumbs. So far as possible, add the water altogether sprinkling it evenly over the surface, (uneven addition may cause blistering when the pastry is cooked). Stir it in with a round-bladed knife until the mixture begins to stick together in large lumps. With one hand, collect it together and knead lightly for a few seconds, to give a firm, smooth dough. The pastry can be used straight away, but is better allowed to 'rest' for 15 minutes. It can also be wrapped in polythene and kept in the refrigerator for a day or two.

When the pastry is required, sprinkle a very little flour on a working surface and the rolling pin, not on the pastry, roll out the dough evenly in one direction only, turning it occasionally. The usual thickness is about 0.3 cm *(⅛ in)*; do not pull or stretch it. Use as required. The usual oven temperature is 200–220°C *(400–425°F)* mark 6–7.

This amount is sufficient to cover a 1.1-l (2-pt) pie dish, a 23-cm (9-in) flan dish, or make a top and bottom crust for an 18-cm (7-in) pie plate. (See also footnote to flan pastry recipe.)

Note For a slightly richer pastry increase the fat to 150 g *(5 oz)*.

Flan pastry

100 g *(4 oz)* plain flour
pinch of salt
75 g *(3 oz)* butter or block margarine and lard
5 ml *(1 level tsp)* caster sugar
1 egg, beaten

Mix the flour and salt together and rub in the fat with the fingertips, as for shortcrust pastry, until the mixture resembles fine crumbs. Mix in the sugar. Add the egg, stirring until the ingredients begin to stick together, then with one hand collect the mixture together and knead very lightly to give a firm, smooth dough. Roll out as for shortcrust pastry and use as required. This pastry should be cooked in the oven at 200°C *(400°F)* mark 6.

To adjust this recipe for various sizes of flan ring or loose bottomed fluted flan tin allow:
100 g (4 oz) flour etc for a 15-cm (6-in) ring
150 g (5 oz) flour etc for an 18-cm (7-in) ring
200 g (7 oz) flour etc for a 20.5-cm (8-in) ring
250 g (9 oz) flour etc for a 23-cm (9-in) ring.
Adjust other ingredients in proportion.
These amounts also apply to shortcrust pastry.

Pâte sucrée (sugar pastry)

200 g *(7 oz)* plain flour
pinch of salt
100 g *(3½ oz)* caster sugar
100 g *(3½ oz)* butter
3–4 egg yolks

Sift the flour with the salt into a pyramid on a working surface. Make a 'well' in the centre of the pyramid and put in the sugar. Cut the butter into pieces and add it with the egg yolks, to the sugar. Using a palette knife, flip the flour from side to side over the yolks and then pinch the mixture together with the finger tips of one hand until all the flour is incorporated. Work the dough quickly and lightly into a smooth pastry, using the 'heel' of the hand, then form it into a small ball, wrap in kitchen foil or plastic film and leave in the refrigerator or a cool place for 1 hour.

This quantity is sufficient for a 23-cm (9-in) loose bottomed fluted flan tin or will make about 24 tartlet cases.

Cheese pastry

100 g *(4 oz)* plain flour
pinch of salt
50 g *(2 oz)* butter or block margarine and lard
50 g *(2 oz)* Cheddar cheese, finely grated
little beaten egg or water

Mix the flour and salt together and rub in the fat, as for shortcrust pastry, until the mixture resembles fine crumbs in texture. Mix in the cheese. Add a little egg or water, stirring until the ingredients begin to stick together, then with one hand collect the dough together and knead very lightly to give a smooth dough. Roll out as for shortcrust pastry. Use as required. The usual temperature for cooking cheese pastry is 200°C *(400°F)* mark 6.

Note Use a well flavoured cheese with a bite when ever possible; a pinch of dry mustard added to the flour with the salt helps to bring out the cheese flavour.

Rich cheese pastry

75 g *(3 oz)* butter or block margarine and lard
75 g *(3 oz)* Cheddar cheese, finely grated
100 g *(4 oz)* plain flour
pinch of salt

Cream the fat and cheese together until soft. Gradually work in the flour and salt with a wooden spoon or a palette knife until the mixture sticks together; with one hand collect it together and knead very lightly until smooth. Cover with greaseproof or waxed paper and leave in a cool place. Use as required.

Bake at 200°C *(400°F)* mark 6.

Note Use a well flavoured cheese with a bite whenever possible; a pinch of dry mustard added to the flour with the salt helps to bring out the cheese flavour.

Suetcrust pastry

200 g *(7 oz)* self raising flour
2.5 ml *(½ level tsp)* salt
100 g *(3½ oz)* shredded suet
about 105 ml *(7 tbsps)* cold water

Mix together the flour, salt and suet. Add enough cold water to give a light, elastic dough and knead very lightly until smooth. Roll out to 0.5 cm *(¼ in)* thick.

This pastry may be used for both sweet and savoury dishes and can be steamed, boiled or baked; the first two are the most satisfactory methods, as baked suetcrust pastry is inclined to be hard.

This quantity is sufficient for a 900-ml–1.1-l (1½–2-pt) pudding basin.

One-stage short pastry

125 g *(4 oz)* soft tub margarine
175 g *(6 oz)* plain flour, sifted
15 ml *(1 tbsp)* water

Place the margarine, 30 ml *(2 tbsps)* flour and the water in a mixing bowl. Cream with a fork for about half a minute, until well mixed. Mix in the remaining flour to form a fairly soft dough. Turn on to a lightly floured board and knead until smooth. Roll out fairly thinly. One-stage pastry is usually baked at 190°C *(375°F)* mark 5. *This amount is enough to line a 20.5-cm (8-in) fluted flan ring.*

Fork-mix pastry
(made with oil)

40 ml *(2½ tbsps)* oil
15 ml *(1 tbsp)* cold water
100 g *(4 oz)* plain flour
pinch of salt

Put the oil and water into a basin and beat well with a fork to form an emulsion. Mix the flour and salt together and add gradually to the mixture to make a dough. Roll this out on a floured board or between greaseproof paper.

This is a slightly more greasy pastry than one made with solid fat, so it is more suitable for savoury dishes than for sweet tarts. Bake in the oven at 200°C *(400°F)* mark 6.

Macaroni cheese (p. 273).

'FLAKED' PASTRIES

Flaky pastry

Probably the commonest of the flaked types, this can be used in many savoury and sweet dishes. The instructions may appear rather complicated at first reading, but are less difficult than they appear and if you follow them carefully, you should be able to obtain really good results.

Rough puff pastry

This is similar in appearance and texture to flaky pastry, though perhaps not so even, but it is quicker and easier to make and can be used instead of flaky in most recipes. Today, bought ready made puff pastry is frequently used to replace home made rough puff. Buy a 212-g *(7½-oz)* packet to replace home made pastry made with 100 g *(4 oz)* flour, and a 368-g *(13-oz)* packet to replace home made pastry made with 200 g *(7 oz)* flour. Bought pastry should be rolled out slightly thinner than your own.

Puff pastry

The richest of all the pastries, puff gives the most even rising, the most flaky effect and the crispest texture, but because of the time it takes, most people make it only occasionally. It requires very careful handling and whenever possible should be made the day before it is to be used, so that it has time to become firm and cool before it is shaped and baked. If you have a freezer, it's well worth while to make up a bulk batch and pack in amounts that are practical to thaw and use. Bought puff pastry, either chilled or frozen, is very satisfactory, but remember to roll it out to a thickness of 0.2–0.4 cm *($\frac{1}{16}$–$\frac{1}{8}$ in)* only, as it rises very well.

'First rollings' are used for vol-au-vents, bouchées and patties, where appearance is important. 'Second rollings' and trimmings can be used for other dishes, such as sausage rolls.

General points for flaked pastries

1. Always handle lightly and as little as possible.
2. The fat for flaky and puff pastries should be of about the same consistency as the dough with which it is to be combined – this is the reason for 'working' it on a plate beforehand. The fat for rough puff pastry should be firm so that the cubes of fat retain their shape while being mixed into the dry ingredients.
3. Remember to 'rest' all flaked pastries, ie to cover them and leave in a cool place for about 15 minutes, both during and after the making and also after shaping and before baking; this will prevent the fat from melting and spoiling the flaked texture when the pastry is cooked.
4. Always roll out lightly and evenly, not taking the rolling pin over the edges of the pastry. Never stretch the dough during shaping, or the finished dish will tend to be mis-shapen.

Roquefort quiche (p. 268).

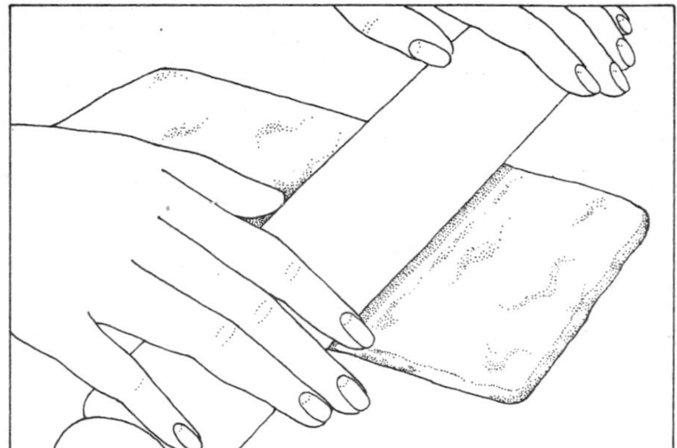

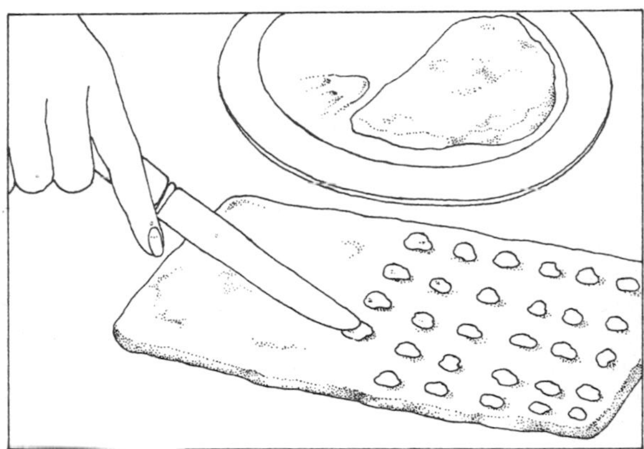

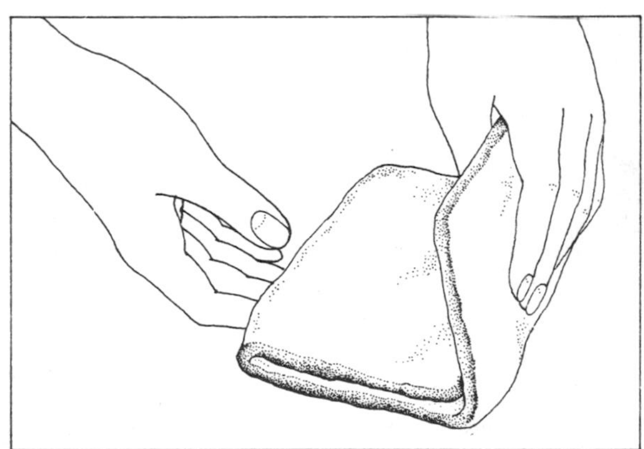

Flaky pastry – first roll the dough into an oblong

Put a quarter of the fat over the pastry, in flakes

Fold the dough into three, with the fat inside

Flaky pastry

200 g *(7 oz)* plain flour
pinch of salt
150 g *(5 oz)* butter or a mixture of butter and lard
about 105 ml *(7 tbsps)* cold water to mix
squeeze of lemon juice
beaten egg to glaze

Mix together the flour and salt. Soften the fat by 'working' it with a knife on a plate; divide it into 4 equal portions. Rub one quarter of the softened fat into the flour and mix to a soft, elastic dough with the water and lemon juice. On a floured board, roll the pastry into an oblong 3 times as long as it is wide. Put another quarter of the fat over the top two-thirds of the pastry in flakes, so that it looks like buttons on a card. Fold the bottom third up and the top third of the pastry down and turn it through 90° so that the folds are now at the side. Seal the edges of the pastry by pressing with the rolling pin. Re-roll as before and continue until all the fat is used up.

Wrap the pastry loosely in greaseproof paper and leave it to 'rest' in a refrigerator or cool place for at least ½ hour before using. This makes handling and shaping the pastry easier and gives a more evenly flaked texture.

Sprinkle a board or table with a very little flour.

Roll out the pastry 0.3 cm *(⅛ in)* thick and use as required. Brush with beaten egg before baking, to give the characteristic glaze.

The usual oven setting for flaky pastry is 220°C *(425°F)* mark 7.

Rough puff pastry

200 g *(7 oz)* plain flour
pinch of salt
150 g *(5 oz)* butter or block margarine and lard
about 105 ml *(7 tbsps)* cold water to mix
squeeze of lemon juice
beaten egg to glaze

Mix the flour and salt; cut the fat (which should be quite firm) into cubes about 2 cm *(¾ in)* across. Stir the fat into the flour without breaking up the pieces and mix to a fairly stiff dough with the water and lemon juice. Turn on to a floured board and roll into a strip 3 times as long as it is wide. Fold the bottom third up and the top third down, then turn the pastry through 90° so that the folds are at the sides. Seal the edges of the pastry by pressing lightly with a rolling pin. Continue to roll and fold in this way 4 times altogether. Leave to 'rest' wrapped in greaseproof paper for about ½ hour before using. Roll out and use as for flaky pastry.

Rough puff gives a similar result to flaky pastry, but the flakes are not usually as even, so where even rising and appearance are particularly important, eg with patties and vol-au-vents, it is better to use flaky pastry. On the other hand, rough puff has the advantage of being quicker to make.

The usual oven setting for rough puff is 220°C *(425°F)* mark 7.

Puff pastry

200 g *(7 oz)* plain flour
pinch of salt
200 g *(7 oz)* butter, preferably unsalted
about 105 ml *(7 tbsps)* cold water
squeeze of lemon juice
beaten egg to glaze

Mix the flour and salt. Work the fat with a knife on a plate until it is soft, then rub a knob of it into the flour. Mix to a fairly soft, elastic dough with the water and lemon juice and knead lightly on a floured board until smooth. Form the rest of the fat into an oblong and roll the pastry out into a square. Place the block of fat on one half of the pastry and enclose it by folding the remaining pastry over and sealing the edges with a rolling pin. Turn the pastry so that the fold is to the side, then roll out into a strip 3 times as long as it is wide. Fold the bottom third up and the top third down and seal the edges by pressing lightly with the rolling pin. Cover the pastry with waxed or greaseproof paper and leave to 'rest' in a cool place or in the refrigerator for about 20 minutes. Turn the pastry so that the folds are to the sides and continue rolling, folding and resting until the sequence has been completed 6 times altogether. After the final resting, shape the pastry as required. Always brush the top surfaces with beaten egg before cooking, to give the characteristic glaze of puff pastry.

The usual oven setting for puff pastry is 230°C *(450°F)* mark 8.

Note Even without a freezer, uncooked home-made puff pastry keeps 2–3 days, wrapped in a cloth or foil in the refrigerator.

MISCELLANEOUS PASTRIES

Choux

To ensure a good result with this special type of pastry, used for éclairs, profiteroles and aigrettes, note these points:

1. All the flour must be added quickly, with the saucepan off the heat.
2. The paste must be cooked until it comes away from the sides of the pan.
3. The eggs must be added gradually, only just enough being used to give a piping consistency.
4. The oven door must not be opened during the cooking.
5. Eclairs and profiteroles should be split open when they are cooked, to dry the inside of the pastry.

Hot-water crust

This pastry is mixed with boiling water, which makes it pliable enough to mould into a raised pie that will hold its shape as it cools and during the baking. It is a 'strong' pastry, fit to withstand the extra handling that it must receive during the shaping and also the weight of the savoury filling it must hold.

If you do not wish to 'raise' the pie by hand, you can use a small cake tin. For a more elaborate raised pie, you can use a special metal mould; various sizes are available but they are all made in two parts, joined by a hinge, so that they can easily be removed when the pie is cooked.

Hot-water crust pastry is used for such dishes as veal and ham pie and game pie.

Choux pastry

50 g *(2 oz)* butter or block margarine
about 150 ml *(¼ pt)* water
120 ml *(8 level tbsps)* plain flour, sifted
2 eggs, lightly beaten

Melt the fat in the water and bring to the boil; remove from the heat and quickly tip in the flour all at once. Beat with a wooden spoon until the paste is smooth and forms a ball in the centre of the pan. (Take care not to over-beat or the mixture becomes fatty.) Allow to cool for a minute or two. Beat in the eggs a little at a time, beating vigorously – this is important – to trap in as much air as possible. A handheld electric mixer is ideal for this and will also enable you to incorporate all the egg easily. Carry on beating until a sheen is obvious. Use as required. Some people prefer to chill a hand-made paste in the bag for about 30 minutes before piping. The usual oven setting is 200–220°C *(400–425°F)* mark 6–7.

Note When beating by hand with a wooden spoon the arm tends to tire, the beating speed is reduced and the final consistency is often too slack to retain its shape. In this case a little of the egg may have to be omitted – and remember to use standard eggs for the hand method.

Hot-water crust pastry

450 g *(1 lb)* plain flour
10 ml *(2 level tsps)* salt
100 g *(4 oz)* lard
150 ml *(¼ pt)* plus 60 ml *(4 tbsps)* milk or milk and water

Mix the flour and salt. Melt the lard in the liquid, then bring to the boil and pour into a well made in the dry ingredients. Working quickly, beat with a wooden spoon to form a fairly soft dough. Use one hand to lightly pinch the dough together and knead until smooth and silky. Cover with plastic film or a damp tea towel. Leave to rest for 20–30 minutes for the dough to become elastic and easy to work. Use as required. See the directions below for the method of shaping a raised pie by hand and in a cake tin. Keep the part of the dough that is not actually being used covered with a cloth or an up-turned basin to prevent it hardening before you can use it.

SHAPING PASTRY

Covering a pie dish

Roll out the pastry to the required thickness and 5 cm *(2 in)* wider than the pie dish, using the inverted dish as a guide. Cut a 2.5-cm *(1-in)* wide strip from the outer edge and place it on the dampened rim of the dish. Seal the join and brush the whole strip with water. Fill the pie dish generously, so that the surface is slightly rounded; use a pie funnel if insufficient filling is available. Lift the remaining pastry on the rolling pin and lay it over the pie dish. Press the lid lightly on to the pastry lined rim to seal. Trim off any excess pastry with the cutting edge of a knife held at a slight angle away from the dish. Seal the edges firmly so that they do not open up during cooking – hold the knife blade horizontally towards the pie dish and make a series of shallow cuts in the pastry edges to give the appearance of leaves of a book. If you wish, scallop the edges (see page 17) and use trimmings rolled thinly as decorative leaf shapes etc. Cut a slit in the centre of the pie crust for the steam to escape.

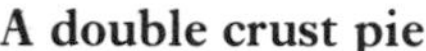

A double crust pie

Divide the pastry into two parts, one slightly bigger than the other. Shape the larger piece into a ball and roll it out to the required thickness. Rotate the pastry as you roll it, to keep it circular; pinch together any cracks that appear at the edge. Roll it out to about 2.5 cm *(1 in)* wider than the inverted pie plate. Fold the pastry in half, position it on the pie plate and unfold; ease it into place without stretching or having any air pockets. Add cold filling, keep the surface slightly rounded. Roll out the remaining pastry for the lid, keeping it about 1 cm *(½ in)* beyond the rim. Brush the pastry over the rim, then lift the lid into position as for covering a pie. Seal the edge either by folding the surplus edge of the lid over the rim of the base pastry or by pressing the two layers together and trimming as for covering a pie. Knock up the edges and make a short slit in the centre for the steam to escape.

A flan case

Choose a plain or fluted flan ring placed on a baking sheet; loose-bottomed flan tin or sandwich tin. Roll out the pastry thinly to a circle about 5 cm *(2 in)* wider than the ring. With a rolling pin lift the pastry and lower it into the ring or fold the pastry in half and position it in the tin. Lift the edges carefully and ease the pastry into the flan shape, lightly pressing the pastry against the edges – with a fluted edge press your finger edge into each flute to ensure a good finish. No air should be left between the container and pastry. Trim the pastry into a plain ring using a knife or scissors, leaving just a fraction of pastry above the rim, neaten by knocking it up with a knife. On a fluted ring roll across the top of the ring with the rolling pin.

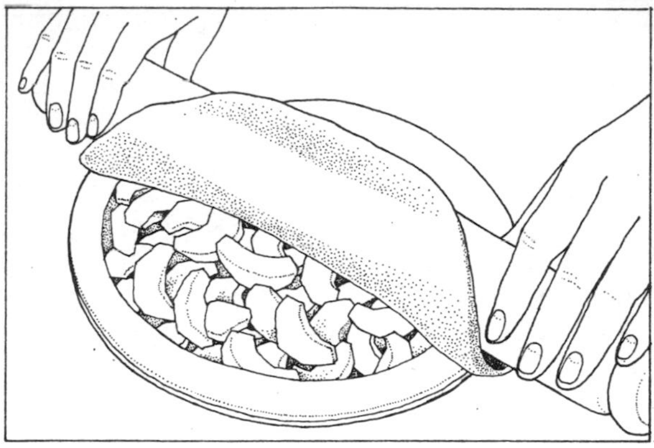

Covering a pie

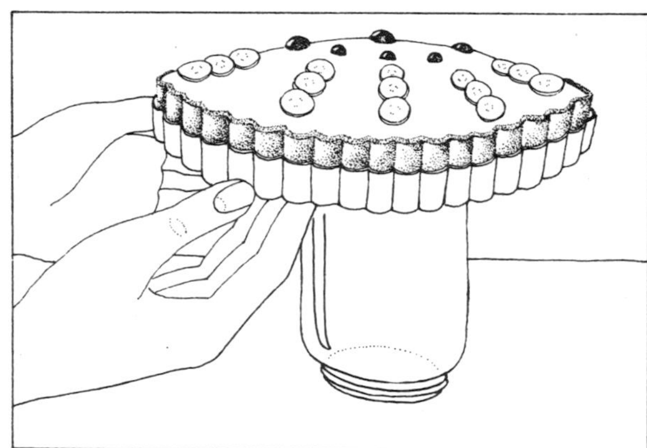

Removing a baked flan from a loose-bottomed tin

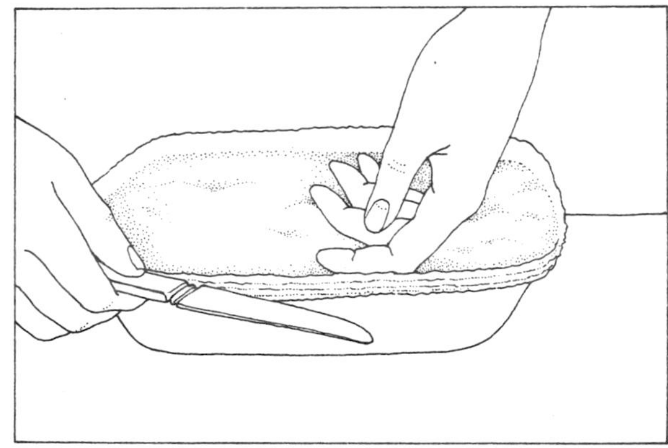

Knocking up

Lining individual tartlet tins

Arrange the tins close together on a baking sheet. Roll out the pastry thinly and cover the whole area of the tins with pastry like a blanket – do not stretch the pastry, which should be loosely positioned. With a small knob of dough press the pastry into each tin. With a rolling pin roll across the complete set of tins and lift the surplus pastry away. Use the finger tips to re-shape the pastry. With a sheet of patty tins, cut rounds of thinly rolled pastry slightly larger than the top of the tin and ease one round into each shape.

To bake blind

Flans and tarts are often 'baked blind' when they are to be filled with a cold or uncooked filling or when they are made in advance and stored for a few days in an airtight tin. Line the pie dish or flan ring with the pastry. Cut out a round of greased greaseproof paper slightly larger than the pastry case – it does not need to be too exact – and fit this, greased side down, inside the pastry, or utilise the wrapper from a block of fat. Half-fill the paper with uncooked dried beans or rice or pasta (let these cool after use and keep them in a special container for use again). Bake the pastry as directed in the recipe for 10–15 minutes, until it has set. Remove the paper and baking beans from the pastry case and return this to the oven for a further 5 minutes to dry out. Use as required. If you make a particular size flan regularly it is worth cutting a round of kitchen foil; keep it handy for using every time.

Small tartlets which are required for filling or storing can also be baked blind. Line tartlet tins with rounds of pastry, prick well with a fork (this is generally sufficient to ensure a good shape with small items) and bake as directed in the recipe.

Making bouchées

Roll out 200 g *(7 oz)* puff pastry (ie made with 200 g *(7 oz)* flour etc) 0.5–1 cm *(¼–½ in)* thick. Using a 4-cm *(1½-in)* plain cutter, cut out 20–25 rounds and put them on a baking sheet. Cut part-way through the centre of each round with a 1-cm *(½-in)* plain cutter. Glaze the tops with beaten egg and bake in the oven at 230°C *(450°F)* mark 8 for 10 minutes, until golden brown. Remove the soft pastry from inside and cool the cases on a rack. Before serving, reheat in the oven at 180°C *(350°F)* mark 4 for about 15 minutes and fill with the hot filling (see also page 34). Individual vol-au-vents are made in a similar way but are cut with a 7.5-cm *(3-in)* plain cutter and a 5-cm *(2-in)* plain cutter for marking the lid.

Making vol-au-vents *see colour plate facing p. 96*

Roll out 200 g *(7 oz)* puff pastry (200 g *(7 oz)* flour etc) about 2.5 cm *(1 in)* thick. Put on to a greased baking sheet and cut into an oval or large round to take in nearly all the pastry. (Try not to cut nearer than 1 cm *(½ in)* to the edge of the slab of pastry.) With a small knife mark an oval or round 1–2 cm *(½–¾ in)* inside the larger one, to form a lid, cutting about halfway through the pastry. Brush the top with beaten egg. Bake in the oven at 230°C *(450°F)* mark 8 for 30–35 minutes, covering the pastry with greaseproof paper when it is sufficiently brown. Remove the lid, scoop out any soft pastry inside and dry out the case in the oven for a further 5–10 minutes.

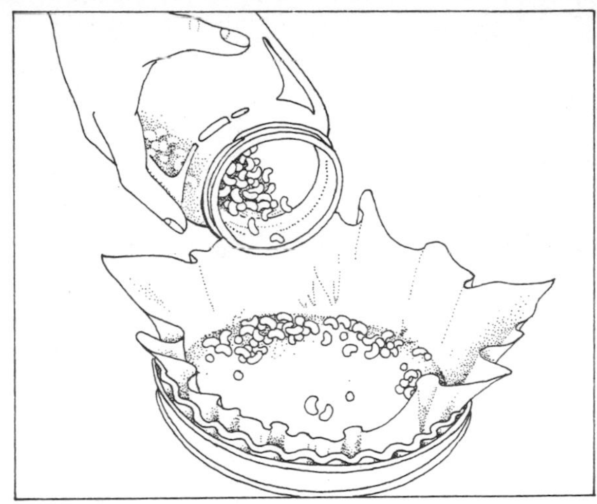

Lining a flan case for baking blind

Serve hot or cold, filled with a savoury sauce as suggested for bouchées on page 34, or make a cold sweet by filling with soft fruit, peaches or apricots and whipped cream.

Shaping a raised pie

Use the recipe amount given under hot water crust.

To shape dough for a large pie, grease a 1.4-l *(3-pt)* hinged pie mould or use a round cake or loaf tin of the same capacity. Place the mould on a baking sheet. Roll out two-thirds of the pastry on a floured surface into an oval 28 cm by 25.5 cm *(11 in by 10 in)*. Keep the remaining pastry covered. Drape the rolled pastry over the rolling pin, lift the pin and unroll it over the tin. Press the pastry into the tin to 0.5 cm *(¼ in)* above the rim. Pack the filling into the pastry shell. Roll out the remaining pastry to fit the top of the mould. Position it over the filling and pinch the edges together and flute. Brush the lid with egg beaten with a little water and a pinch of salt.

For small pies use six 350-g *(12-oz)* or 450-g *(1-lb)* jam jars. Invert the jam jars. Divide two-thirds of the pastry into six. Roll each piece into a 15-cm *(6-in)* round and trim the edges. Place the rounds over the jars, mould into shape (avoid pressing the pastry too thinly) and use your fingertips to smooth down the folds. Cover with a clean tea towel and leave in a cool place for 2 hours. Ease the pastry away from the jar, gently twisting the jar, to give a cup shape. Fill and finish as for a large pie.

All pies Make a fairly large hole in the centre of all pies. For the tassel, roll out pastry trimmings into broad strips. At 0.3–0.5 cm *(⅛–¼ in)* intervals cut almost but not completely across, as if to make a fringe. Roll up and fan out the strips. Chill, then glaze with egg and bake.

Family cakes and scones

Cake making ingredients

Flour

Today we can buy from a wide range of flours and there is a 'right' one for various jobs, even though many people rely on self raising flour to fill every bill. The difference is largely due to the gluten factor – the strength of the flour. Gluten is the substance which makes so much difference to the volume and texture of your dough when baked.

There are two main types of flour available – high-gluten (strong) and low-gluten (weak). A strong flour, often referred to as bread flour, which has a gluten content of 10–15%, and high-raising, water-absorbing qualities, is best for bread and other yeasted goods which need to have a large volume and a light, open texture; it is also best for puff pastry, for Yorkshire batter and for steamed puddings. But we don't always want such a high rise. A soft, starchy flour, with a lower gluten content of 7–10% is best for cakes, biscuits and shortcrust pastry, where a smaller rise and a closer, finer texture is required. Such a flour absorbs fat well and produces a light, soft texture. For biscuits and shortbread, where in fact no rise is wanted, extra starch, such as cornflour or rice flour, or even custard powder, can be added to the soft flour: 200 g *(7 oz)* plain flour and 25 g *(1 oz)* cornflour are the basic proportions. For shortbreads, increase the proportion using 1 part cornflour to 2 parts flour.

Whether soft flour should be plain or self raising is a matter of personal taste. Self raising is popular because it eliminates errors, ensuring a happy balance of raising agents, which are evenly blended throughout the flour. It is fine for all rubbed-in mixtures. With plain flour the quantity of raising agent can be varied to suit the particular recipe and individual methods. If you only have plain household flour, use 225 g *(8 oz)* flour and 12.5 ml *(2½ level tsps)* baking powder to replace self raising.

When less raising agent is called for than in self raising flour, a mixture of plain and self raising is very satisfactory. Once the proportion of fat in the mixture is higher than half fat to flour but lower than equal quantities of fat to flour, replace 225 g *(8 oz)* plain and 7.5 ml *(1½ level tsps)* baking powder by 100 g *(4 oz)* self raising and 100 g *(4 oz)* plain. For a very rich cake, with equal amounts of fat, sugar, and flour, replace 225 g *(8 oz)* plain flour and 2.5 ml *(½ level tsp)* baking powder by 175 g *(6 oz)* plain flour and 50 g *(2 oz)* self raising. The Victoria sponge is a special case. Many people make it with self raising flour, and the result is perfectly acceptable, though the colour is paler and the texture more irregular and open than it should ideally be. To get the traditional appearance, use plain flour and a little baking powder, or half plain and half self raising. And for, say, rich yeast dough, add some soft flour for extra fat absorption; for scones, add some strong flour to give extra rise.

Other speciality flours can be used to add variety – wholemeals are 100% of the wheat (though sometimes a little of the coarse bran has been removed during the milling). Wheatmeals are 85–95% of the wheat and contain all the germ and some of the bran. These bran flours do not store well and should be bought in small quantities. The texture of mixtures based on these flours is close and fairly substantial.

It is also worth noting that by varying the other ingredients in the mix, the cooking and the handling, the glutens in the dough can be toughened or softened to produce the right kind of mixture.

Gluten is toughened by salt (when you forget the salt, the bread dough is sticky), by acidity (from sour milk, as in scones, and from lemon juice used in puff pastry); by all kinds of handling (rolling for puff pastry, kneading for yeast dough, and by mixing).

Gluten in the dough is softened by fat; by sugar; by the enzymes in the yeast and malt, and in bran and germ (as in wholemeal flour).

All this explains why yeasted goods should be well kneaded, to develop the dough strength and offset the softening effect of the yeast, and why puff pastry needs a good deal of rolling to distribute the fat and offset the softening due to the high fat content; why cakes and short pastry should be lightly handled and worked as little as possible to avoid toughening.

Flour that has been sifted (even when there are no other dry ingredients in the recipe) is easier to incorporate.

Flour should be stored in a dry, cool place.

Sugar

Sugar is an important ingredient in all cake baking and is essential in sponges and meringues. Brown sugars and other kinds can give variety and extra flavour, if correctly used.

Caster sugar is, of course, the one most commonly used in recipes, especially for creamed mixtures and whisked sponge mixtures.

Granulated sugar, generally speaking, produces a creamed mixture which is slightly reduced in volume, with a reasonably good texture, apart from a slight grittiness and sometimes a speckly appearance. For rubbed-in mixtures, granulated sugar is quite acceptable.

Icing sugar is the finest of all sugars. Icing sugar is not generally used for basic cake mixtures, the volume produced being poor and the crust hard, but it is favoured for some biscuit and meringue recipes. It is ideal for decorating cakes, and, of course, in the preparation of icing.

Soft brown sugar (moist brown and 'pieces'), whether dark or light, imparts more flavour – a caramel taste – than white sugar and has a slightly finer grain. When it is used to replace caster sugar in sandwich cakes, the volume is good; these sugars cream well.

Demerara sugar is even coarser in the grain than granulated, which it can replace in rubbed-in mixtures. It is more suitable for making cakes by the melting method, such as gingerbreads, where heat and moisture help to dissolve it. It is unsatisfactory for creamed mixtures, because its large crystals do not break down during mixing.

Barbados sugar is a very dark, unrefined sugar of a similar colour to treacle. Too strong in flavour for light cake mixtures, it helps to give a good flavour and colour to rich fruit cakes, and of course to gingerbreads. You can modify the decided flavour of Barbados sugar by using it half-and-half with white sugar.

Other sweeteners

Golden syrup is sweeter than treacle and can be used to replace part of the sugar content in a recipe. It gives a special flavour which is particularly acceptable with spices.

Treacle, dark syrup, not as sweet as golden syrup. A little added to rich fruit cakes gives a good dark colour and distinctive flavour; it is also a traditional ingredient for gingerbreads and for the making of malt bread.

Honey is to be found in some recipes. The ability of honey to absorb and retain moisture and thus retard the drying out and staling of baked goods, is a great help. Only part of the sugar content should be replaced by honey – generally not more than half.

Which fat?

The commonest fats used in baking are butter and margarine, but others such as lard, blended white vegetable fat, dripping and oil may be used. Butter and block margarine are usually interchangeable though butter gives a flavour all of its own, a 'plus' for richer mixtures. Most 'luxury' and soft tub margarines are suited to special all-in-one recipes. Oil is being more often used today, but again specially proportioned recipes are needed for this cooking medium. As a rule, butter and firm margarine should not be taken direct from the refrigerator or cold larder. If the fat to be used in a creamed mixture is firm, beat it alone, then add the sugar and cream together.

What size eggs?

When a recipe says 'take an egg', which do you choose, large or standard, medium or small? Large and standard eggs give similar results in cake baking, although there is a very slightly reduced volume in, say, a Victoria sandwich and a fatless whisked sponge when standard ones are used. When either small or medium eggs are used, an adjustment is necessary in most recipes. Increase the number of eggs used by one-third, ie use 1 extra to every 3 indicated in the recipe.

The liquid

Moisture is required for the evolution of steam. More often than not the liquid in a mixture is milk or water, but brewed tea, cider, fruit juice and beer are included in certain specific recipes, or may be used to taste. It is often practical to use instant skimmed milk instead of fresh. Simply mix the measured milk with the flour and add water as required. Sour milk and buttermilk are called for in certain kinds of bread and scones.

Raising agents

Baking powder usually consists of bicarbonate of soda and an acid-reacting chemical such as cream of tartar. When moistened, these react together to give the gas carbon dioxide. Flour contains a sticky, rubbery substance called gluten, which when wet is capable of holding the gas made by the raising agent, in the form of tiny bubbles. Since all gases expand when heated, these tiny bubbles formed throughout the mixture become larger during the baking, and thus the cake rises. The heat dries and sets the gluten and so the bubbles are held, giving the cake its characteristic texture. However, cake mixtures are capable of holding only a certain amount of gas, and if too much raising agent is used the cake rises very well at first, but then collapses, and a heavy, close texture is the final result.

A combination of bicarbonate of soda and cream of

tartar is sometimes used to replace baking powder. Sour milk is used in some cakes and scones; as it contains an acid, the amount of cream of tartar should be reduced.

By including whisked egg in a cake mixture, we can use air as a raising agent, instead of carbon dioxide. Thus when a high proportion of egg is used and the mixture is whisked, as in sponge cakes, very little, if any, raising agent is needed. In creamed mixtures also the eggs are beaten in and – so long as the correct proportion of egg is used and the mixture is well beaten – little additional raising agent is required. In plain cakes, where beaten egg is added together with the liquid, the egg helps to bind the mixture, but it does not act as the main raising agent.

Spices and essences

Have ready-mixed spices to hand for general flavouring, since they're carefully blended. But for the special recipes – and for your own pleasure, too, it's good to have certain individual spices such as cinnamon, mace and nutmeg to use with discretion on their own or to blend with others.

Many of the common cake flavourings are obtainable in the form of essences. These are usually concentrated, and should therefore be used sparingly. Caramel is again a highly concentrated product and so just a dash is normally sufficient.

Whenever practical, natural flavourings like lemon, or orange, are the most pleasant to use. Remember, when using the rind of any citrus fruit, to grate only lightly, so as to remove just the yellow part – the white pith imparts a bitter flavour. If only a few drops of lemon juice are needed, pierce the fruit with a fork and squeeze out the juice.

Fruit, nuts and peel

Fruit Always choose good-quality dried fruits, plump and juicy. Should dried fruit like sultanas become hard, leave them to plump up in hot water, drain and dry off. You can buy them ready-washed, but it's wise to give them a good looking over. Unwashed fruits are cheaper, though, so if you buy them, wash well, drain and leave to dry spread out over muslin or blotting paper on an open-mesh rack; let them dry thoroughly, but don't put them over direct heat, because this tends to make them hard. Remember that seedless raisins are small and similar in size to sultanas, but ready-prepared seeded or stoned raisins are large and juicy, with an excellent flavour, since the seeds are removed after the fruit has dried. Check them, though, because now and again a stone does turn up. To stone your own raisins, work them between the finger-tips to remove the stones, and occasionally dip your fingers in water. Wash any excess syrup from glacé cherries before use and thoroughly dry.

Peel You can, if you wish, buy 'caps' of candied orange and lemon peel separately and mix them to definite proportions after shredding, grating, mincing or chopping. Ready-mixed chopped peel is no doubt easier and quicker, but there's extra aroma and flavour to be gained by preparing it yourself. The ready-cut peel sometimes needs more chopping to make it finer.

Nuts When you're using almonds, walnuts, hazels and so on in a recipe, check before you start to see whether they are to be blanched or unblanched, whole, split, flaked, chopped or ground. A small point this, but it saves last-minute irritation. Nibbed, ready-chopped almonds are most handy, but may need an extra chopping to make them finer.

Cake decorations

Here's a check-list; keep a selection of these items and you will never be without an instant finish for your cakes. For even more suggestions, look round sweet shops, confectionary counters or large department stores, grocers and supermarkets.

Nuts Shelled walnuts (refresh them in the oven if you've had them a little time), hazel-nuts, pistachio (rather expensive; buy in small amounts, as they tend to lose colour, and always blanch before use), almonds (have a selection of types), pecans (a change from walnuts, smoother in texture, more bland in flavour).

Crystallised violets and roses Buy in small quantities, and keep in a dark place or jar to avoid bleaching.

Angelica Look for a really good colour and not too much excess of sugar. To remove sugar, place the angelica for a short time in hot water, drain and dry well.

Chocolate and coloured vermicelli Buy in fairly small amounts, unless a favourite recipe needs a larger quantity for, say, coating the sides of a cake. Vermicelli stales and becomes speckled.

Silver dragees (balls) Keep in a dry place. It's a good idea to keep two sizes. Use tweezers for handling, if you have damp, warm hands or find them difficult to grip. Dragees also come in a variety of other colours.

Hundreds and thousands Popular with children, useful for a quick decoration for iced buns.

Glacé and candied fruits Probably cherries, ginger and pineapple are the most useful; others are generally left-overs after the Christmas season. Will go sugary if kept too long.

Mock coffee beans (to be found in sweet shops) are unusual and a change for coffee cakes and gâteaux.

Chocolate for making squares and curls. Both plain and milk chocolate are handy for grating; the softer chocolate coverings are useful for grating and melting. For more advanced work, choose special couverture chocolate.

Preparing tins

Follow the manufacturer's special directions regarding non-stick (silicone-finished) tins, which do not usually require greasing or lining.

Greasing

Grease all cake tins lightly with melted white fat (preferably unsalted) or with oil. The quickest method is to brush them over with a pastry brush dipped in the fat or oil. They may also be dredged with flour as an additional safeguard against sticking: sprinkle a little flour in the tin and shake until coated, then shake out any surplus. For fatless sponges use a half-and-half mixture of flour and caster sugar. (If you often make these cakes, it pays to keep a dredger filled with the flour-and-sugar mixture.) The same treatment can be given to a sponge flan tin to produce a crisper crust. When you use a loose-bottomed flan tin for pastry, there is no need to grease it, though it should be greased when it is used for a sandwich mixture.

Lining

With most cakes it is necessary to line the tins with greaseproof paper, which is usually greased before the mixture is put in, or with non-stick vegetable parchment (silicone-treated), which does not require greasing, and can be used several times.

For a Victoria sandwich cake mixture, it is often sufficient to line the base only of the tin.

For rich mixtures and fruit cakes, line the whole tin. The paper is usually doubled to prevent the outside of the cake from over-browning and drying out. (With the extra rich fruit mixtures used for wedding and other formal cakes, which require a long cooking time, it is also advisable to pin a double strip of thick brown paper round the outside of the tin, to help prevent the outside of the cake overcooking.)

Here are the general methods of lining tins:

To line a deep tin Cut a piece (or 2 pieces, if necessary) of greaseproof paper long enough to reach round the tin and overlap slightly, and high enough to extend about 2.5 cm *(1 in)* above the top edge. Fold up the bottom edge of the strip about 2.5 cm *(1 in)*, creasing it firmly, then open out and snip this folded portion with scissors; this snipped edge enables the paper band to fit a square, oblong, round or oval tin neatly. Brush the inside of the paper with melted white fat (though if the cake mixture is very rich with butter, there is no need to grease the paper). Place the strip in position in the greased tin, with the cut edge flat against the base. In a rectangular tin, make sure the paper fits snugly into the corners.

Cut a double round of paper to fit inside the base of the tin (stand the tin on the paper, draw round it and then cut). Put the rounds in place – they will keep the snipped edge of the band in position and make a neat lining; brush

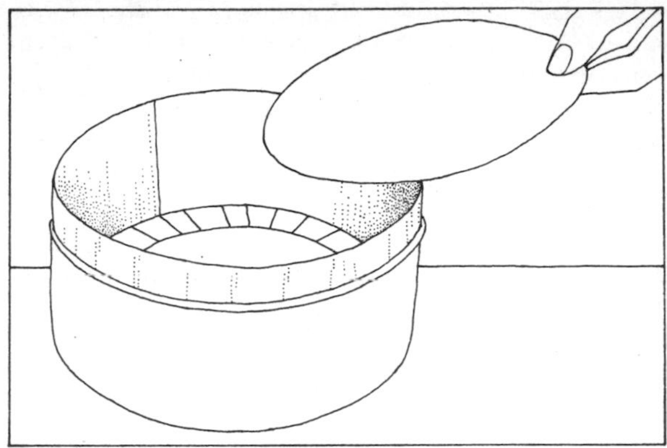

Lining a cake tin with greaseproof paper

the base of the lining with melted white fat – unless the mixture is buttery enough to make this unnecessary.

To line a sandwich tin Cut a round of greaseproof paper to fit the bottom of the tin exactly, as a precaution against sticking. If the tin's sides are shallow and you want to raise them, fit a band of paper inside the tin, coming about 2.5 cm *(1 in)* above the rim.

To line a Swiss roll tin Cut a piece of paper about 5 cm *(2 in)* larger all round than the tin. Place the tin on it and in each corner make a cut from the angle of the paper as far as the corner of the tin. Grease both paper and tin and put in the paper so that it fits closely, overlapping at the corners. Brush with melted fat and, if you wish, dust with a half-and-half mixture of flour and sugar sifted together. Non-stick paper is very satisfactory for lining this type of tin.

To line a loaf tin It is not usually necessary to line a loaf tin fully. Grease the inside, line the base only with an oblong of greaseproof paper and grease the paper also.

To line a sponge flan tin After greasing the inside well, place a round of greased greaseproof paper over the raised part only of the tin.

Baking cakes

Before starting to make cakes, arrange that the oven will be at the correct temperature by the time it is required.

To test whether a cake is cooked

Small cakes should be well risen, golden brown in colour and firm to the touch – both on top and underneath – and they should begin to shrink from the sides of the tin on being taken out of the oven.

Larger cakes present more difficulty, especially for beginners, although the oven heat and time of cooking give a reasonable indication, but the following tests are a guide:

(a) Press the centre top of the cake very lightly with the

finger-tip. The cake should be spongy and should give only very slightly to the pressure, then rise again immediately, retaining no impression.

(b) In the case of a fruit cake lift it gently from the oven and 'listen' to it, putting it closely to the ear. A continued sizzling sound indicates that the cake is not cooked through.

(c) Insert a hot skewer or knitting needle (never a cold knife) in the centre of the cake. It should come out perfectly clean. If any mixture is sticking to it, the cake requires longer cooking.

Cooling

Allow the cake a few minutes to cool before turning it out of the tin; during this time it will shrink away from the sides and is more easily removed. Turn it out very gently, remove any paper and place, right side up, on a wire cooling rack.

Lemon cake

100 g *(4 oz)* butter or margarine
225 g *(8 oz)* self raising flour
pinch of salt
100 g *(4 oz)* sugar
grated rind and juice of 1 small lemon
1 egg, beaten
about 90–120 ml *(6–8 tbsps)* milk

Grease a 15-cm *(6-in)* cake tin. Rub the fat into the flour and salt until the mixture resembles fine breadcrumbs. Stir in the sugar and lemon rind. Make a well in the centre, pour in the egg, lemon juice and some of the milk and gradually work in the dry ingredients, adding more milk if necessary to give a dropping consistency. Put the mixture into the tin, level the top and bake in the oven at 180°C *(350°F)* mark 4 for about 1¼ hours, until golden and firm to the touch. Turn out and cool on a wire rack.

Chocolate and coconut cake

175 g *(6 oz)* self raising flour
pinch of salt
45 ml *(3 level tbsps)* cocoa
100 g *(4 oz)* butter or margarine
100 g *(4 oz)* sugar
50 g *(2 oz)* desiccated coconut
1 egg, beaten
2.5 ml *(½ tsp)* vanilla essence
about 90–120 ml *(6–8 tbsps)* milk to mix

Grease and flour a 15-cm *(6-in)* cake tin. Sift the flour, salt and cocoa together. Rub the fat into the flour until the mixture resembles fine breadcrumbs. Stir in the sugar and coconut. Make a well in the centre, pour in the egg, essence and some of the milk and gradually work in the dry ingredients, adding more milk if necessary to give a dropping consistency. Put into the tin and level the top. Bake in the oven at 170°C *(325°F)* mark 3 for about 1 hour, until well risen and firm to the touch. Turn out and cool on a wire rack.

Cherry cake

100 g *(4 oz)* butter or margarine
225 g *(8 oz)* self raising flour
pinch of salt
100 g *(4 oz)* sugar
100–175 g *(4–6 oz)* glacé cherries, washed, dried and quartered
1 egg, beaten
2.5 ml *(½ tsp)* vanilla essence
about 75 ml *(5 tbsps)* milk

Grease and line the base of a loaf tin measuring 21.5 by 11.5 cm *(8½ by 4½ in)* across the top, 1.3-l *(2¼-pt)* capacity. Rub the fat into the flour and salt until the mixture resembles fine breadcrumbs. Stir in the sugar and the cherries. Make a well in the centre, pour in the egg, essence and some of the milk and gradually work in the dry ingredients, adding more milk if necessary to give a dropping consistency. Put the mixture into the tin and level the top. Bake in the oven at 180°C *(350°F)* mark 4 for about 1¼ hours, until well risen, golden brown and firm to the touch. Turn out and cool on a wire rack.

Fruit cake

100 g *(4 oz)* butter or margarine
225 g *(8 oz)* self raising flour
pinch of salt
100 g *(4 oz)* sugar
50 g *(2 oz)* currants
50 g *(2 oz)* sultanas
30 ml *(2 tbsps)* chopped candied peel
2 eggs, beaten
about 60 ml *(4 tbsps)* milk

Line a 18-cm *(7-in)* cake tin. Rub the fat into the flour and salt until the mixture resembles fine breadcrumbs. Stir in the sugar, fruit and peel. Make a well in the centre, pour in the egg and some of the milk and gradually work in the dry ingredients, adding more milk if necessary to give a dropping consistency. Put the mixture into the tin and level the top. Bake in the oven at 180°C *(350°F)* mark 4 for about 1 hour, until the cake is golden brown and firm to the touch. Turn out and cool on a wire rack.

Sultana cake
Make as above, using 150 g *(5 oz)* sultanas instead of the mixture of fruit.

Seed cake
Make as above, using 25 g *(1 oz)* caraway seeds instead of the fruit.

Farmhouse cake

225 g *(8 oz)* wholemeal flour
225 g *(8 oz)* plain flour
5 ml *(1 level tsp)* mixed spice
5 ml *(1 level tsp)* bicarbonate of soda
175 g *(6 oz)* butter
225 g *(8 oz)* sugar
100 g *(4 oz)* sultanas
100 g *(4 oz)* raisins, stoned
45 ml *(3 tbsps)* candied peel, chopped
1 egg, beaten
300 ml *(½ pt)* milk

Grease and flour a 20.5-cm *(8-in)* tin. Sift the flours, spice and bicarbonate of soda. Rub the fat into the dry ingredients until the mixture resembles fine breadcrumbs. Stir in the sugar, fruit and peel. Make a well in the centre, pour in the egg and some of the milk and gradually work in the dry ingredients, adding more milk if necessary to give a dropping consistency; put the mixture into the tin and level the top. Bake in the oven at 170°C *(325°F)* mark 3 for about 2 hours, until firm to the touch. Turn out and cool on a wire rack.

Tyrol cake

100 g *(4 oz)* butter or margarine
225 g *(8 oz)* plain flour
5 ml *(1 level tsp)* ground cinnamon
50 g *(2 oz)* caster sugar
50 g *(2 oz)* currants
50 g *(2 oz)* sultanas
5 ml *(1 level tsp)* bicarbonate of soda
150 ml *(¼ pt)* milk
45 ml *(3 tbsps)* clear honey

Grease and base-line a 15-cm *(6-in)* cake tin. Rub the fat into the flour and cinnamon until the mixture resembles fine breadcrumbs. Stir in the sugar and fruit and make a well in the centre. Dissolve the bicarbonate of soda in some of the milk, add to the honey and pour into the well. Gradually work in the dry ingredients, adding more milk if necessary to give a dropping consistency. Put into the tin and level the top. Bake in the oven at 170°C *(325°F)* mark 3 for about 1½ hours, until well risen and firm to the touch. Turn out and cool on a wire rack.

Vinegar cake

100 g *(4 oz)* butter or margarine
225 g *(8 oz)* plain flour
pinch of salt
75 g *(3 oz)* soft brown sugar
50 g *(2 oz)* currants
50 g *(2 oz)* sultanas
45 ml *(3 tbsps)* chopped candied peel
5 ml *(1 level tsp)* bicarbonate of soda
15 ml *(1 tbsp)* vinegar
about 45 ml *(3 tbsps)* milk

Grease and base-line an 18-cm *(7-in)* cake tin. Rub the fat into the flour and salt until it resembles fine breadcrumbs. Stir in the sugar, dried fruit and peel and make a well in the centre. Dissolve the bicarbonate of soda in a little milk and pour into the well, add the vinegar and some more of the milk and gradually work in the dry ingredients, adding more milk if necessary to give a dropping consistency. Put the mixture into the tin and level the top. Bake in the oven at 190°C *(375°F)* mark 5 for 15 minutes, then reduce to 180°C *(350°F)* mark 4 and bake for a further hour. Turn out and cool on a wire rack.

Matrimonial cake

75 g *(3 oz)* plain flour
2.5 ml *(½ level tsp)* bicarbonate of soda
50 g *(2 oz)* rolled oats
5 ml *(1 tsp)* lemon essence
100 g *(4 oz)* soft brown sugar
100 g *(4 oz)* butter, melted

For the filling
100 g *(4 oz)* dates, stoned
15 ml *(1 level tbsp)* soft brown sugar
2.5 ml *(½ tsp)* lemon essence
about 150 ml *(¼ pt)* water

In Canada and the United States these fruit-filled slices are traditionally served at the surprise 'shower' parties given for brides-to-be by their girl friends.

Grease an 18-cm *(7-in)* sandwich tin. Begin by making the filling. Chop the dates roughly and put into a pan with the sugar, essence and enough water to cover. Bring to the boil and simmer gently until thick and smooth. Cool before use.

Sift the flour and bicarbonate of soda. Add the oats, lemon essence, sugar and melted butter and stir with a fork until well mixed. Press half this mixture on to the bottom of the tin, spread with the date filling and cover with the remainder of the crumb mixture, patting it down lightly. Bake in the oven at 190°C *(375°F)* mark 5 for 30 minutes, until lightly browned. Cool in the tin. Leave until the next day before cutting.

Rock buns

100 g *(4 oz)* butter or margarine
225 g *(8 oz)* plain flour
10 ml *(2 level tsps)* baking powder
pinch of salt
2.5 ml *(½ level tsp)* mixed spice, optional
grated rind of ½ a lemon
100 g *(4 oz)* demerara sugar
100 g *(4 oz)* mixed dried fruit
1 egg, beaten
about 5 ml *(1 tsp)* milk, optional

Grease two baking sheets. Rub the fat into the sifted flour, baking powder, salt and spices until the mixture resembles fine breadcrumbs. Stir in the rind, sugar and fruit. Make a well in the centre, pour in the egg and a little milk if necessary, to give a stiff crumbly consistency. Bind together loosely using a fork. Use two forks to shape the mixture together in rough heaps on the baking sheets. Bake in the oven at 200°C *(400°F)* mark 6 for 15–20 minutes. *Makes 12.*

Variation

Replace the dried fruit by 100 g *(4 oz)* chopped stoned dates and 15 ml *(1 tbsp)* chopped crystallised ginger.

Raspberry buns

75 g *(3 oz)* butter or margarine
225 g *(8 oz)* self raising flour
pinch of salt
75 g *(3 oz)* sugar
2 eggs, lightly beaten
raspberry jam

Grease a baking sheet. Rub the fat into the flour and salt until the mixture resembles fine breadcrumbs; stir in the sugar. Make a well in the centre, add the eggs and mix well to form a stiff dough. Turn out on to a floured board and form into a roll. Cut into 10 pieces, shape them into balls and place well apart on the baking sheet. Make a hole in the centre of each and fill with a little jam. Close up the opening, sprinkle with a little sugar and bake in the oven at 200°C *(400°F)* mark 6 for about 15 minutes, until golden brown. Cool the buns on a wire rack. Eat really fresh. *Makes 10.*

Almond fingers

100 g *(4 oz)* plain flour
pinch of salt
50 g *(2 oz)* butter or margarine
5 ml *(1 tsp)* caster sugar
1 egg yolk and cold water to mix
For the filling
45 ml *(3 tbsps)* raspberry jam
1 egg white
45 ml *(3 level tbsps)* ground almonds
50 g *(2 oz)* caster sugar
few drops almond essence
45 ml *(3 tbsps)* flaked almonds

Lightly grease a shallow 19-cm *(7½-in)* square tin. Sift the flour and salt and rub in the butter. Stir in the sugar and add the egg and sufficient water to mix to a firm dough. Knead lightly and roll out to a square; use to line the base of the tin. Spread the pastry with the jam, almost to the edges. Whisk the egg white until stiff, fold in the ground almonds, sugar and essence. Spread this mixture over the jam. Sprinkle with flaked almonds and bake in the oven at 180°C *(350°F)* mark 4 for about 35 minutes until crisp and golden. Cool in the tin, then cut into 8–12 fingers and remove with a palette knife.

Mincemeat slices

100 g *(4 oz)* butter or margarine
225 g *(8 oz)* self raising flour
100 g *(4 oz)* sugar
1 egg, beaten
45–60 ml *(3–4 tbsps)* milk to mix
mincemeat
brown sugar for topping

Grease a baking sheet. Rub the fat into the flour till the mixture resembles fine breadcrumbs and stir in the sugar. Make a well in the centre, pour in the egg and 45 ml *(3 tbsps)* milk and gradually stir in the dry ingredients, adding more milk if necessary to give a soft dough. Turn the mixture on to a floured board, divide into 2 and roll out each piece to a 20.5-cm *(8-in)* square. Lift one on to the baking sheet, spread with mincemeat leaving a small border at the edges, place the other piece on top and press down firmly. Brush the top with milk and sprinkle with brown sugar. Bake in the oven at 190°C *(375°F)* mark 5 for about 20 minutes. When cool, cut into 12–14 squares.

Coconut tarts *see colour plate facing p. 337*

For the pastry
50 g *(2 oz)* butter or margarine
100 g *(4 oz)* plain flour
pinch of salt
5 ml *(1 level tsp)* caster sugar
1 egg yolk and cold water to mix

For the filling
raspberry jam
50 g *(2 oz)* butter or margarine
50 g *(2 oz)* caster sugar
1 egg, beaten
50 g *(2 oz)* desiccated coconut
45 ml *(3 level tbsps)* self raising flour

Grease 16–18 patty tins. Rub the fat into the flour and salt until the mixture resembles fine breadcrumbs; stir in the sugar. Make a well in the centre and pour in the egg yolk and enough water to mix to a firm dough. Turn on to a floured board and knead lightly, roll out and cut into rounds large enough to fit the patty tins. Line the tins with this pastry and put a little jam in each. Cream the fat and sugar for the filling until pale and fluffy. Add the egg a little at a time, beating well after each addition. Fold in the coconut and flour, using a metal spoon, and add a little water if necessary to give a soft dropping consistency. Place in spoonfuls in the lined patty tins and bake in the oven at 190°C *(375°F)* mark 5 for 15–20 minutes, until golden and firm to the touch. Lift out and cool on a wire rack.

RICH CAKES

Rich cake mixtures contain higher proportions of fat and sugar and this necessitates a different method of making. The fat and sugar are creamed together, the egg beaten in and the flour then folded into the mixture. This is called the creaming method of cake-making.

The recipes here include Victoria sandwich and Madeira cake, with variations, together with some small cake recipes, such as queen cakes and madeleines.

Victoria sandwich cake *see colour plate facing p. 337*

100 g *(4 oz)* butter or margarine
100 g *(4 oz)* caster sugar
2 eggs, beaten
100 g *(4 oz)* self raising flour
30 ml *(2 tbsps)* jam
caster sugar to dredge

Grease two 18-cm *(7-in)* sandwich tins and line the base of each with a round of greased greaseproof paper. Cream the fat and sugar until pale and fluffy. Add the egg a little at a time, beating well after each addition. Fold in half the flour, using a metal spoon, then fold in the rest. Place half the mixture in each tin and level it with a knife. Bake both cakes on the same shelf of the oven at 190°C *(375°F)* mark 5 for about 20 minutes, or until they are well risen, golden, firm to the touch and beginning to shrink away from the sides of the tins. Turn out and cool on a wire rack.

When the cakes are cool, sandwich them together with jam and sprinkle the top with caster sugar.

Chocolate
Replace 45 ml *(3 level tbsps)* of flour by 45 ml *(3 level tbsps)* of cocoa. Sandwich together with vanilla or chocolate butter cream. For a more moist cake blend the cocoa with water to give a thick paste. Beat into the creamed ingredients.

Orange or lemon
Add the finely grated rind of one orange or lemon to the mixture. Sandwich the cakes together with orange or lemon curd or orange or lemon butter cream. Use some of the juice from the fruit to make glacé icing.

Coffee
Add 10 ml *(2 tsps)* instant coffee dissolved in a little warm water to the creamed mixture with the egg. Or use 10 ml *(2 tsps)* coffee essence.

Victoria sandwich cake (Economical recipe)

50 g *(2 oz)* margarine
50 g *(2 oz)* sugar
1 egg, beaten
few drops vanilla essence
100 g *(4 oz)* self raising flour
30–45 ml *(2–3 tbsps)* milk or water
jam
caster sugar

Grease an 18-cm *(7-in)* sandwich tin and line the base with a round of greased greaseproof paper. Cream the fat and sugar together until pale and fluffy. Add the egg and the vanilla essence a little at a time, beating well after each addition. Fold in half the flour, using a metal spoon, then fold in the rest and add milk or water to give a soft dropping consistency. Put into the tin and bake in the oven at 190°C *(375°F)* mark 5 for about 30 minutes. Turn out and cool on a wire rack. Split and fill with jam. Dredge with caster sugar. Serve the day the cake is made.

Ginger cake

225 g *(8 oz)* self raising flour
10 ml *(2 level tsps)* ground ginger
100 g *(4 oz)* butter or margarine
50 g *(2 oz)* sugar
30 ml *(2 tbsps)* golden syrup
2 eggs, beaten

Grease and line an 18-cm *(7-in)* cake tin. Sift together the flour and ginger. Cream the fat, sugar and syrup together until pale and fluffy. Add the egg a little at a time, beating well after each addition. Fold in half the flour, using a metal spoon, then fold in the rest. Put into the tin and bake in the oven at 170°C *(325°F)* mark 3 for about 1¼ hours, until golden and firm to the touch. Cool on a rack. The ground ginger may be replaced by 100 g *(4 oz)* chopped preserved ginger. For a more festive effect, cover the top of the cake with glacé icing when it is cold; decorate with pieces of crystallised ginger.

Walnut cake

75 g *(3 oz)* shelled walnuts or walnut pieces
225 g *(8 oz)* self raising flour
pinch of salt
150 g *(5 oz)* butter or margarine
150 g *(5 oz)* caster sugar
grated rind of 1 lemon
3 eggs, beaten

Grease and line an 18-cm *(7-in)* cake tin. Keep a few of the walnuts to decorate the cake and chop the rest coarsely. Mix the flour, salt and chopped nuts. Cream the fat, sugar and lemon rind until pale and fluffy. Add the egg a little at a time, beating well after each addition. Fold in half the flour and nut mixture using a metal spoon, then fold in the rest. Put into the tin, place the rest of the nuts on top and bake in the oven at 180°C *(350°F)* mark 4 for 1–1½ hours. Turn out and cool on a wire rack.

Almond cake

175 g *(6 oz)* self raising flour
pinch of salt
45 ml *(3 level tbsps)* ground almonds
30 ml *(2 level tbsps)* ground rice
225 g *(8 oz)* butter
225 g *(8 oz)* caster sugar
2.5 ml *(½ tsp)* almond essence
4 eggs, beaten
milk to mix

Grease and line an 18-cm *(7-in)* cake tin. Mix the flour, salt, almonds and ground rice. Cream the butter and sugar until pale and fluffy. Add the almond essence. Beat in the egg a little at a time. Fold in the dry ingredients, adding a little milk if necessary to give a dropping consistency. Put into the tin, level the top and bake in the oven at 170°C *(325°F)* mark 3 for 2–2¼ hours. Turn out and cool on a wire rack.

Madeira cake

110 g *(4 oz)* plain flour
110 g *(4 oz)* self raising flour
175 g *(6 oz)* butter
175 g *(6 oz)* caster sugar
5 ml *(1 tsp)* vanilla essence
3 eggs, beaten
about 15–30 ml *(1–2 tbsps)* milk
2–3 thin slices citron peel

Grease and line an 18-cm *(7-in)* cake tin. Sift the flours. Cream the butter, sugar and essence until pale and fluffy. Beat in the egg a little at a time. Fold in the re-sifted flour, adding a little milk if necessary to give a dropping consistency. Put into the tin and bake in the oven at 180°C *(350°F)* mark 4. After 20 minutes, put the citron peel across the cake and continue to cook for a further 40 minutes. Cool on a waire rack.

Orange cake
Add the grated rind of 2 oranges to the butter and sugar.

Rich seed cake
Add 10 ml *(2 level tsps)* caraway seeds with the flour. Omit the citron peel.

Dream cake
Add 75 g *(3 oz)* chopped walnuts and 75 g *(3 oz)* quartered glacé cherries with the flour. Omit the citron peel.

Caraway cobbler ring cake

see colour plate between pp. 336 and 337

For topping
50 g *(2 oz)* butter or margarine
50 g *(2 oz)* blended white vegetable fat
75 g *(3 oz)* soft light brown sugar
1 egg, beaten
200 g *(7 oz)* self raising flour
grated rind of ½ lemon
25 g *(1 oz)* cornflakes, crushed
5 ml *(1 level tsp)* caraway seeds

For base
100 g *(4 oz)* butter or margarine
100 g *(4 oz)* caster sugar
2 large eggs, beaten
grated rind of ½ lemon
100 g *(4 oz)* self raising flour

Grease and base-line a 19-cm *(7½-in)* 1.4-l *(2½-pt)* angel ring mould with sloping sides. For topping, cream the fats and sugar. Beat in the egg. Gradually add the sifted flour, lemon rind and half the cornflakes. Combine the remaining cornflakes with the caraway seeds. Lightly flour your hands and shape the dough into small balls. Toss in the cornflakes and caraway coating to cover. Leave in refrigerator until firm.

For the base, cream the fat and sugar until light and fluffy. Gradually add the eggs, beating well after each addition. Stir in the lemon rind. Sift the flour and stir it in gradually. Beat lightly. Spread the mixture in the base of the tin, level the surface. Bake the sponge in the oven at 180°C *(350°F)* mark 4 for about 20 minutes. Remove it from the oven and quickly place the topping balls over the base. Return the cake to the oven and cook for a further 15 minutes. Allow to cool in the tin before easing round the edge with a knife and turning out on to a rack to cool.

Half-pound cake

225 g *(8 oz)* butter or margarine
225 g *(8 oz)* caster sugar
4 eggs, beaten
225 g *(8 oz)* seedless raisins
225 g *(8 oz)* mixed currants and sultanas
100 g *(4 oz)* glacé cherries, halved
225 g *(8 oz)* plain flour
2.5 ml *(½ level tsp)* salt
2.5 ml *(½ level tsp)* mixed spice
60 ml *(4 tbsps)* brandy
few halved walnuts

A practical version of the traditional English pound cake – so called because most of the ingredients were added in 1-lb quantities.

Line a 20.5 cm *(8 in)* round cake tin with double greased greaseproof paper. Cream the fat and sugar together until pale and fluffy. Add the eggs a little at a time, beating well after each addition. Mix the fruit, flour, salt and spice and fold into the creamed mixture, using a metal spoon. Add the brandy and mix to a soft dropping consistency. Put the mixture in the tin, level the top and put on the nuts. Bake in the oven at 150°C *(300°F)* mark 2 for about 2½ hours. Turn out to cool on a wire rack.

Coconut frosted ring

see colour plate between pp. 336 and 337

175 g *(6 oz)* butter
175 g *(6 oz)* caster sugar
3 large eggs, beaten
175 g *(6 oz)* self raising flour
30 ml *(2 level tbsps)* cocoa
45 ml *(3 tbsps)* milk
grated rind of ½ lemon
15 ml *(1 tbsp)* lemon juice
few drops yellow colouring

For frosting
225 g *(8 oz)* granulated sugar
60 ml *(4 tbsps)* water
1 egg white
50 g *(2 oz)* long shred coconut, toasted

Cream the butter and sugar until fluffy. Add the eggs gradually, beating between each addition. Fold in the sifted flour. Divide the mixture into one-third and two-thirds. To two-thirds of the mixture add the cocoa, blended to a paste with milk; mix well. To the remaining one-third add lemon rind, juice and colouring. Mix well. Spread the chocolate mixture round the sides of a greased 1.7-l *(3-pt)* plain ring mould. Put the lemon mixture in a piping bag with a 2.5-cm *(1-in)* plain vegetable nozzle. Pipe a circle in the centre of the chocolate mixture. Level the surfaces carefully with palette knife. Bake in the oven at 180°C *(350°F)* mark 4 for about 40 minutes. Remove from the tin and allow to cool on a wire rack. For the frosting, dissolve the sugar in the water, then without stirring boil to 116°C *(240°F)*. Beat the egg white stiffly. Remove the sugar syrup from the heat, allow the bubbles to subside then pour on to the egg white; whisk all the time until the frosting begins to thicken and shows signs of going opaque. Pour it over the cake and quickly spread and swirl it with a palette knife. Sprinkle at once with coconut.

Orange peel kugelhupf

see colour plate between pp. 336 and 337

225 g *(8 oz)* butter
225 g *(8 oz)* caster sugar
3 large eggs
225 g *(8 oz)* self raising flour
grated rind of 1 orange
50 g *(2 oz)* finely chopped mixed peel
orange syrup (see below)

Brush a 1.7-l *(3-pt)* kugelhupf fancy ring tin with lard. Cream together the butter and sugar until really light and fluffy. Beat in the eggs, one at a time. Gently beat in the sifted flour and then the orange rind and mixed peel. Turn into the ring tin. Place on a baking sheet and bake in the oven at 190°C *(375°F)* mark 5 for about 60 minutes. Turn out and, while still hot, spoon over the orange syrup. Leave until cold, store a day before slicing.

Orange syrup Sift 50 g *(2 oz)* icing sugar into a bowl and gradually blend in 75 ml *(5 tbsps)* orange juice.

Chocolate cake

75 g *(3 oz)* self raising flour
30 ml *(2 level tbsps)* ground rice
100 g *(4 oz)* plain chocolate, grated
100 g *(4 oz)* butter or margarine
75 g *(3 oz)* caster sugar
5–10 ml *(1–2 tsps)* vanilla essence
2 eggs, beaten
chocolate butter icing (see page 384)
chocolate glacé icing (see page 385)
crystallised violets

Grease and line a 15-cm *(6-in)* cake tin. Mix the flour and ground rice. Put the grated chocolate into a small basin, place over a saucepan of hot water and heat gently to melt the chocolate. Cream the fat, sugar and essence until pale and fluffy. Add the melted chocolate (which should be only just warm) to the creamed mixture and mix lightly together. Beat in the egg a little at a time. Fold in the flour, put into the tin and bake in the oven at 180°C *(350°F)* mark 4 for 1–1¼ hours. When cold, split in half and fill with butter icing. Ice with glacé icing and decorate with violets. Alternatively, fill and decorate with coffee butter icing and coarsely grated chocolate.

Divorce cake
Sandwich with rum butter (see page 205) and dust the top with caster sugar.

Dundee cake

100 g *(4 oz)* currants
100 g *(4 oz)* raisins, stoned
100 g *(4 oz)* sultanas
50 g *(2 oz)* whole almonds, blanched
225 g *(8 oz)* butter or margarine
225 g *(8 oz)* soft brown sugar
grated rind of 1 lemon
4 eggs, beaten
275 g *(10 oz)* plain flour
100 g *(4 oz)* chopped mixed peel

Grease and line a 20.5-cm *(8-in)* cake tin. Prepare the fruit and chop the nuts (leaving a few whole for decorating the cake). Mix with the flour. Cream the fat, sugar and lemon rind until pale and fluffy. Beat in the eggs, fold in the flour, fruit, peel and nuts, put into the tin and hollow the centre slightly; arrange the split whole almonds on top. Bake in the oven at 170°C *(325°F)* mark 3 for 2½–3 hours. Cover the top with brown paper if the cake is browning too fast. When quite firm to the touch, remove from the tin and cool on a rack.

Rich cherry cake

225 g *(8 oz)* glacé cherries
150 g *(5 oz)* self raising flour
50 g *(2 oz)* plain flour
45 ml *(3 level tbsps)* cornflour
45 ml *(3 level tbsps)* ground almonds
175 g *(6 oz)* butter
175 g *(6 oz)* caster sugar
3 eggs, beaten
6 cubes of sugar

Grease and line an 18-cm *(7-in)* cake tin. Halve the cherries, wash and dry thoroughly. Sift the flours and cornflour. Stir in the ground almonds and cherries. Cream the butter and sugar until pale and fluffy and beat in the egg a little at a time. Fold in the dry ingredients. Put the mixture into the cake tin, making sure the cherries are not grouped together, and hollow the centre slightly. Roughly crush the sugar cubes with a rolling pin, sift out the larger pieces and scatter these over the cake. Bake in the oven at 180°C *(350°F)* mark 4 for 1–1½ hours, until well risen and golden brown. Turn out on to a wire rack to cool.

Genoa cake

225 g *(8 oz)* sultanas
225 g *(8 oz)* currants
50 g *(2 oz)* chopped mixed peel
100 g *(4 oz)* glacé cherries
40 g *(1½ oz)* whole almonds
225 g *(8 oz)* plain flour
pinch of salt
5 ml *(1 level tsp)* mixed spice
5 ml *(1 level tsp)* baking powder
200 g *(7 oz)* butter or margarine
175 g *(6 oz)* caster sugar
grated rind of 1 lemon
3 eggs, beaten
15–30 ml *(1–2 tbsps)* milk

Grease and line an 18-cm *(7-in)* cake tin. Prepare the fruit and chop the peel. Halve the cherries and wash and dry them. Blanch and chop the almonds, reserving a few for decoration. Sift the flour, salt, spice and baking powder. Cream the fat, sugar and lemon rind together until pale and fluffy. Beat in the egg a little at a time and fold in the flour, followed by the fruit, adding milk if necessary to give a dropping consistency. Put into the tin, decorate with the remaining almonds, halved, and bake in the oven at 150°C *(300°F)* mark 2 for 3–3¼ hours. Turn out and cool on a wire rack.

Sultana almond lattice cake *see colour plate facing p. 337*

100 g *(4 oz)* butter
100 g *(4 oz)* caster sugar
2 large eggs
1 egg yolk
175 g *(6 oz)* plain flour
225 g *(8 oz)* sultanas

For the almond lattice
100 g *(4 oz)* almond paste
50 g *(2 oz)* glacé cherries, halved

Grease a 16.5-cm *(6½-in)* loose-bottomed cake tin. Cream the butter and sugar in the usual way. Gradually beat in the eggs and extra yolk. Fold in the flour, and lastly the sultanas. Turn the mixture into the prepared tin and level the surface.

Roll out the almond paste thinly, cut into strips and use to lattice the top of the cake. Fill each square thus made with a halved cherry. Bake in the oven at 180°C *(350°F)* mark 4 for about 1¼ hours. (A flat tin placed across the top of the cake tin for the first ½ hour prevents over-browning of the almond paste.) Turn the cake out of the tin and cool on a wire rack. Serve plain, or dusted with icing sugar.

Note If testing this cake with a skewer, do not push it through the almond paste as this will be sticky and give a false impression.

Cream cheese and honey slices

100 g *(4 oz)* plain flour
75 g *(3 oz)* butter
100 g *(4 oz)* cream cheese
25 g *(1 oz)* honey
25 g *(1 oz)* sugar
2.5 ml *(½ level tsp)* ground cinnamon
2 eggs, beaten
caster sugar and cinnamon for topping

Sift the flour and chop in the butter; add 15 ml *(1 tbsp)* water, work with a knife to a smooth dough. If necessary chill to make rolling out easier. Use to line a 28.5 by 18.5 by 1.5-cm *(11¾ by 7¾ by ¾-in)* Swiss roll tin. Mix together the cream cheese, honey, sugar and cinnamon and add the eggs. Pour this mixture on to the pastry and sprinkle the top with sugar and cinnamon. Bake in the oven at 180°C *(350°F)* mark 4 for about ½ hour. Cut into slices when cool.

Queen cakes *see colour plate facing p. 337*

100 g *(4 oz)* butter or margarine
100 g *(4 oz)* caster sugar
2 eggs, beaten
100 g *(4 oz)* self raising flour
50 g *(2 oz)* sultanas

Spread 12–16 paper cases out on baking sheets, or for a better finished shape put them into patty tins. Cream the fat and sugar until pale and fluffy. Add the egg a little at a time, beating well after each addition. Fold in the flour and then the fruit, using a tablespoon. Two-thirds fill the cases with the mixture and bake in the oven at 190°C *(375°F)* mark 5 for 15–20 minutes, until golden.

Variations

Replace the sultanas by one of the following:

50 g *(2 oz)* chopped dates
50 g *(2 oz)* chopped glacé cherries
50 g *(2 oz)* chocolate chips
50 g *(2 oz)* chopped or crystallised ginger

Fairy cakes
Omit the sultanas, but otherwise make as for queen cakes.

Butterscotch gâteau

see colour plate between pp. 336 and 337

225 g *(8 oz)* **plain flour**
7.5 ml *(1½ level tsps)* **baking powder**
2.5 ml *(1½ level tsp)* **bicarbonate of soda**
pinch salt
225 g *(8 oz)* **soft dark brown sugar**
100 g *(4 oz)* **butter**
175 ml *(6 fl oz)* **milk**
7.5 ml *(1½ tsps)* **vanilla essence**
2 eggs, beaten

For butter cream
100 g *(4 oz)* **butter or margarine**
30 ml *(2 tbsps)* **black treacle**
10 ml *(2 tsps)* **lemon juice**
225 g *(8 oz)* **icing sugar, sifted**

For caramel
50 g *(2 oz)* **caster sugar**
60 ml *(4 tbsps)* **water**

Grease and base-line a 20.5-cm *(8-in)* diameter 6.5-cm *(2½-in)* deep moule à manqué (sloping-sided) cake tin. Sift together the first four ingredients. Stir in the brown sugar. With an electric mixer, cream the fat until soft, then slowly add the dry ingredients until crumbly. Continue beating, adding milk and essence, for 2 minutes. Add the eggs and beat for 1–2 minutes more. Pour into the tin. Bake in the oven at 190°C *(375°F)* mark 5 for about 1 hour. Turn out and cool on a rack.

Cream the fat, treacle and lemon juice together. Beat in the icing sugar. Cut the cake in half and sandwich with some butter cream. Spread more over the cake and ridge the sides and top with a fork. Pipe the rest of the butter cream round the edge. Finish with caramel.

Caramel Dissolve the sugar in the water. Boil to a brown colour. Pour it on to a greased tin and, when set, break it into small pieces.

Madeleines

100 g *(4 oz)* **butter or margarine**
100 g *(4 oz)* **caster sugar**
2 eggs, beaten
100 g *(4 oz)* **self raising flour**
red jam
desiccated coconut
glacé cherries and angelica

Grease 10–12 dariole moulds. Cream the fat and sugar until pale and fluffy. Add the egg a little at a time, beating well after each addition. Fold in half the flour, using a tablespoon, then fold in the rest. Three-quarters fill the moulds and bake in the oven at 180°C *(350°F)* mark 4 for about 20 minutes, or until firm and browned. Turn them out of the moulds to cool on a wire rack. Trim off the bottoms, so that the cakes stand firmly and are of even height. When they are nearly cold, brush with melted jam, holding them on a skewer, then roll them in coconut. Top each madeleine with a glacé cherry and 2 small angelica 'leaves'.

Note For the traditional French madeleine, Genoese mixture is baked in special fluted shell-shaped tins, well greased.

Coburg cakes

6 blanched almonds
150 g *(5 oz)* **plain flour**
5 ml *(1 level tsp)* **bicarbonate of soda**
2.5 ml *(½ level tsp)* **ground allspice**
2.5 ml *(½ level tsp)* **ground ginger**
2.5 ml *(½ level tsp)* **ground cinnamon**
50 g *(2 oz)* **butter or margarine**
50 g *(2 oz)* **caster sugar**
1 egg, beaten
15 ml *(1 tbsp)* **golden syrup**
60 ml *(4 tbsps)* **milk**

Grease 12 fluted bun tins and place half a blanched almond in each. Sift the flour, bicarbonate of soda and spices. Cream together the fat and sugar until light and fluffy. Add the egg a little at a time, beating well after each addition. Mix the syrup and milk and add alternately with the flour, folding in lightly until evenly mixed. Divide the mixture between the tins and bake in the oven at 180°C *(350°F)* mark 4 for about 25 minutes, until firm to the touch. Turn out and cool on a wire rack.

Viennese tarts

225 g *(8 oz)* **butter or margarine**
50 g *(2 oz)* **icing sugar**
175 g *(6 oz)* **plain flour**
50 g *(2 oz)* **cornflour**
few drops vanilla essence
red jam and icing sugar to decorate

Arrange some paper cases in patty tins.

Cream the butter or margarine with the sifted icing sugar until smooth. Fold in the sifted flour and cornflour and add the vanilla essence. Put the mixture into a piping bag fitted with a 1-cm *(½-in)* star nozzle. Pipe it into the paper cases, starting at the base and working up the sides with a spiral movement, and leaving a slight hollow in the centre of each. Bake in the oven at 180°C *(350°F)* mark 4 for 20–25 minutes, until just golden. When the tarts are quite cold, sift some icing sugar over the top and place a little red jam in the centre of each. *Makes 9–10.*

Linzertorte

150 g *(5 oz)* plain flour
2.5 ml *(½ level tsp)* ground cinnamon
75 g *(3 oz)* butter
50 g *(2 oz)* caster sugar
50 g *(2 oz)* ground almonds
grated rind of 1 lemon
2 egg yolks
15 ml *(1 tbsp)* lemon juice
350 g *(¾ lb)* raspberry jam
whipped double cream for serving

Sift the flour and cinnamon into a bowl and rub in the butter. Add the sugar, ground almonds and the lemon rind. Beat the egg yolks and add with the lemon juice to the flour, to make a stiff dough. Knead lightly and leave in a cool place for 30 minutes. Roll out two-thirds of the pastry and use to line a 20.5-cm *(8-in)* fluted flan ring on a baking sheet. Fill with raspberry jam. Roll out the remaining pastry and cut into 1-cm *(½-in)* strips. Use to make a lattice design over the jam.

Bake in the oven at 190°C *(375°F)* mark 5 for 25–35 minutes. Allow to cool, remove from the flan ring, and serve with whipped cream.

Note Fresh or frozen raspberries can be used in place of the jam: reduce 450 g *(1 lb)* raspberries with 15 ml *(1 tbsp)* water, a knob of butter and a little sugar to taste to a thick purée. Cool before using.

Date bran muffins

100 g *(3½ oz)* plain flour
2.5 ml *(½ level tsp)* salt
15 ml *(1 level tbsp)* baking powder
50 g *(2 oz)* bran
250 ml *(9 fl oz)* milk
30 ml *(2 tbsps)* whipped-up white cooking fat
45 ml *(3 level tbsps)* caster sugar
1 egg, beaten
100 g *(4 oz)* dates, chopped

Grease 12–16 6.5-cm *(2½-in)* deep muffin tins. Sift the flour, salt and baking powder. Soak the bran in the milk for 5 minutes. Meanwhile, cream the fat and sugar until light, add the beaten egg and mix until smooth. Add to the bran mixture and stir. Add the flour mixture and dates, stirring only until just mixed. Fill the muffin tins two-thirds full and bake in the oven at 200°C *(400°F)* mark 6 for 20–25 minutes, until golden and well risen. Cool on a wire rack.

SPONGE CAKES

These mixtures contain no fat but a high proportion of eggs and sugar and are made by the whisking method, that is, the eggs and sugar are whisked together and the flour folded in very lightly. Following the recipes for fatless sponges is the one for Genoese sponge, which includes some butter.

Sponge cake

3 eggs
100 g *(4 oz)* caster sugar
75 g *(3 oz)* plain flour

Grease two 18-cm *(7-in)* sandwich tins and dust with a mixture of flour and caster sugar. Put the eggs and sugar in a large deep bowl, stand this over a pan of hot water and whisk until light and creamy – the mixture should be stiff enough to retain the impression of the whisk for a few seconds. Remove from the heat and whisk until cold. Sift half the flour over the mixture and fold in very lightly, using a metal spoon. Add the remaining flour in the same way. Pour the mixture into the tins, tilt backwards and forwards until it is spread evenly and bake in the oven at 190°C *(375°F)* mark 5 for 20–25 minutes. Turn out to cool on a wire rack.

Note If you are using an electric mixer, no heat is required during whisking.

Sponge fingers

1 large egg
45 ml *(3 level tbsps)* **caster sugar**
60 ml *(4 level tbsps)* **strong plain flour**

Grease a sponge finger tray with melted lard and dust with flour and sugar. Put the egg and sugar in a deep bowl and stand this over hot water; whisk until light, creamy and stiff enough to retain the impression of the whisk for a few seconds. Remove from the heat and whisk until cool. Sift half the flour over the mixture and fold in very lightly, using a metal spoon. Add the remaining flour in the same way. Spoon just enough mixture into each hollow in the tray to reach the top. Bake in the oven at 200°C *(400°F)* mark 6 for about 10 minutes, until golden. Remove the sponge fingers carefully from the tray and cool on a wire rack.

Note If you are using an electric mixer, no heat is required during whisking.

Variation
If you wish, the ends of the fingers may be dipped into melted chocolate, and allowed to harden before using.

Sponge drops

Grease a baking sheet, or line it with non-stick paper. Make the mixture as for sponge fingers. Spoon or use a 1-cm *(½-in)* plain nozzle to pipe small rounds on to the sheet, fairly far apart. Bake in the oven for 8–10 minutes until golden. Remove from the sheet and cool. When cold, dust with icing sugar, sandwich in pairs with whipped cream or dip one side of each drop in melted chocolate.

Swiss roll

3 eggs
100 g *(4 oz)* **caster sugar**
100 g *(4 oz)* **plain flour**
15 ml *(1 tbsp)* **hot water**
caster sugar to dredge
warm jam

Line a Swiss roll tin 33.6 by 22.5 cm *(13 by 9 in)*. Put the eggs and sugar in a large bowl, stand it over a pan of hot water and whisk until light and creamy; the mixture should be stiff enough to retain the impression of the whisk for a few seconds. Remove the bowl from the heat and whisk until cool. Sift half the flour over the mixture and fold in very lightly, using a metal spoon. Add the remaining flour in the same way and lightly stir in the hot water. Pour the mixture into the prepared tin, tilt the tin backwards and forwards allowing the mixture to run over the whole surface. Bake in the oven at 220°C *(425°F)* mark 7 for 7–9 minutes until golden brown, well risen and spongy. Meanwhile, have ready a sheet of greaseproof paper liberally sprinkled with caster sugar. To help make the sponge pliable you can place the paper over a tea towel lightly wrung out in hot water.

Turn the cake quickly out on to the paper, trim off the crusty edges with a sharp knife and spread the surface with warmed jam. Roll up with the aid of the paper, making the first turn firmly so that the whole cake will roll evenly and have a good shape when finished, but roll more lightly after this turn. Dredge the cake with sugar and cool on a wire rack.

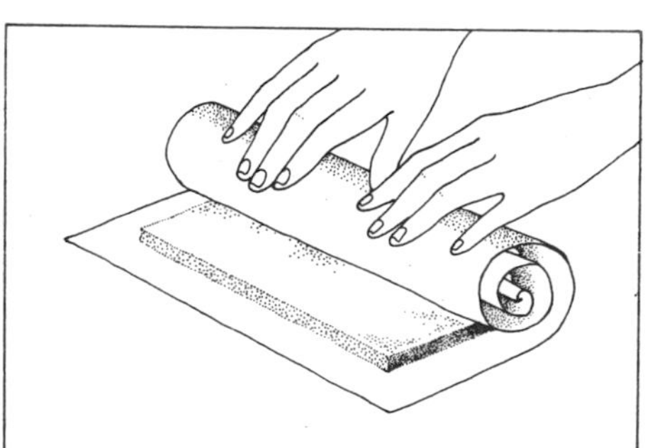

Rolling up a Swiss roll sponge, with a sheet of greaseproof paper inside

Note If you are using an electric mixer no heat is required during whisking.

Chocolate Swiss roll
Replace 15 ml *(1 level tbsp)* of the flour by 15 ml *(1 level tbsp)* cocoa. If you are using a cream filling, turn out the cooked sponge and trim as above, but do not spread with the filling immediately. Cover the sponge with a sheet of greaseproof paper and roll it up loosely. When

the cake is cold, unroll, remove paper, spread with cream or butter cream (see page 384) and re-roll.

Small Swiss rolls
Bake a sponge as above. When it is cooked, turn it out, trim and cut in half lengthways. Spread each half with jam and roll up, starting at the longer sides and making 2 long, thin rolls. When the cake is cold, cut each roll into 3 even lengths. Other fillings may be used, or the rolls may be coated with glacé icing or decorated to make small Christmas logs.

Swiss roll variations see page 388.

Genoese sponge

40 g *(1½ oz)* **butter**
75 g *(2½ oz)* **plain flour**
15 ml *(1 level tbsp)* **cornflour**
3 large eggs
75 g *(3 oz)* **caster sugar**

Grease and line two 18-cm *(7-in)* sandwich tins. Heat the butter gently until it is melted, remove it from the heat and let it stand for a few minutes, for the salt and any sediment to settle. Sift the flour and cornflour. Put the eggs and sugar in a large bowl, stand this over a saucepan of hot water and whisk until light and creamy – the mixture should be stiff enough to retain the impression of the whisk for a few seconds. Remove from the heat and whisk until cool. Re-sift the flour and carefully fold in half with a metal spoon. Make sure the butter is cooled until it just flows and, taking care not to let the salt and sediment run in, pour the butter round the edge of the mixture. Then fold it in alternately with the rest of the flour. Fold very lightly or the fat will sink to the bottom and cause a heavy cake. Pour the mixture into the tins and bake in the oven at 190°C *(375°F)* mark 5 until golden brown and firm to the touch – 20–25 minutes. Turn out and cool on a wire rack. Use as required, for layered cakes and iced cakes.

Note If you are using an electric mixer no heat is required during whisking.

GINGERBREADS

The main difference between these and other types of cake is that the treacle or syrup is heated (sometimes with the sugar and fat) before being added to the dry ingredients. Gingerbreads are both quick and easy to make and very popular.

Everyday gingerbread

450 g *(1 lb)* **plain flour**
5 ml *(1 level tsp)* **salt**
15 ml *(1 level tbsp)* **ground ginger**
15 ml *(1 level tbsp)* **baking powder**
5 ml *(1 level tsp)* **bicarbonate of soda**
225 g *(8 oz)* **demerara sugar**
175 g *(6 oz)* **butter or margarine**
175 g *(6 oz)* **treacle**
175 g *(6 oz)* **golden syrup**
250 ml *(½ pt)* **milk**
1 egg, beaten

Grease and line a 23-cm *(9-in)* square cake tin. Sift the flour, salt, ginger, baking powder and bicarbonate of soda. Warm the sugar, fat, treacle and syrup until melted, but do not allow to boil. Mix in the milk and the egg. Make a well in the centre of the dry ingredients, pour in the liquid and mix very thoroughly. Pour the mixture into the tin and bake in the oven at 170°C *(325°F)* mark 3 for about 1½ hours, or until firm to the touch. Turn out to cool on a wire rack. For a smaller cake, use half quantities, with an 18-cm *(7-in)* square tin; bake for about 1 hour.

Orange gingerbread

350 g *(12 oz)* plain flour
pinch of salt
5 ml *(1 level tsp)* ground cinnamon
10 ml *(2 level tsps)* ground ginger
5 ml *(1 level tsp)* bicarbonate of soda
100 g *(4 oz)* butter or margarine
100 g *(4 oz)* sugar
grated rind and juice of 1 orange
75 g *(3 oz)* chopped mixed peel
100 g *(4 oz)* treacle, warmed
2 eggs, beaten
little milk if necessary

Grease and line an 18-cm *(7-in)* square cake tin. Sift the flour, salt, spices and bicarbonate of soda and rub in the fat until the mixture resembles fine breadcrumbs. Stir in the sugar, orange rind and juice, chopped peel, treacle and eggs; mix to a pouring consistency, adding a little milk if necessary. Put into the tin and bake in the oven at 170°C *(375°F)* mark 3 for about 1¼ hours. Turn out to cool on a wire rack.

Fruit gingerbread

100 g *(4 oz)* butter or margarine
350 g *(12 oz)* plain flour
75 g *(3 oz)* sugar
50 g *(2 oz)* chopped mixed peel
75 g *(3 oz)* sultanas
50 g *(2 oz)* chopped nuts
15 ml *(1 level tbsp)* ground ginger
10 ml *(2 level tsps)* mixed spice
5 ml *(1 level tsp)* bicarbonate of soda
350 g *(12 oz)* golden syrup, warmed
2 eggs, beaten

Line a 20.5-cm *(8-in)* square tin. Rub the fat into the flour until the mixture resembles fine breadcrumbs. Add the sugar, peel, sultanas, nuts, spices and bicarbonate of soda. Make a well in the centre, pour in the syrup and eggs and mix thoroughly. Pour into the tin and bake in the oven at 150°C *(300°F)* mark 2 for 1¾–2 hours. Turn it out to cool on a wire rack. If you prefer, omit the peel and sultanas and substitute 100 g *(4 oz)* chopped preserved ginger.

TRADITIONAL CAKES

This is a small collection of old and regional recipes which are so good that they are well worth reviving.

Maids of honour

568 ml *(1 pt)* milk
pinch of salt
15 ml *(1 tbsp)* rennet
75 g *(3 oz)* butter, softened
2 eggs
15 ml *(1 tbsp)* brandy
45 ml *(3 level tbsps)* nibbed almonds
10 ml *(2 level tsps)* caster sugar
212-g *(7½-oz)* pkt bought puff pastry
few currants, optional

These are small tartlets with a filling made from flavoured milk curds. They originated in Henry VIII's palace at Hampton Court, where they were popular with the Queen's Maids of Honour, and the recipe was a closely guarded secret. However, in George I's reign a lady of the court gave it to a gentleman who set up a shop in Richmond, where the tarts are still made. The recipe was made public in 1951 for a television programme about historic dishes of Britain.

Warm the milk until it feels just warm to a finger, add the salt and rennet and leave to set; when firm, put into a piece of fine muslin, secure with a piece of string and hang it up over a bowl. Allow to drain overnight.

The next day, rub the curds and the butter through a sieve. Whisk the eggs and brandy together and add to the curds, with the almonds and sugar. Line about 12 6.5-cm *(2½-in)* deep patty tins with thinly rolled pastry, press it into the bases. Half-fill with the curd mixture and if you wish sprinkle currants over the top. Bake in the oven at 220°C *(425°F)* mark 7 for 15–20 minutes. Turn out to cool on a wire rack.

Scottish ginger cake

350 g *(12 oz)* **plain flour**
2.5 ml *(½ level tsp)* **salt**
10 ml *(2 level tsps)* **bicarbonate of soda**
15 ml *(1 level tbsp)* **ground ginger**
50 g *(2 oz)* **sultanas**
100 g *(4 oz)* **candied peel, chopped**
50 g *(2 oz)* **preserved ginger, chopped**
350 g *(12 oz)* **black treacle**
175 g *(6 oz)* **butter or margarine**
75 g *(3 oz)* **soft brown sugar**
3 eggs, beaten
30–45 ml *(2–3 tbsps)* **milk**

Line an 18-cm *(7-in)* square cake tin. Sift the flour, salt, bicarbonate of soda and ground ginger. Add the sultanas, peel and preserved ginger. Put the treacle, butter and sugar into a pan and warm gently, until melted. Mix with the eggs and milk, make a well in the centre of the dry ingredients, pour in the treacle mixture and beat very thoroughly. Pour into the tin and bake in the oven at 170°C *(325°F)* mark 3 for about 1¼ hours. Turn out to cool on a wire rack. This cake improves with keeping.

Scotch or black bun for Hogmanay (New Year's Eve)

For the pastry
225 g *(8 oz)* **plain flour**
pinch of salt
100 g *(4 oz)* **butter**
beaten egg to glaze

For the filling
225 g *(8 oz)* **plain flour**
5 ml *(1 level tsp)* **ground cinnamon**
5 ml *(1 level tsp)* **ground ginger**
5 ml *(1 level tsp)* **ground allspice**
5 ml *(1 level tsp)* **cream of tartar**
5 ml *(1 level tsp)* **bicarbonate of soda**
450 g *(1 lb)* **stoned raisins**
450 g *(1 lb)* **currants**
50 g *(2 oz)* **chopped mixed peel**
100 g *(4 oz)* **nibbed almonds**
100 g *(4 oz)* **brown sugar**
1 egg
150 ml *(¼ pt)* **whisky**
about 60 ml *(4 tbsps)* **milk**

Grease a 20.5-cm *(8-in)* cake tin. Make the pastry in the usual way. Take two-thirds of it and roll out into a round about 35 cm *(14 in)* diameter. Line the tin with it, making sure the pastry comes above the top of the sides of the cake tin and distributing the fullness evenly round the sides.

For the filling, sift the flour, spice, cream of tartar and bicarbonate of soda into a large bowl and mix in the raisins, currants, peel, almonds and sugar. Add the egg, whisky and milk and stir till the mixture is evenly moistened. Pack it into the pastry case and fold the top of the pastry over. Roll out the remaining dough to a 20.5-cm *(8-in)* round. Moisten the edges of the pastry case, put on the lid and seal the edges firmly together. With a skewer make 4 or 5 holes right down to the bottom of the cake, then prick all over the top with a fork and brush with beaten egg. Bake in the oven at 180°C *(350°F)* mark 4 for 2½–3 hours; cover with brown paper if the pastry becomes too brown. Turn out to cool on a wire rack.

This cake should be made several weeks or even months before it is to be eaten, so that it may mature and mellow.

Oatmeal parkin

225 g *(8 oz)* **plain flour**
10 ml *(2 level tsps)* **baking powder**
20 ml *(4 level tsps)* **ground ginger**
100 g *(4 oz)* **lard or margarine**
225 g *(8 oz)* **medium oatmeal**
100 g *(4 oz)* **caster sugar**
175 g *(6 oz)* **golden syrup**
175 g *(6 oz)* **black treacle**
1 egg, beaten
60 ml *(4 tbsps)* **milk**

Grease and line a 23-cm *(9-in)* square cake tin or a shallow meat tin. Sift together the flour, baking powder and ginger. Rub in the fat and add the oatmeal and sugar. Heat the syrup and treacle over a very low heat; do not over-heat. Make a well in the centre of the dry ingredients and gradually stir in the liquid from the saucepan and the beaten egg and milk. Pour into the tin and bake in the oven at 180°C *(350°F)* mark 4 for ¾–1 hour. Allow to cool a little in the tin, then turn out to finish cooling. Serve cut into squares or fingers. Keep for about 1 week before eating.

ONE-STAGE CAKES

If you use a soft tub margarine, or a whipped-up white cooking fat, you can make a cake without rubbing in or creaming the fat first – it's wonderfully quick and easy. Mix the ingredients very thoroughly, scraping round the sides of the bowl quite often, but don't over-beat – take particular care if you are using an electric mixer.

Fruit cake

225 g *(8 oz)* **self raising flour**
10 ml *(2 level tsps)* **mixed spice**
5 ml *(1 level tsp)* **baking powder**
100 g *(4 oz)* **soft tub margarine**
100 g *(4 oz)* **soft brown sugar**
225 g *(8 oz)* **dried fruit**
2 eggs
30 ml *(2 tbsps)* **milk**

Grease an 18-cm *(7-in)* round cake tin and line the base with a round of greased greaseproof paper. Sift the flour, spice and baking powder into a large bowl, add the rest of the ingredients and beat until thoroughly combined. Put into the tin and bake in the oven at 170°C *(325°F)* mark 3 for about 1¾ hours. Turn out to cool on a wire rack.

Sandwich cake

100 g *(4 oz)* **self raising flour**
5 ml *(1 level tsp)* **baking powder**
100 g *(4 oz)* **soft tub margarine**
100 g *(4 oz)* **caster sugar**
2 eggs
jam or lemon curd to fill

Grease two 18-cm *(7-in)* sandwich tins and line each base with a round of greased greaseproof paper. Sift the flour and baking powder into a large bowl. Add the other ingredients, mix well, then beat for about 2 minutes. Divide the mixture evenly between the tins. Bake in the oven at 170°C *(325°F)* mark 3 for 25–35 minutes. Turn out to cool on a wire rack and when cool, sandwich with jam or lemon curd.

For more lavish decoration, sandwich together with butter cream and pour chocolate icing over the top, letting it trickle down the sides. (See pages 384 to 387 for icings.)

Orange
Add the grated rind and juice of 1 orange.

Mocha
Sift 30 ml *(2 level tbsps)* cocoa and 15 ml *(1 level tbsp)* instant coffee with 75 g *(3 oz)* flour.

Chocolate, cherry and nut cake
Omit 30 ml *(2 tbsps)* sugar and add 60 ml *(4 tbsps)* grated plain chocolate, 75 g *(3 oz)* chopped glacé cherries and 30 ml *(2 tbsps)* chopped walnuts.

Small buns
Make into 18–20 buns and bake in the oven at 200°C *(400°F)* mark 6 for 15–20 minutes.

Toffee bars

100 g *(4 oz)* **soft tub margarine or whipped up white fat**
50 g *(2 oz)* **caster sugar**
50 g *(2 oz)* **brown sugar**
1.25 ml *(¼ level tsp)* **salt**
5 ml *(1 tsp)* **vanilla essence**
1 egg
100 g *(4 oz)* **self raising flour**
90 ml *(6 level tbsps)* **rolled oats**
50 g *(2 oz)* **plain chocolate**
50 g *(2 oz)* **chopped nuts**

Grease and base line a 23-cm *(9-in)* shallow square tin. Beat the fat, sugars, salt, essence and egg together until light and fluffy. Stir in the flour and oats. Spread the mixture in the tin and bake in the oven at 180°C *(350°F)* mark 4 for 30 minutes. Turn out and cool on a wire rack. Melt the chocolate, spread on the cooled cake and sprinkle with the nuts. Cut into 18 bars.

CAKES MADE USING OIL

Cakes made using oil (corn oil for example) are very easy to mix and very successful. Oil is especially suitable for use in cakes made by the melting method, eg gingerbread, as it blends in so easily with the treacle, etc.

When using oil for making sandwich cakes, it is essential to add extra raising agent or to whip the egg whites until stiff and to fold them into the beaten mixture just before baking. This helps to counteract the heaviness that sometimes occurs when oil is used.

Victoria sandwich cake made with oil

150 g *(5 oz)* **self raising flour**
5 ml *(1 level tsp)* **baking powder**
pinch of salt
125 g *(4½ oz)* **caster sugar**
105 ml *(7 tbsps)* **cooking oil**
2 eggs
45 ml *(2½ tbsps)* **milk**
few drops vanilla essence
jam

Grease two 18-cm *(7-in)* sandwich cake tins and line the base of each with greased greaseproof paper. Sift the flour, baking powder and salt into a bowl and stir in the sugar. Add the oil, eggs, milk and essence and stir with a wooden spoon until the mixture is blended and creamy – not less than 2 minutes. Put into the tins and bake in the oven at 180°C *(350°F)* mark 4 for 35–40 minutes. Turn out to cool on a wire rack. When cold, sandwich together with jam.

Fruit cake made with oil

225 g *(8 oz)* **plain flour**
10 ml *(2 level tsps)* **baking powder**
1.25 ml *(¼ level tsp)* **salt**
150 g *(5 oz)* **caster sugar**
150 ml *(¼ pt)* **oil**
2 eggs
45–60 ml *(3–4 tbsps)* **milk**
275 g *(10 oz)* **mixed dried fruit**
100 g *(4 oz)* **glacé cherries, quartered**
50 g *(2 oz)* **mixed candied peel, chopped**

Grease and line an 18-cm *(7-in)* cake tin. Sift the flour, baking powder, salt and sugar into a basin. Add the oil, eggs and 45 ml *(3 tbsps)* milk and beat thoroughly for 2 minutes. Add the fruit and peel and a little more milk if necessary to give a dropping consistency. Put into the tin and bake in the oven at 170°C *(325°F)* mark 3 for 1 hour, turn down the oven to 150°C *(300°F)* mark 2 and bake for a further 1¼–1½ hours. Leave in the tin to cool for 1 hour, then turn it out. When the cake is cold, store it in an airtight tin for at least one day before cutting.

Chocolate gâteau

150 g *(5 oz)* **self raising flour**
pinch of salt
45 ml *(3 level tbsps)* **cocoa**
150 g *(5 oz)* **caster sugar**
75 ml *(5 tbsps)* **corn oil**
2 eggs, separated
75 ml *(5 tbsps)* **water**

Grease two 18-cm *(7-in)* sandwich tins and line the base of each with a round of greased greaseproof paper. Sift the flour, salt and cocoa into a mixing bowl and add the sugar, oil, egg yolks and water. Beat with a wooden spoon for at least 2 minutes. Whisk the egg whites until stiff and fold in the chocolate mixture. Divide the mixture between the sandwich tins and bake in the oven at 180°C *(350°F)* mark 4 for about 30 minutes. Turn out and cool on a wire rack. When cold, sandwich together with chocolate frosting (below).

Variations

This cake can be made in a variety of flavours, eg orange or lemon. Use 175 g *(6 oz)* self raising flour and omit the cocoa, replace the water by orange juice or lemon juice and add the grated rind of an orange or lemon to the mixture. Sandwich together with vanilla frosting (below) and decorate with crystallised orange or lemon slices.

Vanilla or chocolate frosting

150 g *(5 oz)* **icing sugar**
25 ml *(1½ tbsps)* **corn oil**
15–25 ml *(1–1½ tbsps)* **milk**
few drops vanilla essence

Sift the icing sugar and beat in the oil, milk and vanilla essence until smooth. For chocolate frosting, reduce sugar to 125 g *(4½ oz)* and sift with 45 ml *(3 level tbsps)* cocoa.

Feather sponge

100 ml *(3½ fl oz)* **corn oil**
100 ml *(3½ fl oz)* **water**
2 eggs, separated
150 g *(5 oz)* **plain flour**
45 ml *(3 level tbsps)* **cornflour**
175 g *(6 oz)* **caster sugar**
10 ml *(2 level tsps)* **baking powder**
pinch of salt
whipped double cream and jam to fill

Normal method
Grease and base-line with non-stick paper two 20.5-cm *(8-in)* sandwich tins. Whisk the oil, water and egg yolks together in a bowl. Add the flour, cornflour, 125 g *(4 oz)* of the sugar, the baking powder and salt, sifted together. Beat all well together to form a smooth, slack batter. Beat the egg whites till foamy, then beat in the remaining 50 g *(2 oz)* sugar until the mixture 'peaks'; fold into the batter. Divide the mixture between the tins and bake in the oven at 190°C *(375°F)* mark 5 until well risen and spongy – 25–30 minutes. Turn out on to a wire rack and leave to cool. Sandwich with cream and jam.

Blender method (only suitable for a large blender goblet)
Sift the flour, cornflour, 125 g *(4 oz)* of the sugar, the baking powder and salt through a conical sieve straight into the blender goblet (or sift them onto paper and then tip the mixture into the goblet). Add the oil, water and egg yolks. Switch on and blend to a batter. Whisk the egg whites until foamy, add the remaining 50 g *(2 oz)* caster sugar and whisk again until stiff. Lightly and evenly fold the goblet contents through the egg whites. Divide the mixture between the prepared tins and finish as above.

Cherry cake made with oil

100 ml *(4 fl oz)* **corn oil**
2 eggs, beaten
30 ml *(2 tbsps)* **milk**
150 g *(5 oz)* **caster sugar**
275 g *(10 oz)* **self raising flour**
pinch of salt
225 g *(8 oz)* **glacé cherries, quartered**
grated rind of ½ orange

Grease and line a 18-cm *(7-in)* cake tin. Whisk together the corn oil, eggs, milk and sugar. Sift the flour and salt and add the cherries and grated orange rind. Gradually beat the flour and cherry mixture into the liquid ingredients, using a wooden spoon. Turn the mixture into the prepared tin and bake in the oven at 180°C *(350°F)* mark 4 for 1–1¼ hours. Turn out to cool on a wire rack.

Oaty slices

100 g *(4 oz)* **self raising flour**
100 g *(4 oz)* **rolled oats**
150 ml *(¼ pt)* **corn oil**
100 g *(4 oz)* **black treacle or golden syrup**
100 g *(4 oz)* **demerara sugar**
1 egg
60 ml *(4 tbsps)* **milk**

Grease and line the base of an 18-cm *(7-in)* square tin. Put the flour and oats in a bowl. Gently warm the oil, treacle or syrup and the sugar in a pan until the sugar is dissolved. Beat the egg with the milk. Make a well in the centre of the dry ingredients and pour the liquids into it. Beat well for 1–2 minutes, pour into the tin and bake in the oven at 170°C *(325°F)* mark 3 for 1–1¼ hours. Cool on a wire cooling rack and store for several days before cutting.

SCONES, GIRDLE CAKES, DOUGHNUTS

Home-made scones, sweet or savoury, are quickly and easily made and very popular, whether hot or cold. You can mix and cook them while the rest of the tea is being prepared. The raising agent may be baking powder or bicarbonate of soda and cream of tartar, with fresh or soured milk. Similar mixtures can be used for quick breads made without yeast.

Self raising flour is perfectly satisfactory for scones, although you get a slightly better rise with plain flour and raising agent.

Scones should be eaten the day they are made as they quickly go stale.

Girdle scones

In some parts of the country girdle scones are more frequently made than oven scones. If you do not possess a griddle, you can use a thick frying pan or the solid hotplate of an electric cooker.

To prepare a griddle, rub it with salt and kitchen paper, dust well to remove the salt, and then heat it slowly and thoroughly (10–20 minutes). Before cooking the scones, lightly grease the griddle with a little lard or vegetable fat.

Scone-making faults

The scones are heavy and badly risen This may be because:
1. Insufficient raising agent was used.
2. The handling was heavy, especially during the kneading.
3. Insufficient liquid was used.
4. The oven was too cool or the position for baking was too low in the oven.

The scones spread and lose their shape because of:
1. Slack dough, caused by using too much liquid.
2. Too heavily greased tin. The fat melts on heating in the oven and 'pulls out' the soft dough before it has set.
3. Badly done kneading (especially of the scraps for the second rolling) or twisting the cutter round as the scones were stamped out (such scones are oval instead of round when cooked).

The scones have a very rough surface when cooked because:
1. The kneading was insufficient or badly done.
2. When the scones were transferred from the board to the baking sheet, they were badly handled.

The scones are under-cooked on top and black underneath This occurs if the baking sheet is too large for the oven and does not allow circulation of hot air – the heat hits the sheet and is deflected down, causing over-cooking of the bottom of the scones and insufficient cooking of the top. There should be a gap of at least 5 cm *(2 in)* between the sides of the shelf and the baking sheet, especially over the flame in a gas oven.

Faults with girdle scones

Uneven cooking may be due to using a frying pan with a thin, uneven base.

Spreading happens if the batter is too thin; it should be so thick that it only just pours from the spoon.

Sticking The scones stick if the griddle was dirty or insufficiently greased. It should be 'proved' by being rubbed with salt while it is heating.

Oven scones

225 g *(8 oz)* self raising flour
2.5 ml *(½ level tsp)* salt
5 ml *(1 level tsp)* baking powder
25–50 g *(1–2 oz)* butter or margarine
150 ml *(¼ pt)* milk
beaten egg or milk to glaze, optional

Preheat a baking sheet in the oven. Sift the flour, salt and baking powder together then rub in the fat until the mixture resembles fine breadcrumbs. Make a well in the centre and stir in enough milk to give a fairly soft dough. Turn it on to a floured board, knead very lightly if necessary to remove any cracks, then roll out lightly to about 2 cm *(¾ in)* thick, or pat it out with the hand. Cut into 10–12 rounds with a 5-cm *(2-in)* cutter (dipped in flour) or cut into triangles with a sharp knife. Place on the baking sheet, brush if you wish with beaten egg or milk and bake towards the top of the oven at 230°C *(450°F)* mark 8 for 8–10 minutes, until brown and well risen. Cool the scones on a rack. Serve split and buttered.

Alternative raising agents

If plain flour and baking powder are used instead of self raising flour, allow 15 ml *(1 level tbsp)* baking powder to 225 g *(½ lb)* flour and sift them together twice before using. If you use cream of tartar and bicarbonate of soda in place of baking powder allow 5 ml *(1 level tsp)* cream of tartar and 2.5 ml *(½ level tsp)* bicarbonate of soda to 225 g *(½ lb)* plain flour with ordinary milk or 2.5 ml *(½ level tsp)* bicarbonate of soda and 2.5 ml *(½ level tsp)* cream of tartar with soured milk.

Everyday fruit scones

Add 50 g *(2 oz)* currants, sultanas, stoned raisins or chopped dates (or a mixture of fruit) to the dry ingredients in the basic recipe.

Rich afternoon tea scones

Follow the basic recipe, adding 15–30 ml *(1–2 level tbsps)* caster sugar to the dry ingredients and using 1 beaten egg with 75 ml *(5 tbsps)* water or milk in place of 150 ml *(¼ pt)* milk; 50 g *(2 oz)* dried fruit may also be included.

Cheese scones *see colour plate facing p. 336*

225 g ***(8 oz)*** **self raising flour**
pinch of salt
5 ml ***(1 level tsp)*** **baking powder**
40 g ***(1½ oz)*** **butter or margarine**
75–100 g ***(3–4 oz)*** **mature cheese, finely grated**
5 ml ***(1 level tsp)*** **dry mustard**
about 150 ml ***(¼ pt)*** **milk**

Grease a baking sheet. Sift the flour, salt and baking powder and rub in the fat until the mixture resembles fine breadcrumbs. Stir in half the cheese, the mustard and enough milk to give a fairly soft, light dough. Roll out about 2 cm *(¾ in)* thick and cut into rounds with a 5-cm *(2-in)* plain cutter. Put onto the baking sheet, brush the tops with milk and sprinkle with the remaining cheese. Bake in the oven at 220°C *(425°F)* mark 7 for about 10 minutes. When cold, cut in half and butter.

Wholemeal scone round *see colour plate facing p. 336*

50 g ***(2 oz)*** **plain flour**
pinch of salt
15 ml ***(1 level tbsp)*** **baking powder**
175 g ***(6 oz)*** **plain wholemeal flour**
50 g ***(2 oz)*** **caster sugar**
50 g ***(2 oz)*** **butter or margarine**
about 150 ml ***(¼ pt)*** **milk**

Sift together the plain flour, salt and baking powder into a bowl. Add the wholemeal flour and sugar. Lightly rub in the fat, and mix to a soft but manageable dough with milk. Shape into a flat 15-cm *(6-in)* round. Mark into 6 triangles with the back of a floured knife. Place on a pre-heated ungreased baking sheet and bake at once at 220°C *(425°F)* mark 7, towards the top of the oven, for about 15 minutes.

Note If using wholemeal self raising flour, reduce the baking powder to 5 ml *(1 level tsp)*.

Batch cake

75 g ***(3 oz)*** **lard**
225 g ***(8 oz)*** **self raising flour**
2.5 ml ***(½ level tsp)*** **salt**
5 ml ***(1 level tsp)*** **ground mixed spice**
75 g ***(3 oz)*** **caster sugar**
75 g ***(3 oz)*** **currants and sultanas, mixed**
15 ml ***(1 tbsp)*** **chopped mixed peel**
about 105 ml ***(7 tbsps)*** **milk**

Grease and flour a baking sheet. Rub the lard into the sifted flour, salt and spice until the mixture resembles fine breadcrumbs. Stir in the sugar, fruit and peel, make a well in the centre and pour in some of the milk; gradually work in the dry ingredients, adding a little more milk if necessary to give a soft but manageable, not sticky dough. Put on to the baking sheet and pat the surface to make a round about 2.5 cm *(1 in)* thick. Bake in the oven at 200°C *(400°F)* mark 6 for 20–30 minutes. Cool on a wire rack and serve fresh, cut and buttered.

Plain girdle scones

225 g ***(8 oz)*** **plain flour**
5 ml ***(1 level tsp)*** **bicarbonate of soda**
10 ml ***(2 level tsps)*** **cream of tartar**
5 ml ***(1 level tsp)*** **salt**
large knob of lard or butter
30 ml ***(2 level tbsps)*** **caster sugar**
about 150 ml ***(¼ pt)*** **milk**

Preheat and grease a griddle, hot plate or heavy based frying pan. Sift together the flour, bicarbonate of soda, cream of tartar and salt. Rub in the fat. Stir in the sugar. Mix to a fairly soft, manageable but not sticky dough, with the milk then turn the dough on to a floured board. Divide it into two and knead each piece very lightly if necessary to remove any cracks. Roll out into two rounds 0.5 cm *(¼ in)* thick and cut each into 6 triangles. Cook steadily on the hot griddle for about 5 minutes, until well risen and pale brown underneath; turn them and cook for a further 5 minutes until the other side is browned and the centre is dry.

Fruity girdle scones

225 g ***(8 oz)*** **self raising flour**
pinch of salt
2.5 ml ***(½ level tsp)*** **grated nutmeg**
50 g ***(2 oz)*** **lard, margarine or butter**
50 g ***(2 oz)*** **caster sugar**
50 g ***(2 oz)*** **dried fruit**
1 egg, beaten
milk to mix

Preheat and grease a griddle, hot plate or heavy based frying pan. Sift the flour, salt and nutmeg together and rub in the fat until the mixture resembles fine breadcrumbs. Stir in the sugar and the fruit. Mix with the egg and milk to a firm but not dry dough, roll out to 1 cm *(½ in)* thick and cut into rounds or triangles. Cook on a moderately hot griddle till brown on both sides – about 10 minutes in all.

Scotch pancakes or drop scones *see colour plate facing p. 336*

100 g ***(4 oz)*** **self raising flour**
30 ml ***(2 level tbsps)*** **caster sugar**
1 egg, beaten
125–150 ml ***(about ¼ pt)*** **milk**

Mix the flour and sugar. Make a well in the centre and stir in the egg, with enough of the milk to make a batter of the consistency of thick cream. The mixing should be done as quickly and lightly as possible – don't beat. If a thin pancake is wanted add slightly more milk.

Drop the mixture in spoonfuls on to a hot, lightly greased griddle, hot plate or heavy based frying pan; for round pancakes, drop it from the point of the spoon, for oval ones, from the side. Keep the griddle at a steady heat and when bubbles rise to the surface of the pancakes and burst – after 2–3 minutes – turn the cake over, using a palette knife. Continue cooking until golden brown on the other side – a further 2–3 minutes. Place the finished pancakes on a clean tea towel, cover with another towel and place on a rack to cool. (This keeps in the steam and the pancakes do not become dry.) Serve with butter or with whipped cream and jam. Makes about 15–18 pancakes.

For richer drop scones, add about 25 g *(1 oz)* fat, either rubbing it into the flour or adding it melted with the eggs and milk. If you wish, 50 g *(2 oz)* sultanas may be added. If you prefer, use 100 g *(4 oz)* plain flour, 2.5 ml *(½ level tsp)* bicarbonate of soda and 5 ml *(1 level tsp)* cream of tartar instead of the self raising flour.

Potato sconcs

450 g ***(1 lb)*** **floury potatoes, peeled**
10 ml ***(2 level tsps)*** **salt**
25–50 g ***(1–2 oz)*** **butter**
about 100 g ***(4 oz)*** **flour**

Cook the potatoes in boiling salted water for about 20 minutes, until tender; drain well and mash. Add the salt and butter and work in enough flour to give a stiff mixture. Turn on to a floured board and knead lightly, roll out to 0.5 cm *(¼ in)* thick and cut into triangles or 6.5-cm *(2½-in)* rounds. Cook on a hot greased griddle or in a thick frying pan for about 4–5 minutes on each side, until golden brown. Serve hot spread with butter. Cold cooked potatoes can be used, but the cakes will not be so light.

Northumberland 'Singin' Hinny' *see colour plate facing p. 336*

25 g ***(1 oz)*** **lard**
350 g ***(12 oz)*** **self raising flour**
50 g ***(2 oz)*** **ground rice**
5 ml ***(1 level tsp)*** **salt**
50 g ***(2 oz)*** **sugar**
75 g ***(3 oz)*** **currants**
300 ml ***(½ pt)*** **single cream and milk, mixed**

Rub the lard into the flour, ground rice and salt until the mixture resembles fine breadcrumbs. Stir in the sugar and the currants. Make a well in the centre, pour in the liquid and gradually work in the dry ingredients to give a soft but manageable dough. Roll out about 0.5 cm *(¼ in)* thick and prick all over with a fork. Cut into triangles or 6.5-cm *(2½-in)* rounds, place on a moderately hot griddle and cook for 3–4 minutes on each side, until brown. Serve hot, split and buttered.

Simple doughnuts

225 g ***(8 oz)*** **plain flour**
2.5 ml ***(½ level tsp)*** **bicarbonate of soda**
5 ml ***(1 level tsp)*** **cream of tartar**
pinch of ground cinnamon
25 g ***(1 oz)*** **butter**
50 g ***(2 oz)*** **caster sugar**
1 egg, beaten
milk
deep fat for frying

Sift the flour, bicarbonate of soda, cream of tartar and cinnamon and rub in the butter until the mixture resembles fine breadcrumbs. Stir in the sugar. Make a well in the centre, pour in the egg and gradually work in the dry ingredients, adding a little milk if necessary to give a soft dough. Heat the fat so that when a 2.5-cm *(1-in)* cube of bread is dropped in it takes 60–70 seconds to brown. Drop small balls of the mixture into the fat and fry until a light brown colour, turning them frequently. Lift out, drain on crumpled kitchen paper and sprinkle with sugar. Alternatively, the dough may be made stiffer, turned out on to a floured board and lightly kneaded until free from cracks, then rolled out until 1 cm *(½ in)* thick, cut into rings with two round cutters and fried as before.

For doughnuts made with yeast see page 414.

QUICK BREADS AND BUTTERED CAKES

Quick bread

25 g *(1 oz)* butter or margarine
450 g *(1 lb)* self raising flour, or 450 g *(1 lb)* plain flour and 25 ml *(5 level tsps)* baking powder sifted together twice
5 ml *(1 level tsp)* salt
1 egg, beaten
about 300 ml *(½ pt)* milk or milk and water

Grease a baking sheet. Rub the fat into the flour and salt until the mixture resembles fine breadcrumbs. Make a well in the centre, pour in the egg and some of the milk or milk and water and gradually work in the dry ingredients, adding more liquid if necessary to give a soft but manageable dough. Knead very lightly on a floured board, shape into a round, plait or twist and brush with milk or egg. Place on the baking sheet and bake in the oven at 220°C *(425°F)* mark 7 for about 30–35 minutes. Cool on a wire rack and eat fresh.

Raisin malt loaf

225 g *(8 oz)* plain flour
1.25 ml *(¼ level tsp)* salt
30 ml *(2 level tbsps)* soft brown sugar
5 ml *(1 level tsp)* bicarbonate of soda
150 g *(5 oz)* seedless raisins
50 g *(2 oz)* golden syrup
30 ml *(2 tbsps)* malt
about 150 ml *(¼ pt)* milk

Grease and line an oblong loaf tin about 21.5 by 11.5 cm *(8½ by 4½ in)* top measurements. Sift the flour, salt, sugar and bicarbonate of soda; add the raisins. Melt the syrup and malt in half of the milk. Make a well in the centre of the dry ingredients and pour in the milk mixture; gradually work in the dry ingredients, adding more milk to give a sticky, stiff consistency. Put into the tin and bake in the oven at 170°C *(325°C)* mark 3 for 1–1¼ hours. Turn out to cool on a wire rack and keep for 24 hours before serving sliced and buttered.

Date and raisin tea bread

225 g *(8 oz)* plain flour
5 ml *(1 level tsp)* baking powder
100 g *(4 oz)* butter or margarine
100 g *(4 oz)* stoned dates, chopped
50 g *(2 oz)* walnut halves, chopped
100 g *(4 oz)* seedless raisins
100 g *(4 oz)* demerara sugar
5 ml *(1 level tsp)* bicarbonate of soda
about 150 ml *(¼ pt)* milk

Grease and line a loaf tin measuring 25 cm by 15 cm *(9¾ in by 5¾ in)* across the top. Sift together the flour and baking powder and rub in the fat until it resembles fine breadcrumbs. Stir in the dates, walnuts, raisins and sugar. Mix the bicarbonate of soda and milk in a measure and pour into the centre of the dry ingredients; mix well together to give a stiff dropping consistency. Turn the mixture into the prepared tin and bake in the oven at 180°C *(350°F)* mark 4 for about 1 hour, until well risen and just firm to the touch. Turn out and cool on a wire rack.

Bran tea bread

75 g *(3 oz)* All-bran
225 g *(8 oz)* sultanas
225 g *(8 oz)* soft brown sugar
300 ml *(½ pt)* milk
175 g *(6 oz)* self raising flour
5 ml *(1 level tsp)* baking powder

Place the bran, sultanas and sugar in a bowl, pour the milk over and leave overnight to soak.

The next day, grease and line a loaf tin measuring about 21.5 by 11.5 cm *(8½ by 4½ in)* top measurements. Sift the flour with the baking powder and stir into the bran mixture. Stir well and turn the mixture into the prepared tin. Bake in the oven at 190°C *(375°F)* mark 5 for 1–1¼ hours. Turn out the loaf, remove the paper and cool the bread on a wire rack. Serve sliced and buttered.

Banana tea bread

200 g *(7 oz)* **self raising flour**
1.25 ml *(¼ level tsp)* **bicarbonate of soda**
2.5 ml *(½ level tsp)* **salt**
75 g *(3 oz)* **butter**
175 g *(6 oz)* **sugar**
2 eggs, beaten
450 g *(1 lb)* **bananas, mashed**
100 g *(4 oz)* **nuts, coarsely chopped**

Grease and line an oblong loaf tin, about 21.5 by 11.5 cm *(8½ by 4½ in)* top measurements. Sift the flour, bicarbonate of soda and salt. Cream the butter and sugar until pale and fluffy and add the egg a little at a time, beating well after each addition. Add the bananas and beat again. Stir in the flour and the nuts. Put into the tin and bake in the oven at 180°C *(350°F)* mark 4 for about 1¼ hours, until well risen and just firm. Turn out and cool on a wire rack. Keep for 24 hours before serving sliced and buttered.

Honey and banana tea bread

Reduce the sugar to 100 g *(4 oz)* and the bananas to 225 g *(½ lb)*. Beat 30 ml *(2 tbsps)* honey into the creamed mixture and add 225 g *(8 oz)* mixed dried fruits before putting the mixture into the prepared tin.

Cranberry nut bread

225 g *(8 oz)* **plain flour**
7.5 ml *(1½ level tsps)* **baking powder**
2.5 ml *(½ level tsp)* **bicarbonate of soda**
5 ml *(1 level tsp)* **salt**
50 g *(2 oz)* **margarine**
175 g *(6 oz)* **sugar**
150 ml *(¼ pt)* **orange juice**
15 ml *(1 tbsp)* **grated orange rind**
1 egg, beaten
75 g *(3 oz)* **walnuts, chopped**
100 g *(4 oz)* **cranberries, chopped**

Grease and line an oblong tin about 21.5 by 11.5 cm *(8½ by 4½ in)* top measurements. Sift together the flour, baking powder, bicarbonate of soda and salt. Rub in the margarine and add the sugar. Mix the orange juice, grated rind and beaten egg. Pour into the dry ingredients and mix lightly. Fold in the walnuts and cranberries. Turn into the tin and bake at 180°C *(350°F)* mark 4 for 1–1¼ hours until risen, golden brown and firm to the touch. Turn out and cool. The next day, serve thickly sliced and buttered. Frozen cranberries can be used instead of fresh.

Party cakes

One of the simplest ways of decorating a party cake is to add icing and a little decoration to an ordinary Victoria sandwich, so we begin this chapter with recipes for various icings and frostings and suggestions for using them. See also the frostings given on page 377.

CAKE ICINGS

Butter cream

75 g *(3 oz)* butter
175 g *(6 oz)* icing sugar, sifted
vanilla essence (or other flavouring)
15–30 ml *(1–2 tbsps)* milk or warm water

Cream the butter until soft and gradually beat in the sugar, adding a few drops of essence and the milk or water. This amount will coat the sides of an 18-cm *(7-in)* cake, or give a topping and a filling. If you wish both to coat the sides and give a topping or filling, increase the amounts of butter and sugar to 100 g *(4 oz)* and 200 g *(8 oz)* respectively.

Orange or lemon butter cream
Omit the vanilla essence and add a little finely grated orange or lemon rind and a little of the juice, beating well to avoid curdling the mixture.

Walnut butter cream
Add 30 ml *(2 level tbsps)* finely chopped walnuts, mix well.

Almond butter cream
Add 30 ml *(2 level tbsps)* very finely chopped toasted almonds; mix well.

Coffee butter cream
Omit the vanilla essence and flavour with 10 ml *(2 level tsps)* instant coffee powder blended with some of the liquid or 15 ml *(1 tbsp)* coffee essence used to replace an equal amount of the liquid.

Chocolate butter cream
Flavour either by adding 25–40 g *(1–1½ oz)* melted chocolate, omitting 15 ml *(1 tbsp)* liquid or by adding 15 ml *(1 level tbsp)* cocoa dissolved in a little hot water (this should be cooled before it is added to the mixture.)

Mocha butter cream
Dissolve 5 ml *(1 level tsp)* cocoa and 10 ml *(2 level tsps)* instant coffee powder in a little warm water taken from the measured amount; cool before adding to the mixture.

Glacé icing

Put 100–175 g *(4–6 oz)* sifted icing sugar and (if you wish) a few drops of any flavouring essence in a basin and gradually add 15–30 ml *(1–2 tbsps)* warm water. The icing should be thick enough to coat the back of a spoon. If necessary, add more water or sugar to adjust the consistency. Add a few drops of colouring if required and use at once.

Quick pizza (p. 268).

For icing of a finer texture, put the sugar, water and flavouring into a small pan and heat, stirring, until the mixture is warm – don't make it too hot. The icing should coat the back of a wooden spoon and look smooth and glossy.

This amount is sufficient to cover the top of an 18-cm *(7-in)* cake or up to 18 small cakes.

Orange icing
Substitute 15–30 ml *(1–2 tbsps)* strained orange juice for the water in the above recipe.

Lemon icing
Substitute 15 ml *(1 tbsp)* strained lemon juice for the same amount of water.

Chocolate icing
Dissolve 10 ml *(2 level tsps)* cocoa in a little hot water and use to replace the same amount of plain water.

Coffee icing
Flavour with either 5 ml *(1 tsp)* coffee essence or 10 ml *(2 level tsps)* instant coffee powder, dissolved in a little of the measured water.

Mocha icing
Flavour with 5 ml *(1 level tsp)* cocoa and 10 ml *(2 level tsps)* instant coffee powder, dissolved in a little of the measured water.

Liqueur icing
Replace 10–15 ml *(2–3 tsps)* of the water by liqueur as desired.

American frosting

225 g *(8 oz)* sugar
60 ml *(4 tbsps)* water
pinch of cream of tartar
1 egg white

Note To make this frosting properly, it is necessary to use a sugar-boiling thermometer. If you do not possess one, you can make Seven-Minute frosting (see below).

Gently heat the sugar in the water with the cream of tartar, stirring until dissolved. Then, without stirring, boil to 120°C *(240°F)*. Beat the egg white stiffly. Remove the sugar syrup from the heat and immediately the bubbles subside, pour it on to the egg white in a thin stream; beat the mixture continuously. When it thickens, shows signs of going dull round the edges and is almost cold, pour it quickly over the cake and at once spread evenly with a palette knife. The quantities given make sufficient frosting for an 18-cm *(7-in)* cake.

Orange frosting
Add a few drops of orange essence and a little orange colouring to the mixture while it is being beaten and before it thickens.

Lemon frosting
Add a little lemon juice while beating the mixture.

Caramel frosting
Substitute demerara sugar for the white sugar; follow the same method as above.

Coffee frosting
Add 5 ml *(1 tsp)* coffee essence to the mixture while beating.

Cheese board (p. 263).

Chocolate frosting

150 g *(5 oz)* icing sugar, sifted
1 egg
2.5 ml *(½ tsp)* vanilla essence
25 g *(1 oz)* plain chocolate, melted
25 g *(1 oz)* butter

Beat all the ingredients together in a bowl over a pan of hot water.

Seven-minute frosting

1 egg white
175 g *(6 oz)* caster sugar
pinch of salt
30 ml *(2 tbsps)* water
pinch of cream of tartar

This is an imitation American frosting that does not need a thermometer.

Put all the ingredients into a bowl and whisk lightly. Place the bowl over hot water and continue whisking until the mixture thickens sufficiently to hold 'peaks' – about 7 minutes depending on the whisk used and the heat of the water. The same variations can be made as for true American frosting.

Satin frosting

75 g *(3 oz)* butter at room temperature
350 g *(12 oz)* icing sugar, sifted
45 ml *(3 tbsps)* cream
vanilla essence

Cream the butter and gradually beat in the sugar and cream; when the mixture is smooth, flavour it with vanilla essence.

Maple satin frosting

Replace the cream by maple syrup.

Lemon satin frosting

Omit the vanilla essence and add the grated rind of ½ lemon.

Fudge topping

225 g *(8 oz)* icing sugar
30 ml *(2 level tbsps)* cocoa powder
75 g *(3 oz)* whipped-up white vegetable fat
45 ml *(3 tbsps)* milk
75 g *(3 oz)* sugar

Sift the icing sugar and cocoa into a bowl. Heat the rest of the ingredients gently in a small pan until the sugar is dissolved. Bring to the boil, pour into the icing sugar, stir until mixed, then beat until fluffy. Spread over the cake, using a knife, rough up the surface and leave to set.

Fondant icing

Make the fondant as described in the recipe on page 485 and prepare it for use as follows:

Put the required amount in a basin; the full amount given makes a generous coating for an 18-cm *(7-in)* cake; stand the basin over hot water and melt over a very gentle heat. Take care not to over-heat the fondant, as this makes the texture rough and destroys the gloss. Dilute the melted fondant with sugar syrup (see below) or with plain water to the consistency of double cream – or until the mixture will just coat the back of a wooden spoon. To make sugar syrup, dissolve 225 g *(½ lb)* sugar in 300 ml *(½ pt)* water, then boil without stirring to 110°C *(220°F)*; cool before using. Cakes which are to be coated with fondant icing should be glazed completely with apricot glaze (see below) and then coated with almond paste, to give a really professional appearance. To ice small cakes or pastries, spear them on a fork or skewer and dip them in the prepared fondant.

To ice a large cake, put it on a wire tray with a plate below and pour the icing quickly all over the cake. Don't touch the icing with a knife or the gloss finish will be spoilt. Add any desired decoration and leave the cake to set.

To give a thick topping of fondant on a Victoria, Madeira, cherry cake or similar, pin a band of double greaseproof paper closely round the cake so that it comes 2.5 cm *(1 in)* above the top. Prepare half the amount of fondant, ie make it with 225 g *(½ lb)* sugar and thin with syrup made with 100 g *(¼ lb)* sugar; pour it on to the top of the cake. When the topping is set, ease off the paper collar, using the back of a knife blade and dipping this frequently into hot water.

Apricot glaze

For use under fondant icing and almond paste.

Place 225 g *(½ lb)* apricot jam and 30 ml *(2 tbsps)* water in a saucepan over a low heat and stir until the jam softens. Sieve the mixture, return it to the pan and bring to the boil, boiling gently until the glaze is of a suitable coating consistency. This glaze can be potted as for jam (see page 435) and kept for future use.

DECORATING A SPONGE CAKE

Here are nine easy ways of 'dressing up' a pair of 18-cm *(7-in)* cakes, using plain ones for some versions and chocolate or coffee-flavoured cakes for others. Following these recipes come a couple of slightly more elaborate decorated cakes and ideas for presenting a Swiss roll. For butter cream see page 384.

1. Sandwich the cakes together with lemon curd. Make some lemon butter cream with 100 g *(4 oz)* butter and 200 g *(8 oz)* icing sugar and swirl it over the cake and down the sides. Decorate the top of the cake with mimosa balls and pieces of cut angelica.
2. Make some orange or lemon butter cream with 100 g *(4 oz)* butter and 200 g *(8 oz)* icing sugar. Use half to sandwich the cakes together and the rest to cover the top smoothly. Mark the top in lines or squares with a fork and decorate with small pieces of crystallised orange or lemon slices.
3. Drain a can of pineapple, mandarins or peaches. Sandwich the cakes together with apricot jam. Make some butter cream with 100 g *(4 oz)* butter, 200 g *(8 oz)* icing sugar and including a little of the fruit juice and spread it round the sides of the cake and over the top. Press chopped almonds round the sides and mark the top with a fork. Decorate with pieces of the drained fruit.
4. Make some coffee butter cream, with 75 g *(3 oz)* butter and 175 g *(6 oz)* icing sugar, and an equal amount of chocolate butter cream. Sandwich the cakes with some coffee butter cream. Spread some chocolate butter cream round the sides and swirl with a knife. Spread the remaining chocolate butter cream smoothly over the top. Use the remaining coffee butter cream to pipe whirls closely together round the top edge. (This cake is even nicer if made with a coffee-flavoured Victoria sandwich.)
5. Sieve 90 ml *(6 tbsps)* apricot or raspberry jam. Sandwich the cake with some jam and use the rest to brush round the sides. Holding the cake on its side, roll it in desiccated coconut or chopped nuts until an even layer sticks to the jam. Cover the top with glacé icing made with 100 g *(4 oz)* icing sugar and decorate when half set with chocolate drops or halved nuts.
6. Sandwich the cakes together with walnut butter cream made with 50 g *(2 oz)* butter and 100 g *(4 oz)* icing sugar. Cover the top with chocolate glacé icing made with 100 g *(4 oz)* icing sugar and decorate with chopped or halved walnuts.
7. Sandwich 2 chocolate layers together with chocolate butter cream made with 100 g *(4 oz)* butter and 200 g *(8 oz)* icing sugar and spread the rest round the sides. Roll the sides in chocolate vermicelli. Cover the top of the cake with chocolate glacé icing made with 100 g *(4 oz)* icing sugar. Melt 40 g *(1½ oz)* plain chocolate and pour in a thin stream from a spoon to form a 'scribble' pattern.
8. Make some chocolate butter cream with 100 g *(4 oz)* butter and 200 g *(8 oz)* icing sugar; use some of this to sandwich the cakes and spread the rest roughly round the sides. Cover the top of the cake with white glacé icing made with 100 g *(4 oz)* icing sugar and decorate with chocolate drops.
9. Make any of the frostings given at the beginning of this chapter. Sandwich the cakes together with a little of the frosting and pour the rest over the cake, allowing it to flow down the sides. Using a warmed round-bladed knife, swirl the frosting decoratively.

Feather coconut sandwich

100 g *(4 oz)* butter
100 g *(4 oz)* caster sugar
2 large eggs
100 g *(4 oz)* self raising flour
apricot jam
desiccated coconut

For the white glacé icing
100 g *(4 oz)* icing sugar, sifted
15 ml *(1 tbsp)* warm water, approx

For the pink glacé icing
50 g *(2 oz)* icing sugar, sifted
cochineal
10 ml *(2 tsps)* warm water, approx

Grease and line two 18 cm *(7-in)* sandwich tins. Make up the basic Victoria sandwich cake mixture, following the recipe on page 365. Divide it between the tins and bake in the oven at 180°C *(350°F)* mark 4 for about 30 minutes. Cool it on a wire rack. Sandwich the cakes together with apricot jam. Coat the sides with warmed jam and roll them in desiccated coconut. Make up some white glacé icing and quickly pipe lines of pink icing 1–2.5 cm *(½–1 in)* apart over the surface, using a writing nozzle. Quickly run a skewer or a sharp-pointed knife across the lines and back again, 1–2.5 cm *(½–1 in)* apart, producing the feathered effect.

SWISS ROLL VARIATIONS

Roll up the cake (plain or chocolate) with greaseproof paper inside it (see page 372) and allow it to cool. Fill and decorate in one of these ways:

1. Thaw and drain a small packet of frozen raspberries. Whip 142 ml *(¼ pt)* cream, fold in the raspberries and sweeten to taste. Open out the Swiss roll, spread with the cream mixture to within 1 cm *(½ in)* of the edge and roll up again. Sprinkle with caster sugar.
2. Make peppermint butter cream with 100 g *(4 oz)* butter, 200 g *(8 oz)* icing sugar and 1–2 drops of peppermint essence and spread on a chocolate roll. Re-roll.
3. Whip 142 ml *(¼ pt)* double cream, fold in 10 ml *(2 level tsps)* caster sugar and a few drops of vanilla essence and spread on the cooled Swiss roll. Place 100 g *(4 oz)* plain chocolate and 50 g *(2 oz)* butter in a basin over a pan of hot water and melt over a gentle heat, stirring. Allow the mixture to cool until it thickens sufficiently to coat the back of the spoon. Brush off any sugar from the outside of the roll, coat it with the chocolate and, as it sets, decorate with halved walnuts.

See also the Yule log recipe on page 406.

CAKES FOR A CROWD

Basic small cake mixture

225 g *(8 oz)* butter or margarine
225 g *(8 oz)* caster sugar
4 eggs
225 g *(8 oz)* self raising flour
vanilla essence

Grease and line a shallow tin about 35.5 by 25.5 cm *(14 by 10 in)*. Cream together the butter and sugar until light and fluffy. Beat in the eggs one at a time. Lightly beat the flour into the creamed mixture and then add about 2.5 ml *(½ tsp)* vanilla essence. Turn the mixture into the tin, level the mixture and bake in the oven at 180°C *(350°F)* mark 4 for 35–40 minutes, until well risen and spongy to the touch. Turn out and cool on a wire rack.

If wrapped in kitchen foil, this slab will keep moist for several days.

Chocolate slab

Make up the basic recipe above adding to the creamed mixture 25 g *(1 oz)* cocoa, blended with a little water to a smooth paste.

Pink slab

Add a few drops of cochineal to the basic mixture.

For finishing this selection you will need

900 g–1.1 kg *(2–2½ lb)* **ready-made almond paste**
1.1–1.4 kg *(2½–3 lb)* **icing sugar, for the glacé icing**
jam (preferably raspberry)
flavourings
crystallised rose petals
butter cream made with 350 g *(12 oz)* **icing sugar and flavoured to taste**
walnut halves

Trim the sides of each slab to square the edges. Cut the plain slab lengthwise into three 7-cm *(2¼-in)* strips. Cut the pink slab lengthwise into three 7-cm *(2¼-in)* strips. Cut one 7-cm *(2¼-in)* strip lengthwise from the chocolate slab, then two 4-cm *(1½-in)* strips, leaving one remaining strip.

Battenberg slices

Divide one 7-cm *(2¼-in)* strip of plain slab and one 7-cm *(2¼-in)* strip of pink slab in half lengthwise. Use jam to join the four different strips in a chequerboard pattern. Thinly roll out some of the almond paste into a rectangle the length of the strip and four times the width of one surface; brush it well with jam. Sit the cake on the paste and shape the paste round it, pressing it well on to the cake; make a firm join. Place the cake with the join on the underside. Pinch the top edges; using a knife, mark the surface in a trellis. Leave to firm up before cutting into slices. *Makes 16.*

Rose petal slices

With some plain butter cream, sandwich one 7-cm *(2¼-in)* strip of plain slab and one 7-cm *(2¼-in)* strip of pink slab together. Cover with almond paste as for Battenberg cake. Leave to dry for a few hours, then coat with lemon glacé icing based on 350–450 g *(12–16 oz)* icing sugar. Decorate the top with walnut halves and rose petals placed in position to give 16 slices. Cut when set. *Makes 16.*

Rolled almond slices

With some butter cream, sandwich together one 7-cm *(2¼-in)* strip of chocolate slab and one 7-cm *(2¼-in)* strip of plain slab. Cover with almond paste as for Battenberg cake. Brush the top with jam and place a long roll of almond paste in position along the centre. Coat the whole with chocolate glacé icing based on 350 g *(12 oz)* icing sugar. When this is set, pipe 16 lines of pink glacé icing at an angle across the top. Cut at an angle. *Makes 16.*

Coffee feather bars

Split a strip of chocolate and a strip of pink cake and sandwich them together with butter cream (plain or coffee flavoured). Stand them on a rack. Coat the top with coffee glacé icing; quickly pipe a line of stiffer plain glacé icing and feather it by pushing a skewer or the point of a knife in the opposite direction. Leave to set. *Makes 24.*

SMALL CAKES

Truffle cakes

100 g *(4 oz)* **stale cake or cake trimmings**
100 g *(4 oz)* **caster sugar**
100 g *(4 oz)* **ground almonds**
sherry or rum to flavour
sieved apricot jam
chocolate vermicelli

Rub the cake through a fairly coarse sieve and add the caster sugar and ground almonds. Add enough hot sieved apricot jam to bind. (Flavour with either sherry or rum.) Shape the mixture into small balls and leave to become firm. Dip each ball into the jam and roll in chocolate vermicelli. When dry, put into small paper cases. *Makes 16–18 cakes.*

Coconut pyramids

2 egg whites
150 g *(5 oz)* sugar
150 g *(5 oz)* desiccated coconut

Grease a baking sheet and cover with rice paper. Whisk the egg whites stiffly and fold in the sugar and coconut, using a metal spoon. Pile in small pyramids on the baking sheet, press into neat shapes and bake in the oven at 140°C *(275°F)* mark ½ until pale fawn – about ¾–1 hour. If you wish, the mixture can be tinted pink or green. *Makes about 12 cakes.*

Langues de chat

50 g *(2 oz)* butter
50 g *(2 oz)* sugar
1 egg
50 g *(2 oz)* self raising flour
vanilla butter cream, made with 50 g *(2 oz)* butter, 100 g *(4 oz)* icing sugar
50 g *(2 oz)* plain chocolate

Grease baking sheets. Cream the butter and sugar and beat in the egg. Work in the flour to make a mixture of a consistency suitable for piping. Put into a forcing bag fitted with a 1-cm *(½-in)* plain piping nozzle and force on to the baking sheets in fingers about 6–8 cm *(2½–3 in)* long, spaced widely apart. Bake in the oven at 220°C *(425°F)* mark 7 for about 5 minutes, until the edges of the biscuits are colouring. When the fingers are cold, sandwich them together in pairs with butter cream and dip the ends of each in the melted chocolate. If left plain, these biscuits are good with a rich sweet such as syllabub or soufflé. *Makes about 12.*

Palmiers

100 g *(4 oz)* puff pastry, ie made with 100 g *(4 oz)* flour etc (see page 354) or 225 g *(8 oz)* ready made puff pastry
caster sugar
sweetened whipped cream or jam
icing sugar

Roll the pastry out evenly until it is 0.3 cm *(⅛ in)* thick (0.2 cm, $\frac{1}{16}$ *in*, if bought pastry) and about 50 cm *(20 in)* long, then sprinkle it generously with caster sugar. Fold the ends over to the centre until they meet and press down firmly. Sprinkle generously with more sugar and fold the sides to the centre again; press and sprinkle with sugar. Place the two folded portions together and press; then, with a sharp knife, cut into 0.5-cm *(¼-in)* slices. Place cut edge down on a baking sheet, allowing room to spread, and bake in the oven at 220°C *(425°F)* mark 7 for 6–7 minutes, until golden brown. Turn them and bake for a further 6–7 minutes. Cool on a rack and just before serving, spread sweetened whipped cream on half of the slices, sandwich with the remaining slices and dredge with icing sugar. (If preferred, jam may be used in place of cream.) *Makes about 12.*

Meringues *see colour plate facing p. 464*

2 egg whites
50 g *(2 oz)* granulated sugar and 50 g *(2 oz)* caster sugar or 100 g *(4 oz)* caster sugar
142 ml *(¼ pt)* whipped cream

Line a baking sheet with kitchen foil or non-stick paper.

Whisk the egg whites very stiffly, add the granulated sugar or half the caster sugar and whisk again until the mixture regains its former stiffness. Lastly, fold in the caster sugar very lightly, using a metal spoon. Pipe through a forcing bag (or put in spoonfuls) on to the baking sheet and dry off in the oven at 130°C *(250°F)* mark ¼ for about 3 hours, until the meringues are firm and crisp but still white; if they begin to brown, prop the oven door open a little. Cool them on a wire rack. When they are cool, sandwich them together with whipped cream. *Makes 12–16 meringue shells.*

Variations

1. Tint pink by adding 1–2 drops of red colouring with the sugar.
2. To make coffee meringues, use coffee essence, adding 5 ml *(1 tsp)* to each egg white when the sugar is folded in.
3. For chocolate meringues, add cocoa with the caster sugar, allowing 5 ml *(1 level tsp)* per egg white.
4. Add finely chopped nuts, melted chocolate or a liqueur to the filling.

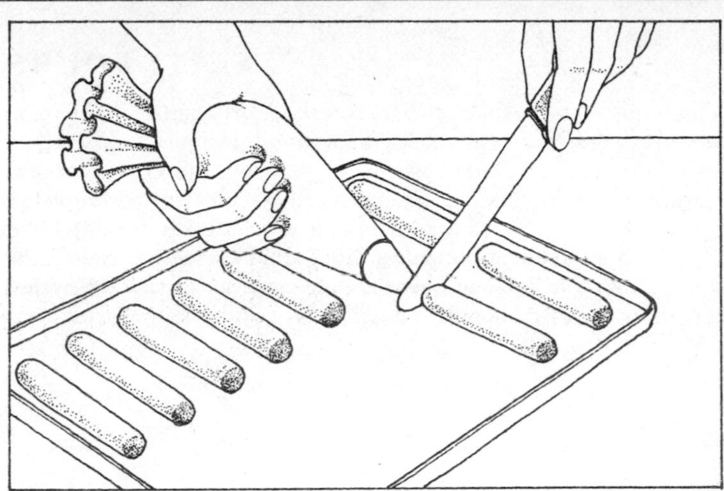
Shaping éclairs

Eclairs

choux pastry, made with 120 ml *(8 level tbsps)* **flour (see page 355)**
142 ml *(¼ pt)* **double cream, whipped with 60 ml** *(4 tbsps)* **single cream, or 150 ml** *(¼ pt)* **confectioner's custard**
choclate or coffee glacé icing, made with 100 g *(4 oz)* **icing sugar (see page 385), or 50 g** *(2 oz)* **melted chocolate**

Put the choux paste into a forcing bag fitted with a plain round nozzle of 1 cm *(½ in)* diameter and pipe in fingers 9 cm *(3½ in)* long on to the baking sheet, keeping the lengths very even and cutting the paste off with a wet knife against the edge of the pipe. Bake in the oven at 200°C *(400°F)* mark 6 for about 35 minutes, until well risen, crisp and of a golden brown colour. Remove from the tin, slit down the sides with a sharp-pointed knife to allow the steam to escape and leave on a cake rack to cool. When the éclairs are cold, and shortly before serving, fill with whipped cream or flavoured custard, then ice the tops with a little chocolate or coffee glacé icing or dip them in melted chocolate. *Makes about 12.*

Cream puffs

choux paste, made with 120 ml *(8 level tbsps)* **flour (see page 355)**
142 ml *(¼ pt)* **double cream, whipped with 60 ml** *(4 tbsps)* **single cream, or 284 ml** *(½ pt)* **whipping cream, whipped**
melted chocolate or icing sugar

The characteristic light, crisp texture and crazed tops of cream puffs are achieved by baking the pastry in its own steam. For this you will need a large, shallow tin with a tightly fitting lid. If this type of tin is not available, use a heavy, flat baking sheet and invert a roasting tin over it, sealing the join with a flour and water paste if the fit is not good.

Pipe the paste into bun shapes 4–5 cm *(1½–2 in)* in diameter 7.5 cm *(3 in)* apart on 2 damp baking sheets and cover. Bake in the oven at 200°C *(400°F)* mark 6 for 45–50 minutes. It is very important not to remove the covering tin during the cooking or the puffs will collapse; to test them, shake the tin gently – if the puffs move about freely, they are cooked. Split them and cool on a rack. When they are cold, fill with whipped cream and dip the tops in melted chocolate or dust with icing sugar. *Makes 8–10.*

Chocolate cases

175 g *(6 oz)* **plain chocolate**
100 g *(4 oz)* **sponge cake crumbs**
15 ml *(1 tbsp)* **raspberry jam**
sherry to taste
142 ml *(¼ pt)* **double cream, whipped**
8 maraschino cherries

Coat the inside of 8 small paper cases with melted chocolate and leave to set overnight; peel off the paper carefully. Mix together the cake crumbs, jam and sherry and fill the cases with this mixture. Top each with some whipped cream and a cherry. *Makes 8.*

PETIT FOURS

This term covers the small, rich, sweet cakes and biscuits served as a dessert at the end of a dinner and sometimes for afternoon tea. They usually include miniature macaroons, meringues, éclairs and piped biscuits (see pages 390, 391, 426, 429) and very small iced cakes. These last are made by cutting a thin slab of Genoese sponge into small fancy shapes – oblongs, squares, rounds, triangles, diamonds and crescents – coating with sieved apricot jam and decorating them. Some of the cakes are coated with glacé icings of different colours. Others may have a roll or knob of almond paste or a complete layer of paste, placed on top before the icing is added. Add crystallised flowers, nuts, pieces of glacé cherry, silver and mimosa balls or piped butter icing. When the cakes are quite dry, put them into small paper cases.

PARTY GÂTEAUX AND CAKES

Uncooked chocolate cake

100 g *(4 oz)* **plain sweet biscuits, petit beurre type**
50 g *(2 oz)* **digestive biscuits**
50 g *(2 oz)* **walnut pieces, chopped**
100 g *(3½ oz)* **butter or margarine**
30 ml *(2 level tbsps)* **caster sugar**
75 g *(3 oz)* **golden syrup**
50 g *(2 oz)* **cocoa**

For the icing
50 g *(2 oz)* **plain chocolate**
75 g *(2½ oz)* **icing sugar**
large knob of butter

Roughly crush the biscuits with a rolling pin and mix with the nuts. Cream together the butter, sugar and golden syrup. Beat in the sifted cocoa and work in the biscuits and walnuts, mixing well. Press this dough evenly into a 20.5-cm *(8-in)* flan ring placed on a flat serving plate or board. Leave overnight in a cold place (a refrigerator is best). The next day remove the ring, spread a layer of icing over the top of the cake and leave to set. To make the icing, put the chocolate, 15 ml *(1 tbsp)* hot water, the icing sugar and butter in a small pan. Heat over a very low heat until the chocolate has melted; stir and use when of a coating consistency.

Sachertorte (Chocolate cake)

100 g *(3½ oz)* **shelled hazel nuts**
100 g *(3½ oz)* **butter**
150 g *(5 oz)* **caster sugar**
5 large eggs, separated
15 ml *(1 tbsp)* **rum**
75 g *(3 oz)* **chocolate dots (cooking chocolate)**
60 ml *(4 level tbsps)* **dried white breadcrumbs**
pinch ground cloves
chocolate glacé icing (see below)
whipped cream

This world-famous Viennese confection, moist-textured, nutty and chocolate-flavoured, is served with lightly whipped cream. It will keep for a day or two.

Grease and line with greaseproof paper the sides and base of a 23-cm *(9-in)* straight-sided sandwich tin; the side band should come 2.5 cm *(1 in)* above the edge. Lightly brown the hazel nuts under the grill, then place in a paper bag and rub to remove the skins. Put them through a Mouli Baby or an electric blender to grind them. Cream together the butter and sugar until light and fluffy. Beat in the egg yolks one at a time. Melt the rum and chocolate in a basin over hot water. Fold the cooled chocolate into the creamed mixture, with the nuts, crumbs and cloves. Lastly, fold in the stiffly whisked egg whites. When all is evenly mixed, turn the mixture into the tin. Bake in the oven at 200°C *(400°F)* mark 6 for 30 minutes, or until well risen and firm to the touch.

Cool the cake on a wire rack. When it is completely cold (or the next day) coat with chocolate glacé icing and decorate with whipped cream.

Chocolate glacé icing Melt 50 g *(2 oz)* cooking chocolate with 30 ml *(2 tbsps)* water over a low heat and add 5 ml *(1 tsp)* glycerine. Stir in enough sifted icing sugar, about 75 g *(2½ oz)*, to give a coating consistency.

Battenberg cake

175 g *(6 oz)* **butter or margarine**
175 g *(6 oz)* **caster sugar**
vanilla essence
3 eggs, beaten
175 g *(6 oz)* **self raising flour**
30 ml *(2 level tbsps)* **cocoa**
milk to mix, if necessary
raspberry jam
350 g *(¾ lb)* **ready-made almond paste**
caster sugar

Grease and line a Swiss roll tin measuring 30.5 by 20.5-cm *(12 by 8 in)* and divide it lengthwise with a 'wall' of greaseproof paper. Cream the fat and sugar together until light and fluffy and add a little essence. Gradually add the eggs a little at a time, beating well after each addition. When all the egg has been added, lightly fold in the flour, using a metal spoon. Turn half of the mixture into one side of the tin. Fold the sifted cocoa into the other half, with a little milk if necessary, and spoon this mixture into the second side of the tin. Bake in the oven at 190°C *(375°F)* mark 5 for 40–45 minutes, until well risen. Cool on a wire rack.

When the cakes are cold, trim them to an equal size and cut each in half lengthwise. Spread the sides of the strips with jam and stick them together, alternating the colours. Press the pieces well together then coat the whole of the outside of the cake with jam. Roll out the almond paste thinly in caster sugar, forming it into an oblong 35.5 by 25.5 cm *(14 by 10 in)*. Wrap the paste completely round the cake and trim the edges. Pinch with thumb and forefinger along the outer edges, and score the top of the cake with a sharp knife to give a criss-cross pattern.

Caramel nut gâteau

3 eggs
90 ml *(6 level tbsps)* **caster sugar**
10 ml *(2 level tsps)* **instant coffee powder**
60 ml *(4 level tbsps)* **self raising flour**
75 g *(2½ oz)* **ground almonds**
coffee butter cream, made with 100 g *(4 oz)* **butter, 200 g** *(8 oz)* **icing sugar etc**
75 g *(3 oz)* **browned flaked almonds**
whole blanched almonds

For the caramel
175 g *(6 oz)* **granulated sugar**
60 ml *(4 tbsps)* **water**

Grease, flour and line the bases of two 18-cm *(7-in)* sandwich tins. To make the cake, beat the eggs, sugar and coffee as for a whisked sponge cake (page 371). Fold in the sifted flour and ground almonds, put into the tins and bake in the oven at 190°C *(375°F)* mark 5 for about 20 minutes. Turn out and allow to cool. Sandwich the cakes together with half of the coffee butter cream and spread most of the remainder round the sides of the cake (reserving a little for decoration); press the flaked almonds into the butter cream on the sides of the cake.

Make the caramel by dissolving the sugar in the water in a pan, then boiling without stirring until golden. Pour on to the top of the cake and mark into 8 portions with a greased knife before the caramel sets. Pipe with the remaining butter cream and decorate with whole almonds.

Glazed pineapple gâteau

see colour plate between pp. 336 and 337

4 large eggs
100 g *(4 oz)* **caster sugar**
100 g *(4 oz)* **butter, melted**
75 g *(3 oz)* **plain flour**
25 g *(1 oz)* **cornflour**

For the filling
175 g *(6 oz)* **apricot glaze**
284 ml *(½ pt)* **double cream**

For the decoration
226-g *(8-oz)* **can pineapple slices**
30 ml *(2 level tbsps)* **caster sugar**
lemon juice
6 glacé cherries
flaked almonds
50 g *(2 oz)* **icing sugar**

Grease and base-line 2 shallow oblong tins measuring 30.5 by 11.5 cm *(12 by 4½ in)*. Make a basic Genoese mixture as in the recipe on page 373. Bake just above the oven centre at 190°C *(375°F)* mark 5 for about 20 minutes, then turn out and cool on a wire rack.

To finish, sandwich the cakes together with a little apricot glaze and the whipped double cream. Brush the sides and top with more apricot glaze. Drain the pineapple. In a saucepan dissolve the sugar in the pineapple juice without boiling, then bring to the boil, add the pineapple slices and slowly simmer for 20–25 minutes, until the fruit is clear and the juice almost completely reduced. Leave until cold. Arrange the pineapple slices on top of the cake, with a cherry in the centre of each. Scatter the flaked almonds over and coat with a thin lemon icing made by blending the icing sugar with the lemon juice.

Devil's food cake

275 g *(10 oz)* plain flour
10 ml *(2 level tsps)* bicarbonate of soda
2.5 ml *(½ level tsp)* salt
75 g *(3 oz)* butter or margarine
250 g *(9 oz)* soft light brown sugar
2 large eggs
100 g *(4 oz)* unsweetened chocolate, melted
200 ml *(7 fl oz)* milk
5 ml *(1 tsp)* vanilla essence

For butter filling
75 g *(3 oz)* butter
175 g *(6 oz)* icing sugar
15 ml *(1 tbsp)* top of the milk

For frosting
175 g *(6 oz)* chocolate dots
450 g *(1 lb)* icing sugar
30 ml *(2 tbsps)* hot water
2 egg yolks
75 g *(3 oz)* butter, melted

Grease and line two 21.5-cm *(8½-in)* sandwich tins, keeping the greaseproof paper round the sides above the rims. Sift together the flour, bicarbonate of soda and salt. Cream together the fat and sugar until pale and fluffy, then gradually add the eggs, one at a time, beating well after each addition. Add the melted chocolate and beat well. Then add the flour alternately with the milk and vanilla essence. Turn the mixture into the tins and bake at 180°C *(350°F)* mark 4 for about 40 minutes. Cool on a wire rack.

To finish, sandwich the cakes together with butter filling and coat with the frosting; finish in swirls using a round-bladed knife. Leave to set, preferably until the next day, before slicing.

Butter filling Cream the butter until soft then gradually beat in the sifted icing sugar with the milk.

Frosting Melt the chocolate dots in a bowl over warm, not boiling, water. Off the heat, stir in the sifted icing sugar and hot water. Gradually beat in the egg yolks, one at a time, followed by the melted butter, a little at a time. Continue to beat until of a spreading consistency.

Hazel nut gâteau

175 g *(6 oz)* butter
175 g *(6 oz)* caster sugar
3 large eggs
150 g *(5 oz)* self raising flour
25 g *(1 oz)* hazel nuts, ground

For the icing
350 g *(12 oz)* icing sugar, sifted
45–60 ml *(3–4 tbsps)* water

For the decoration
25 g *(1 oz)* butter
100 g *(4 oz)* icing sugar, sifted
a little top of the milk
24 whole hazel nuts

Lightly grease and base-line a *moule-à-manqué* cake tin measuring 24-cm *(9½-in)* across the top. Cream the butter and sugar until light and fluffy. Beat in the eggs, one at a time. Sift the flour over the surface and stir into the creamed ingredients, together with the ground hazel nuts. Turn the mixture into the prepared tin and level off. Bake in the oven or just above at 180°C *(350°F)* mark 4 for about 40 minutes. Turn out and cool on a wire rack, narrow side uppermost.

Blend the icing sugar with enough water to give a coating consistency. Pour over the cake and, using a round bladed knife, ease it over the surface to coat evenly. Leave to set. Beat the 25 g *(1 oz)* butter to a cream and gradually beat in remaining sugar, with just enough top of the milk to give a piping consistency. Using a large star nozzle, pipe 8 rosettes, one for each portion of cake. Top each rosette with 3 nuts.

Doboz torte

4 eggs
175 g *(6 oz)* caster sugar
150 g *(5 oz)* plain flour
100–175 g *(4–6 oz)* caster sugar for caramel
3 egg whites
175 g *(6 oz)* icing sugar
225 g *(8 oz)* butter
100 g *(4 oz)* chocolate, melted
crushed biscuits or chopped nuts to decorate

Line 2 baking sheets with silicone (non-stick) paper. Whisk the eggs, add the 175 g *(6 oz)* sugar gradually and whisk over hot water until very thick and fluffy. Sift half of the flour over the mixture and fold in. Add the remaining flour in the same way. Spread some of the mixture out on the baking sheets into large rounds – about 20 cm *(8 in)* across – and bake at 190°C *(375°F)* mark 5 for 7–10 minutes, until golden brown. Loosen from the tins and trim each cake to a neat shape with a sharp knife – a saucepan lid may be used as a guide. Spread some more mixture on the sheets and bake as above; it will make 6–7 rounds. Lift them on to wire racks to cool, then take the round with the best surface and lay it on an oiled rack or tray.

Make the caramel by putting the 100–175 g *(4–6 oz)* caster sugar in a small, heavy saucepan, placing it over gentle heat, allowing the sugar to dissolve without stirring and boiling it steadily to a rich brown. Pour it over the selected biscuit round, spreading it with a knife that has been brushed over with oil. Mark into 8 sections and trim round the edge.

Now make the chocolate filling. Whip the egg whites and icing sugar in a basin over a saucepan of hot water until very thick. Cream the butter until pale and beat the meringue into it gradually; stir in the melted chocolate. Sandwich the remaining biscuit rounds together in one stack with some of the filling and put the caramel-covered one on top. Spread the sides of the torte with some more filling and press the crushed biscuit crumbs or chopped nuts round the sides. Pipe the remaining filling round the top edge to make a decorative border.

Note For a simpler filling, cream 150 g *(5 oz)* butter and gradually beat in 225 g *(8 oz)* sifted icing sugar. Beat in 50 g *(2 oz)* cooking chocolate, melted but not hot.

Orange liqueur gâteau

2 round 18-cm *(7-in)* sponge cakes
30–45 ml *(2–3 tbsps)* Grand Marnier
grated rind of 1 orange
284 ml *(½ pt)* double cream, whipped
chopped walnuts
15–30 ml *(1–2 tbsps)* fresh orange juice
150 g *(5 oz)* icing sugar, sifted
thin slices of orange

Sprinkle each round of cake with Grand Marnier. Add the orange rind to the cream and use about half of the mixture to sandwich the 2 cakes together. Spread a little of it round the sides and roll the cake in the chopped walnuts. Add sufficient orange juice to the sugar to make an icing thick enough to coat the back of a spoon and spread this over the top of the cake. When the icing is set, pipe with whirls of cream and decorate with thin slices of orange.

If preferred, spread the sides of the cake with apricot jam instead of cream; the amount of cream can then be somewhat reduced.

Nusstorte

7 eggs, separated
150 g *(5 oz)* caster sugar
few drops vanilla essence
50 g *(2 oz)* fine dry white breadcrumbs
75 g *(3 oz)* chopped walnuts and toasted almonds mixed, plus a few whole walnuts

For chocolate icing
3 eggs
175 g *(6 oz)* caster sugar
50 g *(2 oz)* chocolate, melted
few drops vanilla essence

Whisk the egg yolks with the sugar until thick and creamy. Whisk the egg whites stiffly. Add the vanilla essence to the egg yolks and sugar, mix together the breadcrumbs and chopped nuts and fold into the egg yolk mixture with the egg whites. Turn it all into three 20.5-cm *(8-in)* greased sandwich tins. Bake at 180°C *(350°F)* mark 4 for about 25 minutes until firm and lightly browned. Allow the cakes to cool in the tins before carefully turning them out.

For the icing, put the eggs and sugar into a double saucepan and stir until the mixture thickens, taking great care not to overheat it or it will curdle. Remove the pan from the heat and stir in the melted chocolate and vanilla essence. Beat until thick, then allow to cool. Divide the icing between the cakes, sandwich them together and then spread the top with more icing. Decorate with whole walnuts.

Caribbean sponge

For the cake
4 eggs, separated
175 g *(6 oz)* caster sugar
100 g *(4 oz)* self raising flour

For the filling
50 g *(2 oz)* butter
100 g *(4 oz)* icing sugar
30 ml *(2 tbsps)* chopped preserved ginger
60 ml *(4 tbsps)* grated plain chocolate
about 15 ml *(1 tbsp)* rum

For the icing
75 g *(3 oz)* plain chocolate
175 g *(6 oz)* icing sugar
30 ml *(2 tbsps)* single cream or top of the milk
15 ml *(1 tbsp)* boiling water

Grease a 20.5-cm *(8-in)* cake tin, line the base with greaseproof paper and sprinkle the inside of the tin with flour and sugar. Whisk the egg whites stiffly. Stir in the sugar and then the egg yolks until the mixture is evenly mixed. Sift the flour on to the mixture and fold it in carefully with a metal spoon. Pour the mixture into the tin and bake in the oven at 180°C *(350°F)* mark 4 for 35–40 minutes. Turn out and allow to cool.

To make the filling, cream the butter and sugar together until pale and fluffy and add the ginger, chocolate and rum to taste. Split the cooled cake in half and sandwich together with the filling.

To make the icing, melt the chocolate in a basin over hot water, stir in the icing sugar gradually and then stir in the cream very slowly; add 15 ml *(1 tbsp)* boiling water and while the mixture is still hot, swirl it over the cake.

Chestnut gâteau

3 eggs
75 g *(3 oz)* caster sugar
75 g *(3 oz)* plain flour, sifted
15 ml *(1 tbsp)* warm water
apricot jam
100 g *(4 oz)* almonds, chopped and toasted
142 ml *(¼ pt)* double cream, whipped
candied chestnut spread (from the tube)

Grease and line a straight-sided Swiss roll tin measuring 30.5 by 20.5 cm *(12 by 8 in)*. Whisk the eggs and sugar until thick enough to leave a trail. Fold in the flour with a metal spoon, along with the warm water. Turn the mixture into the prepared tin and bake in the oven at 230°C *(450°F)* mark 8 for 10–15 minutes, until well risen and golden brown. Turn on to a wire rack and remove the paper. When cold, cut across into three. Sandwich together in layers with apricot jam. Coat the sides with jam and press in chopped nuts. Decorate the top with piped whipped cream and lines of chestnut spread piped straight from the tube.

Frosted walnut cake

3 eggs
75 g *(3 oz)* caster sugar
25 g *(1 oz)* butter, melted
50 g *(2 oz)* self raising flour
40 ml *(2½ level tbsps)* cornflour
45 ml *(3 tbsps)* walnuts, chopped
2.5 ml *(½ tsp)* vanilla essence

For the decoration
7-minute frosting (page 386)
walnut halves

Line an 18-cm *(7-in)* cake tin. Make a cake from the eggs, sugar, fat and the flour and cornflour (sifted together), as for a Genoese sponge (see page 373), then add the walnuts and vanilla essence. Pour the mixture into the tin and bake in the oven at 180°C *(350°F)* mark 4 for about 45 minutes, until golden brown and springy to the touch. Turn it out on to a wire rack to cool.

When the cake is quite cool, split it in half. Make up the frosting. Working quickly, spread some of the icing on one half of the cake and sandwich the two halves together. Stand the cake on a cooling rack with a plate beneath it and pour the remaining icing over the cake; using a palette knife, quickly smooth it evenly over the cake in a 'whirled' pattern. Decorate with the walnut halves.

SEASONAL AND CELEBRATION CAKES

In this section we give first of all some recipes for suitable mixtures to use for special-occasion and wedding cakes, then notes on the quantities of mixture and the cooking times required for different-sized tins, instructions for making and assembling the cakes and hints on cakes of unusual shape, followed by detailed directions for icing a formal cake. There are also a few ideas for different cake designs, including three wedding cakes.

Christmas cake

225 g *(8 oz)* currants
225 g *(8 oz)* sultanas
225 g *(8 oz)* stoned raisins, chopped
100 g *(4 oz)* mixed chopped peel
100 g *(4 oz)* glacé cherries, halved
50 g *(2 oz)* nibbed almonds
225 g *(8 oz)* plain flour
pinch of salt
2.5 ml *(½ level tsp)* ground mace
2.5 ml *(½ level tsp)* ground cinnamon
225 g *(8 oz)* butter
225 g *(8 oz)* soft brown sugar
grated rind of 1 lemon
4 large eggs, beaten
30 ml *(2 tbsps)* brandy

Line a 20.5-cm *(8-in)* cake tin, using two thicknesses of greaseproof paper. Tie a double band of brown paper round the outside. Clean the fruit if necessary. Mix the prepared currants, sultanas, raisins, peel, cherries and nuts. Sift the flour, salt and spices. Cream the butter, sugar and lemon rind until pale and fluffy. Add the eggs a little at a time, beating well after each addition. Fold in half the flour, using a metal spoon, then fold in the rest and add the brandy. Lastly fold in the fruit. Put into the tin. Spread the mixture evenly, making sure there are no air pockets and make a dip in the centre. Stand the tin on a layer of newspaper or brown paper in the oven and bake at 150°C *(300°F)* mark 1–2 for about 3¾ hours. To avoid over-browning the top, cover it with several thicknesses of greaseproof paper after 1½ hours. When the cake is cooked, leave it to cool in the tin and then turn it out on to a wire rack.

To store, wrap it in several layers of greaseproof paper and put it in an airtight tin. If a large enough tin is not available, cover the wrapped cake entirely with aluminium foil. If you like, you can prick the cake top all over with a fine skewer and slowly pour 30–45 ml *(2–3 tbsps)* brandy over it before storing.

Light Christmas cake

175 g *(6 oz)* glacé cherries, halved
175 g *(6 oz)* currants
175 g *(6 oz)* sultanas
100 g *(4 oz)* glacé pineapple
100 g *(4 oz)* mixed candied peel, chopped
225 g *(8 oz)* butter or margarine
225 g *(8 oz)* caster sugar
50 g *(2 oz)* ground almonds
4 eggs, beaten
225 g *(8 oz)* self raising flour
grated rind and juice of 1 lemon
45 ml *(3 tbsps)* brandy

For those who prefer a cake less richly fruited than the traditional type; it should be made 1–2 weeks before eating.

Line a 23-cm *(9-in)* cake tin, using a double thickness of greaseproof paper. If the cherries are very syrupy, wash them and dry well. Clean the currants and sultanas if necessary. Cut the glacé pineapple into small cubes.

Cream the butter and sugar until pale and fluffy and stir in the ground almonds. Add the eggs a little at a time, beating well after each addition. Add 45 ml *(3 tbsps)* of the flour to the fruits and peel mixing well. Fold these ingredients, alternately with the rest of the flour, the grated lemon rind and the lemon juice, into the creamed mixture. Lastly, stir in the brandy. Put the mixture into the tin and bake in the oven at 170°C *(325°F)* mark 3 for about 2½ hours, or till risen and just firm to the touch. Cool and store as for the rich Christmas cake.

Note 1 If a firmer cake is preferred, use 100 g *(4 oz)* self raising flour and 125 g *(4 oz)* plain.

Note 2 As an alternative, use twice the amount of ingredients given for the Genoa cake (page 369) and bake in a 23-cm *(9-in)* round tin.

Economical Christmas cake

225 g *(8 oz)* sultanas
100 g *(4 oz)* currants
225 g *(8 oz)* raisins, stoned
275 g *(10 oz)* plain flour
5 ml *(1 level tsp)* mixed spice
little grated nutmeg
225 g *(8 oz)* margarine
225 g *(8 oz)* caster sugar
little grated lemon rind
few drops vanilla essence
few drops almond essence
4 eggs, beaten
15 ml *(1 tbsp)* marmalade
2.5 ml *(½ level tsp)* bicarbonate of soda
30 ml *(2 tbsps)* milk or water
few drops gravy browning

Line a 20.5-cm *(8-in)* cake tin, using a double thickness of greaseproof paper. Clean the fruit if necessary and mix it with the flour, mixed spice and nutmeg. Cream the fat, sugar, lemon rind and essences together until pale and fluffy. Add the eggs a little at a time, beating well after each addition; add the marmalade and mix thoroughly. Fold in half the flour and fruit, using a metal spoon, then fold in the rest. Dissolve the bicarbonate of soda in the milk or water and stir into the mixture, with a few drops of gravy browning. The mixture should be of a soft dropping consistency. Put into the tin and bake in the oven at 150°C *(300°F)* mark 1–2 for about 4 hours. Cool and store as for the Christmas cake on page 396.

Simnel cake

550 g *(1¼ lb)* bought almond paste
350 g *(12 oz)* currants
100 g *(4 oz)* sultanas
75 g *(3 oz)* mixed candied peel, chopped
225 g *(8 oz)* plain flour
pinch of salt
5 ml *(1 level tsp)* ground cinnamon
5 ml *(1 level tsp)* ground nutmeg
175 g *(6 oz)* butter or margarine
175 g *(6 oz)* caster sugar
3 eggs, beaten
milk to mix
apricot jam or beaten egg to use under almond paste
glacé icing, optional

Originally this cake was baked for Mothering Sunday, in the days when many girls went into service and Mothering Sunday was the one day in the year they were allowed home. It is now more usual to have Simnel cake at Easter.

Line an 18-cm *(7-in)* cake tin. Divide the almond paste into three; take one portion and roll it out to a round the size of the cake tin. Using the remaining ingredients and following the method for Christmas cake, make up the mixture. Put half of it into the prepared tin, smooth and cover with the round of almond paste. Put the remaining cake mixture on top. Bake in the oven at 170°C *(325°F)* mark 3 for about 1 hour, lower the heat to 150°C *(300°F)* mark 2 and bake for 3 hours, until the cake is golden brown, firm to the touch and no longer 'sings'. Allow to cool in the tin.

Take another third of the almond paste and roll out to a round the size of the tin; make small balls from the remaining third – eleven is the traditional number. Brush the top of the cake with apricot jam or beaten egg, cover with the round of paste and place the small balls round the edge. Brush the paste with any remaining egg or jam and brown under the grill. The top of the cake may then be coated with glacé icing, made by mixing 45 ml *(3 level tbsps)* sifted icing sugar with a little cold water until it will coat the back of the spoon. Decorate the cake with a tiny model chicken or a few coloured sugar eggs.

White fruit cake

100 g *(4 oz)* plain flour
100 g *(4 oz)* self raising flour
50 g *(2 oz)* cornflour
100 g *(4 oz)* glacé pineapple
175 g *(6 oz)* glacé cherries
100 g *(4 oz)* mixed glacé fruits
50 g *(2 oz)* crystallised ginger
50 g *(2 oz)* mixed chopped peel
50 g *(2 oz)* angelica
50 g *(2 oz)* blanched almonds
50 g *(2 oz)* shelled walnuts
225 g *(8 oz)* butter or margarine
150 g *(5 oz)* caster sugar
4 large eggs
15 ml *(1 tbsp)* lemon juice
45–60 ml *(3–4 tbsps)* milk

Prepare a 20.5-cm *(8-in)* round cake tin as for a Christmas cake. Sift together the flours and cornflour. Cut the fruit into pieces about the size of half a cherry. Trim the angelica into matchsticks. Chop the nuts roughly. Mix the fruits and nuts together. Dust 30 ml *(2 level tbsps)* flour over all to coat the sticky fruit. Cream together the fat and sugar, slowly beat in the eggs one at a time, with a little flour. Lightly beat in the remaining flour with the lemon juice and milk. Fold in the fruit and nuts. Turn the mixture into the prepared tin, hollow the centre and bake in the oven at 170°C *(325°F)* mark 3 for 2–2½ hours. Leave in the tin for 15 minutes, then cool on a wire rack.

MAKING CELEBRATION CAKES

see colour plate facing p. 529

Make and bake the cake as for Christmas cake (page 396). using the chart opposite as a guide for quantities. With the larger sizes, 25 cm *(10 in)* and upwards, it is advisable to reduce the oven heat to 130°C *(250°F)* mark ½ after two-thirds of the cooking time.

If possible, store the cake for 2–3 months before eating it. If you wish, a little more brandy may be poured over it halfway through the storing period.

WEDDING CAKES

When you are planning a wedding cake, choose the sizes of the tiers carefully, avoiding a combination that would look too heavy. Good proportions for a three-tier cake are 30.5, 23 and 15 cm *(12, 9 and 6 in)*; for a two-tier cake

Quantities and sizes for celebration cakes

If you want to make a formal cake for a birthday, wedding or anniversary, the following chart will show you the amount of ingredients required to fill the chosen cake tin or tins, whether round or square.

SQUARE TIN SIZE		15 cm (*6 in*) square	18 cm (*7 in*) square	20.5 cm (*8 in*) square	23 cm (*9 in*) square	25.5 cm (*10 in*) square	28 cm (*11 in*) square	30.5 cm (*12 in*) square
ROUND TIN SIZE	15 cm (*6 in*) round	18 cm (*7 in*) round	20.5 cm (*8 in*) round	23 cm (*9 in*) round	25.5 cm (*10 in*) round	28 cm (*11 in*) round	30.5 cm (*12 in*) round	
Currants	225 g (*8 oz*)	350 g (*12 oz*)	450 g (*1 lb*)	625 g (*1 lb 6 oz*)	775 g (*1 lb 12 oz*)	1.1 kg (*2 lb 8 oz*)	1.5 kg (*3 lb 2 oz*)	1.7 kg (*3 lb 12 oz*)
Sultanas	100 g (*3½ oz*)	125 g (*4½ oz*)	200 g (*7 oz*)	225 g (*8 oz*)	375 g (*13 oz*)	400 g (*14 oz*)	525 g (*1 lb 3 oz*)	625 g (*1 lb 6 oz*)
Raisins	100 g (*3½ oz*)	125 g (*4½ oz*)	200 g (*7 oz*)	225 g (*8 oz*)	375 g (*13 oz*)	400 g (*14 oz*)	525 g (*1 lb 3 oz*)	625 g (*1 lb 6 oz*)
Glacé cherries	50 g (*2 oz*)	75 g (*3 oz*)	150 g (*5 oz*)	175 g (*6 oz*)	250 g (*9 oz*)	275 g (*10 oz*)	350 g (*12 oz*)	425 g (*15 oz*)
Mixed peel	25 g (*1 oz*)	50 g (*2 oz*)	75 g (*3 oz*)	100 g (*4 oz*)	150 g (*5 oz*)	200 g (*7 oz*)	250 g (*9 oz*)	275 g (*10 oz*)
Almonds	25 g (*1 oz*)	50 g (*2 oz*)	75 g (*3 oz*)	100 g (*4 oz*)	150 g (*5 oz*)	200 g (*7 oz*)	250 g (*9 oz*)	275 g (*10 oz*)
Lemon rind	a little	a little	a little	¼ lemon	¼ lemon	½ lemon	½ lemon	1 lemon
Plain flour	175 g (*6 oz*)	200 g (*7½ oz*)	350 g (*12 oz*)	400 g (*14 oz*)	600 g (*1 lb 5 oz*)	700 g (*1 lb 8 oz*)	825 g (*1 lb 13 oz*)	1 kg (*2 lb 6 oz*)
Mixed spice	1.25 ml (*¼ level tsp*)	2.5 ml (*½ level tsp*)	2.5 ml (*½ level tsp*)	5 ml (*1 level tsp*)	5 ml (*1 level tsp*)	10 ml (*2 level tsps*)	12.5 ml (*2½ level tsps*)	12.5 ml (*2½ level tsps*)
Cinnamon	1.25 ml (*¼ level tsp*)	2.5 ml (*½ level tsp*)	2.5 ml (*½ level tsp*)	5 ml (*1 level tsp*)	5 ml (*1 level tsp*)	10 ml (*2 level tsps*)	12.5 ml (*2½ level tsps*)	12.5 ml (*2½ level tsps*)
Butter	150 g (*5 oz*)	175 g (*6 oz*)	275 g (*10 oz*)	350 g (*12 oz*)	500 g (*1 lb 2 oz*)	600 g (*1 lb 5 oz*)	800 g (*1 lb 12 oz*)	950 g (*2 lb 2 oz*)
Sugar	150 g (*5 oz*)	175 g (*6 oz*)	275 g (*10 oz*)	350 g (*12 oz*)	500 g (*1 lb 2 oz*)	600 g (*1 lb 5 oz*)	800 g (*1 lb 12 oz*)	950 g (*2 lb 2 oz*)
Large eggs	2½	3	5	6	9	11	14	17
Brandy	15 ml (*1 tbsp*)	15 ml (*1 tbsp*)	15–30 ml (*1–2 tbsps*)	30 ml (*2 tbsps*)	30–45 ml (*2–3 tbsps*)	45 ml (*3 tbsps*)	60 ml (*4 tbsps*)	90 ml (*6 tbsps*)
Time (approx)	2½–3 hrs	3 hrs	3½ hrs	4 hrs	6 hrs	7 hrs	8 hrs	8½ hrs
Weight when cooked	1.1 kg (*2½ lb*)	1.6 kg (*3¼ lb*)	2.2 kg (*4¾ lb*)	2.7 kg (*6 lb*)	4 kg (*9 lb*)	5.2 kg (*11½ lb*)	6.7 kg (*14¾ lb*)	7.7 kg (*17 lb*)

Note For icing quantities see page 400.

30.5 and 20.5 cm *(12 and 8 in)* or 25.5 and 15 cm *(10 and 6 in)*. The bottom tier should be deeper than the upper ones, therefore cakes of 25.5–30.5 cm *(10–12 in)* diameter are generally made about 7.5 cm *(3 in)* deep, while those 18–23 cm *(7–9 in)* are 6.5 cm *(2½ in)* deep and 12.5–15 cm, 5 cm *(5–6 in, 2 in)* deep. Don't attempt to make the bigger sizes of cake unless you have a really large oven, as you should allow at least 2.5 cm *(1 in)* space between the oven walls and the tin. For a three-tier cake, bake the two smaller ones together and the largest one separately.

You can expect to cut 8–10 portions of cake from each 450 g *(1 lb)* cooked mixture.

Cake boards

Silver is the usual colour (except for a Golden Wedding cake). The board should be 2.5 cm *(1 in)* larger than the cake, eg for a 20.5-cm *(8-in)* cake use a 23-cm *(9-in)* board. For a very large cake use a board 5 cm *(2 in)* bigger than the cake.

CAKES OF UNUSUAL SHAPE

Fruit cake mixture

150 g *(5 oz)* currants
50 g *(2 oz)* sultanas
50 g *(2 oz)* raisins, stoned
12 glacé cherries, halved
45 ml *(3 tbsps)* chopped mixed peel
100 g *(3½ oz)* plain flour
1.25 ml *(¼ level tsp)* mixed spice
75 g *(3 oz)* butter or margarine
75 g *(3 oz)* soft brown sugar
1½ eggs

Sandwich cake mixture

50 g *(2 oz)* butter or margarine
50 g *(2 oz)* caster sugar
1 egg
50 g *(2 oz)* self raising flour

If you want to make an unconventionally shaped cake, such as a numeral or a heart shape, the amount of cake mixture needed can be worked out from the capacity of the tin. (Remember to fill the tin only as deep as you want the finished cake to be – not necessarily to the very top.)

For every 600 ml *(1 pt)* of water the tin will hold, you will need fruit cake mixture made with the ingredients listed here, so multiply up as required.

If you use Victoria sandwich cake mixture you will need for each 600 ml *(1 pt)* of capacity, ingredients as listed here.

Make either cake in the usual way. Bake the fruit cake mixture in the oven at 150°C *(300°F)* mark 1–2 and the Victoria sandwich in a moderate oven 180°C *(350°F)* mark 4. The time of course varies according to the shape and depth of the cake.

ICING A FORMAL CAKE

Quantities

The amount of almond paste quoted will give a thin layer.

The amount of royal icing should be enough to give 2 coats plus simple decorations.

		15 cm *(6 in)* square	18 cm *(7 in)* square	20.5 cm *(8 in)* square	23 cm *(9 in)* square	25.5 cm *(10 in)* square	28 cm *(11 in)* square	30.5 cm *(12 in)* square
	15 cm *(6 in)* round	18 cm *(7 in)* round	20.5 cm *(8 in)* round	23 cm *(9 in)* round	25.5 cm *(10 in)* round	28 cm *(11 in)* round	30.5 cm *(12 in)* round	
Almond paste	350 g *(¾ lb)*	450 g *(1 lb)*	550 g *(1¼ lb)*	800 g *(1¾ lb)*	900 g *(2 lb)*	1 kg *(2¼ lb)*	1.1 kg *(2½ lb)*	1.4 kg *(3 lb)*
Royal icing	450 g *(1 lb)*	550 g *(1¼ lb)*	700 g *(1½ lb)*	900 g *(2 lb)*	1 kg *(2¼ lb)*	1.1 kg *(2½ lb)*	1.4 kg *(3 lb)*	1.6 kg *(3½ lb)*

Coffee crackle (p. 349).

(Overleaf) Blender berry cheese mousse (p. 335), Iced raspberry soufflé (p. 330), Strawberry foam (p. 316), Red-currant griestorte (p. 318).

Almond paste

225 g *(½ lb)* icing sugar
225 g *(½ lb)* caster sugar
450 g *(1 lb)* ground almonds
2 standard eggs, lightly beaten
5 ml *(1 tsp)* vanilla essence
lemon juice

Sift the icing sugar into a bowl and mix with the caster sugar and almonds. Add the essence, with sufficient egg and lemon juice to mix to a stiff dough. Form into a ball and knead lightly. This makes 900 g *(2 lb)* almond paste.

Boiled marzipan (see page 486) can also be used to cover a cake.

To apply almond paste

Trim the top of the cake if necessary. Measure round the cake with a piece of string. Brush the sides of the cake generously with sieved apricot jam. Take half the almond paste, form it into a roll and roll out as long as the string and as wide as the cake is deep. Press the strip firmly on to the sides of the cake, smoothing the join with a round-bladed knife and keeping the edges square. Brush the top of the cake with jam. Dredge the working surface generously with icing sugar, then roll out the remaining almond paste into a round to fit the top of the cake. Turn the cake upside down, centring it exactly on the paste, and press it down firmly. Smooth the join, loosen the paste from the board and turn the cake the right way up. Check that the top edge is quite level. Leave for 2–3 days before coating with royal icing.

Almond paste decorations

Simple but attractive decorations for an iced cake can be made from almond paste and they are particularly suitable for Christmas or birthday cakes. Draw the chosen shape on stiff paper and cut it out. (Stars, candles, holly leaves, Christmas trees, houses or engines make good designs, as they have bold outlines.) Colour some almond paste by working edible colouring in evenly; roll out very thinly on a board sprinkled with icing sugar, lay the pattern on it and cut round with a sharp-pointed knife. For holly berries, roll tiny balls of red-tinted paste. Leave the shapes on a plate till quite dry, then stick them on to the royal icing (which must be firm), using a dab of fresh icing.

Royal icing

Allow 4 egg whites to every 900 g *(2 lb)* icing sugar; 15 ml *(1 tbsp)* glycerine may be added to give a softer texture. Sift the sugar twice. Separate the eggs, place the whites in a bowl and stir slightly – just sufficiently to break up the albumen, but without including too many air bubbles. Add half the icing sugar and stir until well mixed, using a wooden spoon; beat for about 5–10 minutes, or until the icing is smooth, glossy and white. Cover the bowl with a damp cloth or damped greaseproof paper and leave to stand for at least ½ hour, to allow any air bubbles to rise to the surface.

Gradually add the remaining icing sugar until the required consistency is obtained. When the icing is intended for flat work, stand a wooden spoon upright in it – if the consistency is correct it will fall slowly to one side. For rough icing, the mixture should be stiff enough for peaks to be easily formed on the surface when you 'pull' it up with the spoon. Add any desired colouring. If possible, leave the icing overnight in an airtight container in a cool place before use. To obtain a really smooth result, just before using the icing, remove 15 ml *(1 level tbsp)* of it and mix to a coating consistency with water, return it to the rest and mix until smooth.

Notes 1. Royal icing can be made quite satisfactorily in an electric mixer; set the control on 'medium' speed and whisk the egg whites slightly. Now add the sifted sugar gradually until the mixture is of the

Pineapple cheesecake mousse (p. 334).

required consistency. It is important to avoid over-beating and to allow the icing to stand for 24 hours before using it.
2. When using royal icing, it is advisable to keep the bowl and/or filled forcing bags covered with a damp cloth or a polythene bag, to prevent a crust forming on the icing.

To rough-ice a cake

Place 5 ml *(1 tsp)* of the icing on the cake-board and put on the cake firmly, centring it accurately. Spoon the icing on top of the cake. Working with a palette knife in a to-and-fro motion until the air bubbles are broken, cover the top and sides of the cake evenly. Now draw a clean ruler or palette knife across the top of the cake evenly and steadily, until the surface is smooth. Using a round-bladed knife, draw the icing up into peaks round the sides and in a 4-cm *(1½-in)* border round the top of the cake – or as liked. Before the icing is set, you can put on one or two simple decorations.

If you want a very simply decorated cake, put almond paste on the top only of the cake and then royal icing on the top and down the sides for about 2.5 cm *(1 in)*, so that the almond paste is hidden. Rough-ice the sides and make a border round the cake as above. Decorate as desired and tie a ribbon round the cake below the icing. For this sort of decoration use half the suggested amounts of almond paste and royal icing.

Flat-icing a cake

Place the cake on the cake-board. Spoon about half the icing on top of it and with a palette knife work with a to-and-fro motion across the icing until the air bubbles are broken and the top of the cake is well and evenly covered. Some of the icing will work down the sides of the cake – return this to the bowl. Now draw an icing ruler or the palette knife across the top of the cake evenly and steadily. Draw it across again at right angles to the first stroke until the surface is smooth. If possible, leave the cake for 24 hours. (In this case, put the icing from the bowl into a polythene bag and store in a refrigerator.)

Put the cake and board on an upturned plate or a turn-table and work the remaining icing on to the sides of the cake. Draw a ruler, knife or baker's card round the sides until they are smooth. Smooth out the join between top and sides, then leave to set for at least 24 hours. Finally, remove any unevenness with a sharp knife.

If liked, apply a second layer of icing to give a really smooth finish. Save a little of the royal icing and mix it with a little water to give a coating consistency; pour on to the centre of the cake then, using a knife, spread it over the top and down the sides. Knock the board gently up and down on the table to bring any air bubbles to the surface, so that they can be burst with a pin before the icing sets. Leave to harden for 2–3 days.

PIPED ICING DECORATION

Butter cream, stiff glacé icing and royal icing can all be piped on to cakes. It is usual for each kind to be used on a base of the same type of icing, though butter cream can be piped on to glacé icing. Use butter cream or glacé icing for decorating sponge cakes and royal icing for the formal decoration of fruit cakes.

When you are decorating a royal-iced cake, let the flat coat of icing harden for several days before attempting the next stage. Plan out the scheme on a piece of greaseproof paper of the same size as the cake, lay this on the icing and with a pin prick out the design lightly, to act as a guide.

The icing used for piping must be free of all lumps, which might block the nozzles; it must also be of such a consistency that it can be forced easily through the pipe but will retain its shape.

Special icing pumps can be bought, but are more difficult to manage than paper forcing bags (made as follows) or small polythene forcing bags.

To make and use a paper forcing bag

1. Fold a 25-cm *(10-in)* square of greaseproof or non-stick paper into a triangle.
2. Holding the right angle of the triangle towards you, roll over one of the other corners to meet it. Roll the second corner over in the opposite direction to meet the first at the back of the bag. Adjust the two corners over one another until a point is formed at the tip.
3. Fold over the corners several times, to secure them in position.
4. Cut a small piece from the tip of the bag and drop in the required metal nozzle or pipe.
5. To use the bag, place a little icing in it and fold the top over once or twice. When piping, hold the bag in one hand as though it were a pencil, with the thumb in the centre to give an even pressure. If you are inexperienced, first practise piping on an upturned plate. Remember that icing can easily be removed while it is still soft, so mistakes can be corrected.

The pipes

For a simple design – which is often the most effective – these types of pipes or nozzles are usually needed:

1. Writing pipes in 3 sizes, to make lines, scallops, dots and words.
2. Star pipes for rosettes, zigzags and ropes.
3. Shell pipe.

For advanced work, use a petal pipe for flowers and bows and a leaf pipe for leaves.

Borders, trellis motifs, plaques

Borders Bold patterns such as shells, ropes and rosettes are used at the point where the cake and board meet; delicate lines and dots are used for the sides and top.

Trellis This can be very effective. Using a writing nozzle, pipe parallel lines in one direction across the space to be covered; when these are dry, pipe more lines on top of them, but in the other direction. For a really good finish, pipe another line on top of the second set, using a very fine pipe. If any 'tails' of icing are left at beginning and end of a line, trim them off while still soft. Don't attempt to pipe a line with the nozzle touching the cake, as this results in an uneven finish – hold the tip of the nozzle above the surface of the cake and let the icing fall in a straight line.

Flowers and leaves Various types of flower can be piped, and when coloured they can look most realistic. Make them in advance, so that they can become really dry before being used.

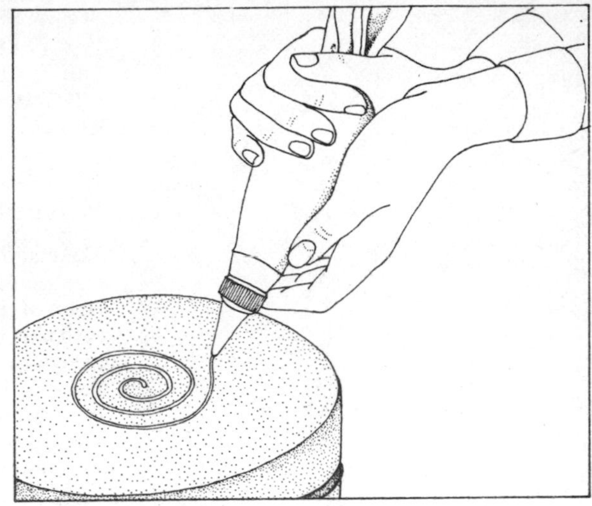

Using a forcing bag

Stick a piece of greaseproof paper to an icing nail with icing and work on this surface.

To pipe a rose, use a petal pipe, held so that the thin edge is uppermost; twisting the stem of the nail between the fingers, pipe a tight centre for the rosebud, then make 5–6 petals round this centre, overlapping them and making them spread outwards.

For a narcissus, work with the thick edge of the pipe to the centre; pipe 5 petals and a centre.

For a pansy, pipe 4 small overlapping petals and one larger one at the bottom.

When the flowers are dry, remove them from the papers. Fix to the cake with a small dab of icing.

Leaves are piped with the special nozzle, often directly on to the surface of the cake.

Plaques of any shape or size can easily be made if you are prepared to spend time and a certain amount of care. They need to be made at least 10 days before the cake is to be assembled.

Flat plaques are the simplest to make, but small curved ones can be shaped on the outside of the tins in which the cakes were baked, so that they will fit the sides of the cakes.

Draw the required shape on a piece of paper, cover this with waxed or non-stick paper and stick it on to a pastry board or to the side of the tin with a little icing. Using a No. 1 or 2 writing pipe, outline the design, then fill in the centre with icing, thinned to a running consistency. Use a hat-pin or a large needle to coax the icing up to the edge and into the corners. Make twice the number of plaques you will eventually need, as they break easily.

When the plaques are dry and firm, after about 2–3 days, add any extra decorations, such as initials or flowers. A week later ease the paper from the back of the plaques to allow the underside to dry out, before sticking them on to the cake.

WEDDING CAKE DESIGNS

First coat the cake as already described with almond paste and royal icing.

Rosebud cake

Make sufficient sugar roses (about 270 for a three-tier cake – see directions already given). Using a No. 1 or No. 2 writing nozzle, pipe 3 layers of fine trellis (see directions already given), covering the top of each tier, but leaving spaces for the pillars. Stick the roses round the top edge of each cake with a little icing and pipe leaves in between the flowers. Tie a ribbon round each tier and stick sugar roses to it at intervals to form a spray; pipe leaves in between the flowers. Pipe a shell edging round the base of each cake on to its board, using the largest pipe for the bottom tier. Put the pillars in position and arrange roses and leaves round the bases. When the whole cake is assembled, top it with a small spray of fresh or artificial roses.

Lace-iced cake

Make 50 sugar roses. Mark 8 scallops on the largest cake by means of a paper pattern; mark 4 scallops on the other cakes. Using a No. 2 or 3 writing pipe, pipe a double line round the scallops, then pipe fine dots between these lines. Fill in the space between the scallops and the edge of the cake with a 'wiggly' line to suggest lace, using a No. 1 or 2 writing pipe. Decorate the sides of the cake with more of the 'lace' pattern. Pipe shell edging round the top edges of the cake and below this pipe a row of fine dots. Pipe a larger shell edge round the bases of the cakes on to the boards. Put the pillars in position and arrange the roses round them. Add a few silver leaves and horseshoes.

Lover's knot cake

Make some plaques for the sides of the cake, 4 for each tier (see directions already given) and decorate with lover's knots piped with a petal pipe.

Pipe a row of large dots round the top edges of the cake. On either side, at the top and bottom of each alternate dot, pipe 2 smaller dots. Repeat this pattern round the bases of the cakes and on to the boards. Stick the plaques into position with a little icing and pipe a row of fine dots round each. Add any silver motifs that are being used and finally assemble the cake.

NOVELTY CAKES

Mushroom cake

100 g *(4 oz)* butter or margarine
150 g *(6 oz)* caster sugar
2 eggs
100 g *(4 oz)* self raising flour
1 egg white
chocolate butter cream, made with 100 g *(4 oz)* butter, 225 g *(8 oz)* icing sugar (see page 384)
small piece almond paste
desiccated coconut
green colouring

Line two 18-cm *(7-in)* sandwich tins. Make a Victoria sandwich cake mixture (see page 365) from the butter, 100 g *(4 oz)* of the caster sugar, the whole eggs and the flour. Bake in the oven at 180°C *(350°F)* mark 4 for about 20 minutes. Whisk the egg white until stiff, whisk in half the remaining 50 g *(2 oz)* sugar, fold in the remainder and form the mixture into small meringues of varying sizes.

When the cakes are cold, sandwich them together with some of the butter cream; spread most of the remainder over the sides and top, then mark with a fork. Make 'stalks' of almond paste and stick them to the base of the meringues with a little butter cream. Using a small writing nozzle, pipe the underside of the mushroom caps with butter cream to represent gills. Tint the coconut with a little green colouring dissolved in water. Place the cake on a board, surround with the coconut and decorate with the meringue mushrooms, placing some of them on the board and some on the cake itself.

Snowman cake

Suitable for the centrepiece at any around-Christmas-time children's party.

175 g *(6 oz)* butter or margarine
175 g *(6 oz)* caster sugar
3 eggs
175 g *(6 oz)* self raising flour, or 150 g *(5 oz)* self raising flour and 45 ml *(3 level tbsps)* cocoa
jam, or vanilla or chocolate butter cream made with 100 g *(4 oz)* butter, 225 g *(8 oz)* icing sugar (see page 384)
chocolate glacé icing, made with 275 g *(10 oz)* icing sugar (see page 385)
12 white marshmallows
6 chocolate drops

Line a 20.5-cm *(8-in)* cake tin. Make a plain or chocolate Victoria sandwich cake (see page 365), using the fat, sugar, eggs and flour, and bake in the oven at 180°C *(350°F)* mark 4 for 45–50 minutes. When it is cool, split it into 3 layers and sandwich together with jam or butter cream. Coat the cake evenly all over with the glacé icing. When this is dry, decorate the edge with marshmallow snowmen (see below) and arrange a group of tiny Christmas trees on the top.

To make the snowmen Use 2 marshmallows for each man. Cut each marshmallow in half through the middle. Two portions form the body and head, while the other 2 are again cut in half lengthwise to make arms and legs. Place in position to form a man, pressing the cut sides on to the icing round the edge of the cake. Use a chocolate drop for a hat. Mark the features with piped butter cream or use silver balls, small pieces of glacé cherry and so on.

Beehive cake

For cake
225 g *(8 oz)* butter or margarine
175 g *(6 oz)* caster sugar
50 g *(2 oz)* clear honey
4 eggs
225 g *(8 oz)* self raising flour

For icing
225 g *(8 oz)* soft tub margarine
450 g *(1 lb)* icing sugar, sifted
15 ml *(1 level tbsp)* instant coffee dissolved in 15 ml *(1 tbsp)* hot water
30 ml *(2 tbsps)* evaporated milk
25 g *(1 oz)* plain chocolate
a little icing sugar, sifted
yellow food colouring
imitation bees

Cream the butter and sugar until light and fluffy. Beat in the honey and add the eggs one at a time, beating well between each. Fold in the flour. Put the mixture in a greased 1.4-l *(2½-pt)* ovenproof pudding basin. Bake at 180°C *(350°F)* mark 4 for about 1 hour. Remove the cake from the basin and cool it on a wire tray. When cool, cut off the top of the cake (the rounded part) to make a flat base. Place the cake on a board or turntable.

Beat the margarine until soft. Add the icing sugar a little at a time, then beat in the coffee and milk. Using a piping bag fitted with a small vegetable nozzle, pipe a continuous spiral to cover the cake. Melt the chocolate in a bowl over hot water and spread thinly on a piece of greaseproof paper. When the chocolate is set, cut out a door for the hive. Mix a little icing sugar with water to give a thick piping consistency. Colour with yellow food colouring. Using a piping bag with a plain nozzle, pipe 'Hunny Home' on the door. Attach the door and bees to the cake.

Yule log

Make a Swiss roll mixture and bake it in the usual way (see page 372). Roll it up without filling, allow to cool, unroll and spread with chocolate butter cream (page 384). Re-roll, coat the outside with more of the chocolate butter cream and fork this to suggest the markings of a tree trunk. Decorate as you wish, adding a model robin if available.

Lilac butterfly cake

For cake
175 g *(6 oz)* **butter or margarine**
175 g *(6 oz)* **caster sugar**
3 eggs
175 g *(6 oz)* **self raising flour**
red, yellow and green food colourings
225 g *(8 oz)* **marzipan**
a little apricot jam

For icing
450 g *(1 lb)* **icing sugar, sifted**
water
purple colouring
1 fruit jelly sweet
liquorice strips

Cream together the butter and sugar until light and fluffy. Add the eggs one at a time, beating well between each addition. Fold in the flour. Divide the mixture into three and colour each with a different food colour. Place spoonfuls of the coloured mixtures in the base of a greased and lined 20.5-cm *(8-in)* square cake tin. Bake at 180°C *(350°F)* mark 4 for 30–35 minutes. Cool on a wire tray. Roll the marzipan out to a 20.5-cm *(8-in)* square, reserving a small piece for the butterfly's body. Brush the cake with apricot jam and place the marzipan on top. Place the cake on a board. Cut as in diagram. Put the wings on a wire tray.

Add sufficient water to the 450 g *(1 lb)* icing sugar to form a thick coating consistency. Reserve 45 ml *(3 tbsps)* of the icing and colour this pale lilac. Put in an icing bag fitted with a plain icing nozzle. Ice each wing with white glacé icing. Immediately pipe 4 lines parallel to the long edge. Using a skewer, draw a line across the lilac piping to give a 'feathered' effect. When the icing has set, arrange the wings on a cake board. Colour the reserved marzipan with purple colouring and mould it into a body shape. Place it in position and put a sweet at the top of the body to represent the head. Use thin strips of liquorice to make antennae. If you wish, pipe whipped double cream or butter cream around the edge.

Candy house cake

For cake
275 g *(10 oz)* **butter or margarine**
275 g *(10 oz)* **caster sugar**
5 eggs
275 g *(10 oz)* **self raising flour**
175 g *(6 oz)* **glacé cherries, chopped**
milk to mix
raspberry jam

For icing
225 g *(8 oz)* **soft tub margarine**
450 g *(1 lb)* **icing sugar, sieved**
30 ml *(2 tbsps)* **evaporated milk**
cochineal

Decorations
1½ pkt pink and white marshmallows
1 cocktail stick
4 red Parkinsons Fruit Thins
pink sugar flowers

Cream together the butter and sugar until light and fluffy. Beat in the eggs one at a time. Add the flour and cherries, stirring until the mixture reaches a dropping consistency adding milk if necessary. Put mixture in a greased and lined 30.5 by 25.5-cm *(12 by 10-in)* slab tin. Bake at 180°C *(350°F)* mark 4 for 40–50 minutes. Remove from the tin and cool on a wire rack. Cut the cake as shown in the diagram. Sandwich roof pieces together with raspberry jam. Spread jam on base and place roof on (see diagram).

Beat the margarine until soft. Beat in the icing sugar a little at a time. Add evaporated milk and mix to a soft consistency. Reserve 15 ml *(1 tbsp)* of icing. Colour the rest with cochineal until a fairly strong pink. Put the cake on a board and spread the icing over. Cut all but two (white) marshmallows through the middle with wet scissors and arrange the pink ones on over-lapping lines on the roof. Cut the white marshmallows in half again and arrange along the eaves. Stick the remaining whole marshmallows on a cocktail stick and use as a chimney on the roof. Place fruit sweets on the front of the house for door and windows. Using the reserved white icing in a piping bag fitted with a plain nozzle, pipe frames on the window and trailing branches around the door. Put sugar flowers on the branches.

Chocolate express

For slab cake
275 g *(10 oz)* butter or margarine
275 g *(10 oz)* caster sugar
5 eggs
275 g *(10 oz)* self raising flour
milk

For Swiss roll
3 eggs
100 g *(4 oz)* caster sugar
100 g *(4 oz)* plain flour
15 ml *(1 tbsp)* water
warm jam

For choclate icing
700 g *(1½ lb)* icing sugar, sifted
175 g *(6 oz)* plain chocolate
60 ml *(4 tbsps)* water

For butter cream
100 g *(3½ oz)* butter or margarine
200 g *(7 oz)* icing sugar, sifted

For decoration
Liquorice Allsorts

Make the slab cake as for Candy House, omitting the cherries.

For the Swiss roll, put the eggs and sugar in a basin over a pan of hot water. Whisk until the mixture is light, thick and forms a trail. Remove from the heat. Sift flour over the surface and fold in gently with a metal spoon. Lightly stir in hot water. Pour the mixture into a lined 30.5 by 23-cm *(12 by 9-in)* Swiss roll tin. Bake in the oven at 220°C *(425°F)* mark 7 for 7–9 minutes. Turn the cake out on to greaseproof paper placed on top of a damp tea towel. Trim off the edges and spread the surface with warm jam. Roll up. Cut thc cakcs as shown in the diagrams. Split the cabin side and front section horizontally through the middle to make four pieces. Cut a small strip from the tender sides (shaded area on diagram). Using a small round cutter, stamp out a funnel from the remaining section.

Put the chocolate and water in a pan and heat gently, stirring until the chocolate has melted. Remove from the heat and stir in the icing sugar until you reach a coating consistency. Add a little extra warm water if the icing is very thick. Use the chocolate icing at once to coat all the cake pieces. Make a butter cream, beating the butter until soft and gradually beating in icing sugar until a smooth consistency is obtained. Cover an oblong board or piece of thick card with foil. Place the largest piece of chocolate iced cake on the board. Spread a little butter cream on the underside of the train body and place it on the base. Spread more butter cream over the cabin end of the body and join one of front sections to this in an upright position. Spread butter cream over the narrow ends and top of one front section and fix the cabin sides to it. Use the other front section as a roof. To make a tender, cover the end of the base with butter cream and join on back section. Spread butter cream along one narrow edge of each side portion and place in position on the base, as shown in diagram. Spread a little butter cream on each wheel and stick in place against the sides of the base. Using a small star nozzle, pipe on the rest of the butter cream. Stick on a funnel and fill the tender with sweets.

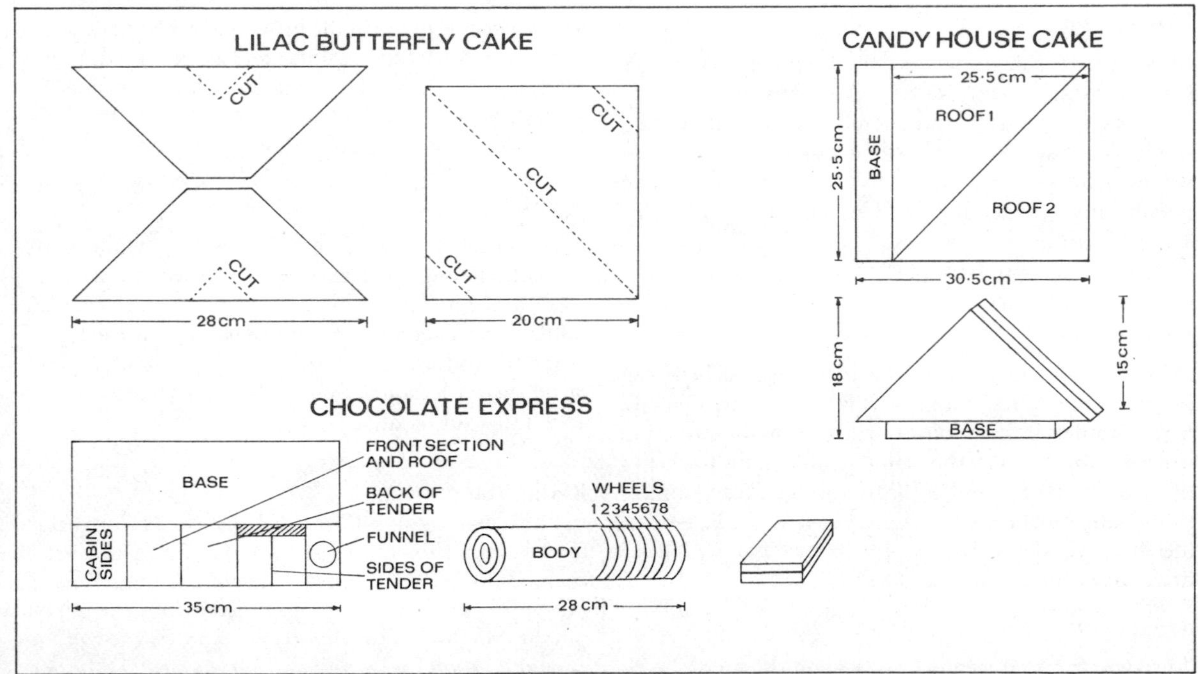

Bread, rolls and buns

Yeast cookery still has a slight aura of mystery, but there is nothing intrinsically difficult about it. The main thing is to realise that yeast, unlike other raising agents, is a living plant, requiring gentle warmth in order to grow. Like any other plant, yeast also requires food and water, and these it obtains from the carbohydrates in the flour and from the moisture used in making the dough. Under these conditions, yeast grows rapidly and as it grows a harmless and tasteless gas – carbon dioxide – is formed. The bubbles of this gas are responsible for the sponginess of the mixture; the growing yeast also produces alcohol, which gives the characteristic yeasty smell and taste to freshly baked bread.

Once you have tackled some simple bread-making, you will almost certainly want to progress to dough cakes, fancy breads, buns and perhaps a continental rum baba or savarin. The taste and texture of home-made bread make it so different from the mass-produced shop variety that you will probably find yourself making it more and more often.

Yeast

Fresh yeast Since this does not keep long it is better bought in small quantities only. It looks rather like putty in colour and texture and should have a faint 'winey' smell. When stored in a polythene bag in a cool place, it will keep for 4–5 days, depending on its freshness when bought; in a refrigerator it will keep for up to a month – again, according to how fresh it was when bought.

As soon as the outside of the yeast becomes dark and the yeast itself is dry and crumbly, it is no longer suitable for use and must be discarded.

Dried yeast, which is available in tins and packets, can be stored for up to 6 months. It is in the form of small, hard granules, fawn in colour. Instructions for activating it are usually given by the manufacturer on the packet or tin. You should remember that it will take 15–20 minutes to activate, longer than for fresh yeast. When substituting dried yeast for fresh you will need 15 ml *(1 tbsp)* dried yeast for 25 g *(1 oz)* fresh.

Flour

The type to use depends of course on the bread being made, but it must always be a plain flour – self raising flour should not be used, as it gives a close, cake-like texture. The best results are obtained by using a 'strong' plain flour. If a 'strong' plain flour is not available, a plain flour is suitable but will not give nearly such a good result.

These are other speciality flours:

Wholemeal 100 per cent wheat.

Wheatmeal 81–95 per cent wheat (ie some of the bran is removed).

Stone-ground More expensive, but of very good flavour, since the heat arising during the grinding 'toasts' the flour slightly. Available as wholemeal and wheatmeal.

Rye flour Gives the typical continental rye bread.

Warmth

For yeast mixtures the bowl, the flour and the liquid used for mixing should all be warmed. Liquids should be at about blood heat, 37°C *(98°F)*, ie so that they feel just warm when tested with the little finger. Once the dough is mixed, it must be kept warm and away from draughts. On the other hand, too great heat kills the yeast, so neither the mixing liquid nor the place where the dough is put to rise must be really hot.

Fat

Fat is not essential for plain mixtures, but the addition of a small amount helps to keep the bread moist. When used, it is generally rubbed into the warmed flour and salt, but in richer mixtures, when more fat is used, it can be melted and added with the liquid ingredients or flaked on to the basic dough, as for flaky pastry. Oil may be added instead of fat.

Rising the dough

All yeast doughs must be risen at least once before baking to allow time for the yeast to work. Doughs must be covered during this stage to prevent the formation of a skin and loss of heat. The easiest way to carry this out is to put the dough to rise in a lightly oiled polythene bag large enough to allow for the rise and loosely tied. At the later, shaped, stage place the tin or baking sheet inside a similarly prepared bag and leave to rise until dough is double in size and springs back when gently pressed with a lightly floured finger. Remove polythene bag before baking.

Tins

When ever reference is made to 450-g *(1-lb)* or 900-g *(2-lb)* loaf tins, the approximate size to use is 20.5 by 10 by 6.5-cm *(8 by 4 by 2½-in)* and 23 by 13 by 7-cm *(9 by 5 by 3-in)* top measurement.

White bread *see colour plate facing p. 544*

700 g *(1½ lb)* strong plain flour
10 ml *(2 level tsps)* salt
knob lard
15 g *(½ oz)* fresh yeast or 7.5 ml *(1½ level tsps)* dried yeast and 5 ml *(1 level tsp)* caster sugar
400 ml *(¾ pt)* tepid water (43°C, *110°F*)

Grease a 900-g *(2-lb)* loaf tin or 2 450-g *(1-lb)* tins, or 2 baking sheets if making rolls.

Sift the flour and salt into a large bowl and rub in the lard. Blend the fresh yeast with the water. If using dried yeast, dissolve the sugar in the water, sprinkle the yeast over and leave until frothy. Mix the dry ingredients with the yeast liquid, adding the liquid all at once. Stir in with a wooden fork or spoon. Work it to a firm dough, adding extra flour if needed, until it will leave the sides of the bowl clean. Do not let the dough become too stiff as it produces heavy 'close' bread.

Turn the dough on to a floured surface and knead thoroughly, to stretch and 'develop' it. To do this, hold the dough towards you, then push down and away with the palm of your hand. Continue kneading until the dough feels firm and elastic and no longer sticky – about 10 minutes. Shape it into a ball.

Put the dough in a lightly oiled polythene bag to prevent a skin forming (the bag must be large enough to allow the dough to rise), tie it loosely and allow to rise until it is doubled in size and will spring back when pressed with a floured finger.

Allow time for the rising of the dough to fit with your day's arrangements, but the best results are achieved with a slow rise. Allow ¾–1 hour in a warm place, ie above the cooker or in the airing cupboard at about 23°C *(75°F)*, 2 hours at average room temperature, up to 12 hours in a cold larder or up to 24 hours in the refrigerator.

Refrigerated risen dough must be allowed to return to room temperature before it is shaped – about 1 hour.

Turn the risen dough on to a lightly floured surface, flatten it firmly with the knuckles to knock out the air bubbles, then knead to make it firm and ready for shaping (do not use too much flour or the colour of the crust will be spoilt). Stretch the dough into an oblong the same width as the tin, fold it into 3 and turn it over so that the 'seam' is underneath. Smooth over the top, tuck in the ends and place in a greased 900-g *(2-lb)* loaf tin. For 2 small loaves, divide the dough into 2 and continue as above; for rolls, divide the dough into 50-g *(2-oz)* pieces and roll each into a ball, place on the baking sheets about 2.5 cm *(1 in)* apart – makes about 18.

Place the tin inside a lightly oiled polythene bag and leave to rise again until the dough comes to the top of the tin and springs back when pressed with a floured finger. Leave for 1–1½ hours at room temperature, or longer in a refrigerator. Leave rolls until doubled in size.

Remove the polythene bag, place the tin on a baking sheet and put in the centre of the oven. Put a pan of boiling water on the oven bottom. Bake at 230°C *(450°F)* mark 8 for 30–40 minutes, 15–20 minutes for rolls, until well risen and golden brown. Rolls will double in size. When the loaf is cooked it will shrink slightly from the sides of the tin, and will sound hollow if you tap the bottom of the tin. Turn out and cool on a wire rack.

Quick white loaf *see colour plate facing p. 544*

15 g *(½ oz)* fresh yeast or 7.5 ml *(1½ level tsps)* dried yeast and 5 ml *(1 level tsp)* caster sugar
about 300 ml *(½ pt)* tepid water
450 g *(1 lb)* strong plain flour
5 ml *(1 level tsp)* salt

Blend the fresh yeast with the water. If using dried yeast, dissolve the sugar in the water, sprinkle the yeast over and leave until frothy. Mix the flour and salt, make a well in the centre and add the yeast liquid. Mix to an elastic dough, adding more water if necessary. Turn on to a floured board and knead for about 5 minutes, until really smooth. Divide the dough into 2 portions and put into 2 small prepared tins; put the tins in lightly oiled polythene bags and allow to rise in a warm place (about 23°C, *75°F*) until the dough fills the tins and springs back when lightly pressed. Bake at 230°C *(450°F)* mark 8 as described above.

The unrisen dough may also be divided in half, made into 2 round cakes, left to rise on a greased baking sheet for 30–45 minutes and baked as for ordinary bread – allow 30–40 minutes.

If the dough is made into rolls, bake for 15–20 minutes.

Quick cheese loaf

Use the above recipe, but add 100 g *(4 oz)* finely grated Cheddar cheese, 5 ml *(1 level tsp)* dry mustard and 2.5 ml *(½ level tsp)* pepper to the flour and salt.

Milk bread

Use the same basic recipe and method as for white bread (basic recipe), but rub 50 g *(2 oz)* lard or butter into the dry ingredients and mix the dough with milk or milk and water. This gives a close-textured loaf with a softer crust.

Wholemeal bread *see colour plate facing p. 544*

50 g *(2 oz)* fresh yeast or 30 ml *(2 level tbsps)* dried yeast and 5 ml *(1 level tsp)* caster sugar
900 ml *(1½ pt)* tepid water
1.4 kg *(3 lb)* plain wholemeal flour
30 ml *(2 level tbsps)* caster sugar
20–25 ml *(4–5 level tsps)* salt
25 g *(1 oz)* lard

Blend the fresh yeast with 300 ml *(½ pt)* of the water. For dried yeast, dissolve 5 ml *(1 level tsp)* sugar in 300 ml *(½ pt)* water, sprinkle the yeast over and leave until frothy. Mix the flour, 30 ml *(2 level tbsps)* sugar and salt; rub in the lard. Stir the yeast liquid into the dry ingredients, adding sufficient of the remaining water to make a firm dough that leaves the bowl clean. Turn it out on to a lightly floured surface and knead until it feels firm and elastic and no longer sticky. Shape it into a ball and put it in a lightly oiled polythene bag to prevent a skin forming. Tie the bag loosely and leave the dough to rise in a warm place (23°C, *75°F*) until doubled in size. Turn the dough out on to a floured surface and knead again until firm. Divide into 2 or 4 pieces and flatten firmly with the knuckles to knock out any air bubbles. Knead well to make it firm and ready for shaping. Shape to fit two 900-g *(2-lb)* or four 450-g *(1-lb)* tins. Brush tops with salted water. Put each one in a lightly oiled polythene bag, tie loosely and leave until the dough rises to the tops of the tins – about 1 hour at room temperature. Bake the loaves in the oven at 230°C *(450°F)* mark 8 for 30–40 minutes. Cool on a wire rack.

Alternative shapings

1. Divide each quarter-portion of dough into 4 smaller pieces, shape into rolls and fit side by side into the tin. Finish as above.
2. Shape each quarter-portion of dough into a round cob, dust with flour and put on a floured baking sheet. Finish as before.
3. Shape all the dough into a round cob and place on a large floured baking sheet. Partly cut into 4 wedges and scatter cracked wheat or

flour over the top. Allow to rise, mark again and bake for 40–45 minutes.

Quick wholemeal bread

15 g (*½ oz*) fresh yeast or 10 ml (*2 level tsps*) dried yeast and 5 ml (*1 level tsp*) caster sugar
about 300 ml (*½ pt*) tepid water
5 ml (*1 level tsp*) sugar
450 g (*1 lb*) wholemeal flour or 225 g (*½ lb*) wholemeal and 225 g (*½ lb*) strong plain flour
5–10 ml (*1–2 level tsps*) salt
25 g (*1 oz*) lard

Blend the fresh yeast with the water. For dried yeast, dissolve 5 ml (*1 level tsp*) sugar in 150 ml (*¼ pt*) water, sprinkle the yeast over and leave until frothy. Mix the sugar, flour and salt and rub in the fat. Add the yeast liquid and remaining water and mix with a wooden spoon to give a fairly soft dough, adding more water if necessary. Turn it on to a floured board and knead well. Divide the dough into two and put into greased 450-g (*1-lb*) tins (or divide in half, shape into rounds and put on a greased baking sheet). Put the tins in lightly oiled polythene bags, tie loosely and leave to rise in a warm place (about 23°C, *75°F*) until the bread fills the tins (or the rounds have nearly doubled in size). Bake in the oven at 230°C (*450°F*) mark 8 for about 15 minutes, reduce the heat to 200°C (*400°F*) mark 6 and cook for a further 30–40 minutes for loaves, 20–30 minutes for rounds.

Apricot and walnut bread

Make up the preceding recipe using half wholemeal and half white flour and adding 100 g (*4 oz*) walnuts, chopped rather coarsely, and 225 g (*8 oz*) dried apricots, cut into pieces; mix the nuts and fruit with the rubbed-in ingredients before adding the yeast and water.

Malt bread

25 g (*1 oz*) fresh yeast or 15 ml (*1 level tbsp*) dried yeast and 5 ml (*1 level tsp*) caster sugar
about 150 ml (*¼ pt*) tepid water
450 g (*1 lb*) plain flour (*not* strong plain flour)
5 ml (*1 level tsp*) salt
60 ml (*4 tbsps*) malt
15 ml (*1 tbsp*) black treacle
25 g (*1 oz*) butter or margarine
sugar and water glaze, optional

Blend the fresh yeast in the water.

For dried yeast, dissolve the sugar in the water, sprinkle the yeast over it and leave until frothy. Mix the flour and salt. Warm the malt, treacle and fat till just melted. Stir the yeast liquid and malt mixtures into the dry ingredients and mix to a fairly soft, sticky dough, adding a little more water if necessary. Turn on to a floured board, knead well until the dough is firm and elastic. Divide into two pieces. Shape both into an oblong, roll up like a Swiss roll and put into 2 prepared 450-g (*1-lb*) loaf tins. Leave to rise in a warm place (about 23°C, *75°F*) until the dough fills the tins; this may take about 1½ hours, as malt bread dough usually takes quite a long time to rise. Bake in the oven at 200°C (*400°F*) mark 6 for 30–40 minutes. When cooked the loaves can be brushed with a sugar glaze of 15 ml (*1 level tbsp*) sugar to 15 ml (*1 tbsp*) water.

Currant bread

15 g (*½ oz*) fresh yeast or 7.5 ml (*1½ level tsps*) dried yeast and 5 ml (*1 level tsp*) sugar
about 400 ml (*¾ pt*) tepid milk
550 g (*1¼ lb*) strong plain flour
10 ml (*2 level tsps*) salt
25 g (*1 oz*) lard
225 g (*8 oz*) currants
30 ml (*2 tbsps*) cut mixed peel
sugar and milk to glaze, optional

Blend the fresh yeast with most of the milk. For dried yeast, dissolve the sugar in half the milk, sprinkle the yeast over and leave until frothy. Mix the flour and salt, rub in the fat and stir in the fruit and peel. Add the yeast liquid and enough of the remaining milk to give a fairly soft dough. Beat well. Turn the dough on to a floured board and knead until it feels firm and elastic. Leave to rise in a warm place (about 23°C, *75°F*) until doubled in size. Knead lightly on a floured board, divide into 2 pieces, flatten each and roll up like a Swiss roll to fit a greased 450-g (*1-lb*) loaf tin. Prove for about 20 minutes, until the dough fills the tins, bake in the oven at 230°C (*450°F*) mark 8 for about 15 minutes, reduce the heat to 190°C (*375°F*) mark 5 and cook for a further 30–40 minutes.

If you prefer, cut the risen and kneaded dough in half and shape each piece into a round, put on a greased baking sheet and allow to prove, then bake as for a loaf, allowing a slightly shorter cooking time.

The top of the currant loaves can be brushed over with a glaze made by dissolving 15 ml *(1 level tbsp)* sugar in 15 ml *(1 tbsp)* milk – do this directly after taking the bread from the oven.

Milk rolls

15 g *(½ oz)* fresh yeast or 7.5 ml *(1½ level tsps)* dried yeast and 5 ml *(1 level tsp)* sugar
about 150 ml *(¼ pt)* tepid milk
225 g *(8 oz)* strong plain flour
5 ml *(1 level tsp)* salt
25 g *(1 oz)* margarine or lard

Blend the fresh yeast with the milk. For dried yeast, dissolve the sugar in the milk, sprinkle the yeast over and leave until frothy. Mix the flour and salt and rub in the fat. Add the yeast liquid and mix to a fairly soft dough, adding a little more milk if necessary. Beat well and knead on a floured board until smooth. Allow to rise in a warm place (about 23°C, *75°F*) until doubled in size, knead lightly on a floured board, divide into 8 pieces and shape in any of the following ways:

Plait Divide the small piece of dough into three, shape each into a long roll and plait together, joining the ends securely.

Twist Divide a piece of dough into two, shape into long rolls, twist together and secure the ends.

Cottage loaf Cut two-thirds off a piece of dough and make into a bun shape; treat the remaining one-third in the same way; damp the smaller one, place on top of the larger one and secure by pushing your little finger right through the centre.

Knots Shape each piece into a long roll and tie a knot.

Round Place the pieces on a very slightly floured board and roll each into a ball. To do this, hold the hand flat almost at table level and move it round in a circular motion, gradually lifting the palm to get a good round shape.

Rings Make a long roll with each piece of dough and bend it round to form a ring; damp the ends and mould them together.

Put the shaped rolls on a greased baking sheet and allow to rise for 15–20 minutes. Bake in the oven at 220°C *(425°F)* mark 7 for about 15 minutes, until golden brown and cooked. The rolls can if you wish be brushed with milk or beaten egg before cooking, to give a glazed finish.

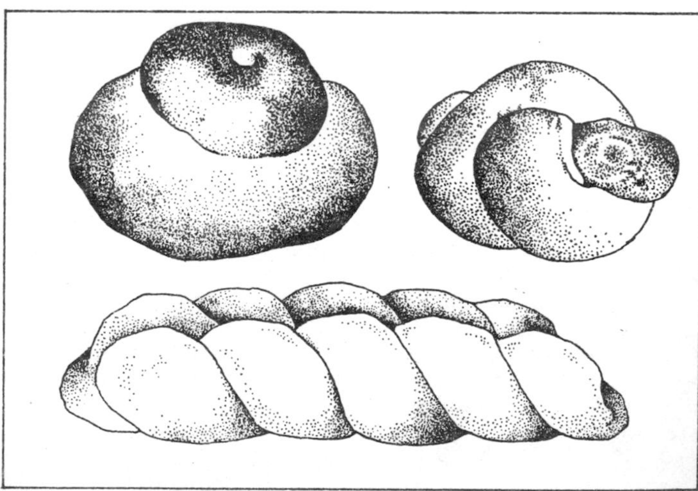

Shaping rolls – cottage loaf, knot and plait

Floury Scotch baps and morning rolls

15 g *(½ oz)* **fresh yeast or 7.5 ml** *(1½ level tsps)* **dried yeast and 2.5 ml** *(½ level tsp)* **caster sugar**
300 ml *(½ pt)* **tepid milk and water, mixed**
450 g *(1 lb)* **strong plain flour**
5 ml *(1 level tsp)* **salt**
50 g *(2 oz)* **lard**

Flour a baking sheet. Blend the fresh yeast with the liquid. For dried yeast, dissolve the sugar in the liquid, sprinkle the dried yeast on top and leave until frothy. Sift together the flour and salt and rub in the lard. Stir in the yeast liquid and work to a firm dough, adding extra flour if needed, until the dough leaves the bowl clean. Turn on to a lightly floured surface and knead for about 5 minutes. Place the dough in an oiled polythene bag and tie loosely. Allow to rise at room temperature for about 1½ hours, or until the dough springs back when pressed lightly with a floured finger. Use two-thirds of the dough to make a large bap. Shape it into a ball and roll out with a floured rolling pin to about 2–2.5 cm *(¾–1 in)* in thickness. Place on a well floured baking sheet and dredge the top with flour.

Divide the remaining dough into 3 or 4 equal-sized pieces, shape each into a ball and roll out to an oval about 1 cm *(½ in)* thick. Place on the floured baking sheet and dredge the tops with flour. Cover with a sheet of oiled polythene or a polythene bag and allow to rise at room temperature until doubled in size – about 45 minutes.

Press each roll and the bap gently in the centre with three fingers, to prevent blisters. Bake in the oven at 200°C *(400°F)* mark 6 for 20–30 minutes for the bap, 15–20 minutes for the morning rolls. Cool on a wire rack.

Bridge rolls

15 g *(½ oz)* **fresh yeast or 7.5 ml** *(1½ level tsps)* **dried yeast and 5 ml** *(1 level tsp)* **sugar**
100 ml *(4 fl oz)* **tepid milk**
225 g *(8 oz)* **plain flour**
5 ml *(1 level tsp)* **salt**
50 g *(2 oz)* **butter or margarine**
1 egg, beaten

Blend the fresh yeast with the milk. For dried yeast, dissolve the sugar in the milk, sprinkle the yeast over and leave until frothy. Mix the flour and salt and rub in the fat. Add the yeast liquid and egg and mix to a fairly soft dough, adding a little extra milk if necessary. Beat well and knead the dough on a floured board until smooth. Leave in a warm place (23°C, *75°F*) until doubled in size. Knead lightly on a floured board, then cut into 12–16 pieces. Make each into a finger or roll shape and place fairly close together in rows on a greased baking sheet. Allow to rise for 15–20 minutes. Bake in the oven at 220°C *(425°F)* mark 7 for about 15 minutes. These rolls can be brushed with beaten egg before cooking, to give a glazed finish.

TRADITIONAL AND RICH YEAST MIXTURES

Lardy cake

15 g *(½ oz)* **fresh yeast or 10 ml** *(2 level tsps)* **dried yeast and 5 ml** *(1 level tsp)* **caster sugar**
300 ml *(½ pt)* **tepid water**
450 g *(1 lb)* **strong plain flour**
10 ml *(2 level tsps)* **salt**
cooking oil
50 g *(2 oz)* **butter**
100 g *(4 oz)* **caster sugar**
5 ml *(1 level tsp)* **powdered mixed spice**
75 g *(3 oz)* **sultanas or currants**
50 g *(2 oz)* **lard**

Grease a tin measuring 25.5 by 20.5 cm *(10 by 8 in)*. Blend the fresh yeast with the water. For dried yeast, dissolve the sugar in the water, sprinkle the yeast over and leave until frothy. Sift the flour and salt into a basin and stir in the yeast mixture, with 15 ml *(1 tbsp)* oil to give a manageable soft dough. Beat until smooth. Leave in a warm place (about 23°C, *75°F*) to rise until doubled in size.

Turn the dough out on to a lightly floured surface and knead for 5–10 minutes. Roll out to a strip 0.5 cm *(¼ in)* thick. Cover two-thirds of the dough with small flakes of butter and 45 ml *(3 tbsps)* sugar, and sprinkle with half the spice and half the dried fruit. Fold and roll out as for flaky pastry. Repeat the process with the lard, 45 ml *(3 tbsps)* sugar and the remaining spice and fruit. Fold and roll once more.

Place the dough in the prepared tin, pressing it down so that it fills the corners. Cover, and leave to rise in a warm place until doubled in size. Brush with oil, sprinkle with the remaining caster sugar and mark criss-cross fashion with a knife. Bake in the oven at 220°C *(425°F)* mark 7 for about 30 minutes. Cool on a wire rack. Serve sliced, plain or with butter.

Sally Lunn

50 g *(2 oz)* **butter**
200 ml *(7 fl oz)* **tepid milk**
5 ml *(1 level tsp)* **caster sugar**
2 eggs
15 g *(½ oz)* **fresh yeast**
450 g *(1 lb)* **strong plain flour**
5 ml *(1 level tsp)* **salt**
sugar glaze (see below)

Thoroughly grease two 12.5-cm *(5-in)* round cake tins. Melt the butter slowly in a pan, remove from the heat and add the milk and sugar. Beat the eggs and add with the warm milk mixture to the yeast. Blend well. Add to the flour and salt, mix well and lightly knead. Put into the cake tins and leave to rise in a warm place (about 23°C, *75°F*) until the dough fills the tins – about ¾–1 hour. Bake in the oven at 230°C *(450°F)* mark 8 for 15–20 minutes. Turn the Sally Lunns out of the tins on to a wire rack, and glaze while still hot.

Glaze Put 15 ml *(1 tbsp)* water and 15 ml *(1 tbsp)* sugar in a small pan, heat to boiling point and boil for a further 2 minutes; use at once.

Doughnuts

15 g *(½ oz)* **fresh yeast or 7.5 ml** *(1½ level tsps)* **dried yeast and 5 ml** *(1 level tsp)* **sugar**
about 60 ml *(4 tbsps)* **tepid milk**
225 g *(8 oz)* **plain flour**
2.5 ml *(½ level tsp)* **salt**
knob of butter or margarine
1 egg, beaten
jam
deep fat for frying
sugar and ground cinnamon to coat

Blend the fresh yeast with the milk. For dried yeast, dissolve the sugar in the milk, sprinkle the yeast over and leave until frothy. Mix the flour and salt and rub in the fat. Add the yeast liquid and egg and mix to a soft dough, adding a little more milk if necessary. Beat well until smooth and leave to rise until doubled in size. Knead lightly on a floured board and divide into 10–12 pieces. Shape each into a round, put 5 ml *(1 tsp)* stiff jam in the centre and draw up the edges to form a ball, pressing firmly to seal them together. Heat the fat to 182°C *(360°F)* or until it will brown a 2.5-cm *(1-in)* cube of bread in 60 seconds. Fry the doughnuts fairly quickly until golden brown (for 5–10 minutes, according to size). Drain on crumpled kitchen paper and toss in sugar mixed with a little cinnamon (if you like). Serve the same day they are made.

Devonshire splits

15 g *(½ oz)* **fresh yeast or 7.5 ml** *(1½ level tsps)* **dried yeast and 5 ml** *(1 level tsp)* **sugar**
about 300 ml *(½ pt)* **tepid milk**
450 g *(1 lb)* **strong plain flour**
5 ml *(1 level tsp)* **salt**
50 g *(2 oz)* **butter**
30 ml *(2 level tbsps)* **sugar**
Devonshire or whipped cream and jam

Blend the fresh yeast with half the milk. For dried yeast, dissolve the sugar in half the milk, sprinkle the yeast over and leave until frothy. Sift the flour and salt, dissolve the butter and sugar in the remaining milk and when at blood heat, stir into a well in the centre of the flour with the yeast liquid. Beat to an elastic dough, turn it out on to a floured board and knead until smooth. Allow to rise in a warm place (about 23°C, *75°F*) until doubled in size, then turn it on to a lightly floured board and divide into 14–16 pieces. Knead each lightly into a ball, place on a greased baking sheet and flatten slightly with the hand. Put to rise in a warm place for about 20 minutes and bake in the oven at 220°C *(425°F)* mark 7 for 15–20 minutes. Before serving, split them and spread with jam and Devonshire or whipped cream, then sprinkle the tops with icing sugar.

Yorkshire teacakes

25 g *(1 oz)* fresh yeast or 15 ml *(1 level tbsp)* dried yeast and 5 ml *(1 level tsp)* sugar
300–400 ml *($\frac{1}{2}$–$\frac{3}{4}$ pt)* tepid milk or milk and water
450 g *(1 lb)* strong plain flour
5 ml *(1 level tsp)* salt
50 g *(2 oz)* butter or lard
30 ml *(2 level tbsps)* sugar
100 g *(4 oz)* currants
30 ml *(2 tbsps)* cut mixed peel
sugar and milk glaze

Blend the fresh yeast with half the milk. For dried yeast, dissolve the sugar in half the milk, sprinkle the yeast over and leave until frothy. Mix the flour and salt, rub in the fat and stir in the sugar, currants and peel. Add the yeast liquid and sufficient of the remaining liquid to give a fairly soft dough. Beat well, turn it on to a floured board and knead until smooth. Allow to rise in a warm place (about 23°C, *75°F*) until doubled in size, turn on to a lightly floured board and divide into 4–6 large or 12 smaller pieces. Knead lightly into rounds and put on a greased baking sheet. Allow to rise for 15–20 minutes and bake in the oven at 220°C *(425°F)* mark 7 for 15–30 minutes, according to size. When the cakes are cooked, brush with a glaze made by dissolving 15 ml *(1 level tbsp)* sugar in 15 ml *(1 tbsp)* milk and return them to the oven for a further 1–2 minutes for the glaze to dry.

Hot cross buns

450 g *(1 lb)* strong plain flour
25 g *(1 oz)* fresh yeast or 15 ml *(1 level tbsp)* dried yeast
5 ml *(1 level tsp)* caster sugar
150 ml *($\frac{1}{4}$ pt)* milk
60 ml *(4 tbsps)* water
5 ml *(1 level tsp)* salt
2.5 ml *($\frac{1}{2}$ level tsp)* mixed spice
2.5 ml *($\frac{1}{2}$ level tsp)* powdered cinnamon
2.5 ml *($\frac{1}{2}$ level tsp)* grated nutmeg
50 g *(2 oz)* caster sugar
50 g *(2 oz)* butter, melted and cooled, but not firm
1 egg, beaten
100 g *(4 oz)* currants
30–45 ml *(2–3 tbsps)* chopped mixed peel
50 g *(2 oz)* shortcrust pastry, ie made with 50 g *(2 oz)* flour (see page 351)

For the glaze
60 ml *(4 tbsps)* milk and water
45 ml *(3 level tbsps)* caster sugar

Flour a baking sheet. Place 100 g *(4 oz)* of the flour in a large mixing bowl and add the yeast and 5 ml *(1 level tsp)* sugar. Warm the milk and water to about 43°C *(110°F)* add to the flour and mix well. Set aside in a warm place until frothy – 10–15 minutes for fresh yeast, 20 minutes for dried.

Sift together the remaining 350 g *(12 oz)* flour, salt, spices and 50 g *(2 oz)* sugar. Stir the butter and egg into the frothy yeast mixture, add the spiced flour and the fruit, and mix together. The dough should be fairly soft. Turn it out on to a lightly floured surface and knead until smooth. Leave to rise until doubled in size – about 1–1$\frac{1}{2}$ hours. Turn the risen dough out on to a floured surface and knock out the air bubbles, then knead.

Divide the dough into 12 pieces and shape into buns, using the palm of one hand. Press down hard at first on the table surface, then ease up as you turn and shape the buns. Arrange them well apart on the floured baking sheet, and put to rise for about 30 minutes. Roll out the pastry thinly on a floured board and cut into thin strips about 9 cm *(3$\frac{1}{2}$ in)* long. Damp the pastry strips and lay two on each bun to make a cross. Bake in the oven at 190°C *(375°F)* mark 5 for 15–20 minutes, until golden brown and firm to the touch. Meanwhile, heat the milk and water and sugar gently together. Brush the hot buns twice with glaze, then leave to cool.

Note If time is short, omit the pastry crosses and mark a cross on each bun with a sharp knife.

Chelsea buns *see colour plate facing p. 577*

225 g *($\frac{1}{2}$ lb)* strong plain flour
15 g *($\frac{1}{2}$ oz)* fresh yeast or 7.5 ml *(1$\frac{1}{2}$ level tsps)* dried yeast
100 ml *(4 fl oz)* tepid milk
2.5 ml *($\frac{1}{2}$ level tsp)* salt
knob of butter or lard, about 15 g *($\frac{1}{2}$ oz)*
1 egg, beaten
melted butter
75 g *(3 oz)* dried fruit
30 ml *(2 tbsps)* chopped mixed peel
50 g *(2 oz)* soft brown sugar
clear honey to glaze

Grease an 18-cm *(7-in)* square cake tin. Put 50 g *(2 oz)* of the flour in a large bowl and blend together with the yeast and milk until smooth. Set aside in a warm place (about 23°C, *75°F*) until the batter froths – 10–20 minutes. Mix the remaining flour and the salt; rub in the fat. Mix into the batter with the egg to give a fairly soft dough that will leave the side of the bowl clean after beating. Turn the dough out on to a lightly floured surface and knead until it is smooth – about 5 minutes. Leave to rise for 1–1$\frac{1}{2}$ hours. Knead the dough thoroughly and roll out to an oblong 30 by 23 cm *(11$\frac{3}{4}$ by 9 in)*. Brush with melted butter and cover with a mixture of dried fruit, peel and brown sugar.

Roll up from the longest side like a Swiss roll, and seal the edge with water. Cut into 9 equal-sized slices and place these, cut side down, in the prepared cake tin. Prove until the dough feels springy – about 30 minutes. Bake the buns in the oven at 190°C *(375°F)* mark 5 for about 30 minutes.

While they are still warm, brush them with a wetted brush dipped in honey.

Bath buns

450 g *(1 lb)* **strong plain flour**
25 g *(1 oz)* **fresh yeast or 15 ml** *(1 level tbsp)* **dried yeast**
5 ml *(1 level tsp)* **caster sugar**
150 ml *(¼ pt)* **milk**
60 ml *(4 tbsps)* **water**
5 ml *(1 level tsp)* **salt**
50 g *(2 oz)* **caster sugar**
50 g *(2 oz)* **butter, melted and cooled, but not firm**
2 eggs, beaten
175 g *(6 oz)* **sultanas**
30–45 ml *(2–3 tbsps)* **chopped mixed peel**
beaten egg and crushed sugar lumps for topping

Put 100 g *(4 oz)* of the flour in a large mixing bowl. Add the yeast and 5 ml *(1 level tsp)* sugar. Warm the milk and water to about 43°C *(110°F)*; add to the 100 g *(4 oz)* flour and mix well. Set aside in a warm place until frothy – about 20 minutes. Sift together the remaining flour and salt and add the 50 g *(2 oz)* sugar. Stir the butter and eggs into the frothy mixture, add the flour, sultanas and peel and mix well – the dough is fairly soft. Turn it out on to a floured surface and knead until smooth. Leave it to rise in a covered bowl until doubled in size. When it is ready, beat well. Place in about 18 spoonfuls on greased baking sheets, cover and leave to rise. Brush with egg and sprinkle with crushed sugar.

Bake in the oven at 190°C *(375°F)* mark 5 for about 15 minutes, until golden; cool on a rack. Serve buttered.

Poppy seed plait

450 g *(1 lb)* **strong plain flour**
5 ml *(1 level tsp)* **caster sugar**
25 g *(1 oz)* **fresh yeast or 15 ml** *(1 level tbsp)* **dried yeast**
250 ml *(8 fl oz)* **warm milk**
5 ml *(1 level tsp)* **salt**
50 g *(2 oz)* **margarine**
1 egg, beaten

For the glaze and topping
beaten egg
5 ml *(1 level tsp)* **caster sugar**
15 ml *(1 tbsp)* **water**
poppy seeds

Put 150 g *(5 oz)* of the flour into a large bowl and blend with the sugar, yeast, and milk. Set aside in a warm place until frothy – about 20 minutes. Mix the remaining flour with the salt and rub in the margarine. Add the egg and the flour mixture to the yeast batter and mix well to give a fairly soft dough that will leave the sides of the bowl clean. Turn the dough on to a lightly floured board and knead until smooth and no longer sticky – about 10 minutes (no extra flour should be necessary). Leave to rise in a warm place (23°C, *75°F*) until doubled in size. Knead the dough lightly on a floured board, divide in half and roll each half into an oblong.

Cut each half into 3 strips lengthwise, keeping the dough just joined at the top. Plait the strips, damp the ends and seal together. Place on a lightly greased baking sheet. Brush with glaze and sprinkle with poppy seeds. Put to rise until doubled in bulk. Bake in the oven at 190°C *(375°F)* mark 5 for 45–50 minutes.

Rum babas *see colour plate facing p. 545*

25 g *(1 oz)* **fresh yeast or 15 ml** *(1 level tbsp)* **dried yeast**
90 ml *(6 tbsps)* **tepid milk**
225 g *(8 oz)* **strong plain flour**
2.5 ml *(½ level tsp)* **salt**
30 ml *(2 level tbsps)* **caster sugar**
4 eggs, beaten
100 g *(4 oz)* **butter, soft but not melted**
100 g *(4 oz)* **currants**
whipped cream

For the rum syrup
120 ml *(8 tbsps)* **clear honey**
120 ml *(8 tbsps)* **water**
rum to taste

Lightly grease about 16 9-cm *(3½-in)* ring tins with lard. Put the yeast, milk and 50 g *(2 oz)* of the flour in a bowl and blend until smooth. Allow to stand in a warm place until frothy – about 20 minutes. Add the remaining flour, the salt, sugar, eggs, butter and currants, and beat well for 3–4 minutes. Half-fill the tins with the dough and allow to rise until the moulds are two-thirds full.

Bake in the oven at 200°C *(400°F)* mark 6 for 15–20 minutes. Cool for a few minutes, then turn out on to a wire tray.

While the babas are still hot, spoon over each sufficient rum syrup to soak it well. Leave to cool. Served with whipped cream in the centre.

Rum syrup Warm together the honey and water and add rum (or rum essence) to taste.

Lemon meringue rice pudding (p. 303).

Savarin

Make up the same mixture as for rum babas, omitting the currants, but put into one large ring tin. Bake at 200°C *(400°F)* mark 6 for about 40 minutes, or until golden and shrinking away from the sides of the tin. Turn out straight away and allow to cool. Soak with rum syrup (see baba recipe), brush with sieved apricot jam and serve on a dish surrounded by fruit salad and topped with whipped cream.

Brioche

15 g *(½ oz)* fresh yeast or 7.5 ml *(1½ level tsps)* dried yeast and 2.5 ml *(½ level tsp)* caster sugar
25 ml *(1½ tbsps)* warm water
225 g *(8 oz)* strong plain flour
a pinch of salt
15 ml *(1 level tbsp)* caster sugar
2 standard eggs, beaten
50 g *(2 oz)* butter, melted
beaten egg to glaze

Blend the fresh yeast with the water. For dried yeast, dissolve the sugar in the water, sprinkle the yeast over and leave until frothy. Sift together the flour, salt and 15 ml *(1 level tbsp)* sugar. Stir the yeast liquid into the flour, with the eggs and butter. Work to a soft dough, turn out on to a floured board and knead for about 5 minutes. Put the dough in an oiled polythene bag and leave to rise at room temperature for 1–1½ hours, until it is doubled in size and springs back when gently pushed with a floured finger. Brush a 1.1-l *(2-pt)* fluted mould with oil.

Knead the dough well on a lightly floured surface. Shape three-quarters of it into a ball and place in the bottom of the mould. Press a hole in the centre as far as the tin base, and put in the middle the remainder of the dough, shaped as a 'knob'; press down lightly.

Place the mould in the oiled polythene bag and leave at room temperature until the dough is light and puffy and nearly reaches the top of the mould – about 1 hour. Brush it lightly with egg glaze and bake in the oven at 230°C *(450°F)* mark 8 for 15–20 minutes, until golden. Turn out and cool.

Note For small brioches divide the dough into 12 pieces, put into deep 7.5-cm *(3-in)* fluted patty tins (oiled), and bake as above for about 10 minutes.

Danish pastries *see colour plate facing p. 576*

The basic dough
25 g *(1 oz)* fresh yeast or 15 ml *(1 level tbsp)* dried yeast and 5 ml *(1 level tsp)* sugar
about 150 ml *(¼ pt)* water
450 g *(1 lb)* plain flour – not strong
5 ml *(1 level tsp)* salt
50 g *(2 oz)* lard
30 ml *(2 level tbsps)* sugar
2 eggs, beaten
300 g *(10 oz)* butter
beaten egg to glaze

Blend the fresh yeast with the cold water. For dried yeast, dissolve the sugar in tepid water, sprinkle the yeast over and leave until frothy. Mix the flour and salt, rub in the lard and stir in the 30 ml *(2 level tbsps)* sugar. Add the yeast liquid and beaten eggs and mix to an elastic dough, adding a little more water if necessary. Knead lightly. Cover the bowl and leave the dough to 'rest' in the refrigerator for 10 minutes. Work the butter with a knife until soft and form it into an oblong. Roll out the dough on a floured board into an oblong about three times the size of the butter, put the butter in the centre of the dough and enclose it, overlapping the unbuttered sides just across the middle and sealing the open sides with a rolling pin.

Turn the dough so that the folds are to the sides and roll into a strip three times as long as it is wide; fold the bottom third up, and the top third down, cover and leave to 'rest' for 10 minutes. Turn, repeat, rolling, folding and resting twice more and use as required.

Crescents Roll out half of the dough thinly and cut out two 23-cm *(9-in)* rounds. Divide each into 8 segments and put a little almond

Cinnamon-apple pancakes (p. 310).

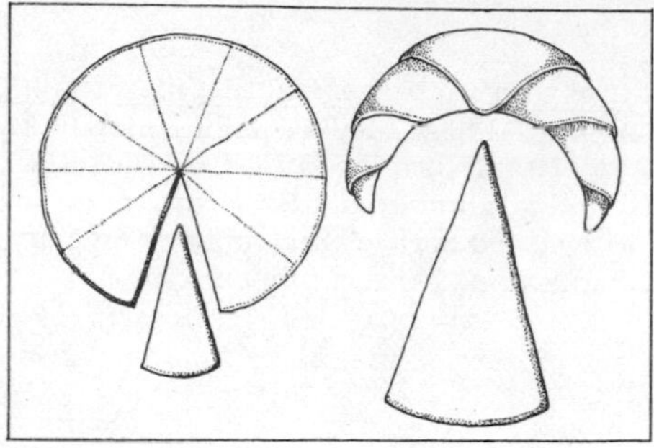
Crescents

Imperial stars

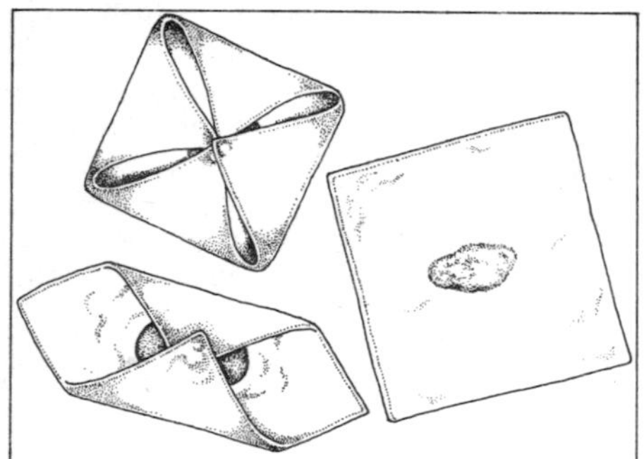
Cushions

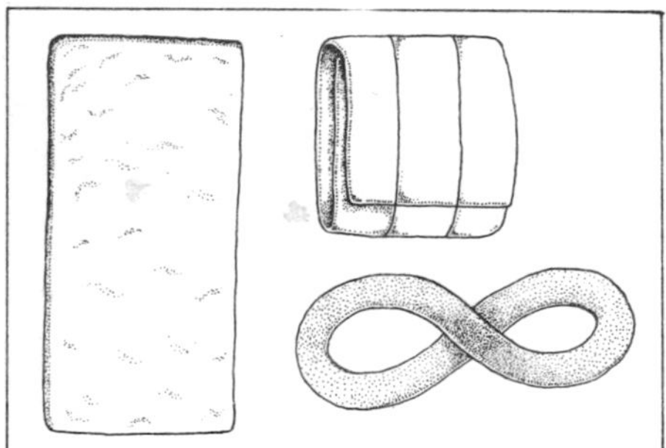
Twists

paste or confectioners' custard mixture at the base of each. Roll up from the base and curl round to form a crescent. *Makes 16 pastries.*

Imperial stars Roll out half of the dough thinly, cut into 7.5-cm *(3-in)* squares and make diagonal cuts from each corner to within 1 cm *(½ in)* of the centre. Put a piece of almond paste in the centre of the square and fold one corner of each cut section down to the centre, securing the tips with a little beaten egg. *Makes about 16 pastries.*

Cushions Using 7.5-cm *(3-in)* squares, put a little almond paste in the centre and either fold over 2 alternate corners to the centre or fold over all 4 corners, securing the tips with beaten egg.

Pinwheels Roll out half of the dough into two oblongs 30 cm *(12 in)* long and 20.5 cm *(8 in)* wide. Spread with cinnamon butter and sultanas, roll up like Swiss rolls, cut into 2.5-cm *(1-in)* slices and place cut side upwards on a baking sheet. *Makes about 16 pastries.*

Twists Roll out half dough as above. Cut each oblong lengthwise to give 4 pieces. Spread with cinnamon butter and fold the bottom third up and the top third down. Cut each across into thin slices. Twist these slices and put on a baking sheet. *Makes about 16 pastries.*

Fillings for Danish pastries

Almond paste

Cream the butter and sugar, stir in the almonds and add enough egg to make a pliable consistency; add a few drops of almond essence if you wish.

Confectioner's custard or pastry cream

Cream the egg yolks and sugar together until really thick and pale in colour. Beat in the flour and cornflour and a little cold milk to make a smooth paste. Heat the rest of the milk in a saucepan until almost boiling and pour on to the egg mixture, stirring well all the time. Return the mixture to the saucepan and stir over a low heat until the mixture boils. Beat the egg white until stiff. Remove the custard mixture from the heat and fold in the egg white. Again return the pan to the heat, add essence to taste and cook for a further 2–3 minutes. Cool before using.

Cinnamon butter

Cream the butter and sugar and beat in the cinnamon.

To finish Danish pastries

After shaping them, prove for 20–30 minutes. Brush with beaten egg and bake in the oven at 220°C *(425°F)* mark 7 for about 15 minutes. While they are still hot, brush with thin white glacé icing (see page 384) and sprinkle them with flaked or chopped almonds which have been lightly browned under the grill. Finish the centres of imperial stars and cushions with a blob of confectioner's custard or red-currant jelly.

Almond paste
15 g *(½ oz)* butter
75 g *(3 oz)* caster sugar
75 g *(3 oz)* ground almonds
1 beaten egg
almond essence (optional)

Confectioner's custard or pastry cream
1 whole egg, separated
1 egg yolk
50 g *(2 oz)* caster sugar
30 ml *(2 level tbsps)* plain flour
30 ml *(2 level tbsps)* cornflour
300 ml *(½ pt)* milk
vanilla essence

Cinnamon butter
50 g *(2 oz)* butter
50 g *(2 oz)* caster sugar
10 ml *(2 level tsps)* ground cinnamon

Biscuits and cookies

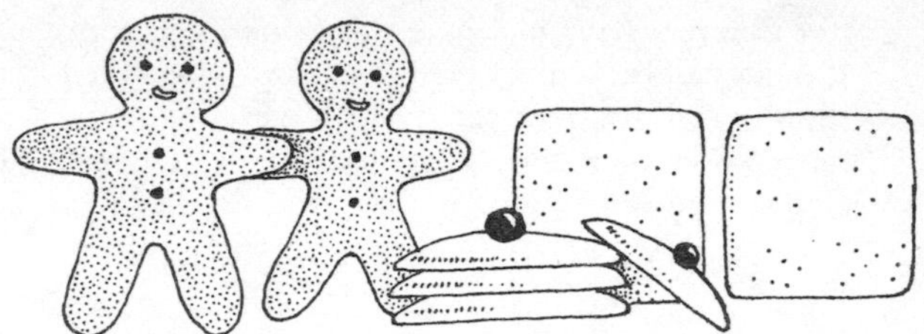

Home-made cookies can be quite irresistible. Dozens of versions can be made from each simple basic recipe, and for every variation on a theme that we suggest here, you will probably conjure up another of your own.

Rolled biscuits are the traditional basic cookies. In every instance, chill the dough slightly if you find it difficult to roll thinly, and roll out between sheets of non-stick or waxed paper. Adding extra flour to stop the sticking will make the biscuit less tender and can spoil the final look. But if you do use flour, be sure to brush away the surplus. In a hot kitchen, handle these doughs a little at a time and leave the rest in the refrigerator to chill.

Drop cookies are made from a soft dough and spooned directly on to the baking sheet. Actually, 'drop' is misleading, since the mixture must be stiff enough to need pushing from the spoon. The texture is variable; it can be soft and cake-like or crisp and even brittle. Drop cookies are often irregular in shape as they tend to spread as they bake, but that is part of their charm.

Shaped cookies are cut from soft doughs that need quick and deft handling, moulded with the palm of the hand into small balls. Dampen your palms if the dough sticks.

Refrigerator cookie doughs are useful to have by you. The cookies they make are always crisp, buttery and flavourful, their individual taste and finish depending on the extra ingredients you add to the basic recipe.

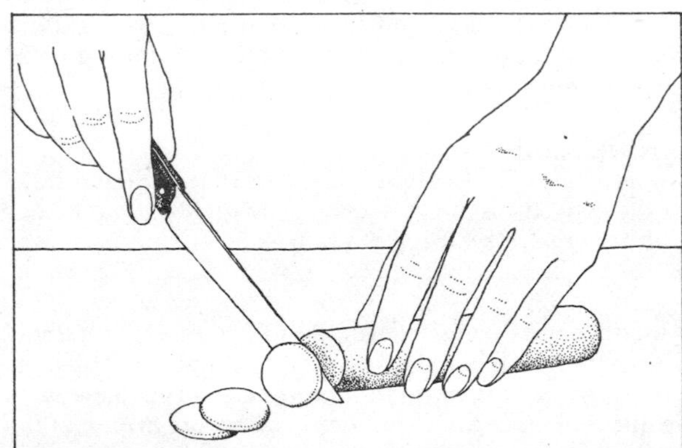

Slicing refrigerator cookie dough

The dough must always be chilled until it is firm, so that it can be sliced as thinly and evenly as possible. The great advantage is that this dough can be kept in the refrigerator ready to be baked as needed for oven-fresh batches on demand.

Piped cookies look very special but don't take any more time to make; they are a good choice when cooking for large numbers. They have a crisp yet melt-in-the-mouth texture, served plain or paired with a filling.

Bar cookies are baked in one large block, cooled, then cut into squares or bars. Flapjacks are probably the best known of these.

For perfect baking

Have all biscuits even in size and rolled to the same thickness for overall browning.

Use a flat baking sheet with hardly any sides. High sides prevent proper browning.

Not enough baking sheets? The back of any large shallow pan may be substituted. Adjust oven shelves to accommodate the extra height if you are using inverted pans this way.

If you are baking one sheet of cookies at a time, place the oven rack at the centre of the oven or just above it. For two sheets, place the racks so as to divide the oven into thirds. If the tops of the cookies don't brown properly, move them to a high position for the last few minutes of baking. Watch carefully.

Check cookies just before the minimum baking time is up. To cool, transfer them with a wide flexible spatula to wire racks. Press down the spatula on the baking sheet and ease it under the cookies.

Some cookies – especially those with syrup or honey as an ingredient – are still soft after baking, so leave them for a few minutes before lifting them off the sheet.

Don't overlap cookies while cooling.

For ideal storing

Line the bottom of an airtight container with waxed or non-stick paper; place a sheet of waxed paper between each two layers of cookies or between each single layer of soft ones.

A slice of apple, changed frequently, helps to keep soft cookies moist in their containers.

Store different types of cookie in separate containers. Bar cookies can be kept in the baking tin and covered tightly with foil to save space.

Store cookies plain, not iced or sugar-dredged. Dress up later as required.

Remember that most home-made varieties will keep for up to two weeks.

If plain cookies lose their crispness, return them to a baking sheet and freshen in oven at 170°C *(325°F)* mark 3 for about five minutes without over-browning.

ROLLED BISCUITS

Shrewsbury biscuits

125 g *(4 oz)* butter or margarine
150 g *(5 oz)* caster sugar
1 egg yolk
225 g *(8 oz)* plain flour
grated rind of 1 lemon

Grease 2 large baking sheets. Cream the fat and sugar until pale and fluffy. Add the egg yolk and beat well. Stir in the flour and lemon rind and mix to a fairly firm dough. Knead lightly and roll out to about 0.5-cm *(¼-in)* thickness on a lightly floured surface. Cut into rounds with a 6.5-cm *(2½-in)* fluted cutter and put on the baking sheets. Bake at 180°C *(350°F)* mark 4 for about 15 minutes until firm and a very light brown colour. *Makes 20–24.*

Spice biscuits
Omit the lemon rind and add 5 ml *(1 level tsp)* mixed spice and 5 ml *(1 level tsp)* ground cinnamon, sifted with the flour.

Vanilla biscuits
Omit the lemon rind and add a few drops of vanilla essence when adding the egg.

Fruit biscuits
Add 50 g *(2 oz)* chopped dried fruit to the mixture with the flour.

Orange biscuits
Replace the lemon rind by the grated rind of 1 orange.

Cherry rings
Omit the lemon rind and add 50 g *(2 oz)* chopped glacé cherries with the flour. Roll out the dough and cut into rounds with a 6.5-cm *(2½-in)* fluted cutter, place the rounds on the baking trays and remove the centre of each biscuit neatly with a 2.5-cm *(1-in)* fluted cutter.

Jumbles
Replace 50 g *(2 oz)* of the flour by 50 g *(2 oz)* ground almonds. Divide the dough into 2 pieces and form each into a roll 1–2 cm *(½–¾ in)* in diameter. Cut off 10-cm *(4-in)* lengths and form into 'S' shapes on a baking sheet. *Makes 12–15.*

Chocolate cream sandwiches
Omit 45 ml *(3 level tbsps)* of the flour and sift in 45 ml *(3 level tbsps)* cocoa. When the cooked biscuits are cool, sandwich them together with vanilla butter cream (see page 384). *Makes 10–12.*

Pinwheels
Make up the mixture and divide it in half. Knead 30 ml *(2 level tbsps)* cocoa into one portion. Roll both halves out into equal-sized oblongs and put the chocolate piece on top of the plain one. Roll up like a Swiss roll and leave in a cool place for 30 minutes, to become firm. Cut the roll into slices 0.5 cm *(¼ in)* thick, put these on a baking sheet, cut side down, and bake.

Fruit squares
Make up the mixture and divide in half. Roll out both portions into oblongs and sprinkle 100 g *(4 oz)* chopped dried fruit over one piece. Cover with the other piece and roll out the mixture 0.5 cm *(¼ in)* thick. Cut into squares. *Makes 18–20.*

Raspberry rings
Roll out the mixture and cut it into rounds, using a 6.5-cm *(2½-in)* plain cutter. Place the rounds on a baking sheet, remove the centres of half the biscuits using a 2.5-cm *(1-in)* plain cutter, and bake. When the biscuits are cool, spread the solid rounds with jam and dip the rings into white glacé icing (see page 000). Place the iced rings on top of the rounds so that the jam shows through. *Makes 10–12.*

Jammy faces
Roll out the mixture and cut it into 6.5-cm *(2½-in)* rounds with a plain or fluted cutter. From half the biscuits remove 2 rounds with a small cutter, to represent eyes, and make a slit to represent a mouth. Bake. When the biscuits are cool, spread the plain rounds with jam and cover with the 'faces'. *Makes 10–12.*

Traffic lights
Roll out the mixture and cut it into oblong fingers. Using a small cutter, cut out 3 rounds, one above the other, from half the oblongs. Bake. When the biscuits are cool, place a little raspberry, apricot and greengage jam on each of the plain biscuits and cover with the others. (If you have no green jam, use apricot jam tinted with a few drops of green vegetable colouring.) *Makes about 12.*

Easter biscuits

100 g *(4 oz)* butter
75 g *(3 oz)* caster sugar
1 egg, separated
200 g *(7 oz)* plain flour
pinch of salt
2.5 ml *(½ level tsp)* ground mixed spice
2.5 ml *(½ level tsp)* ground cinnamon
60 ml *(4 tbsps)* currants
15 ml *(1 tbsp)* chopped mixed peel
15–30 ml *(1–2 tbsps)* milk or brandy
a little caster sugar

Grease 2 baking sheets. Cream together the butter and sugar and beat in the egg yolk. Sift the flour with the salt and spices and fold it into the creamed mixture, with the fruit and peel. Add enough milk or brandy to give a fairly soft dough. Knead lightly on a floured board and roll out to about 0.5 cm *(¼ in)* thick. Cut into rounds using a 5-cm *(2½-in)* fluted cutter. Place on the baking sheets and bake in the oven at 200°C *(400°F)* mark 6 for about 10 minutes. Remove from the oven, brush with beaten egg white and sprinkle lightly with caster sugar. Return to the oven for a further 10 minutes, until golden brown. Cool on a wire rack. *Makes 16–18.*

Pepperkaker *see colour plate facing p. 465*

Swedish ginger biscuits

Makes about 20 angels and 18 Christmas roses

100 g *(4 oz)* butter
100 g *(3½ oz)* demerara sugar
200 g *(7 oz)* molasses or golden syrup
5 ml *(1 level tsp)* ground ginger
5 ml *(1 level tsp)* ground cinnamon
2.5 ml *(½ level tsp)* ground cloves
10 ml *(2 level tsps)* bicarbonate of soda
1 egg
500 g *(1 lb 2 oz)* plain flour
royal icing for decoration

Basic method Roughly cut up the butter and place in a large bowl. In a saucepan, bring the sugar, molasses or syrup and the spices to boiling point. Add the bicarbonate of soda and pour over the butter. Stir until the butter has melted. Beat in the egg and slowly blend in the sifted flour. Knead in the basin to a smooth manageable dough. Roll out about a quarter of the dough at a time and use to make variations. Bake at 170°C *(325°F)* mark 3 for 10–15 minutes. Cool on a wire rack and decorate.

Angels Use half the dough. Roll out to about 0.3-cm *(⅛-in)* thick, if possible between sheets of non-stick or waxed paper. Cut out about 20 rectangles 5 cm *(2 in)* by 7.5 cm *(3 in)* and use the trimmings to shape 20 1-cm *(½-in)* balls for the heads. Place rectangles on greased baking sheets. From the top corners, cut 2 small triangles and replace to form upright wings. Position the heads, pressing on to bodies. Bake as in basic method. Cool on wire racks. Using royal icing of piping consistency, fill a paper icing bag fitted with a No. 2 plain writing nozzle. Outline the angel shape and add a few decorative lines for detail. Leave to dry.

Christmas roses Use half the dough rolled out to about 0.3-cm *(⅛-in)* thickness as for angels. Use a heart-shaped cutter measuring 5 cm *(2 in)* from top to bottom. Stamp out 72 heart shapes. On greased baking sheets, place in fours to form rose shapes, slightly overlapping the tips, press these lightly. Bake as in basic method. Cool on wire racks and decorate with piped royal icing to outline the shape.

Note The thinner you roll the dough, the crisper they bake. If you're in a hurry, roll the dough into an oblong and cut with a sharp knife or pastry wheel into squares or diamonds.

One-two-three biscuits

25 g *(1 oz)* caster sugar
50 g *(2 oz)* butter
75 g *(3 oz)* plain flour
sugar to dredge

Grease one or two baking sheets. Cream together the butter and sugar thoroughly. Work in the flour using a spoon or spatula and finish with the finger tips. Knead lightly to form a ball. Roll out carefully on a lightly floured surface to about 0.3 cm *(⅛ in)* – the mixture will be crumbly and needs knitting together between rollings. Stamp out rounds using a 6.5-cm *(2½-in)* fluted cutter, or cut into fingers. Bake in the oven at 150°C *(300°F)* mark 1–2 for about 25 minutes until lightly tinged with colour. Cool on a wire rack. To serve, dredge with caster sugar. These biscuits keep well in an airtight container. *Makes about 9.*

Christmas extravaganza

see colour plate between pp. 464 and 465

Makes 12 garlands, 12 sugar canes, 12 jam buttons, 18 starry wonders and 16 Christmas tree biscuits

275 g *(10 oz)* butter
450 g *(1 lb)* plain flour
250 g *(9 oz)* caster sugar
finely grated rind of 1 lemon
1 large egg, beaten

Basic method Rub the butter into the flour until the mixture resembles fine crumbs. Stir in the sugar and lemon rind. Bind to a manageable dough with beaten egg.

Christmas garlands Take one-eighth of the mixture and shape it into small balls about the size of a pea. On greased baking sheets press eight balls of cookie dough together into a circle then repeat making a further 11 garlands. Place small pieces of angelica or cherry between the balls, and bake in the oven at 190°C *(375°F)* mark 5 for about 15 minutes. Just before the end of cooking time, brush with lightly beaten egg white and sprinkle with caster sugar. Return to the oven to glaze. Cool on a wire rack.

Jam buttons Shape one-eighth of the mixture into 12 balls. Make an indentation in the centre of each and fill with a little jam or lemon curd. Place on a greased baking sheet and bake at 190°C *(375°F)* mark 5 for about 15 minutes.

Sugar canes Take one quarter of the mixture and divide in 8 equal parts. On a lightly-floured surface roll each piece into a 30-cm *(12-in)* long 'rope'. Cut the 'ropes' into 10-cm *(4-in)* lengths and twist in pairs to make canes. Fold one end round to form a 'hook'. Place on greased baking sheets and bake at 190°C *(375°F)* mark 5 for 10–15 minutes. Cool on a wire rack. When cold dredge with icing sugar. Make up a very little, stiff glacé icing and use to fix pieces of rose petal and crystallized violet to the canes for decoration.

see colour plate facing p. 465

Starry wonders Divide one-quarter of the mixture in half. Work 5 ml *(1 level tsp)* sifted cocoa powder into one-half of the dough. Between non-stick or waxed paper, roll out each mixture to about 0.3-cm *(⅛-in)* thickness. With a 7.5-cm *(3-in)* diameter star cutter, stamp out an equal number of star shapes – about 18. Place on lightly greased baking sheets. Using a 4.5-cm *(1¾-in)* star cutter remove the centre from each star and switch the plain centres with the chocolate ones. Gently press in place to join the edges. Bake at 190°C *(375°F)* mark 5 for about 15 minutes. Cool on a wire rack.

Christmas trees Prepare one-quarter of the mixture as for stars. Stamp out about 16 tree shapes and bake on greased baking sheets at 190°C *(375°F)* mark 5 for 10–15 minutes. Cool on a wire rack. Melt 40 g *(1½ oz)* chocolate and use to coat one side of the plain-coloured trees. Leave to set. Dredge one side of the chocolate trees with icing sugar and decorate with pistachio nuts or angelica.

SHAPED COOKIES

Melting moments

100 g *(4 oz)* butter or margarine
75 g *(3 oz)* sugar
1 egg yolk
few drops of vanilla essence
150 g *(5 oz)* self raising flour
crushed cornflakes

Grease 2 baking sheets. Cream the butter and sugar together and beat in the egg yolk. Flavour with vanilla essence, stir in the flour to give a stiff dough and divide the mixture into 20–24 portions. Form each piece into a ball and roll in crushed cornflakes. Place the balls on the baking sheets and bake in the oven at 190°C *(375°F)* mark 5 for 15–20 minutes. Cool on the baking sheets for a few moments before lifting on to a cooling rack. *Makes 20–24.*

Cherry and nut cookies

225 g *(8 oz)* plain flour
pinch of salt
75 g *(3 oz)* butter or margarine
100 g *(4 oz)* caster sugar
grated rind of ½ lemon
1 egg, separated
45–60 ml *(3–4 tbsps)* milk
100 g *(4 oz)* walnuts, finely chopped
glacé cherries, halved

Grease 2 baking sheets. Sift the flour with the salt, rub in the butter and stir in the sugar, lemon rind, egg yolk and milk to give a fairly firm dough. Form into small balls, dip these in the slightly whisked egg white and roll them in the chopped walnuts. Place the cookies on the baking sheet and top each with a cherry half. Bake in the oven at 180°C *(350°F)* mark 4 for 20–25 minutes, until firm and lightly browned. Cool on a wire rack. *Makes 24.*

Almond crisps *see colour plate between pp. 464 and 465*

125 g *(4 oz)* butter
75 g *(3 oz)* caster sugar
1 egg yolk
few drops almond essence
150 g *(5 oz)* self raising flour
75 g *(3 oz)* nibbed almonds

Cream together the butter and sugar until light and fluffy. Beat in the egg yolk and almond essence and finally the flour to give a smooth dough. Form into a neat log shape and cut into 24 even slices. Shape each into a barrel, then roll in nibbed almonds. Place well apart on greased baking sheets and bake at 190°C *(375°F)* mark 5 for 15–20 minutes. Cool on a wire rack. *Makes about 24.*

Variation
Omit almond essence and nibbed almonds. Sift 5 ml *(1 level tsp)* ground cinnamon with the flour. Roll the mixture lightly into balls and place, well apart, on greased baking sheets. Press half a shelled walnut on alternate cookies. Bake as above. When cold, sandwich in pairs with cinnamon-flavoured butter cream.

Peanut butter cookies

50 g *(2 oz)* peanut butter
grated rind of ½ orange
50 g *(2 oz)* caster sugar
45 ml *(3 level tbsps)* light, soft brown sugar
50 g *(2 oz)* butter
1 standard or medium egg
30 ml *(2 tbsps)* raisins, stoned and chopped
100 g *(4 oz)* self raising flour

Cream together the peanut butter, orange rind, sugars and butter until light and fluffy. Beat in the egg, add the raisins and stir in the flour to make a fairly firm dough. Roll the dough into small balls about the size of a walnut and place well apart on an ungreased baking sheet; dip a fork in a little flour and press criss-cross lines on each ball. Bake in the oven at 180°C *(350°F)* mark 4 for 25 minutes, until risen and golden brown. Cool on a wire rack. *Makes 25–30.*

Nig-nogs

75 g *(3 oz)* plain flour
2.5 ml *(½ level tsp)* bicarbonate of soda
75 g *(3 oz)* caster sugar
75 g *(3 oz)* rolled oats
75 g *(3 oz)* butter or margarine
15 ml *(1 tbsp)* milk
15 ml *(1 tbsp)* syrup

Grease 2 baking sheets. Sift the flour and bicarbonate of soda and stir in the sugar and oats. Heat the butter, milk and syrup together until melted, pour on to the first mixture and mix well. Roll into small balls and place 10 cm *(4 in)* apart on the baking sheets. Flatten slightly and bake in the oven at 150°C *(300°F)* mark 2 for about 25–30 minutes. Cool on the sheets for 2–3 minutes then transfer the cookies to a wire rack to cool completely. *Makes 20.*

Cornish fairings
(Ginger biscuits)

100 g *(4 oz)* plain flour
pinch of salt
5 ml *(1 level tsp)* baking powder
5 ml *(1 level tsp)* bicarbonate of soda
5 ml *(1 level tsp)* ground ginger
2.5 ml *(½ level tsp)* ground mixed spice
50 g *(2 oz)* margarine
50 g *(2 oz)* sugar
45 ml *(3 tbsps)* golden syrup

Grease 2 baking sheets. Sift the flour with the salt, baking powder and other dry ingredients. Rub in the margarine and add the sugar. Warm the syrup and add it to the other ingredients; mix well to a fairly stiff consistency, roll into small balls and place them 10 cm *(4 in)* apart on the baking sheets. Bake at 200°C *(400°F)* mark 6 for about 8 minutes. *Makes 24.*

Ginger nuts

100 g *(4 oz)* self raising flour
2.5 ml *(½ level tsp)* bicarbonate of soda
5–10 ml *(1–2 level tsps)* ground ginger
5 ml *(1 level tsp)* ground cinnamon
10 ml *(2 level tsps)* caster sugar
50 g *(2 oz)* butter
75 g *(3 oz)* golden syrup

Sift together the flour, bicarbonate of soda, ginger, cinnamon and sugar. Melt the butter, and stir in the syrup. Stir these into the dry ingredients and mix well. Roll the dough into small balls, place well apart on a greased baking sheet and flatten slightly. Bake in the oven at 190°C *(375°F)* mark 5 for 15–20 minutes. Cool for a few minutes before lifting carefully from the baking sheet. Finish cooling on a wire rack and store in an airtight tin. *Makes about 24.*

Grantham gingerbreads

250 g *(9 oz)* self raising flour
5 ml *(1 level tsp)* ground ginger
100 g *(4 oz)* butter or margarine
350 g *(12 oz)* caster sugar
1 egg, beaten

Grease 2–3 baking sheets. Sift the flour and ginger together. Cream the butter and sugar and beat in the egg gradually. Stir in the flour and ginger until a fairly firm dough is obtained. Roll into small balls about the size of a walnut and put them on the baking sheets. Bake in the oven at 150°C *(300°F)* mark 2 for 40–45 minutes, until crisp, hollow and very lightly browned. *Makes 30.*

Iced gingernuts *see colour plate between pp. 464 and 465*

50 g *(2 oz)* butter
50 g *(2 oz)* soft, dark brown sugar
100 g *(4 oz)* golden syrup
175 g *(6 oz)* self raising flour
5 ml *(1 level tsp)* ground ginger
glacé icing
stem ginger

Melt the butter and stir in the sugar and golden syrup. Over low heat, stir until just dissolved – do not get too hot. Combine the dry ingredients and sift them into the pan. Mix to a firm paste. Take small spoonfuls and roll in the hands until smooth – about the size of a whole walnut. Flatten the surface and place the cookies well apart on greased baking sheets. Bake at 180°C *(350°F)* mark 4 for about 15–17 minutes. Leave on the sheets to cool. Transfer to wire rack. When cold decorate with a small blob of glacé icing and small slice of stem ginger. *Makes about 32.*

Variation

Omit 50 g *(2 oz)* golden syrup and replace with 50 g *(2 oz)* warm black treacle. Shape as above, flatten surface. Decorate each with a shelled pecan nut before baking.

DROP COOKIES

Orange drop cookies

75 g *(2½ oz)* blended vegetable fat
75 g *(2½ oz)* caster sugar
1 egg yolk
100 g *(4 oz)* plain flour
1.25 ml *(¼ level tsp)* baking powder
1.25 ml *(¼ level tsp)* bicarbonate of soda
grated rind of ½ orange
45 ml *(3 tbsps)* orange juice
caster sugar for dredging
orange butter cream (see page 384)

Lightly grease 2 baking sheets. Cream together the fat and sugar and beat in the egg yolk. Sift the flour, baking powder and bicarbonate of soda and stir into the mixture alternately with the orange rind and juice. When well blended, drop small spoonfuls of the mixture on to the baking sheets, keeping them well apart. Flatten them to about 0.5 cm *(¼ in)* thick and dredge with caster sugar. Bake in the oven at 200°C *(400°F)* mark 6 for about 7–8 minutes until light golden brown. Allow to cool for a minute or two, then put on to a wire rack. Sandwich together with orange butter cream before serving. *Makes 14–16.*

Chocolate cookies *see colour plate between pp. 464 and 465*

75 g *(3 oz)* butter
75 g *(3 oz)* granulated sugar
75 g *(3 oz)* brown sugar
a few drops of vanilla essence
1 egg
175 g *(6 oz)* self raising flour
pinch of salt
50 g *(2 oz)* walnuts, chopped
50–100 g *(2–4 oz)* chocolate chips

Grease 2 baking sheets. Cream the butter with the sugars and essence, then beat in the egg. Fold in the sifted flour and salt, with the nuts and chocolate chips. Drop spoonfuls of mixture on the baking sheets and bake in the oven at 180°C *(350°F)* mark 4 for 12–15 minutes. Cool on the baking sheets for 1 minute, then place on a wire rack to finish cooling. *Makes 20.*

Brandy snaps *see colour plate facing p. 464*

50 g *(2 oz)* butter or margarine
50 g *(2 oz)* caster sugar
50 g *(2 oz)* golden syrup (about 30 ml, *2 tbsps*)
50 g *(2 oz)* plain flour
2.5 ml *(½ level tsp)* ground ginger
5 ml *(1 tsp)* brandy, optional
grated rind of ½ lemon
whipped cream

Grease the handles of several wooden spoons and line 2–3 baking sheets with non-stick paper.

Melt the butter with the sugar and syrup in a small saucepan over a low heat. Remove from the heat and stir in the sifted flour and ginger, brandy and lemon rind. Drop small spoonfuls of the mixture about 10 cm *(4 in)* apart on the lined baking sheets, to allow plenty of room for spreading. Bake in rotation in the oven at 180°C *(350°F)* mark 4 for 7–10 minutes, until bubbly and golden. Allow to cool for 1–2 minutes, then loosen with a palette knife and roll them round the spoon handles.

Leave until set, then twist gently to remove. (If the biscuits cool too much whilst still on the sheet and become too brittle to roll, return the sheet to the oven for a moment to soften them.) Fill the brandy snaps with whipped cream just before serving. Brandy snaps can be stored unfilled for about a week in an airtight tin. *Makes 10.*

Note If you do not have enough baking sheets, it is quite satisfactory to leave the surplus mixture and bake the brandy snaps in batches until all the mixture is cooked.

Coffee kisses

2 egg whites
100 g *(4 oz)* caster sugar
100 g *(4 oz)* ground almonds

For the icing
5 ml *(1 level tsp)* instant coffee
15 ml *(1 tbsp)* hot water
75 g *(3 oz)* icing sugar

For the filling
5 ml *(1 level tsp)* instant coffee powder
5 ml *(1 tsp)* hot water
25 g *(1 oz)* butter
50 g *(2 oz)* icing sugar

Line a baking sheet with silicone (non-stick) paper or rice paper.

Whip the egg whites until stiff and fold in the sugar and ground almonds. Place small spoonfuls of this mixture on the baking sheet and bake in the oven at 190°C *(375°F)* mark 5 until the biscuits are pale brown – about 10–15 minutes. Cool on a wire rack.

While the biscuits are cooling make up the icing by dissolving the coffee in the water and adding enough of this mixture to the sifted icing sugar to give a smooth icing. Use to ice half the biscuits. Make the filling by dissolving the coffee in the water and creaming it with the butter and sugar. Use to sandwich the iced biscuits to the plain ones. Place in paper cases. *Makes 12 pairs.*

Note These coffee kisses are also delicious if the tops are left undecorated.

Nut rocks

125 g *(4½ oz)* icing sugar
2 egg whites
almond or vanilla flavouring
75 g *(3 oz)* chopped blanched almonds or chopped walnuts

Grease and flour a baking sheet. Put the sifted icing sugar with the egg whites into a mixing bowl. Stand the bowl over a saucepan half-filled with boiling water and whisk the mixture until it clings stiffly to the whisk. Add the flavouring and nuts and drop small spoonfuls on the prepared baking sheet. Bake in the oven at 150°C *(300°F)* mark 2 for 20–30 minutes, until crisp outside and soft inside – the nut rocks should hardly colour. Remove and cool on a wire rack. *Makes 12–14.*

Macaroons *see colour plate facing p. 464*

1 egg white
50 g *(2 oz)* ground almonds
100 g *(3½ oz)* caster sugar
2.5 ml *(½ tsp)* almond essence
few split almonds
little egg white to glaze

Line 1–2 baking sheets with silicone (non-stick) paper or rice paper. Whisk the egg white until stiff and fold in the ground almonds, caster sugar and almond essence. Place spoonfuls of the mixture on the baking sheets, leaving plenty of room for spreading. (Alternatively, pipe the mixture on to the paper, using a piping bag and 1-cm *(½-in)* plain pipe.) Top each biscuit with a split almond and brush with egg white. Bake in the oven at 180°C *(350°F)* mark 4 for 20–25 minutes, until just beginning to colour. Cool on a wire rack. *Makes 10.*

Orange peel drops

100 g *(4 oz)* blanched almonds, halved
75 g *(3 oz)* butter or block margarine
100 g *(4 oz)* caster sugar
50 g *(2 oz)* chopped mixed peel
grated rind of 1 orange
30 ml *(2 tbsps)* orange juice
75 g *(3 oz)* self raising flour

Using scissors, roughly snip the almonds crosswise. Cream the butter and sugar until soft and fluffy. Stir in the peel, grated orange rind, almonds and juice. Sift the flour over and fold it in evenly. On greased baking sheets, drop heaped teaspoonfuls well apart to allow for spreading. Bake at 180°C *(350°F)* mark 4 until golden brown – 15–20 minutes. Leave on the baking sheet to cool for a few minutes before transferring on to wire rack. *Makes about 24.*

Florentines

100 g *(3½ oz)* **butter**
110 g *(4 oz)* **caster sugar**
110 g *(4 oz)* **chopped nuts (walnuts and almonds mixed if possible)**
30 ml *(2 tbsps)* **chopped sultanas**
5 glacé cherries, chopped
30 ml *(2 tbsps)* **chopped, mixed peel, re-chopped**
15 ml *(1 tbsp)* **cream**
100 g *(4 oz)* **plain chocolate**

Line 2–3 baking sheets with silicone (non-stick) paper. Melt the butter, add the sugar and boil together for 1 minute. Stir in all the other ingredients except the chocolate and mix well. Drop the mixture in small, well shaped heaps on to the baking sheets, keeping them well apart to allow for spreading – average, 4 per tray. Bake in the oven at 180°C *(350°F)* mark 4 for about 10 minutes, until golden brown.

When you take the biscuits out of the oven, press the edges to a neat shape with a knife. When they are beginning to go firm, remove the biscuits carefully and cool on a wire rack. To finish, spread the backs of the biscuits with melted chocolate and mark lines across with a fork. Store in an airtight tin.

Afghans

200 g *(7 oz)* **butter**
75 g *(3 oz)* **sugar**
175 g *(6 oz)* **plain flour**
15 ml *(1 level tbsp)* **cocoa powder**
50 g *(2 oz)* **cornflakes**
2.5 ml *(½ tsp)* **vanilla essence**
chocolate glacé icing (see page 385)
shelled walnuts to decorate

Cream the butter and sugar and add the flour, cocoa, cornflakes and essence. Drop the mixture in small heaps on greased baking sheets and bake in the oven at 180°C *(350°F)* mark 4 for 15–20 minutes. When cold, coat with chocolate glacé icing and decorate each with a walnut half. *Makes 20–24.*

Anzac biscuits

100 g *(4 oz)* **butter**
15 ml *(1 tbsp)* **golden syrup**
5 ml *(1 level tsp)* **bicarbonate of soda**
30 ml *(2 tbsps)* **water**
75 g *(3 oz)* **plain flour**
225 g *(8 oz)* **sugar**
75 g *(3 oz)* **desiccated coconut**
100 g *(4 oz)* **rolled oats**
25 g *(1 oz)* **walnuts, chopped**
pinch of salt

Melt the butter and syrup in a saucepan and add the bicarbonate of soda dissolved in the water. Mix all the other ingredients in a bowl, add the liquids and mix together. Put on to greased baking sheets in spoonfuls, leaving room for them to spread, and bake in the oven at 180°C *(350°F)* mark 4 for 15–20 minutes. *Makes 25–30.*

BAR COOKIES

Chocolate raisin squares

75 g *(3 oz)* **butter or margarine**
100 g *(4 oz)* **caster sugar**
2 eggs
75 g *(3 oz)* **golden syrup**
50 g *(2 oz)* **plain chocolate, melted**
225 g *(8 oz)* **plain flour**
5 ml *(1 level tsp)* **bicarbonate of soda**
2.5 ml *(½ level tsp)* **cream of tartar**
30 ml *(2 level tbsps)* **cocoa**
30–45 ml *(2–3 tbsps)* **milk**
100 g *(4 oz)* **raisins**
50 g *(2 oz)* **walnut pieces**

Grease and line a tin 28-cm by 18-cm by 4-cm *(11-in by 7-in by 1½-in)*. Cream together the butter and sugar until light and fluffy. Beat in the eggs and then the syrup and melted chocolate (cool, but still flowing). Sift the flour, bicarbonate of soda and cream of tartar. Blend the cocoa to a paste with a little milk. Stir in and, when well blended, add the raisins and walnuts. Beat well. Turn the mixture into the tin, level the mixture and bake in the oven at 180°C *(350°F)* mark 4 for about 40 minutes. Turn out and cool on a wire rack. Remove the paper. Top with frosting and swirl with a knife. When set, cut into bars.

Chocolate frosting Cream 100 g *(4 oz)* butter or margarine, gradually beat in 250 g *(9 oz)* icing sugar, sifted together with 50 g *(2 oz)* plain chocolate, melted, and 15 ml *(1 level tbsp)* warm syrup. *Makes 16.*

Boston brownies

75 g *(2½ oz)* butter or block margarine
50 g *(2 oz)* plain chocolate
175 g *(6 oz)* caster sugar
75 g *(2½ oz)* self raising flour
1.25 ml *(¼ level tsp)* salt
2 eggs, beaten
2.5 ml *(½ tsp)* vanilla essence
50 g *(2 oz)* walnuts, roughly chopped

Grease and flour a shallow 20.5-cm *(8-in)* square tin. Melt the butter and chocolate in a basin over hot water and add the sugar. Sift the flour with the salt and add the chocolate mixture, eggs, vanilla essence and walnuts. Beat until smooth and pour into the tin. Bake in the oven at 180°C *(350°F)* mark 4 for 35–40 minutes, until the mixture is risen and beginning to leave the sides of the tin. Leave in the tin to cool, then cut into fingers. *Makes 12.*

Shortbread

150 g *(5 oz)* plain flour
45 ml *(3 level tbsps)* rice flour
50 g *(2 oz)* caster sugar
100 g *(4 oz)* butter or block margarine

Grease a baking sheet. Sift the flours and add the sugar. Work in the butter with your fingertips – keep it in one piece and gradually work in the dry ingredients. Knead well and pack into a rice-floured shortbread mould or a 18-cm *(7-in)* sandwich tin. If using a mould, turn out on to the baking sheet and prick well. Bake in the oven at 170°C *(325°F)* mark 3 until firm and golden – about ¾ hour. Turn out if necessary. When cool, dredge with sugar. Serve cut into wedges. *Makes 6–8.*

Note The rice flour is a traditional ingredient of shortbread, but it can be omitted, in which case use 175 g *(6 oz)* plain flour.

Date crunchies

175 g *(6 oz)* self raising flour
175 g *(6 oz)* semolina
175 g *(6 oz)* butter or block margarine
75 g *(3 oz)* caster sugar
225 g *(8 oz)* stoned dates, chopped
15 ml *(1 tbsp)* honey
60 ml *(4 tbsps)* water
15 ml *(1 tbsp)* lemon juice
pinch of ground cinnamon

Grease a shallow 18-cm *(7-in)* square tin. Mix the flour with the semolina. Heat the butter with the sugar until the fat is melted and stir them into the flour mixture. Press half of this 'shortbread' mixture into the prepared tin. Meanwhile heat the dates with the honey, water, lemon juice and cinnamon, stirring well, until the mixture is soft and smooth. Spread this filling over the mixture in the tin, cover with the remaining 'shortbread' mixture and press down lightly. Bake in the oven at 190°C *(375°F)* mark 5 for 30–35 minutes. Cut into squares, but do not remove from the tin until cold. *Makes 12.*

Flapjacks

75 g *(3 oz)* butter
75 g *(3 oz)* demerara sugar
100 g *(4 oz)* rolled oats

Grease a shallow 19-cm *(7½-in)* square tin. Cream the butter. Mix together the sugar and oats and gradually work into the creamed butter, until thoroughly blended. Press evenly into the prepared tin with a round-bladed knife. Bake in the oven at 220°C *(425°F)* mark 7 for about 15 minutes, until golden brown; turn the tin half-way through, to ensure even baking. Cool slightly in the tin, mark into fingers with a sharp knife and loosen round the edge; when firm, break into fingers. The flapjacks may be stored in an airtight tin for up to one week. *Makes 12.*

Rich ginger flapjacks

50 g *(2 oz)* butter or block margarine
50 g *(2 oz)* demerara sugar
45 ml *(3 tbsps)* golden syrup
125 g *(4 oz)* rolled oats
2.5 ml *(½ level tsp)* ground ginger

Grease an 18-cm *(7-in)* sandwich cake tin. Melt the butter with the sugar and syrup and pour it on to the mixed rolled oats and ginger. Mix well, put the mixture into the prepared tin and press down well. Bake in the oven at 180°C *(350°F)* mark 4 for 20–25 minutes. Leave to cool in the tin and cut into fingers when cool. *Makes 6–8.*

PIPED COOKIES

Almond petits fours

2 egg whites
175 g *(6 oz)* ground almonds
75 g *(3 oz)* caster sugar
few drops almond essence
glacé cherries and angelica to decorate

Line 2 baking sheets with silicone (non-stick) paper or rice paper. Whisk the egg whites until stiff and fold in the ground almonds, sugar and almond essence. Place the mixture in a piping bag fitted with a 1-cm *(½-in)* star pipe. Pipe in small stars, circles, whirls and fingers on to the baking sheets. Decorate each with a small piece of glacé cherry or angelica and bake in the oven at 150°C *(300°F)* mark 2 for 15–20 minutes, until just beginning to colour. Cool on a wire rack. *Makes 20–24.*

Orange glazed meltaways *see colour plate between pp. 464 and 465*

225 g *(8 oz)* butter
50 g *(2 oz)* icing sugar
grated rind of 1 orange
225 g *(8 oz)* plain flour
30 ml *(2 level tbsps)* apricot jam, sieved
45 ml *(3 level tbsps)* icing sugar
15 ml *(1 tbsp)* orange juice

Cream the butter until soft, sift in the icing sugar and beat until light and fluffy. Stir in the orange rind and flour until well blended. Place the mixture in a nylon forcing bag fitted with a large star vegetable nozzle. Pipe about 40 shell shapes on to greased baking sheets. Chill for ½ hour. Bake in the oven at 170°C *(325°F)* mark 3 for about 20 minutes. Remove from the oven, brush each cookie with a little sieved apricot jam. Combine the sifted icing sugar with orange juice and brush over the jam. Return the cookies to the oven for a further 5 minutes, or until the sugar glaze begins to go slightly crystalline. Cool on a wire rack. *Makes about 40.*

Chocolate Viennese fingers *see colour plate between pp. 464 and 465*

225 g *(8 oz)* butter
75 g *(2½ oz)* icing sugar
50 g *(2 oz)* plain chocolate, melted
225 g *(8 oz)* plain flour
2.5 ml *(½ level tsp)* baking powder
30 ml *(2 level tbsps)* drinking chocolate powder
few drops vanilla essence

Cream the butter, sift in the icing sugar and beat until light and fluffy. Add the chocolate when cool but not set. Sift in the flour, baking powder and drinking chocolate and beat into the creamed mixture with the essence. Using a fabric piping bag fitted with a medium star vegetable nozzle, pipe the mixture into an equal number of finger shapes about 7.5 cm *(3 in)* long on to a greased baking sheet, keeping well apart. Bake at 170°C *(325°F)* mark 3 for about 20 minutes. Cool on a wire rack. When cold sandwich in pairs with vanilla butter cream. *Makes about 18 whole fingers.*

Variation
Omit the plain chocolate and drinking chocolate. Prepare the mixture as above and using the same nozzle, pipe the mixture in two long continuous strips about 6.5 cm *(2½ in)* wide, using a backward and forward zig-zag movement. Bake as above. Whilst warm, mark across into a total of 24 portions, break when cold.

Vanilla shorties

225 g *(8 oz)* butter or block margarine
50 g *(2 oz)* icing sugar
175 g *(6 oz)* plain flour
50 g *(2 oz)* cornflour
few drops vanilla essence

Cream the fat with the sifted icing sugar until light and fluffy. Fold in the sifted flour and cornflour a little at a time with the vanilla essence. Put the mixture into a piping bag fitted with a 1-cm *(½-in)* vegetable star nozzle.

Pipe the mixture into various shapes (eg stars, rounds, whirls, fingers) on to a greased baking sheet. Decorate with pieces of glacé cherry and angelica or walnut. Chill until firm. Bake in the oven at 190°C *(375°F)* mark 5 for 10–15 minutes. Cool on a wire rack.

Alternatively, pipe into an equal number of fingers and bake undecorated at 190°C *(375°F)* mark 5 for 10–15 minutes. Cool on a wire rack. To serve, sandwich together with vanilla butter cream (see page 384) and dip the ends of the fingers into melted chocolate. *Makes 20–24.*

REFRIGERATOR COOKIES

Nut refrigerator cookies

100 g *(3½ oz)* butter or block margarine
100 g *(3½ oz)* demerara sugar
1 egg, beaten
175 g *(6 oz)* self raising flour
75 g *(3 oz)* walnuts or almonds, finely chopped

Cream the butter with the sugar and beat in the egg gradually. Stir in the flour and chopped nuts to give a fairly firm dough. Shape into a long roll, wrap in a polythene bag or in aluminium foil and put in a cool place or in a refrigerator for several hours to chill thoroughly.

To finish, grease 2 baking sheets, cut the roll into 0.5-cm *(¼-in)* slices, place the biscuits widely spaced on the sheets and bake in the oven at 200°C *(400°F)* mark 6 for 10–12 minutes. Cool on a wire rack. *Makes 24.*

Chocolate frosties *see colour plate between pp. 464 and 465*

100 g *(4 oz)* whole unblanched almonds
200 g *(7 oz)* self raising flour
150 g *(5 oz)* caster sugar
1.25 ml *(¼ level tsp)* grated nutmeg
150 g *(5 oz)* butter or block margarine
50 g *(2 oz)* plain chocolate, coarsely grated
1 egg, beaten

Grind the almonds without blanching to a fine crumb. Sift the flour, sugar and nutmeg into a bowl. Rub the fat into the flour mixture until it resembles fine breadcrumbs. Stir in the ground nuts and 25 g *(1 oz)* chocolate. Bind together with egg until smooth. Divide the mixture into two and roll each part into a 30.5-cm *(12-in)* long thin sausage shape, using greaseproof or non-stick paper. Chill in the ice cube compartment of the refrigerator until firm – about 30 minutes. Cut slices off at an angle about 1-cm *(½-in)* thick. Place well apart on greased baking sheets. Bake at 190°C *(375°F)* mark 5 for 15–20 minutes. Cool until just warm then sprinkle the remaining grated chocolate over. Transfer to a wire rack. *Makes about 48.*

Variation
Omit the nutmeg, whole egg and chocolate. Use 15 ml *(1 tbsp)* beaten egg and 7.5 ml *(1½ tsps)* vanilla essence. Shape into rolls about 7.5 cm *(3 in)* long and 1 cm *(½ in)* in diameter. Form into crescents on greased baking sheets. Bake as above. *Makes about 36.*

Coffee chequerboards *see colour plate between pp. 464 and 465*

200 g *(7 oz)* butter
100 g *(3½ oz)* caster sugar
300 g *(10½ oz)* plain flour, sifted
15 ml *(1 tbsp)* coffee essence

Cream together the butter and sugar until light and fluffy. Work in the flour using your fingertips to give a malleable dough. Divide the dough into two equal parts. To one half add coffee essence and work to an even colour using the fingertips. Roll each of the two separate colours into long strips – about 1 cm *(½ in)* wide, cut each in half. Place the strips alternately to form a chequered pattern. Press well together and square up the mixture. Wrap in non-stick paper and leave in the refrigerator until firm enough to slice neatly or keep until needed – up to 2 weeks. With a sharp knife cut off dough in 0.5-cm *(¼-in)* slices and bake on a greased baking sheet at 190°C *(375°F)* mark 5 for 10–12 minutes. Cool on a wire rack. *Makes about 50.*

Sandwiches

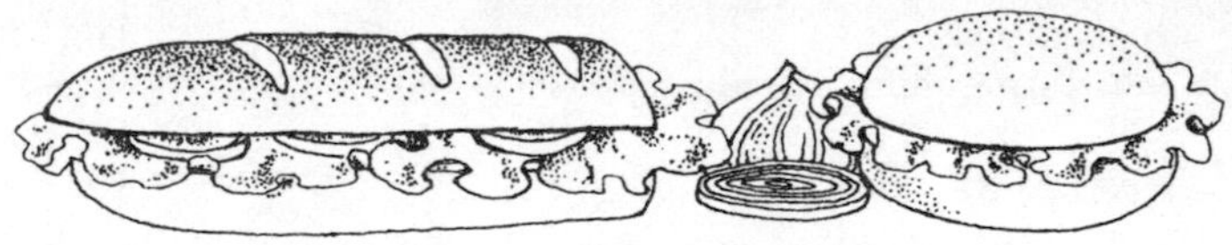

There's no need to stress the good points of the sandwich – we all know it's quick and easy to make, acceptable at almost any hour, capable of endless variation. Moreover, given a touch of imagination and a deft hand, anyone can produce sandwiches that are not just a stopgap, but something to savour and enjoy. And they need not always be cold – on chilly days you can offer piping hot toasted sandwiches; add a cup of soup and you have a satisfying meal.

Here are some reminders about the art of sandwich-making.

Ingredients

Bread Ring the changes on different types of white bread, brown, wholemeal, granary, rye and so on, and vary them with rolls on occasions. Obviously, cut loaves are time-and-labour-saving, but try to get thinly sliced ones. If you slice the bread at home it should preferably be one day old, except for rolled sandwiches, for which the bread needs to be as fresh as possible.

A large 800 g *(28 oz)* loaf cuts into 20–24 slices; if you buy a ready-cut loaf of the same size, it will usually have 24–26 thin slices. A small 400 g *(14 oz)* loaf cuts into 10–12 slices.

Butter This is much easier to spread if it is softened – though not oiled. Spread it all over the slice, right up to the edges (provided the crusts are not going to be cut off). Allow 175–225 g *(6–8 oz)* butter per large loaf.

Fillings The first essential is that the filling must be well-flavoured – anything very delicate or bland is muted to the point of tastelessness when encased in a double layer of bread and butter. Second essential is that the filling must be easy to spread or arrange. Don't use anything very moist unless the sandwiches are to be eaten at once, or it will soak into the bread, producing a soggy effect. Take the filling right to the edges of the slice.

Making and packaging or storing

1. If you are working with anything other than a sandwich loaf, 'pair' the slices accurately to give a neat appearance.
2. Stack up the made sandwiches and cut them in halves or quarters (after first removing the crusts, if you want a more delicate effect). Use a really sharp knife.
3. Wrap the sandwiches in polythene, aluminium foil or greaseproof paper or put them in a plastic box. If they are to be served at home, store them in a cool place until wanted.
4. To keep open sandwiches until required lay them on a tray and cover the whole with a sheet of polythene, foil or greaseproof paper; add any garnish just before serving them.

Ten types of sandwich

Farmhouse

Suitable for lunchbox or picnics.

Cut the bread rather thicker than usual and don't remove the crusts. Use plenty of filling, choosing mixtures such as these:

Minced cooked beef and horseradish cream
Corned beef, chopped watercress or celery and mayonnaise
Mashed canned salmon, chopped cucumber, mayonnaise
Tuna, chopped tomato, mayonnaise
Sardines, lemon juice, watercress
Scrambled egg and chopped chives
Grated cheese, chopped apple, chopped nuts, mayonnaise
Honey and banana

Teatime or cocktail

Slice the bread thinly and cut off the crusts; cut the sandwiches into very small one-mouthful pieces.

Party

Use one of the fillings listed below between thin slices of white or brown bread; remove the crusts and cut the sandwiches into quarters or into fancy shapes – triangles, rounds, fingers. For an attractive effect, use brown and white bread together.

Shrimp, chopped celery, shredded pineapple, mayonnaise
Cream cheese, chopped walnuts, stoned raisins
Chopped ham, sliced hard-boiled egg, chopped pickled gherkin
Minced chicken, minced ham and finely chopped pineapple
Cream cheese, chopped celery, chopped green pepper
Chopped tongue, mayonnaise, a pinch of curry powder, chopped hard-boiled egg

Flaked canned crabmeat, chopped avocado, mayonnaise
Canned pâté, thinly sliced cucumber.

Tiered or decker

Use 3 slices of bread per sandwich, buttering the centre slice on both sides and using 2 different kinds of bread. Typical mixtures:
Flaked canned salmon in one layer, cucumber slices in the second
Chopped ham in one layer, sweet chutney and lettuce in the other
Crisp bacon in one layer, scrambled egg in the other
Cream cheese mixed with chopped parsley in one layer, grated carrot in the other.

Rolled sandwiches

Use thinly cut fresh bread and remove the crusts. Place an asparagus spear, cooked chipolata, roll of ham or slice of smoked salmon on each piece of bread and roll it up Swiss roll fashion.

Pinwheel

Cut the loaf into lengthwise slices and trim off the crusts; butter right to the edges, spread with a colourful filling and roll up like a Swiss roll. Wrap in polythene or aluminium foil and put in a cool place or refrigerator for several hours. Just before serving, cut across in slices.

Cream cheese sandwich loaf

Cut all the crusts off a sandwich or tin loaf and cut it into 4–5 lengthwise slices. Sandwich the slices together, using 3 or 4 different coloured fillings. Coat the outside of the loaf with cream cheese and decorate with sliced cucumber, stuffed olives, etc, and piped coloured savoury butter. Chill. Cut into slices for serving.

Stuffed French loaf

Cut the loaf in half lengthwise and remove the crumb so that the crusts form 2 shells. Butter the insides well and line both halves with a green salad ingredient such as small pieces of lettuce, watercress sprigs or slices of cucumber. Fill up the centre with a moist filling such as scrambled egg, mashed salmon and mayonnaise or cream cheese. Put the halves together and wrap the loaf in greaseproof paper or foil until needed. Serve cut in thick slices. This makes good picnic fare.

Toasted sandwiches

Instead of bread, use 2 pieces of toast, buttering and filling as usual. Alternatively, toast a sandwich made in the ordinary way. Special toasted sandwich gadgets are available, which are very simple to use, so long as you remember to put the bread in buttered side out. Eat toasted sandwiches with a knife and fork.

Some appetising fillings are:
Hot baked beans mixed with horseradish sauce, mustard and crumbled crisply fried bacon
Fried egg and bacon
Fried sliced luncheon meat, sautéed diced tomato and sliced onion
Grilled hamburgers and blue cheese

Rolls and baps

Soft rolls, baps and even plain scones may be used for sandwiches. Cut them nearly in half, butter and fill with any filling. You can also separate the two completely and make open sandwiches; decorate with a sprig of parsley or some simple garnish.

Open (Scandinavian) sandwiches

Use fairly thick slices of any firm bread, butter well, arrange the filling on top and decorate attractively. Choose both fillings and garnishes with an eye for colour. It is usual to eat these sandwiches with knife and fork. Here are delicious mixtures to use in this way:
Slices of cold roast meat garnished with a spoonful of horseradish sauce and a ring of canned red pepper
Cheese slices garnished with chopped radish and chives
Hard-boiled egg slices garnished with anchovy fillets and chopped parsley
Salami slices with scrambled eggs
Shrimps and cucumber cubes mixed with mayonnaise, on a lettuce leaf
Caviare, chopped egg white and chopped onion, garnished with a lemon wedge
Liver pâté, an anchovy fillet and a little horseradish cream, garnished with some parsley
Slices of salt beef with a spoonful of potato salad, decorated with capers
Slices of tomato and hard-boiled egg, garnished with piped mayonnaise and chopped chives
Slices of smoked salmon on lettuce leaves, with a lemon wedge
Cream cheese, garnished with slices of stuffed olive and chopped nuts
Flaked salmon, garnished with a spoonful of cranberry jelly
Scrambled egg, garnished with crisp bacon rolls and sliced mushrooms
Slices of blue cheese garnished with lettuce and halved black grapes
Slices of tongue topped with a green pepper ring filled with cream cheese and garnished with pieces of tomato
Slices of rollmop on lettuce garnished with raw onion rings and tomato wedges
Slices of luncheon meat topped with a spoonful of cottage cheese and garnished with an orange twist

Apple and tomato chutney (p. 448), Piccalilli (p. 453).
(Overleaf) Bakewell tart (p. 292), Fruit cobbler (p. 296).

Jams, jellies and marmalades

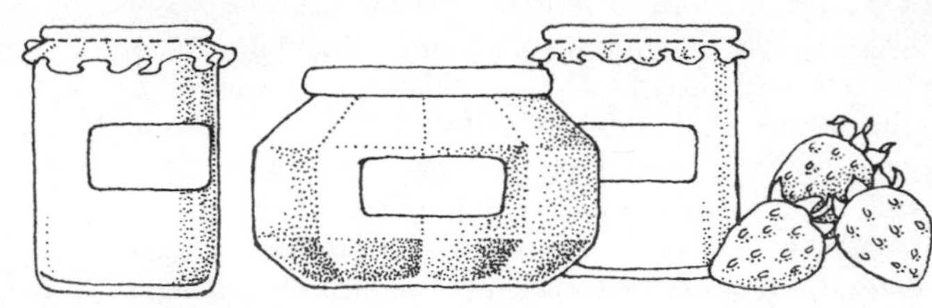

Equipment for jam-making

Some special utensils and tools, though by no means indispensable, make jam-making easier.

Preserving pan

Choose one made from heavy aluminium, stainless steel or tin-lined copper. It should have a fairly thick base or the jam will tend to burn. The pan should be wide enough across the top to allow for good evaporation of the water and deep enough to allow the jam to boil rapidly without splashing all over the cooker. The best overall size will depend on how much jam you make at a time – the jam should preferably not come more than halfway up the pan.

Old-style preserving pans made from unlined copper or brass can be used for jams, jellies and marmalades, providing they are perfectly clean; any discoloration or tarnish must be removed with a patent cleaner and the pan should then be thoroughly washed. Jams made in copper or brass pans will contain less vitamin C than those made in aluminium or stainless steel pans. The preserve must not be left standing in such a pan for any length of time, and a copper or brass pan must not be used for pickles or chutneys, as they are too acidic and would react with the metal.

If you haven't a preserving pan, use a big thick-based saucepan, remembering that since most saucepans are not as wide across as a preserving pan, you may need to allow a longer simmering and boiling period for the fruit.

Slotted spoon

Useful for skimming off any stones as they rise to the surface when you are making jam from fruit such as damsons.

Funnel

A funnel with a wide tube for filling the jars is useful. Failing this, use a jug or large cup.

Cherry stoner

Using a stoner saves much time and prevents the hands from becoming stained with the cherry juice, but a small sharp knife can be used instead.

Sieve

Any sieve that is used in jam-making should be of nylon, not of metal, which might discolour the fruit.

Jam jars

You will need a good supply of jars, which should be free from cracks, chips or other flaws. Jars holding 450 or 900 g *(1 or 2 lb)* are the most useful sizes, as covers are sold for these sizes. Wash them well in warm soapy water and rinse thoroughly in clean warm water. Dry off the jars in a cool oven and use while hot, so that they do not crack when the boiling jam is added.

Jar covers

Most stationers sell packets containing waxed discs, Cellophane covers, rubber bands and labels.

The fruit

This should be sound and just ripe; if necessary, it is better to have it slightly under- rather than over-ripe – at this stage, the pectin (see below) is likely to be most readily available.

Pectin and acid content

The jam will set only if there is sufficient pectin, acid and sugar present. Some fruits are rich in pectin and acid and give a good set; these include cooking apples, gooseberries, damsons, red-currants and black-currants, some plums, also Seville oranges, lemons and limes. Those giving a medium set include plums, greengages and apricots, loganberries, blackberries and raspberries. Fruits that are of poor setting quality include strawberries, cherries, pears, melon, marrow and rhubarb.

The pectin test

If you are not sure of the setting qualities of the fruit you are using, the following test can be made:

When the fruit has been cooked until soft and before you add the sugar, take 5 ml *(1 tsp)* juice, as free as possible from seeds and skin, put it in a glass and when cool add 15 ml *(1 tbsp)* methylated spirit. Shake. Leave for 1 minute; if the mixture forms a jelly-like clot, then the fruit has a good pectin content. If it does not form a

Raspberry jam 1 (p. 438), Apricot jam 1 (p. 435), Orange shred marmalade (p. 444), Lemon curd (p. 439).

single, firm clot, the pectin content is low and some form of extra pectin will be needed. Fruits that lack acid and pectin require the addition of a fruit or a fruit juice that is rich in these substances. Lemon juice is widely used for this purpose, since it aids the setting and at the same time often brings out the flavour of the fruit to which it is added. Allow 30 ml *(2 tbsps)* lemon juice to 1.8 kg *(4 lb)* of a fruit with poor setting properties. Alternatively, use an extract of apple or gooseberry (see below) or include the whole fruit, making a mixed fruit jam. Yet another method is to use a commercially bottled pectin – follow the manufacturer's directions.

Sometimes an acid only is added, such as citric or tartaric acid; these contain no pectin but help to extract the natural pectin from the tissues of the fruit and improve the flavour of fruits lacking in acid. Allow 2.5 ml *(½ level tsp)* to 1.8 kg *(4 lb)* fruit with poor setting properties.

Home-made pectin extracts

Apple Any sour cooking apples or crab-apples may be used for this purpose, also apple peelings and cores and windfalls.

Take 900 g *(2 lb)* fruit, wash it and cut it up without peeling or coring. Cover with 600–900 ml *(1–1½ pt)* water and stew gently for about ¾ hour, until well pulped. Strain through a jelly bag. Make the pectin test to ensure that the extract has a high pectin content. Allow 150–300 ml *(¼–½ pt)* of this extract to 1.8 kg *(4 lb)* fruit that is low in pectin.

Red-currant and gooseberry Make in the same way.

Sugar

Granulated sugar is suitable and the most economical for jam making but less scum is formed with lump sugar and preserving crystals. There is no completely satisfactory substitute for sugar in jam making. If honey or treacle is used the flavour is usually distinctly noticeable. Glucose and glycerine do not have the same sweetening power as cane sugar. If any of these are used not more than half the sugar should be replaced.

Preparation and cooking

Pick the fruit and prepare according to type, then wash it quickly. Put the fruit into a preserving pan or large, strong saucepan, add water as directed in the recipe and simmer gently until it is quite tender. The time will vary according to the fruit – tough-skinned ones such as gooseberries, black-currants or plums, will take ½–¾ hour. Remove the pan from the heat and add the sugar, stir well until this has dissolved; add a knob of butter (this reduces foaming), then return the pan to the heat and boil rapidly, stirring constantly, until the jam sets when tested.

Testing for a set

Temperature test This is the most accurate method. Stir the jam, put in a sugar thermometer and when the temperature reaches 105°C *(221°F)*, a set should be obtained. Some fruits may need 1 degree lower or higher than this, so it is a good idea to combine this test with one of the following:

Saucer test Put a very little of the jam on a cold saucer or plate, allow it to cool, then push the finger across the top of the jam, when the surface should wrinkle. (The pan should be removed from the heat during this test or the jam may boil too long.)

Flake test Remove some jam with a wooden spoon, let it cool a little and then allow the jam to drop. If it has been boiled long enough, drops will run together to form flakes which break off sharply.

Testing for a set – the saucer test

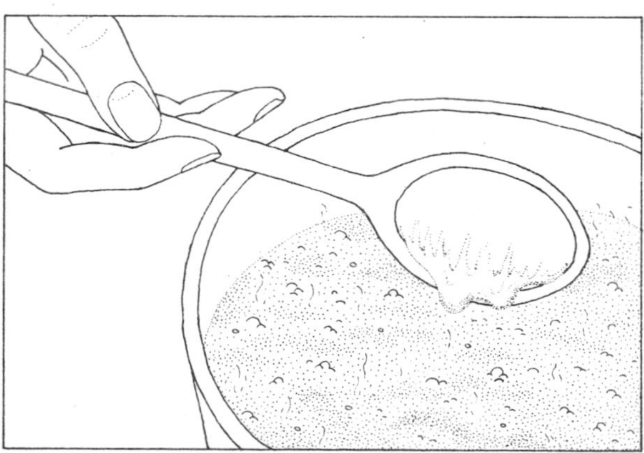

The flake test

Potting and covering

The jars used for jam must be clean and free from flaws and they must be warmed before the jam is put in. As soon as a set has been reached, pour the jam into the jars, filling right to the necks. The only exceptions are strawberry and other whole-fruit jams and also marmalades – these should be allowed to cool for about 15 minutes before being potted, to prevent the fruit rising in the pots. Wipe the outside and rims of the pots and cover the jam whilst still very hot with a waxed disc, wax side down, making sure it lies flat. Either cover immediately with a damped Cellophane round, or leave the jam until quite cold before doing this. Label the jar and store in a cool, dark place.

Apple ginger

1.8 kg *(4 lb)* cooking apples
900 ml *(1½ pt)* water
225 g *(8 oz)* preserved ginger
45 ml *(3 tbsps)* ginger syrup
grated rind and juice of 3 lemons
1.4 kg *(3 lb)* sugar

Peel, core and slice the apples. Tie the cores and peel in muslin and put in a pan with the fruit and the water. Simmer until the fruit is really soft and pulped, remove the muslin bag and mash or sieve the apples. Add the cut-up ginger, the ginger syrup, the rind and juice of the lemons and the sugar. Bring to the boil, stirring constantly, and boil rapidly until setting point is reached. Allow to stand for 15 minutes. Pot and cover in the usual way. *Makes about 2.5–3.2 kg (5½–7 lb).*

Apricot jam 1 *see colour plate facing p. 433*

(Made from dried fruit)

450 g *(1 lb)* dried apricots
1.7 l *(3 pt)* water
juice of 1 lemon
1.4 kg *(3 lb)* sugar
50–75 g *(2–3 oz)* shelled and blanched almonds, optional

Wash the apricots thoroughly, cover with the water and soak for 24 hours. Put the fruit into a pan with the water in which it was soaked, add the lemon juice and simmer for ½ hour, or until soft, stirring from time to time. Add the sugar and blanched almonds, stir until dissolved and boil rapidly until setting point is reached, stirring frequently, as the jam tends to stick. Pot and cover in the usual way. *Makes about 2.3 kg (5 lb).*

Apricot jam 2

(Made from fresh fruit)

1.8 kg *(4 lb)* fresh apricots
400 ml *(¾ pt)* water
juice of 1 lemon
1.8 kg *(4 lb)* sugar

Wash the fruit, cut in half and remove the stones. Crack a few stones to remove the kernels and blanch them by dipping in boiling water. Put the apricots into a pan with the water, lemon juice and blanched kernels and simmer until they are soft and the contents of the pan well reduced. Add the sugar, stir until dissolved and boil rapidly for about 15 minutes, or until setting point is reached. Pot and cover in the usual way. *Makes about 3 kg (6½ lb).*

Quick apricot jam

3 425-g *(15-oz)* cans apricot halves, drained
30 ml *(2 tbsps)* lemon juice
450 g *(1 lb)* sugar

Put the apricots into an electric blender with 300 ml *(½ pt)* of the syrup, the lemon juice and sugar. Mix until smooth, and boil gently in a pan until thick. Pot and cover in the usual way. *Makes about 1.4 kg (3 lb).*

Note If you are using a small blender, process the mixture in small amounts.

Blackberry jam

2.7 kg *(6 lb)* blackberries (not over-ripe)
juice of 2 lemons or 5 ml *(1 level tsp)* citric or tartaric acid
150 ml *(¼ pt)* water
2.7 kg *(6 lb)* sugar

Pick over the blackberries, wash and put them with the lemon juice (or tartaric acid) and water into a pan. Simmer very gently until the blackberries are cooked and the contents of the pan well reduced. Add the sugar, bring to the boil, stirring, and boil rapidly for about 10 minutes, or until setting point is reached. Pot and cover in the usual way. *Makes about 4.5 kg (10 lb).*

Blackberry and apple jam

1.8 kg *(4 lb)* blackberries
300 ml *(½ pt)* water
700 g *(1½ lb)* sour apples (prepared weight)
2.7 kg *(6 lb)* sugar

Pick over and wash the blackberries, put them in a pan with 150 ml *(¼ pt)* of the water and simmer slowly until soft. Peel, core and slice the apples and add the remaining 150 ml *(¼ pt)* water. Simmer slowly until soft and make into a pulp with a spoon or a potato masher. Add the blackberries and sugar, bring to the boil and boil rapidly, stirring frequently, until setting point is reached. Pot and cover in the usual way. *Makes about 4.5 kg (10 lb).*

Bilberry jam

1.1 kg *(2½ lb)* bilberries
150 ml *(¼ pt)* water
45 ml *(3 tbsps)* lemon juice
1.4 kg *(3 lb)* sugar
227 ml *(8 fl oz)* bottle of commercial pectin

This is rather an expensive jam to make unless you can pick the bilberries yourself, but it has a delicious flavour.

Pick over the fruit, removing any leaves and stalks, wash it lightly and put in a pan with the water and lemon juice. Simmer gently for about 10–15 minutes, until the fruit is soft and just beginning to pulp. Add the sugar, stir until dissolved, bring to the boil and boil for 3 minutes. Take off the heat, add the pectin, boil for 1 further minute and allow to cool slightly before potting and covering in the usual way. *Makes about 2.5 kg (5½ lb).*

Black-currant jam

1.8 kg *(4 lb)* black-currants
1.7 l *(3 pt)* water
2.7 kg *(6 lb)* sugar

Remove the stalks, wash the fruit and put into a pan with the water. Simmer gently until the fruit is soft and the contents of the pan well reduced, stirring from time to time to prevent the fruit from sticking to the bottom of the pan. Add the sugar, stir until dissolved and boil rapidly until setting point is reached. Pot and cover in the usual way.

As the skins of currants tend to be rather tough, it is important to cook the fruit really well before adding the sugar. *Makes about 4.5 kg (10 lb).*

Cherry jam

1.8 kg *(4 lb)* cherries (Morello, May Duke)
7.5 ml *(1½ level tsps)* citric or tartaric acid (or the juice of 3 lemons)
1.6 kg *(3½ lb)* sugar

Stone the cherries, crack some of the stones and remove the kernels. Put the cherries, kernels and acid (or lemon juice) in a pan and simmer very gently until really soft, stirring from time to time to prevent them from sticking. Add the sugar, stir until dissolved and boil rapidly until setting point is reached. Pot and cover in the usual way.

As cherries are lacking in pectin, this jam will give only a light set. *Makes about 2.3 kg (5 lb).*

Cherry and red-currant jam

900 g *(2 lb)* dark cherries
450 g *(1 lb)* red-currants
150 ml *(¼ pt)* water
1.4 kg *(3 lb)* sugar

Wash and stone the cherries, wash and string the currants and put the fruit into a pan with the water. Simmer very gently for about ½ hour, or until soft. Add the sugar, stir until dissolved, then boil rapidly until setting point is reached. Pot and cover in the usual way. *Makes about 2 kg (4½ lb).*

Damson jam

2.3 kg *(5 lb)* damsons
900 ml *(1½ pt)* water
2.7 kg *(6 lb)* sugar

Wash and pick over the damsons, put in a pan with the water and simmer for about ½ hour, until the fruit is really soft. Add the sugar, stir until dissolved and boil rapidly until setting point is reached, removing the stones as they rise with a slotted spoon. Pot and cover in the usual way. *Makes about 4.5 kg (10 lb).*

Gooseberry jam

2.7 kg *(6 lb)* gooseberries (slightly under-ripe)
1.1 l *(2 pt)* water
2.7 kg *(6 lb)* sugar

Top, tail and wash the gooseberries and put them into a pan with the water. Simmer gently for about ½ hour, until the fruit is really soft, mashing it to a pulp with a spoon and stirring from time to time to prevent the fruit sticking. Add the sugar, stir until dissolved and boil rapidly until setting point is reached. Pot and cover in the usual way. *Makes about 4.5 kg (10 lb).*

Muscat-flavoured gooseberry jam

A delicious and unusual flavour is given to gooseberry jam by adding 6–8 elderflower heads to each 900 g *(2 lb)* of fruit. Cut off the stems close to the flower, tie the flowers in muslin and add them to the jam when it comes to the boil, removing before it is potted.

Greengage jam

2.7 kg *(6 lb)* greengages
600 ml *(1 pt)* water
2.7 kg *(6 lb)* sugar

Wash the fruit, cut in half and remove the stones. Crack some of the stones to obtain the kernels. Put the greengages, water and blanched kernels in a pan and simmer for about ½ hour, or until the fruit is really soft. Add the sugar, stir until dissolved, and boil rapidly until setting point is reached. Pot and cover in the usual way. *Makes about 4.5 kg (10 lb).*

Note Alternatively, cook the fruit with the stones in and remove them with a slotted spoon as the jam is boiling.

Loganberry jam

1.8 kg *(4 lb)* loganberries
1.8 kg *(4 lb)* sugar

Hull and wash the fruit. Simmer very gently in its own juice for about 15–20 minutes, until soft. Add the sugar, stir until dissolved and boil rapidly until setting point is reached. Pot and cover in the usual way. *Makes about 3 kg (6½ lb).*

Marrow and ginger jam

1.8 kg *(4 lb)* marrow (prepared weight)
1.8 kg *(4 lb)* sugar
25 g *(1 oz)* root ginger
thinly peeled rind and juice of 3 lemons

Peel the marrow, remove the seeds and cut into pieces about 1 cm *(½ in)* square. Weigh, place in a basin, sprinkle with about 450 g *(1 lb)* of the sugar and allow to stand overnight. Press or 'bruise' the ginger with a weight to release the flavour from the fibres, tie it up in a piece of muslin with the lemon rind and place in a pan with the marrow and lemon juice. Simmer for ½ hour, add the rest of the sugar and boil gently until setting point is reached and the marrow looks transparent. Remove the muslin bag and pot and cover in the usual way. *Makes about 3 kg (6½ lb).*

Mulberry and apple jam

1.4 kg *(3 lb)* mulberries
450 g *(1 lb)* apples (prepared weight)
600 ml *(1 pt)* water
1.6 kg *(3½ lb)* sugar

Wash the mulberries and simmer them in half the measured water until they are soft. Peel, core and slice the apples, weigh them and simmer gently in the remaining water until they are really soft and pulped. Combine the mulberries and the apples and add the sugar. Stir until this is dissolved and then boil the jam until setting point is reached. Pot and cover in the usual way. *Makes about 2.3 kg (5 lb).*

Plum jam

2.7 kg *(6 lb)* plums
900 ml *(1½ pt)* water
2.7 kg *(6 lb)* sugar

Wash the fruit, cut in halves and remove the stones. Crack some of the stones and remove the kernels. Put the plums, kernels and water in a pan and simmer gently for about ½ hour, or until really soft. Add the sugar, stir until dissolved and boil rapidly until setting point is reached. Pot and cover in the usual way. *Makes about 4.5 kg (10 lb).*

Note Alternatively, cook the fruit without stoning, removing the stones with a slotted spoon as the jam is boiling.

Quince jam

900 g *(2 lb)* quinces (prepared weight)
1 l *(1¾ pt)* water
1.4 kg *(3 lb)* sugar

Peel, core and slice the quinces and then weigh them. Put them in a pan with the water and simmer very gently until the fruit is really soft and mashed. Add the sugar, stir until it is dissolved and boil the mixture rapidly until setting point is reached. Pot and cover the jam in the usual way. *Makes about 2.3 kg (5 lb).*

Note If the quinces are really ripe, add the juice of 1 lemon with the sugar.

Raspberry jam 1 *see colour plate facing p. 433*

1.8 kg *(4 lb)* raspberries
1.8 kg *(4 lb)* sugar

Wash and hull the fruit and simmer very gently in its own juice for about 15–20 minutes, or until really soft. Add the sugar, stir until dissolved and boil rapidly until setting point is reached. Pot and cover in the usual way. *Makes about 3 kg (6½ lb).*

Raspberry jam 2

1.1 kg *(2½ lb)* raspberries
1.4 kg *(3 lb)* sugar

Wash and hull the fruit and simmer very gently until the juice flows, then bring to the boil and boil gently for 10 minutes. Warm the sugar if possible and add to the fruit. Stir until dissolved, bring quickly back to the boil and boil for 2 minutes. Pot and cover in the usual way.

This jam has only a light set, but has a very good colour and fresh fruit flavour. *Makes about 2.3 kg (5 lb).*

Rhubarb ginger

1.1 kg *(2½ lb)* rhubarb (prepared weight)
1.1 kg *(2½ lb)* sugar
juice of 2 lemons
25 g *(1 oz)* root ginger, bruised and tied in muslin
100 g *(4 oz)* preserved or crystallised ginger

Wipe and trim the rhubarb and weigh it. Put into a large basin in alternate layers with the sugar and lemon juice, cover and leave overnight. Next day, put the mixture into a pan with the root ginger, bring to the boil and boil rapidly for 15 minutes. Remove the bag, add the preserved or crystallised ginger and boil for a further 5 minutes, or until the rhubarb is clear and setting point is reached. Pot and cover in the usual way. *Makes about 2 kg (4½ lb).*

Strawberry jam 1

1.6 kg *(3½ lb)* strawberries
45 ml *(3 tbsps)* lemon juice
1.4 kg *(3 lb)* sugar

(using lemon juice)
Hull and wash the strawberries, put in a pan with the lemon juice and simmer gently in their own juice for 20–30 minutes until really soft. Add the sugar, stir until dissolved and boil rapidly until setting point is reached. Allow to cool for 15–20 minutes then pot and cover in the usual way. *Makes about 2.3 kg (5 lb).*

Strawberry jam 2

(using acid)

1.8 kg *(4 lb)* **strawberries**
15 ml *(1 level tbsp)* **tartaric acid or citric acid**
1.6 kg *(3½ lb)* **sugar**

Hull and wash the strawberries and put in a pan with the acid. Simmer gently in their own juice for 20–30 minutes, or until the fruit is really soft. Add the sugar, stir until dissolved and boil rapidly until setting point is reached. Cool for 15–20 minutes before potting, to prevent the fruit rising in the jars. Pot and cover in the usual way. *Makes about 2.3 kg (5 lb).*

Strawberry conserve

1.8 kg *(4 lb)* **strawberries**
1.8 kg *(4 lb)* **sugar**

Hull and wash the strawberries, keeping them whole, place in a large basin in layers with the sugar, cover and leave for 24 hours. Pour into a pan, bring to the boil, stirring until the sugar dissolves, and boil rapidly for 5 minutes. Return the mixture to the basin, cover and leave for a further 48 hours. Return it to the pan and boil rapidly until setting point is reached. Cool before potting.

This recipe gives a very lightly set jam, with the whole fruit in a thick syrup; it is not practicable to quote a yield, as this varies according to the fruit.

BUTTERS, CHEESES AND MISCELLANEOUS PRESERVES

Fruit butters and cheeses are traditional country preserves which are usually made only when there is a glut of fruit, as a large quantity gives only a comparatively small amount of the finished preserve. Butters do not keep particularly well, so should be made in small quantities and used up fairly soon, but cheeses keep much better. The fruits most commonly used for these preserves are black-currants, damsons, medlars, quinces and apples.

Lemon curd and mincemeat are also included in this section.

With all these preserves it is not so practicable to quote an exact yield as it is for jams.

Preparation and cooking

The fruit needs only picking over and washing, although larger fruits can be roughly chopped. Put it in a pan with just enough water to cover and simmer until really soft. Pass the fruit pulp through a nylon sieve, using a wooden spoon so that the fruit pulp does not discolour. Measure the pulp and allow the following amounts of sugar:

For butters 225–350 g *(½–¾ lb)* sugar to 450 g *(1 lb)* pulp.

For cheeses 350–450 g *(¾–1 lb)* sugar to 450 g *(1 lb)* pulp.

Return the pulp and sugar to the pan, stir until dissolved, then boil gently until the required consistency is reached (see below). Stir regularly, for as the preserve thickens it tends to stick to the bottom of the pan.

Butters should be cooked until they are like thick cream.

Cheeses should be so thick that when a spoon is drawn across the bottom of the pan it leaves a clean line.

Potting

Butters Prepare jars or small pots and cover as for jam (see page 435), or use caps and rings as for bottling. Use or serve as for jam.

Cheeses Brush the inside of some small prepared pots or jars (preferably straight-sided) with olive oil – this enables the preserve to be turned out. Pour in the cheese, cover as for jam and store for 3–4 months before using, as the flavour develops with age. Serve as an accompaniment to meat, poultry and game. Turn out whole and slice at table.

Lemon curd *see colour plate facing p. 433*

grated rind and juice of 4 lemons
4 eggs, beaten
100 g *(4 oz)* **butter**
450 g *(1 lb)* **sugar**

Put all the ingredients into the top of a double saucepan or in a basin standing in a pan of simmering water. Stir until the sugar has dissolved and continue heating, stirring from time to time, until the curd thickens. Strain into small pots and cover in the usual way. *Makes about 700 g (1½ lb).*

Note Home-made lemon curd should be made in small quantities only, as above, since it only keeps for about 1 month. Store in a cool place.

Orange curd

juice and grated rind of 1 large orange
30 ml *(2 tbsps)* chopped mixed peel
100 g *(4 oz)* sugar
100 g *(4 oz)* butter
3 egg yolks

Put all the ingredients into the top of a double saucepan or in a basin standing in a pan of simmering water and stir until the mixture thickens. Pot as for lemon curd. (The mixed peel may be omitted if you prefer.) *Makes about 450 g (1 lb).*

Apple butter

1.5 kg *(3¼ lb)* cooking apples, windfalls or crab-apples
water or water and cider to just cover (about 1 l, *1¾ pt*)
2.5 ml *(½ level tsp)* ground cinnamon
2.5 ml *(½ level tsp)* ground cloves
350 g *(¾ lb)* sugar to each 450 g *(1 lb)* pulp

Wash and chop the apples without peeling or coring, cover with the liquid and simmer gently until really soft and pulpy. Sieve and weigh the pulp and return it to the pan with the spices and the sugar. Stir until dissolved, then boil gently, stirring regularly, until thick and creamy in consistency. Pot and cover as for jam.

Damson cheese

1.5 kg *(3¼ lb)* damsons
150–300 ml *(¼–½ pt)* water
350 g *(¾ lb)* sugar to each 450 g *(1 lb)* pulp

Wash the fruit, remove any stems, put the fruit and water in a covered pan and simmer gently until really soft. Sieve and weigh the pulp and return it to the pan with the sugar. Stir until dissolved, bring to the boil and boil gently until thick, stirring regularly. Pot as usual.

Quince cheese

1.5 kg *(3¼ lb)* quinces
water to just cover
450 g *(1 lb)* sugar to each 450 g *(1 lb)* pulp

Wash and chop the quinces and put them in a pan (including the cores and peel); add the water and simmer gently for about ½ hour, or until really soft. Sieve and weigh the pulp, return it to the pan with the sugar, stir until dissolved and boil gently until thick, stirring regularly. Pot as usual.

Mincemeat

450 g *(1 lb)* currants, cleaned
450 g *(1 lb)* sultanas, cleaned
450 g *(1 lb)* raisins, cleaned and stoned
450 g *(1 lb)* cut mixed peel
450 g *(1 lb)* cooking apples, peeled and cored
100 g *(4 oz)* sweet almonds, blanched
450 g *(1 lb)* soft dark brown sugar
225 g *(8 oz)* shredded suet
5 ml *(1 level tsp)* ground nutmeg
5 ml *(1 level tsp)* ground cinnamon
grated rind and juice of 2 lemons

Finely chop the prepared fruit, mixed peel, apples and nuts. Add the sugar, suet, spices, lemon rind and juice and mix all the ingredients thoroughly together. Cover the mincemeat and leave to stand for 2 days. Stir well and put into jars. Cover as for jam and allow to mature for at least 2 weeks before using.

Note For mincemeat that will keep well, use a firm, hard type of apple, such as Wellington; a juicy apple, such as Bramley Seedling, may make the mixture too moist.

JELLIES

The method is similar to that used for jam, with a few special or additional points. It is not practicable to quote the exact yield in jelly recipes because the ripeness of the fruit and the time allowed for dripping both affect the quantity of juice obtained. 500 ml is used as the metric equivalent of 1 pt in all these recipes. This is adjusted to give the correct consistency.

1. Only fruits giving a good set are really suitable (see page 433). Poor setting fruits can be combined with the better ones to give added colour or flavour.
2. The fruit needs little preparation, though any damaged fruits should of course be removed and large fruits such as apples or plums can be roughly chopped; any skins, cores, stones or pips will be separated from the juice when the pulp is dripping.
3. Cook in water – the juicier the fruit, the smaller the amount of water required; hard fruits need to be covered with liquid. The cooking must be very slow and thorough, to ensure that as much juice as possible is extracted.
4. Leave the fruit to drip in a jelly bag or double thickness of fine cloth (eg a clean tea-towel or cotton sheet). Leave until all dripping has stopped – overnight if necessary – and don't squeeze or poke at the bag of fruit, or the finished jelly will be cloudy.
5. The strained juice – known as the extract – is mixed with sugar and the process is finished as for jam.
6. When setting point is reached, remove any scum with a slotted spoon (or strain the jelly) before quickly potting and covering in the usual way.

Apple jelly

2.5 kg ***(5½ lb)*** **cooking apples**
juice of 2 lemons
water
sugar

Windfalls or cooking apples can be successfully used, but dessert apples should not be used for jelly making. Wash the apples and remove any bruised or damaged portions, then cut them into thick slices without peeling or coring. Put them in a pan with the lemon juice and sufficient cold water to cover (about 1.7 l, *3 pt*). Simmer until the apples are really soft and the liquid is well reduced (by about one-third), then strain the pulp through a jelly cloth. Measure the extract and return it to the pan, with 450 g *(1 lb)* sugar to each 500 ml *(1 pt)* of extract. Bring to the boil, stir until the sugar has dissolved and boil rapidly until a 'jell' is obtained on testing. Skim, pot and cover the jelly as for jam – see page 435.

As the colour of apple jelly is sometimes unattractive, a few blackberries can be added with the apples; or, if preferred, some raspberries, red-currants, cranberries or loganberries may be used instead to give the preserve a better colour.

Blackberry and apple jelly

1.8 kg ***(4 lb)*** **blackberries**
900 g ***(2 lb)*** **cooking apples**
1.1 l ***(2 pt)*** **water**
sugar

Wash the blackberries; wash and cut up the apples, without peeling or coring. Put the fruit in a pan with the water and cook for about 1 hour, until the fruit is really soft and pulped. Strain through a jelly cloth. Measure the extract and return it to the pan with 450 g *(1 lb)* sugar to each 500 ml *(1 pt)* of extract. Stir until the sugar has dissolved and boil rapidly until a 'jell' is obtained on testing. Skim, pot and cover in the usual way.

Bramble jelly

1.8 kg ***(4 lb)*** **blackberries (slightly under-ripe)**
juice of 2 lemons or 7.5 ml ***(1½ level tsps)*** **citric or tartaric acid**
400 ml ***(¾ pt)*** **water**
sugar

Wash the blackberries and pick them over. Put them with the lemon juice (or acid) and water into a pan and simmer gently for about 1 hour, or until the fruit is really soft and pulped. Strain through a jelly cloth, measure the extract and return it to the pan with 450 g *(1 lb)* sugar to each 500 ml *(1 pt)* of extract. Stir until the sugar has dissolved and boil rapidly until a 'jell' is obtained on testing. Skim, pot and cover in the usual way.

Crab-apple jelly

2.5 kg *(5½ lb)* **crab-apples**
1.7 l *(3 pt)* **water**
cloves or bruised root ginger, optional
sugar

Wash the crab-apples and cut into quarters, without peeling or coring. Put into a pan and add the water. Bring to the boil and simmer for about 1½ hours, or until the fruit is mashed, adding a little more water if necessary. A few cloves or some bruised root ginger may be added while the apples are cooking, to give extra flavour. Strain through a jelly cloth, measure the extract and return it to the pan with 450 g *(1 lb)* sugar to each 500 ml *(1 pt)* of extract. Stir until the sugar has dissolved and boil rapidly until a 'jell' is obtained on testing. Skim, pot and cover in the usual way.

Gooseberry jelly

1.8 kg *(4 lb)* **gooseberries**
water to cover
sugar

Wash the gooseberries (but don't top and tail) and put into a pan with just enough water to cover; simmer gently until the fruit is really soft and pulped. Strain through a jelly cloth, measure the extract and return it to the pan with 450 g *(1 lb)* sugar to each 500 ml *(1 pt)* of extract. Stir until the sugar has dissolved and boil rapidly until a 'jell' is obtained on testing. Skim, pot and cover in the usual way.

Black-currant jelly

1.8 kg *(4 lb)* **black-currants**
about 1.4 l *(2½ pt)* **water**
sugar

Wash the currants and remove any leaves, but it is not necessary to remove the stalks. Put into a pan with the water and simmer gently for about 1 hour, or until the fruit is really soft and pulped. Strain through a jelly cloth. Measure the extract and return it to the pan with 450 g *(1 lb)* sugar to each 500 ml *(1 pt)* of extract. Stir until the sugar has dissolved and boil briskly until a 'jell' is obtained on testing. Skim, pot and cover in the usual way.

Japonica jelly

700 g *(1½ lb)* **japonicas**
30 ml *(2 tbsps)* **lemon juice**
1.7 l *(3 pt)* **water**
sugar

Wash the fruit and cut each into 2–3 pieces. Place in a large pan with the lemon juice and water and simmer gently until reduced by about a third, for ¾–1 hour. Strain through a jelly bag. Measure the juice and allow 450 g *(1 lb)* sugar to every 500 ml *(1 pt)* of extract. Dissolve the sugar in the juice over a gentle heat and boil for about 10 minutes, until setting point is reached. Pot and cover in the usual way.

Damson and apple jelly

2.7 kg *(6 lb)* **cooking apples**
1.4 kg *(3 lb)* **damsons**
2.3 l *(4 pt)* **water**
sugar

Wash the apples and chop roughly without peeling or coring. Wash the damsons, remove any stems and put all the fruit in a pan with the water; simmer gently until the fruit is really soft and pulped. Strain through a jelly cloth; measure the extract and return it to the pan with 450 g *(1 lb)* sugar to each 500 ml *(1 pt)* of extract. Stir until the sugar has dissolved and boil rapidly until a 'jell' is obtained on testing. Skim, pot and cover in the usual way.

Red-currant jelly

1.4 kg *(3 lb)* **red-currants**
600 ml *(1 pt)* **water**
sugar

Wash the fruit, but don't remove the stalks; put it into a pan with the water and simmer gently until the red-currants are really soft and pulped. Strain through a jelly cloth, measure the extract and return it to the pan with 450 g *(1 lb)* sugar to each 500 ml *(1 pt)* of extract. Stir until the sugar has dissolved and boil rapidly until a 'jell' is obtained on testing. Skim, pot and cover in the usual way.

Elderberry jelly

900 g *(2 lb)* elderberries
900 g *(2 lb)* cooking apples
600 ml *(1 pt)* water
sugar

Wash the elderberries. Wash the apples and chop roughly without peeling or coring. Cook the fruits separately with just enough water to cover, until they are really soft and pulped. Strain the combined fruits through a jelly bag, measure the extract and return it to the pan with 350 g *(¾ lb)* sugar to each 500 ml *(1 pt)* of extract. Stir until the sugar has dissolved and boil rapidly until a 'jell' is obtained on testing. Skim, pot and cover in the usual way.

Quince jelly

1.8 kg *(4 lb)* quinces
rind and juice of 3 lemons
3.4 l *(6 pt)* water
sugar

Wash the quinces and chop. Simmer, covered, with 2.3 l *(4 pt)* water, the lemon rind and juice until tender – about 1 hour; strain through a jelly bag. Return the pulp to the pan and add the remaining water. Bring to the boil, simmer for ½ hour, then strain. Mix the two extracts together and measure. Bring to the boil and add 450 g *(1 lb)* sugar to each 500 ml *(1 pt)* of extract. Return to the boil and boil vigorously until setting point is reached. Pot and cover in the usual way.

Mint jelly

2.5 kg *(5½ lb)* cooking apples
1.3 l *(2¼ pt)* water
bunch fresh mint
1.3 l *(2¼ pt)* vinegar
sugar
90–120 ml *(6–8 tbsps)* chopped mint
green colour, optional

Wash and roughly chop the apples, put in a large pan with the water and bunch of mint and simmer until really soft and pulped. Add the vinegar and boil for 5 minutes. Strain through a jelly cloth. Measure the extract and return it to the pan with 450 g *(1 lb)* sugar to every 500 ml *(1 pt)* of extract. Stir until the sugar has dissolved and boil rapidly until a 'jell' is obtained on testing. Stir in the chopped mint and a few drops of colouring, if you wish. Skim, pot and cover in the usual way.

MARMALADE

The method of making marmalade is basically very similar to that used for jam, but with the following special points:

1. Seville or bitter oranges should be used; sweet oranges are only used in combination with other citrus fruits, eg in three-fruit marmalade.
2. The peel of citrus fruits is tougher than that of most fruits used for jam-making and therefore the fruit must be evenly shredded, either by hand or in a marmalade cutter. Many recipes suggest cutting up the peel and soaking it in water overnight: this helps to soften the peel, but is not essential.
3. The cooking time is usually much longer than for jams – at least 1 hour – and because of this the quantity of water is usually much larger, to allow for evaporation. The aim is to reduce the contents of the pan by about a half by the end of the first cooking stage and to have the fruit really softened – failure to do this is one of the commonest reasons why marmalade will not set.

Using a slicer to shred the orange peel

4. If the recipe quantities are, say, doubled, it may be necessary to adjust the cooking time and to use an extra large pan.
5. Much of the pectin in the oranges is contained in the pips and membranes. It is important that all this should be extracted. Tie all the pips, and any membrane that has come away from the peel during squeezing, in a piece of muslin. Cook this with the fruit for the first cooking then take it out, let it cool a little and squeeze it as much as possible, letting the pulpy juice run back into the pan. Discard the remaining pips.

Seville orange marmalade

1.4 kg *(3 lb)* Seville oranges
juice of 2 lemons
3.4 l *(6 pt)* water
2.7 kg *(6 lb)* sugar

Wash the fruit, cut it in half and squeeze out the juice and pips. Slice the peel thinly and put in a pan with the fruit juices, water and pips (tied in muslin). Simmer gently for about 2 hours, until the peel is really soft and the liquid reduced by about half. Remove the muslin bag, squeezing it well, add the sugar and stir until it has dissolved. Boil rapidly until setting point is reached – about 15 minutes. Leave to stand for about 15 minutes, then pot and cover in the usual way. *Makes about 4.5 kg (10 lb).*

Orange shred marmalade

see colour plate facing p. 433

900 g *(2 lb)* Seville oranges
2.6 l *(4½ pt)* water
juice of 2 lemons
1.4 kg *(3 lb)* sugar

This marmalade is somewhat more tricky to make than the ordinary kinds and it is essential to test for pectin before the sugar is added. Wash the oranges and peel off enough rind, avoiding the pith, to weigh 100 g *(4 oz)*. Cut the rind in thin strips. Cut up the rest of the fruit and simmer it in a covered pan in 1.4 l *(2½ pt)* of the water and the lemon juice for about 2 hours, until the fruit is really soft. Simmer the shredded rind separately in 600 ml *(1 pt)* water in a covered pan until this also is really soft; drain off the liquid from the shreds and add to the rest of the fruit. Strain the contents of the pan through a jelly cloth and allow to drip into a large bowl for 15 minutes.

Return the pulp left in the cloth to the pan, with the remaining 600 ml *(1 pt)* water, simmer for a further 20 minutes and allow to drip for several hours.

Test the extract for pectin and if the liquid does not clot, reduce it slightly by rapid boiling, then re-test it. Add the sugar and stir until it dissolves. Add the orange peel shreds and boil rapidly until setting point is reached. Allow the marmalade to stand for about 15 minutes and pot and cover in the usual way. *Makes about 2.3 kg (5 lb).*

Grapefruit and lemon marmalade

2 large grapefruit, about 900 g *(2 lb)*
4–5 lemons, about 450 g *(1 lb)*
1.7 l *(3 pt)* water
1.4 kg *(3 lb)* sugar

Wash the fruit, pare off the coloured part of the skin with a knife or peeler and cut it up finely. Peel off the pith and cut up the flesh roughly, removing any pips. Put the peel, flesh, juice and water into a pan, add the pith and pips (tied in muslin) and simmer gently for 1–1½ hours, or until the peel is really soft and the contents of the pan reduced by half. Remove the muslin bag, squeezing it well, add the sugar and stir until it has dissolved. Boil rapidly until setting point is reached. Allow to stand for about 15 minutes before potting. *Makes about 2.3 kg (5 lb).*

Three-fruit marmalade

4 lemons
2 sweet oranges
2 grapefruit
} to weigh a total of about 1.4 kg *(3 lb)*
3.4 l *(6 pt)* water
2.7 kg *(6 lb)* sugar

Wash the lemons and oranges, cut in half and squeeze out the juice and pips. Wash and peel the grapefruit. Remove any thick white pith and stringy parts. Cut up all the peel thinly and cut up the flesh roughly. Put the peel, pulp, juice and water in a pan, with any pith, stringy parts and pips (tied in muslin). Simmer gently for about 1–1½ hours, or until the peel is really soft and the contents of the pan reduced by about half. Remove the bag of pips, squeezing well, add the sugar and stir until it has dissolved. Boil rapidly until setting point is reached, leave to stand for about 15 minutes and pot and cover in the usual way. *Makes about 4.5 kg (10 lb).*

Ginger marmalade

450 g *(1 lb)* **Seville oranges**
3 l *(5¼ pt)* **water**
1.4 kg *(3 lb)* **cooking apples**
3 kg *(6½ lb)* **sugar**
225 g *(½ lb)* **preserved ginger, cut into small dice**
20 ml *(4 level tsps)* **ground ginger**

Wash and peel the oranges and shred the peel finely. Cut up the flesh, removing any tough membrane and pips. Put the peel, flesh, juice and all but 150 ml *(¼ pt)* water into a pan, add the membrane and pips (tied in a piece of muslin) and simmer for about 1½ hours, or until the peel is soft and the contents of the pan are reduced by about half. Remove the bag of pips, squeezing it well.

Peel, core and slice the apples and simmer them gently in the remaining 150 ml *(¼ pt)* water until the fruit is really soft and pulped. Combine the apples with the oranges in the pan, add the sugar and stir until it has dissolved. Add the preserved ginger and the ground ginger and boil rapidly until setting point is reached. Leave for about 15 minutes and pot and cover in the usual way. *Makes about 4.5 kg (10 lb).*

Lime marmalade

700 g *(1½ lb)* **limes**
1.7 l *(3 pt)* **water**
1.4 kg *(3 lb)* **sugar**

For this recipe, weigh the empty pan before you start. Wash the limes and remove the stem end. Place the limes in a pan with the water and cover with a tight-fitting lid. Simmer for 1½–2 hours, until the fruit is really soft. Remove it, slice very thinly, using a knife and fork, and discard the pips. Return the sliced fruit and the juice to the liquid in the pan and weigh. If necessary, boil the mixture until it is reduced to 1.1 kg *(2½ lb)*. Add the sugar and stir until it has dissolved. Boil until setting point is reached, allow to stand for about 15 minutes and pot and cover in the usual way. *Makes about 2.3 kg (5 lb).*

Lemon marmalade

Make in a similar way to lime marmalade above.

Windfall marmalade

2 grapefruit
4 lemons
900 g *(2 lb)* **windfall apples, peeled and cored**
2.8 l *(5 pt)* **water**
2.3 kg *(5 lb)* **sugar**

Wash the citrus fruit, peel off the coloured part of the skin and shred finely. Peel away the pith and chop the flesh roughly. Chop the apples and place with the water, peel and flesh in the pan. Tie the citrus pith, pips, apple peel and cores in a piece of muslin and add to the pan. Simmer gently until the peel is tender and the quantity reduced by half. Remove the muslin bag, squeezing well; add the sugar and stir until dissolved. Boil rapidly until setting point is reached. Allow to stand for 15 minutes before potting and covering in the usual way. *Makes about 4 kg (9 lb).*

Green tomato marmalade

5 lemons
water
900 g *(2 lb)* **green tomatoes**
1.6 kg *(3½ lb)* **sugar**

Wash lemons, halve and squeeze out the juice. Remove the remaining flesh and place it in a large piece of muslin with the pips. Strip away the excess pith and cut the peel into thin strips; place in a pan, add 400 ml *(¾ pt)* water and simmer, covered, for 20 minutes. Meanwhile cut the tomatoes into quarters, remove the core and seeds and add to the lemon pips and flesh in the muslin; tie tightly. Shred the tomato flesh and place in a preserving pan with the lemon juice made up to 1.7 l *(3 pt)* with water. Add the muslin bag, the softened lemon shreds, plus the liquid, and simmer all together until tender – about 40 minutes. Remove the muslin bag, squeezing it well against the side of the pan with the back of a spoon, add the sugar and boil briskly until setting point is reached. Pot and cover in the usual way. *Makes about 2.3 kg (5 lb).*

PRESSURE COOKER PRESERVES

Marmalades and jams

Provided your cooker is one with a three-pressure gauge, it is a good idea to use it for preserving, as it saves quite a bit of time and the fruit retains its flavour and colour.

There are a few points to remember:

1. Always remove the trivet from the pressure pan.
2. Never fill the pan more than half-full.
3. Cook the fruit at medium *(10 lb)* pressure.
4. Reduce pressure at room temperature.
5. Only the preliminary cooking and softening of the fruit must be done under pressure – never cook a preserve under pressure after adding the sugar (and lemon juice, if used), but boil it up in the open pan.
6. You can adapt any ordinary marmalade or jam recipe for use with a pressure cooker by using half the stated amount of water and doing the preliminary cooking of the fruit under pressure. With marmalade, only half the required water is added when the fruit is cooked under pressure, the rest being added with the sugar. These are the times required for different fruits (all at medium, *10 lb*, pressure):

Apples	5 minutes
Blackberries and apples combined	7 minutes
Black-currants	3–4 minutes
Damsons, plums and other stone fruit	5 minutes
Gooseberries	3 minutes
Marrow	1–2 minutes
Pears (cooking)	7 minutes
Quinces	5 minutes
Citrus fruits	20 minutes

Notes Soft fruits such as raspberries and strawberries need very little preliminary softening and are therefore not usually cooked in a pressure cooker.

When two fruits (eg blackberries and apples) are combined, the cooking times may vary somewhat.

Jelly

The fruit used for making jellies can also be softened in the pressure cooker and this method is particularly useful for fruits which have hard skins, pips and so on.

1. Prepare the fruit according to any ordinary jelly recipe.
2. Place it in the cooker (without the trivet) and add only half the amount of water stated in the recipe.
3. Cook at medium *(10 lb)* pressure, then reduce the pressure at room temperature. (See note regarding times.)
4. Mash the fruit well and pour it into the prepared jelly bag. Finish in the ordinary way.

Note Here are examples of the cooking times required:

Apples	7 minutes
Blackberry and apple	9 minutes
Black-currants	4 minutes
Damsons, plums and other stone fruit	5 minutes
Gooseberries	3 minutes
Pears (cooking)	9 minutes
Quince	7 minutes
Citrus fruits	25 minutes

Chutneys, pickles and sauces

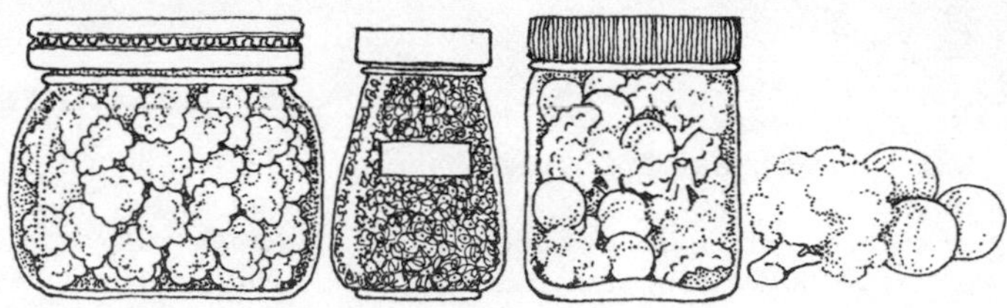

For anyone with a productive garden these preserves are almost as important as jams and bottled fruit. In many of them bruised and poorly shaped fruits and vegetables can be used up, since their appearance is usually of no account in the finished product.

Equipment for pickling

Choose enamel-lined, aluminium or stainless steel pans. Avoid brass, copper or iron, as they tend to impart an unpleasant metallic taste to the preserve. Avoid metal sieves for the same reason and use a nylon one. Jam jars or special pickle jars can be used. Cover them with one of the following:

(a) metal or Bakelite caps, with a vinegar-proof lining,
(b) greaseproof paper and then a round of muslin dipped in melted paraffin wax or fat,
(c) preserving skin (sold in rolls) or vinegar-proof paper,
(d) large corks (previously boiled), covered with a piece of greaseproof paper tied down with string.

If the jars are not adequately covered, the vinegar will evaporate, the preserve shrink and the top dry out.

The vinegar

This is the preserving agent and is almost the most important factor. It should be of the best quality (especially for pickles), with an acetic acid content of at least 5 per cent. 'Barrelled' vinegars are usually of only 4–5 per cent acetic acid content and are not so good. Incidentally, the colour is no indication of strength; further distilling has the effect of rendering vinegar colourless. This 'white' vinegar gives a better appearance to light-coloured pickles such as onions and cauliflower, but malt vinegar gives a rather better flavour. The vinegar is normally given extra flavour by being infused with spices or herbs – see below.

Note Simmer chutneys uncovered, to permit evaporation.

Spiced vinegar

1 l *(1¾ pt)* **vinegar**
30 ml *(2 tbsps)* **blade mace**
15 ml *(1 tbsp)* **whole allspice**
15 ml *(1 tbsp)* **cloves**
18-cm *(7-in)* **piece cinnamon stick**
6 peppercorns

Put the vinegar and spices in a pan, bring to the boil and pour into a bowl. Cover with a plate to preserve the flavour and leave for 2 hours, then strain the vinegar and use as required.

An even better result is obtained if the spices are left to stand in unheated vinegar for 1–2 months.

Notes If the individual spices are not available, use 25–50 g *(1–2 oz)* pickling spice. Different brands of pickling spice will vary considerably, eg some contain whole chilies, and give a hotter result.

For fruit vinegar and tarragon vinegar see page 457.

Sweet spiced vinegar

1.7 l *(3 pt)* **malt vinegar**
450 g *(1 lb)* **brown sugar**
7.5 ml *(1½ level tsps)* **salt**
5 ml *(1 tsp)* **whole mixed spice**
5 ml *(1 tsp)* **peppercorns**
2.5 ml *(½ tsp)* **whole cloves**

Make as for ordinary spiced vinegar.

CHUTNEYS

Apple chutney

1.4 kg *(3 lb)* **cooking apples, peeled, cored and diced**
1.4 kg *(3 lb)* **onions, skinned and chopped**
450 g *(1 lb)* **sultanas or stoned raisins**
2 lemons
700 g *(1½ lb)* **demerara sugar**
600 ml *(1 pt)* **malt vinegar**

This is a light chutney, fruity but not spiced, which is good with pork and poultry. Put the apples, onions and sultanas in a pan. Grate the lemon rind, strain the juice and add both to the pan, with the sugar and vinegar. Bring to the boil, reduce the heat and simmer until the mixture is of a thick consistency, with no excess liquid. Pot and cover. *Makes about 1.8 kg (4 lb).*

Blender apple chutney

1.4 kg *(3 lb)* **cooking apples, peeled, cored and quartered**
1.4 kg *(3 lb)* **onions, skinned and roughly chopped**
2 lemons
450 g *(1 lb)* **demerara sugar**
600 ml *(1 pt)* **malt vinegar**
450 g *(1 lb)* **sultanas**

Put the apples, onions, the juice and thinly pared rind of the lemons, the sugar and vinegar into a large pan. Bring to the boil and simmer until really soft. Pour into the blender goblet a little at a time and blend until smooth. Return the mixture to the saucepan, with the sultanas, and cook for a further 15 minutes, or until thick. Pot and cover. *Makes about 2 kg (4½ lb).*

Apple and tomato chutney

see colour plate facing p. 432

900 g *(2 lb)* **apples, peeled, cored and sliced**
900 g *(2 lb)* **tomatoes, sliced**
350 g *(¾ lb)* **onions, skinned and chopped**
1 clove garlic, skinned and chopped
225 g *(½ lb)* **dried fruit**
350 g *(¾ lb)* **demerara sugar**
15 ml *(1 tbsp)* **mustard seed, tied in muslin**
25 ml *(5 level tsps)* **curry powder**
5 ml *(1 level tsp)* **cayenne pepper**
20 ml *(4 level tsps)* **salt**
900 ml *(1½ pt)* **malt vinegar**

Stew the apples in a very small quantity of water until tender. Put the apples, tomatoes, onions and garlic with the dried fruit, sugar, spices, salt and vinegar, into a pan. Bring to the boil, reduce the heat and simmer until the consistency is thick and there is no excess liquid. Remove the muslin bag, pot the chutney and cover. *Makes about 2.3 kg (5 lb).*

Green tomato chutney

450 g *(1 lb)* **apples, peeled and cored**
225 g *(½ lb)* **onions, skinned**
1.4 kg *(3 lb)* **green tomatoes, sliced thinly**
225 g *(½ lb)* **sultanas**
225 g *(½ lb)* **demerara sugar**
10 ml *(2 level tsps)* **salt**
400 ml *(¾ pt)* **malt vinegar**
4 small pieces dried whole root ginger
2.5 ml *(½ level tsp)* **cayenne pepper**
5 ml *(1 level tsp)* **dry mustard**

A lightly spiced, smooth textured chutney. Mince the apples and onions and put in a pan with the rest of the ingredients. Bring to the boil, reduce the heat and simmer until the ingredients are tender and reduced to a thick consistency, with no excess liquid. Remove the ginger, pot and cover. *Makes about 1.4 kg (3 lb).*

Mincemeat lattice tart (p. 290), Mincemeat surprise pudding (p. 298).

Red tomato chutney

1.8 kg *(4 lb)* **red tomatoes**
30 ml *(2 tbsps)* **mustard seed**
15 ml *(1 tbsp)* **whole allspice**
5 ml *(1 level tsp)* **cayenne pepper**
225 g *(½ lb)* **sugar**
20 ml *(4 level tsps)* **salt**
400 ml *(¾ pt)* **white vinegar**

Prepare the tomatoes by immersing in boiling water for 1–2 minutes and then plunging them into cold; the skins will then peel off easily. Tie the mustard seed and allspice in muslin and add with the cayenne to the peeled tomatoes. Simmer until reduced to a pulp – about ¾ hour – and add the sugar, salt and vinegar. Continue simmering until of a thick consistency, with no excess liquid. Pot and cover. *Makes about 1 kg (2¼ lb).*

Pear chutney

1.4 kg *(3 lb)* **pears, peeled, cored and sliced**
450 g *(1 lb)* **onions, skinned and chopped**
450 g *(1 lb)* **green tomatoes, wiped and sliced**
225 g *(½ lb)* **stoned raisins, chopped**
225 g *(½ lb)* **celery, finely chopped**
700 g *(1½ lb)* **demerara sugar**
1.25 ml *(¼ level tsp)* **cayenne pepper**
1.25 ml *(¼ level tsp)* **ground ginger**
10 ml *(2 level tsps)* **salt**
5 peppercorns, in a muslin bag
1 l *(1¾ pt)* **malt vinegar**

A very dark, smooth, sweet and spicy chutney that is slightly hot.

Put all the fruit and vegetable ingredients into a pan, with no added liquid, and simmer gently until tender. Add the remaining ingredients and simmer until of a thick consistency, with no excess liquid. Remove the bag of peppercorns, pot and cover. *Makes about 1.8 kg (4 lb).*

Spiced pepper chutney

3 red peppers
3 green peppers
450 g *(1 lb)* **onions, skinned and sliced**
450 g *(1 lb)* **tomatoes, skinned and cut up**
450 g *(1 lb)* **cooking apples, peeled and chopped**
225 g *(½ lb)* **demerara sugar**
5 ml *(1 level tsp)* **ground allspice**
400 ml *(¾ pt)* **malt vinegar**
5 ml *(1 tsp)* **peppercorns**
5 ml *(1 tsp)* **mustard seed**

Wash the peppers, halve and remove the seeds. Chop finely or mince the flesh. Place in a preserving pan with the onions, tomatoes, apples, sugar, allspice and vinegar. Tie the peppercorns and mustard seed in a piece of muslin and add to the pan. Bring to the boil and simmer over a moderate heat until soft and pulpy. Remove the muslin bag, pot and cover. *Makes about 1.6 kg (3½ lb).*

Major Marshall's chutney

700 g *(1½ lb)* **freestone plums**
25 ml *(1½ tbsps)* **pickling spice**
2 cloves garlic, skinned and crushed
350 g *(¾ lb)* **onions, skinned and sliced**
900 g *(2 lb)* **tomatoes, skinned and sliced**
900 ml *(1½ pt)* **malt vinegar**
1 kg *(2¼ lb)* **cooking apples, peeled, cored and chopped**
225 g *(½ lb)* **dried apricots, cut-up**
225 g *(½ lb)* **golden syrup**
225 g *(½ lb)* **demerara sugar**
20 ml *(4 level tsps)* **salt**

Wipe the plums, halve and discard the stones. Tie the pickling spice in a muslin bag. Put the plums and all the other ingredients in a large pan, bring to the boil, reduce the heat and simmer uncovered until the ingredients are soft and well reduced. Remove the muslin bag. Pot and cover. *Makes about 2.3 kg (5 lb).*

Choux puffs with plum rum sauce (p. 294).

Banana chutney

900 g *(2 lb)* **cooking apples**
225 g *(½ lb)* **seedless raisins**
225 g *(½ lb)* **dates, chopped**
1.8 kg *(4 lb)* **bananas, peeled and sliced**
225 g *(½ lb)* **onions, skinned and chopped**
10 ml *(2 level tsps)* **salt**
350 g *(12 oz)* **demerara sugar**
30 ml *(2 level tbsps)* **ground ginger**
2.5 ml *(½ level tsp)* **cayenne pepper**
600 ml *(1 pt)* **white vinegar**

Peel, core and roughly chop the apples. Place with the prepared fruit and onions in a preserving pan. Sprinkle with the salt, sugar and spices.

Pour in the vinegar and heat to boiling point. Simmer gently, stirring occasionally until soft and pulpy – about 1 hour. Pot and cover. *Makes about 3.4 kg (7 lb).*

Dower house chutney

700 g *(1½ lb)* **plums**
900 g *(2 lb)* **red tomatoes, skinned and sliced**
900 ml *(1½ pt)* **malt vinegar**
4 medium-sized cloves garlic
350 g *(¾ lb)* **onions, skinned**
1 kg *(2¼ lb)* **apples, peeled and cored**
225 g *(½ lb)* **dried fruit**
450 g *(1 lb)* **demerara sugar**
20 ml *(4 level tsps)* **salt**
25 ml *(1½ tbsps)* **pickling spice**

Wash the plums, halve and remove stones. (If not freestone, leave whole.) Place the plums, tomatoes and vinegar in a large pan and simmer gently until soft. If whole plums were used, remove the stones. Skin the garlic, mince with the onions, apples and dried fruit and add to the plum and tomato mixture with the sugar, salt and pickling spice (the latter tied in a piece of muslin). Simmer until tender and well reduced – about 2 hours. Remove the bag of spices. Pot and cover. *Makes about 2.3 kg (5 lb).*

Plum and apple chutney

450 g *(1 lb)* **sugar**
1 l *(1¾ pt)* **malt vinegar**
450 g *(1 lb)* **apples, peeled, cored and chopped**
1.4 kg *(3 lb)* **plums, stoned and quartered**
450 g *(1 lb)* **onions, skinned and chopped**
225 g *(½ lb)* **stoned raisins, chopped**
225 g *(½ lb)* **carrots, peeled and sliced**
25 g *(1 oz)* **salt**
10 ml *(2 level tsps)* **ground cloves**
10 ml *(2 level tsps)* **ground cinnamon**
10 ml *(2 level tsps)* **ground ginger**
10 ml *(2 level tsps)* **ground allspice**

Put the sugar and most of the vinegar in a pan and bring slowly to the boil. Add the fruit and vegetables. Blend the salt and spices with the remaining vinegar and stir into the ingredients in the pan. Bring to the boil, reduce the heat and simmer until of a thick consistency, with no excess liquid. Pot and cover. *Makes about 2.5 kg (5½ lb).*

Marrow chutney

1.4 kg *(3 lb)* **marrow, peeled and seeded**
salt
225 g *(½ lb)* **shallots, skinned and sliced**
225 g *(½ lb)* **apples, peeled, cored and sliced**
12 peppercorns
2-cm *(¾-in)* **piece dried whole root ginger**
225 g *(½ lb)* **sultanas**
225 g *(8 oz)* **demerara sugar**
900 ml *(1½ pt)* **malt vinegar**

Cut the marrow into small pieces, place in a bowl and sprinkle liberally with salt; cover and leave for 12 hours. Rinse and drain, then place in a pan with the shallots and apples. Tie the peppercorns and ginger in muslin and put in the pan with the sultanas, sugar and vinegar. Bring to the boil, reduce the heat and simmer till the consistency is thick, with no excess liquid. Pot and cover. *Makes about 1.8 kg (4 lb).*

Beetroot chutney

900 g *(2 lb)* **raw beet, shredded or grated**
450 g *(1 lb)* **onions, skinned and chopped**
700 g *(1½ lb)* **apples, peeled and chopped**
450 g *(1 lb)* **seedless raisins**
1 l *(1¾ pt)* **malt vinegar**
900 g *(2 lb)* **sugar**
30 ml *(2 level tbsps)* **ground ginger**

Place all the ingredients in a preserving pan and bring to the boil. Simmer over a moderate heat until soft and pulpy – about 1 hour. Pot and cover. *Makes about 3 kg (6½ lb).*

Rhubarb chutney

2.3 kg *(5 lb)* **rhubarb, washed and cut into small pieces**
450 g *(1 lb)* **onions, skinned and minced**
900 g *(2 lb)* **sugar**
30 ml *(2 level tbsps)* **ground ginger**
50 g *(2 oz)* **ground mixed spice or 15–30 ml** *(1–2 level tbsps)* **curry powder**
10 ml *(2 level tsps)* **salt**
900 ml *(1½ pt)* **vinegar**

Place the rhubarb, onions, sugar, spices, salt and 300 ml *(½ pt)* of the vinegar in a pan and cook slowly until the rhubarb is tender. Add the remaining vinegar and simmer gently until of a thick consistency, with no excess liquid; stir occasionally. Pot and cover. *Makes about 2.7 kg (6 lb).*

Rhubarb and orange chutney

2 oranges
1 kg *(2¼ lb)* **prepared rhubarb**
3 onions, skinned and chopped
900 ml *(1½ pt)* **malt vinegar**
900 g *(2 lb)* **demerara sugar**
450 g *(1 lb)* **raisins**
15 ml *(1 tbsp)* **mustard seed**
15 ml *(1 tbsp)* **peppercorns**
5 ml *(1 tsp)* **allspice**

Squeeze the juice from the oranges and finely shred the peel. Place in a large preserving pan with the rhubarb, onions, vinegar, sugar and raisins. Tie the spices in a piece of muslin and add to the ingredients in the pan. Bring to the boil and simmer until thick and pulpy – about 1½ hours. Remove the muslin bag, pot and cover. *Makes about 3.6 kg (8 lb).*

Indian chutney

450 g *(1 lb)* **cooking apples, peeled, cored and sliced**
225 g *(½ lb)* **onions, skinned and coarsely chopped**
4 cloves garlic, skinned and crushed
20 ml *(4 level tsps)* **salt**
450 g *(1 lb)* **soft brown sugar**
1 l *(1¾ pt)* **malt vinegar**
225 g *(½ lb)* **stoned raisins, chopped**
60 ml *(4 level tbsps)* **ground ginger**
2.5 ml *(½ level tsp)* **cayenne pepper**
45 ml *(3 level tbsps)* **dry mustard**

A curry accompaniment, of a thick sauce consistency and extremely hot. Simmer the apples, onions, garlic, salt, sugar and vinegar until quite soft. Put through a fine sieve. Add the raisins, ginger, cayenne and mustard, mix well and leave in a warm but not hot place until the following day, to thicken. Pot and cover. *Makes about 1 kg (2¼ lb).*

Note If you prefer, increase the amount of ground ginger to 50 g *(2 oz)*, the dry mustard to 50 g *(2 oz)* and cayenne pepper to 20 ml *(4 level tsps)*.

PICKLES

Choose crisp, fresh vegetables and wash and prepare them according to the recipe. They must then be brined (see over) to remove surplus water, which would otherwise dilute the vinegar and render it too weak to act as a preservative for the vegetables.

Ordinary table salt is quite suitable to use for brining. Rinse the vegetables in cold water after brining, or the pickle may be too salty.

Dry brining
For cucumber, marrow, tomatoes and French beans. Layer the prepared vegetables in a bowl with salt, allowing 15 ml *(1 level tbsp)* to each 450 g *(1 lb)* vegetables. Cover and leave overnight.

Wet brining
For cauliflower, cabbage and onions. Place the prepared vegetables in a bowl. Cover with a brine solution, allowing 50 g *(2 oz)* salt dissolved in 500 ml *(1 pt)* water to each 450 g *(1 lb)* vegetables. Put a plate over the surface, to ensure that the vegetables are kept under the liquid, cover and leave overnight.

Finishing
Pack the brined, well rinsed and drained vegetables into jars to within 2.5 cm *(1 in)* of top. Pour spiced vinegar over; take care to cover the vegetables well, giving at least 1 cm *(½ in)* extra to allow for any evaporation which may take place, but leaving a small space at the top of the jar to prevent the vinegar coming into contact with the cover. Cover securely.

Use the vinegar cold for crisp, sharp pickles – eg cabbage, onion – and hot for softer pickles such as plums and walnuts.

Store pickles in a cool, dry, dark place and mature for 2–3 months before tasting, except for red cabbage, which loses its crispness after 2–3 weeks.

Pickled beetroot

Wash the beets carefully, taking care not to damage the skins. Bake in foil in the oven at 180°C *(350°F)* mark 4 or simmer in salted water, with 20 ml *(4 level tsps)* salt to 500 ml *(1 pt)* water, until tender – 1½–2 hours, depending on size. Cool, skin and thinly slice or dice. Pack into jars and cover with spiced vinegar; add 10 ml *(2 level tsps)* salt to each 500 ml *(1 pt)* vinegar if the beets were baked. Cover the jars.

For long keeping, dice the beetroot, pack loosely and cover with boiling vinegar.

Pickled onions

Choose small, even-sized onions – the silver-skin varieties are best. Place without skinning in a brine made from 450 g *(1 lb)* salt to 4.5 l *(1 gal)* water; leave for 12 hours. Peel and then cover with fresh brine and leave for a further 24–36 hours. Remove the onions from the brine and drain thoroughly, pack into jars or bottles and cover with cold spiced vinegar. Cover in the usual way. Leave for 3 months before use.

Pickled red cabbage

1 firm, red cabbage, about 1 kg *(2¼ lb)*
salt
1.3 l *(2¼ pt)* spiced vinegar

Quarter the cabbage, removing the outer leaves and centre stalks. Shred each quarter finely. Place the cabbage in a bowl, layer with salt, cover and leave overnight. Drain the cabbage thoroughly on the following day, rinsing off the surplus salt, pack into jars, cover with cold spiced vinegar and cover the jars.

Use within 2–3 weeks, as the cabbage tends to lose its crispness.

Pickled gherkins

450 g *(1 lb)* gherkins
brine
5 ml *(1 tsp)* whole allspice
5 ml *(1 tsp)* black peppercorns
2 cloves
1 blade of mace
600 ml *(1 pt)* vinegar

Soak the gherkins in brine for 3 days. Drain them well, dry and pack carefully in a jar. Add the spices to the vinegar and boil for 10 minutes. Pour the vinegar over the gherkins, cover tightly and leave in a warm place for 24 hours. Strain the vinegar, boil it up and pour it over the gherkins; cover and leave for another 24 hours, repeating this process until the gherkins are a good green. Pack in wide-necked bottles, cover with vinegar, adding more if required, cork and store.

Pickled walnuts

Use the walnuts green, before the shells have begun to form – test them by pricking with a needle and if you can feel any shell discard them. (The shell begins to form opposite the stalk, about 0.5 cm (*¼ in*) from the end.)

Cover the walnuts with brine and leave to soak for 7 days. Change the brine and soak the walnuts for a further 7 days. Wash and dry them well, spread out and expose to the air until they blacken – about a day. Put into pickle jars, pour hot spiced vinegar over and cover when cold. Store in a cool place for 5–6 weeks before use.

A sweet spiced vinegar may be used.

Green tomato chutney or relish

1.4 kg *(3 lb)* **green tomatoes, sliced**
450 g *(1 lb)* **cucumber or marrow, peeled**
50 g *(2 oz)* **salt**
4 cloves garlic, skinned and chopped
1 large red pepper, seeded and chopped
600 ml *(1 pt)* **malt vinegar**
15 ml *(1 level tbsp)* **dry mustard**
2.5 ml *(½ level tsp)* **ground allspice**
2.5 ml *(½ tsp)* **celery seed**
2.5 ml *(½ level tsp)* **turmeric**

A soft, smooth textured pickle. Place the tomatoes and cucumber in a bowl, sprinkle with the salt, cover and leave overnight; drain well, rinse and place in a large pan. Add the garlic and red pepper to the pan. Blend the vinegar with the dry ingredients, stir into the vegetables and bring slowly to the boil; reduce the heat and simmer for about 1 hour, until the mixture is soft. Pot and cover. Leave for 3–4 months before use.

'Bread-and-Butter' pickle

3 large cucumbers, sliced
45 ml *(3 level tbsps)* **salt**
4 onions, skinned and sliced
600 ml *(1 pt)* **white vinegar**
175 g *(6 oz)* **sugar**
5 ml *(1 tsp)* **celery seed**
5 ml *(1 tsp)* **mustard seed**

This is a relish that goes well with bread and butter – hence its name.

Place the cucumbers, salt and onions in a large bowl, let them stand for 1 hour, pour off the brine, rinse well, then drain. Heat the vinegar, sugar, celery and mustard seed and boil for 3 minutes after the sugar has dissolved. Pack the vegetables into jars, add enough hot vinegar mixture to overflow and seal immediately.

Piccalilli *see colour plate facing p. 432*

2.7 kg *(6 lb)* **prepared vegetables (marrow, cucumber, beans, small onions, cauliflower)**
450 g *(1 lb)* **salt**
4.5 l *(1 gal)* **water**
250 g *(9 oz)* **sugar**
15 ml *(1 level tbsp)* **dry mustard**
7.5 ml *(1½ level tsps)* **ground ginger**
1.7 l *(3 pt)* **white vinegar**
60 ml *(4 level tbsps)* **flour**
30 ml *(2 level tbsps)* **turmeric**

Dice the marrow and cucumber, slice the beans, halve the onions and break the cauliflower into small florets. Dissolve the salt in the water and add the vegetables. Cover and leave for 24 hours.

Remove the vegetables, rinse and drain. Blend the sugar, mustard and ginger with 1.5 l *(2½ pt)* vinegar in a large pan, add the vegetables, bring to the boil and simmer for 20 minutes. Blend the flour and turmeric with the remaining 300 ml *(½ pt)* vinegar and stir into the cooked vegetables. Bring to the boil and cook for 1–2 minutes. Pot and cover.

Mixed pickle

1 kg *(2¼ lb)* **prepared mixed vegetables (cauliflower, cucumber, shallots, French beans)**
brine
1 l *(1¾ pt)* **spiced vinegar**

Break the cauliflower into florets; peel and dice the cucumber; peel the shallots; cut up the beans. Soak the vegetables overnight in brine. Remove, rinse, drain well and dry on a cloth. Pack into jars and cover with cold spiced vinegar. Cover the jars.

SWEET PICKLES

Many people prefer sweet pickles to the more acid type, especially as an accompaniment to cold meat. As well as containing more sugar, they usually have a higher proportion of fruit to vegetables than ordinary pickles. Brining is not usually necessary, since the pickles are cooked and the surplus moisture is evaporated during the cooking.

Pickled apples

30 ml *(2 tbsps)* whole cloves
18-cm *(7-in)* stick cinnamon
30 ml *(2 tbsps)* whole allspice
600 ml *(1 pt)* white vinegar
900 g *(2 lb)* sugar
2.5 ml *(½ level tsp)* salt
900 g *(2 lb)* cooking apples, peeled and cored and cut into quarters

Put all the ingredients except the apples into a pan, heat gently to dissolve the sugar and then bring to the boil. Add the apples and cook gently until soft but not mushy. Drain the apple segments and pack in warm jars.

Boil the syrup till it is beginning to thicken; strain, pour over the apples and seal the jars.

Pickled damsons

1.6 kg *(3½ lb)* damsons, ripe but firm
900 g *(2 lb)* sugar
600 ml *(1 pt)* vinegar
5 ml *(1 level tsp)* ground allspice
15 ml *(1 level tbsp)* ground ginger
5 ml *(1 level tsp)* ground mace
15 ml *(1 level tbsp)* ground cloves

Wash and prick the fruit, put into a pan with the sugar, add the vinegar and spices and cook until tender but not broken. Drain well and put into jars. Boil the syrup for ¼ hour and strain into the jars. The next day pour off the syrup, re-boil and pour over the fruit. Repeat on 4 successive days, then pot and cover the jars in the usual way.

Pickled bananas

2 blades mace
1 small stick cinnamon
6 cloves
300 ml *(½ pt)* vinegar
350 g *(12 oz)* demerara sugar
12 bananas, under ripe

Tie the spices in a piece of muslin and boil with the vinegar and sugar for 15 minutes. Peel the bananas, cut into slices about 0.5 cm *(¼ in)* thick, add to the vinegar and cook gently until almost tender. Lift carefully into hot jars, strain the syrup over the bananas and cover.

Peach pickle

900 g *(2 lb)* granulated sugar
600 ml *(1 pt)* white vinegar
15 ml *(1 tbsp)* whole cloves
15 ml *(1 tbsp)* whole allspice
small piece root ginger
small piece cinnamon stick
rind of ½ lemon, thinly pared
1.8 kg *(4 lb)* freestone peaches, skinned, stoned and quartered

Dissolve the sugar in the vinegar. Crush the spices, tie in a piece of muslin with the lemon rind and add to the pan. Simmer the fruit in the sweetened vinegar until soft. Drain the fruit and pack neatly into warmed jars. Boil the vinegar until it is slightly reduced and beginning to thicken. Pour sufficient vinegar syrup over the fruit to cover, cover the jars and seal. Store for 2–3 months before use.

Pickled orange rings

6 firm oranges, unpeeled but wiped
900 ml *(1½ pt)* vinegar
700 g *(1½ lb)* granulated sugar
20 ml *(4 level tsps)* ground cloves
7.5-cm *(3-in)* cinnamon stick
5 ml *(1 tsp)* whole cloves

This preserve is delicious as an accompaniment to cold ham, turkey, chicken and duck. Slice the oranges into rounds 0.5 cm *(¼ in)* thick. Put the fruit into a pan with just sufficient water to cover and simmer for about 45 minutes, or until the rind is really soft. Drain the oranges and put the juice back into the pan with the vinegar, sugar and spices; bring to the boil, simmer for 10 minutes, then add the drained orange slices a few at a time. Cook gently until the rind becomes clear. Lift the orange rings from the syrup and pack into jars. Continue to boil the syrup until it begins to thicken, cool it and pour over the orange slices. Add a few cloves and cover at once.

Melon pickle

900 g *(2 lb)* prepared melon, cubed
30 ml *(2 level tbsps)* salt dissolved in 2.2 l *(4 pt)* water, for brine solution
400 ml *(¾ pt)* water
150 ml *(¼ pt)* distilled vinegar
1 small stick cinnamon
5 ml *(1 level tsp)* ground cloves
450 g *(1 lb)* sugar
225 g *(8 oz)* cherries (see note)

Soak the prepared melon overnight in the brine solution. Drain. Combine the 400 ml *(¾ pt)* water, vinegar, cinnamon, cloves and sugar and bring to the boil. When the sugar has dissolved, add the melon and cherries. Simmer, covered, for 30–40 minutes, until the melon is clear and tender. Pot and cover.

Note Use either canned cherries or bottled maraschino cherries, well drained.

Pickled melon rind

450 g *(1 lb)* melon rind
100 g *(4 oz)* salt dissolved in 1.1 l *(2 pt)* water
600 ml *(1 pt)* distilled vinegar
300 ml *(½ pt)* water
450 g *(1 lb)* sugar
1 small stick cinnamon
6–8 whole cloves
2–3 drops of green colouring, optional

Cut the thinly pared melon rind into strips, place in the salted water, bring to the boil and simmer for 30 minutes. Drain off the salt water, rinse, cover with fresh water, return to the boil and cook for a further 10 minutes. Change the water and boil gently until the rind is tender. Cover, and leave to stand overnight. Mix together the vinegar, 300 ml *(½ pt)* water and sugar. Add the spices, and heat to dissolve the sugar. Add the drained rind and simmer for 1½ hours, until the syrup is thick and the rind is clear. Remove the spices, add colouring if desired, pot and cover.

Pickled plums

450 g *(1 lb)* sugar
thinly pared rind of ½ lemon
2 whole cloves
a small piece of root ginger
300 ml *(½ pt)* malt vinegar
900 g *(2 lb)* plums

Place all the ingredients except the plums in a saucepan and bring to the boil. Leave until cold, strain and bring to the boil again. Prick the plums with a toothpick, place in a deep bowl, pour the spiced vinegar over and leave covered for 5 days. Strain off the vinegar, re-boil and pour over the fruit. Leave for another 5 days. Pack the plums into jars, reboil the vinegar, pour the boiling vinegar on and cover as for chutney.

Sweet-sour apricots

250 g *(9 oz)* sugar
350 ml *(12 fl oz)* wine vinegar
450 g *(1 lb)* fresh apricots
1 small stick cinnamon

Dissolve the sugar in the vinegar and bring to the boil. Peel the apricots (if the skins are difficult, plunge the fruit into boiling water for a few seconds, then into cold water). Arrange the apricots in a jar, packing as lightly as possible, insert the cinnamon stick and slowly pour the hot vinegar over. Cover as for chutney. Leave preferably for a month before using.

Excellent with meats such as pork, ham and chicken.

Simple sweet pickle

900 g *(2 lb)* hard pears, hard plums or melon flesh
900 g *(2 lb)* sugar
900 ml *(1½ pt)* white vinegar
2 cloves

Prepare the fruit, removing peel, cores and seeds and cutting into pieces. Boil the fruit in water until soft and drain well. Meanwhile boil the sugar, vinegar and cloves for ½ hour. Put the fruit in this liquid and boil for ¼ hour, then pour into jars and cover as for chutney. Keep for 6 months before using.

Mixed sweet pickle

¾ cucumber, washed
450 g *(1 lb)* tomatoes, halved and seeded
700 g *(1½ lb)* marrow, peeled and seeded
900 ml *(1½ pt)* malt vinegar
300 ml *(½ pt)* white vinegar
350 g *(¾ lb)* demerara sugar
20 ml *(4 level tsps)* salt
30 ml *(2 level tbsps)* turmeric
2.5 ml *(½ level tsp)* ground mace
2.5 ml *(½ level tsp)* ground mixed spice
2 large pieces root ginger, bruised
2.5 ml *(½ tsp)* celery seed

Mince the vegetables coarsely. Add the vinegars, sugar, salt and spices and the ginger and celery seed tied in muslin. Stir, bring to the boil and simmer for 3 hours, until dark in colour and of a fairly thick consistency. Remove the bag of spices, pour into warm jars, seal and store in a cool place.

SAUCES, KETCHUPS, FLAVOURED VINEGARS

Home-made bottled sauces usually have one predominating flavour, for instance, tomato or mushroom. Since these sauces are liable to ferment they must be sterilised as described below, after they have been put into the bottles.

Use bottles with screw caps or corks; heat them in a cool oven and boil the caps or corks for 10 minutes. Place the filled and sealed jars in a deep pan with something at the base, such as an upturned plate, a pad of newspaper or a folded cloth. Fill up with cold water to reach the necks of the bottles. Heat to 76°C *(170°F)* (simmering point, if no thermometer is available); maintain this temperature for 30 minutes. Remove the bottles, tighten the screw caps; alternatively, push in the corks, and when the bottles are partly cooled, coat the corks with melted paraffin wax. Secure the corks with wire. Store the bottles in a cool, dry place.

Red tomato sauce

5.4 kg *(12 lb)* ripe tomatoes, sliced
450 g *(1 lb)* sugar
600 ml *(1 pt)* spiced vinegar
30 ml *(2 tbsps)* tarragon vinegar
pinch cayenne pepper
5–10 ml *(1–2 level tsps)* paprika pepper
30 ml *(2 level tbsps)* salt

Place the tomatoes in a pan and cook over a very low heat until they become liquid; reduce by boiling until the pulp thickens, then rub it through a nylon sieve. Replace it in the pan, together with the other ingredients, and boil until the mixture thickens. Pour into warm bottles, sterilise for 30 minutes and seal.

Green tomato sauce

1.4 kg *(3 lb)* green tomatoes
450 g *(1 lb)* apples
2 small onions or shallots, skinned
225 g *(½ lb)* sugar
5 ml *(1 level tsp)* ground pickling spice
2.5 ml *(½ level tsp)* pepper
2.5 ml *(½ level tsp)* dry mustard
10 ml *(2 level tsps)* salt
300 ml *(½ pt)* vinegar
gravy browning to colour

Cut up the tomatoes, apples and onions finely and heat with the other ingredients for about 1 hour, stirring occasionally. Sieve the mixture, re-boil the sauce and bottle while still hot. Sterilise and seal.

Elderberry sauce

1.8 kg *(4 lb)* elderberries
2 medium sized onions
20 ml *(4 level tsps)* salt
600 ml *(1 pt)* spiced vinegar
1.4 kg *(3 lb)* sugar

Wash the fruit and remove the stalks. Skin and chop the onions. Put all the ingredients in a pan and simmer gently until they are well broken down and the onions are tender. Rub the mixture through a sieve, return it to the pan and cook until the sauce has thickened and no excess vinegar remains on top. Bottle while still hot, sterilise and seal.

Plum sauce

3.6 kg *(8 lb)* plums, washed and stoned
450 g *(1 lb)* onions, skinned and sliced
225 g *(½ lb)* currants, washed
1.1 l *(2 pt)* spiced vinegar
450 g *(1 lb)* sugar
50 g *(2 oz)* salt

Place the plums, onions and currants in a pan with 600 ml *(1 pt)* spiced vinegar and simmer for ½ hour. Sieve the mixture, then return it to the pan with the remaining vinegar, the sugar and salt. Simmer for about 1 hour, until of a thick and creamy consistency. Bottle in warm jars, sterilise and seal.

Mushroom ketchup

1.4 kg *(3 lb)* mushrooms, washed and roughly broken
75 g *(3 oz)* salt
5 ml *(1 tsp)* peppercorns
5 ml *(1 tsp)* whole allspice
2.5 ml *(½ level tsp)* ground mace
2.5 ml *(½ level tsp)* ground ginger
1.25 ml *(¼ level tsp)* ground cloves
600 ml *(1 pt)* vinegar

Put the mushrooms in a bowl, sprinkle with the salt, cover and leave overnight. Rinse away the excess salt, drain and mash with a wooden spoon. Place in a pan with the spices and vinegar, cover and simmer for about ½ hour, or until any excess vinegar is absorbed. Press the mixture through a nylon sieve and pour into warm bottles. Sterilise and seal.

Fruit vinegar

These are usually made with raspberries, blackberries or blackcurrants; they are used like a cordial. A fruit vinegar can also be used to replace wine vinegar in salad dressings and so on.

Place the washed fruit in a bowl and break it up slightly with the back of a wooden spoon. To each 450 g *(1 lb)* fruit allow 600 ml *(1 pt)* malt vinegar. Cover with a cloth and leave to stand for 3–4 days, stirring occasionally. Strain the liquid through double muslin and add 450 g *(1 lb)* sugar to each 600 ml *(1 pt)*. Boil for 10 minutes, then cool, strain into bottles and cork.

Tarragon vinegar

Fill a wide-necked jar with freshly gathered tarragon leaves, picked just before the plant flowers. Fill with vinegar, cover and leave in a cool, dry place for about 6 weeks. Strain through double muslin, taste and add more vinegar if the tarragon flavour is too strong. Pour into bottles and cork. Use in making salad dressing.

Note Other herbs – mint, thyme, marjoram or basil – may be used in the same way.

Bottling

Bottling is a process of preserving by sterilisation. The object of preserving fruits and vegetables in bottles is to kill yeasts and moulds already present in surface cells and to prevent others spreading into the container. This is done by heating the fruit or vegetables and then sealing the jars while hot.

Bottling jars

These are wide-necked jars with glass caps or metal discs, secured by screw bands or clips. If the cap or disc has no integral rubber gasket, a thin rubber ring is inserted between it and the top of the bottle. Neither the rubber rings nor the metal discs with fitted seals should be used more than once. Jars can be obtained in different sizes ranging from 450 g *(1 lb)* upwards.

Preparation of jars

Before use, check jars and fittings for any flaw and test to make sure they will be air-tight. To do this, fill with water, put fittings in place, then turn upside down. Any leak will show in 10 minutes. Jars must be absolutely clean, so wash them and rinse in clean hot water. There is no need to dry them – the fruit slips into place more easily if the jar is wet.

What fruit will bottle?

Almost any type – providing you follow the general rules for preparing and processing. As with any other preserving process, the fruit must be fresh, sound, clean and properly ripe – neither too soft nor too hard. Choose fruits of a similar shape, size and ripeness for any one bottle.

Fruit	*Preparation*
Apples	NORMAL PACK Peel, core and cut in slices or rings; during preparation put into a brine solution made with 10 ml *(2 level tsps)* salt to 1.1 *(2 pt)* water, but rinse quickly in cold water before packing into jars. SOLID OR TIGHT PACK Prepare slices as above, remove from brine and dip in small quantities in boiling water for 1½–3 minutes, until the fruit is just tender and pliable. Pack as tightly as possible into the jars.
Apricots	WHOLE Remove stalks, wash fruit. HALVES Make a cut round each fruit up to the stone, twist the 2 halves apart and remove the stone. Crack some stones to obtain the kernels and include with the fruit. Pack quickly, to prevent browning.
Blackberries	Pick over, removing damaged fruits. Wash carefully.
Blackberries with apples	Prepare apples as for Solid Pack (see above) before mixing with the blackberries.
Black-currants	String, pick over and wash.
Cherries	WHOLE Remove stalks and wash fruit. STONED Use a cherry stoner or small knife to remove stones. Collect any juice and include with the fruit. If you like add 10 ml *(2 level tsps)* citric acid to each 4.5 litres *(1 gallon)* of syrup (with either black or white cherries), to improve the colour and flavour.
Damsons	Remove stems and wash fruit.
Figs	Remove stems; peel if you wish. Add 2.5 ml *(½ level tsp)* citric acid to each 600 ml *(1 pt)* of syrup, to give acidity and ensure good keeping. Pack with an equal amount of syrup.
Gooseberries	Small green fruit are used for pies and made-up dishes; larger, softer ones are served as stewed fruit. Top, tail and wash. To prevent shrivelling if fruit is preserved in syrup, the skins can be pricked.
Mulberries	Pick over, handling fruit carefully. Try to avoid washing it.
Pears (dessert)	Peel, halve, remove cores with a teaspoon. During preparation, keep in water containing 10 ml *(2 level tsps)* salt and 7.5 ml *(1½ level tsps)* citric acid per 1.1 l *(2 pints)*. Rinse quickly in cold water before packing.
Pears (cooking)	As these are very hard, prepare as for dessert pears, but before packing, stew gently in a sugar syrup, 100–175 g *(4–6 oz)* sugar to 600 ml *(1 pt)* water, until just soft.
Pineapple	Peel, trim off leaves, remove central core and as many 'eyes' as possible. Cut into rings or chunks.

Fruit	*Preparation*
Plums	WHOLE Remove stalks and wash fruit. HALVES Make a cut round the middle of each fruit to the stone, twist the halves and remove the stone. Crack some of the stones to obtain the kernels and include with the fruit.
Quinces	Prepare as for pears. Always pack into small jars, as they are usually used in small quantities only, eg as flavouring in apple dishes.
Raspberries **Loganberries**	Remove the hulls and pick over the fruit. Avoid washing them if possible.
Red-currants	String and wash.
Rhubarb	As a rule, the thicker sticks are used for made-up dishes and the more delicate forced ones to serve as stewed fruit. Cut rhubarb into 5-cm *(2-in)* lengths. To make it pack more economically and taste sweeter when bottled, it may be soaked first: pour hot syrup over it, leave overnight and use this syrup to top up the packed jars.
Strawberries	These do not bottle well.

Packing the fruit

Put it in the jars layer by layer, using a packing spoon or the handle of a wooden spoon. When a jar is full, the fruit should be firmly and securely wedged in place, without bruising or squashing. The more closely the fruit is packed, the less likely it is to rise after the shrinkage which may occur during processing.

Making sure it's airtight

After processing by one of the methods described below, allow the jars to cool, then test for correct sealing by removing the screw-band or clip and trying to lift the jar by the cap or disc. If this holds firm, it shows that a vacuum has been formed as the jar cooled and it is hermetically sealed. If cap or disc come off, there is probably a flaw in the rim of the jar or on the cap. If, however, several bottles are unsealed, the processing procedure may have been faulty. Use the fruit from the jars at once; it can be re-processed but the result is loss of quality. Store without clips or screw-bands. If you do leave the latter on, then smear each one with a little oil and screw on loosely.

Processing

Bottles can be sterilised in the oven, in a water bath or in the pressure cooker.

The advantages of the oven method are that jars can be processed at one time and no special equipment is needed. It is, however, not quite so exact as the water bath method, as it is not easy to maintain a constant temperature throughout the oven and it is easier to overcook the fruit. The oven method is not recommended for tall jars. If you use this method, use only one shelf of the oven, placed in the centre. Don't overcrowd the jars or the heat will not penetrate the fruit evenly.

Advantages of the water bath method This is the more exact method, but it calls for some special equipment – a large vessel about 5 cm *(2 in)* deeper than the height of the bottling jars, a thermometer and bottling tongs. The vessel can be a very large saucepan, a zinc bath or a zinc bucket; it must have a false bottom such as a metal grid, strips of wood nailed together trellis-fashion, or even a folded coarse cloth. A sugar-boiling thermometer will be satisfactory. Bottling tongs are not essential, but they make it easier to remove the jars from the water bath.

Oven method

Wet pack

Heat the oven to 150°C *(300°F)* mark 1–2. Fill the packed jars with boiling syrup or water to within 2.5 cm *(1 in)* of the top; put on rubber rings and glass caps or metal discs but not screw-bands or clips. Place the jars 5 cm *(2 in)* apart on a solid baking sheet lined with newspaper to catch any liquid which may boil over. Put in the centre of the oven and process for the time stated in the table (on page 460). Remove the jars one by one and put on clips or screw-bands – screwing the bands as tightly as possible. Allow to become quite cold before testing for air-tightness.

Dry pack

Heat the oven to 130°C *(250°F)* mark ½. Pack the bottles with fruit but do not add any liquid. Put on caps but not rubber rings, discs with rings, screw-bands or clips. Place the jars 5 cm *(2 in)* apart on a baking sheet lined as above with newspaper. Process for the time stated in the table, then remove the jars one at a time. Use the contents of one jar to top up the others if the fruit has shrunk during the cooking. Fill up at once with boiling syrup, place rubber bands, caps or metal discs in position and secure with clips or screw the bands on tightly. Leave to cool. When the jars have been filled with fruit and syrup, all air bubbles should be dispelled by jarring each bottle on the palm of the hand; alternatively, pack the fruit and add liquid alternately until the jar is full. Fill the jars to the brim before putting on the fittings.

Note The dry pack oven method is not recommended for fruits which discolour in the air, such as apples, pears and peaches. From the chart on page 460 it will be seen that with both oven methods the time required varies not only with the type of fruit, but also with the tightness of the pack and the total load in the oven at any one time; the load is calculated according to the total capacity of the jars. With fruits such as strawberries and raspberries, these can be rolled in caster sugar before packing dry; the flavour will be delicious but the appearance less attractive.

Times for oven method

These are the temperatures and processing times recommended by the Long Ashton Research Station

Type of fruit	*Wet pack*		*Dry pack*	
	Preheat oven to 150°C *(300°F)* mark 1. Process time varies with quantity in oven, as below			
	Quantity	*Time in minutes*	*Quantity*	*Time in minutes*
Soft fruit, normal pack: Blackberries, Currants, Loganberries, Mulberries, Raspberries, Gooseberries and Rhubarb (for made-up dishes)	450 g–1.8 kg *(1–4 lb)* 2–4.5 kg *(4½–10 lb)*	30–40 45–60	450 g–1.8 kg *(1–4 lb)* 2–4.5 kg *(4½–10 lb)*	45–55 60–75
Apples, sliced	450 g–1.8 kg *(1–4 lb)* 2–4.5 kg *(4½–10 lb)*	30–40 45–60	Not recommended	
Soft fruit, tight packs: As above, including Gooseberries and Rhubarb (for stewed fruit)	450 g–1.8 kg *(1–4 lb)* 2–4.5 kg *(4½–10 lb)*	40–50 55–70	450 g–1.8 kg *(1–4 lb)* 2–4.5 kg *(4½–10 lb)*	55–70 75–90
Stone fruit, light, whole: Cherries, Damsons, Plums	As soft fruit (tight pack)		As soft fruit (tight pack)	
Stone fruit, light, whole: Apricots, Cherries, Gages, Plums	As above		Not recommended	
Apples, solid packs, Apricots, halved, Nectarines, Peaches, Pineapples, Plums, halved	450 g–1.8 kg *(1–4 lb)* 2–4.5 kg *(4½–10 lb)*	50–60 65–80	Not recommended	
Figs	450 g–1.8 kg *(1–4 lb)* 2–4.5 kg *(4½–10 lb)*	60–70 75–90	450 g–1.8 kg *(1–4 lb)* 2–4.5 kg *(4½–10 lb)*	80–100 105–125
Pears	As figs		Not recommended	

Water bath method

Times for water bath method

These are the temperatures and processing methods recommended by Long Ashton Research Station.

Type of fruit	*Slow method*	*Quick method*
	Raise from cold in 90 minutes and maintain as below	Raise from warm 38°C *(100°F)* to simmering 88°C *(190°F)* in 25–30 minutes and maintain as below
Soft fruit normal pack Blackberries Currants Loganberries Mulberries Raspberries Gooseberries and Rhubarb (for made-up dishes) Apples, sliced	74°C *(165°F)* for 10 minutes	2 minutes
Soft fruit tight pack As above, including gooseberries and rhubarb to serve as stewed fruit **Stone fruit, whole** Apricots, Cherries, Damsons, Gages, Plums	82°C *(180°F)* for 15 minutes	10 minutes
Apples, solid pack Apricots, halved Nectarines Peaches Pineapple Plums, halved	82°C *(180°F)* for 15 minutes	20 minutes
Figs Pears	88°C *(190°F)* for 30 minutes	40 minutes

Slow water bath

Pack the jars with fruit and continue as follows:

1 Fill up the jars with cold syrup.
2 Put the rubber bands and heat-resisting glass discs (or metal discs) and screw-bands in place, then turn the screw-bands back a quarter turn.
3 Place the jars in the large vessel and cover with cold water, immersing them completely if possible, but at least up to the necks.
4 Heat gently on top of the cooker, checking the temperature of the water regularly: raise the temperature to 54°C *(130°F)* in 1 hour, then to the processing temperature given in the chart below in a further ½ hour.
5 Maintain the temperature for the time given in the chart.
6 Remove the jars with the tongs (or bale out enough water to remove them with the aid of an oven cloth).
7 Place the jars on a wooden surface one at a time, and tighten the screw-bands straight away.

Quick water bath

If you have no thermometer, this is a good alternative method. Fill the packed jars with hot (not boiling) syrup, cover and place in the vessel of warm water. Bring the water to simmering point in 25–30 minutes and keep simmering for the time stated in the table.

Pulped fruit

Soft and stone fruits can be bottled as pulp. Prepare as for stewing, then cover with the minimum of water and stew until just cooked. While still boiling, pour into hot jars and place the rubber bands and heat-resisting discs (or metal discs) and screw-bands in position.

Immerse the jars in a deep pan and add hot water up to the necks. Raise the temperature to boiling point and maintain for 5 minutes. Remove the jars and allow to cool. If desired, the fruit can be sieved after stewing and before bottling.

Bottling fruit in a pressure cooker

This shortens the time and also ensures that the temperature is controlled exactly. The cooker must have a 'low' *(5 lb)* pressure control. Any pressure cooker will take the 450 g *(1 lb)* bottling jars, but you will need a pan with a domed lid for larger jars.

1 Prepare the fruit as for ordinary bottling, but look at the additional notes in the chart below.
2 Pack the fruit into clean, warm bottles, filling them right to the top.
3 Cover with boiling syrup or water to within 2.5 cm *(1 in)* of the top of the bottles.
4 Put on the rubber bands and caps or metal discs, clips or screw-bands, screwing these tight, then turning them back a quarter-turn. Next, as an extra precaution, heat the jars by standing them in a bowl of boiling water.
5 Put the inverted trivet into the pressure cooker and add 900 ml *(1½ pt)* water, plus 15 ml *(1 tbsp)* vinegar to prevent the pan from becoming stained. Bring the water

to the boil. Pack the bottles into the cooker, making sure they do not touch by packing newspaper between.
6 Fix the lid in place, put the pan on the heat without weight and heat until steam comes steadily from the vent.
7 Put on the 'low' *(5 lb)* pressure control and bring to pressure on a medium heat. Reduce the heat and maintain the pressure for the time given in the last column in the chart. Any change in pressure will cause liquid to be lost from the jars and under-processing may follow.
8 Remove the pan carefully from the heat and reduce the pressure at room temperature for about 10 minutes before taking off the lid.
9 Lift out the jars one by one, tighten the screw-bands and leave to cool.

Preparation and processing

Prepare the fruit as for ordinary fruit bottling, unless otherwise stated. Bring to pressure as described above, and process for the time given in the chart.

Fruit	*Processing time in minutes at 'low'* (5-lb) *pressure*
Apples (quartered)	1
Apricots or Plums (whole)	1
Blackberries	1
Loganberries	1
Raspberries	1
Cherries	1
Red and Black-currants	1
Damsons	1
Gooseberries	1
Pears, eating	5
Pears, cooking (very hard ones can be pressure-cooked for 3–5 minutes before packing in jars)	5
Plums or Apricots (stoned and halved)	3
Rhubarb in 5-cm *(2-in)* lengths	1
Strawberries	Not recommended
Soft fruit – solid pack Put the fruit in a large bowl, cover with boiling syrup 175 g *(6 oz)* sugar to 600 ml *(1 pt)* water and leave overnight. Drain, pack jars and cover with same syrup. Process as usual	3
Pulped fruit, eg apples Prepare as for stewing. Pressure-cook with 150 ml *(¼ pt)* water at 'high' *(15 lb)* pressure for 2–3 minutes, then sieve. While still hot, fill jars and process.	1

Preserving tomatoes

Any method used for bottling fruit is suitable for tomatoes; these are the main variations in the preparation:

Whole unskinned tomatoes (recommended for oven sterilising) The fruit must be small or medium, even in size, ripe yet firm. Remove the stalks and wash or wipe the tomatoes. Pack into jars and fill up with a brine made with 10 ml *(2 level tsps)* salt per 1.1 l *(2 pt)* water.

Solid pack, with no liquid added Any size of fruit may be used but they must be firm. Dip a few at a time first into boiling water, then into cold, and peel off the skins. Small tomatoes may be left whole, but larger ones should be cut in halves or quarters, so that they may be packed really tightly with no air spaces, making it unnecessary to add any water. The flavour is improved if about 5 ml *(1 level tsp)* salt and 2.5 ml *(½ level tsp)* sugar are sprinkled among the fruit in each 450-g *(1-lb)* jar.

In their own juice Peel the tomatoes as above and pack tightly into jars. Stew some extra tomatoes in a covered pan, with 5 ml *(1 level tsp)* salt to each 900 g *(2 lb)* fruit, strain the juice and use to fill up the jars.

Bottling tomato purée

This method enables poorly shaped tomatoes to be used, though they must be sound and ripe. Wash, heat them in a covered pan with a little water and salt and cook until soft. Rub the pulp through a sieve and return it to the pan, then bring to the boil; when it is boiling pour it at once into hot jars and put the rubber bands and heat-resisting glass discs (or metal discs) and screw-bands in place. (It is very important that this process should be carried out quickly, as the pulp deteriorates if left exposed to the air.) Immerse the bottles in a pan of hot water (padded with thick cloth or newspaper), bring to the boil and boil for 10 minutes. Finish and test as usual.

Tomato juice

Simmer ripe tomatoes until soft and rub them through a nylon sieve. To each 1.1 l *(2 pt)* of pulp add 300 ml *(½ pt)* water, 5 ml *(1 level tsp)* salt, 30 ml *(2 level tbsps)* sugar and a pinch of pepper. Process the juice as for tomato purée.

Bottling problems

When the seal fails

Check neck of jar for chips, cracks or other faults. Inspect sealing disc to make sure that there are no faults or irregularities in the metal or the rubber rim. (You must use a new sealing disc every time.) The instructions for

Oven method of sterilising tomatoes

	Wet Pack Pre-heat oven to 150°C *(300°F)*, mark 1, process as below	*Dry Pack* Pre-heat oven to 130°C *(250°F)* mark ½, process as below
Whole tomatoes	450 g–1.8 kg *(1–4 lb)* for 60–70 minutes 2–4.5 kg *(4½–10 lb)* for 75–90 minutes	450 g–1.8 kg *(1–4 lb)* for 80–100 minutes 2–4.5 kg *(4½–10 lb)* for 105–125 minutes
Solid-pack tomatoes (halved or quartered)	450 g–1.8 kg *(1–4 lb)* for 70–80 minutes 2–4.5 kg *(4½–10 lb)* for 85–100 minutes	Not recommended for solid packs

Water bath method of sterilising tomatoes

	Slow Method Raise from cold in 90 minutes and maintain as below	*Quick method* Raise from warm 38°C *(100°F)* to simmering 88°C *(190°F)* in 25–30 minutes and maintain for:
Whole tomatoes	88°C *(190°F)* for 30 minutes	40 minutes
Solid-pack tomatoes (halved or quartered)	88°C *(190°F)* for 40 minutes	50 minutes

Pressure cooker method of sterilising tomatoes

Whole or halved tomatoes in brine (for preparation see ordinary bottling), solid pack	Process the tomatoes for 5 minutes at low *(5-lb)* pressure

each method of sterilising must be followed exactly – it is particularly important to tighten screw-bands immediately after processing.

When fruit rises in the jar
This does not affect the keeping qualities, but it does spoil the appearance. It can be due to over-processing, too high a temperature during the processing, loose packing in the jars, the use of over-ripe fruit or too heavy a syrup.

When mould appears or fermentation takes place
These are caused by poor-quality fruit, insufficient sterilising or failure of the bottle to seal.

When fruit darkens
If only the top pieces are attacked, it can be due to their not being fully covered by liquid or to under-processing. If the contents are darkened throughout, this is probably due to using produce in poor condition, to over-processing or to failure to store in a cool dark place.

Salting beans

Allow 350 g *(¾ lb)* kitchen salt to each 1 kg *(2¼ lb)* French or runner beans, which must be young, fresh and tender. French beans can be left whole, but runner beans should be sliced. Place a layer of salt in a glass or stoneware jar, then a layer of beans; fill the jar with alternate layers, pressing the beans well down and finishing with a layer of salt. Cover with a moisture-proof cover – cork or plastic material – and tie tightly, to allow a strong brine solution to form.

To use Remove some beans from the jar, wash thoroughly in several waters, then soak for 2 hours in warm water. Cook in boiling unsalted water until tender, drain and serve in the usual way.

UNUSUAL PRESERVES

Fruits preserved in brandy or liqueur make a simple but delicious sweet when served with cream or ice cream.

Spiced fruits, which have a slight tartness due to the vinegar used in their preparation, are a good accompaniment to such things as cold roast pork, ham, duck and most game and they look attractive at a buffet meal.

Rose-hip syrup

2.6 l *(4½ pt)* water
900 g *(2 lb)* ripe rose-hips
450 g *(1 lb)* sugar

Have ready 1.7 l *(3 pt)* of boiling water, preferably in an aluminium or unchipped enamel pan. Mince the rose-hips in a coarse mincer, place them immediately in the boiling water and bring this again to the boil. As soon as it re-boils remove the pan from the heat and leave it for 15 minutes, then pour into a scalded jelly bag and allow the bulk of the juice to drip through. Return the pulp to the saucepan, add 900 ml *(1½ pt)* of boiling water, re-boil and allow it to stand without further heating for another 10 minutes, then strain as before. Pour the juice into a clean saucepan, and reduce until it measures about 900 ml *(1½ pt)*, then add 450 g *(1 lb)* sugar and boil for a further 5 minutes.

Pour the syrup while it is hot into clean hot bottles and seal at once. Process for 5 minutes. Cool, and dip the corks in melted paraffin wax.

It is advisable to use small bottles, as the syrup will not keep for more than a week or two once it is opened. 10 ml *(2 tsps)* of this syrup each day is recommended if the diet is lacking in vitamin C.

Brandied peaches

450 g *(1 lb)* fresh peaches or 822-g *(1-lb 13-oz)* can peach halves
225 g *(½ lb)* sugar
about 150 ml *(¼ pt)* brandy or Cointreau

Fresh peaches Skin the peaches by plunging them into boiling water, then gently peeling off the skins. Halve the peaches and remove the stones. Make a light syrup by dissolving 125 g *(4 oz)* sugar in 300 ml *(½ pt)* water and poach the peaches gently for 4–5 minutes. Remove from the heat, drain and cool then arrange the fruit in small jars. Add the remaining sugar to the remaining syrup and dissolve it slowly. Bring to the boil and boil to 110°C *(230°F)*; allow to cool. Add an equal quantity of brandy or Cointreau to the syrup, pour over the peaches and seal as for chutney.

Canned peaches Remove the fruit from the can and drain well, keeping the syrup (this size of can yields about 400 ml *(15 fl oz)*. Reduce the syrup to half the quantity by boiling gently, remove from the heat and cool. Prick the peaches with a fine skewer or darning needle and place in small jars. Add the brandy or Cointreau to the cooled syrup and pour over the fruit; seal as for chutney (page 447).

Brandied pineapple

822-g *(1-lb 13-oz)* can pineapple pieces
3 cloves
a 5-cm *(2-in)* stick of cinnamon
150 ml *(¼ pt)* brandy or Kirsch

Drain the juice from the pineapple and put it in a saucepan; add the cloves and cinnamon and simmer gently together until of a syrupy consistency. Add the pineapple pieces and simmer them for a further 10 minutes. Remove from the heat and add the brandy or Kirsch. Cool, then pack the fruit into a wide-necked bottle. Pour on the syrup and seal.

Meringues (p. 390), Brandy snaps (p. 425), Macaroons (p. 426).
(Overleaf) Almond crisps (p. 423), Iced gingernuts (p. 425), Orange glazed meltaways (p. 429), Chocolate frosties (p. 430), Christmas garlands (p. 422), Chocolate cookies (p. 425), Coffee chequerboards (p. 430), Chocolate Viennese fingers (p. 429), Jam buttons (p. 422).

Brandied cherries

Make a light syrup as for peaches, above. Wash the cherries and prick with a darning needle. Poach them whole and proceed as for peaches.

To vary the flavour, 1 stick of cinnamon may be included in the syrup (remove it before putting the fruit into jars) or 5 ml *(1 level tsp)* ground cinnamon may be added – though this will cloud the syrup.

Spiced pears

900 g *(2 lb)* firm eating pears
400 ml *(¾ pt)* cider vinegar
300 ml *(½ pt)* water
450 g *(1 lb)* granulated sugar
1 cinnamon stick, broken in half
10 whole cloves
small piece of root ginger

Peel, core and quarter the pears. Place in a pan and cover with boiling water; cook gently until almost tender. Drain. Boil together for 5 minutes the cider vinegar, water, sugar, cinnamon, cloves and root ginger. Add the pears and cook until clear. Pack the drained pears into hot jars, cover with boiling syrup; seal with vinegar-proof skin or paper. *Makes about 900 g (2 lb).*

Spiced prunes

450 g *(1 lb)* prunes
cold tea
400 ml *(¾ pt)* vinegar
225 g *(½ lb)* sugar
7.5 ml *(1½ level tsps)* mixed spice

Wash the prunes and soak them overnight in the cold tea. Boil together the vinegar, sugar and spice. Cook the prunes in a little of the tea for 10–15 minutes, or until soft, then drain. Add 300 ml *(½ pt)* of the juice to the vinegar. Put the prunes into small jars and cover with syrup. Cover as for jam (page 435).

Spiced crab-apples

2.6 kg *(6 lb)* crab-apples
900 ml *(1½ pt)* water
2–3 strips of lemon peel
450 g *(1 lb)* sugar
400 ml *(¾ pt)* wine vinegar
1 stick of cinnamon
1–2 whole cloves
3 peppercorns

Wash and trim the crab-apples, then simmer them in the water with the lemon peel until just tender; remove from the heat. Place the sugar and vinegar in a pan and add 900 ml *(1½ pt)* of the liquid from the fruit. Tie the spices in a muslin bag and add to the liquid. Bring to the boil slowly, to dissolve the sugar, and boil for 1 minute. Remove the pan from the heat and add the crab-apples. Simmer gently until the syrup has reduced to a coating consistency (30–40 minutes). Remove the bag of spices after the first ½ hour. Place the fruit in small jars, cover with syrup and cover as for jam (page 435).

Sloe gin

450 g *(1 lb)* sloes
75–100 g *(3–4 oz)* granulated sugar
almond essence
1 bottle gin

Stalk and clean the sloes, prick them all over with a darning needle and put them into a screw-topped jar. Add the sugar and a few drops of almond essence. Fill up the bottle with gin, screw down tightly and leave in a dark place for 3 months, shaking occasionally. At the end of this time, open the jar and strain the liquor through muslin until clear. Re-bottle, cork and leave until required.

Pepperkaker angels and Christmas roses (p. 421–2), Starry wonders (p. 423), Sugar canes (p. 422), Christmas trees (p. 423).

Home freezing

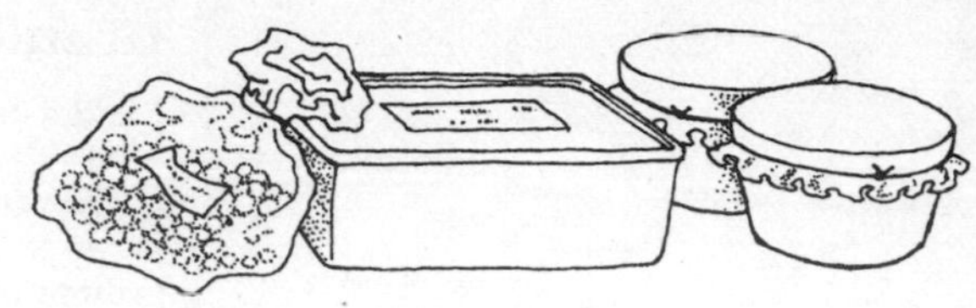

More and more households find it worth while to preserve food by freezing – either to make good use of an abundant supply of fruit, vegetables or other food, or to enjoy the luxury of out-of season delicacies. Bulk buying enables you to buy at the most favourable prices and it is a great convenience to be able to do a large batch of cooking at one time and put some of it by for future use. With the help of a freezer, catering for a party can be spread over the preceding week or two.

If you want to freeze fresh food regularly it is essential that you use either a home freezer or a frozen food compartment with a four-star marking ✱✱✱✱ . Both are capable of temperatures below those of one, two and three star refrigerators (ie −24°C; *−12°F*) and it is essential that food is frozen at or below this temperature.

If you only want to store ready frozen foods, you can use the frozen food compartment of a refrigerator.

Nearly all refrigerators available in this country have a frozen food storage compartment marked with one, two or three stars; these indicate the temperature achieved and the storage life of ready-frozen foods.

One star *	−6°C *(21°F)*	Frozen food will keep for 1 week; ice cream for 1 day
Two stars **	−12°C *(10°F)*	Frozen food will keep for 1 month; ice cream for 2 weeks
Three stars ***	−18°C *(0°F)*	Frozen food will keep for 3 months; ice cream for 1 month. In some refrigerators the 3-star compartment is suitable for freezing small quantities of fresh food, about 1.25 kg *(3 lb)* in 24 hours. Check the manufacturer's instructions.

(No star marking – Store frozen foods for 2–3 days only.)

Types of freezer available

Upright freezers (front opening) vary in size from 50–340 litres *(1.75–12 cu ft)*. Most occupy the same floor space as an equivalent capacity refrigerator. Some small models are designed to stand on top of a refrigerator. Some of the larger models have two doors.

Most upright freezers have at least one shelf with evaporator coils underneath – this is the coldest part and food packages to be frozen must be placed on this shelf. If there are no coils visible, they will be concealed in the sides of the freezer so place the packages against the sides. Pull-out baskets are often provided and many upright freezers have door shelves. Do not use the door shelves for long term storage as these will not be as cold as the main body of the freezer.

Chest freezers (top opening) vary in size from about 100–340 litres *(3.5–12 cu ft)* upwards – usually occupying more floor area than upright models. The evaporator coils are round the sides of the freezer so place food to be frozen against the sides.

Some models have baskets, some have none; sometimes baskets are optional extras. Lids are hinged (sometimes topped with a useful plastic laminated top).

Refrigerator/freezers These are two door models which consist of an ordinary refrigerator with a front opening freezer above or below the main cabinet. The freezer capacity is generally about 96–204 litres *(3.4–7.2 cu ft)*.

Second-hand freezers Second-hand freezers are sometimes available through dealers or advertisements. Check that what you are offered is a genuine home freezer, not an old commercial food conservator. Check also that the temperature will fall to −24°C *(−12°F)* for freezing and can be kept at −18°C *(0°F)* for storage, that the lid or door fits well and that reliable servicing facilities are available.

How to choose a freezer

First decide what type and size of freezer you require. This will obviously depend on the space you have available, how much you are prepared to spend and how much food you want to store in it.

If you are a town dweller and plan to store only small

quantities of commercially frozen food and to do a little home freezing, one of the 114–170 litre *(4–6 cu ft)* upright models or a refrigerator/freezer would probably be big enough. For a small garden owner, or a more ambitious town dweller who plans to take advantage of bulk buying, a 204–340 litre *(7.2–12 cu ft)* model would be more suitable.

As a general rule 28 litres *(1 cu ft)* of freezer space holds about 9–11 kg *(20–25 lb)* of frozen food, though obviously irregularly shaped packages like legs of lamb take up more space than an oblong packet of fish fingers. As a guide, allow 57 litres *(2 cu ft)* of space per member of the family. The cubic capacity as given by the manufacturer is sometimes optimistic; quite a lot of space is taken up by storage baskets in some models, but in time you will get used to judging space.

In many freezers a switch or dial can be set to give a lower temperature or a fast-freeze setting. This should be set for 2 or 3 hours before you put unfrozen food in, so that the freezing process is speeded up, since quick freezing is important. Foods contain water which is progressively converted to ice as the temperature falls. If freezing is slow, then large ice crystals are formed, causing deterioration of the texture, flavour and general appearance. If freezing is rapid, the food will when thawed be close to the original fresh product.

Once the food has been frozen, the setting can be returned to 'normal', maintaining a temperature of −18°C *(0°F)*. Some freezers have a separate 'fast-freeze' compartment; use this for freezing in food, then transfer the frozen food to the main part of the freezer for storage. (Using lower temperatures for storage will do no harm whatever to the food, but the running costs of the freezer will be unnecessarily high.)

It is an advantage if the freezer has a warning device (a light is the most usual arrangement) which comes on when the temperature starts to rise above −18°C *(0°F)*. Alternatively, the electrician who installs the freezer may be able to fit a warning buzzer or light to the plug, which will come on when the current is cut off.

Defrosting

Most freezers are supplied with full instructions for defrosting. If you don't receive this information, we strongly recommend you to contact the maker, as the procedure for different models varies considerably. However, as a general guide, defrosting should be carried out once every 9 months for chest freezers and every 4–6 months for upright freezers – or when the ice coating is about 0.5 cm *(¼ in)* thick on the sides of the cabinet. Choose a time when the freezer contains as little as possible.

Turn off the current at the wall switch, remove any packages, wrap them in several layers of newspaper or a blanket and put them in a refrigerator or somewhere cold. Put a bowl of boiling water in the freezer and close the lid or door. When the ice has started to melt, you can help the defrosting by scraping the sides with a plastic scraper; pick off any loose pieces of frost – it's much easier than dealing with water. Mop up as necessary, drying the sides and base of the freezer well. Turn on the current and leave for 2–3 hours for the temperature to drop before you replace the packages.

Power cuts and breakdowns

1. Do NOT open the freezer door.
2. A fairly full load will stay frozen for at least 12 hours; a lesser load for at least 6 hours.
3. In the case of breakdowns always check wiring, plugs, fuses and switches before calling a service engineer.
4. If the repair is going to take longer than your frozen food will last, check with the service depot for a replacement/loan service or food storage service.
5. As long as food which has begun to thaw out still has ice crystals present it may be re-frozen. Food which has thawed but is still cold to the touch should be used immediately or cooked, cooled and then frozen. Bread, plain cakes, unfilled pastry and fruit can be safely refrozen.
6. Pre-cooked meat, fish and poultry which has thawed should be used immediately.
7. Food which has completely thawed and ceases to feel cold should be discarded; fruit can be used for purées, sauces and jams as long as it looks and tastes alright. Bread, cakes and pastry will be safe to eat.
8. If you have advance warning of a power cut put the fast freeze switch on for about 3 hours beforehand. Fill gaps between the freezer contents with crumpled newspaper or cardboard boxes.

Moving house

1. Always check with the removal firm that they will handle the freezer and state whether it is empty or full.
2. Letting stocks run low before moving day may be a good idea, but on the other hand a good selection of prepared dishes and frozen food is just the thing for a busy moving family.
3. If the move is to be completed within the day, the food should not suffer provided the door is kept shut and the freezer is the last item on the van and the first item off.
4. Make sure you have the new site for the freezer worked out and that there is a plug.
5. It is wise to consult your freezer manufacturer on this subject.

The golden rules of freezing:

1. Always start with good quality foods and freeze them at peak freshness. Food can only come out of the freezer as good as you put it in.
2. Keep handling to a minimum and make sure everything is scrupulously clean. Freezing doesn't kill bacteria and germs.
3. Pay special attention to packaging and sealing. Exposure to air and moisture damages frozen foods.
4. Cool food rapidly if it has been cooked or blanched; never put anything hot – or even warm – into your freezer.
5. Freeze as quickly as possible, and in small quantities.
6. Freeze in the coldest part of the freezer, and don't pack the food to be frozen too closely together – spread it out until it is frozen.
7. Transfer newly added items to the main part of the cabinet once they've been frozen – if a freezer with separate compartments is being used.
8. For large amounts, switch to fast-freeze well in advance; remember to return the switch to normal later.
9. Maintain a steady storage temperature of – 18°C *(0°F)* and don't do anything that will cause temperatures within the freezer to keep fluctuating (eg opening the door too frequently).
10. Label and date food so that you can ensure a good rotation of stock. Ideally, keep a record and tick off items as you use them, then you can tell at a glance which supplies are getting low.
11. Defrost the freezer at a time when stocks are low and if possible on a cold day.
12. Be prepared for emergencies. Make sure you know what steps to take in case of a breakdown or power cut.

Use of the fast-freeze switch: Follow the manufacturer's instructions for the use of this. As a general rule for small quantities, eg for one loaf plus one small casserole, it is probably not necessary to touch the switch at all, simply pop the food in. This should be safe for up to, say, 4 items (perhaps a sponge cake and some biscuits could also be included, but nothing very dense such as a leg of lamb).

For a fairly small amount eg a bulk bake of, say, 4 casseroles and a bulk bake of pies, place the fast freeze switch on for about 2 hours before you put the food in. Leave the switch on for about 4 hours more, totalling 6 hours in all, until the food is really solid.

For a large amount, eg a half-carcass of meat purchased in bulk, fresh, put the fast-freeze switch on for about 6 hours beforehand to ensure the freezer is really cold. Put in the meat and leave for a further 12–24 hours, until solid, depending on the load. This timing is for a full freezer load when you are freezing the maximum your freezer will take. For half your possible maximum load you could obviously use the switch for less time.

These figures are intended only as a guide for those who do not have adequate instructions with their freezer. Only freeze one-tenth of your freezer's capacity in any 24 hours, eg if you have a 285-litre *(10-cu ft)* freezer, you can freeze only 28 litres *(1 cu ft)* of space. 28 litres *(1 cu ft)* of freezer space holds about 9–11 kg *(20–25 lb)* food, so if you have this size of freezer you can freeze 9–11 kg *(20–25 lb)* food in 24 hours.

Food for freezing *see colour plate facing p. 496*

It is possible to freeze almost any food. Most varieties of vegetable and fruit freeze well, except for bananas, whole melons, lettuce and some other salad vegetables. Some fruits tend to lose their colour.

All raw meat, poultry, game and fish may be frozen, also soups, stocks, stews and baked foods, eg pies, cakes, biscuits, bread and sandwiches. Some milk dishes may curdle when frozen and are therefore not generally so satisfactory. Dishes with gelatine alone don't freeze well. Cold soufflés, mousses, cheese cakes are satisfactory.

Packaging

Pack the foods carefully, for faulty packaging results in loss of quality. Allow 1 cm *(½ in)* head space for expansion with liquids and with any foods packed in liquid. Exclude as much air as possible before sealing. Special moisture-proof and vapour-proof packaging materials should be used. Some of the most useful are:

Polythene bags These should be of fairly heavy gauge polythene unless they are to be used for over-wrapping, when thin bags will do. They must be sealed by special covered metal strips or by heat-sealing with an iron. (When using the latter method, shield the polythene with a piece of paper before applying the iron.) Have an assortment of sizes on hand. A self sealing bag is obtainable.

Polythene sheeting Very useful for covering joints of irregular shape and for individually wrapped chops, fish fillets, pies, tarts, cakes, etc. Seal with freezer tape.

Cling film (use freezer quality) is ideal as an inner wrapping for cuts of meat or fish. Overwrap with a polythene bag.

Aluminium foil Use standard thickness foil, rather than thinner brands. Ideal as an inner wrapping to exclude all air from the food. Overwrap with a polythene bag.

Foil dishes and basins Good freezer-to-oven containers for pies, tarts, puddings and casseroles which are to be frozen and reheated.

Polythene boxes Storage boxes with airtight lids can

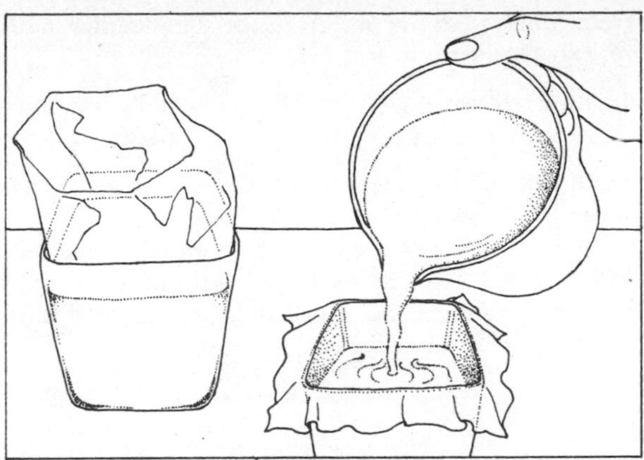

Preforming a liquid package for freezing; when the liquid is frozen, the polythene bag can be removed from the container but will retain a regular shape that is convenient for storing

be used for freezing most foods. Choose the size carefully, so that there is not too much air space round the food. If necessary, seal the lid with freezer tape.

Waxed tubs Firm, round, waxed tubs with airtight lids stack well and are suitable for liquids and for soft, squashable foods, eg soups, sauces, fruit in syrup, purées. Let the food cool before putting it in the tubs.

Waxed cartons Box-shaped containers are usually of a waxed material slightly thinner than that used for tubs; they are used for foods which might squash – fruit, vegetables, cooked carved meats, iced cakes, delicate pastries. The edge of the lid should be sealed with freezer tape.

Waxed paper Useful for separating individual chops, cake portions etc, within a larger pack.

Freezer tape Ordinary adhesive tape will not stick at freezer temperatures. Use the special freezer tape to make packages air-tight.

Labelling

Label all packages carefully with the date of freezing, contents, weight, number of servings, any special processing, etc. Keep account in a notebook of what is in the freezer, and cross off each item as it is used. Use items in rotation. Special freezer adhesive labels can be obtained, but ordinary labels fixed on with freezer tape are equally satisfactory. Tie-on luggage labels can also be used. Waxed containers and foil dishes can be marked with a wax pencil or a waterproof felt-tipped pen. (These markings cannot be removed, so avoid them if you wish to re-use the containers.)

Storing frozen foods

Once it is frozen, food should be stored at a minimum temperature of –18°C *(0°F)*, to prevent any increase in the micro-organisms present. Fluctuating temperatures, or storing at a higher temperature, will cause gradual deterioration, with conditions conducive to growth of spoilage agents.

Freezing fruit

Preparation

Rinse all but soft fruits (such as raspberries) in ice-cold water, a few at a time to prevent undue handling. Drain very thoroughly, as wet fruit dilutes the sugar syrup. Avoid using chipped enamel or iron utensils, which may give the fruit a metallic taste. To prevent fruits such as apricots, peaches, pears and yellow plums from discolouring, keep them covered with water and lemon juice (the juice of 1 large lemon to 1 l, *1¾ pt*, water) during the preparation.

Packing

Fruit may be frozen in one of three ways:
1. As a dry pack 2. In sugar 3. In syrup

Dry pack Suitable for fruit that is to be used for pies or preserves and for small whole fruits (so long as the skins are undamaged) and for those not likely to discolour, eg currants, blackberries, strawberries, gooseberries. Pick over, wash, dry on paper towels and use a rigid container to prevent damage during handling and storage.

Free-flow dry pack This method is suitable for small fruit (or pieces of fruit), eg raspberries, strawberries, cherries, grapefruit segments. Pick the fruit over, prepare as necessary, spread out on a baking sheet and freeze until firm, then pack for storage.

In sugar Particularly suitable for soft fruits. Pick over the fruit but don't wash it unless really necessary. The sugar and fruit can be put into the cartons in layers or they can be well mixed together before being put in. The fruit is more likely to retain its shape if layered, for when it is mixed with the sugar, the juice is drawn out, leaving the fruit almost in purée form when thawed. Use caster sugar.

In syrup Best for non-juicy fruits or for those which discolour during preparation and storage.

The strength of the syrup varies with the fruit being treated.

To make the syrup, dissolve the sugar in the water by heating gently and bringing to the boil; cover and allow to become quite cold before using.

Use approximately 300 ml *(½ pt)* syrup to each 450 g *(1 lb)* fruit – this is normally enough to cover the fruit. Leave 1–2 cm *(½–¾ in)* space for expansion during the freezing. If the fruit tends to float above the level of the syrup in the carton, hold it down with a piece of crumpled waxed paper.

Thawing and cooking fruit

If the fruit is to be served raw, thaw it slowly in the unopened container and eat while still slightly chilled; turn it into a dish only just before serving. Fruits which tend to discolour, eg peaches, benefit by being thawed more rapidly. Stone fruits which tend to discolour should be kept submerged in the syrup while thawing. The times to allow per 450 g *(1 lb)* fruit are as follows (remember that dry sugar packs thaw rather more quickly than fruit in syrup):

In a refrigerator	allow 6–8 hours
At room temperature	allow 2–4 hours

For quick thawing, place the container in slightly warm water for ½–1 hour.

If the fruit is to be cooked, thaw it until the pieces are just loosened. Cook as for fresh fruit, but don't forget when adding sugar that it will already be sweet if it has been packed in dry sugar or in syrup.

Fruit	*Preparation*
Apples, sliced	Peel, core and drop into cold water. Cut into approx 0.5-cm *(¼-in)* slices. Blanch for 2–3 min and cool in ice-cold water before packing. Useful for pies and flans.
purée	Peel, core and stew in the minimum amount of water – sweetened or unsweetened. Sieve or liquidise. Leave to cool before packing.
Apricots	Plunge them into boiling water for 30 sec to loosen the skins, then peel. Either (a) cut in half or slice into syrup made with 450 g *(1 lb)* sugar to 1 litre *(1¾ pt)* water, with some ascorbic acid (vitamin C) added to prevent browning; for each 450 g *(1 lb)* pack allow 200–300 mg ascorbic acid. Immerse the apricots by placing a piece of clean, crumpled, non-absorbent paper on the fruit, under the lid. (b) Leave whole, and freeze in cold syrup. After long storage, an almond flavour may develop round the stone.
Berries, etc. (including currants and cherries)	All may be frozen by the dry pack method, but the dry sugar pack method is suitable for soft fruits, eg raspberries. *Dry Pack:* Sort the fruit; some whole berries may be left on their sprigs or stems for use as decoration. Spread the fruit on paper-lined trays or baking sheets, put into the freezer until frozen, then pack. *Dry Sugar Pack:* Pack dried whole fruit with 100–175 g sugar to 450 g fruit *(4–6 oz to 1 lb)*, mix together and seal.
Blackberries	Dry pack or dry sugar pack – allow 225 g *(8 oz)* sugar to 900 g *(2 lb)* fruit. Leave a headspace, and pack in rigid containers.
Blueberries	Wash in chilled water and drain thoroughly. Can be (a) dry packed; (b) dry sugar packed – about 100 g *(4 oz)* sugar to 450–700 g *(1–1½ lb)* fruit; slightly crush berries, mix with sugar until dissolved and then pack in rigid containers; (c) frozen in cold syrup – 900 g *(2 lb)* sugar dissolved in 1 litre *(1¾ pt)* water.
Gooseberries	Wash and thoroughly dry fruit. Pack (a) by dry method in polythene bags, without sugar; use for pie fillings; (b) in cold syrup using 900 g *(2 lb)* sugar to 1 litre *(1¾ pt)* water; (c) as purée – stew fruit in a very little water, press through a nylon sieve and sweeten to taste; useful for fools and mousses.
Loganberries	Choose firm clean fruit. Remove stalks and dry-pack in rigid containers. Dry sugar pack – see Blackberries.
Strawberries and Raspberries	Choose firm, clean dry fruit; remove stalks. Pack (a) by dry method; (b) by dry sugar method 100 g *(4 oz)* sugar to each 450 g *(1 lb)* fruit; (c) as purée – pass through a nylon sieve or liquidise clean berries; sweeten to taste – about 50 g *(2 oz)* sugar per 225 g *(8 oz)* purée – and freeze in small containers, useful for ice creams, sorbets, sauces or mousses.
Black-currants	Wash and string. (a) Dry and use dry pack method for whole fruit. (b) Purée – cook to a purée with very little water and brown sugar, according to taste.
Red-currants	Wash and dry and string, then freeze on a paper-lined tray in a single layer until frozen. Pack in rigid containers.

Fruit	*Preparation*
Cherries	Remove the stalks. Wash and dry. Use any of these methods: (a) dry pack method; (b) dry sugar pack, 225 g *(8 oz)* sugar to 900 g *(2 lb)* stoned cherries, pack in containers, best used stewed for pie fillings; (c) cover with cold syrup, 450 g *(1 lb)* sugar to 1 litre *(1¾ pt)* water, mixed with 2.5 ml *(½ tsp)* ascorbic acid per 1 litre *(1¾ pt)* syrup; leave headspace. Take care not to open packet until required, as fruit loses colour rapidly on exposure to the air.
Damsons	Wash in cold water. The skins are inclined to toughen during freezing. Best packing methods are: (a) in a cooked purée, to be used in pies; (b) halve, remove the stones and pack in cold syrup, 450 g *(1 lb)* sugar to 1 litre *(1¾ pt)* water; they will need cooking after freezing – can be used as stewed fruit; (c) poached and sweetened.
Figs	Wash gently to avoid bruising. Remove stems, then use one of the following methods: (a) freeze unsweetened, either whole or peeled, in polythene bags; (b) peel and pack in cold syrup, 450 g *(1 lb)* sugar to 1 litre *(1¾ pt)* water; (c) leave whole and wrap in foil – suitable for dessert figs.
Grapefruit	Peel fruit, removing all pith; segment and pack (a) in cold syrup, equal quantities of sugar and water – use any juice from the fruit to make up the syrup; (b) in dry sugar pack – allowing 225 g *(8 oz)* sugar to 450 g *(1 lb)* fruit, sprinkled over fruit; when juices start to run, pack in rigid containers.
Grapes	The seedless variety can be packed whole; others should be skinned, pipped and halved. Pack in cold syrup – 450 g *(1 lb)* sugar to 1 litre *(1¾ pt)* water.
Greengages	Wash in cold water, halve, remove stones and pack in syrup – 450 g *(1 lb)* sugar to 1 litre *(1¾ pt)* water, with ascorbic acid added (see Apricots). Place in rigid containers. Do not open pack until required, as fruit loses colour rapidly. Skins tend to toughen during freezing.
Lemons and Limes	There are various methods. (a) Squeeze out juice and freeze it in ice-cube trays; remove frozen cubes to polythene bags for storage. (b) Leave whole; slice or segment before freezing. (c) Remove all pith from the peel, cut into julienne strips, blanch for 1 min, cool and pack; use for garnishing dishes. (d) Mix grated lemon peel and a little sugar to serve alongside pancakes. (e) Remove slivers of peel, free of pith, and freeze in foil packs to add to drinks.
Mangoes	Peel and slice ripe fruit into cold syrup – 450 g *(1 lb)* sugar to 1 litre *(1¾ pt)* water; add 30 ml *(2 tbsps)* lemon juice to each 1 litre *(1¾ pt)* syrup. Serve with additional lemon juice.
Melons	Cantaloup and honeydew melons freeze quite well (though they lose their crispness when thawed), but the seeds of watermelon make it more difficult to prepare. Cut in half and seed, then cut flesh into balls, cubes or slices and put straight into cold syrup – 450 g *(1 lb)* sugar to 1 litre *(1¾ pt)* water. Alternatively, use dry pack method, with a little sugar sprinkled over. Pack in polythene bags.
Oranges	Prepare and pack as for grapefruit or squeeze out and freeze the juice; add sugar if desired and freeze in small quantities in containers or as frozen orange cubes. Grate peel for orange sugar as for lemon sugar. Seville oranges may be scrubbed, packed in suitable quantities and frozen whole until required for making marmalade. (It is not recommended to thaw whole frozen fruit in order to cut it up before cooking as some discoloration often occurs – use whole fruit method for marmalade. It is advisable to add one eighth extra weight of Seville or bitter oranges or tangerines when freezing for subsequent marmalade making in order to offset pectin loss.)
Peaches	Really ripe peaches are best skinned and stoned under running water, as scalding them to ease skinning will soften and slightly discolour the flesh. Firm peaches are treated in the usual way. Brush over with lemon juice. (a) Pack halves or slices in cold syrup – 450 g *(1 lb)* sugar to 1 litre *(1¾ pt)* water, with ascorbic acid added (see Apricots); pack in rigid containers, leaving 1 cm *(½ in)* headspace. (b) Purée peeled and stoned peaches by using a nylon sieve or liquidiser; mix in 15 ml *(1 tbsp)* lemon juice and 100 g *(4 oz)* sugar to each 450 g *(1 lb)* fruit – suitable for sorbets and soufflé-type desserts.

Fruit	*Preparation*
Pears	It is really only worthwhile freezing pears if you have a big crop from your garden, as they discolour rapidly, and the texture of thawed pears can be unattractively soft. Peel, quarter, remove core and dip in lemon juice immediately. Poach in syrup – 450 g *(1 lb)* sugar to 1 litre *(1¾ pt)* water – for 1½ min. Drain, cool and pack in the cold syrup.
Pineapple	Peel and core, then slice, dice, crush or cut into wedges. (a) Pack unsweetened in boxes, separated by non-stick paper. (b) Pack in syrup – 450 g *(1 lb)* sugar to 1 litre *(1¾ pt)* water – in rigid containers; include any pineapple juice from the preparation. (c) Pack the crushed pineapple in rigid containers, allowing 100 g *(4 oz)* sugar to about 350 g *(¾ lb)* fruit.
Plums	Wash, halve and discard stones. Freeze in syrup with ascorbic acid (see Apricots); use 450 g *(1 lb)* sugar to 1 litre *(1¾ pt)* water. Pack in rigid containers. Do not open packet until required, as the fruit loses colour rapidly.
Rhubarb	Wash, trim and cut into 1–2.5 cm *(½–1 in)* lengths. Heat in boiling water for 1 min and cool quickly. Pack in cold syrup, using equal quantities sugar and water, or dry-pack, to be used later for pies and crumbles.

Fruits not suitable for freezing: Bananas, pomegranates.

Freezing vegetables

Speed is important when dealing with vegetables and they should be frozen only if really fresh, ie not more than 12 hours after harvesting. It is necessary to blanch vegetables (see next paragraph) in order to inactivate the enzymes present, so that the colour, flavour and nutritive value of the vegetables can be preserved during storage. Freeze only young, tender vegetables; it is a waste of space to store old, tough ones.

Blanching

Use a pan large enough to hold a colander or wire basket. Place the vegetables in the basket and immerse this in boiling water using about 3.4 l *(6 pt)* to 450 g *(1 lb)* of vegetables. When the water re-boils, blanch the vegetables for the recommended length of time (see table), then plunge them into ice-cold water; drain and pack immediately.

Don't add salt until the frozen vegetables are cooked for serving. Don't scald more than 450 g–900 g *(1–2 lb)* vegetables at a time; the same water may be used for scalding successive batches of the same kind.

Packing

Cool and drain thoroughly. Pack into rigid containers, leaving a little space for expansion for those vegetables that pack tightly, eg peas, sweet-corn kernels. If freeflow packs are required (peas, beans), then freeze on a tray until just firm before packing.

Thawing and cooking

Put the frozen vegetables in a minimum amount of boiling salted water, about 300 ml *(½ pt)* water and 2.5 ml *(½ tsp)* salt to a 450 g *(1 lb)* package, cover the pan and simmer until tender.

Vegetable	*Preparation*	*Blanching time*
Artichokes Globe	Remove all outer coarse leaves and stalks, and trim tops and stems. Wash well in cold water, add a little lemon juice to the blanching water. Cool, and drain upside-down on absorbent paper. Pack in rigid boxes	Blanch a few at a time, in a large container for 7–10 min
Asparagus	Grade into thick and thin stems but don't tie into bunches yet. Wash in cold water, blanch, cool and drain. Tie into *small* bundles, packed tips to stalks, separated by non-stick paper	Thin stems – 2 min Thick stems – 4 min

Vegetable	*Preparation*	*Blanching time*
Aubergines (Egg plant)	Peel and cut roughly into 2.5-cm *(1-in)* slices. Blanch, chill and dry on absorbent paper. Pack in layers, separated by non-stick paper	4 min
Avocados	Prepare in pulp form. Peel and mash, allowing 15 ml *(1 tbsp)* lemon juice to each avocado. Pack in small containers. Also good frozen with cream cheese to use as a party dip	
Beans – French Runner, Broad	Select young, tender beans; wash thoroughly French – trim ends and blanch Runner – slice thickly and blanch Broad – shell and blanch In each case, cool, drain and pack	 2–3 min 2 min 3 min
Beetroot	Choose small beets. Wash well and rub skin off after scalding. Beetroot under 2.5 cm *(1 in)* in diameter may be frozen whole; large ones should be sliced or diced. Pack in cartons. *Note:* Short blanching and long storage can make beetroot rubbery	Small whole – 5–10 min Large – cook until tender 45–50 min
Broccoli	Trim off any woody parts and large leaves. Wash in salted water, and cut into small sprigs. Blanch, cool and drain well. Pack in boxes in 1–2 layers, tips to stalks	Thin stems – 3 min Medium stems – 4 min Thick stems – 5 min
Brussels sprouts	Use small compact heads. Remove outer leaves and wash thoroughly. Blanch, cool and drain well before packing	Small – 3 min Medium – 4 min
Cabbage Green & red	Use only young, crisp cabbage. Wash thoroughly, shred finely. Blanch, cool and drain. Pack in small quantities in polythene bags	1½ min
Carrots	Scrape, then slice or cut into small dice. Blanch, cool, drain and pack	3–5 min
Cauliflower	Heads should be firm, compact and white. Wash, break into small sprigs, about 2 in *(5 cm)* in diameter. Add the juice of a lemon to the blanching water to keep them white; blanch, cool, drain and pack	3 min
Celeriac	Wash and trim. Cook until almost tender, peel and slice	–
Celery	Trim, removing any strings, and scrub well. Cut into 2.5-cm *(1-in)* lengths. Suitable only for cooked dishes	3 min
Chestnuts	Wash nuts, cover with water, bring to the boil, drain and peel. Pack in rigid containers. Can be used to supplement raw chestnuts in recipe, can be cooked and frozen as purée for soups and sweets	1–2 min
Chilies	Remove stalks and scoop out the seeds and pithy part. Blanch, cool, drain and pack	
Corn on the cob	Select young yellow kernels not starchy, over-ripe or shrunken. Remove husks and 'silks'. Blanch, cool and dry. Pack individually in freezer paper or foil *Note:* There may be loss of flavour and tenderness after freezing. Thaw before cooking	Small – 4 min Medium – 6 min Large – 8 min
Courgettes	Choose young ones. Wash and cut into 1-cm *(½-in)* slices. Either blanch, or sauté in a little butter	1 min
Fennel	Trim and cut into short lengths. Blanch, cool, drain and pack	3 min

Vegetable	*Preparation*	*Blanching time*
Kohlrabi	Use small roots, 5–7 cm *(2–3 in)* in diameter. Cut off tops, peel and dice. Blanch, cool, drain and pack	1½ min
Leeks	Cut off tops and roots; remove coarse outside leaves. Slice into 1-cm *(½-in)* slices and wash well. Sauté in butter or oil, drain, cool, pack and freeze. Only suitable for casseroles or as a base to vichyssoise	Sauté 4 min
Marrow	Young marrows can be peeled, cut into 1–2.5 cm *(½–1 in)* slices and blanched before packing – leave 1 cm *(½ in)* headspace	3 min
Mushrooms	Choose small button mushrooms and leave whole, wipe clean but don't peel. Sauté in butter. Mushrooms larger than 2.5 cm *(1 in)* in diameter suitable only for slicing and using in cooked dishes	Sauté in butter 1 min
Onions	Can be peeled, finely chopped and packed in small plastic containers for cooking later; packages should be over-wrapped, to prevent the smell filtering out *Note:* Small onions may be blanched whole and used later in casseroles	2 min Small whole – 4 min
Parsnips	Trim and peel young parsnips and cut into narrow strips. Blanch, cool and dry	2 min
Peas, green	Use young, sweet green peas, not old or starchy. Shell and blanch, then shake the blanching basket from time to time to distribute the heat evenly. Cool, drain and pack in polythene bags or rigid containers	1–2 min
Mange-tout (Sugar Peas)	Trim the ends. Blanch, cool, drain and pack	2–3 min
Peppers, sweet	Freeze red and green peppers separately. Wash well, remove stems and all traces of seeds and membranes. Can be blanched as halves for stuffed peppers, or in thin slices for stews and casseroles	3 min
Potatoes	Best frozen in the cooked form, as partially-cooked chips (fully-cooked ones are not satisfactory), croquettes or duchesse potatoes. New: choose small even-sized potatoes. Scrape, cook fully with mint and cool. (Appearance similar to that of canned potatoes.) Chipped: Part-fry in deep fat for 2 min, cool and freeze for final frying	–
Spinach	Select young leaves. Wash very thoroughly under running water; drain. Blanch in small quantities, cool quickly and press out excess moisture. Pack in rigid containers or polythene bags, leaving 1 cm *(½ in)* headspace	2 min
Tomatoes	Tomatoes are most useful if frozen as purée or as juice.	–
Purée	Skin and core tomatoes, simmer in their own juice for 5 min until soft. Pass them through a nylon sieve or liquidise, cool and pack in small containers.	–
Juice	Trim, quarter and simmer for 5–10 min. Press through a nylon sieve and season with salt – 5 ml *(1 level tsp)* salt to every 1 litre *(1¾ pints)*. Cool, and pack in small containers	

Vegetable	*Preparation*	*Blanching time*
Turnips	Use small, young turnips. Trim and peel. Cut into small dice, about 1 cm *(½ in)*. Blanch, cool, drain and pack in rigid containers. *Note:* Turnips may be fully cooked and mashed before freezing – leave 1 cm *(½ in)* headspace.	2½ min

Unsuitable for freezing: Chicory, cucumber, endive, kale, lettuce, radishes, Jerusalem artichokes (suitable only as soups and purées).

Freezing meat

If good quality meat is available direct from a farm or at a wholesale price, then freezing is a practical proposition. Many butchers will supply bulk meat at a good discount on normal retail prices, and will butcher it for you which is an advantage. Buying meat that is already frozen is another possibility. Ready-frozen meat is available in bulk packs, sold as whole carcasses, halves or quarters. If required, specified cuts can be bought, but at increased cost.

If you are choosing meat for freezing, remember that very lean meats tend to dry out during freezing, but a layer of fat and good 'marbling' help to prevent this. Too much fat, on the other hand, tends to become rancid. It is important to select the meat carefully.

Preparation of raw meat

Joints Trim off excess fat. Pad any sharp bones to avoid puncturing the wrapping. Don't freeze unnecessarily large amounts of bone.

Steaks and chops Trim as usual. Separate the portions by placing greaseproof or waxed paper between them to prevent them freezing together; alternatively, wrap them individually in polythene sheeting.

Offal Trim as required. If necessary, divide into convenient-sized pieces.

Packing and freezing

This is very important, for incorrect or inadequate packaging will result in rancidity and/or drying out of the meat, with possible freezer burn. Pack in quantities suitable for use. Use a heavy duty polythene bag. Large joints may be given an inner wrapping of cling film or stockinette. Seal carefully. Freeze rapidly.

Thawing and cooking

There is some discussion as to whether or not it is better to thaw meat before cooking. In general, joints cooked from frozen have a better flavour than those that have been thawed first, although when thawed they are on the whole more tender. The only snag about cooking straight from frozen is the difficulty of ensuring that the inside is done without overcooking the outside. (This is no problem, of course, with steaks, chops and other cuts that are 2.5 cm *(1 in)* or less in thickness.) See the more detailed instructions under the heading 'To cook joints from frozen'.

For very large or solid joints, thawing before cooking is the safer bet. As a rough guide, allow 6 hours per 450 g *(1 lb)* in the refrigerator, or 3 hours per 450 g *(1 lb)* at average room temperature; slow thawing results in less drip, so thawing in the refrigerator is much the best. Mince and stewing or braising meats are also best thawed, though in an emergency partial thawing will suffice. Once thawed the meat should be cooked at once; if for some reason it has to wait a short time, be sure to keep it in the refrigerator.

Completely thawed frozen meats are cooked in exactly the same way as their fresh meat counterparts. It is perfectly in order to use frozen meat in making up a dish, and then to freeze this dish in the usual way.

Roasting joints from frozen

It is essential to use a meat thermometer to check the internal temperature of the meat. Insert the thermometer about 30 minutes before the end of the cooking time in the thickest part of the flesh and away from any bones.

Beef Seal in hot fat at 230°C *(450°F)* mark 8 for 20 minutes. Reduce heat to 180°C *(350°F)* mark 4, cover loosely with foil and allow 50 minutes per 450 g *(1 lb)*. Joints on the bone will take about 30 minutes less but check with the thermometer. Thermometer reading: Rare *140°F*; medium *160°F*; well done *170°F*.

Lamb: Seal the joint as above for 20 minutes. Reduce to 180°C *(350°F)* mark 4, cover loosely with foil and allow 60 minutes per 450 g *(1 lb)*. Boneless joints will need extra 30 minutes. Thermometer reading *180°F*.

Pork: Place joint in cold oven set at 220°C *(425°F)* mark 7 and allow 25 minutes per 450 g *(1 lb)* plus 25 minutes from time oven reaches temperature. Thermometer reading *190°F*.

To cook chops, steaks etc from frozen

Grill or fry from frozen over a high heat to brown the meat and seal in juices then lower heat to cook right through.

Freezing chickens
(including capons and poussins)

It is not worth spending your efforts on anything other than young, plump, tender birds. Commercial quick-frozen raw poultry is so readily available it is only an advantage to freeze it at home when the price is very favourable.

If the birds are your own, starve them for 24 hours before killing, and if possible set to and pluck out the feathers while the corpse is still warm – they come out much easier that way.

Hang the chicken for a day before drawing, and be sure to freeze at the lowest possible temperature for your freezer (ideally −32°C *−26°F*) because higher temperatures can give disappointing results. And remember to turn the temperature control down low at least 24 hours before you're planning to freeze a bird – this will give it a chance to get really cold. Once the chicken is frozen, return to the normal freezer temperature.

How you freeze your birds depends on how you're going to cook them. Obviously if you're going to make a chicken casserole, you'll be wasting freezer space if you freeze a chicken whole, instead of cutting it up into more convenient pieces.

And talking of wastage, remember that chicken fat is excellent rendered down for cooking chips in, and that any odd scraps and bones can make fabulous concentrated stocks for using in soups and sauces.

More sizeable remnants of cold roast chicken (carved or not) and poached chicken may be frozen satisfactorily too.

Whole Wipe and dry the bird after plucking and drawing it. Pack the giblets separately instead of inside, because they'll only keep for 2–3 months, while the chicken itself will keep for up to a year. Don't stuff the chicken, as it takes too long to freeze and thaw. If you wish, package any stuffing separately. Truss as for roasting (see pages 152 to 153).

Portions Divide small birds (around 1–1.5 kg, *2–3 lb*), into quarters. With young birds, this can be done with poultry secateurs or a sharp knife. Cut the bird in half, through and along the breastbone. Open the bird out, and then cut along the length of the backbone.

If you want to remove the backbone entirely, cut along either side of it, then lift it out – and don't forget to use it for making stock. If you're using a knife, you'll have to tap the back sharply with a heavy weight to cut through the bony sections.

Either way, once the bird is in two halves, lay these skin side up. Divide each in half again by cutting diagonally across between wing and thigh – allocating more breast meat to the wing than to the thigh, to even out the amount of meat per portion.

Smaller chicken joints When these are to be used in casseroles, etc, cut the thigh loose along the rounded edge and pull the leg away from the body to isolate the joint. Break the thigh backwards so that the knife can cut through the socket of each thigh joint, and loosen the wings from the breast meat in the same way. Divide the legs into two pieces in the centre of the joint.

Lastly, turn over the body of the bird on to its back and carve the breast meat from the breastbone. Both breast portions may be halved, and the back is divided into two or three pieces or used to supplement the stock pot.

Packing

Before packing whole birds in heavy-duty polythene bags, first pad the legs with foil so that they can't spike their way through the wrapping. Exclude as much air as possible before sealing the bag.

With chicken quarters or joints, pack individually in foil or polythene bags, and then combine into a larger package to save time hunting for individual packs.

Cold roast or poached chicken should be cooled as rapidly as possible after cooking. Parcel in foil, with any stuffing packed separately and freeze at once.

Freezing turkeys

In general, these are treated like chickens. But because they are bulky, they take up a lot of valuable freezer space, so it is not good planning to store them for too long. The maximum storage time is 6 months.

Leftover roast turkey may be frozen as for chicken. It's best cut off the bone, and any fat should be discarded, while stuffing should be packed separately. To avoid excessive drying, freeze it with gravy stock, unless it is to be stored only for a very short time.

Freezing game

All game must be hung prior to freezing, for the same length of time as for immediate use and according to individual taste. Prepare and pack as for poultry.

Thawing poultry and game

Poultry and game birds *must* be thawed completely before cooking. To thaw the bird, leave it in its wrapping; the time required depends both on the size of the bird and on the method of thawing. A 1.8-kg *(4-lb)* bird will take 8–10 hours at room temperature or at least 15 hours in a refrigerator. Chicken joints need about 3 hours at room temperature, 6 in the refrigerator. Thaw the chicken in its wrapping. Turkeys should preferably be thawed in the refrigerator; small turkey will take about 2 days to thaw, larger ones 3–4 days. Thaw ducks and geese in their wrapping, allowing about 12 hours at room temperature or 24–36 hours in the refrigerator.

Note Once thawed, the bird should be used as soon as possible.

Freezing fish

Only *very* fresh fish must be used, ie within 12 hours of catching.

Preparation

Clean as usual – that is, scale, remove the fins and gut the fish. Leave small fish whole, but remove the heads and tails of larger fish. Skin and fillet flat fish if you wish, or freeze them whole. Salmon to be frozen whole requires special care. Wash it and remove the scales, gut and wash thoroughly under running water; drain and dry. Place the whole fish (unwrapped and firmly supported) in the freezer, and freeze until solid. Remove, and dip in cold water; this forms a thin ice over the fish; return it to the freezer. Repeat the process until the ice glaze is approx 0.3 cm *(⅛ in)* thick.

Other whole fish can also be frozen this way.

Packaging

Wrap the fish individually in foil or cling film and pack together in polythene bags. Wrap whole ice-glazed fish in heavy-duty polythene and support with a thin board.

Thawing

Thaw slowly in the unopened package in a cool place, continuing just long enough to separate the portions – 45 minutes at room temperature, 3–4 hours in a refrigerator. Small fish may be cooked from frozen, in which case the cooking time must be a few minutes longer than usual. Whole salmon: allow to thaw before cooking. Once thawed, use promptly. Steaks should be cooked from frozen.

Freezing cooked foods

Preparation

In general prepare and cook the foods as if they were to be served immediately, but reduce any strong seasonings, eg curry, garlic. Take care not to overcook the foods, particularly if they are to be re-heated for serving. Adjust seasonings during re-heating.

Chill the foods promptly after cooking and package them as carefully as when freezing fresh foods.

Remember that liquids such as soups and sauces expand, so leave space for this.

Use aluminium foil dishes for foods which will be re-heated for serving, or line a container with foil, freeze, then remove the foil package from the container and overwrap it with polythene. Freeze immediately the food is cool.

Food and storage time	*Preparation*	*Freezing*	*Thawing and serving*
Meat, Raw (leave unstuffed) Beef: 8 months Lamb: 6 months Veal: 6 months Pork: 6 months Freshly minced meat: 3 months Offal: 3 months Cured and smoked meats: 1–2 months Sausages: 3 months	Use good quality, well-hung fresh meat. Removing bones will save space. Butcher into suitable portions. Place polythene sheets or waxed paper between individual chops or steaks	Package carefully in heavy-quality polythene bags. Group in similar types, and overwrap with mutton cloth, stockinette or thin polythene to protect against puncturing and loss of quality	Most meats may be cooked from frozen but with large joints avoid over-cooking meat on outside and leaving it raw at centre. Thaw in the refrigerator, keeping wrappings on, allow about 6 hours per 450 g *(1 lb)*. Small items like chops, steaks, can be cooked frozen, but use gentle heat. Partial thawing is necessary before egg-and-crumb coating, etc
Bacon; smoked joints: 2 months unsmoked joints: 1 month smoked rashers, chops and gammon steaks: 2 months unsmoked rashers, chops and gammon steaks: 2–3 weeks vacuum packed: 20 weeks		Wrap in foil and polythene	
Meat, Cooked Dishes Casseroles, stews, curries, etc: 2 months	Prepare as desired. See that the meat is cooked but not over-cooked to allow for re-heating. Do not season too heavily – check this at point of serving. Have enough liquid or sauce to immerse solid meat completely. Don't add potato, rice or spaghetti, as they acquire a warmed-up flavour and are best added at point of serving; unless otherwise stated same applies to garlic and celery	When mixture is quite cold, transfer to waxed cartons; for dishes with a strong smell or colour, inner-line cartons with polythene bags. Or use foil dishes, or freeze in foil-lined cook-ware	Re-heat food from cartons or polythene bags in a saucepan or casserole dish. Pre-shaped foil-wrapped mixtures can be re-heated in the original dish. When re-heating in a casserole, allow at least 1 hour for heating through at 200°C *(400°F)*, mark 6 then if necessary reduce heat to 180°C *(350°F)* mark 4 until really hot. Alternatively, heat gently in a pan, simmering till hot through
Meat, Roast 2–4 weeks	Joints can be roasted and frozen for serving cold – don't over-cook. Reheated whole joints are not very satisfactory. Sliced frozen cooked meat tends to be dry when re-heated	Best results are achieved by freezing whole joint, thawing, then slicing prior to serving. But small pieces can be sliced and packed in polythene if required to serve cold, or put in foil containers and covered with gravy, if to be served hot	Allow plenty of time for thawing-out – about 4 hours per 450 g *(1 lb)* at room temperature, or double that time in the refrigerator, in the wrapping. Sliced meat requires less time
Meat Loaves, Pâté 1 month	Follow regular recipe. Package in the usual way, after cooling rapidly. Keep for minimum time	When quite cold, remove from tin, wrap and freeze	Thaw preferably overnight, or for at least 6–8 hours, in the refrigerator
Poultry and Game Chicken: 12 months Duck: 4–5 months Goose: 4–5 months Turkey: 6 months Giblets: 2–3 months Game birds: 6–8 months Venison: 12 months	Use fresh birds only: prepare and draw in the usual way. Do not stuff before freezing. Cover protruding bones with greaseproof paper or foil. Hang game desired time before freezing	Pack trussed bird inside polythene bag and exclude as much air as possible before sealing. Freeze giblets separately. If wished, freeze in joints, wrap individually, and then overwrap	Thaw in wrapping, preferably in refrigerator. Thaw a small bird over-night; birds up to 1.8 kg *(4 lb)* up to 12 hours; 1.8–5.4 kg *(4–12 lb)* up to 24 hours; over 5.4 kg *(12 lb)* 48–72 hours. Joints, 6 hours

Fish, uncooked Oily fish including salmon: 2 months White fish: 3 months Smoked salmon: 2–3 months Caviar: do not freeze	Must be really fresh – within 12 hours of the catch. Whole fish: wash and remove scales by scraping tail-to-head with back of knife. Gut. Wash thoroughly under running water. Drain and dry on a clean cloth	For best results, put whole fish unwrapped in freezer till solid. Remove, dip in cold water. This forms thin ice over fish. Repeat process until ice glaze is 0.5 cm *(¼ in)* thick. Wrap in heavy-duty polythene; support with a thin board	Allow to thaw for 24 hours in a cool place before cooking. Once thawed use promptly
Fish steaks	Prepare in usual way	Separate steaks with double layer of cling film; wrap in heavy polythene	May be cooked from frozen
Fish, cooked Pies, fish cakes, croquettes, kedgeree, mousse, paella: 2 months	Prepare according to recipe, but be sure fish is absolutely fresh. Hard-boiled eggs should be added to kedgeree before re-heating	Freeze in foil-lined containers, remove when hard, then pack in sealed bags	Either slow-thaw in refrigerator or put straight into oven at 180°C *(350°F)* mark 4 to heat, depending on type of recipe
Shellfish 1 month	Advisable only if you can freeze within 12 hours of catching		
Sauces, Soups, Stocks 2–3 months: if highly spiced, 2 weeks	All are very useful as stand-bys in the freezer	When cold, pour into rigid containers, seal well and freeze	Either thaw for 1–2 hours at room temperature or heat immediately to boiling point
Pizza, unbaked Up to 3 months baked, up to 2 months	Prepare traditional yeast mixture to baking stage. ie, shaped, with topping. Wrap in foil or polythene. If freezing ready cooked, bake in usual way	Baked or unbaked: freeze flat until solid, then overwrap in ones, twos, threes or fours	Unbaked: remove packaging and place frozen on a baking sheet in cold oven set at 230°C *(450°F)* mark 8 and bake for 30–35 minutes. Baked: remove packaging, place in a baking sheet and reheat from frozen in preheated oven at 200°C *(400°F)* mark 6 for about 20 minutes, or leave in packaging at room temperature for 2 hours before reheating for 10–15 minutes.
Pancakes, unfilled 2 months	Add 15 ml *(1 tbsp)* corn oil to a basic 100 g *(4 oz)* flour recipe. Make pancakes, and cool quickly on a wire rack. Interleave them with lightly oiled greaseproof paper or polythene film. Seal in polythene bags or foil	Freeze quickly	To thaw: leave in packaging at room temperature for 2–3 hours or overnight in the refrigerator. For quick thawing, unwrap, spread out separately and leave at room temperature for about 20 minutes. To re-heat, place stack of pancakes wrapped in foil in the oven at 190°C *(375°F)* mark 5 for 20–30 minutes. To re-heat individual pancakes, place in a lightly greased heated frying pan, allowing ½ minute for each side
Pancakes – Filled 1–2 months	Choose only fillings suitable for freezing. Don't over-season	Place filled pancakes in a foil dish, seal and overwrap	Place frozen in foil packaging in oven at 200°C *(400°F)* mark 6 for about 30 minutes

Food and storage time	*Preparation*	*Freezing*	*Thawing and serving*
Pastry, uncooked Shortcrust: 3 months Flaky and puff: 3–4 months	Roll out to size required (or shape into vol-au-vent cases). Freeze pie shells unwrapped until hard to avoid damage. Use foil plates or take frozen shell out of dish after freezing but before wrapping. Discs of pastry can be stacked with waxed paper between for pie bases or tops. Bulk flaky and puff pastry: prepare to last rolling, pack in polythene bags or heavy duty foil and overwrap *Note:* There is little advantage in bulk-freezing unshaped shortcrust pastry, as it takes about 3 hours to thaw before it can be rolled out	Stack pastry shapes with 2 pieces of cling film or waxed paper between layers, so that, if needed, one piece can be removed without thawing the whole batch. Place the stack on a piece of cardboard, wrap and seal	Shortcrust: Thaw discs at room temperature, fit into pie plate and proceed. Return unbaked pie shells or flan cases to their original container before cooking; they can go into oven from the freezer (ovenproof glass should first stand for 10 minutes at room temperature); add about 5 minutes to normal baking time Bulk flaky and puff: thaw for 3–4 hours at room temperature, or overnight in refrigerator
Pastry Pies, uncooked Double-crust: 3 months	Prepare pastry and filling as required. Make large pies in a foil dish or plate, or line an ordinary dish or plate with foil and use as a pre-former. Make small pies in patty tins or foil cases. Do not slit top crust before freezing	Freeze uncovered. When frozen, remove small or pre-formed pies from containers and pack all pies in foil or polythene bags	Unwrap unbaked fruit pies and place still frozen in the oven at 220°C *(425°F)* mark 7 for 40–60 minutes, according to type and size. Slit tops of double crusts when beginning to thaw
Top-crust: 3 months	Prepare pie in usual way; cut fruit into fairly small pieces, blanch if necessary, and toss with sugar. Alternatively, use cold cooked savoury filling. Cover with pastry. Do not slit crust	Use ovenproof glass or foil dishes. Wrap in foil or plastic film, protecting as for cooked pies	Unwrap and place in pre-heated oven. (Ovenproof glass should first stand for 10 minutes at room temperature.) Cut a vent in pastry when it begins to thaw. Add a little to usual cooking time
Pastry, cooked Pastry cases: 6 months Meat pies: 3–4 months Fruit pies: 6 months	Prepare as usual. Empty cases freeze satisfactorily, but with some change in texture. Prepare pies as directed (using an aluminium foil dish). Brush pastry cases with egg white before filling. Cool completely before freezing	Wrap carefully – very fragile. Protect the tops of pies with an inverted paper or aluminium pie plate, then wrap and seal	Leave pies at room temperature for 2–4 hours, depending on size. If required hot, re-heat in the oven. Flan cases should be thawed at room temperature for about 1 hour. 'Refresh' them if you wish at 180°C *(350°F)* mark 4 for 10–15 minutes
Biscuit Pie Crust 2 months	Not easy to handle unfilled unless the crust is pre-baked. Shape in a sandwich tin or pie plate, lined with foil or waxed paper. Add filling if suitable	Freeze until firm, then remove from tin in the foil wrapping and pack in a rigid container	Filled, to serve cold, thaw at room temperature for 6 hours
Sweets Mousses, creams, etc: 2–3 months	Make as usual; these can be frozen in new toughened tableware glasses by Duralex	Freeze, unwrapped, in foil-lined container until firm, then remove container, place in polythene bag, seal and return to freezer	Unwrap and thaw in refrigerator for about 6 hours or at room temperature for about 2 hours
Ice cream 3 months Commercially made: 1 month	Either home-made or bought ice creams and sorbets can be stored in the freezer	Bought ice creams should be rewrapped in moisture-proof bags before storing. Home-made ones should be frozen in moulds or waxed containers and overwrapped	Put in freezing compartment of the refrigerator for 6–8 hours, to soften a little. Some 'soft' bought ice cream can be used from freezer – keep away from elements, or sides of chest model

Apricot creams (p. 340).

Food and storage time	*Preparation*	*Freezing*	*Thawing and serving*
Cream Whipped: 3 months Commercially frozen: up to 1 year	Use pasteurized only, with a 35 per cent butterfat content, or more (ie double or whipping cream). Whipped cream may be piped into rosettes on waxed paper. Best results are achieved with half-whipped cream, with 5 ml *(1 level tsp)* sugar to 142 ml *(¼ pt)*	Transfer cream to suitable container, eg waxed carton, leaving space for expansion. Freeze rosettes unwrapped; when firm, pack in a single layer in foil	Thaw in a refrigerator allowing 24 hours, or 12 hours at room temperature. Put rosettes in position as decoration before thawing, for they cannot be handled
Cakes, cooked Including sponge flans, Swiss rolls and layers cakes: 6 months (Frosted cakes lose quality after 2 months; since aging improves fruit cakes, they may be kept longer)	Bake in usual way. Leave until cold on a wire rack. Swiss rolls are best rolled up in non stick or waxed paper if to be frozen without a filling. Do not spread or layer with jam before freezing. Use minimum amount of essences, and go lightly with spices	Wrap plain cake layers separately, or together with cling film or waxed paper between layers. Freeze frosted cakes (whole or cut) unwrapped until frosting has set, then wrap, seal, and pack in boxes to protect icing	Iced cakes: unwrap before thawing, then the wrapping will not stick to the frosting when thawing. Cream cakes: may be sliced while frozen, for a better shape and quick thawing. Plain cakes: leave in package and thaw at room temperature Un-iced layer cakes and small cakes thaw in 1–2 hours at room temperature; frosted layer cakes take up to 4 hours
Cake mixtures, uncooked 2 months	Whisked sponge mixtures do not freeze well uncooked. Put rich creamed mixtures into containers, or line the tin to be used later with greased foil, add cake mixture	Freeze uncovered. When frozen, remove from tin, package in foil and overwrap. Return to freezer	To thaw, leave at room temperature for 2–3 hours, then fill tins to bake. Pre-formed cake mixtures can be returned to the original tin, unwrap. Place frozen in pre-heated oven and bake in usual way, but allow longer cooking time
Scones and Teabreads 6 months	Bake in usual way	Freeze in polythene bags in convenient numbers for serving	Thaw teabreads in wrapping at room temperature for 2–3 hours. Tea scones: cook from frozen, wrapped in foil, in fairly hot oven (200°C *(400°F)* mark 6) for 10 minutes. Girdle scones: thaw for 1 hour. Drop scones: thaw for 30 minutes or cover and bake for 10 minutes
Croissants and Danish Pastries Unbaked in bulk: 6 weeks	Prepare to the stage when all the fat has been absorbed, but don't give the final rolling	Wrap in airtight polythene bags and freeze at once	Leave in polythene bags, but unseal and re-tie loosely, allowing space for dough to rise. Preferably thaw overnight in a refrigerator, or leave for 5 hours at room temperature. Complete final rolling and shaping and bake
Baked: 4 weeks	Bake in usual way. (Don't ice Danish Pastries)	Cool, wrap and freeze	Loosen wrappings but leave covered. Thaw overnight in refrigerator, or leave for 5 hours at room temperature. Refresh in oven at 200°C *(400°F)* mark 6 for 5 minutes if required

Soufflé milanaise *(p. 336)*.

Food and storage time	*Preparation*	*Freezing*	*Thawing and serving*
Biscuits, baked and unbaked 6 months	Prepare in the usual way. Rich mixtures – ie with more than 100 g (*¼ lb*) fat to 450 g (*1 lb*) flour – are the most satisfactory	Freeze these either baked or un-baked. Pack carefully. Wrap rolls of uncooked dough or pipe soft mixtures into shapes, freeze and pack when firm. Allow cooked biscuits to cool before packing	Thaw uncooked rolls of dough slightly; slice off required number of biscuits and bake. Shaped biscuits can be cooked direct from frozen: allow 7–10 minutes extra time. Cooked biscuits may need crisping in a warm oven for 5 minutes
Bread and Rolls 4 weeks	Freshly-baked bread, both bought and home-made, can be frozen. Crisp, crusty bread stores well up to 1 week, then the crust begins to 'shell off'	Bought bread may be frozen in original wrapper for up to 1 week; for longer periods, seal in foil or polythene. Home-made bread: freeze in foil or polythene bags	Leave to thaw in the sealed polythene bag or wrapper at room temperature, for 3–6 hours or overnight in the refrigerator, or leave foil-wrapped and crisp it in a fairly hot oven at 200°C (*400°F*) mark 6 for about ¾ hour. Sliced bought bread can be toasted from frozen
Bought Párt-Baked Bread and Rolls 4 months	Freeze immediately after purchase	Leave loaf in the bag. Pack rolls in heavy-duty polythene bags and seal	To use, place frozen unwrapped loaf in oven at 220°C (*425°F*) mark 7 for about 40 minutes. Cool for 1–2 hours before cutting. Rolls: place frozen unwrapped in oven at 200°C (*400°F*) mark 6 for 15 minutes
Sponge Puddings, uncooked: 1 month	Make in the usual way. Use foil or polythene basins, or line ordinary basins with greased foil	Seal basins tightly with foil, overwrap and freeze at once. If freezing pudding mixture in preformed foil, remove from basins when frozen, then overwrap *Note:* Allow room at this stage for later rising	Remove packaging, cover top with greased foil and place, frozen, to steam – 900-ml (*1½-pt*) size takes about 2½ hours. Don't forget to return a pre-formed pudding mixture to its original basin
cooked: 3 months	Prepare and cook in the usual way. Cool thoroughly, cover with foil and overwrap	Freeze quickly	As above – a 900-ml (*1½-pt*) pudding takes about 45 minutes to thaw and re-heat
Sandwiches 1–2 months	Most types may be frozen, but those filled with hard-boiled eggs, tomatoes, cucumber or bananas tend to go tasteless and soggy	Wrap in foil, then in polythene bag	Thaw unwrapped at room temperature or in refrigerator. Time varies according to size of pack. Cut pinwheels, sandwich loaves, etc, in portions when half thawed
Sandwiches for toasting Up to 2 months	Use white or brown bread – cheese, ham, fish are all suitable, but avoid salad foods; season lightly	Interleave for easy separation. Wrap in foil or polythene bags	Place frozen unwrapped sandwiches under a hot grill; thawing will take place during toasting

Marmalade oranges 6 months; useful if it's not convenient to make marmalade when Seville oranges are in season	Wash, dry and freeze Seville oranges whole or prepare marmalade to cooked pulp stage – ie before addition of sugar	Pack whole oranges in polythene bags, pulp in suitable containers	It is not recommended to thaw whole frozen fruit in order to cut it up before cooking as discoloration often occurs. Use whole fruit method for marmalade. Thaw pulp, still wrapped, in refrigerator for 9–12 hours per 450 g *(1 lb)*. It is advisable to add $\frac{1}{8}$ extra weight of oranges for marmalade making to offset pectin loss
Herbs Thyme, sage, rosemary, parsley, mint: up to 6 months	Wash and dry herbs. These can be chopped before freezing, or crumbled when frozen. Prepare bouquet garni, if required	Wrap in small bundles and place in moisture-proof bags. Make individual foil-wrapped packs of chopped herbs	If kept accessible, frozen herbs are as useful as dried, for they can be popped into stews, etc, while still frozen
Fats: Butter, salted: 3 months unsalted: 6 months Margarine: as butter Fresh shredded suet: 6 months	Always buy fresh stock. (If buying farmhouse butter check that it is made from pasteurised cream)	Overwrap in foil in quantities of 225–450 g *($\frac{1}{2}$–1 lb)*	Allow to thaw in refrigerator, 4 hours for a 225 g *($\frac{1}{2}$ lb)* block
Commercially Frozen Foods Up to 3 months as a rule *Note:* The times quoted by the manufacturers are often less than those given for home-frozen foods, because of the handling in distribution, before the foods can reach your own freezer	No further preparation, etc, needed, except for ice cream, which should be overwrapped if it is to be kept for longer than 3 weeks		Follow directions on packet
Eggs separated 8–10 months	Freeze only fresh eggs – yolks and whites separately	Pack in waxed or rigid containers. Yolks – to every 6 yolks mix 5 ml *(1 level tsp)* salt or 10 ml *(2 level tsps)* sugar; use 2.5 ml *($\frac{1}{2}$ level tsp)* salt or sugar when single yolks. Whites need no addition	Thaw in refrigerator or rapidly thaw at room temperature for about $1\frac{1}{2}$ hours
Milk 1 month	Ordinary pasteurized milk does not freeze well. Homogenised is satisfactory	Pack in rigid containers; allow 1 in *(2.5 cm)* headspace. *Do not freeze in bottle*	Thaw in refrigerator. Thawing may be accelerated if milk is to be used in cooking
Yoghurt 6 weeks	Fruit yoghurts are satisfactory but natural yoghurt does not freeze well. Some can be bought ready frozen	Freeze in retail cartons	Thaw for about 1 hr at room temperature
Cheese 6 months	Soft cheeses and cream cheese are suitable for freezing. Hard cheeses become crumbly if stored for too long but are fine grated for cooking. Cottage cheese not suitable for freezing	Wrap in freezer film or polythene bag	Thaw for 24 hr in refrigerator and allow to come to room temperature before serving. Use grated cheese straight from frozen

Home-made sweets

Most home cooks like to try their hand some time at making fudge, toffee and other simple sweets, while the creation of a batch of uncooked peppermint creams or marzipan 'fancies' is a traditional occupation for the children on a wet afternoon.

Remember, however, that true sweet-making doesn't fit in easily with other cookery; it needs your undivided attention, and a hot, steamy kitchen is quite the wrong atmosphere for the job – in fact, a perfectionist will wait for a fine day if the weather is damp!

Equipment

If you want to make more than an occasional batch of sweets, it will pay you to invest in a few pieces of special equipment; they will save time and effort and prevent wasting ingredients. These are the chief requirements:

Sugar-boiling thermometer Necessary for measuring temperature accurately – which often spells the difference between success and failure and makes a good result a matter of certainty rather than luck.

Choose a thermometer which is easy to read and well graduated from 16°C *(60°F)* to 182°C *(360°F)* or 232°C *(450°F)*. These thermometers are usually mounted on brass, with a brass or wooden handle; it is useful to have a sliding clip that fits over the side of the pan.

To 'season' a new thermometer, place it in cold water, bring to the boil and leave in the water to cool.

To check a thermometer, try it in boiling water, 100°C *(212°F)*, and note if it is at all inaccurate.

When using the thermometer, shake it well so that the mercury thread is unbroken and see that the bulb is completely immersed in the mixture. When the thermometer is not actually in the sweet mixture, stand it in hot water. Clean it very thoroughly, as any sugar crystals left on might spoil the next boiling. Always read a thermometer at eye level.

Saucepan This must be strong and thick-based, to prevent burning and sticking. Cast aluminium is a good choice; enamel or non-stick pans are not suitable, as high temperatures may crack the lining.

Spatula A wooden spatula is useful for 'working' fondant mixtures and beating fudges.

Flexible-bladed palette knife One with a stainless steel blade is useful for lifting and shaping sweets.

Marble slab Expensive to buy and not absolutely essential, since an enamelled surface can be used instead. Certain plastic surfaces will also withstand temperatures up to 138°C *(280°F)*, but usually not beyond this.

Equipment for more advanced sweet-making

Rubber fondant mat Consists of a sheet of rubber, 2.5 cm *(1 in)* thick, with fancy-shaped impressions into which liquid fondant, jelly or chocolate is run and allowed to set. When the shapes are firm, they can easily be removed by bending back the rubber.

Cream rings These metal circles are useful for moulding peppermint creams and similar sweets.

Dipping forks Small forks with 2–3 wire prongs or a loop at the end; they are used for lifting sweets out of coating fondant or chocolate, the prongs or loop also serve to make a raised design on the top of the sweets.

Sugar boiling

This process is the basis of all sweet-making. The sugar is first dissolved in the liquid, then brought to the boil, 100°C *(212°F)*. The temperature continues to rise as the water is evaporated; the syrup thickens and then becomes darker in colour as the temperature rises – at 177°C *(350°F)* it is a very dark brown. The table below shows the most important stages.

To measure the temperature really accurately you need a sugar-boiling thermometer (see above), but for simple sweets you can use the homely tests described in the table.

Smooth 102°C–104°C *(215°F–220°F)*: For crystallising purposes. The mixture begins to look syrupy. To test, dip the fingers in water and then very quickly in the syrup; the thumb will slide smoothly over the fingers, but the sugar clings to the finger.

Soft ball 113°C–118°C *(235°F–245°F)*: For fondants and fudges. When a drop of the syrup is put into very cold water, it forms a soft ball; at 113°C *(235°F)* the soft ball flattens on being removed from the water, but the higher the temperature, the firmer the ball, till it reaches the next, firm ball, stage.

Firm or hard ball 118°C–130°C *(245°F–265°F)*: For caramels, marshmallows and nougat.

When dropped into cold water, the syrup forms a ball which is hard enough to hold its shape, but is still plastic.

Soft crack 132°C–143°C *(270°F–290°F)*: For toffees.

When dropped into cold water, the syrup separates into threads which are hard but not brittle.

Hard crack 149°C–154°C *(300°F–310°F)*: For hard toffees and rock.

When a drop of the syrup is put into cold water, it separates into threads which are hard and brittle.

Caramel 154°C *(310°F)*: For praline and caramels. Shown by the syrup becoming golden brown.

Crystallisation

Sugar must be dissolved and boiled with great care, as the syrup has a tendency to re-crystallise if incorrectly handled. These are the main causes of crystallisation:

(*a*) Agitation of the mixture by stirring or beating.

(*b*) The presence of solid particles, eg sugar crystals, during the boiling.

To obtain a clear syrup, note the following points:

(*a*) The pan must be clean.

(*b*) The sugar must be completely dissolved before boiling.

(*c*) If crystals do form, brush the sides of the pan with a brush dipped in cold water.

(*d*) Don't stir the mixture unless the recipe specifically calls for this. You can however use a wooden spatula to tap the grains of sugar on to the bottom of the pan to hasten the process.

(*e*) Once the sugar has dissolved and been brought to the boil, it can be heated rapidly to the required temperature. Remove it immediately from the heat, so that the temperature does not rise any higher.

(*f*) Glucose, honey or golden syrup, 100 g *(¼ lb)* to 675 g *(1½ lb)* sugar or a pinch of cream of tartar or a squeeze of lemon juice may be added; any of these will convert some of the sugar into 'invert' sugar, which does not crystallise so readily. Remember, however, that sweets made with glucose soften more quickly, so that while it is useful in making fondants, cream of tartar is of more use for other types of sweet.

FONDANTS

Fondant forms the basis of a large number of sweets and chocolate centres and is also used for icing cakes. To prepare it, dissolved 450 g *(1 lb)* sugar in 150 ml *(¼ pt)* water and boil the syrup to a temperature of 116°C–118°C *(240°F–245°F)*, following the general directions for sugar-boiling. Cool it on a marble slab or cool surface and 'work' it until it becomes opaque and firm. If necessary, thin it by adding more syrup; you can enrich the fondant by adding cream or milk.

Any fondant that is not required for immediate use may be stored in a covered jar or tin.

Boiled fondant

150 ml *(¼ pt)* water (good measure)
450 g *(1 lb)* granulated sugar
45 ml *(3 level tbsps)* glucose or a good pinch cream of tartar

Put the water into a pan, add the sugar and let it dissolve slowly. Bring the syrup to the boil, add the glucose or cream of tartar and boil to 116°C *(240°F)*. Sprinkle a little water on a marble slab or other suitable surface, pour on the syrup and leave for a few minutes to cool. When a skin forms round the edges, take the spatula and collect the mixture together, then work it backwards and forwards, using a figure-of-eight movement. Continue to work the syrup, collecting it into as small a compass as possible, until it changes its character and 'grains', becoming opaque and firm. Scrape it off the slab and knead it in the hands until of an even texture throughout.

Note If no slab is available, the fondant can be 'turned' in a bowl; leave it in the bowl for ¼ hour to cool, 'turn' it in the bowl until thick, then knead it on greaseproof paper.

Fondant creams

Prepare some fondant and knead it well (particularly if it has been stored for some time). To improve the texture and flavour, add a little cream, evaporated milk or melted butter. (If you are using freshly made fondant, add the cream, milk or butter while the fondant is still melted.) Divide the mixture into portions and flavour and colour as required, eg with lemon, violet, coffee, etc. Roll the fondant out to the required thickness, using a little icing sugar on the board, and cut out with a small cutter or model it by hand.

To obtain fancy shapes, or to make chocolate centres, melt the fondant in a basin over a pan of hot water or in a double saucepan over a very gentle heat; use a little sugar syrup (or a few drops of water) to help to liquefy it. When it is liquid, pour it into moulds in a rubber fondant mat, using a funnel or a teaspoon.

Fondant fruits Cubes of crystallised ginger, glacé pineapple, bunches of raisins or grapes, Cape gooseberries and many other fruits may be dipped in liquid fondant (coloured if liked). Place them in paper cases when dry.

Mocha nuts Flavour the liquid fondant with coffee and dip halved walnuts and whole Brazil nuts in it.

Peppermint creams Knead a few drops of oil of peppermint into the fondant, roll it out 0.5 cm *(¼ in)* thick and cut into rounds with a 2.5-cm *(1-in)* cutter.

MARZIPAN

This is not difficult to prepare and by using edible colourings, moulding the marzipan into different shapes or combining it with other ingredients such as dried or glacé fruit and nuts, you can make a wide variety of sweets.

You can if you prefer use ready-made marzipan, which is cheaper than the home-made kind.

There are two types of marzipan:

1 Boiled – best for flowers and sweets that need a good deal of handling (see recipe below).

2 Unboiled – quicker to make, but needs careful handling to prevent cracking (for recipe see Almond Paste, page 401.

Boiled marzipan *see colour plate facing p. 528*

450 g *(1 lb)* lump sugar
150 ml *(¼ pt)* water
pinch of cream of tartar
350 g *(¾ lb)* ground almonds
2 egg whites
75 g *(3 oz)* icing sugar, sifted

Put the sugar and water into a pan and dissolve over a low heat. When the syrup reaches boiling point, add the cream of tartar and boil to a temperature of 116°C *(240°F)*. Remove the pan from the heat and stir rapidly until the syrup begins to 'grain'. Stir in the ground almonds and egg whites and cook for a few minutes over a low heat, stirring well.

Pour on to an oiled surface (marble or enamelled iron), add the icing sugar and work well with a palette knife, lifting the edges of the mixture and pressing them into the centre. As soon as the mixture is sufficiently cool, knead until smooth. Additional icing sugar may be kneaded in if required.

If necessary, the marzipan may be wrapped in greaseproof paper and stored in a cool place for 2–3 weeks.

Marzipan dates Choose best-quality dessert dates, remove the stones and fill the cavities with coloured marzipan. Roll them in caster sugar.

Marzipan fruits Mould the marzipan to resemble small fruits – for example, oranges, apples, bananas, pears. Paint them with edible sugar.

Marzipan walnuts Colour a small quantity of marzipan, roll it into little balls and press a halved walnut into the top of each.

Neapolitan slices Roll out lengths of marzipan in two contrasting colours and enclose them in a thin sheet of plain marzipan, shaping the whole to resemble a small Battenberg cake about 2.5 cm *(1 in)* across. Cut into 0.5-cm *(¼-in)* slices.

Note Serve all these marzipan sweets in paper cases.

FUDGES

The chief ingredients are sugar, butter and milk or cream; a wide variety of flavourings such as coffee, chocolate and nuts may also be added. Unlike other sweets, fudge mixtures have to be stirred during the cooking, as they have a tendency to burn. Either granulated or caster sugar may be used, but the latter dissolves more quickly. Cooking fudges takes a long time and should not be hurried or the pan base may burn.

Vanilla fudge

450 g *(1 lb)* granulated sugar
50 g *(2 oz)* butter
150 ml *(¼ pt)* evaporated milk
150 ml *(¼ pt)* milk
few drops of vanilla essence

Grease a tin 15 cm by 15 cm *(6 in by 6 in)*.

Put the sugar, butter and milks into a 2.8-l *(5-pt)* heavy-based saucepan and heat gently until the sugar has dissolved and the fat melted. Bring to the boil and boil steadily to 116°C *(240°F)* (soft ball stage), stirring occasionally. Remove the pan from the heat, place on a cool surface, add the essence and beat until the mixture becomes thick and creamy and 'grains' – ie until minute crystals form. Pour it immediately into the tin. Leave until nearly cold and mark into squares with a sharp knife, using a sawing motion. When it is firm, cut into squares. *Makes about 450 g (1 lb).*

Orange fudge

900 g *(2 lb)* granulated sugar
300 ml *(½ pt)* evaporated milk
100 g *(4 oz)* butter
grated rind of ½ orange
60 ml *(4 tbsps)* orange juice

Grease a tin 30.5 cm by 10 cm *(12 in by 4 in)* or an 18-cm *(7 in)* square tin. Put the sugar, milk and butter in a 3.4-l *(6-pt)* heavy-based saucepan and heat slowly until the sugar has dissolved. Add the orange rind and juice, bring to the boil and boil steadily to 116°C *(240°F)* (soft ball stage); stir during the cooking to prevent sticking. Remove from the heat, place the pan on a cool surface and beat until thick, creamy and beginning to 'grain'. Pour into the tin and leave until nearly cold, then mark into squares; when firm, cut with a sharp knife. *Makes about 1.1 kg (2½ lb).*

Lemon fudge Substitute lemon rind and juice for the orange.

Chocolate fudge *see colour plate facing p. 528*

450 g *(1 lb)* granulated sugar
150 ml *(¼ pt)* milk
150 g *(5 oz)* butter
100 g *(4 oz)* plain chocolate
50 g *(2 oz)* honey

Grease a tin 20.5 cm by 15 cm *(8 in by 6 in)*.

Place all the ingredients into a 2.8-l *(5-pt)* heavy-based saucepan. Stir over a low heat until the sugar has dissolved. Bring to the boil and boil to 116°C *(240°F)* (soft ball stage). Remove from the heat, stand the pan on a cool surface for 5 minutes, then beat the mixture until thick, creamy and beginning to 'grain'. Pour into the tin, mark into squares and cut when cold. *Makes about 700 g (1½ lb).*

Marshmallow fudge Add 225 g *(½ lb)* chopped marshmallows to the mixture before beating; continue as above.

Fruit and nut fudge Add 50 g *(2 oz)* chopped nuts and 50 g *(2 oz)* seedless raisins; continue as above.

Date fudge Replace the 150 ml *(¼ pt)* milk by 150 ml *(¼ pt)* water and add 75 g *(3 oz)* finely chopped dates.

Coffee walnut fudge

700 g *(1½ lb)* granulated sugar
300 ml *(½ pt)* evaporated milk
150 ml *(¼ pt)* water
100 g *(4 oz)* butter
25 ml *(1½ level tbsps)* instant coffee
50 g *(2 oz)* walnuts, chopped

Grease a tin 20.5 cm *(8 in)* square. Put the sugar, milk, water and butter into a 3.4-l *(6-pt)* heavy-based saucepan. Blend the coffee with 15 ml *(1 tbsp)* water and add to the pan. Stir over a low heat until the sugar has dissolved. Boil gently to 116°C *(240°F)* (soft ball stage); stir to prevent sticking. Remove from the heat, place the pan on a cool surface, add the nuts and beat with a wooden spoon until thick, creamy and beginning to 'grain'. Pour into the tin and leave until nearly cold; mark into squares. When firm, cut with a sharp knife. *Makes about 900 g (2 lb).*

TOFFEES

A toffee is basically a simple sugar mixture, requiring to be boiled to a high temperature – 138°C–154°C *(280°F–310°F)* according to type. These are important points to remember when making toffee:

1. You must use a large, heavy-based pan, as toffee tends to boil over.
2. Don't stir the mixture unless the recipe definitely states this should be done.
3. Move the thermometer from time to time, as the toffee may stick to the bulb and give an inaccurate reading.
4. Keep the heat very low after the mixture reaches 127°C *(260°F)*.
5. Remove the pan from the heat when the mixture has reached a temperature about 2°C *(5°F)* below the figure required, because the pan holds the heat, so the mixture may be over-boiled. Make sure, however, that the toffee does actually come to the correct temperature.
6. Pour the mixture into the prepared tin as soon as the correct temperature is reached.

Treacle toffee

450 g *(1 lb)* demerara sugar
150 ml *(¼ pt)* water
75 g *(3 oz)* butter
1.25 ml *(¼ level tsp)* cream of tartar
100 g *(4 oz)* black treacle
100 g *(4 oz)* golden syrup

Butter a tin 30.5 cm by 10 cm *(12 in by 4 in)* or an 18-cm *(7-in)* square tin. Dissolve the sugar and water in a 2.3-l *(4-pt)* heavy-based pan over a low heat. Add the remaining ingredients and bring to the boil. Boil to 132°C *(270°F)* (soft crack stage). Pour into the tin, cool for 5 minutes, then mark into squares and leave to set. *Makes about 550 g (1¼ lb).*

Peanut brittle *see colour plate facing p. 528*

400 g *(14 oz)* granulated sugar
175 g *(6 oz)* soft brown sugar
175 g *(6 oz)* corn syrup or golden syrup
150 ml *(¼ pt)* water
50 g *(2 oz)* butter
1.25 ml *(¼ level tsp)* bicarbonate of soda
350 g *(12 oz)* unsalted peanuts, chopped

Butter a tin 30.5 cm by 10 cm *(12 in by 4 in)* or an 18-cm *(7-in)* square tin. Dissolve the sugars, syrup and water over a low heat in a 2.3-l *(4-pt)* heavy-based saucepan. Add the butter and bring to the boil; boil very gently to 149°C *(300°F)* (hard crack stage). Add the bicarbonate of soda and slightly warmed nuts. Pour slowly into the tin and mark into bars when almost set. *Makes about 900 g (2 lb).*

Honeycomb toffee

450 g *(1 lb)* granulated sugar
300 ml *(½ pt)* water
60 ml *(4 tbsps)* vinegar
2.5 ml *(½ level tsp)* bicarbonate of soda

Butter a tin measuring 30.5 cm by 10 cm *(12 in by 4 in)* or an 18-cm *(7-in)* square tin.

Dissolve the sugar in the water and vinegar in a deep, heavy-bottomed pan. Bring to boiling point and boil gently to soft crack stage, 141°C *(285°F)*. Take from the heat. Remove any lumps from the bicarbonate of soda and add to the toffee; stir to mix thoroughly and pour into the prepared tin. Mark into squares or fingers when half-set. *Makes about 450 g (1 lb).*

Hazel-nut toffee

75 g *(3 oz)* hazel-nuts, blanched and chopped
450 g *(1 lb)* granulated sugar
25 g *(1 oz)* butter
10 ml *(2 tsps)* vinegar
150 ml *(¼ pt)* water
pinch of salt
5 ml *(1 tsp)* vanilla essence

Butter a tin measuring 30.5 cm by 10 cm *(12 in by 4 in)* or an 18-cm *(7-in)* square tin.

Warm the nuts. Put all the ingredients except the nuts and the essence into a 2.3-l *(4-pt)* heavy-based saucepan and stir until dissolved. Boil the mixture to 149°C *(300°F)* (hard crack stage). Add the essence, pour half the toffee into the tin, sprinkle the warmed nuts over the surface, then pour the remainder of the toffee over them. Mark into squares when almost set. *Makes about 450 g (1 lb).*

Golden caramels *see colour plate facing p. 528*

225 g *(8 oz)* sugar
50 g *(2 oz)* glucose
15 ml *(1 tbsp)* golden syrup
60 ml *(4 tbsps)* water
60 ml *(4 tbsps)* milk
vanilla essence

Oil a tin 15 cm by 20.5 cm *(6 in by 8 in)*. Put all the ingredients except the essence in a pan, dissolve the sugar and slowly heat to 124°C *(255°F)* (hard ball stage), stirring occasionally. Add a little essence, stir and pour the mixture into the tin. Mark with a knife and break into squares when cold. Wrap individually, in waxed paper if possible. *Makes about 350 g (¾ lb).*

Toffee apples

450 g *(1 lb)* demerara sugar
50 g *(2 oz)* butter
10 ml *(2 tsps)* vinegar
150 ml *(¼ pt)* water
15 ml *(1 tbsp)* golden syrup
6–8 medium sized apples and the same number of wooden sticks

Put the sugar, butter, vinegar, water and syrup into a 2.3-l *(4-pt)* heavy-based pan. Heat gently until the sugar has dissolved and then boil rapidly for 5 minutes until the temperature reaches 143°C *(290°F)* (soft crack stage). Wipe the apples and push the sticks into the cores. Dip the apples into the toffee, twirl around for a few seconds, then leave to cool on a buttered baking sheet or waxed paper.

Nougat

rice paper
75 g *(3 oz)* honey
3 egg whites
50 g *(2 oz)* glacé cherries, chopped
25 g *(1 oz)* angelica, chopped
150 g *(5 oz)* almonds, chopped
350 g *(12 oz)* sugar
150 ml *(¼ pt)* water
50 g *(2 oz)* glucose
vanilla essence

Damp the inside of a tin 30.5 cm by 10 cm *(12 in by 4 in)* or an 18-cm *(7-in)* square tin and line it with rice paper. Melt the honey in a basin over hot water, add the stiffly beaten egg whites and continue to beat until the mixture is pale and thick. Add the cherries and angelica to the almonds. Dissolve the sugar in the water in a small heavy-based saucepan. Add the glucose and boil to 118°C–130°C *(245°F–265°F)*, hard ball stage. Pour this syrup on to the honey mixture, add the vanilla essence and continue beating over hot water until a little of the mixture forms a hard ball when tested in cold water. This may take 30–40 minutes, but is very important if the nougat is to set firmly. Add the fruit and nuts and put the mixture into the tin. Cover with rice paper, put some weights on top and leave until quite cold. Cut into pieces and wrap in waxed paper. *Makes about 550 g (1¼ lb).*

Turkish delight *see colour plate facing p. 528*

(Quick Method)

300 ml *(½ pt)* hot water
20 ml *(4 level tsps)* powdered gelatine
450 g *(1 lb)* sugar
1.25 ml *(¼ level tsp)* citric acid
few drops vanilla essence
few drops almond essence
cochineal
50 g *(2 oz)* icing sugar
45 ml *(1 oz)* cornflour

Put the water in a pan. Sprinkle the gelatine over it, add the sugar and citric acid and heat slowly until the sugar has dissolved. Bring to the boil, boil for 20 minutes, remove from the heat and leave to stand for 10 minutes without stirring. Add the flavourings and divide the mixture, putting half in a tin measuring about 20.5 cm by 15 cm *(8 in by 6 in)*. Add a few drops of cochineal to the second half and pour it over the first layer. Leave in a cool place for 24 hours.

Sift the icing sugar and cornflour together and sprinkle evenly over a piece of paper. Turn the Turkish delight out on to this paper and cut into squares with a sharp knife. Toss well in the sugar mixture, pack in greaseproof paper and store in an airtight tin. *Makes about 550 g (1¼ lb).*

This is a quick method for Turkish delight, but the recipe below produces a more traditional result.

Turkish delight

450 g *(1 lb)* **granulated sugar**
900 ml *(1½ pt)* **water**
1.25 ml *(¼ level tsp)* **tartaric acid**
75 g *(3 oz)* **cornflour**
200 g *(7 oz)* **icing sugar**
50 g *(2 oz)* **honey**
few drops lemon extract
few drops rose water
pink colouring
icing sugar for dredging

Butter a tin 30.5 cm by 10 cm *(12 in by 4 in)*.

Put the sugar and 150 ml *(¼ pt)* of the water into a saucepan, dissolve the sugar without boiling and bring to a temperature of 116°C *(240°F)* (soft ball stage). Add the tartaric acid and leave on one side for the short time required to blend the cornflour. Mix the cornflour and icing sugar with a little of the remaining cold water. Boil the rest of the water, then pour on to the blended cornflour and sugar, stirring hard to prevent lumps forming. Return to the saucepan, boil and beat vigorously until clear and thick. Add the syrup gradually, beating meanwhile over the heat. Continue to boil for 20–30 minutes: the time of boiling must not be shortened, as is it essential that the character of the starch be changed by the prolonged boiling with acid. At the end of 30 minutes the mixture should be of a very pale straw colour and transparent. Add the honey and flavourings and blend thoroughly.

Pour half the contents of the pan into a buttered tin, colour the remainder pale rose pink and pour it on top of the mixture already in the tin. Stand it aside until quite cold. Dip a sharp knife into icing sugar, cut the mixture into neat pieces and toss in icing sugar.

Protect from the dust and leave standing in the sugar for at least 24 hours. Pack in boxes in a generous quantity of icing sugar. *Makes about 700 g (1½ lb).*

This recipe produces a Turkish delight very similar to the genuine oriental variety, but it is impossible to get absolutely identical results without the authentic ingredients.

Coconut ice *see colour plate facing p. 528*

450 g *(1 lb)* **granulated sugar**
150 ml *(¼ pt)* **milk**
150 g *(5 oz)* **desiccated coconut**
colouring

Oil or butter a tin 20.5 cm by 15 cm *(8 in by 6 in)*. Dissolve the sugar in the milk over a low heat. Bring to the boil and boil gently for about 10 minutes, or until a temperature of 116°C *(240°F)* (soft ball stage) is reached. Remove from the heat and stir in the coconut. Pour half the mixture quickly into the tin. Colour the second half and pour quickly over the first layer. Leave until half set, mark into bars and cut or break when cold. *Makes about 550 g (1¼ lb).*

CANDIED, CRYSTALLISED AND GLACÉ FRUITS

Candying is a method of preserving fruits by the use of sugar syrup. They can then be served as a dessert or eaten as sweets. The peel of such citrus fruits as oranges, lemons and citrons can also be candied and is widely used in making cakes, cookies and puddings and in mincemeat and so on.

Candying essentially consists of soaking the fruit in a syrup, the sugar content of which is increased daily over a stated period of time until the fruits are completely impregnated with sugar. They can then be left plain or have a final crystallised or glacé finish.

Candied fruits are expensive to buy because of the labour involved and the amount of sugar used. The process should not however be beyond the skill of the home cook, provided certain basic rules are followed.

The most suitable fruits to treat are those with a really distinctive flavour – pineapple, peaches, plums, apricots, oranges, cherries, crab-apples, pears. Both fresh and canned fruits may be used, but different types should not be candied in the same syrup.

Preparation of the fruit and syrup

Fresh fruit The fruits must be ripe, but firm and free from blemishes. Prepare them according to kind. Small whole crab-apples, apricots and plums should be pricked all over with a stainless fork; cherries must be stoned; peaches and pears are peeled and halved or cut into quarters. The fruits which are peeled and cut up need not be pricked.

Place the prepared fruits in sufficient boiling water to cover them and cook gently until just tender. Overcooking spoils the shape and texture, while undercooking results in slow penetration of the syrup and causes dark colour and toughness. Tough fruits such as apricots may take 10–15 minutes, whereas soft ones need only 2–4 minutes.

Canned fruits Use good quality fruit. Pineapple chunks or small rings, plums, sliced and halved peaches and halved apricots are all suitable.

The syrup Granulated sugar is generally recommended for the preparation of the syrup. Part of the sugar may be replaced by glucose – see chart opposite, which gives full details of the proportion of sugar to liquid at the different stages.

Processing chart for candied fruit

Using 450 g *(1 lb)* prepared fruit (see notes overleaf)

	FRESH FRUIT		CANNED FRUIT	
Day	*Syrup*	*Soak for*	*Syrup*	*Soak for*
1.	Drain 300 ml *(½ pt)* cooking liquid from fruit, add 175 g *(6 oz)* sugar (or 50 g *(2 oz)* sugar and 100 g *(4 oz)* glucose), dissolve, bring to boil and pour over fruit.	24 hrs	Drain off canning syrup and make up to 300 ml *(½ pt)*; add 225 g *(8 oz)* sugar (or 100 g *(4 oz)* sugar and 100 g *(4 oz)* glucose), dissolve, bring to the boil and pour over fruit.	24 hrs
2.	Drain off syrup, add 50 g *(2 oz)* sugar, dissolve, bring to boil and pour over fruit.	24 hrs	Drain off syrup, add 50 g *(2 oz)* sugar, dissolve, bring to boil and pour over fruit.	24 hrs
3.	Repeat Day 2	24 hrs	Repeat Day 2	24 hrs
4.	Repeat Day 2	24 hrs	Repeat Day 2	24 hrs
5.	Repeat Day 2	24 hrs	Repeat Day 2, using 75 g *(3 oz)* sugar.	48 hrs
6.	Repeat Day 2	24 hrs	–	–
7.	Repeat Day 2	24 hrs	Repeat Day 2, using 75 g *(3 oz)* sugar.	4 days
8.	Repeat Day 2, using a further 75 g *(3 oz)* sugar.	48 hrs	–	–
9.	–	–	–	–
10.	Repeat Day 8	4 days	–	–
11.	–	–	Dry in oven at lowest setting or cover lightly and leave in a warm place (this may take from a few hours to 2–3 days) until quite dry; turn them 2–3 times.	–
12.	–	–		–
13.	–	–	–	–
14.	Dry as for canned fruit	–	–	–

Notes

Amount of syrup If the syrup is not sufficient to cover the fruit, make up more in the same strength, but remember that the amount of sugar to add later must be increased accordingly. For example, if you increase the amount used for fresh fruit to 400 ml *(¾ pt)* juice and 250 g *(9 oz)* sugar, on Day 2 you will have to add 75 g *(3 oz)* sugar and on Day 8 add 125 g *(4½ oz)* sugar.

Soaking time It is important that the fruit should soak for a full 24 hours (or as specified) before the next lot of sugar is added.

Days 5, 7, 8, 10 When the added sugar is increased to 75 g *(3 oz)* first dissolve the sugar, then add the fruit and boil it in the syrup for 3–4 minutes.

Day 11 or 14 Once the syrup has reached the consistency of honey, the fruit may be left to soak for as little as 3 days or up to 2–3 weeks, according to how sweet you like the candied fruit to be.

Finishing the candied fruit

When the fruits are thoroughly dried, pack them in cardboard or wooden boxes, between layers of waxed paper, or give them one of the following finishes:

Crystallised finish Take the pieces of candied fruit and dip each quickly into boiling water; drain off excess moisture, then roll each piece in fine caster sugar.

Glacé finish Prepare a fresh syrup, using 450 g *(1 lb)* sugar and 150 ml *(¼ pt)* water, bring to the boil and boil for 1 minute. Pour a little of the syrup into a cup. Dip the candied fruit into boiling water for 20 seconds, then dip them one at a time in the syrup, using a skewer. Place the fruit on a wire rack to dry. Cover the rest of the syrup in the pan with a damp cloth and keep it warm (a double pan is useful for this purpose.) As the syrup in the cup becomes cloudy, replace it by fresh. Dry the fruit as before, turning it from time to time.

Candied peel

Orange, lemon and grapefruit peel are all suitable. Wash or scrub the fruit thoroughly, halve it and remove the pulp. Simmer the peel in a little water until tender – 1–2 hours. (Change the water 2–3 times when cooking grapefruit peel.) Drain well. Make the liquor up to 300 ml *(½ pt)* with water. Add 225 g *(8 oz)* sugar, dissolve over a low heat, then bring to the boil. Add the peel and leave for 2 days. Drain off the syrup, dissolve another 100 g *(4 oz)* sugar in it and simmer the peel in this syrup until semi-transparent. The peel can be left in this thick syrup for 2–3 weeks. Drain off the syrup, place the peel on a wire rack, cover and leave to dry. Store in screw-topped jars.

Chestnuts in syrup

225 g *(8 oz)* granulated sugar
225 g *(8 oz)* glucose or dextrose
180 ml *(¼ pt plus 2 tbsps)* water
350 g *(12 oz)* whole chestnuts, peeled and skinned (weight after preparation) or 350 g *(12 oz)* canned chestnuts, drained
vanilla essence

Put the granulated sugar, glucose or dextrose and water in a pan large enough to hold the chestnuts and heat gently together until the sugars are dissolved; bring to the boil. Remove from the heat, add the chestnuts (drained if canned ones are used) and bring to the boil again. Remove from the heat, cover and leave overnight, preferably in a warm place. On the second day, re-boil the chestnuts and syrup in the pan without the lid; remove from the heat, cover and again leave standing overnight. On the third day, add 6–8 drops of vanilla essence and repeat the boiling process as above. Warm some 450-g *(1-lb)* bottling jars in the oven, fill with the chestnuts and cover with syrup. Seal in the usual way to make airtight. (See page 459.)

Note This recipe gives a delicious result, but the chestnuts are not exactly like commercially prepared Marrons Glacés, which cannot be reproduced under home conditions.

Entertaining

Dinner parties

A successful dinner party brings a warm, intimate sense of well-being to guests and hosts alike. Go about it the sensible way and it will be a pleasure for everybody.

The practical, physical things – like choosing and cooking the food, arranging your home and your table – are the main considerations. But the moment to plan for is not when your first guests are due, but about an hour before. By that time your preparations should be firmly under control and you can, without rush, turn your attention to yourself. Not only to look your best, that follows naturally, but to make the most of your vital contribution to the party – unworried calm and friendly competence. That includes welcoming your guests, introducing new ones to each other with some helpful mention of their work and interests. There must also be time to have an aperitif with them – even if you do then slip off to the kitchen, glass in hand, to ensure the meal doesn't spoil.

As distinct from the casual invitation to a couple of close friends, a dinner party in this context is a firm date fixed at least a fortnight in advance. Composing the menu for four or six guests is fun. The planning can start days ahead, and it is a highly individual exercise. There are so many variables apart from the nature of the occasion and the personal likes and dislikes of both hosts and guests. The time you have, whether you have help to cook and serve, whether you have small children to see off to bed first – these and a dozen other things are different from one household to another. But get things organised properly and none of them is unmanageable.

Planning the menu

A simple, well cooked, three course meal is generally acceptable even for comparatively formal dinner parties at home. Extras might be cheeses, a contrasting selection in small amounts, and fresh fruit. For the single-handed cook-hostess, over elaborate dishes defeat their own object. For the same reason, a dinner party is not the time for experimenting with new dishes. They should be tried out in advance to be sure that you can make them with ease. Thus too, you increase the range of your cooking repertoire.

Meeting your guests' pleasure in the foods you choose also implies avoiding foods which they do not like or cannot eat. There are people who cannot take shellfish, others to whom strawberries are disastrous. Others again avoid this food or that for religious reasons. There is nothing you can do about it once they are gathered round your table, so avoid that shock by finding out in advance, when you're inviting the guests (by phone is less formal). Nobody minds – on the contrary, they'll count you the more thoughtful for it – being asked if there are any must-nots in their eating. If there are, make a note of it. The same enquiry surely will not be appreciated the second time.

Indeed, a record-book of your dinner parties, guests and their comments is always a good idea. It can ensure that you don't give a repeat performance to the same people. More important, it can remind you, perhaps, that the dish that won acclaim was not the soufflé you slaved over, but the delicious way you cooked the potatoes, or dressed a very simple salad.

One standard rule in menu-planning is balance. You don't start with a quiche, go on to steak and kidney pudding and then an apple pie. A solid dessert is only good when preceding courses are light; a rich main course is at its best flanked with, say, a melon starter and a frothy mousse or perhaps a sorbet.

Good planning also means a ready-to-eat first course and no dishes that spoil by waiting or that need too much attention between courses.

Preparation

Having planned your menu in good time – and the wines to go with it – spread other preparations over several days. Make a list of groceries and so on, what you have in the larder and what you have to buy. This goes, too, for the ordering of wines and other drinks which are always better to have in hand at least a day or two in advance. Sort out the table linen and see that it's crisply laundered. See that all serving dishes, glass, cutlery and so on are sparkling bright. Modern oven-to-table ware cuts out the need to transfer food to dinner-service dishes; no matter if one dish doesn't match the others. It is an advantage in serving, however, if your casserole or any other oven-to-table dishes are wide and shallow.

Seeing your table all set with its gleaming glass and silverware and other little elegances is one of the most reassuring sights. So do it as early as you can. Whether you want a centre-piece or not will depend upon the size and shape of your table. If it is on the small side, or narrow, the sense of space can be enhanced by leaving the place settings to speak for themselves. If there is a centrepiece, atmosphere and conversation will be helped if the flower or fruit arrangement is low. Tall, slim candles are the exception and they give a warm and most kindly light.

Another re-assurance is the jot-pad. Use it to work out your time-table for cooking and preparation. Put down on it, as you think of them, all those little things you might fret about forgetting at the last moment; and cross them off as you deal with them. A dinner table for six, for instance, will want two sets of condiments (even though your guests will obviously taste the food before they use them). If there's to be smoking at table there should be, already there, at least three mini ash-trays. And you will want more solid ones strategically placed around the room – or rooms, not forgetting bedroom and bathroom. Which reminds you also to see about guest towels, face tissues and the like. Lest there be a cloud-burst as your guests are arriving, see that you have spare coathangers and allocate some place for wet umbrellas.

Apart from any flowers on the dining table, you will want arrangements in other rooms. If you are not picking them from your own garden it is worth ordering them in advance so that you get the type you want. Your aperitif drinks will remind you of the kind of niblets you want to go with them – crisps, salted nuts, olives and so on – and the little dishes in which you can distribute them around the room before the guests arrive.

Also to be remembered, are the after-dinner things. Good coffee is strong, fresh and piping hot, whether it is served on its own or with brandy or a liqueur. If you want to serve petits fours, liqueur chocolates or chocolate peppermint creams, bring these in unobtrusively in little dishes after that.

Drinks plus

A drinks party offers a fairly cheap way of entertaining large numbers of people without the need to get involved in serious cooking. For a party that is not going to be followed by a meal you will need hand-around snacks to serve with your drinks. Nuts and bolts, crisps and olives are fine for the casual drop-in-for-drinks time but when you have given advance invitations the eats should be a little more elaborate but bite-size. Most people tend to get a bit wide-eyed and greedy when there are home made tid-bits, so offer a variety of four or five goodies served cold plus at least one hot one to help create the party spirit; the nuts, etc, are still thrown in for good measure. A hot choice, like talmouse (see page 31) or beef balls (page 40) can be served straight from the oven on a small baking sheet or in oven-to-table dishes.

As for the drinks, keep them generous but simple. Sherry, vermouth, dry or medium dry white wines, 'bubbly' if you're expansive, are the drinks to home in on. With sherry, fino and the less dry amontillado are essential, and it is safer to have a bottle of sweet as well. With vermouth have an extra dry and a sweeter one. These are pleasant served straight and chilled, with a slice of lemon. It is up to you whether you add the extra kick of gin or vodka. It is usually a good idea to have some beer around for fanciers who never drink anything else, and tonic water, ginger ale, tomato juice or similar for those guests who never drink at all.

Invitations

Send out invitations at least a fortnight before the party. Make it quite clear on the invitation what type of party it will be – whether a sherry party or champagne cocktail, etc. Most drinks parties last from one to a maximum of two hours, and it is essential on a formal invitation to let people know exactly where they stand as regards time.

Preplanning

Order wine and spirits early. If you are not sure how much people will get through, insist on a sale-or-return basis so you only pay for bottles that are opened. If your guests are liable to drink a lot of wine, magnums, half gallons or gallons work out more economical, but remember once opened they cannot be returned, so if the party is drawing to a close beware of opening any large quantity.

Glasses

Most off-licences will lend you glasses free of charge (apart from breakages); if yours does not, pay the hiring charge or evaluate the cost of buying cheaply from Woolworths. Informality about what glass goes with what drink has made life much easier, but for a sherry party it is worth organising a supply of sherry glasses, and tall elegant bubble-trap champagne glasses for a champagne cocktail party. Otherwise it is simplest to cut down requirements to two basic shapes and sizes, a small to medium, stemmed wine glass for cocktails and a flat based, stunted tumbler for spirits, long cocktails and soft drinks.

Freezer

If you have a freezer make use of it by preparing pastry, fillings and garnishes a week or so ahead. Stock up with ice cubes too – a squirt of soda water from a syphon before packing helps to stop these sticking together.

The day before

Get as much of the food ready as possible. Prepare and cook pastry bases, store them in airtight tins. Make fillings and store in sealed boxes or covered bowls in the refrigerator. Prepare garnishes and store them in the refrigerator. Fill the ice trays to ensure plenty of ice on the day. To store additional cubes, empty the trays into a bowl and cover with foil or polythene. Ensure there are clean tablecloths or white sheets for covering the bar table. Make a final check on cocktail sticks, napkins, vital ingredients.

The day itself

Organise coat space and hangers. Arrange fresh towels and soap in bathrooms and cloakrooms. Attack the room itself for large occasions, organise a bar at one end and make sure that there is enough space around it as people tend to congregate in this area, (alternatively this can be arranged in another room, say the dining room). Keep the seating at the other end of the room, grouping the chairs together but arrange only the minimum of seating as drinks parties essentially are to stimulate circulation and conversation and seating tends to inhibit this activity. Preferably have several small tables arranged around the room with plates of canapés and enough space for putting glasses down. Have napkins easily available. Make sure there are sufficient ash trays scattered around the room.

How much will guests eat and drink?

Reckon on 3–5 short drinks each, 4–6 small savouries, plus the usual olives, nuts, crisps.

How many drinks to the bottle?

Sherry, port and vermouth: 12–16 glasses.
Single nips for mixes, vermouths and spirits: 30 a bottle.
Spirits served with soda, tonic or other minerals: 16–20 a bottle.
Split bottle of soda, tonic, ginger ale: 2–3 drinks.
Table wines: 5–6 glasses a bottle.
600-ml *(1-pt)* can fruit juice: 4–6 glasses.
1 bottle fruit cordial diluted with 4 l *(7 pt)* water: 20–26 drinks.
Estimates depend on the appropriate size of glasses.

Cheese and wine party

The friendly trio of pleasant wine, good cheese and warm crusty bread retains its place among the most popular of all entertaining ways. While it can be a non-cooking easy-on-the-hostess affair, such items as a home-made loaf and a couple of creamy, subtly blended cheese dips add to the pleasure.

It is surprising how little cheese gets eaten – don't allow more than 100 g *(4 oz)* per person. This enables you to offer a reasonable selection, so include soft, semi-hard and veined cheeses – say Brie, Boursin, Havarti, Stilton, double Gloucester and Farmhouse Cheddar, are the most popular. Some of the cheeses can be pre-cut into cubes but the cheeses-with-holes and also Danish Havarti and Samsoe are better if cut in wafer-thin slices with a special cheese slice. Arrange cheeses on a wooden board or tray with groups of washed and trimmed radishes (leave the tiny leaves on if they are not wilted), celery sticks in a tall glass, small tomatoes, wedges of cucumber, black olives and mild dill pickles or gherkins. Garnish with crisp lettuce – a variety like Webbs's Wonder or Cos, which doesn't wilt quickly. Covered with polythene film the boards can be made ready well ahead and kept in a cool place – not refrigerated. The cheeses that tend to ooze when really ripe are best kept separately and added to the board at the unveiling time. Fruits like grapes and a crisp juicy variety of apple are also good cheese partners.

A variety of breads looks appetising, a must is crusty French, dark rye is different and little wholemeal cobs scattered with sesame seeds or cracked wheat are a good choice for home-made. Don't leave out bread sticks and cracker biscuits. Have pots of butter soft enough to spread easily; judge the room temperature when the time comes for taking it from the refrigerator. If the butter is cut into cubes or shaped into balls, keep on ice if the room is very warm.

The wines need not be expensive; choose carefully within your price range and avoid those which are over-sweet or rough and vinegary. Ask a reliable wine merchant, or a friend who knows about wine, what is good to buy and have a look at the wines chapter of this book. Inexpensive wine can be bought in gallon or half-gallon bottles. Balance the value of these against ordinary bottles with possibly a discount for a case of 12; there may not be all that much difference in price. If you can obtain the wine on a sale or return basis you will be able to relax, knowing that you will have plenty – but remember not to open too many bottles at a time, or you may be left with a lot of half bottles to be disposed of. Allow a bottle of wine for every two guests and have a selection of red or white; cider or beer could be served too.

Wine and pâté party

This is a variation on a simple wine and cheese party. One of the many pleasant things about pâtés as informal party food is that they positively improve by being made a few days ahead. Make them, cover them and leave them alone to mature in the refrigerator. If you are stuck for time then buy some from a good delicatessen or grocer. Richly sustaining, amply varied in texture and taste, they make a meal in themselves with an assortment of breads, butter, salad stuffs and a glass of wine.

With a dozen or more guests, offer a selection of pâtés, such as a creamy smooth chicken liver pâté that is spooned from dish to plate, for fish fanciers a simple kipper pâté; offer also a rougher textured choice, best sliced in the dish with the first slice eased out, and a bacon wrapped choice for turning out, this too is a slice-it-yourself pâté.

Practically everything in the salad line goes well with pâté. It is simpler and better to serve several kinds of salad separately rather than a mixed one. Chicory spears, celery sticks, watercress sprigs, tomato wedges and carrot sticks all add pleasing freshness and bite. Crispbreads and hunks of oven warmed French bread are fine to put pâté on – freshly made toast too, if you can conveniently manage it. Butter should be firm and there should be plenty of it on the table for people to help themselves. The only props needed for the table are a pile of plates, plenty of knives, napkins, condiments and dressings for salads.

If there is anything else that might be needed in the food line, it is simply a large bowl of the nicest fresh fruits in season. This is not a 'menu' occasion. The choice of suitable wines for a pâté party is as wide as the nature of the pâtés you serve. With the milder ones, a crisp and full bodied white wine will be at home. Beaujolais blanc or Macon blanc, for instance, or one of the fruity and fragrant Traminer wines of Alsace. Many people, however, will still prefer red wine, especially with a robust, coarser recipe. A fresh fruity Château de Julienas or a Fleurie are good buys.

A barbecue party

Summer barbecues are for dusk-to-midnight eating, for youngsters old enough to stay up late and older guests young enough to enjoy them. An oven grid or two on side brick supports, over an open charcoal fire are the basic requirements and quite splendid for barbecues in the confines of the garden. For those who cook this way frequently, sophisticated barbecue equipment can be bought. Foil, throw-away paper plates and extra large absorbent paper napkins save work, and you will need a fork for each guest for eating anything like cole-slaw. Long-handled tongs and forks for turning grilling meals, pastry brushes for basting, a slice for turning griddle scones and thick gloves to protect the hands are among the essential tools of good barbecue cooks.

Amounts of food should always be on the generous side. People with otherwise bird-like appetites often develop man-sized ones with the aroma of out-door cooking to tempt them. Give simplest choice sausages, hamburgers, lamb cutlets (marinated in oil, lemon juice and herbs); bacon and mushrooms can be done by pan-frying or on a griddle. Serve the meat with plenty of warm French bread or toasted buns, jacket potatoes (which could be started in the kitchen oven) and big bowls of salad. For the more elaborate, if there is a spit, whole chickens basted with a barbecue glaze and tandoori chicken are excellent. Foil-roasted corn-on-the-cobs are popular too.

To drink, offer straight *vin ordinaire*, a hot punch if it is cold or a chilled fruit cup or lager. On hand to finish, have fresh peaches, apples, bananas, cookies and coffee.

When you give a barbecue, light the fire about 30 minutes before you start cooking. Feed extra charcoal in small amounts throughout the cooking. The formation of light grey ash means the fire is reaching cooking heat.

A rough guide to cooking times – turning half way: chops, 20 minutes; chicken joints or legs, 25–35 minutes; 2.5-cm *(1-in)* thick steaks, 12–18 minutes; sausages, 20 minutes; hamburgers, 15–20 minutes.

One dish parties

For the times when you feel like having friends to a meal, but don't want to put on a full-scale effort – and for the bed-sitter girl who is pushed for space – the one-dish meal is the answer. The easiest is to have a generous, piping hot casserole, crammed with everything at once – meat, vegetables and herbs so that there is no separate dishing-up to do. Suitable dishes are a hot pot layered with lamb, onion, tomatoes and potatoes, a paella deliciously spicy with saffron and stuffed with chicken, mussels, prawns and peppers, a curry or risotto, even a bumper cottage or cheese pie. All lend themselves to such a meal and when accompanied by a dressed green salad, cheese and fruit make an informal dinner for any guests. Today the choice of oven-to-table dishes is abundant and it is not difficult to find one that tones in with your china and pottery. For one-pot cooking you do need one of ample proportions.

Children's parties

The highlight of any child's year is his or her own party – though the mother doesn't always think so! If possible, stick to suitable age groups (it's not wise to arrange a joint party for your two or three children of varying ages), and invite not more than a dozen guests at once. Five-to-eights generally play together quite well and so do eight-to-twelves; under-fives are almost impossibly difficult to organise – just two or three at a time to tea are enough to cope with.

Receiving an invitation through the post is half the enjoyment for small children, so buy pretty invitation cards and send them out in plenty of time. Small hosts and hostesses love helping to fill in the names on the cards. The invitations should say very clearly what time the children are expected and no less clearly what time they are to go home. Don't be afraid to make the party time short – it is far more fun for children to have a couple of crowded hours than four loose-endish ones. It's a good idea to mention the fact if it is a birthday party, so that guests can bring a small present if they want to and not be embarrassed because they didn't know about it.

Children's parties don't run themselves, but must be most carefully organised. Clear some of the furniture and all precious breakables out of the party room and decorate it with balloons (to take away afterwards) and coloured streamers. Arrange for someone to play the piano or manage the record player for games like Musical Chairs. Make a really long list of games, alternating rowdy and quiet ones. Give small prizes but – like Alice – see that everybody gets one. If organising games seems

Food for freezing (p. 468), Lemon cheesecake (p. 327).
(Overleaf) Autumn luncheon (p. 562).

too much to cope with for the entire time, provide a short programme of cartoon films or a conjuror to keep the children quiet for a little while after tea. When the party is over and parents come to collect their offspring, think twice before offering drinks or coffee – generally it is not necessary and the children will be tired by this time and will get either fractious or over-excited if they are kept waiting.

Serve the food in a separate room from the one where the games are played. Choose easy-to-eat food and keep it simple, as unspillable as possible and in small portions. Most children love savoury sandwiches of scrambled egg, cheese spread or tomato – flavours they meet every day; you can make the sandwiches exciting by cutting them into fancy shapes. Children in the eight-to-twelve year group have enormous appetites, so bridge rolls topped with savoury fillings are a better choice than sandwiches. Small sausages on sticks are always popular (use chipolata sausages, twisted or cut into 3 or 4, and served cold), so are sausage rolls, potato crisps and cheese pastries or scones. Little iced cakes are more appealing when decorated with small sweets, or better still with the initials of each guest. Meringues, éclairs and other rich cakes are best reserved for older children. Chocolate biscuits are a sure bet and so are iced home-made biscuits, in animal shapes or letters. Fruit jelly and ice cream (in waxed containers) vanish like snow in summer.

Tea parties

A tea party may be a purely social occasion or it may arise because a committee is meeting or some other activity is taking place in your home.

In any case, only a light tea is required. Make small sandwiches, filling them with salmon and cucumber, sardine and watercress, egg and tomato, ham and tongue and so on. Try also making some rolled sandwiches, which are easy and popular. Cut thin brown bread and butter, remove the crusts, spread with a creamy filling (such as well-seasoned cream cheese) and roll up the bread. Alternatively, offer tiny bridge rolls, asparagus rolls or small scones. Add an assortment of small cakes and biscuits or fingers of fruit cake. In the winter, hot buttered scones or tea cakes would be welcome.

Provide both China and Indian tea, with milk and sugar and also thinly cut slices of lemon for those who prefer it.

Teenage parties

Teenagers will generally not welcome parental help in arranging their parties; they prefer informality to over-much organisation in any case.

The main task for the mother of a teenage host is simply to see that there is plenty of easily available food and drink and a good supply of plates, glasses, cutlery and paper napkins laid out somewhere where the young ones can easily help themselves as and when they feel hungry – they don't like to be organised into a canteen-like queue. If your kitchen is large enough, that's the ideal place, for spills won't matter, and soup, casseroles and so on can be kept hot indefinitely.

Choose food that is simple to eat. Savoury flans, patties, sausages, risotto, pilau, curries and casserole dishes with savoury rice are all popular, or a delivery of fish and chips from a good local fish fryer can sometimes be laid on. French bread or rolls and butter, with a selection of cheeses, celery, lettuce, chicory and so on, will fill any cracks that may be left.

Don't have too many cakes, jellies and similar sweet things, as these often get left, but a really attractive gâteau and a good fruit salad served with meringues generally go down well.

For drinks you must obviously choose according to the age of the guests, who could be anything from 13 to 18, but have plenty of soft drinks (including some non-fizzy ones), some beer and perhaps a light wine cup, as well as coffee or chocolate in cold weather.

If you have a large garage, cellar or barn for the actual party, so much the better – otherwise it may be as well to remove some of the furniture and any valuable ornaments from the living-rooms and to roll back the carpets, leaving lots of cushions to sit on. A record player is essential, of course, and guests will probably bring discs to supplement their host's collection.

Although parents are not generally welcome at the party itself, in the case of younger teenagers they should be in evidence when the guests arrive and depart, and some grown-up should be available all through the evening in case of any crisis.

Picnics

For some people picnics are a way of life when the days are long and fine. Casual meals by the sea or in the country are relaxing for parents, sheer fun for the kids. Others prefer their outdoor eating no further than the garden, the balcony, or maybe the local common. Choose food that suits the occasion – the travelling distance and mode of transport. And if the weather takes a turn for the worse, don't worry – keep to informality and the same foods are equally delicious indoors, lap service. Pastry-based food is right for outdoor eating; quiches and savoury flans, easy to pack if you keep them in the baking tin overwrapped with clear polythene film, are especially good. Enjoy them with salad greens, potato crisps, cold sausages, plenty of fruit to follow and maybe a slice of cake or a cookie. Salmon patties, made with cheese pastry, are quick to make and fine for impromptu picnics. For a budget version you could use canned tuna instead of salmon. A coarse pâté or meat loaf carries well; served with fresh bread and simple salad ingredients it is nearly

Egg nog (p. 522), Midsummer Night's Dream (p. 514), Irish or Gaelic coffee (p. 520), Russian tea (p. 517).

always enough for the biggest of outdoor appetites. For fresh air people who hike or bike, pack the food individually so that everyone shares the load, and keep wrappings as light as possible. Baked chicken drumsticks, sausages rolled in bread and butter with a spread of chutney, stuffed rolls kept nicely moist, and Scotch eggs all travel well, along with carrot sticks, wedges of cucumber and crisps – not forgetting a twist of salt. Individual thermos containers keep fruit salad chilled. Alternatively, eat fruit yoghurt straight from the carton. Chocolate raisin squares (page 427), wrapped in foil, could be included to fill any odd corners.

Wraps and carriers

If you are only once-in-a-while picnickers, it is not worth investing in elaborate equipment. Polythene wraps and foil for packing the food will do nicely. Picnic addicts, however, like to keep a good selection of rigid plastic containers, large and small boxes, plastic jelly moulds with tight-fitting lids, individual liquid-resistant dishes for soufflés and pâtés and plastic bottles with dispenser lids for dressings and sugar. Don't forget vacuum flasks in varying sizes for hot and cold drinks; the fat, wide-necked type are ideal for hot and cold soups, for carrying ice cubes and for fruit salads. If you add a few ice cubes to the syrup, your fruit salad will stay really chilled in the flask until ready to serve. Picnic hampers can be a mixed blessing. Even if you choose a small square basket with a lid and no internal fittings this is not nearly so useful as a hold-all type carrier. Large insulated zip-fastened bags – some with fitted ice pockets – are worth looking for.

Check list

It can ruin a good picnic if you unpack your feast only to realise that the bottle opener is still in the kitchen drawer. So it is a good idea to have a tick-off list.

Essentials should include: can and bottle opener; corkscrew; damp cloth in a plastic bag for sticky faces and fingers; paper towel roll; first aid kit (including insect repellant); extra empty bags for litter; non-spill salt, pepper and sugar; plates, cups or mugs, glasses for wine; cutlery – including a serrated knife and butter spreader.

Wrap individual place settings of cutlery in napkins and pack the basket in reverse order for unloading, tablecloth (if you're taking one) on top.

Be sure the plates are large enough – it is frustrating to eat a main course from a tea plate.

For obvious reasons it is better not to carry crockery – plastic or disposable things are more practical. But there are people who prefer to drink their tea or coffee from china, and wine really demands clear glasses. Maybe clear plastic ones or heavy tumblers would fill the bill.

Reusable ice packs that are frozen ahead will keep anything cool for a short time. Some foods can be carried frozen to thaw en route.

Keep sandwich spreads fairly soft. Cut a stack of same-filling sandwiches at a time, and wrap the different kinds separately in polythene film to prevent mingling of odours. Bar cakes carry well in their original baking tins.

Weddings

Home catering for more than 100 is beyond the limit that most mothers of the bride feel they can undertake; below this number, with a few recruited helpers and good planning, it is manageable.

Finger foods are ideal – savoury canapés including a variety of sandwiches and a few sweet items. Serve Champagne or a sparkling white wine or as an alternative a white Burgundy or Riesling. Allow $\frac{1}{2}$ bottle per person. Soft drinks should also be available. After the cutting of the cake by the bridal couple it is usual to offer tea or coffee.

MENU

COLD
- Choux cheese balls
- Smoked salmon pinwheels
- Asparagus rolls
- Liver pâté on crackers
- Shrimp tartlets

HOT
- Curried chicken vol-au-vent.
- Tiny meat balls with devilled mayonnaise
- Baby pizza (fried bread rounds with topping of tomato, cheese, herbs, anchovy and olives, oven-browned)
- Hot sausages

SWEET
- Brandy snaps
- Meringues
- Small iced cakes (could be ordered from a local baker)
- Shortbread
- Strawberries and cream in summer
- Fresh fruit salad in winter

A sit-down wedding breakfast is possible for fewer guests. The layout is generally one large table for bride, groom, immediate family, best man and bridesmaids, with guests informally at smaller tables. Service may be provided at the tables if there is adequate staff, otherwise all besides the near family help themselves from a buffet table. Drinks should be the same as for a stand-up reception. If white wine is served through the meal it is customary to serve Champagne or sparkling wine to toast the bride and groom.

MENU

- Melon and grape cocktail
- Cucumber soup or fresh tomato consommé
- Boned duck with orange stuffing
- Salmon trout
- Salads: tossed green
  - dressed mushroom
  - potato and chive
  - tomato with onion

Lemon soufflé
or
Strawberry flan
Wedding cake
Coffee
(It is wise to have something plain like chicken set aside for small child guests).

A check list for planning a wedding is given below; within each heading add your own individual needs.

Venue Well in advance book the hall or room for reception if not at home. At home decide whether a marquee is needed.

Tables and chairs Check that the hall/rooms are equipped and the cloakroom accommodation is good.

Staff Decide whether a toastmaster is required, also waiters, waitresses.

Order invitations to send out 6 weeks in advance. Order service sheets for a church wedding at the same time.

Transport and parking Hire cars as necessary and arrange with friends for more casual help. Check parking facilities at church and hall.

China and silver Consult a hire company well in advance. The yellow pages of the telephone directory are helpful. Hired china is usually returned dirty. Don't forget ashtrays.

Flowers For bouquets, buttonholes, the top of the cake perhaps, church and reception area.

The cake Make up to 3 months ahead or put in a firm order to a baker. Do not forget a cake stand and knife, which can usually be hired from a caterer. Will you need boxes for posting? Out of the ordinary cake boards should be searched out.

Linen Friends may rally round; consider disposables, especially paper napkins. Have plenty of tea towels.

Drinks Arrange for all drinks on a sale or return basis. Most suppliers will lend glasses free, you pay only for breakages. You will also need lemons, ice, bottle opener, corkscrew.

Food Decide the menu well ahead, alongside note the food that can be ordered well in advance and last minute perishables. When a freezer is available prepare as much as possible and make a note of thawing times. Have a conference with helpers and decide who should do what and how the food can be transported. Check facilities at the hall/rooms for storage, eg refrigeration or reheating possibilities. As cooking is larger scale than usual, check that large pans, tins, etc. are available.

How much for how many

Food	*Makes 12 portions*	*Makes 20 portions*	*Practical points*
Soup	2.3 l *(4 pt)*	3.4 l *(6 pt)*	If made ahead, refrigerated and reheated, cream soups may need thinning with stock
Rice	550 g *(1¼ lb)* uncooked	900 g *(2 lb)* uncooked	Allow 10 ml *(2 level tsps)* salt and 600 ml *(1 pt)* water per 225 g *(½ lb)* long grain rice. Cook ahead and reheat in boiling water for 5 min
Mayonnaise	600 ml *(1 pt)*	900 ml–1 l *(1½–1¾ pt)*	For 600 ml *(1 pt)*, use 3 egg yolks, 400 ml *(¾ pt)* oil, 45 ml *(3 tbsps)* vinegar, 7.5 ml *(1½ level tsps)* dry mustard, 7.5 ml *(1½ level tsps)* salt, 5 ml *(1 level tsp)* pepper, 7.5 ml *(1½ level tsps)* sugar
French dressing	300 ml *(½ pt)*	400–600 ml *(¾–1 pt)*	Make in a lidded container and shake together just before serving
Fish cocktail (shrimp, prawn, crab, tuna)	350–450 g *(¾–1 lb)* fish; 1 large lettuce; 400 ml *(¾ pt)* sauce	700 g *(1½ lb)* fish; 2 lettuces; 900 ml *(1½ pt)* sauce	Combine fish and sauce ahead and keep covered in a cool place. Assemble just before serving
Meat (with bone) (boneless)	1.8 kg *(4 lb)* 1.4 kg *(3 lb)*	3.2 kg *(7 lb)* 2.3 kg *(5 lb)*	For buffets: cold cuts, barbecues, cutlets, casseroles, meatballs etc

Food	*Makes 12 portions*	*Makes 20 portions*	*Practical points*
Poultry (turkey)	3.6-kg *(8-lb)* oven-ready bird	6.4-kg *(14-lb)* oven-ready bird	For cold platters with stuffing added
(chicken)	3-kg *(6½-lb)* oven-ready bird	2 2.7-kg *(2 6-lb)* oven-ready birds	
Delicatessen: ham, tongue, salami etc	1.1 kg *(2½ lb)*	1.8–2.3 kg *(4–5 lb)*	For a cold platter
Pâté	900 g *(2 lb)*	1.4–1.8 kg *(3–4 lb)*	As an appetiser or to include in a buffet selection
Ice cream	2 family size blocks	2.3 l *(½ gal)*	Keep at ice cube compartment temperature for easy serving
Cream (single or double)	900 ml *(1½ pt)*	1.1 l *(2 pt)*	To lighten and extend well chilled double cream, add 15 ml *(1 tbsp)* milk to each 142-ml *(5-fl oz)* carton cream before whipping. 142 ml *(5 fl oz)* cream, whipped, gives about 12 individual whirls
Coffee (instant)	40 g *(1½ oz)* coffee; 1.7 l *(3 pt)* water; 568 ml *(1 pt)* milk; 225 g *(½ lb)* sugar	50–75 g *(2–3 oz)* coffee; 3.4 l *(6 pt)* water; 1.1 l *(2 pt)* milk; 450 g *(1 lb)* sugar	Make coffee in jugs as required. Serve milk and sugar separately
(ground)	150 g *(5 oz)* coffee; 1.7 l *(3 pt)* water; 900 ml *(1½ pt)* milk; 225 g *(½ lb)* sugar	250–275 g *(9–10 oz)* coffee; 3.4 l *(6 pt)* water; 1.7 l *(3 pt)* milk; 450 g *(1 lb)* sugar	If you make the coffee in advance, strain it after infusion. Reheat without boiling. Serve hot milk and sugar separately
Sausage rolls	700 g *(1½ lb)* shortcrust or flaky pastry; 900 g *(2 lb)* sausage meat	30 medium or 50 small rolls	Pastry based on 700 g *(1½ lb)* flour, 350–450 g *(¾–1 lb)* fat
Bouchées, vol-au-vents	900 g *(2 lb)* puff pastry; 600 ml *(1 pt)* sauce; 275 g *(10 oz)* prepared filling	50 bouchées, 25 7.5-cm *(3-in)* vol-au-vents	Pastry based on 450 g *(1 lb)* flour, 350 g *(¾ lb)* butter. Fillings: chopped chicken, ham, salmon, prawns, shrimps, mushrooms and sauce
Cheese straws	225 g *(½ lb)* cheese pastry	100 straws	Pastry based on 225 g *(½ lb)* flour, 100 g *(¼ lb)* fat, 100 g *(¼ lb)* cheese
Trifle	2.3 l *(4 pt)* custard; 25 trifle sponge cakes; 1 large can fruit	25 portions	Decorate with cream, glacé cherries, chopped nuts, angelica

Wines and liqueurs

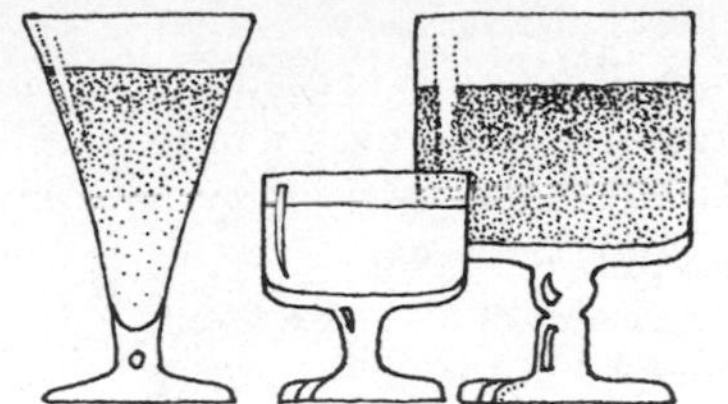
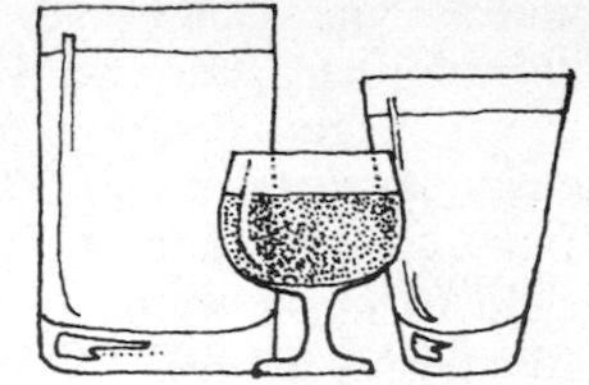

Wine is the juice from freshly gathered grapes, extracted by crushing the grapes and then fermented. The fermentation process turns the grape sugar into alcohol and the juice becomes wine. In table wines, the percentage of alcohol by volume varies from as little as 7 degrees to as much as 14–15 degrees. This measurement of alcoholic strength by volume is known as Gay-Lussac, the name of the French chemist who evolved the system. And this is the way in which alcoholic strength is denoted when it appears on wine labels. When additional alcohol is introduced you have 'fortified' wine, with alcoholic strength from 18–21 degrees or more.

There are many different kinds of grape, grown in various parts of the world, and also different methods of vine-growing and wine-making. The soil, climate and aspect of the vineyards all influence the character of the wine and the quality of the grape juice also varies from year to year according to weather, just as other crops do. So the same wine varies from vintage to vintage.

What's on the label

In the 1970s, wine regulations have undergone considerable revision, so that labels in Britain should now tell you more specifically about the wine inside the bottle. Most important of all from our point of view are the labelling laws of France, Germany and Italy (to which EEC laws have been added) and which apply to sales in Britain. The laws are extremely comprehensive and consequently very complex. (There is helpful information for the consumer about labelling in *Good Housekeeping Book of Wine*.)

France About 15 per cent of the wines of France possess an *Appellation d'Origine Contrôlée* (usually abbreviated to *Appellation Contrôlée, A.O.C.* or *A.C.*). The *appellation* laws for each of the major fine wine regions in France define where the vines are grown; the grape varieties; the way the vines are cultivated; how many can be planted and the yield from particular areas; the amount of wine that can be made, its minimum alcoholic strength and the precise name that can be used for the wine. There are many grades of *appellation*, going in stages from, say, the simple *A.O.C.* Bordeaux or *A.O.C.* Bourgogne to specific commune or district vineyards with their prized *appellation*. For minor wines there is a lower *appellation* known as *Vins Délimité de' Qualité Supérieure (V.D.Q.S.)*. Finally, there are blended wines simply labelled *Vin de table* or Table Wine, Produce of France.

Germany The new German wine law (with more emphasis on quality than the *A.O.C.* quantity-control) now gives more information on the label in simpler terms. It provides three categories. The lowest is *Deutscher Tafelwein* which means German table wine. It need not be made from any particular grape or come from any specific German vineyard and it is not allowed to use a vineyard name. *Qualitätswein bestimmter Anbaugebiete* (or *QbA*) is a wine of quality from a specific region and from specified grapes. *Qualitätswein mit Prädikat* is the top, meaning quality wine with recognised distinction such as *Kabinett, Spätlese, Auslese,* etc. (see pages 505, 506). The grapes and area from which the wine comes are strictly defined and the wine's sweetness is purely dependent on natural grape sugar. The two quality categories must be tasted by an official tasting commission and carry a number to prove this.

Italy Italian wines are controlled by the law of *Denominazione di Origine Controllata* (*D.O.C.*), similar to the French *A.C.* but with a somewhat different system of administration, sometimes more severe. A wine possessing *D.O.C.* clearly states this on the label, where *Classico* means the wine is made in its historic region, *Superiore* that it is matured and of higher alcoholic content and *Riserva* that it has had three to five years maturity, while *Vecchio* means at least two years age. There is now a superior classification, *Denominazione di Origine Controllata e Garantita* (controlled and guaranteed denomination of origin) reserved for the finest Italian wines. Each bottle bears a state stamp and the wines have to comply with stringent requirements. At the time of writing (1975) this denomination has been awarded to only very few wines, one of which is Barolo.

The amount of wine in the bottle from these countries is also now being standardised in centilitres, although bottles still come in a variety of shapes. The larger litre bottles, already standard, are further standardised in multiples of the litre.

The age of the wine

If you are not conversant with the different styles and brands of wine on the market, the reliable wine merchant is still the best adviser. His advice should certainly be sought about vintage wines, particularly if you wish to lay them down for future drinking. Table wines of good and great vintages – notably clarets and red Burgundy, need bottle age that can vary from five to ten years and even more, especially among the great Bordeaux.

Many of the white wines of the Loire, Alsace and Moselle are normally consumed when young – a mere two or three years after bottling. This applies also to Beaujolais.

In the context of this chapter we are not including a list of fine vintage years because to be of continuing value they need wider explanation. With vintages, for several reasons, there are exceptions to the rule. Sometimes, in an otherwise indifferent year, wines from certain vineyards may be remarkably good; in a fine year, wines from some vineyards can be quite ordinary. All the more reason, therefore, to consult a good wine merchant.

How to serve wine

1. All white wines should be served chilled, but not iced. Don't put ice into them.
2. Most red wines are best served at room temperature, but since room temperatures vary, let them stand for a few hours in a 'comfort zone' of around 15–18°C (*60–65°F*). Never subject the wine to fierce, direct heat. Uncork red wines at least an hour or so before serving. Young ones up to 3 hours.
3. The purpose of decanting is twofold; to separate the wine from the lees and, with red wine, to let it take the air. Add to that the pleasure of the sight of wine decanted, whether in a decanter, a carafe or glass jug. It is not, however, *necessary* to decant red wine, so long as the bottle has stood still for an hour or so before serving. If red wine has a very heavy sediment then it obviously needs to be decanted, but this condition is more usually found in old and expensive wines, in which case your wine merchant should advise you how best to treat it.
4. Glasses for wine should be clear, colourless and thin, preferably with a bowl that narrows towards the rim so as to hold the wine's perfume. And ideally it should be a stemmed glass, whether the stem is long or short. The size of the glass should be big enough to swirl the wine around to release its fragrance (holding it by the foot or stem) and the glass should be filled only half-way up or, at most, two-thirds. A 162–175 ml (*5½–6 fl oz*) glass is a good all-purpose size.

How to store wine

All that good wine needs is to be left lying on its side (to keep the cork moist) in a cool, dark, airy, reasonably dry and draught-free place with the minimum of vibration (under the stairs, bottom of a cool larder, hall cupboard, for instance). The bottles can be laid in wine merchants' cardboard boxes or in 'bins' or 'racks' specially made for the purpose. Wine is not all that sensitive to prevailing temperature. While a cellar with a temperature of between 10°C and 13°C (*50–55°F*) is ideal, provided there are no violent fluctuations in the thermometer reading the wine is safe in a reasonably constant temperature between a minimum of 8°C (*45°F*) and a maximum of 20°C (*68°F*). Never lay down a bottle if the wine is beginning to ooze out through the cork. Watch stored bottles and use quickly any bottle that shows signs of 'weeping'.

The wine for the food

The classically accepted partnerships are:
with oysters: Chablis or dry Champagne
with soup: dry sherry or dry Madeira
with fish: dry white wines or dry Champagne
with roasts or game: red Burgundy or full claret
with sweets: Sauternes or fine sweet hock
with cheese: Port, brown sherry or Madeira.

However, there are no rules about wines to be served with food; it is a very personal matter. Helpful guidelines are light wines before fuller ones; dry before sweet; red before sweet white; lesser wines before fine ones. When one wine only is served throughout a meal it should be the wine most appropriate to the main course. Champagne is regarded by some as a suitable wine throughout a meal but many people prefer it as an aperitif.

Dry white wines which stimulate the palate are good as an aperitif or with hors d'oeuvre, shellfish. (Chablis, Muscadet, Portuguese Vinho Verde, Champagne or other sparkling wine if dry.)

Dry or medium dry white wines suit plainly cooked veal, chicken and fish dishes and drink well throughout the meal. (White Burgundy, Sancerre, Alsace Riesling, Moselle, Soave, Verdicchio.)

Rosé wines, of a medium dryness are pleasant summer wines for cold plates and picnic dishes. (Tavel, Rosé de Cabernet.)

Lighter bodied red wine is pleasant with lamb chops, veal escalopes and milder casserole dishes (light clarets, Beaujolais, Valpolicello, Bardolino).

Fuller red wine suits red meats, rich stews, casseroles, game dishes (St. Emilion and Pomerol among the clarets; red Burgundy, Côtes du Rhône, Chianti, Rioja).

Sweet white wines are drunk chilled, on their own or to go with certain sweet puddings and dessert fruits. (Sauternes, sweeter hocks, Muscat de Beaumes de Venise, etc.)

Most wines go well with cheese, especially red wine, which is why in many continental countries the cheese is served before the sweet, allowing the red wine of a main meat course to be finished off with the cheese.

Some foods don't take well to wine – curry and other highly spiced foods are probably better partnered with beer or cider. Chinese food is traditionally served with green tea, though a dry white wine may be suitable. Vinegar is an enemy of wine so when you're serving dressed salads, go easy on the vinegar. A French dressing with five parts oil to one of vinegar will be kind enough to everyday wine but not to fine wines. Citrus fruits and wine don't go. And chocolate desserts are best taken on their own.

BRIEF GUIDE TO THE WORLD'S WINES

France

Bordeaux

This region of south-west France is the most prodigious vineyard in the world for fine wines, through the range of red wines (claret) to the great sweet white wines of Sauternes.

The important red wine grapes are Cabernet-Sauvignon, Cabernet franc, Merlot variety; white wine grapes, Sauvignon blanc, Sémillon and Muscadelle.

The Médoc is where some of the finest red wines come from. Within this district the principle communes or parishes with their own *appellations contrôlées* are:

St. Estèphe, where the wines mature slowly, can have great body and fullness of flavour but often less perfume. Classic clarets, these.

Pauillac is the commune which includes three of the classified First Growths – Châteaux Lafite, Latour and Mouton-Rothschild. Connoisseur wines for halcyon days.

St. Julien has fragrant, elegant wines often described as 'velvety'. They're comparatively easy wines for a beginner.

Margaux in the southernmost stretch of Haut-Médoc, contains the classified First Growth wine of Château Margaux and other fine growths. These wines have a delicacy and a haunting perfume which, to some, makes them the most exquisite clarets of all.

The other main districts of Bordeaux are:

St. Emilion, where the wines can be very fruity and big, and some of them have been called the Burgundies of Bordeaux.

Pomerol produces clarets which have gentleness, richness, deep colour and still a light freshness of character.

Graves, the district south of the Médoc, takes its name from its gravel-and-sandy soil. While known chiefly for its white wines, its greatest reds are equivalent to those of Margaux and Pauillac. Château Haut-Brion is one of the five classified First Growths, and probably the first claret known in Britain came from thereabouts.

Sauternes is the district south of the city of Bordeaux where the greatest sweet white wines of France come from, and it also embraces the smaller area of **Barsac**. The greatest Sauternes, of which Château d'Yquem is the peer, only find rivals in the great wines of Germany, and are made from grapes which have been affected by 'noble rot', or *pourriture noble*. The result is a very sweet, flowery, golden wine, a natural dessert wine. The ordinary Sauternes and Barsacs are just sweet white wines to serve chilled before or after a meal.

Other principally white-wine districts in the Bordeaux region are **Entre-deux-mers, Blaye** and **Bourg**, and they vary from very light and dry to medium sweet. (Bourg also produces some pleasant, fruity reds.) In the Dordogne, Bordeaux's beautiful hinterland, **Bergerac** produces very dry and very sweet white wines, and Monbazillac is the best *appellation,* the wines being rich and golden when mature.

Burgundy

The Côte d'Or is the *département* of the string of little villages and towns whose names are world-famous because they have annexed their names to the great Burgundian vineyards. It is divided into two sections; the more northerly Côte de Nuits and the more southerly Côte de Beaune. Red Burgundies are made from the classic Pinot Noir grape; the whites from the Chardonnay.

The Côte de Nuits Among the outstanding communes are Gevrey-Chambertin where some of the greatest reds, big and very full in bouquet, are found; also Vosne-Romanée, sometimes described as 'holy ground' for it is the home of the wonderful *grands crus* of Romanée-Conti, La Romanée, Richebourg, La Tache. The *appellation contrôlée* wines of Nuits-St. George are dark in colour, crisp and with appreciable bouquet.

The Côte de Beaune red wines are, generally, softer, less full-bodied. Notable red wines come from Aloxe-Corton, Pommard, and Volnay. Red Chassagne-Montrachet (from the predominantly white-wine commune) is a charming, gentle wine.

The communes of Puligny-Montrachet and

Chassagne-Montrachet both share the vineyard of Le Montrachet where superlative white Burgundy is grown – great, round, deep wine with a beautiful bouquet. Then there are the fine white wines from the commune of Meursault, which have something of the flavour of ripe peaches; these and Corton-Charlemagne are gems in the white Burgundy crown.

The **Chablis** district, outside the Côte d'Or, produces a very distinctive white Burgundy, and true Chablis is very light in colour with a greenish glint, sometimes quite big in character but always bone-dry.

The **Côte Maconnais** of south Burgundy is where popular Pouilly Fuissé comes from. It, and other good and genuine white Macons have quite appreciable bouquet, and a greenish tint in their gold. Some of the red wines of Macon – reminiscent of fuller-bodied Beaujolais – and those of the Chalonnais – Givry, Mercurey and Rully, for example, are worth seeking out from a reputable shipper as pleasant value-for-money buys.

Beaujolais, still one of the most popular of red wines of Burgundy, is made from the Gamay grape, which gives it rich bright colour, and fresh fruitiness. There are several grades of Beaujolais and the finer examples are those of the individual communes, which starting at the top are; Moulin-à-Vent, Côte de Brouilly, and Brouilly, Julienas, Fleurie, Morgon, Chenas, St-Amour and Chirouble. Plain Beaujolais is best drunk young. And there is a vogue to drink Beaujolais with phrases like *Vin de l'Année, Nouveau* and *Primeur* appearing on the labels; such wines should definitely be drunk before March of the year following the vintage.

White Beaujolais is a multi-purpose, quite full-bodied wine.

La Champagne

From this carefully defined area of France comes the only true Champagne. Although normally a white wine – there are also some delightful pink ones – Champagne is usually made from a blend of juice from the Pinot Noir and Pinot Chardonnay grapes; the former said to give the wine body, the latter, soul.

Unlike most of the great wines of France, Champagne is usually sold by the name of the house or firm producing it. Vintage Champagne is of a year selected as being of outstanding quality; non-vintage is a blend from different years.

The other sparkling French wines, made by the Champagne method (*la méthode champenoise*), come from the Loire, Alsace, Burgundy and, costing much less than Champagne, are excellent celebration and party drinks.

The Loire

A wide variety of red, white and *rosé* wines, but mainly white, are grown down the length of this great river. And although they are made from four or five different grapes they have similar qualities in common – Loire wines are light, grapy and charming.

Muscadet is a dry white wine from the region around Nantes, near the mouth of the Loire, and the best Muscadet is made in this area, known as Sevre-et-Maine.

Gros Plant is a light, fresh white wine, with the *V.D.Q.S. appellation.*

Pouilly Fumé and **Sancerre**, from the Upper Loire are made from the Sauvignon grape which gives an aroma and palate which is called flinty – crisp, yet fruity and dry. Delicious with summer foods.

Savennières white wines have great distinction, are dry-to-medium, fleshy and full-bodied. Although they are made from the same Chenin Blanc grape, they are in great contrast to the sweet wines of **Côteaux du Layon** to the south and the wines of **Vouvray** to the east, of which even the dry wines (still or sparkling) have a hint of background sweetness.

Anjou Rosé is at its best when it is made from the Cabernet grape, fragrant, medium dry.

Cabernet de Saumur is for those who prefer a drier wine.

Chinon and **Bourgueil** are the classic red wines of the Loire, made from the Cabernet-Franc grape; and with bottle age can be elegant, distinguished wine with a bouquet sometimes described as 'violets and raspberries'.

The Rhône

From this part of France – from just below Lyons extending almost down to Avignon – come a wide range of robust red wines, an increasing number of whites, as well as the most serious *rosés*.

Côte Rôtie is perhaps the most elegant and refined of all Rhône reds; can be drunk young but transforms with age.

Hermitage is the archetypal red; big, characterful, deep-coloured, and when mature, has a marvellous bouquet, described as reminiscent of raspberries and gilly-flowers.

Vacqueyras is a dark red, full flavoured wine with a high alcohol content (13–15 degrees). **Gigondas** is a similar but slower-maturing wine. **Côtes de Ventoux** reds are big and fruity, and achieved an *appellation contrôlée* in 1973.

Chateauneuf-du-Pape the famous, fat and southerly

Rhône wine is a wine with a strict *appellation contrôlée*; softer and quicker-maturing than other red Rhônes, strong and full-flavoured.

White wines of the Rhône to look for include **Lirac Blanc**, delicate but firm; **Crozes Hermitage**, crisp and fruity; **St. Peray Nature**, fresh, full-bodied with a marked bouquet. (There's a sparkling St. Peray, too, made by the *méthode champenoise*.)

Condrieu is an aristocratic – and most expensive – white Rhône wine, with a faintly spicy may-blossom aroma and a delicate, lingering taste.

Alsace

The wines of this 'garden of France' are named for the grapes, notably white.

Riesling, which is the Rhine-Riesling grape is also the finest wine of Alsace, distinguished, delicate, sometimes full-bodied.

Gewürztraminer is fruity, spicy yet can be clean and dry. Ideal with the rich goose and pork dishes of Alsace.

Muscat d'Alsace has a grapy scent but is a clean, dry white wine that makes a good aperitif. Not to be confused with the sweet wine associated with the Muscat grape elsewhere.

Sylvaner is light and sometimes pleasantly tart.

Other French wine regions

From **Provence, Languedoc** and **Roussillon** come two-thirds of France's output of *Vins Délimités de Qualité Supérieure (V.D.Q.S.)*. These wines, red, white and *rosé*, are also grown to strict rules, selected and adjudged by expert local committees. The wines of Minervois, Costières du Gard, Corbières, Côtes de Provence, and Corbières du Roussillon are all trying hard to improve and achieve *A.O.C.* status. Meantime their lower rating generally gives them a price advantage and many of them make pleasant, easy, everyday drinking. The red wines of Cahors on the slopes leading down to the river Lot, the best of which are soft-scented, full of flavour and very sturdy, were once known as the senior *V.D.Q.S.* wines and achieved their *A.O.C.* status in 1971.

Germany

The finest wines of the Rhine and Moselle are made from the classic Riesling grape, as is stated on the label. Many fine wines are also made from successful varieties like Scheurebe, Sylvaner, Traminer and Müller-Thurgau, which names usually appear on the label also. Nowadays many German wines are increasingly made with different varieties and sometimes, for less expensive wines, grape names may not appear on the label.

Rhineland

Hock is still the name most used in English-speaking countries for the white wines of the Rhineland: it is derived from the village of Hochheim. Styles of hock vary considerably, depending among other factors on the areas they come from. The four main Rhine regions are:

Rheingau The wine here, and at its best, is the noblest of all Germany. Slower-maturing, elegant, delicate and with a golden depth of flavour. Among the great estates are Schloss Vollrads, and Schloss Johannisberg – and Kloster Eberbach, sometimes called the headquarters of German wine.

Rheinhessen The bulk of the wine is made from the Sylvaner grape, slightly earthy, soft and sometimes sweetish. It is from here that much of the best Liebfraumilch comes. The other most popular wines of this area are from the Niersteiner vineyards.

Nahe These wines seem to combine the qualities of both the Rhine and the Moselle, the best being flowery, fresh, fruity and well-balanced. The vineyards around Bad Kreuznach and Schloss Böckelheim are notable.

Rheinpfalz (Palatinate) The sunniest, driest, biggest vineyard of Germany produces a wide variety of wines from a number of different grapes. They are generally fuller in style, some of them sweet, all of them partnering well the rich, regional food. Bad Dürkheim is the large and famous wine centre.

Out of the mainstream is **Franconia**, where the best wines are made with the Sylvaner grape and are dry by German standards, rather more French in style. *Steinwein* is the name often given to all Franken wine, much of which is bottled in the flagon-like Bocksbeutel.

Moselle

The spectacular vineyards of the Middle Moselle – around Bernkastel and Piesporter – produce some of the classic wines from the Riesling grape. They can have ineffable fragrance, crispness, and a green delicacy; they are mostly best drunk young. Wines from the Saar and Ruwer tributaries of the Moselle, in good years, have finesse and charm.

German wine styles

It is important to know these terms, which appear on the labels in addition to other names, because each type of wine is very different.

Kabinett This can be translated as 'special reserve', a quality wine carefully tested and tasted for approval.

Spätlese means 'late gathered' so that the grapes are very ripe and the wine made from them has a more intense flavour and aroma.

Auslese means that the finest and ripest grapes have been

specially selected to make a beautiful, fine, slightly sweet wine.

Beerenauslese one step up in which over-ripe or 'sleepy' berries are individually selected to make luscious, golden wine that should be drunk alone, for its own sake.

Trockenbeerenauslese means the grapes have been left until they are semi-dry, almost raisin-like, and the action of 'noble rot' (*Edelfaul*) upon them gives to the wine an ineffable bouquet and intensity of flavour. These wines are among the greatest sweet wines in the world, very expensive and for very special occasions.

Eiswein so-called ice wine is a rarity, when frost freezes the grapes on the vine overnight when, in special years, they've been left until almost Christmas time. A delicate, subtle and beautiful wine results.

Italy

Almost every region of Italy is wine-producing, as are the offshore islands of Sicily and Sardinia. The styles in each region also vary considerably. Don't forget to look for the *D.O.C.* label.

Red wines

Barolo from Piedmont, and bearing a village name, has a very big scent and flavour and great depth of taste; one of Italy's best wines. It is made from the excellent Nebbiolo grape.

Barbaresco also a village-name, from the same region differs only in that it is slightly drier.

Barbera named from the grape, is a very fruity wine, rich garnet colour and with an almost smoky bouquet.

Bardolino is a charming, fresh red wine quite light in style, almost a rosé.

Valpolicella comes, like Bardolina, from the Veneto region. It is cherry-red, sweetly scented with a soft, light flavour. Other red wines, especially in the north of Italy are made from classic grapes such as Cabernet, Pinot and Merlot; well worth seeking out.

Chianti the famous wine of Tuscany is fruity and robust. Vintage Chiantis can be very fine. The best Chianti comes in claret-style bottles; the more common wine in the tubby, familiar flasks.

White wines

Soave, from the Veneto, is an agreeable, fruity, fragrant dry wine.

Verdicchio is a very dry wine with a fair amount of body.

Frascati, wines from the Alban Hills south-east of Rome are honey-coloured, can be dry, slightly sweet or very sweet.

Orvieto a pale golden wine also comes in several styles, the *secco* (dry) and *abbocato* or *amabile* (rather sweet) being the most widely available.

Est! Est! Est! can be dry or slightly sweet, quite fragrant and fresh. It is, like Orvieto, bottled in a wicker-bound flask.

Lacrima Christi, (tears of Christ), is made on the slopes of Vesuvius and has a slightly 'volcanic' hint in taste, in both the dry and sweet versions.

Sardinian wines are coming along and worth watching. Strong, dry white Vernacchia, with a distinct affinity with sherry, is an excellent aperitif; and Nuragus an appetising dry white that's not too strong. Cannonau and Oliena are the best-known reds, probably showing best in their own sunny island.

Sicilian wines are also making progress abroad, notably the good clean reds and white from the Corvo vineyards, from Etna and the sweet white Mamertino.

Spain

Spain is the homeland of sherry but the country is also prolific in table wines, with **Rioja** the 'serious' region. Rioja Baja (the high Rioja) produces the best of them. The red wines are in two styles, one drier, the other fuller and can be quite outstanding when they are estate-bottled. The whites incline to fullness but with a very dry aftertaste. Some quite pleasant white wines also come from **Valdepenas**.

Portugal

The **Douro** is where the wine for port is grown: the two important table wine areas are the **Minho** and **Dao**.

The Minho is celebrated for its *vinhos verdes*, young, low-strength wines with a little natural sparkle or *pétillance*. Called 'green' for youth, not colour, they can be red, white or *rosé*, the whites being best known in this country. Served well chilled they make perfect summer drinking.

Dao is to Portugal what Rioja is to Spain, and from here come the best wines, particularly red. They tend to be hard when young, but a *Reserva*, with good bottle age, can be mellow, subtly scented and quite fine. The whites are quite full-bodied and dry. Mateus *rosé* is the most famous of the pink wines.

Yugoslavia

The white wines of Slovenia, notably Lutomer Riesling and Sylvaner have been the most popular in this country since the last war. Zilavka, a dry, fruity and pungent white wine comes from north of Dubrovnik, Cabernet Brda is a soft, red wine from the Trieste region. Pleasant reds are also made from the classic Pinot Noir grape.

Hungary

The great, sweet wines of **Tokay** are the country's pride: Tokay Aszu the most renowned – delicate, honey-sweet – is a golden dessert wine. Tokay Szamarodni, pale golden, can be dry or medium-sweet.

Pleasant good-value wines for everyday drinking are the **Magyar** Rieslings and the full-flavoured red **Bikaver**, or Bull's Blood.

Other wines

Austrian wines from Wachau, the best-known wine area, include Schluck, a fresh, dry white wine from Sylvaner grapes. Wines with the village name of Gumpoldskirchen are made from the Riesling, Veltliner and Gewürztraminer grapes and vary in style accordingly.

Cyprus, largely because of its sherry-type wine, is Britain's third largest source, though dry white Aphrodite and Arsinoe and the reds, Othello and Afames, are table wines to try. Commandaria, prized by the Crusaders, is the great sweet dessert wine.

Greek table wines to look for include the dry red of Naoussa, the sweet red of Patros, the dry white of Marmarion and the sweet muscat of Samos. The national resin-wine, Retsina is a pleasantly acquired taste.

Switzerland's best wine regions are the Valais and the Vaud, predominantly white-wine vineyards and the wines are named for the grapes. Fendant is among the familiar wines, fruity, quite heady. And Dole is the best of the reds.

Australian table wines include, among their best, those from the Barossa Valley, South Australia, where the delicate white wines are produced from the Rhine-Riesling grape and fine, big reds from the Cabernet grape. Attractive white wines are made in the Hunter River Valley of New South Wales, notably from the Sémillon grape and the Ugni Blanc (or white Hermitage). Fanciers of Australian wines should avail themselves of up-to-date, excellent wine lists from the Australian Wine Centre in London.

South Africa is noted for the best imitation in the world of Spanish sherries. Of table wines, rather dry Rieslings and very dry Steen are interesting.

South America grows about one tenth of the world's wine, though comparatively little is exported. Chilean Cabernet reds and Sauvignon and Sémillon whites can be very good indeed.

California produces a wide range of wines of all types and those from the Napa Valley can be fine by any standards. American wines usually are labelled with the name of the grape or grape variety such as Zinfandel 'California's Beaujolais' among the reds, and the more familiar and classic Sauvignon Blanc.

England and **Wales** show a serious revival in wine-growing, and some 24 vineyards are growing wine on a commercial scale. The wine is mainly white (often made from a cross between the Riesling and Sylvaner grape), with Hambledon in Hampshire the best-known vineyard.

Sparkling wines

Many sparkling wines – Champagne is of its own unique quality and price – are made by the Champagne method, and proudly state this on the label. The other main method is the *cuve close* (or sealed vat). Famous French sparkling wines made by the Champagne method include Vouvray and Saumur; Asti Spumante, the sparkling Italian wines, are made by a process that combines the two methods. Most German *Sekt* (sparkling wine) is made by the *cuve close* method. Good sparkling wines add to the pleasures of party and pick-me-up occasions but should be assessed in their own right and not compared with Champagne.

Fortified wines

The most famous are sherry, port, Madeira and Marsala and strict legislation protects these names in Europe so that sherry can only come from the Jerez region in the south-west of Spain and port from Portugal. The addition of grape alcohol in the wine-making process gives these and other fortified wines alcoholic strength by volume of 18–21 degrees.

Port is made from grapes grown in the upper valley of the Douro river in Portugal and is shipped from Oporto. There are many types of port differing in style, strength, age, sweetness, and colour.

Vintage port is the great wine, unique in style. Unlike all others it spends most of its life in bottle and that can be for 10–20 or even more years for a fine vintage.

Wood ports are blends of wines of different years and ages which are matured in cask; they may be ruby, tawny, 'crusted' or vintage-character. *Ruby* is generally a blend of young wines; *tawny* can be either a fine old matured port which started as a ruby or, down the scale, a blend of ruby port and an older wine. *White port*, made entirely from white grapes, is pale gold, slightly dry and chilled makes a pleasant aperitif.

Sherry comes from the vineyards around the towns of Jerez de la Frontera, Puerto de Santa Maria and Sanlucar de Barrameda, which is on the sea and where, specifically, Manzanilla is grown.

Sherry is a blend of wines, matured by what is called the *solera* system, to ensure a continuing supply of wines of the same style and quality. There are five main types of sherry:

Fino Driest to the taste, pale gold in colour, this is a wine to be chilled, opened and drunk in its beautiful freshness.

Manzanilla is a special type of fino, bone-dry and with a slight sea-breeze flavour to it. Also an admirable aperitif.

Amontillado at its finest is a matured fino, with deep fragrance and a slightly 'nutty' flavour. Other amontillados are blends to achieve what is generally called a 'medium' sherry.

Oloroso Tawny-gold sherry with rich bouquet and not by nature sweet at all, although many are on the sweet side for export markets like ours.

Brown sherries are the sweet, luscious ones often with the name of 'milk' or 'cream', the most famous of which is Harvey's Bristol Cream. The best brown sherries are never cloying and so are any-time drinks as well as splendid dessert wines.

Madeira, named for the Portuguese island where it is made, is fortified by the addition of cane spirit. There are four main types, named for the grapes from which they are made.

Sercial is the dryest and lightest wine, a suitable aperitif, slightly chilled.

Verdelho, medium dry, darker in colour, soft in style.

Bual, velvety, medium-sweet, deep golden-brown, suitable with dessert fruit and nuts.

Malmsey is the great, rich Madeiran dessert wine.

Marsala, the famous wine of Sicily is made from a blend of local wines, brandy and unfermented grape juice. There are dry as well as sweet Marsalas, though the sweet variety used for classic Italian dishes, *scallopine alla marsala* and *zabaglione*, is most widely available.

Aperitifs

Patent aperitifs are either wine-based or spirit based. French and Italian vermouths are among the most widely used wine-based aperitifs. Others, generically called Bitters, are made from distilled spirits of varying alcoholic content flavoured with roots, herbs, barks and with bitterness their common factor.

Vermouths Dry, medium or sweet, they may be served chilled and straight or with ice cubes and/or soda water and a float of citrus; or to make mixed drinks (dry white with gin for a dry Martini; sweet red with whisky for a Manhattan, for instance). Chambery is the most subtle, delightful vermouth of France and has its own *appellation d'origine*. Made from light, dry wine of the southern Alps, its pink version, Chamberyzette, is flavoured with wild strawberries. Noilly Prat is the other bone-dry, pale, best-known French vermouth. Cinzano, Martini and Gancia are famous Italian vermouth names. They can be red (sweet), white (dry) or *bianco* (meaning white, but on the sweet side of medium).

Other patent aperitifs, such as Dubonnet, St. Raphael, Byrrh, Punt e Mes are, like vermouth, made of sweetened wine and often given their characteristic bitter-sweet astringency by the addition of quinine and bitter tree-barks. Some, like Lillet and Pineau de Charente are also fortified with brandy.

Bitters Campari, the best-known Italian bitters, is usually mixed with soda, as is the French Amer Picon. Campari mixed with red Italian vermouth, a splash of soda and a slice of lemon makes the popular drink called Americano. Suze is a very bitter, yellow, gentian-based aperitif, good as a restorative. Fernet-Branca and Underberg are ferocious looking-and-tasting medicinal bitters, good as restoratives, straight or with water; or used, like Angostura, in cocktail mixtures.

Anis drinks – Pernod, Pastis, Ricard, Ouzo – are aniseed/liquorice-flavoured greenish liquors that turn milky when the necessary water dilutant is added.

LIQUEURS AND BRANDIES

Liqueurs are *digestifs*, and so ideal as after-dinner drinks, though increasingly used in cooking sweet dishes, too. Alcohol, an essential ingredient in all liqueurs, may be in the form of grape spirit, grain spirit, fruit spirit. Sweetening is added and the variety of flavourings come from herbs, spices or fruit. Brandy is a spirit distilled from wine and is included here because of its high place among after-dinner pleasures.

The list shows the more familiar liqueurs in this country, although many fascinating local ones can be discovered during travel to regions of their origin.

Advocaat A Dutch liqueur, thick and creamy, made from fresh egg yolks and grape brandy.

Anisette A colourless aniseed flavoured liqueur that comes from France, Spain and Italy. Marie Brizard, from Bordeaux, is the most famous.

Bénédictine The most renowned and popular of herb-based liqueurs, said to have been originally compounded by Don Bernardo Vincelli at Fécamp in 1510.

Brandy There are many grape brandies, and the noble ones come from *Cognac*. From South of Bordeaux comes *Armagnac*, where it is proudly called D'Artagnan's brandy. It has a distinctive herby, sometimes smoky flavour and aroma and the best of it is regarded as equal in quality and finesse to Cognac.

Fruit brandies are sometimes misnamed. The terms 'Cherry Brandy', 'Apricot Brandy', 'Peach Brandy' are established names for sweet *liqueurs* made respectively from the fruits mentioned. Cherry Heering, from Denmark, is the best known import among cherry 'brandies'. *Eaux-de-Vie* (Waters of Life) are truly dry fruit brandies, bottled at higher alcoholic strength than liqueurs.

Calvados (applejack) is an *eau-de-vie*, apple brandy that takes its name from the town of Calvados, the Normandy centre of the French apple orchards.

Cassis A black-currant flavoured liqueur from Dijon, often added to dry white wine for a pretty, cooling summer drink.

Chartreuse One of the most famous herb-flavour liqueurs originally compounded by the Carthusian monks at Chartreuse, near Grenoble. The yellow type is sweeter, the green higher in alcohol, one of the most potent of all liqueurs.

Cointreau is one of the most popular orange curaçaos, colourless and strong; this one a French brand.

Crème de Cacao A very sweet chocolate-coloured and cocoa-flavoured liqueur from the West Indies.

Crème de Menthe Green in colour with a pronounced peppermint flavour. Often served 'on the rocks'.

Curaçao The original orange curaçao was made from citrus fruit from the island of Curaçao but the term is now generic and is used for orange-flavoured liqueurs made from oranges from other countries. Excellent curaçaos are made by Bols and Fockink in Holland.

Drambuie the great Scottish liqueur, golden coloured, with the flavour of whisky and heather honey.

Goldwasser Aniseed-flavoured liqueur from Germany; colourless, with little gold particles in it.

Grand Marnier The best known French brand of orange-flavoured liqueur in the curaçao family.

Kahlua A Mexican coffee liqueur, quite different from Tia Maria, and made for European markets by Heering in Denmark.

Kirsch is an *eau-de-vie*, or stone fruit brandy, in which the crushed kernels are included with the fruit juice – in this instance cherry. Other stone fruit brandies are *Mirabelle* (Mirabelle Plum); *Quetsch* (Switzen Plum); *Prune* (Plum).

Kummel A caraway-flavoured, colourless liqueur of Dutch origin.

Maraschino A bitter-sweet, water white liqueur made with maraschino cherries and their crushed kernels. A very popular addition to many sweets and desserts. It originated in Yugoslavia.

Parfait Amour An exotic, sweet citrus-oil based liqueur made in several colours, mainly violet. It is scented and slightly spiced.

Prunelle A French liqueur, plum-flavoured and pale green.

Royal Mint Chocolate A popular modern liqueur with a subtle flavour blend of peppermint and cocoa; was created by the English wine shipper Dr Peter Hallgarten.

Slivovitz is a colourless, dry plum brandy, notably from the Balkans.

Sloe Gin Rich, ruby red liqueur made by steeping sloe berries in gin. The traditional 'stirrup cup' of Old England.

Soft Fruit Brandies (Eaux de Vie) These delicately flavoured brandies are produced from strawberries, raspberries, blackberries, etc. *Fraise, Fraises des Bois* and *Framboise* are each made in France, Germany and Switzerland.

Strega an aromatic herb liqueur made from a centuries old Italian recipe from the flavours of some seventy herbs and barks.

Tia Maria a Jamaican liqueur rum, based on coffee extracts and local spices.

Triple Sec The name given to a strong white curaçao.

Van Der Hum South Africa's liqueur, tasting of the *naartje*, or tangerine.

(La)Vieille Cure A very potent liqueur with mediaeval origins made in the Gironde from a recipe involving some fifty aromatic plants and roots.

Cocktails, cups and punches

This chapter contains a selection of the many drinks – cocktails, cup, punches both hot and cold, and mulls – which are based on spirits, sherry, port, wine, cider and ale. (The spirits used include whisky, gin, brandy, rum and vodka.) For non-alcoholic punches, cups and so on, see the latter part of the next chapter. Where 'splits' are referred to, these are 240-ml *(8½-fl oz)* bottles.

COCKTAILS

Recipes for a few of the best-known cocktails are given below. In some cases there is more than one accepted recipe and the version you use is a matter of individual taste. If you want to make a cocktail weaker or stronger, increase or decrease the amount of ice you include. Ideally a cocktail should be made in a shaker and transferred to a glass for serving; this ensures that the flavours are well blended. You can of course mix each drink in an individual glass, but do stir them well.

Brandy cocktail

equal measures brandy and French vermouth
crushed ice
lemon rind curls
maraschino cherries

Shake the brandy and vermouth with some crushed ice in a shaker. Pour into glasses and serve each with a curl of lemon rind and a cherry.

Bronx

equal measures dry gin, Italian vermouth and French vermouth
juice of ¼ orange per cocktail
crushed ice

Shake all the ingredients well with the ice in a shaker and strain into glasses.

Champagne cocktail

4 dashes Angostura bitter
1 small sugar lump
juice of ¼ lemon
15 ml *(1 tbsp)* brandy, optional
champagne, chilled in the bottle
lemon slice to decorate

Pour the bitters over the sugar lump and put into a glass. Add the strained lemon juice and brandy if you wish and fill up with champagne. Float a wafer-thin slice of lemon on top.

Manhattan cocktail

broken ice
1–2 dashes Angostura bitters
2–3 dashes curaçao
45 ml *(3 tbsps)* rye whisky
45 ml *(3 tbsps)* Italian vermouth
cherry and lemon peel

Fill a cocktail glass half-full of ice. Mix the liquid ingredients, stir well, strain into the glass, add a cherry and float a piece of lemon peel on top. This is comparatively speaking a very old cocktail, but it is still one of the best-known.

If a dry manhattan is required, use French vermouth instead of Italian. For a medium cocktail use half each of French and Italian.

Daiquiri

juice of ½ lime or ¼ lemon
5 ml *(1 tsp)* sugar
1 measure rum
cracked ice

Mix the fruit juice, sugar and rum and shake well with the cracked ice in a shaker. Dip the edges of the glass in a little more fruit juice and then into caster sugar, to frost the rim, before filling.

Dry martini cocktail

2 parts French vermouth to 1 part dry gin
cracked ice
stuffed olives or lemon rind curls

Shake the vermouth and gin together with some cracked ice in a shaker. Pour into a glass and float a stuffed olive or a curl of lemon rind on top. The proportions of a martini are a matter of personal taste: some people prefer 2 parts of gin to 1 of vermouth, others equal parts of gin and vermouth.

Sweet martini

2 parts Italian vermouth to 1 part dry gin
few drops orange bitters per cocktail (optional)
cracked ice
maraschino cherries

Shake all the ingredients thoroughly together in a shaker and strain into glasses. Serve with a cherry in each glass.

Whisky sour

juice of ½ lemon
5 ml *(1 tsp)* sugar
1 measure whisky
cracked ice

Mix together the lemon juice, sugar and whisky and shake well with the cracked ice. Serve in a whisky tumbler.

Bloody Mary

1 measure vodka
2 measures tomato juice
dash Worcestershire sauce
squeeze of lemon juice
cracked ice

Shake all the ingredients with the cracked ice and serve in a cocktail glass.

Gimlet

3–4 ice cubes
1 part lime juice
3 parts white or golden rum

Put the ice into a jug and pour in the lime juice and rum. Stir well and strain into a chilled martini glass.

Bucks fizz

1 part fresh orange juice
2 parts non-vintage champagne

Chill ingredients and stir well.

Tom Collins

juice of 1 lemon
15 ml *(1 level tbsp)* sugar or sugar syrup
3 measures whisky
soda water

In a shaker, mix 6 ice cubes, lemon juice, sugar and whisky until a frost forms. Pour into a glass and add a slice of orange. Top with soda water and stir.

Pink gin

2–3 drops Angostura bitters
1 measure gin
2–3 measures iced water

Put the bitters into a glass and turn it until the sides are well coated. Add the gin and top up with iced water to taste.

Old fashioned

1 lump of sugar
1–2 dashes Angostura bitters
1–2 ice cubes
1 measure whisky
½ slice orange

Put the sugar cube in a glass and shake the bitters on to it; mix round the glass to dissolve the sugar. Put in the ice, pour over the whisky and float the orange on top.

Negroni

2–3 ice cubes
1 measure Campari
1 measure sweet vermouth
2 measures gin
1 slice of orange
soda water

Put the ice cubes in a tumbler and pour over them the Campari, vermouth and gin. Float the slice of orange on top then top up with soda water to taste.

Screwdriver

1 measure vodka
juice of 1 orange
Angostura bitters (optional)

Put some ice cubes into a tall glass and pour in the vodka and orange juice. Add the bitters and stir lightly.

CUPS AND PUNCHES

When making these drinks, especially the cold cups, it is often convenient to add the sugar in the form of a syrup (see below), which dissolves more readily.

In addition to the wine cups given here, a popular and useful standby is the proprietary long drink sold as Pimms' Cup. This is made with four different bases: No 1 contains gin and bitters; No 2 whisky; No 3 brandy; No 4 rum. The cups are served iced and are often garnished with a sprig of borage or mint.

When serving cups and punches, allow 200 ml *(⅓ pt)* per glass.

Sugar syrup for drinks

450 g *(1 lb)* sugar
300 ml *(½ pt)* water

Put the sugar in a saucepan with the water and dissolve it slowly. Bring to the boil and boil to 105°C *(220°F)*. Cool and bottle. Use as required.

Apple cider cup

2 dessert apples
juice and thinly pared rind of 1 lemon
8 cloves
60 ml *(4 tbsps)* sugar syrup
1 l *(2 pt)* dry cider
½ syphon soda water

Peel, core and slice the apples and put into a bowl with the lemon juice and rind and the cloves. Heat the sugar syrup with about 300 ml *(½ pt)* of the cider; when boiling, pour over the ingredients in the bowl and leave to cool. When cold, add the rest of the cider and the soda water. *Makes about 1.7 l (3 pt).*

Apricot cider cup

820-g *(1-lb 13-oz)* can apricots
1 stick cinnamon, about 5 cm *(2 in)* long
10 g *(½ oz)* sweet almonds, blanched
1 l *(2 pt)* cider
4 'splits' tonic water

Strain the syrup from the apricots, rub the fruit through a sieve and put it into a large jug. Put the cinnamon and almonds with 300 ml *(½ pt)* of the cider in a pan, bring to the boil and leave to stand for about 10 minutes; cool and add to the apricot pulp in the jug. Just before serving add the remaining cider and the tonic water and stir well. *Makes about 1.25 l (2¼ pt).*

Profiteroles (p. 343).

Pineapple cider cup

4.5 l *(1 gal)* cider
1 orange
1 lemon
340-g *(12-oz)* can pineapple pieces, drained
12 maraschino cherries
150 ml *(¼ pt)* sherry
600 ml *(1 pt)* soda water
sprigs of mint

Chill the cider in the bottles. Pare the orange and lemon rind free of all the white pith and put in a bowl with the pineapple pieces, cherries, sherry, orange juice and lemon juice and chill. Just before serving, pour the cider and soda water over this mixture and decorate with sprigs of mint. *Makes about 5.5 l (1¼ gal).*

Brandy cider cup

600 ml *(1 pt)* tea
50 g *(2 oz)* sugar
juice of 2 oranges
90–120 ml *(6–8 tbsps)* brandy
1 l *(2 pt)* cider
1 lemon, thinly sliced

Infuse the tea and strain it on to the sugar in a bowl. Cool and add the orange juice and brandy. Just before serving add the cider and decorate with the lemon slices. *Makes about 2 l (3½ pt).*

Claret cup

150 ml *(¼ pt)* sugar syrup
juice and thinly pared rind of 1 lemon and 2 oranges
2 bottles claret
4 'splits' tonic water
few thin slices of cucumber
sprigs of borage, if available

Put the syrup and the lemon and orange rind in a saucepan and simmer together for about 10 minutes. Cool and add the strained juice of the lemon and oranges, together with the claret; chill. Just before serving, add the tonic water, cucumber and borage (if used). *Makes about 2.3 l (4 pt).*

White wine cup

crushed ice
3 bottles white wine
¾ bottle dry sherry
60 ml *(4 tbsps)* curaçao
4 'splits' tonic water
3 slices of cucumber, a slice of apple and a sprig of borage per jug

Mix all the ingredients together in one or more jugs and chill before serving. *Makes about 3.7 l (6½ pt).*

Honeysuckle cup

1 bottle medium-dry white wine
15 ml *(1 tbsp)* honey, optional
25 ml *(1½ tbsps)* Bénédictine
150 ml *(¼ pt)* brandy
750 ml *(25 fl oz)* fizzy lemonade
2 lemons, sliced
1 peach, sliced
crushed ice

Mix the wine, honey (if used), Bénédictine, brandy and lemonade and pour over the fruit and ice in a bowl. Leave to stand for 1 hour before serving. *Makes about 1.4 l (2½ pt).*

Champagne cup

large piece of ice
25 ml *(1½ tbsps)* apricot brandy
25 ml *(1½ tbsps)* curaçao
50 ml *(2 fl oz)* brandy
1 bottle champagne, chilled
1 'split' soda water
fruit to garnish

Put the ice in a large jug and add the ingredients in the order given. Stir well and decorate with slices of fruit in season. *Makes about 1.4 l (2½ pt).*

Sherry trifle (p. 323).

Midsummer Night's Dream

see colour plate facing p. 497

1 bottle Riesling
1 bottle Beaujolais
750 ml *(25 fl oz)* fizzy lemonade
50 ml *(2 fl oz)* Cointreau
1 dessert apple, cored and sliced
pieces of melon
slices of orange, quartered
a few strawberries
crushed ice
sugar syrup to taste

Pour the wines, lemonade and Cointreau over the fruit and ice in a bowl. Chill and add sugar to taste. Serve ice-cold. *Makes about 2.1 l (3½ pt).*

Chérie

1 bottle rosé wine
crushed ice
1 bottle Sauternes
30 ml *(2 tbsps)* cherry brandy
2 'splits' tonic water
12 fresh or canned cherries, stoned
sugar syrup to taste

Pour the rosé wine over the crushed ice in a bowl. Add the Sauternes and cherry brandy. Before serving, mix in the tonic water and add the fruit, with sugar syrup as required. *Makes about 1.7 l (3 pt).*

Rosy punch

300 ml *(½ pt)* raspberry syrup
2 'splits' tonic water
2 bottles rosé wine, chilled
90–120 ml *(6–8 tbsps)* brandy
1 lemon, thinly sliced
ice cubes

Combine the syrup, tonic water, wine and brandy in a large bowl. Before serving, add the lemon and the ice cubes. *Makes about 2.1 l (3¾ pt).*

Vin blanc cassis – kir

4 parts dry white wine (Chablis or similar)
1 part crème de cassis

Thoroughly chill the wine before combining it with the cassis; serve in a claret glass. This French refresher makes a good mid-morning drink or aperitif.

June cup

1 bottle Beaulolais, chilled
20 ml *(4 tsps)* brandy
a few strawberries, sliced
1 l *(2 pt)* fizzy lemonade, chilled

Pour the Beaujolais and brandy over the strawberries and leave in a cool place for at least ½ hour. Just before serving, add the lemonade. *Makes about 2 l (3½ pt).*

Royal punch

1 l *(2 pt)* China tea
450 g *(1 lb)* sugar
juice of 6 lemons
1 bottle burgundy
1 bottle hock
1 bottle rum
¼ bottle maraschino
1 bottle champagne or other sparkling white wine

Allow the tea to infuse for 10 minutes and strain it over the sugar in a bowl. Add the lemon juice and stir until the sugar has dissolved. Before serving, add the remaining ingredients, all chilled in the bottle. *Makes about 4.5 l (1 gal).*

Hot spiced cider

1 l *(2 pt)* cider
100 g *(4 oz)* sugar
12 whole cloves
4 sticks cinnamon about 5 cm *(2 in)* long
8 whole allspice

Put all the ingredients in a saucepan and heat until the sugar has dissolved. Strain the cider into tumblers. *Makes about 1.2 l (2–2¼ pt).*

Funchal cup (hot)

1 bottle medium Madeira
30 ml *(2 tbsps)* brandy
60 ml *(4 tbsps)* apricot brandy
60 ml *(4 tbsps)* liqueur (eg yellow Chartreuse, Kirsch)
600 ml *(1 pt)* grapefruit juice
2.5 ml *(½ level tsp)* ground cinnamon
300 ml *(½ pt)* water
sugar syrup

Heat the wine, brandies and liqueur together, but do not boil; add the fruit juice and cinnamon and as much water as is needed to bring the cup to the required strength. Adjust the sweetness to taste. *Makes about 1.7 l (3 pt).*

Rum punch

1.7 l *(3 pt)* cold water
450 g *(1 lb)* sugar
1 lemon
4 oranges
300 ml *(½ pt)* strong tea
300–600 ml *(½–1 pt)* rum

Put the water and sugar in a pan with the thinly pared rinds of the lemon and 1 orange. Stir until the sugar is dissolved, bring to the boil and boil for 5 minutes. Remove the pan from the heat and add the juice of the lemon and all the oranges, the tea and the rum. Strain and serve hot or cold. *Makes about 3 l (5–5¼ pt).*

The bishop

2 lemons
12 cloves
1 l *(2 pt)* port
600 ml *(1 pt)* water
5 ml *(1 level tsp)* ground mixed spice
50 g *(2 oz)* lump sugar

Stick 1 lemon with the cloves and roast it in the oven at 180°C *(350°F)* mark 4, for 30 minutes. Put the port into a saucepan and bring to simmering point. In another saucepan boil the water with the spice; add to the hot wine with the roasted lemon. Rub the sugar over the rind of the remaining lemon to remove the zest, put the sugar into a bowl, adding the juice of ½ the lemon, and pour on the hot wine. Serve as hot as possible. *Makes about 2 l (3½ pt).*

Dr Johnson's choice

1 bottle red wine
12 lumps sugar
6 cloves
600 ml *(1 pt)* boiling water
150 ml *(¼ pt)* curaçao
150 ml *(¼ pt)* brandy, optional
nutmeg

This is the classic mull of the eighteenth century.

Pour the wine into a saucepan, add the sugar and cloves and bring to near boiling point; add 600 ml *(1 pt)* boiling water. Pour in the curaçao and the brandy (if used). Pour into glasses and grate nutmeg on top. *Makes about 1.7 l (3 pt).*

Glühwein

600 ml *(1 pt)* red wine
75 g *(3 oz)* brown sugar
2 sticks cinnamon about 5 cm *(2 in)* long
1 lemon stuck with cloves
150 ml *(¼ pt)* brandy

Put all the ingredients except the brandy in a pan, bring to simmering point and simmer gently with the lid on for 2–4 minutes. Remove from the heat, add the brandy, strain and serve at once. *Makes about 700 ml (1¼ pt).*

Julglögg (Christmas wine)

1 bottle aquavit or gin
2 bottles burgundy
75 g *(3 oz)* raisins, stoned
100 g *(4 oz)* sugar
15 ml *(1 level tbsp)* cardamom seeds, optional
6 whole cloves
5-cm *(2-in)* stick of cinnamon
small piece of lemon rind

Pour half the aquavit or gin into a saucepan with the burgundy; add the raisins and sugar. Tie the spices and lemon rind in muslin and add to the pan, cover, bring very slowly to the boil and simmer for ½ hour. Add the remaining aquavit or gin and remove from the heat. Take out the muslin bag of spices and just before serving ignite the mixture with a match. Serve in tumblers or punch glasses. *Makes about 2.4 l (4¼ pt).*

New Year party egg nog

300 ml *(½ pt)* milk
3 eggs, separated
75 g *(3 oz)* caster sugar
90–120 ml *(6–8 tbsps)* brandy
90–120 ml *(6–8 tbsps)* rum
150 ml *(¼ pt)* single cream

Heat the milk without boiling. Whisk the egg yolks and sugar together for a few moments, then add the brandy and rum slowly. Fold in the cream and pour on the heated milk. Whisk the egg whites stiffly and fold into the nog. *Makes 8 servings.*

Hot rumour

1 orange
12 cloves
1 bottle red wine
45 ml *(3 tbsps)* demerara rum
30 ml *(2 level tbsps)* demerara sugar

Stick the orange with the cloves and roast it in the oven at 180°C *(350°F)* mark 4 for 30 minutes. Heat the wine to just below boiling point and add the rum and sugar. Float the orange on the top and simmer for a further few minutes. Remove the orange and serve in punch glasses. *Makes about 900 ml (1½ pt).*

Mulled ale
(Traditional eighteenth-century version)

1 l *(2 pt)* ale
grated rind of ½ lemon
5 ml *(1 level tsp)* ground ginger
5 ml *(1 level tsp)* ground nutmeg
75 g *(3 oz)* soft brown sugar
3 eggs
100 ml *(4 fl oz)* brandy
100 ml *(4 fl oz)* rum

Heat the ale, lemon rind and spices to boiling point. Meanwhile make a poker red-hot; plunge it into the ale and hold it there until the seething subsides. Whip the sugar and eggs till they are frothy. Warm the brandy and rum together in another small pan, pour into the ale mixture and combine with the egg mixture. Pour the whole back and forth from one pan to the other until smooth and creamy. Serve at once. *Makes about 1.7 l (3 pt).*

Mulled ale
(Modern version)

1 lemon
600 ml *(1 pt)* ale
60 ml *(4 tbsps)* brandy
30 ml *(2 tbsps)* rum
30 ml *(2 tbsps)* gin
30 ml *(2 level tbsps)* demerara sugar
300 ml *(½ pt)* water
large pinch ground nutmeg
large pinch ground cinnamon

Pare the lemon thinly and squeeze out the juice. Place the rind, juice and all the other ingredients in a large pan and heat, but do not boil. Strain and serve at once in punch glasses. *Makes about 1 l (2 pt).*

Mulled wine

300 ml *(½ pt)* water
100 g *(4 oz)* sugar
4 cloves
5-cm *(2-in)* stick of cinnamon
2 lemons, thinly sliced
1 bottle burgundy or claret
1 orange or lemon, thinly sliced

Boil the water, sugar and spices together. Add the lemons, stir and leave to stand for 10 minutes. Pour back into the saucepan and add the red wine. Heat but do not boil. Strain the wine into a bowl and serve hot, decorated with the orange or lemon slices. *Makes about 900 ml (1½ pt).*

Mulled claret

1 l *(2 pt)* claret
rind of 1 orange and 1 lemon
12–16 lumps sugar
5 ml *(1 level tsp)* ground cinnamon and ground nutmeg, mixed
2 bayleaves
300 ml *(½ pt)* brandy

Heat the claret with the orange and lemon rind, sugar, spices and bayleaves. Heat the brandy in a separate pan but do not boil. Take both liquids to the guests, pour the wine mixture into a heat-resistant bowl, add the hot brandy, set the mull alight and ladle it into glasses, moving steadily to keep the flames burning. (Incidently, this looks much more effective if the lights are turned out.) *Makes about 1.4 l (2½ pt).*

Tea, coffee and other drinks

We deal here with the two most important 'everyday' drinks and also with milky drinks (both hot and cold), soft drinks and a variety of non-alcoholic party cups and punches.

TEA

Most tea drunk in Britain is of the so-called 'black' type, the leaves being fermented before they are dried, which gives a darkish brown brew. 'Green' or unfermented teas are mainly produced in China and mostly used in a blend.

Indian and Ceylon tea Black tea from India and Ceylon comprises about four-fifths of the total used in this country. Almost all of it is blended here and sold in branded packs. The teas are usually blended to suit the average taste and average water supply, but some firms specialise in making up teas to suit the water of a particular district. It is also possible to buy 'pure' teas from Ceylon, Assam and Darjeeling.

China tea A China tea can be 'pure' (eg Keemun or Lapsang Soochong) but is more usually blended. It is generally made in a weaker brew than Indian or Ceylon tea and is more delicately flavoured. China tea is served with lemon slices, not with milk.

Flower teas Some varieties of tea are mixed with flowers or leaves such as Jasmine, Hibiscus, Camomile, Gardenia, Orange Blossom, Linden, Fennel or Rosehip, to give a delicate and unusual bouquet and flavour. These blends are usually served without milk, in a glass, as a refreshing drink.

Tea-making

Buy tea in small quantities and keep it in an air-tight tin or jar so that the aroma and strength are conserved. The usual amount to allow is 5 ml *(1 level tsp)* per person; when making tea for more than three people, it is usual to allow 5 ml *(1 level tsp)* per person and 5 ml *(1 level tsp)* 'for the pot'. Use freshly boiled water.

Warm the pot, put in the measured quantity of tea, pour on the boiling water and leave to infuse before pouring out. The time required depends on the type of tea used; Indian teas usually require 4–5 minutes, but China teas infuse more quickly and can be poured out 2–3 minutes after being made. In this country tea is generally taken with milk, with or without sugar according to taste, but some people prefer sliced lemon to milk.

Russian tea *see colour plate facing p. 497*

Make a strong infusion of China tea, adding 5 ml *(1 extra tsp)* tea to the given proportions. Half-fill some glasses with tea and fill to the top with hot water. Add slices of lemon and sugar to taste.

This is the traditional way of making Russian tea, but some people just make a weak brew of tea and add the lemon and sugar.

Rum can be used as a flavouring instead of the lemon, if you prefer. In Russia and the Balkan countries, jam is often served with tea.

Iced tea

Make China tea in the usual way and strain it over the back of a spoon into some glasses which have been half-filled with crushed ice. Add sugar to taste and a slice of lemon to each glass. Re-chill before serving.

As a variation, add a sprig of mint before serving.

Hot spiced tea

2.3 l *(4 pt)* water
6 whole cloves
2.5-cm *(1-in)* stick of cinnamon
25 g *(1 oz)* tea
100 g *(4 oz)* sugar
150 ml *(¼ pt)* orange juice or squash
juice of 2 lemons
cinnamon sticks

Add the spices to the water and bring to the boil. Pour on to the tea in a bowl and allow to infuse for 5 minutes. Stir, add the sugar, stir again until dissolved and add the strained fruit juices. If necessary, re-heat before serving, by placing it over a low heat – do not simmer or boil. Strain and serve with the cinnamon sticks. *Makes 10–12 servings.*

Fresh fruit and mint tea punch

600 ml *(1 pt)* boiling water
25 ml *(1½ level tbsps)* tea
175 g *(6 oz)* sugar
150 ml *(¼ pt)* lemon squash
300 ml *(½ pt)* orange squash
ice cubes
½ lemon, sliced
½ orange, sliced
50 g *(2 oz)* strawberries, sliced
mint leaves

Pour the water on to the tea and allow to infuse for 3–5 minutes. Stir, strain into a bowl containing the sugar and stir until this is dissolved. Add the lemon and orange squashes. To serve, pour over the ice cubes in a punch bowl and add the sliced fruit and the mint leaves. *Makes about 1.1 l (2 pt).*

COFFEE

The subtle variations of flavour of individual coffees are endless. It is worth trying them separately and in a blend until you find one you like best. Among the many types of coffee available are:

Brazilian The flavour is very smooth and mild and has no bitterness or acidity.

Chagga Chagga coffee is produced by the Wa-Chagga tribe living on the slopes of Mount Kilimanjaro in Tanzania. The beans are picked and washed in the mountain streams from the Kibo Glacier and then dried in the mountain air. This is a full bodied coffee and usually medium to dark roast.

Colombian Colombian coffee is produced in South America and has a full strong flavour with very little acidity.

Continental blend A blend of dark roasted coffees with a strong flavour. Usually drunk at breakfast.

Java A mature coffee from the East Indies with a subtle, mellow flavour. Is most suitable for drinking 'black' as an after-dinner coffee.

Kenya A very aromatic coffee with a pleasant sharpness. At its best when served 'black' as an after-dinner coffee.

Mocha Mocha is the traditional Turkish coffee. The flavour, traditionally described as gamey, is strong and subtle.

Mysore This coffee is a rich full flavoured coffee from Southern India.

Vienna This coffee is often sold already blended to give a smooth, subtly strong flavour.

Grinding coffee

You can buy roasted beans and grind them at home, or you can ask your supplier to grind them for you to fine, medium or coarse (if he provides this service); alternatively, you can buy ready-ground coffee in a vacuum-sealed pack. It is essential to choose the correct grind for your particular method of making coffee (see below). The pre-packed coffees are generally medium-roasted and medium-ground and are therefore suitable for most methods of coffee-making.

Making coffee

Whichever method you prefer, make sure that you use enough coffee.

Saucepan method Allow 40–50 g *(1½–2 oz)* medium or coarsely ground coffee per 500 ml *(1 pt)* water.

Put the coffee and water in a saucepan and heat gently until almost boiling. Stir and allow to infuse over a low heat for about 5 minutes, but do not allow the coffee to boil or the flavour will be spoiled. Strain into a warmed jug. This method is particularly useful when you wish to make large quantities of coffee.

Jug method Measure out 40–50 g *(1½–2 oz)* medium-ground coffee per 500 ml *(1 pt)* water and warm a jug of known capacity. Put the coffee in the jug and pour in boiling water, stir, cover and allow to infuse for 4–5 minutes; strain the coffee into another warmed jug or straight into the cups.

Some people say that the grounds settle better if a metal spoon is drawn across the top of the coffee just before it is poured out.

Cona or syphon method For this a special Cona or similar syphon type of coffee-maker is needed. Allow 40–50 g *(1½–2 oz)* medium-ground coffee per 500 ml *(1 pt)* water.

Put the water in the lower container and heat it. Place the filter in the neck of the upper container and put in the measured coffee. When the water in the lower container boils, fit the upper container into position: the water will then rise into it. Allow to infuse for 2–3 minutes and draw the coffee-maker off the heat; the coffee will then return to the lower container.

If you like strong coffee, allow it to infuse longer.

Filter method You need a special type of coffee pot which incorporates a metal, china or paper filter. Allow 90 ml *(6 level tbsps)* medium-ground coffee per 600 ml *(1 pt)* water for the types with a metal or china filter, 70 ml *(4½ level tbsps)* finely ground coffee for the model with a paper filter.

Warm the coffee pot and place the filter attachment containing the coffee in position. Pour boiling water through the filter; when you have made sufficient coffee, remove the filter attachment, replace the lid and serve the coffee.

Electric filter coffee makers work on the same principle. The coffee maker usually consists of a main L-shaped body which incorporates the water container, the water boiler and often a hotplate to keep the coffee hot. The coffee is spooned into a filter funnel over the jug, and the water container can be filled with the exact amount needed. The water is heated, pours through the coffee in the filter, and drips into the jug below. A thermostat cuts in to switch off the boiler.

Percolator method Coffee percolators which are heated on top of the stove and also independent electrically heated models are available. Allow 40–50 g *(1½–2 oz)* medium or coarsely ground coffee per 500 ml *(1 pt)* water.

Pour the water into the percolator, put the coffee in the metal basket and put into position. When the water boils it is forced up the centre tube and filters over and down through the coffee grounds. The water should be allowed to percolate through the coffee for 8–10 minutes.

Some electric percolators have a time control which you set to the length of time you require; the coffee will automatically percolate for this period and after that a thermostat will keep the coffee just below boiling point until you need it.

Espresso method Espresso coffee-making machines, which tend to be expensive, make a strong brew. Allow 70 ml *(4½ level tbsps)* finely ground coffee per 500 ml *(1 pt)* water.

The water is placed in the machine and the coffee grounds in the special container. When the water is heated, steam is forced under pressure through the coffee grounds and into the separate jug, where it condenses back to liquid.

Instant coffee Powdered or granulated coffee or liquid essence make a quick drink. Put 5 ml *(1 tsp)* of the instant coffee in each cup and add boiling water, a mixture of heated water and milk or just hot milk. Stir and serve, adding sugar if desired. Liquid coffee essence has added sweetening.

White coffee

The kind most often served at breakfast and mid-morning. Allow 1 part milk to 2 parts coffee. Heat the milk until it is hot but not boiling.

Black coffee

Served in small cups after lunch or dinner. It is made quite strong, 50 g *(2 oz)* coffee being allowed per 500 ml *(1 pt)* water.

Iced coffee

Make some strong black coffee, using 50 g *(2 oz)* ground coffee to 900 ml *(1½ pt)* water. While it is still hot, sweeten to taste. Cool and chill. Pour into glasses, add a cube of ice and top with whipped cream.

Borgia coffee

Combine equal parts of hot Espresso coffee and hot chocolate, top with whipped cream and sprinkle with grated orange rind.

Capuccino coffee

Combine equal quantities of strong coffee and hot milk, pour into mugs and flavour with a pinch of ground cinnamon and nutmeg.

Turkish coffee

The correct utensil to use is a copper coffee pot with a long handle and no lid, but you can of course use a small saucepan.

Allow 15–20 ml *(3–4 level tsps)* finely ground Turkish coffee, 5 ml *(1 level tsp)* sugar, and 150 ml *(¼ pt)* water per person.

Put all the ingredients in the coffee pot or saucepan and heat, stirring, until the mixture boils and looks frothy. Remove from the heat and when the froth subsides, replace on a brisk heat. Bring to the boil 3 times in all. Remove from the heat, add a few drops of rose-water to perfume the coffee and strain it into a warm jug or small cups.

Turkish coffee is drunk black.

Viennese coffee

Use a Vienna blend of coffee. Add warm (not hot) milk to the coffee and just before serving it, float 10 ml *(1 dessertspoonful)* whipped cream on top of each glass.

Creamery coffee

Make 150 ml *(¼ pt)* evaporated milk up to 300 ml *(½ pt)* by adding ice cubes. Stir in 20 ml *(4 level tsps)* instant coffee and 15 ml *(1 level tbsp)* caster sugar. Blend together in an electric blender until the ice is broken. Pour into glasses and top with 15 ml *(1 tbsp)* vanilla ice cream per glass. Sprinkle a little instant coffee powder on top and serve at once. *Makes about 3 servings.*

Coffee with liqueurs

Most liqueurs can be taken with coffee and some can actually be added to it – see below. Coffee used in this way should be made double-strength – that is, with 100 g *(4 oz)* instead of 50 g *(2 oz)* ground coffee per 600 ml *(1 pt)* water.

If cream is poured on top, allow the coffee to stand for a few minutes before drinking it, so that the aroma penetrates the cream. Do not stir the cream and coffee together, but drink the coffee through the layer of cream.

Irish or Gaelic coffee *see colour plate facing p. 497*

You will need 1 part Irish whiskey to 3–4 parts double-strength coffee. Warm some goblets, put 1 measure of the whiskey in each glass and add 5 ml *(1 level tsp)* brown sugar. Pour in black coffee to within 2.5 cm *(1 in)* of the brim and stir to dissolve the sugar. Fill to the brim with chilled double cream, poured over the back of a spoon, and allow to stand for a few minutes.

Liqueur coffee round the world

All the following are made as for Irish coffee. Allow 1 measure of the liqueur or spirit to about 4 measures of double-strength black coffee, with sugar to taste – usually about 5 ml *(1 level tsp)* – and some thick double cream to pour on top; these quantities will make 1 glassful.

Cointreau coffee (made with Cointreau)
Caribbean coffee (made with rum)
German coffee (made with Kirsch)
Normandy coffee (made with calvados)
Russian coffee (made with vodka)
Calypso coffee (made with Tia Maria)
Witch's coffee (made with Strega; sprinkle a little grated lemon rind on top)
Curaçao coffee (made with curaçao; stir with a stick of cinnamon)

Coffee à la brûlot

1 orange
2 sticks cinnamon about 5 cm *(2 in)* long
4 whole cloves
3 lumps sugar
150 ml *(¼ pt)* Cognac
500 ml *(1 pt)* double-strength black coffee

Pare off the coloured part of the orange skin in one long, thin ribbon. Place the rind, cinnamon, cloves and sugar in a pan, pour in the Cognac, warm and ignite it. While the brandy is still flaming, add the coffee; as the flame subsides, ladle the coffee into coffee cups. *Makes 6 servings.*

MILK AND EGG DRINKS

We give here recipes for some favourite cold and hot milk drinks and typical flips and nogs. There are also various proprietary preparations, including cocoa, different kinds of drinking chocolate, Ovaltine, Bournvita, Horlicks and so on; directions for making these are given on the containers.

Milk shakes

Mix the milk with strong coffee, chocolate powder, fruit juice or syrup, or use a special milk shake flavouring; blend until frothy either with a rotary whisk or in an electric blender.

For an ice-cold milk shake, add 15–30 ml *(1–2 tbsps)* ice cream to each glass before serving.

Iced banana shake

300 ml *(1 cup)* milk
1 banana, peeled and mashed
30 ml *(2 tbsps)* ice cream

Whisk all the ingredients together with a rotary whisk until frothy, or blend at maximum speed for 1 minute in an electric blender. Pour into a large glass. The banana may be replaced by 30 ml *(2 tbsps)* raspberries or strawberries, mashed to a purée.

Coffee milk shake

150 ml *(½ cup)* milk
150 ml *(½ cup)* black coffee
30 ml *(2 tbsps)* ice cream

Make as above.

Fruit flip

1 egg
10 ml *(2 level tsps)* caster sugar
juice of 1 orange
juice of 1 lemon

Whisk the egg and sugar together for a few moments. Add the strained orange and lemon juice, strain and serve chilled. *Serves 2.*

Port wine flip

1 egg
5 ml *(1 level tsp)* icing sugar
150 ml *(¼ pt)* port
lump of ice
ground nutmeg

Put the egg, sugar, port and ice into a cocktail shaker or electric blender and shake or blend well. Strain into a glass and sprinkle with a little nutmeg before serving. *Serves 1.*

Egg nog *see colour plate facing p. 497*

1 egg
15 ml *(1 level tbsp)* sugar
50 ml *(2 fl oz)* sherry or brandy
300 ml *(1 cup)* milk

Whisk the egg and sugar together and add the sherry or brandy. Heat the milk without boiling and pour it over the egg mixture; stir well and serve hot in a glass. *Serves 1.*

SOFT DRINKS

Quick lemon squash

juice of ½ lemon
sugar to taste
soda water

Put the lemon juice and sugar into a glass and fill to the top with soda water. *Serves 1.*

'Still' lemonade

3 lemons
175 g *(6 oz)* sugar
900 ml *(1½ pt)* boiling water

Wash the lemons and peel off the rind thinly with a potato peeler. Put the rind and sugar into a basin or large jug and pour on the boiling water. Cover and leave to cool, stirring occasionally. Add the juice of the lemons and strain the lemonade. Serve chilled. *Makes about 1.1 l (2 pt).*

Bitter lemon

3 lemons with peel removed (or 2 whole lemons)
600 ml *(1 pt)* water
100 g *(4 oz)* sugar

Wash the lemons, cut them into pieces, put in a saucepan with the water and bring to the boil. Reduce the heat and simmer gently for 10–15 minutes, until the fruit is soft. Add the sugar and stir to dissolve it. Remove from the heat, cover and cool; strain before using.

This drink is delicious with soda water and/or gin. *Makes about 900 ml (1½ pt).*

Lemon syrup

rind of 2 lemons
700 g *(1½ lb)* sugar
400 ml *(¾ pt)* water
300 ml *(½ pt)* lemon juice

Wash the lemons and grate or pare off the coloured part of the rind very thinly free of all the white pith. Put the lemon rind, sugar and water into a pan and heat slowly until the sugar is dissolved; strain into a basin or jug, add the lemon juice and stir well. Pour into bottles and lightly screw on caps with an acid-resistant lining.

Place the bottles in a deep pan padded with newspaper and fill with water to the base of the caps. Heat the water slowly to simmering point – 75°C *(170°F)* – and maintain this temperature for 20 minutes. Remove the bottles and screw the caps down tightly.

The syrup may be used diluted with water or soda water – allow 1 part syrup to 2–3 parts water, according to taste.

Do not keep home-made syrups from citrus fruits longer than 1–2 months, as the colour and flavour deteriorate.

Orangeade

2 oranges
1 lemon
50 g *(2 oz)* sugar
600 ml *(1 pt)* boiling water

Wash the fruit and thinly pare off the coloured parts of the rinds, free of all the white pith. Put the rinds and sugar into a bowl and pour the boiling water over. Leave to cool, stirring occasionally; add the strained juice of the oranges and lemon. *Makes about 900 ml (1½ pt).*

Orange and grapefruit squash

900 g *(2 lb)* granulated sugar
900 ml *(1½ pt)* water
20 ml *(4 level tsps)* tartaric acid
finely grated rind and juice of 2 large oranges
finely grated rind and juice of 1 grapefruit

Put the sugar and water into a pan and stir over a gentle heat until the sugar has dissolved. Bring this sugar syrup to the boil and simmer for 10 minutes. Put the tartaric acid and the orange and grapefruit rinds in a large bowl or jug, pour on the syrup and leave to stand overnight. Add the fruit juice, strain and bottle. Serve diluted with water or soda water. *Makes about 1.3 l (2¼ pt).*

Lemon barley water

50 g *(2 oz)* pearl barley
water
50 g *(2 oz)* sugar
juice of 2 lemons

Put the barley into a saucepan, just cover with cold water and bring to the boil; strain off the water and rinse the barley under cold running water. Return it to the saucepan, add 600 ml *(1 pt)* water, bring to the boil again, cover and simmer for 1 hour. Strain the liquid into a jug or basin, add the sugar and cool. When the mixture is cold, add the strained lemon juice. Use as required; it will keep indefinitely in the refrigerator.

Note A quicker way of making barley water is to use 'patent' barley.

Grapefruit barley water

Make this as for lemon barley water, above, but substitute the strained juice of 1 large grapefruit for the lemon juice. Sweeten to taste.

Ice cream soda

1 glass soda water per person
15 ml *(1 tbsp)* ice cream per person

Whisk the soda water and ice cream together with a rotary whisk until frothy or blend them at maximum speed for 1 minute in an electric blender. Pour into a large glass and serve at once.

Grapefruit or lime soda

1 cube of ice, crushed
½ glass soda water
30 ml *(2 tbsps)* grapefruit juice or 15 ml *(1 tbsp)* lime juice
15 ml *(1 tbsp)* ice cream

Whisk all the ingredients together with a rotary whisk until frothy, or blend at maximum speed for 1 minute in an electric blender. Pour into a large glass.

Ginger soda

¾ glass ginger beer
¼ glass lemonade
15 ml *(1 tbsp)* ice cream

Make as above.

Home-made ginger beer

To start the ginger beer 'plant'
50 g *(2 oz)* fresh baker's yeast
30 ml *(2 level tbsps)* caster sugar
30 ml *(2 level tbsps)* ground ginger
300 ml *(½ pt)* water

Blend the yeast and sugar until they cream and form a liquid. Add the ground ginger and the water, stir well and place the mixture in a covered jar with a loose-fitting lid.

Each day
Add 5 ml *(1 level tsp)* ground ginger and 5 ml *(1 level tsp)* caster sugar to the 'plant' and stir well.

After 10 days
Dissolve 500 g *(18 oz)* caster sugar in 900 ml *(1½ pt)* water, bring to the boil and cool slightly. Add the strained juice of 2 lemons.

Strain the prepared ginger beer plant through fine muslin and add the strained liquid to the sugar and lemon juice, together with 3.4 l *(6 pt)* water.

Stir well and bottle at once in strong, screw-topped bottles (as used for cider or beer). Store in a cool place (this is essential) and use as required.

To make more ginger beer
Halve the 'plant' (the sediment left on the muslin) and place in 2 separate jars. Add 300 ml *(½ pt)* water, 10 ml *(2 level tsps)* ground ginger and 10 ml *(2 level tsps)* caster sugar to each jar; stir and continue to feed daily as above for 10 days; proceed as before.

NON-ALCOHOLIC CUPS AND PUNCHES

Spicy fruit punch

600 ml *(1 pt)* orange juice
300 ml *(½ pt)* canned pineapple juice
juice and rind of 1 lemon
2.5 ml *(½ level tsp)* ground nutmeg
2.5 ml *(½ level tsp)* ground mixed spice
6 cloves
600 ml *(1 pt)* water
175 g *(6 oz)* sugar
1 l *(2 pt)* ginger ale (chilled in the bottle)
crushed ice

Mix the fruit juices, lemon rind and spices in a large jug. Put the water and sugar into a saucepan and heat gently to dissolve the sugar; cool slightly and add to the other ingredients in the jug. Chill. Strain the liquid and add the ginger ale and some crushed ice before serving. *Makes about 2.8 l (5 pt).*

Citrus punch

juice of 2 grapefruit
juice of 2 lemons
juice of 5 oranges
150 ml *(¼ pt)* canned pineapple juice
150 ml *(¼ pt)* sugar syrup (see page 512)
4 'splits' tonic water (chilled in the bottle)
1 lemon, thinly sliced

Mix the strained fruit juices in a bowl and chill. Just before serving, add the syrup and tonic water and decorate with lemon slices. *Makes approx 1.6 l (2¾ pt).*

Pineapple crush

539-ml *(19-fl oz)* can pineapple juice
juice of 1 orange
juice of 1 lemon
sugar
1 l *(2 pt)* ginger ale (chilled in the bottle)

Combine the fruit juices, sweeten to taste and chill. Just before serving, add the ginger ale. *Makes approx 1.7 l (3 pt).*

Spiced cooler

600 ml *(1 pt)* orange juice
rind of juice of 1 lemon
300 ml *(½ pt)* canned pineapple juice
600 ml *(1 pt)* water
60 ml *(4 tbsps)* sugar syrup (see page 512)
8 cloves
2.5 ml *(½ level tsp)* ground cinnamon
2.5 ml *(½ level tsp)* ground mixed spice
3 'splits' ginger ale (chilled in the bottle)
orange slices, optional

Warm all the ingredients except the ginger ale in a saucepan. Remove from the heat, pour into a jug or bowl and cool. Strain, add the ginger ale and serve decorated with some orange slices, if you wish. *Makes about 1.8 l (3¼ pt).*

Pine-lime sparkle

539-ml *(19-fl oz)* can pineapple juice
45 ml *(3 tbsps)* fresh lemon juice
150 ml *(¼ pt)* lime juice cordial
50 g *(2 oz)* icing sugar
2 'splits' bitter lemon (chilled in the bottle)
pineapple cubes (optional)

Put the pineapple and lemon juices and the lime cordial in a bowl and stir in the icing sugar. Chill. Just before serving add the bitter lemon and some pineapple cubes, if available. *Makes about 1 l (1¾ pt).*

Barbary ale

juice of 8 oranges
rind and juice of 2 lemons
600 ml *(1 pt)* water
175 g *(6 oz)* sugar
5 ml *(1 level tsp)* ground cinnamon
7.5 ml *(1½ level tsps)* ground mixed spice
4.3 l *(7½ pt)* ginger beer

Put all the ingredients except the ginger beer into a bowl and leave for 3 hours. Strain the mixture into a bowl or jug and add the ginger beer just before serving. *Makes about 4.5 l (1 gal).*

Nutrition and special diets

It helps when planning a family diet to know something about what is needed in the way of food nutrients and which foodstuffs contain them. Here are a few brief notes.

Proteins
Proteins are required for growth, the formation of new tissues and the repair and maintenance of the old tissues. They also supply heat and energy.

Sources
Meat, fish, poultry, milk, cheese, eggs, pulses, bread, cereals and nuts.

Fats and oils
These form a fundamental part of all cell structures, provide a concentrated form of energy, and act as carriers for vitamins A, D, E and K.

Sources
Butter, margarine, lard, dripping, vegetable fats and oils, fish oils, meats (especially pork and bacon), cream, cream cheese, eggs.

Carbohydrates
These provide heat and energy for muscular contraction.

Sources
Sugars and starches. Since 50–60% of the total calorie intake is supplied by carbohydrates, we should take care to ensure that the carbohydrate foods taken also contribute other nutrients, eg wholemeal flours and breads, whole-grain cereals, pulses, nuts, potatoes.

Use the following with discretion: white flours, polished rice, puffed or flaked cereals, sugar, jams, biscuits, cakes and pastries.

Minerals
These are necessary for the formation of body structure and for normal body functions. They are widely distributed in foods.

Sources
Calcium Milk, cheese, eggs, green and root vegetables, fortified white flour and bread.

Phosphorus Fish, cheese, milk, eggs, meat, green vegetables, cereals.

Iron Liver, kidney, eggs, whole-grain cereals, heart, meat, fish, pulses, green vegetables and potatoes.

Sodium Salt.

Vitamins
Vitamins are substances required in small amounts in our food to promote the normal health of the body. They can normally be obtained in a good diet of natural foods.

Vitamin A keeps the mucous membranes healthy, also the skin, glands and bones, and is necessary for normal growth and development and for properly functioning eyesight.

Sources
Liver, butter, margarine, eggs, milk, cheese; carrots, spinach and other green vegetables, tomatoes, water-cress, dried apricots and prunes; cod liver oil and halibut liver oil.

Vitamin B (that is the vitamin B complex, including vitamins B_1 B_2, etc.) is necessary for the good condition of the nervous system, for normal appetite and digestion and for other processes.

Sources
Yeast and yeast extracts, whole-grain cereals, wheat-grain cereals and wheat-grain preparations; liver and other offal, lean meat, pork (including ham and bacon), fish, egg yolk, milk, cheese; vegetables, nuts and fruit.

All flour must now by law contain certain quantities of vitamin B_1 and niocin (another constituent of the vitamin B complex).

Vitamin C increases resistance to infection and maintains a healthy condition of the skin (in a deficiency of this vitamin, wounds are slow to heal); it improves the circulation and the condition of the gums and other body tissues. It is found in fresh vegetables and fruits, but the distribution is uneven.

Good sources
Rose-hip berries (as syrup), black-currants, Chinese

gooseberries, citrus fruits and juices. Fresh vegetables are a valuable source, provided correct cooking methods are followed.

Vitamin D ensures the proper utilisation of calcium and phosphorus, directly influencing the structure of bones and teeth.

Sources
Fish liver oils, oily fish, egg yolk, butter, vitamin-enriched margarine. This vitamin can also be manufactured in the body by the action of sunlight and ultraviolet light on the skin surface.

Water
This is an essential constituent of all cells.

Daily diet

All that is required to eat well and wisely is to eat some foods from all of the above groups each day. Energy producing carbohydrates appear at breakfast in the form of cereals, marmalade, bread and sugar; the need for protein is met by bacon, eggs, bread and milk, and for fat by bacon, milk, butter or margarine. At lunch and dinner such foods as meat, fish, poultry, and cheese offer a wide choice of body-building protein; the fruits and vegetables that traditionally go with good eating provide most of the vitamins we need.

The aim of eating well should be to enjoy yourself while having just enough but not one scrap more. You can widen your family's experience by giving them unusual foods occasionally and by serving ordinary foods as attractively as possible. Contrast is important, in colour, in texture and in flavour – as when you serve red tomatoes with white fish, crisp green vegetables with soft mince, fruit after a steak and kidney pudding.

During the day include at least one helping from each of the following groups:
Meat, poultry, fish.
Milk, cheese, eggs.
Fruit and vegetables (at least 2 helpings).
Bread and other cereals.
Butter and margarine.

The menu pattern into which you have to fit the particular dishes is something like this (though there are no hard-and-fast rules about how many meals you should have and when, so arrange them to suit yourself):

Breakfast	Cereal or porridge and fruit juice and/or eggs and bacon or other cooked dish Toast, butter and marmalade, jam or honey
Lunch or Dinner	Meat, poultry or fish Potatoes, green vegetable Dessert
Supper	Savoury dish or salad Bread and butter and cheese Fruit

Breakfast
Give your family a good start to the day – everyone works better after a proper breakfast rather than just a cup of tea or coffee. It need not take long to prepare – fruit, cereal and milk or muesli, toast and marmalade are easy enough.

The true British breakfast always has a cooked dish of some kind. The most popular are eggs and bacon. The eggs may be boiled, poached, baked, fried or scrambled or 'framed' in fried bread (see page 256). Bacon, sausages and kidneys are usually fried or grilled and are often accompanied by tomatoes and mushrooms. Fried bread is another favourite feature – heat some fat in a frying pan and fry bread slices until crisp on both sides.

Fish dishes are almost equally popular, the most usual kinds being kippers, smoked haddock or golden cutlets. Freshly made toast should be served, with butter or marmalade. The usual drinks are tea or coffee.

The Continental breakfast is becoming increasingly popular here and takes the form of coffee, hot rolls, fruit and jam or marmalade. To ensure that the rolls are really fresh and crisp, heat them in the oven for about 10 minutes. Croissants are a pleasant alternative to ordinary bread rolls.

Almost any fresh or stewed fruits are suitable for breakfast, either alone or mixed with breakfast cereals or muesli. Fresh fruit should be prepared just before it is eaten. Fruit juices, fresh, canned and frozen, are popular. They are best if chilled overnight.

Grapefruit served plain Cut the fruit in half, free the flesh from all pith and membranes and remove the centre core and the pips, using a small grapefruit knife. Sprinkle with sugar if you wish.

Grilled grapefruit Halve the grapefruit, remove the pips and cover the flesh with brown sugar. Put under the grill until the sugar has melted.

Oranges Peel the oranges, removing as much as possible of the white pith, then slice fairly thinly across the segments. Flick out any pips with the point of a knife. Sprinkle with sugar if the oranges are sharp.

Dried fruit Apricots, prunes and figs should be washed, then soaked for some hours (or overnight) in fresh water. Cook them in this water, adding 100–175 g *(4–6 oz)* sugar and a piece of lemon rind per 500 ml *(1 pt)*. Stew gently till soft and serve cold.

Lunch or dinner
It is purely a matter of choice and convenience whether you have the main meal in the middle of the day or in the

evening. The traditional meat and two vegetables followed by pudding is quite satisfactory.

Supper

If you have a main meal in the middle of the day all you need for supper is a salad with meat, cheese or fish or a savoury dish like macaroni cheese or kedgeree (see pages 556 to 558 for other ideas) with bread and butter followed by fresh fruit, yoghurt or biscuits and cheese. This is the kind of meal you would choose to have at mid-day if you have a main meal in the evening.

Tea

Afternoon tea, consisting of a variety of thinly cut savoury sandwiches, cake and biscuits, is more of a social occasion than anything else. A more substantial tea with scones, crumpets, bread and butter, honey and jam and a variety of cakes is still a popular meal where there are children coming home hungry from school and in families where a light late supper of soup, a hot milky drink or bread and cheese is preferred.

High tea, when a cooked dish like scrambled eggs or fish cakes is served followed by bread and butter and cakes, is also popular with some families especially those with school children.

A guide to calorie requirements

The following tables show the calorie requirements for a normal diet – these vary according to age and activity – and the number of calories in the most common foods and drinks.

Use them to help plan your meals while following the guide lines for a balanced diet.

Age range	*Occupational category*	*Calories*	*Joules*
Men			
18 up to 35 years	Sedentary	2700	11297
	Moderately active	3000	12552
	Very active	3600	15062
35 up to 65 years	Sedentary	2600	10878
	Moderately active	2900	12134
	Very active	3600	15062
65 up to 75 years	Sedentary	2350	9832
75 and over	Sedentary	2100	8786
Women			
18 up to 55 years	Most occupations	2200	9205
	Very active	2500	10460
55 up to 75 years	Sedentary	2050	8577
75 and over	Sedentary	1900	7950
Pregnancy, 3–9 months		2400	10042
Breast feeding		2700	11297

Age range	*Calories*	*Joules*	*Age range*	*Calories*	*Joules*
Schoolboys			**Boys and girls**		
9 up to 12 years	2500	10460	0 up to 1 year	800	3347
12 up to 15 years	2800	11715	1 up to 2 years	1200	5021
15 up to 18 years	3000	12552	2 up to 3 years	1400	5858
Schoolgirls					
9 up to 12 years	2300	9623	3 up to 5 years	1600	6694
12 up to 15 years	2300	9623	5 up to 7 years	1800	7531
15 up to 18 years	2300	9623	7 up to 9 years	2100	8786

* The energy derived from foodstuffs is expressed in terms of Kilocalories (kcal) or kilojoules (kJ). A kcal is a unit of energy, the amount of heat required to raise 1000 grams of water 1°C. One gram of fat produces about nine kcal (37 kJ). These units are known in everyday speech as 'calories' and 'joules'.

Chocolate fudge (p. 487), Peanut brittle (p. 488), Boiled marzipan assortment (p. 486), Coconut ice (p. 490), Golden caramels (p. 489), Turkish delight (p. 489–490).

(Overleaf) Duck with apricots (p. 169), Black Forest gâteau (p. 343), Smoked salmon mousse (p. 28).

Calorie and carbohydrate content of foods

As well as regulating your calorie intake, try to limit your daily intake of carbohydrate to 60 grams.

	Grams of carbohydrate per oz.	kcal*	kJ*
FRUIT			
Apples	3.5	13	54
Apricots, raw	1.9	8	34
dried	12.3	52	218
Bananas	5.5	22	90
Blackberries	1.8	8	34
Blackcurrants	1.9	8	34
Cherries	3.4	13	54
Damsons	2.7	11	46
Gooseberries,	1.0	5	21
ripe	2.6	10	42
Grapes, black	4.4	17	71
white	4.6	18	75
Grapefruit	1.5	6	25
Lemons	0.9	4	17
Melons	1.5	7	29
Olives in brine	trace only	30	126
Oranges	2.4	10	42
Peaches	2.6	11	46
Pears	3.1	12	50
Plums	2.7	11	46
Prunes	11.4	46	193
Raisins	18.3	70	293
Raspberries	1.6	7	29
Rhubarb	0.2	1	4
Strawberries	1.8	7	
Sultanas	18.4	71	297
Tangerine	2.3	10	42
NUTS			
Almonds	1.2	170	711
Brazils	1.2	183	766
Chestnuts	10.4	49	205
Coconut, desiccated	1.8	178	745
Peanuts	2.4	171	716
Walnuts	1.4	156	653
VEGETABLES			
Artichokes	0.8	4	17
Asparagus	0.3	5	21
Beans, broad	2.0	12	50
butter	4.9	26	109
French	0.3	2	8
haricot	4.7	25	105
runner	0.3	2	8
Beetroot	2.8	13	54
Broccoli	0.1	4	17
Brussels sprouts	0.5	5	21
Cabbage, raw	1.1	7	29
cooked	0.2	2	8
Carrots, raw	1.5	6	25
cooked	1.2	5	21
Cauliflower	0.3	3	13
Celery, raw	0.4	3	13
cooked	0.2	1	4
Chicory	0.4	3	13
Cucumber	0.5	3	13
Leeks, raw	1.7	9	38
cooked	1.3	7	29
Lentils	5.2	27	113
Lettuce	0.5	3	13
Marrow	0.4	2	8
Mushrooms	0.0	2	8
Onions	0.8	4	17
Parsley	trace	6	25
Parsnips	3.8	16	67
Peas, raw	3.0	18	75
boiled	2.2	14	59
dried, cooked	5.4	28	117
Potatoes, old	5.6	23	96
new	5.2	21	88
chips	10.6	68	285
crisps	14.0	159	666
Pumpkin	1.0	4	17
Radishes	0.8	4	17
Seakale	0.2	2	8
Spinach	0.4	7	29
Spring greens	0.3	3	13
Swedes	1.1	5	20
Tomatoes	0.8	4	17
Turnips	0.7	3	13
Watercress	0.2	4	17
MEAT, POULTRY (COOKED)			
Bacon, back (fried)	0.0	169	707
Beef (lean and fat)			
topside, roast	0.0	91	381
sirloin, roast	0.0	109	456
silverside	0.0	86	360
corned	0.0	66	276
Chicken, roast	0.0	54	226
Duck, roast	0.0	89	372
Ham, boiled	0.0	123	515
Heart	0.0	68	285
Kidney	0.0	45	189
Liver, ox (fried)	1.1	81	339
Luncheon meat (canned)	1.4	95	398

Note: 'Trace' indicates that traces of carbohydrate are known to be present; an estimation may or may not have been carried out, but in any case the amount in question is of no quantitative dietetic significance.

Celebration cake (p. 398).

	Grams of carbohydrate per oz.	*kcal**	*kJ**
Lamb, chop, grilled	0.0	36	151
leg, roast	0.0	83	348
Pork leg, roast	0.0	90	377
Rabbit, stewed	0.0	51	213
Sausages, fried	4.5	81	339
black	4.2	81	339
Tongue, sheeps', stewed	0.0	84	352
Tripe	0.0	29	121
Turkey, roast	0.0	56	234
Veal, roast	0.0	66	276

FISH (PREPARED)

	Grams of carbohydrate per oz.	*kcal**	*kJ**
Cod (steamed)	0.0	23	96
Crab	0.0	36	151
Haddock	0.0	28	117
Hake	0.0	30	126
Halibut	0.0	37	155
Herring	0.0	54	226
Kippers	0.0	57	239
Lemon Sole	0.0	26	109
Lobster	0.0	34	142
Mackerel	0.0	53	222
Oysters	trace	14	59
Plaice	0.0	26	109
Prawns	0.0	30	126
Salmon, canned	0.0	39	163
fresh	0.0	57	239
Sardines, canned	0.0	84	352
Shrimps	0.0	32	134
Sole	0.0	24	100

SUGARS, PRESERVES

	Grams of carbohydrate per oz.	*kcal**	*kJ**
Glacé cherries	15.8	137	573
Chocolate, milk	15.5	167	699
plain	14.9	155	649
Chutney, tomato	11.0	43	180
Honey	21.7	87	364
Ice cream	5.6	56	234
Jam	19.7	74	310
Jelly, packet	17.7	73	306
Lemon curd	12.0	86	360
Marmalade	19.8	74	310
Mars Bar	18.9	127	531
Sugar, demerara	29.6	112	469
white	29.7	112	469
Syrup, golden	22.4	84	352
Treacle	19.1	73	305

MILK AND MILK PRODUCTS

	Grams of carbohydrate per oz.	*kcal**	*kJ**
Butter	trace	226	946
Cheese, Cheddar	trace	120	502
Edam	trace	88	368
Blue	trace	103	431
Gruyère	trace	132	552
Cottage	0.6	33	138
Cream, double	0.6		548
single	0.9	62	259
Milk, whole	1.4	19	80
skimmed	1.4	10	42
Yoghurt, low-fat	1.4	15	63
Eggs	trace	46	193
Margarine	0.0		946
Lard	0.0	262	1096
Oil	0.0	264	1105

CEREALS AND CEREAL PRODUCTS

	Grams of carbohydrate per oz.	*kcal**	*kJ**
All-Bran	16.5	88	368
Arrowroot	26.7	101	423
Pearl barley, cooked	7.8	34	142
Bemax	12.7	105	439
Bread, Hovis	13.5	67	280
malt	14.0	71	297
Procea	14.3	72	301
Cornflakes	25.2	104	435
Cornflour	26.2	100	418
Energen rolls	13.0	111	464
Flour 100%	20.8	95	398
85%	22.5	98	410
80%	22.9	99	414
75%	23.2	99	414
Macaroni, boiled	7.2	32	134
Oatmeal porridge	2.3	13	54
Puffed wheat	21.4	102	427
Rice, polished	8.4	35	146
Ryvita	21.9	98	410
Sago	26.7	101	423
Semolina	22.0	100	418
Shredded Wheat	22.4	103	431
Spaghetti	23.9	104	435
Tapioca	27.0	102	427
Weetabix	21.9	100	418

MISCELLANEOUS

	Grams of carbohydrate per oz.	*kcal**	*kJ**
Salt	0.0	0	0
Pepper	19.3	88	368
Vinegar	0.2	1	4

DRINKS

	Grams of carbohydrate per oz.	*kcal**	*kJ**
Bournvita	19.2	105	439
Bovril	0.0	23	96
Cocoa	9.9	128	536
Coffee with chicory essence	16.1	63	264
Lemonade	1.6	6	25
Lucozade	5.1	19	80
Marmite	0.0	2	8
Tea (Infusion)	0.0	1	4
Coffee (Infusion)	0.1	1	4

	Grams of carbo-hydrate per oz.	kcal*	kJ*
ALCOHOLIC DRINKS			
(*Note:* This gives calories, etc. per oz; while the chart which follows gives the figures for an average serving)			
Beer, bitter	0.64	9	38
mild	0.46	7	29
Stout	1.19	10	42
Strong ale	1.74	21	88
Cider, dry	0.75	10	42
sweet	1.21	12	50
vintage	2.07	28	117
Port	3.55	45	188
Sherry, dry	0.39	33	138
sweet	1.95	38	159
Champagne	0.40	21	88
Graves	0.95	21	88
Sauternes	1.67	26	109
Burgundy	0.11	20	84
Beaujolais	0.07	19	80
Chianti	0.05	18	75
Spirits, 70° proof	trace	63	264

Alcohol is a food, producing seven calories (29 joules) per gram, and so the more alcohol your drink contains, the more fattening it will be. Volume for volume, spirits are almost twice as fattening as beer – but of course they are not *drunk in equal volumes. Most people drink spirits in tiny, expensive measures and beer by the half-pint. So, in fact, a pub measure of whisky would be less fattening than a pub measure of wine (usually 120 ml, 4 oz) or 300-ml (½-pt) glass of beer. Beer also contains carbohydrates, which increase its calorie content; there are none in spirits. If, however, your spirit is gin and you add tonic, you are adding more calories. Though many diets recommend cutting out all alcohol, you might find it less depressing to eat less than your diet allows and to make up the difference with a couple of glasses of wine – this would help to combat the greatest threat to the dieter's resolution, monotony.*

	kcal	kJ
BEERS		
Brown ale, bottled, 300 ml (*½ pt*)	80	335
Draught ale, bitter ,,	90	377
Draught ale, mild ,,	70	293
Pale ale, bottled ,,	90	377
Stout, bottled ,,	100	418
Stout, extra ,,	110	460
Strong ale ,,	210	879
CIDERS		
Cider, dry, 300 ml (*½ pt*)	100	418
Cider, sweet ,,	120	502
Cider, vintage ,,	280	1172
TABLE WINES, WHITE		
Champagne, glass, 120 ml (*4 oz*)	84	352
Graves ,,	84	352
Sauternes ,,	104	435
TABLE WINES, RED		
Beaujolais, glass, 120 ml (*4 oz*)	76	318
Chianti ,,	72	301
Médoc ,,	72	301
WINES, HEAVY		
Port, ruby, glass, 60 ml (*2 oz*)	86	360
Port, tawny ,,	90	377
Sherry, dry ,,	66	276
Sherry, sweet ,,	76	318
SPIRITS, 70° PROOF		
Whisky, Gin, Vodka, Rum 0.83 oz (England: ⅙ gill)	53	222
Whisky, Gin, Vodka, Rum 1 oz (Scotland: ⅕ gill)	63	264

(*From* The Composition of Foods, *R. A. McCance and E. M. Widdowson. HMSO.*)

	kcal	kJ
LIQUEURS		
Bénédictine (liqueur glass, 2–3 oz)	69	284
Crème de Menthe ,,	67	280
Anisette ,,	74	310
Apricot brandy ,,	64	268
Curaçao ,,	54	226
COGNAC		
Brandy (1 brandy pony, 1 oz)	73	305

(*From* Modern Nutrition in Health and Disease. *W. G. Wohl and R. S. Goodhart. Philadelphia.*)

The 'kJ' figures given in these tables are approximate metric equivalents of the 'kcal' figures published in the original tables and cannot be attributed to the authorities quoted.

Slimming diet

Your health suffers if you are fat, for it constitutes a strain on many organs when the body has a greater weight to carry around. You tend to become tired and out of breath and are more susceptible to rheumatic diseases, diabetes, varicose veins and heart trouble. If you are seriously overweight see a doctor.

In any case, unless you intend to lose merely a kilogram or so *(2–3 lb)* consult your doctor before dieting.

How it happens

Eating too much and doing too little will make anyone fat – eating too much for *you*, that is. Individual needs vary. The sad fact is that the amount of food that keeps one person slim will make another fat. It is just bad luck if you put on weight on normal sized meals. The reasons given so often, 'heredity' and 'glands', may be true in a way, but even so, you won't put on weight unless you eat more than your particular body can cope with – the excess then becomes fat. Here is a sensible regime to follow.

Daily requirements

Milk:

Pre-school children	900 ml–1 litre *(1½–1¾ pt)*
School children and adolescents	900 ml *(not less than 1½ pt)*
Adults	568 ml *(1 pt)*
Expectant and nursing mothers	1 litre *(1¾ pt)*

Cheese: 25 g *(1 oz)*
Eggs: 1 daily, if possible; 3–5 per week.
Meat, fish: A generous serving daily (have liver or kidneys once weekly, if possible).
Potatoes: A serving daily, especially for adolescents.
Vegetables: Generous servings daily, both cooked and raw.
Fruit: Use raw fruit or tomatoes daily.
Fats: Pre-school children need little.

Adolescents and manual workers need about 40 g *(1½ oz)* daily: this allowance is to include all butter, margarine, oil, used in both spreads and cooking.

Average adult: 25 g *(1 oz)* daily. Adults should restrain their appetite for fatty foods.

Bread: 25–50 g *(1–2 oz)* daily.

How to lose weight

Slimming, like giving up smoking, is easy to start. You have probably done it dozens of times! Why then don't you stay slim? Ask yourself how soon after giving up the diet did you regain the weight loss? How many different diets have you tried? The only way to maintain a loss in weight is to alter your basic eating habits. Choose a sensible diet that suits your metabolism and learn to like it; drop the gimmick diets, crash diets, impossible-to-live-on diets.

Probably the most successful method of slimming is to adopt the low carbohydrate diet. You *can* lose weight by counting the calories of everything you eat and seeing that they never exceed a certain number, but this involves a great deal of tedious calculation. With a low carbohydrate diet you simply cut out all sugar (honey, syrup, jam and all sweets in addition to sugar itself) and reduce starches (bread, potatoes). Cut out also canned fruit, cakes, biscuits and pastry. Speed is not a very important factor when slimming. It is better to think of your diet as six months of controlled but pleasant eating than four weeks of misery.

If you cut down on the carbohydrate don't eat extra protein and fat in its place. Fat is useful in that it takes quite a while to leave your stomach, making you feel less hungry, more satisfied, so don't cut it out altogether. If you cut down carbohydrate foods the fat intake is automatically reduced – you won't be getting the fat in cakes and pastries and you will have less bread on which to spread butter.

To help the slimming process take exercise – not a sudden burst of athleticism, guaranteed to sharpen your appetite, but something steady and regular. Walk to the station, walk up the office stairs, go swimming or dancing instead of watching the television.

The rules of the game

Follow the daily requirements pattern, but reduce the milk to 300 ml *(½ pt)*, butter to 12.5 g *(½ oz)* and bread to 25 g *(1 oz)*.

You may not eat:

Sugar, jam, marmalade, honey and glucose.
Sweets, chocolates and sweet biscuits.
Cakes, puddings and pastries, pasta, rice.
Canned and dried fruits, sweetened fruit juices and squashes or ice cream.
Bottled thick sauces, salad cream and thick soup.
Any fried food.
Beer, wine, cider, spirits.

No nibbling

Remember, a 50-g *(2-oz)* bar of chocolate absent-mindedly eaten between meals supplies about 300 unneeded calories. Missing a meal makes you particularly susceptible to the temptation to nibble, so eat regularly.

Drinks

Alcohol supplies calories and strictly speaking, sherry, wine, beer, spirits, cocktails and liqueurs should not form part of a slimming diet. However, we realise that for many people a social life without drinks is difficult, if not downright dull. Try to make one drink last the evening.

Sample slimming menus

	MONDAY	TUESDAY	WEDNESDAY	THURSDAY	FRIDAY	SATURDAY	SUNDAY
Breakfast	Orange Boiled egg 1 slice crispbread and butter	Hot grapefruit Grilled kidney and bacon 1 slice of toast and butter	Fruit juice Cold ham and tomato 1 slice of brown bread and butter	Fruit juice Poached egg and mushrooms 1 slice of crispbread and butter	Stewed fruit Scrambled egg on 1 slice of toast	Fruit juice Cereal and milk 1 slice of bread and butter	Fruit juice Bacon omelette 1 slice of crispbread and butter
Lunch	Cold tongue Cole slaw Cheese and 2 cream crackers	Cottage cheese and cucumber salad 1 slice of crispbread	Frankfurters and mustard sauce Watercress Sauerkraut Cheese, 2 biscuits and celery	Liver and bacon kebabs Spring greens or broccoli Coffee junket	Meat loaf and salad 1 slice of bread and butter	Soused herrings Tomato salad 1 slice of bread and butter Cheese	Roast beef and horseradish sauce Braised celery Carrots Raspberry and redcurrant purée and yoghurt
Dinner	Grilled gammon Spinach Fresh fruit	Clear soup Grilled fish Runner beans Strawberry yoghurt	Ratatouille Crisp cheese toast	Savoury mince and marrow 1 slice of bread	Cheese soufflé Cauliflower Fresh fruit	Grilled entrecôte steak Tossed green salad Baked apple	Cold roast beef and salad Cheese and 2 cream crackers Glass of milk

Remember No sugar in drinks or in stewed fruit or other sweets; no mid-morning snack (except a cup of tea or coffee); no afternoon tea (except a cup of tea).

If you drink spirits, add water or soda water, not squash, tonic water (unless it's the low calorie variety) or other sweetened drinks.

Of the non-alcoholic drinks, coffee, tea (with milk or just lemon), tomato juice and meat extracts are not fattening. Nor, of course, is water. Nearly all the sweet drinks, fizzy or flat, are fattening and are otherwise valueless. If you must have sweetness use one of the many saccharine based sweeteners.

Slimming aids

There are a number of proprietary slimming aids on the market including flavoured drinks, diet biscuits, soups and snacks. It is important to regard these as substitute foods intended to replace a meal. Follow manufacturers' directions carefully. For instance some diet biscuits should be accompanied by a glass of milk. On the whole these 'aids to slimming' make for a rather dull diet and it is better to get accustomed to eating a normal low carbohydrate diet. However they are useful for occasional use.

Slimming clubs such as Weight Watchers have proved very successful for many people. The group therapy methods followed are most helpful in making slimming a less lonely affair than it usually is.

Sample slimming menus

If you follow this diet, as illustrated in the week's meals in the chart on page 533:
You won't lose 3.2 kg *(half a stone)* in one week and you won't lose even 450 g *(1 lb)* if you cheat by eating cake on the quiet! But you will lose weight steadily and unspectacularly if you literally eat nothing else at all. How honest can you be with yourself?

Alternatives for lunch or dinner include:
Grilled or baked fish with tomatoes.
Roast lamb, veal or pork (no crackling), game or chicken.
Grilled chop, liver, kidneys, bacon with tomatoes or mushrooms.
Omelettes and eggs cooked any way except fried.
Casserole of beef or lamb (not thickened).
With them serve green vegetables or salads and occasionally one *small* potato.

The calorie 'target' varies so much according to age, sex, occupation, etc, that it is not feasible to give an exact figure to aim at, but your doctor will doubtless help you on this point. For most adult women needing to lose weight, a figure between 1000 and 1200 calories per day should mean a steady though undramatic loss in weight.

Diet for putting on weight

It's true, some people need to put on weight! And oddly enough, it's even more difficult to do this than to slim. You need to follow the usual rules of good nutrition, eating plenty of:
Milk, eggs, cheese and meat
Fruit and vegetables
Bread and bread products
Butter and other fats.

Use these foodstuffs in any way you like. (There are plenty of recipes in this book to show you how.) Then add the concentrated calorie foods – see the list on pages 529 to 531. Glucose and sugar, for example, can be sprinkled on cereals or added to puddings. Serve cream with puddings, pour it over fruit and add to soups and sauces. Mash potatoes with plenty of butter or cream and toss vegetables, such as carrots or cabbage, in butter.

Reverse the slimming instructions and take snacks between meals (but not *just before* a meal or you will lose your appetite for it). Take a milk drink with biscuits mid-morning, cake at tea-time and another milk drink on going to bed. Pop a beaten egg into the drink sometimes and make it into an egg-nog. Take wheat germ, or yeast extract such as Marmite, to improve your intake of 'B' vitamins – great appetite-improvers.

Diet in illness

When one is ill there may be some loss of appetite and food likes and dislikes may be exaggerated. So far as possible consider the invalid's preferences and do pay special attention to the appearance and the flavour of the food. Offer small helpings and serve meals fairly frequently – they help to relieve the tedium of illness. Don't however leave food in the sickroom in the hope of tempting the invalid – it usually has the reverse effect.

Even if no special diet is prescribed by the doctor, give light meals, which tax the digestive system less than rich ones. The invalid's requirements of the essential nutrients remain the same as for the healthy person – sometimes indeed they are greater, so you need to provide a variety of particularly nutritious foods. The traditional calf's foot jelly and beef tea don't seem to be so fashionable in the sickroom as they used to be and there is no reason why they should be – still, excellent prepared versions of these and other products are now sold, which save a lot of time. However, we do include a few such recipes in case you want them; in other cases we refer you to suitable recipes included elsewhere in this book.

Calf's foot jelly

1 calf's foot
1.1 l *(2 pt)* water
salt and pepper
1 egg white and egg shell
1 glass sherry
3 cloves
pinch of ground cinnamon
rind and juice of 1 lemon

Wash the calf's foot, blanch it and cut into pieces. Put into a pan, cover with the water and add salt and pepper. Simmer for 3–4 hours, skimming occasionally, until the stock is reduced to half the quantity. Allow to cool and remove any fat. Add the egg white and the washed shell, the sherry, cloves, cinnamon, lemon rind and juice to the stock, return it to the pan and simmer gently for 10 minutes. Strain through a jelly bag and leave to set in a cool place.

Don't keep longer than 24 hours, unless stored in a refrigerator.

Black-currant milk

Pour 150 ml *(¼ pt)* top of the milk into a screw-top bottle, add 15–30 ml *(1–2 tbsps)* black-currant syrup (or rose-hip syrup) and shake well. Serve with cream or ice cream, if desired.

Lemon cobbler

Place the rind of 1 lemon in a pan with 150 ml *(¼ pt)* water and 15 ml *(1 level tbsp)* sugar, boil for 15 minutes, strain and cool; stir in a beaten egg and the juice of a lemon. Serve with soda water or milk.

Vanilla egg-nog

Dissolve 15 ml *(1 tbsp)* glucose in 150 ml *(¼ pt)* milk (warming it slightly if necessary). Beat up 1 egg, stir it into the milk and flavour with vanilla essence (or grated nutmeg) to taste.

Malted brandy shake

Whisk 15 ml *(1 level tbsp)* malted milk powder with 150 ml *(¼ pt)* milk until there are no lumps and add 15 ml *(1 tbsp)* brandy.

Orange cream shake

Add 15 ml *(2 tbsps)* glucose or 15 ml *(1 level tbsp)* caster sugar to 50 ml *(2 fl oz)* single cream and gradually stir in the juice of 1 small orange; add 45–60 ml *(3–4 tbsps)* milk and mix lightly. Serve cold.

Special diets

If one is needed, the doctor will prescribe it. It is dangerous to go on a diet except on a doctor's orders.

'No solids' diet

A fluid diet may be prescribed by the doctor in certain kinds of illness. The calorie, protein, vitamin and mineral needs of the invalid can be supplied quite adequately in the form of fluids, with the help of milk, cream, eggs, butter, glucose, fruit juice, various proprietary foods and water.

Soups and broths Any standard recipe may be useful. Clear soup, beef tea and meat extract drinks are pleasant to drink and stimulate the appetite, but as they contain little protein, they cannot be thought of as a main dish; you can use bouillon cubes to save time when making them. Cream soups are more nutritious, particularly if you add some extra milk, cream, eggs or puréed vegetables.

Puddings and drinks Milk puddings, made rather runny, are very useful, and so are egg custard, yoghurt, ice cream and jelly. Egg-nogs and milk drinks add greatly to the nutritional intake and are no trouble to take. Fruit

Light diet

	SUITABLE FOODS	UNSUITABLE FOODS
Dairy produce	Milk (as much as possible), in the form of milk drinks, junket, baked custard, jellies, puddings and soups. Evaporated, condensed and dried milk, proprietary milk foods, yoghurt. Cream (in moderate amounts). Ice cream. Cheddar cheese, cottage cheese. Butter and margarine.	Strong cheese, eg Gorgonzola, Stilton. Cheese cooked at a high temperature.
Meat, Poultry, Fish, Eggs	Tender cuts – lamb, beef, poultry, simply cooked. Sweetbreads, tripe, liver and brains. White fish – plaice, sole, haddock, cod, turbot, halibut, trout, soft herring roes; steamed, baked, poached, grilled. Canned salmon. Eggs – boiled, poached, scrambled, baked; as soufflés, puddings, drinks and sauces.	Tough meat, fried meat. Made-up dishes using twice-cooked meat. Spiced or highly seasoned mixtures, curries. Coarse or fat meat – pork, heart, duck, goose. Fatty fish – salmon, herrings, bloaters, kippers, sardines, pilchards, eels. Fried fish. Shellfish – lobsters, crab, prawns, shrimps. Fried eggs.
Fruits and Vegetables	Soft raw fruits – ripe bananas, pears, apricots, peaches, oranges, grapes. Stewed fruits – apples, pears, peaches, apricots. Tinned fruit – mandarin oranges, strained baby foods, black-currant purée. Puréed fruit of all kinds. Tomato juice and fruit juices. Potatoes (boiled, mashed, baked in skins); young carrots, etc, marrow, flower part of cauliflower, tomatoes, puréed vegetables, pease pudding.	Hard raw fruits – apples, plums, gooseberries, pineapple. Dried fruit. Fried, roast and chipped potatoes. Fibrous vegetables – onions, leeks, celery, turnips, swedes, cabbage, broad and French beans.
Breads and Cereals (supplementary foods)	White and brown bread, thin crisp toast. Plain, semi-sweet and sweet biscuits. Cornflakes, puffed rice, porridge, white flour, cornflour, rice, sago, tapioca, semolina, macaroni, spaghetti, etc. Plain sponge puddings and cakes.	Wholemeal bread. Nuts. Coconut, rye and wholewheat biscuits. Shredded wheat and any wholewheat cereals (eg coarse porridge). Wholemeal flour. Pastries, hot scones, suet puddings, dumplings.
Miscellaneous	Soup, especially cream types. Preserves – honey, syrup, jam and marmalade. Beverages – tea and coffee; Ovaltine, Horlicks, Benger's and other proprietary milk drinks. Bovril and Marmite. Light wines.	Sauces, pickles and pickled foodstuffs, vinegar, horseradish, curry powder, pepper, mustard. Strong tea and coffee. Spirits.

juices are important to supply vitamin C and they leave a pleasantly fresh taste in the mouth.

Light diet

When this is prescribed, the patient requires simple, easily digested foods. Avoid rich or heavy things such as stew or toad-in-the-hole, or highly seasoned foods like curry, and those which are rich in fat; fats in cooking should also be avoided, and so should roughage. The chart (page 536) lists the main things to include and to avoid.

Bland diet

For an illness involving the digestive system, the doctor may prescribe a bland diet, perhaps calling it a 'gastric' or 'low-residue' diet. Although there are slight differences between the two, basically they both resemble the light diet already given, but excluding foods with woody stalks, tough fibres, pips and skin. This means that fruit and vegetables have to be sieved or purêed or left out altogether. Since the invalid may not get enough vitamin C, he should be given orange or black-currant juice or vitamin C tablets. For a gastric diet the rules are:

1. Take small, regular and frequent meals.
2. Eat slowly.
3. If a meal is missed, take a glass of milk and a few semi-sweet biscuits.
4. Avoid alcohol and smoking.

Suitable main dishes include the following (see recipes elsewhere in the book). Tender cuts of meat, simply cooked.
Veal, lamb or chicken fricassee.
Steamed, poached, grilled or baked fish with white, egg or cheese sauce.
Kedgeree, fish custard, fish pie.
Fish, chicken or cheese soufflé.
Cheese pudding, macaroni cheese.
Hard-boiled, poached or scrambled egg, omelettes.
Roast chicken, veal or lamb.
Chicken in aspic, eggs in aspic.
Creamed sweetbreads.

Suitable puddings, cakes Choose from –
Milk puddings of all kinds.
Jellies, ice creams, meringues, fruit fools.
Queen of puddings (use jelly jam), bread and butter pudding (no dried fruit), trifle, sweet soufflés.
Baked sponge pudding and custard, apple charlotte.
Plain biscuits, meringues, sponge and Madeira cake.

Avoid these things
Coarse cereals, wholemeal bread, oatmeal.
Raw fruit and vegetables (except juice).
Nuts and dried fruit.
Fried foods and fatty fish.
Highly seasoned foods, pickles, ketchup and mustard.
Coarse meat such as beef and pork unless minced.

Restrict
Butter, lard, etc.
Fresh bread.

Low-fat diet

A completely fat-free diet is difficult to achieve and a low-fat one is more usual. It means leaving out obvious fats such as butter, lard and oil and some foods which contain fat. Milk should be skimmed or you can buy dried skimmed milk powder. It is unfortunately a dull diet, as so many dishes depend on fat. You will need vitamin A and D supplements, as they will be lacking in a low-fat diet.

Suitable foods include
Skimmed milk – as much as possible.
Low fat cottage cheese and yoghurt.
Lean meat – boiled or baked lamb, beef, ham, and chicken.
Stews (remove fat when cold).
Fricassees (made without fat).
White fish – haddock, cod, plaice, sole, turbot and halibut – boiled, baked or grilled.
All vegetables and fruit, except avocados.
Macaroni, spaghetti, rice, breakfast cereals.
Milk puddings made with skimmed milk.
Soups (with fat skimmed off).
Day-old bread; meringues. Plain and water biscuits.
Sugar, preserves, boiled sweets.
Chutney, pickles, herbs and spices.
Tea, coffee, Bovril, Marmite, vegetable and fruit juice.

Avoid the following
Fried or braised food. Fat meat, duck, pork sausages.
Herrings, kippers, sardines and salmon.
Whole milk, cream, ice cream, cheese, egg yolk, butter, margarine, cooking fat and oil, suet.
Pastry, biscuits, cakes containing fat.
Mayonnaise, salad dressings, chocolate, coffee, nuts and olives.
Mincemeat and lemon curd.
Cream soups and sauces.
Drinking chocolate, cocoa.

Low-protein diet

Cut down on the protein foods listed below, taking very small helpings only. The doctor will say how much is allowed.
Meat, fish, eggs, poultry.
Cheese, milk and milk products.
Dried pulses, peas and beans.

Bread, breakfast cereals, wheat flour, pasta, nuts, biscuits, cakes.

Eat plenty of vegetables, salads, fruits, arrowroot, cornflour, rice, tapioca, sago, sugar, fats and most preserves.

Low-salt diet

Salt (or its components) is present in most foods, so it is impossible to eliminate it entirely.

A not-too-strict diet will merely involve leaving out salty foods such as bacon and kippers, using no salt in cooking and not adding any at the table. You may need to obtain salt-free butter and bread (some bakers bake it specially).

Use herbs and spices, pepper and mustard to add flavour to savoury food. You may be allowed to use a salt substitute.

Suitable foods for a low-salt diet are:
Most meat, chicken and poultry.
White fish, shellfish, salmon and herrings.
All vegetables and fruit, fruit juices.
Unsalted butter and margarine, olive or salad oil, lard, restricted milk and cream.
Home-made cottage cheese (no added rennet).
Eggs (may be limited to 3 per week).
Pasta, rice, other cereals.
Sugar, preserves, boiled sweets.
Wines and spirits.
Unsalted bread.

Avoid the following
Bacon, ham, sausages, canned meats, bought cooked meats, meat pasties.
Kippers and other smoked fish.
Rollmops.
Fish fingers.
Canned foods (except fruit).
Breakfast cereals, bought biscuits and cakes.
Any cakes containing baking powder or soda.
Cheese, salted butter and margarine, ice cream.
Sauces, chutneys, tomato paste.
Golden syrup, treacle, chocolate, toffees.
Packet mixes.
All powders used for making milk drinks.
Dried fruit except prunes.
Meat and yeast extracts.
Beer.

Vegetarian cookery

Some vegetarians do not eat meat and fish, but eat dairy products, while others (known as 'vegans') will eat no animal products at all. The former can obtain a satisfactory diet from milk, cheese, eggs, butter, vegetables, pulses, fruit, cereals and nuts. The vegans' diet however may be seriously deficient in protein, unless they make a special point of eating a wide variety of cereals, pulses, nuts and vegetables including soya bean products such as TVP (see p. 98) to try to make good this deficiency. Many of the recipes in the chapters on Soups, Vegetables, Salads, Pasta and Rice and Cheese are suitable, though for strict vegetarians they may need some adaptation. Titles of books on vegetarian cookery, may be obtained from the Vegetarian Society, 53 Marloes Road, London, W8 6LD. Health Food stores sell vegetarian foods.

Cholesterol lowering diet

This means cutting out animal fats and dairy products, such as fat meat, cream and butter as these tend to raise the cholesterol level in the blood. They are all classed as saturated fats. Polyunsaturated fats on the other hand help to lower cholesterol level in the blood. These are found in vegetable oils including sunflower seed and corn oil. Some margarines are high in polyunsaturated fats (this is declared on the label) and these are suitable for a low cholesterol diet and can be used for making cakes and pastry. Use any recipe which specifies soft tub margarine, see pages 194, 376. A cholesterol lowering diet is often prescribed for people who have had a coronary attack as there is evidence that a low blood cholesterol level reduces the risk of heart attacks.

Suitable foods
Lean meat, particularly red meat (discard excess fat).
Chicken, turkey.
White fish.
Cottage cheese.
Green vegetables and salads.
Peanut butter.
Fruit and fruit juice.
Skimmed milk.
Most nuts except coconut and cashew.
Bread, crispbreads, and breakfast cereals.
Clear soup.

Avoid the following
All dairy and animal fats.
All offal and shell fish.
Full cream milk (use skimmed) and dairy ice cream.
Cheese other than cottage cheese.
Gravies, rich sauces and cream soups.
Baked foods prepared with egg yolk, butter or whole milk.

Don't eat more than 3 egg yolks a week. Use polyunsaturated fats for all cooking purposes.

Cooking for two

Cooking for two needs the same considerations as cooking for larger numbers. Planning, shopping and preparation are as important when cooking for a small household as for a large one. Cooking for two has problems of its own for most recipes are written for 4–6 people and it is not always a good plan to just halve the quantities and the cooking time – the result will be more successful if you follow a reliable recipe worked out for two people. Another difficulty in the small household is using up oddments of food such as leftover meat from the weekend joint.

Equipment when cooking for small numbers is important as too large pans or dishes will allow liquids to evaporate.

Amounts to buy for two

Meat	100–175 g *(4–6 oz)* boneless, each 225–350 g *(½–¾ lb)* with bone, each
Chicken	350 g *(¾ lb)* each
Fish	175–225 g *(6–8 oz)* each
Beans	350 g *(¾ lb)* for two
Carrots	225–450 g *(½–1 lb)* for two
Celery	1 head for two (Casserole or boil the outside; eat the heart separately with cheese)
Mushrooms	225 g *(½ lb)* for two
Peas in the pod	700 g *(1½ lb)* for two
Potatoes	450 g *(1 lb)* for two
Courgettes	350–450 g *(¾–1 lb)* for two
Tomatoes	225–450 g *(½–1 lb)* for two
Broccoli	350–450 g *(¾–1 lb)* for two
Sprouts	350–450 g *(¾–1 lb)* for two
Cabbage	350–450 g *(¾–1 lb)* for two
Cauliflower	700 g *(1½ lb)* for two

Here are some recipes worked out for two people.

Potted salmon

99-g *(3½-oz)* can red salmon
salt
pepper
pinch mace
50 g *(2 oz)* butter, melted
10 ml *(2 tsps)* lemon juice
30 ml *(2 tbsps)* single cream

Flake the salmon, discarding the skin and any bones. Season lightly with salt, pepper and mace. Beat the fish well with a wooden spoon to give it a smooth consistency. Add half the melted butter, lemon juice and cream, again beating well. Turn into 2 individual dishes and level the surface. Top with the remaining melted butter and garnish with parsley. Chill. Serve as a starter. *Serves 2.*

Cod au gratin

75-g *(3-oz)* pkt instant potato
salt and pepper
milk to mix
1 fillet of cod (about 350 g, *¾ lb*)
20 g *(¾ oz)* butter
30 ml *(2 level tbsps)* flour
300 ml *(½ pt)* milk
100 g *(4 oz)* Cheddar cheese, grated
grated rind and juice of ½ lemon
lemon wedges for garnish

Make up the potato as directed on the packet. Season with salt and pepper. Add enough milk to make of piping consistency. Skin the fish, then poach it for 10 minutes in simmering water. Meanwhile, make a white sauce. Melt the butter in a pan, add the flour and cook for a few minutes off the heat; gradually add the milk, stirring well. Return to the heat and stirring continuously, bring to the boil. Add grated cheese, lemon rind and juice. Season with salt and pepper, cover and keep warm. Spoon the cool potato into a piping bag fitted with a star vegetable nozzle. Pipe a border of potato around a shallow ovenproof dish. Drain the fish and flake it into large pieces. Place it in the potato-bordered dish, and pour the sauce over the fish. Place in the oven at 180°C *(350°F)* mark 4 for about 30 minutes. Serve garnished with lemon wedges. *Serves 2.*

Note If you wish, use freshly boiled potatoes creamed with a little milk and butter for piping. The final cooking can be done under a low grill.

Pasta niçoise

100 g *(4 oz)* twisted pasta
2 firm tomatoes
2 eggs, hard-boiled
113-g *(4-oz)* can tuna fish, drained
½ red pepper, seeded and finely sliced
50 g *(2 oz)* French beans, cooked
8 black olives
few capers
45 ml *(3 tbsps)* garlic flavoured French dressing

Cook the pasta in boiling salted water until tender but not soft. Drain well and rinse at once in cold water. Cool. Quarter the tomatoes, shell and cut the hard-boiled eggs lengthwise into quarters. Flake the tuna fish. Place the pasta, fish, tomatoes, sliced red pepper, French beans, olives and capers in a bowl and mix gently. Add French dressing and toss, using two forks. Spoon on to a serving dish or 2 individual plates, garnish with the quartered hard-boiled eggs. *Serves 2.*

Super kedgeree

2 cook-in-the-bag kippers
2 eggs, hard-boiled
50 g *(2 oz)* butter
100 g *(4 oz)* long grain rice, cooked (see page 277)
15 ml *(1 tbsp)* chopped parsley
juice ½ lemon
salt and pepper
lemon wedges

Cook the kippers, according to the directions on the packet. Discard the skin and bones and flake the flesh. Finely chop the hard-boiled eggs. Melt the butter in a large pan. Stir in the rice and add the parsley and lemon juice. When heated through, add the flaked fish and hard-boiled eggs; continue to heat, stirring gently, for a few minutes until really hot. Adjust the seasoning and serve with lemon wedges. Accompany with a sliced tomato and onion salad. *Serves 2.*

Sausage pie

225 g *(½ lb)* pork sausages or sausage meat
30 ml *(2 tbsps)* cooking oil
1 onion, skinned and thinly sliced
2 tomatoes, peeled and sliced
1 apple, peeled, cored and chopped
1 potato, peeled and diced
salt and pepper
100 g *(4 oz)* shortcrust pastry (see page 351)

Remove the sausage skins and divide each sausage into two, or shape the sausage meat into 8 balls. Heat the oil and lightly fry the onions, tomatoes, apple and potatoes until beginning to brown. Turn into a 900-ml *(1½-pt)* oval pie dish. Season and leave until cool. Roll out the pastry and use to cover the pie. Place it on a baking sheet and bake in the oven at 200°C *(400°F)* mark 6 for about 30 minutes. *Serves 2.*

Stuffed aubergines

2 medium sized aubergines
salt
small knob of butter
½ medium sized onion, skinned and chopped
350 g *(¾ lb)* minced beef
salt and pepper
15 ml *(1 tbsp)* chopped parsley
1 clove garlic, skinned and crushed
4 tomatoes, peeled, seeded and roughly chopped
300 ml *(½ pt)* beef stock

Slice a 'lid' off each aubergine, scoop out the flesh completely, leaving a thin wall, and sprinkle the aubergines liberally with salt; leave them upside down. Retain 100 g *(4 oz)* of the flesh and chop it finely. Heat the butter in a pan. Add the chopped onions and cook until soft. Add the minced beef and cook until browned. Stir in the chopped aubergine and season well with salt, pepper and parsley. Stir in the crushed garlic and chopped tomato flesh. Dry the aubergines with kitchen paper and spoon the mince mixture into the shells. Replace the lids. Place the aubergines in an ovenproof dish and pour stock around. Cover with a lid and bake in the oven at 180°C *(350°F)* mark 4 for about 30 minutes. *Serves 2.*

Beef salad

5 ml *(1 level tsp)* dried basil
30 ml *(2 tbsps)* French dressing (see page 244)
225 g *(½ lb)* cold roast beef, cubed
1 eating apple, peeled, cored and sliced
25 g *(1 oz)* black grapes, stoned
lettuce

Combine the basil and French dressing and leave for the flavours to blend. Pour it over the meat, apple and grapes and toss well. Line two individual salad dishes with lettuce and pile the meat mixture on top. *Serves 2.*

Sunday lamb

1.25–1.5 kg *(2½–3 lb)* shoulder of lamb

For stuffing
60 ml *(4 tbsps)* fresh white breadcrumbs
50 g *(2 oz)* mushrooms, finely chopped
25 g *(1 oz)* finely chopped onion
15 ml *(1 tbsp)* chopped parsley
grated rind of ½ lemon
pinch of dried thyme
salt and pepper
1 egg, beaten

Bone the shoulder or ask the butcher to do this for you. Combine all the stuffing ingredients together. Spread the stuffing over the opened-out joint of lamb. Press it down and roll up the joint. Secure with several bands of string. Weigh the joint and calculate the cooking time, allowing 45 minutes per 450 g *(1 lb)*, put in a roasting tin and place in the oven at 180°C *(350°F)* mark 4.

Note This size joint should give a meal for two hot and one cold, still leaving 225 g *(½ lb)* for a curry later in the week.

Mild lamb curry

25 g *(1 oz)* butter
1 onion, skinned and chopped
1 stick celery, chopped
50 g *(2 oz)* mushrooms, sliced
10 ml *(2 level tsps)* curry powder
10 ml *(2 level tsps)* tomato paste
15 ml *(1 level tbsp)* flour
15 ml *(1 level tbsp)* mango chutney
300 ml *(½ pt)* stock
25 g *(1 oz)* sultanas
225 g *(½ lb)* left-over cold roast lamb, chopped
salt and pepper
1 banana, sliced
100 g *(4 oz)* long grain rice
25 g *(1 oz)* salted peanuts

Melt the butter in a pan and fry the onion, celery and mushrooms until soft. Stir in the curry powder, tomato paste, flour and chutney and cook for further 2 minutes. Gradually stir in stock and bring to the boil, stirring well until it thickens. Add the sultanas and meat. Season well, cover and simmer for 30 minutes. Five minutes before the end of the cooking time add the banana. Cook the rice (see page 277). Serve the curry with rice and garnish with salted peanuts. *Serves 2.*

Lamb sauté

4 lamb cutlets
salt and pepper
25 g *(1 oz)* butter
50 g *(2 oz)* tiny onions, skinned
225 g *(½ lb)* courgettes, topped, tailed and sliced
15 ml *(1 tbsp)* chopped parsley
450 g *(1 lb)* potatoes, boiled and creamed
10 ml *(2 level tsps)* cornflour
150 ml *(¼ pt)* chicken stock

Season the cutlets lightly with salt and pepper. Heat half of the butter in a small heavy based pan and seal the cutlets quickly on both sides. Turn the heat down and simmer, covered, for about 20 minutes. Parboil the onions in salted water and drain. Place the courgettes in a pan of boiling water and cook for about 5 minutes, then drain. Heat the rest of the butter and sauté the courgettes and onions until soft. Toss in chopped parsley. Keep them warm. Using a large star vegetable nozzle, pipe 4 large whirls of potato on to a serving dish, well apart. Remove the cutlets from the pan. Arrange each on a whirl of potato. Place the buttered courgettes and onions around the cutlets and keep warm. Heat the juices in the pan. Slake the cornflour with a little of the stock. Add it to the juices in the pan with the remainder of the stock. Bring slowly to boil, stirring all the time. Check the seasoning and spoon it over the cutlets and serve any remaining sauce in a sauce boat. *Serves 2.*

Gammon steaks with gingered apricots

2.5 ml (*½ level tsp*) dry mustard
5 ml (*1 level tsp*) ground ginger
20 ml (*4 level tsps*) brown sugar
10 ml (*2 tsps*) Worcestershire sauce
30 ml (*2 tbsps*) lemon juice
2 gammon steaks
1 small green pepper, seeded
226-g (*8-oz*) can apricot halves, drained
2 pieces stem ginger, chopped

Combine together the mustard, ground ginger, sugar, sauce and lemon juice. Brush these over the gammon on both sides. Arrange the gammon steaks side by side in a lightly oiled shallow ovenproof dish and pour over any remaining marinade. Cook uncovered in the oven at 190°C (*375°F*) mark 5 for about 30 minutes. Baste with the juices in the dish after 20 minutes. Meanwhile, slice the pepper, blanch in boiling water for 3 minutes and drain. Arrange the quartered apricots down the centre of the dish with the chopped ginger and pepper. Return the dish to the oven for 15 minutes to re-heat. Serve with boiled rice or creamed potatoes and sliced green beans. *Serves 2.*

Pork with wine sauce

4 prunes
salt and pepper
2 boneless pork chops
15 ml (*1 tbsp*) oil
1 orange
150 ml (*¼ pt*) water
90 ml (*6 tbsps*) sherry or Madeira

Pour some boiling water over the prunes and simmer them for 20 minutes until tender. Season the chops and fry slowly in the oil, allowing about 7 minutes on each side. Thinly peel the rind from the orange with a vegetable peeler, cut it into very fine shreds and put these into a saucepan with the water and boil for 5 minutes. Add 30 ml (*2 tbsps*) juice squeezed from the orange and remove from the heat. Remove the chops from the frying pan and pour in the orange liquid, add the sherry or Madeira and heat through. Serve the chops and drained prunes with the juices from the pan poured over. *Serves 2.*

Casseroled chicken with bacon

cooking oil
2 chicken portions
100 g (*¼ lb*) lean streaky bacon, rinded and chopped
100 g (*¼ lb*) carrots, pared and sliced
100 g (*¼ lb*) onion, skinned and sliced
15 ml (*1 level tbsp*) flour
300 ml (*½ pt*) chicken stock
2 tomatoes, peeled and quartered

Add just enough oil to a frying pan to cover the base. When it is hot, add the chicken portions and fry until golden. Drain the chicken. Add the bacon to the pan and cook for a few minutes. Stir in the carrots and onion and cook for 5 minutes then sprinkle over the flour and slowly add the chicken stock. Bring to the boil, stirring. Turn it into a 1.1-l (*2-pt*) casserole, add the fried chicken, cover and cook in the oven at 180°C (*325°F*) mark 3 for about 1 hour. Add the tomatoes for the last 15 minutes. *Serves 2.*

Escalope of chicken

2 chicken breasts
45 ml (*3 tbsps*) fresh white breadcrumbs
15 ml (*1 level tbsp*) grated Parmesan cheese
pinch of dried fines herbes
pepper
½ beaten egg
oil for frying
½ lemon

Place the chicken breasts on a board and beat them out with a rolling pin. Combine the breadcrumbs, cheese, herbs and pepper. On a plate, dip the chicken in the egg to coat evenly. Coat in seasoned crumbs and pat these on well. In a frying pan, heat some oil. Fry the escalopes of chicken until golden brown one side, turn and brown the second side – 7–10 minutes altogether. Cut two slices of lemon and twist for garnish. Squeeze the remainder of the juice over the chicken and serve at once, garnished with lemon twists. *Serves 2.*

Rhubarb fool

150 ml (*¼ pt*) custard – see below
350 g (*¾ lb*) rhubarb
60 ml (*4 tbsps*) orange juice
grated rind ½ orange
50 g (*2 oz*) sugar
pink or red colouring
30 ml (*2 tbsps*) double or soured cream

Make the custard using 15 ml (*1 level tbsp*) custard powder, 15 g (*½ oz*) sugar and 150 ml (*¼ pt*) milk. Cool until luke warm. Slice the rhubarb, cook with the orange juice, rind and sugar until well reduced and with little liquid remaining. Cool. Purée the rhubarb with the custard in an electric blender, or sieve the rhubarb and combine it with the custard. Add colouring to tint an attractive pink. Divide between two bowls or glasses. Chill. When ready to serve, pour on the cream and feather with the handle of a teaspoon. *Serves 2.*

Bananas in orange sauce

25 g *(1 oz)* sugar
1 orange
25 g *(1 oz)* butter
15 ml *(1 tbsp)* Cointreau or other orange liqueur
2 bananas, peeled and halved lengthways

Put the sugar, grated rind of the orange and 45 ml *(3 tbsps)* water in a frying pan. Heat very gently until the sugar has dissolved. Bring to the boil and simmer for 5 minutes. Add the orange juice and butter and continue to cook until the butter has melted. Add the Cointreau and bananas. Cook over a low heat for a further 5 minutes. Serve immediately with cream. *Serves 2.*

Cornish crunchies

25 g *(1 oz)* butter
30 ml *(2 level tbsps)* golden syrup
40 g *(1½ oz)* cornflakes, crushed
2 scoops ice cream
2 pieces stem ginger, chopped
15 ml *(1 tbsp)* stem ginger syrup

Place the butter and syrup in a small pan. Heat and allow to bubble. Remove the pan from the heat and stir in the cornflakes. Place 2 10-cm *(4-in)* flan rings on individual plates. Divide the cornflake mixture between the two rings and press into shallow nests using the back of a wooden spoon. Leave to set for ½ hour. Just before serving, remove the rings and fill the centres with ice cream. Top each with stem ginger and syrup. *Serves 2.*

Zabaglione

2 egg yolks
30 ml *(2 tbsps)* sweet sherry
20 ml *(4 level tsps)* caster sugar

Place the egg yolks, sherry and sugar in a basin. Place over a pan of hot water and whisk until thick and frothy. Turn at once into two individual glasses and serve with sponge fingers. *Serves 2.*

Pineapple meringue pie

100 g *(4 oz)* shortcrust pastry ie made with 100 g *(4 oz)* flour etc (see page 351)
15 ml *(1 level tbsp)* cornflour
312-g *(11-oz)* can crushed pineapple
1 large egg, separated
knob of butter
60 ml *(4 level tbsps)* sugar

Roll out the pastry and use it to line an 18-cm *(7-in)* fluted flan tin placed on a baking sheet. Press the pastry well into the 'flutes'. Bake 'blind' at 200°C *(400°F)* mark 6 for about 15 minutes then remove the baking beans, and return it to the oven for 5 minutes. Meanwhile blend the cornflour with 30 ml *(2 tbsps)* water and stir in the pineapple. Bring to the boil, stirring. Beat in the egg yolk and butter. Turn this into the flan case. Whisk the egg white until stiff, add half the sugar and whisk again. Fold in the remaining sugar and spoon the meringue over the pineapple filling, making sure the meringue meets the pastry. Return the pie to the oven, reduced to 150°C *(300°F)* mark 2, for about 20 minutes. Serve warm or cold. *Serves 2.*

Cheese crumb cocottes

small knob of butter
25 g *(1 oz)* Leicester cheese
60 ml *(4 tbsps)* fresh breadcrumbs, toasted
2 eggs
salt and pepper

Melt the butter and brush the insides of 2 small 150-ml *(¼-pt)* soufflé dishes. Combine the cheese and breadcrumbs. Divide half of the mixture between dishes. Press it lightly round the sides and base of each dish. Break an egg into each. Season well with salt and pepper and sprinkle the remaining crumb mixture on top. Place the dishes on a baking sheet and bake in the oven at 180°C *(350°F)* mark 4 for 8–10 minutes. Serve at once with hot toast. *Serves 2.*

Crumpet pizzas

15 g *(½ oz)* butter
1 onion, skinned and chopped
3 tomatoes, skinned and chopped
5–10 ml *(1–2 level tsps)* mixed dried herbs
4 crumpets
75 g *(3 oz)* Cheddar cheese, diced
few anchovy fillets

Melt the butter and fry the onion and tomato until soft. Add the herbs. Toast the crumpets on one side. Turn them over and cover with the tomato mixture. Top with cheese and anchovy fillets. Place under the grill until golden brown and bubbling. *Serves 2.*

Cooking for large numbers

Entertaining a lot of people should be great fun and can be if you are relaxed and well organized.

So that you don't find yourself saying 'I'll never give another party' you must aim for the greatest effect from the least effort. The first thing to do is to plan menu and preparations very carefully. Choose food that can be prepared well in advance so that all you have to do is add a final garnish or dressing at the last minute. Check that you have the necessary equipment, serving dishes, and utensils and packaging material for freezing.

Plan for smooth service of food so that you don't have to spend too long in the kitchen. Trolleys are very useful for transporting each course and removing used china, glasses, cutlery and dishes.

Here are four scaled menus suitable for various occasions, with some suggestions for storing and freezing (if you are cooking in advance) and for service.

Menu 1 – Buffet supper

Cream of Watercress Soup
Beef and Wine Casserole
Asparagus or French Beans, New Potatoes
Apricot Trifle

Soup: To freeze – process according to quantity. We advise packing in batches sufficient for 10 servings, allowing 6 hours to thaw. The quantity for 50 can be frozen in a 10-litre *(2-gallon)* bucket, but takes 24 hours to thaw. For serving, paper cups are ideal; garnish each with a small sprig of watercress.

Beef and Wine Casserole: For freezing, undercook by ½ hour, and pack in batches for 10 servings, allowing 12 hours at room temperature to thaw. Heating and serving for 10, use a 3–4-litre, *(6–7-pt)* casserole; for 20, two 2.3-l *(4-pt)* casseroles; for 50, two 4-l *(7-pt)* and a 2.3-l *(4-pt)* casserole. Serve sprinkled with chopped parsley.

Vegetables: Canned new potatoes may be used; a 538-g *(19-oz)* can gives 350 g *(12 oz)* drained weight, enough for 4 servings, so multiply as required; heat just before the meal. Rice may replace potatoes if oven space permits. For 10, allow 700 g *(1½ lb)*; for 20, 1.5 kg *(3 lb)*; for 50, 3.6 kg *(8 lb)*. Cook the day before and place in lightly greased baking dishes. Dot with butter and cover with foil; re-heat at 180°C *(350°F)* mark 4 for 30–40 minutes.

Asparagus (or French beans): Follow directions on pack or can.

Apricot Trifle: Serve in 150 ml *(¼ pt)* tumblers, which look attractive and save washing up large serving dishes. Alternatively, use shallow 2.3-l *(4-pt)* dishes; each will give 10 servings. Trifle does not freeze well.

QUANTITIES:	For 10	For 20	For 50
CREAM OF WATERCRESS SOUP			
butter	40 g *(1½ oz)*	100 g *(4 oz)*	225 g *(8 oz)*
onion, skinned and chopped	100 g *(4 oz)*	175 g *(6 oz)*	450 g *(1 lb)*
watercress	1 bunch	2 bunches	5 bunches
stock (well flavoured)	1.1 l *(2 pt)*	2.5 l *(4 pt)*	5.7 l *(10 pt)*
64-g *(2¼-oz)* pkt instant potato	1 pkt	2 pkts	4 pkts
milk	568 ml *(1 pt)*	1.1 litre *(2 pt)*	3 l *(5 pt)*
soured cream	60 ml *(4 tbsps)*	142 ml *(¼ pt)*	284 ml *(½ pt)*

Melt the butter and sauté the onion until transparent, add watercress and cook for 5 minutes. Add stock and simmer for 15 minutes; stir in the instant potato. Place in an electric blender a little at a time and blend until smooth (alternatively, put through a sieve). Pour into a large container and add milk and soured cream; stir vigorously to blend. Cover and chill well.

White bread (p. 409), Wholemeal bread (p. 410), Bread rolls (p. 410).

QUANTITIES:	For 10	For 20	For 50
BEEF AND WINE CASSEROLE			
streaky bacon, rinded and chopped	350 g *(12 oz)*	700 g *(1½ lb)*	1.7 kg *(3¾ lb)*
garlic, skinned and crushed	2 cloves	4 cloves	8 cloves
chuck steak	2 kg *(4 lb)*	3.6 kg *(8 lb)*	9 kg *(20 lb)*
dripping	75 g *(3 oz)*	175 g *(6 oz)*	425 g *(15 oz)*
flour	50 g *(2 oz)*	100 g *(4 oz)*	225 g *(8 oz)*
beef stock	400 ml *(¾ pt)*	900 ml *(1½ pt)*	2.3 l *(4 pt)*
burgundy	400 ml *(¾ pt)*	750 ml *(1¼ pt)*	1.7 l *(3 pt)*
bayleaves	2	4	10
dried thyme	5 ml *(1 tsp)*	10 ml *(2 tsps)*	25 ml *(5 tsps)*
small onions, skinned	225 g *(8 oz)*	450 g *(1 lb)*	1.1 kg *(2½ lb)*
freshly ground pepper	2.5 ml *(½ tsp)*	5 ml *(1 tsp)*	10 ml *(2 tsps)*
mushrooms	225 g *(8 oz)*	450 g *(1 lb)*	1.1 kg *(2½ lb)*
butter	50 g *(2 oz)*	100 g *(4 oz)*	225 g *(8 oz)*

Dice the bacon and fry until the fat runs. Drain and place it in casserole. Mix in the crushed garlic. Cut the meat into 2.5-cm *(1-in)* cubes. Toss in seasoned flour. Melt the dripping and brown the meat quickly, a small portion at a time. Place in the casserole dishes. Add the remaining flour to the pan drippings and cook for a few minutes. Gradually stir in the stock and wine and stir until boiling. Add bayleaves and thyme. Check seasoning before pouring the sauce over the meat. Cover and cook at 170°C *(325°F)* mark 3 for 2 hours. Sauté the onions and mushrooms in butter; drain and add to the casserole. Continue to cook for a further hour.

	For 10	For 20	For 50
Potatoes (ready prepared new)	1.75 kg *(3½ lb)*	3.2 kg *(7 lb)*	8.2 kg *(18 lb)*
Melted butter	50 g *(2 oz)*	100 g *(4 oz)*	225 g *(8 oz)*
Asparagus (or French Beans) Canned or frozen	allowing 100 g *(4 oz)* per head		

	For 10	For 20	For 50
APRICOT TRIFLE			
Sponge cake: 3 eggs 100 g *(4 oz)* caster sugar 100 g *(4 oz)* plain flour 15 ml *(1 tbsp)* hot water	1	2	5
raspberry jam	60 ml *(4 tbsps)*	120 ml *(8 tbsps)*	300 ml *(½ pt)*
apricot halves	1 822-g can plus 425-g can *(1 29-oz can plus 15-oz can)*	2 822-g cans *(2 29-oz cans)*	7 822-g cans *(7 29-oz cans)*
sherry	120 ml *(8 tbsps)*	240 ml *(16 tbsps)*	400 ml *(¾ pt)*
custard	900 ml *(1½ pt)*	1.7 l *(3 pt)*	4 l *(7 pt)*
double cream	284 ml *(½ pt)*	568 ml *(1 pt)*	1½ l *(2½ pt)*
single cream	142 ml *(¼ pt)*	284 ml *(½ pt)*	750 ml *(1¼ pt)*
dark chocolate, grated	5 g *(¼ oz)*	15 g *(½ oz)*	25 g *(1 oz)*

Split the sponge cakes and sandwich with jam; cut in slices and line shallow dishes or individual glasses. Drain the fruit, and add the sherry to the juice. Pour it over the sponge. Add a layer of fruit. Pour over the custard and chill. Beat the creams together. Pipe the cream on to the trifle, allowing each swirl to mark a portion. Sprinkle with a little grated chocolate.

Rum babas (p. 416).

Menu 2 – Summer fork luncheon

Melon and Grape Cocktail
Chicken Galantine and Variety of Meats
Potato Salad   Green Salad
Lemon Cheese Cake

Melon and Grape Cocktail: The evening before, cut out melon balls and seed the grapes; store separately as grapes cause discoloration. Mix and add the dressing just before serving. The dressing can be made several days beforehand and stored in a bottle; shake before using.

Galantine of Chicken: Freezes very well; cool quickly after cooking, but don't cover with aspic jelly. Wrap well in foil and freeze; allow a full 24 hours to thaw. When almost thawed, glaze and decorate with aspic. Allow to set. Slice thinly and arrange with the variety of meats on platters or wooden trays. Garnish with watercress and tomato wedges. Have a choice of chutneys or relishes as accompaniments.

Salads: Green salads can be washed and stored in covered containers in the refrigerator 1–2 days in advance, though chicory heads should not be prepared until the last minute as they discolour. Dressings and mayonnaise can be made beforehand and stored in screw-top jars in the refrigerator; shake well before using.

Lemon Cheese Cake: Freezes very well; allow 6–8 hours for thawing. Decorate before serving. If a 20.5-cm *(8-in)* spring-release cake tin is not available, use a 1.7-l *(3-pt)* ring mould. When making quantities for 50 we would advise making and freezing 1–2 cheese cakes at a time.

Coffee: Allow 200 ml *(⅓ pt)* per person. If ground coffee is used, and made in advance, it must be strained after infusion, then reheated without boiling. Amounts for 10: 150 g *(5 oz)* ground coffee or 40 g *(1½ oz)* instant, 1.7 l *(3 pt)* water, 568 ml *(1 pt)* milk or 284 ml *(½ pt)* single cream, 225 g *(½ lb)* sugar.

Wine: allow 300–400 ml *(½–¾ pt)* per person.

QUANTITIES:	For 10	For 20	For 50
MELON AND GRAPE COCKTAIL			
honeydew melon	1	2	5
black grapes	450 g *(1 lb)*	900 g *(2 lb)*	2.5 kg *(5 lb)*
oil	90 ml *(6 tbsps)*	180 ml *(12 tbsps)*	400 ml *(15 fl oz)*
lemon juice	45 ml *(3 tbsps)*	90 ml *(6 tbsps)*	200 ml *(7 fl oz)*

Using a parisienne cutter, scoop out melon balls and place them in a bowl. Halve grapes, remove pips, add halves to the melon and chill. Mix oil and lemon juice, season and add chives if you wish. Pour over the fruit, toss lightly and serve immediately.

CHICKEN GALANTINE			
1.8-kg *(4-lb)* oven-ready chicken, boned	1	2	5
pork sausage meat	225 g *(½ lb)*	450 g *(1 lb)*	1.1 kg *(2½ lb)*
lean pork, minced	225 g *(½ lb)*	450 g *(1 lb)*	1.1 kg *(2½ lb)*
onion, skinned and chopped	1	2	5
salt and pepper	pinch	2 pinches	5 pinches
Madeira	60 ml *(4 tbsps)*	120 ml *(8 tbsps)*	300 ml *(½ pt)*
sliced ham	75 g *(3 oz)*	175 g *(6 oz)*	450 g *(1 lb)*
sliced tongue	75 g *(3 oz)*	75 g *(6 oz)*	450 g *(1 lb)*
sliced bacon fat	50 g *(2 oz)*	100 g *(4 oz)*	275 g *(10 oz)*
pistachio nuts, blanched and skinned	12.5 g *(½ oz)*	25 g *(1 oz)*	60 g *(2½ oz)*
stock			
aspic jelly	400 ml *(¾ pt)*	900 ml *(1½ pt)*	2 l *(3¾ pt)*

Spread out the boned chicken. Work together the sausage meat, pork, onion, salt and pepper and moisten with Madeira. Slice the ham, tongue and bacon fat into 0.5-cm *(¼-in)* strips. Spread half the meat mixture over the chicken and alternate lines of ham, tongue, bacon fat and nuts. Cover with the remaining meat mixture. Draw the sides of the chicken together and sew firmly.

QUANTITIES:	For 10	For 20	For 50

Wrap in double muslin, tying the ends to make a neat shape. Immerse in stock and simmer about 2¼ hours. Drain, and weight down until cold. Put on a wire rack. Make up the aspic, and when it is on the point of setting, spoon it over the galantine, coating well. Slice when set.

VARIETY OF MEATS

chopped ham and pork	100 g *(4 oz)*	225 g *(8 oz)*	700 g *(1½ lb)*
salami	100 g *(4 oz)*	225 g *(8 oz)*	700 g *(1½ lb)*
continental sausages	225 g *(8 oz)*	450 g *(1 lb)*	900 g *(2 lb)*

POTATO SALAD

potatoes, cooked	1.7 kg *(3¾ lb)*	3.4 kg *(7½ lb)*	8.5 kg *(19 lb)*
celery stalks	4	8	20
hard-boiled egg, diced	2	4	10
mayonnaise	300 ml *(½ pt)*	600 ml *(1 pt)*	1.3 l *(2¼ pt)*

Dice the potatoes and chop the celery; mix them with the diced eggs. Add the mayonnaise, toss lightly, season well and chill before serving.

GREEN SALAD

lettuce	2	4	10
watercress	1	2	5
chicory heads	2	4	10
mustard and cress	1	2	4
green pepper	1	2	4
French dressing	120 ml *(8 tbsps)*	150 ml *(¼ pt)*	300 ml *(½ pt)*

Prepare the ingredients and store them separately. Arrange on a platter or toss in a bowl. Just before serving add the dressing, or serve it separately.

LEMON CHEESE CAKE

lemon jelly	2 pkts	4 pkts	10 pkts
water	60 ml *(4 tbsps)*	120 ml *(8 tbsps)*	300 ml *(½ pt)*
eggs, separated	2	4	10
milk	300 ml *(½ pt)*	568 ml *(1 pt)*	1.4 l *(2½ pt)*
lemons	2	4	10
lemon juice	90 ml *(6 tbsps)*	180 ml *(12 tbsps)*	400 ml *(¾ pt)*
cottage cheese	550 g *(1¼ lb)*	1.1 kg *(2½ lb)*	2.8 kg *(6¼ lb)*
caster sugar	15 g *(½ oz)*	25 g *(1 oz)*	75 g *(3 oz)*
double cream, whipped	142 ml *(¼ pt)*	284 ml *(½ pt)*	750 ml *(1¼ pt)*
digestive biscuits	100 g *(4 oz)*	225 g *(8 oz)*	550 g *(1¼ lb)*
caster sugar for base	50 g *(2 oz)*	100 g *(4 oz)*	275 g *(10 oz)*
butter, melted	50 g *(2 oz)*	100 g *(4 oz)*	275 g *(10 oz)*
cherries and mint to decorate			

Dissolve the jelly in the water in a small pan over low heat. Beat together the egg yolks and milk; pour them on to the jelly, stirring; return the mixture to the pan and heat for a few minutes, without boiling. Take it off the heat, add the lemon rind and juice. Cool until beginning to set. Stir in the sieved cottage cheese (or blend the jelly mixture and unsieved cheese in an electric blender). Whisk the egg whites stiffly, add the sugar and beat well. Fold it into the jelly mixture, followed by the cream. Turn the mixture into 20.5-cm *(8-in)* spring-release cake tins. Crush the biscuits and stir in the sugar and butter. Use this to cover the cheese mixture, pressing lightly; chill. Turn out carefully and decorate.

Menu 3 – Buffet supper

Haddock Mousse
Chicken and Cranberry Curry
Rice
Variety Salads
Choice of Flan Desserts

Haddock Mousse: This can be frozen very successfully. Freeze in the soufflé dish; remove and wrap when solid. Return to the original dish to thaw. Allow 12–15 hours thawing time in a cool place, preferably the refrigerator.

To serve: for 10 guests make up a little more aspic and leave until the consistency of egg white. Decorate with sliced hard-boiled eggs and a little chopped parsley. Spoon over the aspic. For 20–50 guests we suggest serving the mousse as a dip. Place it in small earthenware dishes round the room and provide crackers, crisps and vegetable dunks to accompany.

Chicken and Cranberry Curry: When freezing omit the re-heating after adding the chicken. Cool and pack in quantities for 10. Allow 12 hours at room temperature for thawing. Re-heat in a large pan on top of the stove over a gentle heat. The quantity for 50 will take approximately ¾–1 hour. Alternatively if rice is not being re-heated in the oven, the curry can be put in there at 180°C *(350°F)* mark 4.

Rice: Cook the previous day in boiling salted water for 11 minutes. Drain and rinse thoroughly. Place in a lightly greased baking dish, dot with butter and cover with foil. Re-heat at 180°C *(350°F)* mark 4 for 30–40 minutes.

Flan Desserts: Two recipes are given, each of which provides sufficient for 10.

QUANTITIES:	For 10	For 20	For 50
HADDOCK MOUSSE			
milk	300 ml *(½ pt)*	568 ml *(1 pt)*	1.1 l *(2 pt)*
small carrot	1	2	4
small onion	1	2	4
bayleaf	1	2	4
parsley stalks	3	6	12
peppercorns	6	12	24
smoked haddock	225 g *(8 oz)*	450 g *(1 lb)*	900 g *(2 lb)*
aspic jelly	30 ml *(2 tbsps)*	45 ml *(3 tbsps)*	90 ml *(6 tbsps)*
butter	40 g *(1½ oz)*	75 g *(3 oz)*	175 g *(6 oz)*
flour	25 g *(1 oz)*	50 g *(2 oz)*	100 g *(4 oz)*
eggs, hardboiled	2	4	8
chopped parsley	15 ml *(1 tbsp)*	30 ml *(2 tbsps)*	90 ml *(6 tbsps)*
lemon, rind and juice	1	2	4
double cream	142 ml *(¼ pt)*	284 ml *(½ pt)*	568 ml *(1 pt)*
garnish: hard boiled egg	1	2	4

Pour the milk into a pan and add the peeled carrot, peeled onion, bayleaf, parsley stalks and peppercorns. Bring to the boil, remove from the heat. Infuse for 10 minutes, strain. Poach the fish in water for 15 minutes then drain and flake it with a fork. Make up the aspic jelly by pouring 300 ml *(½ pt)* boiling water on to the crystals, stir to dissolve, then leave in a cool place. Melt the butter, add the flour and cook for 1–2 minutes. Gradually add the strained milk and cook, stirring, until thick and smooth. When the aspic is the consistency of egg white, fold it into the sauce. Shell the eggs and chop these with the parsley. Add to the flaked fish with the grated lemon rind and juice. Whip the cream until fairly stiff and fold into the sauce, then fold into the fish mixture. Pour into a soufflé dish and leave to set. Garnish with slices of hard-boiled egg.

QUANTITIES:	For 10	For 20	For 50
CHICKEN AND CRANBERRY CURRY			
1.6-kg *(3½-lb)* oven-ready chicken	2	4	10
oil to brush			
salt and pepper	pinch	large pinch	2 large pinches
butter	50 g *(2 oz)*	100 g *(4 oz)*	275 g *(10 oz)*
onions, skinned and chopped	2	4	10
garlic cloves, skinned and crushed	2	4	10
flour	40 g *(1½ oz)*	75 g *(3 oz)*	175 g *(6 oz)*
curry powder	60 ml *(4 tbsps)*	105 ml *(7 tbsps)*	75 g *(3 oz)*
tomato paste	60 ml *(4 tbsps)*	120 ml *(8 tbsps)*	140-g and 70-g cans *(5-oz and 2½-oz cans)*
lemon juice	60 ml *(4 tbsps)*	150 ml *(¼ pt)*	300 ml *(½ pt)*
454-g *(16 oz)* cans cranberry sauce	2	4	8
stock	900 ml *(1½ pt)*	1.7 l *(3 pt)*	3.4 l *(6 pt)*
cloves	6	10	30
bayleaf	3	6	15

Brush the chickens with oil and sprinkle with salt and freshly ground pepper. Bake at 200°C *(400°F)* mark 6 allowing 20 minutes per 450 g *(lb)* plus 20 minutes. When cold, strip the flesh from the bones and cut it into thick chunks. Heat the butter in a large pan and sauté the onions until clear. Add the crushed garlic. Remove the pan from the heat and stir in the flour, curry powder, tomato paste, lemon juice and cranberry sauce. Stir well. Gradually add the stock, stirring continuously. Return the pan to the heat, bring to the boil stirring. Add bayleaves and cloves. Cover and simmer for 30 minutes stirring from time to time. Add the prepared chicken and leave over a gentle heat to heat through thoroughly.

RICE			
rice, uncooked	700 g *(1½ lb)*	1.5 kg *(3¼ lb)*	3.6 kg *(8 lb)*
WINTER SALAD			
red eating apples	350 g *(12 oz)*	700 g *(1½ lb)*	2.2 kg *(4¾ lb)*
green apples	350 g *(12 oz)*	700 g *(1½ lb)*	2.2 kg *(4¾ lb)*
lemon juice	2 lemons	4 lemons	6 lemons
French dressing	300 ml *(½ pt)*	400 ml *(¾ pt)*	1.1 l *(2 pt)*
heads of celery	1	2	5
walnut halves, chopped	150 g *(5 oz)*	275 g *(10 oz)*	700 g *(1½ lb)*
watercress to garnish			

Core the apples and dice them without peeling. Toss them in lemon juice. Pour over French dressing. Chop the celery and mix with the walnuts. At the last minute toss all together with the apples and place in serving bowls. Garnish with watercress.

TOMATO AND CUCUMBER SALAD			
tomatoes	900 g *(2 lb)*	1.8 kg *(4 lb)*	2.6 kg *(6 lb)*
cucumber	1	2	4
French dressing	300 ml *(½ pt)*	400 ml *(¾ pt)*	1.1 l *(2 pt)*
chopped chives			

Slice the tomatoes and cucumber thinly and arrange on a platter. Sprinkle with dressing and top with snipped chives.

QUANTITIES:	For 10	For 20	For 50
FLAN DESSERTS			
shortcrust pastry (flour measure)	350 g *(12 oz)*	700 g *(24 oz)*	1.7 kg *(3 lb 12 oz)*
tins: fluted flan rings	2 × 20.5-cm *(8-in)*	4 × 20.5-cm *(8-in)*	5 × 25.5-cm *(10-in)* and 2 × 23-cm *(9-in)*
Filling 1 (Using canned fruit)			
cans of fruit	2 × 425-g *(15-oz)*	4 × 425-g *(15-oz)*	10 × 425-g *(15-oz)*
cornflour	15 ml *(1 tbsp)*	30 ml *(2 tbsps)*	90 ml *(6 tbsps)*
fruit juice	300 ml *(½ pt)*	600 ml *(1 pt)*	1.4 l *(2½ pt)*

Make the pastry up in the usual way and use to line flan rings, placed on baking sheets. Bake blind at 200°C *(400°F)* mark 6 for 20 minutes. Allow to cool. Arrange the drained fruit in the flan cases. Make a glaze by blending the cornflour with a little of the fruit juice in a basin, boil the rest and pour on to the blended cornflour. Return the mixture to the pan and stir until it is cleared and thickened. Use to coat the fruit evenly.

Filling 2 (Using fresh fruit)			
Fresh fruit (eg raspberries or strawberries	450 g *(1 lb)*	900 g *(2 lb)*	2.5 g *(5½ lb)*
Raspberry jelly	½ pkt jelly	1 pkt jelly	2 pkt jelly

Wash the fruit if necessary, drain and arrange in the flan cases. Make up jelly and allow to half set. Pour over fruit when it begins to thicken.

Menu 4 – Informal luncheon

Vegetable soup
Variety Pizza and Quiches
Pineapple and Pepper Salad
French Bread
Caramel Fruit Salad

Vegetable Soup: This can be made on the day of the party. Serve piping hot with croûtons which can be made a few days in advance and store in an air-tight container.

Pizza: These can be frozen ready-cooked. Omit the cheese in the initial cooking and when cool cover the top with a disc of waxed or greaseproof paper. Wrap in foil to freeze. Allow 3 hours to thaw with wrapping removed. Top with cheese and heat through at 180°C *(350°F)* mark 4 for 20 minutes. Pizza should be served warm rather than hot.

Quiches: These freeze well. Cook in the normal way. Cool and freeze. Allow to thaw for 4–5 hours then heat through at 180°C *(350°F)* mark 4 for 30 minutes. Alternatively make these the day before and re-heat. Serve warm.

Caramel Fruit Salad: Freeze in quantities for 10. Allow to thaw for about 5 hours. Or make 1–2 days in advance. Serve chilled.

VEGETABLE SOUP			
butter	50 g *(2 oz)*	100 g *(4 oz)*	225 g *(8 oz)*
frozen mixed vegetables, thawed	900 g *(2 lb)*	1.8 kg *(4 lb)*	3.6 kg *(8 lb)*
onions, skinned and chopped	2	4	10
white stock	600 ml *(1 pt)*	1.1 l *(2 pt)*	2.8 l *(5 pt)*
butter	50 g *(2 oz)*	100 g *(4 oz)*	275 g *(10 oz)*
flour	50 g *(2 oz)*	100 g *(4 oz)*	275 g *(10 oz)*
milk	1.1 l *(2 pt)*	2.3 l *(4 pt)*	5 l *(9 pt)*
salt and pepper			

QUANTITIES:	For 10	For 20	For 50

Melt 50 g *(2 oz)* butter in a saucepan, add the mixed vegetables and onions and sauté gently for 5 minutes without browning. Add stock (can be made from a chicken stock cube) and simmer with the lid on the pan for 10–15 minutes, until the vegetables are almost tender. Meanwhile make a white sauce using butter, flour and milk, in the usual way. Pour the cooked vegetables and sauce into the blender goblet – do this in several parts. Blend until creamy. Return to pan to reheat. Adjust seasoning. Serve really hot with a garnish of chopped parsley.

PIZZA

Basic dough

	For 10	For 20	For 50
strong plain flour	350 g *(12 oz)*	700 g *(1½ lb)*	
salt	7.5 ml *(1½ tsps)*	12.5 ml *(2½ tsps)*	make 5
lard	5 g *(¼ oz)*	15 g *(½ oz)*	amounts
fresh yeast	15 g *(½ oz)*	25 g *(1 oz)*	as for 10
water	200 ml *(7 fl oz)*	400 ml *(16 fl oz)*	
tins: sandwich tins	2 × 20.5-cm *(2 × 8-in)*	4 × 20.5-cm *(4 × 8-in)*	10 × 20.5-cm *(10 × 8-in)*

Mix together the flour and salt. Rub in the lard. Blend the yeast and water and pour into the flour. Hand mix and beat until dough leaves the bowl clean. Knead on a floured board until smooth and elastic. Put the dough in an oiled plastic bag, leave in a warm place to double in size. Turn the dough on to a floured surface and roll to a long strip. Brush with oil and roll up like a Swiss roll. Repeat 3 times. Grease the tins. Roll the dough and fit it into the tins.

Filling 1 – Cheese and Tomato	For 10	For 20	For 50
margarine	50 g *(2 oz)*	100 g *(4 oz)*	275 g *(10 oz)*
onions, skinned and sliced	2 medium	4 medium	10 medium
mushrooms, sliced	225 g *(8 oz)*	450 g *(1 lb)*	1.1 kg *(2½ lb)*
cooked ham, chopped	100 g *(4 oz)*	225 g *(8 oz)*	550 g *(1¼ lb)*
396-g *(14-oz)* cans tomatoes	1	2	5
dried tarragon	2.5 ml *(½ tsp)*	5 ml *(1 tsp)*	12.5 ml *(2½ tsp)*
Cheddar cheese, grated	50 g *(2 oz)*	100 g *(4 oz)*	275 g *(10 oz)*

Melt the margarine and fry the sliced onions until soft. Remove and place them on the pizza dough. Sauté the mushrooms in the rest of the butter, drain well and mix with the chopped ham. Arrange the mushrooms and ham mixture on top of the onions, with the tomatoes, and sprinkle tarragon over the top. Sprinkle with cheese and bake at 230°C *(450°F)* mark 8 for 25 minutes. Reduce the oven temperature to 180°C *(350°F)* mark 4 for a further 25–30 minutes.

Filling 2 – Brisling	For 10	For 20	For 50
onions, skinned and sliced	1 medium	2 medium	5 medium
butter	25 g *(1 oz)*	50 g *(2 oz)*	150 g *(5 oz)*
396-g *(14-oz)* cans tomatoes, drained	1	2	5
99-g *(3¾-oz)* cans brisling in tomato sauce	2	4	10
stuffed olives, halved	16	32	90
Bel Paese cheese, sliced	175 g *(6 oz)*	350 g *(12 oz)*	850 g *(30 oz)*

Sauté the onions in the melted butter until soft. Divide them between the pizza dough, add the drained tomatoes, arrange fish and olives on each and finally top with the sliced cheese. Bake at 230°C *(450°F)* mark 8 for 15–20 minutes. Reduce the temperature to 200°C *(400°F)* mark 6, cover lightly with foil and cook for 30 minutes.

QUANTITIES:	For 10	For 20	For 50
Filling 3 – Haddock			
smoked haddock	450 g *(1 lb)*	900 g *(2 lb)*	2.3 kg *(5 lb)*
peppercorns	3–6	12	25–30
bayleaves	1	2	5
onions, skinned	3 large	6 large	15 large
butter	25 g *(1 oz)*	50 g *(2 oz)*	150 g *(5 oz)*
198-g *(7-oz)* cans of tomatoes	1	2	5
cheese, grated	75 g *(3 oz)*	175 g *(6 oz)*	425 g *(15 oz)*

Poach the smoked haddock with the peppercorns and bayleaf in a little water. Drain, skin and flake the fish. Sauté the peeled and chopped onions in the butter. Divide them between the pizza dough. Purée the canned tomatoes and spoon the purée over the fish filling. Sprinkle with the grated cheese. Bake at 230°C *(450°F)* mark 8 for 15 minutes. Reduce the temperature to 200°C *(400°F)* mark 6, cover lightly with foil and cook for a further 30 minutes.

QUICHES

shortcrust pastry	350 g *(12 oz)*	700 g *(24 oz)*	1.7 kg *(3¾ lb)*
fluted flan rings	2 × 20.5-cm *(2 × 8-in)*	4 × 20.5-cm *(4 × 8-in)*	5 × 25.5-cm *(5 × 10-in)* 2 × 23-cm *(2 × 9-in)*
Filling 1 – Onion			
butter	50 g *(2 oz)*	100 g *(4 oz)*	275 g *(10 oz)*
onions	900 g *(2 lb)*	1.8 kg *(4 lb)*	4.5 kg *(10 lb)*
eggs	4	8	20
milk	568 ml *(1 pt)*	1.1 l *(2 pt)*	2.8 l *(5 pt)*
salt and pepper			
60-g *(2-oz)* can anchovies, drained	2	4	10
black olives, stoned (to garnish)			

Make up the pastry in the usual way and use to line the flan rings, placed on baking sheets. Bake blind at 200°C *(400°F)* mark 6 for about 20 minutes. Melt the butter in a pan and fry the onions until soft. Divide the onions between the flans, and beat together the eggs, milk, salt and pepper and pour over the onions. Arrange anchovies on top in a criss-cross pattern. Place a black olive on each space. Bake at 180°C *(350°F)* mark 4 for 20–30 minutes.

Filling 2 – Cheese and Salmon			
eggs	4	8	20
milk	568 ml *(1 pt)*	1.1 l *(2 pt)*	2.8 l *(5 pt)*
salt and pepper	–	–	–
onions, skinned and chopped	1 large	2 large	5 large
Cheddar cheese, grated	225 g *(8 oz)*	450 g *(1 lb)*	1.1 kg *(2½ lb)*
198-g *(7-oz)* cans of salmon	2	4	10

Line the flan rings and bake as above. Whisk together the eggs, milk, salt and pepper. Then add the onion and cheese and mix well. Divide the salmon between the pastry cases and spoon the cheese custard over. Bake in the oven at 180°C *(350°F)* mark 4 for 20–30 minutes.

QUANTITIES:	For 10	For 20	For 50
Filling 3 – Lorraine			
green back bacon	225 g *(8 oz)*	450 g *(1 lb)*	1.1 kg *(2½ lb)*
onions, skinned and chopped	1 large	2 large	5 large
butter	15 g *(½ oz)*	25 g *(1 oz)*	75 g *(3 oz)*
Cheddar cheese, grated	75 g *(3 oz)*	175 g *(6 oz)*	450 g *(1 lb)*
milk	568 ml *(1 pt)*	1.1 l *(2 pt)*	2.8 l *(5 pt)*
eggs	4	8	20
salt and pepper	–	–	–
parsley, chopped	15 ml *(1 tbsp)*	30 ml *(2 tbsps)*	75 ml *(5 tbsps)*

Line the flan rings and bake as above. Chop the bacon finely and fry with the onions in the butter. Drain well and divide between the flan rings. Add the cheese to the milk and beaten egg mixture. Season well. Add the chopped parsley and spoon the mixture into the flans. Bake in the oven at 180°C *(350°F)* mark 4 for 20–30 minutes.

PINEAPPLE AND PEPPER SALAD

	For 10	For 20	For 50
850-g *(1-lb 14-oz)* can pineapple pieces	1	2	5
green pepper, blanched, seeded and sliced	1 medium	2 medium	5 medium
cucumber, finely diced	¼	½	1¼
sultanas	50 g *(2 oz)*	100 g *(4 oz)*	275 g *(10 oz)*
lettuce, chopped	1	2	5
French dressing	60 ml *(4 tbsps)*	120 ml *(8 tbsps)*	300 ml *(½ pt)*

Drain the pineapple, reserving the juice. Mix the pineapple pieces with the pepper, cucumber, sultanas and lettuce. Combine the French dressing and 30 ml, 60 ml or 150 ml *(2 tbsps, 4 tbsps or 10 tbsps)* pineapple juice. Pour over the salad and toss well.

French Dressing To make 400 ml *(¾ pt)* shake together in screw-topped jar: 2.5 ml *(½ tsp)* salt, 5 ml *(1 tsp)* dry mustard, 2.5 ml *(½ tsp)* freshly ground pepper, 2.5 ml *(½ tsp)* sugar, 150 ml *(¼ pt)* vinegar and 300 ml *(½ pt)* oil.

CARAMEL FRUIT SALAD

	For 10	For 20	For 50
granulated sugar	225 g *(8 oz)*	450 g *(1 lb)*	900 g *(2 lb)*
water	600 ml *(1 pt)*	1.1 l *(2 pt)*	2.3 l *(4 pt)*
vanilla essence			
pears, peeled, cored and quartered	900 g *(2 lb)*	1.8 kg *(4 lb)*	4.5 kg *(10 lb)*
oranges	1	2	5
grapefruit	2	4	10
caramel: sugar	350 g *(12 oz)*	700 g *(1½ lb)*	1.7 kg *(3¾ lb)*
water	180 ml *(12 tbsps)*	400 ml *(¾ pt)*	900 ml *(1½ pt)*

Prepare the syrup by dissolving the sugar in the water and adding a little vanilla essence. Bring to the boil and add the prepared pears, cover, reduce heat and simmer for 5 minutes. Remove from the heat and leave to cool. Remove the rind from the oranges and slice into very fine strips. Simmer in water until tender, drain and rinse. Peel the grapefruit, removing all the pith, and slice then halve. Do the same to the oranges. Place the fruit in a large bowl and add the pears and syrup. To make the caramel, dissolve the sugar in the water and continue to heat over a gentle heat until a deep brown in colour. Pour into a greased tin and leave to set. When set crush and sprinkle over the fruit with the prepared orange rind.

Menus

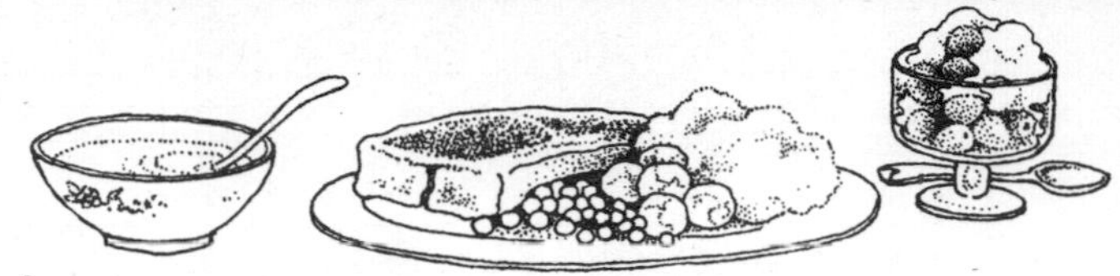

Some sample menus on pages 556–8 will help you plan your family's meals. They can be altered quite easily to suit circumstances – possibly you eat a cooked breakfast at the weekend only, or dinner in the middle of the day and high tea with cake may be your family's usual pattern. Quite often, if the rest of the household is out, you will find yourself eating up leftovers or cheese and biscuits, or boiling an egg.

So much is a matter of choice, but we hope these suggestions will help. The recipes are all in this book.

Special menus
Below are suggestions for lunches and dinners that you may like to use for a family celebration or for entertaining, and for weekend entertaining there are some menus that can be largely prepared in advance.

Two special menus for spring

Luncheon

Cream of Asparagus Soup

*Haddock à la Bistro
Jacket Potatoes
Spinach

*Orange Chiffon Flan

Dinner

*Golden Gate Salad

*Veal à la Crème
Courgettes
Matchstick Potatoes

*Lemon Fluff

Two special menus for summer

Luncheon

*Cream of Cucumber Soup

*Salmon Hollandaise
Green Salad
New Potatoes

*Fresh Raspberry Plate Tart with Cream

Dinner

Melon

*Canard Montmorency
*Pommes de Terre Châteaux
Broad Beans

*Ginger Meringue Creams

Two special menus for autumn

Luncheon

*Clear Tomato Soup

*Oriental Pork Chops
*Onion-topped Potatoes
Green Beans

*Grape Bavaroise

Dinner

Fish Cocktail

*Lamb Cutlets Sautés
Peas Carrots
*Potatoes in Cream

Chocolate Peppermint Crisp Flan

*Starred recipes are included in this chapter

Two special menus for winter

Luncheon	Dinner
*Grapefruit Cups	Globe Artichokes
*Beef and Mushroom Casserole Baked Potatoes Brussels Sprouts	*Chicken and Walnuts Boiled Rice *Bacon-topped Tomatoes
*Mince Pies with Brandy Butter	*Pineapple Sorbet

Menus for a weekend

	SATURDAY	SUNDAY
Breakfast/ Brunch	Muesli* Grilled Sausage, Bacon and Eggs	Melon or Prune Medley* Egg Croustades* Kidney Savouries*
Lunch	Chilled Tomato Juice Glazed Bacon* Spiced Peaches Jacket Potatoes Chicory Salad Lemon Delight*	Tomato Bouillon* Rolled Stuffed Shoulder of Lamb* Roast Potatoes Sprouts Apricot Surprise
Dinner	Kipper Pâté* with Melba Toast Roast Duckling with Grapefruit Sauce* Gâteau Amandine*	Chilled Fruit Cup Lemon Chicken Double Crust Pie* Noodles Rusticana* Tomato Cole Slaw* Pineapple and Grape Salad*

*Starred recipes are included in this chapter.

Spring Menus

	SUNDAY	MONDAY	TUESDAY	WEDNESDAY	THURSDAY	FRIDAY	SATURDAY
Breakfast	Tomato Juice Omelette	Fruit Juice Grilled Bacon and Beans	Fresh Grapefruit Grilled Sausage and Tomato	Poached Egg on Toast	Orange Juice Fried Bacon and Egg	Stewed Prunes Scrambled Egg	Fruit Juice Grilled Kipper Fillets
Lunch or Dinner	Roast Stuffed Chicken and Chipolatas Roast Potatoes Broccoli Rhubarb Betty and Custard	Spanish Omelette Sauté Potatoes Green Salad Jam Roly-Poly and Vanilla Sauce	Grilled Gammon Spinach Potato Croquettes Bread and Butter Pudding	Stuffed Breast of Lamb Roast Potatoes Glazed Carrots Syrup Tart and Custard	Goulash New Potatoes Spring Greens Banana Fritters	Russian Fish Pie Creamed Potatoes Italian-Style Peas Stewed Pears and Chocolate Sauce	Italian Veal Casserole Anna Potatoes Broad Beans Lemon Meringue Pie
Supper	Meat Loaf Salad Fruit Jelly	Beefburgers Spaghetti in Tomato Sauce Peas Cheese and Biscuits	Kedgeree Beetroot Salad Cheese and Biscuits	Macaroni Cheese Baked Tomatoes Fruit	Toad in the Hole Sliced Green Beans Swiss Roll	Cheese Soufflé Salad Niçoise Fresh Fruit	Bacon and Egg Pie Endive and Cucumber Salad

Summer Menus

	SUNDAY	MONDAY	TUESDAY	WEDNESDAY	THURSDAY	FRIDAY	SATURDAY
Breakfast	Fresh Grapefruit Cold Boiled Bacon and Tomatoes	Cereal Scrambled Eggs and Mushrooms	Orange Juice Grilled Bacon	Stewed Apples Kidneys on Toast	Orange Juice Grilled Tomatoes and Sausages	Grapefruit (half) Poached Eggs on Toast	Tomato Juice Grilled Bacon and Fried Eggs
Lunch or Dinner	Roast Leg of Lamb and Mint Sauce New Potatoes Runner Beans Baked Alaska	Swiss Steak New Potatoes Buttered Peas Peach Condé	Soused Herrings Potato Salad Mixed Salad Queen of Puddings	Grilled Lamb Chops, Creamed Potatoes Broad Beans Black-currant Plate Pie and Cream	Chicken Casserole Anna Potatoes Spinach Honeycomb Mould	Fried Plaice Fillets Shrimp Sauce Rissolé Potatoes Garden Peas Summer Pudding	Braised Sweetbreads Jacket Potatoes Mixed Vegetables Apricot Charlotte and Custard

Supper	Quiche Lorraine Tomato and Cucumber Salad Fresh Fruit	Cauliflower au Gratin French Bread Melon Wedges	Liver, Bacon and Onion, Potato Croquettes Fresh Fruit	Stuffed Marrow Spicy Tomato Sauce Cheese and Biscuits	Soup Scotch Eggs Salad	Risotto Waldorf Salad Biscuits and Cheese	Ham Omelettes Grilled Tomatoes Tossed Green Salad Fruit

Autumn Menus

	SUNDAY	MONDAY	TUESDAY	WEDNESDAY	THURSDAY	FRIDAY	SATURDAY
Breakfast	Cereal with Fruit Boiled Eggs	Grapefruit Juice Grilled Bacon and Tomatoes	Tomato Juice Grilled Kippers	Cereal Poached Eggs on Toast	Stewed Fruit Fish Cakes	Orange Juice Bacon and Eggs	Cereal Scrambled Egg on Toast
Lunch or Dinner	Roast Sirloin Roast Potatoes Yorkshire Pudding Cabbage Damson Flan Ice Cream	Moussaka Waldorf Salad Steamed Chocolate Sponge Vanilla Sauce	Mixed Grill Cauliflower and Cheese Sauce Jacket Potatoes Pineapple Upside-down Pudding	Irish Stew Cabbage Mincemeat Tart Custard	Boiled Bacon Parsley Sauce Potatoes Carrots Lemon Meringue Rice Pudding	Stuffed Cod Steaks Mushroom Sauce Potato Croquettes Peas Ginger Sponge and Vanilla Sauce	Chicken and Cranberry Curry Rice Green Beans Apple Snow
Supper	Canneloni with Cheese Sauce Fresh Fruit	Curried Eggs and Boiled Rice Tomato and Cucumber salad Fresh Fruit	Fish Pie Cole Slaw Fresh Fruit	Hot Sausage Rolls Mixed Salad Cheese and Biscuits	Scotch Broth Cheese Pudding Fresh Fruit	Ox-Tail Hot-pot Biscuits and Cheese with Celery	Cold Boiled Bacon Salad Fresh Fruit

Winter Menus

	SUNDAY	MONDAY	TUESDAY	WEDNESDAY	THURSDAY	FRIDAY	SATURDAY
Breakfast	Orange Juice Grilled Bacon and Egg	Cereal Scrambled Egg and Tomatoes	Grapefruit Kipper Fillets	Porridge* Mushrooms on Toast	Stewed Fruit Grilled Sausage and Bacon	Cereal Poached Eggs on Toast	Pineapple Juice Grilled Bacon and Sausages
Lunch or Dinner	Roast Loin of Pork Roast Potatoes Cauliflower Apricot Amber	Cottage Pie Carrots Banana Split	Stuffed Heart Casserole Potatoes Cabbage Syrup Sponge and Custard	Caramelled Gammon Sauté Potatoes Leeks Orange Snow	Braised Beef Jacket Potatoes Brussels Sprouts Baked Ginger Sponge Syrup Sauce	Grilled Herring Mustard Sauce Potatoes, Peas Bakewell Tart and Custard	Lamb Chops Potatoes Fried Cabbage Baked Apples and Custard
Supper	Pizza Winter Salad Fresh Fruit	Vegetable Soup Cold Roast Pork and Chutney Cheese and Biscuits	Fish in Batter Peas Fresh Fruit	Golden Egg Puffs Cole Slaw Fresh Fruit	Ox-Tail Soup Cheese Salad Fresh Fruit	Sausage Bean Feast Celery and Apple Salad Stewed Fruit	Melon Spaghetti Bolognese Cheese and Biscuits

*Starred recipes are included in this chapter

WINTER BREAKFAST

Porridge

This may be made from fine, medium or coarse oatmeal or from rolled oats or 'quick' porridge oats. The consistency and the accompaniments served with it depend on personal taste. If you use coarse or medium oatmeal the porridge is best made the previous evening. Hot or cold milk or cream, brown or white sugar, treacle or golden syrup may be served with any type of porridge – though Scots of course consider that salt is the only permissible flavouring. Water, or a mixture of milk and water, can be used in the cooking.

Using coarse or medium oatmeal To 600 ml *(1 pt)* water, allow 60 ml *(4 level tbsps)* oatmeal and salt to taste. Heat the water and when it is boiling sprinkle in the oatmeal, stirring well with a wooden spoon. Boil for a few minutes, continuing to stir, then allow to simmer until the meal is swollen and quite tender – 20–30 minutes for medium meal and up to 2 hours for coarse. Halfway through the cooking time add the salt.

If a thinner porridge is preferred, add more boiling water. It is easier to cook the porridge over hot water in a double saucepan or in the simmering oven of a solid-fuel cooker.

Using fine oatmeal To 600 ml *(1 pt)* water, allow 60 ml *(4 level tbsps)* meal and salt to taste. Blend the meal to a smooth cream with a little of the water; heat the rest of it and when it is boiling pour on to the blended meal, stirring well. Return the mixture to the pan, bring to the boil and cook for about 5 minutes, stirring all the time. Add the salt.

Using rolled oats To 600 ml *(1 pt)* water, allow about 50 g *(2 oz)* rolled oats and salt to taste. Heat the water and when it is boiling sprinkle in the oats, stirring vigorously with a wooden spoon. Continue to stir and boil for about 5 minutes, then add the salt.

Using special brands of oats
Follow the manufacturer's directions.

SPRING LUNCHEON

Haddock à la bistro

30 ml *(2 tbsps)* olive oil
4 portions fresh haddock fillet, skinned (about 450 g, *1 lb*)
60 ml *(4 tbsps)* dry white wine
30 ml *(2 tbsps)* tomato ketchup
1 clove garlic, skinned and crushed
freshly ground black pepper
1 bayleaf
30 ml *(2 tbsps)* fresh white breadcrumbs
15 ml *(1 tbsp)* chopped parsley

Pour the oil into a shallow ovenproof dish. Arrange the pieces of haddock in the dish and sprinkle with white wine. Sprinkle the ketchup over the fish and add the garlic, black pepper and bayleaf. Finally, cover with the breadcrumbs and chopped parsley and bake in the oven at 180°C *(350°F)* mark 4 for 25–30 minutes. Serve from the dish in which it was cooked.

Orange chiffon flan

200 g *(7 oz)* **flan pastry, ie made with 200 g** *(7 oz)* **flour etc (see page 351)**

For the filling

juice of 2 oranges
lemon juice as required
10 ml *(2 level tsps)* **powdered gelatine**
2 eggs separated
45–75 ml *(3–5 level tbsps)* **caster sugar**
grated rind of 1 orange
60 ml *(4 tbsps)* **double cream**
apricot jam

Roll out the pastry and use it to line a 20.5-cm *(8-in)* plain flan ring, placed on a baking sheet. Bake blind (see page 357) in the oven at 200°C *(400°F)* for 15 minutes, remove the paper and baking beans and return the flan to the oven for a further 5 minutes to dry out. Cool. Make up the filling by measuring the juice from the oranges and making up to 150 ml *(¼ pt)* with lemon juice. Place the liquid in a bowl with the gelatine, the lightly beaten egg yolks and 30 ml *(2 level tbsps)* of the sugar. Put the bowl over a pan of hot water and stir until the mixture is almost at boiling point. Add the orange rind and cool until just before setting point is reached, then whisk the egg whites stiffly and whisk in remaining sugar. Gently beat the cream with a fork until it begins to hold its shape, fold it into the orange mixture and then fold through the egg white mixture until it is evenly distributed. Coat the pastry base of the flan with a thin layer of jam, spoon in the filling and leave it to set.

Serve extra cream separately if you wish.

SPRING DINNER

Golden gate salad

1 lettuce
1 small melon
226-g *(8-oz)* **can crabmeat**
312-g *(11-oz)* **can mandarin oranges**

For the dressing

105 ml *(7 tbsps)* **mayonnaise**
60 ml *(4 tbsps)* **soured cream**
10 ml *(2 tsps)* **chopped parsley**
15 ml *(1 tbsp)* **chopped chives**
6 anchovy fillets, finely chopped
25 ml *(1½ tbsps)* **wine vinegar**
10 ml *(2 tsps)* **lemon juice**
1 clove garlic, skinned and crushed
salt and pepper

Mix all the ingredients for the dressing and chill. Shred the lettuce and arrange on a serving dish. Cut the melon across in 4 thick slices, peel, remove the seeds and place the slices on the lettuce. Drain and flake the crabmeat and mix with the drained oranges. Fill the centres of the melon rings with the crabmeat mixture and just before serving top with a little dressing. Serve the rest of the dressing separately.

Veal à la crème

4 veal escalopes
pepper and salt
15 ml *(1 tbsp)* **lemon juice**
40 g *(1½ oz)* **butter**
100 g *(4 oz)* **button mushrooms**
60 ml *(4 tbsps)* **brandy**
90 ml *(6 tbsps)* **double cream**
parsley to garnish

Flatten the escalopes, season them and sprinkle with some of the lemon juice. Melt 25 g *(1 oz)* of the butter and fry the escalopes in this until they are just brown on both sides. Remove them from the pan and keep warm on a serving dish. Remove the mushroom stalks and chop them. Fry them for 3 minutes in the butter remaining in the pan. Flame 45 ml *(3 tbsps)* of the brandy and when the flames have died, pour it on to the mushroom stalks, adding the cream and the rest of the lemon juice. Stir well to loosen any residue from the pan and cook until the sauce is thick. Season and strain over the escalopes. Slice the mushroom caps and sauté in the rest of the butter; pour 15 ml *(1 tbsp)* flaming brandy over them and use to garnish the escalopes, together with the parsley.

Lemon fluff

3 eggs, separated
125 g *(4½ oz)* caster sugar
juice and grated rind of 2 large lemons
15 ml *(1 level tbsp)* powdered gelatine
45 ml *(3 tbsps)* water
45–60 ml *(3–4 tbsps)* double cream
angelica or grated chocolate for decoration

Whisk the egg yolks and sugar together in a large, deep bowl. Gradually whisk in the lemon juice and continue to whisk until the mixture begins to thicken. Dissolve the gelatine in the water in a bowl over hot water; leave it to cool slightly and then quickly whisk it into the lemon mixture. When it begins to set, fold in the stiffly beaten egg whites and lemon rind. Divide the mixture between 4 sundae glasses and leave to set. Before serving, decorate with swirls of lightly whipped cream and angelica or grated chocolate.

SUMMER LUNCHEON

Cream of cucumber soup

1 cucumber
900 ml *(1½ pt)* chicken stock
5 ml *(1 tsp)* finely chopped shallot or onion
25 g *(1 oz)* butter
30 ml *(2 level tbsps)* flour
salt and pepper
2 egg yolks
60 ml *(4 tbsps)* milk
green colouring
freshly grated cucumber and chopped mint to garnish

Peel the cucumber and cut it into 1-cm *(½-in)* slices. Place the stock, cucumber and shallot in a saucepan and bring to the boil; reduce the heat and simmer for 15–20 minutes, until the cucumber is soft. Either rub the mixture through a fine sieve or purée it in an electric blender. Melt the butter in the pan, stir in the flour and cook over a low heat for a few minutes. Slowly stir in the sieved cucumber and stock, bring to the boil, check the seasoning and simmer for 5 minutes. Cool. Blend the egg yolks and milk together, add a little soup, stir well and pour back into the pan. Re-heat the soup but do not boil it. Colour it a delicate green, garnish and serve.

Salmon hollandaise

butter
700 g *(1½ lb)* middle cut fresh salmon
lemon wedges to garnish
hollandaise sauce (see page 200)

Butter a piece of aluminium foil or thick greaseproof paper thoroughly. Lay the prepared fish in the centre of the paper and join the edges in such a way as to enclose the fish completely. Place it on an ovenproof dish and bake in the oven at 150°C *(300°F)* mark 1–2 for ¾–1 hour; the bone should just show signs of coming through the flesh when the fish is cooked. Unwrap it while warm and carefully remove the skin; leave to cool. When it is cold cut it in half through to the bone, carefully lift on to a serving dish, lift off the bone and cut the lower portion in half. Reassemble and garnish with the lemon wedges. Serve the hollandaise sauce separately.

Fresh raspberry plate tart

175 g *(6 oz)* blended vegetable fat
40 g *(1½ oz)* butter
250 g *(9 oz)* plain flour
a pinch of salt
75 ml *(5 tbsps)* water
450 g *(1 lb)* raspberries
sugar to sweeten
200–300 ml *(⅓–½ pt)* double cream, lightly whipped

Cream the vegetable fat and butter thoroughly and gradually add the sifted flour and salt, beating after each addition. Add the water and mix thoroughly. The mixture will be sticky at first and will be rather difficult to stir. Divide into two and chill until of a rolling consistency. Lightly roll out half the dough on a floured board and line a 20.5-cm *(8-in)* pie plate (preferably metal). Layer in the fruit, sprinkled with sugar. Moisten the pastry edges and cover with the pastry lid, rolled as before. Knock up and flute the edges. Bake in the oven at 200°C *(400°F)* mark 6 for 30–40 minutes. Cool and serve cut in slices and dusted with caster or icing sugar. Serve with cream.

Note If a refrigerator is not available, replace this special pastry by ordinary shortcrust.

SUMMER DINNER

Canard Montmorency

1 duck (about 2.5 kg, *5½ lb*), quartered
5 ml *(1 level tsp)* salt
pepper
25 g *(1 oz)* butter
60 ml *(4 tbsps)* Madeira
396-g *(14-oz)* can stoned black cherries
15 ml *(1 level tbsp)* flour
30 ml *(2 tbsps)* stock made from the duck giblets

Sprinkle the joints with the salt. Melt the butter in a large saucepan and brown the joints on all sides. Remove from the pan and drain off fat; replace the duckling and pour the Madeira and 60 ml *(4 tbsps)* of the cherry juice over. Cover and simmer for 40 minutes, or until tender. Remove the joints from the pan and drain on kitchen paper; keep them warm. Skim the fat from the juice, blend the flour with the stock and stir into the juices in the pan. Bring to the boil, add the cherries and heat through. Adjust the seasoning. Arrange the duckling on a serving dish and coat with the sauce.

Pommes de terre châteaux

700 g *(1½ lb)* even sized new potatoes
40 g *(1½ oz)* butter
2.5 ml *(½ level tsp)* salt

Scrape the potatoes. Heat the butter in a large frying pan and add the prepared potatoes, cover and cook over a low heat for about 15 minutes, shaking occasionally. Turn the potatoes carefully and cook for a further 5–10 minutes, until tender and golden. Sprinkle with salt before serving.

Ginger meringue creams

2 large egg whites
100 g *(4 oz)* caster sugar
142-ml *(¼ pt)* carton double cream
30 ml *(2 tbsps)* finely chopped stem ginger

Line a baking sheet with silicone (non-stick) paper. Whisk the egg whites until stiff, whisk in half the sugar until the mixture is stiff, then fold in the remaining sugar. Spoon the meringue into 4 heaps on the prepared baking sheet, keeping them well apart. Make into flan shapes, with a hollow in the centre of each. Put the cases towards the bottom of the oven set at 130°C *(250°F)* mark ¼ and dry out for 2½–3 hours. Remove from the paper and when cool store in an airtight tin. To finish the sweet, whip the cream lightly and fold in half the chopped ginger; divide the mixture between the meringue shells and top with the remaining chopped ginger.

AUTUMN LUNCHEON

see colour plate between pp. 496 and 497

Clear tomato soup

566-g *(20-oz)* can tomato juice
63-g *(2¼-oz)* can tomato paste
3 whole cloves
1 slice onion
200 ml *(⅓ pt)* chicken stock
5 ml *(1 level tsp)* salt
bayleaf
pinch of ground pepper
pinch of dried mixed herbs
lemon slices to garnish

Place all the ingredients except the lemon slices in a saucepan, bring to the boil and simmer for 5 minutes. Strain, and serve garnished with the lemon slices.

Oriental pork chops

4 loin pork chops
30 ml *(2 tbsps)* soy sauce
15 ml *(1 tbsp)* clear honey
1 small clove garlic, skinned and crushed

Trim off the surplus fat from the chops. Blend together the soy sauce, honey and crushed garlic, pour into a shallow dish, and turn the prepared chops in this marinade. Cover the dish and leave for several hours or overnight in the refrigerator or other cold place.

When you are ready to cook the chops, drain them from the marinade and place them in a shallow casserole. Spoon the marinade over, cover and bake in the oven at 190°C *(375°F)* mark 5 for 40 minutes. Remove the lid and bake for a further 20 minutes.

Onion-topped potatoes

450 g *(1 lb)* potatoes
1 medium sized onion
25 g *(1 oz)* butter
sugar
30–45 ml *(2–3 tbsps)* milk

Peel the potatoes and cook in boiling salted water until tender. Meanwhile slice the onion into 4 rings. Melt half the butter and fry the onion slices gently until tender. Just before serving, sprinkle the rings with a little sugar and turn them once. Drain the cooked potatoes and cream with the remaining butter and milk until light and fluffy. Divide into 4 mounds on the serving dish and top each mound with an onion ring.

Grape bavarois

600-ml *(1-pt)* pkt lemon jelly
15 ml *(1 tbsp)* lemon juice
225 g *(½ lb)* green grapes
150 ml *(¼ pt)* milk
15 ml *(1 level tbsp)* custard powder
10 ml *(2 level tsps)* sugar
142-ml *(5-fl oz)* carton double cream

Divide the jelly tablet into two. Place half in a measure, make up to 300 ml *(½ pt)* with the lemon juice and hot water and stir until dissolved. Leave in a cold place to set to the consistency of unbeaten egg white. Skin and pip the grapes. Fold the grapes into the half-set jelly and spoon them into a 900-ml *(1½-pt)* fancy jelly mould; leave to set. Make a custard, using milk, custard powder and sugar. Leave to cool, stirring occasionally to prevent a skin forming. Melt the remaining half jelly tablet in 150 ml *(¼ pt)* boiling water and leave to cool as above. Whip the cream lightly and fold in the custard. Whisk the jelly and fold it into the cream mixture. Spoon the cream mixture over the set jelly in the mould. Leave to set, then unmould on to a serving dish.

AUTUMN DINNER

Lamb cutlets sautés

75 g *(3 oz)* butter
8 lamb cutlets, trimmed
10 ml *(2 level tsps)* caster sugar

Melt the butter in a large frying pan, add the cutlets and brown them on each side for 2–3 minutes. Sprinkle a little sugar on top of each cutlet, turn and cook for a further 3–4 minutes. Sprinkle the second side with sugar, turn and cook again. Serve with a cutlet frill on the end of each bone.

Potatoes in cream

700 g *(1½ lb)* potatoes
25 g *(1 oz)* butter, melted
1.25 ml *(¼ level tsp)* salt
pinch of pepper
142-ml *(¼-pt)* carton single cream
5 ml *(1 tsp)* chopped parsley

Cook the potatoes in boiling salted water until tender, drain and cool. Dice them and place in a saucepan. Mix the butter, salt, pepper, and cream and pour over the potatoes. Cook slowly without boiling until the cream has thickened and the potatoes are thoroughly warmed through. Sprinkle with chopped parsley.

WINTER LUNCHEON

Grapefruit cups

2 grapefruits
100 g *(¼ lb)* **grapes**
4 maraschino cherries

Cut the grapefruits in half with a sharp knife, making a zig-zag edge, and remove the flesh and core from the skins, leaving the skins unbroken. Peel and pip the grapes and mix with the diced grapefruit flesh. Return the grapefruit and grapes to the cups, chill, and just before serving top each with a cherry.

Beef and mushroom casserole

700 g *(1½ lb)* **chuck steak**
seasoned flour
25–50 g *(1–2 oz)* **dripping**
8 baby onions, skinned
225 g *(½ lb)* **carrots, pared and cut in strips**
225 g *(½ lb)* **turnips, pared and sliced**
100 g *(¼ lb)* **button mushrooms**
30 ml *(2 level tbsps)* **flour**
300 ml *(½ pt)* **stock or water**
salt and pepper

Cut the steak into strips about 7.5 cm *(3 in)* long and dip them into the seasoned flour. Melt the dripping in a pan and brown the meat all over, drain and place in a large casserole. Add the onions to the dripping in the pan, together with the carrots and turnips, and brown them well. Put the vegetables in the casserole with the meat and add the mushrooms. Sprinkle the 30 ml *(2 tbsps)* flour over the dripping in the pan, stir and cook for 2–3 minutes. Stir in the stock or water, bring to the boil, season well and pour over the meat. Cover the casserole and cook in the oven at 170°C *(325°F)* mark 3 for 2–2½ hours. Check the seasoning and if necessary thicken the gravy before serving.

Mince pies

350 g *(12 oz)* **shortcrust or flaky pastry, ie 350 g** *(12 oz)* **flour etc, see pages 351, 354**
350–450 g *(¾–1 lb)* **mincemeat**
milk or egg to glaze

Using shortcrust pastry
Roll out the pastry to about 0.3 cm *(⅛ in)* thick. Cut into about 20 rounds with a 7.5-cm *(3-in)* fluted cutter and 20 smaller rounds with a 5.5-cm *(2¼-in)* fluted cutter. Line 6.5-cm *(2½-in)* patty tins with the larger rounds and fill with mincemeat. Damp the edges of the small rounds and place firmly in position on top of the pies. Make a small slit in the top of each pie and bake in the oven at 220°C *(425°F)* mark 7 for 15–20 minutes, until light golden brown. Cool on a wire rack. Serve warm or cold, dusted with sugar. If preferred, the tops of the pies may be brushed with a little milk before baking.

Using flaky pastry
Roll out the pastry to 0.3 cm *(⅛ in)* thick. Stamp out 16 rounds with a 6.5-cm *(2½-in)* plain cutter. Re-roll the scraps, cut another 16 rounds to use for the bases and place the bases on a damp baking sheet. Put a heaped 5 ml *(1 tsp)* of mincemeat on each, damp the edges of the pastry, cover with the remaining pastry rounds and press the edges lightly together; brush with egg glaze. Bake in the oven at 230°C *(450°F)* mark 8 for about 20 minutes, until well risen and golden brown. Cool on a wire rack.

Serve warm, dusted with icing sugar.

WINTER DINNER

Chicken and walnuts

1.6–1.8-kg *(3½–4-lb)* roasting chicken, jointed, or 6 chicken joints
30 ml *(2 tbsps)* sherry
10 ml *(2 level tsps)* caster sugar
45 ml *(3 tbsps)* oil
225 g *(8 oz)* button mushrooms
170-g *(6-oz)* can water chestnuts
600 ml *(1 pt)* chicken stock
30 ml *(2 level tbsps)* cornflour
100 g *(4 oz)* halved walnuts
25 g *(1 oz)* butter

Place the chicken in a dish, pour the sherry and caster sugar over it and leave it to marinade for 1–2 hours.

Heat the oil in a frying pan and brown the chicken pieces. Slice the mushrooms, drain and dice the chestnuts and put them all in a large casserole. Arrange the chicken pieces on top, pour the chicken juices and chicken stock into the casserole, cover and bake in the oven at 180°C *(350°F)* mark 4 for 2 hours. Drain off the liquor, keep the chicken hot and thicken the liquor with the cornflour. Brown the walnuts in melted butter for 4–5 minutes and drain. Dish up the chicken and vegetables, pour some of the gravy over them (serving the rest separately) and garnish with the browned walnuts.

Bacon-topped tomatoes

450 g *(1 lb)* tomatoes
1 onion, skinned
100 g *(4 oz)* streaky bacon
salt and pepper
10 ml *(2 tsps)* chopped parsley

Skin the tomatoes, cut them into slices and arrange in a shallow ovenproof dish. Chop the onion very finely. Rind and mince the bacon and fry it lightly. Season the tomatoes and sprinkle with the onion and bacon. Bake in the oven at 180°C *(350°F)* mark 4 for 10–15 minutes. Garnish with the chopped parsley before serving.

Pineapple sorbet

369-g *(13-oz)* can pineapple chunks
50 g *(2 oz)* caster sugar
150 g *(5 oz)* corn syrup
grated rind and juice of ½ lemon
400 ml *(¾ pt)* milk
2 egg whites

Chop the drained pineapple very finely and add the caster sugar, corn syrup, lemon rind and juice and the milk. Pour the mixture into 2 polythene or foil dishes and half-freeze to a mush. Turn the mush into a basin and whisk until frothy. Beat the egg whites stiffly and fold them into the pineapple mixture; replace it in the polythene or foil dishes and freeze until firm. Cut into fingers to serve.

WEEKEND MENUS

Swiss apple muesli

60 ml *(4 level tbsps)* rolled oats or medium oatmeal
150 ml *(¼ pt)* fruit juice or water
2 dessert apples
60 ml *(4 tbsps)* cream or top of the milk
15 ml *(1 tbsp)* honey
little brown sugar
50 g *(2 oz)* sultanas or raisins
few chopped nuts

Place the oats and fruit juice or water in a bowl and leave overnight. The next day grate the apples (with their skins on), mix with the rest of the ingredients, except the nuts, put into glasses and sprinkle with the nuts.

Glazed bacon

1.8 kg *(4 lb)* piece of collar or corner gammon bacon
15 ml *(1 tbsp)* clear honey
30 ml *(2 tbsps)* white vinegar
75 g *(3 oz)* demerara sugar

Soak the bacon joint for 2 hours in cold water. Drain. Place it in a large pan and cover with cold water. Bring to the boil and skim. Reduce the heat, cover and simmer gently for 1 hour. Drain the joint, strip off the rind and, using a sharp knife, score in a lattice pattern. Heat the honey and vinegar to combine them, brush over bacon and pat in the demerara sugar well. Place in an ovenproof dish and bake in the oven at 180°C *(350°F)* mark 4 for 20 minutes, basting occasionally. Leave until cold, then wrap in foil and refrigerate. *Serves 8.*

Lemon delight

2 whole eggs
2 egg yolks
50 g *(2 oz)* caster sugar
600-ml *(1-pt)* pkt lemon jelly
juice and grated rind of 1 lemon
150 ml *(¼ pt)* white wine

Whisk together the eggs, egg yolks and sugar in a large bowl over hot water. Whisk until really thick, then remove from the heat and allow to cool. In a small pan dissolve the jelly in 150 ml *(¼ pt)* water. Pour into a measure, add the lemon juice, rind and wine, then make up to 600 ml *(1 pt)* with water. Cool until on the point of setting then whisk the jelly into the cool egg mixture. Turn into a serving dish and chill.

Decorate if you wish with lightly whipped cream and coarsely grated chocolate.

Kipper pâté

350 g *(12 oz)* kipper fillets
90 ml *(6 tbsps)* dry white wine
30 ml *(2 tbsps)* lemon juice
100 g *(4 oz)* butter, softened
black pepper
6 tomato slices
Melba toast

Remove the skin from the kipper fillets. Place in a shallow dish and spoon the wine over. Cover and leave to marinate in a cool place for 4 hours. In a bowl, work the fillets and marinade to a paste with a wooden spoon, or purée them in an electric blender until smooth, adding the lemon juice to make a softer mixture. Beat in the softened butter and season with black pepper. Divide between six 100-ml *(4-fl oz)* ramekin dishes. Smooth over the tops and mark with a fork. Top each with a tomato twist. Serve with Melba toast. *Serves 6.*

Roast duckling with grapefruit sauce

2 1.75-kg *(3½-lb)* ducklings, thawed if frozen
salt
black pepper
30 ml *(2 level tbsps)* plain flour
2 grapefruit
15 ml *(1 level tbsp)* arrowroot
170-ml *(6¼-fl oz)* can frozen concentrated unsweetened grapefruit juice

Joint each duckling into 6. Trim off the excess fat. Wipe and prick the flesh well. Season the joints. Place the joints of duckling on a wire rack in a roasting tin. Cook near the top of the oven at 180°C *(350°F)* mark 4 for 1¼–1½ hours. Baste with the pan juices twice during cooking. 20 minutes before the end of the cooking time, sprinkle with flour and baste again. Remove all peel and pith from the grapefruit and cut the flesh into segments. Make the frozen fruit juice up to 400 ml *(¾ pt)* with water. Blend a little with the arrowroot in a small pan. Add all the juice gradually and bring to the boil, stirring. Transfer the cooked duckling portions to a preheated serving dish. Arrange the fruit segments on top and return the dish to the oven for a few minutes. Drain the fat from the roasting tin, leaving the duckling juices. Add the grapefruit sauce. Heat it through, then strain. Glaze the duckling with some of sauce and serve the rest separately. *Serves 6.*

Prune medley

3 large pears
50 g *(2 oz)* sugar
a sliver of lemon rind
4 large oranges
2 425-g *(15-oz)* cans prunes in syrup
45 ml *(3 tbsps)* lemon juice

Peel and core the pears; slice them thickly. Cover them with 300 ml *(½ pt)* water and the sugar. Add a sliver of lemon rind. Poach them, covered, for about 10 minutes or until transparent. Remove the rind and pith from the oranges and segment the flesh. Discard lemon rind from pears. Lift out pears with a draining spoon and layer with the oranges and drained prunes in a serving dish. Combine the pear syrup with the prune syrup and reduce by boiling uncovered until 300 ml *(½ pt)*. Add the lemon juice. Cool slightly then pour over layered fruit. Chill well before serving. *Serves 6.*

Gâteau amandine

250 g *(9 oz)* pâte sucrée, ie 250 g *(9 oz)* flour, etc (see page 351)
15 ml *(3 level tsps)* powdered gelatine
45 ml *(3 tbsps)* water
568 ml *(1 pt)* milk
100 g *(4 oz)* caster sugar
50 g *(2 oz)* plain flour
20 ml *(4 level tsps)* cornflour
2 large eggs, separated
50 g *(2 oz)* butter
75 g *(3 oz)* ground almonds
icing sugar
apricot jam
25 g *(1 oz)* flaked almonds, toasted
425-g *(15-oz)* can red cherries
142-ml *(¼-pt)* carton double cream
12 cocktail cherries with stems

Divide the pastry in half and roll out both pieces 0.5 cm *(¼ in)* thick. Cut one to fit the base of a 20.5-cm *(8-in)* spring-release cake tin. Prick the base and brush a 1-cm *(½-in)* border with beaten egg. Cut out 14 circles from the remaining pastry with a 6.5-cm *(2½-in)* fluted cutter. Place the circles overlapping round the glazed border, pressing them firmly into position on the base and extending up the side of the tin. Bake 'blind' at 200°C *(400°F)* mark 6 for 25 minutes, then remove the paper and beans and bake for 5 minutes more. Cool and remove from the tin.

Dissolve the gelatine in the water in the usual way. Heat the milk. Blend the sugar, flours and beaten egg yolks together, stir in the milk, return it to the pan and bring to the boil, stirring. Fold in the butter and ground almonds. Mix the gelatine with a little of the custard. Add to the remainder, dust the surface with icing sugar and leave to cool. Coat the outside of the flan with jam and nuts, 2.5 cm *(1 in)* up. Whisk the egg whites till stiff then fold them into the custard. Layer the custard and halved, stoned cherries in the case. Decorate with whipped cream and stemmed cherries. *Serves 6–8.*

Egg croustades

1 large uncut white loaf
fat or oil for deep frying
25 g *(1 oz)* butter
6 large eggs
90 ml *(6 tbsps)* milk
salt and freshly ground black pepper
parsley sprigs

Remove the crusts. Cut the loaf into 8 oblong shapes about 9 by 5 by 2.5 cm *(3½ by 2 by 1 in)*. Cut a small oblong from the centre of each, leaving walls and base intact. Press the base gently down to form a cavity. Heat a pan of deep fat or oil to 182°C *(360°F)*. Fry the bread cases, two at a time, turning once until golden brown. Drain and keep warm. Heat the butter in a small saucepan. Beat together the eggs and milk. Season and add to the saucepan and stir over a moderate heat until the eggs are lightly scrambled and creamy. Remove from the heat and spoon into the bread cases. Garnish with parsley sprigs and serve immediately. *Makes 8.*

Kidney savouries

6 small thick slices white bread
40 g *(1½ oz)* butter
45 ml *(3 tbsps)* corn oil
6 lambs' kidneys
3 rashers streaky bacon, rinded
3 tomatoes, halved
12 pork chipolatas

Using a 7.5-cm *(3-in)* plain pastry cutter, cut 6 rounds from the slices of bread. Heat 25 g *(1 oz)* butter and the oil in a frying pan and fry the bread rounds on both sides until crisp and golden. Drain on kitchen paper and keep warm. Skin, halve and remove the core from the kidneys. Stretch the bacon rashers with the back of a knife. Cut each in half and roll up into 6 rolls. Fry the kidneys, adding extra butter if necessary. Cook for about 8 minutes. Grill the sausages and bacon rolls under a moderate heat for 7–10 minutes, turning once. Grill the tomatoes for 4 minutes. To assemble, place the fried bread rounds on a heated platter. Place 2 sausages across each, then top with 2 kidney halves, a tomato half and finally a bacon roll. Serve immediately. *Makes 6.*

Tomato bouillon

Combine equal amounts of beef consommé and tomato juice, both from a can, and serve hot with a garnish of thinly sliced lemon.

Rolled stuffed shoulder of lamb

175 g *(6 oz)* streaky bacon, rinded
25 g *(1 oz)* fresh white breadcrumbs
45 ml *(3 level tbsps)* chopped fresh mint
salt and freshly ground black pepper
beaten egg
2–2.5 kg *(4–4½ lb)* shoulder of lamb, boned
15–30 ml *(1–2 tbsps)* oil

Finely scissor-snip the bacon and combine it with the breadcrumbs, mint, salt and pepper. Add sufficient beaten egg to bind the ingredients together. Spread out the lamb. Place the stuffing in the cavity where the bone has been removed. Roll up the joint and secure with several bands of string. Weigh the joint. Lightly grease a roasting tin with oil. Place the joint in it and brush with remaining oil. Cook in the oven at 190°C *(375°F)* mark 5. Calculate the cooking time after stuffing by allowing 20 minutes per 450 g *(per lb)*, plus 30 minutes. *Serves 6.*

Apricot surprise

439-g *(15½-oz)* can apricot halves, drained
3 eggs, separated
15 ml *(1 level tbsp)* caster sugar
vanilla essence
483-ml *(17-fl oz)* block vanilla ice cream

Chill a 1.4-l *(2½-pt)* soufflé dish. Put the egg yolks in a large basin with the sugar and vanilla essence and whisk until light and creamy. Place the soufflé dish in a baking dish surrounded by ice cubes. Put the ice-cream in the base and top with apricots. Fold the stiffly whisked egg whites into the yolks and pour over the fruit and ice cream. Place towards the top of the oven at 230°C *(450°F)* mark 8 for 7–8 minutes until golden brown on top. Serve at once. *Serves 6.*

Lemon chicken double crust pie

1.5-kg *(3-lb)* oven-ready chicken
40 g *(1½ oz)* butter
45 ml *(3 level tbsps)* flour
25–50 g *(1–2 oz)* grated cheese
30 ml *(2 tbsps)* chopped parsley
grated rind and juice of 1 lemon
salt and black pepper
350 g *(12 oz)* shortcrust pastry, made with 350 g *(12 oz)* flour, etc. (see page 351)
beaten egg or milk to glaze
225-g *(8-oz)* pkt frozen asparagus spears

Remove the chicken giblets and cook the bird in a roaster bag with the oven set at 190°C *(375°F)* mark 5, for about 1½ hours. Drain off the chicken juices and make up to 300 ml *(½ pt)* with water. Skin the chicken, strip the meat from the bones and roughly chop it. Melt 25 g *(1 oz)* butter in pan, stir in the flour and cook for 1–2 minutes. Blend in the chicken juices to make a sauce; simmer a few minutes then stir in cheese, chicken, parsley, lemon rind and 30–45 ml *(2–3 tbsps)* lemon juice. Adjust the seasoning and allow to cool. Line a 25.5-cm *(10-in)* metal or foil pie-plate with half the rolled pastry. Spread the filling over, damp the edges and top with a pastry lid; seal the edges. Make a slit in centre, brush with egg or milk and bake at 200°C *(400°F)* mark 6 for about 45 minutes. Garnish with freshly cooked asparagus, glazed with melted butter. *Serves 6.*

Noodles rusticana

6 small onions
275 g *(10 oz)* back bacon rashers, rinded
100 g *(4 oz)* butter
275 g *(10 oz)* noodle nests
50 g *(2 oz)* Parmesan cheese, grated
30 ml *(2 tbsps)* chopped parsley
10 ml *(2 level tsps)* mixed dried herbs
freshly ground black pepper
2 270-g *(9-oz)* cans Buitoni tomato sauce
175 g *(6 oz)* mature Cheddar cheese, grated

Peel the onions and parboil in salted water for about 5 minutes. Drain and cut them in half. Cut the bacon into small pieces. Gently fry it until cooked, then remove to one side. Melt 25 g *(1 oz)* butter and fry the onion halves until golden brown, turning carefully to retain their shape. Keep them warm. Cook the noodles in fast boiling salted water for 3–4 minutes then drain well. Melt the remaining butter, add the noodles, bacon, Parmesan cheese, parsley, mixed herbs and pepper. Toss lightly to combine the ingredients. Pile into a shallow heated serving dish. Garnish with onion halves. Sprinkle with more parsley. Serve with a bowl of grated Cheddar cheese and the hot tomato sauce. *Serves 6.*

Tomato cole slaw

450 g *(1 lb)* crisp green eating apples
juice of 1 lemon
450 g *(1 lb)* white cabbage
75 g *(3 oz)* seedless raisins
300 ml *(½ pt)* thick mayonnaise
450 g *(1 lb)* tomatoes
salt and freshly ground black pepper

Wipe the apples. Core and dice them, leaving the skin on. Put the apple in a basin with the lemon juice and toss lightly to coat the pieces evenly with the juice. Finely shred the cabbage. In a large bowl, combine the cabbage with the raisins, mayonnaise and drained apple. Season well. Place two-thirds of the cabbage mixture in a deep serving dish, levelling the surface. Slice the tomatoes crosswise, season, and place half in a layer over the slaw. Cover with remaining cabbage mixture, making a cone shape in the centre. Arrange a circle of overlapping tomatoes around the top edge. Keep in a cool place.

Note If the slaw is made in advance, omit the apple and add before serving. *Serves 6.*

Pineapple and grape salads

2 medium sized ripe pineapples
226-g *(8-oz)* can pineapple rings
250 g *(8 oz)* white grapes, halved, peeled and pipped
50 g *(2 oz)* trifle sponge cakes
30 ml *(2 tbsps)* Kirsch
45 ml *(3 tbsps)* lemon juice
30 ml *(2 level tbsps)* caster sugar

Cut away the top and bottom of each pineapple. Slice each in 3 crosswise. Scoop out almost all flesh from the 'cases' leaving a 'base' intact. Stand each 'case' on a small plate. Cut the pineapple flesh into small pieces. Drain the canned pineapple, reserving the juice. Shred and add it to the fresh pineapple. Combine the pineapple with the grapes. Crush the sponge and divide between the pineapple cases. Mix 90 ml *(6 tbsps)* of reserved pineapple juice with the Kirsch. Spoon this over the sponge. Heat the remaining pineapple juice in a small saucepan with the lemon juice and sugar. Bring to the boil and continue until a syrup is formed. Remove from the heat and set aside to cool. Fill the pineapple cases with prepared fruit and spoon the syrup over. *Makes 6.*

Kitchen planning

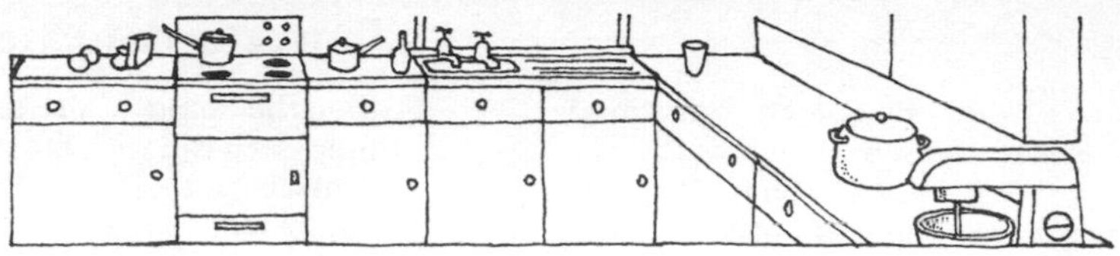

A well-organised kitchen is a pleasure to work in but needs careful thought if it's to suit your requirements. Those lucky enough to start from scratch in a new house usually have less problems than people faced with converting an old kitchen (or other room) where existing conditions have to be taken into account. In this chapter we give rough guidelines on how to set about planning your kitchen. Remember, there are no hard and fast rules and even seemingly identical kitchens on, say, a housing estate, will end up arranged differently because of the users' needs.

Kitchen tasks to consider
Apart from cooking, preparing and serving food and washing up, you may also need to do the laundry and eat some (if not all) meals in your kitchen. Gone for most people are the days of pantries and laundries and in a small house a dining-room may well give way to the need for increased living area. You will also need to store food and cookery utensils, some crockery, cleaning equipment and products in the kitchen.

Arranging things
Aim to do the minimum of walking about, bending or stretching while at your kitchen chores and also aim to make it as attractive a place as possible. You will need to adjust the kind of equipment you buy to the size of the room – a split-level cooker may give more cupboard space but removes a work surface; this is fine in a large kitchen but less good in a small one. Two worktop heights are more comfortable than one. For most people rolling pastry and creaming fat and sugar are more easily done at a lower level than chopping onions. Try and allow for a place where you can sit down to do chores like potato peeling and pea podding – it will make working much more agreeable.

Good lighting is important, both natural and artificial. If you are stuck with poky windows it could be well worth the expense of enlarging them if possible. For the artificial lighting, place fitments where you won't be working in shadow and remember that fluorescent tubes, though more expensive to instal, are cheaper to run.

Ventilation is essential too if you're not to operate amid pools of condensation. Natural ventilation (ie open windows) may be sufficient in summer but in winter you will be glad of an extractor fan and/or cooker hood which remove smells as well as steam.

Sensible surfaces
One way and another, kitchens get a lot of wear and tear so walls, floor and other surfaces should be tough and easily cleaned. Note too that fire is a hazard in every kitchen so it is sensible to instal either a small chemical fire extinguisher, or glass fibre fire blanket within easy reach of the cooker and ensure that every member of the family knows how to operate them in a crisis.

Walls and ceiling should be grease-resistant and easily washable. A good choice is a vinyl emulsion paint which comes in matt or silk finish and has good steam resistance. If condensation presents real problems you can buy special anti-condensation paint. Alternatively use an all-surface polyurethane based paint which dries with a satin finish and can be used for woodwork as well. For a gloss finish, use an oil-based or vinyl gloss paint.

Kitchen walls and ceilings should be cleaned with a damp cloth and mild detergent solution. Stubborn marks and persistent stains can usually be removed by scrubbing. For light soiling clean woodwork with an aerosol cleaner/polish. Heavier marking and grease will need the mild detergent solution and damp cloth treatment.

If you prefer a patterned paper in your kitchen choose a vinyl-faced paper or vinyl wallcovering. These are washable as opposed to wipeable but can be damaged by hot fat splashing so are not really suitable for the area round a cooker, which is better covered with paint or tiles. Tiles in ceramic or stainless steel can be bought in a wide price range and are ideal for wall areas around sink and cooker. Clean them as for paint.

Floor coverings should be as grease-resistant as possible, also non-slip and comfortable to stand and walk on. Buy good quality so it will last and make sure the sub-floor on which you lay it is even and in good condition.

Vinyl is today's most popular choice and comes in sheet or tile form in varying thicknesses – basically the thicker the better. There's a wide price range and vinyls also offer the most extensive choice of patterns and colours. Vinyl asbestos is a cheaper though hard-wearing version in which asbestos is used as a filler and the vinyl content slightly reduced. Manufacturers of both normally supply good care instructions which you should follow for best results.

Linoleum is also hard-wearing but not generally

widely available – you usually have to order it. It comes in sheet or tile form but colours are plain or just slightly flecked or mottled. For a kitchen you should choose the 3.2 mm guage.

Sealed cork tiles are also a good choice as they are warm and comfortable to the feet and spills and stains can be wiped up easily. The latest kind is sealed both on top, underneath and round the edges so there's no question of water or grease seeping underneath the seal at any point and spoiling the finish.

Quarry tiles make a hardwearing floor but can be tiring and cold to stand on. They need some form of protection such as a coating of non-slip wax, applied regularly, or their absorbent surface will quickly become marked.

Ceramic tiles come in marvellous patterns and are virtually indestructible (though fragile china dropped on them won't be) but they tend to be cold and hard on the feet and are also very expensive over a large area.

Carpet, including some in tile form, is available in grades suitable for kitchen use though it is not really suitable for messy families with lots of children or pets. Spillage should be wiped up immediately with a damp cloth – some loose laid tiles can just be taken up and run under a tap to clean. Otherwise they should be treated like ordinary carpet and vacuumed and shampooed as necessary.

Work surfaces should be non-absorbent, grease-resistant and require no more than a wipe over to keep them clean. Laminated plastics are excellent for this and come in a wide range of colours. You can buy the material from DIY shops to cover old wooden and other surfaces. Some laminate worktops have a coved back which means there is no dirt trap at the edge. The only thing to remember with laminated plastic is never to put a hot casserole straight from the oven on to it or you may scorch and damage the surface. Use a rack or trivet.

Stainless steel is another good surface near the cooker as it is completely heat-resistant. Again you must beware of very hot casseroles – these crack if put straight from the oven on to the cold metal. Stainless steel is easy to clean but does tend to scratch and watermark. It can usually be kept in good condition with regular applications of a proprietary cleaner.

Making the most of your equipment

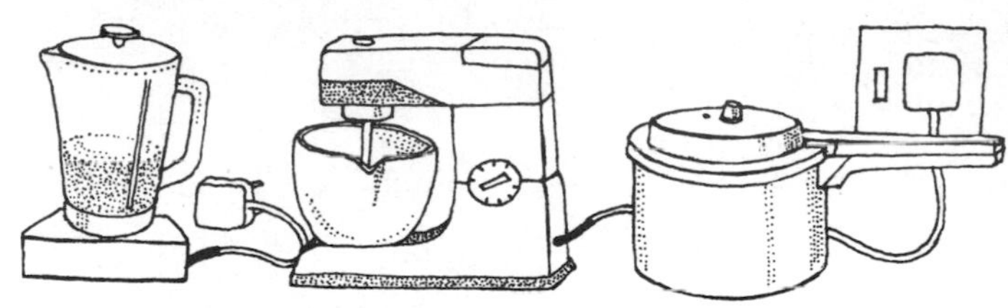

For today's cook the range of equipment on the market can turn a kitchen into a powerhouse of efficiency. Most gadgets and appliances save time and effort for someone but not every cook needs all of them. It is worth assessing carefully what would and wouldn't be a real kitchen aid for you, bearing in mind family size and the kind of food you cook.

In this chapter we deal with the major pieces of cooking equipment you can buy, with the exception of home freezers which are covered on pages 466 to 467.

Choosing a cooker

A cooker is the most important piece of equipment in any kitchen so requires careful thought when it comes to selection.

You may be able to choose what fuel you use – electricity, gas, oil or solid fuel – or you may be stuck with one particular kind which is already supplied to your house and will thus be cheaper than bringing in an alternative.

The basic cooker consists of hob and oven which may be combined in one unit or built into separate, split level, ones. It is possible to vary this combination with equipment such as a split level hob combined with a wall-mounted rotisserie-cum-small oven or an electric frying pan but this is really only suitable when cooking for one or two people and does, to a certain extent, limit conventional cooking style. It's best for general family life to look carefully and extensively at the range of cookers on the market and choose variations within the basic hob/oven framework. Some cookers have three hob rings, others four, while some have double ovens or a grill compartment which also works as a rotisserie/small oven. Split level cookers offer the greatest flexibility in this way and also mean you can combine the use of fuels with, say, a gas hob and electric oven.

Electric cookers have become very sophisticated in recent years and most models now incorporate an automatic timer. These enable you to organise for meals to be cooked when you're not actually there to turn the oven on or off and are a great boon for anyone leading a busy life. Good additional features on electric cookers are duplex (double element) rings so that you don't waste heat when using a small pan and half grill control for when you're grilling just one chop or slice of toast. All models have thermostatic control for precise cooking results (except occasionally in the second oven) and many offer the option of easy-clean linings which save a tedious chore. Some have fan-assisted ovens which give the same temperature throughout the oven – excellent for anyone who does batch cooking for a freezer or large family.

Be careful when choosing a foreign-made electric cooker as these often have their elements in the top and bottom of the oven, whereas British-made ones have side elements. This can mean some slight adjustment in your cooking times and temperatures if you're to get the results you are accustomed to.

Gas cookers have the advantage of instant flame control. When you turn them off they go off. Many now have automatic timers and a useful development with these has been electronic spark ignition which means food left in the oven for any time before automatic cooking starts won't be warmed by the pilot light and possibly develop harmful micro-organisms. You often have a choice of easy-clean linings for the oven and on most models there are large and small hob rings to accommodate different pan sizes.

Oil and solid fuel cookers provide a more limited choice as there are fewer models available and they do have the disadvantage that you have to remember to arrange for the delivery of sufficient supplies of the appropriate fuel – it isn't supplied automatically like electricity and gas.

They are rather like the old-fashioned range and provide constant heat both on top and in the oven. They usually have two large plates on top on which you can place more than one pan at a time and two ovens, one hotter (quick) and one cooler (slow). You need to develop new cooking techniques to get the best from these models but many people swear by them and the constant heat they provide can also be used to heat the domestic water.

Microwave cookers provide a totally different cooking method which copes with most food in minutes. They are still in their infancy as far as the domestic market is concerned and this is reflected in their high price. They are fairly cheap to run because of the short cooking times involved but special techniques are required for ordinary cooking. Their most valuable asset is for thawing and reheating frozen food which is done in a matter of minutes. They are best considered as an addition to conventional cookers rather than a substitute.

Mixers and blenders

These may be one piece of equipment with mixing and blending (plus other) attachments or a separate mixer and blender. The large, many-purpose tabletop models are very powerful and may incorporate such refinements as a shredder, mincer, juice extractor, noodle maker, bean slicer and can opener as well as the blending and mixing attachments. These are suitable for large families and people who cook in bulk for a freezer. They do take up a lot of storage space though and the average household will usually find a satisfactory solution is to have a small, hand-held electric mixer and separate blender. Unless you slice many kilograms of beans each year or extract vast quantities of fruit juice you can do these operations equally efficiently though more slowly with separate manual equipment.

A mixer can be used for the majority of cooking operations. Its most important functions are rubbing in (the fat must be at room temperature), creaming, whisking, making icings and creaming vegetables (use the beaters directly into the saucepan to mash potatoes, etc).

When buying a blender, biggest is certainly best in terms of size and motor power but small may be perfectly adequate for your needs. Very small blenders may be unable to cope with dry work such as chopping chocolate or grinding nuts and will take several goes if you want to blend large quantities. Their most important functions are:

Making breadcrumbs Break bread into cubes and drop a few at a time on to the rotating blades. Empty out the crumbs and repeat. For buttered crumbs, butter the bread before blending. For cheesy crumbs add a few cubes of cheese with the bread. For stuffing, add parsley, lemon rind, herbs and crumbled, cooked bacon to the bread.

Crumbling biscuits, etc. Cracker, biscuit and cake crumbs are made in the same way as bread crumbs.

Mixing instant foods and drinks Use for instant milk drinks, frozen fruit concentrates, instant mashed potato (heat the milk and butter, pour into the goblet and add the potato powder).

Making salad dressings Do not over-blend French dressing as it emulsifies quickly.

Mayonnaise In small quantities, mayonnaise can only be made in a blender if the blades are set low enough to beat the egg yolk. It sometimes helps to add 15 ml *(1 tbsp)* warm water or to use a whole egg. Large quantities are easier.

Puréeing fruit and vegetables Vegetables should not be overcooked before puréeing. For creamed spinach, add egg, cream and nutmeg.

Soft fruits need not be cooked before they are puréed. Harder fruits should first be cooked and stoned. Fruit purées provide the basis for innumerable sweet desserts and sauces.

Some purées (eg blackcurrant, raspberry) will need sieving after blending, to remove seeds.

Chopping raw cabbage, onions, carrots, etc. Half fill goblet with water, add vegetables and blend until the required degree of fineness is reached. Drain. Some models do not require the use of water when chopping vegetables.

Mixing a sauce or binding Blenders can make many sauces. For a white sauce, put flour, fat and milk plus seasonings into the goblet and blend until smooth. Pour into a pan and bring to the boil, stirring continuously. Cook for 4–5 minutes.

For fruit sauces cook first, then blend.

For a binding for meat loaves, hamburgers, potatoes, cakes, etc, use the blender to ensure even mixing. It also gives velvety smoothness to the base of a savoury mousse.

Mixing jellied desserts and savouries If the amount of liquid called for is only a spoonful, dissolve the gelatine in a cup in the usual way, but if the liquid is sufficient to come well above the blades, place half of it in the goblet, sprinkle the measured gelatine over it and leave to swell. Pour on the rest of the liquid, heated to boiling point, and switch on to dissolve the gelatine.

Puréeing soups A blender can take the place of sieving for all but the most smooth textured soups. With these you should first blend, then pass the soup through a fine sieve to remove any remaining coarse particles. Dried pulses like peas and lentils will cook in half the normal time if they are first blended with some liquid or ground when dry.

Other miscellaneous uses Coarse sugar can be powdered for icing or dusting; nuts and chocolate can be chopped or ground; spreads, dips and potted meats can be made.

Tips for getting the best from your blender
Read the manufacturer's instructions carefully for individual directions before using the blender. Always

make sure the lid is in position before switching on.
Cut solid foods into small pieces.
Begin with small quantities when working with heavy or solid foods.
Warm the goblet before blending hot liquids.
Not all blenders will cope with dry foods. Check the instructions supplied by the manufacturer.
Always put in liquids before solids – these help feed the solids into the blade area.
Don't overfill the goblet. Most blenders perform best with the manufacturer's recommended contents – less with thick mixtures. It will be quicker in the end to do more than one batch than to overload.
Never run the appliance for longer than the manufacturer states or you will burn out the motor.
Don't whip cream with your blender – it won't do it; nor will it extract juice or crush ice unless the instruction book says so. It won't mince raw meat, beat egg white, mash home-cooked potatoes, cream fat and sugar or whisk egg yolks and sugar together.
Never try to scrape down the sides of the goblet while it is running; always switch off first.

Pressure cookers

A pressure cooker cuts down lengthy cooking times and saves fuel and money. It is a great help for specific jobs like steaming puddings, cooking pulses, making stock, etc, which will otherwise be very time-consuming.

There is a wide range of pressure cookers on the market today in varying sizes and finishes. Large families and freezer owners will find a big one most useful, otherwise, as a rough guide you'll need a 4.5-litre *(8-pint)* model for a household of 2–3 people; a 5.5–7.5-litre *(10–13-pint)* model for 4–6 people. For preserving and steaming puddings you need a cooker with 3-pressure control (usually called low, medium and high, *or 5, 10 and 15 lb*), while for processing large bottling jars you will require one of the models with a domed lid. If the pan is to be used on a solid hotplate, check that it has a thick, heavy base.

Directions for use vary from make to make so you should read and follow the manufacturer's instructions carefully.

With most cookers the prepared food is put into the pan with the required quantity of liquid, the lid closed and fixed into position and the pressure cooker placed over high heat (unless otherwise stated). When steam flows from the valve on top, the weights are put into place and the contents brought to pressure – recognisable by the muttering noise produced. At this point the heat is reduced and the timing of the cooking period calculated from then.

Getting the best from your pressure cooker

1. Quantities and times here are for use with 4.5–7-litre *(8–12-pint)* models.
2. Do not overfill the cooker – it should never be more than two-thirds full for solid foods and half-full for liquids, cereals and preserves. Models with a domed lid may be filled with solids to within 2.5–5 cm *(1–2 in)* of the pan rim.
3. Cooking times will vary according to the quality of the food and the thickness of the pieces. When in doubt (eg with root vegetables that seem particularly young and tender) cook for a slightly shorter time than stated in the table. If necessary you can always bring the cooker to pressure again for a minute or so but nothing can be done about overcooked food.
4. Before opening the pan, let the pressure drop to normal. This is done either quickly or slowly, according to what is being cooked. For example, cereals and pulses, which tend to froth up and clog the vent, should be allowed to reduce slowly.

   To reduce pressure quickly, take the pan to the sink and run cold water over it for a few seconds without wetting the valve or the vent. Lift the weight gently with a fork to check there is no hissing before removing the weight and the lid. If hissing persists, run more cold water until it stops. To reduce pressure slowly, leave the pan at room temperature until the weight can be lifted without hissing.
5. All pressure cookers should have a safety valve designed to operate and release steam if the pressure rises above 9 kg *(20 lb)*. This may occur if the pan boils dry or the vent becomes blocked by dirt, grease or food. If the valve does blow, inspect the vent, clean it if necessary and see that there is sufficient liquid in the pan before replacing the safety valve, resetting the pressure and cooking again.
6. Pressure cookers should be kept completely clean. The vent should be inspected and washed after each use and the gasket or rubber ring round the lid kept free of grease and food particles. Store the pan with the lid upturned in it.

   If steam escapes round the rim, remove the rubber gasket, rub it with oil, stretch it slightly and replace. Renew the gasket if steam continues to escape.

Stocks and soups

Any recipe may be used though it may be necessary to reduce the liquid to conform with the maximum amount the pan can take. Put all ingredients into the cooker (the trivet should not be used), bring to the boil without putting the lid on, skim the surface and fix the lid. Lower the heat and bring slowly to high *(15 lb)* pressure then reduce the heat and cook for ¾ hour. Except when making soup from pulses reduce the pressure quickly using cold water.

Meat and poultry

You have a choice of three methods.

Boiling is suitable for salt meat such as silverside or brisket. Soak the meat overnight in cold water. Drain, put the meat in the pan without the trivet and add 1 small onion, 1 carrot and a stick of celery and cover with water. Allow 15–20 minutes per 450 g *(1 lb)*, depending on the thickness and size of the joint.

Pot roasting This is the nearest to pot roasting that can be achieved in a pressure cooker. It is suitable for lean cuts such as topside which go a little dry if roasted in the ordinary way in the oven, and fresh silverside or brisket.

Rub some seasoning into the meat and brown it all over in hot fat. Put the meat on the trivet and add water as follows: 300 ml *(½ pt)* for a joint of 1.4 kg *(3 lb)* or less; 150 ml *(¼ pt)* extra for every further 900 g *(2 lb)* of meat. Allow 15–18 minutes per 450 g *(1 lb)*, depending on the size and thickness of the meat.

Braising Prepare the joint of meat and a bed of vegetables as for ordinary braising (see pages 11, 95), add the normal amount of liquid and allow 15–18 minutes per 450 g *(1 lb)* – depending on the size and thickness of the joint.

Chops and liver can be prepared as for a large piece of meat, but are cooked for 7–8 minutes only.

Bacon and ham

All boiling cuts of ham and bacon, particularly the cheaper cuts of bacon (eg collar, flank, streaky), can be treated in this way. Soak for 3–4 hours in cold water and drain. Put in the pan with 300 ml *(½ pt)* of water for a joint weighing 1.4 kg *(3 lb)* or less and an extra 150 ml *(¼ pt)* for each extra 450 g *(1 lb)* above this weight. (It is unlikely that a joint above 2.3 kg *(5 lb)* would fit in the cooker.) Cook for 12 minutes per 450 g *(1 lb)*. A few vegetables such as onion, carrot, celery or turnip, and a bouquet garni, improve the flavour considerably.

Boiling fowl

Pressure cooking is ideal for softening older and tougher birds. Rub seasoning on to the outside, put the bird on the rack, add 300–400 ml *(½–¾ pt)* water, depending on the length of cooking, and cook for 10–12 minutes per 450 g *(1 lb)*, according to size and age. If you wish you can finish the bird by browning it in a hot oven at 220°C *(425°F)* mark 7 for about ¼ hour.

Alternatively, brown the bird in hot fat, put it on a bed of browned vegetables, add just enough water to cover these and cook for 10 minutes per 450 g *(1 lb)*.

Stews and casserole dishes

Most recipes for a stew or casserole can be adapted for use in a pressure cooker; reduce the cooking liquid if necessary so that it does not exceed 600 ml *(1 pt)* and add any thickening (usually in the form of blended flour or cornflour) at the end of the processing in the pressure cooker.

Beef stew The best flavour and colour are obtained if the meat is tossed in seasoned flour and browned lightly before cooking. Cook for about 20 minutes (depending on the quality of the meat).

Irish stew Prepare in the usual way and cook for 15 minutes.

Veal stew Prepare in the usual way and cook for 12–15 minutes.

Steak and kidney for a pudding or pie can receive their preliminary cooking in a pressure cooker. Allow 10–15 minutes (depending on the quality of the meat).

Ox-tail stew Prepare in the usual way and pressure-cook for 40–45 minutes. Leave overnight, skim off the fatty layer and pressure-cook for a further 5–7 minutes before serving.

Stuffed sheep's hearts Prepare in the usual way and allow about 30 minutes.

Tripe and onions Cook the blanched and prepared tripe and onions for 15 minutes. Use the liquid to make the white sauce in the usual way.

Beef olives Prepare in the usual way. Allow about 20 minutes.

Root vegetables

1. Choose vegetables of the same size or cut them into even-sized pieces.
2. Cook at high *(15-lb)* pressure and time them accurately.
3. Use 300 ml *(½ pt)* water for all vegetables except beetroot, which requires 600 ml *(1 pt)*. Sprinkle the actual vegetables with seasoning – it is useless to put this in the water, which does not come into contact with the vegetables.
4. Bring quickly to pressure and reduce the pressure quickly.
5. You can cook more than one type of vegetable at a time, but different types should be put in the special 'separators' or wrapped in pieces of aluminium foil. Put in first the vegetables that require the longest cooking time. After the necessary period, reduce the pressure, open the cooker, add the other vegetables and continue cooking until all are ready.

Cooking vegetables

Vegetable	*Preparation*	*Time*
Artichokes, Jerusalem	Peel and place in water containing lemon juice until required.	5–7 mins., depending on size.
Artichokes, Globe	Not recommended.	
Beetroot	Wash and trim off the leaves.	10–30 mins., depending on size.
Carrots – Old	Peel and dice or cut in rings.	4–5 mins.
Carrots – Young	Scrape and leave whole if small.	5–6 mins., depending on size.
Onions	1. Trim off root; skin and leave whole. 2. Chop or slice.	5–10 mins., depending on size. 3–4 mins.
Parsnips	Peel, core and cut in halves (quarters if large).	5–6 mins., depending on size and age.
Potatoes – Old	Peel. If medium-sized, leave whole. If large, cut in quarters.	4–6 mins., depending on size. 6 mins.
Potatoes – New	Scrape and leave whole, unless large.	5–9 mins., depending on size.
Swedes, Turnips	Peel and dice.	4–5 mins., depending on size.
Pulses	Soak for ½ hour; add 900 ml *(2 pt)* cold water and 5 ml *(1 level tsp)* salt.	20 mins. for haricot beans, butter beans and dried peas. 15 mins. for split peas and lentils.

Puddings

1. Never fill a basin more than two-thirds full.
2. Cover the basin with double greaseproof paper or foil.
3. Stand the basin on the rack in the pan and add 150 ml *(¼ pt)* boiling water for every ¼ hour of the total cooking time, plus 300 ml *(½ pt)*.
4. Cover the pan, heat until the steam flows and allow it to flow freely for the specified time.
5. Put on the weights, bring to pressure and cook for the required time.
6. Reduce the pressure slowly.

Pudding	*Steam without pressure for:*	*Pressure*	*Time at pressure*
Sponge: 600 ml *(1 pt)*	15 minutes	Low *(5 lb)*	25 mins.
Sponge: individual	5 minutes	Low *(5 lb)*	15 mins.
Fruit suet	15 minutes	Low *(5 lb)*	35 mins.
Jam or mincemeat roly-poly (wrap loosely to allow for expansion)	10 minutes	Low *(5 lb)*	25 mins.
Sponge suet	15 minutes	Low *(5 lb)*	35 mins.
Christmas Puddings:			
450 g *(1 lb)*	15 minutes	High *(15 lb)*	1½ hours
700 g *(1½ lb)*	30 minutes	High *(15 lb)*	1¾ hours
1 kg *(2¼ lb)*	30 minutes	High *(15 lb)*	2¼ hours

Before serving Christmas pudding, pressure cook it at high *(15 lb)* pressure, without any preliminary steaming, for a further period: 450 g *(1 lb)* 20 minutes; 700 g *(1½-lb)* 30 minutes; 1-kg *(2¼-lb)* 45 minutes.

Preserving

For the use of a pressure cooker in preserving, see page 446.

Rôtisserie cookery

Modern though this method of cooking may seem, in reality it is a development of the original way of cooking meat, in front of an open fire, instead of in a closed oven as more recently. Apart from the flavour, which some people think is much better than with oven-baked meat, rôtisserie cooking has the advantages that the meat bastes itself as it revolves and that there is little or no splashing and therefore no messy oven to clean.

Rôtisserie units are now fitted on many gas and electric cookers, either in the grill compartment or in the oven – the former being the more satisfactory type. Separate electrically operated models are also available.

A rôtisserie attachment consists of:

A shaft on which the meat, poultry or other food is impaled.

Danish pastries (p. 417–8).

Holding forks which slide on the shaft and can be secured by thumbscrews to hold the food firmly in place.

The motor into which the loaded shaft is fitted; it is driven by electricity or by clockwork.

The tray placed under the revolving shaft to catch the drippings from the meat as it cooks.

General hints for using a rôtisserie unit

1. Prepare the food in the usual way; thaw frozen meat, poultry, etc. Stuff and truss a chicken.
2. Push one of the holding forks on to the shaft and secure it. Place the food on the shaft, pushing this through the centre of the joint or bird. Push on the second holding fork and secure.
3. Turn on the heat and allow the grill or oven to get very hot.
4. Place the loaded shaft in position (the instruction booklet that comes with your cooker will give you full details).
5. Turn on the rôtisserie motor and allow the shaft to revolve several times before leaving it, to make sure that there is no obstruction and that it is turning evenly.
6. Turn down the heat and cook the food as instructed by the makers.

Notes The joint or bird can be basted from time to time with the fat and juices in the tray.

A sliced onion or clove of garlic can be added to the drippings, to give extra flavour. Alternatively, any fat in the tray may be removed and replaced by fruit juice, cider, etc, which can be used for basting and as gravy.

Meat

Any joint – boned or boneless – which is suitable for quick roasting can be cooked on a rôtisserie. It must however be as evenly shaped as possible, so that it will revolve steadily. If it is not a compact shape it must be boned, rolled (after stuffing, if you wish) and tied with string.

Put the joint on the shaft as described above and place it in position with the cut edge towards the heat. Turn on the motor and roast the meat with the heat on full for 5 minutes, to sear the surface; reduce the heat and cook the joint for the necessary time. Individual rôtisserie manufacturers recommend different times, so follow the specific instructions given with your own model.

Here are some special points to note:

Pork If you like a crisp crackling, rub with salt and oil before cooking.

Veal Since this is a dry meat, it is improved by being basted regularly every 15 minutes.

Poultry and game

Any bird, stuffed or unstuffed, or portions of poultry, may be cooked on the rôtisserie. Follow the manufacturer's directions as to timing, etc.

The outside of the bird or joint should be brushed with oil or melted fat before cooking and a whole bird must be trussed into a compact shape.

Very fat birds, such as geese and ducks, should be pricked all over before cooking and roasted with the heat on full for 10–15 minutes, to get rid of the extra fat.

A turkey of up to 5 kg *(12 lb)* can be cooked on some models of rôtisserie, but you must take care to spear it centrally on the shaft and check regularly to see that it is revolving evenly.

Game birds, which tend to be very dry, should have strips of streaky bacon tied over the breast.

Kebab cookery

This way of cooking meat and other foods, which originated in the Middle East, has become popular here and special kebab attachments are now supplied with some rôtisserie units. They consist of a number of skewers which are revolved by means of the rôtisserie motor. The exact manner of assembling the attachment varies with the particular model, but details will be supplied with your cooker.

General hints for using the kebab attachment

1. Choose a mixture of fatty and drier foods and cut them into even-sized pieces.
2. Grease the skewers before use. (Allow as a rule one skewerful per person.)
3. Skewer the food and use the discs provided to hold the pieces firmly in position.
4. Brush the foods over with oil or melted fat.
5. Turn on the heat and let the grill or oven become very hot.
6. Put the kebab attachment in place and turn on the motor. Cook for 10–20 minutes, basting if necessary, until all the foods are done.
7. Serve the cooked kebabs on a bed of rice or risotto or with plenty of French bread and butter and a green salad.

Suggested kebab assortments

Choose 2–3 items from this list and make up each skewerful with 2–3 bite-sized pieces of each foodstuff:

Cubes of beefsteak, veal or lamb
Tiny sausages
Pieces of Frankfurter sausage
Bacon rolls
Chunks of liver
Kidneys (cut up, unless very small)
Cubes of cheese wrapped in ham
Onions (par-boiled small ones are best)
Chunks of green pepper
Tomatoes, small or halved
Mushrooms (cut up if large)

Chelsea buns (p. 415).

Scampi
Prawns
Scallops
Cooking apples, cut in wedges
Thick slices of banana
Peach halves
Pineapple chunks

Marinade

To introduce extra flavour, steep the foods for 1–2 hours in any of the following – used alone or in a mixture – before putting them on the skewers:

Wine or vinegar
Soy sauce
Worcestershire sauce
Lemon juice
Garlic-flavoured oil

Deep fat fryers

For a family that enjoys fried food a deep fat fryer is a way of cooking large quantities quickly and without the attendant spattering and steam that accompany conventional frying. You can control the fat temperature by means of a thermostat so that it never overheats and maintains maximum efficiency for whatever is being cooked.

The deep fat fryer consists of a large pan containing a wire frying basket and a lid. Some models have a built-in filter that removes odour and steam. There is an external thermostat control and means of lowering the frying basket into the fat when it has reached the correct temperature. Food fried by this method cooks much more quickly than in a frying pan since it does not require turning or basting and is also less greasy since it can be drained in the wire basket before serving. It is a particularly good method of cooking things, like Scotch eggs, which are difficult to fry satisfactorily in an ordinary pan.

You will need a large quantity of oil for the deep fat fryer – usually around 4.5 litres *(1 gallon)*. This can, however, be re-used many times provided you strain it between each frying session to remove any bits of food that remain in it. If you don't have a separate container the oil can be stored in the deep fat fryer but you should be careful to remember it's in there when putting it away and getting it out.

A deep fat fryer is a fairly heavy and bulky piece of equipment so is not suitable for use by anyone with weak wrists and will take up a good deal of space in a small kitchen.

Electric frypans

These are sometimes called auto-cookers. They consist of a pan with a lid and work off an ordinary 13-amp socket outlet. They perform many of the functions of a conventional oven while using considerably less fuel so are a good buy for anyone who resents having to turn on a large oven to cook a small quantity of food. In a small kitchen where catering is mainly for 1–2 people, it is possible to substitute an electric frypan for an oven and use it in conjunction with separate hob units.

You cannot grill in an electric frypan but you can roast, bake, steam and make stews, casseroles and soups. You can also use it as a conventional frying pan and the thermostatic temperature control makes it possible to regulate the heat to prevent overheating and smoking.

Some models come with non-stick lining which makes cleaning easier. All can be immersed completely in water once the electric connection has been removed from the pan's socket.

Contact-grills (infra-red)

These are designed for very quick cooking in fairly small quantities. They consist of two hinged plates, each with a non-stick ridged interior. There is also an additional cooking tray, similar to a baking tray, that may be supplied with the grill or bought separately.

The infra-red grills can be run off an ordinary 13-amp socket outlet but the special kind of heat generated penetrates the middle of the food quickly and cooks it right through in considerably less time than conventional radiant cooking methods.

The hinged plates form a double cooking surface for doing steaks, chops and toasted sandwiches. The ridged surfaces give an attractive latticed pattern similar to an outdoor charcoal grill and there is no need to turn food as both sides cook simultaneously.

Using the baking tray between the hinged plates, you can cook wet foods like casseroles and upside-down puddings in just a few minutes.

Infra-red grills make rather a lot of odour and steam so should be used near an extractor fan or cooker hood if possible. They are also rather fiddly to clean since, although the non-stick surfaces wipe down quickly, you cannot immerse the whole appliance but need to keep the electric socket out of the water.

They are real time-savers though, for people who need to prepare meals from scratch in a hurry.

Electric casseroles

These are designed for long slow cooking. They are made of earthenware with an outer case of aluminium and have a low wattage element. They are excellent and economical for stews and casserole dishes, savoury and sweet. They can be left on safely for 6–10 hours without fear of the food becoming over-cooked or the liquid evaporating. It is essential to follow manufacturers' recipes and directions for care.

Kitchen tools

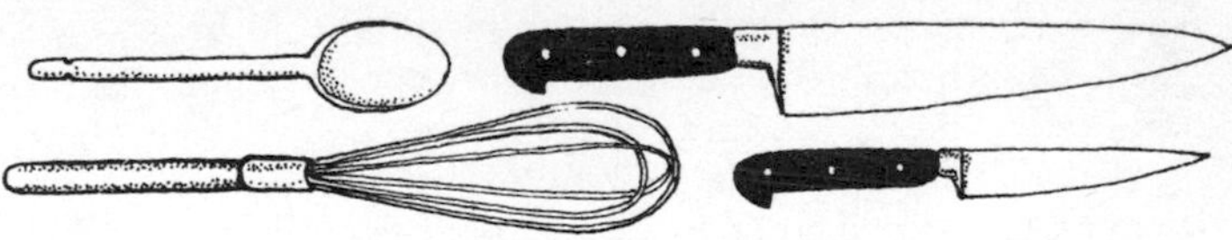

Special gadgets apart, every kitchen needs certain basic tools for essential food preparation tasks. If you buy well-designed, strongly-made equipment and treat it as the manufacturer suggests you should be making a lifetime's investment as well as owning tools which are comfortable and efficient in use.

In this chapter we list the basic equipment needed for an average household of four people and also give detailed notes on choosing saucepans and knives – two essentials where an enormous range and variety makes it difficult to select. Major items of electrical equipment are dealt with on pages 572 to 578.

Choosing saucepans

Cooking services will be strained if you start off with less than one milk pan with a pouring lip or rim and four pans (with lids) holding 1.1 litres *(2 pints)*, 1.7 litres *(3 pints)* – you need two of these – and 3.4 to 4.5 litres *(6–8 pints)*.

The heavier gauge the metal, the less likely is food to stick in the pans. Bases should be flat to ensure even cooking and for electric cookers the diameter of the pans should be similar to that of the hotplate for maximum efficiency and to avoid heat loss. Where a cooker has duplex rings this is easier to achieve.

Look too for a smooth interior that is slightly rounded where sides meet base, to make cleaning easier, and for well fitting lids with heat-resistant knobs. Handles should be firmly fixed and of a convenient length – pans with a capacity of over 4.5 litres *(8 pints)* need a second short handle on the other side to make lifting easy when full.

Aluminium is a good conductor of heat and cooks evenly. Pans made from cast aluminium with a ground base are heavy, strong and particularly suitable for use on solid hotplates. Medium-weight, 10-gauge pans are suitable for all modern gas and electric cookers. Lightweight pans tend to become distorted with use and will then be suitable for use only on gas burners. Even there they won't be very satisfactory as the lid won't fit properly and balance is upset so that the pan can be knocked over easily.

Some aluminium pans have a vitramel (vitreous enamel) finish on the outside which gives an attractive, easily cleaned surface. Alternatively they may be coloured with a sprayed-on polyimide finish which looks like vitramel but is not as durable and may show scratches.

Aluminium tends to discolour in use but this is not harmful and affects only the appearance of the pan, not its cooking ability. Stains can be removed by boiling up a weak acid solution (eg apple peelings in water) in the pan but they will recur. A soaped scouring pad may be used on them but abrasive powders are not advised. The use of soda will discolour aluminium and pit the surface, causing food to stick and burn.

Stainless steel pans are expensive but hard-wearing. Prices vary according to the gauge and quality of the metal. Since steel is not a very good heat conductor the pan bases are usually clad with copper or aluminium to give even heat distribution and some pans have a 3-core sandwich construction throughout which spreads heat well.

Stainless steel pans are easily cleaned and need no scouring. They may stain but marks can be removed with a proprietary stainless steel polish. Pans with copper clad bases will need frequent cleaning to keep them looking good.

Vitramel pans may be made of heavy cast iron, light steel or aluminium with a vitramel (vitreous enamel) coating fused on to it. Best quality vitramel should wear well without chipping. It is available in a wide range of colours and has a hard, glass-like surface which protects against scratching and pitting. One disadvantage is that food tends to stick and burn in vitramel interiors though the heavier-based pans are less susceptible to 'hot spotting'. Abrasive cleaner must not be used.

Copper pans are expensive but hard-wearing too. Copper cooks evenly as it is a good heat conductor. The interior of copper pans is usually lined with tin to prevent chemical reactions occurring between the food and the metal. Some are lined with aluminium, which is also efficient and provides a lighter weight, cheaper solution. A disadvantage is that the outside of copper pans discolours quickly during cooking and requires constant cleaning. This can be done by rubbing with a cut lemon dipped in salt or with a proprietary cleaner.

Non-stick coatings are available on pans of all types. These have been coated with a preparation known as PTFE (trade names Fluon, Teflon or Tefal) to give a surface to which food does not adhere. This finish is particularly useful for milk pans, frying pans and for cooking sauces and sticky foods. It is now possible to use metal utensils on this finish unless the manufacturer specifically states that only wood or plastic should be used. This surface will be spoiled by using abrasives and scourers.

Ceramic glass cookpans can cope with extremes of temperature so will go safely direct from freezer to hot oven. The lids may be of ordinary toughened glass so should not be subjected to rapid temperature changes. Detachable handles and an attractive appearance make them suitable also for oven-to-table use. This material is a poor heat conductor so careful regulation of heat is necessary to prevent 'hot spotting'. It retains heat well and can be used on a low setting. You should avoid using abrasive powders or metal scourers.

Choosing frying pans In general the same points apply as when choosing saucepans. Remember that a heavy pan ensures even heating and a pouring lip is useful for draining off fat as well as pouring out cooked liquids. A 20-cm *(8-in)* base suits the average household.

Choosing kitchen knives

Strong sharp knives that are comfortable to handle speed up food preparation. Most of those on the market have stainless steel blades, some of them the hollow-ground type which retains its sharpness well. It's useful though to have one knife with a non-stainless steel blade as these are excellent for slicing and chopping and can be sharpened to a very fine edge.

Look for durable, firmly fixed handles and always hold a knife to test if it balances well and is comfortable. Choose dishwasherproof knives if you want them to go in a machine. Store kitchen knives where they won't rub against each other and become blunt; a magnetic or hanging rack, special case or baize-lined compartmentalised drawer are best, placed well out of reach of small children.

For sharpening, a steel or carborundum used correctly give the best results though the less adept will get a good edge using a manual or electric knife-sharpening machine.

As well as a general purpose, round-ended knife, most cooks need the following:

Vegetable knife Small with a pointed blade about 7.5–10 cm *(3–4 in)* long. Used for preparing vegetables and boning meat. An additional knife with a serrated or scalloped edge blade is good for slicing fruit and tomatoes.

Cook's or French knife Made in various sizes but always with the blade tapering to a point. Used for cutting and chopping.

Palette knife Not a cutting tool. Has a broad, flexible blade. Used for lifting and turning food.

Carving knife Long and strong, intended to deal with most joints of meat. Special types are made for use with ham and poultry. Always use in conjunction with a well-designed carving fork with an adequate guard.

Bread knife Long-bladed; often with a serrated or saw edge. Used for cutting bread.

Basic kitchen equipment

For cooking and storing

4 saucepans in assorted sizes (see page 579)
1 milk saucepan
1 colander
1 frying pan
1 1.7-litre *(3-pint)* electric or ordinary kettle
1 roasting tin (often supplied with a new cooker)
1 baking sheet
2 sandwich tins
1 cake tin
1 bun tray
1 wire cooling tray
1 mixing bowl
2 or more pudding basins
1 measuring jug (marked metric and imperial)
1 kitchen jug
2 kitchen plates
1 ovenproof plate
2 or more pie dishes
2 or more casseroles
Storage jars and tins; bread bin

Tools and utensils

Set of kitchen knives (see left)
2 kitchen forks
2 kitchen tablespoons
2 kitchen teaspoons
2 wooden spoons
1 perforated frying spoon
1 fish slice
Pastry cutters
Skewers
Set of metric measuring spoons
1 pair scales (marked metric and imperial)
1 rolling pin
1 pastry board
1 chopping board
1 potato peeler
1 apple corer
1 pair kitchen scissors
1 can opener
1 bottle opener, 1 corkscrew
1 egg whisk
1 grater/shredder
1 lemon squeezer
2 sieves
Mincing machine

Useful additions (if you need and can afford them)

For cooking and storing
Double saucepan
Steamer
Omelette pan
Deep fat fryer
Extra wire cooling trays
Extra baking trays
Extra sandwich and cake tins
Plastic storage boxes
Tray of patty tins
1 Swiss roll tin
Dariole moulds
1 flan ring
1 border mould
1 jelly mould
Soufflé dish
1 raised pie mould
Boat-shaped tins
Cream horn tins
Griddle
Pressure cooker
Electric mixer or blender and attachments
Coffee maker, electric or otherwise
Electric frypan or infra-red grill
Electric toaster
Coffee grinder

Tools and utensils
Cook's thermometer
Meat thermometer
Flat whisk
Grapefruit knife
Potato masher
Potato/melon baller
Ladle
Pastry brush
Bean slicer
Garlic press
Tongs
Skewers
Herb and parsley cutter
Wooden spatula
Knife sharpener
Pie funnel
Extra pastry cutters, including a miniature set
Flour dredger
Pestle and mortar
Salad shaker
Trussing and larding needles

Specialised equipment

For cake icing and decoration
Icing bags and assorted pipes
Piping bags and nozzles (plain) for éclairs, meringues, potato, butter icing, etc
Icing turntable
Icing ruler

For jam and jelly making
Preserving pan
Jam spoon
Jam funnel
Cherry stoner
Jelly bag and stand

For bottling
Bottling jars, rings, etc
Thermometer

Food storage

However large or small your kitchen you will need to organise space to store food, including that which you use every day and items which spend longer in the cupboard as they are used only in small quantities or for emergency meals.

Storage for perishable foods, eg meat, fish, dairy products, fruit and vegetables, is of vital importance since these, if kept too long, will develop bacteria, mould and enzymes (called micro-organisms) whose activity will cause these foods to go off. The best place to keep them is in a refrigerator, failing this a ventilated food cupboard or cool larder. If you have neither these products should be bought daily when needed, to ensure safe eating. In general, it is advisable to buy perishable foods as you need them and in small quantities to ensure that surplus doesn't sit around too long before being eaten. Perishable foods intended for long-term storage can be kept in a freezer (see page 466).

The refrigerator

The average domestic refrigerator maintains a temperature of 2°C to 7°C *(35°F to 45°F)* which is sufficiently low to stop micro-organisms developing. It won't destroy any micro-organisms already present in the food so you should take care to buy perishables when they are as fresh as possible and get them into cool storage quickly.

We list here some tips for getting the best out of your refrigerator:

1. Open the door as infrequently as possible. Try to get everything you need out (or in) in one go. The magnetic doors on most of today's models make opening and closing easy – there's no need to bang the door and disturb the contents.
2. Cover all food before you put it in the refrigerator and if it's just been cooked allow it to cool first. Hot or uncovered foods cause the frozen food compartment to become frosted up and this frost forms an insulating layer which prevents the refrigerator from working efficiently.
3. Learn which foods keep best in different parts of the refrigerator:
(a) Raw foods like meat, bacon, poultry and fish should go in the coldest part, directly under the frozen food compartment.
(b) Cooked meats and made-up dishes should go on the middle shelves.
(c) Vegetables and salad ingredients should go at the bottom in the special crisper, if there is one.
(d) The butter compartment is generally inside the door where the temperature is higher so the butter won't get too hard.
4. Remove cooked foods and cheese from the refrigerator half an hour before serving to allow them to come up to room temperature and regain their flavour.
5. Wipe up all spills immediately so they don't have time to solidify. Keep a weather eye open for oddments tucked away in corners and see that they're either eaten quickly or thrown out.
6. Defrost the refrigerator regularly unless it does this automatically. Clean it with a weak solution of bicarbonate of soda in warm water, using a clean cloth. Ordinary soap and detergent tend to leave a penetrating smell which may be absorbed by the stored foods.

The star rating given by refrigerator and frozen food manufacturers is a useful guide to how long you can keep frozen food in the frozen food compartment of a refrigerator or freezer section of a fridge/freezer. It works like this:

✱✱✱✱ is the symbol used to denote the storage temperature of a three star compartment *plus* the ability to freeze a specified weight of fresh food within a 24-hour period at a temperature of −24°C *(−12°F)*. Always check the star markings on commercially frozen food packets.

Maximum temperature of frozen food compartment	Maximum storage time for:	
	(a) frozen foods	(b) ice cream
✱ −6°C *(21°F)*	up to 1 week	1 day
✱✱ −12°C *(10°F)*	up to 1 month	up to 2 weeks
✱✱✱ −18°C *(0°F)*	up to 3 months	up to 3 months

Storing perishable foods in the refrigerator

Food	*How to Store*	*Time*
Milk		
Fresh milk	In bottle or covered container.	3–4 days
Milk sweets, custards, etc.	In covered dishes. Do not freeze.	2 days
Cultured milk	In original container. Do not freeze.	7 days
Fats	Original wrapper, in door compartments	2–4 weeks
Cheese		
Cream, curd or	Original pack, polythene, cling film or foil.	1–2 weeks
cottage cheese	Covered container, polythene or foil.	2–3 days
Poultry		
Whole fresh poultry	Draw, wash, dry and wrap in polythene or aluminium foil. Remove wrappings from ready-to-cook birds.	2–3 days
Cooked poultry	Cool and refrigerate straight away. Remove stuffing, wrap or cover with polythene or foil.	2–3 days
Frozen birds	Leave in original wrapping and refrigerate straight away in the frozen food compartment.	Depends on Star Rating; 2–3 days in main cabinet
Cooked and made-up poultry dishes	Cool and refrigerate in covered dish or container.	1 day
Meat		
Joints	Refrigerate straight away. Rinse off any blood and wipe dry. Cover lightly with polythene or foil.	3–5 days
Steaks		2–4 days
Chops		2–4 days
Stewing meat		2–4 days
Smoked hams		1 week
Offal and mince		1–2 days
Sliced bacon rashers	Wrap tightly in foil or plastic film.	7–10 days
Cooked meats		
Joints	Wrap in foil or polythene or leave in the covered dish they were cooked in or any other covered container.	3–5 days
Casseroles		2–3 days
Made-up dishes		
Fish		
Raw	Covered loosely in polythene or foil.	1–2 days
Cooked	Covered loosely in polythene or foil. Or place in covered container.	2 days
Frozen	In original pack in frozen food compartment.	Depends on Star Rating
Eggs		
Fresh in shell	Small end down.	2 weeks
Yolks	Covered with water if whole.	2–3 days
Whites	Covered container.	3–4 days
Hard-boiled in shell	Uncovered.	Up to 1 week
Yeast, fresh	In loosely tied polythene bag.	Up to 1 month
Packet frozen foods	In original pack in frozen food compartment.	Depends on Star Rating

Food	*How to Store*	*Time*
Fruit and vegetables		
Soft fruits	Clean and refrigerate in a covered container.	1–3 days
Hard and stone fruits	Lightly wrapped or in the crisper.	3–7 days
Bananas	Never refrigerate.	
Salad vegetables	Clean and drain, store in crisper or lightly wrapped in polythene or in a plastic container.	4–6 days
Greens	Prepare ready for use. Wrap lightly or place in the crisper.	3–7 days
Frozen	In original pack in freezer.	Depends on Star Rating

The larder or food cupboard

Ideally the temperature here should not exceed 10°C *(50°F)* and there should be some ventilation. Any outlet or window should be covered with gauze or perforated zinc to keep out insects and it is also wise to draught-proof the door to prevent heat loss from the kitchen and to reduce condensation. Adjustable height shelves are the most useful, though failing this it is best to vary the heights between shelves so that some are suitable for small items, others for large. The shelves should be covered with easily cleaned materials such as self-adhesive plastic, laminated plastic, ceramic tiles or spongeable shelf paper and all spills should be wiped up immediately. Perishable foods should be checked at frequent intervals to make sure they have not become stale or bad and store cupboard cans and packets should be used in rotation. A good way to keep a check on them is to date each one as you buy it and rotate stocks regularly.

Packaged dry ingredients can be kept quite safely in the original packet until opened, after which the contents should be transferred to a storage jar with a well fitting lid. Really airtight lids are essential only for strong-smelling foods like coffee, herbs and spices, which lose their aroma when exposed to the air, and for things like salt and baking powder which absorb moisture and easily become caked.

Cereal products such as flour and semolina keep well but should be watched for insect infestation. Affected foods should be thrown out at once and stocks checked to ensure that damage has not spread. The high fat content of wholemeal flour and oatmeal may cause rancidity so these should not be stored indefinitely.

Dried fruits need cool, dry storage as they are liable to ferment in damp conditions and shrink in a warm atmosphere. Nuts should be used up quickly as their fat content makes them liable to go rancid.

Where there is mould growth on jams or marmalades, scrape it off and use up the remainder as quickly as possible. Throw away any jams or preserves that have fermented. Syrups and honey will crystallise if kept too long but are still usable for sweetening.

Canned fish and meat, with the exception of fish in tomato sauce, are safe to keep for several years, provided the cans remain in good condition. Pasteurised canned hams over 900 g *(2 lb)* should not be stored for longer than 6 months and should be refrigerated. Sterilised hams weighing 900 g *(2 lb)* or less may be kept for 2–3 years. Canned fruit is best used within a year as the contents may deteriorate in colour after this time even though the food value is not altered. Condensed milk will begin to discolour after 6–9 months. Dried full-cream milk will keep for a few weeks after opening but then tends to go rancid.

Always discard any cans that have 'blown' – recognisable by bulging ends and leaking or rusty seams.

Buying in bulk

Both money and time can often be saved, particularly in large families, by buying in bulk. There are specialist organisations dealing in this and a friendly grocer may well be prepared to co-operate with you in doing a special order.

There are some snags though. You have to outlay a large amount of money at one time and you also need a fair amount of storage space *plus* smaller containers for decanting things into once you have opened a large pack. Some bulk bought goods are not of the same high quality as the recognisably branded varieties sold in shops. There is also the possibility that you may be extravagant because you have bought in such large quantities or that you may become tired of something of which there's still a large amount in store.

Where real bargains are to be had it may be more worthwhile to split a bulk load with a friend or neighbour to cut the capital outlay and avoid overstocking.

Bulk buying for the freezer can also save money, particularly if you own a large model. Most vegetables are available in 900-g *(2-lb)* and 2.3-kg *(5-lb)* packs, peas and beans in quantities up to 9 kg *(20 lb)* and there is usually a choice of brands. It is usually more convenient to break down large packs into family-sized portions to save having to hack them up when you're in a hurry. The same rules for sensible buying and storage apply to buying for the freezer as to other buying for storage.

How long will it keep?

Extra long keepers

Canned fish in oil and canned meats (not ham, see above)	5 years
Sugar, cubed, granulated and caster	5 years
Vinegar	2 years
Canned vegetables	2 years
Canned sponge puddings	2 years
Canned soups	2 years
Canned pasta foods in sauce	2 years
Canned meat and vegetable meals	2 years

Long keepers (1 year)

Cornflour, custard powder, blancmange powder, pasta, rice, instant desserts, jams, marmalades, treacle, syrup, dehydrated foods, oils, most canned fruit, canned juices, canned fish in tomato sauce, canned milk, canned milk puddings, icing sugar, cocoa, drinking chocolate, malted milk, instant coffee, packet soups.

Other foods

Flour	up to 6 months
Baking powder, bicarbonate of soda	2–3 months
Dried yeast	up to 6 months
Tea, loose coffee	up to 1 month
Instant low fat/skimmed milk powder	2–3 months
Dried fruit	2–3 months
Nuts, coconut	up to 1 month
Instant potato	9 months
Cake mixes	6 months
Canned ham (over 900 g, *2 lb*)	6 months (keep refrigerated)
Jellies, gelatine	up to 12 months
Herbs, spices, seasonings	up to 6 months
Evaporated milk	6–8 months
Condensed milk	4–6 months
Canned prunes and rhubarb	9 months
Pastry mixes	6 months
Biscuits (according to variety)	3–11 months
Carbonated drinks in cans	6–12 months
Dried peas, beans and lentils	6–12 months

Index